THE DARTNELL MARKETING MANAGER'S HANDBOOK

DARTNELL is a publisher serving the world of business with books, manuals, newsletters and bulletins, and training materials for executives, managers, supervisors, salespeople, financial officials, personnel executives, and office employees. Dartnell also produces management and sales training videos and audiocassettes, publishes many useful business forms, and many of its materials and films are available in languages other than English. Dartnell, established in 1917, serves the world's business community. For details, catalogs, and product information, write to:

THE DARTNELL CORPORATION
4660 N Ravenswood Ave
Chicago, IL 60640-4595, U.S.A.
or phone (800) 621-5463 (U.S. and Canada)

Dartnell Training Limited
125 High Holborn
London, England
WC1V 6QA
or phone 011-44-071-404-1585

Other Dartnell Handbooks:
Advertising Manager's Handbook
Direct Mail and Mail Order Handbook
Office Administration Handbook
Personnel Administration Handbook
Public Relations Handbook
Sales Manager's Handbook
Sales Promotion Handbook

THE DARTNELL MARKETING MANAGER'S HANDBOOK

Sidney J. Levy,
George R. Frerichs,
Howard L. Gordon,
Editors

Third Edition

FIRST EDITION, 1973
SECOND EDITION, 1983
THIRD EDITION, 1994

ISBN 0-85013-203-7

Printed in the United States of America by The Dartnell Press,
Chicago, IL 60640-4595

CONTENTS

Introduction xv

Acknowledgments xix

Special Acknowledgment xx

About the Editors xxi

PART ONE: THE SCOPE OF MARKETING 1

1. Modern-Day Marketing: The Value-Added Era and Its Foundations 4
Dick Berry, University of Wisconsin

2. Marketing Systems: Implications for Marketing Planning 30
Stanley F. Stasch, Loyola University of Chicago
Howard L. Gordon, GRFI Ltd.

3. Implementing the Marketing Concept: Linking Quality, Marketing, and Value 42
Edward J. Kane, Dun and Bradstreet Software Services, Inc.
Eugene J. Kelley, Florida Atlantic University

4. Translating Marketing Strategy: Implementation as Managerial Communication 64
Dennis W. Rook, University of Southern California, Los Angeles

PART TWO: ORGANIZING AND STAFFING THE MARKETING FUNCTION 77

5. Reward Compensation: Marketing's Role 80
Michael T. Higgins, Mike Higgins & Associates, Inc.

6. Staffing the Marketing Function 94
Donald W. Hendon, University of North Alabama

7. Salesperson Performance and Job Satisfaction 106
Steven Brown, Southern Methodist University
Thomas W. Leigh, University of Georgia
J. Martin Haygood, Management Psychology Group

PART THREE: ESTABLISHING MARKETING OBJECTIVES/STRATEGIES 131

8. Setting Marketing Objectives 134
Harper W. Boyd, Jr., University of Arkansas
Jean-Claude Larreche, European Institute of Management (INSEAD)

9. Determining Consumer and Customer Wants and Needs 150
Roger D. Blackwell, The Ohio State University, Management Horizons, Inc.
David T. Kollat, Limited Stores, Inc.
James F. Engel, Wheaton College

10. Brand Dominance: Competitive Advantage Through Consumer Learning 162
Gregory S. Carpenter, Northwestern University
Kent Nakamoto, University of Colorado

11. Segmenting the Market 174
Richard R. Still, University of Georgia

12. Marketing for Professionals 186
Edward W. Wheatley, East Carolina University

13. Green Marketing 220
George Fisk, Emory University

PART FOUR: MARKETING RESEARCH 235

14. What is Marketing Research? 238
Arnold Corbin, New York University
Sol Dutka, Audits & Surveys

15. Communication Research: Continuous Measurement Instruments 254
G. David Hughes, University of North Carolina

16. What is Qualitative Research? 270
Sidney J. Levy, Northwestern University

17. Statistical and Experimental Design 288
Bertram Schoner, Simon Fraser University
Henry H. Rodkin, Maremont Corporation

18. Survey Methods of Data Collection for Domestic and International Marketing Research 300
Naresh K. Malhotra, Georgia Institute of Technology

19. Market-Based Decisions 328
Vincent Barabba, General Motors Corporation

20. Management Science and Model Building 356
James H. Donnelly, Jr., University of Kentucky
John M. Ivancevich, University of Houston

21. Managerial Perspectives on Consumer Satisfaction, Dissatisfaction, and Complaining Behavior 370
J. Barry Mason, The University of Alabama
William O. Bearden, The University of South Carolina

22. Advertising Research and Measurement 398
Darrell B. Lucas, New York University (Retired)

23. Database Marketing 418
Robert C. Blattberg, Northwestern University
Lynn C. Unglaub, Robert C. Blattberg Consultants

24. Sizing Markets 446
Chaim M. Ehrman, Loyola University of Chicago

25. The Marketing Campaign 462
Craig S. Rice, Marketing Dynamics

26. Information Technology in Marketing and Sales 478
Keith Fletcher, Strathclyde University
Alan Crawley, Price Waterhouse

27. Predicting Market Responses to Style Merchandise: Sensory Panels and Sensory Segmentation 508
Russell I. Haley, University of New Hampshire

28. Marketing Theory and Practice 536
Robert Bartels, Ohio State University
Bruce E. Macnab, Kaiser Engineers, Inc.

PART FIVE: DEVELOPING THE MARKETING PLAN 549

29. Market Position Analysis 552
Paul E. Green, University of Pennsylvania
John L. McMennamin, The Carnation Company
Shahrzad Amirani, University of Texas at Arlington

30. Developing the Organization's Marketing Mix 570
William Lazer, Michigan State University,
William Lazer Associates, International
M. Bixby Cooper, Michigan State University

31. The Marketing Decision 588
William F. O'Dell, Market Facts, Inc.
David K. Hardin, Market Facts, Inc.

32. Marketing Strategy 598
Robert A. Lynn, Clark Atlanta University

33. Fostering Ethical Marketing Decisions 606
Gene R. Laczniak, Marquette University
Patrick E. Murphy, University of Notre Dame

34. Ethics in Marketing 626
James M. Hulbert, Columbia University
Bernd Schmitt, Columbia University

35. Government Regulation and the Marketing Manager: Developing a Perspective 636
H. Keith Hunt, Brigham Young University

36. Substantive and Procedural Changes in Antitrust Law: Implications for Marketing Management 644
William L. Trombetta, Fairleigh Dickinson University

37. Managing the Market Planning Process: The Search for Continuous Competitive Renewal 660
Nigel F. Piercy, University of Wales, Texas Christian University
William D. Giles, Strategic Management Resource Centre, Ltd.

38. Marketing to Nonexistent Markets 686
John K. Ryans, Jr., Kent State University
William L. Shanklin, Kent State University

39. Marketing Technology and Consumer Scanning 698
John C. Totten, Nielsen Marketing Research
Mike Duffy, Kraft General Foods, Inc.

40. Evaluating and Controlling Marketing Performance 738
Philip Kotler, Northwestern University

PART SIX: PUTTING THE MARKETING PLAN INTO ACTION FOR CONSUMER PRODUCTS/SERVICES 771

41. The Diffusion of Innovations 774
George R. Frerichs, GRFI, Ltd.

42. Prescription For a Service Quality Revolution in America 786
Leonard L. Berry, Texas A&M University
A. Parasuraman, Texas A&M University

43. Developing and Implementing an Effective
Customer Service Strategy 802
Barry Berman, Hofstra University

44. Social Marketing 824
Karen F. A. Fox, Santa Clara University

45. Strategic Pricing 834
Michael H. Morris, University of Central Florida
George A. Siragusa, Mobil Oil Corporation

46. Pricing 856
Donald V. Harper, University of Minnesota
Jack L. Caldwell, Glenwood-Inglewood Company

47. Getting Things Done:
Customer-Driven Distribution Systems 868
Louis W. Stern, Northwestern University
Frederick D. Sturdivant, The MAC Group, Inc.

48. Product Cannibalism 880
Roger A. Kerin, Southern Methodist University
Dwight R. Riskey, Frito-Lay, Inc.

49. Strategic Planning in Retailing:
Understanding and Responding to a
Dynamic Environment 896
Joel R. Evans, Hofstra University

50. Franchising—A Marriage of System Members 918
Norman D. Axelrad, The Franchising Board, LTD
Your Own Business, Inc.
Robert E. Weigand, University of Illinois at Chicago

51. Yield Management:
New Pricing Strategy 936
James C. Makens, Wake Forest University

PART SEVEN: PUTTING THE MARKETING PLAN INTO ACTION FOR BUSINESS PRODUCTS/SERVICES 943

52. Marketing to Business 946
Thomas V. Bonoma, Harvard University Graduate School of Business Administration
Robert A. Garda, McKinsey & Company, Inc.
Sara M. Roche, McKinsey & Company, Inc.

53. Partnering as a Focused Market Strategy 1010
James C. Anderson, Northwestern University
James A. Narus, Wake Forest University

54. Marketing Raw Materials 1030
H. Robert Dodge, Eastern Michigan University

55. Research on Industrial Products and Services 1042
Richard M. Hill, University of Illinois at Urbana-Champaign

56. Business-to-Business Selling and the Organizational Buying Process 1066
Joseph A. Bellizzi, Arizona State University

PART EIGHT: PROMOTING PRODUCTS AND SERVICES 1081

57. Customer Contacts in an Integrated Marketing Communications Environment 1084
Ronald B. Kaatz, Northwestern University

58. Attack on Many Fronts: Business Communications 1106
Frances B. Emerson, Honeywell Inc.

59. Imagery and Symbolism 1136
Sidney J. Levy, Northwestern University
Ira O. Glick, Ira O. Glick & Associates, Inc.

60. Setting Promotional Marketing Objectives 1146
Joseph P. Flanagan, IMPACT

61. Developing Advertising Message Strategy 1156
S. Watson Dunn, University of Missouri-Columbia
Arnold M. Barban, University of Alabama
Dean M. Krugman, University of Georgia
Leonard N. Reid, University of Georgia

62. Contemporary Advertising Media Planning 1186
Jack Z. Sissors, Northwestern University
James Surmanek, McCann Erickson

63. Public Relations 1196
Harold A. Bergen, Ruder-Finn Inc.

64. Direct Marketing: Modelling Customer-Marketer Relationships in Integrative Marketing Communications 1204
Arch G. Woodside, Tulane University

65. Advertising to the "Other" Culture: Women's Use of Language and Language's Use of Women 1232
Barbara B. Stern, Rutgers, The State University of New Jersey

PART NINE: GLOBAL MARKETING 1249

66. International Marketing Concepts 1252
Illka A. Ronkainen, Georgetown University Helsinki School of Economics

67. Researching Global Markets 1276
Susan P. Douglas, New York University
C. Samuel Craig, New York University

68. Export Marketing 1300
Philip R. Cateora, University of Colorado
Linda J. Shea, University of Massachusetts

69. International Distribution and Selling 1318
Gerald S. Albaum, University of Oregon
Gordon E. Miracle, Michigan State University

70. Barter and Buybacks—Doing Business the Old-Fashioned Way 1344
Robert E. Weigand, University of Illinois at Chicago

71. Unraveling the Mystique of Export Pricing 1356
S. Tamer Cavusgil, Michigan State University

INDEX 1375

INTRODUCTION

If you believe the purpose of a business or organization is to get and keep customers, then you surely regard marketing as a high-priority activity. The end result of marketing is to make things simple for the customer, whether that customer be a purchaser of goods or services, a member of an association, or a citizen trying to get the most from a local, regional, or national government. But achieving that result is not so simple a task.

This Third Edition of the Dartnell *Marketing Manager's Handbook* has been written with the same practical intention as the First Edition in 1973: to make traveling the road to efficient, effective, and *profitable* marketing easier. But today the work of the professional marketer is much more complex.

Marketing is no longer simply a function of the marketing department. Everyone in the organization has a "marketing job," so we as marketers have many more human resources to consider. Customers are more knowledgeable and demanding than their counterparts of twenty years ago. Stability in the marketplace has been shaken to the roots. In the face of this, marketers have at their fingertips techniques that yield seas of data for decisionmaking. (The hard part here is choosing the information that's relevant to the decision.)

These are truly dramatic shifts. They make the work of the professional marketer more challenging—and require a greater flow of creative juices!

For those reasons and others, marketing has in effect *become* the business. It is vital for many folks throughout any business or organization to understand marketing generally and to maintain a customer focus.

Although nearly anyone in a business might benefit from sampling the pages that follow, certain groups of readers will derive greater benefit due to their specific responsibilities on the job. This book should be especially useful for those with marketing titles *and* marketing responsibilities. Some of these groups are members of senior management, marketing managers (including category and brand managers), sales managers, marketing intelligence managers, marketing services staff, merchandising managers, those in charge of the distribution channels, and anyone involved in marketing communications, on either the agency or client side. And, of course, it should be clear that this *Handbook* can be equally valuable to anyone concerned with marketing of products or services working with consumer, trade, professional, technical, or business audiences.

The thinking that drives the format of this new edition of a classic marketing work was to gain access to the leaders in marketing thought and practice—and invite them to write on a topic each believes today's marketers ought to hear about. To do that, we've tapped the expertise and enthusiasm of 112 authors representing 57 universities and 30 organizations. They have responded with 71 chapters covering nearly every key aspect of marketing.

The passage of time since the Second Edition, published in 1983, has produced dramatic changes in the field of marketing, and these changes are reflected in the extensive updating of the book's content. Most of the authors are fresh contributors, some topics have been dropped, and several new topics are included. The ferment in the field of marketing has been vigorous. Old issues have received renewed vitality, and new technologies have created novel opportunities. As a result, this volume now includes new or greater material on such topics as quality, the marketing of services, ethics, global marketing, and database marketing. The section on marketing research has been significantly enlarged. The range of articles is broader than before, in keeping with the need to serve newcomers to marketing and to accommodate the greater sophistication accruing from the intensification of marketing education in recent years.

The book deals with the theoretical to be sure. But it is also of highly practical use because many marketing leaders today move easily between academia and day-to-day business operations as consultants. Many also now run their own businesses that live and die by their ability to *successfully* apply theory to real business situations. This edition has made a serious effort to take advantage of the practical information such crossover work yields. Thus, the book is indeed a rich, diverse collection of marketing thinking, and each chapter is a significant piece in the marketing mosaic.

How can you best use this unique work to serve your needs? You can, of course, read the entire volume through from the first page to the last, which would certainly be a valuable experience. More useful, perhaps, will be for you to use the table of contents or index to focus on a few areas of immediate interest. Think about the marketing opportunities you have right now and find a chapter that relates. Many chapters can be read as worthwhile introductions to a particular topic, even if the chapter has a relatively narrow focus, and as resources offering areas for further study and thought. (To this end, each chapter concludes with suggestions for further reading.) Others offer a more in-depth look at their topics or practical advice that can be readily applied. All of the chapters give insights that can help you make more intelligent decisions about marketing.

There are nine major parts of the *Handbook:*

"Part One: The Scope of Marketing" provides a basic look at the marketing concept and explains its links to the high-priority goal of getting and keeping customers, however they are defined.

"Part Two: Organizing and Staffing the Marketing Function" deals with the many "people issues" of marketing. How do you attract the kind of people you want? How do you reward them?

"Part Three: Establishing Marketing Objectives/Strategies" can help marketers decide which markets to pursue and how to establish and achieve goals that will not only satisfy, but delight, those markets.

"Part Four: Marketing Research" discusses the nature of the information marketers need to make decisions as well as what it takes to go from data to information to the insight that directs action.

"Part Five: Developing the Marketing Plan" talks about the creative process of making marketing decisions.

The next two parts deal separately with the two major customer segments: consumer and business. Part Six is "Putting the Marketing Plan into Action for Consumer Products/Services." Part Seven is "Putting the Marketing Plan into Action for Business Products/ Services." They each offer assistance in how to sharpen tools that will make the marketing process work its hardest for you and your organization.

"Part Eight: Promoting Products and Services" analyzes the range of marketing communications methods and how and when to use them.

"Part Nine: Global Marketing" offers valuable insights on how to think about global business activity as well as how to prepare and implement actions that will build markets in the global village.

As you can see from even this brief overview, this *Handbook* offers a wonderful range of information and assistance to anyone who would better use contemporary marketing techniques to build their business or their organization into all that it can possibly be.

—The Editors

ACKNOWLEDGMENTS

This new edition of the Dartnell *Marketing Manager's Handbook* would not have been possible without the willingness, dedication, and enthusiasm of the more than 100 distinguished authors who contributed to this exciting, but complex, project. They are truly leaders in marketing thought and practice, and our sincere thanks go to each one for sharing his or her expertise and time.

Now, how do you organize such a network of "thought leaders" and keep the communication lines running between authors and editors, especially when the authors are researching, teaching, and performing as professional marketers throughout the world? Lois Gordon had the answer. She put together an efficient, effective system for keeping it all on track during the manuscript collection process and, then, the editing process. She smoothed out many bumps in the road common to a project that depended on so many people to perform so many tasks in pursuit of a single, grand goal. She handled it all with courage and aplomb!

As work first started to shape the new edition, Scott Frerichs used on-line computer databases to search for articles on high-interest subjects. Later, Kathy Frerichs helped draft and edit introductions to several of the nine parts that comprise this book. We appreciate their efforts as well.

Then there was the able assistance of the Department of Marketing support staff at the J.L. Kellogg Graduate School of Management at Northwestern University. They, too, aided the flow of manuscripts through the system and to the editors.

The able and dedicated publishing staff at The Dartnell Corporation provided helpful advice and direction to guide us through the minefield of myriad details peculiar to such a volume. In so doing, they also contributed to the value of this book.

Creating a unique reference work such as this *Handbook* is not easy. But the efforts of all of these folks made it look as if it were.

And thanks, finally, to the readers of this book. Your profitable use of the vast amount of knowledge accumulated here in this single volume will be the most meaningful tribute to everyone who participated in producing the Third Edition of the *Marketing Manager's Handbook*.

—The Editors

SPECIAL ACKNOWLEDGMENT

STEUART HENDERSON BRITT

Steuart Henderson Britt, the originator of the First Edition of The Dartnell *Marketing Manager's Handbook* in 1973, was an extraordinary man. He was a most genial and courteous person but capable of outspoken criticism and intellectual challenge. He had a sharp wit and was an inveterate practical joker. But he was generous and sympathetic as well. He had great curiosity and pursued his studies in many directions. He was a hard worker and highly productive. He earned a law degree as well as a Ph.D. in psychology. He worked as a market researcher in an advertising agency and established his own research firm. He was for ten years the editor of *The Journal of Marketing*. As a researcher and teacher, he was an outstanding member of the faculty of the business school at Northwestern University. He pioneered in the field of consumer behavior—studying it, teaching it, and making significant contributions to the literature on it. He taught advertising and took an inordinate interest in his students, many of whom remain devoted to his memory and attribute to him great influence on their lives.

His concept of the first *Marketing Manager's Handbook* was broad and encompassing. Because he observed a large gap between theory and practice, and wanted to maximize the relevance of the volume, his original design was for each chapter to be prepared by a two-person team of an academic and a practitioner. His vigorous professional participation and his editorship enabled him to tap a wide spectrum of contributors to the book. The *Handbook* was well-received and continued for years to have a steady audience. In 1983, shortly after Britt had died, it was revised by Norman Guess, senior vice president at The Dartnell Corporation, and George Frerichs, Britt's friend and business partner.

Now, the volume has been revised again. We have not adhered closely to the plan for joint authorship because most of the academic authors nowadays have more direct experience with practitioners and often work as consultants. Also, some articles were prepared by practitioners, so there remains a good mix of theory and practical application. However, this latest revision remains true to Britt's dedication to high-quality, thought-provoking work and to his vision of the book as an encompassing look at the many aspects of marketing theory and practice.

We thank Steuart Henderson Britt for his original inspiration for this book, and we believe he would have been pleased with this most recent edition.

—The Editors

ABOUT THE EDITORS

Sidney J. Levy is professor emeritus of Behavioral Science in Management and professor of Marketing at the Kellogg Graduate School of Management at Northwestern University. Previously, he was A. Montgomery Ward Professor of Marketing (1983) and Charles H. Kellstadt Distinguished Professor (1986).

Levy, who earned his Ph.D. from the Committee on Human Development at the University of Chicago, is a licensed psychologist in Illinois, and a member of the American Marketing Association. As a principal with Social Research, Inc., Levy has directed and participated in research for major corporations, media, and various public and private agencies. During 1991, he served as president of the Association for Consumer Research.

Among other distinctions, Levy was named AMA/Irwin Distinguished Marketing Educator in 1988 and, in 1982, received the Fellow Award from the Association for Consumer Research.

Levy's articles have been widely anthologized; those of special significance to marketers include "The Product and the Brand," "Symbols for Sale," "Social Class and Life Style," and "Broadening the Concept of Marketing," and other articles appearing in the *Journal of Marketing* and *Journal of Retailing,* as well as in numerous books on marketing and its effects on society.

George R. Frerichs is the founder of GRFI Ltd. At this firm, he has gained national prominence for his site selection and real estate consulting services; his development of a mathematical model for forecasting sales, profits, and return on investments; his product development marketing research and consulting; and his pioneering work in the area of financial services marketing. Frerichs writes extensively on these and other topics.

Before founding GRFI, Frerichs served as executive vice president of RVI Corporation (formerly Robert Vogele, Inc.), where he developed that firm's financial and marketing consulting services, and in a variety of marketing positions with Earle Ludgin Advertising; BBDO; Leo Burnett Advertising; Abbott Labs; and Pure-Union Oil Company. Frerichs also served as publisher for *Chicago* magazine and as president of the American Marketing Association.

In addition to his experience within the financial and advertising industries, Frerichs has extensive experience in new product idea generation; concept screening and evaluation; product testing; product positioning and perception studies; alternative pricing evaluation; brand name development and testing; packaging and logo design; and market development. He is also active as an expert witness providing testimony in matters pertaining to marketing and distribution and test marketing.

Frerichs received an M.B.A. from the Kellogg Graduate School of Management at Northwestern University and a B.S. degree in economics from Western Michigan University.

Howard L. Gordon is a marketing analyst and teacher with a broad background in developing relevant information and translating results into action. He is a principal of GRFI Ltd., a Chicago-based advertising and marketing firm specializing in research for consumer, trade, professional, and business markets. His work involves "probing the market chemistry" to help clients understand and interpret the marketplace. He directs market evaluations in the U.S., Europe, and Asia.

Gordon has held several faculty posts at Northwestern University. He began his teaching career as a lecturer in marketing and then was appointed associate professor of Advertising at the Medill School of Journalism.

Before joining Northwestern, Gordon served as marketing services vice president for Marsteller Advertising and Burson-Marsteller Public Relations. There he developed new research concepts for identifying market appeals.

As an analyst of buying behavior and motivation, Gordon tracks the values that drive buying decisions. His studies cover such key areas as positioning strategies, customer enthusiasm for products and services, and selling messages.

He chairs the Committee on Lifestyle Evaluation for the Advertising Research Foundation and is a frequent presenter at industry seminars. He also contributes articles to major marketing publications. He is former vice president and director of the American Marketing Association.

Gordon earned an M.S. from Northwestern's Medill School of Journalism and an M.B.A. from Northwestern's Kellogg Graduate School of Management.

PART ONE

THE SCOPE OF MARKETING

PART ONE

INTRODUCTION

As an activity that embodies exchange and competition for existence, marketing has probably been around since the beginning of time. But its modern conceptualization and emergence as a discipline and topic of study started around 100 years ago. It then involved primarily a focus on how commodities moved from their points of origin to reach end consumers. That process is still a central aspect of what marketing is basically about. But the ways of thinking about marketing have altered considerably since those early days. The advances of invention and technology as they affect products and all other aspects of marketing, the growth and elaboration of the media, the great demographic changes, the intensified integration of the global market, and the development of both theoretical and applied attention to the thinking about marketing have all brought about great shifts in the contemporary status of marketing.

From the early days of relatively simple observations of, for example, how winter pears make their way from the Northeast to reach customers in the retail store—essentially a matter of physical distribution involving such issues as packaging, transportation, and storage—to the complexities of marketing cooperatives, company buyer groups, the study of the psychology of consumer segments, analysis of the symbolism of advertising, and other topics, the scope of marketing has kept growing and becoming more elaborate. Under the constant pressure of competition, the need to add value and achieve ever-greater customer satisfaction is critical. The first four chapters of the *Handbook* give an overview of these issues, discussing the character of modern-day marketing in its concern with adding value. A rationale for marketing planning is presented in terms of the way marketing systems operate. Perspectives are provided that relate to implementing the marketing concept, with its emphases on quality and value, and to translating strategies into the actions that express what managers are seeking to communicate.

Dick Berry
Professor Emeritus
School of Business
University of Wisconsin
Madison, Wisconsin

CHAPTER 1

MODERN-DAY MARKETING: THE VALUE-ADDED ERA AND ITS FOUNDATIONS

As we walk, drive, or fly across America, we become aware that a new era of marketing is evolving. It is no longer the era of "pitch and sell" or "price to compete" but an era of "serve and satisfy." Marketing has come of age and has become an exciting profession based on skillful analysis and planning, aimed to position companies for success, profitability, and planned growth. The root of this new thinking and practice is the notion that customer mindedness is the way to do it. What we do in marketing is for the benefit of both the company and the customer. Niche marketing and targeting have become of extreme importance as companies focus on customer needs and wants, providing products and services surrounded by a value-added aura of customer attention and support. You are invited to explore this new era of marketing—looking at the approaches and practices that have evolved and are evolving.

QUESTIONS AND MYTHS ABOUT MARKETING

Questions about Marketing

Question: What is the similarity between a roll of toilet tissue and an airline trip? As an instant reaction, one would say, "None." However, as we probe marketing-related aspects of the question, some interesting things come to light.

The frame of reference for the question is the promotional discourse used by Scott Paper Company for its product ScotTissue and an advertisement for American Airlines' flight services through the Nashville hub. The promotional messages are targeted to the customer, but more importantly, they reflect an understanding of who the customer is, what the customer wants, and what the customer benefits would be.

What we are talking about is the understanding and application of sound marketing principles and practices by companies in their marketing effort. In particular, the messages project benefits that are of importance to target customers but also suggest added values—a key to competitive advantage in today's marketplace. These considerations are surfacing at the onset because of their importance in learning and understanding modern-day marketing and its applications.

The Scott Paper Company has studied the consumer—you and me—determining that as a class of customers we want and value the following in a roll of toilet tissue:

- softness and absorbency,
- long lasting,

- easy start roll, with starter tab, and
- safety for septic systems.

As compared to conventional toilet paper, ScotTissue offers benefits and added values that suggest we purchase and enjoy the product, preferentially to competitive offerings. In current marketing jargon, not only will we be satisfied customers, we will also be delighted—a critical result in today's highly competitive marketplace.

American Airlines, in a full-page newspaper advertisement for its airline services, starts off with the following headline: "Five Reasons to Fly to Nashville, Even When You're Not Flying to Nashville." Hopefully the headline, under the picture of an American jet plane skimming through the skies, will attract the attention of air travelers, creating the desire to read on. The ad offers five supposed benefits to you and me, the target consumers:

- "Scope of service: . . . the convenience and flexibility you need, without the hassle you hate."
- Hassle-free hub: . . . designed with convenience in mind, you don't have to rush to make your next connecting flight."
- "On-time flights: . . . get where you're going, when you need to get there."
- "Admiral's Club: . . . relax between flights in quiet comfort, with your favorite beverage or snack . . . instant access to a host of business tools, including personal computers, fax machines and more."
- "AAdvantage Miles: . . . with our PlanAAhead awards, your first free trip is only 20,000 miles away."

Needless to say, American is trying to sell you air travel. When you glance through the ad, do you become interested in the benefits and added values that are not readily available from other airlines? And when you are planning your next flight, which airline are you likely to consider?

Once again, we are targeted by a company that has done its homework. It has a clear picture of the benefits you are seeking, and with this it offers added values to position the company ahead of the competition. Not only will you end up being a customer and a satisfied customer, but you can expect to be a delighted customer as well.

Myths about Marketing

In summary, the point to be made is that the myth, "marketing is advertising and selling," is the biggest myth and the usual interpretation of marketing by most executives and managers, as well as the general public (Exhibit 1). As demonstrated by the ScotTissue and American Airlines examples, marketing does focus on advertising and selling, but encompasses the information and knowledge about targeted customer groups, with careful planning and implementation of the various strategic and tactical marketing variables, to achieve a desired marketing result.

EXHIBIT 1. Myths about Marketing

- Marketing is selling and advertising.
- We cannot waste time on marketing; we do not have the product designed yet.
- Technology sells . . . the right product will sell itself.
- Purchasing behavior is rational.
- Cost and price are directly related.

Other common myths relate to beliefs from nonmarketing areas of a company, such as the following:

- "We can't waste time on marketing, we don't have the product designed yet." Many technical people have never been exposed to marketing thought and practice so do not have appreciation of the importance of marketing input to the business equation, particularly in new product planning and development.
- "Technology sells . . . the right product will sell itself." Once again we have a technical perspective, based on the thinking that inventiveness and technical superiority will offset the need for careful planning and development of the distribution structure, pricing considerations, and promotional efforts of a venture.
- "Purchasing behavior is rational." This thinking suggests that a product or service can be promoted using purely logical claims and assertions, rather than exploring customer characteristics, to develop and promote a benefit-oriented rationale that offers promise to satisfy customer needs.
- "Cost and price directly related." Arising from the financial areas of a company, this thinking suggests formula pricing, which is in direct conflict with the basic pricing tenant—"what traffic will bear."

As we continue our exploration of the world of marketing, you will gain insight into the theory, thoughts, and practices of modern marketing.

MARKETING DEFINED

Evolution of Modern Marketing

Without question, the early cave man was first to initiate practices of marketing, perhaps limited to bartering and exchanging his earthly possessions and items of food and clothing. The marketing literature describes various eras of marketing leading up to the present day when we appear to have a marketing culture based on the notion of identifying and satisfying customer needs and wants, with the goal to yield a financially sound and profitable outcome. This author attributes the evolution of this marketing orientation to the developments at the General Electric Company, with specification of "The Marketing Concept" in the company's 1952 Annual Report: "the identification and satisfaction of customer needs." In those early years, the author had the

EXHIBIT 2. Definition of Marketing

Marketing is

- a process,
- identifying and satisfying customer needs and wants,
- an exchange of values, and
- achieving mutual satisfaction.

Source: Dick Berry.

good fortune to work with Edward S. "Ted" McKay who headed up GE's marketing services group—one of the earliest departmental structures where marketing services emerged as an organizational entity to plan and implement marketing practices and where company efforts were focused on the marketing concept.

Definition of Marketing

To provide a common frame of reference, a definition of marketing is suggested to assist us through our learning experiences and to provide guidance for future analysis and application (Exhibit 2).

Marketing is a process

- of identifying and satisfying customer needs and wants,
- involving an exchange of values,
- resulting in the achievement of mutual satisfaction.

As a process, marketing can be thought of as being a never-ending series of activities that focus on the desired result of identifying and satisfying customer needs and wants. As the process is implemented, there is an exchange of values between the provider of a product or service offering and a customer, with the expectation that the provider and customer will be mutually satisfied. In other words, the customer will achieve benefits and values that are seen as being equal to or greater than that which was given—usually a monetary consideration. At the same time, the provider is seen to attain values and also to be satisfied. Very simply, if the above conditions are not attained, then one has a faulty outcome, usually resulting in a dissatisfied customer.

DIFFERENTIATION AND COMPETITIVE ADVANTAGE

The ultimate and most desirable outcome to achieve in marketing is to attain an unbalanced situation with competitors—in effect to create imperfect competition. To accomplish this, a provider of products or services must be positioned such that the provider is seen in a more favorable light than competitors. Differentiation (Exhibit 3) is a promotion strategy that is carried out by putting together a combination of

EXHIBIT 3. Product Differentiation

A Way of Creating Imperfect Competition
Perceived differences are promoted to customers to increase demand or deemphasize price.

Differentiation

- is a promotion strategy
- must be perceived by customer . . . to be of value (beneficial)
- allows target marketing to specific market segments
- can be based on
  —product features
  —supportive services
  —intangible benefits (as brand . . . prestige)
  —availability (place considerations)
  —terms (price considerations)

Source: © Dick Berry.

features and benefits such that the customer perceives and values the differences, as compared to competitors. The differences can be based on features of the product or service offering, supportive services, intangible benefits—such as brand name or prestige considerations, availability of the offering, or price considerations. In order for the advantage to be evident, the advantages must be communicated to the target market.

As an example of product differentiation, consider the Disneyland and Disney World theme parks. The aggregation of features and benefits are not matched by any other entertainment offering; thus the differential advantage is very evident. When a parent is considering a vacation trip for the family, an array of possibilities may come to mind, but Disney World and Disneyland stand out as being most desirable alternatives. As these offerings have emerged, they have gained prominence through a variety of publicity and promotional activities sponsored by the Disney enterprises and by a variety of other providers of transportation, housing, entertainment, and other offerings. For example, one quite regularly hears about cruises and tours that focus on Disney World as part of their offerings.

THE CUSTOMER PERSPECTIVE: CUSTOMER NEEDS AND WANTS

Purchase Motivation

An interesting way to gain a better understanding of the suggested definition of marketing and to better understand the notion of "needs" is to look within one's own mind and ask what needs are

EXHIBIT 4. Motiquiz II

An Exercise to Determine Consumer Purchase Motivation

To perform the exercise, identify an investment, product, service, or consumable item that you have acquired or plan to acquire. Next, read the statements on this page . . . *mark those which explain why you have made or plan to make the acquisition.* Review the selected statements . . . *circle numbers of those that most honestly represent your feelings.*

237 To achieve a future economic or social benefit
386 To gain acceptance by other persons
455 To achieve a feeling of importance
229 To achieve a desired arrangement or relationship
551 To contribute in creative expression by yourself
585 To afford an opportunity for personal growth
184 To satisfy a thirst for liquid refreshment within yourself
423 To attain recognition by others
572 To contribute in attaining your full potential in a personal endeavor
131 To provide personal comfort
329 To assist in displaying your love for another person
519 To contribute in fully expressing yourself
313 To enhance your acceptance by another person
497 To gain the admiration of others
278 To provide a measure of security
398 To enhance friendly relations with another person
414 To gain attention of others
143 To provide sexual satisfaction for yourself
246 To achieve a stabilizing effect
564 To satisfy a strong urge, resulting in personal satisfaction
155 To satisfy a craving within you
486 To gain respect from others
361 To gain acceptance by a social group
543 To contribute in your self-expression
116 To provide bodily warmth or cooling for yourself
215 To achieve a measure of protection
538 To take advantage of an opportunity that offers personal reward
129 To provide protection from the elements for yourself
335 To achieve a sense of belonging in a social group
283 To satisfy a custom or procedure
347 To enhance the opportunity to be with others
461 To satisfy a sense of responsibility
527 To satisfy a strong desire, leading to personal satisfaction
374 To gain the love of another person
197 To satisfy your hunger for food
439 To gain the appreciation of others
172 To provide a pleasant feeling for yourself
478 To satisfy a sense of independence
352 To assist in expressing affection for another person
292 To offer protection from danger or hazard
168 To improve your personal health or well-being
596 To provide a challenge
261 To achieve a saving of time or money
442 To satisfy a need for achievement
254 To satisfy an external influence

Explanation of results: The statements are divided into five categories . . . intended to represent the five levels of Maslow's Hierarchy of Needs. The first digit in each statement number indicates the category. These categories are: 1–Physiological, 2–Safety-security, 3–Love-belonging, 4–Self-esteem, 5–Self-actualization. Your purchase motivations are *suggested* by the statement categories.

Source: (C) 1976, Dick Berry.

represented in the product or service purchasing process. The Motiquiz II instrument, Exhibit 4, offers you this opportunity. Think of a product, service, or consumable item that you have acquired or plan to acquire. Next, read the statements in the Motiquiz II and mark those that explain why you have made or plan to make the acquisition. Then review the selected statements and circle the numbers of those that most honestly represent your feelings.

Maslow's Hierarchy of Needs

In making the selections, you have identified those statements that represent your needs, based on the motivational theory of Abraham Maslow. The statements are intended to represent the five levels of Maslow's Hierarchy of Needs, illustrated in Exhibit 5. The first digit in each statement number indicates the category. These categories are 1—Physiological, 2—Safety-security, 3—Love-belonging, 4—Self-esteem, and 5—Self-actualization. Your purchase motivations are suggested by the statement categories.

As an example, assume that Mary has just purchased a new car and selected statement numbers 423, 519, 497, 564, 543, 527, and 172.

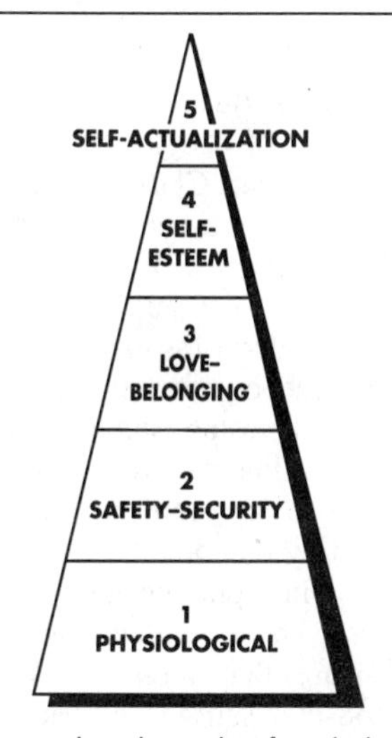

EXHIBIT 5. Maslow's Hierarchy of Needs

Intense job challenge, full potential, full expression, creative expression.

Achievement, respect, recognition, responsibility, prestige, independence, attention, importance, appreciation.

Belonging, acceptance, love, affection, family and group acceptance, friendships.

Security, stability, dependency, protection, need for structure, order, law, tenure, pension, insurance.

Hunger, thirst, reproduction, shelter, clothing, air, rest.

Maslow's hierarchy of needs depicts the five levels of human need as theorized by Abraham Maslow. Most individuals will exhibit needs from the higher levels of the hierarchy. This assumes that the basic needs—physiological and safety-security—have been satisfied. Maslow contended that a person's needs transcend—as lower order needs are satisfied, higher order needs develop.

Why do you think Mary bought the car? What kind of car do you think Mary bought (an economy car, a sports vehicle, a station wagon for the family, etc.)?

If you guessed a sports vehicle, you were probably right, but why? If we analyze the statements we find them to be in the following categories:

- Physiological needs: 172
- Self-esteem needs: 423 and 497
- Self-actualization needs: 519, 564, 543, and 527.

The four selections in Maslow's category of self-actualization suggest a value set to self-actualize—in Mary's case, to do her thing. The two selections in the self-esteem category suggest some concern for respect, recognition, independence, attention, and importance. In other words, when Mary parks the car in the company parking lot or the driveway to her home, she wants everyone to see her new sports car. The single choice of a physiological selection could suggest the need for physical comfort but could also be construed as being a need for a pleasant mental feeling, another form of physical comfort.

Obviously, the Motiquiz approach is not fool proof, but it does help one to understand and appreciate what we are talking about in marketing when we refer to needs and wants.

Needs and Wants

The relationship between needs and wants is illustrated in Exhibit 6 for "you and me," the consumer, and "groups of people," the usual situation in a commercial or industrial situation. Clarifying these relationships is important in developing a targeted marketing effort so that one has a clear understanding of the target audience. When dealing with an individual consumer, one can begin to think about the individual's purchase motivations and use this criteria for planning and implementing the marketing effort. In the case of a commercial or industrial customer, the target audience will be the establishments, with the primary needs being related to the establishments—for example, relating to a target company's business purpose, mission, or financial criteria. Usually growth is a desirable secondary outcome.

The individuals within a company come into play because of the contact relationships in the marketing process. The individuals must be contacted and properly dealt with to ensure that their needs are recognized and satisfied—suggesting a counselor selling approach. In both the case of individual and company customers, it is imperative that the process include consideration of the criteria suggested in Exhibit 6.

In total, the marketing process will involve identifying and understanding needs, transforming these to wants, and completing the process by providing satisfaction from the delivered benefits. In the

EXHIBIT 6. Relationship of Needs and Wants

	Customer Type	
	Consumer "you and me"	**Commercial/ Industrial "groups of people"**
Needs For *vitality and growth* of the organism	• Physiological • Safety-security • Love-belonging • Self-esteem • Self-actualization + Growth	• Attain business purpose and mission • Economic-sales, profit, roi, etc. + Growth (needs of individuals are involved)
Wants Expressed desires	• Products and Services	• Products and services
Satisfactions The result	• Benefits . . . satisfaction of needs	• Benefits . . . satisfaction of needs

Source: © Dick Berry.

majority of cases, satisfaction does not result unless the product or service offering is surrounded by appropriate presale and postsale service offerings.

PURCHASE BEHAVIOR

Understanding Purchase Behavior

It is useful to understand the relationship of human needs to the behavioral process. The human behavior model, Exhibit 7, will be used to develop this understanding. Let us return to Mary and her purchase of a sports car, assuming she has purchased the car. We note that her behavior was predicted by her needs or, conversely, that her behavior exhibits the needs. In both cases, we assume that the Motiquiz selections were reasonably accurate portrayals of her needs.

For the purchase behavior to occur, Mary needed to go through a process of need arousal, as suggested by Maslow's need satisfaction theory. Additionally, Mary's need to purchase the car is the result of a goal-setting process that can be explained by the so-called expectancy theory of human behavior. This theory, simply stated, suggests that "what can be, will be." If it is within the realm of reality for Mary to set and attain a goal to buy a new sports car, and she is so motivated, then it is quite likely that she will buy the car. Contrast this to an individual that lives in a ghetto and is financially strapped—then "what can be" is not likely to include purchasing an expensive sports car.

EXHIBIT 7. Human Behavior Model

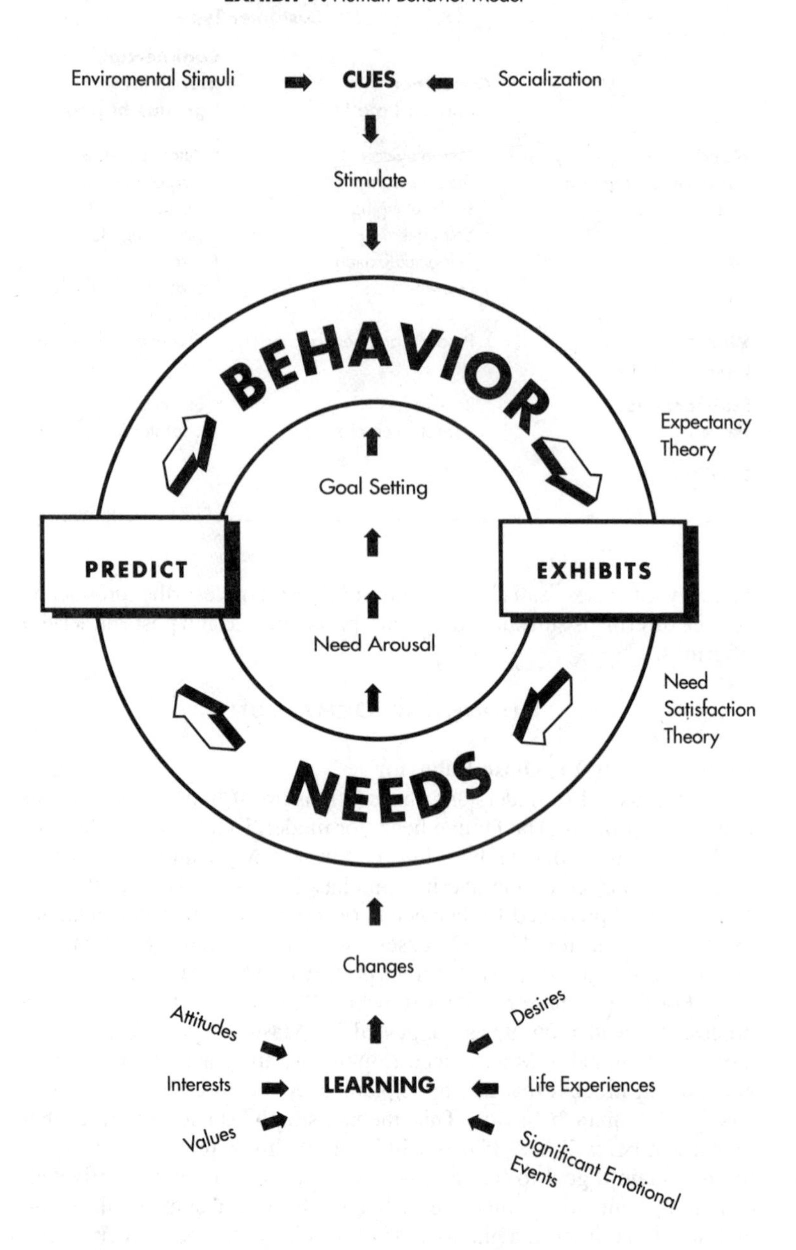

Source: Dick Berry, 1984.

Other aspects of the model are useful in explaining how the specific purchase process works and how one's needs and behavior are altered. Looking at the upper portion of the model, we note that cues stimulate behavior. This is suggestive of the promotional process in marketing. Environmental stimuli could include advertising and publicity messages—for example, a billboard illustration of a sports car. Socialization could include Mary interacting with someone else who has a sports car or, perhaps, with a sales representative, attempting to sell a car to Mary. With regard to the latter, assume how beneficial it would be to the salesperson to understand Mary's underlying motivational needs.

Role of Learning in Purchase Behavior

From the marketing vantage point, another important aspect of behavior will occur after Mary purchases the new car. The purchase will have an impact on her attitudes, interests, and values, probably altering her need system and future behavior. For example, because the new car will become a significant part of her life, she will experience desires that need to be satisfied. It could be that the car has a tape player and she will have a desire for new musical recordings or to explore other offerings, such as better speakers. Thus she will begin to exhibit new behaviors.

Certainly the new car purchase can be looked at as a significant emotional event, with strong impact on her life-style and relationships with others—once again leading to newly emerging needs and behaviors. All of these changes are of importance to the marketing professional who is attempting to sort out information and to plan and implement new marketing programs.

MARKETING STRATEGY AND TACTICS

The Marketing Mix

The archives of marketing contain a multitude of stories and anecdotes about marketing practices and principles. Probably two of the most significant of these are the following:

- Marketers as chefs: presents the notion that marketers concoct menus that formulate combinations of the marketing variables to yield desirable results; and
- The four Ps: suggests that marketers employ four basic variables, designated as the marketing mix, in their work as chefs. The four variables are product, place, price, and promotion.

These ideas—the concepts of marketers as chefs and the four Ps—have been very useful and important in the evolution of marketing. In the following sections, we will build on these conceptualizations as we deal with the notions of marketing strategy and tactics.

A problem with one of the stories became evident to the author about twenty years ago when dealing with presale and postsale services as marketing variables. In suggesting the four Ps, there was the implication that the marketing mix would be limited to the four variables starting with the letter P. If one were to ask, "What about customer service offerings or postsale service support—as warranty services?" the implied response was, "They are part of the product." This, however, does not account for the importance of presale and postsale services when dealing with industrial and commercial product and service offerings. In my understanding, the four Ps version of the marketing mix was introduced by academicians who had a heavy orientation toward consumer goods, as compared to industrial and commercial products. The ideas of presale and postsale customer services are not very evident in this environment, so their response was somewhat acceptable—particularly if they did not want to contradict one of the foundation stones of marketing thought.

In my own work, I have suggested that the marketing mix include four Ps and an S, as we will now discuss in developing the notions of marketing strategy and tactics.

Marketing Doorways to Success

Of critical importance in any marketing effort is success. But how do we measure success? In some situations, it is simply product or service sales, for example, automobiles or real estate. In other situations, it may be a matter of winning over a customer, as in industrial sales where a single customer account may be valued at millions of dollars in repeat sales. In other cases, success comes when a company gains market superiority, with increasing market share or greater share of market, as in consumer goods marketing. In recessive periods, the simple outcome of "staying in business" often spells success. Probably the criteria of significance in most companies is when sales and profitability are as planned.

A company's approach to success is usually to achieve a proper mixture or balance of the strategic and tactical marketing variables, thus overcoming competitive effort and gaining increasing customer allegiance and market share. We will use this frame of reference, exploring approaches to macromarketing and micromarketing using the marketing mix variables.

Going back to the notion that marketers are chefs, let us first go to the cupboard and see what ingredients we have with which to bake our success cake. As shown in Exhibit 8, there are two doors on the cupboard. On the left is marketing strategy and on the right is marketing tactics. It is useful to keep this separation in mind, thinking of marketing strategy as macromarketing and marketing tactics as micromarketing. The importance of this becomes important as one deals with the marketing variables in the context of interacting with various other people in an organization—each with different perspec-

EXHIBIT 8. Marketing Doorways to Success

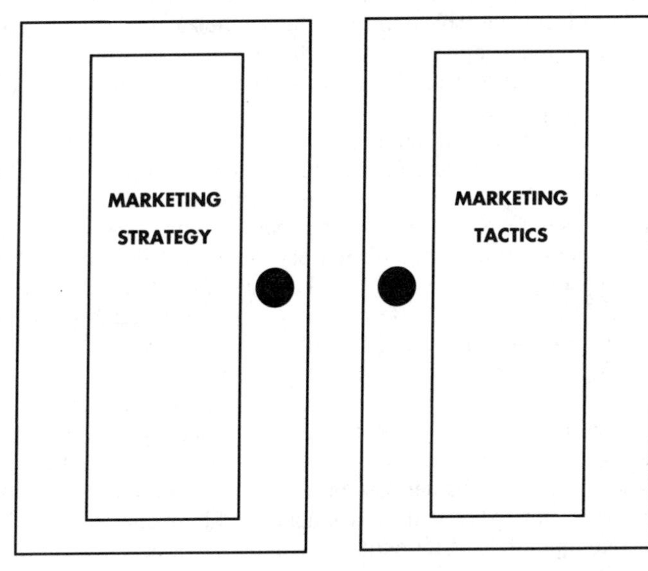

Source: Dick Berry, 1991.

tives of what marketing is all about. The big part of marketing is to use the marketing strategy variables to establish direction and position for a company. The tactical variables are used to tailor a program or plan to reach a specific target audience or to offset competitive effort. Usually most of the variables will be employed, but the balance and emphasis make the difference.

The Marketing Cupboard

Within the cupboard doors we see the strategic variables (ingredients) on the left and tactical variables on the right. Let us first consider an example of how a company sets its direction and position in the marketplace by emphasizing one or more of the strategic variables, such as product, place, price, promotion, or service.

Marketing Strategy and Positioning

In a previous section, the ScotTissue example was highlighted, illustrating how Scott Paper Company appears to be focusing its promotional effort on softness and absorbency, long-lasting characteristics, easy start roll with starter tab, and safety for septic systems. With this information and other background knowledge about the company, it becomes apparent that Scott is using product, place, and promotion as its primary strategic variables. Most of the features and benefits alluded to in the promotional copy relate to product offerings, thus the emphasis on product. The fact that the features and benefits are emphasized, in the toilet tissue's packaging and other promotional efforts, supports the notion that Scott is emphasizing promotion to gain consumer acceptance. Because of the nature of the product and mode of distribution through the retail grocery channel, it is apparent that place is an important strategic variable. But what about price and service?

If one looks at the price for the ScotTissue products on grocery shelves, it becomes apparent that they have a definite price differential as compared to competitive offerings. They are often higher priced by a factor of 30 to 100 percent. Thus they are probably enjoying good margins and profitability but are not using price to gain position and advantage. As far as service is concerned, it is appropriate to say that they may be offering good customer services to the channel members, but there is no special service consideration as far as the consumers are concerned. In summary, toilet tissue has obviously become a commodity item, where low price is usually emphasized by manufacturers. But Scott is attempting to differentiate its ScotTissue as a value-added offering, not as a commodity item, thus positioning it on the high end of the toilet tissue continuum.

As part of this same discourse, what is American Airlines' strategy—as we look back at the previously discussed newspaper advertisement and compare its positioning to other carriers in the airline industry? It would appear that American is attempting to add related offerings to the basic flight services—a product emphasis. The efforts the airline is making relative to scope of services, hassle-free terminal operations, and on-time flights suggests that it has a service emphasis that is "beyond the product." Add to this the promotional emphasis, as evidenced by the newspaper ad, and it begins to appear that it is positioning itself with a strategic combination consisting of product, service, and promotion. Considering the breadth of coverage in the United States and Caribbean areas, with considerable emphasis on destinations served—seventy-three destinations from Nashville alone—it is clear that the airline is also giving considerable emphasis on place considerations as part of its positioning strategy. In the final analysis, it appears that it is emphasizing all strategic variables except price—probably in hopes that it will increase customer traffic, gain market share, and enjoy relatively high margins and profitability, as compared to the competition. Does this sound like a sound marketing approach for an airline company in the 1990s? How about Scott Paper Company's approach?

Marketing Tactics

Tactical marketing cannot be separated from strategic marketing since they are both part of the same game plan. If strategic marketing is the "what," then tactical marketing becomes the "how." For example, if American Airlines decides that strategic emphasis will be given to promotion, then the question becomes, "How will we do it so that our campaigns will be successful, accomplishing specific marketing objectives?"

Referring to Exhibit 9, we note that the various tactical marketing variables are advertising, publicity, and the selling approach. In the interface with customers, American probably can best achieve its air traffic goals by concentrating on media that will reach its target audience, communicating the desired messages effectively. The techniques would best include a publicity campaign to get as much "free advertising" as possible. Thus its public relations staff will write and release appropriate messages to the various media. This would include radio, television, the magazine press, and the news press. If America's story is truly newsworthy, it might schedule a public relations conference, inviting various media representatives to attend. The other part of the advertising campaign will be to budget and schedule various advertisements in the media that would best reach and communicate to the target audience. In the example already mentioned, American chose the newspaper media, with full-page black and white advertisements. Chances are the ads only ran in major newspapers in the southern U.S. markets because of the Nashville hub reference and copy that related to the southern markets. It is also quite likely that the ads ran in *USA Today,* because of the appropriateness of this newspaper to the target audience.

As illustrated in Exhibit 9, the following tactical choices are suggested for the five strategic designations:

- Product: features, reliability, and quality (reliability would be replaced by dependability for a service offering);
- Service: presale service, postsale service, and nonsale service;
- Place: delivery system, locations, facilities;
- Price: price itself, pricing terms, and pricing offers; and
- Promotion: advertising, publicity, and selling.

In executing the desired marketing strategy, the marketing team would select its ingredients from these selections in the marketing cupboard and then bake its cake to achieve desired results. It is useful at this time to reflect on the ScotTissiue and American Airlines programs, thinking about the appropriate tactical choices employed by each of the companies.

In the final analysis, it is most important to realize that the strategic and tactical choices should be made with an understanding of

EXHIBIT 9. The Marketing Cupboard

MARKETING STRATEGY	MARKETING TACTICS
Product	Product Features Product Quality Product Reliability
Service	Presale Service Postsale Service Nonsale Service
Price	Price Itself Pricing Terms Pricing Offers
Place	Delivery System Locations Facilities
Promotion	Advertising Publicity Selling Approach

Source: Dick Berry, 1991.

the marketplace, particularly to have a clear picture of the needs and wants within the target market as well as to understand the positioning of competitors.

CUSTOMER PERCEPTIONS AND THE PRODUCT CONCEPT

Product Concept

The term *product concept* is one that the author has employed for many years as a way to describe the totality of product features and benefits as perceived by the customer. This is inaccurate because the customer sees beyond the product—or service offering—to include aspects of the place, price, promotion, and service that are of consequence. When thinking about a product or service offering, the customer individualizes the product concept as a perception (Exhibit 10). This perception will be relative to competitive offerings and will include both positive and negative characteristics. No two persons have the same perception of the concept. The terms *brand image* and *brand identity profile* have been used similarly to product concept to describe the halo of psychological meanings and feelings that a company

EXHIBIT 10. Product Concept

"The totality of product features and benefits as perceived by the customer."

- Name of the product (or service if a service offering)
- Manufacturer's characteristics and credibility
- Features of the product
- Publicity on the product
- Advertising and collateral material on the product
- Supplier and sales representative
- Word-of-mouth comments about the product
- Historical predecessors of the product from manufacturer
- Price asked for the product
- Price product is sold for
- The way the product is packaged
- The way the product is displayed
- Comparison to other products
- Usefulness of the product
- Service support for the product
- Whether the product is used individually or as a part of a system
- Difficulty or ease of adoption and use

Each customer individualizes a product concept of a *perception*. No two persons have the same perception of the concept.

Source: Dick Berry, 1984.

generates relative to a product or service offering and the array of information and variables that relate to the offering.

It is extremely important for a manufacturer, or other type of provider, to try and have a clear picture of the product concept that it is offering its customers. Not having this awareness can result in serious shortcomings in achieving the desired level of success in its marketing effort. Thus it is important to stand back and look at the marketing effort from the customer perspective to see if changes should be made.

To better realize the importance of the product concept, let us put ourselves in the position of the provider of a health food item called ProLife Acidophilus (PA). The product is composed of friendly bacteria that are encapsulated, bottled (70 capsules per bottle), and offered for sale to health food consumers looking for a supplement to enhance performance of their intestinal systems. The product offsets the deleterious effect of so-called unfriendly bacteria that cause a variety of problems, including constipation, yeast infections, gaseousness, and diverticulosis. The benefits of ingesting PA are essentially the same that result from eating yogurt but with much greater effect. The product is also extremely beneficial to offset the intestinal imbalance that results from taking antibiotic products. The product is sold in a refrigerated package and has a much higher concentration of friendly bacteria than competitive acidophilus-based products.

The provider of PA, HealthLine Products Incorporated, plans to market PA by placing ads in health-related publications, in the form of a coupon and phone number, offering a bottle of the product at a price of $17.95. Alternately, HealthLine Products plans to offer PA through wholesalers at a discount of 50 percent. To support the sales effort, the company will provide a descriptive brochure that highlights product characteristics and nutritional benefits (The Food and Drug Administration does not allow medical claims). The brochure copy will contain several references to various aspects of the bacterial content of the product, the nature of bacterial imbalance problems in the intestinal system, benefits of using PA, and discussion of the functions of the intestinal system, colon, and rectum. Competitors' unrefrigerated products are deemed ineffective by Healthline Products.

Competitive products are offered principally in health-food stores, both in the unrefrigerated and refrigerated packaging, usually without reference to the bacterial content of the product but identifying the class of bacteria contained—Lactobacillus acidophilus—and relying on common knowledge and health-related publications to communicate their desirable aspects. Prices of the established products in health food stores and drug stores are in the neighborhood of $4.50 for 60 unrefrigerated capsules and $7.50 for 100 capsules. Competitive products have appropriate brand names, and reference materials are made available in the health food stores. These publications tend to talk about nutrition and microorganisms, with occasional reference to bacterial aspects of the products and the unfriendly microorganisms in human intestines.

What do think, as a prospective consumer? How do you visualize the product concept for HealthLine Product's ProLife Acidophilus? Referencing the various strategic and tactical variables, what strengths and weaknesses do you see? Will it be successful? What would you do differently if you were marketing director for HealthLine Products?

HOW THE PRODUCT/MARKET SYSTEM WORKS

The Product/Market System

In an attempt to draw a picture of marketing, the illustration in Exhibit 11 was created. It serves the useful purpose of illustrating, in a general way, the various areas of marketing concern to be considered in strategic and tactical planning and analysis. On the left side of the illustration is a typical market with a designated market segment and customer. In the marketing effort an attempt is made to identify with the customer needs and wants and then, through management analysis and planning, to select appropriate strategic and tactical variables, as illustrated on the right side of the diagram. If the analysis and planning effort is carried out advantageously, the provider of the product or service will communicate perceived value and utility to the target market segment, and the customer will receive delivered benefits and satisfactions.

This construct has proven to be particularly useful as a reference checklist in diagnosing marketing problem situations and in developing marketing plans and programs. The footnotes on the illustration serve to point out some of the differences in terminology and the application in service marketing, as compared to product marketing. The main point is that such a reference can be extremely useful in dialoguing with executive groups and planning teams—involving persons who may not be familiar with or well informed in marketing terminology and relationships.

What Is the Problem?

To illustrate the use of the product/market system illustration, let us consider HealthLine Products and its proposed new product PA—looking at the proposal to offer PA through wholesalers to the health food market. To begin your analysis, visualize the product concept and shortcomings of the proposed program. Start out by identifying the market segment, the "typical customer," and what the needs and wants might be. Then consider the product offering and other strategic and tactical variables as proposed by HealthLine Products. Be sure to give attention to the competitive and environmental influences. Does it help

EXHIBIT 11. The Product Market System

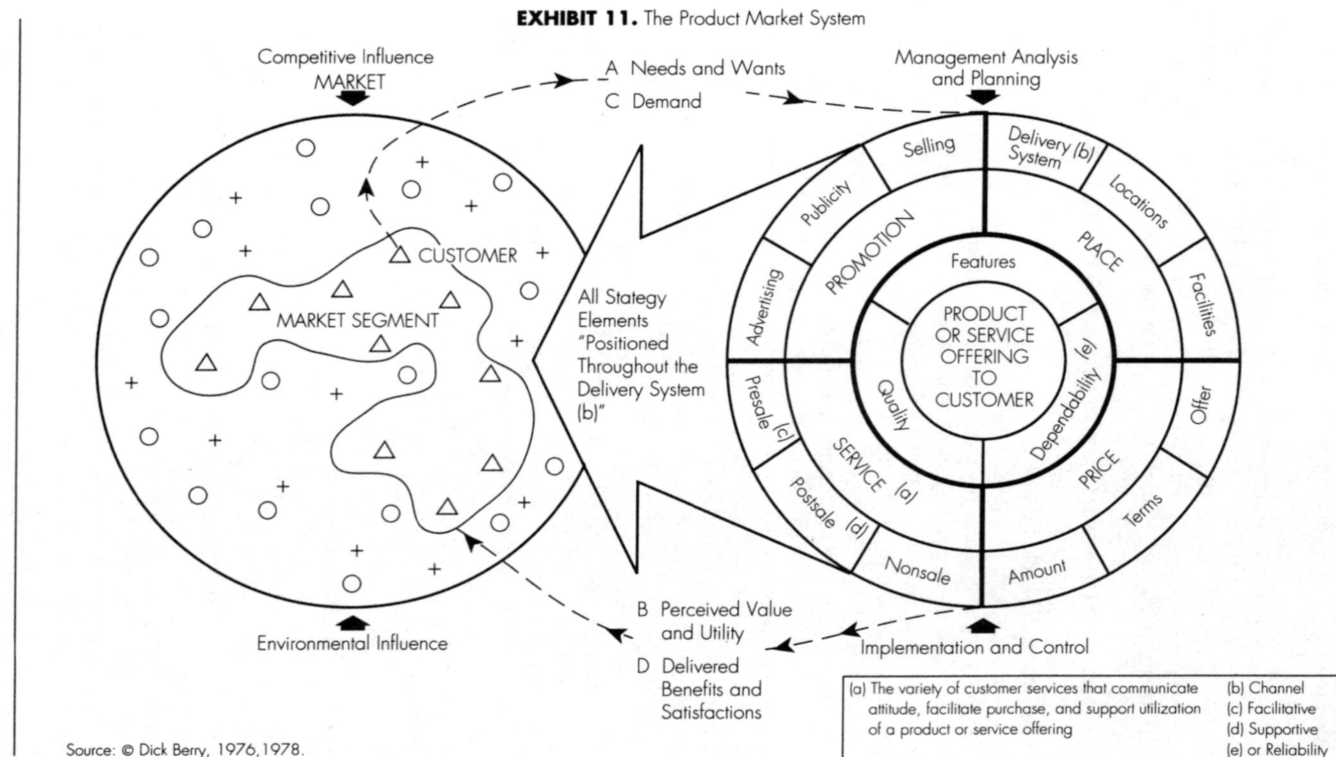

Source: © Dick Berry, 1976, 1978.

you to use the diagram in your analysis? Are the opportunity and related marketing concerns coming into sharper focus? What needs to be done in terms of positioning the strategic and tactical elements throughout the delivery system? In other words, what will the distributors and stores do in the marketing effort, and how will HealthLine Products support them?

MARKET SEGMENTATION, NICHING, AND TARGETING

Framework for Market Segmentation

The critical requirement in any marketing effort is to properly identify with the market being served and to communicate and distribute effectively to the target market. In broad terms, most marketing efforts are directed to a segment that is identified by several characteristics, such as the Standard Industrial Classification (a U.S. government designation), the geographic area being served, the product or service offering, and the buying characteristics of the designated market (Exhibit 12). A wide variety of government publications are available to assist in this classification, and this is usually the starting point for

EXHIBIT 12. Framework for Market Segmentation

Product Characteristics
- Product Type
- Distinguishing Characteristics

Geographic Characteristics
- Region
- Metro/rural
- Climatic

Buying Characteristics
- Mode of Distribution
- Servicing Requirements
- Terms . . . lease/buy

Market Characteristics
- SIC Primary Group
- SIC Product Class

Source: © Dick Berry.

segmentation. Beyond this, the segmentation variables are usually somewhat specific for the company itself, particularly if one is talking about consumer products for a specific type of customer, designated by the geographic area or location, as a retail trading area.

Niching

Putting various of the previously described combinations together results in the practice of niching. In niching, a company such as HealthLine Products will visualize a variety of product-market combinations, designated as niches, with tailoring of the marketing effort to each niche. As an example, HealthLine Products might desire to market PA to older adults, through promotion in adult-oriented publications, on a national basis with sales offers through a coupon advertisement. This would be a niche that would differ from the sale of PA through independent sales agents to health food stores in the Midwestern states, anticipating purchase by health advocates, another niche.

Targeting

Targeting is usually thought of as directing the marketing effort to a specific, well-defined market segment. Considering the broad variety and scope of promotional media and geographic coverage, targeting is extremely important in controlling cost-related aspects of a marketing effort.

CUSTOMER SATISFACTION AND THE NEW MARKETING

Restocking the Marketing Cupboard

In the early 1990s, the author has been conducting research to determine the changing nature of marketing effort—particularly successful marketing approaches. This has included studies on the nature of the marketing mix and customer satisfaction variables employed in the practices of marketing professionals. As a result of this effort, the marketing cupboard has been revised to include the variables shown in Exhibit 13. The most important realization from this work is that customer-related factors have jumped to the forefront in the minds and efforts of marketers as they strive to achieve marketing results and to deliver customer satisfaction.

In determining the shift in emphasis, a national mail survey was conducted of senior executives, marketing managers and professionals, customer service managers, and product support managers. The respondents were asked to rate the importance of the previously described strategic and tactical marketing variables and customer satisfaction criteria in their continuing marketing activities.

EXHIBIT 13. The Marketing Cupboard, Part 2

MARKETING STRATEGY	MARKETING TACTICS
Customer Treatment	Employee Attitude Customer Treatment Response to Customers
Product	Product Quality Product Reliability Product Features
Customer Convenience	Customer Availability Customer Convenience Selling Approach
Service	Postsale Service Presale Service Customer Convenience
Price	Price Itself Pricing Terms Pricing Offers
Place	Accessibility of Provider Provider Facilities Customer Availability
Promotion	Advertising Publicity Selling Approach Pricing Offers

Source: Dick Berry, 1991.

One of the most exciting findings of the work resulted from using a research process called *factor analysis* to see how the variables grouped in importance and in relationship to one another. In effect, this resulted in the suggestion of a new marketing mix, as shown in Exhibit 13. It is thought that those who are following trends and practices in marketing will feel comfortable with the new combinations.

The New Marketing Mix

The marketing mix for the 1990s appears to have four Ps, an S, and two Cs. The configuration, arranged in order of importance, as suggested by the research findings and factor analysis, is as follows:

- Customer sensitivity: employee attitude, customer treatment, and response to customers;
- Product: product quality, reliability, and features (the reliability variable would be thought of as dependability of a service offering);
- Customer convenience: customer availability, customer convenience, and selling approach;
- Service: postsale service, presale service, and customer convenience;
- Price: price itself, pricing terms, and pricing offers;
- Place: accessibility of provider, provider facilities, and customer availability; and
- Promotion: advertising, publicity, selling, presale services, and pricing offers.

As you look through this list thinking about your experiences in marketing, does it seem important that customer-related factors are at the top of the list and that they should be strongly considered in devising marketing strategy and tactics for a marketing plan or program? The answer is obviously *yes.* Hopefully this evolving information will provide guidelines for you in your work and studies in marketing.

Where Do You Go from Here?

The first part of your marketing curriculum has been prepared and arranged to provide information and guidelines as to the nature of marketing efforts and practices. The following materials contain detailed information and suggestions to plan and carry out marketing programs—to identify and satisfy customer needs and wants. Good luck with your experiences and explorations in marketing!

Stanley F. Stasch
The Charles H. Kellstadt Professor of
Marketing
Loyola University of Chicago

Howard L. Gordon
Principal, GRFI Ltd.
Chicago, Illinois

CHAPTER 2

MARKETING SYSTEMS: IMPLICATIONS FOR MARKETING PLANNING

Firms in the United States utilize marketing systems that vary from the relatively simple to those that are quite complex. Executives should recognize that most marketing activities form a part of a larger marketing system, and they should attempt to understand the role played by each activity in helping the overall marketing system achieve its objectives. With such an understanding, they will be better prepared to develop effective marketing plans that will help their firms attain their objectives.

Most marketing-oriented firms sell their products in many different markets. Because such situations are especially conducive to helping marketing executives learn more about the marketing systems they employ, the following discussions assume such a marketing situation. Additionally, two assumptions are that (1) the manufacturer's product quality is comparable to competition's, and (2) the products involved are not new, but ones that have been available for at least a year or two.

Marketing systems come in a variety of forms, five of which are discussed in this chapter. The marketing executive must be interested in these different system forms because they represent alternative choices to a decision that must be considered from time to time. Therefore, marketing executives must be able to recognize these different forms, to understand the variation in complexity they represent, and to understand the planning implications associated with the varying degrees of complexity. In the following discussions, each system is displayed symbolically with the product's manufacturer on the left, the final buyer of the product on the right, and all other system participants in between. Each participant's marketing efforts are also shown symbolically in the illustrations.

INDUSTRIAL PRODUCTS

Perhaps the most simple system is that utilized by the manufacturers whose products are used up—that is, consumed—during the production of some other product. For example, steel producers sell to office furniture manufacturers and chemical processing firms sell to detergent manufacturers. The system typically used by such firms may be similar to that illustrated in Exhibit 1. The manufacturer's principal marketing stimuli are sales calls made by the sales force, the price, and the speed and reliability of delivery time. In recent years, more manufacturers are offering their customers computerized reordering capabilities, which give the customers the added benefit of faster response to their orders, and which help the customers reduce their costs of carrying inventory.

EXHIBIT 1. System for an Industrial Goods Producer

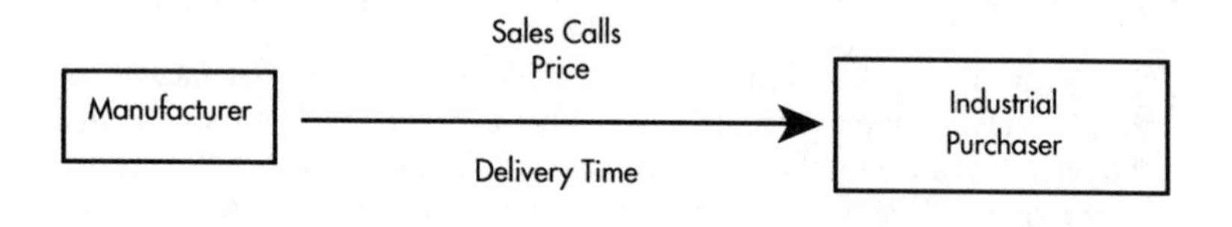

For economic reasons, in the last five years or so, U.S. companies have been cutting back on staff and other personnel and generally downsizing in a variety of ways. Because managers in such companies are now finding that their own time has become a more scarce commodity, the effect of such downsizing has been that companies are looking to outside sources for products and services and expertise that they used to handle in-house. The outside sources most likely to be successful will probably be the companies that can supply the products, services, and expertise the downsized companies are looking for.

The overall effect for the downsized companies is that their managers want to use their time to concentrate on managing high-value activities that are likely to yield the good streams of revenues needed to build the business. This, in turn, means that these companies will place greater reliance on their suppliers and other outside sources in order to run their businesses successfully. They will want better relationships with fewer suppliers, but these relationships will be based on high-value, quality services, as well as on lasting and trusting commitments between seller and buyer.

It seems likely that these types of relationships will develop between all business-to-business marketing situations over the next five to ten years. During the following descriptions of the marketing systems presented in Exhibits 3, 4, and 5, the reader should bear in mind that the developments described in the previous two paragraphs probably apply to all of the business-to-business situations found in those marketing systems.

VERTICALLY INTEGRATED CONSUMER GOODS

Some manufacturers of consumer goods—men's shoes and suits, for example—market their products through their own retail stores. Exhibit 2 shows that such a system can be more complex than that used by the industrial product manufacturer discussed in the above paragraphs. Since the retail outlet is owned by the manufacturer, the latter does not have to expend marketing effort on the former. Instead, the manufacturer—through the retail outlet—uses as marketing stimuli the store's location, price, and advertising to attract consumers to its products.

EXHIBIT 2. System for Vertically Integrated Manufacturer

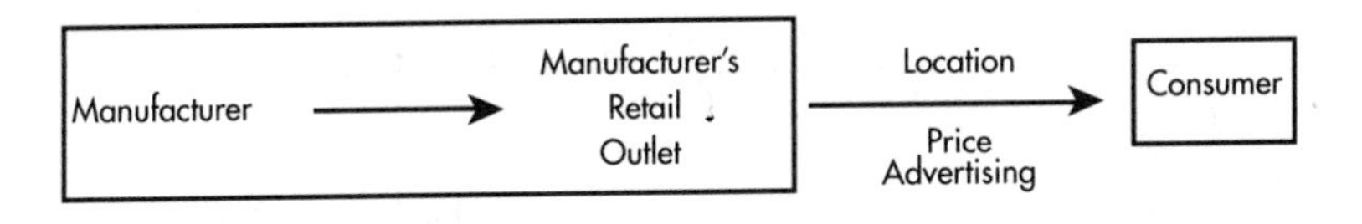

EXHIBIT 3. System Using Independent Retailers

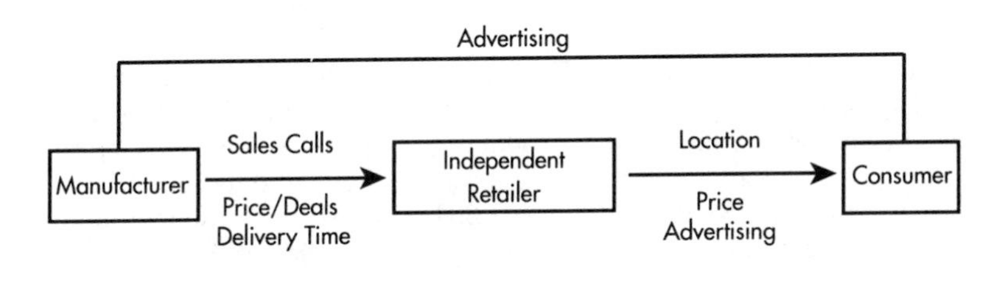

SYSTEM WITH ONE INDEPENDENT MIDDLEMAN

An even more complex system is the one used by some manufacturers of electrical appliances. Instead of using their own retail outlets, as in Exhibit 2, most appliance manufacturers sell their products to independent retailers, who then sell to consumers. Exhibit 3 illustrates such a system. In this case, the manufacturer applies different marketing stimuli toward each of the two-system participants—sales calls, price/deals, and delivery time toward the retailer and advertising toward the consumer. As before, the retailer employs store location, price, and advertising to attract consumers. The increased complexity of the system, compared to the one in the previous paragraph, involves a second set of marketing efforts *in series* with the retailer's marketing efforts and the *parallel* advertising effort used by the manufacturer.

SYSTEM USING CHAIN RETAILER

A fourth system is one that is used by many package food producers who sell through chain organizations. The type of system they use is illustrated in Exhibit 4. Although this system is similar to the one discussed above, it represents greater complexity from the manufacturer's point of view due to the fact that the latter is now separated from the final consumer by the chain's wholesaling and retailing operations.

In recent years, two new developments have occurred in these types of systems. One is that the chain organizations have gained such economic power that they can now demand that manufacturers pay them a fee (called "slotting fees") for just providing them with retail

EXHIBIT 4. System for Items Sold Through Chains

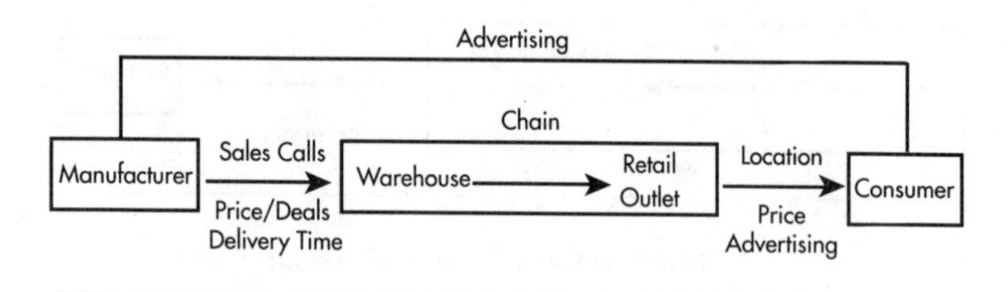

shelf space for their products. The second development is that a number of large package food manufacturers have begun to develop computerized databases of the names and addresses of consumers of their products. They then use the databases to promote directly to those people—usually by mail. Such firms believe that doing so will result in more efficient promotions, compared to using mass media.

SYSTEM WITH TWO INDEPENDENT MIDDLEMEN

Exhibit 5 illustrates a fifth system—one involving a manufacturer, an independent wholesaler, an independent retailer, and the consumer. Such a system is commonly used for nonfood consumer products. Although similar to the two previous systems, it represents an additional degree of complexity due to the introduction of a new set of marketing stimuli between the wholesaler and the retailer. Because of the system's manufacturer-to-consumer length and because of the sets of series and parallel marketing stimuli, this system is the most complex of those discussed here.

Two recent developments that have had an effect on such systems are the great increase in the number of print and over-the-air communication media and improved distribution technology. The increase in the number of communication media has made the manufacturer's advertising task a much more difficult one than it has been in the past, when fewer media vehicles were available and each media vehicle tended to reach a broad market. Improved computers, software, and electronic and computerized communication devices now allow much greater coordination and cooperation between the inventories held by retailers, wholesalers, and manufacturers in such systems, with the added benefits that inventory costs tend to be reduced while delivery times tend to be shortened.

Still other systems of even greater complexity could be discussed here if space permitted. These five systems should be sufficient, however, to illustrate that marketing systems come in different forms with varying complexity and that the system's complexity has important planning implications for the marketing executive.

Exhibit 5. System Using Two Independent Middlemen

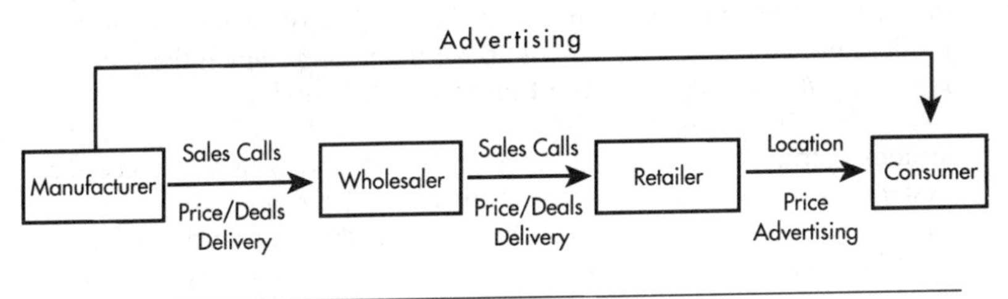

Exhibit 6. Consumer Package Good System

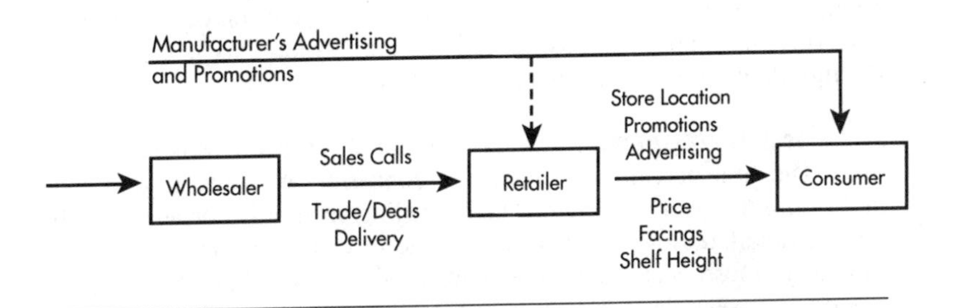

SYSTEM STRUCTURE AND SYSTEM INTERRELATIONSHIPS

After the executive has identified the type of marketing system being used, he or she must delve further into its structure and into the various interrelationships that must be known in order to develop effective marketing plans. For example, consider a consumer package good being sold through a system of independent wholesalers and retailers. Part of such a system is illustrated in Exhibit 6.

The retailer's purchase decision in this system is directly influenced by the wholesaler's sales calls, whatever trade deals might be offered, and delivery capabilities. The retailer's decision may also be indirectly influenced by the manufacturer's consumer-directed advertising and promotions. If all other things are equal, the retailer may feel that it is advantageous to buy larger quantities of a product that is more heavily advertised and promoted. Or, if the choice is between two products similar in all other respects, the retailer may choose to stock only the more heavily promoted one.

The consumer in this system is subjected to a number of marketing stimuli. The manufacturer's advertising and promotions—coupons, cents off, etc.—attempt to influence the consumer's purchase decision. The retailer, through store location and advertising and promotion, will try to attract the consumer to his or her store. Once in the store, the consumer's decision to purchase or not to purchase the manufacturer's product will be influenced by price, the number of facings given the product by the retailer, the height above the floor at which the product is displayed, and the presence of an in-store promotion.

This brief discussion illustrates the detail needed within the system's structure and the interrelationships found within it. Once the system's structure and interrelationships have been properly and carefully detailed, the executive can begin to concentrate on those things (that is, marketing stimuli) that must be included in the product's marketing plan in order to encourage all system participants to function properly on behalf of the firm's product. In order to do the best job of planning, the executive must know which marketing stimuli can be applied to the various participants and how the participants will perform when those various stimuli are employed. This is essentially the input/output aspect of marketing systems.

INPUT/OUTPUT OF SYSTEM PARTICIPANTS

The first part of this chapter is concerned with identifying and describing the overall system. The preceding section is concerned with a more detailed view of the system—one in which the structure of the system is more accurately described, especially the interrelationships existing between various system participants. This section is concerned with the input/output relationships associated with each system participant—that is, how each system participant transforms the inputs it receives (marketing stimuli) into the output it generates (how it performs after having received certain marketing stimuli).

Exhibit 6 is an enlarged view of portions of the system illustrated in Exhibit 5. In trying to understand input/output relationships of system participants, it is helpful to work with an even bigger enlargement of each of the participants shown in Exhibit 6. In the following paragraph, an enlarged view of the consumer as an input/output participant will be discussed. This discussion is followed by a similar view and discussion of the retailer.

Consumer Input/Output

The consumer who purchases a package good represents a system participant whose output is a purchase. This same consumer has probably been subjected to all or most of the inputs illustrated in Exhibit 7. For example, the consumer patronizes the retailer's store partly due to its location, the retailer's overall advertising and promotion, and other reasons. Once the consumer is in the store, the decision to purchase a particular brand of product may be influenced by the price set by the retailer, the number of facings displayed, the shelf height of the display, and in-store promotion. In addition, the consumer's purchase decision may have been influenced prior to the shopping trip by

EXHIBIT 7. The Consumer as an Input/Output Participant

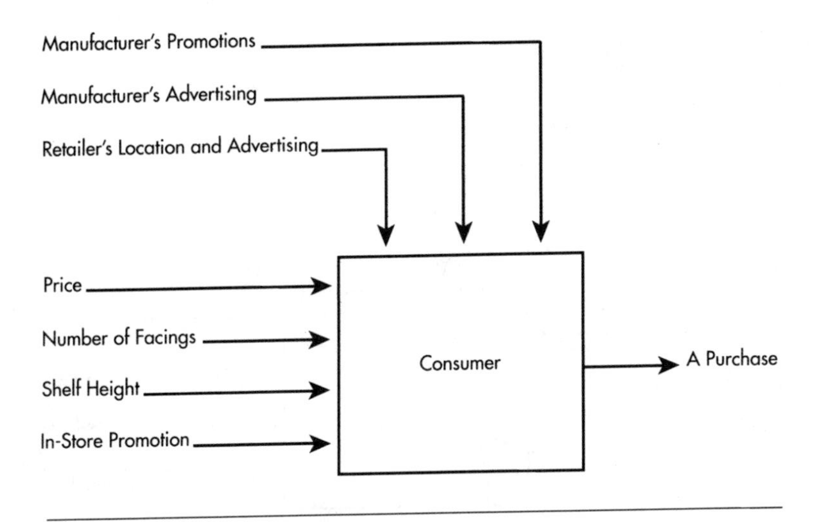

the manufacturer's advertising, which may have caused in the consumer an awareness of and perhaps even preference for the manufacturer's brand. If the manufacturer is using a coupon or cents-off promotion, the consumer may even begin a shopping trip with the intention of making a trial purchase. Thus the consumer may receive as few as two or three inputs or as many as six or eight inputs that are then somehow transformed into one output—a purchase.

Retailer Input/Output

The retailer is another system participant with an input/output relationship (see Exhibit 8). From the package goods manufacturer's point of view, the pertinent retailer outputs are the price at which he sells the package good, the number of facings and their height, and the presence of in-store promotion. Since the manufacturer has only limited influence regarding the retailer's overall advertising and promotion program, these represent outputs that are not easily altered by the manufacturer in the short run. However, the manufacturer may be able to alter some of the marketing stimuli directed to the retailer in the hope of favorably changing the retailer's outputs that apply to the package good. For example, in addition to paying the retailer slotting fees, the manufacturer's consumer-directed advertising and promotion may indirectly affect the retailer in such a way that the package good's price, facing display, shelf height, and in-store promotion will be favorable in

EXHIBIT 8. The Retailer as an Input/Output Participant

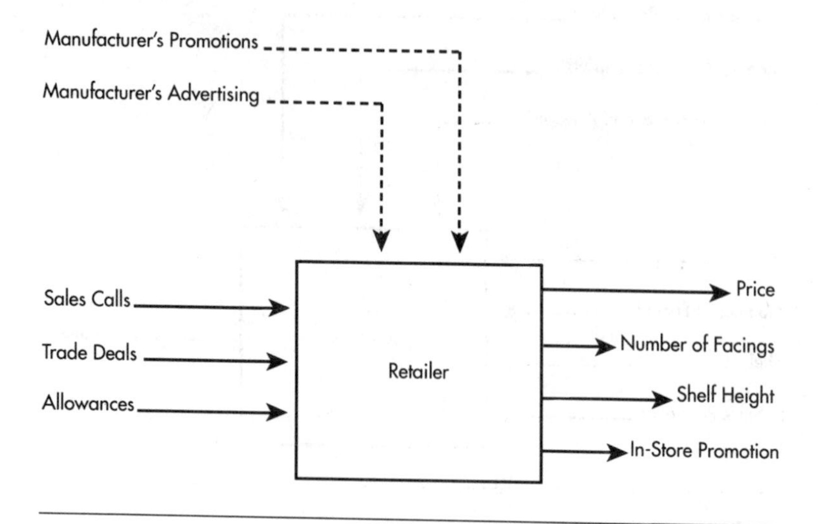

the consumer's eyes. Through the wholesaler's inputs to the retailer—sales calls, allowances, etc.—the manufacturer also may be able to influence the retailer's outputs that make the package good more appealing to consumers. Thus the retailer also acts as an input/output participant in this system, and the manufacturer must recognize this and attempt to employ stimuli that most favorably affect the retailer's output.

INPUT/OUTPUT AND SYSTEM CONTROL

The above discussion illustrates that the consumer's output—a purchase—is influenced by a number of inputs or stimuli, some of which are the retailer's outputs and some of which are the manufacturer's outputs. The retailer's outputs are influenced by a number of inputs or stimuli, some of which are the wholesaler's outputs and some of which are the manufacturer's outputs. The wholesaler's outputs are affected by inputs that are the manufacturer's outputs. Thus the manufacturer's outputs represent inputs to other system participants. These outputs should be so organized that the output of *each subsequent participant* will enhance the marketing position of the manufacturer's product. The implication of these observations is that the manufacturer must have some knowledge of the input/output response of each system participant. That is, if the manufacturer is to control the system to best advantage, he or she must know what output to expect from a system participant for any given input, whether it is a single stimulus or a combination of stimuli. Furthermore, there must be such knowledge for *each system participant* because if the manufacturer does not have such knowledge, any one system participant might perform in a way that will not be to the manufacturer's best interest. When this occurs, the system will not be as effective as the manufacturer would like it to be.

Each input/output response represents a consumer, a retailer, a distributor, or a wholesaler. Each is influenced by one or more inputs, and the output or outputs are a response to these inputs. Thus each participant represents not an unknown "black box" of some kind but a definable segment that will react predictably to given inputs, at least to some extent. This suggests that each participant can be studied and analyzed. Three ingredients of such an analysis are described in the following paragraphs.

ANALYSIS OF MARKETING SYSTEMS

It follows from the preceding discussion that the analysis of a marketing system requires historical data-collection activity. If management must have some knowledge of each system participant's input/output relationship, the historical data collection activity should compile information concerning each participant's input and output. With respect to the inputs received by a participant, records should be kept of both the dollar cost of the input and the actual input units themselves—for example, the number of advertisements placed, the deals and allowances given retailers, and the number of calls made on wholesalers. Similarly, the units of each participant's output should be recorded—for example, the quantity and frequency of purchases by consumers, the retailer's price, the number of facings displayed, and the shelf height used. Both of these data sets can be helpful in attempting to construct a participant's output response to various input levels—one such response perhaps appearing as shown in Exhibit 9.

Two managerial inputs must accompany the historical data collection activity. The first of these is an adequate description by management of a theory of input/output response that can be used to guide the historical data collection activity. Someone must indicate which input and output data are to be collected and how, and this should come from management after they have clearly described the theory they believe to be appropriate. The second managerial input is an attitude that reflects a willingness to experiment.

Management must bear in mind that they sell (1) in many different geographic markets and (2) in many different end-user markets and that these sales (3) occur in one time period after another. Thus their data collection activity can be viewed as occurring along these three dimensions. If management is to obtain information helpful

EXHIBIT 9. Input/Output Response

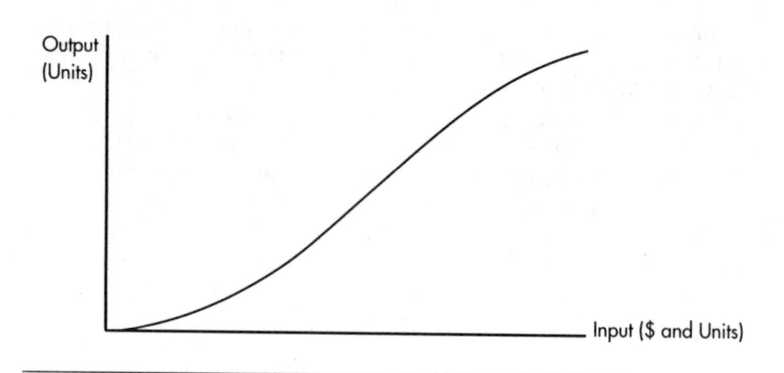

to them when estimating responses similar to that illustrated in Exhibit 9, they should collect data from all the various end-user and geographic markets in which they sell during each time period. Furthermore, they must see to it that the inputs to the various markets in the various time periods *are not always the same.* If management is not willing to experiment—that is, to allow some variations in inputs to various markets and participants—they will not be able to observe variations in outputs and hence will be unable to obtain the information needed to estimate the types of responses illustrated in Exhibit 9.

IMPLICATIONS FOR MARKETING PLANNING

There are four marketing planning implications that can be derived from the preceding discussion.

1. The marketing executive must identify a total system overview that includes the structure of all system participants and the interrelationships existing among them. If the executive omits from the overview any participant or interrelationship, the omitted item may not be taken into consideration when the marketing plan is being developed. Such omissions are likely to result in marketing plans that are less effective than they could be.
2. The marketing executive must identify the input/output characteristics of each system participant. If little is known about how a participant's performance is affected by different marketing stimuli, it will not be possible to include within the marketing plan certain stimuli that could persuasively influence that participant to perform in a desired manner.

3. In order to estimate the input/output response of a system participant, management must have available a data collection activity that records the units of input (marketing stimuli) directed at each system participant and the output performance that resulted. The marketing executive can use such data to study and learn about the input/output response of each system participant.
4. To facilitate input/output response estimation, (1) the historical data collection activity should be guided by theories that are appropriate to each participant's input/output response, and (2) the marketing executive should allow variations in each participant's inputs so that variations in its outputs can be observed. In this way, the data collected historically should reflect various input levels and various output levels, resulting in a more complete data bank for input/output response estimation.

Edward J. Kane
Vice President
Quality and Management Systems
Dun and Bradstreet Software Services, Inc.

Eugene J. Kelley
Distinguished Professor of Marketing
Director, Center for Services Marketing and
Management (CSMM)
Florida Atlantic University
Boca Raton, Florida

CHAPTER 3

IMPLEMENTING THE MARKETING CONCEPT: LINKING QUALITY, MARKETING, AND VALUE

The marketing concept is a customer- and market-driven philosophy of business. It focuses corporate resources on the profitable production of customer satisfaction and values. Companies operating under the marketing concept focus marketing resources and effort, and the support of other corporate departments, on satisfying customer needs. The marketing concept is simple in principle but complex in implementation. The conceptual and philosophical bases of the marketing concept are often understood by management; however, failure to integrate and continually adjust to changes in key factors such as competitive actions and marketplace behavior can force the best strategy to fail in its implementation.

THE FOUNDATION: A CUSTOMER-ORIENTED DEFINITION OF THE CORPORATE MISSION

The starting point for an organization operating under the marketing concept is to define its corporate mission in customer satisfaction and marketplace terms. Customer-need satisfaction and service excellence hold a top priority position in the marketing concept company. Taking advantage of its natural or developed capabilities, the marketing concept organization anticipates change and disciplines itself to the management of that change.

All successful businesses follow the path of customer orientation to some extent. The new element is the integrated application of the marketing concept in companies that have grown in size beyond the point where the decision makers can achieve firsthand knowledge of consumer needs. This application is also new in companies whose traditional products no longer fill marketing needs and who now define the entire business in market-driven terms of customer needs and satisfactions, rather than in product or industry terms (for example, entertainment, not movies; transportation, not railroads; problem solving, not computers). No successful company can continue to be successful if it does not meet the needs of its customers and is not aware of changes in its marketplace.

Marketing Management

A system is needed to implement this new emphasis in corporate decision making. Conscious corporate effort is required to translate the theory into practice. Implementation may be complex enough to incorporate a market research department with the services of a battery of consultants and service companies. Or it may be as simple as a marketing manager with vision and a staff with authority to manage the changes that are occurring. This is the essence of marketing management; it requires new thinking, new skills, and often new organization to perform the activities identified in Exhibit 1, which portrays typical marketing management activities that are grouped by the functions of planning, direction, and control with feedback illustrated.

Marketing concept executives are environmentalists. They are dedicated first to identifying the roles and opportunities of the organization in the changing environment and then to identifying the specific customer set. These tasks lead to setting goals about the relationship that will be established between the organization and its customers. Of particular importance is the conscious selection of customer needs to be fulfilled by the organization. The services and support to be provided and the policies and practices to be established are key decisions that must be made by marketing executives early in the product design and development process.

The customer orientation must be supported by a total marketing effort. This is generated with the objective of maximizing customer satisfaction within the profit objectives established for the company. This way, company objectives are coordinated with the marketing concept philosophy.

Two primary methods of achieving high-profit returns in any marketplace are (1) ensure that the company is the low-cost producer (including all costs, distribution as well as manufacturing); and (2) differentiate the company products sufficiently so that a high-profit market niche is established. Either method has to be managed to ensure that the strategic competitive advantages achieved are sustainable over a period of time.

In the first instance, volume is the key ingredient to maintaining such a position, and nearly every industry shares this characteristic. This concept has been a prime source of opportunity in creating a share shift in foreign markets, such as the Japanese competition in automobiles, steel, and electronics.

There are many examples of companies who differentiate their products or appear to specialize niches. One area of concentration combines differentiation with the attempt to take advantage of a new market as well: sales to women. Handguns, a typically masculine market, in 1989 saw Smith and Wesson introduce "Lady Smith," a line of guns specifically for women. By changing the profile of the gun to suit women, sales to women over the next two years increased from 5 to 18 percent of total company revenues. Niche marketing was a significant factor in improving profitability over the period.

For many years marketing to women was focused almost exclusively on cosmetics, fashions, and packaged products. Today, in

EXHIBIT 1. Marketing Management Activities

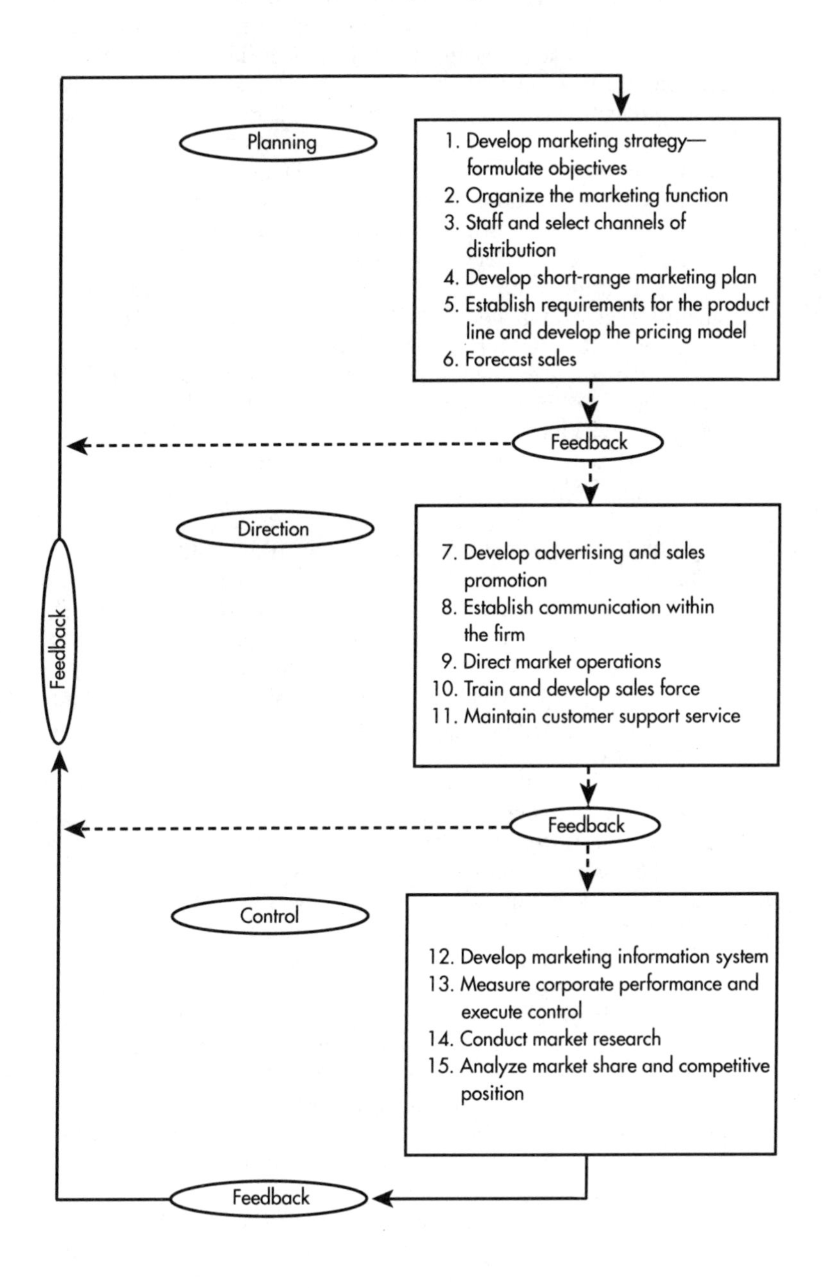
Planning
1. Develop marketing strategy—formulate objectives
2. Organize the marketing function
3. Staff and select channels of distribution
4. Develop short-range marketing plan
5. Establish requirements for the product line and develop the pricing model
6. Forecast sales
Feedback
Direction
7. Develop advertising and sales promotion
8. Establish communication within the firm
9. Direct market operations
10. Train and develop sales force
11. Maintain customer support service
Feedback
Control
12. Develop marketing information system
13. Measure corporate performance and execute control
14. Conduct market research
15. Analyze market share and competitive position
Feedback
Feedback

recognition of the changes in the source of household income, women account for over 50 percent of imported automobiles and 55 percent of major appliances (e.g., refrigerators, washing machines, microwaves). Twenty percent of Nike's revenue in 1991 was generated from women's products. In this case, in particular, much effort had to be devoted to producing products better suited to women as well as advertising Nike's understanding and care about women's athletic needs. Continuous awareness of such changes in preferences and needs of target segments can offer opportunities for corporations to increase market share and profitability.

An important point often overlooked is that even if a company has decided to clearly differentiate its products, unless it possesses a near monopoly it must stay close to its competitors in the area of price (and therefore costs). It would do little to produce the world's best tennis racket that sells for $1,000 since it will find few buyers. Similarly, if the aim is to be the cost leader, the product must still fulfill the basic need and offer sufficient features to ensure usability and value. Regardless of which markets and competitive position we strive to establish, as we will see again and again, the prime focus is on change in the marketing concept company.

Linking Quality and Marketing (The Concept of Value)

The quality movement that has gathered great momentum has mainly focused on two areas: (1) producing better products that satisfy customer needs and expectations, and (2) improving internal operations.

Another related but broader application of quality principles offers greater reward for those in marketing who embrace the concept of value. This is frequently referred to as *value marketing* but we should be clear that we are not referring to "positioning the marketing message" or "selling the sizzle." The value we refer to is real, as expressed in the customer's terms. It is achieved by providing products that are designed with customer input for maximum utility and useability. These products are combined with enhanced services and information access and are offered to customers at competitive prices, often with guarantees for satisfaction.

Value in this sense necessitates the application of total quality throughout the organization. Control of costs is critical. This is attained by aiming to eliminate failure cost (e.g., scrap, rework, warranty cost, administrative failure, poor communication, "unadministratable" contracts) and by minimizing appraisal costs (e.g., tests, inspections, duplication of source data entry). The cost of quality then largely becomes preventive (e.g., training, good procedures, skills matching, communication improvements), a cost of providing good quality rather than a cost of correcting poor quality.

Another key area, identified in the marketing concept cycle is ensuring that good customer input is received early enough to impact the design and development of the product or service and not after the fact (See Exhibit 2). The marketing concept cycle, by its very dynamic nature, embraces the notion of delivering quality to enhance the customers' utility and value. In other words, the cycle has in its framework captured the notion of market-driven quality (MDQ), a recent orientation that many successful corporations have adopted to be more competitive.

By properly focusing on eliminating non-value-adding activities and by listening to the voice of the customer early and often, value is provided. Profit margins as well as competitive pricing are maintained or improved. Examples abound of global companies who use this philosophy, making it more difficult for those who live with the inefficiencies and ineffectiveness of poor quality in their organizations.

Wal-Mart, for example, has outdistanced Sears (an earlier hallmark of quality) by becoming a more efficient operator and offering brand name products at lower prices. Sears attempted to focus its efforts on financial services rather than on its traditional business. The company has recently tried to bolster its value image through the marketing of the Discover credit card (a financial service that fits well with retailing) and Kidvantage. Discover uniquely offers a 1 percent discount for purchases with the card, and Kidvantage incorporates a wear-out guarantee.

Toyota and Honda began by offering value in the low-end price auto market to the dismay of U.S. manufacturers. This was achieved in good measure by a dramatically lower unit cost, the ability to accomplish model changeovers in hours rather than weeks, and by helping the North American consumer define quality in values that played to the strength of the Japanese producers. More recently, both companies have challenged the luxury auto segment by providing high-performance autos at 20 to 30 percent lower prices than Mercedes Benz and BMW.

In the industrial marketing field, Corning, Inc., awakened at one point to discover that the ceramic catalytic converter, one of Corning's most important automotive industry products, was being offered by a Japanese competitor at a price below Corning's cost. Almost since that day Corning, to its great credit, has become a laboratory for total quality focus, technology and marketing alliances, and work force empowerment and experimentation. Corning has become a global force in high-profile markets such as optical fiber, laboratory services, and specialty materials.

Strategic Alliances

Combinations between large competitive firms have become commonplace in global markets. Banks, drug companies, and airlines are but a few industries where American companies have entered into mega-mergers. These consolidations frequently reflect the concern about

EXHIBIT 2. Implementing the Marketing Concept Cycle

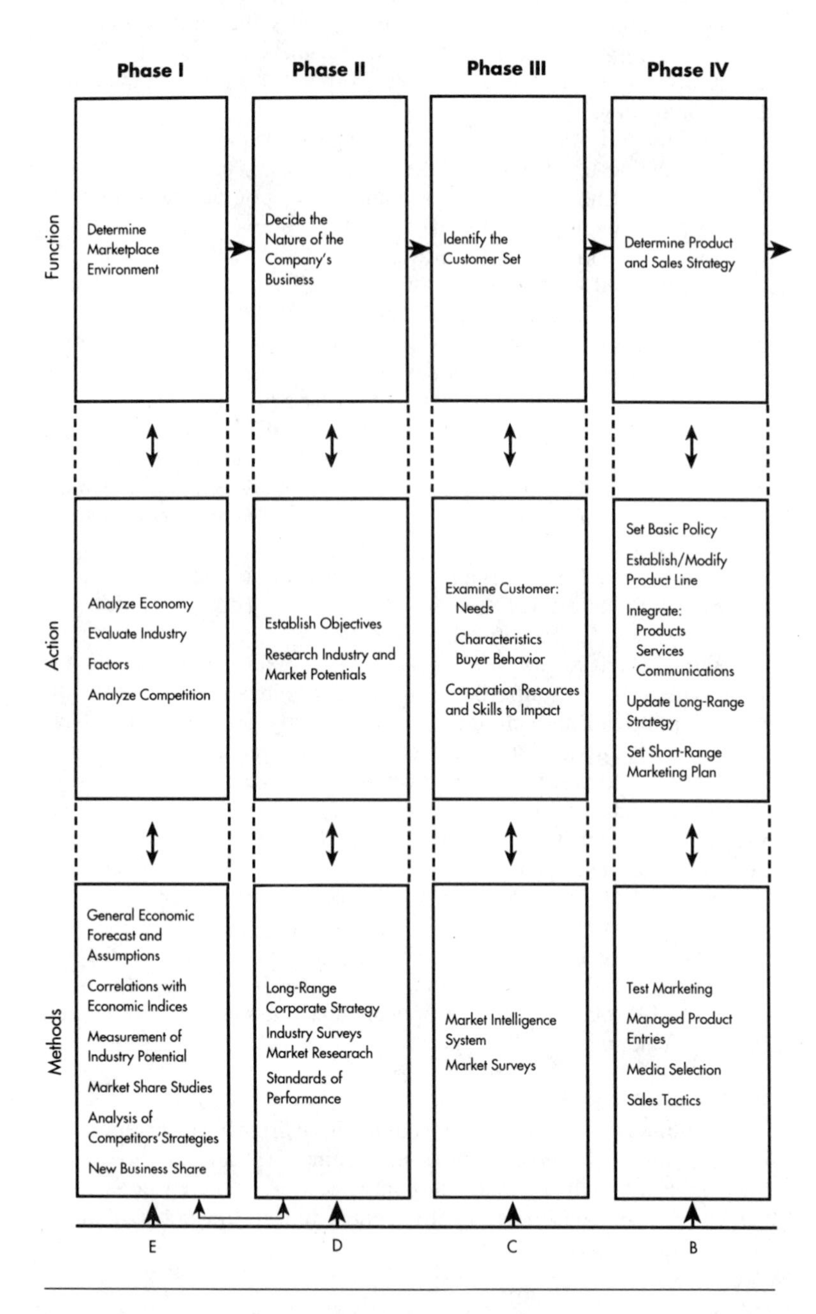
Phase I
Phase II
Phase III
Phase IV
Function
Determine Marketplace Environment
Decide the Nature of the Company's Business
Identify the Customer Set
Determine Product and Sales Strategy
Action
Analyze Economy
Evaluate Industry
Factors
Analyze Competition
Establish Objectives
Research Industry and Market Potentials
Examine Customer:
Needs
Characteristics
Buyer Behavior
Corporation Resources and Skills to Impact
Set Basic Policy
Establish/Modify Product Line
Integrate:
Products
Services
Communications
Update Long-Range Strategy
Set Short-Range Marketing Plan
Methods
General Economic Forecast and Assumptions
Correlations with Economic Indices
Measurement of Industry Potential
Market Share Studies
Analysis of Competitors' Strategies
New Business Share
Long-Range Corporate Strategy
Industry Surveys
Market Researach
Standards of Performance
Market Intelligence System
Market Surveys
Test Marketing
Managed Product Entries
Media Selection
Sales Tactics
E
D
C
B

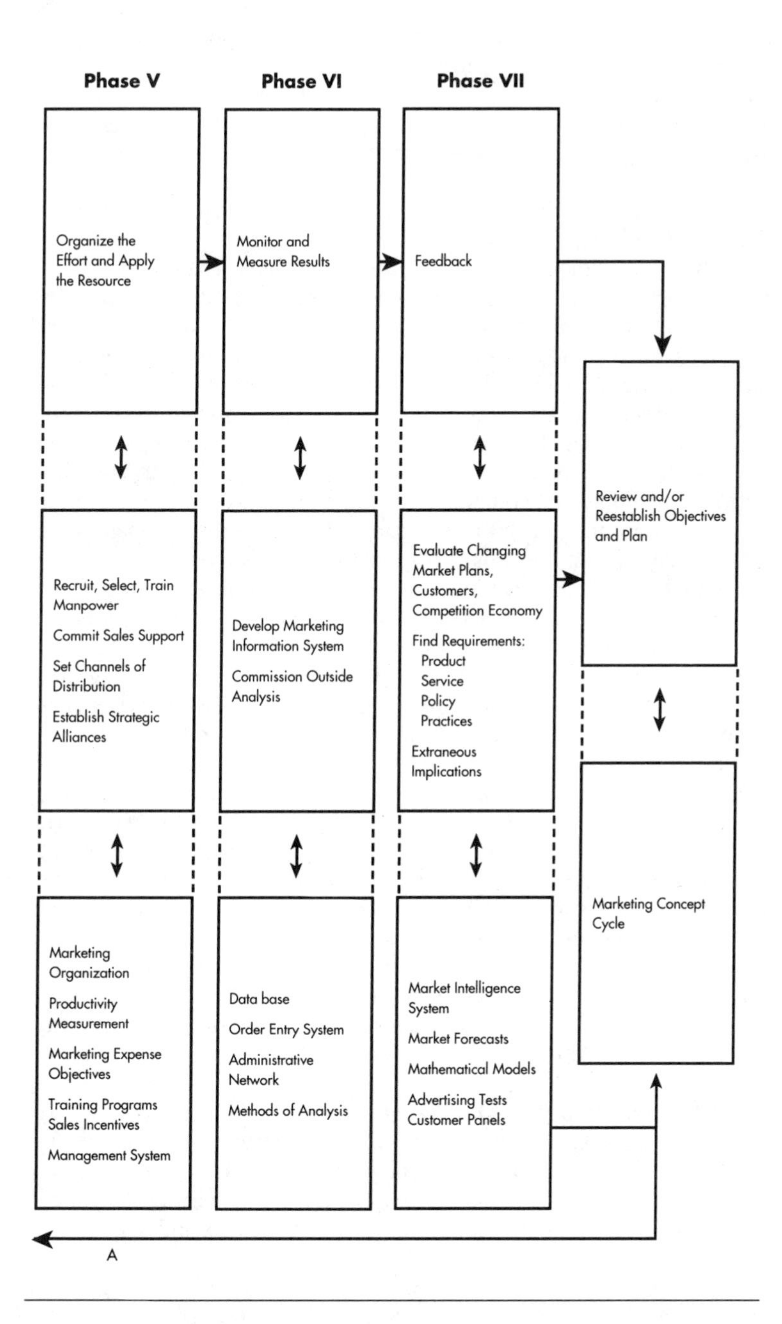
Phase V
Phase VI
Phase VII
Organize the Effort and Apply the Resource
Monitor and Measure Results
Feedback
Review and/or Reestablish Objectives and Plan
Recruit, Select, Train Manpower
Commit Sales Support
Set Channels of Distribution
Establish Strategic Alliances
Develop Marketing Information System
Commission Outside Analysis
Evaluate Changing Market Plans, Customers, Competition Economy
Find Requirements:
Product
Service
Policy
Practices
Extraneous Implications
Marketing Concept Cycle
Marketing Organization
Productivity Measurement
Marketing Expense Objectives
Training Programs
Sales Incentives
Management System
Data base
Order Entry System
Administrative Network
Methods of Analysis
Market Intelligence System
Market Forecasts
Mathematical Models
Advertising Tests
Customer Panels
A

Japanese *keiretsu* and European competitive combines, developed through government encouragement and involvement. As a result, U.S. antitrust enforcement, so relevant in the '60s and '70s, has slackened and many direct consolidations have been unopposed, apparently to encourage global competitiveness by U.S. firms. It remains to be seen whether bigger translates to better in global markets or whether too much is lost by the attendant weakening of domestic markets that have always served as a strong foundation for building national competitiveness.

While the headlines have been monopolized by such alliances as the Chemical Bank/Manufacturers Hanover merger, the Apple/IBM joint effort, and the American, United, and Delta absorption of key international air routes, a more significant marketing principle may be emerging. With the need for global competitiveness, a higher premium is placed on maintaining cost control as discussed in the preceding paragraph and on getting products to market more quickly. This may require a focus on alliances with vendors and competitors short of consolidation. It may take the form of agreements regarding integration of technology, research, distribution channels, and joint supplier/customer planning and commitment. While this has been utilized in the past, it will become much more commonplace and most companies are well advised to consider this as part of their core strategy. It is present to the highest degree today in industries with dynamic technology such as software, drugs, and semiconductors. But even industries where base technologies are not changing rapidly must also look to information technology advancements such as electronic data interchange and client/server technology as they reengineer their internal systems to become more effective in the services they offer and in reducing costs. It would appear that alliances will become essential to any company that wishes to become competitive in global markets.

Strategic alliances result in larger corporations due to synergies in key functional and product areas, successful management of which enhances the capability of the firm to be competitive globally. Greater coordination standardization in operating procedures and effective internal communication of the mission of the enterprise would aid the corporation in its new challenge in the global marketplace. To encounter the vastness of changes occurring worldwide politically, technologically, and culturally, a culture of continuous adaptation and receptivity to change is called for.

Social Responsibility in Marketing Management

The solution of certain societal problems may constitute a key objective for the marketing concept organization. This objective does not arise from basic altruism (although some companies may strongly hold that objective), but because the companies understand that serving their customers' needs, not only as individuals or firms but as consumer-citizens, will ultimately serve the corporation's best interests. Social responsibility should be particularly evident in large companies that have a broad base of users and enough resources to make a major impact on social problems. Marketing management in companies operating under the marketing concept must integrate three areas of organizational concern:

1. customer satisfaction,
2. company profit, and
3. social responsibility.

In the 1990s and beyond, there will be heightened interest in the social responsibility of the company operating under the marketing concept. The last decade has witnessed an unprecendented concern among the publics that a marketing firm serves about social responsibility. An oil spill in Alaska and an industrial disaster in Bhopal, though overseas, received global attention and criticism. The public was unforgiving and the media attention was unrelenting. Given these conditions and a new-found, enlightened self-image of the consumer, the '90s and the next century will demand that a company operating under the marketing concept treat social responsibility with care and diligence.

The marketing concept, therefore, may be defined as a customer-focused orientation that guides all business functions within the organization toward the profitable achievement of corporate objectives through satisfaction of the economic and social needs of the customer.

THE MARKETING CONCEPT CYCLE

Management of Change

If the activities identified in Exhibit 1 are to be meaningful, the company must be

1. environmentally oriented,
2. an anticipator of future trends and changes,
3. organizationally flexible enough to change, and
4. a critical and systematic auditor of all policies and practices relating to the consumer.

Proper implementation of the marketing concept for many remains more of a goal than a reality. For this reason the key question becomes, How can the marketing concept be applied? In other words, How can marketing management more effectively achieve the consumer satisfaction objectives of the firm?

Market-related activities of management must be accompanied by an attitude of continuous awareness of change and the opportunity it creates. For example, many companies today envision a requirement for change that has led them to product-line diversification of a general and dramatic nature. Philip Morris Inc.'s anticipation of the changes in social mores in its major marketplace led to its strategic and aggressive move into food products. The cash flow provided by its tobacco operations was used to acquire General Foods in 1985, Kraft in 1988, and Jacobs Succhard A.G. in 1990. As a result, in 1991 approximately 60 percent of revenues accrued from nontobacco operations.

Diversification is one type of change. Another involves the search (often globally) for new markets when traditional (or domestic) markets stagnate. One example from a mature and previously exclusively American industry is sour mash whiskey. From 1975 sales of all bourbon in the United States dropped from 30 million cases per year to approximately 17 million in 1990. Several of the old-line companies took advantage of the worldwide acceptance of some American products to aggressively introduce and market their products in new markets. They selected the most affluent cultures where U.S. products were in vogue.

As a result, in five years the top distiller, Jim Beam Brands, tripled its exports, and others enjoyed similar success. Japan was the initial target market and grew 50 percent per year in the late '80s. When it fell to a more modest growth in the teens in 1990, marketing began in earnest in Australia and the United Kingdom. Jack Daniels is currently experiencing foreign market growth at a rate of over 25 percent per year, and in 1991 Makers Mark Distillery estimated that it alone exported 21 million cases. In 1992 the industry looked to the rest of Europe as a virtually untapped market.

Changes occur primarily in two ways: environmentally and technically. The marketing concept company is characterized by a conscious effort to recognize and capitalize on *both* types of change. Anticipating the direction and timing of these changes provides the corporation with a valuable competitive edge in the marketplace. Imbued with this attitude, the organization may apply the marketing concept in many different ways; however, some activities should be common to all applications. Exhibit 2 graphically shows the seven phases of functions, action programs, and methods that are part of any marketing concept implementation program.

Marketplace Environment

The marketing concept company must focus on the environment in which it operates because this is where the opportunities for consumer satisfaction are found. In establishing its specific product and market objectives, the company must carefully evaluate the economic condition of the world, the country, and its own industry. Basic strategies must be determined and objectives set for the planned period. Objectives and strategies are used to establish a standard against which marketing results may be evaluated. This actual versus expected comparison may suggest modifications in the current corporate strategy.

Business environmental scanning, as related to the industry, competitors, and customers thus is a matter of primary concern to the company. With the rapid pace of change, a firm needs to develop an early warning system to monitor, anticipate, and preempt changes. Such a system needs to work on a continuous basis and assist the management in defining and directing the competitive strategies and programs for achieving the long-range objectives set forth in the strategic plan. However, the existence of such a system does not guarantee the achievement of objectives. It merely guides the organization in the right direction. Whether the organization is able to move in the desired direction or not depends on (1) the organization's thrust in that direction, and (2) environmental turbulence.

General economic indicators may then be used to shape the boundaries of strategy and determine rough target objectives. These targets must be sharpened and modified through many iterations. Modifiers include competitive "benchmarking," evaluation of existing product lines, audit of support services, and identification of customer needs.

To illustrate the importance of the environment and these modifiers, it is useful to look at the current trends and at history. In the strong economy of the 1960s, corporate strategy was characterized by market expansion, diversification and *organization restructuring.* In the 1970s more turbulent economic conditions produced a general shift in corporate emphasis toward margin improvement, more sophisticated analysis and use of resources, and *market restructuring.*

The 1980s saw increased globalization of markets and therefore greater dependence and interrelationship between the markets. Fluctuating exchange rates had a great effect on the profitability of international companies. In the 1990s a continuation of these trends is expected. With the continued opening of major markets (e.g., European single market beginning in 1992; pressure to reduce free trade barriers in Japan), opportunities will rise as will competitive presence and market restructuring. The opening of markets in Eastern Europe and Russia due to major political upheavals offer avenues for U.S. corporations to market their products in these countries. Careful market selection and appropriate strategies for products and services go a long way in adding to the bottom line. Appropriate hiring of personnel to manage products in these countries is an important task for most corporations.

Not all markets will grow, so cautious long-term strategies are called for. For example, the cost of German reunification and the permanent downsizing and restructuring of major companies in the United States in the early '90s will create shifts in market share and rates of growth.

It is clear that business strategy is the key to gaining a greater share of the market. The war for share foretells a hostile environment where only those who strategically plan can succeed in establishing sustained growth and profitability. Analytical tools are a necessity. Financial models, analysis of competitive strategies, and creative approaches to preempt or combat those strategies will determine market leadership. The essential point is that these factors be evaluated in a comprehensive approach aimed at identifying corporate opportunities. Only then can realistic objectives be set.

Determining the Nature of the Company's Business

Phases I and II of the marketing concept cycle are closely related in that each has great impact on the other in terms of goal setting and the selection of choices. That is, an overall corporate objective might be to grow at a 20 percent controlled growth rate (CGR). When a study of the environment is made, however, it is determined that the current product line or business area focus is insufficient to produce this kind of growth. The next step may be to extend the traditional product line, to diversify into entirely new business areas, or to concentrate on gaining a greater share from competitors. Another alternative is some combination of these actions.

A start is made then by a broad determination of the business in which the company has decided to compete. This will depend on the resources the company brings to bear, its corporate culture, and its analysis of marketplace trends. These influences result then in an iterative process between the first two phases until the corporate objectives are set. (See the previous "Marketplace Environment" section).

Little needs to be said about the realities of marketing myopia; that is, the many companies that have failed to realize what business they are in. The task here is essentially the setting of broad corporate strategic objectives and the challenge of achieving them. These strategic objectives must be based on realistic information about the marketplace. Whatever method is used, the result should be a documented, long-range strategy that clearly communicates the agreed-on corporate objectives. Successful implementation of the marketing concept demands commitment, and good management requires documentation. The strategic plan must be comprehensive and explicitly expressed in writing to ensure that

1. the plan has been clearly and thoroughly thought out and analyzed, and
2. the plan becomes a working document that has been developed and agreed on by those who will implement it.

The process of plan development may follow either the command model (top down) or the incremental model (bottom up). The two models will yield morphologically diverse plans. The command model fits the box metaphor used by Hurst. *Boxes* are the hard-edged, rigid structures that give rational meaning to strategies. The result is an easily understood, regimental plan to be adhered to by all levels of the organization, with a lack of adaptability or creative contextual flexibility. By contrast, *bubbles* have flexible, transparent boundaries that can easily expand and enjoin other bubbles—the major advantage being a shared vision and a team effort to both adhere to and ensure the success of the plan. These are the two extremes of the planning process continuum that an organization needs to decide within. For the larger company, support for the long-range strategy must be found in both external and internal industry surveys and market research reports.

Identification of the Customer Set

The third phase of activity in the application of the marketing concept is closely allied to the first two. In defining the company's business, the customer set is narrowed. In studying the marketplace environment, an attempt is made to identify basic customer needs. Now the task is to identify the product line to be developed or modified. Determination of the action to be taken will demand a detailed examination of the characteristics, needs, and buyer behavior of the selected customer set. Definition of the consumer set must be very current; therefore, this phase of the marketing concept will be reviewed often.

There are many influences on the customer. He or she is not only a customer for the company's product but also for the competitors' product and for other product lines. He or she is influenced by socioeconomic forces and changes in life-style. He or she has certain buying preferences that will influence the seller's decisions on selection of marketing channels. Modern marketing research must assist us in identifying these dynamic trends. An aware, well-disciplined sales force will also be of assistance in identifying customer requirements. The area that requires the greatest effort is that of anticipating new customer needs and innovating the products to satisfy them.

As stated before, change occurs through technological discovery and social or environmental change. For this reason, a market intelligence system must account for both forces. The marketing concept company must be sensitive to the marketplace in order to detect changing attitudes and new demands. This feedback process should be the primary basis on which new products and services are developed. The organization must also recognize that some wants and desires may not manifest themselves until new products or technologies are made available. For example, it is questionable whether the need for vast amounts of information was recognized prior to the invention of the electronic computer.

It is important to search for new opportunities from advanced technological efforts and from changing social values of the marketplace. Market intelligence systems for different companies will vary in structure and complexity. However, most will combine marketplace requirements by integrating the output from development research for the introduction of new products and the modification of existing ones.

Product, Sales, and Distribution Strategy

Entry into phase four marks the mainstream of the marketing concept cycle. Each planning period will necessitate an in-depth analysis of company plans, strategies, and objectives. Depending on where in the cycle the organization is, it may be introducing new products and/or modifying existing ones. Long-range strategies and plans must be updated frequently to ensure their viability and active use. Marketing plans should specify sales by territory and reflect the expectations from promotional efforts and sales campaigns.

Selection and development of the most appropriate distribution channels are particularly significant since the low-cost producer of the future may well be the company that can establish itself as the low-cost distributor. Establishing the right channels in order to preempt competition is essential if the strategy is to result in an increase in share of market.

Contemporary literature in sales management has been concerned with conflicts in the channels and a power struggle for channel captaincy. The growing strength of retailers spells out reduced control on channels for manufacturers. This shift in power balance should be of concern to the firm. A marketing-concept-oriented company is responsible for customer satisfaction and a well-balanced and satisfied distribution channel system. Maintaining fruitful relationships with channel members and resolving conflicts at all levels of the distribution channel, yet not losing sight of the consumer, are complex tasks. The company committed to the marketing concept will be required to walk this tightrope.

Similarly, the promotion and advertising strategy will play a key part, depending on the share of market presently held and the objectives established for the desired share.

An example of an important change in the distribution strategy is the Japanese entry into the information processing field. After several attempts to pursue marketing activities through acquisitions or collaboration agreements (e.g., Fujitsu with Amdahl and TRW; Hitachi with Itel), the Japanese computer manufacturers appear to be universally abandoning that strategy. Japanese culture places high priority on direct control, and many of the past attempts in dealing through U.S. channels have been disappointing. It appears that the emphasis by Japanese computer manufacturers is clearly on direct marketing. This is clear in the decisions by Fujitsu and NEC in establishing direct sales forces in major foreign markets.

In looking at products, the Japanese companies are clearly focused on expansion and product-line extension. Examples are Fujitsu's entry into minisupercomputers and parallel processors and Canon Inc.'s digital integration of copiers, printers, and facsimile machines into a single unit. NEC is also extending its considerable resource to overseas markets. Up until 1989, only 25 percent of revenues were from markets outside of Japan. By 1993 NEC's plans called for 50 percent, with 60 to 70 percent of the products sold overseas being manufactured locally.

Japanese companies are also consistent in their advertising strategy in establishing direct brand identification (e.g., Mita copiers, RICOH and Canon copiers and facsimile machines, and Fujitsu and Hitachi computer systems).

Specific elements of the product, sales, and distribution strategy that relate to the achievement of marketing objectives are

1. basic policy and practices—terms and conditions, accounts receivable, order entry;
2. product line—test marketing new products;
3. channels of distribution (see Phase V);
4. anticipated competitive actions and counter strategies;
5. inventory management;
6. pricing strategy;
7. promotion and advertising; and
8. maintenance and service.

Organizing the Effort and Applying Resources

The fifth phase of the marketing concept cycle is vital to the achievement of marketing objectives. It incorporates research, planning, organization, and strengths and weaknesses of personnel in determining the structure and function of the organization.

Good management principles must be applied in directing the marketing organization. Once the product line has been established along with the marketing plan, much needs to be done to direct the sales force (or alternate channels) toward achieving the objectives. The sales force must be recruited, selected, trained, and organized for maximum field coverage in order to realize territory potential and achieve revenue and profit objectives.

A highly motivated field force is needed to achieve the optimistic results for which marketing concept executives strive. Depending on the company and the industry, sales people will come from varied backgrounds, will have different amounts of experience, and will have responsibility for many different job duties. Such a situation makes it difficult to generalize exactly what constitutes prime sales motivation. There are, however, three important motivating factors for most sales jobs: money, recognition, and advancement. The marketing concept manager must use all of them.

Historically, money has been recognized as one of the key motivating factors for sales personnel. Incentive compensation plans have been popular for just this reason; however, they require frequent evaluation to keep them consistent with company objectives. This is particularly true in a company that operates in fast-changing market environments, such as technological instruments and data processing equipment. In such a case, there may be many incentive plans within each individual sales force.

Recognition of the individual is a powerful motivating force and should not be underestimated by the marketing concept executive. Topflight sales representatives are usually the aggressive individual performers who want to be and need to be recognized as leaders.

Advancement may or may not be a prime motivator depending on the company's hiring policy and career planning programs. The IBM Corporation, for example, has tried in the past to hire computer sales people whose primary interest was to become top executives. The sales people were encouraged to think in terms of advancement and to strive for promotion out of the sales ranks as quickly as possible. Companies that are expanding less rapidly (now including IBM) or have different management selection criteria may have a different hiring policy. Such a company may wish to hire people who are interested in selling as a career. In each case, the company policy toward hiring should directly reflect the corporate objectives.

Employee motivation is an important key to success and should, therefore, occupy a good part of an effective manager's time. The use of management specialists can be very helpful in developing the basic plan and in providing maximum experience within a short time.

If an indirect sales force is to be utilized either exclusively or in addition to a direct field force, additional considerations must be assessed; for example, whether the alternate channel may sell competing products; education, training, and support provided; degree of product exclusivity within a channel relationship and compensation plan sharing with the direct sales force; competitiveness of multiple channels to one another; and consistency with long-term goals and how well these practices fit with the culture of the organization.

Monitoring and Measuring the Results

The effective marketing manager must periodically evaluate the progress of the organization in achieving its objectives. There must be relevant information about all operations. Too much data can be confusing and stifling, and incomplete data can be deceiving. Both situations result in poor decision making. A marketing manager needs information that is timely, allowing him or her to identify the problem, formulate corrective alternatives, and choose a course of action.

Control can be achieved through data-processing techniques. Display terminals may be installed to provide spontaneous information regarding orders and inventories. The question the marketing manager must answer is, "How much sophistication is needed?" An answer to this question requires considerable knowledge about the company's operation and marketplace. Information must be timely enough to enable the marketing manager to take corrective action.

The marketing manager must be involved in the development of the system so that the results can be measured against planned objectives on a periodic basis. Data sources such as order entry, administrative reporting, and inventory analysis must be identified and integrated into the system to ensure complete analysis of the various markets. Techniques of communicating the information must be developed. A simple form letter or handwritten report may serve to inform the marketing manager about what product, what territory, or what class of customer is involved in the problem. Again, the purpose is to identify problem areas and take corrective action.

Some marketing functions are not easily measured. Promotional and market development may well require marketing research to provide adequate analysis. If the marketing manager's system is sophisticated, he or she may utilize a model with which to simulate the results from various alternatives, thereby determining their impact before committing the company's resources. In any case, effective marketing management must incorporate an effective control system to monitor the achieved results and measure them against those forecast. This process allows the marketing manager to concentrate attention and effort on the exceptions, which are usually problem areas.

Feedback

The final test for an organization using the marketing concept is to determine how well its products and services have been accepted in the marketplace and whether it has achieved its corporate objectives. The organization must depend on its marketing intelligence system to provide information on changes in the marketplace and on the acceptance of its products by customers within each of the various markets. These data are necessary to properly evaluate changes in the needs and wants of customers. Corporate management must evaluate how these needs translate into product requirements by analyzing competitive actions and reactions and interpreting their impact on the company's marketing strategy. The sales force, customer panels, market surveys, and advertising tests may all be used to obtain the information needed to modify mathematical models of the business system. Only in this way can the organization remain consistent with the environment yet sensitive to changes. However used, and through whatever vehicles, a system of feedback and forecast must be established as an integral part of the marketing concept cycle.

SUMMARY

The key point in applying the marketing concept is that the activities are cyclical and that the organization cannot afford to be static. The corporation must be dynamic, continually updating and reevaluating its position in relation to the industry, the economy, and its customers. The marketing manager must, therefore, be dedicated to the management of change and must adapt accordingly. A system must be developed that helps the marketing manager incorporate the marketing concept into the job today and assists in predicting tomorrow's changes.

Implications

For the marketing concept company, the implications of the preceding discussion may be summarized as follows.

Acceptance of Change and Environmental Orientation

Organization personnel must be trained and motivated to manage change in order to adjust to the accelerating rate of environmental change being imposed on all organizations. Every organization has traditions and policies that have stood through the years. The marketing concept, with its focus on changing environmental conditions, customer needs, and competitive strategies, requires that all processes and activities of the company be subject to systematic analysis and reexamination. Globalization warrants a change in outlook of frontline managers, an awareness of political, economic, and sociocultural changes in order to design products to match customer needs.

Customer Determination of the Marketing Concept Company's Survival

The focus on customer needs is central to all marketing decisions in particular and to all business functions in general. Demographic, sociographic, and psychographic analysis of both present and potential customers is necessary if the company is to be responsive to customer demands.

Linking Quality and Marketing

The application of quality principles to marketing has great potential for improving the competitiveness of the company. Creating real value in the customer's terms through better products, enhanced service, and information that allows easier use will do more than improve sales. Successful implementation of quality principles in product and service design ensure long-term customer franchises. It will create long-term partnerships that are based on the company's understanding of customers' needs and expectations.

Importance of Disciplined Planning

Marketing activity must not only be planned, but the plan must also be integrated and updated with the execution of marketing functions. The plan must be an active description of the marketing action that is taking place.

Use of a Market Intelligence System

A marketing intelligence system must provide current customer and competitive information that the company can use in planning its efforts to satisfy marketplace requirements.

Product Planning and Development

Data from the marketing intelligence system is integrated with internal information inputs, such as product and technological developments, and serves to modify the basic strategy. In this way, the marketing concept company manages the internal as well as the environmental change.

Monitoring and Measuring the Results

It is essential that an effective control system be designed and established to monitor and measure the progress that the organization is making toward achievement of its objectives. It must focus on problem exceptions rather than on corporate activity that is effectively achieving the objectives as planned.

Strategic Alliances

All forms of alliances and joint efforts between companies and their customers, suppliers, competitors, and governmental agencies appear destined to grow and become more important to the marketing concept company.

Social Responsibility

The marketing concept organization must recognize that service to its customers involves a much broader objective than merely satisfying economic desires. The corporation has a responsibility to satisfy the social needs of all consumers, not just their own customers. Marketing objectives should be established with consideration for their impact on social problems. Objectives and programs designed under a marketing concept orientation must satisfy consumer needs, while remaining consistent with the long-run profit objectives of the business.

SUGGESTIONS FOR FURTHER READING

Bartels, Robert. 1977. The general theory of Marketing. In B. A. Greenberg and D. N. Ballenger (eds.): *Contemporary Marketing Thought.* Chicago: American Marketing Association.

Bartels, Robert. 1970. *The History of Marketing Thought.* Homewood, IL: Irwin.

Berry, Leonard L., and A. Parasuraman. 1991. Marketing services: In: *Competing Through Quality.* New York: The Free Press.

Day, George S. 1990. *Market-Driven Strategy: Processes for Creating Value.* New York: The Free Press.

Fox, Karen S. A., and Philip Kotler. 1980. The marketing of social causes: The first ten years. *Journal of Marketing* 44 (Fall):24–33.

Gronroos, Christian. 1990. Services management and marketing. In: *Managing the Moments of Truth in Service Competition.* Lexington, MA: Lexington Books.

Hunt, Shelby D. 1976. The nature and scope of marketing. *Journal of Marketing* 40 (July):17–28.

Hurst, David K. 1984. Of boxes, bubbles and effective management. *Harvard Business Review* 62 (May-June):78–88.

Kotler, Philip. 1991. *Marketing Management: Analysis, Planning, and Control,* 7th ed. Englewood Cliffs, NJ: Prentice-Hall, Inc.

Lazer, William, and Eugene J. Kelley. 1974. *Managerial Marketing Perspectives & Viewpoints,* 4th ed. Homewood, IL: Irwin.

Porter, Michael. 1985. *Competitive Advantage: Creating and Sustaining Superior Performance.* New York: The Free Press.

Wheelright, Steven. 1984. Strategy, management and strategic planning approaches. *Interfaces* 14 (Jan-Feb):19–33.

Dennis W. Rook
Assistant Professor of Marketing
School of Business
Administration
University of Southern California,
Los Angeles

CHAPTER 4

TRANSLATING MARKETING STRATEGY: IMPLEMENTATION AS MANAGERIAL COMMUNICATION

Fuzzy Vision and Sound Strategy

Over the course of an annual planning cycle, managers typically devote hundreds of hours to crafting effective marketing strategies for their products and brands. Large sums are spent on consumer, competitive, and cost analyses; expensive consulting services are procured; and product task forces often retreat to isolated resort venues to brainstorm and assemble the next year's strategic plan. The core purpose behind these considerable investments is to support the creation of marketing strategies that promise some competitive advantage. In addition to a plan's specific objectives and its executional details, a sound strategy needs to provide an all-embracing "vision" that facilitates both internal and external implementation of the new strategy (Day 1990). Too often, this vision is both unclear and uncompelling for those involved, thereby thwarting even the best-laid plans.

Recent thinking about why fuzzy strategic vision emerges concludes that marketing managers tend to place too much emphasis on front-end analytical aspects of their strategies and too little on issues related to a strategy's real-time implementation and control (Bonoma 1984a). One response to this problem has been the development of better and more timely performance measures for assessing a plan's strengths and weaknesses earlier in the implementation process. A second remedy directs managers to "walk around" more at important implementation sites and to observe and interact with the key participants in executional activities and programs (Peters & Austin 1985). These improvements generally enhance corporate controls, facilitate emergent learning, and allow management to modify things midstream. Yet they do not automatically confront what may be the heart of the problem: a fuzzy strategic vision. As the subsequent examples suggest, serious problems arise when strategy designers and implementers appear motivated by the same strategy, when in fact they are working in divergent directions.

Strategy Implementation as Communication

Almost everyone has played the childhood game "Country Telephone," in which a relatively complicated message is whispered by the first player into the ear of a second and passed on down the line until it reaches the last child. Invariably, the final player reproduces a garbled and amusing variant of the original message. Marketing strategies are vulnerable to a similar phenomenon. Strategies that originate within top management circles must also be passed along an extensive and diverse line of players as they make their way to the marketplace. A marketing strategy task force commonly includes brand managers and their assistants; sales managers and the field force; product research and development personnel; advertising agency and promotional support groups; research providers; networks of distributors; and, ultimately, the consumer. With so many lines of communication, opportunities for miscommunication abound.

Unlike the outcome of Country Telephone, a garbled marketing strategy message is not amusing, and penalties for losing the strategy game can be severe. Also, the source of poor managerial communication is often not so much a failure to *reproduce* the message accurately as it is a failure to *understand* it. Such basic communication breakdowns are generally traced to one or more of these factors: (1) an internal strategic focus, (2) the primacy of implementation, (3) "generic" strategy articulation, and (4) ambiguous, unfocused strategy language.

Problem 1: Internal Strategic Focus

Marketing is distinguished from other managerial functions by its external focus on a company's customers, competitors, and environment. Students of marketing are universally instructed in a "marketing concept" that is grounded in historical, case-based evidence of the benefits that accrue to firms that adopt and maintain externally oriented marketing systems and programs. Despite this view, marketing strategies are often expressed in terms that reflect an internal focus and preoccupation. For example, such strategic directives may emphasize the goals of further increasing the market share or sales. Conversely, firms or brands in trouble often stress the need to reverse their declines. Internally oriented strategies commonly emphasize product improvements; for example, Ford's "Have You Driven a Ford Lately?" slogan. While these directions may be logical foundations for marketing strategy, they are (literally) miles from the real action.

Exactly who and where are the sources of incremental sales? What are these targets supposed to think about a company's needs and solicitations for their patronage? What are the customers expected to do in the marketplace?

Solution 1–A: Strategy "Maps"

Effective marketing strategy relies on the translation of internal objectives into behavioral goals and expectations for specific customers, suppliers, distributors, and other key agents. At its core, this process is a communication exercise in which internal directions are recast as expressions that focus managerial activities on the desired responses of explicit targets. A simple strategy "map" helps management filter and translate its internal strategy into externally oriented

EXHIBIT 1. Hypothetical Strategy Mapping

Internal Strategic Objectives	**External Expression of Strategic Objectives**		
	Customer Target(s)	Idea Objectives	Action Objectives
Reverse Sales Decline	Former users	Induce nostalgia preferences	10% coupon redemption
	Key retailers	Induce "comeback" perceptions	35% co-op advertising buy in
Increase Market Share	New users	Encourage trial and purchase	25% awareness of first-time-buyer program
	Nonexclusive brokers	Increase push efforts	Hawaii trips sales awards

ideas and activities. This process is illustrated in Exhibit 1, with a mapping of two common marketing strategies.

In both hypothetical situations, the mapped strategy moves the managerial dialogue beyond an internal focus toward specific consumer targets; it also translates internal directives into more specific idea and action objectives. Without these communication refinements, managers lack the critical milestones and performance measures they need to evaluate a strategy's implementation. More generally, when managers map their strategy onto the external environment, they can "reality check" their plans. For example, is a 10 percent coupon redemption goal too optimistic or insufficiently aggressive? What behavioral assumptions underly this target figure? Are these assumptions realistic?

Solution 1–B: Strategy Site Visits

When managers map their strategy, they can then identify the situations and marketing locations where the strategy will materialize or, as expressed in a currently popular phrase, "where the rubber meets the road." This knowledge should encourage managers to spend considerable time not merely as supervisors but as naive observers, listeners, and learners (Peters & Austin 1985). This prescription is easy to implement, and it provides a relatively fail-safe mechanism for generating valuable marketplace information. For example, on-the-scene involvement encourages both the specification and gathering of early-stage strategy performance measures (e.g., salesforce enthusiasm, distributor readiness), which further support emergent strategy refinements.

Examples of successful uses of strategy site visits are summarized by Peters and Austin (1985) and in McQuarrie and McIntyre (1990).

Although simple in concept, the idea of getting out of the office is often blocked by intraorganizational barriers. A marketing manager's request to spend two weeks in the field would meet with disapproving raised eyebrows in most companies. Yet an increased commitment to strategy site visits could begin on an incremental basis. Marketing managers already spend some time away from their offices, and they could be more opportunistic in these already-sanctioned situations. For example, a typical focus group junket requires two days away from the headquarters, and focus groups commonly convene in the evening. Some daytime hours might be devoted to local retailer and distributor visits or to opportunistic interactions with consumers. Even the many hours of managerial downtime in airports abound with observational possibilities for studying service encounters, complaining behavior, or other relevant issues.

These tactics are easily woven into a manager's ongoing travel itinerary with little additional cost in time or money. One barrier to conducting more site visits is simple inertia, which individual initiative can overcome. A more serious obstacle arises from anxiety about the relatively unstructured nature of strategy site visits. Managers tend to feel more secure in formal, structured, predictable situations; yet these often provide the illusion rather than the substance of productivity. Increasing the number and frequency of field visits, is compelling: the field is where the bulk of a strategy's implementation occurs.

Problem 2: The Primacy of Implementation

When a strategy is articulated primarily in terms of internal objectives, its external focus and translation may fall short. An opposite problem arises when a myriad of executional details causes managers to lose sight of the strategic big picture. This is a common and difficult situation. Strategy is relatively intangible, materializing in shared ideas, documents, and written directives. Implementation, on the other hand, occurs in the marketplace and emerges in concrete activities and visible tools such as advertising and promotion. As Bonoma (1984a) notes, this disparity between a strategy and its implementation creates diagnostic difficulties. For example, brilliant execution may mask what is really an inappropriate strategy and may actually accelerate progress in the wrong direction. Conversely, poor implementation is frustrating and may cause management to abandon an otherwise sound strategy. One remedy lies in more explicit identification of the organizational "layers" that bridge a strategy's initial design with its implementation.

Solution 2: "Layered" Strategy

Both in its design and execution, a marketing strategy flows through departments within the organization and across a complex network of suppliers, distributors, and facilitating agents. In a top-down organization, strategy originates among senior corporate and/or divisional executives and then moves down to the brand level and out the door to research suppliers, ad agencies, creative boutiques, and other key supporting players. In an incrementalist, bottom-up firm, strategy generation begins with line personnel and generally flows in the opposite direction. Regardless of a marketing strategy's directional flow, at least three "layers" of strategy emerge and reflect the differing tasks and perspectives of those involved.

"Layering" marketing strategy provides a communication link between those who design and those who implement a particular strategy. Each strategy layer varies in terms of its primary strategic focus and the organizational level where key activities occur. (Day 1990). The top or core strategy identifies the central marketing thrust and objectives. A second strategy layer translates the top layer into supportive functional strategies, such as those involving pricing, distribution, the sales force, research and development, etc. Finally, the third layer articulates the strategy in terms of tactical details that involve budgets, schedules, and controls.

The following example of "layered" strategy borrows from Michelob beer's "The Night Belongs to Michelob" promotional campaign. Exhibit 2 summarizes the layers of ideas, activities, and personnel associated with this strategic thrust. As a "dowager" brand in its super-premium category in the mid-1980s (Levy & Rook 1991), Michelob was losing sales and share to a variety of new and old brand competitors. The core strategy was two pronged and emphasized both brand repositioning and customer switching behavior. Before the advent of high-priced import beers, Michelob was perceived and priced above "regular" beer brands. It was positioned as beer for special occasions such as weekend parties, dates, and nights on the town. This position was eroded by both high-image imports and light beer brands that appealed to contemporary, young adult life-styles. Michelob's new brand strategy aimed to revive its "specialness" image. At the same time, it sought to boost its sales not by stealing share from the import brands but by convincing regular beer drinkers to trade up to Michelob in "special" consumption situations.

Advertising's role was particularly critical in the second, or functional, strategy layer. Here the core strategy was translated into an effort to appeal to a key beer drinking segment: "contemporary," young adult males (21–30 years). The advertising theme that integrated and supported this direction was captured in the slogan, "The Night Belongs to Michelob." The basic idea was to depict appealing, night-on-the-town occasions where a customer's request for a Michelob expressed the specialness of the situation. At the third, or tactical, strategy level, glamorous rock-video-style commercials attempted to deliver the strategy. Famous rock groups and stars (Genesis, Wang

EXHIBIT 2. Layering Strategy: Michelob's "The Night Belongs" Campaign

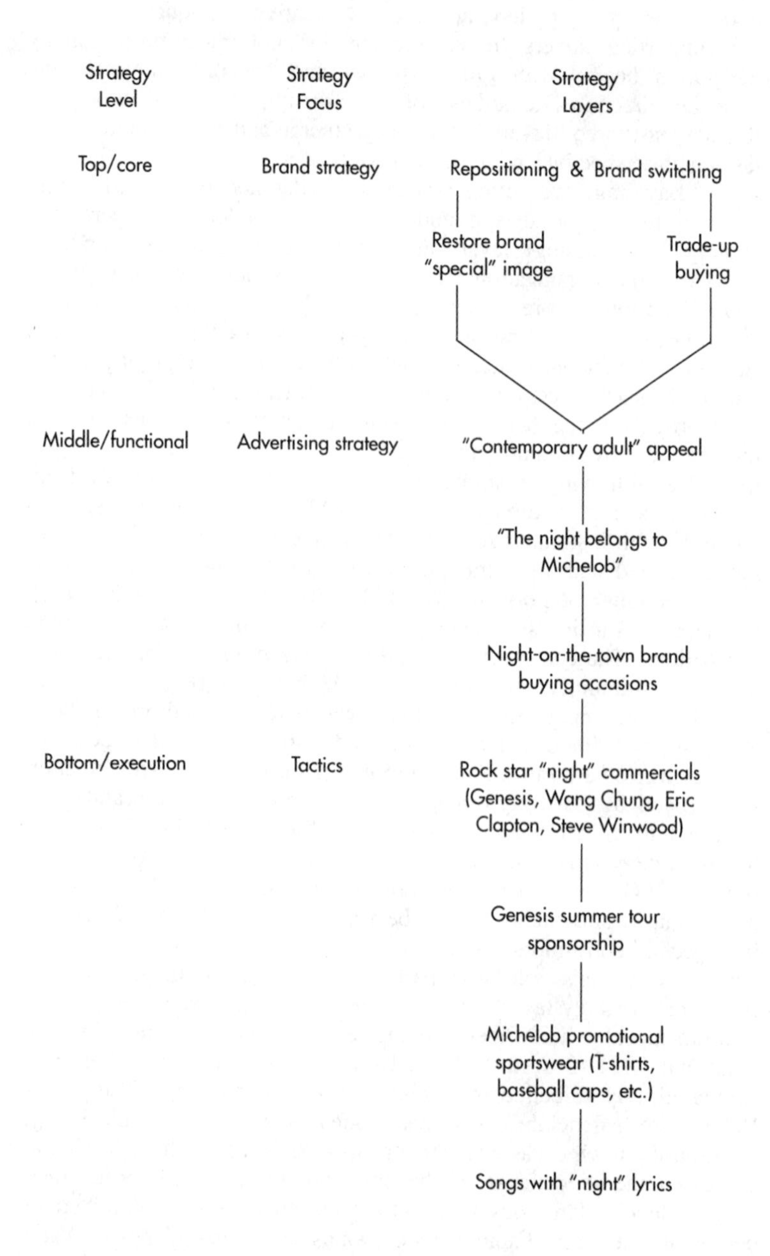

Chung, Eric Clapton, Steve Winwood) appeared singing songs with "night" lyrics that were resonant with the "Night Belongs" campaign.

These award-winning commercials made positive inroads toward the core objective of brand repositioning; yet their impact on actual Michelob sales was negligible. The executional success of the "Night Belongs" advertising clouded the other key objective: trade-up brand switching. It is likely that this second objective needed more support in the distribution system and at points of purchase. As Bonoma (1984a) suggests, successful implementation probably blinded many to the strategy's weak spots. By layering the strategy, managers would have been more likely to see where things were working and where more effort was needed.

Layering a marketing strategy is a useful planning tool with several distinctive benefits. First, it deals with the tendency to get lost in executional details, while the big picture slips away. Managers—just like other individuals—are subject to "fast forgetting." Because the daily managerial swirl is more likely to be preoccupied with executional details than with a brand's core strategy, managers may forget their ultimate destination. Second, layered strategy encourages emergent modifications of either the core, functional, or tactical elements. Brilliant execution may cover up bad strategy, but it can also stimulate revision of the core strategy. For example, a promotional campaign may succeed with a different segment than the one initially targeted. Finally, layering strategy prevents the tail from wagging the dog. For any core strategy there are numerous executional possibilities; rather than digging into tactical elements that are not working, a layered strategy encourages managers to explore alternatives for implementing the main strategic thrust.

Problem 3: "Generic" Strategy Articulation

Many marketing plans today look as if they were cut from the same cloth. Despite the move toward targeting microsegments, as well as the growing need to carve out distinctive positionings in crowded competitive markets, many strategy documents are undifferentiated and essentially generic in content and appearance. One arena where generic-seeming strategy often emerges is in so-called "quality" strategies, several examples of which are provided in Exhibit 3.

Quality claims may support a "heritage" positioning strategy (e.g., Kelly Tires), yet "quality" can be a pernicious marketing abstraction whose meaning, appeal, and intended impact are often unclear. In some communications it seems simply redundant. For example, few would expect Betty Crocker to offer low-quality kitchen accessories, so the advertising quality message really delivers no new information. Quality messages sometimes seem to reflect limited creative thinking. Couldn't anyone at Kraft generate a more relevant, meaningful, and original message for its venerable Velveeta cheese spread?

EXHIBIT 3. "Quality" Marketing Strategies

Company/Brand	Message/Slogan
Velveeta	Outstanding quality . . . outstanding savings
Del Monte	Quality has never been a better value
Buick	The new symbol for quality in America
Russell Athletic	Heritage . . . quality . . . performance
Ford	Quality is job 1
Kelly Tires	Quality since 1894
Betty Crocker	A host of quality accessories
Motorola	Quality means the world to us

Solution 3: In-depth Analysis

Obviously, there are real situations that dictate a broad, quality-oriented marketing strategy. After massive sales and share losses, U.S. automobile manufacturers discovered the need to improve both the actual and perceived quality of their cars. Despite this common industry direction, corporate and individual brands would be expected to execute their quality repositionings in distinctive ways. Yet, by harping on quality, the manufacturers actually reinforce negative consumer memories or arouse counterarguing. Executional similarities blunt the core strategies, making them generic, plain-wrap commodities.

Pontiac's sales successes illustrate the benefits of breaking away from generic strategy. Frustrated by declining sales, Pontiac commissioned extensive research to investigate the meanings of the brand to its current and former customers. Memory traces of Pontiac as a "sexy . . . exciting" automobile were discovered. This finding was translated into Pontiac's "We Build Excitement" campaign, which is credited with boosting brand sales and improving its image among consumers (Mitchell 1986). Although afflicted by "quality" problems similar to other U.S. manufacturers, Pontiac avoided translating the problem *literally* and went on to execute a break-away strategy that sharply distinguished it from other brands.

Problem 4: Unfocused and Ambiguous Strategy Language

The Pontiac success story begs the question, "How can managers avoid generic strategy?" One critical context in which this is problematic involves the core process of identifying a strategy's intended target(s). Within a strategy document, the specified target reflects prior analysis and conceptualization. Managers then communicate the target, along with other strategic elements, to key supporting players. Four common problems often confound this strategy translation process.

First, targets are sometimes *underspecified,* providing only a few census-like facts about current or prospective customers. Today, one still encounters consumer marketing plans that identify targeted customers primarily with demographic, usage frequency, and volume data. Such an approach often defies the marketing concept. Although it may do little damage in some situations (e.g., where demand exceeds supply and competition is weak), more richly detailed target specifications generally increase the likelihood that managers will correctly interpret the target and envision it not as a statistical abstraction but as a "real" person or company.

A second communication problem arises when target descriptions are too *inclusive*. A large number of packaged goods consumer targets are characterized in strategy documents as "female heads of households, aged twenty-five to forty-nine years, and living in an SMSA community." This description covers so wide a population territory that it tends to frustrate efforts to focus and target a specific, meaningful segment. Such broad definitions are relics of mass marketing and are at odds with current perceived needs to sharpen the competitive focus. While it is often literally true that one's customers range in age (for example, from twenty-five to forty-nine years), it is unlikely that the best customers are evenly distributed across such a wide spectrum. They are probably concentrated within a narrower segment of the continuum.

A shotgun approach to targeting generally blunts attempts to gain a sharper focus. When managers see their target "reduced" (hypothetically) to females between the ages of twenty-eight to forty years, they tend to panic at lost sales opportunities among both older and younger consumers. This myopic reaction misses the point. A marketer is more likely to hit the overall target when he or she aims toward the bull's-eye in the center rather than toward the periphery. The bull's-eye should identify the best and most profitable prospects for a positive response to a strategy's objectives.

Even when a customer target is richly detailed and sharply focused, *nondynamic identifiers* often fail to generate the enabling, shared vision that sound strategy requires (Day 1990). A customer target profile moves from static description (e.g., "blue collar") toward an activating dynamic when it includes motivational elements (e.g., "upward mobility aspirations") that converge with a product's perceived benefits and expectations (e.g., "classy," "prestigious"). Knowing the descriptive fact that a young customer is image conscious is relatively meaningless without also learning about what specific images (e.g., Michael Jordan or Axl Rose) he or she aspires to and why.

A final communication problem arises when a target's identity rests on *ambiguous terms*. Marketers often take the meanings of common target identifiers for granted; for example, "active," "upscale," "convenience oriented." Serious implementation problems arise when interpretations of the same strategy language vary within the marketing task force. Individually or together these common communication problems generate strategic directions that are unfocused and have little impact.

Solution 4: Eliminate Ambiguity

The following case history illustrates how these communication problems emerge and what marketing pitfalls they present. In the mid-1980s, Brand X, a light beer, was introduced in order to capitalize on the growing popularity of lower-calorie beverages and to offset sales declines of the beer's parent brand. Extensive research generated a profile of the primary target for Brand X's marketing strategy (Exhibit 4). On the surface, the target profile appeared reasonably focused and detailed; it *looked* OK. More importantly, its depiction of a young, hard-working and hard-playing urban male professional led to widespread agreement that the target was a cultural icon of the 1980s: the "yuppie."

This proved to be an enormous interpretive and communication error. Many key agency creative personnel were themselves young, successful, six-figure professionals leading sophisticated metropolitan lives. Many seemed to be yuppies themselves, and consequently it seemed as though they would be especially adept at communicating to their own kind. Yet they drew the circle too tight and aimed too high. Commercials depicted Brand X beer consumption in elite stratospheres: in a New York nouvelle cuisine restaurant, as a break during do-it-yourself rehabbing of an urban brownstone *pied a terre,* and as a (delayed) reward for a predawn run across the Brooklyn Bridge. These executions of the yuppie strategy were far "too cool for the room," and they went right over target members' heads. In focus group research, target beer drinkers were confused and mildly irritated by these unfamiliar and remote situations, and they registered little interest in a beer brand that seemed intended for other people.

Threatened with the likely loss of a large account, the agency (internally) acknowledged that it was off target and sought to remedy the situation. The key point at which the strategy began to veer off

EXHIBIT 4. Initial Consumer Target: Light Beer Brand X

Demographic Characteristics

- Male
- Young (age 21–30)
- Single
- Urban
- College graduate
- High income
- White collar

Psychographic Characteristics

- Active life-style
- Trendy
- Humor-oriented

Beer Consumption

- 6+ servings per week
- mostly light beer

Summary Target Profile

The male "yuppie" (young urban professional)

course was when it assumed that the yuppie target profile was univocal, when in fact it was open to quite different, alternative interpretations. Reflecting the communication problems identified earlier, the term "yuppie" is ambiguous, too inclusive, and weakly linked to beer-drinking dynamics. Exhibit 5 illustrates the theoretical extremes to which yuppie interpretations can be taken.

Agency personnel tended to see the target yuppie as an individual emerging from the left column in Exhibit 5. They aimed their thinking toward a somewhat older, more sophisticated, affluent, and educated consumer who works and lives in city centers. Consequently, creative efforts were biased toward the top of the beverage hierarchy (Levy 1986) and resulted in commercials that were better suited for cognac than for light beer. In fact, the real Brand X target was closer to the interpretations in Exhibit 5's right column: younger, more macho, less affluent, and not working in the professions. When the agency regained this perspective, it was then able to generate commercials that were more meaningful. New creative executions depicted Brand X consumption in more relevant social settings: apartment parties, dance clubs, and rock concerts. These images reached the target, stimulated more interest in the brand, and saved the business for the agency.

MANAGERIAL COMMUNICATION AS STRATEGIC GLUE

George Day compares marketing strategy to "conceptual glue" that provides common meanings to the functional activities and programs that support a company's core strategic direction (1990). This

EXHIBIT 5. Alternative Interpretations of Initial Target

Demographic Characteristics	Alternative Interpretations		
Male	Low	"Testesterone Level"	High
Young (age 21–30)	30	25	21
Single	Semidomesticated		Party animal
Urban	"Gold coast"		Fringe suburb
College graduate	Princeton		Community college
High income	Affluent		"Above average"
White collar	Brooks Bros.		Marshall's
Psychographic Characteristics			
Active	Triathelete		Brew ball
Trendy	*Vanity Fair*		*People*
Humor oriented	Billy Crystal		Andrew Dice Clay
Beer Consumption			
6+ servings/week	7		24
Mostly light beer	Exclusively		Weak majority

metaphor is vivid and provocative; it also alludes to the critical role managerial communication plays in connecting and cementing the ideas, activities, and people involved in designing and executing a marketing strategy. Although numerous problems commonly arise in translating strategic communications within and across organizational boundaries, effective measures are available to prevent or counter them. Improved strategy translation is not simply a question of "wordsmithing"; it is a managerial "craft" (Mintzberg 1987) that leads toward a strategic vision that is meaningful, enabling, and shared. Finally, most of the alternatives presented here are conceptually simple and easy to implement. They are generally quite low in incremental cost, and they reflect the common wisdom that an ounce of prevention is worth a pound of cure.

REFERENCES

Bomona, Thomas V. (1984a). Making your marketing strategy work. *Harvard Business Review.* March-April, pp. 69–76.

______. (1984b). *Managing Marketing.* New York: The Free Press.

Day, George S. (1990). *Market-Driven Strategy: Processes for Creating Value.* New York: The Free Press.

Levy, Sidney J. (1986), Meanings in advertising stimuli. In Jerry Olson and Keith Sentis (eds.): *Advertising and Consumer Psychology,* vol. 3. New York: Praeger.

Levy, Sidney J., and Dennis W. Rook (1992). Defending the Dowager: Competitive Communication Strategies for Declining Main Brands. Working paper, Northwestern University, Evanston, IL.

McQuarrie, Edward F., and Shelby McIntyre. (1990). Implementing the Marketing Concept through a Program of Customer Visits. Report no. 90–107, Marketing Science Institute, Cambridge, MA.

Mintzberg, Henry. (1987). Crafting strategy. *Harvard Business Review.* July-August, pp. 66–75.

Mitchell, Russell. (1986). How Pontiac pulled away from the pack. *Business Week.* August 25, pp. 56–57.

Peters, Tom, and Nancy Austin. (1985). MBWA (managing by walking around). *California Management Review* 28 (Fall):1–18.

PART TWO

ORGANIZING AND STAFFING THE MARKETING FUNCTION

PART TWO

INTRODUCTION

Marketing must be prepared to utilize the employees of today. Businesses are not created from machines and raw materials, so businesses are not simply the sum total of the people who comprise them. They are much more, and the success of a business depends upon the capabilities of its personnel. Simply put: The better the staff, the better the organization.

People in business have changed because value systems have changed. No longer do employees feel married to a company that will take care of their careers. Remaining silent, waiting your turn, and blindly following orders are concepts of the past. New employees will speak out, take chances, and become the controllers of their own careers. Employers should expect personnel turnover to escalate in the future as people make changes that will best suit their own career development.

Profits or losses result from the decisions and practices of people in the organization. The quality of the people hired and the quality of their performances determine the future of the firm. Because marketing is a "people-intensive" function, staffing is of critical importance. Consider the firm that, in a period of economic uncertainty, is turning in solid business gains. While some—including its competitors—will attribute these gains to good fortune, more likely this performance is due to consistently sound performance on the part of certain key managers. Indeed, perhaps the greatest leverage for improved business performance lies more in the people of the firm than in any other element of the marketing mix.

Part Two seeks to answer the questions: How do I find good marketing people? How do I determine their performances? Staffing is neither an intuitive act nor a science, but a combination of subjective and objective approaches. The increasing presence of professionally trained marketing decision makers and wider use of behavioral science techniques in staffing suggest both approaches will be more precise in the future.

Organization is still more of a skill than a science; it is an art in which thinking is more important than doctrine, and common sense more important than rigid adherence to rules. Experience has shown that an organizational structure that works effectively and successfully in one company may be a complete failure in another. And it follows that no one marketing organization has been found to be "best" o "ideal." Because the organization problem is so complex and of such concern to most businesspeople, it is hoped that in the chapters that follow, the principles detailed and the problems discussed will help in the setup of a more definitive marketing organization that is "custom-built" for a particular business.

Michael T. Higgins
Mike Higgins & Associates, Inc.
Lincoln, Nebraska

CHAPTER 5

REWARD COMPENSATION: MARKETING'S ROLE

The primary purpose of every business enterprise is to get and keep customers. If the enterprise is to fulfill this basic purpose, the responsibility for customer acquisition and customer retention must belong to everyone. Therefore, how we compensate all of our people has a direct impact on whether or not the organization achieves its fundamental reason for existing.

In many organizations, human resources and compensation management are the direct responsibilities of marketing. In other companies, the responsibility is isolated from marketing. In either case, it is absolutely essential for the marketing manager to ensure that a consistent compensation package including rewards for both sales and sales support is coordinated throughout the organization.

This is not a simple task because traditional compensation as well as reward compensation methods are no longer valid in a highly competitive global marketplace. The prevalent corporate mind-set today is centered on short-term goals, and its main expression has been through rewards for short-term achievement. As a result, there has been virtually no long-term, strategic focus nor any appreciation for long-term strategic management.

What are the implications of this corporate mind-set? An incredible—and overwhelming—dichotomy between short-term needs and long-term value has evolved, with dire consequences for both the company's shareholders and its own future viability. First, management's focus on short-term shareholder value (profit) has been maintained at the expense of long-term shareholder value. Second, the emphasis on short-term profitability has eclipsed the priority of serving the marketplace, which has resulted in a significant loss of market share. The resulting inability to compete effectively has further eroded *both* short-term and long-term shareholder value.

MASTER STRATEGY

This short-term focus can best be understood within the context of a corporation's master strategy. The master strategy is the organization's ultimate objective and plan of action. An organization can effectively pursue only one of four master strategies: maximize profit, maximize growth, balance profit with growth, or merge or sell (see Exhibit 1).

Each master strategy requires different priorities, and, therefore, each will lead the organization in a different direction. For example, if the organization's master strategy is to *maximize profit* (the term here is

EXHIBIT 1. The Four Master Strategies of an Organization

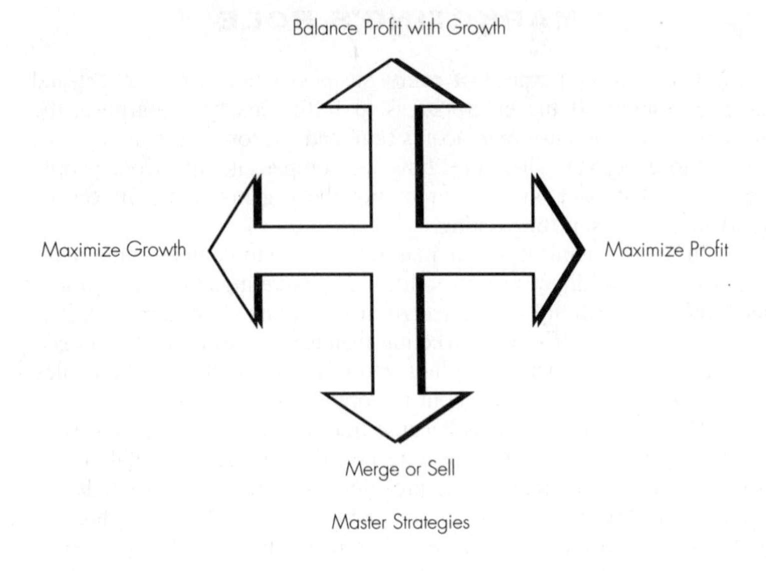

to *maximize,* not emphasize), then management's priorities will include tactics to raise prices at the expense of market share and to sell off fixed assets at the expense of investing in systems, training, facilities, special skills, and expertise. This master strategy is short term because a company cannot maximize profit for too long without driving all of its customers away.

The master strategy that is the opposite of maximizing profit is *maximizing growth.* Here the priority is to gain market share. The company will likely create action plans to lower prices and/or invest in facilities, acquire products, and invest in additional skill, expertise, and systems—all at the expense of profitability. An organization that operates under a master strategy to maximize growth for too long will likely acquire an abundance of customers but will not have enough retained earnings to continue serving its expanded client base.

For obvious reasons, the master strategy to merge or sell the organization is also a *very* short-term strategy.

All three of the foregoing master strategies relate to maximizing short-term shareholder value. The only master strategy that will maximize long-term shareholder value is the strategy to *balance profit with growth.* This master strategy can emphasize profit over growth or emphasize growth over profit, depending on the required, predetermined balance necessary to achieve the organization's priorities.

In most industries it is equally important to balance profit and growth with *quality and productivity.* The implications of productivity are obvious. Quality can be expressed through product quality, production quality, asset quality, and/or service quality. It is also important to note that maximizing profit precludes quality considerations, while maximizing growth precludes an organization's ability to incorporate productivity as a priority.

DICHOTOMY BETWEEN THE SHORT AND THE LONG VIEW

An incredible dichotomy has evolved in which American business has pursued a course of maximizing short-term profit or growth, thus excluding any possibility of improving long-term shareholder value.

The dichotomy is evident everywhere. For example, the vast majority of management bonuses, profit-sharing programs, and pension plans are based on goals to maximize profit. A sales or support staff's growth or volume goals have also been short-term because rewards have been measured in terms of short-term gain. Rarely are growth goals coordinated with reward systems that are intended to maximize profit. The conclusion can be made that reward compensation programs in the United States have traditionally been created and funded by short-term master strategies to either maximize profit or maximize growth.

Long-term shareholder value is based on the master strategy of balancing profit with growth. The levels of achievement to balance profit and growth must also be balanced with productivity and quality. Therefore, the contemporary approach to compensation, recognition, and reward programs must be based on *multiple goal achievement,* that is, a predetermined balance of four elements: profit, growth, productivity, and quality. Each of the four influences must be mathematically weighted rather than arbitrarily weighted to ensure that the reward value is explicitly tied to the level of increased performance.

TRANSITION TO MULTIPLE GOALS

Such a comprehensive program is complex in design; however, it must remain simple to implement, to administer, and to be understood by all participants. The program originates with the creation of incentive models based on multiple goal achievement. These must be mathematically weighted to provide rewards that represent a share of the improved contribution from each of the four critical influences.

The importance of including measurement and reward for all four influences now becomes obvious. If you reward for profit only, you do so at the expense of volume, quality, and productivity. Similarly, if you reward for volume or growth only, people will concentrate on volume at the expense of profit, quality, and productivity. As long as rewards are limited to fewer than all four of these critical influences, producers will always concentrate on what they are being rewarded for and will ignore the other equally critical influences.

This concept of multiple goal achievement was tested for five years in several companies located in different regions of the United States. Once having instituted a multiple goal achievement program, failing companies turned around in six to twelve months, and profitable companies that had difficulty growing maintained their level of profitability and experienced 20 to 30 percent annual growth. Growing companies that had experienced low earnings became high performers (see Exhibit 2). Employees received an additional 20 to 25 percent of their base salaries in performance compensation the first year the program was implemented, and they have improved on that in every subsequent year. Several companies opted to stabilize base salaries and place all base compensation adjustments in the incentive pool. In fact, the employees demanded it. All this occurred while shareholders retained at least 80 percent of the additional contribution to earnings from the improved performance.

A banking institution in southern California was ranked as the twentieth most consistently profitable bank in the United States. In his letter to shareholders, the bank president noted this ranking was

> *. . . an envious accomplishment in our industry under even normal circumstances.*
>
> *It is our opinion that this was a direct result of our Incentive Compensation Program. . . . That program also places us among the leaders in the industry in setting a portion of total compensation on the basis of performance. . . ."*

PARTICIPATION

Maximizing long-term shareholder value to ensure the future viability of a company requires an understanding of and a commitment to strategic priorities throughout the entire organization. This is contrary to the belief of many who consider themselves specialists in compensation programs. They recommend significant reward programs be limited to management only. Others recommend including customer-contact and sales people in the reward program. Restricting recognition and rewards is very shortsighted.

Yet many companies are still adamant about limiting reward opportunities. The absurdity of this mind-set can best be illustrated by imagining the San Francisco Forty-Niners' locker room several years

EXHIBIT 2. Growth of a Midwest Bank

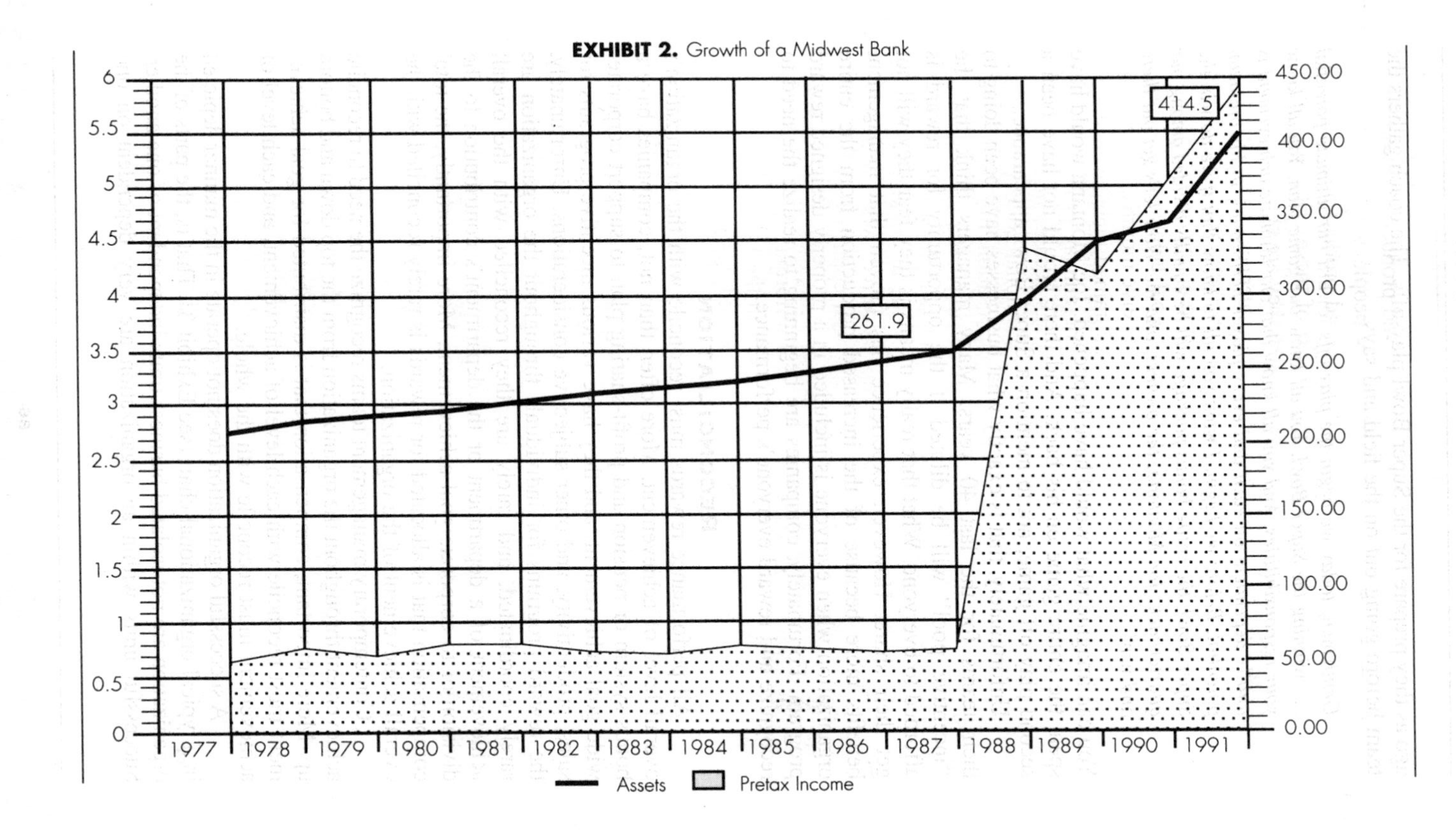

ago as they prepare for the Super Bowl play-offs. The coach gathers the team before going out on the field and says,

> *Gentlemen, today we begin the play-offs toward our ultimate potential . . . winning the Super Bowl. You all know our game plan. You all know your responsibilities. And you all know that our ultimate achievement is totally dependent on each and every player performing to his optimum potential. Before we begin, I want you all to know that if we do win the Super Bowl, the entire bonus package will be equally divided among our quarterback, Joe Montana, the owners, and me. Now let's get out there and win!*

You can imagine what would have happened. Joe Montana would have spent the entire game on his back. And there would not have been a second play-off game, not to mention a Super Bowl appearance.

Unfortunately, that is exactly what businesses have been doing to their teams for the last 40 years. Many managers think that the "incentive pool" will be diluted if the opportunity for reward is afforded to everyone. What that really means is they fear they will not get their share. However, experience has proven that management benefits more because of the increased production from the entire organization when everyone is included in a properly designed reward program. Fortunately, companies are beginning to realize the need to recognize and reward everyone's performance.

RECONCILIATION

All performance rewards must reconcile with the organization's overall level of achievement. More often than not, companies have a bonus system or pension and profit-sharing plan to support corporate-wide goal achievement, and they have various incentive programs for sales, productivity, and other subjective considerations. Unfortunately, the reward programs for individuals throughout the organization are rarely coordinated, and rarely are they reconciled with the overall achievement of a department or the department's contribution to the division or to corporate goal achievement. More importantly, the total compensation that is allocated for rewards is rarely reconciled with the overall achievement of the organization.

Contemporary management teams recognize the need to reconcile achievement throughout the organization from the top down and bottom up. More important, compensation that is distributed for goal achievement must reconcile with each level of achievement, and each level of achievement must reconcile with the whole.

A successful organization does not operate in the manner depicted in a typical organizational chart (see Exhibit 3). That is, the parts of the organization are not isolated business units independent of one another. Successful units within an organization are very dependent on one

EXHIBIT 3. The Traditional Organizational Chart

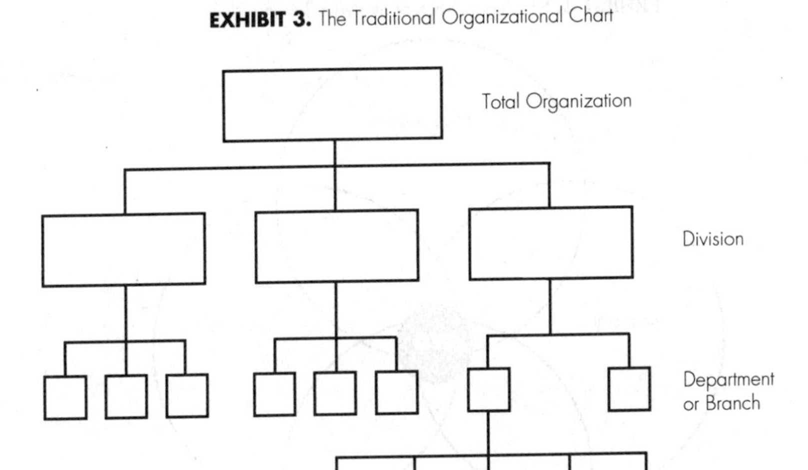

another. An organization operates as a group of interdependent strategic business units (SBUs), and its success usually depends on the success and support of other SBUs (see Exhibit 4).

Many of America's corporate managers are still driven by a World War II mentality that was necessary to win the war; i.e., the need to achieve short-term, maximum results. This mentality emphasized managers who had to be stern task masters and were required to stay aloof and distant from their staff. Although this thinking is still prevalent today, it has no place in a highly competitive environment. Today, in order to maximize everyone's contribution, companies must function so that decision making is the focal point around which everything else revolves. The result is centrally focused, organizational functions that maximize the potential of the company's limited financial, physical, technological, and personnel resources. Rewards, therefore, must be linked to team performance first and then—and only then—to individual contribution.

High achievers and highly productive people—for example, the most effective customer-contact and service quality people—will demand an environment wherein performance specifications are explicitly defined and achievement is tangibly rewarded.

To fully appreciate the notion that high achievers want to work where performance specifications are defined, one need only ask: Who stays in an environment in which people are compensated for tenure

EXHIBIT 4. Interdependence of Strategic Business Units

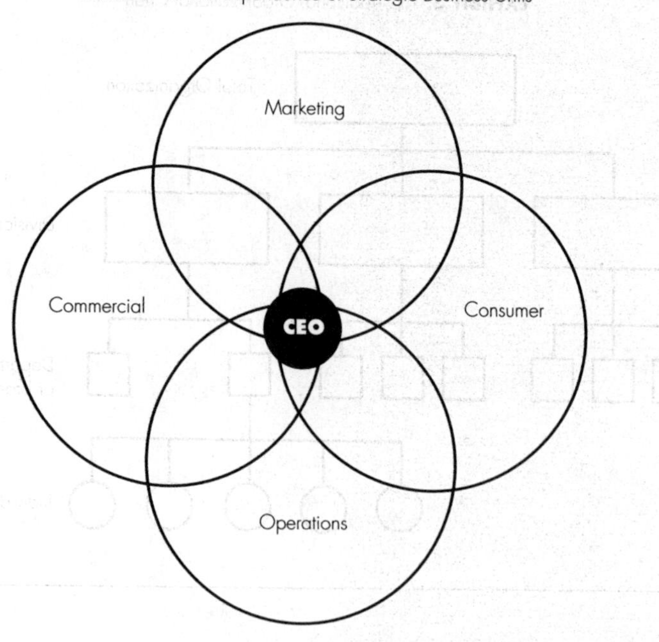

and experience? The answer is: people who cannot, or are not inclined to, perform. Who stays in an environment in which people are compensated for performance? High performers! Therefore, the ultimate goal for those who wish to maximize long-term shareholder value and the future viability of their companies is a commitment for the next three to five years in which 25 to 50 percent of their total compensation will be based on performance.

REACHING PERFORMANCE POTENTIAL

Most organizations conduct subjective annual reviews of their employees. However, subjective performance measurement typically does not result in significantly increased performance; therefore, it cannot justify the payment of significant amounts of performance compensation (see Exhibit 5).

Some organizations base their performance rewards on an arbitrary measure of contribution to corporate profitability. Even though the basis for the reward—profitability—is objective, the value of each individual's contribution to corporatewide profitability is subjective. Research has proven that this type of arbitrary reward, such as distributions to pension and profit-sharing plans or employee stock

EXHIBIT 5. Reward Compensation as a Percentage of Base Salary

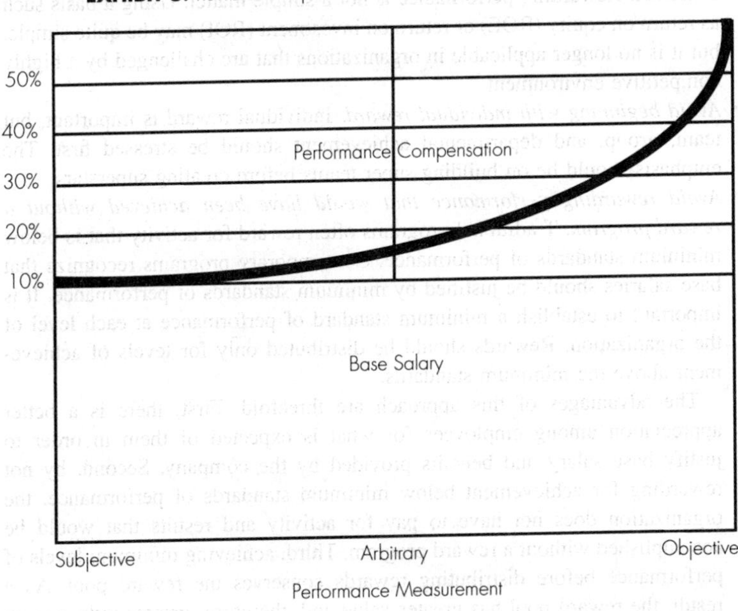

ownership plans (ESOPs) and 401(k)s, has very little influence on performance. As a result, arbitrary rewards for corporate profitability do not trigger significant performance gains.

Objective performance measurement—that is, performance measurement based on quantitative goal achievement—has a significant influence on increased performance. For that reason, significant performance compensation can be rationalized. The key is to drive measurement down through the entire organization and to ensure that objective performance measures always balance profitability and growth achievement with productivity and quality considerations.

PITFALLS

Even if you institute objective performance measures and apply them to everyone in the organization, you will not necessarily be assured of achieving long-term shareholder value. There are several additional pitfalls you must avoid to ensure the maximization of long-term shareholder value:

- *Avoid oversimplification.* A performance compensation system must be easy to implement, easy to administer, and easy to communicate to all participants.

That is precisely why successful reward programs are complicated to construct. Rewarding performance is not a simple matter. Using a basis such as return on equity (ROE) or return on investment (ROI) may be quite simple, but it is no longer applicable in organizations that are challenged by a highly competitive environment.

- *Avoid beginning with individual reward.* Individual reward is important, but team, group, and departmental achievement should be stressed first. The emphasis should be on building super teams before creating superstars.
- *Avoid rewarding performance that would have been achieved without a reward program.* Traditional programs often reward for activity that is below minimum standards of performance. Contemporary programs recognize that base salaries should be justified by minimum standards of performance. It is important to establish a minimum standard of performance at each level of the organization. Rewards should be distributed only for levels of achievement above the minimum standards.

  The advantages of this approach are threefold. First, there is a better appreciation among employees for what is expected of them in order to justify base salary and benefits provided by the company. Second, by not rewarding for achievement below minimum standards of performance, the organization does not have to pay for activity and results that would be accomplished without a reward program. Third, achieving minimum levels of performance before distributing rewards conserves the reward pool. As a result, the reward pool has greater value and, therefore, greater influence on increased performance above minimum standards of performance.
- *Avoid rewarding for activity.* Rewarding for activity is subjective and has little to do with results. Think in terms of the achievement of goals in support of strategic priorities. Rewards should not be based on action plans (activity) by individuals, teams, or strategic business units. Rather, rewards should be based on the individual, team, or SBU contribution to results.
- *Avoid arbitrary rewards.* To have value, the rewards must reflect explicitly quantifiable contributions to the organization. Arbitrary rewards typically have a negative influence on motivation, and they definitely impair the development of a long-term commitment to high performance.
- *Avoid unnecessary expense.* Reward programs should not cost the organization anything. Rather, once minimum levels of performance (plan or budget) are established to justify base salaries, performance rewards should be created by sharing 10 to 30 percent of the increased performance with the people who contributed to the higher level of achievement.

PROGRAM DESIGN

To properly design a performance compensation program that maximizes long-term shareholder value and the future viability of the company, specific expectations must be defined. The most important objective, of course, is to maximize long-term shareholder value. Supporting objectives should include

- improving communications by
  —focusing staff on priorities,
  —reinforcing key objectives,
  —providing explicit direction, and
  —reinforcing primary job functions;
- improving quality relationships and quality products or services;
- increasing work flow and accuracy;
- providing salary administration flexibility;
- stabilizing base salaries;
- rewarding high performers; and thereby
- retaining high-performance personnel.

A reward program that does not achieve all of these objectives will fall short of the need to maximize long-term shareholder value.

CONSEQUENCE IS A CRITICAL ELEMENT

Traditional compensation programs reward people for achieving various levels of performance but rarely, if ever, include a consequence for not achieving minimum levels of performance. However, the lack of consequences or penalties is the single most important reason why individuals, teams, and SBUs are often not motivated to achieve high performance.

An effective performance compensation methodology establishes a minimum level of performance for multiple goal achievement to rationalize or justify base salaries. A series of improved levels of performance is then specified, enabling one to create a matrix of multiple goal achievement. The matrix shows the participants' ability to increase their performance compensation based on the level of performance achieved for various goals. Typically, this requires seven to nine goal line items, which we call key performance indicators (KPIs). Each of the KPIs must be mathematically (not arbitrarily) weighted to allow payment for different levels of achievement.

An equally important facet is the creation of a matrix to relate penalties for achieving a level of performance below minimum standards. The weighting value for each KPI then reduces the incentive pool by the appropriate amount, which is tied to the value of each key performance indicator. By deducting from the incentive pool for results that do not adequately balance profitability and growth with quality and productivity, a significant motivation is introduced for people to achieve above minimum standards of performance.

CONCLUSION

This decade will present a level of domestic and global competitiveness beyond anyone's comprehension. In order for companies to compete—even to survive—a new level of commitment to managing strategic priorities must emerge.

The focus must be on a company's long-term viability and, therefore, on long-term shareholder value. The key is to balance profit and growth with quality and productivity through a program of multiple goal achievement. Expectations for performance must be weighted accurately—and not arbitrarily—to ensure that everyone throughout the organization understands the strategic focus. Ultimately, management's most important challenge will be to demonstrate its commitment to tie its greatest overhead expense—compensation—to long-term strategic goals rather than to short-term tactical goals.

Donald W. Hendon, Ph.D.
Professor of Marketing
University of North Alabama
Florence, Alabama

CHAPTER 6

STAFFING THE MARKETING FUNCTION

INTRODUCTION

This chapter is about the people who make up the marketing organization. It covers responsibilty for staffing; planning ahead for personnel needs; determining what kind of marketing personnel are needed; recruiting, screening, selecting, and testing; integrating personnel into the marketing organization; training and development; appraising and appropriately rewarding performance; and understanding, motivating, and managing.

RESPONSIBILITY FOR STAFFING

In large firms the personnel department has the major responsibility for staffing. Personnel departments have great expertise in planning ahead, recruiting, screening, testing, selecting, training, developing, appraising, compensating, and motivating all personnel, including marketing personnel. Marketers should rely on the advice, counsel, and suggestions of these staff experts before making their final decisions on who to hire. The *line* marketing department must make the final decision, however, on who to hire, terminate, and so forth. In small organizations staffing is just one of many responsibilities of line marketing managers, who must make staffing decisions based on limited information, expertise, and assistance.

Although marketing managers should not rely entirely on their own judgment in staffing matters, neither should they delegate their entire responsibility to the personnel department. Both are needed for successful staffing.

PLANNING FOR PERSONNEL NEEDS

Four variables influence the need for additional marketing people: (1) employee turnover, (2) the nature of the present work force, (3) the nature of the labor market, and (4) the firm's growth rate.

Turnover occurs because of voluntary resignations, discharges, and retirements. With adequate records, turnover can be predicted and new employees can be run through the entire recruiting process in time to meet the company's needs. These records include (1) organization charts, which identify personnel who are ready for promotion, who are promotable at specific future dates, and who are not promotable; (2) replacement tables, showing incumbents and first and second choices for replacement for each position; and (3) management and development schedules for each employee, showing his or her actual and potential progress.

Consider the nature of the company's work force in relation to its changing needs. If the firm is changing drastically—new product lines substituted for old, new technological changes occurring, etc.—then it must retrain present workers and/or bring in new personnel from outside. Companies should pay particular attention to the labor market's overall supply, its mobility, prevailing wage rates in the industry and geographic region, and so forth. Although "promotion from within" is usually a good policy to follow for motivation's sake, it is not necessarily feasible. Therefore, the outside labor market should be monitored continuously to determine its capacity for new hires.

In addition, consider the firm's growth rate. This is influenced by management policy, competition in the marketplace, and the state of the local, national, and world economy. The rate of growth or decline will affect future personnel needs.

DETERMINING WHAT KINDS OF PERSONNEL ARE NEEDED

All marketing jobs can be placed into four groups: (1) various types of sales personnel; (2) management; (3) technical personnel, including market researchers, engineers, and other technical personnel in marketing, nonmanagerial advertising, and so forth; and (4) clerical, secretarial, transportation, and warehousing workers.

RECRUITING

Recruiting is the process of identifying a group of candidates from which to make the final selection. The personnel department should handle the initial recruiting, screening, and testing process using detailed input from the marketing manager concerning the qualifications for the position. The personnel department weeds out many applicants, and the marketing manager then selects from the few who qualify.

It is important that the marketing manager give very specific details about the position requirements to the personnel department. One way to do this is to use *quartile analysis.*

First, rank order all employees. Do this by determining who are your best and worst incumbents in the particular job category. These are your benchmarks. Then place all other employees in rank order in relation to the best and worst. Make certain you quantify the criteria of effectiveness you use in order to comply with federal and state agency guidelines. In the United States, the most important agency is the Equal Employment Opportunity Commission (EEOC). Otherwise, you may run into trouble with affirmative action laws. For example, for sales reps, firms are relatively safe in using sales volume, number of calls made per day, sales quotas attained, number of displays built, and profitability as criteria for effectiveness. Make certain that the criteria you use are objective.

Once you have ranked your incumbents from best to worst, divide them into four groups in order to perform quartile analysis. Look at the top 25 percent and the bottom 25 percent. Ignore the middle two quarters. Compare the top 25 percent with the bottom 25 percent to determine the significant differences between the two groups. If your company keeps its personnel records up-to-date, then personnel clerks can simply search out and find significant differences in as many categories as they can find. For example, if the average age of those in the bottom quartile is twenty-five and those in the top quartile is forty-five, then the marketing manager should instruct the personnel department to look for older applicants instead of younger ones. (This would help win legal battles if your firm is charged with age discrimination.) Perform quartile analysis annually for best results.

Recruiting in the United States is more complicated than in many other nations because federal, state, and local governments involve themselves in the process. The EEOC has the power to institute civil actions in federal courts to prohibit all forms of employment discrimination based on race, religion, color, sex, age, or national origin. Most organizations are under its jurisdiction. Many organizations are also under "affirmative action" rulings, and so they must actively seek out minorities to fill certain vacancies. In many cases, members of the minority group are given preference because of affirmative action laws. The organization should consult an attorney specializing in this area, since federal, state, and local regulations change often.

Many firms have a "promotion from within" policy. Most of these firms review personnel records and appraisal forms to find qualified candidates, while some post job vacancies in the office where employees can see them. Other sources include public and private employment agencies; unsolicited applicants at the company's employment office; advertising in newspapers and trade publications; posting vacancies at universities, trade schools, and high schools; referrals from business associates, present customers, and professional associations; and asking present employees to recommend applicants. Labor unions also have job pools for marketing jobs including transportation, storage, and clerical help.

SCREENING, SELECTING, AND TESTING

Most firms follow nine basic steps immediately following recruiting applicants: (1) applicant is received in the employment office, (2) personnel representative conducts preliminary interview, (3) applicant completes application, (4) applicant completes selection test, (5) personnel representative conducts main employment office interview, (6) personnel representative investigates applicant's background, (7) applicant undergoes medical examination, (8) manager or supervisor conducts final selection interview, and (9) candidate is chosen and hired.

The first six steps make up the screening process itself, and identify the small cadre of candidates who are most qualified to fill the position.

Applicants should be interviewed several times. If your firm uses several interviews, and if you correlate answers to similar questions, you can uncover discrepancies if they exist. In interviews, use questions from the application blank to see if verbal and written inconsistencies occur. Investigate all discrepancies.

Use quartile analysis in designing the application blank. You may want to eliminate elements that were not significantly different between the top and bottom quartiles. It is a good idea—and a simple process—to assign weights annually to the different parts of the application blank, reflecting their relative importance. Assigning weights can also facilitate a numerical cutoff point.

Since the advent of affirmative action legislation, testing has become controversial. Some firms have abandoned testing entirely in light of validation requirements made evident in several U.S. Supreme Court decisions. Ask your attorney for the latest EEOC guidelines. An important guideline concerns establishing validity of tests. You will need to show a significant relationship between test scores and specific measures of job performance. This is called "empirical statistical validity." The relationship must be significant at the .05 level—that is, where there is only one chance in twenty (5 percent) that the correlation was obtained by chance. Furthermore, EEOC guidelines require separate validation studies for each minority group.

If you decide to test after all these caveats, there are many commercial tests you can choose. Some of the main intelligence tests are Science Research Associates' Adaptability Test, Psychological Corporation's Wechsler Adult Intelligence Scale and Wesman Personnel Classification Test, and E. F. Wonderlic's Wonderlic Personnel Test. Personality tests include Sheridan Psychological Services' Quilford-Zimmerman Temperament Survey, Consulting Psychologists Press's California Psychological Inventory, Institute for Personality and Ability Testing's Sixteen Personality Factors Questionnaire, and Psychological Corporations' Edwards Personal Preference Schedule and Minnesota Multiphasic Personality Inventory. Some interest tests are Science Research Associates' Kuder Preference Record Vocational Form CP, Stanford University Press's Strong-Campbell Interest Inventory, and Consulting Psychologists Press's Holland Vocational Preference Inventory.

Four sources for background information about applicants are (1) school and university officials, (2) previous employers, (3) character references supplied by the applicant, and (4) other sources, such as neighbors, retail credit bureaus, police records, and so forth. No matter which sources you use, be careful not to violate privacy laws. Court decisions in the United States in the late 1980s and early 1990s have held references who have said or written uncomplimentary things about applicants liable for damages. As a result, most references will only say good things about applicants. Therefore, references are generally unreliable. If you do use references, it is best to make follow-up phone calls or visit the references in person. Psychologically speaking, phone calls are more accurate than in-person visits. This is because references often feel they are talking to nothing more than a disembodied voice over the air, not in person to another human being. As a result, you can usually get more honest answers this way.

If your applicant passes all your screening hurdles along with the medical exam, then the line marketing manager selects or rejects the applicant. Whether or not an applicant accepts your offer depends in large part on how serious and fair the total selection process is. This may be the applicant's first exposure to your firm, and first impressions are important and lasting.

INTEGRATING NEW EMPLOYEES INTO THE ORGANIZATION—INDUCTION AND ASSIMILATION

Whether the applicants you select stay with your company depends on how well your induction process assimilates them into your organization. Explain the details of the job to your new employee, including company policies. Make sure your new employee meets fellow workers.

TRAINING AND DEVELOPMENT

Training is the process of maintaining and improving an employee's operating efficiency in present assignments. Good training brings increased productivity, higher morale, reduced supervision and accidents, and a more flexible and stable organization. There are three basic levels of training: initial, ongoing, and refresher training. Initial training occurs immediately after employment begins. It orients the new employee and covers specific areas that he or she did not learn in school. Continuing training lets an employee reach full potential and keep pace with changes in the industry.

You can use many different techniques to train marketing employees, including lectures, conferences, case studies, role-playing, job rotation, coaching, and on-the-job training. Each has its advantages and disadvantages. For each technique you consider, ask five questions:

1. Is it oriented to the specific needs of trainees?
2. Does it let trainees use many of their senses?
3. Does it reward trainees for changes in behavior?
4. Does it give regular and constructive feedback to trainees?
5. Does it help trainees when they encounter obstacles?

The goal of all training is to develop employees into better employees. However, there is another aspect to this: executive development (or management development). Only a small percentage of marketing employees are groomed for top positions. Those who aspire to these need special management development training, since top jobs are much more complicated than lower-level marketing jobs.

Executive jobs are typically fragmented, open-ended, interpersonal, active, and verbal. The following are six approaches to develop the necessary skills: (1) To improve decision-making skills, use business games and case studies. (2) To improve interpersonal skills, use role-playing and sensitivity training. (3) To improve job knowledge, use on-the-job experience, coaching, and understudy techniques. (4) To improve organizational knowledge, use position rotation and multiple management. (5) To improve general knowledge, use special courses, meetings, seminars, and selective reading lists. (6) To improve specific, individual areas, use special projects and selected committee assignments.

Without this kind of training, a top-notch sales rep, for example, may fail miserably as a sales manager.

APPRAISING AND REWARDING PERFORMANCE

Performance appraisal is the systematic evaluation of employees with respect to their job performance and their potential for development. The evaluation is usually made by immediate supervisors and reviewed in turn at the next higher level of management. Most companies evaluate employees once or twice a year, but they evaluate new employees more often.

Be on guard against five common errors: (1) halo effect, when just one aspect of an employee's character or performance influences the entire evaluation in either a positive or negative manner; (2) central tendency, when all or almost all employees are appraised as average; (3) constant errors, when "easy" appraisers give consistently high marks and when "harsh" appraisers give consistently low marks; (4) length of service or position errors, when long-time employees and those with high-status jobs in the firm get higher marks than other employees; and (5) prejudice errors, when biases against employees because of their race, religion, nationality, age, or sex play an important role.

There are eight major types of appraisal systems: (1) *Rating scales* involve appraisers placing marks somewhere along a continuum, as in Exhibit 1, or checking boxes that pertain to descriptions of the employee, as in Exhibit 2. (2) *Employee comparisons* involve ranking employees from best to worst on an overall basis according to their job performance and value to the firm (as in quartile analysis). Each employee could also be compared with every other person in the group, one at a time (paired-comparison techniques). (3) The *weighted checklist* is a series of many different statements. Each statement, as the name implies, has a weight attached to it. The appraiser checks all statements that most closely describe the employee's performance. (4) The *forced-choice checklist* contains many groups of four statements each. For

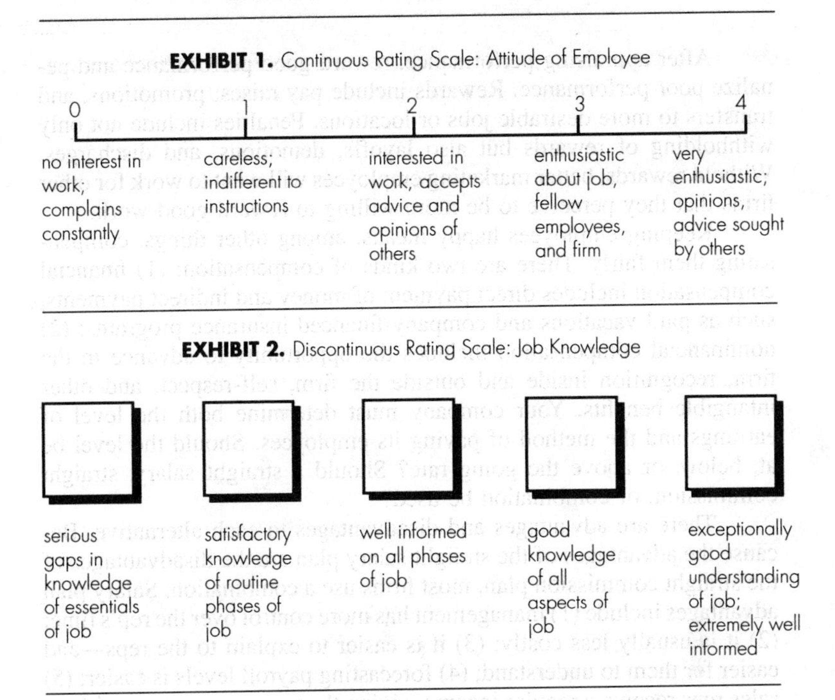

each group, the appraiser indicates the one statement that is most descriptive of the employee's performance and the one statement that is least descriptive. Each statement has a weight attached to it, but the appraiser does not know the weight. The personnel department does the final scoring of this checklist. (5) In the *critical incident method,* a supervisor makes timely records in a notebook of all significant incidents he or she notices that indicate an employee's good and bad performance. (6) Appraisers simply write down impressions of employees on sheets of paper in the *free-form essay method.* (7) The employee's immediate supervisor and three or four other supervisors who know the employee's work performance form a committee to evaluate him or her in the *group appraisal method.* (8) *Management by objectives* emphasizes a joint determination of objectives by supervisor and subordinate, followed by a participative but joint evaluation of success in periodic appraisal interviews.

The most important thing to remember is that the appraisal ratings must be made by the immediate marketing supervisor, with the personnel department assuming the responsibility of monitoring the system. Although the personnel department should not change any ratings made by the supervisor, it does have the obligation to point out inconsistencies.

After appraising performance, reward good performance and penalize poor performance. Rewards include pay raises, promotions, and transfers to more desirable jobs or locations. Penalties include not only withholding of rewards but also layoffs, demotions, and discharges. Without rewards, better marketing employees will want to work for other firms that they perceive to be more willing to reward good work.

Keeping employees happy means, among other things, compensating them fairly. There are two kinds of compensation: (1) financial compensation includes direct payment of money and indirect payments, such as paid vacations and company-financed insurance programs; (2) nonfinancial compensation includes the opportunity to advance in the firm, recognition inside and outside the firm, self-respect, and other intangible benefits. Your company must determine both the level of earnings and the method of paying its employees. Should the level be at, below, or above the going rate? Should a straight salary, straight commission, or combination be used?

There are advantages and disadvantages to each alternative. Because the advantages of the straight salary plan are the disadvantages of the straight commission plan, most firms use a combination. Salary plan advantages include (1) management has more control over the rep's time; (2) it is usually less costly; (3) it is easier to explain to the reps—and easier for them to understand; (4) forecasting payroll levels is easier; (5) sales reps receive a regular income, giving them more security; (6) there is even morale throughout the sales force. The disadvantages of the straight salary plan include (1) sales reps have very little incentive to excel; (2) during business downswings, there are higher expenses (inflexibility); (3) sales reps have no special incentive to exploit business upswings; (4) managers face tough adjustment questions on three things—ability, length of service, and rising cost of living; and (5) it is hard to attract self-starters and hard-driving sales reps.

Finally, it is important to realize that management wants to have control, economy, and simplicity in its sales compensation plan, while sales reps want income regularity, rewards for above-average performance, and fairness. It is difficult but not impossible to reconcile these two points of view.

UNDERSTANDING, MOTIVATING, AND MANAGING MARKETING PERSONNEL THROUGH COMMUNICATION

Empathize. Put yourself in your employee's place. Think as your employee does. If you can identify with your employee in this way, you are in a better position to motivate him or her, and this will improve your leadership ability. Each marketing employee is different, but each has the same varying levels of the same needs: (1) innate physiological needs of food, water, shelter, temperature control, rest, air, waste elimination, sex,

EXHIBIT 3. Number of People and Amount of Information at Five Levels in a Firm

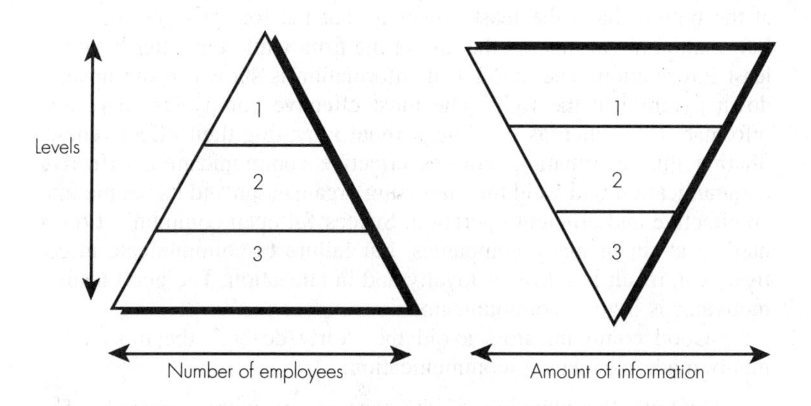

and preservation of self; (2) socially acquired needs of companionship, gregariousness, love, affection, belongingness, being wanted, esteem or respect of others, security, and safety; and (3) egoistic acquired needs of self-significance, self-respect, self-expression, self-accomplishment, acquisition of possessions, independence, and freedom. The best leader-motivator will seek out and learn the needs that are most important to each employee and attempt to satisfy those needs through the working environment and the work itself. Money is a relatively poor motivator in economically advanced nations. Once people make a certain amount of money to satisfy most needs, extra money will not motivate them to produce more. The wise leader-motivator will try to appeal to the employee's social and egoistic acquired needs. (Many psychologists include the need for money as an innate physiological need.) As marketing personnel make more and more money, the relative importance of money as a motivator diminishes somewhat—unless the pay raises do not keep pace with inflation.

Relationships among people are impossible without communication. Successful marketing managers—those who do the best job in motivating their people—are much better communicators than the unsuccessful ones. Exhibit 3 illustrates why it is so difficult to communicate in organizations. The pyramid on the left shows a firm with three levels: top managers, middle managers, and employees. The few at the top have the most power. The bottom level contains the most people, but they have the least power. Knowledge is power, and one of the main reasons the few at the top have the most power and the many at the bottom have the least power is that the former have the most information about matters that affect the firm, while the latter have the least information. The amount of information is shown in the upside-down pyramid at the right. The most effective companies share this information as much as possible without impairing their effectiveness. Sharing this information requires effective communication. Effective communication will weld the marketing organization and its people into an effective and efficient operation. Successful open communication is hard to attain in many companies, but failure to communicate effectively can result in a loss of loyalty and in alienation. The good leader-motivator is a good communicator.

Good communicators avoid the "dirty dozen," the most commonly made mistakes in communication:

1. Thinking the meaning of the message is within yourself. The meaning that counts is that within the other person.
2. Thinking the other person's frame of reference is always the same as yours.
3. Thinking your words mean the same to you as they do to the other person. There are many nuances in language.
4. Thinking what you have to say is all that is worth saying. Be greedy for feedback from the other person—what he or she has to say is very important.
5. Forgetting at times that communication is a shared experience.
6. Thinking that static or noise in the communication process comes from disagreement about clearly defined causes of action. It really comes from different perceptions of the same situation.
7. Forgetting that apparent understanding can lead to later static or noise if both you and the listener are not on the same frequency. (For example, you might think you and the other person have agreed on a 10 percent profit margin. He or she is thinking 10 percent gross profit, and you are thinking about 10 percent net profit. Your assumptions are quite different.)
8. Thinking that you communicate when you speak. Communication only happens when the other person accepts, understands, and is influenced by your words.
9. Thinking communication is primarily saying the right things in the right way. An often-quoted study found that only 7 percent of the meaning comes from a person's words, 38 percent comes from a person's tone of voice and inflection, and 55 percent comes from a person's facial expression and body language.

10. Thinking the other person is giving you his or her undivided attention. In reality, the other person listens to what is real for him or her.
11. Thinking communication is a process of unilateral bludgeoning, not a dialogue. The opposite is true.
12. Concentrating so much on what you are saying that you disregard the emotional impact you are making on the other person. Again, be greedy for feedback.

SUGGESTIONS FOR FURTHER READING

Alexander, Francine. 1989. Performance appraisals. *Small Business Reports*, March, pp. 20–29.

Brown, A. 1985. Employment tests: Issues without clear answers. *Personnel Administrator*, 30:43–56.

Buzzotta, V. R. 1988. Improve your performance appraisals. *Management Review*, August, pp. 40–43.

Dumaine, Brian. 1987. The new art of hiring smart. *Fortune* August 17, pp. 79–81.

Flippo, Edwin B. 1984. *Principles of Personnel Management,* 6th ed. New York: McGraw-Hill.

Hartley, Robert F. 1989. *Sales Management.* Columbus, OH: Merrill.

Henderson, Richard I. 1985. *Compensation Management: Rewarding Performance,* 4th ed. Reston, VA: Reston.

Jenks, James M., and Brian L. B. Zevnik. 1989. ABCs of job interviewing. *Harvard Business Review*, July-August, pp. 38–42.

Keys, Bernard, and Joseph Wolfe. 1988. Management education and development: Current issues and emerging trends. *Journal of Management*, 14:205–229.

Kotler, Philip. 1991. *Marketing Management: Analysis, Planning, and Control.* Englewood Cliffs, NJ: Prentice-Hall.

Kravetz, Dennis J. 1989. *The Human Resources Revolution.* San Francisco: Jossey-Bass.

Leap, Terry L., and Michael D. Crino. 1989. *Personnel/Human Resource Management.* New York: Macmillan.

Melohn, Thomas. 1987. Screening for the best employees. *INC.*, January, pp. 104–106.

Milano, Carol. 1989. Reevaluating recruitment to better target top minority talent. *Management Review*, August, pp. 29–32.

Walton, M. S. 1985. How to draft a sales compensation plan. *Personnel*, June, pp. 71–74.

Steven P. Brown
Southern Methodist University
Dallas, Texas

Thomas W. Leigh
University of Georgia
Athens, Georgia

J. Martin Haygood
Management Psychology Group
Atlanta, Georgia

CHAPTER 7

SALESPERSON PERFORMANCE AND JOB SATISFACTION

Scenario: One hundred sales recruits are identified, hired, trained, and assigned to sales territories. Several years later, management finds that many salespeople have departed and that the sales performance levels of the remainder vary considerably. Management's intuition is that job satisfaction varies among the sales force as well.

Wouldn't it be interesting and useful to examine these 100 salespeople and their territories to determine what factors influence their performance, satisfaction, and retention? Couldn't a company also enhance its cost effectiveness by identifying the personal characteristics and qualities that predict sales performance and satisfaction? Sales managers and academic researchers have long sought to identify the determinants of sales performance. In large part, the riddle remains unsolved. Despite a large number of studies, most of the variance in sales performance remains unexplained. Similarly, a considerable body of research has investigated the linkages between performance and work attitudes among sales personnel. The conclusions of this research also remain controversial.

Our purpose in this chapter is to provide an update on the status of our understanding of the antecedents and consequences of sales performance and job satisfaction. We also suggest directions for future research in the quest to improve our understanding and management of sales force productivity and satisfaction.

DETERMINANTS OF SALES PERFORMANCE

Churchill, Ford, Hartley, and Walker (1985)[1] reported the results of a meta-analysis of more than 116 articles spanning 75 years of research concerning sales performance. They summarized all of the available empirical studies concerning the prediction of sales performance. Their review goes beyond the typical interpretive summary to provide a quantitative evaluation of the evidence regarding factors that affect sales performance.

The conclusions of this meta-analysis are quite revealing but problematical for those seeking a simple solution. There is no "simple and sovereign" explanation of sales performance. The average correlation for any *single* predictor and sales performance is only .19. This means that, on the average, only 4% of the variation in sales performance across sales personnel is accounted for by any one factor.

The fact that sales performance is such a complex phenomenon may not surprise even the casual observer. However, few studies have attempted to model these expected complexities. The failure to come to grips conceptually with these complexities appears to be a major gap in the sales performance literature. Evidence regarding the six summary categories of factors affecting performance (i.e., aptitude, personal attributes, skill levels, motivation, role perceptions, and organizational-environmental factors) suggests several other critical gaps. Each of these six categories is briefly reviewed below.

APTITUDE

Aptitude includes the innate abilities or enduring personal characteristics relevant to sales performance. This category would include native intelligence (math and verbal), cognitive abilities such as reasoning, memory, and speech fluency, and specific psychological traits related to sales aptitude. Psychological traits such as responsibility, dominance, need for achievement, and empathy have frequently been related to sales performance. The weighted-average correlation for these variables with performance is only .14. Aptitude variables, on the average, explain less than 2% of the variation in sales performance.

Thus, aptitude measures are generally poor predictors of sales performance. However, in a limited set of special cases, they may predict well. Careful attention and systematic investigation is therefore required to identify the special circumstances in which aptitude may predict sales performance. Differences across selling contexts in factors such as product type, job type, selling process, or customer type might be likely to affect the aptitude-performance linkage. This issue will be addressed in more detail below.

PERSONAL ATTRIBUTES

A variety of personal factors such as age, height, sex, weight, race, appearance, and marital status have been related to sales performance. The weighted-average correlation with performance is only .16. Thus, on the average, these general personal factors account for less than 3% of the variance in sales performance.

SELLING SKILLS

Selling skills include a variety of acquired proficiencies related to a particular job or task. Examples would include selling style, technical or product knowledge, objection handling or closing skills, and so forth. Reported studies of selling skills are surprisingly rare. However, the weighted-average correlation between selling skills and sales performance was .27. Thus, on the average, selling skills explain slightly more than 7% of the variance in sales performance.

The fact that this proportion of explained variance is higher than that for aptitude confirms the intuition that selling skills should be more closely related to sales performance. It is also likely that the selling skills measures were more specifically developed with relevant selling contexts in mind. The fact that for some studies the correlations between selling skills and sales performance were actually quite high suggests that selling skills are strong predictors in some sales contexts. As with aptitude, research attention to situational moderating factors would be worthwhile.

MOTIVATION

Motivation refers most generally to the expressed willingness or desire to put effort into the job. A variety of different measurement approaches to motivation have been attempted (in sales force research, primarily cognitive and personality approaches, as will be discussed further below). Across the variety of studies using these different approaches, the weighted-average correlation between motivation and sales performance is .18. Thus, on the average, motivation accounts for about 3% of the variation in sales performance. Motivation is not as good a predictor as might have been expected given the centrality of motivation in sales performance models.

ROLE PERCEPTIONS

Role perceptions (specifically role conflict, role clarity, and role ambiguity) have proven to be significant determinants of sales performance. The weighted-average correlation of these role perceptions with performance is .29, explaining, on the average, approximately 9% of the variance in sales performance. This relatively strong association with sales performance, combined with the fact that managerial actions can be undertaken to enhance them, make role perceptions an important focus for sales managers.

ORGANIZATIONAL AND ENVIRONMENTAL VARIABLES

Finally, the effects of a variety of organizational and environmental variables (i.e., sales territory workload and potential, supervision, and marketing policies) on sales performance have been investigated. The weighted-mean correlation for these variables is only .10. Thus, less than 1% of the variation in sales performance is explained by these variables. The fact that many companies systematically manage or balance sales potential and workload across sales personnel may serve to minimize sales territory differences.

CONCLUSIONS ON PERFORMANCE DETERMINANTS

The major conclusion of this research summary is that, on the average, no single predictor explains a large proportion of the variation in sales performance. More general types of variables, such as aptitude and personal characteristics, are especially limited in their contribution. Caution against overreliance on any particular physical, personality, or aptitude criterion for recruiting purposes is thus warranted. Moreover, little research-based guidance is available concerning how these general measures may act in concert. Industrial psychologists collect and interpret a variety of employee data and judgmentally combine it to provide recruiting assessments. Because these assessments will continue to be made, even in the absence of solid research evidence, a subsequent section of this chapter suggests guidelines for effective recruiting.

The fact that role perceptions, selling skills, and motivation explain the highest proportions of variation in sales performance is somewhat reassuring. The common practice of hiring salespeople with a successful track record in the industry, or a closely related industry, may be wise in the absence of other predictors. More importantly, role perceptions, selling skills, and motivation are, in large measure, actionable and at least potentially under management's control. The selection decision is thus only part of the sales performance equation. What matters more appears to be the personal resources, direction, and motivation brought to bear on the specific sales tasks at hand.

Perhaps the most important conclusion is that the determinants of sales performance may be job specific. Hence, the identification of general personality traits or personal attributes for recruiting and selection should be made with an eye toward the particular elements of the sales job to which these traits or attributes may be especially related. Furthermore, a reasonable expectation is that selection criteria or measures that are designed with a particular sales job in mind will provide stronger predictive power.

To the degree that salespeople's ability to perform effectively is job specific, the development of generalizable models will be difficult. However, as the subsequent discussion will illustrate, job-specific factors can be incorporated into performance models as moderators of simple (or main effect) relationships between predictor variables (e.g., sales aptitude, motivation) and sales performance. For example, if industry-specific training is identified as a moderator of the sales aptitude-performance relationship, one would expect to find that aptitude was strongly related to performance when industry-specific training was provided but only weakly or not at all when such training was not provided.

Sales performance models might also be improved by the addition of intermediary psychological or behavioral constructs as *mediators* of expected relationships between personal characteristics and sales performance. That is, the ability to predict sales performance may increase when *process* variables (primarily cognitive and/or behavioral variables) that link predictors to performance are accurately specified. For example, the surprisingly weak link between motivation and sales performance might be strengthened when the behaviors that translate motivation into accomplished work (e.g., effort invested in aspects of the selling task) are explicitly considered. Although the predictive ability of the direct motivation-performance link may be weak, that of the motivation-effort-performance chain is likely to be stronger. Both the moderator and mediator approaches imply the development of greater theoretical knowledge of personal selling processes.

TOWARD A BETTER UNDERSTANDING OF SALES PERFORMANCE

More precise specification of sales performance models is needed to illuminate the determinants of sales performance and to improve sales management practice. Clearly, prior research has found personal characteristics lacking in predictive and explanatory power. The purpose of this section is to suggest directions for improvements in the sales performance models.

One direction for future investigation is to undertake a more stringent analysis of the general personality variables themselves. Trait theory has made a recent comeback in the closely related field of leadership studies. Kirkpatrick and Locke,[2] for example, note that leaders differ from nonleaders on six trait dimensions: drive, desire to lead, integrity, self-confidence, cognitive ability, and knowledge of the business. Barrick and Mount,[3] furthermore, suggest that trait research has been hampered by the lack of a well-accepted taxonomy for classifying personality traits. They suggest a five-factor taxonomy of extraversion or surgency, adjustment or emotional stability, likability or agreeableness, conscientiousness or prudence, and intellect or culture. In each case, the notion is that more systematic investigation of a *core* set of personality traits and their relationship to both subjective and objective measures of employee performance is required if trait theory is to become more predictive of occupational performance.

The same wisdom appears appropriate for sales performance studies. The low *average* correlations between personality traits and sales performance may be at least partly attributable to the wide range of personality traits that have been investigated. Although the predictive ability of some of the above-noted traits may be high, the average correlations are low because of the many traits that have failed to predict performance reliably. The development of a core taxonomy of personality variables conceptually relevant to specific selling contexts appears to be a minimal condition for the advancement of trait theory. Candidate core traits include responsibility, dominance, need for achievement or intrinsic rewards, self-esteem, need for power or extrinsic rewards, sociability, and creativity.[4] The "big five or six" core personality traits from the leadership literature also deserve attention in sales, given the presumed similarities between these performance contexts.[5]

A second important issue is the need to identify conceptually and evaluate empirically situational moderators of the personality trait and sales performance linkage. Varying levels of personal ambition, integrity, or cognitive ability merely endow the salesperson with performance potential. Some sales jobs require and reward high levels of these personal attributes. Others either may not require high levels of these personal qualities or may actually reward salespeople who are relatively low on these attributes. The fundamental research question is why should a specific personal characteristic, trait, or (more likely) trait pattern be expected to influence sales performance in a particular type of sales job? Attention to this research question would allow the identification and measurement of specific conditions likely to determine whether personal attributes translate into effective sales performance.

Sales jobs differ from each other in a variety of ways. The product line represented may be relatively limited or extensive. Products may be simple or complex. Similarly, customers may be relatively homogeneous or heterogeneous in their needs, expertise, buying procedures, and so forth. Hence, the failure to find significant correlations between general personality traits and sales performance may be integrally related to differences in the specific requirements across sales jobs.

Some evidence for such moderator effects was reported by Churchill, et al.[6] Product type moderated the relationship between sales performance and personal factors and personality traits. In other words, the effect of personal characteristics on sales performance varied depending on the type of product being sold. Product type also moderated the effect of skill level, role perception, motivation, and the organizational-environmental factors on sales performance. Surprisingly, product type did not moderate the effect of aptitude on sales performance. Further research concerning the role of product differences as a moderator variable is needed.

Customer type did not significantly moderate the strength of association between sales performance and personal characteristics, aptitude, or skill level. However, the effect of role perceptions, motivation, and organizational-environmental factors on sales performance did vary with the type of customer being sold. Hence, customer distinctions are worthy of further research. This is especially true if customer type differences can be conceptually related to other more specific differences across sales jobs such as the length of the buying cycle, simplicity or complexity in buying center membership or involvement, requirements on the salesperson for servicing and follow-up activities, or the degree to which competing vendors are played off against each other.

Each sales job may be, to some degree, unique in its product, customer, and selling process conditions. However, the development of fundamental categories of product, customer, or selling process categories is a prerequisite for theory advancement.[7] Moncreif's[8] pioneering research examining the activity content of sales jobs deserves follow-up in this regard. Drawing on the sales literature, personal interviews, and focus group sessions in a variety of industries, Moncreif built a taxonomy of 121 selling activities. Sales personnel were then asked to rate the frequency with which they performed each of these activities in their day-to-day sales jobs. The relative frequency of these selling activities is instructive in and of itself.

What is more important to our purpose is that Moncreif was able to identify (using factor analysis) 10 activity groups to form a selling activity taxonomy. The core activities in this taxonomy are: performing the selling function, working with orders, servicing the product, information management, servicing the account, attending conferences and meetings, supporting company recruiting and training efforts, entertaining, out-of-town travel, and working with distributors. Furthermore, he was able to identify (using cluster analysis) five generic sales job types that varied in their selling activity content: the institutional seller, the order taker, the missionary seller, the trade servicer, and the trade seller. The typology is recognized to be preliminary—technical selling, for example, is noted as a missing category. However, the important point is that sales jobs may vary systematically in their activity content. Hence, further conceptual development of the sales job taxonomy, scale refinement, and empirical testing is indicated.

The third, and in our view, most important development required in modeling sales performance is the identification and measurement of psychological and behavioral mediators of the relationships between the more general predictors, such as aptitude and personality, and sales performance. Common sense would suggest a modest relationship between generic personal attributes and sales performance. While such general trait variables as sociability or a high energy level may be expected to be prerequisites for success in sales, salespeople must possess certain skills and exercise them through specific actions to be successful. As Kirkpatrick and Locke note for the leadership context, "Possessing the appropriate traits only makes it more likely that such actions will be taken and be successful."[9] In other words, possession of such generic traits as sociability, forcefulness, or cognitive abilities provides the raw material for sales effectiveness. The individual salesperson, the sales manager, and the sales organization must supply the positive charge for this potential to affect sales performance.

The rest of the trait story, as Kirkpatrick and Locke[10] note, is to be found in the specific capabilities and activities that mediate the trait-performance linkage. In our view, these mediators exist at two distinct levels. First, there are specific cognitive or psychological state variables that are narrower in scope than the typical traits studied in sales contexts. Included in this category would be such individual difference variables as sales knowledge and skill, interpersonal relations skills, job-specific self-efficacy (i.e., confidence in one's competence), role clarity and commitment, motivation to perform the sales job, and goal-related ambitions and commitment. The exact set of these intermediary salesperson capacities is necessarily tentative. Our purpose, in the next section of the chapter, is to exemplify the likely role of such variables in sales performance models and suggest a candidate list of variables for consideration. Development of an exhaustive typology of these variables and specification of the theoretical linkages between personal traits and sales performance is beyond the scope of this chapter.

The second set of mediators, which we posit to be causally consequent to the cognitive or psychological-state variables, are behavioral in nature. These behavioral variables are posited to mediate relationships between mental and psychological variables and sales performance. They include effort, persistence, and direction (or focus). These are commonly suggested in the sales performance literature,[11] but their conceptual and empirical linkages to antecedent and consequent variables have not been established.

In summary, the typical sales performance study has made a conceptual leap in relating relatively general personal background or trait variables to the very specific criterion of sales performance. These relatively general predictors have not performed well with respect to performance in specific sales contexts. Perhaps they should not have been expected to be good predictors given the task at hand and the relatively unsystematic approach that has typically been taken.

We suggest that more powerful and refined of models of sales performance can be developed by better specification of predictor, moderator, and mediator variables. Identification of smaller sets of core traits that are likely to be related to specific selling behaviors in specific contexts can provide managers with powerful tools for improving recruiting and selection procedures. A related and equally powerful improvement can be brought about by identification of specific moderating influences present in various aspects of selling situations. A third type of refinement of sales performance models can be fostered by specification of the *processes* by which personal characteristics and cognitive and psychological state variables influence selling behaviors, which in turn influence sales performance. The following section conceptually defines some of these candidate psychological and behavioral variables that are likely to mediate relationships between personal characteristics and sales performance.

CONCEPTUAL SUMMARY AND GUIDELINES

A summary of the candidate variables related to sales performance is presented in Exhibit A. We present these variables in three categories: general personal background and trait variables, more specific cognitive and psychological-state variables, and behavioral variables. All three types of variables are posited as antecedents of sales performance and other work outcomes. We do not presume to specify

EXHIBIT A. Conceptual Sketch: Factors Affecting Sales Success

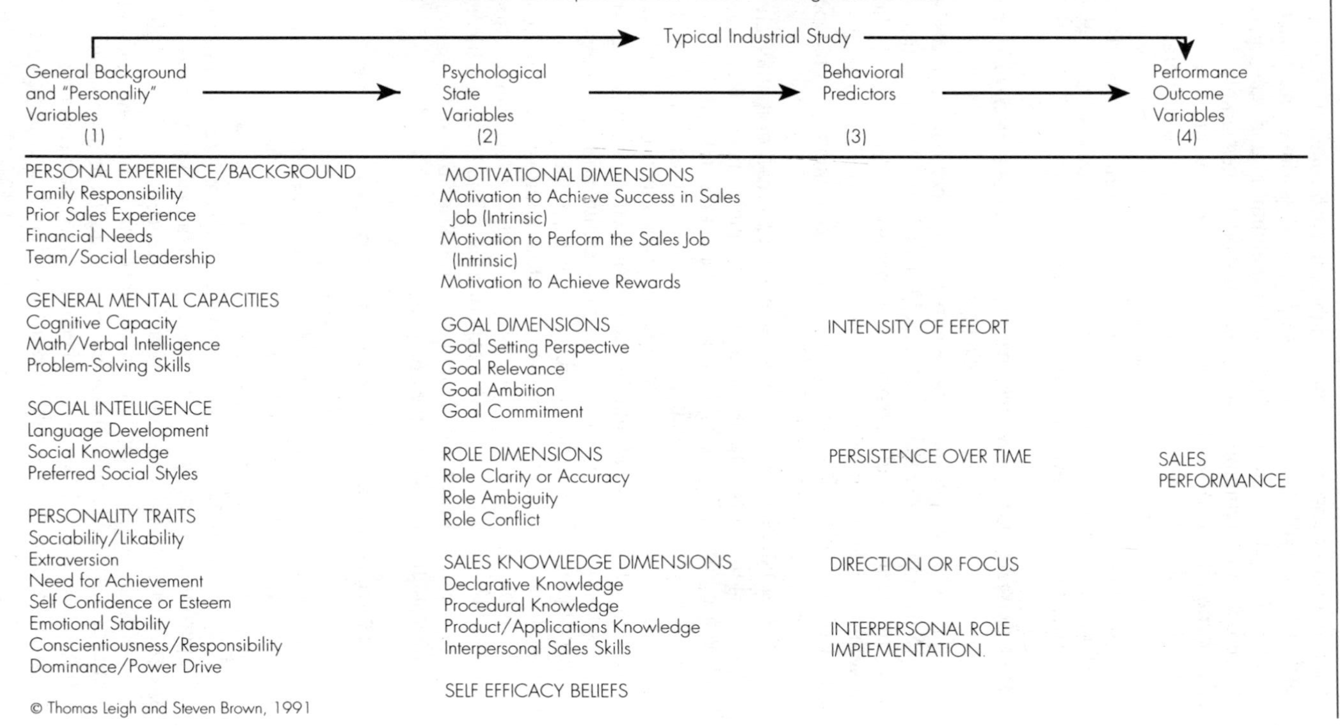
Typical Industrial Study
General Background and "Personality" Variables (1)
Psychological State Variables (2)
Behavioral Predictors (3)
Performance Outcome Variables (4)
PERSONAL EXPERIENCE/BACKGROUND
Family Responsibility
Prior Sales Experience
Financial Needs
Team/Social Leadership
GENERAL MENTAL CAPACITIES
Cognitive Capacity
Math/Verbal Intelligence
Problem-Solving Skills
SOCIAL INTELLIGENCE
Language Development
Social Knowledge
Preferred Social Styles
PERSONALITY TRAITS
Sociability/Likability
Extraversion
Need for Achievement
Self Confidence or Esteem
Emotional Stability
Conscientiousness/Responsibility
Dominance/Power Drive
MOTIVATIONAL DIMENSIONS
Motivation to Achieve Success in Sales Job (Intrinsic)
Motivation to Perform the Sales Job (Intrinsic)
Motivation to Achieve Rewards
GOAL DIMENSIONS
Goal Setting Perspective
Goal Relevance
Goal Ambition
Goal Commitment
ROLE DIMENSIONS
Role Clarity or Accuracy
Role Ambiguity
Role Conflict
SALES KNOWLEDGE DIMENSIONS
Declarative Knowledge
Procedural Knowledge
Product/Applications Knowledge
Interpersonal Sales Skills
SELF EFFICACY BELIEFS
INTENSITY OF EFFORT
PERSISTENCE OVER TIME
DIRECTION OR FOCUS
INTERPERSONAL ROLE IMPLEMENTATION.
SALES PERFORMANCE

causal linkages between specific variables in each category. We simply note that the typical sales force study specifies direct relationships between the general personal variables (column 1) and sales performance outcomes (column 4). Our general model notes simply that this relationship is likely to be mediated by a variety of cognitive or psychological state variables, as well as by specific behavioral variables. Specification of these mediating links is likely to increase the power of prediction and explanation of sales performance models, and we offer the present conceptual schema as a framework that may be more specifically elaborated in further research.

PERSONAL CHARACTERISTICS AND PERSONALITY TRAITS

The general personal characteristics and personality traits are derived from prior research in sales and leadership.[12] The definitions of most of these personal factors are generally understood, so little attention will be devoted to them here. It is important to note that cognitive capacity and mental abilities have been found to be independent of general personality traits.[13]

Social intelligence is the social analog of verbal or mathematical cognitive skills. The argument is that people vary in their social intelligence just as they do in their more abstract mental abilities. Social intelligence presupposes that people will vary considerably in their knowledge concerning kinds of people, kinds of situations, and kinds of social episodes.[14] Social intelligence supposedly drives social role enactments, including typical goals, strategies, intentions, feelings, and expected results. There is also some evidence that people vary in their preferred styles of processing social information—how they make social attributions or evaluations, how they monitor social interactions, and how they cope with everyday experiences.[15] The social intelligence concept seems to be potentially a highly useful addition to the personal variables studied in sales force contexts.

COGNITIVE AND PSYCHOLOGICAL-STATE VARIABLES

The thoughts, feelings, and drives that salespeople experience have important effects on their performance. This fact has led to a booming industry in seminars and motivational books and tapes. The cognitive and psychological-state variables that are likely to influence sales performance include their general motivational state, their goals, role perceptions, and their procedural knowledge.

Motivation. The relationship between motivation and sales performance has already been discussed and will not be belabored here. The two primary approaches that have been taken to salesperson motivation are cognitive (or process) theories of motivation and personality (or content) theories of motivation. Cognitive approaches (e.g., expectancy value theory) consider the values that salespeople attach to particular rewards and the salespeople's estimates of the probability that exerting efforts in specific job tasks will lead to outcomes that trigger those rewards. These models have demonstrated reasonably good predictive validity but have been criticized for not realistically representing actual cognitive processes.

Content theories of motivation posit that need for achievement is a personality trait on which people differ. Those high in need for achievement, in general, tend to perform better in sales and other work contexts. More specific achievement motives have also been identified. These include mastery needs, work orientation, and competitiveness. Mastery needs refer to an inclination to undertake and complete challenging tasks and to put one's best creative efforts into task performance. Work orientation refers to a tendency to work doggedly on tasks even when they are not interesting or challenging. Competitiveness refers to a desire to exceed the performance of one's peers. The typical pattern of results related to these dispositional traits reveals positive relationships between mastery needs and work orientation and performance. Effects of competitiveness have been more complex. In some contexts, competitiveness is positively associated with performance whereas in other contexts it is not. In contexts in which task performance involves intricate or complex behavioral processes, competitiveness is likely to be less positively related to performance. Overall, the validity of content theories of motivation has been somewhat disappointing. As previously indicated, we believe that their validity can be improved by specifying moderator and mediator variables that indicate *in what contexts* strong effects are likely to occur and *the process through which* the effects are likely to be exerted.[16]

Goal Dimensions. An extensive stream of research has investigated the effects of goal properties on effort and task performance. This research has indicated that goals are effective motivators when they are clear, specific, measurable, challenging yet realistic, and when the individual is committed to the goal. Under these conditions, goals appear related to greater levels of effort and performance.[17]

Product and Selling Expertise. Product knowledge is presumed to be critical for all except the most rudimentary sales jobs. Recently, knowledge of *how to sell* has received greater research attention. This interest has been motivated by research in a variety of task domains demonstrating that experts perform better because their knowledge structures are qualitatively different from those of novices.[18] Specifically, experts bring more information to bear on a task and use patterns of information to solve problems more quickly and accurately.[19]

In sales contexts, both declarative (e.g., product knowledge) and procedural knowledge (e.g., knowledge regarding how to approach different types of prospects, how to handle objections, and how to close) are likely to be important. Declarative knowledge includes information relevant to the definition of categories of sales situations and customer types. Procedural knowledge defines the set of action sequences relevant to these categories of selling situation or customer types. Greater declarative and procedural knowledge is likely to enable salespeople to categorize prospects and situations and adapt their strategies and self-presentations more effectively to the dictates of specific situations.

Self-Efficacy Beliefs. Belief in one's competence and ability to do the job at hand is important to salespeople as well as to other types of workers. This is the essence of self-efficacy, which Bandura defines as the judgment of one's "capabilities to organize and execute courses of action required to attain designated types of performances."[20]

Sales calls require the capacity to generate and attempt new and creative selling approaches as novel situations or customer types are encountered. Self-efficacy for sales personnel would appear to be a necessary complement to sales knowledge. Salespeople high in self-efficacy beliefs are likely to persist in situations where their initial efforts meet with resistence or failure.

BEHAVIORAL VARIABLES

Sales performance has been described as a matter of working hard and/or working smart. The behavioral mediators of sales performance that we posit consitute an attempt to capture conceptually these "working hard" and "working smart" dimensions of sales performance.

Effort. In conceptual terms, effort represents the force by which motivation is translated into accomplished work. Effort includes two dimensions—intensity, or the amount of exertion per unit of time, and persistence, or the total amount of time invested in the task. All else being equal, exertion of greater effort along these two dimensions will result in higher levels of sales performance.

Direction (or Focus). The effectiveness of effort in determining higher levels of sales performance is likely to be conditioned in large part by the decisions the salesperson makes about how to use his or her most valuable asset, time. This is an integral component of the "working smart" component of sales performance. Carefully qualifying customers before spending valuable time and money to make a full sales presentation, adequately preparing for sales calls and presentations, and taking time to develop high-potential prospect lists exemplify some of the many ways that choices regarding allocation of time can impact sales performance.

Interpersonal Role Implementation. To be a top performer, a salesperson needs well-developed interpersonal and selling skills. Handling objections smoothly and persuasively and to closing the sale are important skills that must be performed again and again. The salesperson's role performances sometimes resemble those of an actor. Knowing the script is necessary but not sufficient for success; the part must be played with skill and conviction "on stage." Thus, the salesperson's face-to-face selling skills importantly determine his or her level of performance.

GUIDELINES FOR EFFECTIVE RECRUITING

In light of existing research, with the inconsistencies and limitations that have been noted, recruiting an effective sales force appears to be a daunting task. Few solid and reliable criteria exist for effectively predicting sales performance. However, sales managers should consider several factors before proceeding with purely subjective selection decisions.

First, several natural factors restrict the predictive power of most of the measures discussed. Few, if any, sales force studies have been conducted by taking a large random pool of candidates, testing them with selection instruments, and assigning them to sales jobs based on the results. In the real world, a strong self-screening element exists. Relatively few shy and socially retiring people apply for sales jobs. Sales candidates as a group are likely to be above average in extraversion, have a greater interest in business than the general population, and be more driven by strong financial motives.

Even the roughest screening of candidates through informal interviews and reference checks tends to eliminate individuals with very poor social skills, low cognitive abilities, or impaired communication skills. The survivors of this initial rough screening and self-selection process are far more homogenous with respect to the traits associated with sales success. This greatly restricts the range of variation of predictor variables and attenuates their correlations with sales performance. Although it is likely that an extrovert will be more successful than an introvert, it is by no means clear that an extreme extrovert will be more successful than a moderate extrovert.

The sales manager is like a handicapper in a horse race. He or she can readily eliminate the draft horse from consideration; the subtler task is to select among thoroughbreds. While every race is important, the smart handicapper tries to influence the odds over the long term. A number of steps can be taken to enhance the probability of success in sales force selection.

The first and foremost requirement is to develop a good understanding of the sales job. Job analysis is routinely used by industrial psychologists to identify the knowledge, skills, abilities, and personal characteristics required for success. If a sales job is primarily oriented toward cold calling, persistence, effort, relatively high tolerance for rejection, and a direct and forthright style are critical. If the sales relationships tend to be of long duration, these factors may be sacrificed in the interest of social sensitivity, service orientation, and relationship-building skills.

The product or service the salesperson will be selling is also important. If the product is a highly complex and technical item sold on an application basis, then cognitive skills become more important. The ability to formulate a strategy, to understand the unique needs of the customer and the product's fit with those needs, and to convey these articulately are vital to long-term success. If the product is a commodity, sales tend to occur through personal relationship-building skills. Credibility, extroversion, and social savvy tend to become more important for success.

With a job analysis in hand, the sales manager's job is somewhat simpler. The old saying "if you don't know what you want, almost anything will do" contains a large kernel of truth. The job analysis can be used to select appropriate testing instruments, to design interview formats, and to focus the attention of multiple assessors on the same key variables.

In general, interviews should be highly structured so that all candidates are asked the same questions in roughly the same order. Questions should also have a behavioral basis and should ask the person to describe (for example) "a time when . . ." or "a situation where . . ." Asking the person, "Are you responsible?" invariably draws an affirmative response from the prospective candidate. A response to a statement such as, "Describe a time when you had to be very responsible in your job," is more informative. First, the person's selection of an experience, reveals what he or she thinks being responsible really means. Second, the candidate lays the behavior out for the interviewer's evaluation, rather than providing a closed-ended (and largely predetermined) self-evaluation. With a little practice, these types of questions are relatively easy to formulate.

Testing is another sensitive issue. A vast number of tests exist that purport to assess sales ability. The main virtue of some of these is the marketing skill of their developers, rather than the predictive power of the test itself. Tests should be selected on the basis of fit with the job analysis and then only if they meet certain minimal standards of reliability and validity. In general, sales testing houses are not the best sources of reliable and valid tests. A number of test distribution companies require that tests meet the standards established by the American Psychological Association. Sometimes a psychologist with testing expertise can provide valuable service in selecting an initial test battery.

It is often as important to *exclude* tests as it is to include them. Screening people on the basis of tests scores that do not effectively predict success is wasteful at best and a potential source of litigation at worst. Requiring a person to score well on a test of abstract spatial reasoning for a job selling industrial solvents will be likely to screen out a number of individuals who could potentially be successful, while at the same time potentially discriminating against some segments of the population. Again, a job analysis is very helpful.

Another important point to consider is the selection ratio. If almost every applicant is ultimately hired, a recruiting problem, not a selection problem, exists. If the selection system is only marginally efficient, the larger the selection ratio, the better the outcome. An example may help to clarify this.

Assume that for any particular job, 50% of the applicants are likely to perform successfully. Now, let us assume that a selection criterion has been developed that is 60% accurate. That is, for every 100 applicants achieving a passing score on relevant test criterion, 60% will succeed and 40% will fail. Because the criterion score is correlated with performance, raising the cutoff score and increasing the number of applicants will improve selection accuracy.

A final point should be made here. Experience suggests that organizations fall into one of two categories. Many organizations put a tremendous emphasis on the selection process and then turn the new recruit loose with relatively little in the way of training or support. The second type hires with relatively little sophistication and then invests heavily in the training and development process for new recruits. Indeed, they sometimes find themselves trying to "make silk purses out of sow's ears." Only a few of the best companies combine both strategies. They place an early emphasis on the selection of talent, but follow up that effort with effective training and development. This tends to maximize success. While it is true "you can't teach a pig to sing, you'll just frustrate yourself and annoy the pig," it is also important to remember that even opera stars take singing lessons.

OTHER SALES WORK OUTCOMES

Although the performance of salespeople is of primary interest to sales managers, it is by no means the only work outcome worthy of consideration and managerial attention. Job-related attitudes, intentions, and behaviors, such as satisfaction with the job and its various facets, commitment to the organization, intentions to leave the organization, and actual turnover, play important roles in the smooth and efficient operation of a sales organization. The following part of the chapter considers the causes and consequences of these job attitudes and develops managerial implications from a summary of research findings.

JOB SATISFACTION

Job satisfaction is one of the most frequently studied outcomes of sales work. The large amount of research on salesperson job satisfaction and its antecedents and consequences reflects its importance in determining such important attitudes and behaviors as commitment to the organization, intentions to leave the organization, and actual turnover.

Job satisfaction, according to Edwin A. Locke, is "a pleasurable or positive emotional state resulting from the appraisal of one's job or job experiences."[21] Job satisfaction differs from morale in having an individual rather than a group referent and a temporal orientation toward the past rather than toward the future. Churchill, Ford, and Walker defined the conceptual domain of salesperson job satisfaction as "all characteristics of the job itself and the work environment which [industrial] salesmen (sic) find rewarding, fulfilling, and satisfying, or frustrating and unsatisfying."[22]

Satisfaction has typically been defined in operational terms as the salesperson's affective appraisal of various job facets, including the work itself, supervisor, pay, promotion opportunities, and coworkers. The most commonly used measures of job satisfaction include separate rating scales for each facet. This permits managers and researchers to consider separately the effects of such variables as organizational characteristics, managerial behaviors, and role perceptions on salesperson satisfaction with specific job facets. Responses to these "by facet" scales are often summed or averaged to form a composite measure of overall job satisfaction. Other measures of job satisfaction divide the construct into "intrinsic" and "extrinsic" components. The intrinsic component represents those psychological rewards of sales work that the salesperson mediates for himself or herself (such as satisfaction with the challenge of the job itself and with personal growth from doing the work). The extrinsic component refers to rewards that are mediated by others, such as the sales manager, and include monetary compensation, recognition, and promotion opportunities.

Still other measures merely consider global satisfaction with no separate consideration of facets. A recent meta-analysis has indicated that by facet measures tend to produce slightly stronger observed relationships between job satisfaction and its correlates but that the differences are typically not large enough to be of much substantive importance.[23]

JOB SATISFACTION AND OTHER WORK OUTCOMES

Much of managers' and researchers' interest in salesperson job satisfaction stems from its relationships with other work outcomes, such as sales performance, organizational commitment, and turnover.

Sales Performance. A large volume of research has investigated the question of whether "a happy worker is a productive worker," or vice versa. Typically, studies of the relationship between sales performance and job satisfaction have found a modest positive relationship between the two constructs. Most often, this weak relationship has been interpreted to mean that successful sales performance to some extent *causes* job satisfaction. Another possible explanation for the modest positive association between performance and satisfaction is that the two are not causally related, but both variables are related to common antecedent variables. This possibility has received support from several empirical studies and from a meta-analytic integration of empirical studies investigating the issue.[24] Thus, the accumulated research evidence appears to support the view that sales performance and job satisfaction are *not* causally related.

Organizational behavior researchers Iaffaldano and Muchinsky, reviewing the accumulated findings of 217 studies of the performance-satisfaction relationship, arrived at a similar conclusion. Noting that the vast majority of studies found very modest relationships between performance and job satisfaction, they concluded that "few other empirical relations have embraced the null hypothesis so often yet continued to foster additional research."[25] They suggested that the practical importance of performance and satisfaction outcomes and a dogmatic belief that productive workers must be happy workers (or vice versa) has continued to foster volumes of research despite the increasing accumulation of disconfirming evidence.

The finding of no relationship between sales performance and job satisfaction or turnover has important practical implications. Many sales managers assume that top performers in their sales forces are necessarily satisfied with their jobs and may do little to enhance their satisfaction or commitment to the sales team. In a similar vein, managers view turnover as a benign force, believing that poor performers are more likely to leave on their own due to a lack of job satisfaction. The accumulated evidence does not support these assumptions. Sales managers need to focus actively on the job satisfaction and organizational commitment of their top performers and should not assume that successful performance is a panacea for all of the negative influences on salespeople's job attitudes (e.g., role ambiguity and conflict, rejection, isolation, etc.). Successful salespeople tend to have more and better alternative job options than less successful salespeople, to the effect that reward and appreciation of their efforts is necessary to keep them. Managers also need to assess the *functionality* of turnover in their sales forces to make sure they are turning over more low performers than high. A reasonable amount of turnover benefits the organization when lower performers are replaced with higher performers but can be devastating when irreplaceable top performers move on to greener pastures.

Although sales performance appears not to be causally related to job satisfaction or, for that matter, to other work outcomes such as organizational commitment or turnover, the same cannot be said of job satisfaction. Satisfaction appears to be an important determinant of salespeople's commitment to their companies and turnover.

Organizational Commitment. Organizational commitment represents the salesperson's attachment to the organization. It has been viewed in two somewhat distinct ways by researchers. One perspective considers organizational commitment as the result of the salesperson's *investments* of time and effort on behalf of the organization. Through these investments, the individual comes to consider his or her goals and objectives congruent with those of the organization. Another perspective simply regards organizational commitment as a strong and stable attitude toward one's relationship with the organization.

Researchers have long debated whether job satisfaction leads to organizational commitment or vice versa. The accumulated research evidence strongly suggests that job satisfaction is causally antecedent to organizational commitment rather than the reverse. Brown and Peterson's meta-analysis, based on all available empirical correlations between salesperson job satisfaction and organizational commitment, found that a model representing satisfaction as a cause of commitment fit the accumulated data much better than a model representing commitment as the antecedent.[26] Thus, perhaps not surprisingly, research indicates that salesperson job satisfaction leads to increasing psychological attachment to the organization. Satisfied salespeople appear to have a better sense of being part of a team, a feeling that many sales managers strive to foster in their sales forces.

Turnover. The high costs of salesperson turnover make understanding its relationships with job satisfaction and other work outcomes an important concern of managers and researchers. Researchers have described turnover as the result of a process of thinking about leaving the organization, developing an attitude toward leaving, comparing alternative prospects outside the organization with the current job situation, and developing a behavioral intention to leave.

The accumulated research evidence suggests that both job satisfaction and organizational commitment are important determinants of turnover. Findings of path-analytic research indicate that the effect of job satisfaction on turnover occurs mostly indirectly, i.e., through the mediation of organizational commitment, although satisfaction also appears to affect turnover more weakly through a direct path.[27] Thus, more-satisfied salespeople tend to build commitment to the organization and this commitment constitutes a strong disincentive to begin the process of thinking about leaving the organization, comparing alternatives with the present situation, developing an intention to leave, and actually quitting.

The observation that salespeople who like their jobs tend to become more committed to their organization and less likely to leave is a commonsensical one. Many factors that influence job satisfaction are under management's control. Providing clear goals, reducing ambiguity, rewarding achievement, displaying respect, and being actively involved with salespeople are critical. A good boss can help make a happy employee. Things that managers can do to increase job satisfaction are discussed below.

ANTECEDENTS OF JOB SATISFACTION

Given that job satisfaction importantly influences work outcomes such as organizational commitment and turnover and that, at least for managers with a humanistic bent, it constitutes an important end in itself, consideration of its determinants is likely to provide managerially useful insights. This section considers factors that affect salesperson job satisfaction and ways that job satisfaction can be improved.

Many specific variables have been studied as antecedents of salesperson job satisfaction. This multiplicity of specific antecedents can be systematically organized into a smaller number of summary categories. These general categories of antecedent variables include role perceptions, supervisory behaviors, job-task characteristics, and individual differences. These categories of antecedent variables are described here in the order of their average strength of association with job satisfaction as assessed over many empirical studies.

Role Perceptions. Three specific salesperson role perception constructs have been investigated in a number of studies. These include role conflict, role ambiguity, and role clarity. Both role conflict and role ambiguity have consistently been negatively related to job satisfaction, whereas role ambiguity has consistently been positively related to satisfaction. Averaging across these three relationships over many empirical studies, the correlation between role perceptions and salesperson job satisfaction is .36. This indicates that the reduction of role conflict and/or role ambiguity (or the enhancement of role clarity) tends to result in substantial improvements in salesperson job satisfaction. These effects on job satisfaction then have additional concomitant effects on organizational commitment and turnover. Some ways that sales managers can reduce role conflict and enhance role clarity are discussed in the next two sections.

Supervisory Behaviors. Effects of a number of supervisory behavior variables on salesperson job satisfaction have been investigated. These include closeness of supervision, consideration, job feedback, contingent rewards, amount of communication, and arbitrary punishment. All of these supervisory behaviors except arbitrary punishment have been positively related to salesperson job satisfaction. The average correlation with job satisfaction across these supervisory behavior variables was .30. This suggests that greater closeness of supervision, amounts of communication, consideration, job feedback, and contingent rewards all tend to promote greater job satisfaction. Of these supervisory behaviors, the three most effective in terms of enhancing job satisfaction appear to be contingent rewards, consideration, and closeness of supervision.

Some evidence suggests that these supervisory variables exert their effects on job satisfaction primarily through the mediation of reductions in role conflict and role ambiguity. That is, contingent rewards, consideration, closeness of supervision, etc., tend to reduce role conflict and/or role ambiguity, and thus job satisfaction is enhanced.

These results suggest several important considerations for managers. To enhance salesperson job satisfaction, managers should provide specific, accurate expectations about job duties and requirements. What appears detailed and specific to the manager may *not* appear that way to a fledgling sales rep. Thus, to the fullest extent possible, seeing things from the perspective of the new sales rep will help to make expectations about duties and performance levels clear and thus reduce role ambiguity. Empathy for the many difficulties that sales reps encounter in their day-to-day selling also helps create and maintain high levels of satisfaction. The fact that most sales managers tend to come from the ranks of the sales force and thus to have "been there" tends to help in this regard. Frequent communication and feedback are also very conducive to salesperson job satisfaction. The sales manager provides the primary link between the field salesperson and the organization, and frequent direct communication helps to guide and focus selling efforts and to coordinate each individual's activities into a team effort.

Job-Task Variables. Study of job design features and their effects on worker productivity and satisfaction has constituted an important stream of sales force research. Job-task variables that have been investigated in relation to job satisfaction include task autonomy, task significance, task variety, participation (i.e., in the decision-making process), influence over standards, innovativeness required, job involvement, value congruence, and pay. The accumulated research has indicated that all of these variables are positively related to job satisfaction. That is, more significant, varied, and involving jobs tend to be more satisfying. Likewise, greater autonomy, participation in the decision-making process, and challenge to provide innovative problem solutions appear to be associated with greater job satisfaction. Finally, higher pay and the congruence of values between the salesperson and the organization are associated with greater salesperson satisfaction.

Innovations in job-task design features to improve sales productivity and job satisfaction typically fall within the scope of responsibility of executive level sales management. Enhancing sales jobs in terms of autonomy, variety, challenge, participation, innovativeness required, etc. also implies improving levels of skill, motivation, and training in the sales force. Empowering sales personnel to provide custom-tailored product-service packages to fit the special needs of individual customers requires highly skilled, trained, and self-confident salespeople. Deployment of a sales force consisting of this type of salesperson also represents a large investment to the firm. Returns on this investment come back in the form of greater sales force productivity, profitable long-term customer relationships, and reduced costs of turnover.

Upgrading the status of the sales function carries important implications for other functional areas of the business. Greater autonomy and decision-making authority in the field must be accompanied by coordination and cooperation between sales and other functional areas to assure that arrangements concluded between salespeople and their customers are effectively implemented. Thus, managerial actions taken to enhance the content and upgrade the status of sales jobs tend to have far-reaching organizational consequences.

Individual Differences. Individual difference variables that have been related to salesperson job satisfaction include both demographic (e.g., age, sex, education, sales experience, and organizational tenure) and personality variables (e.g., work motivation, general and specific self-esteem). No demographic variable has been found to be consistently significantly related to salesperson job satisfaction. Although only a small number of personality variables have been studied in relation to job satisfaction, three (work motivation, general and specific self-esteem) have been found to have modest positive relationships with job satisfaction. It is not clear whether the significant correlations between these personality variables and job satisfaction are direct causal relationships, whether other variables mediate the relationships, or whether the correlations are spurious and attributable to common relationships with third variables. What does appear clear is that more highly motivated salespeople and those with higher generalized self-esteem and greater esteem for themselves in the role of salesperson tend to be more satisfied with their jobs.

SOME FINAL OBSERVATIONS AND IMPLICATIONS

These observations further underscore the importance of selecting salespeople with "the right stuff." Salespeople with higher levels of motivation are likely to demonstrate higher levels of job satisfaction and organizational commitment. Similarly, individuals who feel good about themselves and about their sales abilities are likely to be more resilient to the vicissitudes that are an inherent part of sales work.

Other factors that are less directly under the control of a field manager include the nature of the job itself and the organization's corporate culture. Jobs that provide greater challenge, opportunity for personal contribution, and reward are inherently more satisfying. Likewise, companies that tend to create a "we vs. they" climate of conflict with customers (with the salesperson caught in the middle trying to mediate) tend to create greater dissatisfaction and turnover in the sales force.

A comparison of two companies' sales forces with marked differences in turnover rates exemplifies these points. One company's sales force has experienced a 70% annual turnover rate. The company has a history of shifting priorities (e.g., company size of the target customers, importance of new business vs. business retention, and changing performance measures), and this has created significant ambiguity for the salespeople about what is expected of them. Management's philosophy has emphasized seeing customers as untrustworthy and the sales force as a group of "hired guns." It is not surprising that few salespeople survive long in such an environment. Management, however, persists in regarding turnover as a "selection" problem.

The second company competes in the same industry (telecommunications), but its sales force is effectively focused on serving the needs of larger customers. Its turnover has been quite low throughout the life of the company despite pressures created by explosive growth. Management espouses a philosophy of "partnering" with customers and provides a high level of autonomy and respect for the salesperson. Management's primary goal has been to provide all necessary support for complete customer satisfaction, and the salesperson plays a key role in delivering essential value-added services. The relative lack of conflict and ambiguity, the challenge of the job, and the positive relationship between management and the sales force has led to a highly committed sales team and a low turnover rate.

CONCLUSION

In today's increasingly competitive markets, the importance of the sales force as a source of competitive advantage is increasing. The role of the salesperson is becoming more professional and demanding, and the cost of maintaining a highly trained and motivated team of salespeople in the field is mounting steadily. These trends point up the importance of understanding the forces that determine the performance and job attitudes of salespeople. Only through such understanding can wise decisions be made regarding recruitment, selection, training, and management of the sales force.

This chapter has summarized decades of empirical research on these questions and drawn managerial implications from the accumulated findings. Despite the large amount of research effort that has been invested in these questions, much of the variance in salesperson performance and job attitudes remains unexplained. We have suggested some directions for future research designed to account for this as-yet-unexplained variance. Future progress in these directions can have a major impact on improving the theory and practice of sales management.

FOOTNOTES

1. Churchill, Gilbert A., Jr., Neil M. Ford, Steven W. Hartley, and Orville C. Walker, "The Determinants of Salesperson Performance: A Meta-Analysis," *Journal of Marketing Research,* May 1985, pp. 103–118.

2. Kirkpatrick, Shelley A. and Edwin A. Locke, "Leadership: Do Traits Matter?" *The Executive,* May 1991, pp. 48–60.
3. Barrick, Murray R. and Michael K. Mount, "The Big Five Personality Dimensions and Job Performance: A Meta-Analysis," *Personnel Psychology,* January 1991, pp. 1–26.
4. Ford, Neil M., Orville C. Walker, Jr., Gilbert A. Churchill, Jr., and Steven W. Hartley, "Selecting Successful Salespeople: A Meta-Analysis of Biographical and Psychological Selection Criteria," *Review in Marketing,* Michael J. Houston (ed.), Chicago: American Marketing Association, 1988, pp. 90–131.
5. Weitz, Barton A., "Effectiveness in Sales Interactions: A Contingency Framework," *Journal of Marketing,* Winter 1981, pp. 85–103.
6. Churchill, et al., "Determinants of Performance."
7. Hunt, Shelby D., *Marketing Theory: Conceptual Foundations of Research in Marketing,* Columbus, Ohio, Grid, Inc.
8. Moncrief, William C., III, "Selling Activity and Sales Position Taxonomies for Industrial Salesforces," *Journal of Marketing Research,* August 1986, pp. 261–270.
9. Kirkpatrick and Locke, "Leadership," p. 49.
10. Kirkpatrick and Locke, "Leadership."
11. Ingram, Thomas N. and Raymond W. LaForge, *Sales Management: Analysis and Decision Making,* 2nd ed., Fort Worth, The Dryden Press, 1992.
12. Comer, James M. and Alan J. Dubinsky, *Managing the Successful Sales Force,* Lexington, Massachusetts, Lexington Books.
13. Barrick and Mount, "The Big Five."
14. Cantor, Nancy and Walter Mischel, "Prototypes in Person Perception," in Leonard Berkowitz, (ed.), *Advances in Experimental Social Psychology,* Vol. 12, New York, Academic Press, 1979, pp. 3–52.
15. Cantor and Mischel, "Prototypes."
16. McClelland, David C., *Human Motivation,* New York, Cambridge University Press, 1987; Spence, Janet T. and Robert L. Helmreich, *Masculinity and Femininity: Their Psychological Dimensions, Correlates, and Antecedents,* Austin, University of Texas Press, 1978.
17. Locke, Edwin A. and Gary P. Latham, *A Theory of Goal Setting and Task Performance,* Englewood Cliffs, New Jersey, Prentice-Hall, 1990.
18. Chase, W.G. and K.A. Ericsson, "Skilled Memory," in J. R. Anderson (ed.), *Cognitive Skills and Their Acquisition,* Hillsdale, New Jersey, 1981.
19. Weitz, Barton A., Harish Sujan, and Mita Sujan, "Knowledge, Motivation, and Adaptive Behavior: A Framework for Improving Selling Effectiveness," *Journal of Marketing,* October 1986, pp. 174–191; Leigh, Thomas W. and Patrick F. McGraw, "Mapping the Procedural Knowledge of Industrial Sales Personnel: A Script-Theoretic Investigation," *Journal of Marketing,* January 1989, pp. 16–34.
20. Bandura, Albert, *Social Foundations of Thought and Action: A Social Cognitive Theory,* Englewood Cliffs, New Jersey, 1986.
21. Locke and Latham, *A Theory.*

22. Churchill, Gilbert A., Jr., Neil M. Ford, and Orville C. Walker, Jr., "Measuring the Job Satisfaction of Industrial Salesmen," *Journal of Marketing Research,* August 1974, pp. 254–260.
23. Brown, Steven P. and Robert A. Peterson, "Antecedents and Consequences of Salesperson Job Satisfaction: Meta-Analysis and Assessment of Causal Effects," *Working Paper,* University of Georgia, 1992.
24. Behrman, Douglas N. and William D. Perreault, "A Role Stress Model of the Performance and Satisfaction of Industrial Salespersons," *Journal of Marketing,* Fall 1984, pp. 9–21.
25. Iaffaldano, Michelle T. and Paul M. Muchinsky, "Job Satisfaction and Performance: A Meta-Analysis," *Psychological Bulletin,* March 1985, pp. 251–273.
26. Brown and Peterson, "Antecedents and Consequences."
27. Brown and Peterson, "Antecedents and Consequences."

PART THREE

ESTABLISHING MARKETING OBJECTIVES / STRATEGIES

PART THREE

INTRODUCTION

Knowing your market is important! Market understanding enables management to set realistic goals and objectives and to formulate effective marketing strategies.

What should be done to get and keep a customer? To answer this question, a business must ask itself other questions: What capabilities do we have? Where are existing opportunities? How can we match our capabilities to those opportunities? How can we meet the needs of our customers? How do we fulfill their hopes and dreams?

Successful marketing programs make every possible effort to talk to the correct audience or audiences, either consumers or businesses. Considerable skill is required, not only to select the appropriate market, but also to prepare the program and to select the messages that will have both a positive and somewhat lasting effect upon the target markets.

Once marketers have correctly identified to whom the key elements of the program should be directed, the marketers are then in a position to measure the effectiveness of that program by measuring, or auditing, the responses and actions of the target groups. But identifying the target markets for any given marketing program is only the first step in achieving a successful marketing effort.

The marketer must also seek to achieve the correct mix for his or her products or service(s) in terms of unit sale size, price, promotion, and channels of distribution in an effort to maximize the likelihood of product purchase or service use.

A review of Part Three of this *Handbook* should provide considerable insight as to the factors that are needed in any viable marketing program to successfully market to virtually any user segment: young or old, consumer or business, professional or laborer, in terms of satisfying their needs and desires.

Harper W. Boyd, Jr.
Donaghey Distinguished Professor of Marketing
College of Business Administration
University of Arkansas (Little Rock)

Jean-Claude Larreche
Professor of Marketing
European Institute of Management (INSEAD)
Fontainbleau, France

CHAPTER 8

SETTING MARKETING OBJECTIVES

The setting of the firm's objectives is the first step in the strategic planning process. It is critically important since objectives serve as guidelines for all levels of managers in their decision-making activities and particularly those relating to the allocation of the firm's resources. Over the years business scholars have argued about what constitutes a set of viable objectives for a firm. These scholars represent four different schools of thought—those taking an economic point of view, those advocating a market or customer stance, those favoring social benefits, and those representing an organizational approach. Our discussion will focus on the first two concepts although all four must be utilized if the firm is to be successful.

Corporate objectives impact both strategy and operating decisions. In the case of the former, they do so largely in terms of the nature and scope of the businesses the firm pursues over time. From this emerges a definition of the business which is based largely on how the firm perceives the opportunities and threats facing its various product-market entries. Since, for a variety of reasons (e.g., the product life cycle) the firm will likely alter its investment emphasis with respect to one or more of its entries, its business definition will change over time. This, in turn, may affect the firm's choice of objectives. Thus, there is a strong interrelationship between objectives, strategy, and business definition.

Operating decisions are influenced by corporate objectives in the way managers formulate objectives for their areas of responsibility in their efforts to attain higher level objectives. There is, therefore, a hierarchy of objectives in any business organization. If, for example, a firm deems it necessary to sell a full line of products to the total U.S. market (business definition) in order to obtain its profitability objectives, then this will surely affect those decisions pertaining to channels of distribution, the sales force, advertising, and physical distribution.

It has long been recognized that corporate objectives influence both strategic and operating decisions. It has only been recently, however, that the linkages between objectives, business definition, and strategy have been explored in any depth. While each of these subjects is a worthy topic of discussion in its own right, it is their totality that is critical to the most managers. The purpose of this chapter is, therefore, to explore these linkages and to do so from the point of view of how they direct the firm's resource allocation process as well as serve as the basis for the organization's structure and its direction, motivation, and control.

GOALS VERSUS OBJECTIVES

There is considerable confusion in the literature between *goals* and *objectives.* Some writers use the two terms interchangeably along with *purposes* and *ends.* Others differentiate on the basis that objectives serve as the means by which goals are obtained while still others argue just the opposite. For our purpose a goal is defined as an open-ended statement which is expressed in broad terms describing some "state" the firm wishes to achieve. It is not bounded in time nor is it specific in any measurement sense. Such statements as being "a good corporate citizen," "a fair employer," "serving customers with high-quality products," and a "maximizer of profits" are examples.

Objectives, on the other hand, are measures of desired results and, as such, are comprised of four components—the desired attribute or result, a progress index, a target measure, and the time frame within which the target is to be achieved. Hofer and Schendel provide examples of some typical business objectives in Table 1.

The main value of a goal is that it is useful as a way of arriving at an objective. For example, the goal of a high quality product can be made into an objective by indicating its specific attributes or, as in the above table, relating it to competition. Goals also have merit in

TABLE 1.

Possible Attributes	Possible Indexes	Targets and Time Frame		
		Year 1	Year 2	Year 3
Growth	$ Sales Unit sales	$100 mil. X units	$120 mil. 1.10 X units	$140 mil. 1.20 X units
Efficiency	$ Profits Profits/sales	10 mil. .10	12 mil. .10	15 mil. .10
Utilization of resources	ROI ROE	.15 .25	.15 .26	.16 .27
Contribution to owners	Dividends EPS	$1.00/share $2.00/share	$1.10/share $2.40/share	$1.30/share $2.80/share
Contribution to customers	Price, quality, reliability	Equal or better than competition	Equal or better than competition	Equal or better than competition
Contributions to employees	Wage rate employment stability	$3.50 @ hr. < 5% turning	$3.74 @ hr. < 4% turning	$4.00 @ hr. < 4% turning
Contributions to society	Taxes paid, scholarships, etc.	$10 mil. $100,000	$12 mil. $120,000	$16 mil. $120,000

Source: Charles W. Hofer and Dan Schendel, *Strategy Formulation: Analytical Concepts* (New York: West Publishing Company, 1978), p. 21.

providing motivation to managers and employees. The AT&T goal of building a "... good, cheap, fast, worldwide telephone service for everyone" is cited as such an example.[1]

Most firms have multiple objectives. Drucker, in an effort to balance the long run versus the short run, advocates that firms have objectives in eight key areas. These are market standing, profitability, innovation, productivity, physical and financial resources, manager performance and development, worker performance and attitude, and public responsibility.[2] The use of multiple objectives raises the question of internal consistency; that is, the obtaining of one objective must not preclude the obtaining of any other objective. For example, an improvement in market share in a fast growth situation is not likely to be accompanied by increased profits and a more positive cash flow. Further, objectives must be consistent with "reality"; e.g., if the ROI objective is twice that experienced on average by the industry, then there would be good reason to question its validity. In a similar vein the objectives must be "logical" in terms of the firm's resources and the anticipated dynamics of the environments in which it operates.

ECONOMIC OBJECTIVES

Typically the firm's overriding objectives are stated in economic terms. This assumes that profit maximization is the firm's primary consideration or rationale for existence. This is understandable, given that historically the firm has been viewed as an economic unit—the efficiency of which is measured on the basis of the returns generated by the capital invested. Indeed, the very essence of micro-economic theory is premised on the assumption that the rational firm will seek to maximize the return on its capital. Disagreement among those who adhere to the profit maximization school is mainly centered on which efficiency measures to use.

There are, of course, many business scholars who assert strongly that a firm's social responsibility goes far beyond profit maximization. They challenge Friedman who believes that any business objective other than that of profit maximization will undermine the foundation of our free society.[3] The social objectives argument that the market place should not be the sole means for judging the contributions made by a firm to society is hard to ignore.[4] The problem is that if the firm's primary objective is not economic, then how does it determine how best to allocate its resources?

Given the depth and complexity of social problems, most firms would be hard pressed to determine what would be the best way to attempt to solve them. Thus, we urge that social responsibilities over and beyond those concerned with the firm's legal (regulatory) framework not be made part of its business objectives. Rather, we suggest that the firm *first* strive to maximize its profitability and *second* to undertake to discharge those social responsibilities—either alone or in concert with others—which are acceptable to its various stockholders.

PROFITABILITY MEASURES AS ALLOCATION CRITERIA

Economic objectives are usually expressed in terms of one or more profitability measures such as return on investment (either equity or total assets), earnings per share, profit after taxes, and profits as a percentage of net sales. Some companies state their longer term objectives in the form of variables which, if achieved, will lead to greater profits; e.g., increased sales or market share. Some elaborate their objectives in the form of debt-equity ratios, dividends, and debt retirement. Most factor a per annum growth rate into their sales and profit-after-taxes measures. Because of the high cost of capital and inflation, more and more companies are including cash flow among their set of economic objectives. Some managers will trade off a higher cash flow for a lower rate of return given the difficulty of effecting change without cash. When the firm's future environment is uncertain, managers will opt for flexibility objectives which typically include R & D strength, number of fertile technologies in which the firm has expertise, number of independent segments serviced, and liquidity.

While almost all companies use a variety of economic measures, the dominant one is concerned with profitability as determined on the basis of either equity or total assets employed. Any chief executive officer has to have as one of the primary objectives a "satisfactory" return to the stockholder. This is typically expressed as a return on equity or earnings per share. A return on assets employed or managed measure is used as a way of guiding and evaluating the firm's profit center or strategic business unit managers. The logic here is that the manager of such a unit should be responsible for earning a satisfactory return on the assets granted to the division. Thus, the manager and the subordinates are highly motivated to generate maximum profits—and, of course, expect to be rewarded accordingly.

Given the firm's overall profitability objective—a return on investment measure—the typical procedure is to factor it into the firm's capital budgeting system in an attempt to discriminate between investment requests within and between strategic business units. Inevitably, the use of a single rate of return measure will mean that some divisions will not be successful in obtaining their "share" of the corporation's resources. This will prove dysfunctional to those divisions which are mandated to grow or "turn around" as a result of the strategic plan which is based largely on the opportunities and threats emerging from the changing environment. Quite obviously the overall rate also affects the decision as to what businesses the firm wishes to pursue; i.e., its business definition. Thus, we note the interdependence between objectives and business definition and the need to link them strategically.

There is also the operational question of how the assets managed figure is derived. One obvious problem is that the use of a single rate of return measure of a strategic business unit's performance is that it does not discriminate between investments which bear different risks; e.g., an inventory build-up can typically be liquidated more easily than can an increase in machinery and equipment. Nor does a single rate treat costs as part of an interdependent system. Thus, new machinery could well improve quality and thereby lower sales and service costs. Further, when a gross book value is used as the basis for determining the worth of assets employed, the manager involved could improve performance by scrapping a fixed asset which still has a value or by lowering his inventory even if this lowered sales. If net book value is used, then a unit's investment base declines over time, thereby providing an automatic increase in the division's return on investment.

The use of such measures as the basis for reward and punishment causes many unit managers to take actions which are more oriented towards the short than the long run. Thus, managers may sacrifice future earnings to show a satisfactory short-term profit by reducing R & D, sales, and advertising expenses.

MEASURING FUTURE PROFITABILITY

The inherent problem with the use of "long-run profit maximization" (the present value of future profits) as the firm's primary economic objective is that at best it is difficult to measure *present* profits. Even when this is accomplished satisfactorily, the results may not be a good indication of future profits. As we have earlier noted, it is not overly difficult to improve short-term profitability in ways which may seriously endanger longer-term profits.

In the long run a firm's profitability is largely a function of how it copes with the impact of environmental changes on its investment units. It does so by altering its present allocations between units and by adding and/or subtracting products, markets, or both. In making its investment decisions the firm is guided by its assessment of the investment climate for each unit as well as its relative ability (distinctive competency) to exploit it. If we define investment units as product-market relationships, then what is needed is a measure of the relationship between them. Market share is increasingly used as such a measure since it ties the product directly to the market served and, in the process, tells something about the firm's competitive position. Market share can, therefore, be used as a strategic market objective in its own right and as such is directional in nature in terms of the investments to be made.

Market share is determined by dividing company sales of a given product by industry sales for the market served. Share data can be computed using physical units or dollars. While the former "method" is preferred because of the precision possible, the latter is often used because of its ready availability from secondary sources. The difficulty here is that one is not always sure of what level of product-type aggregation is involved.

For market share to serve as a valid indicator of longer-term profitability, it would have to be highly correlated with return on investment. While it has long been believed that such was true, it was not until the PIMS (Profit Impact of Marketing Strategies) study that we had strong empirical evidence over a wide range of businesses to not only verify this conclusion, but to shed light on why it occurred.[5]

The PIMS study found that absolute market share was strongly correlated with product profitability as measured by pretax ROI. On the average each difference of 10 share points is associated with a difference of about 5 ROI percentage points (see Exhibit 1 for these relationships).

There are several commonsense explanations why we would, on average, expect high share businesses to yield higher ROI's than low share businesses. First, there is the assumed inverse relationship between share and per unit costs due to scale and learning effects. The Boston Consulting Group has combined these two effects into what they call the "experience curve." Their proposition is that every time

EXHIBIT 1. Relationship between Market Share (Absolute) and Pretax ROI

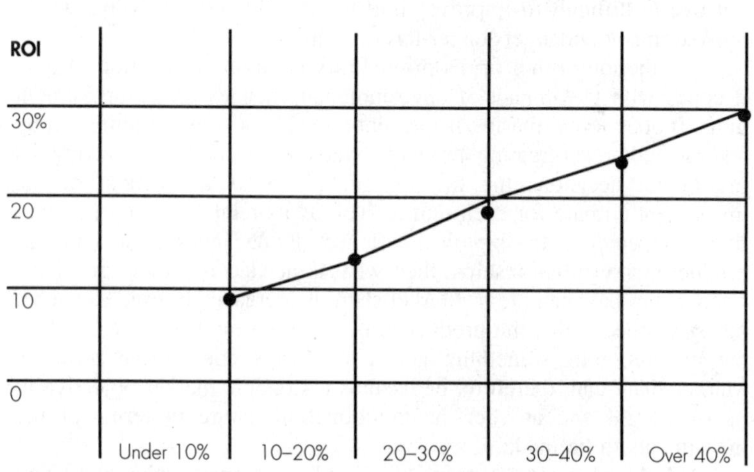

Source: Robert D. Buzzell, Bradley T. Gale, and Ralph G.M. Sultan, "Market share—A Key to Profitability," *Harvard Business Review*, January-February, 1975, p. 98.

the firm's accumulated sales double per unit costs (based on value added) drop between 20 and 30% as expressed in real dollars. Thus, cumulative relative share (firm's share divided by that of the industry leader) will be closely correlated with relative per unit costs and have a direct bearing on profitability.

A second reason why higher profitability derives from high share is a better "fit" between the product and the served market. This can be due to higher product quality in a physical sense and/or better services. Often the higher perceived quality permits charging a premium price. And, third, there is the possibility of market power which enables the dominant firm to earn higher profits because of its ability to police the industry (administer prices) and bargain more effectively with suppliers.

It must be noted that the above fails to take into account the position of the product in the life cycle. Yet stage in the life cycle should affect both profitability and cash flow. Thus, products with high shares during the growth stage will tend to generate negative cash flows and lower profitability than will the same product during the mature stage. Also, different kinds and amounts of expenditures are associated with different stages in the product life cycle. This is certainly the case with such marketing costs as those having to do with product development, advertising, channel/account development, and the building of a sales force.

Despite this difficulty market share is used by some managers as a proxy measure for future profitability and hence serves as the basis for setting objectives. The latter are stated in the form of "change"; i.e., increasing, holding, or harvesting share. The former is most likely to be adopted when the market is growing while the holding or maintaining relates to a stable market situation. Harvesting or disinvestment is recommended mainly when the market is declining or when the firm cannot finance the necessary growth required to make the product viable on a relative cost basis.

The use of market share measures as objectives, however, inevitably gives rise to the thorny question of how the firm defines its business, and, in particular, its served markets. Without such a definition a market share measure cannot even be calculated. It is also true that business definition affects the choice of a given share objective as is the case when a firm redefines its product-market scope to take advantage of opportunities presented in the form of new segments. Under such conditions the firm would inevitably set new share and cash flow objectives. This is not to suggest that objectives do not affect business definition since profitability is at the heart of any investment decision relating to the scope and direction of the business. Because objectives and business definition are so highly interrelated, it is necessary to discuss the latter subject further. This is the purpose of the next section.

BUSINESS DEFINITION

Objectives are important in setting the level of economic performance the firm seeks to attain. For them to be used effectively requires a resource allocation process which permits the firm to deploy its resources across its investment centers in its efforts to achieve success. In the aggregate these centers define the firm's business. Thus, from an operational point of view, objectives and a definition of the business are inseparable.

Business definition—sometimes called business purpose or concept of the business—has long been of interest to marketing scholars. Drucker and Levitt, in particular, have advocated the dominance of the market place in such a definition. The former argues persuasively that the purpose of the firm is to ". . . create a customer."[6] Levitt elaborates this notion by urging firms to define themselves not in terms of the products they sell, but by the functions such products perform. Since needs remain relatively constant over time while products are often rendered obsolete by technological change, such a concept helps ensure the firm's continuing vitality. Thus, it is argued, had the railroads conceptualized themselves as being in the transportation rather than in the railroad business, they would have continued to prosper.[7]

The difficulty with defining a business solely on the basis of product function lies in its lack of specificity. To define a firm's business as being "transportation" is to do so in such a generalized way as to make it impossible for management to formulate strategy. Does being in the "transportation" business imply a product line consisting of trains, cars, trucks, ships, airplanes, taxis, busses, and helicopters serving a variety of customer groups including individuals, families, business firms, and the government?[8]

The strategy literature—starting in the mid 1960's—sought to provide greater specificity by defining a business in terms of its product-market scope. Following along these lines the end goal of the strategic planning process was conceptualized as being a best yield portfolio or mix of products and markets.[9] This view of the business and the strategic planning process implicitly recognizes product-market relationships as investment units; further, that their aggregation represents a definition of the business which changes over time.

BUSINESS DEFINITION DIMENSIONS

In more recent years attempts have been made to define the business in ways which will provide the firm with a competitive superiority based largely on the dynamics of the firm's product-market environment. In particular, there has been increasing awareness of market segments as a way of defining and understanding market opportunities and threats. For the most part the dimensions used include customer groups (market segments), customer needs, products, and technology. The use of these dimensions is an extension of product-market scope since markets can be defined in terms of needs and products in terms of their technology. This elaboration is, however, important since it provides a way of integrating products and markets and, in the process, understanding their relationships from the customer's point of view.

If segments can be defined, first, in terms of their needs and, second, on the basis of their identifying characteristics (e.g., demographics, lifestyle, and geographical location), then the first two dimensions can be merged. Needs can be defined in either broad (generic) or specific terms. The more general the need is stated the more difficult it is for the firm to deploy its resources; e.g., almost everyone needs "transportation," but in what form?

A definition of needs—if it is to be useful—must be specific as to what goals/objectives the consumer wishes to attain and/or what problem solutions are being sought. Since most consumers use a system consisting of labor, products, and machines to "solve" a problem, the ascertainment of needs—there is usually more than one—in measurable form is rarely easy. Further, needs will often vary depending upon the use environment.

Some illustrations may help clarify the above. Consumers, in general, have the need to clean their teeth. They do so in an effort to attain such goals as those pertaining to appearance (white teeth), health (tooth decay prevention), and social acceptance (lack of mouth odor). In the case of overseas travel such needs as time in route, safety, comfort, and the convenience and punctuality of departure and arrival times, are presumably critical to most passengers. In a similar way food packers have a need to protect their product in transit and in storage against damage, loss of freshness and appearance, taste deterioration and shrinkage.

In an effort to solve a problem, the consumer (either household or industrial) employs a decision process which matches products to needs. This consists of the development of choice criteria by which needs are translated into a set of ideal choice criteria. The latter reflect the product characteristics or attributes the consumer feels are necessary to meet his/her needs. Product alternatives are, therefore, evaluated on the basis of whether they possess the desired attributes as well as the extent to which each is of value to the consumer. For certain needs, the above process takes place within different use settings, thereby giving rise to different choice criteria.

Given the above, need segments can be derived at a number of different levels of aggregation; e.g., use environment, product class, product type, and brand levels. In the case of our transportation example, segments (groups of potential customers) could be structured around business versus vacation and international versus domestic travel (different use situations), product class (airplane, ships, railroads, and automobiles), product type (international versus domestic carrier and plane type—747/DC10/L1011 versus 707/DC8), and brand (TWA, Pan Am, BA, and Air France). The existence of a given segment would be based on the extent to which a sufficient size group possessed a different set of choice criteria. The size of the segment would depend upon the extent to which the firm deemed it necessary to have high homogeneity within versus heterogeneity between segments. One can, of course, carry segmentation too far. Segments must be large enough to justify the economics required to be treated differently.

If we first segment on the basis of different choice criteria (presence of different attributes and/or different values attached to individual attributes), then we need to identify the individuals belonging to each segment. The resulting groups are called operational segments. For consumer goods these are mostly based on demographics, lifestyle, and geography while for industrial products these are based on account size and geography.

The choice criteria of the various segments provide the basis for the firm's product line decisions as well as those pertaining to the physical (including price) and service dimensions of the individual product. The closer the product's characteristics are perceived to be similar to the choice criteria of the target segment, the higher the probability of its being purchased. Brand share should, therefore, be closely tied to the brand's relative rating vis-à-vis the choice criteria.

Technology in a broad sense can be thought of as the resources (including skills) required to design, manufacture, and market that "utility package" which best meets the needs (choice criteria) of a customer group (segment). It needs to be emphasized here that technology does apply to marketing. This is particularly true for many consumer goods where the determinants of market share are largely those skills related to product design and product development, advertising, and merchandising. Thought of in this light the choice of products and their characteristics become a function of how technology is applied to meeting needs. Thus, we can drop product(s) as one of the business definition dimensions.

Hopefully, the above discussion has provided a way of linking customer groups, customer needs, and technology both conceptually and operationally. Collectively they serve as the essence of how a business defines itself. The tighter the linkages the more precise the definition and the greater the chance for the business definition to be successful. What has not yet been discussed, however, is the extent to which the firm wishes to engage in serving multiple customer needs and customer groups. Usually referred to in terms of "scope," such decisions clearly affect the business definition and are the subject of the next section.

SCOPE AND BUSINESS DEFINITION

Most business definitions have typically relied on some kind of a product-market *scope* measure. Abell elaborates this concept by advocating that businesses be defined by applying scope and differentiation measures to the three dimensions. "Scope" he defines on the basis of being focused or narrow with respect to customers served, their needs, and the technologies employed.[10] Differentiation has two meanings; first, the extent to which a business treats one or more of the three dimensions differently and, second, the extent of difference between the offerings of two or more competitors. Clearly the first meaning is simply another way of implying broad scope.

Perhaps a more meaningful way of looking at a way of classifying alternative business definitions is to apply only the focus and differentiation (first meaning) to the three dimensions. This simpler typology omits the extent to which the firm differentiates itself from competitors. One can argue that the decision to do this makes no great difference since competitive offerings have already been taken into account in the way the firm has differentiated its offerings across its segments. Further, a firm will take competitive offerings into account in deciding which business definition to opt for.

The modified typology contains eight different ways of defining the business as follows:

Business Definition Category	Customer Groups	Customer Needs	Technologies
1.	Focused	Focused	Focused
2.	Focused	Focused	Differentiated
3.	Focused	Differentiated	Focused
4.	Focused	Differentiated	Differentiated
5.	Differentiated	Focused	Focused
6.	Differentiated	Focused	Differentiated
7.	Differentiated	Differentiated	Focused
8.	Differentiated	Differentiated	Differentiated

Most businesses start out by using a highly-focused approach. Some firms continue to employ such a narrow scope even though it involves high risk since a change in any of the dimensions can pose a substantial threat. Examples here include specialized suppliers to the automobile industry. Success is largely a function of volume, the ability to reap the benefits of the experience curve, and a product which is closely linked to buyer specifications. The more unique the need and tailored the product, the greater the protection afforded the high share seller since little or no cost advantages will accrue to firms servicing broader groups and/or needs.

Category two consists of using two or more technologies to service a customer group, the members of which have the same needs. This can happen when a business is in a state of transition regarding its technologies (e.g., electronic versus mechanical). The use of more than technology is present in tennis today where players are confronted with an array of wood, plastic, and metal rackets. In such a case one could argue that groups and their needs are too broadly defined; that segments exist, but cannot be defined operationally.

Category three is concerned with servicing the multiple needs of a single customer group using a single technology. Examples here include the increased versatility built into hand-held calculators, hi-fi units which both record and play, and security systems which guard against fire and theft. Closely-related technologies are used by many companies to generate a host of products serving different yet related needs of the same group; e.g., laundry and cleaning products.

Category four is less focused than the earlier three since different technologies are used to service different needs of the same customer group. Examples include many household products companies which sell a variety of product classes to the American housewife; e.g., P & G which sells laundry, paper, food, and beverage items; Gillette which sells razors and personal care items to men, and General Electric which sells both small and major appliances besides radios and television sets to much the same households.

Category five involves selling essentially the same product to meet the same needs of a variety of customer groups. Examples include firms selling such products as office supplies, paper, metals, plastics, electric motors, and computers across customer groups (end users). Most large packaged food and beverage companies sell to both households and commercial customers.

Category six involves the use of different technologies to service the same need of multiple groups. Of necessity this definition requires a broad definition of need. The use of specially formulated paints (protective coatings), and the production of a variety of floor (cork, vinyl, and wood) and wall coverings (paint and wallpaper) are examples here.

Category seven seeks to serve the multiple needs of more than one customer group via one product. Versatility is the order of the day here; e.g., tractors which can fulfill a variety of needs for farmers and road builders. The last category involves differences across all three dimensions and is more likely to apply at the corporate rather than the business level.

The weakness in the business definition classification scheme discussed lies in its inability to specify the degree of difference existing between multiple customer groups, needs, and technologies. The broader the definitions the less the differences. In contrast the more a firm tends to define its customer groups on the basis of their choice criteria the more precise will be the business definition and the greater the number of customer groups.

Business definitions can and do change over time primarily because of market evolution. Thus, a focused definition is appropriate early on in the product life cycle, but its relevancy decreases over time as market fragmentation occurs. Clearly, the more differentiated the firm the more life cycles are involved, thereby in turn affecting business definition. In any event, using the same framework as discussed above enables the firm to redefine itself. Thus, change can occur in seven ways:[11]

1. In customer groups
2. In customer needs
3. In technologies
4. In customer groups and customer needs
5. In customer groups and technologies
6. In customer needs and technologies
7. In all three

When thought of in terms of change, the business mix the firm aspires to becomes an objective in its own right. It is certainly directional in nature with respect to investments even to the extent of defining—at least broadly—where and how they must be made. If strategy is thought of largely as a change in product-market scope, then any change in business definition derives from strategy. The two—strategy and business definition—are, therefore, intimately related.

A precise definition of the business is critical if the proper functional area strategy decisions are to be made. The more broadly a firm defines itself the greater the impact is likely to be on marketing. This is particularly true with regard to its advertising, sales, and distribution strategies. If segments are defined using choice criteria, then the strategies relating to the servicing of the need(s) are more easily defined; i.e., the basis used for linking customer groups and their needs is highly diagnostic and facilitates the development of viable R & D, product and product line, price, channels, advertising, and personal selling decisions.

SUMMARY AND CONCLUSIONS

Marketing plays a key role in the establishment of the firm's objectives. Traditionally, these have been defined using a variety of economic measures of which some index of profitability is the single most important measure. Because of the difficulties inherent in forecasting future profitability, many firms have turned to the use of market share as a proxy measure of future profitability. Thus, objectives are often stated in terms of increasing share, maintaining share, and harvesting. The PIMS report shows that there is a high positive correlation between market share and pretax return on investment.

Market share measures require a precise understanding of both products and markets serviced. These, in turn, form the basis for the way the business defines itself. Indeed, without such a definition it is hardly possible for the firm to determine market share and the profitability of its product-market investment units. Thus, there is a strong interrelationship between objectives and business definition.

The most recent thinking centers on the use of three dimensions (customer group, customer needs, and technology) as the bases for defining a business. When scope (focus versus differentiation) measures are applied to these three dimensions, then seven different business definitions emerge, each of which has its own advantages and disadvantages.

The tighter the firm is able to link the three dimensions the more likely it is to have a business definition which leads to success and is capable of changing to meet new opportunities and threats. Further, business definition is essential if the proper functional area strategies are to emerge. This is particularly true in marketing where critically important strategic decisions pertaining to product, price, channels, advertising, and personal selling must be made.

NOTES

1. Charles H. Granger, "The Hierarchy of Objectives," *Harvard Business Review,* May-June, 1964, p. 66.
2. Peter F. Drucker, *The Practice of Management,* (New York: Harper and Row, 1954).
3. Milton Friedman, *Capitalism and Freedom* (Chicago: The University of Chicago Press, 1962), p. 133.
4. Andrew Shonfield, *Modern Capitalism: The Changing Balance of Public and Private Power* (New York: Oxford University Press, 1965), p. 227.
5. Robert D. Buzzel, Bradley T. Gale, and Ralph G. M. Sulton, "Marketing Share—A Key to Profitability," *Harvard Business Review,* January-February, 1975. Also see Strategic Planning Institute, "Market Position: Build, Hold or Harvest," Pimsletter number 3 (Cambridge, MA, 1977).
6. Drucker, *op. cit.,* p. 37.
7. Theodore Levitt, *Innovation in Marketing: New Perspective for Profit and Growth* (New York: McGraw-Hill, 1962), pp. 63–71.
8. H. Igor Ansoff, *Corporate Strategy* (New York: McGraw-Hill, 1965), p. 107.
9. Charles O. Rossotti, "Two Concepts of Long-Range Planning: A Special Commentary" (Boston: The Boston Consulting Group, N.D.).
10. Derek F. Abell, *Defining the Business* (Englewood Cliffs, N.J.: Prentice-Hall, Inc., 1980), Chapter 7.
11. *Ibid.*

REFERENCES

Roger W. Brooksbank, *Marketing Intelligence and Planning,* "Marketing Planning: A Seven-Stage Process," 1990, pp. 21–28.

Yash P. Gupta, Subhash C. Lonial, W. Glynn Mangold, *International Journal of Operations and Production Management,* "An Examination of the Relationship between Marketing Strategy and Marketing Objectives," 1991, pp. 33–43.

Roger D. Blackwell
Professor of Marketing
The Ohio State University
Affiliated Consultant, Management
Horizons, Inc.

David T. Kollat
Senior Vice President
Limited Stores, Inc.

James F. Engel
Professor
Graduate School of Communications
Wheaton College

CHAPTER 9

DETERMINING CONSUMER AND CUSTOMER WANTS AND NEEDS

Difficulty in determining consumer wants and needs increases as a function of increasing discretionary income and wealth. In an economy where the incomes of most consumers barely exceed that required for survival (or doesn't even reach that level), predicting consumer needs and wants is easy—just market more basic food and shelter. In an affluent society, most of the population has great discretion in spending their money. The more discretion, the more difficult it is to understand exactly what products will be purchased in preference to other attractive alternatives.

Some persons will spend their discretionary funds on education, others on boats, improved housing, leisure and travel, stereo, clothing, good restaurants, religious activities, personal services for the maintenance of lawns, and so on. In other words, people's choices vary greatly concerning what they want most. Because of this, it is proper to think of airlines in competition with home builders, stereo marketers in competition with boat marketers, and universities in competition with churches. Perhaps some persons believe that as incomes rise, marketing competition lessens. Quite the opposite is true.

Marketing executives, government administrators, church boards, and others should have learned one very important principle over the past few decades: *Consumers spend their dollars on what they want most.* Any assumption that consumers spend their money on what is "best" for the greater social good or only on what they "ought" to buy (according to someone else's criteria) is naive and empirically unfounded. Customers are self-satisfying, adaptive problem solvers who will buy the products they believe give them personally the most pleasure and value. Any type of organization that is dependent on money from consumers (i.e., business, government, churches, schools, and the like) had better learn well how to determine what it is that consumers really want if the organization hopes to survive and prosper.

THE ROLE OF THE CONSUMER

Consumers have two vital roles. First, they determine the nature of resource allocation in an economy. Second, consumers determine the success of specific organizations within a society.

Understanding the Needs of a Society

The needs and desires of a society—or of the consumers who comprise a society—are not static. They cannot be considered "given" in any realistic economic science. Marketing activity is a process by which the demand structure for economic goods and services is anticipated or enlarged and satisfied through the provision of those goods and services. The study of consumers has as its focus, therefore, the determination of what those needs may be, how they are formed, and how they are influenced by marketing activity.

Marketing in advanced economies is a group behavior process in which millions of individual consumers and industrial organizations are linked together with countless institutions. When one considers the hundreds of thousands of production and distribution decisions that must be made for consumers to get the products they want and for industrial buyers to produce and sell the goods required for the process to be effective, it is obvious that *it is essential to understand how consumers' preferences are formed.*

Improving Marketing Management

Marketing management is sometimes conceptualized as interpreting what customers want, providing the goods and services that evolve from those wants, and the follow-up activities necessary to ensure that the desired satisfaction was obtained from the goods. Several important marketing managerial benefits associated with these activities are particularly dependent on the beginning activity of interpreting customer wants.

Locating New Market Opportunities. New market opportunities are determined by discovering customer groups with unmet needs. Unmet needs alone are not enough, however. Groups with unmet needs must have enough *income* to make it *profitable* to supply those needs. Additionally, marketing management must evaluate *whether unmet needs and wants in general* (such as desire for pleasurable use of leisure time) *can be channeled into specific products* (such as boats or skiing equipment). This requires analysis of the probability of the firm's promotional program effectively communicating to the consumer the match between unmet needs and the product's benefits. It also requires analysis of whether the product, which may meet a consumer's unmet need, can be produced and marketed at a *price within the customer's range of acceptance,* and *whether distribution channels can be induced to carry the new goods.*

New market opportunities arise for a variety of reasons in industrialized societies. One is *geographical mobility.* People live where they did not live before and thus create new markets. The aggressive business firm recognizes these new markets and builds new supermarkets, new discount houses, and new shopping centers in suburbia and interurbia.

Another source of new markets is *social mobility.* As people become more educated and acquire a more sophisticated social milieu, their interests change, frequently resulting in markets for new products. A third cause of new market opportunities is *psychic mobility,* when people change their conception of themselves and their environment along with physical and social mobility. In this new conception, a person's inner self is no longer fixed and immutable. Personality is free to deviate from rigidly prescribed social norms, and people can express their desires in many ways. In a society in which people have the income to purchase much of what they want, understanding this phenomenon is a key to success for the "growth" firm.

Developing Segmentation Strategies. No two people are exactly alike. This conclusion is readily accepted when the FBI is speaking of fingerprints, but it is also true when describing consumer preferences for products. This reality is in contrast to the implicit assumption to the contrary that characterizes much of traditional economic and marketing thought. Determining consumer wants and needs must become increasingly detailed if products are to be developed that truly satisfy the consumer's desires for manifold variations in color, style, durability (matched with price), benefit, size, and so forth.

Rarely can products be designed exclusively for the tastes of one individual, however. For production and marketing efficiency, groups of consumers must be determined whose tastes are sufficiently similar that they can be grouped together as "market segments." Segmentation does not typically center on *one* of the preferred characteristics, however. Consumer researchers usually must determine the distribution of preferences of *various* product characteristics. This fact enormously complicates the determination of consumer wants for specific products but is essential to effective segmentation strategies.

Improving Marketing Programming. Marketing programmers (advertising, channels of distribution, pricing strategies, and so forth) are most likely to be effective when they are related closely to a thorough understanding of customer wants and needs. With promotional strategies, understanding the underlying reasons for purchase and use of a product is essential to developing proper themes for advertising. In designing the features of a product, consideration should be given to the evaluative criteria that truly distinguish one product from another in the consumer's mind and provide a differential advantage over competitors. Improved retailing performance can be expected from understanding the degree to which consumers have well-formulated preferences for products (and thus prefer self-service) and the degree to which they need advice and specific information (and therefore prefer sales assistance).

The Role of the Industrial Producer

Industrial purchasing processes have the same functional character as consumer decision processes and thus probably have more similarities than differences to consumer purchasing. Older books often described industrial buying as "rational" or economic in nature in contrast to consumer buying, and generally neglected the social-psychological factors that are important in understanding how industrial buying decisions actually occur. It is increasingly recognized that the needs and wants of both consumers and business organizations are basically derived from individuals who are adaptive, information-desiring problem solvers.

Markets are increasingly understood as an integrated process derived from the wants and needs of ultimate consumers. As consumers change in their preferences for products and services, changes must occur in the inventories of retailers and wholesalers who supply them. This pressure is felt immediately on consumer manufacturers who in turn change their requirements (their "wants" and "needs") from industrial manufacturers of components, materials, supplies, and business services. As a marketing tactic, industrial firms increasingly conduct research on the market needs of their customers' customers.

While the parameters vary substantially between industrial and ultimate customers, the basic processes are similar. Industrial buyers do not cease to be human in organizations but retain similar psychological drives, desires, urges, and reference group pressures. Selling cannot be done to an organization; it can be done only to individuals within an organization.

A MODEL FOR DETERMINING CUSTOMER WANTS AND NEEDS

There are three basic approaches to understanding customer wants and needs empirically. These approaches are (1) a *distributive* approach, focusing on the outcome of behavior; (2) a *morphological* approach, which describes the way a decision is made; and (3) an *analytical* approach, which is similar to the morphological approach except that it assesses the impact of various influences on purchases (such as advertisements or displays). The latter two are similar and are more frequently referred to jointly as the *decision process* approach.

The Decision Process Approach

The decision process approach views *purchase as one point in a process* of action undertaken by the customer. To know what it is that a customer wants and perhaps will purchase requires an examination of behavior as more than a discrete act. The concern is as great with how a decision is reached as it is with the decision itself and thus provides a much richer information base with which to devise effective marketing strategies and product satisfaction.

The decision-making formulation used here to understand customer wants consists of five processes linked in a sequence: (1) problem recognition, (2) search, (3) alternative evaluation, (4) choice, and (5) outcomes.[1] This is an attempt to describe the behavioral processes that intervene from the stage at which consumers recognize that some decision is necessary through purchase to the point at which there is postpurchase evaluation of an alternative and its attributes.

Interpreting customer wants and needs requires a "multi-mediation" model. This term refers to the fact that many processes intervene between exposure to a stimulus and final outcomes of behavior. As a result, there are a number of factors that serve to mediate or affect the outcome if an analyst is to understand realistically the relationship between customer wants and demand for specific products and services.

A multi-mediation model of consumer behavior is displayed in Figure 1. Although it refers specifically to the behavior of ultimate consumers, the process with minor modification can also be applied to individuals functioning in industrial and distributive organizations.

The Individual's Psychological Make-Up

At the heart of customer behavior is the *central control unit* (CCU), which is the psychological command center, including both memory and the basic facilities for thinking and direction of behavior. The primary components for purposes of understanding consumer desires and needs are information and experience, evaluative criteria, and attitude, which, in turn, are affected by personality. These variables interact to form what may be called a "filter" through which incoming stimuli are processed.

It is particularly important in determining customer wants and needs to focus attention on a customer's *evaluative criteria.* Evaluative criteria are specifications used by the consumer to compare products and brands. Examples include price, performance, and durability. They reflect the individual's goals and basic desires with respect to purchase and are shaped by his basic attitudes, personality, past experience and learning, and by interaction with others in his family and social environment.

The function of evaluative criteria is to serve as standards or guidelines against which alternatives are compared and evaluated. The criticality in knowing these criteria stems from the condition that products that fail to meet these specifications are unlikely to be considered as alternatives in the purchase process. When a strategist begins analyzing customer needs, he or she does not usually find specific "needs" for a new product or brand. Rather, a "bundle" of evaluative criteria is found, which, given satisfactory communications and distribution of the product, may result in the consumer "wanting" the offered product enough to buy it.

The Perceptual Process

The matching of "products offered" with "products wanted" must pass through a perceptual or "sizing up" process by the consumer. The perceptual process is shown in Figure 1 as consisting of four distinct phases: (1) exposure, (2) attention, (3) comprehension, and (4) retention.

Exposure. Individuals are constantly bombarded with physical and social stimuli that must pass through the five senses (sensory receptors) to have any potential of communicating a matching of need and solution.

FIGURE 1.
A Multi-mediation Model of Consumer Behavior

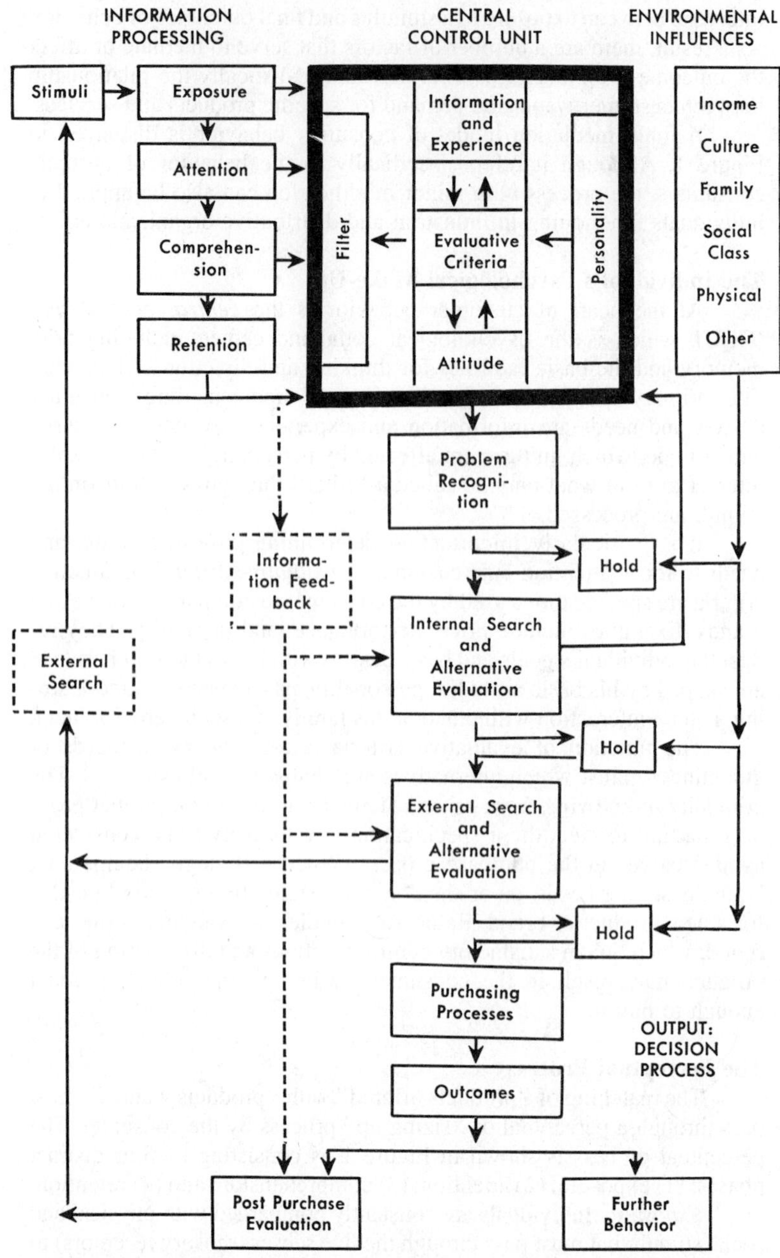

Source: James F. Engel, David T. Kollat, and Roger D. Blackwell, *Consumer Behavior*, Copyright © 1968, 1973 by Holt, Rinehart and Winston, Inc., Adapted and reprinted by permission of the publisher.

Attention. Consumers give attention to some stimuli and ignore others. This process is known to be highly selective, dependent on the attributes of the communication (its ability to stimulate attraction, intensity, and so forth), need activation, resistance of attitude change, and other variables. The consumer will be especially alert to information that strikes a responsive chord among felt needs, desires, and interests. Conversely, he or she tends to ignore stimuli, that do not unlock a need or interest or that tend to conflict with the present product and brand choices that already are satisfactory. Thus, it is essential that a marketing strategist understand thoroughly the underlying attitudes, feelings, interests, and preferences of any consumers with whom he or she wants to communicate that a product solves an unmet need for the consumer.

Comprehension. The filter also serves to distort stimuli in such a manner that certain attributes are amplified whereas others are diminished or ignored. This distortion usually occurs in such a way as to make the stimulus more consonant with the individual's predispositions. This distortion occurs even though the consumer is exposed to and has attended the message.

Retention. Perception is selective in a third way. The set of stimuli that finally becomes stored in conscious memory and which therefore relates a product to unmet needs tends to be a much smaller set than the initial set. Retention can be measured, using question-answer methods at various periods after exposure.

Problem Recognition

Behavior is initiated when an individual perceives a difference between an ideal and an actual state of affairs. This is called problem recognition and is the first stage of decision making, shown in Figure 1. It is the key to understanding customer needs and wants.

Problem recognition may occur through *need activation* in which the individual becomes alert, responsive, and vigilant because of a feeling of discomfort or dissatisfaction triggered by sensory receptors. The result is arousal or a state of *desire* which provides for an energizing of need-satisfying action. For example, the consumer becomes hungry, meaning that the system is activated. Whether this will move toward purchase of a particular food product depends on the many other variables described here, but problem recognition is the essential stage. Without it, demand for products does not occur.

Marketing strategists must be aware that problem recognition can also occur through awareness of an external stimulus, such as an advertisement. An ad for a large, cool drink can help the customer feel thirsty and thereby initiate behavior. It should be noted that something about the ad may conflict with current preferences and lead that person to ignore or distort the input, however, and therefore not lead to problem recognition.

Action can be constrained by the intervention of external constraints such as those shown in Figure 1. A family may recognize that a new automobile is needed, but perhaps a strike has caused uncertainty about income in the future. This may cause a *hold* in the process. Many factors operate as constraints such as cultural values and conflicting family desires.

Search Processes: Information Processing

After a problem is recognized and no constraints intervene to halt the decision process, customers determine whether the alternatives for action are adequately evaluated. The initial step will be internal search in the memory or experience of the consumer. If the consumer considers the alternatives to solving the problem to be adequately known and evaluated, he or she will proceed immediately to purchase. When stored information is not adequate, further information is sought.

Alternative Evaluation

Frequently consumers perceive a problem to exist and conclude that they do not know enough about the alternatives for action. They *search for information, either passively or actively.* That is, they become more receptive or interested in information that they "happen" to see and in other instances, they aggressively seek information from friends, advertising, product-rating agencies, and retail outlets. Varying degrees of search will occur depending on the psychological makeup of the customer and the amount of stored information. It is essential that a marketing strategist conduct research defining the sources of information used for each type of product by various customer segments in their search behavior.

Customers become involved in a process called alternative evaluation. This process is the comparison of evaluative criteria, or the specifications by which people choose a product as relative to their needs, and their beliefs about the ability of a brand or store to satisfy those evaluative criteria. This comparison process involves the attitudes, beliefs, and intentions which are a result of previous experiences and accumulated assimilation of information from values, lifestyles, and other influences. It is most important for a firm to understand the evaluative criteria of target markets so that the store or brand can focus its scarce resources of providing benefits that are those that will satisfy the most important criteria of customers. A knowledge of evaluative criteria also provides the guideline for focusing promotional activity and adjusting such things as commissions for sales activity, appeals, and products featured in advertising, store hours, and other elements of the marketing mechanism.

Choice Processes and Outcomes

After passing through earlier stages, the consumer arrives at a decision to purchase that may be acted on immediately or at a later period. A great many variables affect the outcome of purchasing behavior. The effectiveness of retail sales clerks, availability of credit terms, selection of colors and models, delivery capability, and installation assistance are just a few of the variables that affect the match between consumer wants and marketing offerings. The decision-process approach enables the marketing strategist to observe, for example, that a consumer may have a want that is satisfied by a particular brand of a product. The consumer may develop favorable attitudes toward that brand, be satisfied in internal and external search that this is the best brand, but not find that brand available at the preferred retail outlet, or that the price or credit terms make that brand less preferred than other alternatives. In some cases, an effective sales presentation during purchasing may switch the consumer to an alternative.

Post Purchase and Further Behavior

It is believed that once a purchase occurs, a customer becomes sensitive to further information that confirms the choice and reduces post-decision dissonance. The customer may seek out such information. The purchase may also trigger additional action, such as further purchases of home furnishings after an initial purchase of carpeting is made or lessons after sports equipment is purchased.

It should be pointed out that the process described here is the most complete type, called extended problem solving. Simpler forms called limited or habitual decision-process behavior are also frequently encountered.

Implications

Marketing strategists should recognize the adaptive character of the needs and wants of problem-solving customers. Consumers are not inert individuals capable of being manipulated. Instead, consumers should be understood as information seekers who evaluate communications and product choices in terms of their drives and aspirations. When products are consonant with their problem-solving strategies, consumers choose these products. When products are unsatisfactory, they choose alternatives.

In an affluent economy, the ever-changing, adaptive nature of consumer wants and needs are released in continuously updated product choices. This breeds disaster for rigid marketing organization but breathes dynamism into the firm that plies and plans with consumer behavior.

NOTES

1. Roger D. Blackwell, James F. Engel, and David T. Kollat, *Consumer Behavior* (New York: Holt, Rinehart and Winston, Inc., 3rd edition 1978).

SUGGESTIONS FOR FURTHER READING

Henry Assael, *Consumer Behavior and Marketing Action* (Boston: Kent, 1987).

Roger D. Blackwell, James F. Engel, Wayne Talarzyk, *Contemporary Cases in Consumer Behavior* (New York: Holt, Rinehart and Winston, Inc., 1977).

Gerald Celente, *Trend Tracking* (New York: Warner Books, 1991).

Richard P. Coleman, "The Continuing Significance of Social Class to Marketing," *Journal of Consumer Research,* December 1993, pp. 265–80.

James F. Engel, Roger D. Blackwell, David T. Kollat, *Consumer Behavior,* 3rd ed. (New York: Holt, Rinehart and Winston, Inc., 1978).

James F. Engel, Roger D. Blackwell, and Paul W. Miniard, *Consumer Behavior,* 7th ed. (New York: Dryden Press, 1993).

John A. Howard, *Consumer Behavior: Application of Theory* (New York: McGraw-Hill Book Company, 1977).

Sidney J. Levy, "Symbolism and Life Style," *Toward Scientific Marketing,* ed. Stephen A. Greyser, Chicago: American Marketing Association, 1964, pp. 140–50.

A. Maslow, *Motivation and Personality* (New York: Harper and Row, 1954).

Patrick Murphy and William Staples, "A Modernized Family Life Cycle," *Journal of Consumer Research,* June 1979, pp. 12–22.

Faith Popcorn, *The Popcorn Report* (New York: Harper Business, 1992).

Joseph T. Plummer, "The Concept and Application of Life Style Segmentation," *Journal of Marketing,* January 1974, p. 34.

Jagdish N. Sheth, *Models of Buyer Behavior* (New York: Harper & Row, 1974).

Michael R. Solomon, *Consumer Behavior* (Needham Heights: Allyn and Bacon, 1992).

Arch G. Woodside, Jagdish N. Sheth, Peter D. Bennett, *Consumer and Industrial Buying Behavior* (New York: North-Holland, 1977).

Gregory S. Carpenter
Associate Professor of Marketing
Richard M. Clewett Research Professor
J. L. Kellogg Graduate School of Management
Northwestern University
Evanston, Illinois

Kent Nakamoto
Assistant Professor of Marketing
Graduate School of Business
University of Colorado
Boulder, Colorado

CHAPTER 10

BRAND DOMINANCE: COMPETITIVE ADVANTAGE THROUGH CONSUMER LEARNING

Introduction

In many markets, competition produces a remarkable outcome: one brand outsells all others not just for a short time but sometimes for decades. Wrigley's chewing gum, Gerber baby food, Kleenex tissues, and others have retained the largest shares of their markets for years. Empirical studies demonstrate that this observation is true among brands that dominate a market early in its life—so-called market pioneers (Robinson and Fornell 1985; Urban, et al. 1986)—and among high market share brands in general (Hambrick, MacMillan, and Day 1982).

The persistent dominance of these brands challenges the traditional view of competition, in which successful brands attract new competitors offering improved products or, at the very least, equivalent products at lower prices, eventually reducing the dominant brand's market share. Indeed, dominant brands retain their high market shares *despite* successful new product introductions, shifting consumer tastes, and changing technology. Some even thrive as a result of new competition. Coca-Cola's market share, for instance, *increased* following the initiation of the so-called cola wars by Pepsi with its Pepsi Challenge.

We explore what creates and sustains such an enduring advantage in this chapter. Our explanation focuses on consumer preference and choice. The traditional view of consumer choice in markets dominated by a single brand is that buyers choose brands based on actual or perceived attributes and price relationships according to their (fixed, predetermined) preferences (Schmalensee 1982). Of course actual consumer behavior in these markets is much more complex. The dominant brand is perceptually distinctive, adding complexity to simple assessments of attributes and price. Buyer preferences are affected by the order in which buyers learn about brands (Carpenter and Nakamoto 1989), and consumer tastes are neither predetermined nor fixed (Tversky, Sattath, and Slovic 1988). We are not born with brand preferences but *learn* our preferences through experiences with brands. This process, called *preference formation,* is central to the creation of buyer preferences, resulting in a persistent competitive advantage for a dominant brand. The following paragraphs describe this preference formation process and how brand dominance influences it, creating such an advantage.

Once a competitive advantage is created one must ask, What sustains it? What protects a dominant brand, for instance, from low-priced competitors offering equivalent products (so-called me-too brands)? We turn to the competitive implications of consumer preference formation to address this question. At the heart of any explanation for dominant brand advantage is a model of consumer decision making. In the traditional view of competition where buyers choose based on simple attribute-price relationships according to fixed preferences, a high market share can be sustained if competitors offering more value can be deterred from entering the market (Encaoua, Geroski, and Jacquemin 1986).

In contrast, a consumer preference formation view of competition suggests a very different competitive process. Rather than having fixed, predetermined preferences, buyers *learn* their preferences, and the process of preference formation creates a preference structure favoring the dominant brand. This learning process, more complex than simple attribute-price comparisons, is strongly influenced by the dominant brand. It can *define* the ideal product and become the standard of comparison for all other brands, affecting the perceived value of every brand. Moreover, this preference structure, once created, is difficult to alter. Therefore, consumer learning yields a preference structure that favors the dominant brand, is slow to change, and is difficult for competitors to alter, producing a persistent dominant brand advantage.

We will explore consumer preference formation and its competitive implications in three stages. First, we will consider how brand dominance influences the formation of consumer preferences. We will consider how initial experiences with a brand influence subsequent brand preference and the role of brand dominance in that process. Next, we will discuss how that same process creates consumer preferences that make reducing the high share of the dominant brand difficult for competitors. Finally, we will explore the strategic implications of consumer preference formation and the competitive advantage it creates.

CONSUMER PREFERENCE FORMATION

Consumer Learning

Memory for product information or past usage experience has a profound impact on consumer decisions. For example, knowledgeable consumers appear to rely more heavily on brands as foci for organizing product information and on categories and subcategories as bases for grouping brands (Bettman 1986; Johnson and Russo 1984; Sujan 1985). In addition, choice experience results in selective retention of brand information favoring chosen brands (Biehal and Chakravarti 1982). This selective retention continues to favor previously chosen brands even if a previously inferior brand is improved through addition of a new attribute (Biehal and Chakravarti 1983). Thus choice affects memory, and memory in turn affects choice.

Because of this ongoing interaction of experience and preference, the order of a consumer's product experiences can affect choices over time. Changing the order of experiences, even if they are the same in aggregate, changes product perceptions and preferences. Brands a consumer is exposed to first influence the structure of the consumer's preferences in the category and can become perceptually and preferentially dominant for the consumer. Two archetypal situations in which order of experience plays a significant role are especially interesting. In the first case, consumers enter a market consisting of a largely fixed set of brands; in the second case, brands sequentially enter a largely stable market of consumers. The first case is typical of mature markets, and the second case is more likely to be found in emerging markets or emerging segments of mature markets.

Sequential Consumer Entry. Consider a market in which new consumers enter, older ones exit, but the available brands are largely stable. One example is the toothpaste market; although new brands have successfully entered, the major brands remain largely the same, and new consumers are constantly entering the market. If one brand dominates such a market, an entering consumer's initial product experiences are likely to include it because of its wide availability and common use. An extreme version of this would occur if one's experience were limited to a single brand for an extended period of time. For instance, one might grow up in a household where one brand is regularly used for whatever reason (e.g., a "Crest household"). Exposure to a dominant brand will bias learning. Growing up in a Crest household will lead to a different learning experience with regard to toothpaste than growing up in a household where either a variety of brands or one other brand was regularly used.

Sequential Brand Entry. Another important situation is that presented by brands sequentially entering a market consisting of a static set of customers. Consumers' initial experiences will be limited to early entering brands by default. These brands can significantly affect the consumer learning experience. In the nondairy dessert toppings market, for instance, eighteen years elapsed between the introduction of Cool Whip and a comparable competitor. The category was defined by Cool Whip, and consumers' knowledge of it was biased by that limited definition of the category. Regardless of whether learning is biased by buyers or brands sequentially entering the market, early consumer experience is limited to a specific subset of the brands ultimately available and experienced in the category.

Consumer Learning and Preference

Consumer learning about the category is likely to bias preferences in favor of this subset of brands for two reasons. First, prior to experience, consumers may know little about the importance of attributes or their ideal combination. For example, one hundred years ago, few people were likely to have strong opinions about how sweet or carbonated a cola should be. A successful early entrant can have a major influence on how attributes are valued and on the ideal attribute combination. Coca-Cola, for example, may have had a significant impact in its early years on the formation and evolution of individuals' preferences for colas. This influence shifts individuals' preferences to favor the brands tried first.

Second, these brands are likely to be strongly associated with and highly representative of the category and, therefore, highly salient. Exemplar theories of categorization (Medin and Schaffer 1978; Medin, Altom, and Murphy 1984) suggest that these brands become exemplars or "standards" against which new brands are compared. Moreover, for goal-directed categories (of which product categories would be one example), the "goodness" of an item as a member of the category is a function of the relative proximity of an object's features to category ideals and the frequency with which an item has been experienced as a member of the category (Barsalou 1985). Brands experienced first will likely be seen as ideal (because preferences form around them) and they will have been experienced more frequently than others, so they can become strong standards of comparison.

This is especially true in product categories where the contribution of product attributes or features to overall brand value and the ideal attribute combination are ambiguous. For example, if one purchases a down quilt and receives a certain measure of value from it, the contribution of the percentage of goose down fill to that overall value is ambiguous. Other examples include the flavoring of soft drinks, features of computer programs, and combinations of ingredients in vitamins. Under these conditions, brands that consumers sample first, whether because of a brand's early market entry or its current high market share, will be favored. The impact of experience on consumer preferences will be much lower if the value of attributes and their ideal combination are unambiguous or readily observed.

Preference Structure

To see how early trial affects preference more formally, consider a consumer's experience before and after trial. Prior to trial, consumer preferences are likely to be weakly formed because the category is novel. The value of an individual attribute or the superiority of one attribute combination over another may not be obvious even if buyers have objective information on brand attributes (Howard 1989; Howard and Sheth 1969). Consider home robots, an emerging market. Few buyers know much about the relative value of home robot attributes or of the ideal combination of them. As a result, individuals may be indifferent about alternatives within a relevant range. In a two-attribute market the distribution of ideal points or vectors across consumers would be approximately uniform, as shown in Exhibit 1a. The average ideal will be located in the center of the market, as shown in Exhibit 1b. Attribute weights used to value brands will also be tentative.

Buyers update their preferences through trial. Sampling an early entrant in an emerging market or the dominant brand in an established market, a consumer may associate a successful outcome with the attribute combination of the tried brand, lacking information to the contrary (Meyer 1987). In doing so, buyers develop a naive theory relating brand attributes to value, which advertising and repeat purchasing reinforce (Hoch and Ha 1986; Deighton 1984). Having used one home robot model that is highly rugged for extensive outdoor use, for instance, one might infer that one's satisfaction is due in large measure to the robot's unique attributes; continued use and advertising reinforce this belief. Thus buyers learn through trial how to value attribute combinations, but if a trial is limited to a dominant brand, updated preferences will favor it.

Consumer learning leads individuals to shift their ideal points toward the position of the tried brand, as shown in Exhibit 2. Both the

EXHIBIT 1. Hypothetical Prior (a) Taste Distribution and (b) Corresponding Perceptual Map with Average Ideal Point

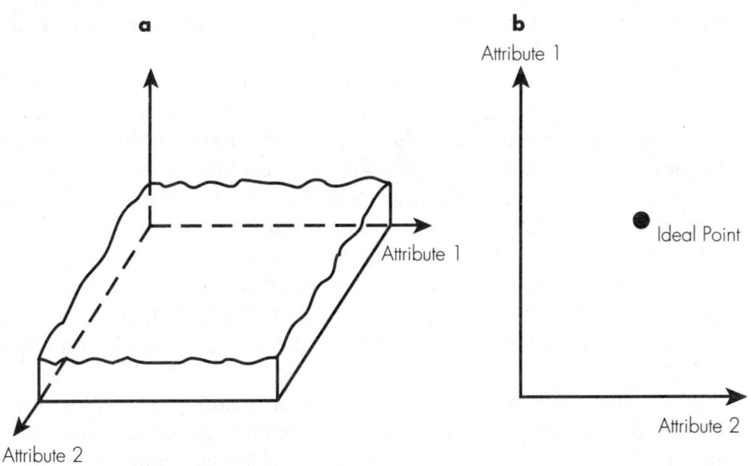

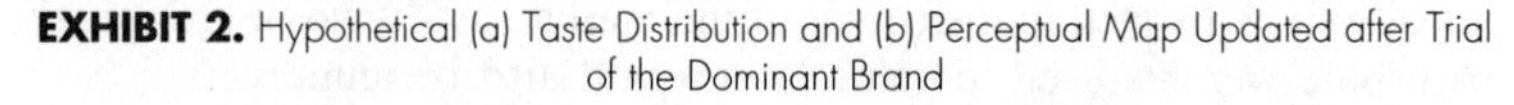

EXHIBIT 2. Hypothetical (a) Taste Distribution and (b) Perceptual Map Updated after Trial of the Dominant Brand

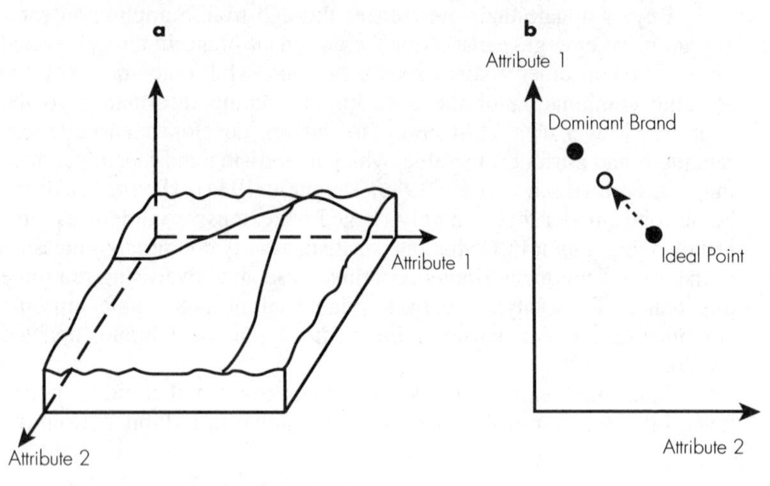

taste distribution and average ideal point shift toward the brand's location. This shift occurs *independent of the brand's characteristics* because of the ambiguity in attribute valuation.

This shift in preferences also defines attribute trade-offs buyers use, which is the relative importance of attributes in product evaluation. For example, in Exhibit 2, the location of the dominant brand implies that attribute 1 should be more important in evaluation than attribute 2. Again, the attribute importances favor the trade-offs adopted by the dominant brand. Consistent with this mechanism, Carpenter and Nakamoto (1989, Study 1) found that the location of the average ideal point for consumers shifts in the direction of the location of the dominant (or pioneering) brand. In addition, they showed (Study 2) that the relative importance weights of attributes reflect the strengths of the dominant brand.

In sum, the processes of consumer learning and preference formation lead to rules of competition, reflecting consumer preferences, slanted in favor of a dominant brand. The dominant brand has not so much *found* a preferred position as *created* one.

COMPETITIVE ADVANTAGE

Perceptual Distinctiveness

Dominant brands have an additional important advantage over later entering competitors—perceptual distinctiveness. Because they are experienced, first, and perhaps more often, dominant brands attain *category dominance* (Farquhar, Herr, and Fazio 1990). They are more naturally salient for the typical consumer—strongly associated with and highly representative of the product category. Indeed, they are often *cognitively inseparable* from the category and come to mind more quickly and reliably than other brands when the category is mentioned (e.g., Kleenex tissues, Levi's jeans). As such, these brands become *cognitive referents* for consumers (Medin and Schaffer 1978; Sujan 1985).

Recent studies present evidence consistent with this general view. Kardes and Kalyanaram (1990) cite information integration findings showing that the amount of information in memory regarding a brand will influence the extremity of its evaluation and the consumer's confidence in that evaluation. They show that the brand first encountered has an advantage both in terms of recall of brand information and preference over later encountered brands, even if a later encountered brand is superior. Consumers simply have more information about dominant brands in memory, and it is more accessible, increasing evaluation of these brands at the cost of later entering brands about which consumers retain less information.

Competitive Implications

The competitive implications of category dominance are profound. It makes the preferred position occupied by the dominant brand very difficult to assail. A me-too product, despite its similarity to the dominant brand, will suffer in comparison. The more similar the me-too and dominant brands, the *greater* the relative prominence of the dominant brand. Thus preferences for the dominant brand are *asymmetric;* greater similarity between a competitor and the dominant brand *increases* valuation of the dominant brand and *decreases* valuation of the competitor. In the case of a me-too brand, this is because the me-too brand derives its identity from the dominant brand, and this similarity reduces any distinctive value of the me-too brand. It is different simply because it is not the dominant brand, but since it has no distinctive competence it is inferior.

Consistent with this analysis, Carpenter and Nakamoto (1989, Study 1) found that the greater the perceived similarity between the dominant brand and a later entrant, the greater the preference advantage of the dominant brand. Moreover, compared to differentiated later entrants, me-too brands' price discounts were less valued (Study 2).

Brown and Lattin (1990) found further consistent evidence in market data—the longer a dominant brand preceded its competitors in the market, that is the longer consumers learned about it alone, the greater its competitive advantage.

Persistence

Once this preference structure is established, why does it persist? At one level the preference structure can be viewed as a schema, and once established consumers have no incentive to relearn these preferences. For instance, once we learn how to value home robot attributes, we have no incentive to revisit our decision and change preferences. Moreover, schema are difficult to alter even if consumers are confronted with disconfirming information (Bettman 1986; Fiske and Taylor 1984). If a competitor seeks to change the preference structure by suggesting that consumers are using the "wrong" criteria to evaluate brands, consumers will be reluctant to change preferences. Effecting change requires that a competitor present consumers with *overwhelming* evidence that a new preference structure is needed. For a nondominant brand, presenting such evidence is a daunting task. The preference structure established by the dominant brand often persists as a result.

An Example

This preference formation process and the resulting competitive advantage are well illustrated by Vaseline, which was introduced in 1880 and advertised as a healing agent of unsurpassed purity. Sampling Vaseline, a translucent, highly pure gel, buyers learned that its attributes produced an effective wound preparation and, generalizing from this observation, inferred that the effectiveness of petroleum jelly lies in its translucence and purity (in contrast to the competing black coal tar derivatives of the time). Subsequent trials and advertising of course confirmed this conjecture. Thus translucence came to be favored over opacity and gained more importance in brand evaluation. Moreover, all later brands were compared to Vaseline and found wanting even if identical simply because they were not Vaseline. This has produced a lasting competitive advantage.

STRATEGIC IMPLICATIONS

The implications of consumer preference formation for competitive marketing strategy are significant. Competitive advantage is traditionally viewed as arising from entry or mobility barriers erected by established firms through capacity expansion, advertising, or other strategic investments designed to make competition more costly for later entrants and thus deter competition (Encaoua, Geroski, and Jacquemin 1986; Porter 1985). So long as a cost differential persists, competitors will be deterred, and a high market share will be sustained.

Entry barriers can arise from a number of sources including product positioning (Lane 1980; Prescott and Visscher 1977). An early entrant may adopt the "best" market position, leaving smaller or less attractive segments for others. Located in less attractive positions, these smaller brands are at a competitive disadvantage, leading to the continued dominance of one brand if they cannot easily reposition. Switching costs created by uncertainty about later entrants' quality can have a similar impact on competition. If trial of the dominant brand is successful, trying an alternative is risky, forcing later entrants to cut prices or offer some premium to compensate for risk and induce trial. So long as trial of later entrants remains low and their quality remains unknown, the dominant brand will retain its high market share (Schmalensee 1982).

Empirical studies show that entry barriers are an important source of competitive advantage (Robinson and Fornell 1985), but they also show that dominant brand advantages exist in markets where traditional entry barriers do not exclude competition. For example, Urban et al. (1986) show that Miller's Lite Beer retains its advantage even though conventional entry or mobility barriers did not deter competitors such as Budweiser and Schlitz. Buyers are aware of both brands, and brands can reposition. Thus competitive advantage must be sustained by something more than entry or mobility barriers.

Competitive advantage, in a consumer preference formation framework, arises because a brand influences the evolution of preferences and creates a *preference asymmetry* in doing so. Achieving market dominance, possibly by early successful entry, provides the opportunity to define the ideal combination of attributes and to create an asymmetric preference structure that limits the impact of competitors on the dominant brand's market share. The resulting competitive advantage persists even in cases where strategic investments are ineffective at creating cost differences and entry barriers in the traditional sense.

A particularly vivid example of the difference in approach is provided by the case of me-too brands. Conventional analysis argues that me-too brands fail because of ruinous price competition; picking a position near the dominant brand and competing on price leads to lower prices for all and the elimination of high profits. In contrast, in a consumer learning framework, me-too strategies do not provoke a disastrous price war. Having positioned near the dominant brand with a low price, a me-too brand earns low profit. In fact, it poses no real threat to the dominant brand; it derives its identity from the dominant brand, but offering nothing unique except a low price (and that is not of central importance), a me-too brand will sell poorly (Carpenter and Nakamoto 1990). Thus me-too brands do not "fail" so much as languish.

CONCLUSION

Consumer preference formation suggests a view of competition and strategy that differs significantly from the conventional view. Brand dominance, in that view, indicates exceptional profits, attracts new competitors, leads to lower prices, and eliminates dominant brand advantage. Brand strategy is designed to erect barriers to that competition.

A consumer-learning view reflects a very different world. Brand dominance influences the evolution of buyer preferences and creates a *preference asymmetry* that persists because of the persistence of that learning. Competitive entry places little pressure on a dominant brand. Preferences are asymmetric, so greater similarity between a competitor and the dominant brand *increases* rather than *decreases* the dominant brand's market share. The dominant brand's market share advantage persists as a result.

Most fundamentally, this suggests a different view of competition in which brands *battle over* consumer preferences rather than simply responding to them. Competition in such a world becomes a struggle to define consumer preferences with the winner receiving a tremendously valuable asset—a favorable, asymmetric preference structure—producing a persistent dominant brand advantage.

REFERENCES

Barsalou, Lawrence W. 1985. Ideals, central tendency, and frequency of instantiation as determinants of graded structure in categories. *Journal of Experimental Psychology: Learning, Memory and Cognition,* 11 (October):629–55.

Bettman, James R. 1986. Consumer psychology. *Annual Review of Psychology,* 37:257–89.

Biehal, Gabriel, and Dipankar Chakravarti. 1983. Information accessibility as a moderator of consumer choice. *Journal of Consumer Research,* 10 (June):1–14.

______. 1982. Information presentation format and learning goals as determinants of consumer memory-retrieval and choice processes. *Journal of Consumer Research,* 8 (March):431–41.

Brown, Christina L., and James L. Lattin. 1990. Pioneering Advantage in Packaged Goods: The Headstart Effect. Working paper, Graduate School of Business, Stanford University, Stanford, CA.

Carpenter, Gregory S., and Kent Nakamoto. 1990. Competitive strategies for late entry into a market with a dominant brand. *Management Science,* 36:1268–78.

______. 1989. Consumer preference formation and pioneering advantage. *Journal of Marketing Research,* 26 (August):285–98.

Deighton, John. 1984. The interaction of advertising and evidence. *Journal of Consumer Research,* 11 (December):763–70.

Encaoua, David, Paul Geroski, and Alexis Jacquemin. 1986. Strategic competition and the persistence of dominant firms: A survey.

In J. E. Stiglitz and G. G. Mathewson (eds.): *New Developments in the Analysis of Market Structure.* Cambridge, MA: MIT Press.

Farquhar, Peter F., Paul M. Herr, and Russell H. Fazio. 1990. A relational model for category extensions of brands. *Advances in Consumer Research,* 17:856–60.

Kardes, Frank, and G. Kalyanaram. 1990. Consumer Learning and the Pioneering Advantage: An Information Integration Perspective. Working paper, College of Business Administration, University of Cincinnati, OH.

Hambrick, D. C., I. C. MacMillan, and D. L. Day. 1982. Strategic attributes and performance in the BCG matrix—A PIMS based analysis. *Academy of Management Journal,* 25:510–31.

Hoch, Stephen J., and Young-Won Ha. 1986. Consumer Learning: Advertising and the ambiguity of product experience. *Journal of Consumer Research,* 13 September:221–33.

Howard, John A. 1989. *Consumer Behavior in Marketing Strategy.* Englewood Cliffs, NJ: Prentice-Hall.

Howard, John A., and Jagdish N. Sheth. 1969. *The Theory of Consumer Behavior.* New York: Wiley & Sons.

Johnson, Eric J., and J. Edward Russo. 1984. Product familiarity and learning new information. *Journal of Consumer Research,* 13 September:221–33.

Lane, W. J. 1980. Product differentiation in a market with endogenous sequential entry. *Bell Journal of Economics,* 11 (Spring):237–60.

Medin, Douglas L., and Marguerite M. Schaffer. 1978. Context theory of classification learning. *Psychological Review,* 85 (May):207–38.

Meyer, Robert J. 1987. The learning of multiattribute judgment policies. *Journal of Consumer Research,* 14 (September):155–73.

Porter, Michael E. 1985. *Competitive Advantage.* New York: The Free Press.

Prescott, Edward C., and Michael Visscher. 1977. Sequential location among firms with foresight. *Bell Journal of Economics,* 8 (Autumn):378–93.

Robinson, William T., and Claes Fornell. 1985. Sources of market pioneer advantages in consumer goods industries. *Journal of Marketing Research,* 22 (August):305–18.

Schmalensee, Richard. 1982. Product differentiation advantages of pioneering brands. *American Economic Review,* 27:349–65.

Sujan, Mita. 1985. Consumer knowledge: Effects of evaluation strategies mediating consumer judgments. *Journal of Consumer Research,* 12 (June):31–46.

Tversky, Amos, Shmuel Sattath, and Paul Slovic. 1988. Contingent weighting in judgment and choice. *Psychological Bulletin,* 95:371–84.

Urban, Glen L., Theresa Carter, Steve Gaskin, and Zofia Mucha. 1986. Market share rewards to pioneering brands: An empirical analysis and strategic implications. *Management Science,* 32 (June):645–59.

Richard R. Still
Professor of Marketing & International Business
The University of Georgia

CHAPTER 11

SEGMENTING THE MARKET

Discussion in this chapter focuses on key aspects of market segmentation. The first three sections clarify the concepts of market and market segmentation and explain the two main approaches to market segmentation: demographic and psychographic. The fourth section considers certain problems in segmenting consumer and industrial markets. The fifth section analyzes marketing characteristics of goods and services as they influence the bases on which markets can be meaningfully segmented. The sixth section sets forth the implications for marketing decision makers.

MARKETS AND MARKET SEGMENTATION

Two of the most important and basic marketing concepts are those of "a market" and "market segmentation." A "market," according to the American Marketing Association, is the aggregate demand of the potential buyers of a product or service.[1] A market, in other words, represents the total demand of all those who might conceivably buy a particular product or service. But an aggregate demand, or total market, also is the sum of the demands of different *segments* of the market, each containing a group of buyers (or buying units) who share qualities or characteristics that make the segment different from other segments and of significance to the marketer. Thus, a market is not only the aggregate potential demand for a product but the sum of various demand subtotals, each representing the potential demand of a particular market segment.

Diversity, not uniformity, characterizes the markets for all products. No two buyers or potential buyers of any product are ever exactly alike in all respects. But groups of buyers do share certain characteristics that are meaningful to the marketer and which have implications for both the setting of market objectives and the formulation of marketing strategies. By grouping buyers sharing characteristics of marketing significance into market segments the marketer attains some degree of homogeneity, facilitating the analysis of each market segment's unique needs, wants, and desires and the tailoring of marketing strategies accordingly.

Meaning of Market Segmentation. The term "market segmentation" is used in two different senses. Many use the term to describe specific types of marketing strategies (or programs) designed to cultivate chosen market segments.[2] Others use the term to describe the process of identifying subsets of buyers with different buying desires or requirements.[3] "Market segmentation" is used here in the second sense, i.e., to refer to the marketer's efforts in searching for improved insights on markets.

Market segmentation is an analytical process that precedes market targeting, i.e., deciding which market segments to cultivate. It involves dividing up a product's total market into smaller and more homogeneous segments, any one or more of which might be designated as market targets requiring individually tailored marketing strategies. The distinctive features of each identified market segment, in other words, *may* make it profitable for the marketer to adapt the product and/or marketing programs so as to meet more precisely each segment's requirements. Market segmentation provides the marketer with improved insights on the market's nature, hence assisting in selecting target markets and in designing optimal marketing strategies.

Principle of Segmentation. One management consultant suggests a "principle of segmentation" that provides a helpful guide for practical marketers: *Segmenting the market is the process of grouping individuals whose expected reactions to the producer's marketing efforts will be similar during a specified time period.*[4] Thus, the aim of market segmentation is to identify groups of potential buyers who can be expected to respond similarly to given marketing moves (i.e., to changes in products, distribution, promotion, and price). Similar responses may be forthcoming for any of various reasons including comparable needs, wants, attitudes, interests, and lifestyles. Furthermore, the skilled segmenter recognizes that the characteristics of any market segment change over time because of shifts in needs, wants, competition, and other variables. A currently useful market segment in terms of response homogeneity can become relatively heterogeneous within a short time; therefore, in planning the cultivation of a given market segment, a definite limit should be set on the time period for implementation of marketing efforts.[5]

Whatever the basis used for segmenting the market, the resulting market segments should be groups of prospective buyers who are more like each other within the groups on all relevant dimensions than they are to members of other groups. Segmentation should aim for minimizing within-segment variance and maximizing between-segment variance.[6]

Requirements for Meaningful Market Segmentation. One key step in segmenting a market involves selecting the criteria to use in dividing up the market into segments, i.e., in determining the characteristics of prospective buyers that will produce the most meaningful and useful market segments. Kotler suggests three requirements for effective segmentation. The first is *measurability,* or the degree to which the size and purchasing power of the resulting segments can be measured. The second is *accessibility,* or the degree to which the resulting segments can be effectively reached and served. The third is *substantiality,* or the degree to which the segments are large and/or profitable enough to justify separate cultivation.[7] Bell suggests an important fourth requirement for meaningful segmentation—chosen segments should differ in their responsiveness to marketing efforts;[8] unless market segments respond uniquely to given marketing moves, they do not justify the expenditures required for planning and implementing individualized marketing strategies.

DEMOGRAPHIC SEGMENTATION

The most common approach to market segmentation seeks to identify groups of prospective buyers sharing selected demographic characteristics. Demographic segmentation, in other words, seeks to answer the question, "Who is the market?" Consumer markets are segmented on the basis of such demographic variables as geographic location, rate of product usage, income, age, sex, education, stage in the family life cycle, religion, race, and social class. Industrial markets are segmented demographically according to such variables as geographic location, kind of business, rate of product usage, and size of user.

Geographic Segmentation. The most widely-used form of demographic segmentation groups customers and prospects according to their geographic locations. Department stores in large cities, for instance, generally group their customers into local and out-of-town accounts. Some manufacturers selling regionally or nationally usually classify their customers by region—e.g., into those located east and west of Denver.

For many products, sufficient variations exist from place to place in buyer needs, wants, and preferences to justify geographic market segmentation. Furniture manufacturers, for instance, recognize that consumer preferences for different styles of furniture vary considerably region by region. Southern consumers typically exhibit a much stronger preference for traditionally-styled furniture than do Midwesterners, while large groups of consumers in the Far West prefer furniture styles showing oriental or Scandinavian influences. Similarly distinctive regional preferences exist for many grocery products, items of clothing, floor coverings, and paint.

Climatic differences justify geographic market segmentation for some products. Areas with long hot summers, for instance, are the most fertile markets for home and auto air conditioners. Areas with considerable snow and long winters are the best markets for winter sports equipment and snow blowers. Geographical differences in climate, in other words, sometimes cause variations in product-usage rates and the proportions of the population who need or want a particular product.

Regional variations in income cause some products but not others to find more fertile markets in some areas than they do in others. While to the maker of garbage cans, income differentials are of little significance, to the maker of garbage compactors, the higher income regions definitely represent the best market targets.

But statistics on regional income generally relate to per capita income; thus, even the maker of garbage compactors may find "pockets" of good prospects within a region that has low per capita income. Interregional variations in income are not as great as the differences between urban and rural incomes within a single region. Differences in per capita incomes in Atlanta and Philadelphia, for example, are not so great as differences in per capita incomes of residents of Atlanta and rural Georgia.

Segmentation by Rate of Product Usage. Many marketers segment their markets according to the amount of product consumed by different buyers. A grocery products manufacturer, for instance, divides the total market into five segments:

- present heavy users
- present light users who are potential heavy users
- present light users who are confirmed light users
- nonusers who are potential heavy users
- nonusers who are potential light users

For many consumer products, considerable variation exists in the product usage rates of heavy and light users. Most people, for instance, drink soft drinks occasionally, but less than a third of the population drink them at the rate of one glass or more per day, and this heavy-user group accounts for more than three-quarters of soft drink sales. Under a fifth of the homemakers use flour once a day or more, but they account for more than half of the flour used. Under 15% of the population make almost 75% of the long distance telephone calls.[9]

Companies segmenting their markets by rates of usage must identify the reasons for usage variations. Often the differences trace to such demographic factors as age, income, size of household, or stage in the family life cycle. The Quaker Oats Company, for example, found that the housewife's age and family size were the two main variables differentiating heavy from light users of Life, a ready-to-eat breakfast cereal. Housewives under 40 in families of five or more members were identified as "extremely important targets" (i.e., heavy users), while those 50 and over in families of one or two members were classed as "very inferior targets" (i.e., as either nonusers or very light users).[10]

PSYCHOGRAPHIC SEGMENTATION

Psychographic segmentation involves breaking down a market according to the life styles, personality characteristics, or buying motives of buyers. Distinctive life styles characterize the members of various subcultures, with new life styles continually developing and older life styles becoming obsolete with the passage of time. One writer describes a life style as "a vehicle through which we express ourselves" and "a way of telling the world which particular subcult or subcults we belong to."[11] Some life styles, e.g., the Hippie, the Yippie, the Surfer, the Executive, and the Black Militant, are fairly easy to identify. Other life styles, e.g., the Sports Fan, the Do-It-Yourselfer, and the Compulsive Shopper, are somewhat more difficult to recognize.

Psychographic research aims to describe the human characteristics of consumers influencing their responses to marketing variables—products, packaging, media, and the like—that demographic characteristics alone do not explain.[12] Two major approaches to psychographic analysis have emerged. The first focuses on individual consumption patterns on the assumption that an individual expresses personality and projects chosen life style(s) through the products consumed. The second analyzes the individual in terms of activities, interests, opinions, and values as measures of life style. It has seen increasing use in supplementing demographic descriptions of consumer groups, but psychographic researchers differ as to the appropriate dimensions of life style.[13]

Most psychographic studies involve asking respondents to indicate on rating scales their degree of agreement with various statements. For instance, one researcher asked housewives to rate their agreement on a scale ranging from five to one with such statements as:

If there's a flu bug going around, I'm sure to catch it.
Once you've got a cold, there is very little you can do about it.

This study resulted in descriptions of four segments of the market for cold remedies:

Realists—not health fatalists, nor excessively concerned with protection or germs; view remedies positively, want something that is convenient and works, and do not feel the need for a doctor-recommended medicine.

Authority Seekers—doctor-and-prescription oriented. Neither fatalists nor stoics concerning health, but prefer the stamp of authority on what they do take.

Skeptics—have a low health concern, are least likely to resort to medication, and are highly skeptical of cold remedies.

Hypochondriacs—have high health concern, regard themselves as prone to any bug going around and tend to take medication at the first symptom. They do not look for strength in what they take, but need some mild authority reassurance.[14]

ULTIMATE CONSUMERS AND INDUSTRIAL USERS

The first step in segmenting the market for any product is to divide its prospective buyers into two broad categories: ultimate consumers and industrial users. The sole basis for classifying a buying unit as an ultimate consumer or an industrial user is the general reason for buying. Ultimate consumers buy for either their own or their households' personal consumption, while industrial users buy to further the production of other goods and services. The mass of ultimate consumers makes up the "consumer market" and the mass of industrial users the "industrial market."

Ultimate consumers and industrial users differ considerably in their buying patterns and behavior. Ultimate consumers buy in much smaller quantities and for consumption over shorter time intervals than do industrial buyers. Ultimate consumers are not as systematic buyers as are industrial users; some industrial users are profit-seeking enterprises, thus encouraging systematic buying procedures, while others are non-profit organizations whose operations are audited by outside authorities, which also encourages systematic buying procedures. Typically, too, ultimate consumers are part-time buyers, while industrial users employ professionals who devote their main efforts to buying. Furthermore, ultimate consumers spread their buying skills over a wide range of goods and services, while professionals specialize and have more chance to perfect their buying skills.

Segmenting Consumer Markets. In segmenting many consumer markets, the household is a more significant analytical unit than the individual. Some products, such as most groceries, although usually bought by individuals, are consumed by all household members. Other products, such as household appliances and automobiles, are purchased jointly by two or more members of a household and are used by all household members. In such instances, market segmentation, either according to demographic or psychographic variables, should be based on differences among households rather than among individuals.

Some consumer markets, however, are meaningfully segmented according to differences among individual consumers. Market segmentation along sexual lines, for instance, is meaningful for a wide variety of cosmetics, grooming aids, and clothing, with male and female market segments requiring different marketing strategies.

Talley reports an interesting case of market segmentation according to differences in individual consumers. The case concerns a producer of crystal glassware which had long focused its marketing efforts on the bride-to-be market, but its sales had topped out. After studying the market more closely, management concluded that three market segments existed for crystal: (1) the bride-to-be, (2) the matron, and (3) the "rich aunt." The matron market segment consists of women who had not been affluent enough to buy crystal at the time of marriage but whose buying power had grown subsequently to the point where they now could afford this type of purchase. The "rich aunt" market segment is made up of well-to-do relatives who buy gifts for brides. Marketing efforts were redirected, the two new market segments were tapped, and company sales and profits resumed their growth.[15]

Segmenting Industrial Markets. The four most common bases for segmenting industrial markets are (1) geographical location, (2) kind of business or activity, (3) customer size, and (4) usual purchasing procedure. Geographic segmentation generally is according to geographic clusters of buyers or by sales territories. Segmentation by kind of business or activity often is effected through the SIC system, which classifies all industrial users into 10 major categories which, in turn, are broken down into finer divisions. The SIC system is a way to break down an industrial market by kind of business or activity into relatively small, medium-size, or large market segments.[16] Most governmental agencies use the SIC system in presenting statistical data of interest to market analysts.

Industrial market segmentation by customer size is important. Industrial users range all the way from one- and two-person shops to huge organizations employing hundreds of thousands. Consequently, the size of industrial purchases varies greatly, and many industrial marketers segment their markets by customer size and use different marketing strategies to reach the individual segments.

When some buyers buy the product as original equipment and others buy it for replacement purposes, market segmentation according to usual purchasing procedure is meaningful. Original equipment buyers follow more complex buying procedures than if they were buying for replacement. Because of relative unfamiliarity and lack of experience with the product, the original equipment buyer demands fuller and more technical product information, oftentimes conducts an exhaustive study of possible suppliers and their offerings, and requires more company executives to "okay" the purchase. By contrast, when an item is being bought as a replacement, the buying decision is reached through routine procedures. Thus, adequate reasons exist for some marketers to divide their markets into original equipment (O.E.M.) and replacement market segments, and to individualize marketing strategies for each segment.

MARKETING CHARACTERISTICS OF GOODS AND SERVICES

Numerous marketing characteristics of goods and services influence the bases on which their markets can be meaningfully segmented, but three are important in so many situations as to deserve mentioning here. One concerns the degree of "customization" of the product. At one extreme, certain products, such as special-purpose machine tools and custom-tailored clothing, are literally "one of a kind" designed to fit each buyer's unique requirements; in such cases, each potential buyer, in effect, is a separate market segment. At the other extreme, some products, such as cement, are so highly standardized that it is meaningful to segment the market by grouping an extremely large number of buyers into a very few market segments according to such bases as buyer size and geographic location.

Brand loyalty is a second marketing characteristic that frequently provides a meaningful basis for segmentation. Most brands have certain customers who are extremely loyal, thus constituting a core market segment. But the brands also have other buyers who switch from brand to brand, and these comprise the fringe market segment. Whenever a brand has both brand-loyal and fringe buyers, segmentation on the basis of brand loyalty may prove meaningful in setting marketing objectives and in formulating strategy for the two quite different markets.

The product's stage in its life cycle is a third marketing characteristic that provides a meaningful basis for segmentation. At different stages in a product's life cycle, changes occur in the relative size and importance of different groups of buyers. In the market introduction or pioneering life cycle state, the product is bought by a small group of "innovators," those who are first to accept a radically-new type of product. They are followed by the "early adopters," who, though not venturesome enough to try the adoption first, want to be among the early buyers. Gradually, members of groups making up the mass market (i.e., those in the "early" and "late" majorities) buy the product and it finally reaches market saturation. Others—the laggards—buy the product very late in its life cycle, after its market has begun to decline. Thus, it is often meaningful to identify target market segments at each stage in a product's life cycle. In the market pioneering stage, for instance, money and marketing effort are wasted if the marketer attempts simultaneous cultivation of the total market. Usually, it is more effective and less costly to concentrate early marketing efforts on the innovators, and shift later to the early adopters and to each of the following groups, one at a time.

IMPLICATIONS

For the marketing decision maker, there are six main implications of the preceding discussion.

1. Recognition that diversity, not uniformity, characterizes the total market and is a necessary preliminary to the realistic setting of marketing objectives and to the formulation of effective marketing strategy.
2. Market segmentation is most profitable when members of individual segments are alike in terms of their likely responses to different marketing moves. Unless market segments respond uniquely to given marketing moves, they do not justify expenditures for individually-tailored marketing strategies.
3. Demographic segmentation is most useful in answering the question "Who is the market?"
4. Psychographic segmentation is useful mainly in supplementing demographic descriptions of customer groups, since it helps in understanding and predicting buyer behavior.

5. Generally different approaches should be taken to the cultivation of consumer and industrial markets.
6. Various marketing characteristics of goods and services influence the bases on which their markets can be profitably segmented.

NOTES

1. Committee on Definitions, *Marketing Definitions* (Chicago: American Marketing Association, 1960), p. 15.
2. For example, see Wendell R. Smith, "Product Differentiation and Market Segmentation as Alternative Marketing Strategies," *Journal of Marketing,* Vol. 21 (July 1956), pp. 3–8.
3. For example, see Philip Kotler, *Marketing Management,* fourth edition (Englewood Cliffs, N.J.: Prentice-Hall, Inc., 1980), p. 195.
4. Steven C. Brandt, "Dissecting the Segmentation Syndrome," *Journal of Marketing,* Vol. 30 (October 1966), p. 25.
5. Brandt, same reference as footnote 4.
6. Martin Christopher, "Cluster Analysis and Market Segmentation," *British Journal of Marketing,* Vol. 3 (Summer 1969), p. 99.
7. Kotler, same reference as footnote 3, at pp. 205–206.
8. Martin L. Bell, *Marketing: Concepts and Strategy,* 3rd Ed. (Boston: Houghton Mifflin Co., 1979), p. 125.
9. Fred D. Reynolds and William D. Wells, *Consumer Behavior* (New York: McGraw-Hill Book Company, 1977), p. 390.
10. "The Quaker Oats Company—Life Cereal" case in Milton P. Brown, Richard N. Cardozo, Scott M. Cunningham, Walter J. Salmon, and Ralph G. M. Sultan, *Problems in Marketing,* 4th Ed. (New York: McGraw-Hill Book Company, 1968), pp. 181–182.
11. Alvin Toffler, *Future Shock,* Bantam Edition (New York: Bantam Books, Inc., 1971), p. 314.
12. Harold W. Berkman and Christopher Gilson, *Consumer Behavior* (Boston: Kent Publishing Company, 1981), p. 63.
13. Ronald E. Frank, William F. Massy, and Yoram Wind, *Market Segmentation* (Englewood Cliffs, N.J.: Prentice-Hall, Inc., 1972), pp. 58–59.
14. Ruth Ziff, "Psychographics for Market Segmentation," *Journal of Advertising Research,* Vol. 11 (April 1971), pp. 4–6.
15. Walter J. Talley, Jr., *The Profitable Product* (Englewood Cliffs, N.J.: Prentice-Hall, Inc., 1965), pp. 93–94.
16. For an explanation of the S.I.C. system, see Office of Management and Budget, *Standard Industrial Classification Manual,* 1972 (Washington: U.S. Government Printing Office, 1972).

SUGGESTIONS FOR FURTHER READING

Norman L. Barnett, "Beyond Market Segmentation," *Harvard Business Review,* Vol. 47 (January-February 1969), pp. 152–166.

Harold W. Berkman and Christopher Gilson, *Consumer Behavior* (Boston: Kent Publishing Company, 1981).

Kate Bertrand, "Market Segmentation: Divide and Conquer," *Business Marketing,* Vol. 74 (October 1989), pp. 48–54.

Paul N. Bloom and Philip Kotler, "Strategies for High Market-Share Companies," *Harvard Business Review* (November-December, 1975), p. 63.

E. Raymond Corey, "Key Options in Market Selection and Product Planning," *Harvard Business Review,* (September-October, 1975), p. 119.

James F. Engel, Henry F. Fiorillo, and Murray A. Cayley, *Market Segmentation Concepts and Applications* (New York: Holt, Rinehart and Winston, Inc., 1972).

Kenneth M. Freeman, "Target Marketing: The Logic of It All," *Journal of Consumer Marketing,* Vol. 9 (Summer 1992), pp. 15–18.

Peter J. LaPlaca and Newton Frank, *Marketing Strategies for a Tough Environment* (Chicago: American Marketing Association, 1980).

David J. Luck and O. C. Ferrell, *Marketing Strategy and Plans* (Englewood Cliffs, N.J.: Prentice-Hall, Inc., 1979).

Fred D. Reynolds and William D. Wells, *Consumer Behavior* (New York: McGraw-Hill Book Co., 1977).

William D. Wells and Douglas J. Tigert, "Activities, Interests, and Opinions," *Journal of Advertising Research* (August 1971), p. 27.

Gordon and Julian Wills, "Journey to Marketing Clubland," *Marketing Intelligence and Planning,* Vol. 10 (1992), pp. 22–36.

Edward W. Wheatley, Ph.D
Chair/Professor
Department of Marketing
East Carolina University
Greenville, North Carolina

CHAPTER 12

MARKETING FOR PROFESSIONALS

INTRODUCTION

Who are "professionals"? Should professionals market? What are the key characteristics that differentiate services marketing in the professions from consumer and industrial product marketing? How can professionals respond to take advantage of these differences? How should the marketing function be structured? What are the responsibilities/qualifications of a professional firm's marketing manager? How can professionals analyze their practice from the marketing management prospective? What are the key steps in developing, implementing, and controlling marketing programs? This chapter will address these topics and more.

This chapter is written for professionals interested in integrating marketing into their ongoing practice management operations. It will also be helpful to marketing specialists seeking to assist professionals and professional firms develop and implement marketing programs. The intention of the chapter is not to introduce professionals to what marketing is. This background can be gained from other readings in the *Marketing Manager's Handbook.* Rather, the chapter is dedicated to showing professionals how to apply marketing to their professional service settings. Finally, the chapter is not an end in itself but a beginning. In the 1970s and 1980s numerous books and articles were written on the topic of marketing for the professions. The work has taken two forms: the application of marketing to the professions and marketing applied to individual professional specialities such as accounting, law, health care, architecture, dentistry, and so forth. To enhance your knowledge and skills and leverage the benefit of the *Marketing Manager's Handbook,* the following approach is recommended:

1. Read *Marketing Managers' Handbook* chapters for general marketing background in the field.
2. Read this chapter for an understanding of marketing in the professions.
3. Read at least one of the general marketing professional services books listed at the end of this chapter.
4. Read a specialty book dedicated to marketing in your specific profession; examples are listed at the end of this chapter.
5. Implement a computer-based periodical title search to locate specific articles related to marketing your individual professional skills. Request abstracts of articles whose titles appear relevant. Request and read reprints of those articles that best fit your needs. Using the *Marketing Manager's Handbook* as a guide and following these recommendations, you will become both knowledgeable and current on the application of modern marketing principles and practices to the professional service environment.

WHO ARE THE "PROFESSIONALS"?

This chapter is directed toward individuals and organizations who meet traditional criteria for professional designation. These criteria include the following:

1. controlled entrance requirements to the professional field based on precise criteria;
2. advanced specialized higher education;
3. an apprenticeship experience;
4. certification by a rigorous examination prepared and administered by members of the profession;
5. continuing education;
6. a code of ethics or professional oath endorsed by each professional and enforced by the professional association; and
7. a specialized relationship with clients based on dedication to service and confidentiality.

Examples of professions that meet the traditional definition include medical, health care, law, public accounting, engineering, dentistry, architecture, the clergy, research scientists, and education.

SHOULD PROFESSIONALS MARKET? ETHICAL AND PRACTICAL CONSIDERATIONS

Most definitions of marketing have several common characteristics including the following:

1. understanding the legal, political, competitive, ethical, social, cultural, and technical environment of the marketplace;
2. analyzing buyers' needs and desires as well as market opportunities;
3. developing and managing service offerings that match current and emerging market needs;
4. implementing personal and nonpersonal communication flows to inform markets, to secure customers, and to maintain customer goodwill and patronage loyalty;
5. managing service operations such that services are conveniently available at the appropriate place, price, and time; and
6. maintaining communications between service encounters to meet after the sale service needs and reinforce repurchase loyalty and recommending behavior.

Should professionals market? To one degree or another professionals have always marketed their services. In serving their clients they have been mindful of the functions of marketing and have sought, through training or intuition, to match their service offerings to the needs and desires of the market. What is different today is the wider adoption of the marketing concept by professionals, the developing sophistication of professional service marketing practices, and the integration of the marketing function into the ongoing practice management operations of professional organizations.

Ethical codes define the shoulds and should nots of professional behavior. Until the late 1960s professional ethical codes had changed little. In the past, professional codes generally forbade the "solicitation" of clients. Advocates of this prohibition believed that the public should be protected from professionals who might abuse their special position of public trust to unduly influence buyer behavior. However, proponents of professional marketing believed that the public would be better informed and better served by a more open competitive marketplace. In response to competitive pressures, many professionals and professional firms have become actively involved in this marketing revolution. The trend toward the integration of marketing by the professions will continue to accelerate into the next century.

The key ethical question is not *Should* professionals market? but rather *How* should professionals market? The professional designation is unique and important in its differentiation. This special status should be cherished and protected by members of the professions. Professional marketing should remain professional. It should emphasize informational rather than persuasive promotional appeals, emphasize fact-based communication rather than puffery, and take care not to manipulate the market through the use of fear appeals or the misuse of the special knowledge and unique relationships that professionals have with their clients. I subscribe to and recommend the American Marketing Association code of ethics (Exhibit 1) as a rule of conduct that can be used to supplement individual professional codes, guide professional marketing policies and practices, and guide marketing specialists who work with professionals.[1]

THE PROFESSIONAL SERVICE ENVIRONMENT—CRITICAL SERVICE CHARACTERISTICS

Before analyzing a specific service market and developing a marketing program it is important to understand certain fundamental and critical characteristics of services. Each characteristic presents an opportunity for improved professional service marketing performance. The following listing presents a brief description of key service characteristics and identifies actions professionals can take to deal with their unique environment.

1. *Lack of tangibility.* Many products are durable and tangible. Many services have highly intangible components (e.g., the advice given by an attorney, the review of a client's tax situation by a CPA, the diagnostic process utilized by a skilled physician in identifying an illness and prescribing a treatment). Inexperienced buyers of professional services frequently are not able to readily identify what they received for their investment. Augmenting a service encounter with

EXHIBIT 1. American Marketing Association Code of Ethics

Members of the American Marketing Association are committed to ethical, professional conduct. They have joined together in subscribing to this Code of Ethics embracing the following topics:

Responsibilities of the Marketer

Marketers must accept responsibility for the consequences of their activities and make every effort to ensure that their decisions, recommendations, and actions function to identify, serve, and satisfy all relevant publics: customers, organizations, and society.

Marketers' professional conduct must be guided by:

1. The basic rule of professional ethics: not knowingly to do harm;
2. The adherence to all applicable laws and regulations;
3. The accurate representation of their education, training, and experience; and
4. The active support, practice, and promotion of this Code of Ethics.

Honesty and Fairness

Marketers shall uphold and advance the integrity, honor, and dignity of the marketing profession by:

1. Being honest in serving consumers, clients, employees, suppliers, distributors, and the public;
2. Not knowingly participating in conflict of interest without prior notice to all parties involved; and
3. Establishing equitable fee schedules including the payment or receipt of usual, customary, and/or legal compensation for marketing exchanges.

Rights and Duties of Parties in the Marketing Exchange Process

Participants in the marketing exchange process should be able to expect that:

1. Products and services offered are safe and fit for their intended uses;
2. Communications about offered products and services are not deceptive;
3. All parities intend to discharge their obligations, financial and otherwise, in good faith; and
4. Appropriate internal methods exist for equitable adjustment and/or redress of grievances concerning purchases.

It is understood that the above would include, but is not limited to, the following responsibilities of the marketer:

In the area of product development and management,

- disclosure of all substantial risks associated with product or service usage;
- identification of any product component substitution that might materially change the product or impact on the buyer's purchase decision;
- identification of extra cost-added features.

physical documents can help demonstrate what the professional did in arriving at final recommendations or in delivering the service. For example, a physician can provide a bound, personalized printout containing the results of an annual physical examination. This, along with a detailed descriptive invoice and clearly explained billing procedures, can provide increased tangibility and a competitive

In the area of promotions,

- avoidance of false and misleading advertising;
- rejection of high pressure manipulations, or misleading sales tactics;
- avoidance of sales promotions that use deception or manipulation.

In the area of distribution,

- not manipulating the availability of a product for purpose of exploitation;
- not using coercion in the marketing channel;
- not exerting undue influence over the reseller's choice to handle a product.

In the area of pricing,

- not engaging in price fixing;
- not practicing predatory pricing;
- disclosing the full price associated with any purchase.

In the area of marketing research,

- prohibiting selling or fundraising under the guise of conducting research;
- maintaining research integrity by avoiding misrepresentation and omission of pertinent research data;
- treating outside clients and suppliers fairly.

Organizational Relationships

Marketers should be aware of how their behavior may influence or impact on the behavior of others in organizational relationships. They should not demand, encourage, or apply coercion to obtain unethical behavior in their relationships with others, such as employees, suppliers, or customers.

1. Apply confidentiality and anonymity in professional relationships with regard to privileged information;
2. Meet their obligations and responsibilities in contracts and mutual agreements in a timely manner;
3. Avoid taking the work of others, in whole, or in part, and represent this work as their own or directly benefit from it without compensation or consent of the originator or owner;
4. Avoid manipulation to take advantage of situations to maximize personal welfare in a way that unfairly deprives or damages the organization or others.

Any AMA members found to be in violation of any provision of this Code of Ethics may have his or her Association membership suspended or revoked.

benefit for the professional. Providing more tangibility can also reduce fee objections and improve collections (Wheatley 1992).

2. *Problem psychology.* In many instances professionals are consulted by clients experiencing problems or by clients forced to consult with them concerning some complex pending matter. Clients may be tense and even resent the need or requirement to retain the professional.

This psychological environment may create a negative overtone. It is important for professionals to not only respond to clients' technical service requirements but also the emotions being experienced by clients. Sensitivity training and the development of interpersonal skills is an important professional asset.

3. *Uneven demand and peak load periods.* The programming of professional service delivery is not as orderly as the programming of a production line making watches. Professionals often experience episodic or seasonal increases and decreases in demand. Peak load periods create stress for the professional staff members and may result in delays for clients or reduction in service quality. Demand engineering is a function that should be programmed into every professional practice. At a minimum, professionals should analyze demand patterns and use discretionary staff to offset peak loads. Cross training of professional staff members will allow for absorption of uneven demand patterns. Waiting time strategies can be implemented and incentives can be identified that can shift demand away from peak loads and into periods of lower activity. Professionals who do not practice demand engineering may have activity patterns that range from boredom to chaos. Minimizing these extremes will improve clients' satisfaction and loyalty.
4. *Internal clients.* Effective service delivery is not only a function of the individual professional but also of the performance given by each member of the staff. For example, in a large medical practice patient experience is as much a function of the performance of the x-ray technician, the receptionist, the billing and insurance clerk, the nurse, and the lab technician. In turn, each of these staff members serves and supports the other. Professional practices whose staff members serve each other well usually serve clients well. Where there are cliques, personality conflicts, poor organization/supervision, or other barriers, client service suffers. Careful recruiting, selection, training, compensation, motivation, and evaluation of the professional team is a critical ongoing function.
5. *Highly personal.* In most cases services are performed by people for people. Service evaluations are based on how the client feels about the professional. One way to differentiate the practice is to give special attention to recruiting and training client contact personnel. Training should emphasize nontechnical aspects of client service as well as technical skills. In addition, client feedback should be solicited on a regular basis to monitor service satisfaction and client perception levels.
6. *The producer/service unity.* The channel of distribution for services is often direct—example, person to person. You may not like a particular Chrysler dealer, but you still may be a loyal Chrysler car buyer. On the other hand, if you are dissatisfied with the project

manager assigned by your architectural firm, it is doubtful that you will use that firm again or recommend it to other potential clients. In essence, the person delivering the service is the service organization. It is imperative that professionals realize that every individual with whom the client has contact affects the client's image of the practice. Initial and continuous training in the development and projection of a positive and professional image is important. Ongoing training at all levels of the customer contact spectrum is also critical.

7. *Compressed time factor.* Of necessity and sometime by design, service providers seek to optimize their time spent with clients. A buyer's experience with a home computer may take place over many years. A client's experience with a consulting engineer may be over in a matter of hours or days. A service encounter should be carefully planned, implemented, and controlled. Service delivery systems and methods should be designed, documented, implemented, and monitored to maximize client results and satisfaction.
8. *"Unfair" (nontechnical) evaluation.* Most professional service consumers do not have the technical background or qualifications to establish and apply objective criteria in evaluating professional service performance. This does not, however, deter them from evaluating professionals. Successful professionals carefully and clearly explain and demonstrate what they are doing. In addition, they are careful to meet the emotional needs of clients. They understand that while some clients cannot understand what was done, they do have strong opinions about how they were treated.
9. *The influencers.* The majority of new professional clients come by referrals from others. Identifying influencers and expanding the referral network is critical to professional practice growth and survival.

Being responsive to the unique characteristics common to the professional service marketing environment can give a professional a competitive edge resulting in increased client satisfaction, higher gross revenue, practice growth, and an expanding referral base. The addition of practice marketing and management skills to the technical portfolio will greatly enhance the probability for and longevity of commercial success.

ORGANIZING FOR MARKETING

Adding the marketing function to a professional firm does not require the establishment of a new department or hiring a large full-time staff. Marketers do not market professional services; professionals do. Unlike the large sophisticated marketing departments found in consumer and industrial product service organizations, most professional firm marketing assistance is provided by a combination of outside consultants and a small internal staff. Consultants and/or the internal marketing specialists develop marketing materials and programs and act as staff assistants in the implementation of marketing activities carried out by members of the professional staff.

The responsibility for bringing marketing to the firm can be given to or assumed by a senior partner, a junior professional, the practice administrator, a marketing/practice development committee, or a task force. Let us examine each alternative.

1. *Senior partner (s).* Since the senior partner(s) has the authority and hopefully respect of the professional staff, the marketing effort will get wide attention. However, senior personnel may lack marketing skills. In addition, if the practice's efforts are to be successful, more than one person will have to be committed to and involved in marketing. Overinvolvement of senior personnel may also divert practice leadership energy away from important practice management tasks and policy development. While highly visible commitment and support of the marketing effort is required by the senior professionals, they should not shoulder sole responsibility for the marketing effort.
2. *Junior professional.* A junior staff member may not have the authority or respect to lead the firm in new directions. While a junior person may have the enthusiasm and energy, and in some cases natural talent for marketing, it is doubtful that long-range success can be achieved through this alternative.
3. *Practice administrator.* Many practice administrators have business training. They also know the professional staff well, including staff strengths and weaknesses. However, primary responsibilities usually encompass financial, operations, and human resources management. While practice administrators hold a key post, they seldom enjoy true peer status with professional staff members. Also, they have little if any line authority and do not seriously affect decisions concerning promotion and salary.
4. *Development committee.* The committee approach involves several people, leverages creativity, and provides representation for marketing program development at all levels. However, committees have bad reputations as dead-end assignments, where effort and time go unappreciated and unrewarded. Committees also suffer from a perceived lack of authority.
5. *Task force.* A task force has the advantages of the committee with few of its disadvantages. To make the task force work,
   a. keep the size manageable (three to five persons);
   b. give it clearly defined objectives;
   c. publicly announce task force formulation and support its ongoing operations with top management authority;
   d. specify a fixed life (e.g., six to twelve months);
   e. specify a timetable for the completion of the task force's objectives;

f. appoint the best people at each level; be sure the managing partner and the practice manager are *ad hoc* members;
g. monitor progress closely, with the task force reporting on a monthly basis to the managing partner; and
h. tie task force performance to the staff review and evaluation process.

Next, identify and select a consultant. The consultant assists the task force in assessing the firm's current marketing position, developing future strategy, and creating a specific professional service marketing plan. In selecting a consultant, experience and expertise are important. However, the ideal resource is a marketing specialist who is sensitive to the professional environment and can adjust to the diverse personalities and levels of marketing interest common to professional organizations. While the consultant brings expertise to marketing plan development, it is critical that task force members play an active role and interact with the consultant on a regular basis. A program developed in isolation by the consultant typically results in severe problems with program approval and implementation.

The next organizational step involves plan implementation and management of the ongoing marketing effort. In a smaller practice the senior or managing administrative partner usually assumes responsibility for controlling program implementation. Consultants may be used to conduct quarterly or semiannual marketing program reviews. Recommendations for program modifications are usually made and the program is adjusted based on actual experience. As the practice grows, professional firms often consider hiring a full-time marketing manager. The specific title, qualifications, and duties are different based on the type of professional firm and the practice environment. However, having a clearly written detailed position description and definition of duties is the key starting point. Developing the position description is often a joint effort between the consultant and the marketing task force. Time taken in this task will pay off in effective recruiting, screening, and selection. The importance of good interpersonal skills, mutual respect, and acceptance by the professional staff cannot be overemphasized. In some cases, it is actually better to seek a less experienced marketing specialist in the formative stages of his or her career. This allows him or her to grow with the practice and minimize the existence of preconceived "right" approaches and solutions. On the other hand, a large well-established, multioffice professional practice might be best served by bringing in a highly experienced marketer with professional service firm experience. Larger firms have the practice management expertise and intrastructure necessary to implement structured programs more effectively.

Institutionalizing the marketing position is generally a controversial step. To minimize any negative psychological impact of establishing this staff position, a participatory approach and a "softer" position

EXHIBIT 2. Marketing Coordinator Position Description

Reports To:	Managing Partner
Position Concept:	A "one-person marketing department" working with the managing partner and other firm members as appropriate. The marketing coordinator is responsible for analyzing the practice environment and past, current, and potential client information and identifying marketing opportunities and drafting a positioning statement. Based on these results the marketing coordinator will develop and execute practice marketing programs designed to increase market awareness, reinforce client loyalty, and increase practice revenues.

* * * * *

1. *Initial Duties:* Become familiar with the profession, industry, firm, and market by identifying, acquiring, and reviewing relevant external and internal data.
   After a thorough orientation, develop a written one-year marketing plan. The initial plan will focus on increasing general market awareness and focused marketing efforts in the market segments identified. Duties will include:
   a. Conceptualizing, writing, and coordinating production of client service brochures.
   b. Distributing new brochures with appropriate cover letters from the professional staff.
   c. Developing, writing, packaging, and submitting proposals. Coordinating proposal response strategy, preparation, presentation, and follow-up.
   d. Organizing and maintaining a marketing database and information systems.
   e. Developing, maintaining, and updating client, referral, community, and professional relations mailing lists.
   f. Establishing specific action plans for market targets and performance goals (e.g., leads developed, proposals presented, gross sales).
   g. Developing leads, organizing, screening, and ranking as appropriate. Ensuring appropriate staff are informed, scheduled, and equipped to make the contacts.
   h. Maintaining a marketing log to track leads, proposals, interviews, and projects.
   i. Identifying and leveraging public relations opportunities through preparation and dissemination of news releases concerning firm, client, project, or staff activities such as awards received and projects completed.
   j. Remaining informed concerning firm project status and progress and providing assistance as requested with client inquiries, problems, and complaints.
   k. Developing specific sales support materials as needed for specific sales calls or presentations.

title such as marketing coordinator could help. Exhibit 2 illustrates an actual position description developed for a large southeastern U.S. professional firm. Specific position descriptions and experience requirements will differ based on the professional setting. However, this position description contains elements that are common to the majority of professional service firms.

l. Developing and implementing an ongoing personal/telephone/written contact program for appropriate staff. Targets include current, past, and potential clients.
m. On an ongoing basis updating the managing partner concerning marketing activities. On a quarterly basis preparing a written report detailing activities, accomplishments, and needs. This report will serve as the basis for an annual progress review and evaluation conducted by the managing partner.
n. At the appropriate time, planing and executing a "grand opening" reception at the new office for clients, former clients, prospects, referral sources, and community members.

2. *Ongoing Duties:* In addition to these first year duties, ongoing responsibilities include:
   a. Creating and distributing an intermittent written communication piece to the practice mailing list to maintain awareness and contact.
   b. Developing a practice graphics identity program that creates and integrates the practice logo, color, and presentation scheme in all written communications from routine correspondence to proposals. Registering service marks.
   c. Conducting client perception and satisfaction research, recommending activities as indicated by the findings.
   d. Monitoring professional and market trends and recommending appropriate firm responses such as new market targets, new services, and new marketing approaches.
   e. Performing other marketing related duties as assigned.

3. *Qualifications:*

Education:	College degree in marketing, communications, technical writing, or related field.
Experience:	Some work experience in marketing, sales, advertising, public relations, or communications.
Skills and Abilities:	Strong written and interpersonal communications skills. PC literacy, desktop publishing capabilities a plus, ability to organize and maintain client and project databases, develop and coordinate marketing plans; creative, positive attitude. Will represent firm well to clients and external public.
Work Style:	Dependable, flexible, self-confident, sets and achieves objectives. Personal style and work product convey high-level professional image.

ANALYZING YOUR PRACTICE— THE MARKETING AUDIT

The marketing professional services (MPS) audit is a self-administrated diagnostic test (Wheatley 1983). The audit consists of a series of questions dealing with both professional practice management and current marketing practices.

The audit that follows is divided into eight sections:

1. the practice environment;
2. client analysis and opportunities;
3. practice philosophy, positioning, and targeting;
4. the service mix;
5. professional fees;
6. personal communication;
7. written communication; and
8. MPS control and evaluation.

Before you respond to the questions in each section, please review the brief introductory comments.

In addition to answers, the audit questions will stimulate further questions. This is to be encouraged. These questions will be of two types: branches and probes. Branching questions will arise when a basic audit question suggests a second or third question related to the first. Branching may occur when the audit question does not exactly fit your circumstances but stimulates a question or series of questions that do. Probing questions usually develop when an audit question is directly related to your practice or to an area of interest involving your practice. In a probe you get deeper and deeper and usually more specific in the level of detail than called for in the basic audit question.

I suggest you copy the questions, then cut them out and paste them to the type of writing surface most comfortable to you—a medical pad, legal pad, or loose-leaf notebook. Not every audit question will apply to every professional or every organization, but beware of the "NA" (not applicable) syndrome. An easy way to avoid critical self-evaluation is simply to say, "Well that's not applicable in our case." The real question is Could it be applicable? and Should it be applicable? At the very least, every question should be evaluated in the light of the potential contribution it could make to client retention, growth, and profitability.

I. Your Practice Environment

Your practice environment is the real world in which you operate. It includes both macro and micro variables. Macro variables include national and regional governmental policies and regulations and the national and regional economic situation. Micro variables are those that are more closely and directly related to your everyday opportunities and constraints. They consist of local regulations, local economic conditions, the composition of your practice market, and so on. In consumer and industrial product and service marketing, we refer to this portion of the environment as the external environment or uncontrollable variables. Although each of us has some opportunity to have an effect on our practice environment, the impact on any one individual or firm is usually slight. The most successful professionals are usually those who can adjust to and often profit from changes.

1. Do you have a practice management plan?
2. Do you have a marketing professional services plan?
3. Is your practice organized so that a specific individual has the authority and responsibility for practice management operations?
4. Are your practice management operations evaluated on a routine basis? How often, by whom, and with what effects?
5. Are there any laws that have significant regulatory impact on your practice?
6. Are you in compliance with these requirements?
7. What are the current ethical codes of your profession?
8. Do you have copies of the specific ethical codes that affect you?
9. Are you appropriately involved with the key professional associations that affect your practice environment?
10. What specific actions have been taken by you to consider, modify, or enforce your ethical codes?
11. Are there any immediate or future political developments that might significantly affect your professional environment, including those of other professionals, your clients, your staff, and referral sources?
12. What agencies, boards, commissions, committees, and so on have had or could have significant impact on your professional environment?
13. Are you aware of and appropriately involved with any political or public organizations that affect your professional environment?
14. Who are your direct competitors?
15. Who are your indirect competitors?
16. Can you describe the client base of your most significant competitors?
17. What do you know about the fee structure of significant competitors?
18. What do you know about competitors' strengths and weaknesses?
19. Are you in a position to assess size, structure, and potential for future growth for key competitors?
20. Do competitors know what you want them to know about you?
21. Describe the current economic situation and how it affects your practice environment.
22. How might future economic scenarios affect your practice?
23. Have you developed at least one offensive and one defensive strategy to cope with significant economic changes?
24. How does your natural environment (regional location, climate, topography) affect your current and future practice environment?
25. Can you enumerate the key technological advances associated with your profession over the past few years? Include those that directly affect your clients, such as new medical hardware for physicians, and those that indirectly affect clients, such as minicomputer billing and administrative systems.

26. Which technologies are you using or not using? Why?
27. How are you tracking and evaluating potential future service delivery or administrative technology?
28. Identify any key cultural shifts in your practice environment, such as significant in- or out-migrations.
29. Do you have an operating budget appropriately developed and controlled?
30. Do you receive and review detailed, accurate, and understandable regular reports concerning the financial condition of and trends in your practice?
31. Do you have a human resources plan and program that identifies long-range goals, inventories, strengths, and weaknesses of existing staff and provides for training and growth, feedback, and consultation?
32. When was the last time you evaluated the physical and atmospheric environment of the practice (e.g., office locations, design, decor, ease of access, parking, reception areas, professional and staff offices, and support facilities)?

II. Client Analysis and Opportunities

If you are a new professional, these questions are designed to get you thinking in an organized way about client analysis. If you are currently involved in an individual or group practice, these questions will help you see where you are and where your practice might develop in a new and interesting way.

1. In addition to your individual working client files, have you established an independent set of client analysis files?
2. Is new client information routinely collected and posted to the client analysis files?
3. Is client information summarized in matrix form by key practice variables, such as client type, size, primary and secondary services provided, billings, collection experience, profitability, growth potential, referral potential, and so on?
4. Does the posting, review, and reporting of client information take place on a routine and regular basis?
5. Are you able to identify high-assay (current and potentially high-profit clients) and low-assay clients?
6. Do high- and low-assay clients fall into any identifiable segments or groups?
7. What discrete segments emerge or seem to be emerging from your client analysis? For example, if you are a CPA, are more of your clients small industrial businesses, self-employed professionals, or commercial firms?
8. Considering your present high-assay client bases and the strengths of your practice, what is the potential client base you would

like to serve? For example, if you are the administrator of a health maintenance organization, do you have a detailed list of potential individual and organizational members?

9. Are any environmental developments forecast that could create opportunities for new client acquisition? An example might be a county or state government program to bring a certain type of industry to your area.
10. Have you developed a client purchasing model? Such a model is a diagram or description of the actions your clients take from the time they are aware of the need for professional service until they actually locate and retain a professional.
11. Do you routinely solicit, record, analyze, and act on client input and evaluation of your professional services?
12. Do you or members of your staff conduct exit interviews with clients who are terminating or have apparently terminated their relationship? Do any patterns exist that might indicate areas of weakness, improvement, or opportunity?

III. Philosophy, Positioning, and Targeting

The questions in this section will assist you in considering how you and your practice can become actively and appropriately involved in marketing your professional services.

1. Have you and/or your staff thoroughly discussed your philosophy concerning marketing?
2. Has this philosophy been reduced to writing and communicated to all professionals and staff?
3. Has a positioning statement been drafted, discussed, reduced to writing, and communicated?
4. Based on your analysis in sections I and II and the development of an appropriate positioning statement, have you identified specific client targets for service expansion?
5. Based on your analysis in sections I and II and your position statement, have you identified specific targets for new client acquisition?
6. Are your client targeting plans in actionable form? For example, does detailed information concerning the client target exist?
7. Is a specific individual charged with the responsibility for client development?
8. Are objectives quantified where possible, including time for accomplishment and projected costs and revenues?

IV. Your Service Mix

Your service mix refers to the combination of services you offer to clients. These services may include those that are directly professional, such as the preparation of a will by an attorney, and services that are not directly professional, including credit, the mailing of information or news releases, or client parking. Please note that the audit sections are based on the assumption that you have responded to the first three sections. The main thrust of the service mix review is to ensure that you are matching your services to client needs and market opportunities.

1. Are service mix analysis, planning, development, and termination a regular part of your management activities?
2. Do you have a written description of services you currently provide and services you prefer to handle by referral?
3. Are you able to provide clients with written information concerning the services available from your referral sources?
4. How well does your current service mix match the present and potential market opportunities you have identified?
5. Have you objectively assessed your own current level of qualifications to provide the services offered?
6. How often do you assess the level and currency of qualifications of your staff relative to your service mix offerings?
7. Do you have an ongoing program that provides for upgrading service delivery skills?
8. Are continuing professional education and development activities matched to your marketing opportunities and targets?
9. Have you identified areas for potential service expansion for existing clients?
10. Have you identified potential new service offerings for potential clients?
11. Is your staff recruiting and training program matched to service expansion and new service development objectives and opportunities?
12. Do you have a systematized service delivery operation or procedure?
13. How often is your service delivery system reviewed critically?
14. What are the significant strengths and weaknesses of your service delivery system?
15. Which items in your service mix are candidates for deemphasis, sell-off, or termination?

V. Professional Fees

Marketing professionals are concerned about the economic and emotional components of fees. In the industrial and consumer product and service fields, marketing professionals are intimately involved in establishing and communicating prices. The following questions are designed to help you assess the current fee structure in your own practice.

1. What is the normal fee structure or range of fees in your practice environment?
2. Do you solicit client feedback concerning your fee structure on a regular basis?

3. How do your fees compare with those of direct competitors? with professional fees in general?
4. On what basis do you justify fees that are lower and higher than competitive norms?
5. How do you establish fees?
6. What procedures exist for fee structure review?
7. Does your current management system allow you to match costs to revenues by client or engagement?
8. Do you maintain a record of fee-related problems, such as failure to get or retain clients; direct complaints or disputes; billing writedowns, writeups, and writeoffs?
9. How and when are prospective clients made aware of your fee structure and policies?
10. Do clients receive a separate written document discussing fee policies, or is this discussion part of your practice brochure or client information booklet?
11. Does your management system provide for control so that fee proposals, billing, and collection procedures are consistently applied by all staff?
12. Has a fee policy been developed and documented? Would you describe your practice as fee-competitive, competitive on other than fee dimensions, or flexible?
13. How are clients notified of revisions in your fee structure?

VI. Personal Communication

The personal communication review includes not only your personal interactions with clients but also those of your staff. Interpersonal communication provides a unique marketing opportunity and permits confirmation that the client has indeed made the right selection of the professional and the professional organization.

1. Do you hold regular staff meetings characterized by open, two-way communication?
2. How often do you meet with your staff members individually?
3. Are staff members willing to take you into their confidence on occasions when they have pressing personal problems that have affected or might affect their performance?
4. Are appropriate staff members briefed and assisted in carrying out their client, professional, and communication relations roles?
5. Has the initial client or prospective client consultation procedure been carefully developed and utilized?
6. Are client contact personnel, from receptionist to professionals, evaluated and trained in image development and interpersonal relationships?
7. Have you sought objective evaluation of your own interpersonal skills?

8. What areas of strength and weakness do you think exist in your own inventory of interpersonal communication skills?
9. How has your service delivery system been adjusted to compensate for staff strengths and weaknesses?
10. Do you solicit direct client feedback concerning perceptions of your staff on a regular basis?
11. Are current and potential referral sources identified in writing and catalogued by level of referral activity?
12. Does a system exist for personal acknowledgment and follow-up of all referrals?
13. How often do you call/see regular referral sources?
14. Do you maintain a written record of related professionals to whom you refer?
15. How do you follow up your referrals to ensure that your colleagues are aware of your importance to their practice?
16. List the activities you and/or your staff conduct to stimulate referrals—seminars, workshops, mailings, luncheons, visits, and so on.
17. Have you prepared or caused to be prepared a written analysis of the community infrastructure, noting relevant clubs, boards, committees, and so on?
18. Have you developed a community relations plan and targeted key organizations for active involvement by you and your staff?
19. Do you offer staff personnel as expert speakers to relevant professional, industry, and community organizations? Are professional staff members trained in presentation skills? Does the firm support presenters with appropriate materials, handouts, media preparation, etc.?
20. Does your benefit and compensation program provide for specific recognition of associates or staff members who generate new clients?
21. Does your benefit and compensation program provide for associates and staff members whose activities create positive visibility for the practice?
22. Do clear and generous reimbursement policies exist for staff members who participate in approved community and professional activities?
23. Are the expense policies for staff marketing efforts well documented and communicated?

VII. Written Communication

Professionals who are investigating marketing frequently focus on advertising as the primary form of written communication. But typical mass-media advertising may not be at all suited to professional marketing objectives. In this audit section, we will review many other types of written communication that can affect client and prospect perception.

1. Have you selected a practice image objective?
2. Is the image you wish to convey congruent with all aspects of your practice, such as client base, service mix, staff, location and facilities, and fee structure?
3. Have you selected a practice identifier or logo consistent with your image?
4. Are all printed and typed communications centrally reviewed and controlled before release?
5. Does your practice identifier or logo appear on every piece of written communication generated by your practice?
6. Has an appropriate type style been selected to match your image goals?
7. Is this distinctive type style used on all printed communication?
8. Have appropriate paper stock and colors been selected and used to build practice identity?
9. Identify, collect, and review all current written communication vehicles, such as stationery, envelopes, receipts, invoices, purchase orders, cards, proposals, pamphlets, brochures, appointment cards, billing reminders, client data sheets. Are they consistent in appearance, quality, and use of logo?
10. Have you reviewed all self-completion client forms for clarity, diplomacy of questions, and mechanical problems, such as room to write?
11. Has some form of client brochure or information and service document been developed and circulated?
12. If your practice involves proposals, are proposals carefully prepared and reviewed from an objective marketing perspective for form, content, and presentation?
13. Are you up-to-date concerning new technology for proposal preparation/delivery (e.g., video taping, computer-generated graphics, and desktop publishing)?
14. Is the decision to publish informational communications verified by client, prospect, or referral source need?
15. What printed media, such as journals, convention or conference programs, and trade or professional magazines, are read by your clients, prospects, and referral sources?
16. Are staff members authoring articles in areas of their expertise for appropriate professional/trade publications?
17. Are any general or mass newspapers and magazines consistently read by clients, prospects, and referral sources?
18. Is media advertising (informational, institutional, or persuasive) congruent with your marketing philosophy and image?
19. Have existing informational pieces such as newsletters and updates been critically tested for value to clients and prospects?

VIII. Control and Evaluation

1. Is the marketing program reduced to a written document that specifies objectives, time frames, resources, expected results, and responsibilities?
2. Are all staff members participating in program implementation within their comfort zones?
3. Does a regular, periodic review of the marketing program progress take place?
4. Is program contribution part of the total review process for monetary and nonmonetary staff compensation?
5. Do you maintain a concise, permanent record of marketing ideas and activities that failed as well as those that succeeded?
6. Does your management system provide sufficient current data to permit development of a marketing information system that will isolate program activity costs, client information, and profitability analysis?

DEVELOPING THE MARKETING PLAN

Most marketing plans have several things in common. First is an external assessment. Prior to developing actions to be taken, the planner needs to assess and forecast the most likely conditions that will prevail during the planning period. This environmental scan includes economic, political, legal, ethical, competitive, technological, and managerial factors. You will note that the Marketing Professional Services Audit contains several questions that should be considered in evaluating your practice environment.

The second step common to marketing planning involves the analysis of marketing opportunities and the targeting and analysis of specific client groups. It is a true axiom in marketing that we pay too much attention to developing new clients at the expense of providing optimum service to existing clients. It is therefore important that specific marketing efforts be aimed at existing clients in order to reinforce their loyalty and potential recommending behavior. Potential clients are usually identified as a group (e.g., a specific industry). This industry was roughly classified as film and TV production. This new area citizen was then segmented into its various components (e.g., sound studios, creative houses, video production facilities, distribution organizations). These segments were then ranked in priority order based on their likelihood of need for accounting, tax, and consulting services. Finally, the market with the highest assay potential (the potential for building the highest fee revenue and profits) was targeted for specific marketing activities during the following year's planning period.

Following the environmental scan and client analysis and targeting, the firm will seek to define the position it wishes to achieve in the market. Positioning is the process of defining where the firm fits in the competitive spectrum of other professional service organizations.

Developing a practice positioning statement provides the mechanism for focusing the professional's specific and unique skills on a market niche that is not being well served or for which the professional has a unique competitive advantage. The following two sections present two contrasting positioning statements—one for a prestigious law firm, another for a low-priced accounting bookkeeping service. The competitive positioning defined in these actual examples provides clear direction as well as limitations for the marketing activity (Wheatley 1983).

Following the environmental scan, market targeting and practice positioning planners normally review the specific service offerings in the practice's "service mix." The emphasis here is on whether existing services truly match the targeted markets and the conditions expected in the practice environment during the planning period. Service mix modifications may be suggested and implemented. In addition, new services may be developed to match the unmet needs of new target customers.

Fee management involves three distinct areas. First, fee should be established for new services and reviewed for existing services to test whether they need to be increased, decreased, or remain the same. Second, the professional should review how well fees and fee setting and collection practices are understood by clients. Serious collection or write-down problems, as well as potential clients lost due to fee objections or misperceptions indicate the need for greater attention to communicating fee policies and practices. Finally, collection methods and success should be reviewed since these mechanics directly affect clients.

The Professionals' Professional

Let us assume you are the senior partner in a small law firm, Smith, Gomez, and Smith. Your positioning statement might read this way:

1. Smith, Gomez, and Smith's goal is to become known as a firm of exceptionally skilled negotiators and litigation specialists.
2. Our area of emphasis is commercial practice, concentrating on corporate clients. Within that area of practice, we are deeply skilled in negotiation and litigation arising from major real estate transactions.
3. Within the area of real estate, our primary area of expertise and experience lies in representing real estate developers and development corporations.
4. We are an extremely professional firm. We seek to be respected by other nonlitigating and litigating attorneys in the field of real estate as well as related real estate referral sources.
5. Our acceptance of new clients will be on a selective basis. Partner emphasis will be on the pursuit of the practice development objectives of specialization. We do not seek to become all things to all people or a general legal practice.
6. Our fees are to be established and maintained at the level of other high-quality litigating law firms. In accepting any engagement, fee

level must be carefully assessed in order to permit us to provide the degree of personalized service and partner involvement congruent with our highly professional image.

7. At Smith, Gomez, and Smith, a partner will always have significant direct involvement in any major matter. Partner presence is a key variable in our service mix.
8. We do not seek to become a large law firm. Our size will be controlled in order to maximize our flexibility, responsiveness, and partner presence in client matters.
9. We are aggressive and systematic in the development of our specialized practice. In seeking to become recognized by other professionals and referral sources, partners and associates are active in professional and trade associations. They speak and publish in their respective areas.
10. When a matter outside our direct professional expertise comes to our attention, we will refer the matter to another professional who meets our high standards rather than attempt to stretch our time and expertise to matters we cannot service as satisfactorily as we would like.

You will notice that this positioning statement says as much about what the firm will not do as what it will do. The statement provides focus, specificity, limitation, and philosophy. It touches on many areas of the marketing mix, including services, market analysis and targeting, the role of MPS in the organization, and pricing.

The Everyone's Professional

The following positioning statement might be developed for a growing CPA firm seeking to penetrate the small business market and nonusers or light users of accounting services in the middle and lower classes. We will call this firm Elwood and Everything.

How to Position Your Services

1. Elwood and Everything is the complete accountant for the small organization or individual. Our practice development plan is based on securing a high volume of smaller accounts and providing these individuals and organizations with fairly routine and repetitive accounting and tax services.
2. Our services are clearly specified in our client information brochure. We do not provide exotic financial or tax services such as corporate mergers and acquisitions, complex estate tax planning, elaborate systems analysis, and computer feasibility studies. Rather, our emphasis is on preparing individual and small business income tax returns, providing basic bookkeeping and compilation services, and conducting annual year-end closings and audits.

3. The use of standardized, completely documented routines, as well as the preparation of simplified tax returns by paraprofessionals and by minicomputer, will permit us to be price competitive with local, regional, and national CPA firms.
4. Our pricing structure and competitive position will be between those of franchised tax preparers and bookkeeping services such as H&R Block and local, regional, and national CPA organizations.
5. All work will be performed under the supervision of a CPA; however, whenever possible, work will be performed by paraprofessionals.
6. We are aggressive marketers and price competitors. Our use of mass media, particularly newspapers, direct mail, and radio, is congruent with the market targets we have selected.
7. Since we are striving to become known as your "neighborhood accountant," it is not essential that partners and associates be highly visible in state and national associations. Partners and associates are expected to be extremely active in local civic, service, and social clubs and organizations.
8. Our future growth strategy is based on replication of existing small offices through branching rather than the development of a large, centralized service complex.

The Communication Stage

Now that the target markets have been selected and defined and adjustments made as necessary to the service mix and service pricing, the professional moves to the communications phase of the marketing plan. Personal communication is the traditional, and, in the opinion of many, the most effective means of marketing professional services. In developing their personal contact programs with new clients, inexperienced professionals often neglect three other important audiences. These include members of the internal professional and support staff, existing clients, and referral sources. Since professional services are essentially marketed by professionals, it is critical that internal staff and professional firm members be well trained, enthusiastic, and knowledgeable concerning the firm's capabilities. Helping every staff member become marketing minded will also sensitize them to the opportunity for new business development as they perform day to day work for clients. Unfortunately, current clients are often taken for granted. The majority of new business for professionals comes from referrals and the majority of those referrals come from existing clients. At the very minimum, the professional should focus on understanding the perceptions of existing clients concerning service performance. Professionals should correct misperceptions, solve actual problems that exist, and take the extra steps necessary to ensure long-term client retention and recommending behavior.

Developing and retaining an expanding base of outside referral sources is another important strategy for growing the practice. Referral contact and ongoing relationship programs must be established to ensure that the referral network remains healthy and expands.

Written communications programs are the final component of the marketing plan. Again, the audiences are similar, including internal staff and professionals and external audiences of current clients, new clients, and referral sources. Written communications include three major categories: operational, institutional, and competitive communications.

Operational. Any and every piece of written/printed communication says something about the firm. Collectively, the quality of these routine communications affect client perception of the firm's image. Stationary, envelopes, invoices, purchase orders, checks, correspondence, business cards, sinage, rate schedules, job summaries, expense reports, and so forth should all be designed and produced to convey an appropriate, positive, and consistent image.

Institutional. Various brochures, newsletters, press release forms, special reports or client bulletins, advertising, directory listings, holiday cards, and so forth must be designed, produced, and distributed to reflect the image adopted in the practice positioning statement.

Competitive. Sales letters, responses to proposal requests, presentations, proposals, brochures targeted to a specific client or industry group, and so forth should be developed based on careful analysis of potential client needs and buying behavior and tailored to the strongest needs and motivations of the client. Competitive communications are a blend of technical and marketing content.

Finally, the plan must have formality and clear structure so that tasks may be delegated, schedules monitored, and success evaluated. Exhibit 3 (shown on pages 212–213) illustrates the flow and relationships common to the professional service marketing planning activity. By now you may have recognized that this planning model follows the major sections and steps involved in the marketing audit. Specific audit questions within each section will help you identify and initiate planning activities. Detailed recommendations for developing marketing programs are available in the many references cited at the end of this chapter.

The important thing is to investigate a practice marketing approach, develop an integrated structure from which to proceed, and implement portions of the marketing plan that are appropriate and feasible. Develop a broad and energetic plan. Do not let your creativity be constrained by current resource or personal problems. You do not have to, and probably will not, implement the entire plan. However, you will have a blueprint for the future as well as some building blocks for the present. You will have alternatives that can be given priorities and acted on as future time, opportunities, and resources permit (Wheatley 1983).

INTERNAL BARRIERS TO PRACTICE MARKETING

In most business organizations, marketing is a driving force. CEOs often come from a marketing career background. Corporate VPs of marketing have substantial authority, power, and budgets. Marketing is relatively new to the professions. Marketing was formerly viewed as "unprofessional." Given this background, professional firms may have operating philosophies and practices that can impede marketing success. These self-imposed barriers include the following:

1. *The philosophical barrier.* Does the practice have a carefully developed, written, clearly communicated, and continuously supported marketing philosophy and commitment? The firm's philosophy should be evident in a practice positioning statement and/or in practice management short-term and strategic plans.
2. *Unclear marketing expectations.* Include realistic expectations and responsibilities for practice development in written job descriptions for each staff level. Never assign such responsibilities to others unless your firm has also accepted its own responsibility for proper training and support.
3. *Lack of recognition.* Marketing is not a short-term panacea that will create instant practice growth and revenue. Professional service marketing is less direct, is information based, and is dependent on establishing, building, and maintaining positive relationships with past, current, and future clients and referral sources. Success requires focused, consistent, and long-term efforts. Return on marketing effort may take months to years to materialize. Ongoing staff marketing efforts should be acknowledged, formally recognized, and reinforced by senior professionals and practice management on a continuing basis or the program will atrophy.
4. *Staff compensation.* Ultimately, professional staff activities are directly responsive to the firm's compensation system. If these efforts are not recognized and rewarded in a consistent, tangible way, practice development efforts will falter.
5. *Insufficient training.* Many enlightened firms have expanded their in-house training programs to include internal marketing and practice development. Internal marketing should be designed to enhance
   a. knowledge of the firm's product-service mix;
   b. pride in the firm's unique talents, expertise, and capabilities;
   c. awareness of opportunities for new service and business expansion; and
   d. specific marketing skills.
6. *Expense reimbursement policies.* Effective practice development costs money. Restrictive policies and stringent expense controls quickly convey the wrong message to staff members. Active practice development means higher expenses.

EXHIBIT 3. The Marketing Planning Process

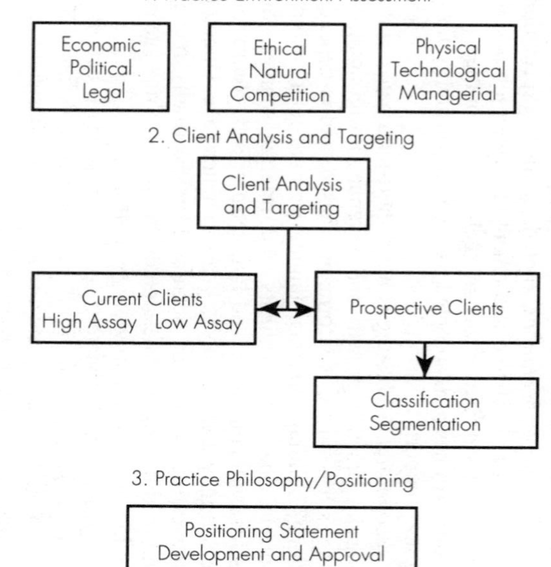

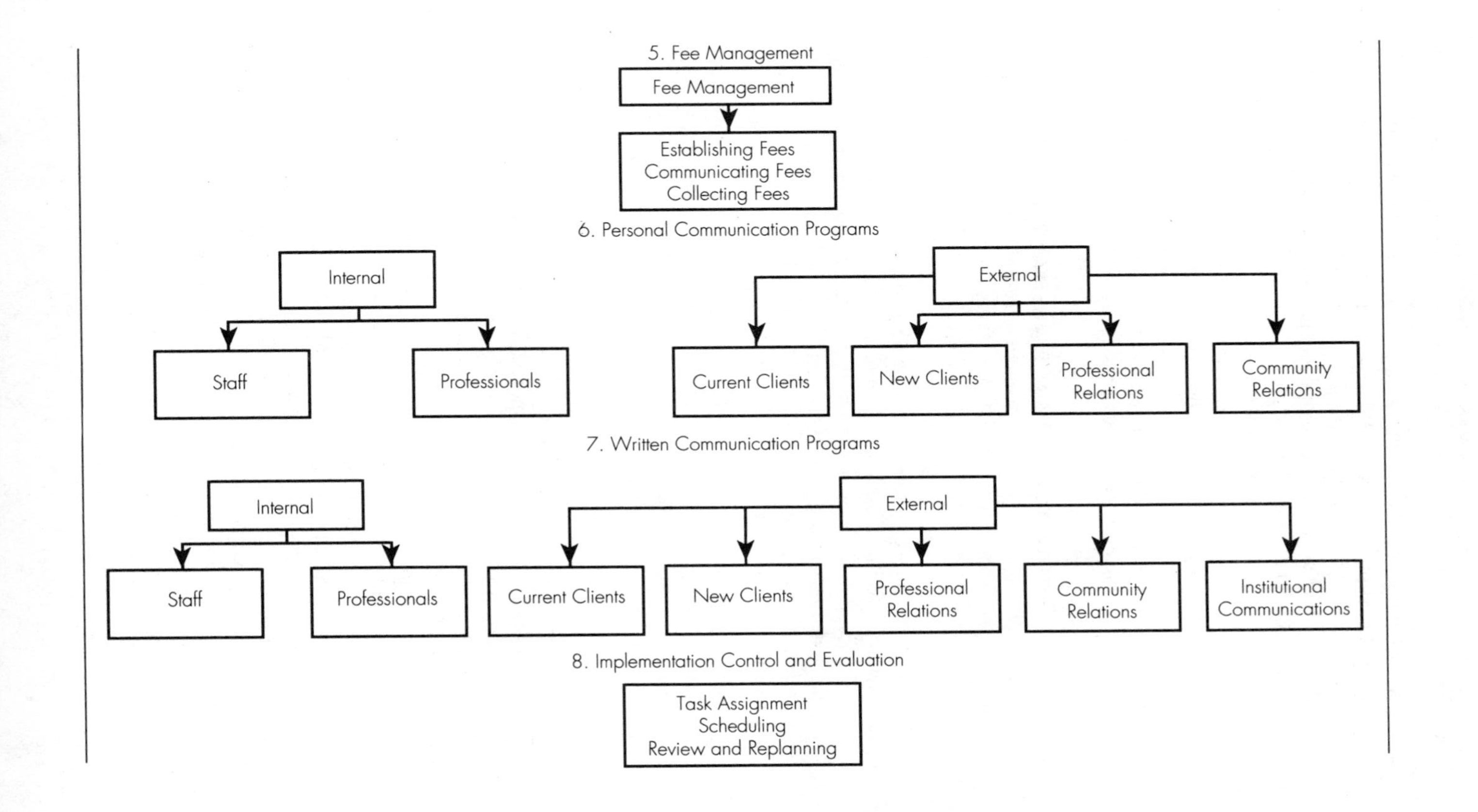
5. Fee Management
Fee Management
Establishing Fees
Communicating Fees
Collecting Fees
6. Personal Communication Programs
Internal
Staff
Professionals
External
Current Clients
New Clients
Professional Relations
Community Relations
7. Written Communication Programs
Internal
Staff
Professionals
External
Current Clients
New Clients
Professional Relations
Community Relations
Institutional Communications
8. Implementation Control and Evaluation
Task Assignment
Scheduling
Review and Replanning

7. *Lack of guidance.* Experience plays a major role in professional career development. Successful "rainmakers" have learned how to build client and referral relationships and market services. Unfortunately, the organizational culture of some professional firms isolates junior staff members until they "prove themselves." To minimize these problems, a mentoring program is helpful. Younger associates can learn successful techniques and tips from their more senior colleagues. Mentors can analyze failures and give moral support to associates. While younger associates are colleagues, they are nevertheless competing against one another. Having a senior mentor gives the associate someone to relate to outside the peer group (Wheatley 1989).

GROW YOUR OWN RAINMAKERS

Managing executives and managing senior partners in professional service firms have at least one thing in common (Wheatley 1987). They all agree that a major criterion for promotion to executive or partnership status is the ability to generate new business. The name given to these all too rare new business developers is revealing: "rainmakers." Rainmakers make things happen.

If the competitive environment is getting tougher and rainmakers continue to be in short supply, what can a professional service firm do to increase its probability of success? Develop, implement, and maintain an internal professional development program for associates.

1. Integrate marketing into the firm's practice management structure and operations. If the firm has not already done so it should conduct a marketing audit, draft a positioning statement, and develop and implement a professional service marketing program.
2. Centralize the personnel management function. If the recommendations that follow are to be implemented, there must be a focus of authority and responsibility for their execution.
3. Identify the areas of practice specialization for each firm associate. Professionals have only one thing to sell: their expertise. All associates will spend a major part of their time doing the firm's basic and fundamental work. However, work should be related to their area of interest and future specialization. Professionals cannot sell something until they have knowledge that goes beyond the normal basic technical proficiency that all competing professional firms possess. Specialized knowledge and abilities are key to successful professional service marketing.
4. Each associate should be assigned to a specific professional development partner/manager. This senior individual should be working in the area of the associate's future specialty. In addition to their working relationship, the practice development partner/manager should schedule nonworking contact on a regular, bi-

monthly basis. These informal visits will hopefully permit the development of a personal as well as a professional relationship with a firm leader.

5. Plan and implement a continuing professional development program. This program has two objectives: technical and internal marketing.
6. Budget 25 percent of annual continuing professional development hours to practice development (marketing) topics.
7. Involve associates in the firm's marketing program *now.* Marketing-related activities should be programmed into the associate's career development along with the technical development.
    a. Develop a menu of associate practice development activities.
    b. Require each associate to buy into the program he or she finds most comfortable. This agreement to participate should be a formal, written commitment. Associates should be encouraged to capitalize on their natural strengths, interests, and abilities. It is therefore essential that a wide variety of activities be included in the associates' client development menu.
    c. Provide the resources necessary for each associate to participate in whatever activity he or she selects.
    d. Require frequent informal reporting to the associates' professional development partner/manager. Informal feedback and suggestions can leverage the experience of senior people and provide a buffer for the rejections or frustrations experienced as the associates develop.
    e. The report should review the objective of the professional development activity as well as a cost/benefit analysis of the progress toward that objective. This report should be part of the associates' annual or semiannual review.
    f. Promotion and compensation should be based in part on a weighted scoring system that includes participation (not simply results) in marketing programs. In addition, the associate's attendance, involvement, and progress in continued professional development training programs should also be scored.
    g. Ongoing continuing professional development programs should give associates the "how to do it" help they need in the client development activities selected.
8. Involve associates wherever possible in the practice development activities of their professional development partner/executive and other firm personnel. As a minimum, they should have an opportunity to observe the implementation of marketing programs by more experienced personnel.
9. Keep associates informed. As new associates read the reported activities of their senior firm members, they begin to understand the purpose of this role model reporting.

10. Enrich the associates' continuing professional development program with outside stimuli. Assign required readings followed by discussions. Utilize special seminars sponsored by industry or professional associations. Consider required seminar attendance at programs sponsored by universities or private seminar firms. Require attendance at industry conferences that fit the associates' areas of specialization. Have associates attend seminars and workshops sponsored by various referral network organizations.

CONCLUSION

The formal and ongoing integration of marketing into the practice management structure of professional firms continues at an increasing rate. Professionals and professional firms that have not yet seriously investigated marketing may find their future success threatened by competitors who have already developed and implemented ongoing marketing programs. This chapter, other *Handbook* readings, and the additional references that follow will help you evaluate the relevance of marketing for your practice.

NOTES

1. American Marketing Association, 250 S. Wacker Drive, Chicago, IL 60606-5819.

REFERENCES

Wheatley, Edward W. 1992. Creating tangibility makes your service more valuable to patients. In: *Practice Economics.* New York: KSF Group Publications.

Wheatley, Edward W. 1989. Internal barriers to developing a practice. *Journal of Accountancy* 167 (1):124–30.

Wheatley, Edward W. 1987. Rainmakers, mushrooms and immaculate conception—Internal marketing for professional firm associates. *Journal of Professional Services Marketing* 2 (4):73–82.

Wheatley, Edward W. 1983. *Marketing Professional Services.* Englewood Cliffs, NJ: Prentice-Hall.

SUGGESTED READING

Key Journals and Conference Proceedings

Journal of Professional Services Marketing, published quarterly by the Haworth Press, Inc., 75 Griswald Street, Binghamton, NY, 13704.

Journal of Services Marketing, published quarterly by Grayson Associates, 108 Loma Media Road, Santa Barbara, CA 93103.

Services Marketing Conference Proceedings, published annually by the American Marketing Association, 25 S. Wacker Drive, Chicago, IL, 60606-5819.

General

Bateson, John E.G. 1989. *Managing Services Marketing*. Hinsdale, IL: The Dryden Press.

Berry, Leonard, and A. Parasuraman. 1991. *Marketing Services: Competing Through Quality*. New York: The Free Press.

Bly, Robert W. 1991. *Selling Your Services: Proven Strategies for Getting Clients to Hire You (or Your Firm)*. New York: Holt.

Czepiel, John A., Carole A. Congram, and Jim Shanahan (eds.). 1987. *The Services Challenge: Integrating for Competitive Advantage*. Chicago: American Marketing Association.

Designing a winning service strategy. 1989. *Seventh Annual Services Marketing Conference Proceedings* (Arlington, VA, 1988). Chicago: American Marketing Association.

Gronroos, Christian. 1990. *Service Management and Marketing: Managing the Moments of Truth in Service Competition*. Lexington, MA: Lexington Books.

Gummesson, Evert. 1981. How professional services are bought. In Michael Rines (ed.): *Marketing Handbook*. London: Gower Press.

Johnson, Eugene M., Eberhard E. Scheuing, and Kathleen A. Gaida. 1988. *Profitable Service Marketing*. Homewood, IL: Irwin.

Kotler, Philip and Paul N. Bloom. 1984. *Marketing Professional Services*. Englewood Cliffs, NJ: Prentice-Hall.

Lovelock, Christopher H. 1991. *Services Marketing*, 2nd ed. Englewood Cliffs, NJ: Prentice-Hall.

______. 1988. *Managing Services: Marketing, Operations, and Human Resources*. Englewood Cliffs, NJ: Prentice-Hall.

McCaffrey, Mike and Jerry Derloshon. 1983. *Personal Marketing Strategies: How to Sell Yourself, Your Ideas, and Your Services*. Englewood Cliffs, NJ: Prentice-Hall.

Venkatesan, M., Diane M. Schmalensee, and Claudia Marshall (eds.). 1986. *Creativity in Services Marketing: What's New, What Works, What's Developing*. Chicago: American Marketing Association.

Wheatley, Edward W. 1983. *Marketing Professional Services*. Englewood Cliffs, NJ: Prentice-Hall.

Wilson, Aubrey. 1972. *The Marketing of Professional Services*. London, NY: McGraw-Hill.

SPECIFIC SERVICES

Accounting

Denney, Robert W. 1983. *Marketing Accounting Services*. New York: Van Nostrand Reinhold Company.

Listman, Robert J. 1988. *Marketing Accounting Services*. Homewood, IL: Irwin.

Mahon, James J. 1982. *The Marketing of Professional Accounting Services: A Practice Development Approach*. New York: John Wiley and Sons.

Architecture

Coxe, Weld. 1982. *Marketing Architectural & Engineering Services*, 2nd ed. New York: Van Nostrand Reinhold Company.

Consulting

Connor, Richard A. Jr., and Jeffrey P. Davidson. 1990. *Marketing Your Consulting and Professional Services*, 2nd ed. New York: John Wiley and Sons.

Friedman, Lee A., and David H. Rothman. 1988. *Zero Defect Marketing: The Secrets of Selling High Tech Services*. Homewood, IL: Irwin.

Financial

Beitman, Hartford. 1990. *Financial Services Marketing: Proven Techniques for Advertising, Direct Mail, and Telemarketing*. Blue Ridge Summit, PA: Liberty Hall Press.

Donnelly, James H., Jr., Leonard L. Berry, and Thomas W. Thompson. 1985. *Marketing Financial Services: A Strategic Vision*. Homewood, IL: Irwin.

Seglin, Jeffrey L. 1988. *Marketing Financial Advisory Services: A Hands-On Guide*. Englewood Cliffs, NJ: Prentice-Hall.

David B. Zenoff (ed.). 1989. *Marketing Financial Services*. Cambridge, MA: Ballinger.

Health Care

American Hospital Association. 1982. *Planning Hospital Health Promotion Services for Business and Industry*. Chicago: American Hospital Association.

Cooper, Philip D., Karen M. Jones, and John K. Wong (eds.). 1984. *An Annotated and Extended Bibliography of Health Care Marketing*. Chicago: American Marketing Association.

Cooper, Philip D., and Larry M. Robinson. 1983. *Health Care Marketing Management: A Case Approach*. Germantown, MD: Aspen Systems Corp.

Flexner, William A., Eric N. Berkowitz, and Montague Brown. 1981. *Strategic Planning in Health Care Management*. Germantown, MD: Aspen Systems Corp.

Gerson, Richard F. 1989. *Marketing Health/Fitness Services*. Champaign, IL: Human Kinetics Books.

Kotler, Philip, and Roberta N. Clarke. 1985. *Marketing for Hospitals and Health Care Institutions*. Englewood Cliffs, NJ: Prentice-Hall.

Rubright, Robert, and Dan MacDonald. 1981. *Marketing Health & Human Services*. Rockville, MD: Aspen Systems Corp.

Washington, Rev. 1987. *Marketing Psychological Services: A Practitioner's Guide, Task Force on Marketing and Promotion of Psychological Services of the APA Board of Professional Affairs*. Washington, DC: American Psychological Association.

Winston, William J. (ed). 1985. *Marketing Ambulatory Care Services*. New York: Haworth Press.

______. (ed.). 1984. *Marketing Long-Term and Senior Care Services*. New York: Haworth Press.

______. (ed.). 1984. *Marketing for Mental Health Services*. New York: Haworth Press.

Government and Social Services

Crompton, John L., and Charles W. Lamb, Jr. 1986. *Marketing Government and Social Services*. New York: John Wiley and Sons.

Montana, Patrick J. (ed.). 1978. *Marketing in Nonprofit Organizations*. New York: Amacon Publishers.

Legal

Denney, Robert W. 1984. *How to Market Legal Services*. New York: Van Nostrand Reinhold Company.

Gilson, Christopher C., Linda C. Cawley, and William R. Schmidt III. 1979. *How to Market Your Law Practice*. Germantown, MD: Aspen Systems Corp.

George Fisk
Emory University

CHAPTER 13

GREEN MARKETING

Since managers are finding superior growth and profit opportunities by formulating "green marketing" programs, emphasis is on enhancement of side effects that can promote a sustainable society and diminution of negative environmental spillovers affecting health, safety, and quality of life. Green marketing is the new cornerstone on which a growing number of future marketing strategies will be predicated.

Green marketing considers marketing in terms of environmental impacts on customers, regulatory agencies, and other publics with which every management must interact. In the planning stage, strategic green marketing options that contribute to sustainable society goals from which the firm can extract profits are identified. In the implementation stage, elements of green marketing strategy are blended. Finally, in the control stage, benefit/cost performance is measured, monitored, and communicated to impacted publics. The goal of this process is to gain continuous improvement in cost/effectiveness of green marketing programs.

This analysis applies to market directed industrial democracies having well organized private sector marketing networks and infrastructures, and characterized by legal and social sanction systems for deterring activities deemed harmful to public and consumer interests.

Until recently, prevailing practice debited the future for environmental depletion costs. Now, as environmentalists point out, symbolic green marketing gestures will not deal with the mounting problems of environmental deterioration. Since the era of free resources is being replaced by the era in which all economic activity needs to serve the goals of a sustainable society, marketing responses to competitive challenges is no longer adequate unless it adopts a green marketing perspective. Marketing managers must acknowledge constraints on their freedom of action imposed by environmental costs: air is not free; water is not free; natural resources are not free. Someone pays for the social externalities of their use. Governments are increasingly insisting that those who incur environmental costs have to bear a share of spillover cost amelioration.

WHAT IS GREEN MARKETING?

Many managers believe that simply complying with legal requirements for environmental protection constitutes an adequate green marketing effort. Others acknowledge ill-defined social responsibilities, but have no coherent strategic orientation to green marketing. The viability of firms whose production and use of resources requires a vision of green marketing as "moving beyond the law and ahead of its industry" in order to design the green marketing strategies is considered here (Kleiner 1991). As innocuous as this sounds, it demands that managers implement a more proactive concept of green marketing that includes reformulation of products for recycling, reuse, or harmless disposal and it may require undertaking extensive research and development to replace or conserve the use of products with spillover environmental impacts.

In summary, four principles distinguish green marketing from non-green marketing:

1. Green marketers will not produce or distribute products yielding environmentally high impact side effects;
2. Green marketers will seek to enhance rather than harm the viability of the environment in designing, producing, and distributing products;
3. Green marketers will take a proactive rather than reactive stance toward legal requirements, seeking to exceed rather than simply to comply with legally mandated environmental requirements; and
4. Producers will help to share the social costs of whatever environmental spillovers are created by their manufacture and marketing of products for sale and use.

Impact Audit

Managers seeking to reap the advantages of green marketing as well as those hoping to avoid crippling social sanctions will find help in collecting information required to identify publics with whom they interact by completing an impact audit. Avoiding legal and social sanctions is not always as straightforward as eliminating offending practices revealed by an impact audit because programs introduced to replace environmentally objectionable operations must also be examined for spillover effects that impacted publics find objectionable.

The first step in developing a green marketing program is to assemble evidence on the nature of these marketing spillovers and the various publics receiving their effects, both beneficial and unwanted. Desirable spillovers can then be extended and those that are unwanted can be minimized.

To complete the first step, data are collected from news media, monitoring agencies, and surveys. Next they can be assembled into a spreadsheet (see Exhibit 1). Although Exhibit 1 does not define green marketing for any particular firm, it shows the kind of information needed to develop a green marketing program in light of the firm's marketing impact.

Every marketing manager needs to identify current and potential publics with power to exercise sanctions. For example, any product using plastics and chemicals can create a high level of community environmental pollution. Public reactions may range from ill will and refusal to work for the company to effective consumer boycott and

EXHIBIT 1. Matrix for Constructing an Impact Audit for Green Marketing by a Particular Firm

	Strategic Impact Area		
Public Receiving Spillover Impact	**Conservation of Resources**	**Recycling and Remanufacturing**	**Pollution Prevention and Abatement**
Community residents			
Consumers of the product			
Taxpayers			
Government agencies			
Internal publics: employees, stockholders			
Other publics			

stockholder action against management. Consequently, a basic question to be asked before developing green marketing programs is, "Who will face serious environmental consequences if a particular practice is undertaken by our marketing department?" Identifying publics who could be harmed sufficiently to mobilize sanctions against a particular firm should be attempted even if there is no assurance that they can be recognized in advance.

For example, one public seldom recognized are banks who can retroactively impose *greenlining,* a refusal to grant loans to firms seeking to use as collateral property containing previously created hazardous waste dumps (Hector 1992). Greenlining consists of refusing loans to firms believed to have been in violation of the Comprehensive Environmental Response, Compensation, and Liability Act. Public interest groups and governmental regulators can also impose additional sanctions such as boycotts and fines on firms whose past behavior has demonstrably polluted groundwater or soil. The severity of sanctions now aimed at firms whose processes pollute water, air, and soil are increasing to the point that by definition, such firms can no longer be assured of access to either private or public financial resources.

Illustrating the practice of examining proposed remedies for objections to existing practice is the experience of McDonald's in replacing styrofoam with plastic cups in fast food stores. McDonald's yielded to a letter writing campaign by school children. Instead of recycling polystyrene clamshell hamburger boxes and cups, it substituted paper containers in its restaurants. Prior analysis had convinced management that polystyrene was more recyclable than paper, but shortly after the decision to use paper containers was adopted, an impact analysis of single use paper versus polystyrene cups in *Science* revealed that the environmental benefits of the styrofoam cups relative to their costs exceeded the benefit/cost ratio of the paper cups that McDonald's used to replace the plastic (Hocking 1991). This case illustrates the need to evaluate benefits versus costs of proposed changes relative to the benefit/cost ratios of existing practice to determine if improvements could result from the changes proposed.

Using Exhibit 1 as a guide, impact audits may prove valuable in assessing the spillover benefits resulting from green marketing efforts. Firms new to green marketing may want to discover which of their strategies yield the most desirable consequences and those that are not sufficiently effective in advancing sustainable society goals to be worth the cost. The same procedure may be used for identifying publics who receive benefits. When benefits and costs are reasonably well identified, their ratios may often be estimated in monetary or physical terms before relating these results to social goals.

DESIGNING AND LAUNCHING A GREEN MARKETING STRATEGY

Once a firm knows its environmental benefits and costs with reasonable accuracy, it is in a position to design a *proactive green marketing strategy.* The initial step is to conceptualize what dimensions of green marketing imply for the firm. Every green marketing strategy contains elements of conservation, appropriate disposal of wastes and reuse, and remanufacture or recycling of resources incorporated in the good or service produced. Blending these strategic elements of green marketing is directly related to every firm's environmental benefit/cost impacts. For example, firms that produce large volumes of air pollution can put research and development effort into developing alternative energy sources. Firms responsible for generating large amounts of packaging waste can work on reducing packaging volume, recycling, or both, and so on.

Multiplying regulatory restrictions and sales losses befalling firms that fail to respect these requirements suggests that penalties will be even more severe in the future. For example, by ignoring the solid waste crisis to which they were contributing, plastics manufacturers faced enactment of laws requiring packaging taxes, degradability requirements, and other restrictions that raised the cost of making products with plastics (Sherman 1989).

Similarly General Motors has been warned in the press to stop reacting to environmentalist and regulatory concerns, and instead to anticipate future demands by performing beyond what was expected because it is environmentally necessary (Matthews 1992). Politically expedient resistance to raising automobile fuel economy standards on the grounds that it will only displace automobile workers and drive investment away from the industry provides an example of why business loses when it ignores environmental realities. In this example, diminishing oil supplies and the need to move to cost efficient alternative fuels and transportation methods is generating research on technological substitution for the automobile. Before the automobile industry drives itself out of business, it needs to anticipate future demands for transportation in a densely populated society.

Proactive Strategy

A proactive green marketing strategy begins by anticipating and understanding demand because marketing is said to begin with the consumer. The rising chorus of consumer complaints about needlessly wasteful packaging or shoddy products that have to be discarded because of their high costs of repair offer clues to future developments. Many consumers are eager to conserve—to save costs of energy consumption—because they are concerned about the environment as well as their pocketbooks. Yet they purchase new but unwanted replacement products because the market offers few viable alternatives.

Many synergies between consumer demand and supplier marketing effort can be achieved via green marketing. These range from the use of string bags to replace plastic and paper containers in grocery shopping to the development of vast recycling and pollution abatement programs. As in all marketing strategies, the first question to ask is, "What do consumers want us to do about this idea?" Proactive—in contrast to reactive—strategy seeks to raise the spillover benefit cost ratios of existing marketing programs. Procter & Gamble, an early target of environmentalists, was able to recoup and become the standout leader reported in an *Advertising Age* survey to find the most environmentally conscious marketer in the United States. By reducing the volume of diapers entering landfills, introducing nontoxic inks on its packages, reducing package wastes and related measures dictated by customer reactions, Procter & Gamble—once a leading contributor to the garbage problem—began instead to contribute to its solution (Chase 1991). By seeking proactively to establish contact with the press, environmentalists, and consuming publics, Procter & Gamble recovered its long-held leadership image in the public mind.

The merit of a proactive strategic posture is further exemplified by American Electric Power (AEP), long opposed to restrictions on air pollution contained in the Clean Air Act. Recognizing that public opinion supports energy conservation and restrictions on coal-burning power plants, AEP promoted a high efficiency light bulb, reclaimed strip mines for fishing and wildlife habitats, and spent over a billion dollars to retrofit its coal-burning plants with pollution control equipment to comply with Clean Air Act standards. AEP is also developing very high efficiency power generation and transmission facilities. Although progress is slower than many environmentalists desire, the basic change in management attitudes presages efforts to develop new kinds of electrical energy power plants (Wald 1992).

As noteworthy as a switch to a proactive "green" posture may be, the most persuasive case is based on the superiority of green marketing in raising marketing benefit/cost or effectiveness cost ratios. For example, "in a plot twist worthy of Hollywood, Green Crusader John Bryson became chairman of the nation's second largest utility. Now he plans to clean up the place," says Peter Nulty (1991). Immediately upon his appointment as chairman of Southern California Edison, Bryson reportedly initiated a "demand side" management program. By offering customers promotional deals on the purchase of energy-saving florescent bulbs and the purchase of energy-efficient replacement motors for industrial applications, Bryson eliminated the need to add a new 1,000 megawatt plant. Not only did he initiate conservation measures, but he cut emissions of carbon dioxide when Southern California Edison initiated construction of geothermal and other nonfossil fuel energy generation facilities. In one of the most environmentally vulnerable industries, Bryson successfully developed a coordinated program to get ahead of regulatory requirements, not simply to meet them.

Bryson and American Electric Power show that business, which frequently loses when it challenges legal expressions of the public interest, can also win its case when it garners public support and customer allegiance by serving environmental protection demands.

Nevertheless, although strong, the case for proactive green marketing must face the realities that green programs may increase cost. Yet, even here the correct emphasis is on the ratio of increased cost to increased benefit. If their costs exceed their benefits, the programs are rarely warranted on other grounds, but if their benefits exceed their costs, there are good grounds for pursuing green marketing programs.

Illustrating this point in the metal refining field is a highly visible polluter, Doe Run, the largest lead smelter in the United States. In this case the key public was internal: the company's employees. By anticipating where trouble could occur and reporting performance to employees, Doe Run was able to motivate pollution control performance improvements (Nulty 1991). Green marketing can induce behavior change in many firms when management includes in its communication network the employees responsible for correcting environmentally harmful practices.

BLENDING ELEMENTS OF GREEN MARKETING STRATEGY

Managing environmental impacts calls for three kinds of green marketing strategies:

1. Conservation of resources used in production and marketing;
2. Recycling or remanufacturing; and
3. Pollution prevention and abatement.

The blending of these three elements of green marketing strategy varies with the frequency and severity of spillover impacts not only between industries, but between and within firms in each industry.

Conservation

Conservation sounds like a way to lose customers and shrink sales. It may indeed produce these effects in the short run for specific products, but it is often a force for redefining the firm's product offering and even redefining its core competency and business mission. If marketing managers ask the question, "How do I help customers save money through conservation?" they may discover demands for new products unrecognized in the course of daily business.

Sparing use or substituting more plentiful for scarcer resources is a conservation strategy that must be used when technological means are unavailable to remove manufacturing and marketing bottlenecks. The most widely practiced means for inducing conservation behavior among customers is to raise prices. Another means is to change legal requirements requiring substitution of an environmentally less harmful material for a more harmful one: refrigerator manufacturers are routinely substituting natural gas for chloroflourocarbons formerly used as refrigerants. Similarly, substituting packaging that is biodegradable for packaging that is not, or enforcing returnable beverage container legislation by means of a bottle deposit requirement illustrates that conservation may also be achieved by legislatively mandated substitution.

Examples of technologically driven substitution appear in current energy conservation practice: "The world's houses and apartments consume one-sixth of all energy—more energy than all the oil Middle Eastern nations pump out of the ground every year . . ." (During 1988). If consumers could economize, they would retrofit homes with energy-saving equipment if the cost savings could be shown to exceed the direct cost. By installing insulation, retrofitting ceiling insulation and storm windows, and installing temperature control systems, high efficiency furnaces, air conditioners, and thermal window glass and shades, most households that have retrofitted to conserve energy have indeed saved on energy expenditure while creating new and growing opportunities for utilities and equipment suppliers alike.

Technology driven conservation strategy is applicable to a broad spectrum of substitute processes and materials. Selling benefits is standard marketing practice, but in the case of conserving scarce and expensive resources, it is far easier to demonstrate that the cost of operating inefficient energy systems exceeds the costs of installing high performance energy savings equipment.

Recycling

Reusing energy conserves it, so in this sense recycling can sometimes achieve conservation objectives. Recycling is a far-reaching concept that includes remanufacturing such complex products as engines and computers and renovating industrial structures. When they think of recycling, many people mention consumers returning glass bottles and newspapers for resource recovery and returning plastic bottles to collection centers. In several European countries, recycling centers in local neighborhoods and in market locales collect anything people discard for reprocessing. Recycling also requires reverse distribution channels for hazardous chemicals and other dangerous industrial wastes that are reprocessed.

Costs of recycling are currently an important barrier to its more widespread adoption. Many community efforts to recycle have been thwarted by lack of markets for recycled materials. When governments establish regulatory requirements such as beverage container return legislation, consumers recycle to retrieve their deposits. Some communities regularly recycle municipal garbage on a sufficiently large scale to earn revenues that may be deducted from their tax burdens. Simply securing contracts with local government for procurement of products manufactured from recycled materials is often sufficient to organize the continuous markets needed to attract recycled materials.

Environmentally proactive firms recognize that they can give products a second life by keeping them out of landfills. They develop new uses for products in joint ventures with trade associations or government and univeristy research centers. In the energy industry, for example, legally mandated electrical energy cogeneration permits utility customers to earn credit by feeding power back into the energy-producing plants by using steam to operate turbines or even by the generation of solar energy. Some households offer opportunities to marketers of solar panels and wind turbines by home energy generation, still a joke to most public utilities, but for a few consumers, a cost-effective means of conserving power.

Volkswagen and other automobile producers are beginning to seek ways to use their old recycled cars for resource recovery, including a product recovery charge to dispose of old automobiles and appliances. Chrysler has designed an experimental model specifically for easy disassembly and reuse or recycling of parts. Product recovery is also spreading into redesigned office buildings such as Audubon House in New York. Chutes running from floors above will separate and collect organic materials for composting, glass, newspapers, white paper, and mixed paper as well as aluminum cans and plastic containers (Muschamp 1992). Any producer whose product wastes are still entering landfills in large volume needs to consider what a proactive recycling or product recovery strategy could offer in the way of new marketing opportunities.

Eastman Kodak, for example, remanufactures disposable cameras from materials recovered from cameras returned for film processing.

Up to 85 percent of the materials in a disposable camera are reused in this way, enabling Kodak to charge substantially less than if materials were not recaptured for reuse.

Recycling of scarce water is also finding acceptance via green marketing. In areas such as California and Arizona, new landscaping opportunities are emerging for replacement of large green lawns by more climatically appropriate landscaping requiring far less water. In other cases, the newest approach is to relocate residential population into different living arrangements that provide only limited lawn area or to use "grey water" not fit for human consumption to water existing lawns.

The processing, exporting, remanufacturing, and marketing of urban wastes present new opportunities for creating new jobs, new firms, and industries (Renner 1992). To make the greatest contribution to green marketing, reductions in energy use equivalent and toxic waste releases via recycling should be considered by firms in industries where these problems have serious environmental consequences. Recycling can contribute to conservation efforts and to pollution abatement as well.

Pollution Control

Renner has shown that just three industries accounted for almost 85 percent of manufacturing toxic releases in 1987–88 (Renner 1992). When refining and coal products manufacturers are added to these three industries—chemicals, paper, and primary metal—the total rises to 88.2 percent of manufacturing toxic releases. Although the numbers vary slightly from year to year, this concentration of industries regularly accounts for the most industrial pollution.

For firms in the industries responsible for high proportions of pollution, the message is clear: develop nonpolluting manufacturing processes or curb pollution to gain access to new plant location sites. An economy-wide step for reducing pollution is to substitute development of new products that provide employment in industries other than those responsible for heavy pollution. This strategy is being pursued by economic development authorities in many communities now plagued by heavy pollution. Such proactive green marketing can save jobs, investments, and communities.

The two pollution control options of recycling wastes or conserving resource use have been increasingly recognized by product and packaging planners in marketing and engineering departments everywhere. Just as plastics manufacturers have developed recyclable plastics and auto manufacturers have developed recyclable auto parts, the oil industry has funded the development of oil-eating bacteria to consume ocean oil spills.

Removing the source of pollution is even more effective than developing processes for recycling wastes or pollution abatement, according to executives of Tetrapak, a major supplier of food and drug packages. Again conservation is one means for reducing pollution at the source. Another—favored by Tetrapak—is engineering pollution out of the manufacturing-use-disposal process. Both approaches have developed favorable cost/benefit ratios to meet environmental regulations.

GREEN MARKETING PROGRAM CONTROL

Improving Cost/Effectiveness

The search for continuous performance improvement consists of calculating revenues and costs of alternative courses of action, then comparing their relative profitability or their cost effectiveness in attaining desired goals. Thus green marketing is a search for improvements among environmentally desirable marketing practices to find those offering the highest ratios of profitability.

Green marketing program control takes place in four stages:

1. Measurement of social benefits and social costs of potentially profitable strategies are calculated;
2. Monitoring of program costs and benefits of programs that are implemented to obtain cost inputs and benefit outputs;
3. Calculation and evaluation of benefit/cost and cost/effectiveness ratios for ongoing programs; and
4. Choice of programs for further support or discontinuation is communicated to impacted publics concerned with the side effects they experience.

The statistical database for green marketing program control consists of unsought spillover costs and benefits. These are far more difficult to quantify and trace than such accounting concepts as cost of goods sold and average inventory turnover. Because environmental impacts of goods moving through distribution channels spill over on people not participating in market exchanges, measures must be created that are appropriate for specific environmental problems facing each firm.

However, difficult does not mean impossible. Four kinds of externalities can be monitored and fed back to management responsible for controlling green marketing activities. First, wastes resulting from consumption activities can be measured in either physical or monetary units. Externality costs ranging from the discard of packaging to the discard of used product and the economic costs of processing these wastes can be compared to offsetting benefits of employment, income, and tax revenues generated by production and marketing activities to assess economic benefit cost ratios for a particular activity. The results can be fed back to impacted publics via regulatory hearings, legal proceedings, public relations programs, and internal management controls.

Second, different kinds of environmental impacts can be identified for a time period during which wastes produced by manufacturing and marketing campaigns continue to present measurable problems in maintaining environmental quality.

More difficult to measure but important to assess are the gains from recycling or reuse and the foregone pollution or resource depletion resulting from conservation of energy, water, or materials. Cost savings earned by using retrofitted electrical appliances are one striking example of such numbers. These difficult assessments may warrant the employment of consulting engineers, economists, and ecologists. Extra costs of estimation may often be justified by their use in environmental impact statements to government as well as in public relations and for internal management control efforts as illustrated by the Doe Run smelting example cited earlier.

Third, quality of life benefits and costs for which social indicators are available can be constructed from social statistics such as health statistics or habitability indexes. Changes in the quality of life are often describable by consumers and residents of communities affected by the manufacturing and marketing activity being monitored. For example, coal-burning utilities not only affect the communities in which the coal is mined, but also communities in which the energy is consumed. Health statistics for residents of other communities exposed to the acid rain and pollution resulting from coal-fired electricity generation can reflect the long-run impact of coal on personal health histories. In nations of Eastern Europe, the incidence of health-related problems arising from coal burning is so high that a number of industrial communities are facing depopulation.

Green marketing program control can also lead to discontinuation of existing practices. Examples include infant death following improper use of the Nestle infant milk formula in developing nations and the sale of nonbiodegradable disposable diapers that overburden landfills. To deal with such social externality problems, quality of life impact audits can monitor package design and marketing managers can organize reverse marketing channels for the return of discarded products or to attract recycling via incentive programs.

A final type of benefit/cost measurement is one more familiar to marketers: the use of image studies to find out where the green marketing efforts of the firm have positioned the individual products or the firm itself in the minds of consumers. For example, while American Electric Power is winning recognition as a green marketer, products as innocent as the Ivory Soap trademark have called some groups into boycott activities against imagined cabalistic symbolism. Members of some communities vote their anxieties rather than their knowledge of a marketer's efforts to meet and exceed mandated legal environmental requirements. It may be less costly to discover such positioning perceptions by periodic market audits than to launch a public relations program to rectify an action sanctioned by aroused public opinion.

IS GREEN MARKETING WORTH THE COST AND EFFORT?

A *Wall Street Journal* article notes that "Green Product Sales Seem to be Wilting" (Reitman 1992). Recycling bins in many U.S. supermarkets and shopping centers are often neglected trash heaps whose content lacks market value. Cynical marketers can market nonbiodegradable packages as biodegradable or make other claims sure to be challenged by the government or by environmental activists. Evidence that interest in green products is lagging is traceable to their relatively high prices as the incomes of potential customers continue to shrink. Should green marketing be relegated to history as another passing fad?

Simply posing this question under current conditions in which environmental compliance efforts are at an unprecedented level and increasing in intensity and scope should give the potential investor confidence in investing in green marketing. It is evident that the impact of modern industrial technology on the environment has not been recognized in business circles to the same degree as in the scientific community. Although the power of renewal and revival of nature is clearly awesome, industrial processes are creating so many environmental problems that massive measures are required to retard their spillover consequences.

Green marketing that encourages consumers to be more efficient in their use of energy, water, and materials presents such an array of appealing marketing opportunities for growth and profit, that with a spread of concern for the environment, uncollected waste materials can be systematically reprocessed through reverse marketing channels once markets can be organized. (Exhibit 2 illustrates a few technically possible applications.)

Growing concern of local and central government for the consequences of contemporary industrial processes is driving many nations

EXHIBIT 2. Marketing Opportunities Resulting from Demands for Solutions to Environmental Problems

Problem	Marketing Opportunities
Contamination and exhaustion of landfill space	Recovery of gases, usable materials, and energy
Packaging litter and wastes	Reuse or elimination of packages
Creation of demand for environmentally high-impact products	Redesign of recyclable or reusable product components
Pollution of air, water, and soil	Development of nonpolluting fuels, fertilizers, water purification, and reuse systems

toward investment to exploit opportunities such as are portrayed in Exhibit 2. Recognition of the need for global cooperation on environmental issues is being driven by public demands for a habitable planet. Using the technologies of marketing, the vision of a sustainable growth society can certainly spur the search for new job and investment opportunities.

Business managers who maintain traditional accounting profit and loss perspective while rejecting the concept of social externalities risk more than the loss of their competitive vitality because new challenges to environmentally damaging business activity are tilting the social benefit/cost ratios toward adoption of green marketing (*Business Week,* October 19, 1992). Hence these practices are not just good citizenship, but represent far-sighted growth strategy as well.

REFERENCES

Business Week, "Tree Huggers vs. Jobs: It's Not That Simple," October 19, 1992, pp. 69, 71.

Dennis Chase, "P&G Gets Top Marks in an AA Survey," *Advertising Age,* January 29, 1991, p. 8.

Alan During, "Setting Our Houses in Order," *World Watch,* May-June, 1988, p. 27.

Gary Hector, "A New Reason You Can't Get A Loan," *Fortune,* September 21, 1992, pp. 107–112.

Martin B. Hocking, "Paper Versus Polystyrene: A Complex Choice," *Science* 251, February 1, 1991, pp. 504–505.

Art Kleiner, "What Does It Mean to Be Green?" *Harvard Business Review* 69, July-August, 1991, p. 38.

Jessica Matthews, "Build Us the Green Machine," *International Herald Tribune,* January 15, 1992, p. 7.

Herbert Muschamp, "Beyond Organic Architecture: The Office as Oasis," *The New York Times,* July 26, 1992, p. 26.

Peter Nulty, "Finding A Payoff in Environmentalism," *Fortune,* October 21, 1991, p. 61.

Peter Nulty, "Doe Run: How to Clean Up on the Cheap," *Fortune,* December 1991, p. 68.

Michael G. Renner, "Saving the Earth, Creating Jobs," *World Watch,* January-February, 1992, pp. 10–17.

Valerie Reitman, "Green Product Sales Seem to Be Wilting," *The Wall Street Journal,* May 18, 1992, p. B1.

Stratford P. Sherman, "Trashing a $150 Billion Dollar Business," *Fortune,* August 28, 1989, p. 64.

Matthew L. Wald, "A Coal Burning Utility That's Trying to Paint Itself Green," *The New York Times,* July 26, 1992, p. 4.

PART FOUR
MARKETING RESEARCH

PART FOUR

INTRODUCTION

This revision of the *Handbook* markedly increases its coverage of the topic of marketing research. The rise of the marketing concept, with its emphasis on meeting customer needs, made it an imperative in modern marketing to gather data about customers. Nowadays, in fact, many managers take that imperative for granted. Still, many others give lip service to the necessity for research but neglect to budget for it adequately. This neglect is an implicit overconfidence in one's knowledge of the marketplace that is likely to be challenged by the changes in the market with its proliferation into ever-novel segments. The mysteries of the economy and its impact on customers, the pressure of international trade and competition, the excitement of innovations, and the force of demographic shifts in age and ethnicity, for example, are all sources of problems and opportunities for marketing managers. Research that inquires into such matters in general and in the specific ways they affect one's company, product, brand, and use of the marketing mix is an important way to cope with the problems and to explore the opportunities.

Marketing research is basically a way of interacting with customers. The cliché expression,"the information highway," is an anticipation of a heightened future of such interaction. Travel on this highway is under way. The research field has burgeoned, and sophisticated managers recognize the necessity of developing and maintaining a flow of information to facilitate their decision making. Since the last edition of the *Handbook*, there has been a quantum leap in growth in both the kinds of information sought and the methods of acquiring that information.

Traditionally, the main kinds of research data have been gotten from conducting a simple survey: This method remains a standard one and is, of course, discussed in this part of the *Handbook*. Many organizations also need to keep constant tabs on sales and inventories, and there are routinized services that make such information available. There are also variations on these methods: special designs that answer complex questions by means of statistical techniques and experimental designs, and that take advantage of the rich technology provided by the computer and its many applications. The use and ramifications of quantitative methods are taken up in this part by several authors, indicating the role of research in relation to such topics as competition, advertising, customer satisfaction, and predicting market response. The recent widespread interest in database marketing focuses on a special example of how the marketing research field has taken advantage of the new means of gaining information. The new chapter on database marketing, by Robert Blattberg, is an outstanding contribution to our understanding of this subject.

Part Four also gives fresh attention to the topic of qualitative research. This form of marketing research is usually thought of as taking the form of "focus groups," which have become well-known, and are widely and casually used. Before focus groups came into such vogue, other qualitative methods were fashionable. Recently, the need for richer and more diverse kinds of insights into the marketplace has led to a revival of interest in them. These now include such approaches as one-on-one interviews, varieties of projective techniques, and ethnographic studies.

Arnold Corbin
Professor Emeritus of Marketing
Graduate School of Business Administration
New York University

Sol Dutka
President
Audits & Surveys

CHAPTER 14

WHAT IS MARKETING RESEARCH?

As more firms recognize the importance of operating with the marketplace as the central focus, the transcending importance of basing planning and decision making upon solid informational feedback from the marketplace is becoming increasingly apparent.

Hence there is a growing importance being accorded the research function by marketing management.

ROLE OF MARKETING RESEARCH

The role of marketing research, as the science of feedback, should be *to integrate, organize, and interpret the various data "flows" so as to provide marketing intelligence that will improve the quality of managerial decision-making throughout the firm.*

The primary orientation of marketing research must be toward the information needs of top management decision makers, although there is ample opportunity also to contribute to the solution of many problems that arise in every portion of the marketing system. But marketing research must define its own efforts in terms of the *needs of the marketing system,* rather than in terms of its problem-solving tools and capabilities, as it too often has in the past.

Marketing research should be regarded as a supplement to executive judgment. It provides the essential ingredient of feedback, both internal and external, and helps in narrowing the area for intuition and hunch. Yet it should not replace judgment seasoned by experience (and even within certain steps in the research process).

Relationship of Goals and Objectives to Research Strategy and Functions

The general marketing goals of a corporation determine its corporate marketing research strategy, both long term and short term.

Broadly speaking, corporate marketing research strategy makes its contribution to the achievement of these marketing goals by means of the following overlapping functions:

1. *Control:* Provides a corporation with measures of feedback on the marketplace and the company's specific performance within it.
2. *Developmental:* Provides the company with an organized method for seeking out new corporate opportunities and/or directions.

A company's marketing research strategy should be an optimization of its goals and the resources allocated to its marketing research functions. These resources consist of:

1. the corporate goals and objectives themselves;
2. the company's marketing goals and objectives;

3. the dollar resources it can allocate within this framework;
4. the manpower capabilities it has, or can obtain;
5. other facilities, such as computer capabilities; and
6. the corporate climate, that is, the organizational structure and environment within a company in which marketing decisions are made.

Figure 1 outlines the functions of corporate marketing research as it operates within the framework of corporate marketing goals. This diagram also includes the tactics by which these strategies are achieved.

The Developmental Function

The functions of marketing research can be separated into areas of developmental and control concerns. The developmental area includes the research and developmental processes that mediate between the possibilities offered by the state of technology and customer needs to bring new consumer and industrial products or services to the marketplace.

Marketing research operates in four major spheres in this area: in *need* discovery—to ferret out unsolved problems or unsatisfied needs that offer opportunities; in *concept testing*—designed to assay the feasibility of an idea to capitalize on a discovered opportunity; in *product-testing*—to measure the extent to which the suggestions of the concept tests are realized in the product; and in *test marketing*—to determine if the market is ready and willing to accept the new product as readily as the company's marketing and profit goals require.

The second part of the development process concerns tracking those characteristics of the customer—product, media, and related traits and behavior, which imply changing needs and desires that could be satisfied by new product development. This segment of effort serves to feed suggestions into a company's R&D laboratories.

The Control Function

While the *development* area focuses on the future and is concerned with bringing the company into it as smoothly and as profitably as possible, the *control* function is more concerned with seeing to it that the *present* does not get out of hand.

Control has two major subsections into which the marketing research operations are organized: *barometric measurements*—to gauge the corporation's progress toward the achievement of marketing and communications goals; and *long-range monitoring*—to examine changes in markets, consumer behavior, and needs insofar as these changes can affect the current product mix and stance of the company.

The investigation of specific problems uncovered by any of the barometric checks or through other sources is related to both develop-

FIGURE 1. The Functions of Corporate Marketing Research

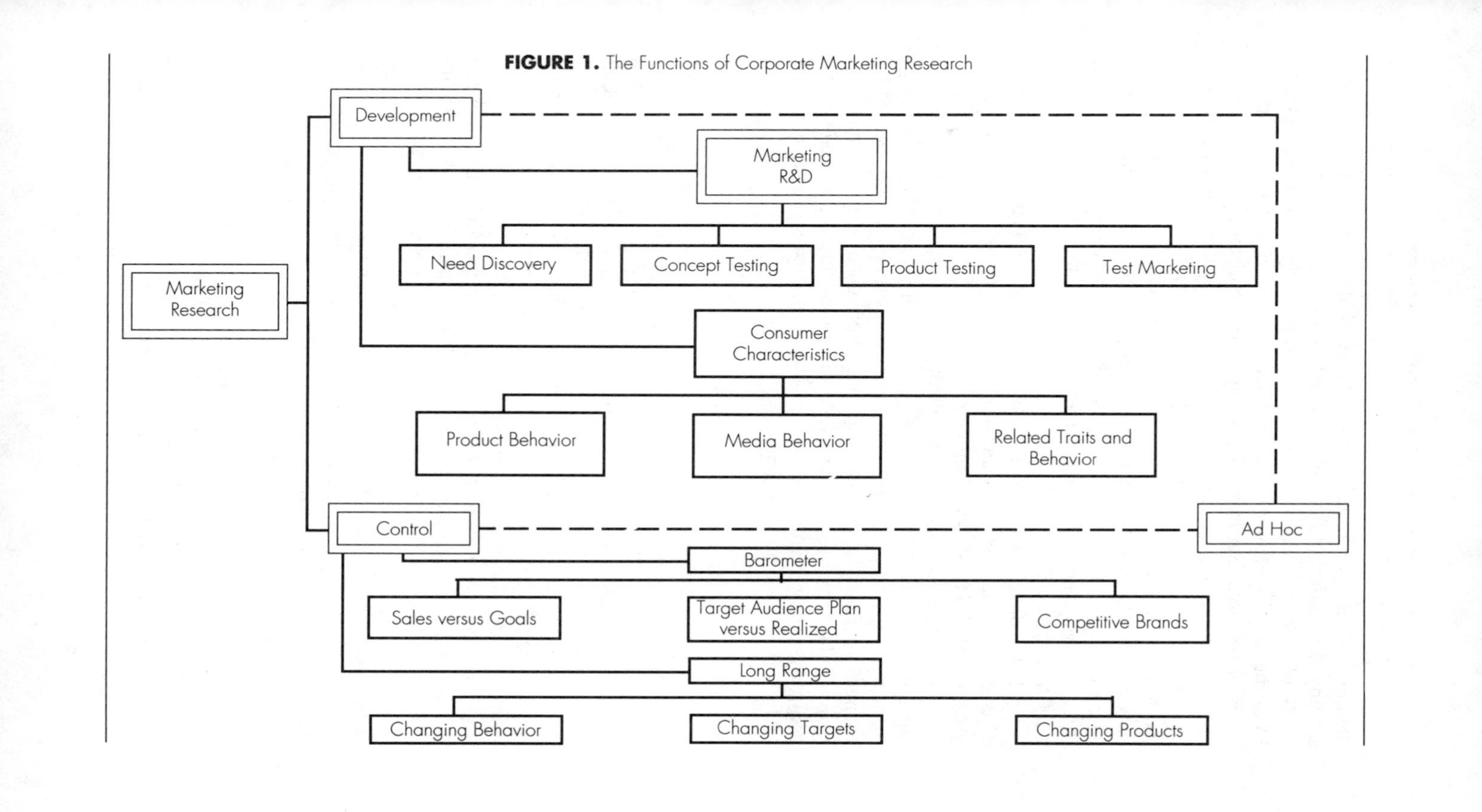

mental and control research to indicate that it may be effectively employed in either or both of these activities.

While these two areas are related, separating the control function from the developmental is a convenient way to view these two major types of research. For example, the appearance of an aerosol dispenser in a field previously committed to liquid formulations may be discovered in one of the barometric checks and trigger a study to investigate the relative appeals of the two formulations. This study is part of the developmental process in that its findings give direction to the design of a new product if management decides that such a new product is viable.

Development and *control* appear to be quite similar and differ only in emphasis.

In the developmental area, one of the concerns is the investigation of consumer characteristics, including *product behavior, media behavior,* and *related traits and behavior.*

Control's *long-range* assignment covers much the same areas—changing behavior, changing targets, and changing products. Development thus may focus on new product areas as they may be affected by changes in lifestyle, product use, and preference. Control may deal with similar concerns, but they tend to be directed to the products the company is now manufacturing and marketing and so serve as distant early warning signals of change.

Monitoring Environmental Changes

There is one area of change that can be monitored by either of these two main functions of corporate marketing research—that is, the changes in the environment that may affect the ways in which a company operates. The detection of signals of such change is difficult because the change may make itself felt in a number of ways.

Some examples that are common today are (1) concern with environmental pollution, thus affecting the kind of containers soft drink bottlers use—aluminum vs. steel cans, the returnable vs. the nonreturnable bottle; and (2) increasing informality of American eating habits, particularly among the young, making it more difficult for established hot drinks to thrive and easier for cold soft drinks to flourish. It is moot as to which function (control or developmental) would have discovered these changes first, but both certainly would play a role in discovering, diagnosing, and providing suggestions for solutions to the problems.

Acquisitions

There is, finally, an additional area of the development function—the problems of acquisitions—what kinds of product lines should be sought, whether they fit the company's objectives, and how effective they might be toward enhancing the corporation's growth and development. Regular barometric data on the sales of a corporation's products would also provide data on its distribution by type of outlet. The potential fit and effectiveness of a contemplated acquisition could then be determined by examining the degree of overlap of the candidate firm's product line and the corporation's existing product line. High distribution overlap would indicate that the company under consideration might be a better candidate for acquisition, all other things equal, than a company whose product line has low overlap.

By way of example, a company in the toiletry and cosmetic field was recently interested in acquiring another firm whose product line complemented its own. One of the anticipated benefits of such an acquisition was the fact that it could use its already existing sales force to distribute the products of the acquired company and eliminate the acquired sales force.

A relatively simple retail distribution study conducted prior to the final negotiations revealed that the retail distribution patterns of both companies had little overlap. The acquiring company, as part of its corporate distribution strategy, had set up its distribution patterns to distribute mostly in those areas outside of major metropolitan centers. Its marketing strategy was designed to dominate the cosmetic and toiletry counters in these particular areas.

The firm it was thinking of acquiring had for years used television advertising in major metropolitan areas and had set up its distribution accordingly. Thus, the potential saving that would have been effected by the elimination of one sales force would not have come about.

Both of the two areas mentioned above—environmental analysis and corporate development (acquisitions)—represent examples of the way in which progressive companies are enlarging the scope of the corporate marketing research function. They illustrate the "macro" use of research to serve the fact-finding needs that flow from ever-widening corporate concerns in today's dynamic business world. Here, the research function is not narrowly confined, in a "micro" sense, to specific projects in marketing. Quite the contrary, in the "macro" sense, research strategy may be effectively deployed to improve decision making in nonmarketing functions of the company.

NATURE AND SCOPE OF MARKETING RESEARCH

In seeking ways to define marketing research comprehensively and meaningfully, it is not easy to avoid a discussion of Marketing Research—Is It Art or Science? The generally accepted polarized starting points for the protagonists in such a discussion appear to be either the acceptance of art as completely the product of the emotional storage of an individual or science as a cold, intellectual, rational display.

Further, art is taken as synonymous with creativity, and science with logic. But in the philosophy of science we find that most scientists have abandoned this attempt at compartmentalizing the resources of the mind, and have come to appreciate that both areas exist and serve each other in meeting the individual's needs to know.

Marketing research, just as any other branch of the behavioral sciences, can earn its place as a scientific discipline if its procedures can be properly classified as scientific.

First, then, consider the concept of scientific method. This involves a sequence of steps whose starting point is not always fixed. A problem, a question, or just curiosity, leads to a tentative explanation of an observed phenomenon. This explanation, usually labeled "hypothesis," dictates a form of test that will permit the verification or rejection of the hypothesis. Data are then collected to permit the test to be carried out. The verification of the hypothesis leads to additional experiments, repeated verification, if possible, and the label of "law." Rejection of the hypothesis leads to further thought concerning an explanation, adoption of a new hypothesis, collection of additional data, and so on.

Considering these elements of *hypothesis, data collection, testing,* and *generalization* and how this plan relates to marketing research, one must deal with two factors:

1. the role of creativity in scientific research; and
2. the lack of similarity between the behavioral (social) sciences and the physical sciences.
   a. the nature of the test subjects; interactions between observed and observer;
   b. the time dimension in behavioral research; observations time-dependent in the behavioral science, time-independent in the physical sciences; and
   c. the fact that physical laws are more advanced and sophisticated than social laws.

The physical sciences, with a long tradition of reliance on mathematical techniques and with a history of dealing with the immutability of nature, have been held up as standards of comparison for the "scientific-ness" of social and behavioral research. However, once one recognizes the basic differences between physical and behavioral research, one ceases to make comparisons with the one as the standard and the other as striving to achieve the standard. Instead, the standard should be the principle of scientific method as sketched briefly above. The continued progress of behavioral and marketing research will depend on adherence to these principles, not with how closely one can adapt specific techniques (for example, the differential calculus) to problems of behavioral research.

Differences between Market Research and Marketing Research

The difference between market research and marketing research is more than a semantic one. They can be distinguished on at least two substantive grounds. In the first place, they differ in scope. Market research is research about the market: its size, composition, structure, and so on. In contrast, marketing research is research about any problem in marketing, not just the market; for example, in the area of a salesperson's compensation or channels of distribution. Thus, the term "marketing research" is much broader in scope, and is therefore preferable.

Another basis for distinction is that market research emphasizes measurement; it concentrates on quantitative dimensions. In contrast, marketing research emphasizes creativity; it concentrates on qualitative aspects. It seeks to discover unsatisfied consumer needs and wants; it tries to ferret out unsolved problems in the marketplace, the so-called "holes" in the market that offer significant opportunities for bringing innovation and change to it. The objective is to disturb the equilibrium in the market in the company's favor. The resulting increase in market share redounds to the innovator as a reward for detecting problems, frustrations, difficulties or dissatisfactions, and then providing solutions that are perceived by the market as true solutions. This is the heart of the developmental type of research referred to previously. It focuses on what could be, rather than on what is.

A few examples of this highly creative use of marketing research to seek holes in the market may be in order at this point. The opportunity which U.S. Time Company capitalized on so successfully was discovered through the application of market segmentation techniques, based not on demographic criteria, but on more sophisticated and relevant criteria, such as value. The research revealed "three distinct segments, each representing a different value attributed to watches by each of three different types of consumers."[1] Yet the principal companies making better watches were inadvertently concentrating exclusively on only one of these three segments, thus "leaving the bulk of the market open to attack and exploitation" by U.S. Time Company through its low-priced line of Timex watches.

The dramatic and successful entry of Xerox into the copying market in the late '50s is another classic example of the use of creative marketing research to discover and develop a huge, unexploited market opportunity. The two principal companies then in the market, Kodak (Verifax) and 3M (Thermofax), not only had inferior technology but required users to purchase their machines outright and to use only paper made exclusively by them. Defined this way, the market for copying machines (and copying) remained relatively small. If Xerox had used mere market research, it might have concluded, "The market is too small; why bother?"

However, its marketing research revealed the true potential for a company that could bring real innovation to the market, not only in technology (xerography), but in marketing strategy as well. It said, "We'll lend you our machine, and you can use any paper you wish!" The wedding of superior technology and superior marketing produced a striking synergistic effect; when copying was made easy, the market exploded! Xerox was not interested in what the market was but what it could be as a result of the constructive contribution Xerox could bring to it.

These examples are but two of many that could be cited to demonstrate the tremendous potential underlying the creative use of marketing research to ferret out problems in the marketplace, and thus provide market-oriented guidance for the internal development of viable solutions. The objective is to find markets seeking products, rather than the reverse, which frequently characterizes the routine type of market research.

THE MANAGER-RESEARCHER RELATIONSHIP

The success of marketing research efforts in a company is dependent on the maintenance of a healthy, continuing relationship between the decision makers who use research and those who do the research. In many companies, this relationship is far from ideal.

The Researcher's Point of View

C. Theodore Smith of the American Telephone & Telegraph Company, in a study conducted for The Conference Board polled some 66 members of the Board's Council of Marketing Research Directors about the problems they encounter in dealing with their management associates. His findings indicated that the single thing that bothered researchers most and that occurred most frequently was that of not thinking of the researcher as a full member of the team. The next three complaints cited, in order of frequency and irritation, were (1) not using research findings effectively, (2) not allowing enough time to do a good job, and (3) not taking the research approach seriously. He noted, too, a tendency to attack findings at variance with preconceived notions and to use research to prove a point, rather than to find facts.

Suggestions for Improving the Relationship

It is clear that there is work to be done on both sides. A continuing partnership relationship needs to be built on each partner's understanding and to contribute to the needs and functions of the other. For example, the manager, in addition to defining the problem correctly, specifying the information needed to resolve it, and indicating how the results of the research will be used also can make other useful inputs during the research process. He or she can suggest sources for obtaining information, comment on early data feedback, specify the most useful form of report, and so on.

Another means for improving the relationship is to distinguish between the technical and the management aspects of the research functions. Because the skills of the professional specialists who actually design or do the research studies are quite distinct from the skills required to understand the needs of management and to communicate the results in management terms, there seems to be a niche for a research generalist who can act as a catalytic agent between the two groups and work effectively with both of them. The goal of such a research manager should be to assure that the technological weapons of research are effectively concentrated on the right targets and that the research produces informational feedback framed in management's terms of reference and oriented toward improvement of its decision-making process.

To facilitate this process, the marketing research manager should be a regular, fully-accredited member of the marketing team. This implies that he or she should be considered not only as a research specialist who can make useful input to the information base for planning, but also as a marketing generalist who can contribute to the decision making of the marketing team. Thus that individual can help formulate objectives, strategies, and action programs with respect to products and markets, within the framework of overall corporate goals and objectives.

Such recognition of the marketing research person as a fully equal member of the marketing team with peers in the other marketing functions will go far to alleviate a principal source of frustration.

Far more effective research planning will result if the research manager is regarded as a marketing expert, as well as a researcher. If he or she is accorded this status and does participate in the running and decision making of the marketing operation, that person can gain a truly first-hand appreciation of what is going on in the marketplace with customers and their marketing executives, with customers' customers, and so on down the line.

Operating at these "grass-roots" levels, he or she will be stimulated to generate research projects to meet the needs of the operation as they are detected, based on first-hand evidence, instead of waiting solely for second-hand requests from others. His or her role in initiating research thus changes from a passive one to an active one. He or she gains a greater insight into research needs and opportunities and therefore can plan and program research activities with greater realism and effectiveness on a longer-range time scale and within a broader frame of reference.

This approach to planning research is in strong contrast to the present situation in many companies where marketing research is managed by crisis rather than by objective, and where it is set up as a purely staff activity on the 19th floor to which marketing executives address their "Request for Research" forms and hope that someone sometime will get around to working on them.

Problems and Limitations

While there are differences among companies in the way marketing research resources are strategically deployed, one might venture a few generalizations that characterize a number of companies today. The main criticism to be leveled at current use of research is its narrowness in terms of time span, scope of activities, and technique.

Preoccupation with the Present

In the first place, there is a tendency for research to be preoccupied with maintaining the momentum of the present: doing more of what we are already doing, putting out "fires," responding to emergency requests for studies; in other words, concentrating on urgent, day-to-day operational projects. Relatively little time is devoted to integrating current activities with a long-range strategic research plan for optimizing its potential contributions to the achievement of corporate goals and objectives. The strategic forest is being lost while excessive attention is accorded the tactical trees. The emphasis tends to be more on "doing the thing right" than asking "Are we doing the right thing?"

A typical corporate research budget reinforces this conclusion concerning the obsessive concern with today at the expense of "what we might do tomorrow." This company manufactures health and beauty-aid products, with a total sales volume of over $100,000,000 and an advertising budget of $15,000,000. Its total budget for market research is $275,000. Of this amount, $200,000 (or 73%) is spent on only one kind of barometric research, that is, sales data on its own and its competitors' products.

If the setting of goals and the direction of efforts to achieve these goals makes any sense, then the allocation of a good share of the budget for the measurement of the rate of goal fulfillment also makes sense. But the failure to allocate funds to the other control, as well as to the developmental research functions, is dangerous in an age when change is dominant. One characteristic of this acceleration of change is that the turnover of things in our lives grows ever more frantic.

Excessively Narrow Scope

The scope of research also tends to become excessively narrow in many companies in at least two senses. In the first sense, researchers often concentrate more on collecting isolated facts, or bits and pieces of information, than on building an integrated body of knowledge relevant to the broad, long-range problems and strategic decisions facing management. One of the ironies of the large investment made by so many companies in marketing research is that the results of this effort do not become part of a systematic body of knowledge in the company that can be useful in judging the viability of new ideas. This data bank, which could serve as a valuable first screening for the evaluation of suggestions, can be expected to come closer to reality as computer storage and information-seeking algorithms become more sophisticated and available.

In the second sense, the bulk of the specialized individual studies is preoccupied with solutions to *ad hoc* crises, or with providing barometric feedback measurements on the marketplace and the position of the company's entries in it. They tend to focus on the descriptive or the "what is" more than on the creative or the "what could be." As Alfred Politz emphasized, ". . . to be creative, research must be predictive . . ."

Admittedly, the developmental, R&D type of research that seeks to discover unsatisfied needs is much harder to do, but it can be potentially much more rewarding in terms of opportunities for quantum leaps forward in market penetration, sales, and earnings growth. Unfortunately, it often receives too small a share of total marketing research resources; the scales of the balance tend to tip heavily in favor of the more applied type of *ad hoc* research. Perhaps if the wider perspective of the systems approach to research planning and control presented below is adopted, this imbalance in the deployment of research resources may be redressed and a more effective mix achieved.

Looking Inward to Elegance of Techniques

Finally, there is a tendency for researchers to look inward too much toward refining their techniques, and to look outward too little toward providing useful inputs to the solution of problems faced by managers or to discovering new opportunities in the marketplace. Too many researchers look for ways to bend the problem to the technique of the day than to view the problem and its solution as the goal of the research.

These myopic love affairs with new techniques tend to isolate "ivory tower" research specialists from the mainstream of management, thus creating a gulf that militates against the optimum utilization of research resources. However, management sometimes encourages this tendency by its compartmentalizaton of research and by its failure to recognize the role of research as part of corporate marketing strategy.

Implications

What is a viable approach to dealing with some of the difficulties presented above? The solution may well lie in establishing a total, long-range strategic research plan for the company, for each of its organizational components, and for its principal products and markets.

As Adler recommended some time ago, "This program would be used to guide the design of individual studies so that they not only contribute knowledge for the short term but also contribute to the evolution of a unified body of information needed to implement the marketing concept over the long term."[2]

In designing such a long-range strategic *research* plan, the developmental steps should be integrated with those applicable to the strategic *marketing* plan, which in turn should be tied to and flow from the strategic *business* plan for the company as a whole, and for each of its major components.

The planning and control process should embrace the following steps.[3]

1. Formulate specific long-term marketing objectives, based on long-term corporate objectives.
2. Spell out in detail the policies and programs required to achieve the marketing objectives.
3. Identify roadblocks in the way of attaining objectives and specify where further information or research is needed.
4. Define what and how marketing research can contribute to the discovery of unsatisfied needs, to problem solving, and to information gathering.
5. Get inputs and commitments from all members of the marketing team regarding objectives, strategies, plans, and programs.
6. Formulate a priority order and a timetable for the research projects agreed on by the team.
7. Allocate the necessary funds, personnel, and facilities for implementing the research program according to the weights decided by the team.
8. Include provisions for checkpoints and yardsticks for measurement, feedback, control, analysis of variations from plan, and plan revisions during the implementation process in order to "close the loop" on the system.

NOTES

1. Daniel Yankelovich, "New Criteria for Market Segmentation," *Harvard Business Review,* Vol. 42 (March-April, 1964), pp. 83–90.
2. Lee Adler, "Phasing Research into the Marketing Plan," *Harvard Business Review,* Vol. 38 (May-June, 1960), pp. 113–122.
3. Ibid.

SUGGESTIONS FOR FURTHER READING

Lee Adler and Charles S. Mayer, *Managing the Marketing Research Function* (Chicago: American Marketing Association, 1977).

Tom Suraphol Apaiwongse, "Factors Affecting Attitudes Among Buying-Center Members Toward Adoption of an Ecologically-Related Regulatory Alternative: A New Application of Organizational Theory to a Public Policy Issue," *Journal of Public Policy & Marketing*, Vol. 10 (Fall 1991), pp. 145–160.

Danny N. Bellenger, et al., *Qualitative Research in Marketing* (Chicago: American Marketing Association, 1976).

George B. Breen, *Do-It-Yourself Marketing Research* (New York: McGraw-Hill, 1977).

John P. Dickson and Douglas L. MacLachlan, "Fax Surveys? Study Finds the Time May Be Right for Business Research," *Marketing Research: A Magazine of Management & Applications*, Vol. 4 (September 1992), pp. 26–30.

Ronald A. Fullerton, "The Art of Marketing Research: Selections from Paul F. Lazersfeld's 'Shoe Buying Zurich' (1933)," *Journal of the Academy of Marketing Science*, Vol. 18 (Fall 1990), pp. 319–327.

Thomas S. Gruca and Charles D. Schewe, "Researching Older Consumers," *Marketing Research: A Magazine of Management & Applications*, Vol. 4 (September 1992), pp. 18–24.

John G. Keane, "Some Observations on Marketing Research in Top Management Decision Making," *Journal of Marketing*, Vol. 33 (October 1969), pp. 10–15.

Arthur Koestler, *The Act of Creation* (New York: The Macmillan Company 1964).

M.H.B. McDonald, "Technique Interrelationships and the Pursuit of Relevance in Marketing Theory," *Quarterly Review of Marketing*, Vol. 15 (Summer 1990), pp. 1–11.

David D. Monieson, "Intellectualization in Macromarketing: A World Disenchanted," *Journal of Macromarketing*, Vol. 8 (Fall 1988), pp. 4–10.

James H. Myers and A. Coskun Samli, "Management Control of Marketing Research," *Journal of Marketing Research*, Vol. 6 (August 1969), pp. 267–277.

James H. Myers and Richard R. Mead, *The Management of Marketing Research* (Scranton, PA: International Text Book Company, 1969).

Terrence V. O'Brien, "Data Management and Analysis," *Marketing Research: A Magazine of Management & Applications*, Vol. 4 (September 1992), pp. 58–60.

Anastasios Papathanasis and Christopher Vasillopulos, "Task and Job: The Promise of Transactional Analysis," *American Journal of Economics & Sociology*, Vol. 50 (April 1991), pp. 169–181.

J. Paul Peter, "Realism or Relativism for Marketing Theory and Research: A Comment on Hunt's 'Scientific Realism,' " *Journal of Marketing*, Vol. 56 (April 1992), pp. 72–79.

Melvin Prince, "Choosing Simulated Test Marketing Systems," *Marketing Research: A Magazine of Management & Applications*, Vol. 4 (September 1992), pp. 14–16.

N. Mohan Reddy, "Defining Product Value in Industrial Markets," *Management Decision*, Vol. 29 (1991), pp. 14–19.

Alvin Toffler, *Future Shock* (New York: Random House, 1971).

Lewis C. Winters, "International Psychographics," *Marketing Research: A Magazine of Management & Applications*, Vol. 4 (September 1992), pp. 48–49.

Gordon A. Wyner, "Uses and Limitations of Conjoint Analysis—Part II," *Marketing Research: A Magazine of Management & Applications*, Vol. 4 (September 1992), pp. 46–47.

George M. Zinknan, Marilyn Y. Jones, Sarah Gardial, and Keith K. Cox, "Methods of Knowledge Development in Marketing and Macromarketing," *Journal of Macromarketing*, Vol. 10 (Fall 1990), pp. 3–17.

G. David Hughes
Burlington Industries Professor of Business Administration
University of North Carolina
Chapel Hill, North Carolina

CHAPTER 15

COMMUNICATION RESEARCH: CONTINUOUS MEASUREMENT INSTRUMENTS

Marketing managers want to know if their advertising, personal selling, and public relations copy and execution will meet their communication goals. This is a difficult question because most of these media provide a continuous stream of stimuli. Diagnosing the effective and ineffective parts of the stimulus stream can be accomplished three ways. First, subjects can be asked to recall scenes, but their recall error is high due to faulty memory and recency effects. Second, the commercial can be stopped and subjects asked their opinion after each scene, but this destroys their thought processes and therefore the total effect of the commercial. The third approach uses response devices that allow subjects to respond continuously, in real time, without interruption from the researcher. Some systems feed subjects' responses back to them immediately for their explanations.

A Brief History of Continuous Instruments

Instruments for continuous research began with Dr. Frank Stanton of CBS and Professor Paul F. Lazersfeld of Columbia University, who were interested in analyzing radio, and later television, programs. Their "Program Analyzer" was a modified polygraph in which a paper tape moved under eleven paired sets of pens (Peterman 1940). Each subject held two buttons—one for each hand. The subjects pressed the green button in the right hand if they liked a part of a program and the left, red button if they disliked it. The analysis consisted of summing the likes and dislikes on the paper tracing. The system could examine eleven subjects at a time. Variations of this two-button system still exist today. Such systems were installed in theaters and were used to test television programs, commercials, and movies. CBS had its own theater and made such tests until the late 1980s. Tests of the reliability and validity of these measures are difficult to find. In 1940, Horace Schwerin did an exploratory study of the reliability of the Lazersfeld-Stanton system by correlating across two groups the linking rankings of sections of a program. There were nineteen subjects in each of the two groups. He found correlations of 0.90.

Dr. George Gallup, who founded the Gallup Poll, developed a system that was used in the late 1930s to edit the movie *Gone with the Wind.* It was also used to measure audience reactions to the Kennedy-Nixon debate.[1] The system was abandoned by Gallup and later taken over by a company that turned it into a theater testing operation.

Theater systems, with subjects pushing buttons, turning a dial, and moving pens across a polygraph remained until the 1980s when microcomputer technology made its impact. The systems became portable and enabled more sophisticated analysis. The response devices now vary. The PEAC/Viewfacts system uses a five-button device. McCollum/Spielman Research uses a similar device. A dial-type device is used in the Perception Analyzer, from Columbia Information Systems, and by the Preference Analyzer II system by ORTEK Labs. QuickTally uses a keypad and a slider for continuous evaluations. The SpeedBack system from Decision Labs, Ltd., has a full alphanumeric keypad, a one-to-one hundred dial, and a two-line screen (Fenwich & Marshall 1991; Porado 1989).[2]

Not all continuous measurement procedures use electronic devices. The warmth that is elicited by a television commercial has been tested by having subjects move a pencil down a page at a constant speed while watching the commercial (Aaker, Stayman, Hagerty 1986). Young and Robinson (1989) examined the "rhythms" of recall by having subjects first view a commercial and then sort pictures from scenes according to their recall. The frequencies of recall determine the shape of the curve for the group.

All of these measurement approaches require a conscious response by the subject. Other continuous measures have used continuous, unconscious, physical responses, such as skin resistance, heart rates, breathing rates, eye tracking, the dilation of the pupil, and analysis of brain waves. For example, Thorson and Lang (in press) used phasic decelerative heart rate patterns to determine the effect of videographic insertions when a lecture consisted of a talking head. These insertions enhanced the learning of familiar material and seemed to inhibit the learning of unfamiliar material. The authors see clear applications for advertising strategies: "These results extend the idea that attention to television exhibits limited attentional capacity, and suggests that there is a trade-off between people's ability to attend to structural and informational aspects of the television stimulus."

Inner Response, Inc., uses electrodermal measures to test commercials. It found that ". . . even as strong a spokesperson as Bill Cosby will not hold an audience's attention, if the basic message is not of interest to them."[3]

The Department of Advertising Research at Vienna University (Austria) uses a combination of conscious and unconscious response devices. Unconscious devices include eye movement tracking, electrodermal measures, and measures of breathing rates. In the conscious category, they have two devices for the program analyzer: the two-button approach and a joy stick. They also use a hidden camera to track behavior while watching television and a system known as the campagnon test. In this test, the subject pages through a magazine that is on a mirror-top table. A hidden camera records the pages of the magazine and eye movement as reflected in the table.[4]

INSTRUMENT RELIABILITY AND CONSTRUCT VALIDITY

Reliability

To have confidence in any measurement system we need to know if it is reliable—that is, if it will give similar results across similar groups and if it will give similar results after repeated measures on the same group. There have been very few reliability tests of continuous response devices reported in the literature. There was the Schwerin test noted in the previous section that was done in 1940. In 1990 Hughes and Lennox (284–288) conducted a study primarily to test the reliability of the SpeedBack(R) system. They had a test group of fifty-two persons watch television commercials and a weather report the first week, dialing on a scale of one to one hundred, with measures in fractions of a second. One week later, this group repeated the experiment along with a control group of fifty-one persons. The curves for the test group during the first week were plotted over their curves during the retest the second week and, except for advertising wearout and wearin, which will be discussed, the two curves were very close. The first-week test group curve was very close to the control group the second week. Thus the authors concluded that for both a test-retest and a matched-group test, the system had high reliability.

In 1991 Fenwick and Rice reported a reliability test of the PEAC system, which had measured responses in either two- or three-second intervals. Using data that had been generated for client tests, they did an *ad hoc* match of groups according to age and sex. A repeated measures analysis of variance found that only one in the ten cases examined had significantly different traces. The authors concluded that the matched sample design demonstrated high reliability.

Construct Validity

Construct validity occurs when a new instrument and familiar ones are used in the same experiment and their measures are correlated in predictable ways. The SpeedBack(R) system was subjected to two tests of construct validation with very encouraging results (Boyd & Hughes 1991; Plum, Cohen, Hughes 1992). This kind of validation is important to academics, but marketing practitioners want to know if the instrument is valid if it will help develop better strategies.

MANAGEMENT APPLICATIONS

Diagnostics

One of the primary uses of continuous measures is to diagnose the copy and the execution of a television commercial. Exhibit 1 illustrates such an application among eighty primary grocery shoppers who used any product in the category three or more times per week. They responded using the PEAC system using five buttons. The scale was very negative (VN), slightly negative (SN), neutral (N), slightly positive (SP), and very positive (VP). Measures were made every two seconds, so there were fifteen measures for the thirty-second commercial.[5] The first three measures revealed a positive response to the music, but the next two measures in the seven-to-ten second segment showed negative responses toward the unrealistic way that the woman acted while cooking. The next two measures (eleven to fourteen seconds) showed positive responses to the ingredients and the possible reaction of the children. The fifteen-to-twenty-two second segment revealed negative responses to the portrayed behavior of the children. In the last segment, the mother seems to be back in charge and the children seem to like the product, ending the commercial on a happy note. Given this diagnostic, the creative staff can develop ways to end the commercial on an even higher note. For example, they could replace the negative interaction of the mom and kids in the fifteen-to-twenty-two second segment with a segment on the family liking the end results.

How do heavy drinkers, light drinkers, and nondrinkers evaluate a commercial? This question is addressed in Exhibit 2. Sharp's, a nonalcoholic beer, had just been introduced and two fifteen-second commercials were being aired. Subjects were eighty-seven seniors at a southeastern university that prided itself in its beer drinking habits. Subjects viewed the commercials twice, first dialing along a favorability scale and then along a usefulness scale.[6] The SpeedBack(R) system took measures every one-fifth of a second on a scale of one to one hundred, with fifty as neutral. The system produces seventy-five measures for the fifteen-second commercials and one hundred fifty for thirty-second ones, thereby catching subtle responses. The students also saw an Army recruiting commercial (fifteen seconds) and a Bud Lite beer commercial (thirty seconds), thereby providing a comparative norm from a well-known, effective beer commercial. Prior to seeing the commercials, the subjects used the keypad on the SpeedBack(R) system to enter their demographics, including how frequently they drank beer—weekly, monthly, or not at all—which created three subgroups for the following.

In Exhibit 2, we see that all three groups dialed downward at the start of the two Sharp's commercials, responding negatively to the graphics. The nondrinkers continued to dial downward, but four

EXHIBIT 1. The Viewfacts PEAC System Sample Diagnostic Analysis

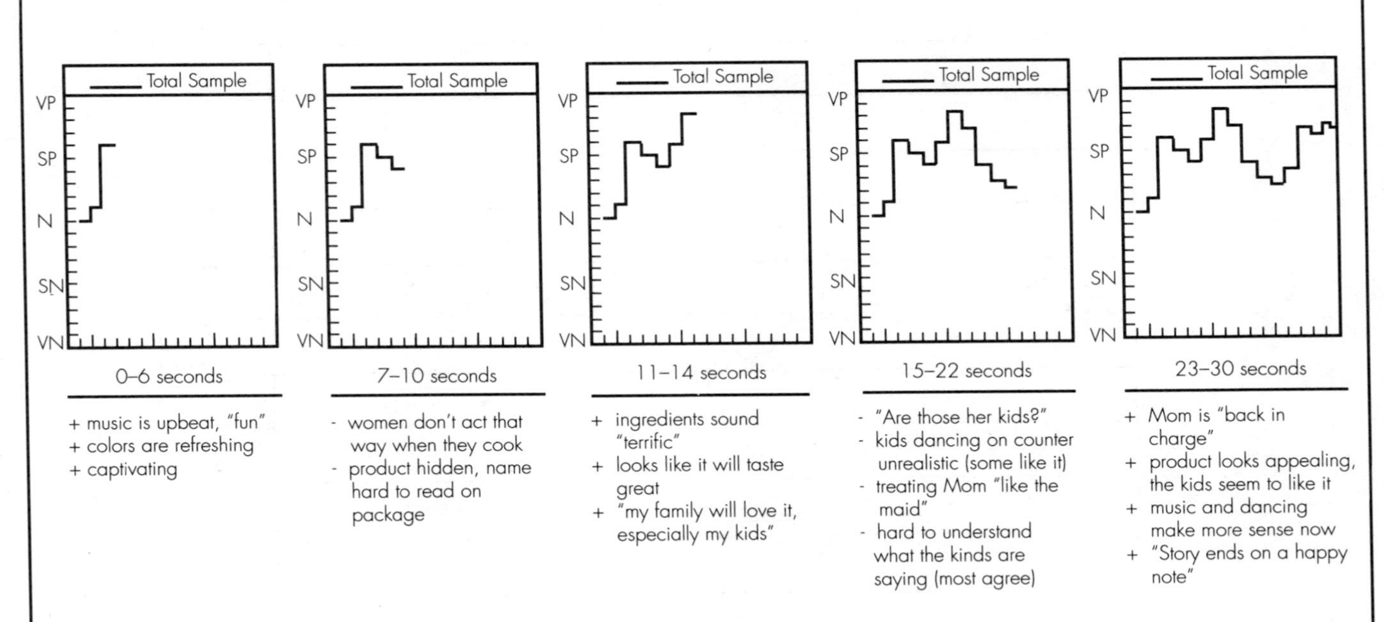

Key: The horizontal axis hatch marks indicate intervals of two seconds.
The five points on the vertical axis run from very positive on top to neutral in the center to very negative at the bottom.

EXHIBIT 2. Cognitive Evaluation of Beer Ads

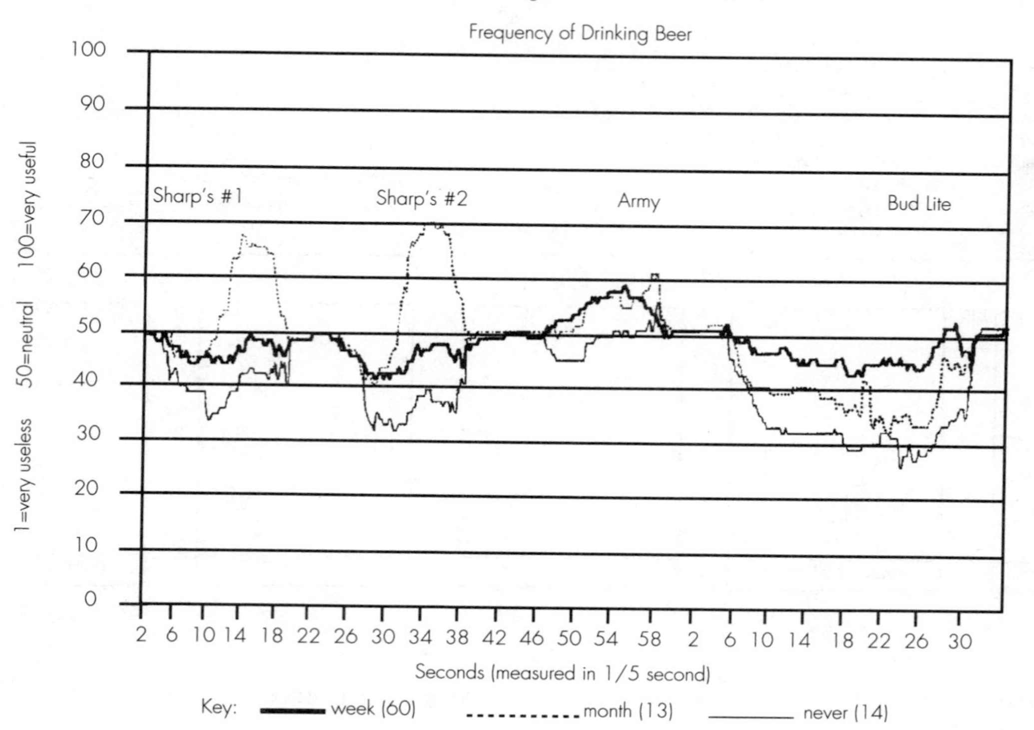

seconds into the commercial the weekly drinkers produced a flat curve and then moved to about neutral. This pattern indicates they had mentally tuned out the commercial. The monthly drinkers, in contrast, went sharply upward at this point because they found the cognitive information, nonalcoholic content, useful. Was this a good commercial? It depends on the communication goal. If it was to convince heavy drinkers to drink Sharp's, it is doubtful that much persuasion took place. The nondrinkers do not want it to appear that they are drinking beer. Which leaves the light drinkers, who want to look macho but not get drunk.

The Army recruiting commercial was favored by the heavy and light beer drinkers, but the nondrinkers were slightly negative, ending in neutral. Perhaps there is a shared macho element in beer drinking and military risktaking. Comparing the Sharp's commercials with the Bud Lite commercial we see that little information was gained about Bud Lite. The commercial merely showed the familiar beach scene with young, attractive people having fun and drinking Bud Lite. These students knew from experience all they needed to know about this brand. But such was probably not the goal of the campaign. Instead the commercial wanted students to feel good about partying with Bud Lite. To test that goal, they should have dialed along the affect dimension, unfavorable-favorable in this case.

Exhibit 3 illustrates that the affect (favorability) curve can be climbing while the cognitive (usefulness) curve is declining. When defining communications goals, it is important to note that subjects can distinguish between these two dimensions. It is the interaction of these two curves that seems to enhance week-after recall (Hughes 1992). For both Sharp's commercials, the heavy drinker and the nondrinker were about equally unfavorable—but for different reasons. The light drinker remained around neutral in effect. All user categories were equally neutral about favorability regarding the Army commercial. The Bud Lite commercial, however, seemed to be right on target if it was designed to make viewers feel good about partying. The weekly drinkers moved rapidly to eighty-five and remained there throughout the commercial. While the nondrinkers scored 75, they dropped off when beer was shown at the end of the commercial. Because these are typical college student scores for the Bud Lite campaign, we can feel confident about using them as a benchmark to evaluate the Sharp's commercials.

The system used for this test immediately created a new videotape with superimposed curves and demographic breakouts over the commercials so that responses were directly related to the stimuli. This overlay tape was immediately played back to the panelists for them to explain their responses. This part of the session is extremely useful because it provides a deeper probe than the typical focus group

EXHIBIT 3. Affective Evaluation of Beer Ads

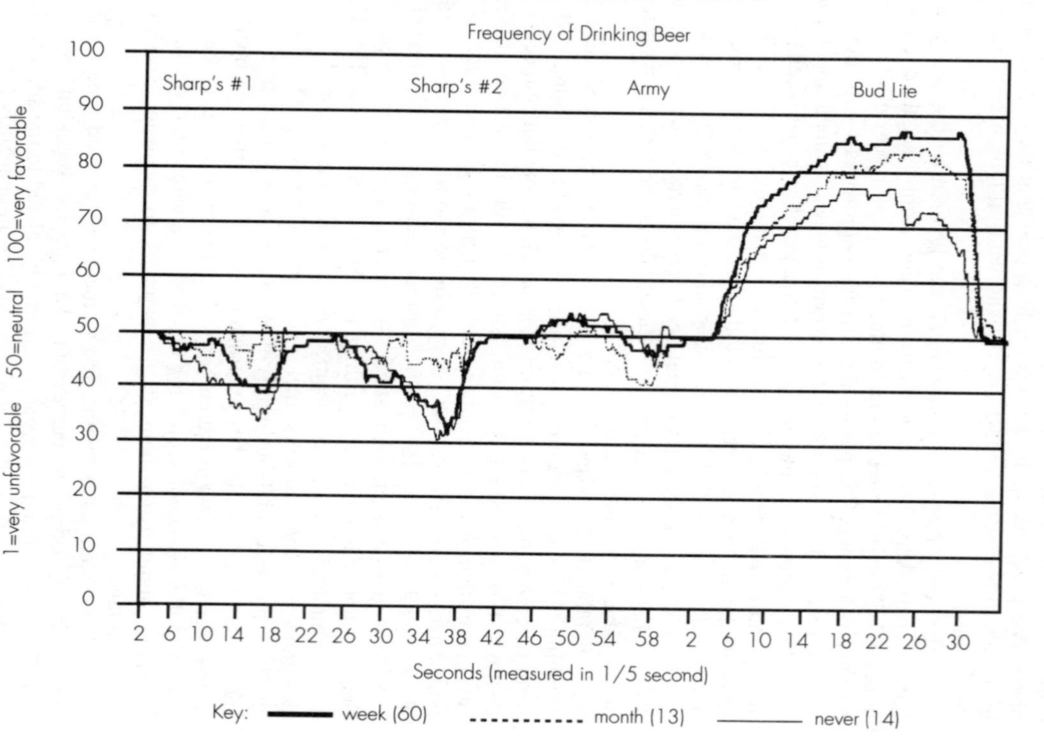

discussion. It also provides explanations in the words of the panelists rather than the research analyst.

The movement toward regional strategies raises the question about whether television commercials must be regional too. Hughes (1992) has shown that there can be significant regional differences between response curves. A McDonald's commercial and a Rice Krispies commercial were used to warm up focus group panels around the country. The panelists, mothers with young children, were professionally recruited for a company that wanted to test a new consumer product concept. The warm-up commercials showed significant differences between the eighty panelists in the Midwest and the forty panelists in Chicago. Because the scale was in units of one to one hundred, it was, possible to do a significance test each one-fifth of a second. In this way, the precise stimulus that triggered this difference could be examined. One interesting difference occurred in the Rice Krispies commercial. Chicago mothers responded positively to the child playing with the toy gun that came in the package as he shot it at the father.

What to Test

Continuous research has been used to test new product concepts, copy strategies, graphics, spokespersons, different executions, print advertisements, speeches, and music. Continuous measures need not wait for the production of the final commercial. In fact, the greatest benefit can come from testing as early in the development of a commercial as possible. The author is familiar with tests of storyboards by a grocery manufacturer to settle an argument between it and its advertising agency. They could not agree on which of four executions was appropriate for the middle ten seconds of a thirty-second commercial. Four focus groups of twenty persons each saw videotapes of the commercials in storyboard format, with the middle section rotated across groups. There was high replication across groups and it became clear which executions were the winners and which were the losers. Similarly, Spaeth and Feldman (1991) found that likability scores for rough and finished commercials were not significantly different. They cautioned, however, that their samples were not matched.

Differences in the responses to lecture and drama formats in commercials were examined by Alwitt (1992). In a lecture format, a speaker addressed the audience directly, using persuasive arguments. In a drama commercial, characters spoke to each other, rather than directly to the audience. Alwitt found that evaluations of lecture commercials by highly involved viewers rapidly became positive, while evaluations of drama commercials built slowly and then surpassed the lecture commercials. This is another example of how it is possible to test different executions.

Copy tests can identify some specific fatal flaws. For example, one statement in a three-minute presentation by a presidential candidate switched a substantial segment of viewers from being strongly for the candidate to being strongly against him. This study also revealed that a negative statement by a candidate had twice the negative effect as a positive statement had a positive effect. Thus, to break even, he had to make two positive statements to overcome the negative one (Hughes 1990).

In addition to testing the content and execution of a commercial, continuous response measures can also be used to identify when a commercial wears out. Continuous measures identify those points in a commercial when long-term memory clicks in and mental processing clicks out. They also reveal that wearing can occur when the cognitive component requires several exposures to be understood (Hughes 1992). Response patterns measured over several executions could identify when a thirty-second commercial could be reduced to a fifteen-second one and which parts to retain in the shorter version.

Validating with Links to Other Response Variables

Cases in which continuous measures have been linked to other variables, such as recall, and finally to behavior, such as buying, are difficult to find in the literature. In the few cases when they have been conducted, they have been for consulting purposes and a detailed release of findings has not been possible. Thus we must be content with disguised cases.

Young and Robinson (1989) required subjects to sort fifteen to twenty scenes from a thirty-second commercial into remembered and not-remembered piles. The frequencies with which scenes were remembered were plotted along the time line for the commercial. They then compared the shapes of these curves with independent measures of recall. Commercials with high recall had a common curve pattern: they had a strong positive slope at the beginning, a positive trend line, and peaks in the curve where there was a picture of the product or a clear statement of a problem or product benefit. These patterns were confirmed when subjects used the SpeedBack(R) system. In the first week, they dialed for favorability toward the commercials. The following week, unaided recall was used to collect their reports of the best commercials (Hughes 1992). Thus we see confirmation of the links between continuous measures and recall using two different measurement methods—one a hand sort and one an electronic dialing.

One of the more interesting validations occurred when the author was testing political television commercials. In one case, continuous measures clearly showed that a candidate running for the U.S. Senate was more effective than the hired actor. The candidate became the spokesperson for all of his commercials and went on to win. In another case, congressmen were being criticized for voting a pay raise for themselves. An attack and five defensive commercials were tested. The resulting strategy was used by one congressman who went on to win. A candidate who did not use the strategy lost severely. In a third case, a candidate for governor was losing ground due to an attack commercial. This commercial along with several rebuttal commercials were tested. Various spokespersons were tested. One commercial was selected and run the next week. A week later, an opinion poll showed the numbers reversed, in favor of the candidate who was tested. Several weeks later, he went on to win. Not all political results are so favorable. There was the candidate who hardly moved the panelists off neutral. He lost by a wide margin. Political commercials are a good means for validation because there are so few alternatives, in contrast to the grocery brands.

Viewfacts conducted several studies to link its second-to-second (S-T-S) measures to closed-end questions after the test and to direct response data that had been generated from running the commercials nationally (Polsfuss & Hess 1989). The products were Dr. Pepper soft drinks, Volkswagen cars, and subscriptions for different magazines offered by Time, Inc. Time used direct-inward-response television commercials. These commercials require viewers to order by dialing an 800 number and using their credit cards.

The dependent variable for each Dr. Pepper commercial was the average scale score for the following statement: "Makes you want to buy the brand." For each Volkswagen commercial, the dependent variable was the average score for the following statement: "Effectiveness of the commercial in persuading you to consider the brand." The independent variables were transformations of the S-T-S data that reduced the continuous measures to a single number. Viewfacts reported using the mean area under the curve and the mean number of button pushes. Some of these measures were specific to events in the commercial, such as when the car was shown and when the character drank the soft drink. The best correlation coefficients between the dependent and independent variables were reported and they ranged from 0.40 to 0.75. They also used several of their S-T-S measures as independent variables in a regression model and reported an R square of 0.60. Because they did not show the equation, it was not possible to determine the extent of multicolinearity between these independent variables.

Ten commercials were used for Time, Inc. Five were classified as successful and five were classified as failures, based on each commercial's cost per order as determined by direct-inward-response data. The dependent variable was zero or one, indicating whether the commercial was a success or not. Independent variables were the area under the S-T-S curve, the number of key depressions, and closed-ended questions. The model correctly classified nine of the ten commercials with only the S-T-S data. Adding the closed-end questions resulted in ten of the ten correctly classified.

The author also tested three television commercials that solicited magazine subscriptions. Using the SpeedBack(R) system and fewer than twenty panelists, he was able to correctly rank order the commercials according to their productivity. He also identified the most productive commercial for a fast food chain and for an insurance company.

ASI Market Research (Japan), Inc., has reported that it uses key measures from its test of commercials in a model to project how much trial the commercial will stimulate. The repeat purchase level is estimated using price and quality information. These two estimates are then used to forecast market share.[7]

CONCLUSION

Continuous response measures are becoming more common for the evaluation of advertising, personal selling, and promotions. Their primary application is a diagnostic one in that they can identify fatal flaws in strategies and executions early in the development of a strategy.

Continuous measures can increase the amount of information that is gathered from a focus group because they allow panelists to respond privately and continuously. The private inputting of data reduces group effects (Baggaley 1987). The dominant member of the group does not influence the shy panel member. If an overlay tape is played back to the group for a deeper discussion, the shy panelist gains courage when he or she sees the frequency distribution of responses and realizes that a large part of the group shares the same opinion. Thus more information is produced because more people participate and because probing is in greater depth. Furthermore, the data can be more valid because they represent individual opinions, not those of a dominant member of the group. The increase in the quantity, quality, and depth of information can reduce the number of panelists needed and therefore offset the cost of running an "electronic" focus group. Many users have found that critical problems can be identified with thirty to sixty panelists.

While the validation studies tend to come largely from consulting data, there is growing evidence that continuous response measures are linked to other measures of behavior. Future research with continuous measures will link these data to other steps in the buying process, such as liking, recall, trying, and repeat purchases, so marketing strategists will have another tool for making their marketing efforts more productive.

NOTES

1. Alec Gallup, personal communication, July 18, 1990.
2. Philip Porado, company promotional materials.

3. John A Schimell, Jr., personal correspondence, February 12, 1992.
4. Demonstration videotape, Department of Advertising, Vienna University, Austria.
5. Promotional material, Videofacts, Inc.
6. Data are from unpublished studies by Decision Labs, Ltd.
7. ASI Market Research (Japan), Inc., corporate promotional material.

REFERENCES

Aaker, David A., Douglas Stayman, and Michael Hagerty. 1986. Warmth in advertising: Measurement, impact and sequence effects. *Journal of Consumer Research* 12(4):365–81.

Alwitt, Linda F. 1992. Online Viewer Evaluations of Lecture and Drama Commercials. Working paper, DePaul University, Chicago.

Baggaley, Jon. 1987. Continual response measurement: Design and validation. *Canadian Journal of Education Communication* 16(3):217–38.

Boyd, Thomas C., and G. David Hughes. 1991. Validating realtime response measures. *Association of Consumer Research Proceedings.*

Fenwich, Ian, and Marshall D. Rice. 1991. Reliability of continuous measurement copy-testing methods. *Journal of Advertising Research* February/March, pp. 23–29.

Hughes, G. David. 1992. Realtime response measures redefine advertising wearout. *Journal of Advertising Research* May-June.

Hughes, G. David. 1990. Diagnosing communications problems with continuous measures of subjects' responses: Applications, limitations, and future research. In James H. Leigh and Claude R. Martin (eds.): *Current Issues and Research in Advertising*. Ann Arbor, MI: University of Michigan.

Hughes, G. David, and Richard D. Lennox. 1990. Realtime response research: Construct validation and reliability assessment. In William Bearden, et al. (eds.): *Enhancing Knowledge Development in Marketing*. Chicago: American Marketing Association.

Peterman, Jack N. 1940. The "Program Analyzer": A new technique in studying liked and disliked items in radio programs. *Journal of Applied Psychology* 24:724–41.

Pham, Michael, Joel B. Cohen, and G. David Hughes. 1992. Separating Affective and Evaluative Responses to Advertising Stimuli: The Use of Realtime Response Measures. Working paper, Center for Consumer Research, University of Florida, Gainesville.

Polsfuss, Mark, and Michael Hess. 1989. The Relationship Between Second-to-Second Response and Direct Response: What Is the Link? Sixth Annual ARF Copy Research Workshop, New York, May 22–23.

Porado, Philip. 1989. Finding faster feedback. *Campaigns & Elections* 10 (December):34–37.

Schwerin, Horace. 1940. An exploratory study of the reliability of the "Program Analyzer." *Journal of Applied Psychology* 24:742–45.

Spaeth, James, and Gary Feldman. 1991. Integrating Evaluative and Diagnostic Measures: Know More About How Your Advertising Works. Copy Research Workshop, The Advertising Research Foundation, September 11.

Thorson, Esther, and Annie Lang. ——. The effects of television videographics and lecture familiarity on adult cardiac orienting responses and memory. *Communications Research.*

Young, Charles E., and Michael Robinson. 1989. Video rhythms and recall. *Journal of Advertising Research* 29 (June-July):22–25.

Sidney J. Levy
J. L. Kellogg Graduate School of Management
Northwestern University

CHAPTER 16

WHAT IS QUALITATIVE RESEARCH?

Qualitative research has been important in marketing research for over fifty years, but it is still unevenly known and understood. *Qualitative research* is a general term that needs discussion because it is not used consistently. In the marketing trade press, qualitative research is sometimes used to refer only to "focused group interviewing." John Lofland (1971) uses a broader definition, referring to "field" or "qualitative" research, and indicates that its two basic techniques are intensive interviewing and participant-observation, but he does not exclude other techniques. The term "qualitative" naturally implies non-quantitative, as if enumeration and calculation were excluded, but despite this name and occasional controversy about the matter, qualitative research is *not* opposed to quantitative research and is *not* conducted without regard to quantities.

In the chapter on the design of the study called *Boys in White,* Howard S. Becker and his associates contrast the qualitative methods they used with conventional techniques of analysis that depend on data gathered in a standardized way for systematic comparison and statistical tests.

> *Since our data do not permit the use of these techniques, we have necessarily turned to what is ordinarily vaguely referred to as "qualitative analysis." Qualitative analyses of field data are not new in social science; indeed, many classics of social research have been based on such analyses. But the methods of arriving at conclusions have not been systematized and such research has often been charged with being based on insight and intuition and thus not communicable or capable of replication (1961).*

The report of their study attempts to show by its explicit and careful presentation that qualitative analysis can be made communicable and replicable. Although their report includes various charts and 45 tables, it is mainly a verbal presentation that integrates observations and interview data, citing field notes, verbatim quotations, and input from various personnel (observers, faculty, students, etc.). The various levels of analysis, results, findings, conclusions, implications, and recommendations are interwoven to create a complex interpretation of the situation being studied.

Comparing Approaches

When research is made an issue of quantitative versus qualitative, workers who emphasize the quantitative approaches often derogate other methods as non-scientific, to which defensive responses are made, as shown in this example:

> *I am surprised that Frazier quotes the statement . . . that the only way to solve these problems . . . is by large computers. A man as experienced as Frazier should know what every scientist knows, namely that no scientific problem is ever solved by computers. Problems are solved by human patience and imagination and nothing else. A computer comes in when it is a matter of getting quantitative information once a problem has been qualitatively understood. I think it is fair to say that the problem about which Frazier reports has not yet been solved. Nothing could be more useless in this state of affairs than a computer (Elsasser).*

Similarly, E. J. Hobsbawm takes occasion to make this point even more generally in a review of Lewis Mumford's book *The Myth of the Machine: The Pentagon of Power:*

> *. . . (T)here are some things for which the prevailing scientific orthodoxy can more plausibly be blamed . . . it deliberately narrows the scope of what we can "know" to what we can measure and state quantitatively, reproduce or falsify experimentally, or formulate mathematically . . . The results of this distinction between "hard" and "soft" knowledge, the former being regarded as in some sense more real when it is only more manageable, are perhaps most dangerously absurd in the social and life sciences . . . If human beings and societies were reducible to a limited bundle of quantifiable motivations and aims, as corporations can be reduced to rational profit maximizers . . . it would eliminate precisely those problems to which the solution purports to apply, those of men in societies (1970).*

It is evident that there are many approaches to gaining information and understanding. Quantitative and qualitative approaches will here be regarded at times as supplementary or complementary, overlapping or redundant, and mutually exclusive or contradictory. That is, the kinds of learning each provides may be different but fit together so that using both approaches would give a fuller or more rounded outcome; or the two sets of data may seem to explain each other. They may appear to be two different but compatible views of the phenomena. The findings may be basically the same, providing verification or reinforcement or merely a superfluity of information. The findings may differ in ways that seem incompatible, leading to the belief that (charitably) both are correct "at different levels" or that one of them is invalid. Which method is valid in such cases is often difficult to judge; people are likely to argue for their preferred answer or their preferred methods, and the usual conviction carried by numbers—even those that are inaccurate—commonly takes precedence.

A way of coming closer to the present goal of understanding the qualitative approach is not to engage in such antagonism as suggested above, but—for clarity's sake—to define the basic character of the two approaches and to compare and contrast them. This contrast has been well accomplished by Robert S. Weiss (1966) in an article titled, "Alternative Approaches in the Study of Complex Situations." He distinguishes there between the *analytic* and *holistic* (or qualitative) approaches, making these main points:

1. There are two quite different approaches to the task of making a complex situation understandable: one that can be characterized as analytic, and one that can be characterized as holistic. In research designs, the analytic aim leads naturally to the survey; the holistic aim to case studies, small sample studies, or, if the situation permits, to a field experiment.
2. In the analytic approach, investigators are prepared to see a complex situation as a tangle of related elements. They take as their task the isolating of elements from each other, or perhaps, the identification of a small number of linked relationships. This approach requires the identification of the important elements of the complex situation and, almost invariably, some attempt at quantitative measurement leading to a statement of their interrelations. For example, it having been decided that convenience is an important element in the decision to open an account at a bank, the survey may show how that variable is related to the place of residence of respondents. The two elements, convenience and place of residence, were identified prior to the survey.
3. In the holistic approach, investigators see a complex situation as containing within itself—perhaps hidden from casual view—a system of interrelated elements constituting its underlying structure, in terms of which the phenomena of the situation are to be understood. They are concerned with identifying the nature of the system rather than with focusing on particular independent-dependent variable relations. The chief interest might be phrased as "Taking it all together, how does the whole thing work?" Rather than relating convenience to place of residence, the problem might be, what is the pattern of money management in the family that leads to various forms of savings placement?
4. Neither of these two approaches is preliminary to the other. It is sometimes argued that the holistic approach is essentially exploratory, hypothesis generating, and therefore preliminary to the more definitive, hypothesis testing, analytic approach. In practice, either approach may support the other; identified regularities may help to clarify the whole system, or examining the system may help reveal some regularity.
5. The careful study of a single case is the most promising strategy for understanding how elements are organized in at least one instance, even though the problem of generalization remains. The holistically-oriented investigator finds in such close study a density of empirical

detail (sometimes called a "thick description") that makes the approach ideal for the development and testing of complex models of the organization of the case elements.

6. There are several grounds for generalizing from a case study. If the values of essential elements of the system are given, then the system as a whole must result; the particular case serves partly as an argument for the theory and partly as an illustration of its application. The generalization is to a theoretical level rather than to a descriptive level, and there is no suggestion regarding the frequency with which the organization occurs. That is, the single case follows the laws that have produced the organization of the system. If a survey had come before, the frequency of the cases may already be known.
7. Small sample studies are natural extensions of the case study approach. They usually lead to groupings of cases that display similar organization and to the development of typologies. Summaries of such findings are generalizations concerning the consistent organization to be found within a series of real instances, where the consistency is believed to be not simply fortuitous, but rather a reflection of the basic structure and dynamics of these instances.

Another way of comparing research approaches and their value for providing different kinds of information is suggested by Morris Zelditch, Jr. (Vol. 67). He notes the interaction of three types of information with three types of methods. The three types of information are:

- *Type I: Incidents and Histories.* An incident might be a log of events during a given period—a description of a shopping trip or preparation of a meal—including the complex of ideas and explanations that went on. And a history is a sequence of incidents—both incidents and histories are configurations of several properties of the object or event being studied.
- *Type II: Distributions and Frequencies.* These report observations that are identical, such as the number of people who own a given product, who have seen a given advertisement, etc.
- *Type III: Generally Known Rules and Statuses.* This kind of information tells what the customs of the group are, the rules of behavior governing who does what, the expected procedures, and the norms to which people are supposed to conform.

Three broad classes of methods are: (1) participant-observation; (2) informant-interviewing; and (3) enumeration and samples. The criteria for judging the value of the procedures are defined as *informational adequacy* (accuracy, completeness of data) and *efficiency* (cost of added information). Exhibit 1 sums up an evaluation of the three methods, in terms of these criteria, indicating how well they provide the three types of information.

EXHIBIT 1. Methods of Obtaining Information

Information Types	Enumerations and Samples	Participant-Observation	Interviewing Informants
Frequency Distributions	Prototype and best form	Usually inadequate and inefficient	Often, but not inadequate; if adequate, it is efficient
Incidents, Histories	Not adequate by itself; not efficient	Prototype and best form	Adequate with precautions, and efficient
Institutionalized Norms and Statuses	Adequate but inefficient	Adequate but inefficient except for unverbalized norms	Most efficient and hence best form

In marketing, the interview is a central method; some participant-observation is used. Not included in Exhibit 1 are projective techniques and other psychological methods, although depending on their form and handling, they can be used for each of the types of information.

THE PHENOMENOLOGICAL PERSPECTIVE

In the process presented here, the basic intention of qualitative research is to understand the behavior at issue as incidents, histories, norms, and statuses, putting to the side distributions and frequencies, except as they are included in the configuration of properties. To reach that understanding, it is regarded as imperative to *interpret* the data gathered.

The qualitative researcher interprets what the people in the sample are like, their outlooks, their feelings, the dynamic interplay of their feelings and ideas, their attitudes and opinions, and their resulting actions. Doing so requires a theory or a theoretical orientation that guides the researcher. The conduct of surveys tends to be predicated on a theory that accepts the reported data largely at face value. The data may be taken as an estimate rather than literally, and cautions are offered about sources of error. But practically speaking, most marketing research survey reports give tables of percentages with little or no qualification, and the figures are usually dealt with as matters of plain fact, even if at times puzzling. The research report may sum up the numbers that stand out as large or small, thereby interpreting that they are important. Beyond that, interpretation of the results is often left to the receiver of the report.

Qualitative analysis usually emphasizes a *phenomenological perspective.* That is, a basic theoretical assumption is made that human behavior is the result of people's perceptions of themselves and their environment. Most qualitative analysis is thus an interpretation of how the people being studied interpret the objects, communications, and other people that are involved in the topic being researched.[1]

The main features of qualitative research with regard to marketing are:

1. The marketing problems studied are—in some sense—general ones, broad questions, or patterns of behavior in the marketplace rather than specific details and variables.
2. When specific details and variables are focused on, the main aim is still to understand how they fit together to make sense of the whole situation.
3. The researcher inevitably has hypotheses in mind to guide the study, but may not specify them or their importance. He expects to "discover" what variables are important rather than to go in thinking he knows them. Lofland points to the central nature of this issue, in observing that qualitative study of people is a *process of discovery.*

   It is of necessity a process of learning what is happening. Since a major part of what is happening is provided by people in their own terms, one must find out about those terms rather than impose upon them a preconceived or outsider's scheme of what they are about. It is the observer's task to find out what is fundamental or central to the people or world under observation (1971).

4. The study is thus likely to be intensive rather than extensive, to learn "in depth" about what people do, what they think and feel, and why, rather than or in addition to how many do it.
5. The basic tasks, then, are those of interpreting, integrating, and synthesizing, rather than measuring, although measurements may be used as inputs. Qualitative study is a way of thinking, not merely the absence of measurement.
6. Relatively small samples—sometimes even single cases—are used in qualitative research because the usual assumptions governing statistical surveys are not required. Some thinkers believe that qualitative research is not part of the scientific method; it is accused of relying on subjective interpretation and may not use precise measurement. This view is not a reasonable one. The words and events being interpreted are data in the real world and, handled in organized ways, can lead to the discovery of what are regarded to be fresh facts and fresh knowledge. If such scientific requirements as publicity, disinterest or objectivity, and critical consensus are aimed for, the use of qualitative research is an important part of scientific method in gathering and analyzing empirical information about people.

Qualitative research may be used at various levels of inquiry or for various purposes. When research is termed basic or universalistic and is aimed at larger generalizations about human behavior, the qualitative approach can play an important scientific role. It is also useful in studying specific or particularistic problems that are more limited in their situations or purposes; thus, it cuts across the procedural problems that distinguish the two directions of generalizations.

Because qualitative marketing research deals with people, and because it tries to understand them in their personalities, incidents, and histories, it is an intriguing research approach. Also, because it looks for internal relationships and candidly relies on interpretation of what often seems to be a welter of kinds of data (rather than avoiding these problems through the use of statistical units), it is a controversial method. For the same reasons, it lacks familiar formal algorithms and therefore seems a difficult method. As with other work, the difficulty is reduced by careful study and practice to further the explicitness and realism that will promote the state of the art. The following brief history of qualitative research in marketing may serve as a step in the direction of this understanding.

A BRIEF HISTORY

Gathering intelligence about the marketplace on an informal basis has gone on as long as there have been marketplaces. Marketing research can include any forms of acquiring, recording, and analyzing market information, and there have always been explorers, scouts, runners, agents, representatives, salesmen, spies, tax gatherers, census takers, and other government functionaries with vital statistics, etc., to provide word of the status of the market.

Recently, Donald M. Hobart told how modern marketing research began at the Curtis Publishing Company:

> *There was a time when marketing research did not exist. About the year 1910, an idea was born. It was one of those ideas, simple in themselves, which are destined to move men along new paths of endeavor. The father of this idea was Mr. Stanley Latshaw, at that time the advertising representative in Boston for The Curtis Publishing Company.*
>
> *He was not satisfied with the way in which he and his salesmen sold advertising space. Neither they nor their customers knew much about markets and the wants and habits of consumers and dealers.*
>
> *But such information did not exist. That fact is difficult of realization by the modern business man with a wealth of facts and figures to guide him. How was it to be obtained? Mr. Latshaw devised a plan, and not too easily, sold it to Mr. Curtis. The plan to implement the original idea was as simple as the idea itself. The plan was to hire a competent man, turn him loose with a roving commission, and then see what happened. The man whom Mr. Latshaw hired for this untried work was the late Charles Coolidge Parlin, a schoolmaster from a small city in Wisconsin . . . (Hobart 1950).*

The Growth of Surveying

This marketing research activity was part of the general rise of social surveys in the United States. Following the tradition of the first U.S. Census in 1790, and spurred by the English work of Charles Booth in 1886, many large scale projects were carried out (Young 1939; Parten 1950). By the 1920s, community studies were flourishing, with growing demand for sociological measurements. Similarly, the growth of psychological testing, stimulated by the use of intelligence measurement in World War I, added to the general interest in gathering data about members of the public. Concern with public opinion and the factors impinging on it led to studies of the mass media—notably radio—then later other broadcast and print media. Awareness of the role of public opinion grew with studies of the nature of the public in the writings of Walter Lippmann in the 1920s; studies of newspapers and their readers especially emphasized political implications. In the 1930s, psychologists (notably Gordon W. Allport and Hadley Cantril) examined the role and impact of radio. The 1940s and 1950s were a kind of golden age of communications study as psychologists, sociologists, political scientists, historians, and journalists (and many others, especially under the leadership of Samuel A. Stouffer, Robert K. Merton, Paul F. Lazarsfeld, and Bernard Berelson) delved into the various media.

The role of communications in influencing voter behavior, the effects of propaganda, and public opinion polling were all part of the climate that fostered marketing research into buyer behavior. For example, in 1926, General Foods Corporation established a panel of homemakers that acted as a consumer jury for testing new products; in 1932, the Psychological Corporation set up what was probably the oldest continuous poll of buying behavior.

A great deal of this survey work was aimed at measuring the characteristics of audiences, their awareness of information, their ownership of goods, their purchasing actions, their voting intentions, and their listening and readership habits. Much emphasis was placed on learning *what* people did and the statistical differences among them in terms of age, sex, education, income, occupation, marital status, and so forth. The goal of *understanding behavior* was central, of course, but it took a lot of time, energy, and ingenuity to find out what the actions were, *per se,* as an important first step. By comparing the characteristics of groups that did different things, some understanding was gained. It is meaningful to know that the average age of the user group is higher than that of the non-users, that the heavy users are in the lower income brackets, and that the election victory is due especially to the votes of a certain ethnic group. The reasons why these relationships existed were not much studied, but the findings could be speculated about and taken to affirm or question previously-held hypotheses.

The Rise of Qualitative Analysis

During this period of growth in polling and surveying, research was directed at the dimensions of the market. The idea was to learn especially about the size of the market, its major divisions, its distribution in space, and to obtain estimates of the demographic characteristics that sensibly related to the buying and selling actions at issue. In the 1930s, hints began to appear in the marketing literature that some people were dissatisfied with those research aims. The information being gained seemed too descriptive and mechanical, insufficiently explanatory. The psychological profession was flourishing in its own movement from a measurement phase to an interpretive phase. Personality analyses and the use of projective techniques came to the fore, expressing a clinical attitude in addition to the traditional laboratory focus. Instead of IQ measurement—as in World War I—qualitative personality assessment was given main emphasis by the Office of Strategic Services (OSS), the precursor to the CIA.

Similar interests arose in the marketing research field, partly through its own evolution and partly through diffusion from the behavioral sciences. Psychological theories, insights, and methods began to enrich marketing thinking in general as well as its research. In 1935, Paul Lazarsfeld wrote, "The Art of Asking Why in Marketing Research." It was a landmark article that may fairly entitle him to credit as one of the fathers of the application of behavioral science methods and thinking to modern marketing research. (Elsewhere [Levy 1978] I have suggested the sire was Malinowski; no doubt there were several fathers.) Consumer goods companies pioneered, using outside research organizations and consultants, including academicians interested in applying behavioral science ideas to business problems. In 1939, Ernest Dichter carried out qualitative analyses of Ivory soap and Plymouth cars.

Having some traditional receptivity to psychology, advertising agencies were aware of the explorations that were going on in the communications field (Strong 1913; Poffenberger 1925). They played an important role in the growing competition among brands and were increasingly aware of the resulting segmentation in the marketplace. In trying to account for the segmentation, demographic information was not always sufficient or satisfying. Sometimes, for example, there were no significant differences between two user groups in their age, sex, and income distributions, so those characteristics did not appear to account for their different marketing behaviors. Often too, the reasons users gave for their different brand preferences did not discriminate among the brands, a fact referred to as the long recognized problem that there are discrepancies between what people say they do or think or like and what they actually do, think, or like. The reasons people give may not be all the reasons, and they may not understand their own behavior well enough to explain it.

The study of consumers was intensified in several directions after World War II. The needs of the time and the growth of social science technology found expression in the work of many pioneers. Building on the interests of W. Lloyd Warner (social stratification and symbol systems), Burleigh B. Gardner (human organization), and William E. Henry (analysis of fantasy), Social Research, Inc. was established in 1946. Ernest Dichter gained increased prominence as a psychological consultant with insightful and provocative analyses of consumer behavior. The same year, the Survey Research Center embarked on annual Surveys of Consumer Finances, providing data for the economic psychological analyses of George Katona and his associates. Companies increasingly commissioned more and more qualitative kinds of marketing research projects.

The results of the early work on social-psychological aspects of consumer behavior gradually worked their way into the academic literature; initially, reports of commercial studies were more likely to be found in various trade publications such as *Advertising Age, Tide, Printers' Ink,* and *Advertising & Selling.* In 1947, the *Harvard Business Review* published Ernest Dichter's "Psychology in Marketing Research," asserting and illustrating the importance of distinguishing between the usual "rationalized" explanations for actions and customers' deeper, unconscious reasons. Such admonition reflected the attempts in the late 1940s to get past the "lists of motives" that had previously made up much of the psychological approach to explaining customer behavior (Kronhauser 1923; Copeland 1924; Duncan 1940; and McGregor 1940).

Indirectness and Depth

The idea that direct answers to direct questions give results that are misleading, incomplete, inaccurate, or superficial naturally turned thoughts toward indirect methods of eliciting information. The use of projective techniques, which were flourishing in psychology, seemed promising. They were used richly in the work of Social Research, Inc., with adaptations of the Thematic Apperception Technique, incomplete sentences, word associations, and other methods. For example, *Tide,* a newsmagazine of advertising, marketing, and public relations, reported on Social Research Inc.'s work in analyzing the symbolic meanings of greeting cards and soap operas, using methods adapted from the disciplines of social anthropology and psychology (*Tide,* October 17, 1947, December 5, 1947). The kind of indirectly derived insight that a projective approach might yield was dramatized for the marketing profession by a single simple experiment reported by Mason Haire in 1950. He showed samples of women a brief shopping list and asked for a description of the woman who had prepared the list. The list was varied by including or omitting a brand of instant coffee. The respondents who saw instant coffee on the list projected their ideas about instant coffee by tending to describe the buyer as less oriented to home and family, compared to the descriptions given by those who saw the list without instant coffee (Haire 1950).

Because the usual structured questionnaire was often found to be insufficiently informative, research workers found it useful to develop more conversational interviews. Sometimes these interviews were carried out by psychiatric or psychological personnel and were compared to the free association sessions connected with psychoanalytic therapy. Because of this, such interviews came to be called *depth interviews*. Also, in the late 1940s and after, the work of Carl R. Rogers gained prominence for the *non-directive interview*. Despite theoretical differences between these approaches, both rely on the subject freely, introspecting and talking so that thoughts and feelings are explored and brought forth more fully. It is further believed that mental content will then emerge that is less superficial, less guarded, and that reveals more of the person's actual state of affairs.

Motivation Research

The wave of interest in marketing research using behavioral science methods and principles that began to grow around 1940 seemed widespread by the mid 1950s. The work that was most intriguing tried to link marketplace behavior with personality traits, to explore consumer motivations, and to analyze perceptions of products and brands. *The Chicago Tribune's* Pierre Martineau commissioned a series of basic product studies (beer, cigarettes, soaps and detergents, and automobiles) that he subsequently publicized via numerous industry presentations. (In these presentations, Martineau was often challenged by surveyors because the sample sizes—e.g., 300 respondents—seemed small to them; he asked how to defend himself. I told him that we were exploring motivations, not measuring frequency distributions of known variables. He said, "Then let's call it motivation research," and so it was.) As the subject became popular within the industry, the literature on the topic grew. Numerous articles discussed motivation research, and books by Martineau (1957), Joseph W. Newman (1957), George Horsley Smith (1954), Harry Henry (1958), and Vance Packard (1957) presented concepts, methods, applications, defenses, and criticisms.

At times, hostility to the new methods and practitioners was intense. Motivation researchers were accused of offering false panaceas—or conversely, dangerously effective insights. Allegedly, they used inadequate or improper techniques and samples, were arrogant, and ignorant of business. They used language the critics said was obscure jargon; they came up with ideas that were condemned as irrelevant or impractical—or just silly. The vice of subjectivity, with its supposed lack of validity and reliability of findings, was especially emphasized. The sound of battle can be heard in some titles of articles of the period:

- "Politz Tags Motivation Research 'Fake,' 'Hah!' Hahs Dichter Group," *Advertising Age,* September 19, 1955, p. 3.
- "Battle of Embittered Ph.D.s," *Advertising Age,* 1955, September 19.
- "Research Rivals Trade Blows," *Business Week,* 1955, October 29.
- "Is Motivation Research Really an Instrument of the Devil?" William D. Wells, 1956.

The trade press publicized amusing interpretations from Ernest Dichter, such as a convertible car represents a mistress, teenagers use soap to wash off sexual guilt, and baking a cake is analogous to delivering a child. Some thought these were "large doses of Freud & Co. (Carlson 1953)," although the insight about cakes seemed less ludicrous when The Pillsbury Company translated it into the successful jingle, "Nothin' says lovin' like somethin' from the oven."

By 1958, the pros and cons had been pretty thoroughly reviewed and exhausted. A good compendium of these views was compiled by Robert Ferber and Hugh G. Wales in *Motivation and Market Behavior.*

Although there was no clear consensus as to what constituted motivation research, Newman (1957) provided a comprehensive view. Using a case approach, he shows the breadth of understanding that was sought in so-called motivational studies. Other writers focused on specific techniques, giving the impression that motivation research was synonymous with certain psychological methods. James Vicary specialized in the use of word associations; others used systematic personality tests to correlate personality variables with marketing behavior. Franklin Evans tested whether Ford and Chevrolet owners had different personality patterns on the Edwards Personality Inventory. J. Walter Thompson advertising company used this same test to measure personality variables among members of its consumer panel, to determine, for example, whether scores on the innovativeness variable correlated with consumers' innovative behavior in the supermarket. Kassarjian has thoroughly reviewed the results of personality studies (Kassarjian 1975).

Much motivation research was in actuality a full expression of qualitative research, and at times it was called that, to avoid some of the confusion about it or to compound it. The latter name was aimed at showing that all the methods of the behavioral sciences—not just the survey and attendant statistical techniques—could be used to illuminate a problem.

During the 1960s, the interest in motivation research subsided. It became fashionable to think of such research as having been a fad of the 1950s. That was true to some degree, as the experimenting with projective techniques declined, and the full-scale use of formal personality instruments was largely abandoned. The criticisms of motivation research—despite being in many instances defensive and unreasonable—took their toll. Also, the surge of behavioral science personnel who had moved into the marketing research field did not continue to grow at the same rate. Two sets of pioneers had been especially important in fostering the initial wave of motivation-qualitative work. Such figures as Ernest Dichter, Burleigh B. Gardner, Steuart Henderson Britt, Harriett Bruce Moore, Dietrich Leonhard, Hal Kassarjian, Louis Cheskin, Herta Herzog, Virginia Miles, William D. Wells, and several others, were not succeeded by comparably significant workers.

The second group who played a special role were the daring business people who had the curiosity and imagination to support innovative research projects, and who were willing to learn about methods that were unconventional and seemed quantitatively insecure. These included George Reeves and Sandy Gunn of J. Walter Thompson; Henry O. Whiteside of Gardner Advertising; J. Walter Thompson, Hugh McMillan, and Jack Bowen of Campbell-Ewald; Leo Burnett of Leo Burnett Advertising; Pierre D. Martineau of *The Chicago Tribune*; Gerhardt Kleining of Reemstma in Germany; Dudley Ruch of Pillsbury; John Catlin of Kimberly-Clark; Robert Gwynn and Dan Bash of Sunbeam Corporation; George Stewart of Swift and Company; Beland Honderich of the *Toronto Star*; and many more. In many organizations, such individuals were not present, and their numbers did not easily multiply.

In addition to the slow growth of knowledgeable and interested personnel, qualitative research moved out of the limelight. It was absorbed into the more routine activities of some research departments and companies, as each of these came to claim to "do it" too. Burgeoning interest in the use of computers and cognitive processes put it in the shade. And it tended to be assimilated into the general field of consumer behavior, which had by then crystallized into the main form in which marketing teachers and practitioners thought about the application of behavioral science concepts to marketing. About a dozen years of related work culminated in the substantial integrations by Engel, Kollat, and Blackwell in 1968 with their text, *Consumer Behavior*, and by Howard and Sheth in 1969 with *The Theory of Buyer Behavior*.

On the practitioner side, the 1970s saw the rise of the marketing research method called the focus group. The method was not new, having a history in the study of group dynamics (Lewin 1947), small groups (Bales 1950), and convenient survey methods (Parten 1950). The shift from the open-ended but focused individual interview to using a similar procedure with groups was discussed by Merton, Fiske, and Kendall in 1956. It shortly found its way into the marketing literature with such articles as "Group Interviews Reveal Consumer Buying Behavior" by Munn and Opdyke in the *Journal of Retailing* (1961), an article by A. E. Goldman in the *Journal of Marketing* called "The Group Depth Interview" (1962), and a story in *Printers' Ink,* "Market Testing by Group Interview" (1962). By the 1970s, use of the focus group had swept through the business community. It had become the preferred and prevalent method for doing qualitative research. In many organizations, it was—and is—considered synonymous with qualitative research and was the only method used to get qualitative information. Over the years, there was toying with the use of participant observation and attempts at creating ethnographies and thick descriptions. The latter methods have rich potential, and in the 1980s, this anthropological influence became more substantial, if still short of flourishing.

In the early 1990s, the situation of qualitative research in marketing may be summed up as follows: applied and scholarly work continue to interweave. In applied work, the focus group method is entrenched and in widespread use for various reasons and with various difficulties. Other methods are used unevenly and sporadically, or not at all. The use of one-on-one interviews is increasing again because of the fullness and richness of the information that can be obtained. Here and there one or another projective technique is applied: for example, matching pictures of people with brands of beer drinkers, getting people to tell stories to pictures and to relate various kinds of fantasies, etc. (Levy 1985). Ethnographic approaches—participant observation and detailed descriptions—have been found useful.

NOTES

1. Although Weiss equates "analysis" with a non-qualitative approach, it is also used in its general way to refer to the handling of any data.

REFERENCES

"Battle of Embittered PhD.s," *Advertising Age*, September 19, 1955.

Becker, Howard S., Blanche Geer, Everett C. Hughes, and Anselm L. Strauss, *Boys in White*, University of Chicago Press, 1961.

Belk, Russell W., *Highways and Buyways: Naturalistic Research from the Consumer Behavior Odyssey*, Association for Consumer Research, 1991.

Copeland, Melvin T., *Principles of Merchandising*, Chicago: A. W. Shaw Company, 1924.

Dichter, Ernest, "Psychology in Marketing Research," *Harvard Business Review*, Summer 1947, pp. 432–443.

Duncan, Delbert J., "What Motivates Business Buyers," *Harvard Business Review*.

Elsasser, Walter M. "Computers No Panacea," *Science News*, Summer 1940, pp. 448–454.

Ferber, Robert and Hugh G. Wales, *Motivation and Market Behavior*, Irwin, 1958.

Haire, Mason, "Projective Techniques in Marketing Research," *Journal of Marketing*, April 1950, pp. 649–656.

Henry, Harry, *Motivation Research*, London: Crosby Lockwood & Son, Ltd., 1958.

Hobart, Donald M. (ed.), *Marketing Research Practice*, New York: The Ronald Press, 1950.

Hobsbawm, E. J., "Is Science Evil?" *The New York Review*, November 19, 1970, p. 15.

Kassarjian, Harold and M. J. Sheffet, "Personality and Consumer Behavior: One More Time," in E. Mazze (ed.), *Combined Proceedings*, Chicago: AMA, 1975, pp. 197–201.

Kornhauser, Arthur W., "The Motives-in-Industry Problem," *Annals of the American Academy of Political and Social Science*, September 1923, pp. 105–116.

Lazarsfeld, Paul, "The Art of Asking Why in Market Research," *The National Marketing Review*, Summer 1935, pp. 26–38.

Lofland, John, *Analyzing Social Settings*, Wadsworth Publishing Co., 1971.

Levy, Sidney J., "Dreams, Fairy Tales, Animals, and Cars, *Psychology and Marketing*, Summer 1985.

McGregor, Douglas, "Motives as a Tool of Market Research," *Harvard Business Review*, Autumn 1940, pp. 42–51.

Martineau, Pierre D., *Motivation in Advertising*, New York: McGraw-Hill, 1957.

Newman, Joseph W., *Motivation Research and Marketing Management*, Cambridge, Mass: Harvard University, 1957.

Packard, Vance, *The Hidden Persuaders*, New York: Pocket Books, 1957.

Parten, Mildred, *Surveys, Polls, and Samples: Practical Procedures*, Harper Bros., 1950.

Poffenberger, Albert T., *Psychology in Advertising*, Chicago: A. W. Shaw Company, 1925.

"Politz Tags Motivation Research 'Fake,' 'Hah!' Hahs Dichter Group," *Advertising Age*, September 19, 1955, p. 3; "Research Rivals Trade Blows," *Business Week*, October 29, 1955.

Scott, Walter Dill, *Psychology of Advertising*, Boston: Small, Maynard & Company, 1917.

Smith, George H., *Motivation in Advertising and Marketing*, New York: McGraw-Hill, 1954.

Strong, Jr., E. K., "Psychological Methods as Applied to Advertising," *Journal of Educational Psychology, 1913*, p. 393.

Weiss, Robert S. "Alternative Approaches in the Study of Complex Situations," *Human Organization*, Fall, 1966, pp. 198–206.

Wells, William D., "Is Motivation Research Really an Instrument of the Devil?" *Journal of Marketing*, October 1956, pp. 196–198.

Young, Pauline V., *Scientific Social Surveys and Research*, Prentice-Hall, 1939.

Zelditch, Morris Jr., "Some Methodological Problems of Field Studies," *American Journal of Sociology*, 67, pp. 566–67.

Bertram Schoner
Professor of Marketing
Simon Fraser University

Henry H. Rodkin
Vice President, Marketing, International Operations
Maremont Corporation
Carol Stream, Illinois

CHAPTER 17

STATISTICAL AND EXPERIMENTAL DESIGNS

Ultimately there is one and only one reason why a marketing executive would wish to employ any of the techniques discussed in this chapter—he or she has to make a marketing decision and has inadequate information available. For example, the concern may be whether or not to introduce a new frozen specialty food, say hors d'oeuvres, into a regional market. The consumers could be expected to be families with incomes over $25,000 per year who entertain frequently. Thus it would be important to know the number of such families in the particular region in order to predict sales.

While available data may yield the percentage of families who meet the income criterion, frequency of entertainment data is not available. Taking a census, i.e., a complete survey of every family in the region, would be inordinately expensive. What is required is some technique for selecting a sample of families from the region such that one could be reasonably assured that the proportion of potential consumers in the sample provides a good estimate of the proportion in the region.

Sample survey research is essentially passive in nature. One wants to draw inferences about a population from the data in the sample. Experimentation, on the other hand, is active. Some sort of experimental treatment or treatments must be performed in order to predict whether or not the treatment yields some desired effect. In our frozen food example, one might place the hors d'oeuvres in package A in one set of stores and in package B in a matched set of stores in order to predict which package would lead to greater sales. Finally, the Bayesian approach directly incorporates judgment, survey or experiment results, and economic payoffs into the decision structure.

Statistical problems are essentially of two types—estimation problems and hypothesis testing problems. For the headnote example, it may be necessary to *estimate* the number of high-income families, in some region, who entertain frequently. Presumably, if this number is above some value, the firm would market their new frozen food; if below that value, the firm would not market the frozen food. Thus one approach to the problem would be to generate a sample survey from which the proportion of high-income families would be estimated. If this proportion is sufficiently high (ignoring other considerations), the decision would be to market the frozen food.

A closely related decision strategy would be to employ *hypothesis testing*. Suppose we believe that marketing our new frozen food would be warranted if 10% or more of our *target population* (the population of the region from which the sample was selected) meet the criteria of income and frequency of entertaining. Two hypotheses may be formed, which are labeled H_1 and H_2.

H_1: the percentage of the population that meets our criteria is less than or equal to 10%.

H_2: the percentage of the population that meets our criteria is greater than 10%.

The company's problem would be to decide on the basis of sample information which hypothesis to accept. The advantage of hypothesis testing is that it permits probabilities to be associated with making incorrect decisions. For example, the researcher can answer the question "How probable would it be that we would observe 11% or more in a sample who meet the income and entertainment criteria, given that 10% or less of the target population actually meet these criteria?"

The passive nature of the sample survey procedure is evident. Test marketing two package designs and estimating the future sales of each, or testing the hypothesis that package A sells more than package B, would be illustrations of making inferences on the basis of experimental treatments.

Sample Bias

There are two sources of error in a sample—systematic and random. *Random error* arises because (with respect to the variable of interest) the sample differs from the target population by chance alone. For example, if measuring family income, by chance the mean income of the sample may be less than that of the target population. If more samples were selected, one could expect this chance variation to average out.

A *systematic error* arises because the method of selecting the sample, in effect, makes the sampled population (known as the *sample frame*) differ from the target population. To the degree to which the sampled population differs from the target population, a *bias* is introduced.

In the frozen food example, suppose the sample were selected from the telephone book. The sample frame would contain three sources of bias. First, families without a phone would not be in the frame. Second, recently arrived families would not be in the frame. And third, families with unlisted numbers would not be in the frame. Since one might expect families in the three categories above to differ from the target population, both with respect to income and frequency of entertaining, the research results would be in error even if a census of the sample frame were undertaken.

Sample Design

The simplest *probability* sample is known as a random sample. In this design, every possible sample of a particular size has an equal probability of being selected. (One implication of this design is that every member of the frame has an equal probability of being selected.) Assuming that the frame and target populations are identical, probability statements may be made that some measure of the sample, say the sample mean, will differ by so many units (e.g., dollars of income) from the corresponding measure of population. The larger the sample, the smaller the probability that the difference will be as great as some given value.

Thus, in the frozen food example, probability statements such as "What is the probability of observing 11% or more *of our sample* with average income greater than $25,000, given that the percentage of families *in the region* with average income less than $25,000 is 10%?" are possible.

The cost of a true random sample can be exorbitant if the information must be collected by personal interviews. *Clustering,* or bunching the observations, permits a larger sample size for the same cost. Thus, if one were collecting information from 100 personal interviews in a city, each city block could be regarded as a cluster. One procedure would be to select randomly ten blocks from a population of city blocks, and ten families to be interviewed on each block. Such a design is more subject to random error than a random sample because one would expect families within each cluster to be somewhat alike. Thus, if by chance, three blocks in the sample came from unusually rich neighborhoods, the sample would not be representative.

In some instances, random error can be reduced by a process known as *stratification.* For example, it is well known that there is a positive correlation between education and income. Suppose one were interested in average income, and it was known that 20% of the heads of families in a population had completed college, an additional 50% had completed high school, and 30% had not completed high school. If a random sample by chance happened to contain, say, 50% of the respondents who had completed college, it is virtually certain that average income would be overestimated. One could guard against such an outcome in advance by randomly selecting 20% of the sample from college graduates, 50% from high school graduates, and 30% from those who had not completed high school. The extra cost of such a procedure would generally be more than compensated for by the much smaller component of random error.

Both cluster and stratified sampling can be combined to achieve the smallest possible random error for a given expenditure. Suppose, in the frozen food example, a survey were to be taken of 100 cities. One would want to ensure that cities of varying size were in the sample of cities selected. The following procedure could be adopted.

1. Stratify cities by size. Each city represents a cluster of families.
2. Within each stratum, randomly select a sample of cities.

3. Within each city in the sample, form a set of clusters by census tract.
4. Stratify the tracts by average household income.
5. Randomly select tracts from each stratum.

Experimental Design

The elements of an experiment are the following. First, there is a number of *experiment units* (e.g., stores and customers) and two or more *experimental treatments* (e.g., package designs and promotional campaigns) to which the experimental units will be exposed. Second, there is a hypothesis to be tested against one or more alternative hypotheses. Third, the hypothesis is of the form that there is a difference between the effects of the various treatments (possibly in a certain direction). The hypothesis could be that package A will sell better than package B. The competing hypothesis would be that package A does not sell better than package B.

In a *true* experiment, the experimenter has control over which experimental treatments will be assigned to which experimental units, when they will be assigned, and when the dependent variable of interest will be measured. The experimenter designs the study so as to exclude systematic differences in observed effects that arise from causes other than the treatments. The "error" in the observations of the experiment should arise by chance alone.

An illustration of a poor experimental design, which would not qualify as a true experiment, should clarify the concepts. Suppose that an industrial manufacturer feels that a mailing of an illustrated brochure to customers will result in increased sales. Fifty customers who had not made purchases within the past two months are selected for the experiment, and brochures are mailed to them. If 20 (or any other number) of the customers place orders within the next 60 days, can the manufacturer conclude that the brochure is effective?

The answer, of course, is a flat no. Many factors other than the mailing could account for the orders. One possibility is that the increase in sales can be attributed to economic conditions within the industry. If sales overall are increasing, we could expect purchases by any particular group of customers to increase also.

Another explanation lies in the method of selection of the experimental units. Since the sample was selected according to some criterion, rather than randomly, the experimental units differ from the total population of customers in a systematic manner. Therefore, it cannot be argued that the brochure, even if effective on the sample selected, would be effective on customers in general. For example, the customers who had not ordered in 60 days may have been those who had not been visited by the firm's salespeople during that period. Customers receiving regular sales calls may be inclined to ignore brochures and place orders only when the salesperson calls.

Still another cause for doubt arises by virtue of the fact that the sample was selected on the basis of a *low* frequency of past orders. Suppose that all customers average, say, $500 per month in purchases, but purchases in any month vary around that figure; thus at any one time, some will be purchasing below their average and some above their average. If we then selected only customers who in the previous two months have bought little or nothing, we would find that their future purchases would tend to increase to their average. This would be so regardless of whether or not the firm engaged in some special effort to increase sales.

The reader can find, without difficulty, numerous other explanations as to why sales to the sample increased. The implication is that it is difficult to conclude that a mailing of the brochure to other customers of the firm would affect sales in any way. Therefore, the research is virtually useless.

A far better approach would have been for the firm to have chosen randomly a sample of customers, to have sent the brochure to this sample, and then to have compared average sales of the sample over the period with sales of the customers to whom no brochure was sent. This procedure would control any of the counter-explanations argued above. The only remaining source of error would be chance variations.

More complicated problems might require more complicated designs. But the basic approach of randomly assigning treatments to experimental units remains the same. And if the only source of error is chance, it becomes possible, on the assumption that a hypothesis is true (or, on the assumption that it is false) to assign probabilities to an error being made.

Quasi-experimental Designs

The strict controls of a true experiment may not always be possible, particularly if the experiment is to be conducted in the field and not in the laboratory. In such cases, *quasi-experimental designs* may be employed. Such designs are possible when the experimenter can control the taking of observations, even though the assignment in treatments cannot be controlled.

Let us extend the previous example. Suppose that the fixed costs associated with designing and producing a brochure are such that there is a strong incentive to mail the brochure to all customers and potential customers. For future reference, the firm would still like to have a reasonable idea as to whether or not any increase in sales could be attributed to the brochure.

Many of the previous problems of competing hypotheses are eliminated because the whole population, rather than a sample, is selected. Certainly there is no problem associated with the sample being systematically different from the population in some manner. But what cannot be controlled is that the test period itself may be atypical. Depending on the nature of the product, factors ranging from unusually pleasant weather to optimism produced by some presidential announcement may account for the sales increase. Nevertheless, the firm may look at sales during a number of periods prior to the brochure mailing and a number of periods subsequent to the mailing. If there appeared to be a definite shift in the pattern of sales at the inception of the mailing, it is reasonable to accept the hypothesis that the mailing caused the shift. Should something highly unusual have occurred at the same time as the mailing, the experimenter, presumably, should be aware of it.

Again, other more complicated quasi-experimental designs may be preferred in some situations. Such designs are generally characterized by a series of observations, sometimes associated with a series of administrations of the experimental treatment.

Analysis of Data

In this section, a brief description of the techniques of (a) cross-classification analysis, (b) correlation analysis, and (c) regression analysis are discussed.

Cross-classification analysis is most useful in exploratory research, but can be useful in many advanced studies. It serves to provide insight into problems where two or more variables interact to produce an effect that one alone does not produce, or where the apparent effects of one variable are in reality produced by a correlation of that variable with the true causal variable.

For example, a magazine study of readership may indicate that its audience is primarily high income. But a further breakdown, by *both* income and education, may show that it is higher education, and not income, that differentiates its readers. This is illustrated in Table 1.

While the implication of Table 1 may have been discovered by examination of the education variable alone, Table 2 illustrates a case where both variables must be examined together to show that readers are almost entirely high-income high school graduates or moderate to low-income college graduates.

TABLE 1. Magazine Readership

Income	Education			
	Grade School Percentage	High School Percentage	College Percentage	Total Percentage
Greater than $35,000	1	4	55	60
Less than $35,000	1	3	35	40
Total	2	7	90	100

TABLE 2. Magazine Readership

Income	Education			
	Grade School Percentage	High School Percentage	College Percentage	Total Percentage
Greater than $35,000	5	40	5	50
Less than $35,000	5	5	40	50
Total	10	45	45	100

Correlation analysis is used to measure the degree to which two variables move together (or in opposite directions). Thus education is positively correlated with income, which indicates that one would expect, in general, to see high education associated with higher income. No causal relationship may be inferred from correlation, as can be noted from the fact that automobile production in the United States is positively correlated with population growth in China.

Regression analysis is employed to estimate one variable by the use of one or more other variables. For example, in Table 3, sales of a certain product are plotted against city size, and a linear "best fit" employed to show the relationship between the two. Given no other information, if the product were marketed in a city with 100,000 residents, a good guess of sales would be $15,000.

There are many other statistical techniques in use that cannot be described here because of their complexity and because of space limitations. To cite a few, discriminant analysis may be employed to predict in which of two or more categories (say, heavy or light product users) consumers may fall on the basis of other information (income, education, attitudes, etc.). Factor analysis is used to reduce many variables to a few underlying factors. Multidimensional scaling is useful in establishing product images.

BAYESIAN ANALYSIS

Bayesian versus Classical Assumptions

In classical statistics, it is important to distinguish between those things that may and those that may not have probability statements attached to them. In particular, the classical reasoning asserts, population parameters are *not* random, and thus cannot have probability measures defined on them. For example, the proportion of families in a given area that meet the criteria for potential purchasers of frozen hors d'oeuvres is some unknown number, but the fact that the number is unknown does not make it random. A *sample* mean has a probability associated with it since different samples (selected by some probabilis-

TABLE 3. Sales vs. City Size

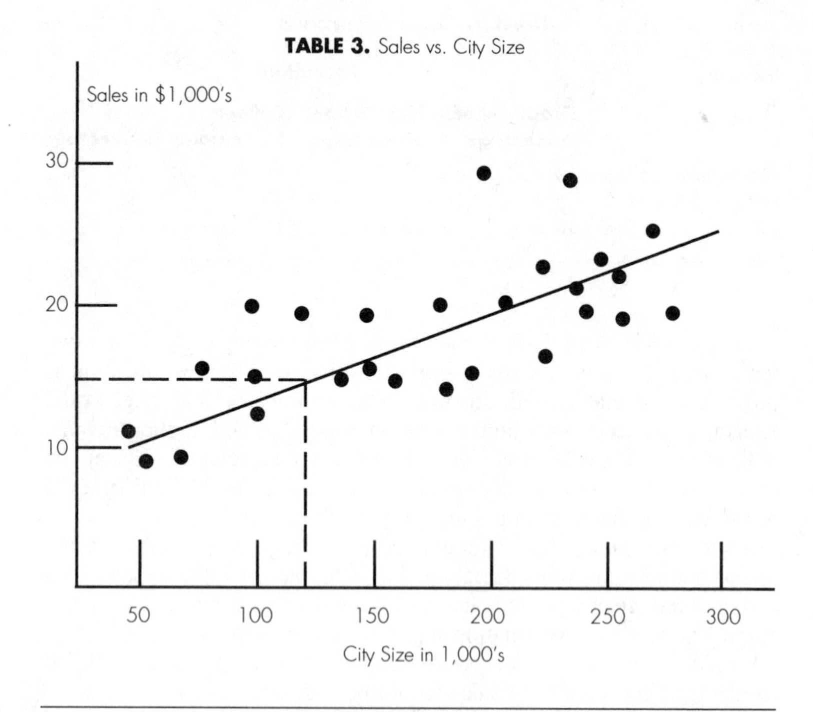

tic process) will yield different sample means. A *population* mean, however, is what it is, and is unaffected by sampling.

This may appear to be an esoteric quibble at first blush. Unfortunately the implications for practical problems are enormous. Classical statisticians are willing to assign a probability of observing a particular sample or experimental result *given* a population parameter. But the market researcher really needs a probability assigned to possible values of the parameter, given a sample result.

Finally, it should be noted that the techniques of confidence intervals and hypothesis testing are formulated to avoid attaching probability measures to population parameters. *Bayesian procedures do attach probabilities to parameters.* Thus the analysis of decision problems by the Bayesian is markedly different from the analysis of the same problem by a classical statistician.

An Example

The following example is considerably oversimplified, but illustrates the approach that would be employed in a Bayesian analysis. A company is considering two sales presentations for use by its salesmen.

The first (type A) presentation costs \$10. The second (type B) employing "give-aways," costs \$12.

The company has considerable experience with type A presentations and knows that 40% of such presentations yield sales, each sale generating a contribution to profit of \$40. Thus, on the average, a presentation yields 0.4 × \$40, or \$16 gross contribution to profit per presentation. Subtracting the \$10 cost of the presentation, the type A presentation has a net "expected" contribution to profit of \$6.

After considerable discussion, the director of marketing assigns a probability of 0.8 to the proportion of sales in a type B presentation remaining at 40%, and a 0.2 probability to the percentage rising to 50%. Table 4 portrays what is known as the decision tree. If the proportion of sales remains 0.4, expected net contribution to profit with the type B presentation is \$4. If the proportion is 0.5, however, the expected contribution is (0.5 × \$40 – \$12), or \$8. The net expected profit of the type B presentation is thus (0.2 × \$8 + 0.8 × \$4), or \$4.80.

The type A presentation, worth \$6, is preferred. This is because the probability of the type B presentation being superior to the type A is low. How high would it have to be for the type B presentation to be preferred? The expected value of the presentation would have to be greater than \$6. Thus we have

$$p \times \$8 + (1 - p) \times \$2 > \$6$$

where p is the probability that type B presentation is successful half the time. Solving yields p must be greater than two-thirds.

The sales manager decides to try an experiment. The type B approach is to be tried on ten prospects. It may be shown by a theorem of statistics (Bayes theorem) that if six or more prospects place orders, the probability of the underlying proportion of orders (over many sales) being 0.5 is greater than two-thirds. Thus the decision would be to convert to the type B presentation. With five or fewer orders, the decision would be to retain the type A presentation.

The above example illustrates the three essentials of an economic decision under uncertainty employing Bayesian Decision Theory. First, judgment is required in assessing the "prior" probabilities of the true "state of nature" (0.2 and 0.8 in the example). Second, these probabilities may be changed by survey or experimental data. And third, possible economic consequences are weighted by their appropriate probabilities in reaching a decision.

The preceding example does not illustrate one other extremely useful feature of Bayesian analysis—the expected value of information. It is possible to compare the expected value of improvement in a payoff by virtue of sample or experimental information with the cost of the research. Thus one can select from several research designs that design which yields the highest expected net return.

TABLE 4. A Decision Tree

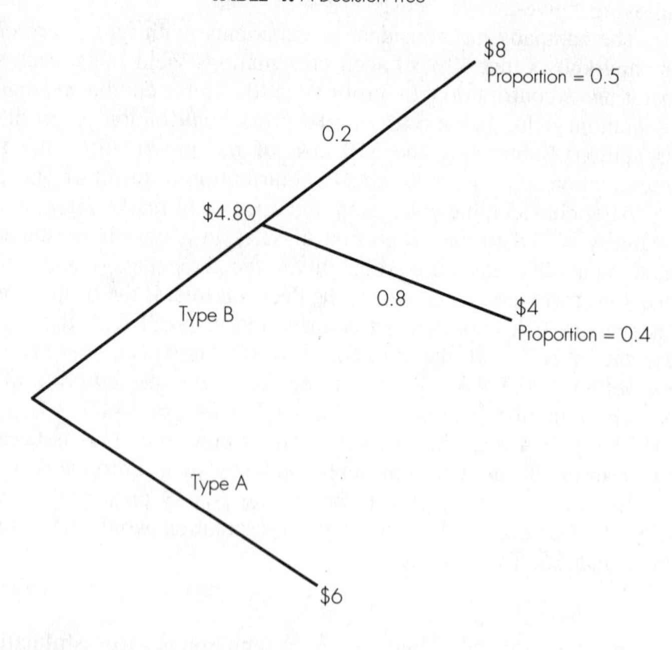

Implications

The purpose of this chapter is to provide some insight into how various research techniques can be of use to the marketing manager. Research studies cannot be employed to replace experience and good judgment, but rather to provide better information to the decision maker.

SUGGESTIONS FOR FURTHER READING

David A. Aaker, *Multivariate Analysis in Marketing: Theory and Application* (Belmont, California: Wadsworth, 1971).

Selwyn W. Becker, *Innovations in Organizations* (New York: Elsevier-North Holland Publishing Co., 1978).

Donald T. Campbell and Julian C. Stanley, *Experimental and Quasi-Experimental Designs for Research* (Skokie, IL: Rand McNally, 1963).

Keith K. Cox and Ben M. Enis, *Experimentation for Marketing Decisions* (Scranton, PA: International Textbook, 1969).

Anil Gaba and Robert L. Winkler, "A Bayesian Model," *Management Science,* Vol. 38 (July 1992), pp. 913–925.

Marvin E. Goldberg, "A Quasi-Experiment Assessing the Effectiveness of TV Advertising Directed to Children," *Journal of Marketing Research,* Vol. 27 (November 1990), pp. 445–54.

Paul Jedemus and Robert Frame, *Business Decision Theory* (New York, NY: McGraw-Hill, 1969).

Taro Yamane, *Elementary Sampling Theory* (Englewood Cliffs, NJ: Prentice-Hall, 1967).

Naresh K. Malhotra
Regents' Professor and Coordinator of
Marketing and Management Science
School of Management
Georgia Institute of Technology
Atlanta, Georgia

CHAPTER 18

SURVEY METHODS OF DATA COLLECTION FOR DOMESTIC AND INTERNATIONAL MARKETING RESEARCH

In this chapter, we focus on the major methods employed in survey research. Survey—or communication—methods are briefly discussed and classified by mode of administration as traditional telephone interviews, computer-assisted telephone interviews, personal in-home interviews, mall-intercept interviews, computer-assisted personal interviews, mail interviews, and mail panels. We describe each of these methods and present a comparative evaluation of all the survey methods when collecting data for domestic marketing research. Next, we focus attention on international data collection and evaluate these methods from that perspective. We conclude with some observations on the use of different survey methods.[1]

SURVEY METHODS

The survey method of obtaining information is based on the questioning of respondents. Respondents are asked a variety of questions regarding their behavior, intentions, attitudes, awareness, motivations, and demographic and lifestyle characteristics. These questions may be asked verbally, in writing, or via computer, and the responses may be obtained in any of these forms. Typically, the questioning is *structured*—the degree of standardization imposed on the data collection process. In structured data collection, a formal questionnaire is prepared and the questions are asked in a prearranged order, thus the process is also direct. Whether research is classified as direct or indirect is based on whether the true purpose is known to the respondents. A direct approach is nondisguised; the purpose of the project is disclosed to the respondents or is otherwise obvious to them from the questions asked.

The structured-direct survey—the most popular data collection method—involves administering a questionnaire. The survey method has several advantages. First, the questionnaire is simple to administer. Second, the data obtained are reliable because the responses are limited to the alternatives stated. The use of fixed-response questions reduces the variability in the results that may be caused by differences in interviewers. Finally, coding, analysis, and interpretation of data are relatively simple.

Disadvantages are that respondents may be unable or unwilling to provide the desired information. For example, consider questions about motivational factors. Respondents may not be consciously aware of their motives for choosing specific brands or shopping at specific department stores. Therefore, they may be unable to provide accurate answers to questions about their motives. Respondents may be unwilling to respond if the information requested is sensitive or personal. Also, structured questions and fixed-response alternatives may result in loss of validity for certain types of data such as evolving beliefs and feelings. Finally, wording questions properly is not easy. Yet, despite these disadvantages, the survey approach is by far the most common method of primary data collection in marketing research. Survey methods can be classified based on the mode used to administer the questionnaire. These classification schemes help distinguish among survey methods.

SURVEY METHODS CLASSIFIED BY MODE OF ADMINISTRATION

Survey questionnaires may be administered in three major modes: (1) telephone interviews, (2) personal interviews, and (3) mail interviews (see Exhibit 1). Telephone interviews may be further classified as traditional telephone interviews or computer-assisted telephone interviews (CATI). Personal interviews may be conducted in-home, as mall-intercept interviews, or as computer-assisted personal interviews (CAPI). The third major method—mail interviews—takes the form of ordinary mail surveys or surveys conducted using mail panels. Of these methods, telephone interviews are the most popular in the United States, followed by personal interviews. Mail interviews are the least popular. We now describe each of these methods.

TELEPHONE METHODS

As stated earlier, telephone interviews can be typed as traditional and computer-assisted.

Traditional Telephone Interviews

Traditional telephone interviews involve phoning a sample of respondents and asking them a series of questions. The interviewer uses a paper questionnaire and records the responses with a pencil. Low-priced WATS (wide area telephone service) lines have made nationwide telephone interviewing from a central location practical. With the popularity of WATS lines, the use of local telephone interviewing has decreased in recent years (Frey 1983).

Computer-Assisted Telephone Interviewing (CATI)

Computer-assisted telephone interviewing from a central location is now more popular than the traditional telephone method. Computer-assisted telephone interviewing (CATI) uses a computerized question-

EXHIBIT 1. A Classification of Survey Methods Based on Method of Administration

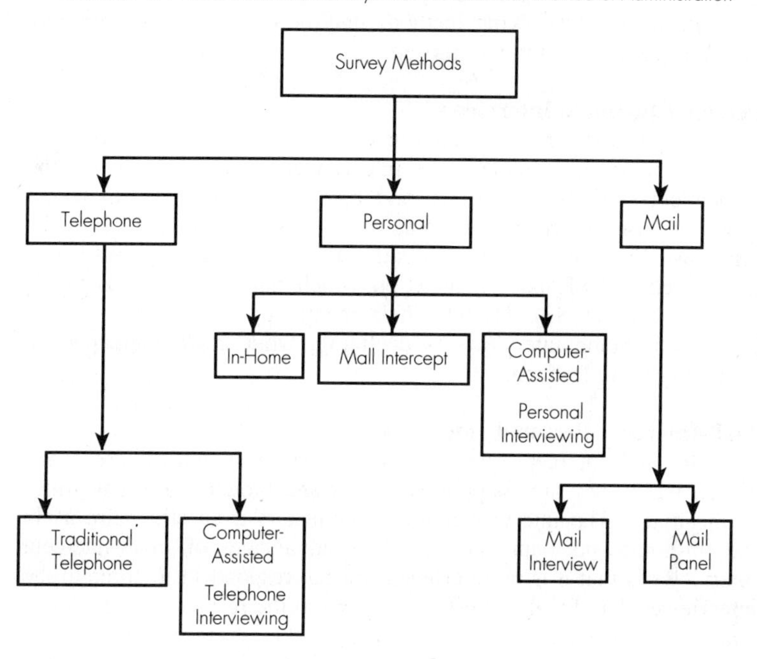

naire administered to respondents over the telephone. A computerized questionnaire may be generated using a mainframe computer, a minicomputer, or a personal computer. The interviewer sits in front of a CRT (cathode ray tube) terminal and wears a mini-headset. The CRT replaces a paper and pencil questionnaire and the mini-headset substitutes for a telephone. On command, the computer dials the telephone number to be called. When contact is made, the interviewer reads questions posed on the CRT screen and records the respondent's answers directly into the computer memory bank.

The computer systematically guides the interviewer and only one question at a time appears on the CRT screen. The computer checks the responses for appropriateness and consistency and uses the responses as they are obtained to personalize the questionnaire. The data collection flows naturally and smoothly. Interviewing time is reduced, data quality is enhanced, and the laborious steps in the data collection process—coding questionnaires and entering the data into the computer—are eliminated. Because the responses are entered directly into the computer, interim and update reports on data collection or results can be provided almost instantaneously.

PERSONAL METHODS

Personal interviewing methods may be categorized as in-home, mall-intercept, or computer-assisted.

Personal In-Home Interviews

In personal in-home interviews, respondents are interviewed face-to-face in their homes. The interviewer's task is to contact the respondents, ask the questions, and record the responses. In recent years, the use of personal in-home interviews has declined due to its high cost. Nevertheless, they are still used, particularly by syndicated firms, such as the Roper Organization, which maintains omnibus panels (Market Facts 1983). Despite their many applications, the use of personal in-home interviews is declining, while mall intercepts are becoming more frequent.

Mall-Intercept Personal Interviews

In mall-intercept personal interviews, respondents are intercepted while they are shopping in malls and brought to test facilities in the malls. The interviewer then administers a questionnaire as in the in-home personal survey. The advantage of mall-intercept interviews is that it is more efficient for the respondent to come to the interviewer than for the interviewer to go to the respondent (Bush and Hair 1985; Rafael 1984). This method has become increasingly popular and there are several hundred permanent mall research facilities. Mall intercepts are especially appropriate when the respondents need to see, handle, or consume the product before they can provide meaningful information.

Computer-Assisted Personal Interviewing (CAPI)

In computer-assisted personal interviewing (CAPI), the respondent sits in front of a computer terminal and answers a questionnaire on the CRT screen by using the keyboard or a mouse. There are several user-friendly electronic packages that design questions that are easy for the respondent to understand. Help screens and courteous error messages are also provided. The colorful screens and on- and off-screen stimuli add to the respondent's interest and involvement in the task. This method has been classified as a personal interview technique since an interviewer is usually present to serve as a host or hostess and to guide the respondent as needed.

CAPI has been used to collect data at shopping malls, product clinics, conferences, and trade shows. However, you may wonder, how does CAPI compare with the traditional method of conducting personal interviews? The experience of several firms, such as the First National Bank of Chicago, has been very positive (Liefeld 1988).

MAIL METHODS

Mail interviews, the third major form of survey administration, can be conducted via ordinary mail or the mail panel.

Mail Interviews

In the traditional mail interview, questionnaires are mailed to preselected potential respondents. A typical mail interview package consists of the outgoing envelope, cover letter, questionnaire, return envelope, and possibly an incentive (Conant, Smart, and Walker 1990; James and Bolstein 1990). The respondents complete and return the questionnaires.

However, before data collection can begin, the respondents need to be at least broadly identified. Therefore, an initial task is to obtain a valid mailing list. Mailing lists can be compiled from telephone directories, customer rosters or association membership rolls, or purchased from publication subscription lists, or commercial mailing list companies. Regardless of its source, a mailing list should be current and closely related to the population of interest. The researcher must also make decisions about the various elements of the mail interview package (see Exhibit 2).

Mail Panels

A mail panel consists of a large, nationally representative sample of households that have agreed to participate in periodic mail questionnaires, product tests, and telephone surveys. The households are compensated with various incentives. Some marketing research organizations that maintain mail panels include National Family Opinion, Market Fact's Consumer Mail Panel, Marketing and Research Counselors' National Neighborhood Panel, and Home Testing Institute.

Mail panels can be used to obtain information from the same respondents repeatedly. Thus they can be used to implement a longitudinal design that examines changes over time. Remember, however, that not all survey methods are appropriate in a given situation. Therefore, the researcher should conduct a comparative evaluation to determine which methods are appropriate.

A COMPARATIVE EVALUATION OF SURVEY METHODS

Exhibit 3 (shown on page 307) compares the different survey methods across a variety of factors. For any particular research project, the relative importance attached to these factors will vary. These factors consist of flexibility of data collection, diversity of questions, use of physical stimuli, sample control, control of the data collection environment, control of field force, quantity of data, social desirability,

EXHIBIT 2. Some Decisions Related to the Mail Interview Package

Outgoing Envelope	
Outgoing Envelope: size, color, return address	
Postage	
Method of addressing	
Cover Letter	
Sponsorship	Signature
Personalization	Postscript
Type of appeal	
Questionnaire	
Length	Layout
Content	Color
Size	Format
Reproduction	Respondent anonymity
Return Envelope	
Type of envelope	
Postage	
Incentives	
Monetary vs. nonmonetary	
Prepaid vs. promised amount	

obtaining sensitive information, potential for interviewer bias, response rate, perceived anonymity, speed, and cost.

Flexibility of Data Collection

The personal interview, whether conducted in-home or as a mall-intercept interview, allows the highest flexibility of data collection. Because the respondent and the interviewer meet face-to-face, the interviewer can administer complex questionnaires, explain and clarify difficult questions, and even utilize unstructured techniques.

The traditional telephone interview, by contrast, allows only moderate flexibility because it is more difficult to use unstructured techniques, ask complex questions, or obtain in-depth answers to open-ended questions over the telephone. CATI and CAPI allow somewhat greater flexibility because the researcher can use various question formats, personalize the questionnaire, and handle complex skip patterns (directions for skipping questions in the questionnaire based on the subject's responses). Because the mail questionnaire allows for no interaction between the interviewer and the respondent, mail surveys and mail panels have low flexibility.

Diversity of Questions

A wide variety of questions can be asked in a personal interview because the interviewer is present to clarify ambiguities. Thus in-home,

EXHIBIT 3. A Comparative Evaluation of Survey Methods for Domestic Research

Criteria	Telephone Interviews	CATI	In-Home	Mall Intercept	CAPI	Mail Surveys	Mail Panels
Flexibility of data collection	Moderate	Moderate to high	High	High	Moderate to high	Low	Low
Diversity of questions	Low	Low	High	High	High	Moderate	Moderate
Use of physical stimuli	Low	Low	Moderate to high	High	High	Moderate	Moderate
Sample control	Moderate to high	Moderate to high	Potentially high	Moderate	Moderate	Low	Moderate to high
Control of data collection environment	Moderate	Moderate	Moderate to high	High	High	Low	Low
Control of field force	Moderate	Moderate	Low	Moderate	Moderate	High	High
Quantity of data	Low	Low	High	Moderate	Moderate	Moderate	High
Response rate	Moderate	Moderate	High	High	High	Low	Moderate
Perceived anonymity of the respondent	Moderate	Moderate	Low	Low	Low	High	High
Social desirability	Moderate	Moderate	High	High	High	Low	Low
Obtaining sensitive information	High	High	Low	Low	Low to moderate	High	High
Potential for interviewer bias	Moderate	Moderate	High	High	Low	None	None
Speed	High	High	Moderate	Moderate to high	Moderate to high	Low	Low to moderate
Cost	Moderate	Moderate	High	Moderate to high	Moderate to high	Low	Low to moderate

mall-intercept, and CAPI allow for diversity. In mail surveys and mail panels, less diversity is possible. In traditional telephone interviews and CATI, the respondent cannot see the questions while answering and this limits the diversity of questions. For example, in a telephone interview or CATI, one could not ask respondents to rank 15 brands of automobiles in terms of preference.

Use of Physical Stimuli

Often it is helpful or necessary to use physical stimuli such as the product, a product prototype, commercials, or promotional displays during the interview. For the most basic example, a taste test involves tasting the product. In other cases, photographs, maps, or other audio visual cues are helpful. In these cases, personal interviews conducted at central locations (mall-intercept and CAPI) are preferable to in-home interviews. Mail surveys and mail panels are moderate on this dimension because sometimes it is possible to mail the facilitating aids or product samples. The use of physical stimuli is limited in traditional telephone interviews and CATI.

Sample Control

Sample control is the ability of the survey mode to reach the units specified in the sample effectively and efficiently (Childers and Skinner 1985). At least in principle, in-home personal interviews offer the best sample control. It is possible to control which sampling units are interviewed, who is interviewed, the degree of participation of other members of the household, and many other aspects of data collection. In practice, to achieve a high degree of control, the researcher has to overcome several problems. It is difficult to find respondents at home during the day because most people work outside the home. Also, for safety reasons, interviewers are reluctant to venture into certain neighborhoods and people have become reluctant to respond to strangers at their door.

Mall-intercept interviews allow only a moderate degree of sample control. While the interviewer has control over which respondents to intercept, the choice is limited to mall shoppers, and frequent shoppers have a greater probability of being included. Also, potential respondents can intentionally avoid or initiate contact with the interviewer. Compared to mall-intercept, CAPI offers better control because sampling quotas can be set and respondents randomized automatically.

Moderate to high sampling control can be achieved with traditional telephone interviews and CATI. Telephones offer access to geographically-dispersed respondents and hard-to-reach areas. These procedures depend on a sampling frame—a list of population units with their telephone numbers (Czaja, Blair, and Sebestik 1982; O'Rourke and Blair 1983). The sampling frames normally used are telephone directories, but telephone directories are limited because (1) not everyone has a phone; (2) some people have unlisted phone numbers; and (3) directories do not reflect new phones in service or recently disconnected phones. While the telephone has achieved an almost total penetration of households, there are some variations by region and within regions. The percentage of households with unlisted numbers is about 31% and varies considerably by geographical region. In large metropolitan areas, it may be as high as 60%. The total of unpublished numbers and new phones in service since the directory was published can account for as much as 40% of total telephone households in some metropolitan areas (Survey Sampling 1992).

The random digit dialing (RDD) technique is used to overcome the bias of unpublished and recent numbers. RDD consists of selecting all ten telephone number digits at random (area code, prefix or exchange, and suffix). While this approach gives all households with telephones an approximately equal chance of being included in the sample, it has some limitations. It is costly and time consuming to implement because not all possible telephone numbers are in service: although there are 10 billion possible telephone numbers, there are only about 86 million actual household telephone numbers. Also, RDD does not distinguish between telephone numbers that are of interest and those that are not (in a consumer survey, for example, business and government numbers are not of interest). There are several variations of RDD that reduce wasted effort. One variation randomly selects a working exchange and adds a block of four-digit random numbers. In random digit directory designs, a sample of numbers is drawn from the directory. These numbers are modified to allow unpublished numbers a chance of being included in the sample. The popular approaches for modification of numbers include (1) adding a constant to the last digit; (2) randomizing the last r ($r = 2, 3,$ or 4) digits; and (3) a two-stage procedure. These procedures are described and illustrated in Exhibit 4. Of these three methods, adding a constant to the last digit—particularly Plus-One sampling—results in high contact rates and representative samples (Blair and Czaja 1982).

Mail surveys require a list of addresses of individuals or households eligible for inclusion in the sample. Mail surveys can reach geographically-dispersed respondents and hard-to-reach areas (Biner and Barton 1990). However, mailing lists are sometimes unavailable, outdated, or incomplete. Typically, telephone and street directories are used for a listing of the general population. Problems with these types of lists have been discussed already. As illustrated in Exhibit 5 (shown on page 311), catalogs of mailing lists contain thousands of lists that can be purchased.

Another factor outside the researcher's control is whether the questionnaire is answered and who answers it. Some subjects refuse to respond because of lack of interest or motivation; others cannot respond

EXHIBIT 4. Random Digit Directory Designs

Addition of a Constant to the Last Digit

An integer between 1 and 9 is added to the telephone number selected from the directory. In Plus-One sampling, the number added to the last digit is one.

Number selected from directory: 953–3004 (exchange-block). Add one to the last digit to form 953–3005. This is the number to be included in the sample.

Randomization of the *r* Last Digits

Replace the *r* (*r* = 2, 3 or 4) last digits with an equal number of randomly selected digits.

Number selected from directory: 881–1124. Replace the last four digits of block with randomly selected numbers 5, 2, 8, and 6 to form 881–5286.

Two-Stage Procedure

The first stage consists of selecting an exchange and telephone number from the directory. In the second stage, the last three digits of the selected number are replaced with a three-digit random number between 000 and 999.

Cluster 1

Selected exchange: 636
Selected number: 636–3230
Replace the last three digits (230) with randomly selected 389 to form 636–3389.
Repeat this process until the desired number of telephone numbers from this cluster is obtained.

because they are illiterate (Conant, Smart, and Walker 1990). For these reasons, the degree of sample control in mail surveys is low (Erdos 1974; Hubbard and Little 1988).

Mail panels, on the other hand, provide moderate to high control over the sample. They provide samples matched to U.S. Bureau of the Census statistics on key demographic variables. It is also possible to identify specific user groups within a panel and to direct the survey to households with specific characteristics. Specific members of households in the panel can be questioned. Finally, low incidence groups—groups that occur infrequently in the population—can be reached with panels, but there is a question of the extent to which a panel can be considered to be representative of the entire population.

Control of the Data Collection Environment

The degree of control a researcher has over the environment in which the respondent answers the questionnaire is another factor that differentiates the various survey modes. Personal interviews conducted at central locations (mall-intercept and CAPI) offer the greatest degree of environmental control. For example, the researcher can set up a special facility for demonstrating the product. In-home personal interviews offer moderate to good control because the interviewer is present.

EXHIBIT 5. Sample Mailing Lists

List Title	Number on List	Price*
Advertising agency executives	31,000	$45/M
Banks, branches	40,100	$45/M
Boat owners	567,400	$50/M
Chambers of commerce	6,885	$60/M
Personal computer owners	2,300,000	Inquire
Families	81,000,000	Inquire
Hardware wholesalers	14,600	$45/M
Magazines, consumer	1,385	$85
Photography clubs	930	$85
Sales executives	97,300	$45/M
Wives who work	250,000	Inquire
Yuppies	115,000	$45/M

*Price shown is per 1,000 names (/M), except where noted.
Source: Alvin B. Zeller, Inc., *1990 Catalog of Mailing Lists.*

Traditional telephone and CATI offer moderate control. The interviewer cannot see the environment in which the interview is being conducted, but he or she can sense the background conditions and encourage the respondent to be attentive and involved. In mail panels and especially in mail surveys, the researcher has little control over the environment.

Control of Field Force

The field force consists of interviewers and supervisors involved in data collection. Because they require no such personnel, mail surveys and mail panels eliminate field force problems. Traditional telephone interviews, CATI, mall-intercept, and CAPI offer moderate degrees of control because the interviews are conducted at a central location, making supervision relatively simple. In-home personal interviews are problematic in this respect. Since many interviewers work in many different locations, continual supervision is impractical (Guengel, Berchman, and Cannell 1983).

Quantity of Data

In-home personal interviews allow the researcher to collect large amounts of data. The social relationship between the interviewer and the respondent, as well as the home environment, motivate the respondent to spend more time in the interview. Less effort is required of the respondent in a personal interview than in a telephone or mail interview. The interviewer records answers to open-ended questions and provides visual aids to help with lengthy and complex scales. Some personal interviews last for as long as 75 minutes. In contrast to in-home interviews, mall-intercept and CAPI provide only moderate amounts of data. Because these interviews are conducted in shopping malls and other central locations, the respondent's time is more limited. Typically, the interview time is 30 minutes or less. For example, in recent mall-intercept interviews conducted by General Foods, the interview time was limited to 25 minutes.

Mail surveys also yield moderate amounts of data. Fairly long questionnaires can be used since short questionnaires have not been shown to generate higher response rates than long ones. Mail panels, on the other hand, can generate large amounts of data because of the special relationship between the panel members and the sponsoring organization. For example, the author has used the Market Facts panel to administer a questionnaire that took two hours to complete.

Traditional telephone interviews and CATI result in the most limited quantities of data. They tend to be shorter than other surveys because respondents can easily terminate the telephone conversation at their own discretion. These interviews commonly last about 15 minutes, although longer interviews may be conducted when the subject matter is of interest to the respondents (Sudman 1976). Studies indicate that respondents tend to underestimate the length of telephone interviews by as much as 50 percent—this suggests that telephone interviews may be conducted for a longer duration than is currently the practice.

Response Rate

Survey response rate is broadly defined as the percentage of the total attempted interviews that are completed. Personal, in-home, mall-intercept, and computer-assisted interviews yield the highest response rate—typically more than 80%. Problems caused by not-at-homes can often be resolved by calling back at different times. Telephone interviews—traditional and CATI—yield response rates between 60 and 80%. These modes also suffer from not-at-homes or no-answers. Higher response rates are obtained by call-backs; many telephone surveys attempt to call back at least three times.

Mail surveys have the poorest response rate. In a mail survey of randomly selected respondents, without any pre- or post-mailing contact, the response rate is typically less than 15%. Such low response rate can lead to serious bias (nonresponse bias) because whether a person responds to a mail survey is related to his or her interest in the topic. The magnitude of nonresponse bias increases as the response rate decreases. However, use of appropriate response-inducement procedures can increase the response rate in mail surveys to 80% or more. Response rates in mail panels are typically in the 70–80% range because of assured respondent cooperation.

A comprehensive review of the literature covering 497 response rates in 93 journal articles found weighted-average response rates of

81.7, 72.3, and 47.3% for personal, telephone, and mail surveys respectively (James and Bolstein 1990; Yu and Cooper 1983). It was also found that response rates increase with:

- either prepaid or promised monetary incentives;
- increase in the amount of monetary incentive;
- nonmonetary premiums and rewards (pens, pencils, and books);
- preliminary notification;
- foot-in-the-door techniques—these are multiple request strategies. The first request is relatively small, and all or most people agree to comply. The small request is followed by a larger request, called the critical request, which is actually the target behavior.
- personalization (sending letters addressed to specific individuals); and
- follow-up letters.

Perceived Anonymity

Perceived anonymity refers to the respondents' perceptions that their identities will not be discerned by the interviewer or the researcher. Perceived anonymity of the respondent is high in mail surveys and mail panels and low in personal interviews (in-home, mall-intercept, and computer-assisted). Traditional telephone interviews and CATI fall in the middle.

Social Desirability/Sensitive Information

Social desirability is the tendency of the respondents to give answers that are socially acceptable, whether or not they are true. Because mail surveys and mail panels do not involve any social interaction between the interviewer and the respondent, they are least susceptible to social desirability. Evidence suggests that such methods are good for obtaining sensitive information such as financial or personal behavior. Traditional telephone interviews and CATI are moderately good at avoiding socially desirable responses and good for obtaining sensitive information (Aneshensed, et al. 1982). Personal interviews, whether in-home, mall-intercept, or computer-assisted, are limited in this respect, although the problem is somewhat mitigated in the case of computer-assisted interviews.

Potential for Interviewer Bias

An interviewer can bias the results of a survey by the manner in which he or she (1) selects respondents (interviewing somebody else when required to interview the male head of household); (2) asks research questions (omitting questions); and (3) records answers (recording an answer incorrectly or incompletely). The extent of the interviewer's role determines the potential for bias (Cannell, Miller, and Oksenberg 1981; Miller and Cannell 1982). In-home and mall-intercept personal interviews are highly susceptible to interviewer bias. Traditional telephone interview and CATI are less susceptible, although the potential is still there. For example, with inflection and tone of voice, interviewers can convey their own attitudes and thereby suggest answers. Computer-assisted interviews have a low potential for bias; mail surveys and mail panels are free of it.

Speed

Traditional telephone interviews and CATI are the fastest ways of obtaining information. When a central telephone facility is used, several hundred telephone interviews can be done per day. Data for even large national surveys can be collected in two weeks or less. Next in speed are mall-intercept and computer-assisted interviews, which reach potential respondents in central locations. In-home personal interviews are slower because there is dead time between interviews while the interviewer travels to the next respondent. To expedite data collection, interviews can be conducted simultaneously in different markets or regions. Mail surveys are typically the slowest—it usually takes several weeks to receive completed questionnaires and follow-up mailings take even longer. Mail panels are faster than mail surveys because little follow-up is required.

Cost

Personal interviews tend to be the most expensive mode of data collection per completed response, while mail surveys tend to be the least expensive. In general, mail surveys, mail panel, traditional telephone, CATI, CAPI, mall-intercept, and personal interviews require progressively larger field staff and greater supervision and control. Hence, the cost increases in this order. However, relative costs depend on the subject of inquiry and the procedures adopted.

SELECTION OF SURVEY METHOD(S)

As is evident from Exhibit 3 and the preceding discussion, no survey method is superior in all situations. Depending on such factors as information requirements, budgetary constraints (time and money), and respondent characteristics, none, one, two, or even all methods may be appropriate. Remember that the various data collection modes are not mutually exclusive. Rather, they can be employed in a complementary fashion to build on each other's strengths and compensate for each other's weaknesses. The researcher can employ these methods in combination and develop creative methods. To illustrate, in a classic project, interviewers distributed the product, self-administered questionnaires, and return envelopes to respondents; traditional telephone interviews were used for follow-up. Combining the data collection modes resulted in telephone cooperation from 97% of the respondents. Furthermore, 82% of the questionnaires were returned by mail (Payne 1964).

SURVEY METHODS IN INTERNATIONAL MARKETING RESEARCH

The selection of a survey method is even more complex when the research is being done in an international setting.

Telephone Interviewing and CATI

In the United States and Canada, the telephone has achieved almost total penetration of households. This factor, along with the speed and cost considerations has resulted in telephone interviewing as being the dominant mode of administering questionnaires to respondents. In Canada, 48% of the interviews conducted in 1986 were telephone interviews (Monk 1987); telephone interviews constitute 48% of all the interviews conducted in the United States (Honomichl 1984). The same situation exists in some of the European countries. In Sweden, the number of telephones per 1,000 inhabitants exceeds 900; in Stockholm, the figure is even higher (Kaiser 1988). Along with its low cost, this has led to a sharp increase in the use of telephone interviews, which now amount to 46% of the interviews conducted and are the dominant interviewing method (Kaiser 1988). In other countries, like the Netherlands and Switzerland, the number of telephone interviews exceeds the number of personal interviews, although the amount of money involved in telephone interviewing is less than the amount involved in personal interviewing. In the Netherlands, the ratio of telephone interviews to personal interviews is 1 to 1.5, when expressed in the value of commissioned research (Oostveen 1986). Yet, even in these countries, the sampling of respondents for telephone interviewing may pose serious problems.

In many other European countries, telephone penetration is still not completely limiting the use of this method. Telephone penetration in England is only about 80%, and many are still skeptical of the value of telephone interviewing, especially for voting intention measurement (Worcester 1987). Only 11.2% of the interviews in Finland are conducted by telephone (Vahvelainen 1987); in Portugal, telephone penetration is still low (33.6%), except in the Lisbon area (76%). For this reason, only 17% of the interviews conducted are telephone interviews (Queiros and Santos Lima 1988). There is very little telephone interviewing in Greece because there are still a substantial number of households without a telephone. Yet, the use of telephone interviewing appears to be growing as more and more households are getting telephones. For example, the use of telephone interviews in Spain is increasing—about 67% of the homes have telephones, but in some metropolitan areas (Madrid and Barcelona), this reaches 100%, making telephone interviews very reliable (Garrido 1987).

In NICs (newly industrialized countries) such as Hong Kong, 96% of households (other than on outlying islands and on boats) can be contacted by telephone. With some persistence, evening telephone interviewing can successfully achieve interviews with 70 to 75% of selected respondents. Residents are uninhibited about using telephones and relaxed about telephone interviews. Yet, given the culture, this is not the most important mode of data collection (Davies, et al. 1987).

The use of telephone interviewing in developing countries poses serious problems because very few households have telephones. Telephone incidence is low in Africa (Corder 1978); India is a predominantly rural society where the penetration of telephones in households is less than 1% (Sopariwala 1987); and in Brazil, the proportion of households with telephones is low—30% in large cities—(Pinheiro de Andrade 1987). Even in countries such as Saudi Arabia, where telephone ownership is extensive, telephone directories tend to be incomplete and outdated. In many developing countries, telephone interviewing may represent additional problems. Daytime calls to households may not be productive because social customs may inhibit housewives from talking with strangers. This situation could be alleviated somewhat by using female telephone interviewers; however, in cultures such as Saudi Arabia, the employment of women is very difficult and can take place only under special conditions. Also, in many cultures, face-to-face relationships are predominant. All of these factors severely limit the use of telephone interviewing in developing countries.

In sum, telephone interviews may be more appropriate when the respondents are relatively upscale consumers who are accustomed to business transactions by phone, such as lawyers or doctors, and consumers who can be reached by phone and can express themselves easily. With the decline of costs for international telephone calls, multicountry studies can be conducted from a single location. This greatly reduces the time and costs associated with the organization and control of the research project in each country. The additional costs of making international calls may not be significant (De Houd 1982). Furthermore, international calls obtain a higher response rate and the results have been found to be stable, the same results being obtained from the first 100 interviews as from the next 200 or 500. It is necessary to find interviewers fluent in relevant languages, but in most European countries, this is rarely problematic.

CATI facilities are well developed in the United States, Canada (Monk 1987), and in some European countries such as Germany (Marcotty 1985). As the use of telephone interviewing is growing, they are becoming popular in other countries such as the Netherlands, Switzerland, and Sweden (Saris and de Pijper 1986). However, we do not expect that CATI will become popular in developing countries in the near future. While CATI facilities are available in Brazil, they are not popular (Pinheiro de Andrade 1987).

Personal Interviews

Due to high cost, the use of in-home personal interviews has declined in the United States and Canada. In 1986, only 24.3% of the interviews conducted in Canada were in-home (Monk 1987). The corresponding percentage for the United States is even smaller—13% (Honomichl 1984). However, they are still the dominant mode of collecting survey data in many parts of Europe and in the developing world. For example, in-home personal interviewing is the dominant interviewing method in Switzerland (Demby 1990).

At least in principal, in-home personal interviews offer the best sample control. It is possible to draw a representative sample of households using a probability sampling scheme. For this purpose, a list of sampling units is not necessary. It is also possible to control which sampling units are interviewed, who is interviewed, the degree of participation of other members of the household, and many other aspects of the data collection process. In practice, to achieve a high degree of control, the researcher has to contend with several problems even in developed countries. It may be difficult to find respondents at home during the day—in the United States, nearly half the women work outside the home. Making callbacks is time-consuming and expensive. For safety reasons, interviewers are reluctant to venture into certain neighborhoods and people have become reluctant to respond to strangers at their door.

In-home interviews require the availability of a large pool of qualified interviewers, which could be problematic. The contractual arrangements with interviewers may vary considerably. For example, in France, there are three categories of interviewers: interviewers with annual guarantee for a specified duration, interviewers with annual guarantee for an unspecified duration, and freelance interviewers with no salary guarantee. Furthermore, the overheads can also vary: in France, the employer and the interviewer must pay large social security contributions; in Belgium, the interviewers are self-employed and pay their own social security contributions; and in England, although both the employer and the interviewer pay national insurance contributions, these tend to be small—10.45% of salary for employer and 9% of salary for interviewer (Bigant and Rickebusch 1985).

In many developing economies, it is difficult, if not impossible, to draw probabilistic samples. Listings that serve as sampling frames for representative samples may not be available. For example, in Saudi Arabia, there is no officially recognized census of population. Because there are no elections in this country, voter registration records do not exist (Tuncalp 1988). Moreover, accurate maps of population centers are not available. Due to the fast pace of urbanization, maps drawn by municipalities become outdated very quickly. Therefore city blocks cannot be used as the basis for cluster, area, or stratified random sampling. Even if it were possible to draw random samples, the unapproachability of women in many cultures would make the probability sampling procedures biased and nonrepresentative. In-home personal interviews may be further hindered by many people who consider their homes to be off limits to strangers. In Mexico, upper socioeconomic classes are difficult to reach because of the housing structures of walls, gates, and intervening servants. In addition, dwelling units may not be numbered and streets unidentified, making it difficult to locate predesignated households. Several family units may be inhabiting one dwelling unit and many relatives may be sharing a house due to extended family structures, making it difficult to select a specific respondent. More than one person in the household may qualify for participation in the interview based on pre-established quota sampling requirements (Yavas and Kaynak 1980).

In spite of these limitations, in-home personal interviews are popular in many European countries, NICs, and developing countries. In England, the ratio of personal to telephone interviews is 4.8 to 1.0, expressed in the value of commissioned research. Political opinion polls commissioned in England one evening can be conducted nationally the next day, with representative samples of over 1,000 respondents, using face-to-face personal interviews and reported back the same afternoon to be released on that evening's television news (Worcester 1987).

In Portugal, face-to-face interviews make up 77% of the total interviews conducted (Queiros and Santos Lima 1988) and are the most commonly used interviews in Spain (Garrido 1987). Personal interviews are also used for electoral polls in Italy, Greece, Japan, and India. Most of the interviews done in Hong Kong, India, Brazil, and Africa are personal interviews.

Mall Intercept and CRT Interviews

The North American type of retailing, plus the inclement weather for several months of the year, have made enclosed shopping malls very common in the United States and Canada. Many marketing research organizations have permanent facilities in such malls, equipped with interviewing rooms, kitchens, observation areas, and other devices. Mall intercepts constitute 15.2% of the interviews in Canada (Monk 1987) and 19% in the United States (Honomichl 1984). Even in these countries, mall intercepts and computer-administered personal interviews conducted in central locations offer only a moderate amount of sample control. While the interviewer has control over which respondents will be intercepted, the choice is limited to mall shoppers (or those present in the central location). Thus frequent shoppers have a greater probability of being included in the sample. Also, contact with the interviewer can be intentionally avoided or initiated by a potential respondent. As compared to mall intercepts, computer-administered interviews offer better control because sampling quotas and respondent randomization can be accomplished automatically.

While mall intercepts are being conducted in some European countries such as Sweden (Kaiser 1988), they are not that popular in Europe and in developing countries. However, central location/street interviews are popular in some European countries; they constitute the dominant method of collecting survey data in France and the Netherlands (Demby 1990).

Similar remarks apply to computer-administered CRT interviews that are conducted in central locations. However, some interesting developments with respect to CRT interviewing are taking place in Europe. An interviewing program for the home computer has been developed in the Netherlands (Saris and de Pijper 1986) and has been used in panel studies. Each household participating in the panel gets an MSX computer and a modem, and the questionnaires are received and dispatched electronically. The Dutch Gallup Institute, NIPO, maintains such a panel—called tele-interview panel—of more than 1,000 households (Saris and de Pijper 1986).

Mail Interviews

Because of low cost, mail interviews continue to be used in most developed countries where literacy is high and the postal system is well developed. Mail interviews constitute 6.2% of the interviews in Canada (Monk 1987) and 7% in the United States (Honomichl 1984). Literacy is close to maximum in the Nordic countries (Denmark, Finland, Iceland, Norway, and Sweden), and the educational level of the population is extremely high (Vahvelainen 1985). Hence, mail interviews are commonly used. For example, 24.9% of the interviews in Finland are mail interviews and an additional 6.3% are semi-mail (Vahvelainen 1987). Mail interviews comprise 22% of the interviews conducted in Sweden (Kaiser 1988) and are very popular in the Netherlands, comprising 33% of all data collection. In Sweden, 23% of all interviews are conducted by mail (Demby 1990).

The problems of using mail interviews are further compounded in developing countries because illiteracy in many countries is high. The culture is such that households do not normally correspond by mail. (In many countries, such as in Southeast Asia, the household utility bills are paid in person rather than by mail). Hence, even literate respondents would make bad correspondents. This would result in very low response rates. Given the slow pace of life and the low value of time, mail surveys would take inordinately long, particularly if reminders or callbacks are used.

Another major problem is that in many developing countries the mail system is not very efficient or reliable. Street addresses may not be fully in place. In some countries, such as Saudi Arabia and Nicaragua, there is no postal delivery of personal mail to homes. People living in the cities rely on post office boxes for the delivery of mail (Tuncalp 1988). Mail surveys are also hazardous in countries such as Brazil, where it has been estimated that 30% of the domestic mail is never delivered. The postal system is still more inefficient, and may even break down in villages and rural areas.

In Africa, Asia, and South America, the use of mail surveys and mail panels is low because of illiteracy and the large rural population. In NICs such as Hong Kong, mail surveys have been tried with varied success with businessmen. Mail surveys are typically more effective in industrial international marketing research. Mailing lists such as Bottin International, or directories for specific industries, are available. The problem, however, is to identify the appropriate respondent within each firm and to personalize the address, thereby increasing the likelihood of response.

Mail Panels

Mail panels are well developed and are often used along with other panels such as scanner panels in the United States and Canada. Panels are being extensively used in England, France, Germany, and the Netherlands (Bigant and Rickebusch 1985). Mail and diary panels are also available in Finland, Sweden, Italy, Spain, and other European countries.

Mail panels provide moderate to high control over the sample. In the United States, they provide samples matched to U.S. Census Bureau statistics on key demographic variables. It is also possible to identify specific user groups within a panel so that the survey can be directed at households with specific characteristics. Specific members of households in the panel can be questioned and low incidence groups can be reached. However, there is a question of the extent to which a panel can be considered to be representative of the entire population.

Use of panels may increase with the advent of new technology. For example, in Germany, two agencies (A. C. Nielsen and GfK-Nurnberg) have installed electronic scanner test markets, based on the Behavior Scan model from the United States. Nielsen will use television; GfK will use cable (Marcotty 1985). However, such panels have not yet been developed in Hong Kong (Davies, et al. 1987) and most of the developing countries.

EVALUATION FOR USE IN INTERNATIONAL MARKETING RESEARCH

The factors that have been considered in domestic survey research are helpful in providing a general evaluation of the different methods of administering a survey questionnaire. However, the evalu-

EXHIBIT 6. A Comparative Evaluation of Survey Methods for Use in International Marketing Research

Criteria	Telephone	Personal	Mail
High sample control	+	+	−
Difficulty to locate respondents at home	+	−	+
Inaccessibility of homes	+	−	+
Unavailability of a large pool of trained interviewers	+	−	+
Large population in rural areas	−	+	−
Unavailability of maps	+	−	+
Unavailability of current telephone directory	−	+	−
Unavailability of mailing lists	+	+	−
Low penetration of telephones	−	+	+
Lack of an efficient postal system	+	+	−
Low level of literacy	−	+	−
Face-to-face communication culture	−	+	−

ation of the different methods could change rather dramatically in an international marketing research context taking into account the stage of economic, technological and business development; population distribution; educational level; and culture of the country in which the research is being conducted. The major interviewing methods are now evaluated in light of additional factors that are also relevant in conducting research in different countries. Special attention is given to conducting research in North America, Europe, and developing countries. The criteria used in evaluating the different methods focuses on locating, contacting, and obtaining information from the respondents.

A comparative evaluation of the major modes of collecting quantitative data in the context of international marketing research is presented in Exhibit 6. In this table, the communication methods of Exhibit 1 are discussed only under the broad headings of telephone, personal, and mail interviews. The use of CATI, CRT interviewing, and mail panels depends heavily on the state of technological development in the country. Likewise, the use of mall intercept interviewing is contingent on the dominance of shopping malls in the retailing environment. The major methods of interviewing are discussed with respect to the criteria given in Exhibit 6.

If a high degree of sample control is required, mail surveys are not a viable option. If several families are living under one roof, as in some cultures, it may be difficult to identify the respondent by mail. Even if that were possible, poor response rate is very likely to result in a final sample that deviates significantly from the characteristics of the initial sample.

The difficulty of reaching respondents at home may make the use of personal interviews infeasible. This difficulty may arise due to a number of reasons. Both spouses may be working, the homes may be off limits to strangers, or it may not be possible to approach women at home, particularly during the day when they are alone.

The unavailability of a large pool of trained interviewers is another factor that would hinder the use of personal interviews. Typically, personal interviews require a far greater number of interviewers as compared to telephone interviews. In addition, the supervision of telephone interviewers is relatively easy as the interviews are conducted from one or a few central locations. On the other hand, interviewers conducting personal interviews are geographically scattered, making supervision difficult. Of course, the problem of training and supervision is eliminated in mail surveys because there are no interviewers. However, if a large percentage of the survey population lives in rural areas, personal interviews become the favored mode. In many nations, particularly in developing countries, it is difficult to reach the rural population by telephone or mail.

Maps are essential to personal interviews and mailing lists. Telephone directories are essential to conduct both telephone and mail surveys. In many parts of the world, postal zip codes are not commonly used, so the complete address must be obtained from a telephone directory. The unavailability of any of these aids to sampling frames used to identify and locate respondents would hinder the use of the corresponding methods of interviewing.

A low penetration of telephones in the homes would make telephone interviewing infeasible for most consumer surveys. Likewise, the lack of an efficient postal system would argue against the use of mail surveys.

The levels of literacy should be taken into account while selecting a data collection method. Low levels of literacy would favor the use of personal interviews. Although literacy levels in developed countries are typically 99%, they are much lower in other countries. They could be as low as 5% in Upper Volta and 12% in Afghanistan. Linguistic heterogeneity is yet another factor that should be considered—the questionnaire may have to be administered in countries speaking a diversity of languages. For example, 159 languages are spoken by at least one million people, 12 languages are spoken by more than 100 million people, and 14 languages are spoken by at least 40 million people (Douglas and Craig 1983).

In addition to understanding the language, we must understand the habit, culture, social behavior, and consumption patterns of the country in which the research is being conducted. There may be difficult barriers in religion, customs, social etiquettes, and laws that may have to be carefully navigated. In many parts of the world, the culture is such that face-to-face communication is preferred, favoring the use of personal interviews. The availability of different communication media varies from country to country. Differences exist between the highly developed nations of North America and Western Europe, and the developing nations of Asia, Africa, and Latin America, but there are also differences within these regions.

SELECTION OF SURVEY METHODS IN INTERNATIONAL RESEARCH

In addition to the factors considered under domestic research, a very important consideration in selecting the methods of administering questionnaires is to ensure equivalence and comparability across countries. Different methods may have varying reliabilities in different countries. In one country, for example, a mail survey may be known to have a given level of reliability; in another country, in-home interviews may have an equivalent level of reliability. Thus, mail surveys should be used in the first country while in-home interviews should be conducted in the second country. In collecting data from different countries, it is desirable to use techniques with equivalent levels of reliability rather than the same techniques (Douglas and Craig 1983).

CONCLUSION

In this chapter, we consider the use of survey methods in domestic and international marketing research. Internationalism and global thinking is on the increase and this will further increase the demand for knowledge and information leading to increased marketing research (Goodyear 1985). Increasingly, marketing research projects will require the collection of data in an international or global setting. For administration of the survey questionnaire, suitable infrastructures must exist. In large overpopulated agglomerations with one language (like London, Paris, or Zurich), personal interviews become more feasible (Marcotty 1985). Yet, the best data collection method may vary even in countries that are located in the same geographic region. Personal in-home interviews are the dominant mode in England and Switzerland; central location/street interviews are dominant in France; in the Netherlands, mail and central location/street interviews are the most popular; and in Sweden, telephone interviewing is the dominant method of collecting survey data (Demby 1990). Despite the many advantages of telephone and mail surveys, these modes may be practically ruled out in many developing countries because of the low number of telephone subscribers, overloaded telephone lines, high illiteracy rates, postal inefficiencies, and low response rates (Yavas and Kaynak 1980).

The costs of different methods of questionnaire administration could vary considerably from country to country. In many developing countries, the marketing research infrastructure may be lacking, which might impose substantial costs in developing sampling frames, selecting and training qualified interviewers, and compiling other basic information. Personal interviewing tends to be the dominant mode of questionnaire administration outside of the United States (Barnard 1982); although it may have the greatest cost associated with it, in international marketing research, it may also be the most cost effective. In many situations, low wage rates, higher response rates, improved quality of data, and representativeness of the target population may offset the higher costs.

In some places like the Far East, Pacific Basin, and Middle East, any method of interviewing may not be fully acceptable. However, some of the methods could be creatively modified to overcome the country-specific barriers. For example, it has been suggested that in Saudi Arabia, graduate students could be employed to hand-deliver questionnaires to relatives and friends (Tuncalp 1988). These initial respondents could be asked for referrals to other potential respondents, and so on—this snowball sampling approach should result in a large sample size. This process should also yield a high response rate since the personal efforts of the graduate students are involved in each round. The quality of data would be high because the students, who make good field workers, would be available to address respondents' questions.

In international marketing research, the country has traditionally been used as the relevant unit of analysis. However, this need not necessarily be the most appropriate. In administering the questionnaire, it may be desirable to select a geographic region or country grouping as the unit of analysis. For example, it may be appropriate to design marketing strategies for geographic regions such as Western Europe, Eastern Europe, or the Far East. To illustrate, the automobile industry often defines target markets in terms of groupings of countries due to economies of scale and the need to integrate small markets (Douglas and Craig 1983). On the other hand, it may be desirable to select subgroupings within countries, such as cities, communities, or cultural groups as the unit of analysis. This may be appropriate if the countries are heterogeneous with regard to language, socioeconomic and technological development, social cohesion, and other factors affecting the behavior of interest.

NOTES

1. This material is drawn from Chapters 7 and 25 of Malhotra, N. K. (1993), *Marketing Research: An Applied Orientation,* Englewood Cliffs: Prentice Hall, Inc.; and Malhotra, N.K. (1991), "Administration of Questionnaires for Collecting Quantitative Data in International Marketing Research," *Journal of Global Marketing,* Vol. 4, No. 2, 1991, pp. 63–92.

REFERENCES

C.S. Aneshensed, R. R. Frerichs, V. A. Clark, and P. A. Yokopenic, "Measuring Depression in the Community: A Comparison of Telephone and Personal Interviews," *Public Opinion Quarterly,* (Spring 1982), pp. 110–21.

P. Barnard, "Conducting and Coordinating Multicountry Quantitative Studies Across Europe," *Journal of the Market Research Society,* (1982), pp. 24, 46–64.

J. Bigant and Y. Rickebusch, "Marketing Research in France," *European Research,* (January 1985), pp. 4–11.

Paul M. Biner and Deborah L. Barton, "Justifying the Enclosure of Monetary Incentives in Mail Survey Cover Letters," *Psychology and Marketing,* (Fall 1990) pp. 153–162.

J. Blair and R. Czaja, "Locating a Special Population Using Random Digit Dialing," *Public Opinion Quarterly,* 46 (Winter 1982), pp. 585–590.

A.J. Bush and J. F. Hair, Jr., "An Assessment of the Mall Intercept as a Data Collection Method," *Journal of Marketing Research,* (May 1985), pp. 158–67.

C. F. Cannell, P. U. Miller, and L. Oksenberg, "Research on Interviewing Techniques," in S. Leinhardt, ed., *Sociological Methodology,* San Francisco: Jossey-Bass (1981).

Terry L. Childers and Steven J. Skinner, "Theoretical and Empirical Issues in the Identification of Survey Respondents," *Journal of the Market Research Society,* 27 (January 1985), pp. 39–53.

Jeffrey S. Conant, Denise T. Smart, and Bruce J. Walker, "Mail Survey Facilitation Techniques: An Assessment and Proposal Regarding Reporting Practices," *Journal of Market Research Society,* (UK), 32 (October 1990), pp. 569–580.

C. K. Corder, "Problems and Pitfalls in Conducting Marketing Research in Africa," in B. D. Gelb, ed., *Marketing Expansion in a Shrinking World,* Philadelphia 1978, pp. 86–90.

R. J. Czaja, J. Blair, and J. P. Sebestik, "Respondent Selection in a Telephone Survey: A Comparison of Three Techniques," *Journal of Marketing Research,* 19 (August 1982), pp. 381–385.

R. W. B. Davies, C. J. W. Minter, M. Moll, and D. T. Bottomley, "Marketing Research in Hong Kong," *European Research,* (May 1987), pp. 114–120.

M. De Houd, "Internationalized Computerized Telephone Research: Is It Fiction?" *Marketing Research Society Newsletter,* 190 (January 1982), pp. 14–15.

E. H. Demby, "ESOMAR Urges Changes in Reporting Demographics, Issues Worldwide Report," *Marketing News,* 24(1), (January 1990), pp. 24–25.

S. P. Douglas and C. S. Craig, *International Marketing Research,* Englewood Cliffs, N.J.: Prentice-Hall, Inc. (1983).

P. L. Erdos, "Data Collection Methods: Mail Surveys," in R. Ferber ed., *Handbook of Marketing Research,* New York: McGraw-Hill, (1974).

James H. Frey, *Survey Research by Telephone,* Beverly Hills, CA: Sage Publications (1983).

G. Garrido, "Marketing Research in Spain: A Promising Future," *European Research,* (May 1987), pp. 99–113.

J. R. Goodyear, "The UK Market Research Industry: Past, Present, and Future," *European Research,* (July 1985), pp. 116–123.

P. G. Guengel, T. R. Berchman, and Charles F. Cannell, *General Interviewing Techniques: A Self-Instructional Workbook for Telephone and Personal Interviewer Training,* Ann Arbor, Mich.: Survey Research Center, University of Michigan (1983).

J. J. Honomichl, "Survey Results Positive," *Advertising Age,* 55 (November 1984), pp. 23.

Raymond Hubbard and Eldon L. Little, "Promised Contributions to Charity and Mail Survey Responses: Replications with Extension," *Public Opinion Quarterly,* 52 (Summer 1988), pp. 223–230.

Jeannine M. James and Richard Bolstein, "The Effect of Monetary Incentives and Follow-Up Mailings on the Response Rate and Response Quality in Mail Surveys," *Public Opinion Quarterly,* 54 (Fall 1990), pp. 346–361.

B. P. Kaiser, "Marketing Research in Sweden," *European Research,* (February 1988), pp. 64–70.

John P. Liefeld, "Response Effects in Computer-Administered Questioning," *Journal of Marketing Research,* 25 (November 1988), pp. 405–409.

T. Marcotty, "Mysterious Germany," *European Research,* (October 1985), pp. 148–150.

Market Facts, Inc., *Consumer Market Research Technique Usage Patterns and Attitudes in 1983,* Chicago: Market Facts, Inc., (1983).

P. U. Miller and C. F. Cannell, "A Study of Experimental Techniques for Telephone Interviewing," *Public Opinion Quarterly,* 46 (Summer 1982), pp. 250–269.

D. Monk, "Marketing Research in Canada," *European Research,* (November 1987), pp. 271–274.

D. O'Rourke and J. Blair, "Improving Random Respondent Selection in Telephone Interviews," *Journal of Marketing Research,* 20 (November 1983), pp. 428–432.

J. C. J. Oostveen, "The State of Marketing Research in Europe," *European Research,* (1986), pp. 100–135.

S. L. Payne, "Combination of Survey Methods," *Journal of Marketing Research,* 1 (May 1964), p. 62.

P. Pinheiro de Andrade, "Market Research in Brazil," *European Research,* (August 1987), pp. 188–197.

L. Queiros and J. L. Santos Lima, "Marketing Research in Portugal," *European Research,* (August 1988), pp. 185–191.

Quirk's Marketing Research Review, (April 1988), p. 20.

J.E. Rafael, "Self-Administered CRT Interview: Benefits Far Outweigh the Problems," *Marketing News,* (November 1984), p. 16.

W. E. Saris and Marius W. de Pijper, "Computer Assisted Interviewing Using Home Computers," *European Research, (1986), pp. 144–151.*

D. Sopariwala, "India: Election Polling in the World's Largest Democracy," *European Research,* (August 1987), pp. 174–177.

S. Sudman, "Sample Surveys," *Annual Review of Sociology,* (1976), pp. 107–120.

S. Tuncalp, "The Marketing Research Scene in Saudi Arabia," *European Journal of Marketing,* 22 (May 1988), pp. 15–22.

T. Vahvelainen, "Marketing Research in the Nordic Countries," *European Research,* (April 1985), pp. 76–79.

T. Vahvelainen, "Marketing Research in Finland," *European Research,* (August 1987), pp. 62–66.

R. M. Worcester, "Political Opinion Polling in Great Britain: Past, Present, and Future," *European Research,* (August 1987), pp. 143–151.

U. Yavas and E. Kaynak, "Current Status of Marketing Research in Developing Countries: Problems and Opportunities," *Journal of International Marketing and Marketing Research,* (May 1980), pp. 82–83.

J. Yu and H. Cooper, "A Quantitative Review of Research Design Effects on Response Rates to Questionnaires," *Journal of Marketing Research,* 20 (February 1983), pp. 36–44.

Vincent P. Barabba
Executive-in-Charge
Business Decision Center
General Motors Corporation
Detroit, Michigan

CHAPTER 19

MARKET-BASED DECISIONS

This chapter is based on the premise that competitive edges are to be found in how and when market information is used. The true customers of market information are all groups within a firm and those with whom a firm has strategic alliances that affect the firm's market performance. While this is a very broad mandate, it is an accurate reflection of the many groups that need market information to help guide their decisions.

The premise that competitive edges determine the use of market information raises a significant issue about how traditional market research functions have been traditionally positioned with a firm's organizational structure. David Packard, co-founder of Hewlett-Packard Co., has commented that "Marketing is too important to be left solely to the marketing department." Because the marketing staff is only one of many groups that actually do the firm's marketing, it should be treated as only one—albeit an important one—of many groups in need of market information.

For those who question this position, consider the following:

> *A generally accepted definition of marketing is that it is the process of planning and executing the conception, pricing, promotion, and distribution of ideas, goods, and services to create exchanges that satisfy individual and organizational objectives.*[1]

Now answer the following question:

> *What portion of a company's decisions relative to these marketing functions are made solely by the marketing department?*

The answer, of course, is that the marketing department makes only a small portion of all the company's marketing decisions.

This observation does not necessarily reflect poorly on marketing departments. In fact, in many market-based companies, it is simply recognition that the marketing concept has been fully integrated into all functions of the firm.

In a recent study conducted for the Marketing Science Institute,[2] John C. Narver and Stanley F. Slater found that business units with a market orientation (market based) had a much higher probability of being more profitable. Given the following description of "market based" provided by Narver and Slater, the results should not be surprising:

a. the degree to which buyers' preferences are understood and a unit's continuous focusing on activities that increase the perceived value among customers of its offerings;

b. the extent to which there is an ongoing assessment of the business unit's offerings and capabilities relative to the competition; and
c. the degree of interfunctional coordination, i.e., the degree to which "information on buyers and competitors is shared throughout the business, decisions are made interfunctionally, and all functions contribute to the creation of buyer value."

Point (c) is particularly important in any organization that must make decisions across several units or functions. Part of the problem of making good decisions or being market based is due in large part to the existence of isolated functional silos. Just as farms have different silos for separating different grains, many large companies have organizational silos that house functional specialists. The concept of silos refers to the vertical alignment with an organizational hierarchy. In the organizational context, connections are made naturally within the silos. Connection means the resolution of conflicting visions or frames of reference necessary for action to occur throughout the organization. And, vision means a sense of how the world works, or a sense of what causes things to happen.

While vertical connections are natural and relatively easy, what is really needed is connection in the horizontal sense—that is, alignment with the purpose and vision of the entire enterprise. This requires connection across the functional silos, viable only if the firm's leadership has developed connection and functional integration across the tops of the silos. Otherwise, they should not expect to achieve effective discussion and integration from silo to silo at the working level.

This is not limited to any one sector of our society. Management and staff in every type of organization—farms, factories, government—need to understand how each person or functional area relates to the enterprise's unified vision of how to create long-term customer satisfaction. If that does not occur, the viability of the enterprise is at great risk. The result will be abandoned farms, companies with shuttered factories, and overturned or thrown-out governments, all because they have lost sight of their real purpose for being—to get connection across their functional expertise to serve the customer. Large organizations are not immune from the consequences of not solving this problem; just consider the leaders of the former Soviet Union.

The market-based enterprise (market information is integral to cross-function decisions that create long-term customer relationships) is better positioned to be more profitable than those that are not market based precisely because the activities and attitudes involved in being market based have a direct impact on the quality of thinking within a unit. This, in turn, affects the quality of decision making, which subsequently impacts customer perceptions of the relative value of a firm's offerings.

A MANAGEMENT DILEMMA

Management across all functions of organizations are faced with a continuing dilemma. They are aware of the need to be more sensitive to the voice of the market, yet are conflicted because they have had negative experiences in using market information or have been told by others about negative experiences. Despite their awareness of the need for its use, managers in all functional areas are still not making full and proper use of market information.

The Need for Better Information Use

There are several factors that stimulate the need for more frequent and effective use of market information.

- All competitors have access to the same data because of advances in the availability of quality and timely data.
- Because of the more diverse and changing customers in the marketplace, not only is a broader array of market information necessary, but also the standard ways of interpreting data may be inadequate.
- As lead times for new products shorten and firms enter new markets more quickly than in the past, the time available for reaching decisions is shortening.
- Rapid changes in the marketplace render pertinent information outdated more quickly. Managers need to respond quickly in examining market conditions and taking necessary actions.
- More developmental or exploratory—rather than confirmatory—market research is needed to deal with the many options available in addressing an issue, particularly in determining the right thing to do and how to do it right.

The need for better use of market information does not mean that firms should be guided solely by that information. If that were the case, and if they were all equally competent in using market information, a firm would not differ significantly from those of its competitors who are also only responding to market needs.

Factors Discouraging Better Information Use

There are several conditions that inhibit the collection and efficient use of market information. For example, there is a tendency of some people to confine their thinking to the immediate time period. Much market research also focuses on current issues rather than on those of the future. This is sometimes referred to as the "90-day syndrome." Just as there is a short-term focus on issues, there is also a problem of manager turnover. The frequent management turnover does not allow companies to develop an institutional memory. Only infrequently in this country are a manager's accumulated experiences left behind to benefit the replacement manager.

The timing of research is crucial to obtain the best results to use in decision making. Often research is done to justify a project that has already been initiated, rather than to provide fresh information to the decision process.

Information technology used in the provision of market research has become more ubiquitous and user friendly, resulting in an enormous improvement in the ability of managers to access and use the information on their own. The danger lies in the misuse of information by managers because they lack understanding of the limitations of the data and/or the analytic tools.

There are two trends causing changes in the status of the research function. The first is the movement toward the contracting out of research, with the in-house market researchers serving primarily as purchasing agents. This lessens the chance that they conduct consistent and business environmental scanning that is so important in identifying emerging issues. The other trend is that, although internal market research groups perform a high quality and much needed function, they often lack the stature in the organization that would allow them to participate fully in the decision process.

Other inhibiting factors include difficulty in justifying market research expenditures, impediments created by the difference in viewpoints between users and researchers, and the often unfounded assumption that because we live in a market we understand it and need not study it further.

THE MYTHS OF INFORMATION USE

Although a variety of factors are making it more necessary for firms to improve their sensitivity to market information, other factors are interfering with their doing so. Traditional research functions, where they exist at all, are generally unable to solve this dilemma. Part of the problem are the myths that surround information use.

The first myth concerns the dangers of letting market research either lead to unsuccessful product concepts or get in the way of new and creative ideas. The second myth is the textbook account of recognizing the need for information, to its acquisition, and on to its decision application.

The Myth of Market Research Failures

This myth describes the disasters wrought by market research and the "successes" its absence can bring. One of the most frequently and persistently told examples of the market research disasters is that of the Edsel. This story, now nearly 30 years old, was resurrected in an article in the May 31, 1989 issue of *Investor's Daily:* "Then again, the infamous Edsel was the most heavily researched vehicle of its day. Yet it turned out to be perhaps the auto industry's biggest bomb."[3] It is true, of course, that after three years (1960) the Edsel, kept alive through two model changes, was allowed to pass into extinction. Interested observers, who have heard about the extensive market research conducted before the Edsel's introduction, have concluded that inasmuch as the Edsel's development was so thoroughly "market researched," its failure must be related in some way to the inability of market research to provide timely and accurate information.

A review of the literature on the Edsel's failure, however, leaves open the question of exactly how much research was actually conducted, but is very clear on how well it was used. John Brooks, in an extremely revealing two-part series published in the *New Yorker,* in November and December of 1960, points out that the only research completed before introduction of the Edsel was on its name—the conclusions of which were ignored by the Ford Executive Committee—and two interview studies, each involving 800 consumers, conducted in Peoria, Illinois and San Bernardino, California, probing people's feelings about many different types of cars.[4]

In another account, William Reynolds, writing in *Business Horizons* in 1967 states, "If one goes through the bound volumes of Edsel research in the Ford archives, one is struck—after a somewhat eerie feeling is overcome—by the sophistication of the techniques used and the perspicacity of the findings. No styling research was conducted, but, as noted at the time, no one in the industry was doing such research. Otherwise, the research was comprehensive in the areas of market delineation, product characteristics and image, competition, copy strategy, and other aspects of the marketing plan."[5]

If there is any disagreement between the two authors of the Edsel story on how much market research was actually done, there is, however, little question between them about the extent to which it was used. Brooks makes the point quite clear:

> *For although the Edsel was supposed to be advertised, and otherwise promoted, strictly on the basis of preferences expressed in polls, some old-fashioned snake-oil-selling methods, intuitive rather than scientific, crept in. . . . As for the design, it was arrived at without even a pretense of consulting the polls, and by the method that has been standard for years in the designing of automobiles—that of simply pooling the hunches of sundry company committees. The common explanation of the Edsel's downfall, then, under scrutiny, turns out to be largely a myth, in the colloquial sense of that term. (emphasis added)*[6]

But, as indicated earlier, the notion behind this myth is persistent. In the February 12, 1990 edition of the *Detroit Free Press,* the article rekindles the vision of the market research failure myth from a slightly different perspective:

> *Telnack (vice president of design at Ford) led the team that shaped the Ford Taurus, a car that has reaped many international design awards, spawned a host of imitators and helped Ford become the most profitable*

> *manufacturer of the Big Three. This came despite early research which indicated some would react violently against the car's design. Telnack stood his ground, and was rewarded. (emphasis added)*[7]

Again, there appears to be "the other side of the story!" In a 1989 book, "Reinventing the Wheels," the authors support the notion that there was some market research conducted that surfaced some negative reaction to the Taurus aero design.

> *Ford researchers also knew that a certain percentage of the American driving population would adamantly dislike the Taurus styling. These would be the types of people . . . who are almost always unreceptive to anything new or different. Ford designers labeled them "Johnny Lunch-buckets" and, for all practical purposes, these customers were written off as being unreachable—at least for the first model year or two.*[8]

The authors also identify specific actions that were taken to improve the product. For example, in April 1981, more than a year after development had begun, the overall size of the car was drastically changed. As Lewis Veraldi, Ford Motor Company executive, put it, "We scrapped the whole car . . . the car was re-engineered to be bigger than originally intended, and this was done because of a perceived change in the targeted market. . . . The small prototype of Taurus was expanded in all dimensions. Its wheelbase was enlarged, its track was widened, and its overall volume was increased."

So here are two myths published in the popular press: The first, that market research conducted for the Edsel contributed to an error of the first type; that is, indicated the product was right when it was wrong. The second myth was that market research contributed to an error of the second type, indicating a product was wrong when it was right. Interestingly, other, more detailed accounts on both subjects indicate just the opposite.

But the popular press is not alone in perpetuating the concept of the market research folly. In a 1980 article in the *Harvard Business Review,* "Managing Our Way to Economic Decline," the authors state,

> *In the past 20 years, American companies have perhaps learned too well a lesson they had long been inclined to ignore: Business should be customer oriented rather than product oriented. . . . "We have got to stop marketing makeable products and learn to make marketable products." At last, however, the dangers of too much reliance on this philosophy are becoming apparent. As two Canadian researchers have put it: "Inventors, scientists, engineers, and academics, in the normal pursuit of scientific knowledge, gave the world in recent times the laser, xerography, instant photography, and the transistor. In contrast, worshippers of the market concept have bestowed upon mankind such products as newfangled potato chips, feminine hygiene deodorant, and the pet rock."*[9]

Although the bias of these authors is obvious in their selection of market-based examples, they are also biased (or perhaps only ignorant) in their presentation of technological examples.

The success of xerography was a function of not only Chester Carlson's technical invention—exciting and innovative as it was—but also of the ability and foresight of Joseph Wilson in its marketing. He fit the product into a market that was not aware it needed it. Based in part on market research, Wilson considered selling copies through a lease program, rather than machines, leading to Xerox Corporation's success in the use of xerography. Although it may not have been visible, decisions leading to Xerox's success were based on market research.

Market research is likely to have played a role in the success of instant photography. When Land introduced instant photography, the photography industry was already mature. It would be naive to assume that no information existed about the preferences of consumers pertaining to time and resources for processing film. In addition, if the success of instant photography could be attributed to Land's omniscience about the future success of a product, what happened to his omniscience in bringing instant movies (Polavision) to the market?

There is always the debate between those who think the best path to product innovation is through the creativeness and foresight of the designers and those who think the path is through the consumers' expressed wishes. The path is undoubtedly between the two extremes. Akio Morita, founder of Sony, has said, "Our plan is to lead the public to new products rather than ask them what they want. The public does not know what is possible, but we do." While we must give consideration to such a statement from such a successful firm, how do we treat their major miscalculation about the market's response to Sony Beta format versus VHS format for video magnetic tape?

The Myth of the Textbook Project

The second myth surrounding the use of market information is the stuff of which textbooks are made. While it presents an ideal explanation of how market research can be done, it bears little resemblance to reality.

The textbook description of the use of market research starts with the product management team who wants to reassess its positioning strategy in the wake of a competitor's unexpected success with a new product. The entire team is in agreement and motivated to prepare the best strategy possible; there is adequate time to collect the needed information to prepare the proposal; all the team members bring considerable experience to the process that they are willing to share with the other members of the team; extensive relevant information exists in tracking studies, the media, etc., that the team is using as a guide in conducting their research; and the team has decided it is worthwhile to conduct market research to obtain more specific information on their own and competing products on certain attributes and features and market potential.

With the expertise and enthusiasm of the product team in full swing, the director of market research is also working hard on the problem. She is familiar with the problem, has brought together relevant information from existing studies, and is asked to develop a proposal and a budget for the project. She develops a proposal, and because of the adequate lead time available, does not incur any unexpected costs and is able to ask most of the important questions.

The managers of the project and the director of market research have worked together in the past, understand each other, and have a good understanding of the limitations and benefits of market research. In addition, the market research director understands how these managers make decisions and the form in which they like to receive information.

The outside supplier of the market research, a firm trusted because of its superior track record, conducts the research and delivers on schedule. The market research staff prepares a draft report of the findings and circulates it to the product team and then meets with the market research staff for a presentation and discussion of results. The managers feel that they gained great insight from the research and decide to change the fundamental direction of the project in accordance with the results of the study.

A few weeks later, the project team reaches a decision based—among other things—on their confidence in the market research. The research also validated and reinforced other information the project team had. If they had been asked, the project team would have said that the research was well worth the cost and realized that without it, a costly mistake would have been made.

There are a number of assumptions underlying the textbook myth. First, the list of assumptions could be extended considerably. These assumptions are, for the most part, valid most often with respect to relatively routine decisions. However, when even just one assumption is compromised, there is a domino effect whereby other assumptions are compromised as well. For example, if the need for research is not identified and conveyed to researchers early enough, accuracy may be lost as the project is implemented hurriedly. This, in turn, may impede the development of a consensus as to what the information really means and lessens confidence in the effectiveness of particular decision options. This may have the further effect of eroding personal rapport between managers and researchers.

Second, recall that there are routine and non-routine decisions and that the non-routine ones are the more difficult. Consider that the assumptions above hold for non-routine decisions and that in the case of non-routine decisions, all bets about them are off. If even one assumption of this set is not met, there is a good chance of failure of the process because of the domino effect. If the lead time is not adequate, errors can easily be made or important parts of the research not considered. This could lead to inadequate research, the development of mistrust between members of the project team and the research staff, and in general, an eroding of the process by which market research is done and decisions made.

Because of the ease with which such domino effects occur, the storybook version of information use is not common for routine decisions. However, the problems are compounded, and very different patterns of information use develop when decisions

1. are not routine;
2. have a high degree of uncertainty and risk;
3. involve different groups within a firm;
4. have major long-term consequences for the firm;
5. involve substantial current financial outlays;
6. are urgent; or
7. do not have the benefit of much existing information.

You can almost count on problems compounding and very different patterns of information use developing.

Finally, a critical assumption to the premise of this chapter is that the quality of thinking about an issue prior to the collection of data is the major determinant to the quality of thinking after the data have been collected. This approach is one that is in the best interests of both market information users and providers of market information. It increases the chances of doing the right thing and doing it right, thus enhancing the value of information for users and their appreciation of the market information.

THE PERSPECTIVES OF INFORMATION ACQUISITION AND USE

The most fundamental difference between the technologies for doing research and those for improving its use is people orientation.

- Data acquisition and processing technologies are oriented toward "people proofing." That is, they are oriented toward eliminating or at least isolating and defining human bias by establishing "objective" guidelines for experimental design, sampling procedures, the construction and administration of questionnaires, reliance on formal analytic procedures, and so on.
- The process of using information is more a judgmental matter. In fact, it's not desirable to try to make information use non-judgmental since the effective application of research relies heavily on the decision maker's experience related to the problem under study. As we move from data collection, processing and storage to information use, we move from systematic procedures to one dominated by art or craft. Thus, technologies for improving research use must be "people involving."

We cannot hide from the fact that the conversion of intelligence into knowledge is necessarily a human process. No group of technical specialists or computer can do it alone. This means identifying core behavioral processes that are operating and then lessening their negative consequences and augmenting their positive consequences.

THE INQUIRY CENTER

In this chapter, the term "*inquiry center*" is used to describe the "ideal state of mind within a company for effectively and efficiently reconciling differences between those who provide information and those who use it."[10] By design, the inquiry center is not *precisely* defined. Experience shows that it is more likely that ideas, like the inquiry center, will be adopted if they can be easily adapted to the realities of those who will be required to use them.

The inquiry center describes a particular way of learning about the marketplace and using the resulting knowledge. While the term "center" denotes an organizational unit, it is as much an attitude, ethic, or creed as it is a formal entity. Of course, all firms and their divisions or departments and individual employees have ways of learning about their markets and ways of using this information, but few take the trouble to check how well their learning systems work and whether they can be improved. The inquiry center concept fosters the development of an enterprise-wide attitude essential in becoming a market-based organization that is sensitive to the voice of the market.

The Voice of the Market

The first step in developing this attitude is to understand where and how information fits into the process that leads to decision making. A concept that is sometimes used to show this relationship is the familiar information triangle shown in Exhibit 1. The triangle implies a large number of facts—normally generated from transactions—that are distilled into information that is eventually used to develop strategy. The potential flaw in this concept is in taking the relationships illustrated in the triangle literally because the triangle implies that

1. strategy and information "automatically" come together, and
2. strategic information can be created in the absence of policy direction.

There is strong evidence that these two implications are not correct because there are complex interrelationships existing throughout the hierarchy. Knowledge creation, dissemination, and application are themselves not separable processes. They are further complicated by the integrated sets of assumptions, truth tests, expectations, and decision rules we possess and which make up our viewing lens.

EXHIBIT 1. Traditional Information Triangle

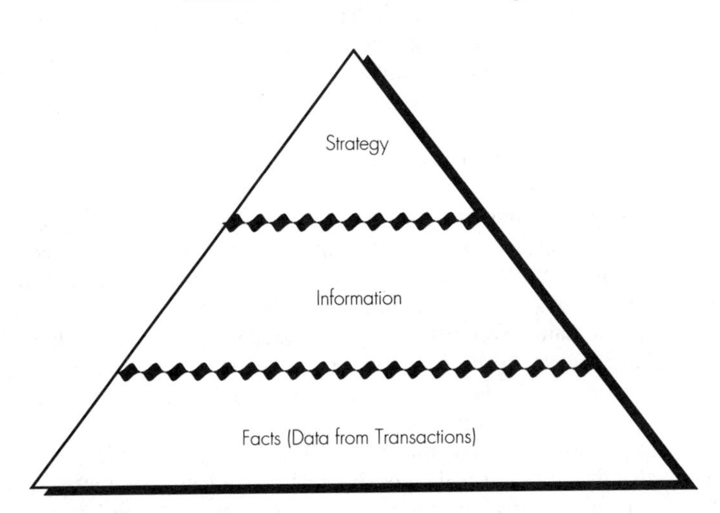

The Law of the Lens

Viewing lenses are rooted in our existing knowledge and usually lead us to find what we are looking for—this is the *law of the lens.* The law of the lens manifests itself in many ways. For example, new product management teams, when assessing the feasibility of introducing new products, tend to favor their introduction with a frequency that is unwarranted by subsequent commercial performance. Analysis of many new product failures points to a tendency to both design research and interpret research results in a way that does not allow equal opportunity for evidence to arise that runs counter to a new product launch decision.

The need to avoid these obstacles is found in contrasting two analytical conditions that lead to conflicts over approving programs or selecting among alternatives.

Constructive Conflicts. In the first analytical condition, those involved in the decision have differing interpretations of an agreed-to set of facts. Conflicts of this type are *constructive* and beneficial to decision making because they sharpen the analytical skills and encourage use of the intuitive and experiential strengths of the participants.

Destructive Conflicts. In the second analytical condition, those involved have failed to establish a common set of facts to interpret. Usually power—and not necessarily merit—dictates the final decision, if a timely decision is made at all. This is a *destructive* type of conflict, which is both time consuming and potentially costly.

Given that we have both conditions operating throughout the public and private sector, how do we go about ensuring that, at least as it relates to the market research function, we operate in the mode of the first analytical condition (i.e., interpreting an agreed-to set of facts) almost exclusively?

A suggested first step to encourage these changes among decision makers is to improve our understanding of the knowledge concept by modifying the traditional information pyramid to make clear that there is a decision-making domain that is different from the information-producing domain. We must also acknowledge, however, that although these domains are different, they should be integrated and not separated. Because of the law of the lens, however, there are considerable forces that encourage separation.

To enhance both our understanding of the role of information in knowledge development and a positive role for a "lens," we must expand the traditional information hierarchy. Exhibit 2 expands the information hierarchy and introduces a distinction between the role of the information providers and the role of the decision and/or policy makers in the development of knowledge. The primary effort of information providers is to transform data to information and information to intelligence. The primary effort of decision and/or policy makers is to transform intelligence to knowledge and the knowledge to quality decisions. We must acknowledge, however, that although these domains are different, they are integral to each other, although the forces of the law of the lens will encourage separation.

Because of their view of the world and their experiences, decision makers have their own perception of reality that has direct impact on how they interpret, accept, reject, or synthesize intelligence reports. Similarly, the information providers have their own view of the world and how information can be collected and analyzed that will color the intelligence reports they bring forward. The point is that neither of these two groups are right or wrong, but that they have different ways of looking at and interpreting information. To prevent a disconnect in the development of knowledge, this information hierarchy includes explicit overlap at the intelligence level to allow for explicit surfacing of any differences in assumptions or expectations.

Incorporating the work of Steve Haeckel to the information hierarchy adds the construct of the law of the lens (see Exhibit 3, shown on page 342). In this case, a complex multiple glass lens is intended to refine and focus at each level in the information hierarchy and, in the process, to decrease the volume of information and objectivity while increasing clarity and value.[11]

EXHIBIT 2. The Modified Information Pyramid

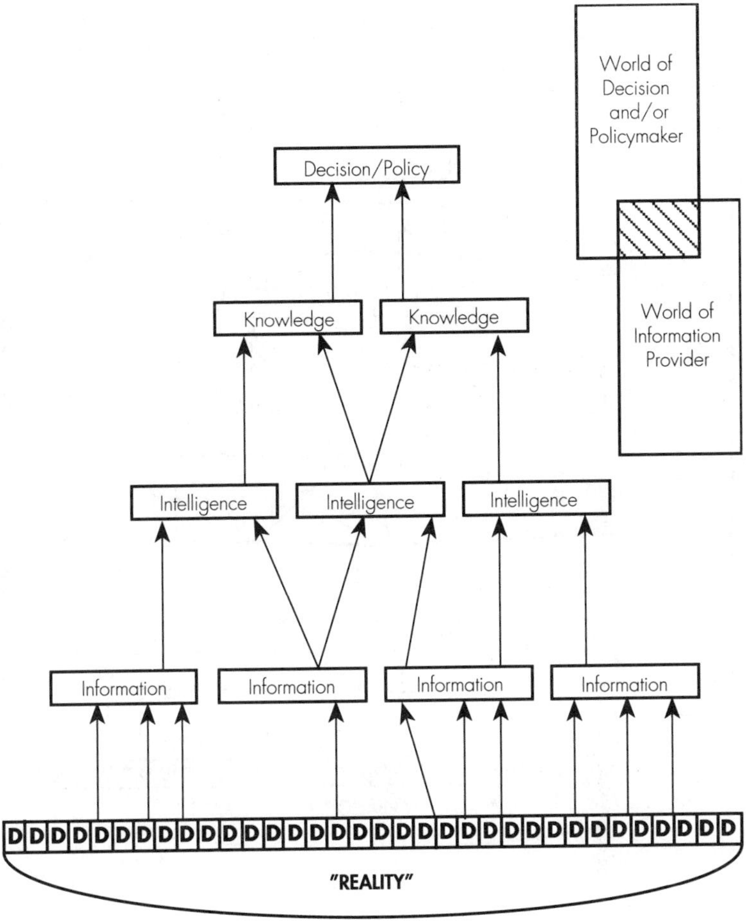

World of Decision and/or Policymaker

Decision/Policy

World of Information Provider

Knowledge

Knowledge

Intelligence

Intelligence

Intelligence

Information

Information

Information

Information

DDDDDDDDDDDDDDDDDDDDDDDDDDDDDDDDDD

"REALITY"

EXHIBIT 3. Modified Haeckel's Hierarchy

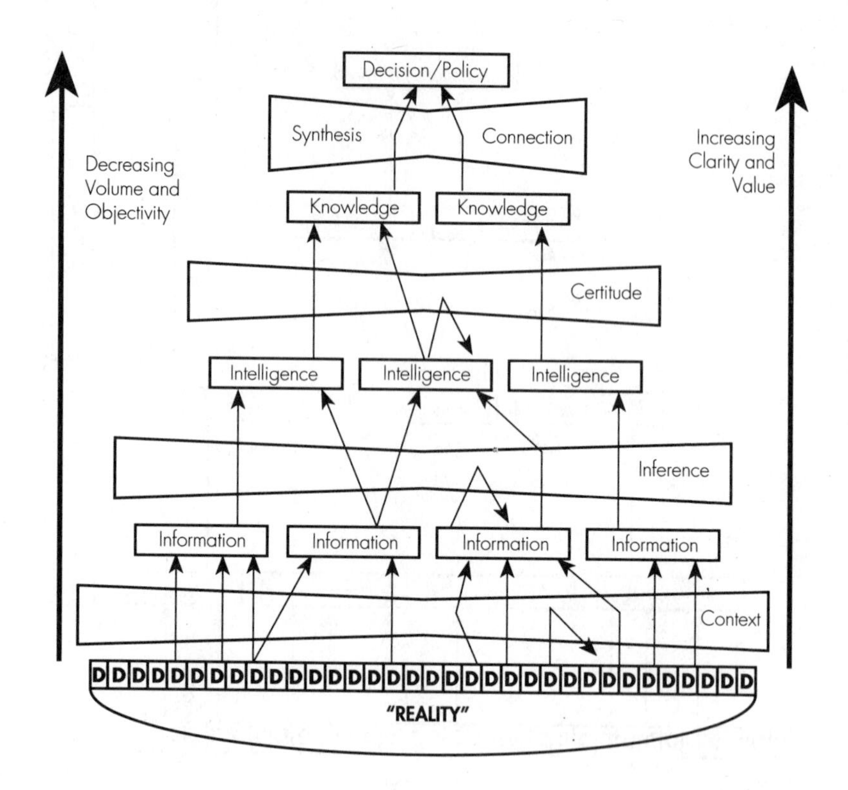

Data. Data may take many forms: rumors, forecasts derived from complex mathematical models, intuitive feelings, personal observations, recommendation, opinions, and almost anything else that purports to describe or relate to a past, current, or future situation. Data are representations of reality that may or may not have meaning, accuracy, or believability. Data are often referred to as raw material, facts, and statements. When put into context—to make its meaning clear or more relevant—data become *information.* If we do not know what data mean in context, they are uninformative. Inferring how the information relates to a specific issue or decision positions information as *intelligence.* To be intelligence then, the information must be

- clear, because it is understandable to those who must use it;
- timely, because it gets to them when they need it;
- reliable, because diverse observers using the same procedures see it in the same way (although they may draw different conclusions); and
- valid, because it is cast in the form of concepts and measures that capture congruence with established knowledge or independent sources.[12]

Intelligence is what we believe to be true from a decision-focused analysis of information. Intelligence does not become *knowledge* until both the decision makers and providers warrant the intelligence as certified. Knowledge is interpretation of intelligence and its connection to how our business operates. It is a model of how the business runs. It is the wherewithal of the enterprise business model. The inquiry center allows decision makers to connect "what we know" with "what we need to do," i.e., synthesize and connect knowledge and *decisions.*

While Exhibit 3 shows a single information hierarchy, in large companies with many functions, it is likely that functional information silos have also developed. Consequently, it is highly unlikely that the same types of "lenses" have been applied. For effective sharing of information across functions, it will be critical that functions connect at each level to understand how each has placed their data in context. It will not be possible for management to provide good policy decisions if the intelligence brought forward is based on different contexts and inferences. For example, a good decision on product advertising will be virtually impossible if the information providers in advertising and in product development have made different inferential assumptions about the products' target customers.

What is needed is a process that allows us to make—if not perfect business decisions—at least the best possible decisions. The goal is defined in terms of reducing the complexity of the overwhelming amount of data and other input that managers have at their disposal. However, past strategies that have been used to achieve the goal (namely, increasing the amount and analysis of information) are actually compounding the problem.

In addition to adding significant insight to the concept of the information hierarchy, Haeckel also noted:

> *The serious business issue behind this is that there is no value theory for the increasingly important asset called information. It seems clear that the value of information is enhanced by structure, organization and context, but how much is it worth to provide the structure and how should one price the result?*

Finding the answer to Haeckel's question is not easy. On the other hand, one does not need to spend much time considering the value of reducing the amount of corporate and societal waste generated every day in the councils of government and corporate boardrooms because sincere and dedicated individuals are left wanting in their understanding of significant issues. Relevant market information is at least as valuable as the value associated with the promise of advertising and merchandising techniques. And although we spend considerable resources on them, our measured understanding of their value is no better than our understanding of the value of relevant information to the decision process.

As indicated earlier in this chapter, in today's complex world, it is no longer of value for a manager to only seek the "right" decision. Rather, the greatest value is in managing the decision-making process in a way that increases the chances of choosing the best decision among the available alternatives—given all the circumstances at that time. This type of decision-making process will require appropriate tools, expertise, and innovative momentum to achieve quality decisions in the complex world of today and tomorrow. If the inquiry center is to help in this new decision-making process of the organization, it must be integrated into that process. That is, it must be adaptable to the environment in which it will operate and be considered an appropriate inquiring tool of the decision maker.

A successful inquiry center must also be capable of integrating multiple perspectives. It must integrate (1) the logical analysis, (2) the connection across silos, and (3) the creation of new solutions by those who will affect, or be affected by, the outcomes.

Logical Analysis

Management is very comfortable with the logical/analytical perspective that is dominated by familiar theories, tools, and techniques. They are accustomed to decision making as an extension of a logical, analytical process. At the heart of this approach is the process of separating or breaking up a whole into its parts so as to find out their nature, proportions, functions, relationships, and so on. In using this dimension, however, we have been taught that to better understand a problem, we need more information. To deal with more information, we need more people, more sophisticated techniques, and more state-of-the-art technology. As stated earlier, however, more is not necessarily better unless it is put into context with appropriate judgment applied and is accepted and synthesized with other knowledge.

Connection

The second perspective within the inquiry center is the connection across silos. Decision making and implementation in virtually any organization is a collective process. It is shaped by the factors and dynamics that underly human behavior in social settings. Sharing information from various perspectives is a start. However, the highest level that can be achieved in this dimension is when the interaction occurs in such a manner that not only do better ideas come forward, but they are developed in such a way that their implementation is prompt and consistent.

Creating New Solutions

The third perspective within the inquiry center is creating new solutions. People with access to diverse experiences and viewpoints can be the key to generating the best possible range of alternatives to solve an important, complex problem. As a concept, creating new solutions encompasses the full range of what is truly creative within the human psyche—whether it is called intuition, fantasy, inner imagery, or even inspiration.

To help decision makers to use information to move beyond the realm of facts and analytical thinking to the higher altitude of vision or improved decision quality and wiser decisions is the significant challenge of the inquiry center concept. To do this, we need to somehow integrate the logical analysis, connection across silos, and create new solution dimensions in such a way as to design a three-dimensional conceptual space representing each of these perspectives.

THE FUNDAMENTAL VALUE OF THE INQUIRY CENTER

At the top of the information hierarchy, it is suggested that knowledge plus synthesis creates wisdom (see Exhibit 4). Robert Waller offers a keen insight into the role of the inquiry center concept in assisting to synthesize knowledge to wisdom.

> *Complexity is composed of elements and intricate relationships among these elements. When humans confront complexity, they must discover these relationships and (in organizational life) communicate them to one another in an intelligible form. Conscious manipulation of elements and relations, however, is a function of the short-term memory. As was noted earlier, this part of the human cognitive apparatus suffers from some severe limitations.*

EXHIBIT 4. Three-Dimensional Construct of Inquiry Center

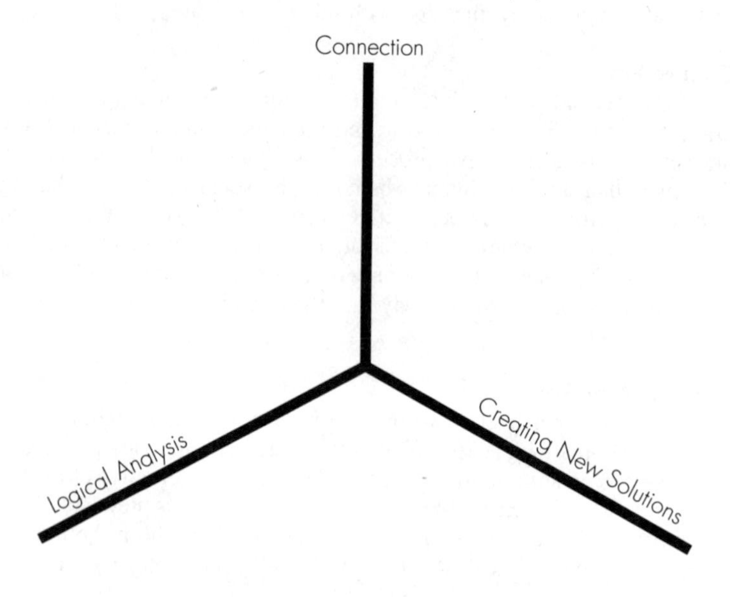

This comes down to a design problem. On the one hand is complexity in all of its richness. On the other hand, we see the human, restricted in terms of short-term memory, but with marvelous capabilities for long-term information retention, for judgment, for utilizing experience, for intuition, and, yes, for passion. Somehow, then, a way must be found that recognizes the central features of complexity and yet takes into account both the strengths and weaknesses of human cognition.

Human cognitive abilities cannot be modified to fit the demands of complexity. But neither can complexity be changed. If a problem situation is simplified to bring it within range of human capacities, then we are no longer dealing with the original problem (in fact, this sort of "under-modeling" probably occurs all the time, since we are unable to grasp the relational abundance of complex situations with our cognitive abilities).

Since neither the human nor complexity can be changed, a way must be found to link the two without changing either. In engineering terminology, an interface device must be sought that will link humans and complexity, while preserving the original properties of each. (emphasis added).[13]

An Example of Implementing an Inquiry Center

At the 1989 General Motors Market Research Conference, the GM position on linking the firm and the market was stated.

> *And if you bring together the voice of the customer, the voice of the dealers, the voice of the public, you might look at that as the voice of the market. . . . Another important area [is that] when we listen to the voice of the market, [we need to remember] the customers are not going to give us all the solutions to their needs and wants. That means we also have to listen to the voice of GM. You have to work at the balance between the market pull and the technology push.*

That comment and direction led to agreement within the market and product planning community to use the following definitions in developing action strategies and education programs relative to the use of market research in the product and market development process at General Motors.

> *VOICE OF THE MARKET is "what the market indicates it needs and wants and is willing to pay for." By market we mean where exchange takes place. In this context, "voice of the market" includes all types of customers as well as entities that can affect our product; voice of the customers (external), regulators, competitive manufacturers, etc. (market pull).*
>
> *VOICE OF GENERAL MOTORS (the firm) is "what GM is capable of and willing to provide to the market." In this context, GM is considered in the broadest business sense to include all the different functional areas within GM that are responsible for providing the product or service; voice of the design staff, engineering, manufacturing, marketing, finance, etc. (company push).*
>
> *MARKET-BASED GM is a GM where decision making is based on effectively and efficiently reconciling any differences between the voice of the market and the voice of GM. [The term "based" versus "driven" is used here to emphasize the point that this is a reconciliation between the two voices and not being driven solely by either one] (Balance of market pull and company push).*

Exhibit 5 reflects the relationships of these three concepts.

To accomplish the effective and efficient reconciliation of the differences between the voice of the market and the voice of GM, a process was needed that would cause the appropriate interaction between the providers of information and the users of information for any given decision. Exhibit 6 illustrates the process model for representing the continuous interaction between the providers and users, with shifting levels of responsibility, as they move through the following stages: data management, "what do we know," to the analysis stage, "what does it mean?," and through to the implications stage, "what should we do?"

EXHIBIT 5. Reconciling the Voice of the Market and the Voice of General Motors

Market Pull
What the market indicates it needs and is willing to pay for
"Voice of the Market"
Quality Market-Based Decisions
Simultaneously consider both voices, aiming to effectively and efficiently reconcile any differences between them resulting in . . .
GM Developing Innovative Products and Services
Company Push
What GM is capable of and willing to provide to the market
"Voice of General Motors"

EXHIBIT 6. Reconciling the Voice of the Market and the Voice of General Motors: The Process Model

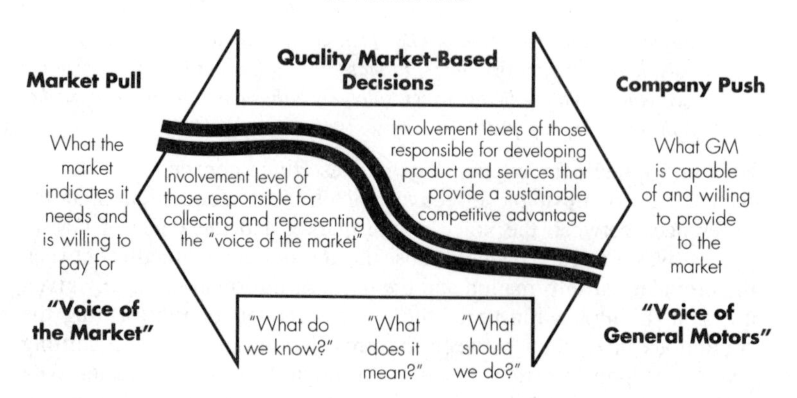

Market Pull
What the market indicates it needs and is willing to pay for
"Voice of the Market"
Quality Market-Based Decisions
Involvement level of those responsible for collecting and representing the "voice of the market"
Involvement levels of those responsible for developing product and services that provide a sustainable competitive advantage
"What do we know?"
"What does it mean?"
"What should we do?"
Company Push
What GM is capable of and willing to provide to the market
"Voice of General Motors"

An implicit assumption of the illustration is that no group in the company owns or has sole use of the voice of the market. It is important that all affected parties understand that all users—not just the marketing department—own the voice of the market. The market research function, as the provider, is empowered to stand as a representative of the voice of the market, with the added responsibility of ensuring that the voice is relevant to general as well as specific issues facing all functions of the company.

The relevance of this illustration to the inquiry center concept is highlighted in the shaded area in Exhibit 6, and represents the area where information users and providers work together in an environment conducive to the effective interplay of logical analysis, connection, and the creation of new solutions. This notion of working environment is required if we accept the belief that for the effective development and use of information, individuals on cross-functional teams are required to cross the functional line between user and provider to ensure there is clear understanding of the issues being addressed, as well as clear communication of the findings across all relevant functional areas (engineering, marketing, design, finance, market research, etc.).

Presented this way, the inquiry center is a place where tools or ideas exist that help in the conduct and dissemination of market research. These are tools that management—working with researchers—can use to ensure that information collected is of value and is actually used.

One set of ideas that help to get the most out of information are directed at the need to manage and overcome—not ignore—certain behaviors among information users that can lessen the value of research. Six behaviors of special importance are presented below. They can all be related to one another through a concept called avoiding post-survey regret.

What is meant by post-survey regret? Following the collection of information, there is often regret that certain questions were not asked or not asked differently (solving the wrong problems by failing to ask the right question). It is reflected by such statements as, "I wish we had asked . . . ," "Why wasn't 'X' included as a question?" "It's too bad we didn't include . . . ," "Why did we bother asking this?," "We should have included 'Y' as a possible response," and "It's too bad we didn't use a 'Z' scale instead of . . ." Some post-survey regret is unavoidable. It can be a positive sign that we've learned something as a result of the study. More often it reflects a failure to think about the use of information early enough in the research process. Had we thought about what information we might use to answer one question, we might realize that it would be necessary to ask another. Significant post-survey regret need only occur a few times—in some cases only once—before some managers become discouraged about the potential value of market research.

STEPS TO ENSURE MARKET RESEARCH IS OF GREAT VALUE AND IS ACTUALLY USED

Step One: Ask Managers to Predict Important Data Outcomes

Symptoms of a Problem: Often market research users make such statements as, "I could have told you that," "I already knew that," or "That's a pretty obvious result." This is sometimes referred to as pseudo-clairvoyance. The dynamics of pseudo-clairvoyance work something like this: (a) a particular result (e.g., the number of people expressing satisfaction with a product or service attribute) triggers thinking about what might have caused this result; (b) with the benefit of hindsight, these casual factors become more obvious, i.e., more heavily weighted; (c) managers conclude that they would have given these factors much greater weight in comparison to factors producing other outcomes; and (d) from this they conclude that had they been asked to predict an outcome, they would have correctly given special attention to the factors causing the actual outcome and hence would have correctly predicted it.

Pseudo-clairvoyance is generally an honest event; it is frequently an unconscious process that produces the conscious thought, "I could have told you that!" However, there are also instances where managers may claim they already knew something when they know they did not. They describe as "pretty obvious" a result that surprises them. The reasons for this kind of response are quite numerous. Perhaps the most common reason is not wanting to appear unknowing.

Idea: A way of overcoming these symptoms is to ask managers to predict important data outcomes before the research is actually started. This serves two closely related purposes. The first is to document for the individual manager the difference between what she or he predicted and the actual outcome—giving her or him a better sense of the value of the research. The second purpose is to be able to calculate the value of individual questions and of the overall project to managers.

Step Two: Determine Comfort Zones of Managers Prior to Conducting the Research

Symptoms of a Problem: Comfort zones refer to the expected and acceptable ranges for research findings. For example, a manager might expect that, among all respondents, about 50% will like a certain product feature. If many more than half the respondents dislike the feature, a manager might not feel comfortable with the research result. Such a finding does not ring true with his or her other knowledge. The manager's discomfort with these findings causes him or her to question the validity of the research. The tendency by the manager in such cases is to find out the source of the error (e.g., an improper wording of the question, a biased sampling plan, etc.), and to dismiss the result because of this perceived error.

Idea: The suggestions that follow are not designed to change the results of market research findings, but to make sure they are both valid and reliable and, most importantly, that they are used. A first step would be to determine the comfort zones of affected managers prior to conducting research. Ask them, for a given research question, what results they would find surprising or difficult to believe. It is important to understand just how broad or narrow comfort zones are among managers with respect to important research findings. Sometimes the more knowledge or expertise managers have with respect to an issue, the narrower their comfort zones. Thus, an inexperienced manager may expect a "satisfactory" rating between 45% and 55%, whereas an experienced manager might expect a rating between 48% and 52%.[14]

Knowing whether managers have broad or narrow comfort zones may help researchers design the research sampling plan, as well as decide how to present results. For instance, if a finding falls outside the comfort zone of a key decision maker, it will be important for the researcher to re-verify and be prepared to discuss the technical validity of the result. The researcher might also want to present other evidence supporting the finding, such as other findings that are quite believable and also consistent with the surprising data.

It is important for researchers to have a good sense of their clients' comfort zone for yet another reason. One of the many bases for establishing personal trust between researchers and managers is a manager's knowledge that the researcher will not spring an embarrassing surprise on him or her. That is, if there is an unexpected result, managers know they will be informed privately in advance of any open discussion among other managers. While the information is still discussed in a group meeting or in a report, the manager is not caught by surprise and may be better prepared to discuss the information.

Step Three: Identify Early the Likely Areas of Uncertainty after the Research Is Completed

Symptoms of a Problem: Doing research is like piecing together a jigsaw puzzle. We never have the time or the funds to collect and position all the pieces, but we can place just enough of them to give us a sense of the true picture. We fill in the remaining pieces from our other knowledge and experience about variables not formally researched. Most of the information used in the decision-making process is derived from these experiences. (In a very technical sense, it is the data missing from these experiences that are sought through formal research.) Research results are generally evaluated and then translated into action based on assumptions about variables not directly addressed by the project. Frequently, these assumptions are not made explicit, and they are sometimes the source of conflict about the accuracy, meaning, and use of specific research findings. When they are not made explicit, they are difficult to examine for accuracy or relevance, though central to a decision. Failure to identify differences of opinion about the missing data early in a research project means that an opportunity to resolve these differences in the formal research effort is lost.

Just as there is important knowledge available from other relevant experiences, so too are there important areas of uncertainty that cannot be cleared up significantly by experiential knowledge or knowledge provided by a formal research effort. Ultimately, managers must act as if they were certain about these issues. This uncertainty gets absorbed and is represented by a best guess about the real status of the factor or issue. Managers seem to appreciate those researchers who are willing to join with them in absorbing uncertainty.

Idea: Identify early in the research process the likely areas of thinking where uncertainty will persist even after formal research and other relevant experiences are brought forth. Decisions can be made as to whether resources should be (re)allocated to reduce any of these uncertainties rather than those being addressed by the planned research. Also, a common understanding between managers and researchers about what uncertainties will remain reduces certain post-survey regrets and better prepares the researcher to deal with these uncertainties when asked to do so. For example, some issues can be pursued in exploratory research that might help interpret data later on, even though these issues could not be pursued in the more formal project.

Step Four: Develop Simulated Data

Symptoms of a Problem: Thinking without the added stimulus of meaningful and relevant data is likely to be less successful than thinking with data; it tends to be less creative and less comprehensive than data-rich thinking. There is a tendency to think differently and much more comprehensively about an issue when it is illustrated with relevant data. This is true even when relevant data are hypothetical or simulated rather than actual data.

Idea: The stimulus to thinking provided by simulated data helps identify important differences in perspectives among managers. By thinking about specific empirical outcomes well in advance of actual findings, managers and researchers are better prepared to interpret final research results and can do so more quickly, perhaps shortening the decision time. They are also better prepared to translate research results into specific actions. When managers have thought about alternative decisions early in the research process using relevant simulated data, they develop a consensus more quickly about what final data mean, their validity, and what actions to take. Thus, the likelihood of doing the right thing and doing the thing right is considerably higher when pre-research thinking is information-rich rather than information-poor.

Step Five: Perform Action Audits

Symptoms of a Problem: One of the most common sources of post-survey regret occurs when research results suggest a novel decision or action but do not provide sufficient data for its evaluation since it had not been anticipated. For example, interviews with hospital purchasing agents resulted in a suggested shipping container design that management had not contemplated, even though the purpose of the study concerned purchasing agent dissatisfaction with delivery problems and the incidence of damaged goods being received. Had more thought been given to what might be done with answers to the single question than had been raised about the containers, more helpful information about improving them might have been obtained initially. Instead, a follow-up study was required.

Idea: Performing an action audit—an enumeration of alternative actions or decisions prior to the design of a questionnaire—provides a wide array of possible actions and better information when managers explicitly consider (a) the importance of a question, (b) the question's utility in developing an action, and (c) what else is needed for a given question to be useful in choosing or implementing a decision. It is important to elicit—perhaps using simulated results—an array of actions that might be suggested by the research beyond those already identified. The researcher should identify the questions that relate to various actions and the kind of analyses that will be done with the final data. Managers should then have the opportunity to indicate where the data may be insufficient and/or excessive for evaluating these actions.

Step Six: Anticipate Unwelcome Results

Symptoms of a Problem: An equal-opportunity research methodology is one that gives an unwelcome (bad news) answer the same opportunity to show up as it does a more welcomed (good news) answer. An unequal-opportunity methodology generally favors the more welcomed answer. Unequal-opportunity methodologies are not usually the result of a deliberate effort to skew results. They are more often a consequence of not thinking carefully about potential answers, including unwelcome ones. If an important potential response—welcomed or not—is not anticipated, it is not likely to show up in a research project even if it is a real phenomenon in the marketplace.

When unequal-opportunity methodologies surface, it is almost always unintentional. There may be an honest conviction that a particular answer is correct and therefore all that is necessary is research that verifies this judgment. In this case, the research is used as an insurance policy against the highly unexpected outcome that a decision or assumption is wrong. The research may be designed adequately to allow the disproof of this judgment, but little or no allowance is made to find out what the alternative answers might be. Typically, in such cases, modest or weak support for the expected answer is obtained partly because respondents could not, in effect, "vote" otherwise.

Idea: Develop working teams designed to look at the problem from diametrically opposed points of view and develop simulated results based on their research plan. Have each team review the simulated results of the other teams' research plan with the objective of challenging whether their opponents have designed their research to avoid an unwelcome result.

There are, of course, many other tools and ideas that should find a home within an inquiry center. Indeed, each enterprise should develop the set of tools that will have the most beneficial impact for them.

CONCLUSION

This chapter begins with the belief that all groups within a firm do marketing and concludes with the notion that earning customer commitment to the firm will be a major goal of the 1990s. By helping groups throughout a company make better decisions through use of better information, the inquiry center concept can increase the likelihood that firms will earn that commitment. These observations are summarized below.

GIVEN:

Marketing—particularly as experienced and understood by the marketplace—is a company-wide activity.

THEREFORE:

The internal "customers" for market research are located throughout a company.

THE INQUIRY CENTER MUST:

Provide all internal customers with appropriate voice of the market information and with the support necessary to use this information effectively in the decision-making process.

AS A RESULT:

The quality of company-wide marketing is enhanced by the use of voice of the market.

THIS IS IMPORTANT BECAUSE:

The quality of company-wide marketing affects customer perceptions of a firm's long-term commitment to providing high value in its product/service offerings.

AND:

Customers' commitments arise from their perception of the company's own commitment to providing high value in product/service offerings.

NOTES

1. Zaltman and Park.
2. John C. Narver and Stanley F. Slater, "Superior Customer Value and Business Performance: The Strong Evidence for a Market-Driven Culture," Report No. 92–125, *Journal of Marketing Research,* November 1993.

3. Paul A. Eisenstein, "Car Makers Fine-tune Market Research Use," *Investor's Daily,* May 31, 1989.
4. John Brooks, "The Edsel" (Annals of Business), *The New Yorker,* November 26, 1960 and December 3, 1960.
5. William Reynolds, "The Edsel Ten Years Later," *Business Horizons,* Fall 1967, p. 39.
6. Brooks, op. cit.
7. Richard Ratliff, *Detroit Free Press,* February 12, 1990, p. 29.
8. Alton F. Doody and Ron Bingaman, *Reinventing the Wheels,* Cambridge, MA: Ballinger Publishing Co., 1988.
9. Robert H. Hayes and William J. Abernathy, "Managing Our Way to Economic Decline," *Harvard Business Review,* July–August 1980, pp. 67–77.
10. Vincent P. Barabba and Gerald Zaltman, *Hearing the Voice of the Market,* Harvard Business School Press, Boston, MA: 1991.
11. Provided courtesy of S. H. Haeckel, IBM.
12. Harold L. Wilensky, "Organizational Intelligence: Knowledge and Policy in Government and Industry," New York: Basic Books, 1967.
13. Robert J. Waller, 1983. "Knowledge for Producing Useful Knowledge and the Importance of Synthesis." *Producing Useful Knowledge for Organizations,* Ralph H. Kilman, et al., New York: Praeger Publishers.
14. Vincent P. Barabba and Gerald Zaltman, *Hearing the Voice of the Market,* Part IV.

James H. Donnelly, Jr.
Turner Professor of Marketing
University of Kentucky
Lexington, Kentucky

John M. Ivancevich
Dean, College of Business Administration
University of Houston
Houston, Texas

CHAPTER 20

MANAGEMENT SCIENCE AND MODEL BUILDING

Every day marketing decision makers face an unending sequence of decision problems, each of which can have a tremendous impact on the success or failure of a product or service. Their task is to develop marketing plans and programs and monitor their outcomes so that when unwanted deviations occur, corrective measures can be taken. This chapter presents a managerially-oriented discussion of how management science contributes to more effective marketing decisions by providing a formal, disciplined approach to problem formulation and analysis.

TRADITIONAL BASES FOR MARKETING DECISIONS

Given the vast domestic and international complexities associated with marketing decisions, how do marketing decision makers finally reach a decision in which they can place a great deal of confidence? The general answer to this question is, "They usually don't." This is because a systematic body of normative marketing theory is not available to marketing decision makers. How then do the marketing executives resolve the majority of the product, distribution, promotion, and pricing decisions in the face of so much uncertainty? Traditionally they have utilized one or a combination of the following approaches.

Tenacity. Here the manager uses as a basis for a decision a premise that has "always been known to be true." For example, if a software manufacturer used certain media to advertise its products because "they have always been the best way to advertise software," it would be utilizing this method. The unfortunate thing about this method is that frequent repetition of such "truths" often enhances their validity in the eyes of many people.

Authority. This method centers around "established beliefs." With the passage of time many companies tend to let these evolve to the point where they may become policies or procedures to guide decision makers. For example, a product manager may be given an advertising budget that reflects a safe historical ratio of advertising to sales. What often happens in this case is that something that starts off sound may outlive its relevance or usefulness. Another example of this method is small or medium-sized firms basing their key marketing decisions on what the larger firms in the industry are doing.

A Priori. This approach to making decisions is sometimes referred to as the method of intuition. Many times a manager will rely on hunches or intuition in making marketing decisions. This may be especially true for an experienced decision maker. Because of many years of experience, the marketing manager believes he or she can "feel" when the time is right to introduce a new product. In fact, there are undoubtedly numerous marketing executives who believe that experience is the best or only teacher. However, as valuable as experience may be it has one great fault: it is unique in every person. As a result, each person perceives a situation based on that person's own experience and personality. Thus it is not surprising to find that a production manager attributes more power to product design and a sales manager attributes more power to personal selling.

THE GROWTH OF MANAGEMENT SCIENCE

While it is true that these methods play an important role in marketing management, there are many marketing problems that can benefit from a more formal research approach. Management science is one formal research approach that many companies have used to solve a variety of management and marketing problems.

While the methods and techniques of the management scientist are mathematical and specialists in this field are trained in mathematics, the basic concepts of most management science models can be completely comprehended and appreciated with an understanding of only very basic mathematics. The purpose of this chapter is to present a managerially-oriented overview of selected management science models, not to teach marketing managers to be management scientists. There is no more reason for a marketing manager to be a technically proficient management scientist than for a physician to be a bacteriologist. However, the manager must know what to expect of management science, understand its strengths and weaknesses, and know how to use mathematical models as *tools,* just as the physician must know what to expect of bacteriology and how it can serve as a diagnostic tool. Readers should keep this in mind as they read about management science.

BOUNDARIES OF MANAGEMENT SCIENCE

As is often the case with an emerging body of knowledge, there is much confusion over just what it includes. Since its early development is rarely a consciously planned effort, there may even be numerous approaches to studying phenomena that differ little except perhaps in name. This appears to have been the case with management science. Over the years, numerous synonyms for the term "management science" have appeared, such as operations research, operational research, operations analysis, and systems analysis. They all share in common the desire to apply scientific analysis to managerial problems in all organizations.

While it is difficult to place clear boundary lines around management science, it is possible to distinguish certain characteristics of its approach. It is generally agreed that most management science applications possess the following characteristics (Turban and Meredith 1981):

1. *A primary focus on decision making.* The principal end result of the analysis must have direct implications for management action and follow through.
2. *An appraisal resting on economic effectiveness criteria.* A comparison of the various feasible actions must be based on measurable values that reflect the future well-being of the organization. Examples include costs, revenues, and rates of return on investment.
3. *Reliance on a formal mathematical model.* These models are actually possible solutions to the problems, which are stated in mathematical form.
4. *Dependence on a computer.* This is actually a requirement necessitated by either the complexity of the mathematical model, the volume of data to be manipulated, or the magnitude of computations needed to implement the model.

THE ROLE OF THE COMPUTER IN MANAGEMENT SCIENCE

Computers have fostered most of the advances in the management science approach over the past two decades. In fact, it is not coincidental that computer technology developed in a parallel fashion with the field of management science. Undoubtedly there would be negligible interest right now in the field of management science (except perhaps for some applied mathematicians) if it were not for the computer. The computer has gone through its own stages of development from a point where it could only process routine data to a point where it can now effectively assist in the conduct of management science studies. The increasing availability, understanding, and use of computers in decision support systems has made it possible to turn heretofore theoretical mathematical models into everyday, here-and-now, practical decision aids.

THE PRACTICAL VALUE OF MATHEMATICAL MODELS FOR MARKETERS

Before discussing mathematical models, let us make one important point. It is rare, if ever, that a manager can perform what would be considered a *bona fide* scientific experiment to test the feasibility of taking a particular action. The practicalities of the real world preclude any manager from doing this. In other words, a manager cannot usually experiment with inventory to determine which level minimizes carrying costs and ordering costs or cannot experiment with the advertising budget to determine which combination of media (for example, radio,

TV, magazines) produces the most favorable sales results. However, an accurately constructed mathematical model enables the decision maker to experiment with possible solutions without interrupting the ongoing system. If the model accurately represents the ongoing system, it will provide the decision maker with the results of proposed solutions. In other words, it will react as the real system would react; therefore, the decision maker can simulate the behavior of the real system. It is this experimental role of mathematical models that makes them useful to marketing managers.

Understanding the role of mathematical models in management science, we can now define exactly what a mathematical model is: *A mathematical model is a simplified representation of the relevant aspects of an actual system or process.*

At this point, the value of a simplified representation may be questioned. That is why the definition includes the two words "relevant aspects." It is obvious that the value of any model depends on how well it represents the system or process under consideration. A highly simplified model that accurately describes a system or process will provide a more clearly understood starting point than a vague conception that a manager mentally creates. Such a model forces the manager to consider systematically the variables in the problem and the relationships among the variables. Thus forcing the manager to formalize thinking reduces the possibility of overlooking important factors or giving too much weight to minor factors.

In reality, readers are probably more familiar with models for decision making than they think. The accounting equation $A = L + C$ is a mathematical model. In fact, it is the oldest decision-making model showing a simplified relationship between assets, liabilities, and capital. It does not resemble the actual system physically; but it does behave as the real system behaves. It is an abstraction of the financial condition of a particular enterprise at a given moment. On the other hand, the income statement is also a mathematical model that is an abstraction of the operations of a business over a period of time.

In conclusion, instead of studying the actual system, managers can study a mathematical model or representation of the system. This enables them to experiment using the model in order to determine the effects such changes will have on the overall performance of the actual system.

TYPES OF MATHEMATICAL MODELS

Before managers can understand, evaluate, and utilize mathematical models, they must be aware of the major types of these models. Mathematical models may be classified by the purpose of the model (descriptive or normative) and/or by the types of variables included in the model (deterministic or probabilistic).

Purpose of the Model: Descriptive or Normative

A *descriptive model* is one that describes how a system works. That is, it describes things as they are and makes no value judgments about the particular problem being studied. Many times a model is constructed solely to be a description of a real-world phenomenon in mathematical terms. This model can then be used to display the situation more clearly or to indicate how it can be changed. Descriptive models display the alternative choices available to the decision maker and, in some cases, help the decision maker determine the consequences or outcomes of each alternative. However, a descriptive model does not select the best alternative.

A *normative (or prescriptive) model* selects the best from among alternatives based on some previously determined criteria that are also included in the model. It tells how the system should be in order to achieve a particular objective. These models are also referred to as optimizing models and decision models since they seek the optimum from among all the possible solutions.

Types of Variables in the Model: Deterministic or Probabilistic

A model is *deterministic* when the law of chance plays no role. In other words, the model contains no probabilistic considerations. For example the model, Profit = Revenue – Costs, is a deterministic mathematical model. All of the factors taken into account in the model are exact or deterministic quantities, and the solution is determined by this set of exact relationships. In other words, in a deterministic model, we assume conditions of certainty.

Once chance or random variables are introduced, conditions of uncertainty exist and the model is said to be a *probabilistic* model. Probabilistic models are based on the mathematics of statistics. Conditions of uncertainty introduced in the model are often based on observations of real-world events. For example, insurance companies make heavy use of actuarial tables that give the probability of death as a function of age. These tables can be considered probabilistic models.

Exhibit 1 summaries our discussion of this point. It indicates that a mathematical model may be either descriptive or normative in purpose and contain either deterministic or probabilistic variables. At this time, let us briefly examine some of the more popular management science models that are useful to marketers.

POPULAR MANAGEMENT SCIENCE MODELS

Decision-Theory Models

Decision theory is firmly rooted in the fields of statistics and the behavioral sciences and has as its goal to make decision making less of an art and more of a science. Decision theory focuses on certain elements

EXHIBIT 1. Types of Mathematical Models

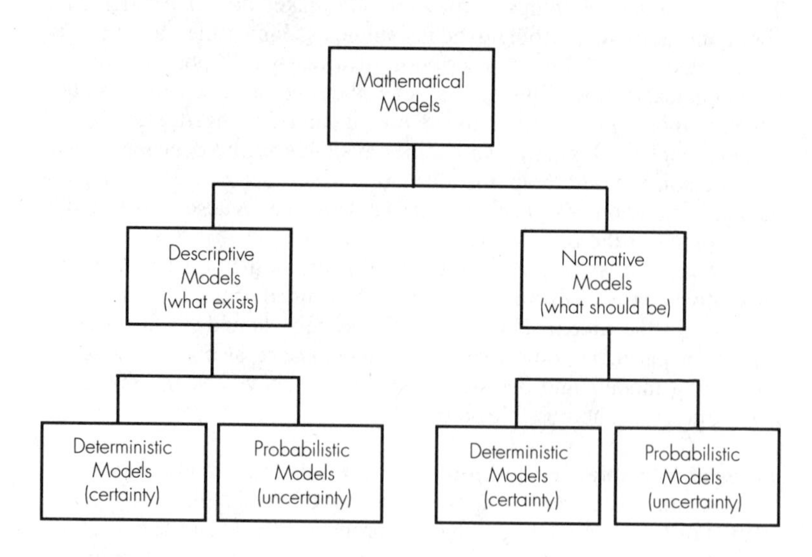

that are common to all decisions and provides a framework that enables a decision maker to better analyze a complex situation containing numerous alternatives and possible consequences. Decision-theory models are normative in purpose and contain probabilistic variables.

Break-Even Models

One widely-used mathematical model is known as the break-even model. While it did not originate specifically with the management science approach, it is included here because it is mathematical in nature. Its major function is to determine the break-even point for the firm as a whole or any of its specific products or services. The break-even point is that particular level of operations where total revenue equals total cost, and profit is zero. It can also be utilized to determine what levels of profits or losses will be achieved at a particular level of output. The break-even model is descriptive in purpose and contains deterministic variables.

Inventory Models

Inventory models provide answers to two questions: "How much?" and "When?" Just as a business is concerned with obtaining goods to be sold at the most favorable price, it must also be concerned with the point at which orders are placed for repeat goods and the quantity of each order. On the one hand, enough inventory must be available at all times to ensure that there are no lost sales or loss of customer goodwill due to stockouts; on the other hand, frequent orders result in increased costs such as the storage costs from carrying an excessive inventory. The costs of ordering and carrying an inventory behave in such a way that one increases while the other decreases. Inventory models that are normative in purpose and contain deterministic variables enable the manager to determine the economic order quantity (EOQ) and the optimum reorder point. Because they can be applied wherever inventories are kept, they have also found wide use in nonbusiness organizations.

Allocation Models

Allocation models are used in a variety of situations in which numerous activities are all competing for limited resources. These models enable the decision maker to allocate scarce resources to maximize some given objective. The resources may in certain departments include labor time that the production manager must allocate to several different products to maximize the objective or profit. The resource may be an advertising budget that the marketing manager must allocate over several different advertising media to maximize the objective of the most exposure for the product(s). In each case, the manager wishes to find the optimum way to allocate the scarce resources, given certain objectives (profit, exposure for the product) and certain constraints (available time, dollars).

One of the most widely used allocation models is the linear programming model. Linear programming expresses the objective to be achieved in the form of a mathematical function, the value of which is to be maximized (for example, profits) or minimized (for example, costs). The constraints are introduced that reduce the number of feasible alternatives. A powerful linear programming procedure known as the simplex method searches the feasible alternatives to find the particular one that maximizes or minimizes the value of the objective function. The linear programming model is normative in purpose and contains deterministic variables.

Network Models

Network models are extremely useful in planning and controlling both simple and complex projects. The two basic and most common types of network models are PERT (Program Evaluation and Review Technique) and CPM (Critical Path Method). PERT is a method of planning and controlling nonrepetitive projects—projects that have not been done before and will not be done again in the same exact manner (for example, product development projects). CPM is a planning and control technique used in projects for which some past cost data are available. Network models are normative in purpose and contain probabilistic variables.

Brand-Switching Models

One of the most important measuring devices used by marketing executives in determining the success or failure of their efforts is the share of the market secured by a product. Obviously, marketing managers constantly seek ways to increase their product's share of the market or to at least prevent the existing share of the market from declining. To do this, they must have some idea of the behavior of consumers, both in terms of their brand loyalty and their switching from one brand to another. Brand-switching models provide such information. Brand-switching models can be considered descriptive in purpose and contain probabilistic variables.

Waiting-Line Models

In the production department, workers waiting in line to requisition needed tools or raw materials cost money. Their managers would like to minimize idle time, but on the other hand, they cannot afford to provide a great number of service facilities. Thus they must strike a balance between the costs of additional facilities and worker idle time. There are many other examples of processes that generate waiting lines. Customers must often wait in lines in a supermarket, in a bank, and at an airline ticket counter. Waiting-line models, which are descriptive in purpose and contain probabilistic variables, enable managers to reach effective solutions to these and similar waiting-line problems.

Simulation Models

Simulation means to have the appearance or form of something without the reality. In many situations, management problems are so complex that they cannot be depicted by a standard mathematical model. Simulation involves constructing a model that replicates some aspects of the organization's operation and then performing step-by-step computations with the model, thus duplicating the manner in which the actual system might perform. An individual simulation can be thought of as an experiment on a model. Numerous trials or experiments are performed until a workable satisfactory solution, rather than an optimal solution, is reached. This experimental nature of simulation is an important advantage because the system can be studied under a wider variety of conditions than would be possible using the actual real-world system. In this respect, all mathematical models involve some degree of simulation. Simulation models are descriptive in purpose and contain probabilistic variables.

CONSTRUCTING MANAGEMENT SCIENCE MODELS

At this point, we shall examine the steps management scientists take to ensure a logical approach for formulating and constructing mathematical models. While several general approaches are available, the following series of steps is widely accepted:

1. Define and formulate the problem.
2. Construct the model.
3. Solve the model.
4. Test the solution.
5. Develop necessary controls for the solution.
6. Implement the solution.

Define and Formulate Problem

This first step in the model-building process lays the foundation for all of the following steps. If a problem is ill-defined or loosely formulated, any model constructed on such a foundation will be of little or no value. A problem that is well defined and formulated is one in which all of the elements are clearly delineated. This includes determination of the objective(s) to be achieved, identification of alternative courses of action, and all known components of the particular problem.

The types of problems faced by marketing executives will vary in complexity. For example, some will be relatively *structured,* with easily identifiable variables that are known to behave with a high degree of certainty. Others will be *unstructured,* containing a large number of variables that behave with a high degree of uncertainty. Thus managers face problems that range from the relatively simple and structured to the complex and unstructured. Most problems will fall somewhere along a continuum between these two extremes. As an illustration, let us examine some hypothetical points on this continuum.

Structured Problems. A structured problem may have few or several variables, but all of the variables are deterministic (behave with certainty).

1. *Few deterministic variables.* These types of problems are probably in the minority. They contain only a small number of variables that behave with a high degree of certainty. Some inventory problems are of this type, where all variables such as demand, ordering costs, and carrying costs are all known or determinable quantities.
2. *Many deterministic variables.* These kinds of marketing management problems contain many variables, but all of the variables behave with a high degree of certainty. Allocation problems where a number of activities are all competing for limited resources are one group of problems that usually fall into this category.

Unstructured Problems. An unstructured problem may have a few or many variables, but all of the variables are probabilistic (behave with uncertainty). In some extreme cases, the manager may not even be able to define all the variables present.

1. *Few probabilistic variables.* Marketing management problems of this type contain a small number of variables, but they behave with a high degree of uncertainty. A banker trying to decide whether to introduce a new senior citizen package account faces this type of problem. Although not knowing what competitors will do, the manager does know that whatever they do is going to influence the outcome. Decision theory models have been useful for some problems of this type.
2. *Many probabilistic variables.* These kinds of marketing management problems contain a greater number of variables, and all of them behave with uncertainty. An example of such a problem is launching a new product or advertising campaign. The reader can imagine that constructing mathematical models for such problems is extremely difficult even with the aid of a computer. Network and simulation models can and have been used successfully for problems of this type. Exhibit 2 summarizes our discussion on the types of problems faced by marketing managers.

Construct Model

After the problem has been clearly formulated and defined, the model construction phase begins. This involves expressing the elements of the problem in mathematical form. Clearly, this is a vital phase. What is important here is that the model constructed responds in the same fashion as the real system. There are three basic elements of every mathematical model:

1. *Components.* These are the parts of the model. They may be firms, households, warehouses, costs, media, and other phenomena that are a part of the real system.
2. *Variables.* These relate in one way or another to the components of the model. They are often classified as *input variables,* which arise outside the component and must be fed into it (for example, inventory, raw materials); *status variables,* which describe the state of a component (for example, income, education, age); and *output variables,* which are anything generated by a component (for example, costs, demand).
3. *Relationships.* These specify how the values of different variables are related to each other. For example, inventory models specify the relationship between ordering costs and carrying costs.

Solve Model

Once the model has been constructed, the next step is to arrive at a solution to the model. For a normative model, this involves math-

EXHIBIT 2. Types of Problems Faced by Marketing Managers

Type of Problem	**Structured**		**Unstructured**	
Number of variables	Few	Many	Few	Many
Types of variables	Deterministic (certainty)	Deterministic (certainty)	Probabilistic (uncertainty)	Probabilistic (uncertainty)
Example of useful management science technique	Inventory control model	Linear programming model	Decision theory	Netword and simulation models

ematical techniques for arriving at the best strategy or alternative. In the case of complex linear programming problems, this may involve numerous computations. In the case of a descriptive model where usually there is no solution, the model can be termed "solved" when it accurately describes the system under study.

Test Solution

Once the model is solved, the solution should be tested before it is applied to a large segment of the organization's operations. The reason for this should be clear: testing the solution enables management to determine the effect of the model on a small scale, and if any errors are discovered, the model can be altered accordingly and a new solution obtained. For example, the solution to an inventory problem could be tested on a small scale using perhaps one warehouse or store. In this way, one can gain some insight into the value of the solution and adjust accordingly if changes are necessary. Then and only then should the solution be applied on a full-scale basis.

Develop Controls

Once the model is constructed and solved, there must be a provision for control. In other words, the model must be carefully and continually reexamined to ensure that the variables and relationships have not changed. Whenever there is a change in any of the variables included in the model, it may be necessary to completely revise it. There are also many forces at work that affect management decisions but over which the manager has little or no control. Thus the need for tight monitoring of the model is vital. Imagine, for example, the impact of past fuel shortages and the political unrest in the Middle East on the models used by oil companies for allocating fuel to service stations.

Implement Solution

After the model has been solved and tested, the solution should be implemented by or recommended to the manager in cases where staff analysts have constructed the model. In any case, the manager must be aware of the objectives, assumptions, omissions, and limitations of the model. After this is done, further reformulation of the problem may result because of some previously overlooked factor that is considered important. Before the solution is finally implemented, all personnel who will use the solution produced by the model should be made aware of the basic rationale behind the model and the advantages to be gained by implementing the solution. The manager must keep in mind at all times the behavioral ramifications involved in implementing change. A well-constructed model may not provide its true benefit if individuals in the organization resist implementation or pay only token service to the solution provided by the model. Thus behavioral factors can vitally affect the success of management science solutions. The entire process for constructing management science models is illustrated in Exhibit 3.

EXHIBIT 3. Constructing Management Science Models

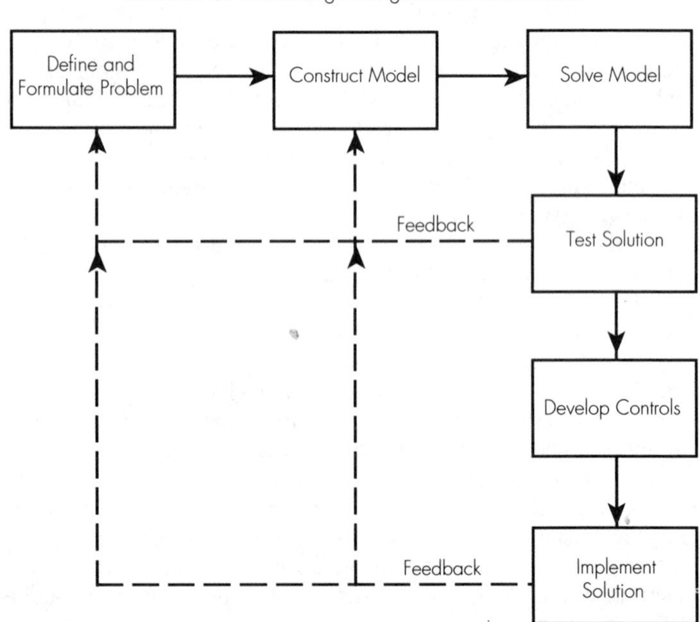

IMPLICATIONS

To operate effectively in an environment that is becoming more complex and dynamic, marketing management can benefit from a more formal approach. Management science is an attempt to apply scientific methods to large-scale management problems. It seeks to express these problems in mathematical form to enable either solution or experimentation. While management science in marketing has already made useful contributions, it appears that the surface has only been scratched in applying mathematical techniques and tools to marketing problems.

REFERENCE

Turban, Efraim, and Jack R. Meredith. 1981. *Fundamentals of Management Science.* Dallas: Business Publications, Inc.

SUGGESTIONS FOR FURTHER READING

Dyer, Robert F., and Ernest H. Forman. 1991. *An Analytic Approach to Marketing Decisions.* Englewood Cliffs, NJ: Prentice-Hall, Inc.

Nutt, Paul C. 1989. *Making Tough Decisions: Tactics for Improving Managerial Decision Making.* San Francisco: Jossey-Bass Publishers.

Nylen, David W. 1990. *Marketing Decision-Making Handbook.* Englewood Cliffs, NJ: Prentice-Hall, Inc.

Souder, William E. 1987. *Managing New Product Innovations.* Lexington, MA: Lexington Books.

J. Barry Mason
The University of Alabama
Tuscaloosa, Alabama

William O. Bearden
The University of South Carolina
Columbia, South Carolina

CHAPTER 21

MANAGERIAL PERSPECTIVES ON CONSUMER SATISFACTION, DISSATISFACTION, AND COMPLAINING BEHAVIOR

The social environment is being subjected to increasingly close scrutiny by management. Many executives talk about shifting consumer attitudes as much as changing economic conditions—an indication that management considers consumer attitudes a key factor regardless of economic conditions. These shifts in attitudes and behavior are manifested in new life-styles and, therefore, new consumer desires and new consumer demands.

A prominent concern of management when thinking about today's consumer is the continuing high level of consumer dissatisfaction with products and services. By some standards, however, the quality of goods and services available today may be higher than ever. The marketing system is also working at an ever greater level of efficiency. Still, consumer dissatisfaction, even in the face of these circumstances, is as apparent as ever and raises the issue of whether consumers can ever be completely satisfied. This chapter highlights what we know about the characteristics of dissatisfied consumers, the nature of complaints expressed, and from whom consumers seek complaint resolution and proposes a summary model of the antecedents of overall consumer satisfaction/dissatisfaction. Finally, guidelines are presented for positive company responses to these issues.

CONSUMER SATISFACTION IN PERSPECTIVE

Consumer satisfaction is a primary goal for all successful enterprises. Many executives have long had a tradition of recognizing the importance of the consumer as reflected in the adage that "the consumer is always right," except of course when the consumer shoplifts, switches price tags, or engages in other antisocial behavior. Still, many consumers today feel relatively powerless in the marketplace, especially when dealing with large complex institutions. Thus a stronger focus by management on consumer satisfaction, dissatisfaction, and complaining behavior remains worthwhile for a variety of reasons: (1) consumer activism is a signal that all consumers are not docile, happy, well-adjusted customers of the marketplace; (2) the discontented consumer is an unsatisfied consumer and, therefore, is probably worthy of special effort and attention from marketing executives; and (3) militant consumers are usually characterized as active, vocal, and semiorganized participative critics of the marketing system and firm behavior (Singh 1990).

When a few consumers express dissatisfaction, they typically reflect the opinions of a much larger number of people (Albrecht and Crego 1987). Research conducted by the Technical Assistance Research Program (TARP), specialists in consumer research, for example, found that 31 percent of consumers facing an average potential loss of $142 because of defective products or services still did not complain (Anton 1988). Consumers who do complain provide a clear signal that all is not well with the marketplace. Such complaints can provide useful feedback about dissatisfaction with company offerings and allow management to take needed actions. Resolving consumer dissatisfaction is good business. Depending on the industry, companies can improve profits from 25 to 85 percent by reducing consumer defection just 5 percent (Reichheld and Sasser 1990). Consultant Laurel Liswood has calculated that the lifetime value of a supermarket customer averages $250,000 (Focus on Customer Retention . . . 1990). Resolving consumer complaints quickly and efficiently has the effect of salvaging substantial future cash flows. Finally, TARP research has found that the average return from investments in problem-handling systems ranges from 100 percent for manufacturers of durable goods such as washing machines and refrigerators to 170 percent for banks (Sellers 1988; Stewart 1991).

Consumerist Goals

Consumer dissatisfaction and complaining behavior are not new phenomena. Consumers have been active in the United States for more than 100 years. At various times, they have pursued at least three sets of objectives affecting management: changes in political or economic institutions, support of new business institutions, and modifications of existing business establishments (Hollander 1972-1973).

Changes in Political or Economic Institutions. Consumers often use purchasing power in efforts to cause changes in political or economic institutions. Familiar examples include boycotts of stores distributing merchandise produced by nonunion workers, protests against retail outlets selling animal fur products, and boycotts of firms conducting business with South Africa. Boycotts of stores that allegedly discriminate in employment against minorities are also well known.

Support of New Institutions. Consumers traditionally have supported such activities as consumer cooperatives and shopping services designed to reduce the costs of distribution.

Modifications of Existing Business Practices. Perhaps the best-known efforts of consumers in pushing to change existing business practices were those fighting legislation against chain stores during the 1930s and 1940s. The so-called Green movement of the 1990s is similarly causing firms to use new forms of packaging, modify product ingredients, recycle waste products, and help clean up the environment.

Forces Behind Consumer Dissatisfaction

A new era in the history of consumerism is emerging. The outlook and values of today's consumer are different from those of consumers in the 1970s and 1980s, although the consumer movement continued in the 1990s in a quieter, mature stage. Many of the issues around which consumers first rallied in the 1960s and 1970s have been addressed, if not remedied. Consumer concerns that have persisted include complaints about false or misleading advertising and labeling, deceptive price comparisons, and high-pressure selling tactics. One manifestation of the current consumerism is the increasing number of mandatory deposit laws for beverages. The laws mark a fundamental shift in food marketing away from an energy- and materials-intensive system toward one that is more heavily focused on recycling. Similarly, concerns about the accuracy of product nutritional claims, weight loss claims, and similar issues are hallmarks of consumer concerns in the 1990s.

Today, local organizations that can provide direct tangible benefits to socially conscious consumers seem to be more effective vehicles for change than national groups. An example of a local organization's success was the Massachusetts-based animal welfare group that pressured McDonald's and Burger King to boycott Canadian fish products in protest of that nation's seal hunting.

Some people see a new rise in consumer militancy that will extend the consumerism of the past decades into a new realm. This militancy, they contend, will especially reach those with money but little discretionary time. One expert has observed that such people are not going to put up with poor service, poor-quality products, lack of concern for them, or anything that eats away at their time or money. If they believe no one else will help them, "they will take the law into their hands" (Sheth 1987). Examples of this militancy include attacks on airline personnel by passengers who have been bumped from their flights, hostility toward life-style discrimination in business practices, physical assaults against persons wearing fur, and boycotts of various sorts (Litman 1991; If you Light up . . . 1991).

The Extent of Consumer Satisfaction/Dissatisfaction

Most dissatisfied customers never complain. Instead, they simply switch stores or brands (Richins 1987). Research has shown that customers who have a bad experience tell approximately eleven people about it; those with good experiences tell just six (Hart, Heskett, and Sasser 1990; Madden 1988). Simply cutting defections in half could more than double the average company's growth rate (Reichheld and Sasser 1990).

Additionally, a comparison of the results of two studies separated by thirteen years shows that we still have a long way to go in meeting the expectations of consumers who do complain (Berry and Parasuraman 1991). Research in 1975 revealed, as shown in Exhibit 1, that only one-third to one-half of consumer complaints were resolved to the customer's satisfaction compared to one-half to two-thirds in 1988. The 1988 study, however, investigated the performance of five companies acknowledged to be the best in their industries. Satisfaction resolution likely would be less common in the general population of firms. Regardless, the sobering dimension of the 1988 research is that 33 to 50 percent of the leading companies in the United States are failing to resolve customer complaints satisfactorily.

Executives too often still have a tendency to perceive customers as adversaries. The president of TARP has established that premeditated rip-offs by complaining consumers represent only 1 to 2 percent of the incidents in most organizations. He goes on to observe, however, that most organizations defend themselves against such customers by ". . . . treating the 98 percent of honest customers like crooks to catch the 2 percent who are crooks" ("Improving Service . . ." 1990).

Most Common Types of Complaints. Unprofessional workmanship, poor quality of parts or materials, and failure to perform work on time are among the most frequently voiced reasons for dissatisfaction. All of these reasons are under the control of management and probably could be reduced without undue expense or difficulty.

Consumer dissatisfaction, however, is not necessarily limited to an overall poor postpurchase reaction to the quality of a product or service. Rather, consumer dissatisfaction is often much broader and may concern advertisements, pricing practices, installation practices, and delivery or credit that may be in no way related to the quality of the product. Complaints thus should be viewed as a process that includes consumer shopping, purchasing, and consuming. Dissatisfaction may occur at any or at all of these stages and should be monitored by management for potential sources of customer frustration.

Precise information on the nature and frequency of dissatisfaction following a purchase is difficult to develop. However, some generalizations are possible. For example, a statewide survey in Michigan discovered that retail stores were cited most often as sources of consumer anger, with 32 percent of the respondents reporting bad experiences with them (More Than a Third. . . . 1987). The research established that service was a common source of complaints, followed by bad experiences with personnel, inadequate complaint handling, poor quality products or services, and the cost of voicing concerns.

An analysis of the records of 172 Better Business Bureau offices, which handle approximately ten million consumer complaints and inquiries a year, revealed the top ten categories of complaints (Council of Better Business Bureaus 1986), as shown on page 376.

EXHIBIT 1. Customer Satisfaction and Problem Resolution: 1975 vs. 1988

Authors and Year of Study	Nature of Study and Sample	Type of Service	Sample Size‡	Percentage of Sample Indicating Satisfactory Problem Resolution
Andreasen and Best 1975*	Customer-satisfaction study of a random sample of households in major metro areas in the United States; customer-satisfaction data on a variety of general product and service categories were collected	Home repair	78	53
		Car repair	261	50
		Credit	69	50
		Film developing	84	45
		Appliance repair	107	36
		Medical/Dental care	84	35
		Car parking	47	30
Berry, Parasuraman, and Zeithaml 1988†	Service-quality study of random samples of customers of five nationally known companies; data on customer assessment of various facets of each company's services were collected	Telephone repair (Co. 1)	148	67
		Insurance (Co. 2)	137	59
		Insurance (Co. 3)	73	50
		Banking (Co. 4)	122	

*The service-category labels and numbers in this part of the exhibit are from Exhibit IV in Alan R. Andreasen and Arthur Best. 1977. Consumers complain—Does business respond?" *Harvard Business Review.* July-August, pp. 93–101.

†Source: Leonard L. Berry and A. Parasuraman. 1991. *Marketing Services: Competing Through Quality.* New York: The Free Press, p. 36.

‡Number of respondents who experienced a problem in each category.

	Number	Percentage
1. Ordered product sales	60,883	30.6
2. Home remodeling/improvement companies	36,083	18.2
3. Auto repair shops	27,171	13.7
4. Franchised auto dealers	21,806	11.0
5. Home furnishings stores	10,599	5.3
6. Financial companies	10,084	5.1
7. Direct selling companies	9,189	4.6
8. Department stores	7,791	3.9
9. Insurance companies	7,753	3.9
10. Dry cleaning/laundry stores	7,427	3.7

From Whom do Consumers Seek Satisfaction? Consumers do seem to talk to other consumers in expressing their dissatisfaction, as noted earlier. This situation can cause a major ripple effect. The types of actions taken by consumers in an effort to resolve their dissatisfaction in the marketplace can vary widely, however. Informal actions may reflect a decision to stop buying a product, to boycott the seller, or to warn friends about the product and/or seller. More formal complaining efforts include a complaint to private or governmental agencies, legal action, or an effort to obtain redress directly from the business firm.

Consumers who get upset are most likely to complain personally or else do nothing. They appear to be least likely to boycott the store or product or go through channel intermediaries. The most frequent action is a personal complaint to the store manager, salesperson, clerk, or similar person.

Reasons for Taking No Action. Primary reasons normally given for not complaining are, (1) "I didn't think it was worth the time and effort;" (2) "I wanted to do something about it but never got around to it;" (3) "I didn't think I could get anyone to do anything about it;" and (4) "I didn't know what to do about it or where to go for help" (Day 1980). These findings reflect a lack of adequate response mechanisms for both identifying and resolving product- or service-based dissatisfaction by management. Such dissatisfaction often translates into lost customer goodwill, lost revenue, and an eroded customer base.

Consumers are becoming increasingly conscious of what they need to know about products and services and are more careful in seeking sources of information. Consumer-oriented businesses can thus greatly strengthen customer loyalty by interpreting and serving these specific needs. In a climate where needs are increasingly well structured, delivering the proper information in the right format has the potential of being a powerful differential advantage in the marketplace. Firms may need to give a great deal more emphasis in the future to serving the information needs of the consumers whose products needs they hope to satisfy.

Management thus needs to shift from thinking about what competition is doing to what consumers are thinking (Robert 1988). From a company's point of view, for pragmatic or noble reasons, what is too often missing is a user mentality (Bitner 1990). When management looks at new programs, its approach is usually fairly traditional and third-party sensitivity is not readily evident.

A variety of studies have discovered that many organizations fail to respond at all to the complaints they receive (Gilly 1987). Response rates to complaints were found to vary from a high of 79 percent (Kendell and Russ 1975) to a low of 56 percent (Resnik, Gnauck, and Aldrich), as shown in Exhibit 2. Equally important is the issue of how organizations respond. The most frequent response by retailers in a study by Kelly (1979) was to do nothing or to tell the customer to take the problem to the manufacturer. The manufacturer's most frequent response was to replace the items.

Various steps can be taken to influence consumer reaction to dissatisfaction. Three variables seem to primarily influence such reactions: the sellers' reputation for quality and service, the nature of the circumstances surrounding the sale, and the responsiveness of the marketing channel in providing redress to dissatisfied consumers. A strong reputation for quality and service is likely to encourage dissatisfied consumers to express their dissatisfaction since they expect fair treatment in addition to a satisfactory product (Bitner, Booms, and Tetreault 1990). Consumers are less likely to respond affirmatively when dealing with an organization with a weak or unknown reputation.

Sales pressure also influences a consumer's reaction when dissatisfaction occurs. An adverse reaction is more likely to occur after a hard sell than if the dealer had pointed out both the advantages and disadvantages of the product and worked to assure the "best buy" for the consumer. A good reputation for standing behind the merchandise sold is particularly important. A prompt and cheerful exchange by a local retail outlet can go a long way toward mitigating dissatisfaction with a product, for example.

Additionally, various circumstantial factors affect the tendency to complain (Folkes, Koletsky, and Graham 1987). Complaints are most likely to occur about such major durables as automobiles. Such items are perceived as both essential and expensive. Inexpensive items are not as likely to generate complaints (Richins 1985). Also, the more difficult the complaining process, the less likely such an action will occur. Government regulations and activities such as those of the Consumer Products Safety Commission can also greatly influence the tendency to complain, as can adverse publicity about a product. The poorly informed consumer is more likely to experience problems and should be a target of management efforts to provide consumer information and education. Lack of knowledge about how to buy and use products can lead to dissatisfaction and frustration for all parties involved.

EXHIBIT 2. Summary of Major Postcomplaint Studies

Study Reference	Product(s) Studied	Data Collection Method	Response Rate to Complaints%	Satisfaction with Complaint Response	Other Postcomplaint Variables Measured
			Complaint Letters		
Kendall and Russ (1975)	Consumer packaged goods	Wrote letters of complaint to manufacturers	79	70% answered in a "presumably satisfactory manner"	—
Pearson (1976)	Consumer products	Students asked to write letters (complaint or praise) to business firms	74	80% of complaint letter writers were satisfied with the response received	—
Resnik et al. (1977)	Consumer products	Students asked to write genuine letters of complaint	56	50% of those receiving a response were satisfied; 27% of all letter writers satisfied	—
			Surveys		
Andreasen and Best (1977)	Consumer products	Random telephone survey of U.S. households	—	30%-81% of complainants were satisfied with the response received, depending on product	—
Gilly and Gelb (1982)	Oil Co.	Survey of complainants to an oil company	—	50% satisfied if complained about nonmonetary problem; 79% satisfied if complained about monetary loss	Repurchase behavior

Kelly (1979)	Clothing	Survey of complainants to a clothing manufacturer	—	40% satisfied with retailer response; 85% satisfied with manufacturer response	Intentions to shop at store; intentions to buy brand; word-of-mouth
Lewis (1982)	Hotel	Survey of consumers who communicated with a hotel	—	Mean of 3.1 on a 5-point satisfaction scale	Word-of-mouth; intentions to patronize
TARP (1979)	Consumer products	National consumer survey asking about their most serious consumer problem	—	23% who complained were completely satisfied with the response received; additional 20% found the solution to be acceptable	Intentions to repurchase
			Experiments		
Dwyer and Dornoff (1981)	Shoes	Consumers asked to evaluate complaint letters and recommend responses	—	Respondents recommended manufacturer's actual response 30%-70% of the time	—
Resnik and Harmon (1983)	Building materials	Consumers asked to examine complaint letters and manufacturer's responses	—	71% of the time consumers believed manufacturer's response would be satisfactory	—

Source: Mary Gilly. 1987. Post complaint processes: From organizational response to repurchase behavior. *Journal of Consumer Affairs* 21 (2): 295.

Who is Most Likely to Complain. People who complain are not typical of the population but also are not part of a lunatic fringe (Cadotte and Turgeon 1988). Various personality, attitudinal, and life-style variables affect whether a person will complain and the action he or she will take. The principal findings in profiling the dissatisfied and complaining consumer have generally been convergent. Complainers tend to be younger, have more education, have a higher income, and work in managerial/professional capacities more often than does the general public (Singh 1990).

Less research has been done on noncomplainers. However, noncomplaining but dissatisfied consumers appear to be unsure of the response called for, feel powerless to act, or simply feel that complaining is not worth the effort. Noncomplainers also tend to have lower incomes, lower levels of education, less political involvement, more pessimism about the interest of government in consumer problems, and less confidence in the future of the nation than complainers (Singh 1990). Other research has shown that persons who blame themselves for their dissatisfaction are also less likely to complain (Folkes 1988). Finally, complaining is also less likely when the dollar costs are low and the problem is judgmental as opposed to a manifest defect (Richins 1985).

SUMMARY MODEL OF CONSUMER SATISFACTION/DISSATISFACTION

A basic understanding of consumer satisfaction/dissatisfaction and complaining behavior is possible through a model of the constructs and determinants of such behavior. Such a model is depicted in Exhibit 3. The model can serve as a basis for understanding the factors behind the descriptive data that have been presented to this point. The model depicts complaining behavior as but one stage in the overall purchase experience that includes past purchase experiences, prepurchase and search, purchase, use, evaluation of the postpurchase experience, and some form of response to the experience.

As shown, a basic understanding of consumer satisfaction can begin by starting with the prepurchase experiences of the consumer. Consumers sometimes begin with a needs assessment that the product or service can satisfy and then seek information about the total costs of such a purchase including the monetary costs, shopping costs, and maintenance and up-keep costs. Such prepurchase perceptions about a particular product or service are also partly a function of past experience. During the shopping/purchase/use stage, information about source of the product, service, and warranties is needed in addition to product information.

Following purchase and use, postpurchase evaluation occurs. Such evaluation is in the context of an initial standard that exists in the

EXHIBIT 3. A Model of Complaint Behavior

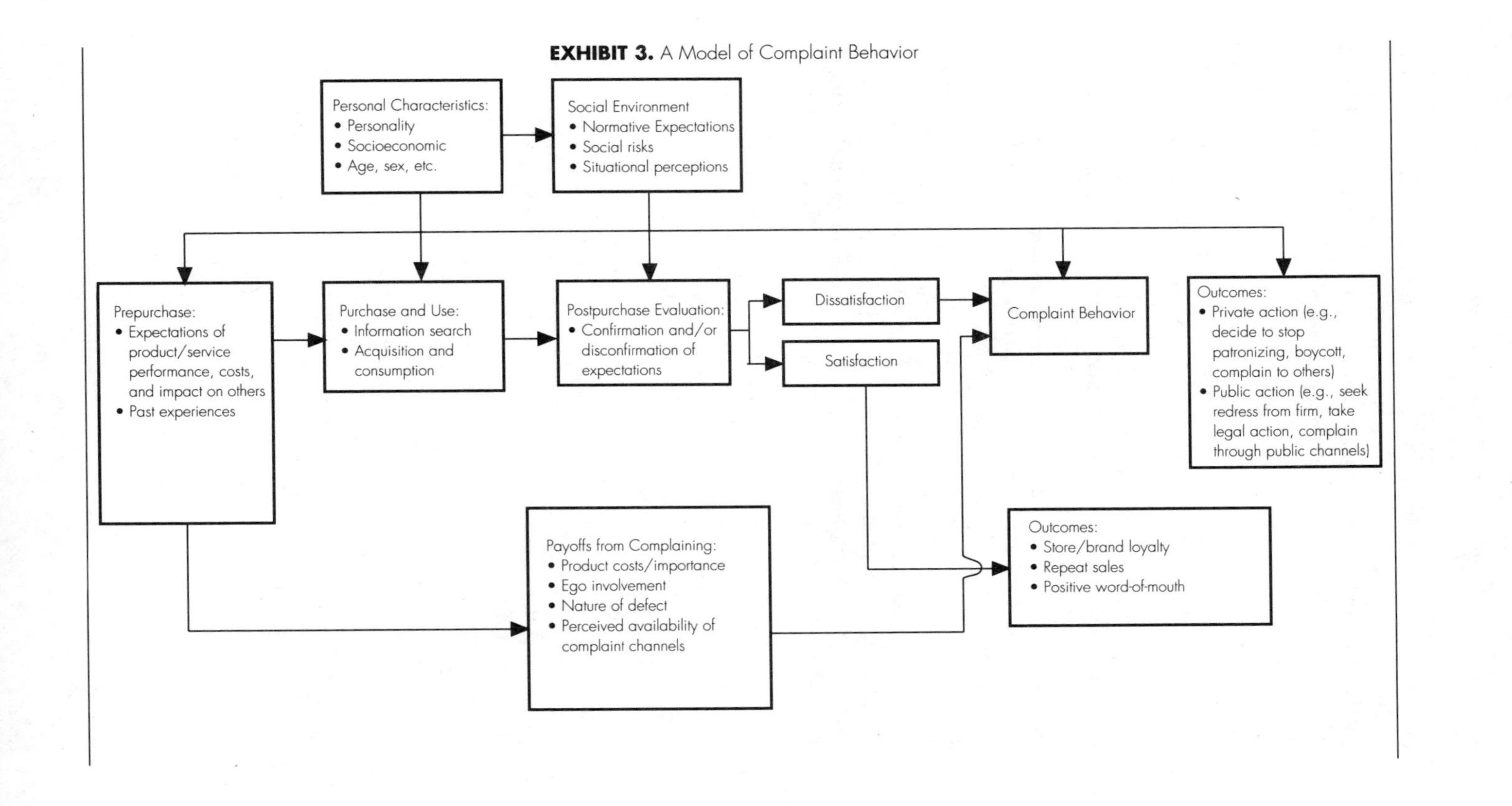

consumer's mind and discrepancies, if any, from this reference point. Expectations about a product in effect serve as a frame of reference against which one can make a comparative judgment (Oliver and Swan 1989). Experiences that are poorer than expected (negative disconformation) or better than expected (positive disconformation) may result. Expectations about the product as reflected in the postpurchase experience are a function of both personal characteristics and characteristics of the social environment. Such features include prior product experience, brand perceptions, individual characteristics, and communications that have occurred with salespersons, social referents, and others.

A positive disconformation of expectations is reflected in satisfaction with the purchase experience that can result in increased store or brand loyalty, repeat purchase, and positive word of mouth among the consumers' centers of influence. Negative disconformation can lead to dissatisfaction that may be either expressed or unexpressed. Expressed dissatisfaction may take some form of complaint behavior, as previously noted. Specifically, the consumer may take public or private action. The perceived payoffs from complaining affect whether a formal complaint is expressed. As observed earlier, manifest defects in a product, high-cost products, products perceived as necessities, relative ease in complaining, or products with a high degree of ego involvement are more likely to trigger a complaint on the part of the consumer.

ORGANIZING FOR CUSTOMER SATISFACTION

Research on customer loyalty by the Forum Corporation found that only 14 percent of customers who stopped patronizing businesses did so because they were dissatisfied with the quality of what they bought. More than two-thirds defected because they found customer support personnel to be indifferent or unhelpful (Schlesinger and Heskett 1991). Still other research has shown that 75 percent of all incidents of dissatisfaction could be traced to customer expectations that exceeded the capacity of service delivery systems (Niquist, Bitner, and Booms 1985).

A close link exists between resolving a customer's problem on the spot and the customer's intent to repurchase (Hart, Heskett, and Sasser 1990). When customers experience minor problems, 95 percent say they will repurchase if the complaint is resolved speedily. If the resolution process takes even a little time, however, the number drops to 70 percent. A spread of 25 percentage points can easily mean the difference between spectacular or mediocre operating performance (Schlesinger and Heskett 1991).

Similarly, research done for the U.S. Office of Consumer Affairs found that in households with service problems with a potential cost of more than $100, 54 percent would maintain brand loyalty if their problems were satisfactorily resolved. Only 19 percent would repeat their purchase if they were unhappy with the problem resolution. For less expensive problems ($1 to $5), 70 percent would maintain brand loyalty if their problems were resolved satisfactorily. Only 46 percent would repurchase if the problem was not fixed (U.S. Office of Consumer Affairs 1986).

Defensive marketing strategies, designed to retain customers, are thus becoming more important in today's competitive, saturated markets. In summary, evidence suggests that "(1) a dissatisfied customer, once persuaded to stay, is loyal and, thus, more valuable than before; (2) responsive complaint management is likely to generate positive consumer word-of-mouth communication; and (3) consumer complaints can be useful sources of . . . quality control" (Zemke and Schaff, 1989). Research has shown, however, that consumer expectations are higher and tolerance zones narrower for recovery actions than for the initial encounter (Parasuraman, Berry, and Zeithaml 1991).

Management must work to reduce the cycle of failure that results in customer dissatisfaction. Managers too often create and run "a self-reinforcing system that establishes an inevitable cycle of failure. Ironically, the system's assumptions and operating practices virtually guarantee the degradation of the services that business exists to provide" (Schlesinger and Heskett 1991).

Operational Response Mechanisms

Management has taken a variety of actions in recent years to generate higher levels of consumer satisfaction with the purchase experience. The actions include open dating of food, nutritional labeling, unit pricing, voluntary trade regulation guidelines, and "hot lines" to trade associations that can investigate and act on consumer complaints. What, however, can be done at the level of the individual firm in a more aggressive response to consumer dissatisfaction?

Before rushing into consumer education and other response programs, management needs to be sure that it possesses the organizational capability to respond to consumer concerns. Consumer satisfaction programs take a lot of time and effort to develop, but they can pay off richly in company profits and increased customer satisfaction.

A Consumer Affairs Office. An effective consumer affairs office ideally has input into several activities. These activities include (1) policy input into areas that directly affect consumers—for example, advertising and credit decisions; (2) development of guidelines for handling consumer complaints; (3) analysis and dissemination of information at all levels on consumer complaints and on policies for resolving complaints; and (4) continuous efforts to maintain dialogue with consumer citizens' groups, consumer affairs specialists, and trade association personnel. Management should review existing procedures and policies affecting consumers and initiate changes when appropriate.

In-Store Consumer Consultants. The use of in-store staff consumer consultants, a more recent development than corporate staff consumer consultants, is also becoming increasingly popular. In some instances, in-store consumer advisers operate on the sales floor. They not only keep people happy by giving straight answers but also enable management to keep a constant finger on the pulse of their customers.

Information Feedback. To keep better informed of consumer problems, management can use any of several approaches. These may include maintaining an 800 number consumer "hot line" to handle complaints. The idea of consumer advisory panels is also growing in popularity. These panels are typically composed of representative cross-sections of community citizens: men and women, average shoppers, senior citizens, and members of various ethnic groups. Although the payback from such programs cannot be measured directly, they do provide effective communication with the consumer.

Employee Commitment. Management should strive to instill stronger commitment to consumer satisfaction. An effective motivator is economic incentives. Other incentives are also important, but most of us have yet to meet the person who is not interested in money. Management too often pays the lowest wages to the very persons who represent their company to the consumer (Bitner, Booms, and Tetreault 1990). Paying better wages to attract, retain, and reward good personnel can reduce both turnover and related consumer problems.

Employee turnover and customer satisfaction are directly correlated (Schlesinger and Heskett 1991). Management should consider granting some type of merit increase at the ultimate consumer level for those persons who go beyond what is normally expected of them. In addition, management should consider the use of flex-time. Although retired persons and others, such as housewives, may not be able to work conventional 8:00 to 5:00 hours, they may desire to work several hours during the day simply to get out of the house. Such persons can make superior employees.

Economic incentives can also be established to encourage more positive actions over the long run (Hart, Heskett, and Sasser 1990). A possibility is an incentive at the end of each quarter for the person who receives the fewest customer complaints or merchandise returns.

Monitoring Consumer Satisfaction

Management should not rely solely on complaint letters received as valid expressions of the extent and nature of consumer satisfaction. Rather, management can do a better job of listening to customers by developing a carefully structured series of studies on satisfaction, dissatisfaction, and complaints about products and services (Sterschic 1990; Parasuraman, Berry, and Zeithaml 1990). Such studies should be conducted periodically to help management assess consumer satisfaction and the extent to which voluntary complaints received are indicative of the customer base as a whole.

The following guidelines can be helpful in developing a system for effectively anticipating and responding to customer complaints and dissatisfaction (Berry and Parasuraman 1991):

1. Make it easy for customers to express their dissatisfaction, for example, by establishing a toll-free number with sufficient telephone lines to handle the calls.
2. Conduct customer satisfaction research at every opportunity and use consumer focus groups to ferret out unhappiness.
3. Train employees to respond to customer dissatisfaction by enhancing their communication and stress management skills. Empower them to resolve customer problems with a minimum of hassles, and reward employees who make special efforts to resolve consumer problems.
4. Take steps to minimize customer hardships when a problem occurs by providing a fast response and doing something extra for customers who encounter problems with the organization.
5. Identify the core causes of customer dissatisfaction. Customer complaints are typically symptoms of a breakdown within the organization.
6. Establish and continually update a problem-tracking system to identify patterns in customer problems and opportunities for modifying the system to avoid difficulties in the future.

STRATEGIC DIMENSIONS OF CUSTOMER SATISFACTION*

Firms with strong customer satisfaction ratings share the following six attributes: (1) they set themselves "impossibly high" standards; (2) they are obsessive about knowing, even better than the customers themselves, what the customers want; (3) they create and manage customers' expectations; (4) they design their products or services to maximize customer satisfaction; (5) they commit resources to meet their commitment to customers, virtually regardless of the cost; and (6) they make customer satisfaction everybody's business (Lele 1987).

Customer-focused organizations realize that every dimension of the firm must be structured from the customers' point of view. Long-term customer satisfaction results from the interaction of four distinct variables: the product, sales activity, after-sales support, and the culture of the organization, as shown in Exhibit 4.

The Product

Most of us can probably remember such phenomenally successful products as the Volkswagon Beetle, the IBM Selectric typewriter, and the first generation Apple computer. They excelled in product design

EXHIBIT 4. Components of Customer Satisfaction Fundamentals

Product	Design —Messages —Sales and support effectiveness Feedback and incentives Sourcing and manufacturing —Customer contact —Quality —Cost
Sales Activity	Messages —Overt —Covert Attitudes —Salesforce training —Salesforce rewards Intermediaries —Incentives —Selection —Training —Monitoring
After Sales	Support services —Coverage —Quality and performance Feedback and restitution —Coverage —Responsiveness
Culture	Formal symbols and systems —Mission statements —Performance standards —Compensation Informal symbols and systems —Beliefs —Values

Source: Milind Lele. 1987. *The Customer is the Key.* New York: John Wiley and Sons, p. 84.

and product quality. Similarly, the Lotus spreadsheet program swept the market because it was user friendly.

Customers define product value in the context of functions, features, and packaging. Value is also reflected in communication and promotion programs, atmospherics, and quality of sales personnel. Value in use, for example, includes user friendliness and performance, while value in disposal focuses on what can be done with the product when it is no longer of value to the customer. Responsive customer feedback systems, continuing innovation in meeting or exceeding customer expectations, and understanding customer needs by design, engineering, and manufacturing personnel are important (Dougherty 1990).

Sales Activity

Sales-related activities communicate implicit and explicit messages that influence customer attitudes and expectations prior to, during, and after the sale. The full array of promotional programs as part of a marketing plan communicate both explicit and subconscious messages about the business unit's attitude toward customers. Product literature, advertising, and mailings are important as overt messages. Atmospherics, design, and layout, salespersons' attire, and even store location send subtle, perhaps subconscious, messages.

Expectations are affected by each person with whom the customer comes in contact, ranging from the telephone receptionist to the service technician. The attitudes of customer contact personnel are reflected in their product knowledge, courtesy, and sales focus. Training has an important role in improving salesperson response, especially if it includes a focus on customers and on knowledge of competitors' products and applications. Too often, training is limited to providing knowledge about the business units' products or services, not those of competitors.

Incentives are also important in assuring that sales personnel work to create and maintain long-term customer satisfaction. For example, charging product returns against a salesperson's account can help discourage an overly aggressive, short-term sales focus.

The choice of intermediaries as channel partners is also important because they are often the primary point of customer focus with the parent organization and its products or services. Careful attention should be directed to the selection of channel members in providing their staffs with the appropriate training and in making sure customers are treated in ways that are compatible with management's image for the product or service. Such designers as Liz Claiborne, for example, have developed the "store within a store" concept in which they have total control over the sale and display of their merchandise. Responsive intermediaries are also important in providing after-sale support and in handling customer complaints. Successful marketers understandably regard channel members as partners, not nuisances.

After Sales

After-sales customer satisfaction activities can assume a variety of forms including toll-free numbers, recall notices, warranties, training for customer personnel, and similar activities. After-sales activities are of two types: (1) *support services,* such as warranties and parts, and (2) *feedback and restitution,* which involve refunds, refund policies, complaint resolution, and complaint handling (Lele 1987).

Astute organizations focus on after-sales support as a primary way of strengthening customer relationships. Problems occur when business unit managers are not aware of customer support needs or do not understand how their needs affect the type of after-sales support needed. The appropriate levels and types of after-sales support vary by type of product or service. Important types of support for packaged goods and products, for example, include hot lines for answering questions and easy refunds. Important after-sales support for durables include a strong inventory of spare parts, technician training, and warranty services.

Culture

The culture of an organization, as embedded in corporate values, is a primary driver of product functions, features, and pricing, in addition to sales activity and after-sales support. Firms with a strong commitment to maximizing customer satisfaction will synchronize these activities to ensure long-term success.

The values underlying corporate culture consist of two primary components: formal values as reflected in corporate mission statements, action plans, and policies and procedures, and (2) informal values as reflected in corporate actions. The informal values are the true measure of a firm's intentions and commitment to customers. They reflect the extent to which a focus on customer satisfaction permeates all levels of an organization.

DIAGNOSING CUSTOMER SATISFACTION SHORTFALLS

Management cannot address the issue of customer satisfaction unless it understands the multiple dimensions of customer expectations (Zeithaml, Parasuraman, and Berry 1990): Customer expectations can be understood in the context of five dimensions (see Exhibit 5):

1. *tangibles*—visible facilities, equipment and apparatus;
2. *reliability*—ability to perform dependably and accurately;
3. *responsiveness*—willingness to provide strong customer satisfaction;
4. *assurance*—knowledge and courtesy of employees and their ability to inspire trust and confidence; and
5. *empathy*—sharing and individualized attention to customers.

Differences between customer expectations and perceptions (Gap 5 in Exhibit 5) result from four organizational gaps: (1) not knowing what customers expect (Gap 1), (2) the wrong customer satisfaction standards (Gap 2), (3) an expectations-performance gap (Gap 3), and (4) promises that do not match delivery (Gap 4). Each of the four internal organizational gaps is caused by inadequate performance on one or more of the five dimensions of tangibles, reliability, responsiveness, assurance, and empathy.

EXHIBIT 5. The Extended Gaps Model of Customer Satisfaction

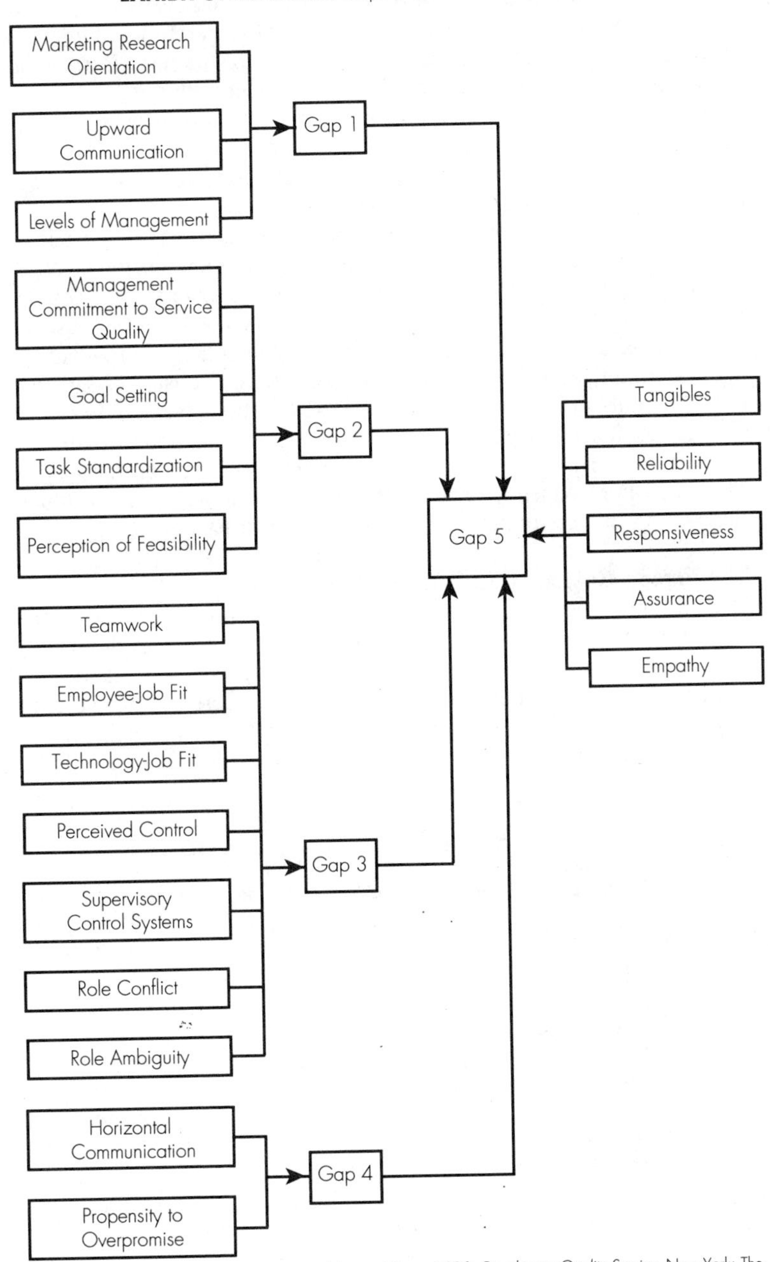

Source: Valerie Zeithaml, A. Parasuraman, and Leonard Berry. 1990. *Developing Quality Service*. New York: The Free Press, p. 131.

Not Knowing What Customers Expect

The reasons management does not know what customers expect are diverse but often occur because of a lack of research-based findings in structuring customer support programs (Parasuraman, Berry, and Zeithaml 1990). Additionally, a failure to interact with customers on a continuing basis can contribute to problems, as can a lack of intense, continuing communication between customer contact personnel and management. Excessive layers of bureaucracy often separate customer contact personnel from top management.

Progress in closing the gap is achieved by making strategic use of customer complaints. Top management should review customer complaints on a regular, perhaps daily, basis and help customer contact personnel learn how to resolve the issues. As noted earlier, use of customer panels chosen from target markets can be helpful in identifying opportunities for improvement, as can assessing customer satisfaction with individual purchases. A service satisfaction research *process* is needed, not just an occasional study. Snapshots at one point in time are not sufficient. Rather, continuing assessments over time are necessary. The types and frequency of research appropriate in assessing customer satisfaction in a continuing context are shown in Exhibit 6.

The Wrong Customer Satisfaction Standards

Simply understanding customer expectations is not sufficient. Standards that meet customer expectations must also be developed and implemented. An internal as opposed to an external orientation, resource limitations, an obsessive focus on market share or sales volume, or a culture in which customer satisfaction is not really a high priority can lead to a gap between management specifications of standards for

EXHIBIT 6. Research-Based Customer Satisfaction Assessments

Type of Research	Frequency
Customer complaint solicitation	Continuous
Posttransaction follow-up surveys	Continuous
Managers telephoning customers for informal feedback	Weekly
Customer focus groups	Monthly
"Mystery shopping" of service providers	Quarterly
Employee surveys	Quarterly
Total market service quality surveys	Three times/year
Special purpose research	As needed

Source: A. Parasuraman, Leonard L. Berry, and Valarie Zeithaml. 1990. Guidelines for conducting service quality research. *Marketing Research: A Magazine of Management and Applications* 2 (4):43.

customer satisfaction and customer expectations. This gap can be closed by establishing goals based on customer requirements and expectations rather than on internal business unit standards that may not be important to customers. Other steps include standardizing tasks by implementing policies and procedures that can be readily implemented and routinized, improving work methods by taking advantage of technology, maintaining data bases on important customers to help management be more responsive to their needs, and continuously measuring and reviewing internal standards compared to customer expectations.

An Expectations Performance Gap

A performance gap occurs when management is unable to deliver service at the level of customer expectations. The reasons for the gap can include role ambiguity, role conflict, poor employee-job fit, poor technology-job fit, inappropriate supervisory control systems, an inappropriate evaluation/compensation system, employee perceived lack of control, or lack of team work (Zeithaml, Parasuraman, and Berry 1990).

Role ambiguity can occur when employees do not have the information or perhaps the training needed to perform their jobs. As a result, they are unsure what management expects and/or how to meet the expectations. Training can eliminate role ambiguity, but lack of role clarity may still exist. Communication, confidence, feedback, and competence are important in establishing role clarity. Employees must understand their role by receiving specific and continuing communication from management about the products offered, target customers and their expectations, and the strategies and philosophies of the business unit. Role conflict can be avoided by helping customer-contact personnel understand what counts above all else in dealing with customers.

Promises That Do Not Match Delivery

Management must be careful not to establish unrealistic customer expectations in communications such as advertising, personal selling, or public relations. Otherwise, disappointed customers will be the result (Zeithaml, Parasuraman, and Berry 1990). Differences between promises and delivery can occur because of a lack of standardized policies and procedures or inadequate communication between product development personnel, customer contact personnel, operations personnel, and media personnel.

Effective horizontal communications are necessary to ensure that promises match delivery. Sales personnel must have detailed information about promises in media campaigns. Also, employee selection, training, and incentives need to be aligned with customer satisfaction expectations.

CLOSING THE EXPECTATIONS/PERFORMANCE GAP

Customer satisfaction requires a fundamental commitment from top management, middle management, and first-line supervisors. Top management helps create the culture and vision for the organization. Middle management becomes the linch pin because it is the link between top management and first-line supervisors (Stershic 1990). First-line supervisors help build the team perspective between product management, sales, and media with a core focus on customer satisfaction.

A program for closing the expectations/performance gap consists of four distinct steps (Day 1990):

1. Assessing the present orientation of the business unit and identifying the barriers to becoming market driven.
2. Demonstrating top management's commitment to a more market-driven orientation.
3. Aligning the customer support strategy with the organizational structure and human resources.
4. Encouraging and rewarding market-driven behavior at all levels of the organization.

Assessing the Current Situation

Key questions to ask include the following (Shapiro 1988):

1. What do our customers think of us relative to the competition?
2. What do we, as a management team, think of our performance as an organization? Are we market driven, and if not, where do we fall short?
3. What are the barriers to becoming more market driven?

Developing an externally focused customer satisfaction orientation begins with data. A helpful device is a "user friendly" audit that can identify problems and opportunities. An audit, such as the one shown in Exhibit 7, may reveal the absence of strong, credible leadership at the top. Inadequate communications may also be found to hinder the implementation of customer satisfaction programs. Similarly, management may be encouraging customer-contact personnel to be overly rigid in adherence to policy on such issues as returns and handling of complaints.

Demonstrating Top-Management Commitment

All employees must believe that customer satisfaction is a top priority with senior management. Such a commitment is demonstrated in how they allocate their time and whether management is willing to measure the performance of the business unit against the toughest competitors in the target market segment. Continuing emphasis on customer needs, requirements, and trends is critical, as is a willingness

EXHIBIT 7. Self-Examination Checklist

1. Are we easy to do business with?
   Easy to contact?
   Fast to provide information?
   Fast to order from?
   Make reasonable promises?
2. Do we keep our promises?
   On product performance?
   Delivery?
   Installation?
   Service?
3. Do we meet the standards we set?
   Specifics?
   General tone?
   Do we even know the standards?
4. Are we responsive?
   Do we listen?
   Do we follow up?
   Do we ask "why not," "why"?
   Do we treat customers as individual people?
5. Do we work together?
   Share blame?
   Share information?
   Make joint decisions?
   Provide satisfaction?

Source: Benson Shapiro. 1988. "What the Hell is Market Oriented? *The Harvard Business Review.* November-December, p. 125.

to invest resources in research designed to provide a better understanding of customers and competitors and in training to help customer-contact personnel more effectively meet customer needs.

Aligning Strategy, Structure, People, and Programs

Management may find that the business unit is too internally focused on products and systems instead of customers. An audit may also determine that product personnel and customer-contact personnel do not communicate in sharing information about product lines, promotion programs, pricing, and needed research. A team perspective between all divisions is necessary. Employee training should cover all functions within the business unit and provide detailed knowledge of customer segment requirements. Periodic meetings with all departments also should be held to identify ways for improving customer satisfaction.

Encouraging and Rewarding Market-Driven Behavior

The reward structure within the organization must clearly signal that the customer comes first. A truly customer-driven culture will not emerge within the organization if the primary emphasis continues to be on sales volume, cost control, and reducing inventory, for example, to the possible detriment of customer satisfaction.

CONCLUSION

Management needs to develop a total customer response program if it is to respond effectively to consumer dissatisfaction. Simply developing how-to-shop booklets or similar materials does not represent a sufficient response to the information needs of today's consumer. Population growth is slowing. Thus, increasing volume in the future will likely come at the expense of competition. A high quality and comprehensive customer response program can be one way of increasing sales volume at limited cost.

In summary, today's consumers more than ever are seeking clear labeling, better disclosure of conditions in terms of credit, honesty in advertising, and similar dimensions that would make it easier for them to function as informed consumers. Consumer activism can be the hope of an alert management. Historically, when the service institutions of society have not adequately served customers, new institutions have evolved. Since this is the case, management can never go wrong in adopting a philosophy of better service to their customers.

NOTES

*The remaining portions of this article are reproduced with modifications from *Marketing Management* by J. Barry Mason and Hazel Ezell. Copyright (c) 1993 by Macmillan Publishing Company. Reprinted by permission.

REFERENCES

Albrecht, Karl, and Edwin T. Crego, Jr. 1987. What every consumer wants. *Laventhol and Horvath Perspective* 3 (2):2–5.

Andreasen, Alan R., and Arthur Best. 1977. Consumers complain—Does business respond? *Harvard Business Review* 55 (4):93–101.

Anton, Jon. 1988. Why it pays to solicit consumer complaints. *Telemarketing* 7 (5).

Berry, Leonard L., and A. Parasuraman. 1991. *Marketing Services: Competing Through Quality*. New York: The Free Press.

Bitner, Mary Jo. 1990. Evaluating service encounters: The effects of physical surroundings and employee responses. *Journal of Marketing* 54 (April):69–82.

Bitner, Mary Jo, Bernard M. Booms, and Mary Stanfield Tetreault. 1990. The service encounter: Diagnosing favorable and unfavorable incidents. *Journal of Marketing* 54 (January):71–84.

Cadotte, Ernest R., and Normand Turgeon. 1988. Dissatisfiers and satisfiers: Suggestions from consumer complaints and compliments. *Journal of Consumer Satisfaction, Dissatisfaction and Complaining Behavior* 1:74–79.

Council of Better Business Bureaus. 1986. *Newsletter of the American Council of Consumer Interests* 34 (October):1.

Day, George S. 1990. *Developing Market Driven Strategy*. New York: The Free Press.

Day, Ralph. 1980. Research perspectives on consumer complaining behavior. In Charles W. Lamb, Jr., and Patrick M. Dunne (eds.): *Theoretical Developments in Marketing*. Chicago: American Marketing Association.

Dougherty, Deborah. 1990. Understanding new markets for your products. *Strategic Management Journal* 11:59–78.

Dwyer, F. Robert, and Ronald R. Dornoff. 1981. The congruency of manufacturer redress actions and consumer redress norms and expectations. In Kenneth L. Bernhardt, et al. (eds.): *The Changing Marketing Environment: Theories and Applications*. Chicago: American Marketing Association.

Focus on customer retention is a proven profit strategy. 1990. *The Service Edge* June, p. 2.

Folkes, Valerie. 1988. Recent attribution research in consumer behavior: A review and new directions. *Journal of Consumer Research* 14 (March):548–61.

Folkes, Valerie, Susan Koletsky, and John L. Graham. 1987. A field study of causal inferences and consumer reaction: The view from the airport. *Journal of Consumer Research* 13 (March):534–39.

Gilly, Mary C. 1987. Post complaint processes: From organizational response to repurchase behavior. *Journal of Consumer Affairs* 21 (2):293–313.

Gilly, Mary C., and Betsy D. Gelb. 1982. Post-purchase consumer processes and the complaining consumer. *Journal of Consumer Research* 9 (December):323–28.

Hart, Christopher W. L., James L. Heskett, and W. Earl Sasser, Jr. 1990. The profitable art of service recovery. *Harvard Business Review* July-August, pp. 148–56.

Hollander, Stanley C. 1972-1973. Consumerism: A historical perspective. *Journal of Retailing* 48 (Winter):6–21.

If you light up on Sunday, don't come in on Monday. 1991. *Business Week* August 26, pp. 68–69.

Improving service doesn't always require big investments. 1990. *The Service Edge* July-August, p. 3.

Kelly, J. Patrick. 1979. Consumer expectations of complaint handling by manufacturers and retailers of clothing products. In Ralph L. Day and H. Keith Hunt (eds.): *New Dimensions of Consumer*

Satisfaction and Complaining Behavior: Proceedings of the Third Annual CS/D and CB Conference.

Kendell, C. L., and Frederick A. Russ. 1975. Warranty and complaint policies: An opportunity for marketing management. *Journal of Marketing* 39 (2):36–43.

Lele, Milind M. 1987. *The Customer Is the Key: Gaining an Unbeatable Advantage Through Customer Satisfaction.* New York: John Wiley & Sons.

Lewis, Robert C. 1982. Consumer complaints—What happens when business responds? In Ralph L. Day and H. Keith Hunt (eds.): *International Fare in Consumer Satisfaction and Complaining: Proceedings of the Seventh Annual CS/D and CB Conference.*

Litman, Joanne. 1991. Consumers seek escape from captive-ad gimmicks. *Wall Street Journal* September 13, p. B1.

Madden, Charles. 1988. The costliest customer of all. *Baylor Business Studies* Winter, pp. 9–11.

More than a third of Michigan consumers have been so burned that they stay away from some businesses. 1987. *Marketing News* April 24, pp. 20.

Niquist, Jody D., Mary Jo Bitner, and Bernard H. Booms. 1985. Identifying communication difficulties in the service encounter: A critical incidents approach. In John Czepiel, Michale R. Solomon, and Carol Suprenant (eds.): *The Service Encounter: Managing Employee/Customer Interaction in Service Business.* Lexington, MA: Lexington Books.

Oliver, Richard L., and John E. Swan. 1989. Equity and disconfirmation perceptions as influences on merchant and product satisfaction. *Journal of Consumer Research* 16 (December):372–83.

Parasuraman, A., Leonard L. Berry, and Valarie A. Zeithaml. 1991. Understanding customer expectations of service. *Sloan Management Review* 32 (Spring):39–48.

Parasuraman, A., Leonard L. Berry, and Valarie A. Zeithaml. 1990. Guidelines for conducting service quality research. *Marketing Research: A Magazine of Management and Applications* 2 (December):34–44.

Pearson, Michael M. 1976. A note on business replies to consumer letters of praise and complaints. *Journal of Business Research* February:61–67.

Reichheld, Frederick F., and W. Earl Sasser, Jr. 1990. Zero defections: Quality comes to services. *Harvard Business Review* September-October, pp. 105–113.

Resnik, Alan, and Robert R. Harmon. 1983. Consumer complaints and managerial response: A holistic approach. *Journal of Marketing* 47 (Winter):86–97.

Resnik, Alan, Bryan Gnauck, and Rodney Aldrich. 1977. Corporate responsiveness to consumer complaints. In Ralph L. Day (ed.): *Consumer Satisfaction, Dissatisfaction and Complaining Behavior: Proceedings of the Second Annual CS/D and CB Conference*.

Richins, Marsha. 1987. A multivariate analysis of responses to dissatisfaction. *Journal of the Academy of Marketing Science* 15 (3):24–31.

Richins, Marsha. 1985. Factors affecting the level of consumer-initiated complaints to marketing organizations. In Keith Hunt and Ralph Day (eds.): *Consumer Satisfaction, Dissatisfaction and Complaining Behavior*. Bloomington, IN: School of Business, Division of Research.

Robert, Michael. 1988. *The Strategist CEO: How Visionary Executives Build Organizations*. New York: Quorum Books.

Schlesinger, Leonard A., and James L. Heskett. 1991. The service-driven service company. *Harvard Business Review* 69 (September-October):71–81.

Sellers, Patricia. 1988. How to handle customers' gripes. *Fortune* October 24, pp. 88–100.

Shapiro, Benson. 1988. What the hell is market oriented? *Harvard Business Review* 66 (November-December):119–25.

Sheth, Jagdish N. 1987. Changing demographics and their impacts on consumer behavior. *In Proceedings of the Division of Consumer Psychology*. New York: American Psychology Association.

Singh, Japdish. 1990. A typology of consumer dissatisfaction response styles. *Journal of Retailing* 66 (Spring):57–99.

Sterschic, Sybil F. 1990. The flip side of customer satisfaction research. *Marketing Research: A Magazine of Management and Applications* December, pp. 45–50.

Stewart, David. 1991. The customer as annuity. *USC Business* 2 (Summer):48–52.

TARP. 1979. *Consumer Complaint Handling in America: Summary of Findings and Recommendations*. Washington, DC: Technical Assistance Research Programs.

U.S. Office of Consumer Affairs. 1986. *Consumer Complaint Handling in America: An Update Study, Part II*. Washington, DC: Technical Assistance Research Programs.

Zeithaml, Valarie, A. Parasuraman, and Leonard L. Berry. 1990. *Delivering Quality Service*. New York: The Free Press.

Zemke, Ron, and Dick Schaff. 1989. *The Service Edge*. New York: New American Library.

Darrell B. Lucas
New York University (retired)
New York, New York

CHAPTER 22

ADVERTISING RESEARCH AND MEASUREMENT

Most advertising research deals either with copy and commercials or with the media in which they circulate. While the messages and their media work together, research has usually been quite different for both. The purpose of copy tests is often to determine the rank order of alternate themes and executions of advertisements. Media research, by contrast, concentrates on quantitative measurement of some aspect of the media function. This means that, while the function of the advertising message is to have a maximum qualitative impact, the primary function of the medium is to reach or expose the message to a maximum number of the right kinds of people. Hence, the frequent reference to media research as a numbers game.

Basic Considerations

Advertising is a business expense or investment, and its cost must be regained through increased sales or profits that would not have occurred without it. Much advertising research is done without any clear reference to sales. The designer of research may leave it entirely up to the interpreter or user of the results to rationalize any relationship between the results and ultimate profitability. Many copy tests deal with only one aspect of the total advertising function, and they are often lacking in validity. To refer to the winner of such a tenuous test as the *best* or *most effective* advertisement can only reduce the possibility or proper interpretation and application of the findings. Instead of concluding that one advertisement is *better* than another, it may be more accurate to say that it probably was noticed by more people, or perhaps read or remembered by more. There are other functions, aspects or elements with which conclusions might deal in contrast with measurement of the overall impact of an advertisement or campaign.

Definitions and Planning

Terminology is important at all stages of advertising research. Even such a common term as memory requires definition, for it may be simply a claim of recognition or demonstration of ability to recall, with or without aids. Attitude is often defined narrowly as predisposition to act, although this is not universally accepted. Terms in media research also require definition, usually beyond ordinary dictionary usage. Media audience (defined later), for example, is a useful term only insofar as users agree on an arbitrary definition. All advertising research has special need for definition, for so many of its terms are used colloquially in a different sense.

Good research requires careful planning at all stages. Intelligent planning can begin only after the problem has been sharply defined. Then the method has to be decided on. Planning includes the technical design in detail. Even the planning for reporting should be worked out clearly in advance of the research. Just how far the research planners should go in the interpretation of results should be anticipated early. Much research is reported by technical people in a manner suited only to other technical people. There are levels of understanding all the way from the research department to the chief executive officer, and from the sales staff on through trade channels to the ultimate consumer. Research findings will be most useful and will be applied most effectively only to the degree that they can be understood in the form in which they are reported.

Exhibit 1 shows the hierarchy of advertising performance measures along with the spectrum of job functions and responsibilities for people involved in the creation, management, and use of advertising. For example, a copywriter may be interested in learning the consumer or business decision maker emotional reaction to a print ad or commercial, e.g. How much does it cause the reader to perspire (basal skin response)? At the other end of the spectrum—which emphasizes the 'big picture approach'—marketing directors will be more interested in the sales/market share effects of advertising efforts. (While the services and measures shown in the exhibit are useful in general, it is not meant to imply that all are equally valid for purposes of level-to-level prediction of advertising performance).

SCIENTIFIC METHOD

Scientific method involves measurement and often calls for the design of an experiment. The ideal experiment is carried on under completely controlled conditions, with only one or possibly two or three causal elements being manipulated at a time. This greatly constricts advertising experiments or tests, for it puts emphasis on the control of normal or natural conditions of exposure of the message or medium being measured. When natural exposure is not feasible and when too many variables are operating at the same time, it is practically impossible to arrive at unequivocal conclusions. Much advertising research is criticized for lack of natural test conditions. Likewise, there is criticism for making the blind assumption that uncontrolled or unknown variables are going to remain equal when other things may not be equal at all.

Basic aims of advertising research are to determine causes and to determine the amount of the effects. It is seldom safe to assume that, when two variables correlate closely, one of the variables is the cause of variation by the other. Much of the research on broadcast media, which has often shown a striking correlation between media usage and

EXHIBIT 1. Communication evaluation and advertising effectiveness*

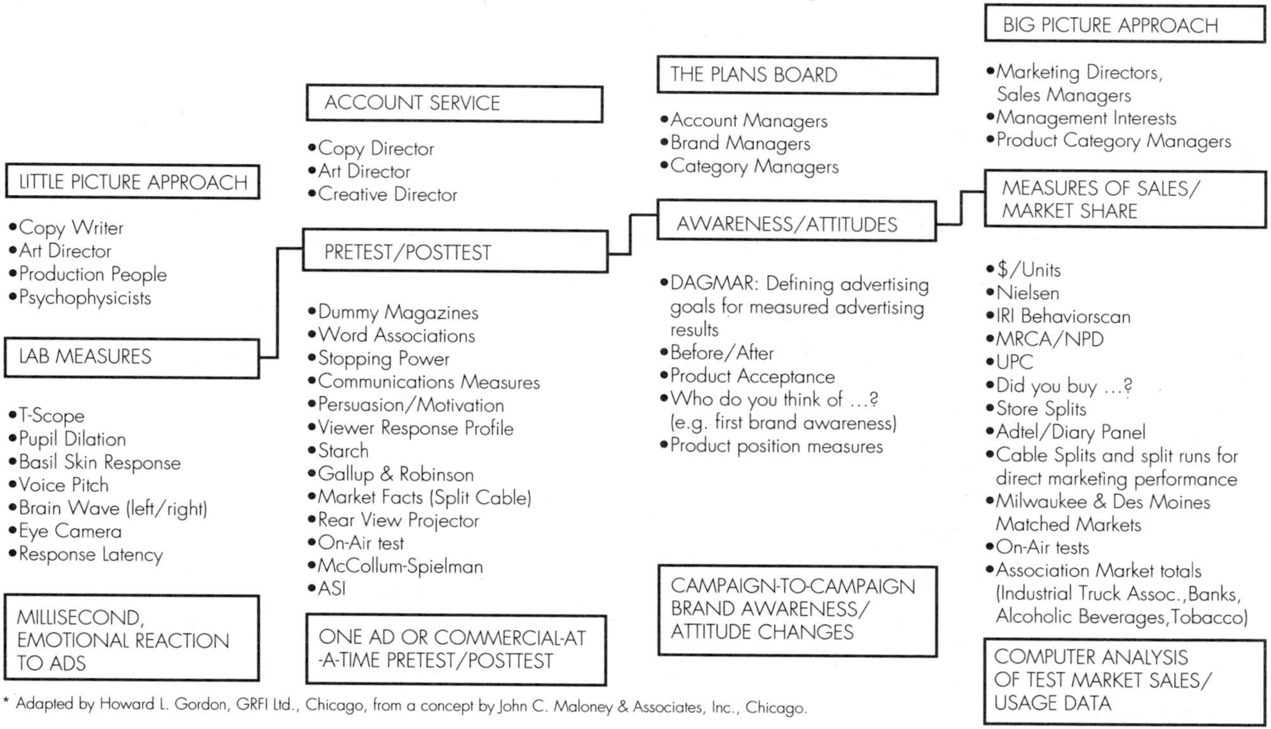

LITTLE PICTURE APPROACH
- Copy Writer
- Art Director
- Production People
- Psychophysicists

ACCOUNT SERVICE
- Copy Director
- Art Director
- Creative Director

THE PLANS BOARD
- Account Managers
- Brand Managers
- Category Managers

BIG PICTURE APPROACH
- Marketing Directors, Sales Managers
- Management Interests
- Product Category Managers

LAB MEASURES
- T-Scope
- Pupil Dilation
- Basil Skin Response
- Voice Pitch
- Brain Wave (left/right)
- Eye Camera
- Response Latency

PRETEST/POSTTEST
- Dummy Magazines
- Word Associations
- Stopping Power
- Communications Measures
- Persuasion/Motivation
- Viewer Response Profile
- Starch
- Gallup & Robinson
- Market Facts (Split Cable)
- Rear View Projector
- On-Air test
- McCollum-Spielman
- ASI

AWARENESS/ATTITUDES
- DAGMAR: Defining advertising goals for measured advertising results
- Before/After
- Product Acceptance
- Who do you think of ...? (e.g. first brand awareness)
- Product position measures

MEASURES OF SALES/ MARKET SHARE
- $/Units
- Nielsen
- IRI Behaviorscan
- MRCA/NPD
- UPC
- Did you buy ...?
- Store Splits
- Adtel/Diary Panel
- Cable Splits and split runs for direct marketing performance
- Milwaukee & Des Moines Matched Markets
- On-Air tests
- Association Market totals (Industrial Truck Assoc.,Banks, Alcoholic Beverages,Tobacco)

MILLISECOND, EMOTIONAL REACTION TO ADS

ONE AD OR COMMERCIAL-AT -A-TIME PRETEST/POSTTEST

CAMPAIGN-TO-CAMPAIGN BRAND AWARENESS/ ATTITUDE CHANGES

COMPUTER ANALYSIS OF TEST MARKET SALES/ USAGE DATA

* Adapted by Howard L. Gordon, GRFI Ltd., Chicago, from a concept by John C. Maloney & Associates, Inc., Chicago.

consumer ownership of advertised brands, has been generally rejected by researchers and also by the buyers of media time and space. This does not mean that there is never a causal relation when two variables correlate; it means that one must be very cautious in making such an assumption. When both the well-trained scientist and the experienced practitioner share a gut feeling that there must be a significant causal relationship in an advertising situation, that is about the maximum assurance that can be achieved.

THE PLACE FOR SCIENTIFIC SAMPLING

Precise measurement of effects of advertising must relate to a clearly-defined market or population. If the research calls for projection to a total market or population, then the sample must be designed to match the universe at which the research is aimed. Scientific sampling requires that everyone in the particular universe has a known probability or chance of being selected for the survey. Over a period of a quarter of a century after commercial introduction of known-probability sampling around 1948, the advertising business came to accept and even to demand such scientific sampling methods before accepting population projections in promotional research. That standard continues.

Probability sampling is often expensive, and there are advertising tests that do not justify the cost of such scientific precision. Copy tests, intended to discover rank order of themes or designs, may rely on samples that are parallel but may not represent the total population of the intended market. If the leading advertisement or element achieves a big enough advantage, it may be concluded that it is probably superior with regard to the quality under test; the safety of that conclusion may never be known.

When the purpose of testing is not to measure, but rather to discover characteristics, the size and design of the sample may not be very important. Depth interviews or informal (focus group) discussions may turn up unsuspected factors or indicate that they are important enough to justify later measurement. In one instance, when a leading mass marketer of economy products bought up a small prestige product, it was a group discussion that first warned the creative writers against prominent display of the name of the new owner in the advertisements. A number of those in the informal discussions suggested that they had been much more impressed with the prestige product than by the giant maker of economy products. Through similar informal discussions, the manufacturer of soups was reminded that, while a family might look on the serving of a clear soup as a special, extra treat, they might have the impression that soups-with-solids are a substitute kind of food made from leftovers or solids of inferior quality. Examples like these show that there is a place for exploring with less-than-scientific samples, though never for projecting such findings to definable populations.

BACKGROUND CONSIDERATIONS REGARDING COPY AND COMMERCIAL TESTING

The testing of advertising copy and commercials has an instructive history. Beginning around 1930, academic and commercial research people experimented and sought to design a valid test of specific pieces of copy, and later, commercials as broadcasting came into prominence. Despite early optimism, real progress was minimal. Repeatedly, someone or an agency announced success in designing a highly valid copy or commercial test, or even a formula for evaluating copy without the need for a test. Before the end of 50 years of testing, most people in the business had concluded that it is unlikely that a universal copy gauge will come to light for some time, if ever. Anyone who ventures into the field of copy testing without a clear picture of the past is likely to run into many frustrations, and even to spend money wastefully on some untried or already tried faulty panacea.

If copy testing is such an elusive pursuit why, then, should it not be abandoned completely? Many answers could be suggested, but the demand for measurement is so great, costs are so low, and the stakes are so high that the effort cannot and should not be abandoned. One reason for this conclusion is that it is generally conceded that a good advertisement can be 10 times as productive as the next best alternate. Low cost is especially evident where a test depends on using alternate advertisements in publications that make no charge for running two or more different designs in as many alternate copies in the press run. Another important reason for copy and commercial testing is that the advertising process has some *sine qua nons,* to be mentioned later, which do yield to fairly simple measurement.

Before going into specific copy and commercial tests, it should be pointed out that there are some serious constraints unique to advertising. The presidential forecaster, for example, is finally proved right or wrong. The copy and commercial tester, by contrast, who deals with general advertising, may never know the profitability or effectiveness of individual advertisements or even of a campaign. Pretesting is especially precarious if advertising exposure cannot be made sufficiently natural or if the lapse of time between testing and final release invalidates the findings. Nevertheless, most agencies and their clients do pretesting as a regular day-to-day practice. Yet, while most will agree that profitability has to be the justification for all advertising costs, the industry is almost equally divided on the question as to whether the contribution of advertising to sales should be the basic criterion of effectiveness.

THEORETICAL STAGES IN THE ADVERTISING PROCESS

An examination of the advertising process reveals a number of points on which nearly all advertising people and research authorities agree. For example, one of the *sine qua nons* referred to earlier is that an advertising message has to be noticed, or at least exposed, in order to have possible effect. Some advertising messages have to be read or heard and perhaps listened to in order to contribute to the sales process. Even the establishment of relevant selling points capable of later recall may often be a desirable goal. So far, so good.

Carrying on further into the advertising process begins to bring complications. There are many advertisements for which recall of verbalized sales points seems very secondary to the ability to convey a mood or a desire capable of determining a purchase or a brand choice. For some advertisements, comprehension of the message may be vitally important; for others conviction or intent to buy may be more important.

A few advertisers, and especially some giants with heavy spending, are committed to the evaluation of their advertisements on the basis of separate tests of the kinds of factors just mentioned. Others are as definitely committed to the search for the final payoff. It is clear that copy and commercial testing must be guided by complete agreement and, hopefully, complete understanding of the goals that pretesting, or evaluation after the fact, is designed to evaluate.

DIRECT AND INDIRECT SALES MEASURES

Mail-order advertisers are among those most clearly committed to sales or profits for evaluating each advertisement. Usually they are in a position to trace the sales resulting from each copy insertion. This is usually done by keying each advertisement in such a way that every written or telephoned response can be identified with the particular piece of copy. While this procedure is more common on printed advertisements than in broadcasting, the same basic principle can be used in either medium.

Testing of mail-order copy by splitting the press run of a publication into two or more alternate segments appears to be simple and logical. If every second or nth copy carries a different advertisement, it ensures that the prospective buyers in each audience are very much alike. In practice, it usually takes experience to judge whether each piece of copy gives equal opportunity to the element or elements being tested. Also, it is essential to ensure that the scheduling of insertions gives equal opportunity to each variation of copy. One technique is to run the same piece of copy as a control for every split press run. Another useful control is to run the same piece of copy both at the beginning and again at the end of the test period. This may show whether the campaign is losing, or possibly gaining, momentum during the test. There are also seasonal and market variables to be considered to best evaluate the findings. There remains the question as to whether the winning advertisement in one test publication will perform best in other publications.

Another method of sales testing, especially adapted for pretesting, is to make a series of trial runs of different copy in different cities or markets. Store audits, if properly handled, provide an objective method for checking sales differences. Even this simple test procedure carries enough hazards to justify the employment of an experienced supervisor and, at best, calls for caution in drawing conclusions. The selected stores must be representative, they must carry adequate stock, cooperating dealers must keep accurate invoices, personal selling activity and all promotion by competitors must remain steady and the amount of advertising should not be too atypical. These are only a few considerations and, after a winner is declared, it may still fail to fit market conditions at some later date of general release. While this once popular test method has declined in use and in confidence, it should still be kept in mind for possible use on occasions when it has promise of providing useful information.

Some attempts to evaluate the sales effects of advertising have been based on trends where all advertising has been suspended. Two important reasons cast doubt on using this approach to evaluating the effects of advertising. First is the likelihood that advertising requires some time lag before its effects are completed. Second, and more important, is the fact that eliminating advertising is seldom a realistic alternative to running a campaign. Usually, when advertising is completely stopped, there are marketing problems that are not typical. Those who have tried to analyze advertising effects on the basis of complete elimination of advertising sometimes fail to point out why advertising was dropped. No firm conclusions should be based on such a situation.

The arrival of cable television brought great promise of the possibility of comparing sales effects of alternative commercial messages. Where large groups of households are served by the same antenna, there is opportunity to connect alternate households, or alternate groups of homes, separately. While many households may be attending to the same program at the same time, the commercial interruptions can be used for alternate advertising messages. Then, if the households will cooperate in keeping purchase diaries, the results may reflect differing sales impact of the varied commercials. While such facilities are commercially available, there must be insistence that the samples of cooperating homes represent definable markets. There is much to recommend this method for testing television commercials, but sampling limitations and cable costs are inherent in its use.

There is a recurring question as to whether or not the general advertiser might assess sales effects on the basis of intensive statistical analysis. Some advertisers have, on occasion, been in a position to estimate the sales impact of a clearly identified campaign. To do so requires that detailed records be kept of the complete marketing process and that all forms of promotion other than advertising be kept constant. It is very important to monitor all competitor activity and to estimate competing expenditures. Then, if the advertiser agrees to make a deliberate change, either in total advertising expenditure or in the campaign itself, the statistician may succeed in isolating some evidence of sales impact. Many times, the successful advertiser is in the position of wanting to know whether or when to change what appears to be an effective campaign. Most of the models in current use are incapable of giving much guidance in that situation.

There is one particular test method that can be tried without going into the market and which, if valid, can pretest sales effectiveness in advance of general circulation. The test audience is gathered in a studio or auditorium and advertisements are exposed in a more or less natural editorial environment. Before the program begins, each subject may be invited to choose a free sample from several brands of the test product. Again, after exposure of the copy or commercial, in a suitable context, the same subjects are given another opportunity to take a second product sample. Careful noting of the expected increase of choice of the advertised brand is used to evaluate the likely sales impact of the advertisement. Variations of the test advertisement can be tested with different audiences. If the product is too expensive or not adapted to free sampling, various devices such as lotteries are used to motivate and measure effects.

Representative sampling is the main problem with this test method. Even if the invited audience is a systematic selection from a defined universe, a large proportion may not appear for the test. A partial solution is to build a demographic balance in the tabulating process, but this is hard to defend. Even more serious charges are made against the test method itself, although proponents have made strong claims of proof of validity based on later sales.

This does not exhaust the many approaches that have been made or can be made for evaluating the sales effects of advertising. The discussion should make it clear that there is no simple, universal, valid method for testing the sales contribution of single advertisements, or even whole campaigns. If the advertiser is committed to the principle that sales effects are the only proper criterion for evaluating copy and commercials, the company and those who do its research will find that there are many obstacles to achieving the goal of valid measurement, either before or after general circulation. The danger is not only in failure to reach the goal, but also in accepting invalid evidence leading to misguided decisions.

ATTENTION, COMMUNICATION, AND COMPREHENSION

If one is willing to abandon the quest for sales measures, there are still copy and commercial tests that many consider to be more proper gauges of advertising effect. First in the advertising process would be the noting of, or exposure to, the message. Magazine advertisement noting has been reported on a syndicated basis almost from the beginning of copy research. The scores on noting are obtained as claims made by admitted issue readers after looking into the magazine under normal reading conditions. If there is no control on guessing or confusion, the claims are subject to great possible exaggeration or even deflation. While noting and reading scores on advertisements have been used very extensively, they are not highly regarded from a research standpoint.

More dependable evidence that advertising messages have at least been exposed, in print or broadcasting, comes from page exposure research and broadcast program audience measurement. The most objective method for measuring page exposure involves the use of tiny spots of glue between magazine pages. Breaking the spots is strong evidence of page opening, and questioning techniques have been developed to substitute for glue. Individual advertisers may find the cost too great for testing single advertisements, but publishers have used the method to establish high probability of exposure of their own advertising pages.

The measurement problem is somewhat simpler as applied to radio and television commercials. Unlike magazines, where there may be much competition for attention to particular pages, the broadcast program interrupts and suspends competition while advertising is injected. The people in the audience can avoid advertising exposure only by making an effort. Existing evidence shows that only a small minority do so. Thus, by making a small discount, the advertiser can use the measured program audience as a rough guide to the size of the number exposed to the advertising.

Broadcast advertising is better adapted to measurement of recall than is the case for magazines. The precise time of exposure of the commercial to the audience is known, making it relatively easy to use telephone calls to check later recall while impressions are fresh. Minimal memory of any element exclusive to the commercial can be used to estimate exposure; detailed playback of the commercial can evaluate both recall and communication. Magazines, by contrast, are read in such a manner that it is not practical to measure recall while all impressions are fresh. The recall scores on individual advertisements tend to be small, but whatever is retained stands as proof of exposure, recall, and communication. For this reason, the recall of both printed advertisements and broadcast commercials has come into wide use and is respected by most.

Recall probably has its greatest practical use in demonstrating the level and thoroughness of communication. Where the message includes a number of new sales points, recall can establish just which points have been best communicated. If no aids to memory are given, it is proper to motivate recall by offering money or other rewards for each recalled sales point. It is also proper to aid recall by recreating the context in which the advertisement appeared or was heard. To many advertisers, this sort of demonstrated recall of the sales message is a significant measure of probable effectiveness.

Closely related to this kind of feedback of selling ideas is the degree of clear communication of the meaning of the message. Comprehension has long been stressed by copy and commercial testers as one of the most important elements in advertising effect. Since measures of comprehension are so pervasive in formal education, it is surprising how little application of comprehension testing has found its way into advertising research. One reason may be the fact that research people, creative writers, and clients may differ so much as to what meaning was intended to be conveyed. There are many situations where tests of comprehension could well be applied, providing the three disparate parties can reach agreement among themselves.

CONSUMER PREFERENCES AND ATTITUDES

Not all creative advertising efforts are designed solely to convey logical, rational ideas. Many advertisements, which are probably very effective, do not impart to their audiences impressions capable of being readily verbalized. To ask a test subject to give a verbal report of the effect of the advertisement may lead to a meaningless reply or, worse yet, a misleading response. In a somewhat similar way, to ask the respondent whether the advertisement is liked, or which of two is liked better, has long been rejected as a productive method of copy test. Where feelings and attitudes are involved in copy research, there is little available methodology that is dependable.

Shortly after World War II, there was a popular effort to introduce profound psychological methods into research on motivation. The findings were reported in the form of interpretations of verbalized responses obtained in interviews. No numerical counts or statistical analysis was required. Of more importance was the fact that there was no single, accepted method of analysis just as there is no universally accepted Freudian approach. It was difficult to determine whether the reported conclusions were valid or not. After more than a decade, this form of motivation research was relegated largely to the discovery of new hypotheses. It was observed that generalized conclusions from such investigations were likely to be statements of the obvious or very controversial concepts or conclusions that could be reached more easily by simpler methods of inquiry.

Attitude research, used to predict sales and sometimes to compare alternate advertisements, lacks some of the controversy associated with psychological motivation research. Questions are generally aimed at such points as belief in advertising claims, evaluation of the importance or uniqueness of an advertising claim, or expression of likelihood of buying the brand. Attitude research is probably useful in keeping an index of attitudes toward a company or toward a prominent product. Its application to the evaluation of specific advertisements or campaigns has not been fruitful. Consumer responses regarding whether advertising claims are believed, whether the copy convinces prospects that the brand is their first choice, and whether they are most likely to buy that brand on their next purchase all are usually of limited value.

TESTING IN THE LABORATORY

Several laboratory devices have been employed to test advertising copy. They include an instrument similar to a lie detector for recording skin moisture, cameras for recording pupillary dilation and also for recording eye movements of an observer or reader, and a binocular instrument for testing which of two competing visual images is actually perceived. There was also a device for precisely-timed flashes of light, to be used in conjunction with both the recognition and the recall methods of exploring impressions made during brief exposure. For the armchair copy tester, there was even a 27-point rating scale with each point weighted to provide a total score. None of these approaches has survived the brief days of welcome for any untried innovation.

CHOOSING A METHOD OF TESTING AND EVALUATING

Selection of the best test method or methods for general advertising depends heavily on judgment and experience. The simplest problem is to test advertising aimed at a single, easily-measured function. For example, the manufacturer of a newly-invented textile fiber concluded that the immediate, quick objective of advertising should be to gain awareness of the product and its name. He gave it a brand name and set up a budget intended to gain the desired level of awareness of the name and general purpose of the product. The advertiser and the agency were able, based on previous experience involving a mathematical model, to estimate quite accurately how much time and money would be required. And they achieved their goal on schedule without exceeding the budget. This was a relatively easy assignment and it measured the effect of a whole campaign. Similar tests of single advertisements may sometimes be possible and desirable, if time permits. It may also be desirable to experiment first in a single selected market.

Other advertising objectives or intermediate goals short of sales impact may also lend themselves to measurement. Some of the methods already discussed lend themselves logically to measuring success in accomplishing certain objectives. Other objectives may be more difficult to evaluate by known test procedures, or may even be hard to define clearly enough to be tested. Many times the impact of a single advertisement is too limited to adapt to copy testing or even to evaluate after circulation. Complete campaigns are likely to be more easily evaluated, especially after circulation. An example was the problem of a manufacturer of automotive equipment whose brand name was easily confused with a better-known, competing brand. After launching a campaign with special copy emphasis on clear brand identity, the company had no difficulty in obtaining research to gauge their success in clearing up the brand confusion.

In summary, there are many considerations in choosing the best method or methods for testing desired advertising effects. The first consideration is, obviously, the objective of the advertisement or campaign. There follow such factors as cost, time required, the validity of the test method, and the question as to whether the purpose is to pretest or to evaluate at some later date following circulation.

Creative writers typically resent or resist copy testing, often asserting that findings are wrong. Their attitude cannot be explained away by pointing out that they naturally want to protect their brain children. The fact is that the creative writer may be right. There is a history of faulty copy tests and of unsupported claims of test validity. There are many examples of advertisements that were generally considered to be brilliant and probably effective, and that would never have survived most copy tests. Copy testing should not dictate decisions. Client management usually determines whether advertisements should be approved and should always reserve the right to make such decisions.

MEDIA MEASUREMENT

Whereas copy testing has been subject to wide differences of opinion as to proper objectives, media research has enjoyed much greater agreement as to intermediate and final objectives. The stages assigned to most major advertising media are usually agreed on, both in definition and in sequence. It is also agreed that the primary function of most media is to bring the advertisements into contact with a maximum number of the right people.

There are other media functions, such as providing a favorable atmosphere surrounding the advertisements, which are conceded to be important but, nevertheless, secondary. After considering all functions, the media buyer as well as those who design and test advertisements, makes a conscious or an implied judgment as to the expected profitability of the advertising investment. Most advertising dollars are spent for time or space, and the money the advertising agency spends on creating and testing advertisements is absorbed in the media investment. Many advertising agencies have turned to a fee system to cover their costs and profits, but the money the agency invests in creative work and copy testing within the agency usually does not differ much from the discounts that media normally grant to recognized agencies.

The evolution of advertising has brought complications to all advertising research, and especially to media research. When the bulk of national advertising dollars was spent on less than a dozen magazines and just three national broadcasting networks, at one time broadcasting their programs simultaneously across the nation, evaluating the quantitative dimensions of media was relatively simple. As mathematical models came into use, it appeared feasible to design a model for optimal media schedules. But, as advertisers turned to emphasis on individual markets, as national media began to offer local or regional coverage, as magazines and broadcast channels begin to multiply, and as the time and frequency of advertising exposure became beyond easy grasp, the problems of media measurement were magnified greatly. There is no sign that the complexity of media scheduling will decrease; in fact, technical invention promises to revolutionize all forms of communication. Each revolutionary change in media will pose more intricate problems for research.

Despite all of the growing complications in media, there has been substantially more progress in media evaluation than in evaluating advertising copy. Again, one important reason is that there is general consensus that the primary function of a medium is to reach a maximum number of the right people. And quantitative measurement is inherently easier to achieve than any meaningful measurement of characteristics usually identified as qualitative.

QUANTITATIVE EVALUATION OF MEDIA

Quantitative evaluation of major media begins with the fact that each medium has some definable physical unit. Publications have copies and can count numbers sold or delivered to potential readers. Radio and television depend on receiving sets that originally were counted to ensure that there were a sufficient number sold to reach an adequate audience. However, the advertisers using broadcasting soon began to demand that there actually be a significant number of listeners or viewers to justify the costs. At first, audiences were rated on a comparative basis, but later the demand turned more specifically to a count of the size and demographic description of the audience.

This leads to the second quantitative stage in media evaluation, which aims at measurement and classification of total publication and broadcast audiences. One key element is the definition of audience, a definition that has been generally and arbitrarily agreed on. Definitions differ for various media. A member of the audience of a specific issue of a particular magazine is anyone, above a certain age, who has seen or looked at a minimum of one major editorial item. This seems superficial, but it implies that the individual has at least opened and looked into a copy. Exposure beyond that point almost defies definition. A member of the audience of a broadcast program is, again, confined to those above a minimum age and must have attended, or been exposed, for at least a minimum length of time. Nearly all of a newspaper audience is assumed to be accumulated within 24 hours after delivery. The measured audience is made up of those who claim to have read an issue yesterday, in response to a set of carefully-designed questions.

There was a time, after the three major national advertising media had achieved almost complete dominance in that field, that their audiences could be measured with widespread acceptance within the advertising industry. Even though media, themselves, paid most or all of the research costs, the measurements made by independent research firms became almost standardized.

The first projected magazine audience studies took couples into the field before publication to measure and later discount confused claims of reading. A second survey was then required, after publication, to measure total audience claims. This dual measurement permitted audience adjustment or correction and the published figures were widely accepted. Later, it was found that putting the survey emphasis on editorial interest, rather than issue reading, would deflate reading claims to about the same net totals as produced by the dual process. Television measurement of households tuned to programs reached the height of objectivity when the electronic meter (Audimeter) came into use. Approval of measurement of newspaper audiences was achieved more simply when claims of reading during the 24-hour period of yesterday were accepted for the purpose of surveys of daily newspapers.

Revolutionary changes in media caused complications in audience measurement, followed by declining confidence in the reported findings. This was especially true of magazines. The editorial-interest technique, designed to measure a few mass magazines in a single set of interviews, lost credibility when applied to the scores of special interest magazines which had replaced the defunct mass giants. An attempt to solve the research problem by combining the accepted technique with a dubious recall method on the many small circulation magazines utterly failed to win the confidence of space buyers and advertisers. As the number of new publications increases, so does the problem of measurement.

Electronic measurement of television program tuning could provide estimates of human audiences only when supplemented by a related sample supplying subjective reports of program viewing. As households began to use two or more receiving sets, the problem of collecting information on set tuning together with a count of viewers and their demographics grew more complicated. Meanwhile, the introduction of cable television, satellite transmission, increases in licensed channels, and a variety of home recording instruments already threaten to pose great challenges to audience research. The potential for many new developments in transmission is hard to reckon with, either in communication or in audience measurement. If newspapers are converted largely to electronic form, they must share the research problems of the electronic media.

Even as the problems of media audience measurement grow, advertisers are aware that such audiences are not the final gauge of media effectiveness. A third quantitative stage, after the medium reaches its audience, is to expose advertisements to as many in that audience as possible. Exposure of magazine pages, as mentioned earlier, has been investigated with some success. Since most national advertising messages reach their audiences only as a result of other primary incentives, such as magazine editorial matter, exposure of the advertisements can be credited almost entirely to the medium. Some authorities believe that exposure should be considered as the final stage of accomplishment of the medium on behalf of the advertiser. If so, there can be assurance in that available exposure evidence indicates that well over four out of five in the media audience see or are exposed to the typical magazine or television advertisement.

Probably most advertisers have the opinion that the advertising function of the medium should carry on to a fourth stage, which is actual awareness of the advertisement. Otherwise, based only on exposure, such cost factors as size, duration, and color would all have the same score. On the other hand, performances by individual advertisements in gaining audiences must be credited to the nature of the advertisement as well as the medium. Crude measures of the advertising audiences achieved in magazines and newspapers have been carried on for many years. If the medium is to be evaluated on the basis of such scores, it would probably be based on averages for each cost unit. Better yet, when accurate measures are available, the medium would be rated according to average scores only on advertisements addressed to the total audience of that magazine or newspaper. Certainly, low scores on poor copy or on selected audience segments should not be blamed on the medium.

There remain two possible further stages in evaluating advertising media. The next stage would require measurement of the ability of the medium to communicate the advertising message. A possible final stage would require measurement of actual increased sales or profitability of the advertising. These two stages, like the fourth stage of gaining advertising awareness, involve the effectiveness of the advertising message as well as the contribution of the medium. Therefore, while the profitability of each media investment would be an ideal gauge of the medium, the probability of achieving such a solution is remote. In fact, each medium may have unique qualitative values, as well as quantitative potential, which would be reflected in such a comprehensive appraisal. The concept of quality will follow next, and qualitative research has led to many conflicting claims. This should not cloud the fact that, regardless of conflicting research, the media buyer always consciously or unconsciously attempts to judge the profitability of each media purchase. And, because media costs account for most advertising dollars, it is in wise media selection that there lies the greatest opportunity for increasing the effectiveness of advertising dollars.

QUALITATIVE EVALUATION OF MEDIA

Quality of media refers not only to the contribution of the medium to making effective advertising impressions, but also to the quality of the audience that the medium attracts. The mechanical advantages that each medium offers to advertisers are usually self-evident. Measurement of the effect of the general atmosphere with which a medium surrounds its advertisements is much more elusive. While it seems universally agreed that some media provide a more favorable atmosphere for advertising than others, very little of the research in that area has provided convincing evidence.

The quality of the measured audience of a medium, in terms of the common demographic breakdowns, is usually easy to determine. Age, sex, and economic level can be recorded at the time of a personal interview, and are likely to be reported reliably by telephone. These familiar characteristics contribute heavily to media decisions. Their measurement has taught media buyers some unexpected generalizations. The economic levels and education of readers of a picture magazine may be just as high as for text magazines. The audience of a magazine edited for men may have a large proportion of women in it. The reader of one women's service magazine may be as likely as any other woman to read a second or even a third women's service magazine. The list could go on.

Attempts have been made to measure psychological characteristics of the audiences of different media and programs. Whether the audience of one medium is more venturesome, hedonistic, or inclined to follow the leader than other audiences has been explored. While the research has shown some interesting tendencies, there is usually a big problem in selecting media to fit desired psychological audiences. As advertising media develop more and more according to special interests, it may become more practical to fit media to psychological characteristics.

MEASURING MEDIA PROFITABILITY

The ultimate purpose of media research is to bring advertising judgments closer to an intelligent appraisal of the contribution of media to sales effects. A few companies have made changes in their media schedules on the basis of research on sales effectiveness. Two of the companies are among the biggest advertisers, and at the time were spending more than 90% of their advertising dollars in television. The one financed extensive research through an independent operator, and the evidence pointed toward a greater share going into magazines. The other was confronted by research conducted by one of the biggest magazines and concluded that more money should go into magazines. Ironically, the small change in investment went into competing magazines.

An interesting experiment, at little cost, was conducted by one of the leading American automobile manufacturers. Two of the most prominent magazines were persuaded to make a split run of some of their issues. Every other copy of the press run carried a full-page advertisement of the car; alternate copies carried no advertisement for that car. The manufacturer reported all purchases of the car made in a period following introduction of the series of advertisements. The publishers then used their subscription lists to check which purchases were made in the households that got the advertisements as compared with those who received none of the advertisements. This was really a comparison between advertising and no advertising. The gain among those probably exposed over those not exposed was sufficient to pay for the cost of the half-run of advertisements. Actually the comparison involved only fractional percentage points. There can be argument as to whether this was a meaningful test of sales impact of either the medium or the particular advertisements. The favorable findings did not appear to result in any changes in the established advertising schedule.

IMPLICATIONS

Those who share the belief, advanced here, that copy or commercial testing must relate directly or indirectly to sales effectiveness of advertising, have to face many frustrations. Measurement of the degree of this relationship is not usually feasible even after money for time and space has been spent; and even less feasible beforehand. A half century of claims that one copy testing method or another will produce solid evidence of advertising effectiveness has produced so much contradictory evidence that the field remains wide open.

The intermediate steps of communication, all the way from initial advertising exposure to ultimate sales or profits, include some stages that can be measured. Since some of these steps appear to be logically essential to advertising effect, it is not surprising that much copy and commercial testing has dealt with intermediate points in the advertising process. Some of the most logical and measurable involve memory and include such cognitive functions as awareness, recognition (if controlled for guessing), recall, and comprehension. Other elements, which may be equally important for certain advertisements, are feelings and attitudes. Feelings are difficult to measure or to relate to profitability.

Since there is no accepted theory of the advertising process, it is not now feasible to specify all of the factors that may relate to advertising effect.

Media research has advantages in that the primary function is quantitative and that there is general agreement on the stages of the media function. When there were few national advertising media, and when advertisers treated the whole United States as one great market, the problems of media research were relatively simple. As media multiplied in numbers and variety and as national advertisers began to concentrate on single cities or markets, there has been a growing complexity in research.

Research is still the only source likely to give media planners and buyers the guidance needed for intelligent planning of schedules. As long as the variety of media resources continues to grow, the difficulties and the costs of media research will grow accordingly. Advertisers are faced with the fact that individual advertisers can seldom finance thorough research on each medium they may consider using. In fact, only a few of the largest media can afford to finance research of their own properties. The field for meaningful exploration of both quantitative and qualitative exploration of their values remains open. Future advertising research is faced with growing challenges.

SUGGESTIONS FOR FURTHER READING

Dutka, Solomon (Original edition by Russell Colley, 1962) *Defining Advertising Goals for Measured Advertising Results* (DAGMAR), Association of National Advertisers, Inc., 1994.

Fletcher, Alan D. and Thomas A. Bowers, *Fundamentals of Advertising Research,* 2nd ed., Grid Publishing, Columbus (OH), 1983.

Greene, William F., "Observations: What Drives Commercial Liking? An Exploration of Entertainment vs. Communications," *Journal of Advertising Research,* Vol. 32, March/April 1992, pp. 65–68.

Lucas, Darrell B. and Steuart H. Britt, *Measuring Advertising Effectiveness,* McGraw-Hill, NY, 1963.

Mick, David G., "Levels of Subjective Comprehension in Advertising Processing and their Reaction to Ad Perceptions, Attitudes and Memory," *Journal of Consumer Research,* Vol. 18, March 1992, pp. 411–24.

Schwerin, Horace S. and Henry H. Newell, *Persuasion in Marketing,* John Wiley & Sons, Inc., NY, 1981.

Sissors, Jack Z. and Lincoln Bumba, *Advertising Media Planning,* NTC Publishing, Lincolnwood (IL), 1990.

Trout, Jack and Al Reis, "The Positioning Era Cometh," *Advertising Age,* April 24, 1972, p. 38.

Zielske, Hugh A., "The Remembering and Forgetting of Advertising," *Journal of Marketing,* Vol. 22, January 1959, pp. 239–43.

Robert C. Blattberg
Polk Brothers Distinguished Professor of Retailing
Kellogg Graduate School of Management
Northwestern University
Evanston, Illinois

Lynn C. Unglaub
Vice President
Robert C. Blattberg Consultants
Chicago, Illinois

CHAPTER 23

DATABASE MARKETING

The use of data for marketing is as old as direct mail and catalog marketing. In the early days, direct mail marketers and catalog companies kept customer records on index cards. With the advent of computer technology, the industry leaders shifted their customer records to mainframe computers. The shift to database marketing came when firms began to use the power of the information to design and monitor marketing programs directed to these customers. Because it has been touted as a more efficient form of marketing, many traditional marketers have considered transforming themselves into database marketers.

The purpose of this chapter is to help the reader understand what database marketing is and what is required for a firm to use database marketing effectively. To help establish a perspective, the chapter begins with a brief history of database marketing. Database marketing is then defined and contrasted to traditional marketing. Next the key elements of database marketing are described. Inhibitors to becoming a database marketer are discussed and the chapter concludes by showing how the marketing function will need to change if the firm and its service providers want to become effective database marketers.

THE ANTECEDENTS OF DATABASE MARKETING

The foundation was laid for database marketing with the dawn of the mail order industry in the last century. As early as 1872 with the launch of the Montgomery Ward catalog and Richard Warren Sears' first sales of gold watches to railroad agents in 1886, companies were employing public delivery to inform potential customers of their offerings, to receive orders, and to deliver merchandise. Although the industrial revolution of the late 1800s made the mass production of consumer goods possible and brought down prices to the point where a majority of households could afford a variety of products manufactured outside the home, most consumers lived far away from major metropolitan areas where department stores were located. However, mail delivery was becoming increasingly reliable. Firms that began as small operations quickly blossomed into some of the biggest businesses in the United States.

By 1910, catalog companies had developed the "12-month prune rule" whereby customers who had not purchased anything for the past year were dropped from the mailing list. This was the beginning of database marketing. Over the next few decades, catalog companies realized that many households who purchased a few small items each year were unprofitable whereas a customer who purchased a major item every two years might be very profitable. Catalogers and direct mailers quickly learned that a detailed customer file became very important to reducing mailing costs.

To target prospects, R. L. Polk and Reuben H. Donnelley began to compile customer lists from external sources, including telephone directories, automobile registrations, and driver's license records. Although the information was rudimentary, Old American Insurance was successful during the 1940s at targeting older Americans with direct mail solicitations for life insurance through driver's license records. The records listed age, and people who drove cars were assumed to be affluent and mobile (and therefore in reasonably good health).

Unlike the mass appeal used by general merchandise companies, the efficient identification of new prospects was of profound importance to the direct mail industry. Companies like Market Compilation and Research Bureau and The Kleid Company emerged to help firms increase their customer base by selling them the lists of other companies' customers who were direct-mail responsive for related products.

THE EMERGENCE OF COMPUTER TECHNOLOGY

In 1963, the U.S. Postal Service introduced zip codes and rules requiring third-class mailers to not only label each piece of mail with the proper zip code, but to sort outgoing mail in zip code sequence. The labor costs required to comply with the new rules promised to be enormous. The industry adopted computerization of mailing lists as a solution. The introduction of computers in the direct mail industry led to major industry innovations in the ensuing decades. Many experts cite the computerization of the industry as the beginning of "true" database marketing.

In the 1960s, a number of direct mailers began to experiment with using zip codes and census tract information to predict buying behavior. From the 1960 census, the U.S. Census Bureau divided certain parts of the nation into 180 groupings and released basic demographic information on each one. O.E. McIntyre, a list management company, developed a system it created SIFT (Selection by Individual Families and Tracts), which combined geographical demographics with individual data from their list of 40 million names.

In the late 1960s, merge/purge programs became publicly available. Prior to this, it was almost impossible to avoid sending more than one solicitation to the same consumer or to abstain from sending acquisition offers to current customers. Merge/purge programs not only saved companies money by avoiding the mailing of duplicates, but they also changed the way direct mailers could target. Previously, mass direct mailers rented only large, broadly targeted mailing lists because combining a number of small lists resulted in many duplicates. With a merge/purge program, these marketers could combine many small lists and weed out duplicates, thereby permitting them to prospect a new universe of lists previously deemed too inefficient. Computerization also brought a deluge of personalized, computer-generated letters. Letters personalized only with a "Dear Mr. Jordan" salutation pulled as many as six times the responses as nonpersonalized offers in the mid 1960s. While creative approaches to personalization continue to work fairly well, complaints from a growing number of consumers over a perceived threat to their privacy is discouraging marketers from using personal information in their copy.

THE GROWTH OF STATISTICAL SOPHISTICATION

A number of factors converged in the late 1960s and 1970s to make direct marketing much more scientific. Increasing postage costs made it impractical to send out mailings on a mass basis. More "niche" catalogs and mail order companies went into business, making the targeting of good prospects essential. A number of mathematicians became interested in the field, leading to more sophisticated statistical and financial analyses. These new techniques included lifetime value models that directed the level of investment a company could profitably make in each customer segment and scoring models developed using multiple regression, AID, or CHAID, which predicted the responsiveness of customers to new offers. Most of the new analytical techniques and technology were used on a piece-meal basis until the 1980s, when further reductions in computing costs and the sharing of information allowed companies to begin to implement more sophisticated, integrated programs.

The pace of innovation in computer technology quickened in the 1980s. Relational database technology made the storage, retrieval, and manipulation of massive warehouses of customer information feasible. The introduction and rapid growth of personal computers allowed marketing managers to conduct sophisticated analyses at their desktops. Not only did companies collect additional customer data, they began to use this information to understand their customers and predict their behavior. The era of database marketing had begun.

THE DAWN OF A NEW ERA

In the 1990s, the focus of database marketing has begun to shift to relationship marketing. The concept suggests that by better understanding customers on an individual level and by delivering to them information and products targeted to their specific needs, marketers can develop long-term annuity streams that translate into substantial profits. This concept differs from traditional direct marketing that targets customers in segments and focuses more on attracting new customers than on retaining old ones. Relationship marketing uses improved technology to regularly communicate with the firm's customers and to base product offerings on the consumer's buying behavior. The saturation of products in the marketplace, increasing costs of targeting a mass audience, and consumer concerns over the environment and personal privacy require firms to concentrate on selling more to current customers and retaining those customers already loyal to the firm. Otherwise, the firm's marketing costs will skyrocket, putting the firm at risk economically.

DEFINITION OF DATABASE MARKETING

Database marketing is extremely difficult to define. If the definition is too narrow, it excludes many potentially interesting uses of databases for marketing; if it is too broad, all firms using any type of data will be considered database marketers. In this chapter, two definitions will be given and the reader can decide which is most appropriate. The first is a broad definition that encompasses more than just the use of a customer database to send promotional materials. The second definition is more narrow and more traditional. At the end of this section, we indicate which definition will be used throughout the remainder of this chapter.

Broad Definition of Database Marketing

> *The creation and use of databases in conjunction with information technology to improve the efficiency and effectiveness of marketing activities.*

In examining this definition, we see that it includes the use of electronic point-of-sale (POS) data, not only customer-specific information, as well as other relevant marketing data used to design and develop marketing programs. Thus Procter and Gamble, Kraft-General Foods, and other leading package goods companies who use electronic POS data for measuring the effectiveness of marketing activities such as pricing and promotions are "database marketers" using this definition. This definition does not require database marketing to use a database to deliver marketing programs to the customer nor to use it to communicate with the customer. It does not even require that a customer database be employed. Thus employing this definition, any firm using databases to improve the efficiency and effectiveness of the marketing function is a database marketer.

It is important to recognize that using the broad definition greatly expands the types of activities that fit under the umbrella of database marketing. Promotional analysis, baseline development, and price elasticity modeling all conform to this broader definition. Marketing research is included in this definition. Many of the quantitative marketing models that have been created over the last twenty years would be tools of database marketing.

What is excluded from this definition? The answer is any research or marketing activity that does not directly translate into more efficient and effective marketing programs. For example, firms who use salespersons to call on accounts are *not* database marketers. If, on the other hand, the firm targets accounts and uses information to design the customer-salesperson interaction, then it fits this definition of database marketing.

Narrow Definition of Database Marketing

The use of internal and external customer databases in conjunction with information technology to develop and communicate individualized marketing programs.

The narrow definition of database marketing requires that a customer database be used to deliver marketing programs. The delivery may be through mail, phone, or direct contact. By using detailed internal customer files and external lists, firms can develop highly customized marketing programs directed to their customers. The factor that differentiates database marketers from direct marketers is the sophisticated use of information to design individual marketing programs. By obtaining and managing detailed customer behavior data in conjunction with promotional histories, database marketers can infer the types of products and services the customer is likely to buy, create targeted promotions directed to the customer based on historical responses, and produce special pricing. Traditional direct marketers do not have these capabilities because of their inability to process information rapidly and cost effectively. With a detailed customer history file, database marketers can create marketing programs that are highly individualized. The enabling factor is computer technology. While theoretically this can be done without computer technology, it is almost impossible to execute it. The major change that has made database marketing possible is low-cost, high-powered computer systems and software that make accessing the databases far easier. Statistical analysis programs have been developed which allow database marketers to score and target individual customers in much greater detail than was feasible for direct marketers twenty years ago.

Contrasting the narrow definition with the broad definition, the narrow definition greatly limits what activities fit under the umbrella of database marketing and who is a database marketer. It also raises the question of how revolutionary database marketing really is. This definition is clearly an extension of direct marketing with a greater emphasis on computer technology.

Definition Used in This Chapter

The definition that will be used throughout this chapter is the narrow definition. By limiting the scope of the chapter, we can focus on how information technology in combination with selected marketing programs can be used to create highly efficient, very targeted marketing programs that are only beginning to be used in a wide variety of industries. While this approach to marketing will not fit every company, as the cost of database development declines and as the ability of firms to learn how to use one-on-one marketing strategies and tactics increases, the number of firms using database marketing will increase. Ironically, computer technology is enabling firms to revert back to the type of one-on-one marketing that firms conducted before it became cost-effective to mass market. The difference is that computer technology, not individual sales personnel, is designing and delivering the marketing "pitch."

DATABASE MARKETING VERSUS CONVENTIONAL MARKETING

Database marketing differs from conventional marketing both strategically and tactically. This section will focus on the strategic differences and the next section will focus on the tactical differences.

Focusing on the Lifetime Value of a Customer

One of the primary advantages of database marketing is that it enables the firm to compute the lifetime value of the customer, which is the discounted net profit the firm makes from a customer. The advantage of computing lifetime value of a customer is that it changes the focus and mission of the firm from product orientation to customer orientation. Concepts like brand equity and product positioning, which are at the heart of traditional marketing, while still very important, become less of a focus to the firm than the value of the customer franchise and how to maximize it. The firm's marketing and product activities are directed toward how it can change the customer's long-term value. This means that the firm will make or buy products or services that will enhance the relationship with the customer, and the firm will price and promote based on the long-term relationship with the customer.

To compute the lifetime value of a customer requires information such as the customer's purchase history, promotional history, and projected future purchases (dollars and frequency). The source of this information is a detailed customer history file that conventional marketers do not maintain, and hence they cannot compute the lifetime value of their customers.

We will consider an example to demonstrate the differences in decision making between a traditional marketer and a database marketer that can compute the impact of its marketing activities on the lifetime value of the customer. Consider a firm that issues an FSI (free standing insert) coupon that costs $7 per thousand and has a face value of $.40 plus $.10 handling charges. The coupon generates 20 purchases for every 1,000 sent. Of the 20 responses, 10 are customers who would have bought the product without the coupon, 5 are totally new customers to the product, and 5 are switchers from other brands who historically have bought the brand. The initial purchase made by a customer is $2.00. The retailer pays the manufacturer $1.50 for the product, and the incremental profit for the manufacturer is 67% resulting in a profit of $1.00. If one computes the initial profitability of the customer to the firm, we see that only ten purchases were incremental, and so they generate $10 in profits (to the manufacturer); but we must subtract the coupon redemption and distribution costs of $10 and $7, respectively, resulting in a net loss of $7 per thousand coupons issued. If one simply looks at the initial net profitability of the coupon, it is easy to conclude that it should not be run. However, there is also the long-term profit generated from the five new customers. Assume each of these customers will buy six more times, on average, over their lifetime, resulting in a net profit of $30 (6 × 5 × $1) minus the initial loss to acquire these customers of $7, which generates $23 in profit per thousand. However, without being able to calculate the long-term value of the program by tracking the buying behavior of individual customers, the firm will fail to determine the relevant economic return and reject the program. Thus the lifetime value calculation is critical to the economic analysis of marketing activities. Without it, the firm is far more likely to reject programs that generate long-term profits, which adversely affects the profitability of the firm.

Installed Base Marketing

Another critical difference is the firm's focus on the importance of selling more to existing customers. A rule of thumb is that it costs seven times as much to acquire a new customer as it does to sell additional products to an existing customer. The source of this rule of thumb is the economic analysis of direct mailers who separate their acquisition costs from their ongoing marketing costs. It is also known that multiple-time purchasers have much lower promotional and marketing costs than one-time buyers. Thus once a customer consistently does business with the firm, he or she has signalled a satisfaction level with the firm and is comfortable with its position, value, and customer service level.

Using the heuristic just described, it is clear that the firm should try to sell more to existing customers, which is called *installed base marketing*. Customer relationships have significant value because it is less expensive to sell new products and services to the firm's customers than to acquire new customers. Firms who try to understand how to sell more to existing customers because of the affinity they have established with them are likely to have lower marketing costs. Database marketing facilitates this strategy because through the availability of a detailed customer database, the firm is able to target current customers without having to invest in untargeted promotions and advertising. The smart database marketing firm is likely to focus on new products or services that it can sell to its customer base rather than developing new products or services for which its current customer base is not a particularly good target.

While selling to existing customers may seem obvious, contrast it to Procter and Gamble. It sells Tide to the household but does not necessarily sell additional products and services to the same customers. It uses, instead, the brand's franchise to create spin-off products such as Tide with Bleach. The difference is that Procter and Gamble is focused on the brand's equity and what else can be sold using the image and positioning of the brand versus using an installed base marketing strategy that focuses on the customer and how to sell more to the existing customer base. Clearly both can be successful strategies, but the database marketing firm has an advantage because it can always continue to expand its product line (brand equity) as well as acquire other products and services that appeal to its existing customer base (customer equity).

Shift From Mass to One-on-One Marketing

Marketing is entering a new era in which communication will no longer be one way from the manufacturer or seller to the customer but can become two way, when the buyer's needs can be directly or indirectly communicated to the seller. While this occurs now between a salesperson and a prospective customer, there is no systematic communication based on the historical customer-seller relationship. There is also no memory trace showing the promotions and marketing communications received by the consumer and the resulting behavior.

Because computers can be linked with telecommunications and other communication vehicles, it is now possible to begin developing one-on-one marketing vehicles that relate specifically to the customer's needs. The computer maintains and analyzes the information and then uses it to send customers information. Thus mass marketing tactics such as FSIs and network television are necessary only to the extent that targeted, specialized messages do not increase response rates enough to cover the higher distribution costs of targeted vehicles. Newspapers, network television, and even mass promotions have begun to feel the increased competition from one-on-one marketing campaigns designed around detailed customer information.

An example will help clarify the concept. Spiegel, a leading U.S. catalog company, can target customers based on recent purchase behavior. A customer that purchases a purse from Spiegel will receive different types of promotional material than a customer who purchases housewares from the catalog. Targeting based on purchase behavior leads to higher response rates and hence more efficient marketing execution.

The concept of developing a marketing program based on customer needs is not unique to database marketing but it is more cost-effective today because storage and access of customer purchase information is much cheaper. Ironically, good salespeople in prior generations kept card files of customers and then knew when to call the customer and what to offer. The difference is that through database marketing, one-on-one marketing can actually be executed for a mass market. Tailored products, advertising, copy, pricing, and promotions are based on historical information gathered and maintained about customers' behavior.

Efficiency and Effectiveness of Marketing Expenditures

As was implied in its definition, database marketing can lead to more efficient and effective marketing programs. Efficiency means that the same sales are generated through lower marketing expenditures; effectiveness means that the marketing program produces a higher response. Both are important.

Efficiency is created through detailed customer information. Suppose you were working for a securities firm selling stocks and bonds. You have two customers, both with a net worth of one million dollars: One owns a large portfolio of stocks and bonds ($500,000) and the other a portfolio of rare antiques and modern art ($500,000). Which one will be more responsive to a new stock offering? The odds clearly favor the customer with the stock and bond portfolio. Knowing customer behavior increases the firm's ability to target the relevant customers. Customer information directly affects marketing efficiency.

Effectiveness is improved through database marketing because it allows the firm to determine the relevant communications, products, pricing, and promotions to customers based on their past purchase and promotional responsiveness and relevant customer characteristics. American Express can offer cruise customers different types of promotions and copy based on their past behavior. If a customer has gone to the Caribbean every year for the last five, it is easy to target very specific types of promotions and copy to that customer. A customer who has changed venue every year but has also taken a yearly cruise will receive different copy and promotions. Effectiveness, just like efficiency, is enhanced with information.

Efficiency and effectiveness are enhanced through analysis of past marketing campaigns. Database marketing facilitates this because it focuses on the collection, maintenance, and analysis of response data. Time-Life is able to determine the cost-effectiveness of different television ads for its magazines because it can track the responses for each insertion through the toll-free numbers. By matching the toll-free number with the insertion ads, the lowest cost per order can be determined. Database marketing firms like Time-Life are able to produce more effective ads (higher response rates) and more efficient marketing programs (lower cost per thousand) because they are able to track their customers' buying behavior. This clearly gives them an advantage.

In summary, database marketing affects the strategy of the firm because it

- focuses the firm on the lifetime value of the customer,
- concentrates on selling more to existing customers,
- makes it possible to use one-on-one marketing tactics to a mass market, and
- improves the effectiveness and efficiency of the firm's marketing programs.

A detailed customer database makes all of this possible. Conventional marketing firms are at a strategic disadvantage because they cannot execute the same strategies that a database marketing firm can.

ELEMENTS OF DATABASE MARKETING PROGRAMS

The components of a database marketing program—the media, offer, and package—are elements that distinguish database marketing from traditional marketing. The purpose of this section is to describe the major options in each of these areas and to discuss their application. In conventional marketing, the retail outlet is the marketplace; in database marketing, the media defines the marketplace. The various media options include direct mail, telemarketing, newspapers, magazines, co-ops, broadcast, and electronics. The offer is the motivation for the prospect to buy the product or service. Knowledge of the target audience is critical to structuring a successful offer. The alternatives in creative packages are limitless and therefore only the major types of packages will be discussed in this section.

The tactics used by database marketers are almost identical to those used by direct marketers. The difference is in database marketers' ability to target, customize, and monitor marketing programs. Analysis of internal customer files or external data sources provide database marketers with more sophisticated targeting. The ability to customize the messages or offers depends on the amount of information the firm has about the customer or prospect, and clearly database marketing expands the firm's ability to customize. Monitoring again is enhanced by tracking customer responses to specific marketing programs. Database marketing improves the efficiency and effectiveness of marketing tactics but does not change the vehicles used. The one caveat is that database marketers must monitor the response from any marketing programs.

The Media of Database Marketing

Telemarketing. Marketers are often surprised to learn that the telephone is probably the largest advertising media with over $45 billion a year in total expenditures. Experts estimate that this number is fairly evenly divided between outbound calls for selling and sales support activities and inbound calls for orders, inquiries, and customer service. Stone defines telemarketing as "the planned, professional, and measured use of telecommunications in sales and marketing activities" (1984). Each of these adjectives—*planned, professional, measured*—is important since successful telemarketing is not a boiler-room operation where ill-prepared operators canvass untargeted lists to push products. Although integration of telecommunication into a marketing program can dramatically increase its effectiveness, telemarketing is not inexpensive and therefore must be carefully planned and measured.

It is important to realize what benefits telemarketing can provide when deciding to incorporate it into a marketing program. Telemarketing provides immediate customer feedback so that the marketer can measure and project the effectiveness of the program. Because the communications are interactive, the caller can collect diagnostic information from the prospect to allow the marketer to modify the script or offer to improve the response rate. When integrated with a field salesforce, telemarketing can improve customer service and reinforce customer relationships.

The critical component that distinguishes a telemarketing program from other database marketing programs is the script. In writing the script, each contact should be viewed as a sales call and should contain each of the elements required for a call. These elements include

- removing the curse from the call and breaking the preoccupation barrier,
- introducing the caller and the company,
- qualifying the contact so that the call is not wasted,
- describing the product or service,
- summarizing the major benefits to the prospect,
- presenting the offer and trial close,
- handling objections and answering questions,
- repeating the order and all relevant information, and
- thanking the customer for the order.

A good script is flexible and provides a framework for the call but does not sound like a "canned pitch."

Although telemarketing is used for both consumer and business products, it has become especially important to business-to-business firms as they attempt to reduce selling costs. Although inbound telemarketing has long been recognized as an efficient means of handling leads, taking orders, and servicing customers, outbound telemarketing can also be integrated into the territory and account management activities of the sales force. Outbound telemarketing is an efficient means to generate and qualify leads, reactivate accounts, cross-sell new products, monitor inventory levels, and notify customers about special promotions or price changes.

Direct Mail. Mailing lists provide the media for direct mail. The list that generally proves most responsive and profitable is the company's own customer file, often referred to as the house list. The information maintained on the customer database is used to profile and segment the customers into groups that reflect their responsiveness to the company's assortment of products and offers. Profiles of customer segments are used to acquire external mailing lists with similar characteristics in order to prospect for new customers. There are two basic types of external lists: lists of customers, prospects, or subscribers from other companies and compiled lists. Lists from other direct response companies have one key advantage when compared to compiled lists—the names are those of direct response buyers. However, if your market is college students or new mothers, compiled lists will offer the largest universe.

The rental of names is generally negotiated through a list broker. The broker works for both the company that owns the list and the company renting the list, although his or her fee is paid by the list owner when a rental is arranged. With literally thousands of lists available, the broker can provide valuable insights into which lists represent the market the mailer is targeting. Names are rented for a one-time use; only the responders may be added to the company's in-house files. Firms that rent their house lists frequently or have many lists available for rent have begun to use list managers to deal with the numerous details associated with promoting and managing the rental process. The list manager handles contacts with brokers, bills the broker and collects payments, approves mailing pieces and dates, maintains the list, and processeses rental orders. The price range for most list rentals in 1992 was $40 to $60 per thousand names.

Magazine. Selection is the key to using magazines as the media for database marketing. Just as the location, whether Rodeo Drive or an outlet mall, creates an image and attracts a particular type of customer to a retail store, the readership of a magazine defines a market. High ticket collectibles may do well in *Smithsonian* and the *New Yorker* while moderately priced fashions perform well in publications like *Seventeen* and *Cosmopolitan.* Magazines provide a high number of exposures at a relatively low cost; however, the response rate, average order, and bad debt rate must be carefully tracked to manage the media profitably.

Broadcast. As the average American household substitutes its consumption of print media (i.e., newspapers and magazines) with hours of exposure to broadcast media (i.e., TV, cable, and radio), database marketers have adapted their media plans, offers, and strategies. Broadcast is now employed for all the classic database marketing tactics—direct selling, lead generation, support of other media, and outlet locator programs. Network broadcast TV can be extremely expensive and is rarely the most effective option for database marketing. The cost is based on the rating (i.e., percentage of households viewing the program), length of the ad, and time of day. An 18 rating means that 18 percent of the television households are watching the program. When the ratings for all the time periods in a schedule are combined, the sum is called the gross rating points or GRP. Advertisers focus on two measures of effectiveness: reach and frequency. *Reach* refers to the number of *different* households that see the message in a given timeframe and *frequency* refers to the number of times the message will be viewed. Broadcast time may be purchased by specific time slot—the most expensive—or ROS (run of station) with or without specified time of day. If demand for TV time is relatively low, it may also be purchased based on PI (payment per inquiry) or bonus to payout.

Radio offers an economical low-reach, high-frequency media. There are many more radio stations than TV stations in a market and each offers its own type of audience based on its programming. Understanding the profile of your customer or prospect is critical in selecting successful outlets and time of day. The relatively low cost of air time and commercial production also makes radio an attractive alternative for many database marketers.

Cable TV. The fastest growing media alternative in terms of dollars spent by all advertisers is cable TV. Cable TV looks like network broadcast but offers the database marketer an important advantage in that the cable TV audience is well defined. Cable operators maintain customer records that can be matched with demographic and psychographic information to profile their subscribers. There is also the chance to market the product, the audiences through the special interest cable channels like Arts & Entertainment or ESPN. Because cable time is more widely available and cheaper than network time, longer commercials can be created that tell a more complete story. This trend has led to the phenomena of "infomercials" that may be 30 minutes in duration.

Newspapers. In 1965, Time-Life Books proved that preprint was a viable direct marketing medium. Preprints now abound in four-color single-page and multipage formats. With daily circulation of over 70 million, newspapers offer an attractive channel for products with a mass appeal. Syndicated Sunday supplements such as *Parade* and *Family Weekly* offer a vehicle to reach millions of households in both primary and secondary metro markets at a relatively low cost. A third form of newspaper advertising is called ROP (run of paper). It is widely used by retailers, but has only proven cost-effective for database marketers who run small-space, low-cost ads over a long period of time with high frequency so that the number of impressions accumulate rapidly compared to cost.

Co-op. The largest mail co-op in the U.S. is Carol Wright, which is owned by Donnelley Marketing and distributed to more than 24 million households selected from the 70 million on Donnelley's household database. Carol Wright is primarily used by consumer packaged goods manufacturers to distribute cents-off coupons. Although direct mail is much more expensive on a cost-per-thousand basis to circulate coupons when compared to newspapers and FSIs, the redemption rate is generally two to three times greater. Instead of Carol Wright, database marketers tend to use mail order co-ops arranged by a consortium of database marketers and distributed to households that have proven to be mail responsive. Other database marketers have developed their own in-house co-op mailings, which spread their mailing costs across several offers. In general, co-op mailings pull one fourth the response rate of solo mailings, but they likewise cost about one fourth of a solo mailing.

Electronic Media. Stand-alone electronic media such as video cassettes, video discs, and computer discs including CDs have ushered in a revolution in database marketing. Database marketers are just beginning to tap the exciting potential of two-way electronic media such as Videotext, Prodigy, and two-way cable television.

The Offer in Database Marketing

The proposition the marketer makes to the prospect is referred to as *the offer.* The basic components of the offer for a product or service include product description, price, premium or incentive, guarantees, time limit, credit options, future obligations and options, additional charges, and optional features. Variations of these components that are used to motivate the prospect to buy include incentives such as sweepstakes and free gifts. Even the way an offer is stated can effect response rates. *Buy one get one free* generally draws a higher response than *50 percent off.*

With the wide variety of options available in creating the offer, it is important to clearly establish the objective of the program. The best offer to generate a sales lead may be very different from the most effective offer to attract new customers. It is also important to understand why a prospect is motivated to respond. The marketer can use a positive option like social approval or sensory gratification or a negative option like problem removal or avoidance.

The Package in Database Marketing

The classic direct mail package includes an outer envelope, letter, brochure, order form, reply envelope, and other inserts such as a free gift slip or product sheet.

Solo. The simplest form of a promotional offer is the solo. With this appeal, the marketer must explain the product and motivate the customer to respond with one exposure. The typical solo package includes a letter, brochure, reply card, or order form and return envelope.

Multistep. A variation of the solo promotion is the multistep promotion. For products that are too complicated or expensive to sell through a single mailing, it is often possible to generate a list of interested prospects through direct mail, magazines, or TV with responses provided by toll-free numbers, bingo cards, or reply cards. The sale is generally completed through a direct contact. Products typically sold in this manner include encyclopedias, financial services, and expensive exercise equipment.

Catalog. With a catalog, the marketer can offer an assortment of hundreds of products within a single mailing. Circulation costs are spread across many items, and the probability that the customer will find an appealing item is increased. Catalogs also enjoy a longer shelf life in the home than solo mailings. There are four basic types of catalogs: business-to-business catalogs, which primarily offer office equipment and supplies; full-line merchandise catalogs; retail catalogs like Neiman-Marcus, which are designed primarily to support store traffic; and specialty catalogs, which now form the most competitive, fastest growing segment of the catalog industry.

Continuity. An important and extremely profitable segment of the traditional direct marketing industry is continuity programs. Under these programs, the customer is shipped a product periodically against regular payments. Most continuity programs operate as a negative option under which the company continues to send products to the customer until the customer cancels the program. Books, records, video cassettes, and recipe cards are frequently sold through continuity programs. Leading companies in this segment include Time-Life Books and the Franklin Mint.

THE ECONOMICS OF DATABASE MARKETING

Database marketing is not viable for every firm. There are certain economic conditions required before a firm should invest in database marketing. This section will offer a brief example to illustrate when database marketing pays and when it does not. Some general principles are then identified when database marketing has the highest potential payout.

Example

Two alternative scenarios show when a detailed customer database increases the firm's profitability. We will use a traditional FSI coupon drop versus a database marketing targeted coupon to analyze the payout.

Scenario 1—We will return to our example from the "Database Marketing versus Conventional Marketing" of this chapter. An FSI coupon was dropped at a cost $7 per thousand, the face value of the coupon was $.40 plus $.10 handling costs, and the response rate was 2 percent. The profit for the manufacturer was $1.00 per unit sold. Fifty percent of the sales were incremental. For the current example, we will not assume any new buyers were attracted by the coupon. Under scenario 1, traditional couponing, the costs were $7 per 1,000 for distributing the coupon and $10 for redeeming it, totalling $17. The profits were $10 from incremental units sold and so the coupon drop resulted in a $7 loss.

Scenario 2—Suppose the firm was able to obtain a detailed list of its customers along with their purchasing behavior and then use this list to mail the coupon to infrequent users. The cost of this mailing is $250 per thousand. The response rate is 15%, and 90% of the units sold are assumed incremental. For scenario 2, the response rate increased significantly, but so did the cost of distributing the coupon. The coupon generated 150 responses per thousand. The distribution cost is $250 and the redemption cost is $75. The profit generated before distribution and redemption costs was $135 from the incremental units sold. After subtracting distribution and redemption costs, the net loss was $190. Thus while the direct mail coupon was more effective, it was less efficient and profits declined. Clearly database marketing did not pay off.

Using scenario 2, assume that the firm modifies its program to mail five different coupons for five unique products to a selected set of customers based on their buying behavior. The cost of the coupon distribution drops to $50 per coupon per thousand. What is the payout? It goes from a loss of $190 to a profit of $10. If the promotion cost drops significantly, then the use of database marketing can pay off.

When Is Database Marketing Most Effective and Efficient?

The previous example highlights one issue: the cost of targeting. However, there are several conditions required to make database marketing feasible:

1. The cost of targeting relative to mass marketing must not be inordinately high.
2. The average price of the product or service or its gross margin relative to the marketing cost must be high, which implies that database marketing is far less effective for low-ticket items unless there are multiple purchases made from the same promotional event.
3. The ability to group promotions (e.g., through catalogs, co-op mailings) is critical to the efficiency of database marketing because it decreases the cost of targeting.
4. The more rapid the repeat purchasing, the higher the economic payout of database marketing.

Given these requirements, which types of firms will be most effective at database marketing? The answer is firms such as catalog companies that can promote multiple items, thus decreasing promotional cost per item and increasing the average expenditure per promotional mailing; credit card and financial services companies that have long-term relationships with their customers and rapid repeat usage cycles; and business-to-business marketers such as Dell Computer that sell items such as microcomputers through the mail can succeed because the cost of promotion is low relative to the price of the item.

Firms can restructure their marketing strategies so they can meet the four requirements described. DEC is beginning to sell computers directly. Many business-to-business marketers are developing catalogs to substitute for direct selling. Procter and Gamble, Kraft, and Ocean Spray are testing a frequent-user card so that multiple promotions can be sent to customers based on their purchase behavior.

The economic equation of database marketing determines its viability. The clever firm restructures its marketing strategy to make the economic equation work for its products and services.

EXAMPLES OF DATABASE MARKETING FIRMS

The following section provides two case studies in database marketing. Each outlines the objectives of the company for its database marketing program, how the company created its database, and general applications.

Industry: Insurance
Company: USAA (United Services Automobile Association)
Case: Alternative sales channel and customer support

Background

USAA, founded in 1922, is a large insurance and diversified financial services firm based in San Antonio, Texas. It is made up of fifty-six subsidiaries and affiliates, and owns and manages over $20.1 billion in assets. Some of its products include property and casualty, life and health, and automobile insurance; no-load mutual funds; real estate investments; discount brokerage services; credit cards; deposit services; and consumer loans. USAA members insure one another and share in any profits realized by the company.

USAA's membership consists of active and former military officers and their dependents, which at present number over two million. While property and casualty insurance and the organization's buying services are only available to its members, the majority of remaining products are available to the general public. Although products are available to the general public, the mission of the company is to provide products and services that satisfy the needs of its members.

USAA's Objectives

According to the company, USAA's standing as one of the premier financial services providers is largely due to its emphasis on information technology. From its inception, USAA has conducted most of its business by mail and currently has no independent selling agents. The reason for this was necessity. The company was formed by a few military officers to provide each other with automobile insurance. The officers were having difficulty obtaining reasonable rates for their coverage because the traditional insurers felt that military officers were a significant risk. Because the officers were stationed throughout the United States and abroad, business had to be conducted by mail. This practice has proven to be an efficient, cost-effective means of serving its members. Because the target customers of the firm are military officers, the majority of whom are on active duty, stationed throughout the world and constantly being relocated, mail communication has proven not only cost-effective but logical. The firm sees its databases as vital in its pursuit of providing the lowest cost, highest quality products and services.

Collecting and Maintaining Database Information

As mentioned previously, USAA has been building customer files since its inception. Additional customers are largely recruited through word-of-mouth endorsements by the company's current members. This is possible because of the trust that exists between military officers. New client names are also obtained through university ROTC programs, the various military academies, and the direct commissioning offices. The company does not purchase commercial lists because they do not exist for its target market segment.

The company feels the quality and breadth of its data is unmatched within the industry. The reason for this is the willingness of its members to share extensive personal information with the company. This occurs because of the trust the company has developed with its members and because the company makes it clear to its members that the information is necessary to provide them with the best service possible. To foster this trust, USAA does not share data with any outside firms.

Initially, there are fifteen critical pieces of data collected. Database maintenance then becomes a constant and ongoing process. Every contact with its members and customers is a chance to update database information. In addition, to ensure the integrity of its data, the company sends out data update forms to 20 percent of its customers every year. The analogy the company uses is that database maintenance is like painting a bridge; you start at one end and by the time you finish, it is time to start again.

General Uses of Database Marketing

Because of their integrated information technology, all departments can access the central database that supports many applications including research and development, product promotion, and new product solicitation. The company strategically orients itself around "lifecycle needs" because it views its customers as being clients from "cradle to grave" (for twenty-five years or longer). The lifecycle need concept associates the company's products and services with different stages in its members' career and life. Therefore, product managers can target promotions toward that segment of the database that falls within the most likely user category of their product or service.

Information collected from customers can also provide vital input for the process of new product development. For example, feedback from members stored in the database showed that most of its members were using services provided by the American Automobile Association (AAA). USAA developed a travel product that was more competitively priced than AAA for its members. Another example of the powerful new product development application of the company's databases is the buying services provided by the company. Through database analysis, it was clear that the company's customers wanted low-cost, long-distance telephone service. Once the company was aware of this demand, USAA approached Sprint and obtained a low-cost primary service deal for its customers. USAA is the ultimate database marketer in that it leverages its relationship with its customers (affinity group) to offer new products and services as demanded by its members (installed base marketing).

Problems

The greatest challenge for USAA is providing quality customer service worldwide. It is the company's use of information technology that has enabled it to offer the range of products and services that its members demand.

Another challenge is the development of affinity between members and USAA, not specific agents. Because of the personalized nature of selling financial services, the company is organized so that a customer can speak with the same agent regarding any product if he or she so desires. While each agent cannot be an expert in every product, an agent can act as the point person with a particular customer and direct questions to the appropriate agents. Each promotion gives a toll-free number to call, or the customer can call any agent, including the one he or she has used previously, for information. Again, the information maintained in its databases allows the company to provide expert service. Its technology allows every agent to have access to the purchase and policy records of every member; therefore, regardless of which agent answers the call, he or she can speak intelligently to the customer about needs, previous products purchased, and the relationship of the new product or service to the customer's other products and services.

Industry: Catalog
Company: Spiegel
Case: Strategic repositioning

Background

In 1905, Joseph Spiegel began operating from a location in Chicago selling inexpensive, utilitarian household goods and furniture to the working-class, immigrant population. By offering easy financing with low downpayments and reasonable monthly installments to the expanding middle class, the Spiegel catalog enjoyed steady growth throughout the first half of the century. Although Spiegel grew to become the fourth-largest catalog company in the United States (behind Sears, Montgomery Ward, and J.C. Penney), by the 1970s new forces were eroding Spiegel's traditional market. The number of working class families as a percentage of the population was beginning to decline, and discount stores and mass merchandisers were offering stiff competition for the remaining market.

Spiegel's Objectives

In 1976, Hank Johnson, the firm's new CEO, recognized a need for change more radical than merely altering the merchandise assortment or developing more efficient and effective tactics for marketing to the current customer base to shore up short-term profits. Johnson identified four trends—computers, toll-free numbers, working women, and accelerating social and economic change (Johnson 1990)—that shaped his strategy for transforming Spiegel from a downscale, me-too catalog to an upscale, unique specialty book. Johnson's objective was for Spiegel to become "the ultimate, convenient way to shop for the upper third of the households in the country, providing fashionable merchandise for adult women in those households."

Spiegel moved its headquarters to an upscale Chicago suburb to revitalize its image with its employees, suppliers, customers, and market. The 200 retail stores were closed. Hundreds of items including top sellers were dropped in order to stress fashion and quality rather than price. New catalogs were designed with a more lavish appeal and expensive appearance. The apparel books featured apparel from leading designers like Liz Claiborne, Norma Kamali, and Yves St. Laurent. Goods from Laura Ashley, Henredon, and Fieldcrest were featured in the home fashions catalogs.

Uses of Database Marketing

To acquire their new target customer, Spiegel had to go beyond the traditional catalog customer lists. Eighty percent of Spiegel's customer file did not fit the profile of the new target customer so Spiegel began compiling lists of relatively affluent, working women from other sources such as upscale magazine subscription lists. A preview catalog, "Discover Spiegel," which contained its best merchandise at the lowest possible cost, was used to entice the initial response. Catalog circulation was augmented with sophisticated print ads in fashion and interior design magazines that projected Spiegel's new image and offered the preview book (Johnson 1982).

Databases were critical in allowing Spiegel to track its customers, segment them, and determine their buying preferences. Spiegel began to offer specialty books that focused on a particular type of merchandise. Women who bought shoes were sent books featuring shoes and accessories. Customers who ordered linens were sent the housewares books. Target marketing to the upscale, working woman was becoming a reality for catalogers. Circulation was reduced from forty million to twenty million, but increasing response rates and order amounts drove higher earnings. Between 1976 and 1982, response rates rose from two to four percent and the average order tripled. By the mid 1980s, the desired minimum household income for a target household was $25,000 and the median income was $35,000 (Spiegel 1984).

Spiegel began to extend database marketing techniques beyond the traditional segmentation of customers based on RFM or the type of merchandise purchased. Spiegel surveyed a sample of its customers about their lifestyles, family structure, careers, and attitudes and then clustered the customers based on their answers. The clusters reflected a sense of style from the classic, traditional woman to the avant garde. The firm then analyzed the specific items that the women in each cluster had purchased. With the clustered items, Spiegel could look at the purchases of all the customers in its database and assign each customer to an appropriate style. Catalogs were then developed that offered an assortment of merchandise reflecting a particular style rather than a particular type of merchandise.

INHIBITORS TO SUCCESS

In addition to the economic obstacles described previously, the successful implementation of a database marketing program can be affected by a number of factors—some of which are beyond the control of the firms conducting these programs. The firm must recognize these inhibitors and ascertain whether they make it impossible for the firm to become a successful database marketer.

Acquiring Customer Information

Although many consumers are unclear about the amount and types of personal information that are being collected by credit bureaus, database marketers, and list compilers, their concern about the potential for invasion of privacy is growing. The language of the U.S. Constitution does not refer to any "right of privacy" in the commercial context, and it has never been articulated by any decision of the U.S. Supreme

Court. In fact, the court has taken the position that the flow of information is crucial to a free economy (Posch 1988). However, legislation restricting invasive telemarketing practices and controlling the dissemination of data is being considered in almost every state. Congress is currently considering bills that would restrict access to credit agencies' databases and establish a federal data protection board that would regulate privately held databases. This growing level of concern among consumers may soon cut off some of the most important sources of data about customers. The three major credit agencies and the database marketing industry are working with the U.S. Office of Consumer Affairs to address these concerns through voluntary measures.

If sources are limited, data acquisition will become much more expensive. This places a premium on firms with large, detailed customer databases because these firms will be able to market to existing customers using purchase history information. Database marketing firms will have an advantage because they will have the information to concentrate on installed base marketing and will not need to rely on customer acquisition strategies.

Limitations Due to the Quantity and Quality of Data

Beyond the pending legislative restrictions on the exchange and collection of customer data are the practical obstacle of obtaining and retaining customer data. With order entry systems in catalog companies and scanner systems tied to frequent buyer programs in retailer companies, it is possible to capture and analyze the buying behavior of each customer. However, the massive size of these databases makes them expensive to store and process. Citicorp faced this problem when it tried to create frequent user programs for grocery retailers. The sheer size of the database was beyond its computer processing capabilities.

In addition to buying behavior, personal information about the customer such as his family structure, financial condition, lifestyle characteristics, attitudes, and demographics are required to complete an accurate profile. Some of this information can be purchased from data suppliers such as Donnelley Marketing and R. L. Polk, but the most accurate data usually come from self-reports through survey responses or telemarketing. Intensive effort is required to capture this information and then maintain its accuracy. Until marketers learn to use these data to create more accurate and predictive profiles of their customers, response rates to database marketing programs will stall and economic barriers to the implementation of these programs will remain intact.

Computer Literacy in the Marketing Organization

As cited in the brief history of database marketing that introduced this chapter, computerization is a necessary component. Many of the innovations in the field were driven by technology. Economic barriers to the adoption of powerful computer systems are decreasing as distributed processing capabilities are appearing on the manager's desktop. The constraining factor in the implementation of these capabilities is now the lack of computer literacy among marketing managers. The information systems department in an organization often lacks the experience in marketing applications required to fill this gap. Companies often turn to software and services provided by vendors and consultants to augment their internal expertise. However, the firms that develop analytical and computer skills within the marketing organization where critical decisions are made will build the strongest competitive advantage.

Marketing Organizations Are Slow to Change

Database marketing presents a new paradigm for the organization. Visions of marketing to the masses must be supplanted by marketing to the individual. In addition to new analytic skills and computer literacy, the organization must learn to develop new creative approaches, adopt new measurements and economic models, and work with new types of media to communicate to targeted customers. Service providers such as some advertising agencies have also had great difficulty in designing effective one-on-one programs. New paradigms are needed in pricing, communications programs, and product design. These types of systemic changes will diffuse slowly through the organization.

THE ORGANIZATIONAL IMPACT OF DATABASE MARKETING

If a firm makes a commitment to become a database marketer, it can no longer conduct business using the old organizational paradigms. This section begins by describing the organizational changes necessary for a firm to be an effective database marketer and ends with a table summarizing this section.

The New Marketing Organization: Customer Retention and Customer Acquisition Specialists

The marketing function has traditionally been focused on managing elements of the marketing mix such as pricing, promotions, advertising, and channel management, and there are staff departments whose responsibility it is to manage these activities (e.g., the advertising department). This will need to change as a firm moves to become a database marketer. The marketing function will need to be reorganized around (1) current customers and (2) customer acquisition. This bifurcation is necessary because each type of customer requires different types of marketing programs. Marketing to current customers requires concentrating on customer retention and installed base marketing. Marketing to prospects requires sophisticated offers, cost-effective media selection, and quality copy. The skills and programs necessary to market to these two segments is different and implies the need for separate organizations.

The New Marketing Research: Measurement and Management of Customer Affinity

The past thirty years have seen a strong orientation in marketing to product positioning. Many brands have developed a distinct positioning and this has catapulted them to category dominance. One such case is Marlboro cigarettes. Customers develop an image of a firm that is similar to its positioning but is usually softer and less focused. Sometimes this image is managed by the firm and sometimes it evolves by itself. Harley-Davidson has a very distinctive image that has evolved over time, and now the firm is using this image to its advantage. It markets accessories consistent with the Harley Davidson image. A database marketing firm must learn to manage the affinity the customer has with it because this affinity offers an opportunity to develop a strong installed-base marketing program.

The need to understand the customer's affinity with the firm will require marketing research to shift its activities from brand attitudinal research to determining customer affinity. Affinity refers to the "unique" relationship the customer develops with the firm. AARP (American Association of Retired Persons), for example, has developed a very strong affinity with its members. It is quite different from a positioning that focuses the customer on the individual product or service. While attitudinal research is oriented toward advertising and understanding how it works, customer affinity research requires evaluating the types of products and services that are consistent with the customer's affinity with the firm. Can Toys Я Us create summer camps for children? Can McDonald's sell clothing for children? Can L. L. Bean create a line of sports clothing to compete with Nike and Reebok? The answer depends on the affinity created by the firm with its customer. Since affinity is not tangible, the type of research required may be far less quantitative than current marketing research and may be more in the tradition of linguistic research which tries to understand the meaning of symbols and words that have connotations not easily discerned. Thus uncovering the boundaries of customer affinity is likely to be subtle and complex and less amenable to "scientific" discovery. Yet, it has significant consequences for the firm.

The New Marketing Services Function: Knowledge-Based Systems Experts

Database marketing, as its name implies, is very data intensive. This requires the ability to analyze and use information for decision making. In the consumer packaged goods industry, firms are beginning to use knowledge-based systems (related to expert systems) to help them work with the massive quantities of data that their brand managers and sales force must use. Cover Story and Sales Partner produced by Information Resources, Inc., and knowledge-based systems by McCann and Gallagher (1990) provide graphical computer-generated information that serves as the basis for marketing decisions. These systems take the information, use rules to search through the information for certain types of events, and then access statistical models to produce recommended marketing and sales actions. While in their infancy, these systems allow marketing mangers to identify key findings in the data without having to peruse the massive databases being generated.

As databases become larger, which is inevitable, the need for "smart systems" will increase. Database marketing firms, to take full advantage of their customer and marketing databases, need to develop automated analytical systems that can assist decision makers and analysts in working more effectively with the data. One important inhibitor to the successful use of marketing databases will be the inability of marketing managers to analyze them to develop tactics and strategies. Expert systems, artificial intelligence, and knowledge-based systems will be the primary way many firms will be able to gain a competitive advantage from their databases.

What does this imply about the types of information systems the organization will need to supply? The answer is that marketing will need a "knowledge-based systems" team to translate and transform data into computer delivery systems that simplify working with data. These systems are more sophisticated than traditional marketing decision support systems because they use expert systems/artificial intelligence to recommend decisions, not simply to provide easy access to data. Obviously, this expertise rarely exists in any organization and definitely not in marketing. Yet, it is critical to managing the use of information—the key to effective database marketing.

The New Agencies: Retention and Acquisition

As database marketing matures, there will be agencies who specialize in designing tactics and strategies to utilize (1) the firm's customer database and (2) outside data sources for customer acquisition. This implies that advertising and promotional agencies will be forced to change their orientation to concentrate on either retention or acquisition marketing so that they have the skills to be expert in a given type of marketing. New types of services firms with different names such as retention specialists or acquisition specialists will evolve. This change will redirect the strategies and tactics used. While concepts like positioning will still be important, so will special programs that "tie" the customer to the firm through frequent user cards, special services provided to customers, and regular communications focused on the customer's specific needs. This bifurcation of marketing activities implies that a fundamental change is required—agencies must recognize the differences in retention and acquisition marketing. Separate account teams, separate services, and separate (but integrated) strategies are needed. Can one agency provide these services? It is unlikely.

The New Accounting: Lifetime Value of the Customer

As discussed earlier, database marketing focuses the firm on customer retention and its importance to the long-term success of the firm. Firms will quickly learn that any erosion of its customer base is of paramount importance, and the firm must orient all of its activities around maintaining its customer base. General Motors, who in the 1980s lost significant market share while maintaining its short-run profitability, is a perfect case in point. In the 1970s, product quality slipped and the percentage of GM customers who purchased a second or replacement vehicle dropped. Had the firm had an accounting system that tracked the long-term value of General Motors' customers, the financial community and its directors would have learned that the company was in serious trouble. Unfortunately, profits lagged changing customer retention levels.

If a balance sheet item and a flow statement (similar to an income statement) were added that showed the value of the firm's customer franchise, executives would be forced to focus on customer retention and satisfaction to a greater extent than currently exists. The role of accounting is to provide this type of statement. This would then focus the marketing, production, and operations functions on retention strategies that include improved customer service, improved product quality, better value of the firm's products and service, relationship pricing, and other factors that determine whether the customer is willing to continue the relationship he or she has with the firm.

The New Focus of Product Development: Installed-Base Marketing

Installed-base marketing becomes critical to maximize the lifetime value of the customer. The integration of marketing and new product development is very important in being able to market successfully to an installed based. Marketing must be able to identify products and service the customer base wants and needs. New product development must concentrate on acquiring new products or services, rather than creating and producing them. Thus new product development must expand its flexibility to become a "systems integrator," which means taking components from other sources and putting them together as a product or service provided to the customer. Managing outsourcing for product development becomes a critical new function within the firm.

Operations and production must also be more closely aligned with marketing because they both greatly affect the lifetime value of the customer. If either provides poor value to the customer because its costs are too high, or because product or service quality is too low, then the long-term relationship with the customer is jeopardized. Currently,

Comparison of the Old Marketing Organization to the New Database Marketing Organization

Function	Traditional Marketing	Database Marketing
Marketing	Organized around the marketing mix	Organized around customer retention and customer acquistion
Marketing Research	Focused on consumer research and market size analysis	Focused on the measurement and management of customer affinity
Marketing Services	Directed to manage the firm's agency and outside vendor relationships	Provide knowledge-based system expertise
Outside Agencies	Organized around marketing mix functions	Organized around retention and acquisition
Accounting	Product oriented	Analyze and provide statements about the lifetime value of a customer
New Product Development	Product oriented	Become specialists in the acquisition and management of products to be sold to the installed customer base

marketing is responsible for external relationships and production and operations for internal systems. The problem is that the two functions must be more tightly linked. Without a closer linkage through greater understanding of the customer's evaluation of the products and services of the firm, a key asset of the firm, the customer lifetime value will decline.

REFERENCES

Johnson, Hank. 1990. *The Corporate Dream: Making It Big in Business*. New York: Carol Publishing Group.

Johnson, Henry. 1982. Spiegel's new winnin' spirit based on target marketing. *Direct Marketing*. August.

McCann, John M., and John P. Gallagher. 1990. *Expert Systems for Scanner Data Environments*. Boston: Kluwer Academic Publishers.

Posch, Robert J., Jr. How the law(s) of "privacy" impact your business. *Direct Marketing*. October, pp. 74–82.

Spiegel, Edward. 1984. Spiegel's turnaround–Net sales rocket to $516 million. *Direct Marketing*. April, pp. 40–57.

Stone, Bob. 1984. *Successful Direct Marketing Methods*. Chicago: Crain Books.

Chaim M. Ehrman, PhD
Marketing Department
Loyola University of Chicago
Chicago, Illinois

CHAPTER 24

SIZING MARKETS

INTRODUCTION

The term *sizing markets* is the combination of two separate terms: *sizing* and *markets*. The term *size* is defined as "physical magnitude, extent, or bulk: relative or proportionate dimensions" (Webster's 1985). *Market* is defined as a group of actual or potential customers for a particular product or service (Zikmund and D'Amico 1989). The term, *sizing markets* refers to assessing the magnitude or the number of actual or potential users or purchasers for a given good or service. The relationship between market segmentation and sizing is described in the next few paragraphs.

Market segmentation consists of dividing a market into smaller, homogeneous submarkets. This division can be based on several variables, such as consumption patterns (heavy users versus light users), demographics, psychographics, etc. The term *target market* refers to the market segment to which the organization decides to direct its marketing plan (Zikmund and D'Amico 1989). In order to select a target market, it is important and even crucial to ascertain that the segmentation of this market is based on relevant and meaningful dimensions.

A heterogeneous market can be divided into homogeneous market segments using any variable to segment or subdivide the market. For example, one can segment the beer-drinking market by males born on October 1. This segment is not meaningful, since the consumption patterns of males born on October 1 should be identical to that of males born on any of the other 364 days of the year. Therefore, this segment is not meaningful. Similarly, this segment cannot be targeted with any rationale, since the segment is not meaningful.

In order to establish a meaningful segment, which is a prerequisite for selecting a viable target market, there are four requirements that must be satisfied in segmenting any market. These requirements are the following:

1. The segment must have a distinguishing feature that is important.
2. The segment must have a significant size.
3. The segment must be accessible through channels of distribution.
4. The segment should respond favorably to marketing mix variables.

Item number 2, market size, is a crucial ingredient in market segmentation and in defining a target market. Ignoring market size can generate segments that are not meaningful at all.

Methods for sizing markets using secondary data as well as forecasting are discussed later on in this chapter. However, the initial thrust of this chapter is focused on the need for sizing with respect to marketing mix variables. When sizing markets becomes interrelated with marketing mix variables, the sizing task becomes very focused and easier to solve.

MOTIVATION FOR SIZING MARKETS

There are many significant reasons why sizing markets is important. In order to present structure to this section, the importance of sizing markets is classified along the marketing mix variables: product, price, channels of distribution or place, and promotion. Each of the four Ps is dealt with separately in its own subsection.

Motivation for Sizing Markets—Product

In the area of new product planning and development, sizing markets is the basis for the launch decision. Many creative, innovative product ideas have not been commercialized simply because the market size was not sufficiently large for the firm. Sizing markets gives the "bottom line" information for new product introduction.

In the area of foreign investment and international marketing, the literature is replete with examples showing that the key determining factor for foreign direct investment as well as international marketing is the size of the market.

The size of a market represents potential sales, earnings, profits, and return on investments. As the size of the market increases, chances for success increase. As a critical mass increases in size, the likelihood of success increases.

In addition to likelihood of success, there is another reason why market size is such a crucial barometer in the product planning and development decision process. It is known that in production, economies of scale do exist. As the quantity of units produced increases, the cost of production on a per-unit basis decreases. Therefore, a larger market size, in marketing terms, can herald a lowering of costs and a higher figure of total sales.

In mathematical terms, it can be shown very easily that profit impact increases significantly once variable costs decrease. Recall that variable costs are those costs that change with respect to production, such as wages, raw materials, maintenance expense, and so forth. Fixed costs are those costs that do not change with respect to production, such as property taxes, plant and equipment rentals, top managements' salaries, advertising, and so forth. One can compute profit impact, total revenues minus fixed and variable costs, as follows.

$$\text{Profit Impact} = (\text{Sales in Units}) \times (\text{Price} - \text{Variable Costs}) - \text{Fixed Costs}$$

As sales increase, profit impact increases. As variable costs decrease, profit impact increases. As sales increase *and* variable costs decrease, profit impact increases dramatically.

A large market size can justify a reduction in variable costs. Plant expansion or acquisition of cost-saving efficient machinery, which contribute to reduction in variable costs, are feasible only when market size is large enough to warrant this expansion.

Finally, the experience curve is another reason why size is crucial. The experience curve is a significant factor once the market size becomes large. The experience curve effect refers to the fact that the time and effort needed to complete a job decreases with repetition. One becomes more adept at job completion, cutting down on work time and effort, as the job is repeated over time. A large market size allows for the experience curve effect to kick in, since the repetition issue becomes a factor. This effect is not allowed to reach fruition when there is only a small market size for the given product at hand.

To recapitulate, market size is a crucial ingredient in practically every decision in the area of product planning and development. The size of a given market determines whether the new product idea is to be launched or not. The size of a market determines whether a firm will go international or remain domestic. The size of the market determines which particular product attribute should be offered and which particular attributes should be dropped. Positioning of a product is largely determined by the size of the market.

Motivation for Sizing Markets—Price

In this subsection, the importance of market size is addressed in the context of price. It is known that elasticity of demand directly determines whether a price increase will reduce total revenue or increase total revenue. The term *elasticity* simply measures how responsive consumers are to changes in price. In the case of a product with a demand curve that is highly elastic, sales will drop significantly when prices rise and sales will rise significantly when prices fall. Conversely, a product with an inelastic demand curve will show relatively small changes in sales regardless of whether prices rise or fall.

One of the important criteria for measuring price elasticity is the Total Revenue (TR) test. TR is measured by price per unit (P) multiplied by the number of units or quantity (Q) sold. Mathematically, TR = (P) × (Q). The rule for elasticity is the following:

- If a price increase generates a loss in TR, the demand is elastic.
- If a price increase generates a gain in TR, the demand is inelastic.
- If a price increase generates no change in TR, demand is unit elastic.

The term TR includes price and quantity sold, which is directly determined by the size of the market. Therefore, price elasticities are a function of the size of the market. A simple illustration is given in the following paragraph to highlight the importance of market size with respect to pricing and market selection.

Consider the following. A commodity has a given market size of Q1 at a given price of P1. The same commodity has a different market size, Q2, at a different price, P2. The decision maker has to decide, Should the price be P1 or P2? In terms of earnings, the issue is, Is market Q1 more lucrative or is market Q2 more lucrative? Assuming we have accurate measurements, the answer is very simple. Compute TR1 for market Q1 and TR2 for market Q2. If TR1 is greater than TR2, then pursue market Q1 at price P1; if TR2 is greater than TR1, pursue Q2 at price P2. This relationship can be shown mathematically as follows.

TR1 = (P1) × (Q1)	TR2 = (P2) × (Q2)
If TR1 > TR2, Price = P1 Select Market Q1	If TR2 > TR1, Price = P2 Select Market Q2

The decision to price a product or service is directly dependent on the size of the given market. If a market is sufficiently large, a price decrease can be justified due to increased total revenues. A small market size may not justify a drop in price since the incremental total revenues may be too small and total revenues will drop because of the price decrease. The pricing decision for any commodity or service is affected by the size of the markets for each of the respective prices.

Motivation for Sizing Markets—Place

In the question of channels of distribution, market size plays a pivotal role in determining levels of distribution. There are three levels of distribution: intensive (place the product at every possible outlet), intensive (place the product at a few select outlets), and exclusive (place the product at only one outlet). The decision variable that is used to determine the appropriate level of distribution is the size of the market. Intensive distribution is appropriate only when there is a large market size. Exclusive distribution is appropriate when the size of the market is much smaller.

In a similar vein, the mode of distribution is determined by the size of the market. Reliance on the wholesaler can be directly related to the size of the market. A small market size dictates greater reliance on intermediary channels, such as wholesalers.

Success in channels of distribution is determined by the size of the market. For example, retailers' performance is measured by turnover (twelve divided by the number of months needed to sell the entire inventory). A high turnover indicates good performance. As the size of the market increases, the chances for high turnover increase. The likelihood of success in retailing is clearly dependent on market size.

Motivation for Sizing Markets—Promotion

In the area of promotion, market size plays a crucial role. For example, media selection is directly dependent on market size. A product with mass market size would be well-suited for a television campaign. Conversely, a product with a small regional market size would be better suited by advertising through print media. Sizing markets is a necessary step for the media selection decision.

Other forms of promotion are also dependent on sizing the market. For example, personal selling is justified only if the market size is large enough to cover the expenses and training of salespeople. In a similar vein, direct marketing is justified only if market size is sufficiently large. If the market is very small and product price is low, the cost of purchasing a mailing list may not be recovered.

A promotional campaign can be a viable option only if market size is adequate, that is, large enough that incremental sales, attributed to the promotional effort, will be able to pay for promotional costs and have some revenues left over. If the market size is small, there are very few options available. Perhaps in-store promotions may do the job of promoting the product, since these costs are fairly low.

These last few sections have underscored the need for sizing of markets. This responsibility should be viewed as crucial. Market size has impact on segmentation and on all facets of the marketing mix. The importance of this decision area cannot be overstated. There are so many decision areas in marketing that are based on market size information. In the next section, the appropriate units for market size are discussed.

THE APPROPRIATE UNIT FOR SIZING MARKETS

The term *size* can refer to different units. For instance, one can define size to be the number of individuals in a given market segment or the number of households in a given and defined market segment. An airline company defines its market size in terms of business travelers (individuals), family travelers (households), and corporate travelers (companies).

An important issue to be resolved in any market sizing problem is, What are the appropriate units for sizing? Size can be geographic based by city, county, state; it can be population based by individual, household, or family; it can be income based, by employees of the same corporation. The appropriate unit for sizing clearly must be resolved before any attempt at sizing takes place.

In order to answer this question, it is important to understand the inputs in any buying decision. In the next subsection, three inputs for a buying decision are given. The appropriate unit for sizing is resolved once the key input for the buying decision is identified.

Inputs Affecting Buying Decisions

In the marketing literature, it has been shown that many buying decisions can be characterized as having inputs from three major players: the user, the decision maker, and the purchaser. Sometimes all three inputs are generated by the same individual. (Some texts further subdivide the decision maker category into three: gatekeeper, decider, and influencer) (Zikmund and D'Amico 1989). In this discussion, the original three are adequate.) Examples are given for consumer goods and industrial goods, in which the user, decision maker, and purchaser are separate entities.

In a toy-buying scenario, a child wants to play with a given toy (user), the parents decide on a particular toy (decision maker), and the grandparents purchase the toy (purchaser). We see that three separate inputs are involved in the decision to purchase a toy.[1] This example deals with consumer goods.

In the area of industrial goods, we find the same basic division. For instance, a secretary may want a new software package for word processing (user), the office manager may target a few brands as acceptable (decision maker), and the purchasing officer may select a brand that the company has already established as a source (purchaser). It is obvious that these three players have key inputs in consumer as well as industrial buying decisions.

Sizing markets can effectively be done for three separate entities. One can measure the market size of the user, the decision maker, and the purchaser. The decision to assess market size must be preceded by the following: Which one of the three inputs is most important for the marketer? The answer allows the marketer to identify precisely the particular entity that is to be "sized" for the given product or service.

Identifying the Key Input for Sizing Markets

Sizing a market can address the user market, the decision maker market, and the purchaser market. The objective for sizing determines which is the appropriate one for sizing. If an objective for sizing is to assess production requirements, then the user market is most important. If the objective is to assess direct marketing requirements, that is, the number of promotional pieces to be sent through the mail, then the decision maker market is most important. If the objective is to assess the number of freebies to be sent to purchasing agents, then the purchaser market is most important.

Once the key input is defined, the unit for sizing is defined as the unit most appropriate for the key input. Consider the airline example mentioned earlier. If the key input is the decision maker, there are many appropriate units for sizing: individual (single traveler decides alone), household (one decision is made for the household), and company (one decision is made by the travel department for employees traveling).

If the airline company wants to size its passenger market to determine if there is a need for larger planes, then the correct unit or measure of interest is the number of individual travelers, excluding children under two years of age, who do not occupy a seat. In order to present a sequential decision process to define the appropriate unit for sizing, three basic steps are presented in the next section that give structure to the unit-to-be-sized issue.

Prerequisites for Sizing Markets

The decision maker interested in sizing markets is advised to go through this preliminary exercise to help define the key input in the buying decision that is most important and the appropriate unit to be used when sizing a market. The questions are the following:

1. Why do you want to size your market?
   - Market segmentation
   - Product related
   - Price related
   - Place related
   - Promotion related
2. Which key input is of most importance to you?
   - User
   - Decision maker
   - Purchaser
3. Which unit is crucial for the key input described in step 2?
   - Individual
   - Household
   - Company

The total possibilities for each item in the marketing mix are the following:

	Key Input		
	User	Decision Maker	Purchaser
Unit to Be Sized:			
Individual			
Household			
Company			
Other			

The first question helps determine objectives for sizing markets. Segmentation or marketing mix variables can be objectives for sizing a market. Once the objective for sizing markets is known, the second question helps determine a key input in buying decisions: Is it the user, the decision maker, or the purchaser? Each of these three inputs have their respective unit that is most appropriate. Some key inputs have multiple units, such as the decision maker for air travel. Typically, there is one appropriate unit: individual level, household level, company level, or any other level. Therefore, the answer to question 2 gives information for identifying the unit for sizing, which concerns question 3. We have already discussed objectives markets and unit selection for sizing. We will now consider techniques for sizing.

SIZING MARKETS

Techniques for sizing, mentioned in this section, stress the use of secondary data, that is, published data that can be readily accessible in a good library. Generating new and unpublished data is in the domain of marketing research.

Sizing Markets—Using Census Data

Markets can be sized using census data. In fact, the federal government has published a handbook on how to size markets (Department of Commerce 1974). The next few paragraphs use the example provided in the handbook.

Say a firm is interested in sizing the market for industrial lubricants in Cook County, Illinois. A quick analysis of the industry shows that there are three major users of the product: apparel products manufacturers, chemical manufacturers, and fabricated metals manufacturers. *County Business Patterns* is a publication that classifies employees by county and by industry. In 1974, employment figures for Cook County were the following: apparel—18,066, chemicals—32,661, fabricated metals—87,101. These numbers give us a total number of employees per industry. It is now necessary to measure consumption on an employee basis.

Purchasing agents provide necessary information on annual consumption of industrial lubricants on a pounds-per-employee basis. The following data were gathered: apparel—30 pounds, chemicals—50 pounds, fabricated metals—65 pounds. The total market size in industrial lubricants for Cook County is 7,836,595 pounds per year. The calculations are summarized below as follows:

Industry	Employees	Pounds-per-Employee	Total
Apparel	18,066	30	41,890
Chemicals	32,661	50	1,633,050
Fabricated metals	87,101	65	5,661,565
Total			7,836,595

This example is a fairly straightforward illustration on how to size a market for an industrial product. In order to have access to the census data, it is important to understand the standard industrial classification (SIC) system and how it operates.

SIC System and Its Application for Sizing Markets

The United States Government has categorized industry segments based on their economic activity. The first major division consists of ten different areas: agriculture, mining, construction, manufacturing, transportation and utilities, wholesale trade, retail trade, finance and insurance, services, and public administration. Each number describes a further refinement and narrowing down of the given industry classification.

Consider the following example described in the Fisher-Price case.[2] Assume we are looking at the size of the writing tablet market. The SIC number is 26482. This number has a hierarchy that explains its roots. This hierarchy is presented below.

2
26 = Paper manufacturing
264 = Paperboard mills
2648 = Stationery products
26482 = Tablets and related products

The rule is very clear: As the number of SIC digits you use increases, the degree of focus on subcategories within that industry increases.

The usage of the SIC system allows the marketer to tap into vast data banks of information. For example, the *U.S. Census of Manufacturing, Census of Retailing, Economic Statistics, County Business Patterns,* and *Statistical Abstracts* are just a few of the many publications from the census and commerce departments that make wide use of the SIC system. Therefore, SICs should be considered an indispensable tool in assessing and evaluating market size for a given product or service.

The discussion on sizing markets has focused on usage of secondary data to get appropriate information. However, the need to size markets is not restricted to products and services currently on the market. A key factor in the decision to launch a new product or service is the size of the potential market. Sizing markets also plays a pivotal role in the selection of new ideas for research and development.

Sizing Future Markets

Data given by the census and commerce departments are crucial for sizing when the given product or service is current. However, if a new product feature is added to an existing product, this addition may precipitate a major change in user market size. U.S. census information only reports data based on products or services that are currently in use but not potential usage.

In a similar vein, if one contemplates introducing a totally new product or service, census data may be of little value in estimating size of this new potential market. Therefore, one must go outside governmental sources to determine the size of a market.

Forecasting—Using Demographic and Economic Data. One approach to assessing the size of a market for a new good or service is to follow the population trends of the given market segment. A demographer studies size, composition, and distribution of human populations (Zikmund and D'Amico 1989). Consider, for instance, age distribution of the U.S. male population in the forty to forty-nine age bracket. Estimated projections are documented as follows.

Given Year	Estimated Size
1975	12mm
1985	14mm
1995	18mm
2005	20mm

If a firm sells products to the target market of males in the forty to forty-nine age group, such as antibaldness creams, it can readily be shown that this market size will increase 150 percent over the next twenty years. This estimate is a simple extrapolation of increases in previous years.

A straight-line extrapolation, based on population change, entails three steps.

1. Compute total product sales as a percentage of population.
2. Estimate your population size for the year(s) of your choice.
3. Multiply the figure in step 1 by the figure in step 3.

This number is your estimated market size for the desired year(s). In mathematical terms,

Size of market (time = t + k) = Sales (Time = t)/
Segment population (time = t) × Segment population (time = t + k)
Key: t = annual sales this year;
k = a given number of years in the future

The assumption is that consumption patterns remain constant. Therefore, the term *straight line* is used because a straight line has a fixed slope. Clearly there are many more complex alternatives to straight-line projections.

Another variable that is usually linked with market size is economic activity. Most consumer goods are characterized by a demand curve that is elastic. A drop in real disposable income signifies that the same price may, in reality, cost more for the consumer since income levels decreased. Consumer goods that cost more experience a drop in sales, as described earlier. In terms of forecasting, it is of utmost importance to get information about future economic activity. There are some variables, known as lead variables, that herald future economic activity, and they are described in the next paragraph.

There are many lead indicators that are used to forecast future economic activity. Some examples include the number of new housing permits, machine-tool sales, and direction (+,–) of the Dow Jones industrial average. These variables are a harbinger of future economic activity. New housing permits indicate future construction. A builder would not apply for a housing permit if there were no plans for construction. Similarly, a manufacturer would not purchase machine tools unless there were a number of firm orders for manufacturing jobs.

These industries provide derived demand, which in turn generates demand for many other industries. The automobile manufacturing industry provides demand for the upholstery, steel, tire, paint, and plastic industries. The same is true with the construction industry. A positive change on the Dow Jones average indicates that there are more buyers than sellers. Consumers, the backbone of the economy, typically purchase when they are optimistic about the future and sell when they are pessimistic about the future. An optimistic consumer buys more than a pessimistic consumer.

These lead variables are instrumental in predicting market size for the future. If machine tool sales, retail sales, construction, and the Dow Jones average are all pointing upward, then the economy should be entering a growth phase. The estimation of market size would go awry if these indicators were not taken into consideration.

The exact magnitude of the impact economic and demographic variables have on market size clearly varies from product to product. For example, the cable television industry can define its market size as all households owning a television. Some variables meaningful for market segmentation are age (negatively related), income (positively related), home ownership, and so forth. It has been shown that these demographic and economic variables have different impacts at different geographic locations.[3]

There are mathematical tools, such as linear regression, that can measure for each targeted market the precise input these variables can have on sizing future markets. There are many computer packages that can generate a regression output, showing the magnitude of input the economic and demographic variables can have. Computers can generate output for regression in an equation format. For example, in the cable TV example, the output may look like this:

Size of market =
Constant + A(Income) + B(Age) + C(Family size) + D(Apartment)

The letters A, B, C, and D are coefficients that serve as weights on the magnitude of this relationship, and the constant is a fixed number. In this section, the focus is on the input economic and demographic variables can have on sizing markets.

Forecasting—Using Time Series Data. In sizing markets, one may find a situation for which government data are unavailable and economic and demographic data are also not readily available. This scenario is possible when one must make a decision very quickly and there is not enough time to collect data. This scenario is not unusual. Consider new product introduction. A firm wants to capture "first mover" advantage, that is, being the first to introduce a new product. The time necessary to size the market may jeopardize the first-mover advantage. Two approaches toward forecasting are presented below.

One approach in sizing markets in the absence of other variables is to use subjective data. "Experts" in the field can be called for their opinion as to what the size of the market is. This technique is called "jury of execute opinion." Alternatively, one can question marketing people who are in close touch with the consumer and are familiar with their particular wants and buying habits. This panel of experts would include top salespeople, retailers, and wholesales in the given field.

A second approach is to use quantitative data, based on previous sales of a product or service. This approach is known as time series, and the key variable to be forecasted is sales with respect to time. Of course, other variables such as household population can be estimated using these same basic techniques.

Time series can be a linear extrapolation, as mentioned earlier in the context of economic and demographic variables. The relationship between sales from year 1 and year 2 is measured and extended to the next year. This equation would read,

$$\text{Sales (Year 3)} = \text{Sales (Year 2)} \times \{\text{Sales (Year 2)/Sales (Year 1)}\}.$$

For instance, if sales in year 1 were $1,000, and sales in year 2 were $1,200, then sales in year 3 should be $1,440. Although this approach is simplistic, it gives a number to go by when sizing markets.

The method described above assumes a fixed annual rate of change. Once this rate has been computed, it can be extended for future years. Most data, however, do not have a fixed rate of change. For example, sales can be high one year due to a tax rebate, and this boost will not continue into next year's sales.

One method to smooth cyclical changes in sales or other variables is known as moving averages. Sales or population data are collected for three or five years added, and divided by the number of years collected. This number becomes the forecast for the following year. Once the data are available for that year, the moving average moves down a year, the new data are added, and the last of the three- or five-year data is dropped. The following is an illustration of a three- and five-year moving average.

Year	Sales	Three-Year Moving Average	Five-Year Moving Average
1	100		
2	115		
3	85	100.0	
4	120	106.7	
5	130	111.7	110.0
6	100	116.7	110.0
7	75	101.7	102.0
8	95	90.0	104.0
9	100	90.0	100.0
10	95	96.7	93.0

It is interesting to note that as the number of years included in a moving average grow, the fluctuations decrease. The three-year moving average has a range from a high of 116.7 to a low of 90.0, and the five-year moving average has a smaller range, from a high of 104 to a low of 93. The range of the original data was over 55 points, from a high of 130 to a low of 75. Therefore, one can readily see the smoothing tendencies of moving averages.

A final comment on forecasting using time series data: the forecast is based on previous data, measuring the rate of change from one year to the next and projecting it to the future. The straight linear extrapolation approach analyzes the ratio change from one year to the next. The moving average approach collects data from several years and then projects the figures to the future. There is equal weighting of data using the moving average approach. However, the recency effect may often be a factor: data that are more recent should be weighted heavier than data that are distant and may have little bearing on the forecast.

The technique that weights recent data more heavily is known as exponential smoothing. Since the weights are no longer equal, the forecast is no longer a linear extrapolation. It is the responsibility of the researcher or demographer to assign the appropriate weights for both recent data and distant data.

In order to demonstrate the exponential smoothing approach, assume a weight of 50 percent for last year's sales and a weight of 50 percent on the five-year moving average estimate of sales. The data used earlier to demonstrate the three- and five-year moving average is presented on the following page to show exponential smoothing in action.

We note that the exponential smoothing was closer to the noticeable drop in sales in year seven than any other technique. It also is closer to the peak that was reached in year five than any other technique. The reader is encouraged to read the chapter on forecasting to gain further insights in this challenging and vital field of sizing markets.

Year	Sales ($)	Three-Year Moving Average	Five-Year Moving Average	Exponential Smoothing 50 percent (Last Year) 50 percent (Five-Year Moving Average)
1	100			
2	115			
3	85	100.0		
4	120	106.7		
5	130	111.7	110.0	120.0
6	100	116.7	110.0	105.0
7	75	101.7	102.0	88.5
8	95	90.0	104.0	99.5
9	100	90.0	100.0	100.0
10	95	96.7	93.0	94.0

CONCLUSION

The area of sizing markets is a fundamental component in segmentation and the marketing mix. It has been shown that without proper sizing, the marketer may not be aware if he or she has a meaningful segment and if the target market has any chance of success. Furthermore, sizing is crucial in deciding on product decisions, pricing decisions, and place and promotion decisions. The reader is encouraged to pursue the area of sizing both in terms of demographic variables, economic variables, and forecasting techniques in general. A fringe benefit is that sizing is crucial in other areas beside marketing. For example, portfolio analysis has an important component known as "industry attractiveness" (GE/McKinsey model). The first variable that is used to measure industry attractiveness is market size. This variable also has one of the highest weights among twenty-six other variables used to measure industry attractiveness. Therefore, it is indeed a worthwhile endeavor to develop expertise in sizing markets—not only for marketers also but for business decisions in general.

NOTES

1. Fisher-Price Case, Harvard Case Studies, Cambridge, Mass.
2. Harvard Case Studies, Cambridge, Mass.
3. TransAmerica Cable Case, Harvard Case Studies, Cambridge, Mass.

REFERENCES

U.S. Department of Commerce. 1974. *Measuring Markets: A Guide to the Use of Federal and State Statistical Data*. Washington DC: U.S. Government Printing Office.

Zikmund, William, and Michael D'Amico. 1989. *Marketing*. New York: John Wiley.

Craig S. Rice
President, Marketing Dynamics
Former Corporate Marketing Director of ConAgra
Omaha, Nebraska

CHAPTER 25

THE MARKETING CAMPAIGN

The right to encourage the purchase of a brand has existed, in one degree or another, for centuries. A somewhat oversimplified definition of our current economy might be that it is one in which people are reasonably free to buy and sell things, within protective regulatory limits, using money as a medium of exchange.

Implicit here is the right to offer goods and services for sale and . . . primary to our purpose . . . the right to *encourage people to buy these goods and services.* This, above all, is the underlying assumption of this chapter as to any marketing campaign.

The marketing campaign can be effectively compared with a political campaign. At the cash register, customers "vote" with dollars for their favorite brand and, just as a thorough, organized drive is the kind that often wins an election, a comprehensive marketing campaign, tying in many factors, is usually essential to success in today's sophisticated markets.

Because the cost of a marketing failure today is so staggering, all reasonable steps must be taken to avoid it. A thorough insight into sound marketing-campaign planning and execution greatly helps to maximize the chances of marketing success.

The rationale behind this planning and programming is being adapted more and more to the selling of many major brands. This is not surprising, since the basic strategy is an outgrowth of trial and error encountered over recent years in day-to-day marketing experience. Trial, correction, and continuation are, together, reasonably good evidence of actual campaign effectiveness.

WHAT IS "THE MARKETING CAMPAIGN"?

There is much confusion about the terms "marketing," "advertising," "selling," etc. Nearly every authority and manager has a definition. This is a problem in semantics and not a very serious one, except that, for the good of all marketing personnel, it is well to use words correctly. Difficulties and errors can be avoided if we all talk the same language.

"Marketing" is generally accepted as the overall function: the moving of product from the factory, through the channels of distribution, to the consumer. Major consultants believe it begins before the plant starts to produce. It begins in an analysis of the market (market research) to determine what *should* be produced.

In moving the merchandise, advertising, promotion and personal selling are used. Hence, marketing is the overall function of movement, in contrast to research, advertising, promotion and salesmanship, which are parts or steps in this movement.

The marketing campaign is simply the execution of a marketing plan, which is made up of various special plans, such as a research plan, selling plan, and advertising plan. The marketing campaign planner is a kind of "marketing architect."

The marketing campaign plan, from a physical standpoint, is a written plan that runs between 10 and 50 pages. It comprises several dozen paragraphs, each covering some important factor such as prevailing circumstances, financial objectives, product, advertising, merchandising, and testing.

The planning concept is a strange idea. Except to the military commander or the upper management group, it is strange because it deals with three abstractions, which have important, realistic, and quite practical meanings:

Situation (meaning "where are we?"),
Objective (meaning "where are we going?") and
Strategy (meaning "how are we going to get there?").

This simply represents an approach, a pattern, or way of figuring things out. The whole idea, small but potent, is by far *the most important concept of this volume.* Significantly, these same terms, situation-objective-strategy, are used continuously by the military as well as in the mathematical "theory of games," and are common denominators of planning by management of many major companies.

The planning concept meets the test of common sense and application to everyday life. When anyone takes action or faces a problem, almost always he or she looks at the situation, conditions or problem . . . decides what to accomplish . . . then, fixes on some sort of plan (be it ever so simple) to reach this goal. Example: These papers keep falling apart (problem situation) . . . they should be kept together (objective) . . . so, staple them together (strategy).

The situation leading to a marketing campaign is usually one of the following:

- A decline in sales and/or market share.
- A static, unsatisfactory situation.
- An inadequate growth in share and/or sales.
- A sudden market change that represents an opportunity.
- Another year has rolled around with no particular situation in mind, other than "business as usual" (most common lead-in).
- A new, promising product.
- Unusual action or inaction by competition.

The objectives of the campaign are often one or several of these:

- To stop a decline in sales and/or market share.
- To increase sales, share or profits to X$ or X percent share.
- To increase total sales through increasing the market.

- To take advantage of competitive weakness or opportunities.
- To *maintain* business as usual.
- To introduce and make profitable a new product.
- To respond, protect, or maintain the brand against competition.

Some confusion over "situation" and "objectives" is common—usually the confusion between a problem and the desire to solve it. "Declining sales" is a "situation," certainly not an objective. To end the decline is an "objective." A simple way to keep these straight is to recognize that the situation is the prevailing, current condition. The objective is the goal or the thing to be accomplished.

There is even greater confusion between "objectives" and "strategies." While the objectives are the goals to be reached, the strategies are the methods used to get there. Advertising, promotions, sampling, etc. are almost never objectives. They are means (or strategies) to reach an end.

The objective is usually the most important, yet least considered, factor in campaign planning. Certainly the strategy, which forms the bulk of the plan, is completely dictated by the goal. A quite different approach (strategy) would be used to introduce a product than to maintain status quo . . . both are logical objectives.

Advertising objectives should be identified specifically, as advertising is a key factor in the marketing campaign. Some planners tend to follow the lazy route of assigning to advertising the same objectives as the overall marketing campaign. This can produce rather ridiculous objectives for advertising, such as "to make a new brand profitable." It can be a marketing objective, but would hardly be the objective of advertising alone.

Basically, there are only two fundamental objectives of advertising:

1. To convince a prospect to *try the product* (before trying, he or she is fair game and a prime target for advertising, but after trying it, there is very little that the advertising can tell about the product that he or she does not know better than anyone).
2. To *reassure users* that other people are still using the product; that it still has prestige and acceptance.

Taken together, these two points make strong rationale for the "wave theory" of heavy, then light, advertising scheduling.

The campaign financial objective, from an overall standpoint, is generally like that of almost any other major capital commitment: to maximize the long- and short-run profit per dollar invested.

"Advertising can sell anything," some critics say. That may be true, but will it sell enough to pay for the product, advertising, and other expenses, and leave a profit to serve as a return on the marketing dollar invested? The marketing campaign should be planned to provide an answer in the affirmative, in most cases.

Planning the campaign and determining the strategy should be a simple, chronological procedure in the situation-objective-strategy planning pattern to be most efficient. This is only sensible since the situation will influence the selection of objectives and the establishment of objectives will affect and guide the strategies to be used for reaching these goals.

The preparation, then, should begin with the best possible assessment of the external and internal situations within the practical boundaries and limits of available time and budget.

The external situation will include market size, trends, distribution channels, relative quality of competitive products, competitive prices, promotion activity, and any other significant marketing factors, such as consumer habits and opinions.

The internal situation includes the present product quality, price structure, sales level, profit picture, marketing history, marketing budget, etc., or, briefly, what is available with which to work both inside and outside the company.

The next step is to realistically establish the financial, sales, and marketing goals. Follow this with the strategy—a program, plan, or policy for each marketing-advertising factor, such as product, package, price, promotion, copy theme, media, publicity, testing, etc.

Who Prepares the Plan?

This is a subject of growing debate and will be for some years ahead.

When formalized marketing planning first began to grow in popularity, it was usually assigned to the advertising agencies, possibly on the basis that here were thinkers, writers, and people familiar with the marketing problems, programs, and results in many companies. Furthermore, agencies often offered higher salaries and attracted particularly well-qualified persons.

More recently, advertisers have been importing able marketing planners and taking over the planning function. The feeling here is that no one knows the company's strengths, weaknesses, problems, opportunities, and available tools as well as members of that company. This is probably true, no matter how closely the agency or marketing consultants may work with the firm. However, sound and effective plans can be produced either way, by the company or by the agency.

The best system is to decide, between the two groups, which one is better qualified and let that group prepare the initial plan. Then permit the other group to review and suggest revisions to it. But always, in the last analysis, the final responsibility for the plan and for the results must rest with the company.

When the plan is prepared within the agency, it should be drafted by the account executive or an able assistant. This plan then is reviewed by the account supervisor, agency head, plans board, and/or marketing people before it is presented to the client company.

When the plan is prepared by the company, it should be drafted by the marketing manager or the staff, then reviewed by top management before being sent to the agency for comment.

A. THE SITUATION .... (Summary of market facts)	History ... past and recent ... of product and market. Business sources ... sizes, trends, opinions, problems, opportunities.
B. THE OBJECTIVES	Sales, profits, market share, distribution, image ... by year. Short range. Long range.
C. THE STRATEGY..........	Basic statement ... one-page summary of all strategies. Strategy for product ... improvements. Packages. Selling ... training. Pricing. Promotions. Sampling. Advertising. Copy theme. Media scheduling. Publicity. Theme. Projects. Schedule. Market research. Data needs. Plan. Schedule. Finance. Sales. Costs. Profits. Timetable. Market testing. Cities. Costs. Strategy. Results.

Plan adjustment almost invariably is necessary, with differences of opinion as to various elements of the plan. If the fact-gathering process is done carefully and thoroughly, the conflicts on the situation section are rare. The objectives section is also usually an area of easy agreement and most groups concur on the desirable.

It is the strategy, or methods area, that brings the most conflict. Members of both groups are likely to have their own concepts. Rarely can each element of the plan be assessed on an accurate, quantitative scale.

The best management policy is to use every effort to maintain an open-minded, common sense approach, weighing and judging all data objectively and impartially, yet still holding firmly to any strong feelings and beliefs. This is most essential.

Agency and company personnel often do themselves and their companies a disservice by giving in too quickly on their own strong convictions, particularly when these are backed with good evidence, facts, and/or experience. However, there is such a thing as "holding on too long." So, in the interest of progression and internal harmony, a compromise must eventually be reached. Ultimate decisions will be made through a *combination* of data, logic, and personal conviction.

Elements of the campaign strategy within the plan are applications of the available factors (such as products, salespeople, management, and money), plus the intangibles (*ideas* on products, promotions, selling themes, etc.) toward reaching the agreed-upon objectives in light of the situation facing the planner and executives. This means using available tools to reach a goal in spite of, or because of, prevailing problems. A major element of the campaign strategy is the development of a program that delivers a strong selling message to the right prospect at the right time.

Some executives tend to believe that all the marketing strategy needed is to lay out an advertisement and run it. This may have been true at one time, and still exists in relatively undeveloped, inefficient marketing situations. However, to reach the basic common objective of maximizing results per dollar invested, the plan must represent a thorough, comprehensive integration of dozens of marketing elements, such as package types, pricing, product, promotion, copy themes and slogans, display signs, print, mail, outdoor, radio, TV advertising, media selection, strategic scheduling for seasons and holidays, sampling, sales training, public relations, testing, and many elements *within* these elements.

The initial plan document may or may not include copy and visuals of proposed advertisements. However, these usually follow after the basic document has been reviewed.

"Selling" the Plan. When the ads and promotional material have been prepared, an extremely effective step, and one too often ignored by smaller or less successful marketing groups, is to prepare a flipchart version of the campaign. This should be used for presentation to management groups and key elements of the distribution channel: major retailers, chains, wholesalers, brokers, and salespeople. In this way, these key groups see and grasp the whole plan and are then more likely to become interested in it and support it.

Feedback and Adjustment. As the campaign is executed, feedback of results, opinions, problems, acceptance, sales into retail, sales out of retail, and other similar information should be stimulated to flow through sales reps, dealers, brokers, and other members of the distribution system to the marketing management. This flow should not only be encouraged, but the marketing manager should be ready, willing, and able to act when action is indicated.

The role of management is to handle available capital to provide a satisfactory return to the stockholders. As personal selling for the manufacturer is limited to action with wholesalers or retailers, management must rely on the marketing-campaign to win consumer acceptance and preference for his brand. This effort usually concentrates on convincing the consumer that the product provides more satisfaction per dollar than does a competitive product.

But the cost of marketing is rarely cheap. One ad can cost $50,000. The primary role of management in the marketing campaign is to select, balance, and shape each element to produce maximum profit for each dollar invested.

Two common management errors are (1) failure to recognize that maximizing sales does not necessarily maximize profits or return on investment, if costs are excessive; and (2) the marketing campaign must maximize *both* long- and short-term profits. A "fast killing" in the short run can destroy a firm's long-run prospects, but collapse in the short run may mean that there will be no long run.

The Role of the Retailer. It may come as a surprise to most manufacturers that retailers will normally do almost nothing to sell one brand over another, unless they have some incentive. A typical dealer comment is: "I really don't care how good your product is. What are you going to do to move it off those shelves?" Unit movement is the major source of profits. Given sufficient incentive, the dealer *can* greatly stimulate movement off shelves by special display and advertising. Because of the sharp growth of larger retailers, dealer support can often spell the difference between product success and failure.

There are two solutions to the dealer incentive problem. The first is alerting him or her to the details of the marketing campaign, covering such factors as special pricing, sampling, new packaging, new product features, publicity, contests, as well as advertising in an interesting, perhaps flip-chart form, especially designed for presentation to the dealer (this can and *has* resulted in strong dealer support). Secondly, there are retailer deals, offers, cash incentives, contest sharing, co-op advertising, or display purchasing, particularly if part of a strong, complete, initial marketing campaign that can be very effective dealer incentives.

Thereafter, dealer support (display) depends on movement out of retail, not on fancy plans.

Factors in campaign success are:

- Value . . . a real or apparent, favorable price/quality ratio.
- Product availability (distribution).
- Strong, clear, motivating promotions and/or advertising, in tune with market conditions, with sufficient reach and frequency to affect the market.
- A marketing investment that is in reasonable ratio to the market size, competition, and sales objective.
- A situation in which receipt of a marketing message is likely to have some influence on a prospective customer.

Ideally, all of these factors have been tested and are found to be present with results of the program known and measured. The degree to which these factors do *not* exist is the degree to which the campaign is likely to *not* maximize profits in relation to the investment made.

It is a common amateur misconception that advertising can sell anything, including shoddy products. This happens on rare occasions, but more usually it does not.

There is a saying in marketing circles that a good advertising campaign will put a poor product out of business faster than a poor advertising campaign simply because more people will try the product and the dissatisfaction will spread faster.

Reader Benefit, Opportunity, and Reward. A great income opportunity faces the marketing individual of today. This opportunity grows out of the presence of a marketing problem, a problem that *can* be solved and can bring benefit to those who solve it.

Only a small percentage of today's marketing-advertising personnel has much understanding of marketing-campaign planning and execution. Yet, in the face of this fact, there is an increasing demand for just such knowledge by hundreds of major advertisers, plus hundreds of advertising agencies. The result of such a demand has been a series of individual efforts by marketers to set up their own version of a marketing campaign outline. Some of these are good and workable. Most, at best, are incomplete. At worst, they are naive, unrealistic, and neither good selling nor planning tools.

The opportunity for reward lies in the mastery of marketingcampaign planning and execution, a fairly complex activity, but easily grasped by people of reasonable intelligence. Those who grasp and apply these procedures can make an important contribution to building company sales.

The purpose of this chapter, then, is to summarize the key marketing-campaign elements. These elements are almost never covered in this particular practical manner by current texts, not because the authors are not learned and diligent, but simply because not many have had any *actual* experience at meeting the demand for a good return on the marketing dollar invested.

We do not attempt to cover basics of advertising, typography, or creative copy development, or sales management functions such as selection, training, and motivation of salespeople. We concentrate on broad-scale marketing campaigns from a business management's standpoint of research, planning, and execution to make a marketing investment develop a profit.

Before the actual presentation of a campaign document, two objectives should be accomplished within the plan:

- to provide a written program for maximizing the return on the marketing investment; and
- to show good evidence to management, who may also be major stockholders, that this campaign is a truly sound proposal and a good investment.

A major part of both objectives is achieved when the plan is thorough, comprehensive, orderly, logical, and easy to read and understand. There is a danger of dogmatic "must-do" outlines that force each campaign into the same mold. No single form is ideal for all campaigns, just as no single architectural plan is ideal for all buildings. But there is a difference between form and content. All good architectural plans will account for certain important key factors, and these are usually many in number. An architect or a marketing planner will often work from a checklist of several hundred items. Even the top-flight professionals sometimes forget a critical item.

It is difficult here to define "critical." What may seem insignificant at the planning stage may become vital as the program is executed. This is perhaps the best rationale for being somewhat more thorough, comprehensive, detailed, and calculating as to content than many informal planners usually are. The format should be indefinite and flexible. It should be adapted to the specific needs and prevailing circumstances of market and product. However, some general formats work well for nearly all plan documents. Thus good plans for selling steel pipelines to engineers, drugs to physicians, soft drinks to teenagers, or hamburger rolls to mothers are likely to differ widely in content, but not nearly so radically in format, subject, and points covered. The outline for a marketing campaign suggested in this chapter is just such a flexible form that it may be used for many products.

Basically, there is only one good criterion for both format and content . . . will it do the job with maximum or near maximum efficiency?

Sources for the outline recommended were campaign courses taught at some of the major graduate business schools, campaign formats and contents used by leading management consultants, principal advertisers and major agencies, all conducted in recent years. More important, the best elements of these plans have been consolidated into this outline and found to be highly effective in scores of actual marketing programs on widely varying product types in the United States and Canada.

Preparatory Data. Considerable research and fact-gathering are advisable and usually essential before a sound plan can be constructed. One of the most frequent errors is to initiate vast projects with only half the pertinent data. At best, this leads to error-ridden plans that are executed with resultant inefficient use of capital and low return on investment, or plans that must be redone. At worst, this can lead to an abortive campaign with serious loss of invested funds.

One good method for obtaining data for the agency and marketing group is to circulate a letter to all concerned listing data needed, names of people who should have this information, and stating due dates.

The data that should be available includes the following items:

Product data, specific products to be advertised, current packaging sizes and prices. An accurate, objective assessment should be made of product quality, relative to competition. While this is obviously a key factor, unfortunately it is often painful and so is ignored. Competitive product types, prices, promotions, advertising themes, and investment volumes are certainly pertinent. Yet, these are subjects that planners often do not bother to learn thoroughly or accurately even though these data are relatively easy to secure.

Distribution levels of the product and of competitive products are significant facts. They will definitely affect the goals and the strategies to be planned.

The new market facts that should be gathered include market size in actual, annual, and retail dollars; the market potential if all valid prospects purchased the item; and the market trend in dollar and percentage changes in recent years. The planner should have at least some understanding and preferably a keen insight into prospect and dealer opinions, likes and dislikes relative to the product, packaging, and company, as compared to competition. Consumer readership of past advertising on this or similar products and their opinion of various-purposed ads can be very helpful in preparing the basic theme as well as an advertising and media plan.

The customer, of course, is king, queen, president and boss . . . all rolled into one! He or she is usually a soft-spoken despot who will simply ignore a product, package, or marketing program that he or she dislikes. Attempts to force the despot to accept something that he or she has repeatedly rejected are frequent marketing errors that can result in sharply reducing returns on the marketing investment.

A deliberate forcing upstream against prospect preference will sell some products, but it is unlikely to sell enough to pay all marketing and product expenses and still leave a satisfactory profit. Even well-conceived plans often fail, contrary to the belief of most beginners. Ill-conceived programs have little chance of success.

Background or historical data are very useful in preparing an effective campaign, just as knowing the strengths, weaknesses, victories, and defeats of an army helps in designing future strategy. The planner should check past sales and profit history, the most successful and least successful programs, past market-test results, historic channels of distribution, problems, opportunities, and alternatives.

Objectives should be spelled out for short term and long term—for sales, profit, distribution, brand, and company image. These may not be final objectives. Initial or preliminary ones are often unrealistically conservative or excessively optimistic, but they do form a very useful "going-in" hypothesis, a sort of "where-we-would-like-to-end-up-if-at-all-feasible" statement.

Strategy sections should now spell out just what is to be done to *reach* objectives. This should include any proposals for more market or product research, product or package or price changes, promotions to be used, selling themes, media, dealer and salesperson incentives, publicity, financial plans, testing programs, etc.

Thoroughness is essential and the lack of it is a grave error in most marketing campaigns, reducing return on marketing investment. The planners no doubt can think of other factors that should be covered in addition to those just mentioned. The specific situation will probably suggest these, particularly any trouble spots to be remedied.

The main point here is that the planner should check every conceivable aspect that can influence the success of the campaign. Frequent plan and procedural errors have already been pointed out. Lack of thoroughness is the worst error. This is caused mainly by insufficient training, but partly by a strange belief, common with amateur planners, that no one is really going to read the plan very carefully; instead, it will simply be rubber-stamped into existence. Nothing could be further from the truth. Every page and every sentence are read and reread by several, perhaps a dozen, seasoned agency and advertiser executives who have seen many plans before and know where to look for errors. Every single point may be questioned to be certain that the proper reasoning and evidence supports the proposal.

Planners frequently forget that the campaign often involves a heavy financial investment. The job security of several managers, including the planner, may depend on the success of the plan. That alone is good reason for checking it thoroughly and for making it a complete, careful, and well-conceived plan in the first place. When planners say "The campaign was shot down in flames," they usually mean that a number of errors were found that made the plan unacceptable. These may be poorly developed concepts, but more often are errors of omission.

Sequence of events should be understood in preparing the document since this can save effort by avoiding false starts. A step that is taken out of order can be a waste of time because later steps may negate it. The typical sequence is:

1. A decision is made by the advertiser that a marketing campaign plan is needed. A tentative marketing budget should be designed at this point unless circumstances suggest that more information should be obtained first. If the agency is to play a partnership role in the planning, as assumed here, it should now be notified.
2. A preliminary data list and marketing campaign outline should now be prepared and a planning meeting held with key people, those

immediately involved, to review this list and outline and obtain suggestions for changes with general agreement on such changes.

3. At this point, facts should be collected. When the agency personnel have completed their data requirements, or reasonably so considering budget and time limits, they should say so and present a plan for getting any remaining essential data. Here is another point of weakness. Agency personnel rarely wish to risk displeasing the client by asking for more time and more spending prior to preparing the plan, even though sometimes this might be a wise investment. So they often hastily gather what data are conveniently available and proceed with insufficient information. This is not to the ultimate good of either the advertiser or the agency. Sound client and agency executives usually can discuss the situation and decide on a time extension. Any necessary additional data should now be obtained.
4. Now the preliminary plan should be prepared following the approved outline. When completed it should be reviewed, page by page, by the marketing group. Ideally, copies should be made available to all concerned, at least a day or two prior to the review meeting. Changes should be made in the plan wherever the meeting chairman believes them to be necessary.
5. At last the final plan can be prepared. This may require only minor changes to the preliminary plan, or an extensive re-do with major changes in each section.
6. It is time then for the final plan to be approved with perhaps minor changes. The planner should note also that unlike an architectural plan, which should be executed precisely as drawn, the marketing plan is often subject to change to a greater or lesser degree as plans proceed and market circumstances indicate.
7. Now the various parts of the plan can be put into action by appropriate marketing groups, with a system for feeding back data established and making adjustments or revisions when advisable.

The proper, constructive attitude by all parties can result in rapid preparation of highly effective marketing campaigns. This attitude can develop a "go-go" and "can-do" spirit that not only brings out the best talent in those involved, but can lead to that extra effort, extra thought, and very special extra spark that is frequently the difference between mediocrity and supreme excellence.

Common and expensive errors by marketing directors are to give the planner too much direction, too many restrictions, too little time to gather facts and make plans, and too little patience to hear out the plans and the rationale. Such actions tend to sharply reduce the return on the marketing investment.

Obviously, the whole sequence is a matter of give and take. For each step and element, there should be only one basic criterion: *Is this a sound decision for maximizing progress toward the established goal, with the available budget?* Logic, a good attitude, and sound judgment must prevail. In the final analysis, much depends on the planner's willingness and ability to understand the situation and to prepare efficient and effective strategies for reaching the approved objectives. Perhaps of even greater importance is the planner's ability to see this talent in others.

A common error that planners make is to treat the program investment rather lightly or superficially. An excellent method of avoiding this is for the planner to take the attitude that it is *his* or *her* money, *his* or *her* investment, and *his* or *her* time that are at stake, and to a substantial degree that is usually true.

The writing style should be very short, terse, and telegraphic. Absolutely no unnecessary words should be used. Never take ten words to say what can be said in five. Readers are usually very busy and time is at a premium. They will appreciate brevity.

Mechanically, the marketing campaign document is usually 10 to 50 pages, double-spaced, typewritten, mimeographed, and bound in a paper cover. Since most good plans cover from 50 to 200 items, they are not likely to be less than 10 pages, except for small individual portions of an annual marketing plan, such as a two-month special in-store promotion of one-package size.

A flip-chart presentation summarizing and highlighting the plan can be an effective tool just prior to distributing the final document. The advantages are that it tends to sell the overall plan to the group. It can visualize, explain, and tie the whole program together. This is particularly useful when the plan is involved and must be presented to many associated executives who cannot spend the time to read the document thoroughly. Also, it can help develop agreement on basic concepts and allow objective and open discussion, which is not as easy to do when working from the typed document.

The flip-chart presentation is also good when there is strong need to cover certain key points, hold to a given sequence or pattern, and avoid getting held up on details, or when there is danger that listeners' attention will lag. Viewers will watch and listen with interest, particularly when the presentation moves along briskly, with about one chart every 10 to 40 seconds.

On the other hand, many careful executives tend to be a bit skeptical of the flip-chart, considering it to be something of a forced-feeding, stampeding, or pressure device that is more appropriate for giving what otherwise might be confusing instructions (such as management might do with salespeople), than for presenting a proposal that may be shot through with errors, omissions, inaccuracies, and poor logic. These errors may go by largely unrecognized if the presentation is made so rapidly that the audience has little time for thought on each item. Also, it can give individuals the often false impression that audience silence means agreement. Some executives are reluctant to disagree with a chart. The result can be that the plan is challenged less than it ought to be. The net analysis of flip-chart presentation: a good tool for the presenter but one that the audience should view with care and not hesitate to question wherever it may seem advisable to do so.

SUGGESTIONS FOR FURTHER READING

Chip R. Bell, *The Marketing of Change* (Austin, TX: Learning Concepts, 1982).

Martin L. Bell, *Marketing: Concepts and Strategy* (Boston: Houghton-Mifflin Company, 1979).

Jay Diamond and Gerald Pintel, *Principles of Marketing* (Englewood Cliffs, NJ: Prentice-Hall, Inc. 1980).

Tom Eisenhart, "Carving Out a Trade Show Niche with TV Spots," *Business Marketing*, July 1992, p. 42.

Carrie Goerne, "Business Marketers Find Increased Success as They Turn to Direct Mail," *Marketing News*, July 6, 1992, pp. 3, 5.

Jan Jaben, "Finding a Happy Medium," *Business Marketing*, July 1992, pp. 40–41.

John Sinisi, "KGF's New Dressing," *Brandweek*, September 28, 1992, pp. 10–15.

Keith Fletcher
Professor of Business Administration
Strathclyde University Graduate School of
Business
Glasgow, Scotland

Alan Crawley
Senior Consultant
Price Waterhouse
New York, New York

CHAPTER 26

INFORMATION TECHNOLOGY IN MARKETING AND SALES

INTRODUCTION

Information technology (IT) has three main strands—computing, microelectronics, and telecommunications—that are combined to provide a wide variety of products and services. The UK Department of Industry definition of IT is the "acquisition, processing, storage and dissemination of vocal, pictorial, textual and numeric information by a microelectronics-based combination of computing and telecommunications."

Such a wide definition clearly incorporates many diverse industries and products, and IT will therefore be used by most managers in one form or another. Its most well-known business application is in the field of office automation where major changes have taken place over the last ten years. These changes frequently have provided the impetus for other changes within the organization.

While IT is sometimes narrowly seen as computer hardware or information systems, it includes much more than these two important elements. Information networks, on-line databases, and expert systems are all now becoming relevant to managers, but other products and services such as fax machines, mobile telephones, cable and satellite television, facilities for electronic banking and payment at point of sale, and automatic article identification at warehouses and supermarkets all spring from a common technological base and have the potential to change drastically the way a firm operates.

IT is thus not just a collection of new products and services but a new way of conducting industrial, commercial, educational, and administrative business. It has been predicted that IT will affect every household and occupation, changing patterns of employment, lifestyles, and spending patterns and creating new jobs and markets.

As with most office-based functions, the way in which the marketing tasks are performed is also likely to change with the introduction of the new technology.

Marketing is concerned with customer relationships, and IT is having a major impact in this area by changing both the nature of the relationship and the balance of power. Marketing is concerned with satisfying customers' needs by providing products and services that give benefits the customers value. IT allows new benefits and enhanced value to be incorporated into products and services. In industries like insurance and banking, effective use of information technology can provide very clear and distinct competitive advantages with the IT infrastructure providing a solid technological foundation around which the organization can function.

In the UK, we are seeing a further technological revolution in retail banking, with every aspect of its operation becoming more and more dependant on IT. Much of this is directed at understanding customers, their needs, and the relationship they want with the bank and finding improved mechanisms and methods for managing this relationship. Finally, marketing is concerned with communicating to the market through advertising media and direct marketing, and IT is changing the channels and methods available to do this. The practice of marketing thus needs to be studied to ensure that the firm is conducting its activities in the most efficient and effective manner.

Marketing is also concerned with defining and managing the interface between the firm and its markets. The way in which these markets change, the opportunities and threats created in the environment, and the developments in the marketing system and infrastructure are important as they affect the exchange relationships between suppliers, manufacturers, intermediaries, retailers, and customers. They are all therefore external factors of relevance to the marketing department. It is an essential aspect of a marketing manager's job to monitor these changes and to ensure that the correct strategic position is adopted, as well as modifying the marketing mix as necessary.

The ease with which an effective internal and external appraisal can be conducted has changed as the quality and sophistication of information systems have improved. The development of powerful but cheap personal computers (PCs) has encouraged individual managers to become users, and "user-friendly" software, such as that pioneered by the Apple Macintosh, has created a new breed of computer users who interact directly with databases rather than through computer intermediaries. This, more than anything else, has encouraged managers to consider how IT could improve their own effectiveness and efficiency.

The new generation of user-friendly computers is empowering middle managers to carry out sophisticated analyses with relative ease and improve the quality and speed of important decision making. For instance, a major European pharmaceutical company is currently investing in information systems designed to minimize the time required to develop and launch new products. With development times of 10–12 years, even a two-year reduction can provide considerable competitive advantage in a market where the first or second to launch a new product dominates.

There is thus a key role for personal computers in achieving corporate goals. The ability of managers to make informed, quality decisions is enabled through the use of IT.

The introduction of computers into selling is not a new development. Many of the problems of sales management appear well suited to quantitative and hence frequently computer solutions. The determination of optimum sales force size, size and structure of territories, and sales quotas have all been achieved using computer models. Other packages have been written to aid the selling process by developing customer targets and call norms, allocating time between customers, precall planning, and qualifying leads. As selling has increased in sophistication it has become increasingly marketing oriented, taking a longer-term view of profits and considering the longer-term satisfaction of customers, rather than immediate sales targets. There is thus no need, particularly with business-to-business selling, to attempt to move the potential customer through all the stages of the purchase decision in one "hard sell" presentation. If the aim is to build long-term sales relationships, then IT can be used at each stage to support the sales activities.

This concept of proactively managing customer relationships can be seen in the activities of a major UK telecommunications company that has invested considerable amounts of money in the development of telephone account management for their small- and medium-sized business accounts. The principle is straightforward. The company has a very large customer base and a sales force that is unable to service all customers adequately.

The sales force can be directed at larger accounts while telephone account managers can proactively develop and manage relationships with a very large number of smaller accounts. Although individually they represent low volumes of equipment and network sales, taken together they are worth many hundreds of millions of dollars in sales.

Effective use of information technology has enabled the company to unlock the massive potential that lay dormant for so long. Perhaps even more important is the capability to defend market share in a sector that is subject to increasingly aggressive competition during a period of rapid market deregulation.

Computer-generated mailshots, or advertising aimed at obtaining literature requests, will help generate leads helping to avoid the need for cold calling. A personalized follow-up letter, information sheet, or brochure will help stimulate interest and a telemarketer call can help prepare the ground for the actual contact.

At the actual presentation, portable videos and other audiovisual equipment are increasingly being used, such as compact daylight viewers/projectors for slide-based presentations. These are now often the size of a briefcase, they have remote control, and they have high-definition screens at a low cost.

The combination of lower prices and high power of micros encouraged Ciba-Geigy Pharmaceuticals to supply BBC B Micros to its sales force to be used in conjunction with printed promotional support materials and videos. The software program was mainly educational and provided a focus for the discussion and later sales presentation. Philips Lighting and British Gas similarly bought Hewlett Packard portable computers for their sales engineers to take on building sites. The machines were programmed to allow the salesperson to produce a quotation on site, without the need for a 24-hour delay while design and support staff were consulted. The software was designed to prompt the salesperson to ask for all relevant information and provide the quotation while interest was still high. Many other organizations have cut the time between the salesperson stimulating desire and being able to initiate action by allowing sales details of the visit to be entered directly onto a portable. The information can then be transmitted back to the company in the evening via a modem and home telephone. The central computer automatically accepts the data, allowing overnight updating of records and transaction checks. After a sale is made, the computer also contributes to the cultivation of long-term customer relationships and hence repeat and cross-selling opportunities. A computerized record system therefore allows the company to maintain customer loyalty and satisfaction and contribute to future sales activities.

The use of the computer in sales should not be seen simply as a method of increasing efficiency with the sole aim of reducing costs. Instead they should be used as a long-term investment in competitive advantage, allowing the sales force to be more effective in the sales situation while also allowing a much closer customer relationship. An example of the way in which IT can "lock" in third-party distributors is found in the motor finance industry.

Finance houses will partially fund computers and software for motor dealers. Facilities enable dealers to rapidly process finance applications and speed up payment of commissions. This has a beneficial effect for the finance house of creating a barrier to switching from one finance house to another. Information technology provides the basis of a mutually beneficial and profitable relationship.

ISSUES AND PROBLEMS IN INFORMATION USE

It has been said that "to manage a business well is to manage its future, and to manage the future is to manage information." This point has been emphasized by Liam Strong, director of marketing and operations for British Airways, who stated,

> *You know your competitors have the same information as you do, so the issue becomes how you use it. IT becomes a question of speed, skill, and understanding. It is not a question of information being power. It is about analysis and how you use it to integrate the business.*

Information is increasingly being seen as a strategic resource, and as such the business justification for investing in IT is changing. In the 1970s and 1980s, information was regarded as an administrative tool to be used for such automated functions as accounting, inventory control, and payroll. As companies begin to use information strategically, by integrating information systems strategy with a company's business and marketing strategy, managers need to make a conceptual transition from data to information, to information as a resource, to information as a competitive weapon (Synott 1987).

However, a number of studies have suggested that firms are not ready to make this transition. A 1983 study of leading firms in UK industry (based on similar United States research by Cox, Good, and Amstutz) found that only 54 percent of the firms claimed to have a marketing information system and that UK firms lagged behind the United States. It was also clear that the systems that did exist had a very low level of analytical and computational ability and were often used purely for storage and retrieval (Fletcher 1983). A 1990 survey by Price Waterhouse found that firms were still oriented to "back office" benefits of cost savings and coping with increased data, although this was declining, and it predicted that in the future greater attention would be paid to "front office" applications such as defense of existing customers and expansion of business through IT-enabled strategy, product improvements, etc. (Price Waterhouse 1990). Price Waterhouse noted, however, that while marketing applications—particularly of a strategic nature—were predicted to rise, a number of problems were likely to hinder this trend.

A major problem identified of relevance to marketing was the difficulty of integrating IT plans with corporate plans. Brancheau and Wetherbe (1987) had earlier noted that the top-ranked issue facing information managers was strategic planning, followed by competitive advantage and other studies have confirmed the importance of integrating these two areas of IT and strategic marketing planning. Oasis, a UK IT consultant firm, reported research findings that 75 percent of managers were dissatisfied with the management of marketing information caused by the lack of integrated systems and data control. Those firms most successful in managing marketing information were oriented first to strategy, second to information needs, and last to technology (Oasis 1989). They also found that poor communication and a low level of respect between marketing and IT departments was disrupting joint operations. A later Oasis survey investigated the main obstacles in helping marketing exploit IT potential more fully (necessary for the transition to front-office strategic applications), and found a high level of agreement between marketing and IT managers (Exhibit 1).

The study also noted an increasing trend toward creating mechanisms for joint planning between marketing and the IT department, which should go some way to resolving the problem, identified in the Price Waterhouse survey, of integrating IT with corporate plans.

A recent study in a major UK telecommunications company investigating the use of IT in marketing corroborated the OASIS findings and identified further impediments to the use of IT in marketing.

EXHIBIT 1. Management of Marketing Information

What are the main obstacles in helping marketing exploit IT potential more fully?

	IT Manager	Marketing Manager	Joint
1 Poor appreciation at board level of potential	1	2	1
2 Poor training for marketing staff in IT	3	1	2
3 Difficulty justifying major IT expenditure on strategic grounds	2	4	3
4 Poor understanding of marketing requirements by IT Department	4	3	4
5 Hardware/software shortcomings	5	6	5
6 Lack of vehicle for joint IT/marketing planning	6	7	6
7 Rapid pace of technological change	8	5	7
8 Rapid pace of change in competitive environment	7	8	8

Source: Oasis 1990.

The problem of "competition for functional responsibility" was cited as a cause of dissipation of data between different functions as well as duplication of development efforts. In this case, the finance department saw itself as the logical and obvious place to develop a customer-oriented information system. Marketing sales and corporate planning all disagreed.

The point is of course that an information system should support all those key functions with information covering all aspects of the customer's relationship with the company.

A further problem was the lack of a cohesive and integrated model of marketing. In the absence of a clear vision of marketing within a wider business system, IT for marketing has resulted in a series of diffuse and fragmented systems that fail to provide the necessary support for managers.

This feature has been recognized as a fundamental shortcoming of post-IT marketing developments, and now the company invests considerably more time understanding the detailed business processes from which IT requirements can be identified.

They recognize that databases in themselves cannot offer any real solutions. System functionality *and* data must fit with business strategy, management approach, and processes if real and sustained benefits are to be realized.

Gibson and Nolan (1974) suggested EDP growth would go through a life cycle of initiation, contagion, control, and maturity which seems to have gained wide acceptance, and others have adapted this model for electronic office information systems and IT (Earl 1989). Earl suggests that the S curves of learning seem to be repeated for the new technologies but that some of the curves seem to be much shorter than those for the more complex technologies. As firms are likely to locate themselves on different stages of the different technology curves, the problem for IT managers of integrating and managing the technology is great. There is a need to build bridges between the different technologies and their applications as many strategic applications will be based on visionary use of integrated technologies (Earl 1990).

INFORMATION PROVISION AND IT

The provision of customer-related information should be one duty of marketing information systems, yet the conclusion from the research suggests that the majority of firms have not reached a sufficient level of sophistication in their general market and information acquisition and usage to allow them to benefit from data-based marketing. Information systems tend to follow a hierarchy (Sprague and Watson 1979) with low-level electronic data processing (EDP) systems being the first stage. An EDP system would have a basic data processing function with no common database. It could classify, sort, add, and delete information and thus act as an electronic filing cabinet. Next comes an integrated data processing system where users can access information from different sources. If this includes a marketing database, rather than simply financial and sales figures, and has the ability to analyze data and run simple models, then it enters the marketing information system (MIS) of the hierarchy. At the peak are decision support systems (DSS) or strategic information systems (SIS) that, as the name implies, are capable of aiding the decision maker in making strategic decisions, and as such require sophisticated software, decision models, and information flows.

The ideal marketing information system thus differs from lower-level systems in that the database being collected is transformed into information relevant to decisions the marketer has to make. The role of analysis is therefore critical in affecting this transformation. The marketing information must provide software and functionality to enable analysis to take place. These decisions themselves tend to be of different types, ranging from the simple structured decisions involved in controlling the marketing function (such as checking sales trends, salespeople quotas, etc.), to the much more unstructured, qualitative decisions relating to strategic planning.

At the strategic planning level, executives are making decisions as to which markets to attack, the nature of competition and competitive advantage, as well as allocating resources to allow the firm to position itself effectively. The information to aid strategic planning decisions therefore tends to be qualitative, general, future oriented, and externally focused. Information for control purposes will tend to be quantitative, detailed, past and present oriented, and internally focused. An information system for marketing purposes should therefore be capable of handling all types of data and analytical requirements.

Technology that can facilitate data acquisition, processing, and communication is therefore a key management concern. The cost of these activities has, in the past, been a justifiable excuse for many firms who did not want to invest in an information system. Today, however, due to developments in IT and deregulation of telecommunications, these constraints have been reduced, if not removed. The developments of local and wide area networks means it is no longer meaningful to talk about information processing and communications as independent activities. The roles of computing and communications are so entwined that their business value depends on the total system (Hammer and Manqurian, 1987).

The provision of huge external databases that are easily accessible and do not have geographic constraints has created opportunities for even the smallest firm. The reluctance of industry to adopt this technology and make use of value-added data services (VADS) provoked the UK government, in association with British industry, to launch VANGUARD in 1986. This was a consortium of sponsors, Department of Trade and Industry (DTI), the Telecommunications Managers Association, and the IT Users Standards Association, whose main purpose was to promote the uptake of VADS in UK businesses (HMSO, 1988). VADS embraces a wide range of time- and cost-saving facilities for transferring information electronically rather than on paper. It is typically categorized into electronic data interchange (EDI), electronic mail (E-mail), and on-line information services.

It is increasingly the case that it is what a company knows and how it manages this knowledge base, rather than its physical assets, that will determine its market value. The use of VADS is therefore more than just an aid to manipulating the marketing mix, but it is a strategic marketing resource. There are now over 4,000 commercially accessible on-line databases worldwide. These can be accessed through host organizations such as Lockheed Dialog, Datastart, IRS-Dialtech, SDC-Orbit, Pergamon-Infoline, and Datastream. The user, by means of a dial-up telecommunication link to a remote computer, interactively searches the database using key words or questions. The output can be displayed on the terminal or printed out as necessary.

The information providers (IPs) are made up of organizations such as publishers, trade associations, governments, and commercial organizations such as Reuters, Dow Jones, Financial Times, Dun & Bradstreet, etc. They gain the benefit of being able to continually update their material in a way that is not possible with printed copy. Marketing managers can therefore check for the most recent research or information to help their decision making, without the delay this would normally entail. Specialized databases exist that list published research and data on over 130 countries with forecasts, market trends, and industry comment.

The disadvantage of VADS to the firm is that there is an initial outlay of equipment and database charges for a connection fee and then additional charges for data obtained, which can make the search an expensive process and can cause an inexperienced user to incur high costs. This may encourage firms to put on-line access under the control of an information specialist, but the trend is toward "end-user" computing and distributed systems that allow the organization's members to gain experience and ensure the system meets the needs of the users rather than computing technicians.

At present, the main UK users of VADS are advertising agencies and retail organizations who wish to monitor specific markets through access to such things as Mintel, MEAL (Media Expenditure and Analysis Ltd), and BRAD (British Rate and Data) through MAGIC (Marketing and Advertising General Information Centre) and MAID (Media Analysis and Information Database). They also have the marketing sophistication required to make use of the information once it is acquired.

It is not possible for an organization lacking in marketing skills to gain them through the purchase of technology. If a firm does not know how to use a business information library to conduct an environmental analysis, then providing the information on-line will not bring any advantages. If a firm does not have a customer orientation, then its customer database will be little more than a mailing list.

While there are many examples of successful use of IT to gain competitive advantage, there are just as many examples of firms who have failed to gain the benefits expected from investing in IT.

The barriers to the successful use of information systems and IT have been noted by Kemerer and Sosa (1988). Often IT opportunities are not exploited due to a nonsupportive corporate environment, particularly when the benefits are qualitative or diffused throughout the organization as with decision support systems. The high initial investment in hardware, software, and training is beyond the reach of many companies, especially when the technology is at the leading edge and unproven.

For smaller companies, this may even extend to the use of personal computers for sales and marketing purposes and often reflects a fundamental lack of understanding of the benefits of IT in this area. Optimally managing customer relationships is as much, perhaps more, of a commercial imperative for small companies as it is for larger ones.

The difficulties created by the failure of technology to fulfill the salesperson's or vendor's promises can lead to major losses if the functioning of the organization is hindered, but most firms cannot afford to run duplicate systems until the bugs are removed. Kemerer and Sosa give the example of Federal Express Corporation of America, which was forced to stop its Zapmail electronic document transmission because of service after a plague of telecommunication equipment difficulties.

> *The telephone lines performed extremely poorly, and transmissions were slow and noisy, making repeat transmissions necessary. This of course caused Federal Express to incur large, unexpected costs. The company nevertheless decided to continue the project and upgrade it. They set up satellite transmission facilities at customer sites and installed rewritten software and more mainframe switching stations around the country. The company also had to request the use of a communications satellite. The FCC approved a satellite launch, but the Challenger Space Shuttle disaster caused the cost of satellites to "skyrocket" and their launching to be delayed. All of these problems contributed to Zapmail's failure, which in the end meant a $200 million loss for Federal Express.*
>
> *(Kemerer and Sosa 1988)*

Even after the IT idea has been successfully developed and implemented, other problems arise. It may be copied by competitors, as with ATMs, such that the competitive advantage is lost. The gains in this case may not last long enough to justify the investment, but if competitors use the idea themselves, the firm will still have to make the investment simply to catch up.

The system may often be much more expensive to maintain than initially predicted as maintenance, training, and enhancement costs are met. Indeed the very success of the system may cause problems as latent demand is unleashed, which makes the system oversubscribed almost immediately.

The design of an information system for marketing managers therefore requires an analysis of the uses to which it is to be put and the benefits a firm hopes to acquire. To make full use of the marketing opportunities that come from the application of IT, the focus should not simply be on the cost benefits available from greater efficiency, but on ways in which IT can be used to give a long-term, sustainable competitive advantage. This requires the marketing manager to consider the strategic role of IT.

IT AND MARKETING STRATEGY

IT is having an influence on the way in which marketing managers conduct their jobs through the availability of computers and software. These allow manipulation of data and better analysis of market conditions and demand. The provision of networks to transmit information regardless of the geographical distances involved, and at a fraction of the cost or time previously involved, has also created new opportunities both for suppliers and users of information.

EXHIBIT 2. The Three Levels of IT's Impact

Industry Level	
IT changes industry:	Products and services Markets Production economics
Firm Level	
IT affects key competitive forces:	Buyers Suppliers Substitution New entrants Rivalry
Strategy Level	
IT affects a firm's strategy:	Low-cost leadership Product differentiation Concentration on market or product niche

Source: Parsons, 1983.

Many firms, particularly in the United States, have realized that the investment in IT should be seen not simply as a corporate overhead to be absorbed as part of the cost of doing business, but as a competitive weapon in its own right. This requires senior managers to view IT not as a part of the infrastructure servicing the rest of the organization to be left to computer specialists, but as a strategic resource.

Marketing managers in financial services and other service-oriented companies are increasingly viewing their customer information systems as a corporate resource of strategic importance. IT helps unleash the real business potential of the customer base through the ability to identify important customer segments utilizing a wide range of data and implementing marketing programs specific to these clearly defined groups of customers.

A framework for studying the potential impact of IT on a firm's business has been provided by Parsons (1983). He suggests that senior management must understand how IT might impact the competitive environment and strategy of the business if they are to allocate sufficient resources to IT. The three areas he focuses on are industry level, firm level, and strategy level (Exhibit 2).

INDUSTRY-LEVEL IMPACT OF IT

At the industry level, IT changes the nature of the industry itself, shortening industry life cycles, changing the nature of the products and services, opening up new markets by erasing geographical limitations, and meeting emerging needs with new products and innovative services such as home banking. By changing the economics of production, as with the newspaper industry or the nature and efficiency of distribution, many traditional and fundamental assumptions within the industry must change. This macroenvironmental review is a major part of strategic planning and in some industries such as banking is likely to highlight substantial opportunities or threats created by IT. This has forced some firms to reevaluate their mission statement or definition of their business.

WHAT BUSINESS ARE WE IN?

One of the essential elements of the strategic process is the answer to the question "What business are we in?" This definition should then be used to guide the activities of the firm while making strategic choices. One of the consequences of IT is that it encourages, and in some cases forces, a redefinition of the firm's business. As IT allows institutions to offer new services, their traditional view of their business becomes increasingly restrictive. American Express reportedly views itself not as being in the financial services business but as being in the information business.

American Airlines is an example of a business that has gained a major competitive advantage by selling not only airline seats but information. In 1975, United Airlines offered to link travel agents directly into its Apollo booking system. American Airlines followed with SABRE, which had the added attraction of listing over 400 competitors' flights as well. Since virtually all America's travel agents book through computerized reservation systems and travel agents provide the majority of the airline business, any system that attracted them would potentially benefit the operating airline. In SABRE's case, the attraction for travel agents was that there was now no need to shop around for information since American Airlines provided it through its alphabetical listing of airlines. The fact that American Airlines, listed as AA, came first in the list and was thus most likely to be accessed for details of seat availability was a fortunate coincidence. As competitors offered their own systems, the American government was forced to step in and regulate the area, banning some of the more obvious bias. In a bid to attract the travel agents, the airlines improved their systems by including more information—this time on hotel reservations and car rental. The cost of these systems became a major barrier to entry since no airline could exist without access to one. Some decided it was cheaper to use SABRE than build their own, and with a charge for each booking, American Airlines recognized that what had started as an aid to efficiency could become a profit center and marketing tool in its own right. The reservation system allows airlines to recognize frequent fliers, identify traffic trends, and in minutes identify underbooked flights, allowing immediate marketing responses. The effectiveness of marketing tactics used to attract identified target segments can also easily be monitored, all at a fraction of the time and cost possible without the system. The UK airlines have their own system, Travicom, which links with the reservation systems of 49 different airlines, including BA's booking system Babs, with 97 percent of travel agents using it. In 1987, American Airlines objected to the merger of BA and British Caledonian (the owners of Travicom) alleging that B-Cal would stop issuing its tickets through SABRE, that Travicom was biased towards BA, and that B-Cal did not list U.S. rivals, making it difficult for AA to operate in the UK. BA also bought an 11 percent stake in Apollo, the United Airlines system, and the biggest competitor to SABRE, which brought accusations of unfair competition.

The trend seems to be for consortia to form to develop even more advanced reservation systems, and this has increased the pressure for an international code of conduct. What is clear is that to define a business in terms of the product or basic service being sold is an error since it restricts corporate vision.

It has been suggested (Abell 1980) that to specify what business a firm is in, a firm must look at three important areas. First, which customer groups are being satisfied? Second, which customer needs are being satisfied? Third, what technology is being employed to satisfy the customer?

The definition of *customer groups* tends to be a "What is at present" rather than a "What might be" question. Unless the customers have unique characteristics, in terms of geography, size, or other features that add to switching costs, then poaching by other firms is extremely likely. Similarly, with customer needs, competitive advantage can be gained by identifying an unmet need or by satisfying it to a greater degree than competitors, as did American Airlines. However, these gains are often transient. In the past, it has frequently been the third criterion, the differing technological base and experience of suppliers, which has allowed firms to identify their competitors and thus position themselves. The ubiquitous nature of IT has meant that previously unrelated industries are being brought together by a common technology, making even this criterion redundant. The boundary lines between the technology of information handling and transmission, telephone, newspapers, printing, photocopying, broadcasting, and computers, are decaying as IT develops. Facsimile machines now photocopy and transmit, telephones can be used to communicate between computers, electronic newspapers and video magazines are available, and cable networks link television sets and computers. Information is frequently a common denominator of many industrial practices and exchanges since telecommunications and computers link them all. A definition of a business must therefore be based not on what the supplier thinks is being sold, but what the customer thinks is being bought.

ELECTRONIC MARKETS

The potential benefits of IT include enhanced communication, increased efficiency in decision making, and better information flows. This allows the extension of markets across geographical and industrial boundaries and improved relationships between elements of the supply chain.

This can be seen in the creation of electronic markets where computer-to-computer buying and selling takes place. For computer-to-computer trading to take place, a common communications standard needs to exist, either as an industry standard or by the vendor providing the suitable software and equipment. The creation of an electronic market reduces inefficiencies and improves buyers' access to sellers while disseminating full, accurate, and immediate information. Electronic trading is not new, but the most recent development is the network of computer terminals allowing large numbers of people access to remote centralized markets. Perhaps one of the most well-known electronic markets is the buying and selling of stocks and shares. The 1987 stock market crash focused attention on the dangers of "program trading" where individual traders program their systems to automatically buy or sell shares when prices reach predetermined levels. It was suggested that this automatic selling contributed to the crash when computers themselves created a drop in prices, by their prior decisions, resulting in further automatic sell-offs. During this period of extreme volume and volatility, 9 of the 12 computer systems of the New York Stock Exchange broke down at some point, adding to the panic and confusion.

IT makes it so much easier to exchange information that it encourages the growth of geographically dispersed markets, as did its predecessors the telegraph and telephone. For each exchange to take place, a cost is incurred and the more exchanges that take place the greater the potential for cost savings. The customer benefit comes from making more advantageous matches between buyers and sellers. IT can help both buyer and seller link their needs more closely through a mutual understanding of product or service availability and customer needs. By the constant exchange of information, stocks can be reduced and delivery improved, giving benefits to both parties and improving the general efficiency of the market.

Malone et al. (1989) believe that this evolutionary computer-aided buying and selling will disrupt conventional marketing and distribution patterns. Those companies who use electronic markets wisely will emerge as winners in the competitive landscape. The losers are those who are unwittingly eliminated from the distribution chain and those who try to lock in customers through obsolete arrangements. They give an example of Teleaction, an electronic home shopping system launched by JC Penney in 1988, where customers can get detailed information about products by using a push-button phone. IBM and Sears have jointly created Prodigy, which is a home shopping and entertainment system that can be accessed through personal computers. The Comp-U-Card system involves buyers calling an operator to order a wide range of consumer goods listed in a database. Buyers can get information on products, and once an individual decides to buy an item, the system selects it at the lowest price and it is directly shipped and charged to the buyer. Comp-U-Store provides a similar service for computer users.

A further example is given by the Royal Bank of Scotland's Royline system. This provides remote access from a customer's premises to all that customer's bank accounts. The customer is able to make payments, move money between accounts, amend standing orders, and so on.

The principal advantage to the customer is that he or she has direct control of his or her banking and cash management facilities. In developing this facility the Bank has considerably improved the levels of customer service in the important small business sector.

The system utilizes several aspects of IT, computers, and telecommunications to deliver a service based on electronic trading which delivers real competitive benefits to the Bank.

FIRM LEVEL IMPACT OF IT

The second level of Parsons's three-level impact of IT focuses on the firm itself. Porter (1985) describes five basic competitive forces that determine a firm's profitability and the nature of competition. These are

1. the threat of new entrants;
2. the threat of substitute products or services;
3. the bargaining power of suppliers;
4. the bargaining power of buyers; and
5. rivalry among existing firms.

Munro and Huff (1985) have shown how IT has the power to change these competitive forces as shown in Exhibit 3.

Many of the potential changes brought about by IT require the cooperation of suppliers, buyers, or the intermediaries supporting the firm's interaction with buyers, and these change the complex relationship between the participants. This can affect relative bargaining power in negotiations over price, product, and other decisions during the exchange process.

EXHIBIT 3. Competitive Forces and Potential Impact of IT

Force	IT Potential
Buyers	Buyer power is reduced by increasing switching costs to buyers—for example, linking technology systems with home banking, computer-to-computer ordering, locking in buyers.
Suppliers	Supply chain management by retailers and JIT manufacturing systems demand much more from suppliers and transfer costs. Suppliers of information, as with EPOS systems controlled by retailers, gain power.
Substitutes	IT creates substitutes for many products and services, as with electronic mail and hard copy letters and communications. IT can be used to shorten NPD processes to duplicate or replace products and by adding benefits can create unique packages.
New Entrants	Existing entry barriers are often negated and new ones created by the requirements for investment in computer telecommunication networks.
Rivals	IT changes rivalry as in IT-based consortia (eg. Unichem) using shared databases and ordering facilities. New rivals are created.

Source: Modified from M. Munro and S. Huff 1985.

BUYER/SUPPLIER POWER DURING EXCHANGE

The ability to identify and switch between suppliers can do much to reduce a manufacturer's costs. A few suppliers of labor, energy, components, or whatever can force concessions from a buyer if no choice is available. Conversely, strong buyer groups can force concessions from suppliers if they are the dominant or only users of the producer's products.

There has been considerable interest shown in the changing power balance between suppliers, manufacturers, and retailers. Power reflects the degree to which one firm can influence the actions and decisions of another and has been classified into reward, coercive, expert, reference, and legitimate power. Its application to the relationship between manufacturers, retailers, and buyers has been shown by Guiltman and Paul (1982) in Exhibit 4.

From the seller's point of view, the three most important kinds of power are reward, referent, and expertise. The use of coercion to force the other party to accept the exchange, as when the buyer takes the majority of a supplier's production and threatens to change supplier, is unlikely to achieve commitment or satisfaction. IT has allowed greater rewards, or benefits, to be bundled into an offering, thereby increasing reward power. It allows access to databases and expert knowledge through information systems, thus increasing expert power. Similarly, by allowing retailers to conduct direct product profitability analysis of

EXHIBIT 4. Alternative Power Bases Available to Manufacturers, Distributors, and Buyers

Power Base	To a Manufacturer	To a Buyer or Distributor
Reward	Ability to offer product with low prices, quantity discounts, or extra benefits	Ability to offer large buying volume
Coercive	Ability to withdraw product (with the loss of sales) when no comparable alternative is available to the buyer	Ability to reject offer (with little of no loss of sales) when no equivalent distribution or buyers are available to sellers
Expert	Ability to offer superior or needed technical assistance	Ability to provide unique distribution support
Referent	Ability to offer prestige brand name	Ability to offer image of quality retail outlet or serve as prestige example of satisfied buyer
Legitimate	Contractual provision that requires distributor to carry full line	Contractual provision that requires seller to provide warranty repair and exclusive distribution

Source: Guiltman and Paul, 1982, 282.

individual items, by the analysis of EPOS scanning data, they now have more information than manufacturers, allowing them to use coercive power in refusing shelf space, leveraging one supplier's goods against another, and insisting on just-in-time (JIT) delivery and flow-through distribution.

Some retailers in the United States and Britain have been able to increase the power they exert over suppliers and customers through the extension of EPOS to recognize customers and relate purchases to individuals. This is achieved using "smart cards."

The benefit to customers is that they can be offered discounts based on an analysis of their own buying behavior. Discounts offered to the customer are read from the card and money off purchases automatically given. This facility gives the retailer considerable power through the ability to progressively influence buyer behavior by reinforcing purchase decisions through careful discounting. The retailer is able to exert more coercive power through a detailed understanding of consumer preferences, which enhances the degree of leverage they have with manufacturers.

The installation of up-to-date scanning equipment has also helped stores improve their image of efficiency and reliability in the same way that robotics and on-line ordering can improve the image and status of manufacturing firms. Legitimate power only plays a part when the participants of an exchange agree to a long-term relationship to justify the cost of investment.

The parties that take part in an exchange are each attempting to maximize their own utility. If a long-term orientation to the firm's activities is taken, and if future exchanges are valued, then the well being of both parties is an essential aspect of the exchange. This mutual dependence is an essential aspect of such IT linkages as JIT manufacturing and supply chain management. JIT requires the supplier to produce and deliver to the original equipment manufacturer (OEM) the necessary units in the correct quantities at the correct time, within agreed performance specifications every time (Hayes 1981). Supply chain management looks at the total supply chain, usually from the retailer's viewpoint, and integrates it using modern electronic data processing and telecommunication tools to support systems integration, functional integration, and optimization of inventory and capacity utilization (Houlihan 1982).

It has been suggested that JIT exchange relationships have the greatest degree of dependency and risk with a tangled web of relations and the need for high communication of both formal and informal nature (Frazier, et al 1988). While JIT has received considerable attention in the purchasing, materials, and logistics literature, marketing academics do not seem to have recognized the importance of JIT to them. An example of the impact of information technology on IT in retail affecting the manufacturer end of the channel is illustrated by Dawson and Sparks (1986). With the use of JIT and production to order by clothing manufacturer, the dyeing of cloth is only done after detailed knowledge from the marketplace is analyzed in order to know what colors are selling. This reduces considerably the amount of unsold stock and thus results in the potential for a more efficient "cost structure" in the process of production. They point out that the Benetton franchise operation efficiently utilizes this type of information and Montgomery and Hausman (1985) believe it is this rapid response system, using CAD for cutting and design, that has given them an edge over their less responsive competitors.

The introduction of JIT requires reliability from suppliers in delivering quantity and quality, and this changes the mix of suppliers who can meet the standards or want to. Similarly, the use of single sourcing makes a manufacturer vulnerable if commitment is required, considering the added costs and skills necessary for the supplier to integrate with the manufacturer systems.

The benefits from this cooperation and commitment can be substantial. An example (Stevens 1988) is one firm that achieved a reduction of inventory from 2.8 months to 1.3 months and a labor reduction of 30 percent. Space was reduced by 5 percent, work in progress was reduced from 22 days to 1 day, and production increased by 200 percent. Stevens gives examples of other UK firms making similar savings.

If links are made with interorganizational information systems, then other major improvements in efficiency can be made. General Motors tied its CAD/CAM and order entry systems to its suppliers' production systems. The suppliers' computers communicate directly with General Motors robot-based assembly lines in an integrated flexible manufacturing system (Cash and Konsynski 1985). Another example is a large retailer that has linked its materials-ordering system with the primary supplier's order-entry system. The supplier with the lowest cost automatically gets the order, and the retailer's computer continually monitors the supplier's finished goods inventory, factory scheduling, and commitments to ensure sufficient inventory will be available to meet unexpected demand from the retailer (MacFarlan 1984).

Houston and Gassenheime (1987) remind us that good marketing management emphasizes the building of long-term relationships, which results in a well established set of expectations about the nature and outcomes of exchange. This requires a balancing of the various, often conflicting, functional objectives participating firms will have. Relationships are likely to evolve as each party to the exchange develops a dependence and discrete transactions are transformed into more durable associations supported by shared goals, planning, and commitment to the relationship (Dwyer, et al 1987).

JIT and supply chain management could not exist without improved information flow between the participants, and IT has provided the technology and software to make this possible. In 1988, agreement was reached on EDIFACT (electronic data interchange for administration, commerce, and transport). This created an internationally agreed-on common language necessary for communication. Previously, a domestic common language had been agreed on called TRADACOM (Trading Data Communications). This standard had been promoted by the UK Article Numbering Association (ANA) to improve data exchange between companies allowing direct computer-to-computer communications between otherwise incompatible systems. It is estimated that 80 percent of all electronic data interchange (EDI) transactions passing between British companies in 1988 were based on TRADACOM.

COMPETITION

The remaining three competitive forces identified by Porter relate to competition and the threat of new entrants, the threat of substitute products or services, and rivalry among existing firms.

New entrants are a constant threat to existing firms as they reduce market shares and, by increasing competition, often reduce profitability as they attempt to gain a foothold. In growing industries, demand may increase sufficiently to accommodate the new entrants, but in a mature industry, reduced market shares and sales can well result in the departure of one or more of the less efficient founder firms. Entry barriers, such as the high cost of manufacturing plants, the investment required to build distribution networks, and building reputations or low-cost structures based on experience, all deter new entrants. IT is changing the cost of entry, particularly manufacturing costs.

Mass production with undifferentiated products is no longer necessary to gain economies of scale. Increasing use of computer-controlled manufacturing processes means that greater production variability can be achieved with little or no sacrifice of scale economies. A standard "core" product can be created with the customization of end products, even if they are configured from identical components. IT has made diversity as cheap as uniformity.

In retail banking, use of sophisticated customer information systems enables specific tailoring of services and products around a basic core concept or offering to meet the particular needs of customers. IT provides the mechanism that makes this managable.

Similarly, a new entrant can invest in new technology, learning from the experiences of existing producers, and leapfrog them in terms of cost, reduction, and productivity. By the time the other firms have caught up, the new entrant may be firmly established in the market and may dominate certain key segments.

THE CREATION OF NEW BUSINESSES WITHIN OLD

Porter and Millar (1985) state that information technology creates new businesses within old ones, pointing out that a company that embeds information technology in its activities may have excess capacity or skills that can be sold to outside organizations. They point out that Sears has utilized skills in credit-card processing and provides a similar service to others, selling credit authorization and transaction processing services to Phillips Petroleum and retail remittance-processing services to Mellon Bank. Worthington (1988) believes that there is only a short step from offering in-house credit to offering other financial services to the retailer's credit card list. He points out that banks have to fear that retailers might take advantage of EFTPOS and enter into direct competition with banks by offering financial services. The Burton group has the largest retail credit card group in the UK, Storecard, which was launched in 1986, covering Habitat, Mothercare, BHS, Savacentre, and Richard Shops. Worthington points out that Storecard holders receive special offer sales previews and other customer incentives. Also in 1987, Storecard linked up with Comp-U-Card and offered Discount Shopping Service, which was a computerized home shopping service.

Worthington argues that a retailer such as Marks and Spencers, who launched its own charge card in 1985, could translate its expanding and successful credit card base combined with its "longstanding relationship of mutual trust with its customers" into providing financial services. He states that in June 1987, Marks and Spencers acquired from Citibank Savings a further 130,000 budget card accounts. These pay interest on credit balances and Marks was able to take them over because in early 1987 they had acquired licensed deposit-taker status from the Bank of England.

Worthington believes that this created the opportunity for Marks and Spencers to achieve the status of a fully fledged bank, giving an example of how a new business may arise from within a company's existing operations.

IT also creates substitutes for many products and services. Electronic databases allow quick searching by key words and are replacing library research, consultancy firms, and electronic newspapers (such as the experiment in the UK by the Birmingham Mail and Post). Electronic journals and magazines already exist although they have met with limited market success. IT has mainly been used as a component of a larger product, such as with speedometers in cars and control mechanisms in washing machines, their incorporation bringing cost reductions and improved performance. In some products, such as quartz watches, the cost and performance improvements have been much more drastic, making previous products and most of the Swiss watch industry redundant. IT often enables a simplicity of design or construction, which allows the cost savings to support aggressive pricing strategies. Alternatively, added functions or benefits can be incorporated into the product, increasing its value over competitors in the eye of the consumer.

While rivalry is an essential aspect of competition, most managers have, consciously or unconsciously, learned acceptable and unacceptable rules of competition to ensure profitability levels are kept adequate for all. These cozy arrangements may lead to the formation of cartels and cooperative agreements to keep out new entrants. The danger of new entrants is that they may disrupt the agreements or disturb the passive state of mind of existing firms. This negative, reactive approach ensures potentially disruptive marketing strategies are not attempted.

IT, by changing the market environment and creating new opportunities and threats, tends to disrupt relationships between market participants. IT allows greater coordination and control of activities regardless of location. The restructuring of operations is frequently possible to allow better matching of competitive strategy and market needs. As discussed earlier, suppliers, manufacturers, intermediaries, and customers may find that it is worthwhile to enter into mutually beneficial agreements. Some competitors may similarly find that they can use each other's facilities, as with American Airlines' reservation system and the sharing of ATMs by banks, in a way that improves efficiency while maintaining competition. The balance between cooperation and competition can be a difficult one for firms to achieve and encourage vertical or horizontal integration and takeovers.

STRATEGY LEVEL IMPACT OF IT

The third level suggested by Parsons relates to the effect of IT on a firm's strategy and how it attempts to satisfy the market. Marketing emphasizes that the product bought by the consumer is not simply the tangible physical object but the totality of benefits and values that are perceived as flowing from ownership and use of the product. Thus the value of a product is derived from all aspects of the firm's operations, which synthesize into the aspects visible to the consumer, summarized in the marketing mix.

Value has been defined as the amount buyers are willing to pay for a product or service. A business is profitable when the value it creates exceeds the cost involved in performing all the firm's operations necessary to bring the product into being. Moriarty and Swartz (1989) argue that marketing and sales productivity systems (MSP) enhances a company's efficiency: "They support more intense product or service differentiation, improved customer service, reduced operating costs, and more streamlined operations" (10).

MSP systems boost the efficiency of sales and marketing staff, and the collection and analysis of marketing information results in improved timeliness and quality of sales and marketing executive decision making. Porter (1985) has popularized the idea of the value chain to illustrate how a firm creates value. He classifies the activities of a firm into the primary activities involved in the physical creation of the product (such as manufacturing, delivery, sales) and the support activities that service the primary activities and allow them to take place (such as general management, accounting, personnel). All of these independent activities are linked in various ways and contribute to the end product as purchased by the consumer. The efficiency with which they are performed determines the cost and value created. The firm's activities are also part of a wider set of activities that together form the value system. Suppliers, intermediaries, and end users have their own value chains that link together to form a channel transforming raw materials into the final product and transporting it to the end user.

The firm, to gain competitive advantage, must look for ways of improving its own activities, the linkages between activities, or the linkages between elements of the wider value system. Porter gives examples of how IT is permeating the value chain at every point and transforming both the way in which value activities are performed and the nature of linkages among them.

Management is being improved through information systems and various computer models that improve decision making. Computer-aided design, computerized accounting and costing procedures, electronic mail, on-line search procedures, and electronic data interchange all improve the information processing components of the support activities. The primary activities have similarly been affected by such things as automated warehousing, automatic identification techniques, computer-aided manufacturing, automatic order processing, database marketing and telemarketing, portable computers for salespeople, computerized fault identification for after-sales services, etc.

The introduction of IT is frequently cost led rather than market led, resulting in long-term strategic advantage often being lost. Wiseman and MacMillan (1984) have suggested that a "strategic target" should be chosen on which to focus the advantage gained by IT. They suggest that companies should focus on the value systems of suppliers, customers, or competitors. Suppliers include those who provide raw material, capital, labor, and services. Customers include users, retailers, wholesalers, and distributors. Competitors include existing rivals, potential new entrants, substitute products, or any firm competing for scarce resources. They recognize that the linkages in the value system mean that changes in one area will have impact on another, allowing multiple targets.

Once a target has been chosen, the strategic thrust or approach must be chosen. Two major generic approaches frequently cited are differentiation and cost. IT can reduce costs in any part of the value chain by reducing waste, improving productivity, identifying marginal customers, and so forth, and this is frequently the spur to IT adoption. In following a differentiation strategy, IT is used to add unique features or benefits or to contribute to existing aspects of the mix in a way that will set it apart from competitors. Parsons (1983) argues that firms pursuing a differentiation strategy are most successful when they establish uniqueness in several categories and gives examples of cost and differentiation strategies as in Exhibit 5.

The enhanced value given to a product or service that differentiates it from competition can help lock in customers, particularly if the switching cost is high. Once a relationship has been built up and time, money, and effort has been invested in the relationship, then the emotional as well as the financial cost of change can be high. The reduction in cost in any part of the value chain may also be used offensively if it allows flexibility on price structures. An example is an airline seat reservation system where day-to-day price changes are possible as demand changes.

The choice of a low-cost strategy against a differentiation strategy should be based on how well the application matches the strategic needs of the company and competitive conditions. Wiseman (1988)

EXHIBIT 5. IT applications That Support Generic Strategies of Firms

	Generic Strategies	
	Low Cost	**Product Differentiation**
Product design development control	Product engineering systems Project control systems	R & D databases and professional work project stations electronic mail CAD custom engineering systems Integrated systems for manufacturing
Operations	Process engineering systems Process control systems Labor control systems Inventory management systems Procurement systems Quality monitoring systems	CAM Systems for suppliers Quality assurance systems Quality monitoring systems
Marketing	Streamlined distribution system Centralized control systems Econometric modeling systems	Sophisticated marketing systems Market databases Graphic display systems Telemarketing systems Competition analysis systems Modeling systems Service-oriented systems Distribution systems
Sales	Sales control systems Advertising monitoring systems Systems to consolidate sales function Strict incentive/monitoring systems	Differential pricing systems Office/field communications Customer/sales support systems Custom order entry Dealer support systems Customer order entry systems
Administration	Cost control systems Quantitative planning and budgeting systems Office automation for staff reduction	Office automation to integrate functions Environment scanning and nonquantitative planning systems Teleconferencing systems

Source: G. Parsons, IT: A new competitive weapon. *Sloan Management Review,* 1983 p. 12.

points out that while a strategic thrust may initially be very successful, it often has the effect of destabilizing the entire industry. The creation of competitive advantage by the use of IT signals a new era of megacompetition, in which competitors wage a counterattack by adopting the technology themselves and offering similar or better benefits. Wiseman puts forward the axiom that successful strategic use of IT spurs strategic responses.

An excellent example of Wiseman's point is provided by the general insurance market in the UK. During the 1980s, the Royal Bank of Scotland established Direct Line insurance to sell personal insurance lines (motor, household, etc). The company trades directly with end consumers using direct-response advertising and telemarketing.

The huge success of the venture has prompted a number of the major insurers to follow—notably General Accident which has established a new company to compete head on with Direct Line in this market.

These businesses are viable only through the use of IT to provide the basic infrastructure delivering cost and efficiency advantages and to deliver the competitive advantage these early entrants into this new area of the general insurance market currently enjoy.

It therefore becomes important to capitalize on being first, despite the risks of so doing. In deciding on whether to launch a preemptive strike, the response lag of competitors must be considered to determine the duration, vulnerability, and value of competitive advantage derived from the thrust.

Other strategies include concentrating on a market niche, distinguishing the firm by unusual cost or product features. Porter calls this a focused strategy, while marketers will recognize it as a concentrated rather than differentiated segmentation strategy. As with the differentiated strategy, the firm must ensure its competitive advantage is sufficiently entrenched, or the entry barriers and switching costs are sufficiently high, to ensure other larger firms will not be attracted into the segment. Substitution will always be a threat to a firm following this strategy, particularly if competitors are allowed to close the competitive gap by their own investment in IT and marketing strategies.

Innovative offerings, which better satisfy the customer, and increased cooperation between suppliers and customers can improve efficiency and hence customer service. A focus strategy therefore uses both low cost and differentiation to satisfy a particular niche in a novel way.

CONCLUSION

Firms are constantly seeking the competitive equivalent of the Holy Grail. They search for the one technique, philosophy, or concept that gives them a unique insight into their industry or the nature of their operations or allows them by adopting the technique, to gain such an advantage that they may, unlike their less fortunate or less astute competitors, find the clear path to corporate salvation and long-term security. In search of such a technique, many false gods are enthusiastically embraced, only for the adherents to realize that the benefits are not as great as claimed or that negative aspects exist that reduce the overall worth of the idea. Often, these early converts are moving away from the technique even as they are being promoted as disciples of the new order.

Many managers quite rightly suspected that the hype surrounding IT disguised yet another "flavor of the month" fad, which would be absorbed into existing practices without major effect. While the successes of IT were widely promulgated, the failures received less publicity and many firms made unwise investments that did not create the competitive advantage expected.

Failure to create competitive advantage often results from a lack of understanding on the part of marketing and IT managers of the need for a clear and defined link between business process and function and IT. This is even more initiated in marketing applicants where the business processes involved may be unclear, at least to the extent of development.

Investment in IT for marketing often highlights key organizational and functional issues that have to be addressed before IT can help to deliver competitive advantage.

It is therefore interesting to note that the growth of IT, and its incorporation into business practices, has continued despite the problems met. This has resulted from a two-fold pressure. First, the successful use of IT has created such competitive advantage that other firms have been forced to follow if they wish to remain in the industry. The new IT-based practice thus becomes the industry standard.

Second, IT is not based on any one technology or technique but on an integrated collection of technological advances that allow multiple applications in many different areas of business practice. These tend to be self-supporting, creating a synergistic benefit as the firm moves along the experience curve. Disappointment in one area is often compensated by unexpected benefits elsewhere. This is often the case when a cost-driven improvement in efficiency gives improved customer service on which the firm can then capitalize.

IT is not a panacea for an inefficient or uncompetitive firm. It will not allow a reactive, production-oriented firm to gain major competitive advantage at a stroke. It will not even give long-term competitive advantage if not used as part of an integrated marketing strategy.

What it does offer—for firms of all sizes, in whatever industry, selling products or services—is an opportunity to integrate all its business operations in a way that creates maximum added value for the customer, while keeping in constant touch with the marketplace to identify new opportunities and threats as they arise. It therefore allows firms with a customer orientation to stay level, if not ahead, of its competitors by ensuring that to the best of its ability it is focused on giving maximum customer satisfaction.

It is often said that marketing is too important to be left to the marketing department. Equally, IT is much too important to be left to information technologists. IT and marketing are both integrating approaches that are most successful when accepted throughout an organization and used for both operational and strategic purposes. Marketing managers should therefore consider as a matter of urgency how IT can be used within their own organizations.

REFERENCES

Abell, D. (1980), *Defining the Business: The Starting Point of Strategic Planning*, Prentice Hall.

American Marketing Association (1989), *Marketing News*, Vol. 23, No. 9.

Brancheau, J.C., Wetherbe, J.C. (1987), "Key Issues in Information Systems Management," *MIS Quarterly*, March, p. 27.

Cash, J., Knosynski, B. (1985), "IS Redraws Competitive Boundaries," *Harvard Business Review*, March/April, pp. 134–42.

Dawson, J.A., Sparks, L. (1986), "New Technology in UK Retailing," *Journal of Marketing Management*, Vol. 2, No. 1, pp. 7–22.

Dwyer, F., Schurr, P., Oh, S. (1987), "Developing Buyer-Seller Relationship," *Journal of Marketing*, Vol. 52, April, pp. 11–27.

Earl, M. (1989), *Information Management: The Strategic Dimensions*, Oxford University Press.

Earl, M. (1990), "The Pitfalls of Partial Solutions," *View 90*, Anderson Consulting, pp. 40–41.

Fletcher, K. (1983), "Information Systems in British Industry," *Management Decision*, Vol. 21, No. 2, pp. 25–36.

Frazier, G., Spekman, R., O'Neal, C. (1988), "Just-in-Time Relationships in Industrial Markets," *Journal of Marketing*, Vol. 52, No. 4, pp. 52–67.

Gibson, C., Nolan, R. (1974), "Managing the Four Stages of EDP Growth," *Harvard Business Review*, January/February, pp. 76–87.

Guiltman, J., Paul, G. (1982), *Marketing Management: Strategies & Programmes*, McGraw Hill.

Hammer, M., Manqurian, G. (1987), "The Changing Value of Communications Technology," *Sloan Management Review*, Vol. 28, No. 2, pp. 65–71.

HMSO (1988), Vanguard: Opportunities for education and training to accelerate the update of value added and data services in the UK.

Houlihan, J. (1982), "Supply Chain Management in the Modern Approach to Logistics," *Focus: The Journal of the Institute of Physical Distitution Management*, Vol. 1, No. 3, pp. 12–16.

Houston, F., Gassenheimer, J. (1987), "Marketing & Exchange," *Journal of Marketing*, Vol. 51, October, pp. 3–18.

Kemerer, C., Sosa, G. (1988), "Barriers to Successful Strategic Information Systems," *Planning Review*, Vol. 16, September/October, pp. 20–23, 46.

MacFarlan, F.W. (1984), "Information Technology Changes the Way You Compete," *Harvard Business Review*, May/June, No. 3, pp. 93–103.

Malone, T.W., Yates, J., Benjamin, R.I. (1989), "The Logic of Electronic Markets," *Harvard Business Review*, May/June, No. 3, pp. 166–82.

Montgomery, D., Hausman, W. (1985), "Managing the Marketing Manufacturing Interface," *Journal of Management*, Vol. 2, No. 2.

Moriarty, R., Swartz, G. (1989), "Automation to Boost Sales & Marketing," *Harvard Business Review*, January/February, No. 1, pp. 100–108.

Munroe, M., Huff, S. (1985), "Information Technology and Corporate Strategy," *Business Quarterly*, Vol. 50, No. 2, pp. 18–24.

Oasis (1989), "A Report on the Management of Marketing Information Oasis and Chartered Institute of Marketing Report" (Second Report 1990).

Parsons, G.L. (1983), "Information Technology: A New Competitive Weapon," *Sloan Management Review*, Vol. 25, No. 1, pp. 3–14.

Porter, M. (1985), *Competitive Advantage,* New York, Free Press.

Porter, M., Viller, V. (1985), "How Information Technology Gives You Competitive Advantage," *Harvard Business Review*, July/August, pp. 149–60.

Price Waterhouse (1990), *International Information Technology Review*.

Sprague, R., Watson, H. (1979), "Bit-by-Bit: Toward Decision Support Systems," *California Management Review*, Vol. 22, No. 1, pp. 61–8.

Stevens, G. (1988), "Can JIT work in the UK?" *Logistics Today*, Vol. 7, No. 1, pp. 6–9.

Synott, W.R. (1987), *The Information Weapon—Winning Customers & Markets with Technology*, John Wiley & Sons, NY.

Wiseman, C., MacMillan, O. (1984), "Creating a Competitive Weapon from Information System," *Journal of Business Strategy*, Vol. 5, No. 2, pp. 42–9.

Wiseman, C. (1988), "Attack and Counterattack: The New Game of Information Technology," *Planning Review*, Vol. 16, September/October, pp. 6–14.

Worthington, S. (1988), "Credit Cards in the United Kingdom—Where the Power Lies in the Battle Between the Banks and the Retailers," *Journal of Marketing Management*, Vol. 4, No. 1, pp. 61–70.

Dr. Russell I. Haley
The Whittemore School of Business and Economics
University of New Hampshire
Durham, New Hampshire

CHAPTER 27

PREDICTING MARKET RESPONSES TO STYLE MERCHANDISE: SENSORY PANELS AND SENSORY SEGMENTATION

BACKGROUND

Interest in market segmentation continues unabated. By now it is a well-known fact that every market consists of a number of segments, some of them large enough to represent attractive targets for major marketers. As our ability to reach them through direct marketing has grown, companies have become interested in smaller and smaller segments and subsegments. So these days few companies are thinking in terms of total markets and the "average" consumer. Almost everyone recognizes that, as a minimum, in every product category there is a price market and a quality market with quite different needs and wants. And, of course, it is accepted practice to look at alternative geographic, demographic, geodemographic, psychographic, and behavioral segments and, where possible in marketing planning activities, to take their differences into account.

Fueled by the growth of interest in segmentation possibilities, the last three decades have seen substantial progress in marketing research approaches to understanding segmented markets. But despite progress elsewhere, one major product type has remained largely intractable—that of sensory merchandise.

Sensory merchandise, as the term is used here, refers to any merchandise for which product choices hinge importantly on sensory benefits—benefits that concern agreeable responses from one or more of our five senses. Examples of such merchandise abound. For taste, there are soft drinks and flavors of ice cream; for touch, upholstery fabrics and shaving products; for sound, recorded music and high fidelity speakers; for smell, fragrances and deodorants; and for sight, dinnerware and watches.

Our lack of progress in this area is certainly not related to the fact that these are categories of minor importance. To the contrary, sales of style merchandise alone, merchandise in which product styling plays a key role in choice, are, among consumer markets, second in sales only to food. And, while health and nutrition considerations are increasingly important in mealtime selections, taste is by no means a minor factor in food choices.

Why then the slow progress in this area? The central problem is that for sensory merchandise, respondents have trouble both in recognizing and in articulating the true reasons for their preferences. Preferences depend heavily on executional details, and those are very difficult to communicate with words alone. It is impossible, for example, to say "blue" and have everyone think of the same color.

Some people will envision a light blue, some a primary blue, some a dark blue, and some a turquoise. It is even more difficult to describe a musical selection in such a way that a person who has not heard it will receive the same kind of emotional impact that exposure to the music itself would cause.

Unfortunately, most popular current market research methods center on questionnaires, and those in turn are based on obtaining the responses to words and phrases of the people being interviewed. But words are slippery things when it comes to communicating sensory elements. And it is there that the root of the problem lies. Questionnaires that rely on verbally communicated sensory stimuli are very loose instruments.

This problem is especially severe when the respondents are ordinary consumers. Ordinary consumers learn to use words somewhat differently and each has a somewhat different vocabulary. Professional taste testers can be another matter.

At one major coffee manufacturer, for example, it has been found that professional taste testers can be taught a special and precise vocabulary to describe the variety of taste sensations associated with coffee. Using a vocabulary of about 15 words (including adjectives such as woody, green, and caramel), it is possible to profile different blends of coffee beans so reliably that the profiles do not depend on the person doing the profiling. But the training process is an extended one requiring the trainee to go repeatedly from physical stimuli to words and back again until the trainee is able to make identifications that are both accurate and reliable. In contrast, ordinary consumers—when asked to profile coffee taste—use a limited vocabulary centering on such words as strong, smooth, and bitter. And it is extremely difficult for production people to use those untrained observations to determine how best to improve taste.

Which brings us to the purpose of this chapter. In it, two research approaches are suggested specifically for dealing with sensory merchandise. Each has proven to be helpful in practice. One is termed *sensory panels* and represents a translation of the sort of taste testing panel just described into other areas of aesthetics and sensory response. The other is an extension of the well-known technique of *benefit segmentation* (Haley 1968) to sensory merchandise. This new approach is labeled *sensory segmentation.*

While the following discussion could, logically, center on products involving any of our five senses, the printed page lends itself most readily to examples in the area of sight—in marketing terms what is sometimes called *style merchandise.* However, it should be remembered that the techniques suggested are equally applicable to any area in which ordinary research respondents have difficulty recognizing and articulating the true reasons underlying their preferences.

PROBLEMS OF MARKETING STYLE MERCHANDISE

One central problem for style merchandise is how to obtain accurate demand forecasts. Typically, in the style merchandise situation, a line of offerings must be selected from a large number of alternative design possibilities. The penalties attached to poor choices of individual items are not large. However, the financial success of the selector depends on his or her ability to make a high proportion of good choices.

This general kind of problem arises in a large number of business settings. For example it extends to

- a department store clothing buyer selecting the fall clothing line from the offerings of a large number of clothing manufacturers;
- a clothing manufacturer deciding which of a variety of designs submitted by his design department should be included in his offerings;
- a brand manager deciding which of the advertising executions submitted by her advertising agency should form her commercial pool;
- a greeting card manufacturer trying to decide which of the large number of designs and verses created by his artists and writers should be incorporated into his line;
- a dinnerware manufacturer trying to decide which of a large number of possible patterns should decorate the four alternative settings she plans to offer the public;
- a watch manufacturer balancing his line by the size of watch face, the type of metal used, and the watch strap style;
- a catalog house deciding which of a large variety of swim suits should be featured in a small and fixed amount of catalog space; and
- a silverware manufacturer planning to introduce six new designs. The question is which six?

These are not theoretical situations. Each represents a specific client situation that has arisen in recent years. They have in common the fact that anticipating consumer response to style is a central problem element, the fact that a limited number of selections must be made from a relatively large number of candidate designs, the fact that the choices must be made within a fairly restricted time period (sometimes a day or two), and the fact that the process is repetitive—it will recur at fairly regular intervals, sometimes several times a year, sometimes only once every two or three years.

The traditional packaged goods approach to new product problems is a series of research steps ranging from focus groups to concept tests and product tests and finally to sales tests and real or simulated market tests. The combination of the large number of items to be evaluated plus time constraints prevent this from being a practical research model for marketers of style merchandise.

A review of the sparse literature relating to goods characterized by the attributes of color, line, and design suggests that little progress in research methodology has been made since the situation was summed up by John Mertes almost 20 years ago (Mertes 1968). Yet the importance of fashion goods is undeniable. Among consumer markets their dollar sales volume is second only to food. Moreover, as individuality has become an increasingly important consumer value, style has been playing an increasingly important role in product acceptance. This is true not only of the kinds of merchandise already mentioned but of automobiles, appliances, luggage, television sets, radios, and stereos. Even packaged goods styling has exerted some influence on sales through packaging and labeling. Yet in comparison to its influence on consumer choices it has received little attention in the marketing research literature.

In part, this has been because our methods have not been adequate to the problems posed. Most frequently, when marketing research has been asked to help with the problem of preevaluating style merchandise, the suggested method has been some form of survey, either at the consumer level or at the trade level. However, the success record of such preevaluation efforts has been spotty. This can be partly attributed to the aforementioned need for obtaining results inexpensively and quickly enough to capitalize on rising consumer enthusiasm for a particular style and partly to some rather severe limitations on the applicability of the research designs customarily used. Often, so many compromises have to be made that survey methods become impractical.

For example, it is unusual to have an actual production run of the merchandise you wish to evaluate available for testing. So it is often necessary to resort to devices such as handmade samples, mock-ups, three-dimensional slides, color photographs, or line drawings. While these may allow the research to be conducted, they necessarily distort consumer reactions to the extent that they do not accurately represent the merchandise that will finally be marketed.

In addition, there is the problem of obtaining a representative sample of consumers at an affordable cost. Few manufacturers have such a large investment in one or two designs that they can afford to research them thoroughly. More often there will be a substantial number of items in the manufacturer's line. And while it may be possible to have inferior styling on one or two items and still survive, the overall styling of the line must be at least equivalent to competition if the manufacturer is to retain his or her market position.

Also, it is often difficult to find consumers who are in a true buying frame of mind and thus consumers who can provide responses that will be predictive of their actual buying behavior in the future. Too frequently, meaningless responses are extracted from consumers who are really not very interested in the subject and as a result give off-hand answers to the questions put to them. Then, too, there is the opposite danger that consumers will become overly involved in the interview situation and will turn themselves into what they perceive to be styling experts. Or they may be so concerned with the self-image being painted by their responses that they will only make selections that they feel will reflect unquestionable good taste rather than what they themselves might buy.

Still another difficult problem is that of finding some reasonably realistic simulation of the way styles are accepted. Often, before a style becomes a genuine hit, it is discussed by people in a long interlinked chain of social groups and subgroups. Its final acceptance depends on the net result of these exchanges and interactions. The kind of friendly relaxed talk that occurs among friends, relatives, and acquaintances in real life is very hard to imitate in a research environment.

Then too there is the problem of timing. Styles are too frequently a perishable commodity. It is by no means unheard of to have the principal competitor of the originator of a style beat him to market with it. And usually the manufacturer who gets to the market first with a hot new item is the one who reaps the greatest rewards. All this puts an extremely high premium on fast research. From the standpoint of a marketer who has what he believes to be a real money maker on his hands, it is very risky to wait four to ten weeks, or even more, for research results that he knows from experience are apt to be somewhat less than definitive.

Finally, there is the issue of secrecy. Exposing designs that are under serious consideration to a sample of consumers for research purposes runs the risk that one or more of those consumers may be employed by a competitor. In one well-documented case, new product research was being conducted on behalf of a major U.S. manufacturer. For purposes of competitive security, in addition to the standard screening questions that are supposed to eliminate people working for competitors and their advertising agencies, initial interviews were conducted in a small town in British Columbia, Canada. As luck would have it, the very first household contacted was that of the regional sales manager for Western Canada of their leading competitor. Needless to say, the respondent showed a great deal of interest in the designs being evaluated.

ONE NEW DIRECTION—THE SENSORY PANEL

One purpose of this chapter is to suggest an empirical approach to the preevaluation of style merchandise, an approach that circumvents many of the difficulties of traditional methods, yields quick results, is competitively secure, and, at the same time, is affordable even for the smallest manufacturer. The approach had its genesis in a problem of a somewhat different nature which arose a number of years ago. A well-known department store was wrestling with the problem of selecting competent buyers. The performance records that they kept on their buyers suggested that a few buyers were highly proficient at selecting styled items that would sell well, while others were only moderately effective at best. Furthermore, despite a substantial amount of research, it had not been possible to identify background variables that could be used to identify accurately persons with this ability to pick winners.

The performance records, however, showed that it was an undeniable fact that there *was* a select group of buyers who consistently out-performed the larger group of ordinary buyers in anticipating the styling preferences of consumers. The merchandise they selected regularly outsold the merchandise selected by the other buyers. This raised a number of questions in addition to the basic one of trying to develop some means of identifying people who possessed this skill—a skill that was dubbed the "common touch." How many people must be tested to find individuals with this ability? Is an individual's ability restricted to certain sensory subgroups of merchandise, or does it cut across a wide range of style merchandise? Does this ability last indefinitely or does it wear out? Does it operate all of the time, or is it intermittent? Can it be systematized and harnessed? To provide answers to these and other questions, it was decided to conduct a series of experiments to explore the phenomenon of the common touch.

The procedure that was envisioned was a form of sensory or aesthetic "taste testing" that would generally parallel the kind of physiological taste testing frequently carried out in the research laboratories of large food and beverage manufacturers. Normally they administer a series of tests, such as triangle tests,[1] (Little 1958) aimed at measuring the discriminatory powers of their subjects. When a sufficient number of people with the ability to discriminate have been identified, they are used as a taste testing panel. In this capacity, they screen new product possibilities to be sure that they are discriminably different from products they already market. Also, in companies such as General Foods, such panels have the responsibility for making sure that coffee brands such as Maxwell House, Sanka, and Yuban retain their exact current flavor. This cannot be done without human intervention because even coffee beans grown on the same hillside in two successive years do not produce coffee with an identical flavor. The culprit is differences in growing conditions. Variations in amounts of sunlight and rainfall can result in significant flavor variations. So for each growing season, a portion of the blended coffee is saved and new blends from the next season are systematically tested against it until the taste testing experts on the taste panel are unable to tell the difference between the new and old blends. At that point and only at that point authorization is given to go into mass production with the new blend.

The objectives we had in mind for our sensory taste testing panel were somewhat different from traditional organoleptic panel tests such as physiological taste or scent tests. Organoleptic testing generally concentrates on *discrimination* ability. Thus the primary interest is not so much whether flavor A is better than flavor B but rather whether professional taste testers are able to note consistent differences of some sort between flavor A and flavor B. Larger samples of ordinary consumers are normally used to supply evaluative information at a later point and as a separate phase of the new product research program.

It was hypothesized, instead, that there were people in the general population who had what was termed the common touch. In other words, when they liked a style, lots of people would like that style and vice versa. If this was the case, then a sensory taste testing panel made up of people with the common touch might well be able to do a better job of selecting fast selling designs than either an ordinary marketing executive or an executive team selected for that purpose.

From early experiments in product categories for which sales data were available, it was quickly learned that the common touch was not quite so common as had been hoped. Perhaps as a function of category involvement, people who clearly demonstrated their ability with dinnerware were markedly less effective when it came to judging wearing apparel and vice versa. However, once again it was discovered that in *each* product category there *was* a group of people who consistently outperformed the remainder of the population available for testing. Moreover, as time passed and subsequent tests were run and validated, it became evident that the "Common Touch" was not a transitory ability and that the people who possessed it were apt to retain their ability over substantial periods of time.[2]

SELECTING COMMON TOUCH PANEL MEMBERS

The approach, then, is essentially one of systematizing executive judgments. And while it relies on a rigorous testing procedure, it has some philosophical similarities with Bayesian approaches, with the Delphi[3] technique and perhaps even with clairvoyance. Conceptually, it is quite simple. It involves selecting a panel of persons whose ability to anticipate styling preferences has been objectively tested and using these people to preevaluate style merchandise.

In selecting panels, one of the first questions to arise is who should be eligible for participation. Obviously, some practical considerations will enter at this point, such as who will have time available when panel judgments are needed and who can be counted on for long-term efforts on the company's behalf. However, experience suggests that, because the common touch may be found in almost anyone, the testing base should be as broad as possible. The more people tested, the higher the probability of discovering proficient judges. And since the testing procedure itself is quite inexpensive, the net dollar payoff from a good panel can be impressive.

One school of thought argues that, as a minimum, judges should be purchasers or consumers of the products being evaluated. It would hold, for example, that women's fashions should be evaluated only by woman judges. Other respondents, because they are assumed to be less knowledgeable, are considered somewhat suspect, even though they may score well in a test. However, on the pragmatic side of the argument, judges have sometimes been shown to have outstanding ability to predict consumer tastes, even though they themselves have never bought the product in question. Despite conflicting evidence, most companies have a strong intuitive leaning toward judges who are also consumers. And, of course, it is especially convenient if the judges are full-time or part-time employees of the company that wishes to make the styling evaluations.

The next question concerns the appropriate testing procedures for selecting able judges. There are, of course, a large number of alternative approaches to this problem. The procedure utilized most frequently is a test-retest design. Under this approach, potential judges are first asked to evaluate a series of items that are currently being or have recently been offered for sale. Since the sales rates of these products are already known, they can be used as one standard for evaluating the quality of the prospective panel members' judgments.

Ideally, the items to be evaluated in the test should include some of the very best selling items in the line and some of the very worst, in about equal quantities. The number of judgments depends importantly on how many judgments will be obtained at each rating session when the panel is in regular operation. Ideally, the test should be about the same length as is anticipated for normal rating sessions of the expert panel once it is in operation. Fatigue is also a factor. Too many items can warp a respondent's judgment. But, where interest is high, a surprising number of judgments can be gathered without any measurable deterioration in judging power. In the absence of other criteria, as a rule of thumb the test should probably be no longer than 20 minutes or about 50 judgments, whichever is shorter.

In instructing people who are about to take the qualification test, it is important that they be told to make their judgments on the basis of their personal likes and dislikes, rather than by attempting to predict what the general public is apt to like and buy. This puts them in an entirely natural framework. The alternative approach, that of asking people directly whether they think an item will sell well, places panel members in the role of experts and they may predict a bright success for a design to which they have a personal aversion. This kind of expertise has been found to be relatively unstable. Conversely, people's personal judgments and tastes have been found to be very stable indeed. Interestingly, it has been discovered that, as a generalization, quick judgments are more likely to be accurate predictors than considered judgments.

In selecting panels, the problem of rater reliability must also be dealt with. While high scores on the prediction ability test are an encouraging factor, they can sometimes be obtained by luck alone. The customary procedure for insuring against this is the retest. Persons who have scored well on the first test are asked to repeat their success. Usually this is accomplished by asking prospective panel members to take the qualification test again after enough time has elapsed so that it is unlikely that the respondent will *remember* accurately the preferences he had indicated previously.

Considerations of reliability often pose a dilemma. Is it preferable to select a panel member who picks 80 percent winners in the original test and a *different* 80 percent in the retest, or is it better to pick a person who selects the *same* 75 percent as winners in both the test and the retest? Ideally, all members should be both accurate and reliable. In practice, some members score higher on accuracy, while others do better on reliability. Fortunately, however, the number of cases in which this kind of conflict arises is small. And there is always the possibility of breaking such "ties" with a third test.[4]

Another problem concerns panel balance. Should the panel be composed simply of people with the highest overall scores? Or should the test be stratified by the types of merchandise to be evaluated (e.g., sensory segments) and efforts made to balance panel membership by where their errors are made?

Relative costs of errors for the various types of merchandise involved can be taken into consideration in arriving at this decision. If all of the merchandise to be evaluated is of the same basic sensory type, members can be chosen on the basis of unweighted scores. On the other hand, if errors in some categories are more costly than others, weighted scores can be developed. Alternatively, it is possible to set up entirely separate panels for special purposes (e.g., one for each sensory type). A factor analysis of rater scores across several classes of merchandise may provide some guidance on whether it is reasonable to expect that several types of prejudging ability will exist in the same individuals or whether separate groups should be established.

A supplementary question concerns panel size. How large should the panel be? Use of too few panel members may result in unreliable ratings, while too many may generate unnecessary cost. Although some product categories may be exceptions, it is usually true that panels of between 10 and 15 members represent the best compromises between cost and reliability.

OPERATING THE PANEL

Some helpful rules of thumb concerning the operation of the panel include the following:

- Items should be submitted in random order rather than in sets of highly similar items. This minimizes carry-over effects from one item to the next and increases the amount of discrimination among the judges.

EXHIBIT 1. Typical Purchase Intent Scale

- Definitely would buy
- Probably would buy
- Might or might not buy
- Probably would not buy
- Definitely would not buy

- Voting should be made independently by individual judges. Experiences with groups and with theater settings suggest that the so-called "contamination" effect can be quite powerful. In other words, when some judges know the opinions of other judges, their own opinions may be distorted. If most selections of style merchandise in the marketplace are made on the basis of individual taste, gathering judgments individually is somewhat more true to life.[5]
- Rating sessions should not exceed 20 minutes.

Nor should respondents be asked to make evaluations more frequently than about once a week. In both cases, the point at issue is respondent fatigue. Too-frequent interviews or interviews that are too long can cause "conditioning" of the judgment of panel members and substantial losses in the predictive accuracy of their votes.

NATURE OF THE VOTING

Voting usually takes the form of some kind of rating scale (Exhibit 1). A full discussion of alternative evaluative scales is beyond the scope of this chapter. A thorough review of the alternatives was made by the Arrowhead #9 Committee of the Advertising Research Foundation some years ago (Haley and Case 1979). In general, the following was concluded:

- Scales that do not result in a large proportion of highly positive ratings are desirable.
- Scales with more than seven points were less discriminating as were those with fewer than four.
- Unbalanced scales are preferred to balanced scales.
- Among the monadic scales tested, the verbal purchase intent scale did best.

Perhaps even more important than the choice of the proper rating scale is the way in which the scale is scored and the ratings combined. By now it is well established that almost all scales should be weighted by some sort of power function. In other words, the upper end of the scale has more predictive power than the lower part. One simple way to take account of this fact is the so-called "top box" method of scoring rating scales. This rough approximation assigns the top box a weight of one and the remaining boxes weights of zero. Exhibit 2 illustrates the curvilinear relationship between scaled ratings and purchase behavior.

EXHIBIT 2. Brand Share by Rating Scale Point

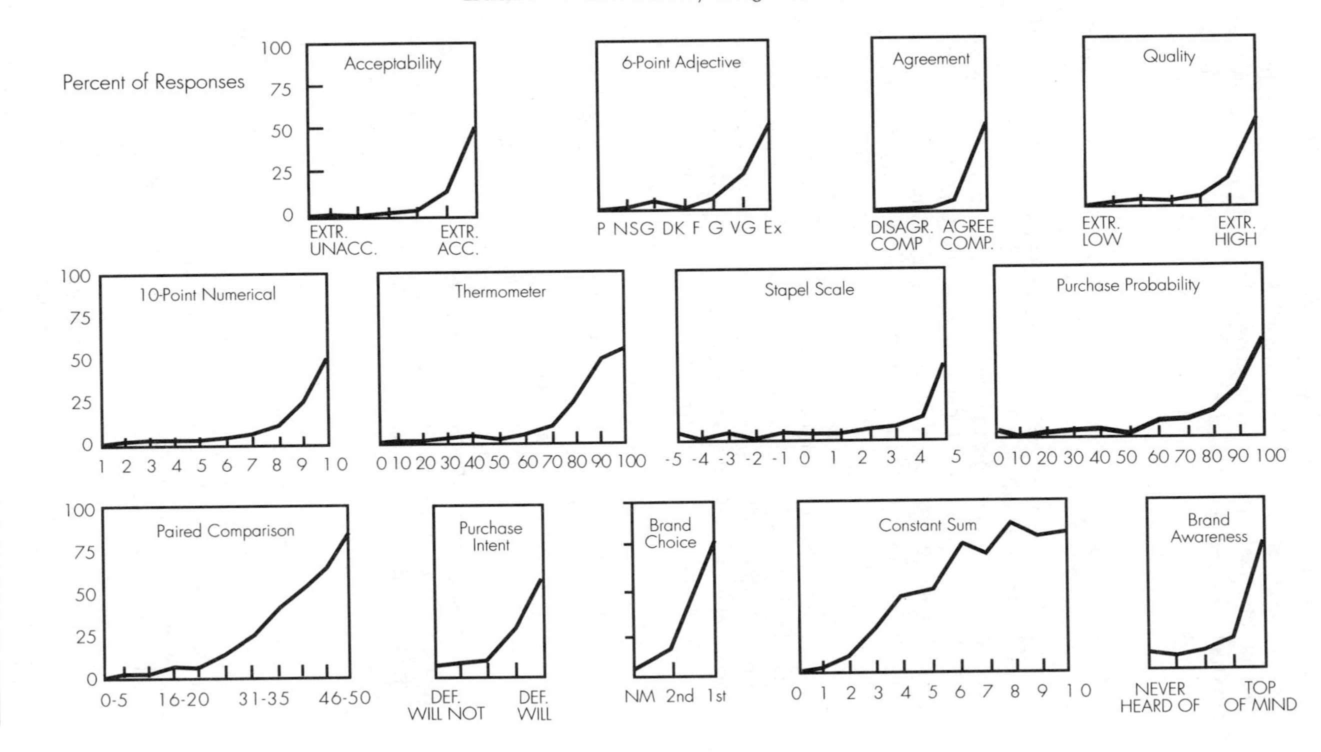

VALIDATING THE PERFORMANCE OF PANEL MEMBERS

A number of possibilities are available for evaluating the performance of panel members. One possibility is to make further use of current sales records. This approach poses the question of whether the high qualifying scores obtained by panel members can be extended to items not included in the test.

The same current sales records that were used to design the screening test can be employed for additional testing, simply by selecting a new sample of items and measuring the ability of the panel to discriminate between additional good and poor sellers in that set.

A second possibility, which has only been explored in a limited way because of its expense, is to design a special sales test to provide a short-term validation of panel judgments. Under this approach, a small production run of new merchandise is made. Panel members make judgments, and the merchandise is made available to a limited number of customers. The judgments of panel members are then compared to sales performance.

A final approach, and the one most often employed, is to delay final selection of the panel until, in the normal course of things, the new items that have been judged enter the line. Sales performance at that time provides an empirical guide to the most effective panel members.

No matter which method of validation is chosen, the "expert panel" method of preevaluating style merchandise is most effective when it is adopted as a continuous system. This permits regular testing of new potential panel members at specified intervals to replace people who become inaccessible or for some reason drop out. Also a panel wear-out factor has been observed. The judgment of a small minority of the panel members seems to become distorted and lose its predictive power after they have participated in a number of evaluation sessions. These people must be identified and weeded out. Of course, it is possible that a part of this "wear out" phenomenon may be attributable to the fact that a few people manage to slip through the screening tests through good luck in guessing rather than through possession of the common touch. Or perhaps they have just become tired of coming to panel sessions or being visited by panel moderators and have lost interest. Whatever the reason, it is desirable to check the ability of current panel members from time to time to make sure that each panel member is making a worthwhile contribution to the accuracy of the group's evaluations. For example, in one instance it was found that checks at six-month intervals were sufficient to spot the one or two members who needed replacement.

THE TRACK RECORD

The final question to be considered is the pragmatic one of how well the system works in practice. Exhibit 3 shows the results of expert

EXHIBIT 3. Predicted Sales*

		High	Medium	Low	
Actual Sales	**High**	28.0	10.8	0.4	39.3
	Medium	7.9	27.9	2.0	37.8
	Low	3.9	3.9	15.0	22.9
		39.8	42.7	17.5	100.0

*Columns and rows do not add exactly to marginal totals because of rounding.

panel preevaluations of over 700 items of styled merchandise, all of which eventually reached the market and thus established sales performance records.

In this case, the management decision was a choice between three alternative sizes of a production run. If it was anticipated that the item would be extremely popular, an especially large production run would be authorized. If, on the other hand, there were severe doubts about the ability of the item to generate sales, a short production run would be made.[6] Finally, if evaluations fell in between these two extremes, a normal production run size would be selected. Past experience had established appropriate levels for heavy, medium, and small runs for the various classes of merchandise involved.

The data shown in each cell of Exhibit 3 are the percentages of all items evaluated. Thus, on the basis of panel predictions, it was anticipated that 39.8 percent of the items would sell well enough to justify heavy production runs. Of these items, 70.4 percent (28.0/39.8) eventually sold at high rates.

There are a number of ways of analyzing these data statistically. However, whatever approach is chosen, the ability of the panel to anticipate sales performance is clearly significant. As shown in Exhibit 4, the success record of expert panel preevaluations far exceeds the laws of chance. If the judgments summarized here had been randomly dispersed across the table, the probability of a correct prediction would have been about .33. The actual level of predictive accuracy was .71. Thus the expert panel was more than twice as effective as a random selection process would have been.

It may well be asked how seasoned marketing executives would have performed under these circumstances had the decisions been left to them. In this instance, we are fortunate in that the company to which these data apply had traditionally used a group of top executives to make their style selections and continued to do so during the period to which these data apply. Their correct prediction percentage was 52.0 percent with their errors due largely to excessive optimism about future sales performance. While at first glance this may look little better than a coin flip, remember that the random standard is 33 percent (or about

EXHIBIT 4. Overall Predictive Accuracy of the Expert Panel

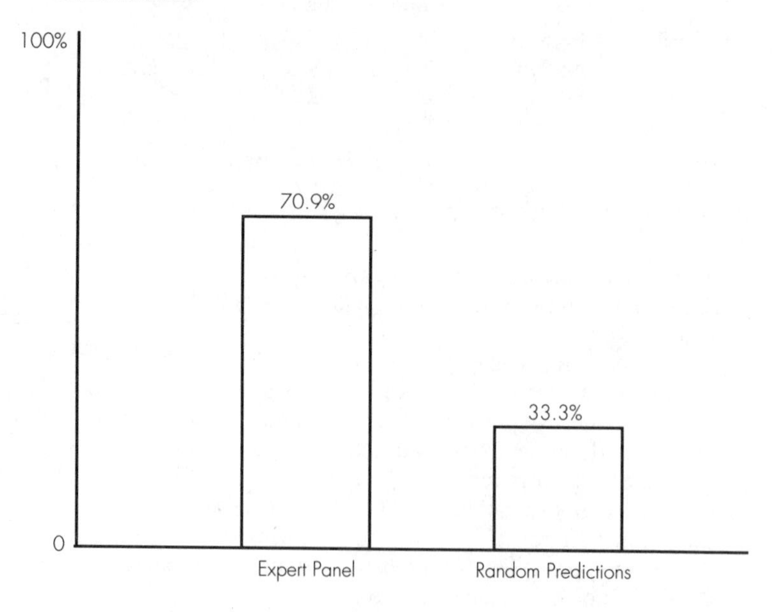

35 percent if allowance is made for the uneven distribution of the row marginals).

Another interesting implication of the prediction data is that it is easier to identify potentially poor selling items than potentially outstanding ones. As Exhibit 5 shows, judges who have passed the selection test are rarely mistaken when they show a unanimity of negative opinion. Also, the variance of judges' opinions concerning items that eventually turn out to be slow sellers is substantially less than for items that ultimately sell well. Thus it can be hypothesized that expert panels may make their greatest contribution to marketing efforts in helping to avoid costly mistakes.

This kind of phenomenon is by no means unique to this kind of panel. It may well be pervasive in all marketing research. In other words, it may be true that marketing research in general is more effective in preventing poor decisions than in selecting best decisions. The same superior ability to identify potential "losers," which is so evident in these panels, has been observed in such varied fields as copy research, taste testing, product testing, and market tests. Bad items are simply easier to spot than good ones, and it is easier to get agreement

EXHIBIT 5. Predictive Accuracy by Type of Prediction

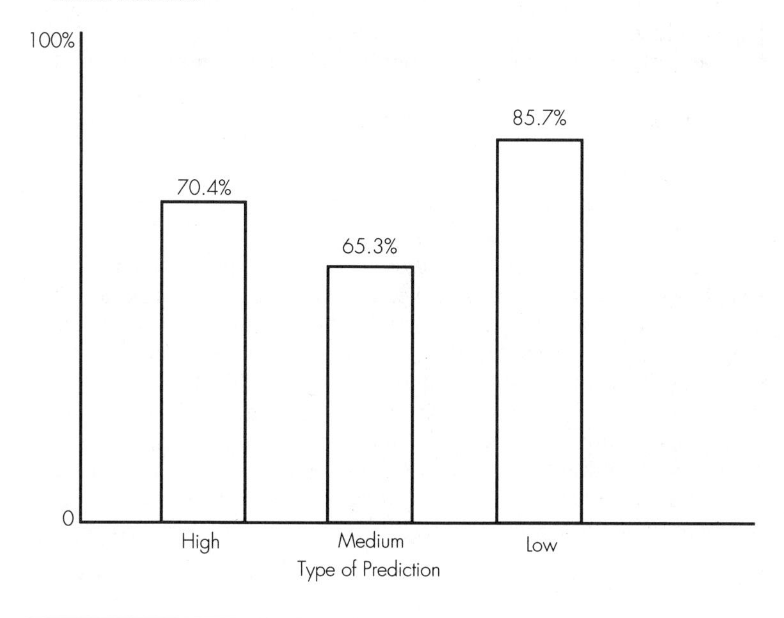

that an item is going to be a failure than that it is going to be a noteworthy success. Panel experience puts this into clear focus.

As a sidelight, it might be mentioned that the original problem of selecting potentially good department store buyers for style merchandise was also solved as a byproduct of the developmental work that was done on the "expert panel" concept. While no demographic or personality factors were found that could explain a substantial proportion of the variance in buyer performances, the same testing procedures used in selecting panel members can be and were used as a direct test of styling judgment and incorporated into the normal battery of personnel department tests.

In practice, panels have proved to be efficient screening devices. While they do misclassify individual items, their overall record is encouraging. In addition, they are a flexible instrument in that both panel size and acceptance score levels can be adjusted to provide acceptance and rejection rates that are affordable. In other words, it is possible to balance the two traditional kinds of sampling errors (the risks of rejecting a good item and of accepting a bad one) to yield a practical balance to the screening procedure.

One final implied result is that systematically quantified judgments from a small sample of judges of proven ability may have been underutilized in general as a research tool. In fact, one researcher even has concluded on the basis of his researches that there is a correlation between superior management ability and extrasensory perception (ESP) (Wright 1969). However this may be, panels of tested experts represent a constructive step toward remedying the historical deficiency in preevaluations of style merchandise.

A SECOND NEW DIRECTION—SENSORY SEGMENTATION

Sometimes, especially in those circumstances in which fast research results are not a pressing need, a strategic study—one aimed at uncovering and providing detailed descriptions of attitudinal segments—will prove to be a very wise use of research dollars. There are many examples in the marketing literature of cases in which undiscovered or poorly understood segments have been brought into clear focus through proper application of market segmentation techniques (Haley 1985).

The traditional approach to this kind of problem is benefit segmentation. Briefly, a full-fledged benefit segmentation study calls for three research phases:

- A qualitative phase aimed at developing a full list of the benefits, lifestyles, and beliefs that might underlie the existence of attitudinal segments in the marketplace
- A data reduction phase that reduces the first phase list to a manageable size
- A measurement phase in which the attitudes of a projectable sample of customers is measured on the reduced set of items, and multivariate techniques are used to identify and describe major market segments

However, a retrospective review of the utility of 20 years of experience with benefit segmentation methodology (Shapiro, Dolan, Quelch 1985) highlighted one significant weakness. While the method works very well in categories in which the primary benefits are *rational,* it works considerable less well when the primary benefits are *sensory* or emotional.

The reasons for this are not hard to find. As noted earlier, sensory benefits are extremely difficult—some would say virtually impossible—to capture fully in words. And traditional marketing research relies heavily on obtaining meaningful reactions to consumer ratings of such things as the perceived importance of often lengthy lists of benefits expressed in words and phrases. Despite the difficulty of dealing with them in a traditional marketing research framework, differences in the relative appeal of sensory benefits are just as likely to cause a variety of sensory segments to exist in categories of sensory merchandise as individual differences in the importance of rational

benefits are to cause benefit segments to exist in more rationally oriented categories.

Most of the earlier discussion about estimating demand for style merchandise via sensory panels implicitly assumed one broad universe of styles with all styling executions being potential substitutes for each other. Occasionally that is the situation. But more frequently we are dealing with styling *typologies,* and consumers are in fact making *two* decisions instead of one. Their first decision is which of several *types* of styles they prefer. And having made that decision, they then choose a specific styling execution within the preferred styling type. A few examples will illustrate that situation.

The first concerns dinnerware. Extensive work has been done in establishing styling typologies in that category. For example, Exhibit 6 shows the type called formal.

Exhibit 7 shows one called informal.

There is a parallel situation in watches. The first basic style division is into watches perceived as women's watches and those perceived as appropriate for men. Each of these two categories is in turn divided—women's watches into dress watches and everyday

watches and men's watches into sports watches and everyday watches (Exhibits 8, 9, 10, and 11).

There are also typologies in greeting cards—mood typologies such as humorous cards versus conventional cards or informal affectionate cards versus formal more remote cards. Whenever such typologies exist it is *very* important that they be recognized and taken into consideration in line planning. Returning to dinnerware, let us examine the reasons.

For the purpose of simplicity, let us assume that there are only two types of dinnerware patterns—formal and informal. And let us further assume that two thirds of potential dinnerware purchasers prefer formal patterns and the other third prefer informal patterns.

To make the problem clear, let us assume that the manufacturer is trying to decide which of eight designs to manufacture. Four of the designs are formal and four are informal. But for reasons of production and inventory efficiencies, the manufacturer can only make two of them.

The evaluation procedure is seemingly straightforward. The manufacturer exposes a reasonably representative group of consumers to the patterns, asks their preferences, and then manufactures the two

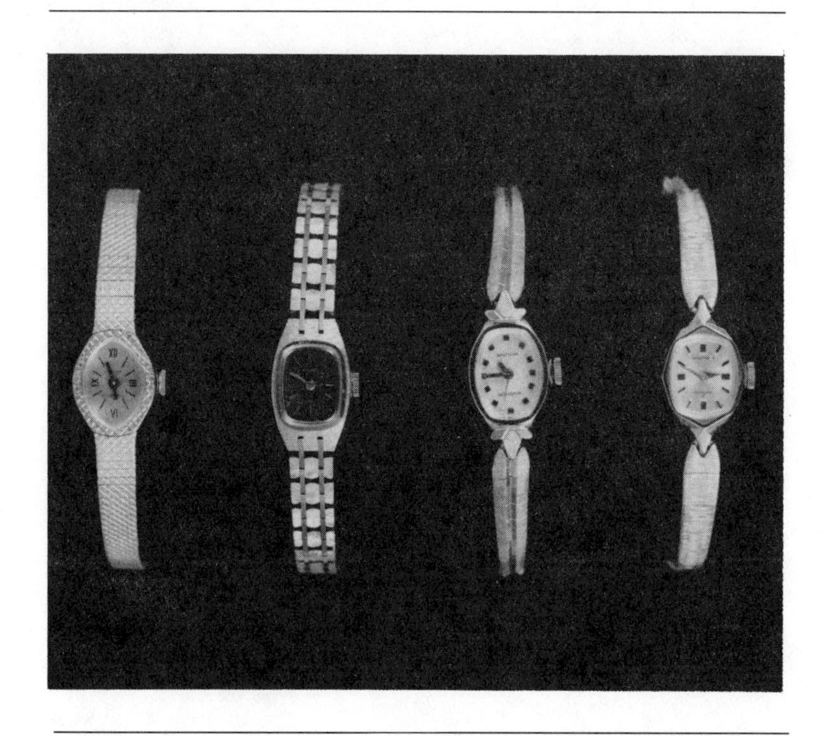

most preferred designs. While this seems to make intuitive sense, it results in a less than optimal design selection. In this case, greater volume may be obtained from the designs ranking second and fourth in preference than from the designs ranking first and second. This is *not* intuitively obvious, but it may well be true.

If all respondents evaluate all patterns, none of the informal patterns will be chosen. Remember that only one third of the population prefers that type. They will always be outvoted by the two thirds who prefer formal patterns.

But the problem is even more serious. When the people who prefer informal patterns are asked to evaluate formal patterns, they are likely to rate the most informal of the formal patterns as the most attractive of that type. But this will not be the one preferred by the people who will actually buy formal designs. They prefer very simple designs—the simpler the better.

Thus when the votes of the people who prefer formal designs are combined with those who prefer informal designs, the winning designs are compromise designs that are not completely satisfactory to either segment. So if the design that ranks second for the total sample is the first choice of the formal segment, and if the design that ranks fourth overall is the first choice of the informal segment, those two designs will outsell the two that rank first and second among the total sample. This is the essence of sensory segmentation and niching.

Here is one final example of the perils of ignoring sensory segmentation. Because this is a current study it is necessary, for competitive reasons, to disguise the product category. However, it is style merchandise. Typical displays may contain 50 to 60 different designs.

In this case, the manufacturer had first done a typology study of his and competitive items offered for sale. He identified 13 basic types of sensory merchandise and four consumer targets. Because this category involves frequent gift giving, persons identified as likely gift givers were asked which of 52 items (about 4 per type) they would select as gifts for each of the four targets. First choice results are shown in Exhibit 12. Sensory types are presented in the rank order obtained by aggregating results across the four targets. The point to be noted is that the type that receives the greatest number of first choices in total is *not* the *first* choice for *any* of the four potential targets.

While this discussion concerns manufacturers who use consumers to evaluate their designs, consumer preferences are not the only ones at issue here. As noted earlier, a legitimate question is if sensory segments exist whether an "expert" judge for one styling type can serve effectively as a judge for another type.

In greeting cards, the answer in at least one instance is "no." Expert judges for humorous cards are by no means expert when it comes to judging conventional cards. In other product categories such

EXHIBIT 12. Rank Orders of First Choices

Sensory Type	Total Sample	Target I	Target II	Target III	Target IV
A	1	4	3	6	3
A	1	4	3	6	3
B	2	6	1	12	4
C	3	1	4	3	8
D	4	2	6	8	12
E	5	3	2	5	6
F	6	7	7	4	1
G	7	10	9	1	9
H	8	11	11	2	5
I	9	8	8	9	2
J	10	5	12	13	7
K	11	12	10	10	10
L	12	9	5	7	11
M	13	13	13	11	13

as dinnerware, the evidence is more hopeful. The best judges seem to have preference patterns that extend across several style types.

The area being discussed is, in effect, a new form of segmentation, one that might most appropriately be labeled "sensory segmentation." In some product categories, notably those in which styling plays a dominant role, there is limited value in the standard kinds of word scales that are customarily used in benefit segmentation studies. Moreover, the utility of sensory segmentation extends far beyond style merchandise. It applies to all merchandise where sensory cues have a strong bearing on product choice. Among categories in which sensory segmentation has already been applied are the following:

Silverware patterns	(sight)
Greeting cards	(sight)
Bathing suits	(sight)
Sewing patterns	(sight)
Watches	(sight)
Dinnerware	(sight)
Clothing	(sight)
Pop records	(sound)
Fragrances	(smell)
Ice cream flavors	(taste)
Coffee	(taste)
Soft drinks	(taste)
Fabric textures	(touch)

The critical consideration for marketers attempting to do marketing research on sensory merchandise is that if accurate evaluations are to be obtained, it is necessary to approach people with reasonably close simulations of the sensory elements that will be contained in the merchandise when it reaches its final form.

To discover sensory segments, it is necessary to go even further. Because preference distributions across a single sensory dimension are often bipolar rather than unimodal, it is necessary to expose respondents to a wide array of *sensory* stimuli, measuring preference intensity levels as you go. These substitute for the *verbal* stimuli normally used in consumer surveys conducted for market segmentation purposes. But, aside from that very critical change, normal benefit segmentation procedures apply.

Several research tools are available for analyzing sensory data. If consumer survey research is the choice and the underlying dimensions of preference can be hypothesized with confidence, the technique of conjoint analysis can be used to identify optimal preference points. Alternatively, if a sufficiently diverse set of stimuli can be assembled, the technique of factor analysis can be used to identify primary dimensions and the tool of cluster analysis can be used to discover relatively homogeneous subgroups of respondents whose preference patterns differ from those of the general population.

There is an interesting parallel here between the discovery that special approaches (e.g., sensory segmentation), ones that extend beyond traditional benefit segmentation, are required to deal with sensory merchandise and trends in current thinking in copy research. Copy these days is often characterized as being either rational cognitive, on the one hand, or emotional, sensory, and mood related on the other. Standard copy testing approaches seem appropriate where copy is primarily rational. But something special is called for when it is not. So typology work is progressing with the objective of defining nonverbal copy types beyond the rational/emotional dichotomy. At the University of New Hampshire, for example, trained judges have been coding copy executions by nonverbal as well as logical elements, and analysts have been clustering the results. The coded profiles of the resultant types of commercials have been found to be both reliable and reasonably good predictors of the persuasion, recall, and brand salience scores obtained from copy tests.

To sum up, in the area of strategic research, benefit segmentation can be expected to do a good job when copy executions are to communicate benefits that are primarily rational. However, the kinds of sensory segmentation approaches advocated by this chapter are likely to be both more appropriate and more powerful when the forces determining sales success are primarily emotional or sensory.

NOTES

1. In a triangle test, the respondent is given three items, two of which are identical, and asked to identify the item most different from the other two (Little 1958).
2. In one instance, about 10 percent of an original sample of 500 employees qualified as panel members. Six months later, the original panel members were retested along with the people who had not qualified on the first test. Nearly 90 percent of the original panel members requalified.
3. The Delphi technique is a method of pooling expert judgment through several rounds of questionnaires to carefully selected specialists (Best 1974, Brown 1968, Dunlap and Collier 1980, "An Experimental Study . . ." 1969, Jolson and Rossow 1971a and 1971b, Linstone and Turoff 1975).
4. As a sidelight, in the testing that was undertaken, one man's judgment was found to be so accurate *in-reverse* that he became a panel member although he was never told exactly how his evaluations were being used. When he liked a design, it was *unlikely* to be accepted and vice versa. Fortunately, however, this kind of situation has proved to be highly unusual.
5. One manufacturer was able to successfully combine some of the advantages of group assemblages and individual voting by installing a specially wired central board of electric lights outside the room in which respondents were asked to record their votes. Each panel member was equipped with a small hand box with push buttons that registered his opinions on the outside light panel where they were in turn recorded. This has the advantage of gathering a number of votes instantaneously while maintaining the secrecy of votes among the voters themselves.
6. Not running the item at all was not economical once the investment required for the test run had been made.

REFERENCES

Best, R.J., "An Experiment in Delphi Estimation in Marketing Decision Making," *Journal of Marketing Research,* Vol. 11, November 1974, pp. 448–452.

Brown, B.S., "Delphi Process: A Methodology Used for the Elicitation of Opinions of Experts," Santa Monica, CA: The Rand Corporation, 1968, pp. 2–3.

Bruner II, Gordon C., "Music, Mood and Marketing," *Journal of Marketing,* Vol. 54, No. 4, October 1990, pp. 94–104.

Bunn, D.W., "The Synthesis of Predictive Models in Marketing Research," *Journal of Marketing Research,* Vol. 16, May 1979, pp. 280–283.

Cox, Anthony D., and Summers, John O., "Heuristics and Biases in the Intuitive Projection of Retail Sales," *Journal of Marketing Research,* August 1987, pp. 290–297.

Dunlap, W.R., and Collier, E.V., "A Fortran Computer Program for Delphi Calculation," *Educational and Psychological Measurement,* Vol. 40, No. 3, Autumn 1980, p. 797.

Edell, Julie A., and Chapman Burke, Marian, "The Power of Feelings in Understanding Advertising Effects," *Journal of Consumer Research,* Vol. 14, No. 3, December 1987, pp. 421–433.

"An Experimental Study of Group Opinion: The Delphi Method," *Futures,* Vol. 1, No. 5, September 1969, pp. 408–426.

Givon, Moshe, "Taste Tests: Changing the Rules to Improve the Game," *Marketing Science,* Vol. 8, No. 3, Summer 1989, pp. 282–290.

"Group Feedback Analysis: A Method of Field Research," *Psychological Bulletin,* Vol. 72, 1975, pp. 108–117.

Haley, Russell I., "Benefit Segmentation: A Decision Oriented Tool," *Journal of Marketing,* Vol. 32, July 1968, pp. 30–35.

Haley, Russell I., *Developing Effective Communications Strategy: A Benefit Segmentation Approach,* John Wiley & Sons, Inc., New York, 1985.

Haley, Russell I., and Case, P.B., "Testing Thirteen Attitude Scales for Agreement and Brand Discrimination," *Journal of Marketing,* Vol. 43, Fall 1979, pp. 20–32.

Haley, Russell I.; Richardson, Jack; Baldwin, Beth M.; "The Effects of Non-Verbal Communications in Television Advertising," *Journal of Advertising Research,* Vol. 24, No. 4, pp. 11–18.

Holbrook, M.B., "Aims, Concepts, and Methods for the Representation of Individual Differences in Esthetic Responses to Design Features," *Journal of Consumer Research,* Vol. 13, No. 3, December 1986, pp. 337–347.

Holbrook, Morris B., and Batra, Rajeev, "Assessing the Role of Emotions as Mediators of Consumer Responses to Advertising," *Journal of Consumer Research,* December 1987, pp. 404–420.

Hornik, J., "Experts' Estimates for Advertising Pretesting," *Current Issues & Research in Advertising,*" University of Michigan, 1981, pp. 29–42.

Hornik, Jacob, and Rubinow, Steven C., "Expert-Respondents' Synthesis for International Advertising Research," *Journal of Advertising Research,* June/July 1981, pp. 9–17.

Jolson, M.A., and Rossow, G. L., "The Delphi Process in Marketing Decision Making," *Journal of Marketing Research,* Vol. 8, November 1971a, pp. 443–448.

Jolson, M.A., and Rossow, G. L., "The Delphi Process: A Methodology for Solving the Consensus Problem," Combined Proceedings, 1971b Spring and Fall Conferences, American Marketing Association, edited by F.C. Allvine, pp. 518–522.

Kotler, P., "A Guide to Gathering Expert Estimates," *Business Horizons,* Vol. 13, 1970, pp. 79–87.

Linstone, H. A., and Turoff, M., "The Delphi Method, Techniques and Applications," Addison-Wesley Publishing Co., 1975.

Little, Arthur D., Inc., *Flavor Research and Food Acceptance,* Reinhold Publishing Corporation, New York, 1958.

Lurie, A., *The Language of Clothes,* Vintage Books, New York, 1981.

Mertes, John E., "Taste, Variety and Change—Yesterday and Today," *Business Perspectives,* Fall 1968, pp. 4–11.

Middlestadt, Susan E., "The Effect of Background and Ambient Color on Product Attitudes and Beliefs," *Advances in Consumer Research,* Vol. XVII, 1989, pp. 244–.

Morris, P.A., "Decision Analysis Expert Use," *Management Science,* Vol. 20, May 1974, pp. 1233–1241.

Press, S.J., "Qualitative Controlled Feedback for Forming Group Judgments and Making Decisions," *Journal of the American Statistical Association,* September 1978, Vol. 73, No. 363, pp. 526–535.

Savage, L.J., "Elicitation of Personal Probabilities and Expectations," *Journal of the American Statistical Association,* December 1971, Vol. 66, No. 336, pp. 783–801.

Shapiro, Benson P.; Dolan, Robert J.; Quelch, John A.; *Marketing Management Readings: From Theory to Practice,* Richard D. Irwin, Inc., Homewood, Illinois, 1985, Vol. III, pp. 18–29.

Some Views on the Use of Expert Judgment for Forecasting, *Technological Forecasting and Social Change,* Vol. 3, 1972, pp. 279–289.

Stayman, Douglas M., Aaker, David A.; Bruzzone, Donald E.; "The Incidence of Commercial Types Broadcast in Prime Time," *Journal of Advertising Research,* June/July 1989, pp. 26–33.

Stewart, David W., Hecker, Sid; Graham, John L.; "It's More Than What You Say: Assessing the Influence of Nonverbal Communication in Marketing," *Psychology & Marketing,* Vol. 4, No. 4, Winter 1987, pp. 303–322.

Studying Expert Informants by Survey Methods: A Cross-National Inquiry, *Public Opinion Quarterly,* Vol. 31, Spring 1967, pp. 9–26.

Wasson, Chester R., "How Predictable are Fashion and Other Product Life Cycles," *Journal of Marketing,* July 1968, Vol. 32, No. 3, pp. 36–43.

Winkler, R.L., "The Consensus of Subjective Probability Distributions," *Management Science,* Vol. 15, No. 2, October. 1968

Wright, Robert A., "E.S.P., Not Science, Rules Decisions, Professor Says," *New York Times,* August 31, 1969.

Robert Bartels
Professor Emeritus of Marketing
College of Administrative Science
The Ohio State University
Columbus, Ohio

Bruce E. MacNab
Vice-President for Sales
Kaiser Engineers, Inc.
Oakland, California

CHAPTER 28

MARKETING THEORY AND PRACTICE

NATURE AND ORIGIN OF THEORY

For only a few years, attention has been given to understanding marketing theory, while for many years much attention has been given to understanding marketing practice. Although both theory and practice have developed concurrently, they have developed somewhat apart, for they have been regarded as different modes of thought. Yet, as practice is the essence of theory and theory finds expression in practice, their unity should be apparent. Considering this statement, one is led to ask: Is marketing theory being practiced, and is marketing practice being theorized?

This question has far-reaching implications. It asks:

- Is our knowledge of marketing a formative influence on practice, or is it merely a chronicle of past and present marketing practices?
- Who contributes to marketing theory—theorists or practitioners?
- Is marketing thought more than the sum of marketing experience?
- Is marketing theory to be derived inductively from observed experience, or deductively from selected concepts and assumptions?

These and similar questions are significant to both theorists and practitioners.

It is commonly believed that theory and practice are separable—that practice may be unsupported by theory and that theory is unrealistic and impractical. If this were so, one might conclude that if theory were influential only when explicitly stated and consciously administered, then, unless theory is consciously applied, no theory is being practiced.

The opposite conclusion must be the truth, namely, that in every act of marketing, some theory is applied. Action is indicative of thought, and every thought is part of the sum total of human intelligence. Every act of marketing practice expresses some element of general intelligence, which if it were articulated would be a general theory of marketing. The fact that such a theory has not been formally stated does not deny the potential organization, structure, consistency, and unity of such thought. Ideas expressed in practice may appear to be fragmentary, isolated, and contradictory, but through their antecedents and implications they are related, coherent, and consistent. Practices represent ideas which, like pieces of a large jig-saw puzzle, have relationships even before they are connected. As the overall picture is glimpsed but not fully represented by scattered parts, so an undeveloped theory of marketing is suggested by the ideas expressed in marketing practice. Thus, *some* theory *is* always being practiced, but *what* theory?

It is the work of theorists to discover what theories are being practiced. This they do by theorizing practice—by analyzing it, conceptualizing experience, organizing ideas, drawing inferences of causality, and generalizing thought. In this sense, theorists *discover* the theories implicit in practice. Deriving first lesser theories, they progress toward integrations that must finalize in a general theory of marketing. Appreciation of these facts would show theorists the stage of their progress and show marketers that their practices have more rationale than they think.

To the extent that theory parallels practice, developments in theory depend on the state of practice. Thus, progress in theorization has reflected progressive change in marketing practice. Early thought was less reflective of individual entrepreneurial practice and more reflective of the collective practice of marketing in the general economy. Later, generalization on a level called "principles" was attained, furnishing some guidelines for practice, usually on an operational or functional level rather than for marketing management. More recently, theorization has dealt with marketing management of a broader scope, both within and outside the company.

The marketing literature has reflected the prevailing dominant types of practice, appearing throughout several decades under functional and institutional titles.

- *Advertising*—dealing with creation and presentation of commercial messages in various media; with budgets and expenditures; with social and economic consequences of advertising.
- *Salesmanship*—dealing with means of making personal selling more effective and reflecting changing concepts of the buyer mentality and of sales tasks.
- *Sales Management*—dealing with personnel, functional, and general marketing management in the firm.
- *Credit*—dealing with finance as an auxiliary to selling, from the standpoints of both functional and top management.
- *Research*—presenting a language technology whereby analysis, information retrieval, and interpretation have been emphasized.
- *Retailing and Wholesaling*—dealing with decision and control processes in operating the respective types of establishments.
- *General Marketing*—dealing with the overall process of marketing in the economy and with problems and policies confronting those engaged in the marketing work.

Despite the fact that there has been theorization in these areas since the beginning of the twentieth century, surprisingly little progress has been made in the statement of acknowledged marketing theories. One reason for this is that the levels of practice dealt with did not lend themselves to comprehensive or general theories. Also, theorization was more productive of basic concepts and simpler statement of cause and effect, on which synthesis and broader generalizations would ultimately be built. Moreover, because achievement of desirable cost-volume-profit relationships was the prime consideration, attention was given to the factors affecting these economic variables. As other goals and variables were recognized, ways were opened for exploration of more comprehensive theories.

However, all marketing theory is not simply theorization of existing marketing practice. Theory has been evolved by other means also, particularly when based on concepts from other disciplines. Viewed in the light of concepts from psychology, sociology, communication theory, engineering, biology, anthropology, and other fields, marketing has a different appearance than when viewed wholly as an economic phenomenon. Employing nonmarketing concepts, theorists have perceived marketing as social action (as society in general evolving the institutions, values, and processes for meeting its consumption needs), as patterns of personal and interpersonal behavior (as persons acting unilaterally and multilaterally in the performance of distributive role functions), as flows of products, services, and messages (as the movement of various elements multidirectionally between suppliers and users in the market). Built on these concepts, theories have brought new insight to marketing practice. Thus, theories concerning marketing systems, environmentalism, internationalism, and social responsibility have been introduced.

In general, technical or economic marketing theories seem to have been drawn mainly from practice; theories concerning human relationships and behavior in marketing have more often been based on concepts drawn from other disciplines.

MARKETING THEORIES

No attempt can be made here to suggest the entirety of the theoretical structure currently implicit in all marketing practice or in the prevailing body of marketing thought. It may be useful, however, to identify some of the areas in which theorization has attained a degree of form and acceptance. Recognizing the present level and nature of marketing theory, both practitioners and theorists may gain confidence in the structure of our knowledge and thus become better able to proceed from the foundations that have already been laid. The following, therefore, are proposed as some of the areas of theory that are currently identifiable.

Theory of Market Gaps. Marketers describe their role as the distributing of products, but theorists see it as the removing of various gaps or separations between producers and consumers. Basically, the two groups are separated by the fact that one has products and the other needs them. Not only products, but time, space, lack of information and means of payment, need for service, and some legal elements also separate these two ends of the market.

To close these gaps is the purpose of marketing. Advertising, selling, and buying bridge the information gaps; financing and credit granting, the payment gap; and transportation and storage, the space and time gaps, respectively. The only justification for an activity is the fact that it eliminates some phase of the separation between parties in the market.

This concept of marketing can be extended to broad and comprehensive theories useful for formulation of public policy as well as for justification of policies and practices within a given firm. With this view of the marketing task, practitioners may discover in their market new gaps resulting from social change, new refinements of their own marketing offering, and new means for analysis and control of their present marketing activity.

Theory of Value. In the eyes of the public, because of the intangibility of the "product" created by marketing activity, justification for it is needed. This justification has taken the form of a theory of value whereby marketing activity is deemed to be of value or to have "utility." Utility is defined as usefulness having economic value and is classified as time, place, possession, information, availability, and service utility. Thus, worth or value is attributed to the activities by which the marketing gaps are closed. Examples of the value placed on these marketing activities are found in buyers' willingness to pay for having goods available at the time and place that they want them, and in the assortment and atmosphere desired. They willingly pay for credit service, making possible immediate possession and utilization of the goods. And they pay in money as well as in time and effort to obtain information essential to a satisfying purchase.

Value creation is a manageable marketing function. In practice, managers select the utilities they create, find alternatives to creating marketing utilities, and seek means by which the costs of utility creation are reduced or their values in the minds of customers are enhanced.

The value concept in marketing also has implications other than those for management. Value created by marketing activity is a recognized component of the gross national product. It is a concept useful for determining the productivity of marketing effort at different levels or stages of distribution. Value added by marketing is, moreover, a base for taxation, for pricing structures, and for the shifting of marketing functions forward and backward in the distribution channels.

Theory of Specialization and Integration. Another marketing theory explains the institutional structure creating the utilities that close the market gaps. It is a theory to guide practitioners in determining what contribution to make to the marketing effort.

This theory relates institutional inputs to the functional outputs required by the marketing task to be performed. It rests on two assumptions: (1) that the marketing task and inherent functions are determined by market circumstances, and (2) that while the functions to be performed may not be eliminated, they may be shifted or allocated to a variety of types and combinations of institutions. A marketing institution, conceptually viewed, is some combination of economic factors that determine the nature of the contribution it makes to the marketing task. It is characterized by the lines of goods handled, by its organizational structure, capital strength, space and facilities, number of store units, its services, and price lines. The capacity to perform the needed marketing functions may be found in one institution or in a series of them, but the total input must equal the total output demanded.

All types of wholesale and retail institutions illustrate this principle of specialization and integration. The multiple lines of general wholesalers and department stores are in contrast to single line and specialty line distributors; chains, in contrast to independent operators; straight retailers, in contrast to those combining retailing with sales to wholesale, industrial, and institutional customers. Additions and deletions of the component elements describe the multiplicity of the institutional structure.

This theory provides practitioners the option to select their role in the distributive system. By eliminating or minimizing some of the characterizing factors, they become specialists and reduce their input or by adding integrating factors they increase their input. The selection may depend on both external and internal factors.

Theory of Environmentalism and Adaptivity. The marketing process is explained only in part by the theory of specialization. More is accounted for by a theory concerning external or environmental influences to which management of internal factors must be adapted. The environment largely determines the marketing task to be performed, but a conceptual view of environment must be obtained before its relevance can be appreciated.

The environment is a complex of physical and spiritual factors. It is made up of things and people; economic and noneconomic factors; the past and the present; attitudes, values, and customs; and private and public sectors. Above all, it is subject to change.

External factors influence the marketing of both consumer and industrial goods. In retailing, increased use of personal automobiles, greater consumer price consciousness, and emphasis on time-saving shopping patterns afforded opportunities for application of such merchandise techniques as relocation of outlets, reduction of services, and uncommon combinations of product lines, thus producing supermarket or discount type operations successively in foods, electrical appliances, clothing, drugs, and furniture. Similarly in industrial marketing when, in German and Japanese postwar environments of devastation, intense nationalism, and close government-business cooperation, Western techniques of market research, product planning, and promotion were adaptively applied, new institutions, channels, and marketing patterns emerged to redefine the competitive field. The prominence of both German and Japanese business in world markets is due in great measure to the opportunities and necessities provided by their environments.

Theory of Differential Advantage. In addition to the theories concerning internal and general external considerations in marketing practice, still another deals with a special external influence, namely competition, or management's lateral trade relationships. A long-held theory is that by differentiating offering through individualization, one tends to remove the practice from direct competition and to monopolize the position in the market.

The roots of this theory extend into traditional economic theory, which reasons that behavior in markets characterized by undifferentiated offerings is competitive, cooperative, and sometimes collusive, but that behavior may be more free of competitive constraints when offerings are unique. Differentiation of vendors is achieved by individualization of one's products, by claims concerning their quality, and by services, personal relationships, and resource controls.

Product differentiation is dependent on product planning, and this planning takes into account both horizontal and vertical relationships of the planner. Product planning may differentiate one's products from those of a competitor, thus achieving a horizontal differentiation and advantage in serving a market. However, product differentiation on one level of production and distribution may impose commensurate planning by subcontractors and resources from whom materials, parts, and components are obtained for assembly in the final differentiated product. Automobile manufacturers, for example, differentiate their cars in both significant and insignificant ways to gain a competitive advantage. In changing their models to extend this differentiation, they at the same time compel their suppliers to make corresponding changes and differentiation in *their* products.

While the practice of differentiation is pervasive, it is not universal. Vendors in less developed countries differentiate themselves by lines of goods handled but less by other marketing tactics, thus competing for cost and volume advantages. In more developed markets, differentiation of products within lines is commonplace, aggressive, and sometimes even antisocial. Public constraints may be imposed to correct the excesses, as is often done through legislative or administrative rulings.

Theory of "The Marketing Concept." In recent years, a change in marketing theory has resulted from consideration of whether the marketing process in unidirectional or circular. Marketing has generally been regarded as a flow of goods and services from producers to consumers, with only payment flowing in return. As research of markets increased, the return flow of information was also acknowledged as important. When ascertainment of market needs and desires became the starting point for profit goals in production and distribution, a new theory of marketing was implied. The role of the consumer was elevated, and marketing was viewed as the supplying of goods and services to meet predetermined needs, rather than simply the supplying of goods and services.

Acceptance of this policy has been slow, progressing gradually throughout the 20th century. Increasing adoption of it has been evident in the conscientious efforts often made to ascertain customers' problems, needs, desires, limitations, and habits before planning, producing, and distributing products. Impetus is further given to adoption of this policy by consumer groups and government agencies who speak with determination that consumers' interests come first.

If this concept is carried to its logical conclusion, namely, that service and market satisfaction are primary, many marketers will indeed follow a theory causing them to *begin* their marketing activity where that of their predecessors *ended,* namely, with the consumer.

Theory of Consumer Behavior. In the rising concern for consumers, several theories have been undertaken to explain their motivation and behavior. The analyses have generally employed concepts from allied social and behavioral disciplines. The consumer has been variously conceived as an economic person, a mental mechanism, a social animal, a problem solver, or a decision maker.

Explanations of consumer behavior differ not only as to concept of the consumer but also in the intricacy of the variables employed to describe the consumption process. Some explanations are a straight description of sequential steps proceeding from felt needs to information seeking, to choice among alternatives, and ultimately to purchasing. Others attempt to match variables to show the relationships between internal factors in the decision process and external influences on those internal factors. Choice alternatives, degrees of satisfaction, realization, and reevaluation of experience for subsequent decisions are also taken into consideration.

Advertising, personal salesmanship, product planning, service policies, and other management decisions rest heavily on theories of consumer behavior, and the concepts inherent in different theories should be taken carefully into consideration.

Theory of Marketing Role Behavior. As behavioral concepts applied to consumer analyses have been used also to interpret other aspects of marketing, marketing has been interpreted as a social process, or as an economic process conducted by people as social beings, not merely as economic beings.

The behavioral concepts on which this view of marketing is built include those of marketing role, participants, role function, power, expectations, obligations, and modes of behavior such as conflict, cooperation, competition, leadership dominance, and emulation. Individuals are seen to act in these various ways within the social system organized for the accomplishment of the marketing task. Motivation by goals not exclusively economic are perceived to be the basis of behavior; the sanction of role expectations by society is a guide to behavior. The explanations of behavior thus drawn from other concepts of people and other concepts of marketing have been applied to interpretations of interpersonal behavior both within organizations and in external relations, particularly in the distribution channels.

The business person who on Monday morning doffs identification with family, church, social peer groups, patriotism, and conscience and dons only an identity as an "economic person" is not understandable in terms of social role theory. But he or she is so understandable who brings to bear on business decisions the influences pressed by all of these affiliations. This latter person represents the "whole" person, who is engaged in business; the former, the business technician, who away from work becomes socialized. Each is enacting an entirely different theory of business behavior.

Theory of Social Responsibility. Once a social concept of marketing is accepted, more than one new theory may be derived from it. Whereas economic theory has for centuries acknowledged the responsibility of entrepreneurs almost solely to themselves, now with rising social consciousness and with adoption of behavioral analytical techniques, responsibility to others is also recognized, including consumers, employees, competitors, and society in general.

Responsibility to consumers is widely accepted as a principal obligation of business personnel, particularly marketers. This responsibility is imposed, however, not only on retailers who deal face-to-face with consumers. It is more lately extended to producers of the goods that retailers sell, thus assigning responsibility not merely to the *participants* in a transaction but to the *contributors* thereto.

By still further extension of the concept of responsibility, the entire community in a collective sense is embraced. Thus marketers are held responsible for the general welfare in ways formerly not expected of them. To them therefore is imputed responsibility for maintaining inventories adequate for emergency needs, for withdrawing defective or harmful products from marketing channels and even from users, from contributing to waste accumulation resulting from packages and products not easily disposed of after use, from polluting the public with detrimental child influences, with superficial value standards, and with fears and phobias demeaning to the human personality.

A theory of social responsibility has arisen not so much from marketing practice nor from purely hypothetical theorization, but rather from social change and the different social context in which the marketing process is viewed. Such a theory is not yet fully articulated, but some of its principles are becoming apparent as, for example, that inasmuch as any marketing system exists only because it is socially sanctioned, society has a right to demand that its performance be consistent with the welfare and expectations of society as a whole. The assumptions underlying such a conclusion are congruent with other aspects of marketing theory, and the implications of a broadened application of this conclusion are worthy of consideration by both theorists and practitioners.

IMPLICATIONS

Is marketing theory being practiced? Yes, it *is,* in the sense that the thought behind every marketing decision or action is a portion of a structure of thought including premises, logic, and conclusions which together constitute a theory. No thought or act is separate from its antecedents and its implications. The practice of marketing, however, is not always recognized to have such theoretical backing, but rather is regarded simply as "policy," "customary procedure," "according to the rules," or even "accidental." There is little assurance of action's consequences apart from the reasoning in which the action is held. Nor is there the opportunity for progressive development which is afforded by objective rationality.

From another point of view, it must be said that marketing theory is *not* being practiced as much as it should. A considerable body of knowledge about marketing has been developed and, whatever its stage of theory may be, it is being communicated extensively through technical schools, colleges, and various executive development programs. It is doubtful that this knowledge is sufficiently received as "theory" or that the advantages of a "theoretical" understanding are appreciated. It is more often received simply as a descriptive statement of what is being done and therefore what should be done. Moreover, specialization of work positions has reduced the responsibility for understanding much more than a narrow segment of what is known about marketing. Such levels of practice do not require knowledge of theory, but rather of procedure. On high levels of management, there is more awareness of guiding principles relevant to the total operation, but there is also continued need for appreciation of ideas that are being derived from new theoretical premises.

Is marketing practice being theorized? It has been said that the work of the theorist is to probe practice and to discover the theories implicit therein. This is being done, but research is often of such detailed character that the true theoretical import of studies is lost in the technicalities of the research. Failure to bring research to a significant level of generalization is a reason that practitioners are insufficiently aware of the existence and usefulness of theory. Marketing thought has long been criticized for the low level of its intellectual character. This too, is attributable to failure to carry theorization beyond simple generalizations, leaving anything further unsaid. Certainly clarification of concepts, definition of terminology, ascertainment of facts, identification and scaling of variables, and the postulation of principles are all important, even indispensable in the development of a discipline, but until theorization attains the status of theory and lesser theories are integrated into more general theories, the ultimate in scholarly contribution to practice is not attained.

The great need is for theory generalists more than for theoretical specialists, if marketing theory and practice are to advance most rapidly. Few individuals have attempted to formulate general theories, and fewer have reduced their thoughts to writing. More today are resorting to fresh conceptions outside the traditional body of marketing thought for their insights, but these, too, must not only be carried to the level of theory but they must be integrated with all else that is known about marketing.

The prospect ahead is encouraging, if those in the practice of marketing realize that they are applying and must apply theory to their practice, and if those in the theorization of marketing dedicate themselves to the formulation of theories, particularly to those on a higher and more general level of integration.

SUGGESTIONS FOR FURTHER READING

Henry Assael, (ed.), *Early Development and Conceptualization of the Field of Marketing* (New York: Arno Press, 1978).

Joseph V. Anderson, "Power Marketing: Its Past, Present, and Future," *Journal of Services Marketing,* Fall 1987, pp. 27–35.

Robert Bartels, *The History of Marketing Thought* (Columbus, OH: Grid, Inc., 1976, 2nd ed.).

Robert Bartels, *Marketing Theory and Metatheory* (Homewood, IL: Richard D. Irwin, Inc., 1970).

David Besanko and Wayne L. Winston, "Optimal Price Skimming by a Monopolist Facing Rational Consumers," *Management Science,* May 1990, pp. 555–567.

Paul D. Converse, *The Beginning of Marketing Thought in the United States and Fifty Years of Marketing in Retrospect* (New York: Arno Press, 1978).

Reavis Cox, et al. (eds.), *Theory in Marketing* (Homewood, IL: Richard D. Irwin, Inc., 1964).

D. F. Dixon and I. F. Wilkson, "An Alternative Paradigm for Marketing Theory," *European Journal of Marketing* (UK), 1989, pp. 59–69.

Jerome B. Kernan and Montrole S. Sommers (eds.), *Perspectives in Marketing Theory* (New York: Appleton-Century-Crofts, Inc., 1968).

William Lazer, "Some Observations on the 'State of the Arts' of Marketing Theory" in Eugene J. Kelley and William Lazer (eds.), *Managerial Marketing: Perspectives and Viewpoints* (Homewood, IL: Richard D. Irwin, Inc., 3rd ed., 1967), pp. 707–717.

Robert Skipper and Michael R. Hyman, "Marketing and Logical Deduction," *Journal of Marketing,* April 1990, pp. 89–92.

Ralph B. Thompson and John H. Tarecy, *A Selected and Annotated Bibliography of Marketing Theory* (Austin, TX: University of Texas, 1958).

PART FIVE

DEVELOPING THE MARKETING PLAN

PART FIVE

INTRODUCTION

Some people say that developing a marketing plan for today's fast-paced business is almost futile. By the time a plan is formulated, it is almost certainly out-of-date. Because the pace of change and technological advancements are accelerating, the difficulty of this challenge will only continue to increase.

However, the true professional knows that the development of a marketing plan or business plan, as some firms are now referring to it, is still an essential element of any successful business strategy. Even though some managers incorrectly, in our opinion, indicate that the written plan may no longer be a necessity, the planning process is considered by most to be very important. Customers are always changing, and their priorities are changing as well. A successful business must be sensitive to its customers, and a continuous process of planning and adapting to change is the way to keep pace.

A successful business or marketing operation must rest on a carefully thought-out plan. The strategic aspects of this plan center on ways to use available resources to secure differential advantages over competitors and to move toward attainment of the firm's objectives. To realize the strategy of the business, the marketing plan must reflect all aspects of the market. Above all, it must anticipate the actions and reactions of competitors.

Marketing has long been considered by many to be an art. The marketing manager measures success in terms of creativity and imagination as much as sales, brand share, and profits. Simulation-based systems are becoming the mechanisms through which many managers test their intuitive, creative strategies against the realities of the marketplace. As such, these systems are catalysts for a more orderly, if not scientific, approach to marketing management.

Some practitioners consider the impact of simulation-based systems on management, thinking it to be as important as the substantive results achieved. Such systems enable management to examine the implications of their insights, judgments, and suspicions about the market and competitive processes. They provide logical answers to management's "What if" questions: "What will happen if we adopt a particular campaign strategy; or if our competition follows one of several open courses of action; or if the basic market conditions change?" They motivate the manager to consider alternative strategies and to examine the implications of a broad range of contingencies. This, in turn, leads to more organized planning, earlier detection of deviations from "expected conditions," and greater sensitivity to the market processes responsible for sales and profits.

Another important aspect in the marketer's quest for sales and profits is ethics. Today's businessperson must ask if today's competitive pressures conflict with ethical considerations. Also, does the legal system provide too many or too few ethical constraints on the marketer? While most marketers have always been conscious of ethical considerations, today's climate of consumerism renders many traditional attitudes obsolete. Marketers must adopt a more broadly based view of ethics if they truly want to understand and meet the needs of today's customers.

All of these factors not only influence the development of today's business marketing plan, but they are also extremely important for us to evaluate in terms of the level of our performances.

Paul E. Green
University of Pennsylvania
Philadelphia, Pennsylvania

John L. McMennamin
The Carnation Company
Los Angeles, California

Shahrzad Amirani
University of Texas at Arlington
Arlington, Texas

CHAPTER 29

MARKET POSITION ANALYSIS

Measuring the position of a firm's product or service in the minds of consumers—if not the touchstone to successful marketing—is crucial to the planning of most strategic efforts. Chemically similar products, for example, brands of aspirin or Vitamin C, may be perceived quite differently by the consumer. Conversely, chemically (or physically) differentiated brands might be perceived similarly if their differentiation occurs along dimensions that are not salient to the potential buyer.

Not surprisingly, managers are interested in buyers' perceptions of their brand, particularly if there are misperceptions that cast the product/service in an unfavorable light. Misperceptions can often be corrected through advertising/promotion. Interest in relationships between perceptions and "true" product profiles is becoming all the more important, given the growing trend toward comparative advertising. Indeed, the strategy of brand positioning is based on finding meaningful (and deliverable) advantages over competing brands.

Furthermore, brand preferences are obviously dependent on perceptions, since being able to distinguish between brands is a necessary condition for preferring one brand to another. Not surprisingly, consumers' preferences (and perceptions) are rarely homogeneous. The strategy of market segmentation attempts to capitalize on differences across submarkets in brand perceptions and preferences.

This chapter is concerned with the application of new procedures for measuring buyers' perceptions and preferences for brands and the implications of these measurements for the design and control of marketing strategy. First, a few brief examples are presented. Next, one problem—concerned with the development of promotional strategy for a laundry-type product—is discussed in some detail. The import of these new measurement techniques on the development of new products or services and the control of existing ones is briefly described.

The methodology to be discussed in this chapter has the rather esoteric name of *multidimensional scaling*. Without delving into technical details, these relatively recent techniques, developed by psychometricians and mathematical psychologists, permit the researcher to portray buyers' perceptions and evaluations geometrically. Brands (or suppliers) are represented as points in a geometric space whose axes can be described as frames of reference along which brands are compared perceptually.

People (e.g., consumers, retailers, corporate salespeople) can also be represented in these spaces. In this case, the point locations represent their perceptions of the *ideal* amounts of each dimension of the perceptual space—that is, those levels that they would most prefer to have in a product or service.

Over the last decade, multidimensional scaling and similar methods have undergone a rapid expansion in the variety of models and techniques. In particular, *correspondence analysis* has emerged as a popular type of scaling procedure. We conclude the chapter with a discussion of some of these newer developments and their role in market positioning.

SOME EXAMPLES

Soft Drink Slogans

A prominent producer of soft drinks wished to consider the adoption of a new slogan—one that would connote the distinctive features of the brand. The firm's advertising department had prepared 15 candidate slogans and the problem was which one should we choose?

A study of consumers' perceptions of these slogans and their association with various brands of soft drinks was undertaken. The study indicated that 11 of the 15 slogans were perceived as more closely associated with the images of one or more competitive brands than the firm's own brand. Had no comparison of brand-slogan congruence been attempted, it is conceivable that a slogan might have been chosen that would be more closely associated with a competitor's brand than with the company's own brand.

Computer Firm Images

A large producer of computers was concerned with the relationship between the physical characteristics of its hardware and data processors' perceptions. Computer models—the firm's and its competitors'—were first positioned geometrically in performance space (how long it would take the computer to perform multiplication, size of core, etc.). Perceptual judgments of computer model similarity were also obtained from the firm's sales personnel, its customers, and its noncustomers.

The sales personnel's perceptions agreed most closely with the objective (performance) positioning of the computer models. However, the firm's customer perceptions disagreed in significant ways with the sales personnel's perceptions, suggesting that the salespeople were not emphasizing certain performance characteristics of the company's line that would enhance customer satisfaction. Perceptions of the firm's noncustomers had relatively little correspondence with the true performance characteristics of its computers. Quite to the contrary, noncustomers perceived the firm's computer line as more or less undifferentiated from those of other firms.

The firm's noncustomers, to a large extent, evoked criteria other than physical performance in evaluating competitive models. Noncustomers were chiefly concerned with the prominence of the computer firm, the size of its technical support staff, and the various marketing services it could offer. Performance/cost ratios, which were quite favorable for the models marketed by the sponsor of the study, meant relatively little to its noncustomers. Not surprisingly, the firm's noncustomers tended to be less technically sophisticated data processors—ones who would be attracted to a large, well-established (albeit higher-priced) computer supplier.

High-Nutrition Cereals

A marketer of a high-nutrition brand of cereal was becoming increasingly concerned over the relevance of its advertising toward promoting a cereal that both tasted good and had high nutritional value. Discussions with advertising agency personnel led to a new campaign that humorously stressed qualities of good taste and high nutrition. The firm's marketing personnel wondered if this new message was getting across to the consumer.

A study of housewife perceptions of the firm's brand in comparison to other cereals was undertaken. The study indicated that the advertising goals *were* being achieved: while perceived as a high-nutrition cereal the firm's brand plotted closer in "perceptual space" to good-tasting cereals than did any of the other high nutrition brands. That is, consumers were perceiving the hybrid advertising appeal in ways desired by the company. In this case, perceptions were measured for the purpose of monitoring the results of a basic change in advertising appeal.

A New Drug Product

A well-known pharmaceutical manufacturer had developed a new over-the-counter item that would be more effective but higher priced than existing items. Marketing management's problem was to determine the copy points to utilize in the introductory phase of commercialization. Since the product was one whose initial acceptance was assumed to be heavily influenced by physicians' recommendations, the perceptual study was directed to this "specifier" group first.

Five sets of copy appeals were examined. Contrary to the supposition of the firm's marketing personnel, the most popular appeal stressed one simple, prominent copy point—an appeal that the firm thought would be too "soft sell." The firm's favorite appeal (before the study) was perceived by the physicians as being more relevant to the current leading (competitor's) product than it was to the firm's new entrant.

A DETAILED ILLUSTRATION OF MARKET POSITION ANALYSIS

The preceding capsule descriptions, while illustrating the nature of market position analysis, are too brief to give the reader a feel for the nature of the methodology. In this section of the chapter, we describe a more detailed example—one dealing with the selection of promotional appeals for fabric softeners.

The sponsor of this study was one of several manufacturers of fabric softeners. The firm's marketing research personnel were becoming increasingly concerned with two basic strategic questions regarding the market positioning of their product: (1) How can the total market for fabric softeners be expanded and (2) How can their share of this expanded market be increased? At the time the study was initiated, all fabric softener manufacturers were using promotional appeals that emphasized the tactual or feel-like benefits associated with the use of the product.

Given the rather experimental nature of multidimensional scaling methodology, the firm's marketing research personnel elected to launch a small pilot study whose purpose was to see how fabric softener users (of any brand) differed in their perceptions from nonusers of fabric softeners.

Method

The first step in the pilot study was to develop a list of activities that a housewife would view as naturally associated with her daily world. From a much larger initial list, the 43 activities shown in Exhibit 1 were finally selected. Note that two items of interest here are activities 12 ("Using a fabric softener in your wash") and 38 ("Wearing soft clothes").

Two small samples (60 respondents) of fabric softener users and nonusers were recruited by a screening-type telephone interview. Each sample was matched roughly with regard to demographics, according to data assembled by the firm's personnel. Since the respondents were asked a varied series of product usage questions in the screening phase, they did not know the specific purpose of the follow-up interview. In the follow-up interview all respondents—identified from the screening interview as users or nonusers—were shown a set of cards on each of which appeared the name of one of the activities shown in Exhibit 1.

After looking through the cards (spread out randomly on a table in front of her), the respondent was asked to group the activities into clusters that represented activities that seemed to "go together" or be related to each other. The respondent was asked to make up ten such groups (with no need to equalize the number of items per cluster) that represented activities that seem to be highly similiar within the cluster.

EXHIBIT 1. List of Activities (Stimuli)

Number	
1	Sunbathing
2	Baking a cake for the family
3	Sewing buttons on husband's shirt
4	Receiving an admiring glance from a man
5	Relaxing in a warm bath with bath oil
6	Receiving help from dinner guests with the dishes
7	Smoothing on hand lotion
8	Going to church
9	Drinking a cool drink on a hot day
10	Sleeping on freshly ironed sheets
11	Cooking a fancy dinner for guests
12	Using a fabric softener in your wash
13	Peeling potatoes
14	Saving up some "mad money"
15	Going to the beauty parlor
16	Using a cream rinse after shampoo
17	Moisturizing your face with special cream
18	Doing volunteer charity work
19	Shopping for new clothes for yourself
20	Putting fresh flowers on the table
21	Using a room freshener spray
22	Putting on perfume or cologne
23	Buying a new plant for living room
24	Cleaning out the closets
25	Letting your husband pick the movie to see
26	Hanging freshly cleaned curtains
27	Burning incense
28	Opening windows to air out the room
29	Receiving praise from your family
30	Feeling like a good mother
31	Knowing you are an excellent housewife
32	Serving a special treat to the family
33	Receiving an affectionate kiss from your husband
34	Getting someone else to do your work
35	Sleeping late in the morning
36	Reclining in a soft chair
37	Smelling flowers in a garden
38	Wearing soft clothes
39	Wearing an attractive outfit (new)
40	Receiving an achievement award
41	Powdering the baby
42	Healing a diaper rash
43	Making love

Analyzing the Data

A rather simple measure of perceived interactivity similarity can be developed by merely counting, across respondents, the number of times any pair of activities are grouped together. These frequency counts were made separately for users and nonusers. The resulting tables showed the incidence (across respondents) with which any pair of activities were grouped together.

Two (complementary) methods were used to analyze these frequency data. First, for users and nonusers separately, the data were scaled multidimensionally, leading to the two geometric patterns shown in Exhibits 2 and 3.

Second, the same incidence tables were submitted to a numerical clustering program that groups highly similar activities together in a hierarchical fashion—that is, one in which small clusters of highly related items are progressively grouped into larger and larger clusters, containing less similar items, until all items are merged into one large cluster. The results of this step appear in Exhibits 4 and 5.

Scaling Results

Looking first at the *gross* patterns of activity grouping, we note in both Exhibits 2 and 3 that some evidence for a dimensional interpretation is apparent. Insofar as the horizontal axis is concerned, we note that family-connected activities tend to plot on the left of the origin, while personal activities tend to plot on the right.

Insofar as the vertical axis is concerned, we see that outside activities ("Going to church," "Doing volunteer work") tend to plot above the origin, while inside activities ("Buying a new plant for the living room") tend to plot below the origin. We tentatively conclude that the horizontal axis might be labeled "family-personal" while the vertical axis might be labeled "outside-inside" in terms of the major characteristics of the activities.

It seems clear at this point that between-group differences must be sought at a finer level of structure. That intergroup differences do exist is brought out by examining selected activities. For example, we first focus our attention on activity 12, "Using a fabric softener in your wash."

If we look at the activities in Exhibit 2 (user group) that are near activity 12, we see activities like (1) "Using a room freshener spray," (2) "Opening windows to air out the room," (3) "Putting fresh flowers on the table," and (4) "Hanging freshly cleaned curtains." Thus, for users the activity of "Using fabric softener in your wash" appears to exhibit a cleanliness and freshness theme in terms of the activities perceived to be similar to it. Note that activity 38, "Wearing soft clothes," plots rather distantly from activity 12, suggesting that these activitites were not highly associated with each other.

EXHIBIT 2. Two-Dimensional Activity Configuration—Users*

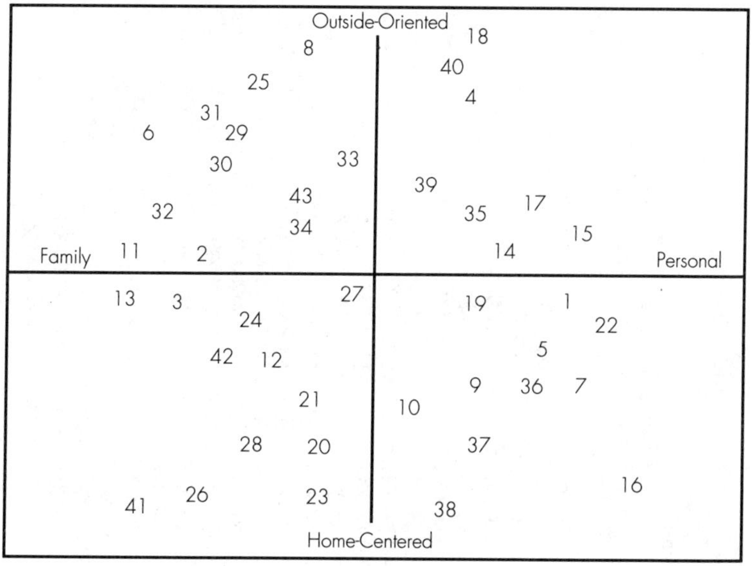

Outside-Oriented
8 18
40
25
4
31
6 29
30 33
39
43
32 17
35
34
15
Family 11 2 14 Personal
13 3 27 19 1
24 22
42 12 5
9 36 7
21
10
28 20 37
16
41 26 23 38
Home-Centered

*See Exhibit 1 for legend.

EXHIBIT 3. Two-Dimensional Activity Configuration—Nonusers*

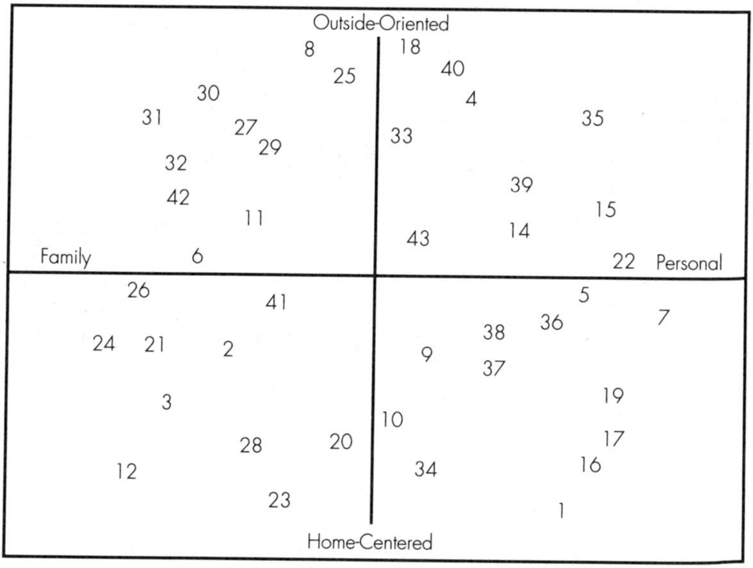

Outside-Oriented
8 18
40
25
30
4
31 35
27 33
29
32
39
42
15
11
43 14
Family 6 22 Personal
26 5
41
36 7
38
24 21 2 9
37
3 19
10
17
28 20
12 34 16
23
1
Home-Centered

*See Exhibit 1 for legend.

EXHIBIT 4. Hierarchical Clustering of 43 Activities by User Group*

```
                              Activities
0 3 3 1 3 1 0 0 1 1 2 0 3 1 1 3 2 2 2 2 2 1 2 2 4 4 2 3 3 0 1 0 3 0 3 0 1 4 0 2 3 4
9 6 7 0 8 5 5 7 6 7 2 1 5 4 9 9 0 3 7 4 6 2 1 8 1 2 9 0 1 3 1 2 2 6 4 8 8 0 4 5 3 3

○ ○ ○ ○ ○ ○ ○ ○ ○ ○ ○ ○ ○ ○ ○ ○ ○ ○ ○ ○ ○ ○ ○ ○ XXX ○ ○ ○ ○ ○ ○ ○ ○ ○ ○ ○ ○ ○ ○ ○ XXX
○ ○ ○ ○ ○ ○ ○ ○ XXX ○ ○ ○ ○ ○ ○ ○ ○ ○ ○ ○ ○ ○ ○ XXX ○ ○ ○ ○ ○ ○ XXX ○ ○ ○ ○ ○ ○ ○ XXX
○ ○ ○ ○ ○ ○ ○ ○ XXX ○ ○ ○ ○ ○ ○ ○ ○ ○ ○ ○ ○ XXX XXX ○ ○ ○ ○ ○ ○ XXX ○ ○ ○ ○ ○ ○ ○ XXX
○ ○ ○ ○ ○ ○ ○ ○ XXX ○ ○ ○ ○ XXX ○ ○ ○ ○ ○ ○ XXX XXX ○ ○ ○ ○ ○ ○ XXX ○ ○ ○ ○ ○ ○ ○ XXX
○ ○ ○ ○ ○ ○ XXX XXXXX ○ ○ ○ XXX ○ ○ ○ ○ ○ ○ XXX XXX ○ ○ ○ ○ ○ ○ XXX ○ ○ XXX ○ ○ ○ XXX
XXX ○ ○ ○ ○ XXX XXXXX ○ ○ ○ XXX ○ ○ ○ XXX ○ XXX XXX ○ ○ ○ ○ ○ ○ XXX ○ ○ XXX ○ ○ ○ XXX
XXX ○ ○ ○ ○ XXXXXXXXX ○ ○ ○ XXX ○ ○ ○ XXX ○ XXX XXX ○ ○ ○ ○ ○ ○ XXX ○ ○ XXX ○ ○ ○ XXX
XXX ○ ○ ○ ○ XXXXXXXXX ○ ○ ○ XXX XXX ○ XXX XXXXX XXX ○ ○ ○ XXX ○ XXX ○ ○ XXX ○ ○ ○ XXX
XXX ○ ○ ○ ○ XXXXXXXXX XXX ○ XXX XXX ○ XXX XXXXX XXX ○ ○ ○ XXX ○ XXX ○ ○ XXX ○ ○ XXXXX
XXX ○ ○ ○ XXXXXXXXXXX XXX ○ XXX XXX ○ XXX XXXXX XXX ○ ○ ○ XXX ○ XXX XXX XXX ○ ○ XXXXX
XXX ○ XXX XXXXXXXXXXX XXX ○ XXX XXX ○ XXX XXXXX XXX ○ XXX XXX XXXXX XXX XXX ○ ○ XXXXX
XXXXX XXX XXXXXXXXXXX XXX ○ XXX XXX ○ XXX XXXXX XXX ○ XXX XXX XXXXX XXX XXX ○ ○ XXXXX
XXXXX XXX XXXXXXXXXXX XXX ○ XXX XXX ○ XXX XXXXX XXX XXXXX XXX XXXXX XXX XXX ○ ○ XXXXX
XXXXX XXX XXXXXXXXXXXXXXX ○ XXX XXX ○ XXX XXXXX XXX XXXXX XXX XXXXX XXX XXXXX ○ XXXXX
XXXXX XXX XXXXXXXXXXXXXXX XXXXX XXX ○ XXXXXXXXX XXX XXXXX XXX XXXXX XXX XXXXX ○ XXXXX
XXXXXXXXX XXXXXXXXXXXXXXX XXXXX XXX ○ XXXXXXXXX XXX XXXXX XXX XXXXX XXX XXXXX ○ XXXXX
XXXXXXXXX XXXXXXXXXXXXXXX XXXXX XXXXX XXXXXXXXX XXX XXXXX XXXXXXXXX XXX XXXXX XXXXXXX
XXXXXXXXX XXXXXXXXXXXXXXX XXXXX XXXXX XXXXXXXXXXXXX XXXXXXXXXXXXXXX XXX XXXXX XXXXXXX
XXXXXXXXX XXXXXXXXXXXXXXXXXXXXX XXXXX XXXXXXXXXXXXX XXXXXXXXXXXXXXX XXX XXXXX XXXXXXX
XXXXXXXXXXXXXXXXXXXXXXXXXXXXXXX XXXXX XXXXXXXXXXXXX XXXXXXXXXXXXXXXXXXX XXXXX XXXXXXX
XXXXXXXXXXXXXXXXXXXXXXXXXXXXXXX XXXXXXXXXXXXXXXXXXX XXXXXXXXXXXXXXXXXXXXXXXXXXXXXXXXX
XXXXXXXXXXXXXXXXXXXXXXXXXXXXXXXXXXXXXXXXXXXXXXXXXXXXXXXXXXXXXXXXXXXXXXXXXXXXXXXXXXXXX
```

EXHIBIT 5. Hierarchical Clustering of 43 Activities by Nonuser Group*

Activities

```
0 3 2 2 2 3 0 0 3 3 1 0 1 1 0 2 3 1 1 3 0 1 1 2 2 1 2 2 1 0 3 2 3 3 4 4 0 1 4 2 0 3 4
6 4 7 0 3 7 1 9 5 6 5 7 6 7 5 2 8 4 9 9 3 3 2 4 6 0 1 8 1 2 2 9 0 1 1 2 8 8 0 5 4 3 3
o o o o o o o o o o o o XXX o o o o o o o o o o o o o o o o o o o o o o o o o o o o o
o o o o o o o o o o o o XXX o o o o o o o o o o o o o o o o o o o o XXX o o o o o o o
o o o o o o o o o o o XXXXX o o o o o o o o o o o o o o o o o o o o XXX o o o o o XXX
o o o o o o o o o o XXXXXXX XXX o o o o o o o o o o o o o o o o o o XXX o o o o o XXX
o o o o o o o o o o XXXXXXX XXX o o o o o o o o o o o o o XXX o o o XXX o o o o o XXX
o o o o o o o o o o XXXXXXX XXX o o XXX o o o o o o XXX o XXX o o o XXX o o o o o XXX
o o o o o o o o o o XXXXXXX XXX o o XXX o o o o o o XXX o XXX XXX o XXX o o o o o XXX
o o o o o o o o o o XXXXXXX XXX o o XXX o o o XXX o XXX o XXX XXXXX XXX o o o o o XXX
o o o o o o o o o o XXXXXXX XXX o o XXX o o o XXX o XXX o XXX XXXXX XXX o o o o XXXXX
o o o o o o XXX o o XXXXXXX XXX o o XXX o o o XXX o XXX o XXX XXXXX XXX o o o o XXXXX
o o o XXX o XXX XXX XXXXXXX XXX o o XXX XXX o XXX o XXX o XXX XXXXX XXX o XXX o XXXXX
o o o XXX o XXX XXX XXXXXXX XXX o XXXXX XXX o XXX o XXX o XXX XXXXX XXX o XXX o XXXXX
o o o XXX o XXX XXX XXXXXXX XXX o XXXXX XXX o XXX o XXX XXXXX XXXXX XXX o XXX o XXXXX
o o o XXX o XXXXXXX XXXXXXXXXXX o XXXXX XXX XXXXX o XXX XXXXX XXXXX XXX o XXX o XXXXX
o o o XXX o XXXXXXX XXXXXXXXXXX o XXXXX XXX XXXXX o XXX XXXXX XXXXX XXX o XXX XXXXXXX
XXX o XXXXX XXXXXXX XXXXXXXXXXX o XXXXX XXXXXXXXX XXXXX XXXXX XXXXX XXX XXXXX XXXXXXX
XXX o XXXXX XXXXXXX XXXXXXXXXXXXXXXXXXX XXXXXXXXX XXXXX XXXXX XXXXXXXXX XXXXX XXXXXXX
XXX o XXXXX XXXXXXX XXXXXXXXXXXXXXXXXXX XXXXXXXXXXXXXXX XXXXX XXXXXXXXX XXXXX XXXXXXX
XXX XXXXXXX XXXXXXXXXXXXXXXXXXXXXXXXXXX XXXXXXXXXXXXXXX XXXXXXXXXXXXXXX XXXXX XXXXXXX
XXX XXXXXXX XXXXXXXXXXXXXXXXXXXXXXXXXXX XXXXXXXXXXXXXXXXXXXXXXXXXXXXXXX XXXXX XXXXXXX
XXX XXXXXXX XXXXXXXXXXXXXXXXXXXXXXXXXXX XXXXXXXXXXXXXXXXXXXXXXXXXXXXXXX XXXXXXXXXXXXX
XXXXXXXXXXXXXXXXXXXXXXXXXXXXXXXXXXXXXXXXXXXXXXXXXXXXXXXXXXXXXXXXXXXXXXXXXXXXXXXXXXXXX
```

We now turn to Exhibit 3, which shows the activity configuration for nonusers. This time we note that the activities plotted near activity 12 are: (1) "Peeling potatoes," (2) Sewing buttons on husband's shirt," and (3) "Cleaning out the closets." While some of the same activities noted in Exhibit 2 also plot fairly near activity 12 in Exhibit 3, it seems evident that nonusers also associate chore-like activities with the activity of "Using a fabric softener in your wash."

Clustering Results

As another means for comparing activity groupings between users and nonusers, the original similarity table for each group was clustered by means of a hierarchial clustering program. In this way, we are able to check the visually obtained clusterings observed in Exhibits 2 and 3 with a procedure that works directly with the original frequency tables. We note from these clustering results that insofar as users (Exhibit 4) are concerned, activity 12 first groups with activities 21 ("Using a room freshener spray") and 28 ("Opening up windows to air out the room"). This cluster is then joined by activities 24 ("Cleaning out the closets") and 26 ("Hanging freshly cleaned curtains").

In the case of nonusers (Exhibit 5), activities 3 ("Sewing buttons on husband's shirt") and 13 ("Peeling potatoes")—in addition to activities 24 and 26—are most highly associated with activity 12. Again we note the combination of olfactory and chore-like activities in the clustering developed from the nonuser group. Interestingly enough, tactile items like "Wearing soft clothes" do not seem to be highly associated with activity 12.

IMPLICATIONS

The preceding pilot study—coupled with the results of a series of focus-group interviews—essentially indicated that

1. Both users and nonusers associate olfactory-like (rather than tactual) activities with fabric softeners.
2. The nonuser group also associates chore-like activities with fabric softener usage.

From the standpoint of the sponsoring firm's promotional strategy, the pilot study suggested that "softening clothes" was no longer newsworthy and that other benefits—freshness, brightness, clean smell—would appear more interesting to promote. Moreover, in the case of nonusers some means of convincing housewives that (1) their efforts would be appreciated by other family members (prinicipally the husband) and (2) fabric softeners could be conveniently used appeared to be needed. The implications for promotional strategy and/or new product development are apparent, given this information. *And* promotional appeals were changed by the study's sponsors.

MORE RECENT DEVELOPMENTS

In the last decade or so, U.S. marketing researchers have become very interested in a new technique for multidimensional scaling called *correspondence analysis.* This tool had long been popular in Europe, particularly in France.

Correspondence analysis works with two-way (or multi-way) cross tabulations of categorical data—for example, buyers' favorite brands cross-classified by age categories. Typically, such data have been used by marketing researchers to look for associations between two or more categorical variables.

When the cross-tables have many rows and columns, it is difficult to discern patterns from the numbers alone. Correspondence analysis provides a way to portray cross-tabulations in pictorial form. Cells in the table that have differentially high freqencies are represented by row and column points that are relatively close together on the map.

Conversely, a row and column whose cell exhibits a low frequency tends to show the associated points relatively far apart. Assuming that the rows and columns are associated (that is, the joint frequency is not simply proportional to the product of the row and column's marginal frequencies), correspondence analysis tries to find compromise locations of all row and column points that best agree with the table's overall association. As such, it provides explanatory power beyond that of a simple statistical test of row and column independence.

A Numerical Example

As an example, we consider the cross-tabulation shown in Exhibit 6. The input data consist of a 10 x 11 frequencies table obtained by a sample of 404 physicians. A respondent was asked to select those promotional activities (newsletter, clinical reports, etc.) that he/she would most prefer a drug firm to implement in introducing a new antihypertensive drug. A total of 1,375 responses (an average of 3.4 selections per respondent) were obtained. Physicians were also classified by specialty (cardiologist, general practitioner, nephrologist, internist, and family physician) and by proneness to innovate (high versus low), based on their first principal component score developed from responses to five psychographic statements.

Exhibit 6 represents a conventional cross-tabulation of frequencies that can be analyzed by simple correspondence analysis. Exhibit 7 shows the two-dimensional joint space plot of physician segments and promotional activities. As noted, along the horizontal axis the specialty physicians (nephrologists, cardiologists, and internists) are separated from the generalists (general practioners and family physicians). We also observe that the effect of a high versus low "innovativeness" is seen to vary by physician specialty.

EXHIBIT 6. Input Data for Two-Way Correspondence Analysis

	News-letter	Clinical Reports	Use Trials	Ex-hibits	Detail-ing	Dinner Meetings	Direct Mail	Journal Cards	Samp-ling	Sym-posia	Audio/ Visual	Total
Cardiologist												
- Innovative CRD-1	14	43	43	27	25	26	11	8	17	41	16	271
- Noninnovative CRD-2	9	30	29	17	31	17	5	3	6	34	22	203
General Practitioner												
- Innovative GP-1	13	23	23	18	52	34	7	15	15	19	25	244
- Noninnovative GP-2	13	26	25	21	56	29	8	14	17	16	29	254
Nephrologist												
- Innovative NEP-1	2	15	12	10	9	10	3	7	6	14	8	96
- Noninnovative NEP-2	1	5	9	5	6	3	1	3	6	6	4	49
Internist												
- Innovative IM-1	2	8	8	6	3	3	0	2	4	9	3	48
- Noninnovative IM-2	6	11	11	7	6	3	2	5	3	7	1	62
Family Physician												
-Innovative FP-1	2	5	9	3	11	9	2	4	0	3	3	51
- Non-innovative FP-2	8	10	10	4	21	11	6	3	5	8	11	97
Total	70	176	179	118	220	145	45	64	79	157	122	1,375

Attitudinal Statements

1. I like to try new and different things.
2. I often prescribe new medications
3. I go to more medical conventions than most of my colleagues.
4. I spend more of my time keeping up with new medical developments than most doctors.
5. I spend more time reading medical journals than most doctors.

Cluster Analysis of Joint-Space Coordinates

While the two-dimensional map of Exhibit 7 provides some help in interpreting the space, one wonders whether a cluster analysis of higher-dimensional coordinates might provide enhanced interpretive value. To that end, the coordinates of the four-dimensional correspondence analysis solution were clustered via a hierarchical linkage program. Exhibit 8 shows the results.

As observed from Exhibit 8, the higher-dimensional solution provides useful ancillary information, beyond that provided by the map. For example, we observe that innovative cardiologists and nephrologists cluster together, along with the more "scientific" information sources: clinical reports, clinical trials, and exhibits. This cluster is later joined by innovative internists and symposia.

Both innovative and noninnovative general practioners cluster tightly, along with the less "prestigious" information sources of detailing and audiovisual. This cluster is then joined by noninnovative family physicians and direct mail promotion. Rather, isolated clusters are noted in the case of (1) innovative family physicians and dinners; (2) noninnovative nephrologists and samples; and (3) noninnovative internists and newsletters.

EXHIBIT 7. Joint Space Obtained from Correspondence Analysis

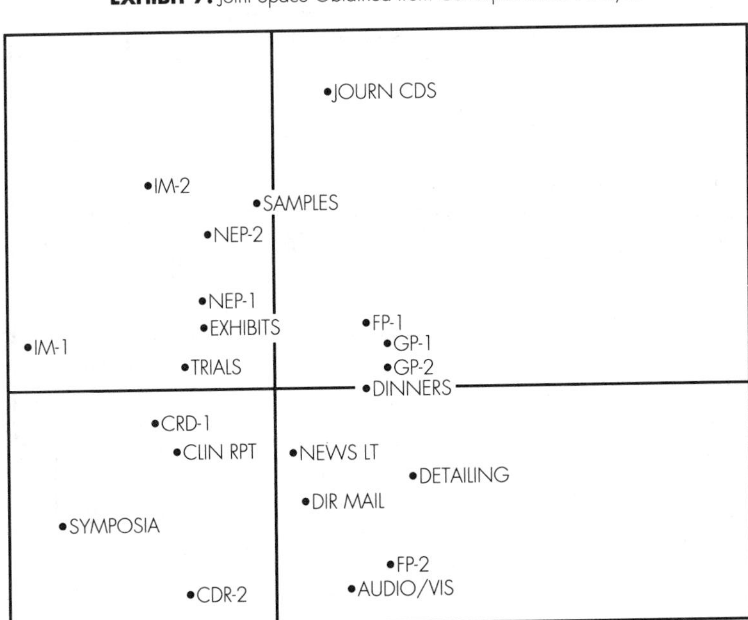

EXHIBIT 8. Cluster Analysis Diagram Based on Four-Dimensional Solution

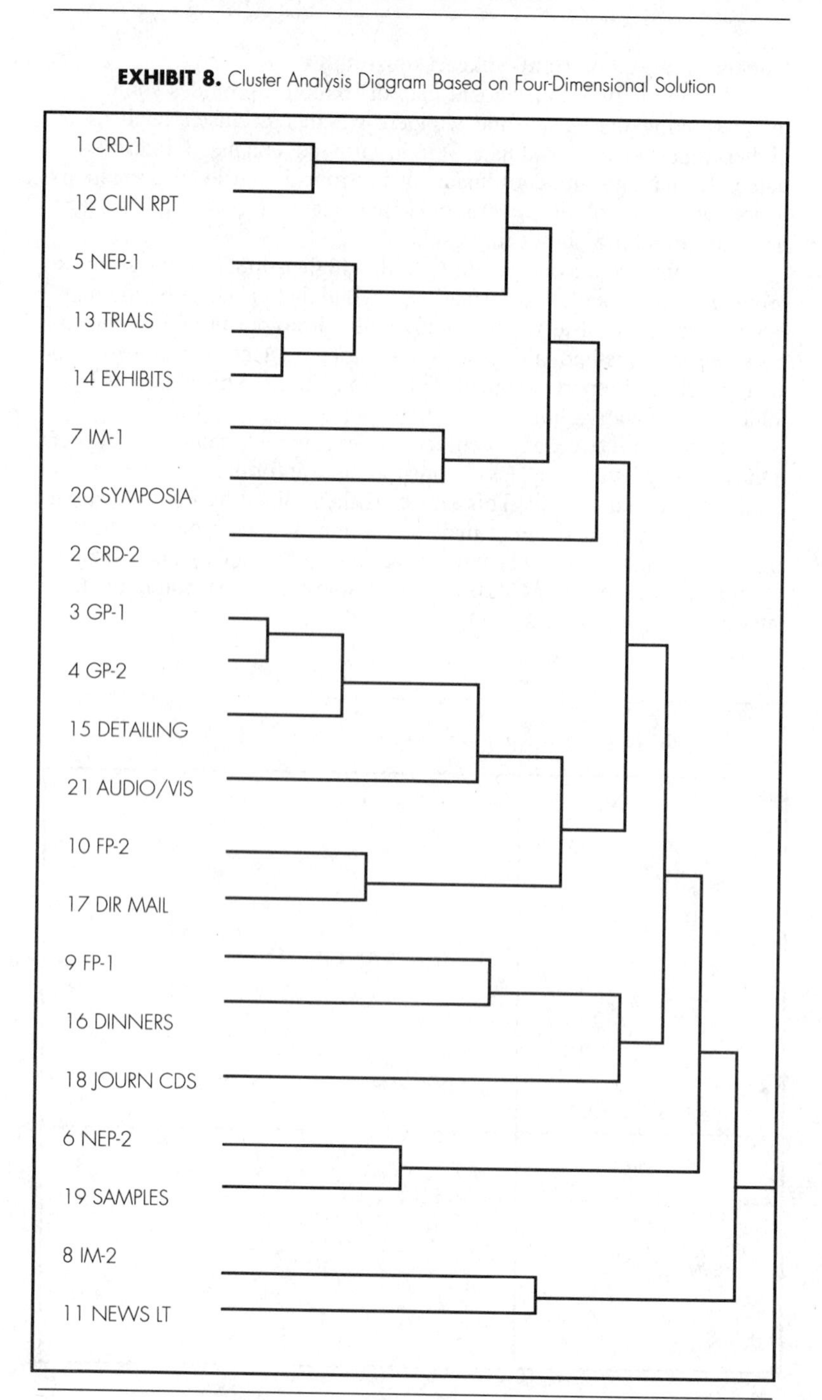

In general, the associated cluster analysis brings out relationships between specialty/innovativeness and preferred promotional activities. At the high end of the prestige scale are clinical reports, clinical trials, exhibits, and symposia; these are typically associated with specialist physicians. General practioners favor detailing and family physicians appear to favor direct mail and dinner meetings. Since the cluster solution entailed four-dimensional coordinates (rather than the two-dimensional coordinates utilized in Exhibit 7), more of the original information was preserved in the cluster solution of Exhibit 8.

Extensions to Higher-Way Data

Correspondence analysis can also be applied to higher-way classification tables such as promotional activities by physician specialty, or by physician's most-used antihypertensive brand. The resulting map would show all three sets of points, rather than the two sets illustrated in Exhibits 7 and 8.

Correspondence analysis has gained enough proponents that many computer program packages are now available for implementing the technique. It has now become routine to supplement numerical cross-tables with the pictorial output of correspondence analysis.

CONCLUSION

From a somewhat more general viewpoint, market position analysis—using multidimensional scaling, correspondence analysis, and clustering techniques—provides help in understanding one's place in the market, as perceived and evaluated by actual or potential customers. In addition, one can assess the position of competitive products. These positions can be monitored over time as a firm changes its product offerings or promotional strategy.

As a diagnostic tool, this methodology can also provide some insights regarding the wisdom of changing the perceptions of buyers' brands, the saliences of customers' perceptual dimensions, and the relevance of the dimensions themselves.

From a strategic viewpoint, both traditional multidimensional scaling and correspondence analysis show how a market (or submarket) perceives brands or services as similar or different. Respondent preferences can also be accomodated. Managers often use the resulting maps to find "gaps" in the market where a new product could be located near a group of consumers who would be attracted to its specific features. As such, perceptual and preference mapping plays a role in product line development.

By the same token, perceptual and preference differences are often noted within the larger market. In this case, niche marketing strategies can be followed to appeal to the needs of different submarkets.

SUGGESTIONS FOR FURTHER READING

Phipps Arabie, J. Douglas Carroll, and Yoram Wind, "Overlapping Clustering: A New Methodology for Product Positioning," *Journal of Marketing Research,* Vol. 18 (1981), pp. 310–317.

J. Douglas Carroll and Phipps Arabie, "Multidimensional Scaling," in *Annual Review of Psychology,* ed. M.R. Rosenberg and L.W. Porter (Palo Alto, CA: Annual Reviews, 1980).

Lee G. Cooper, "A Review of Multidimensional Scaling in Marketing Research," *Applied Psychological Measurement,* Vol. 7 (Fall 1983), pp. 427–450.

Wayne S. DeSarbo and Ajay Manrai, "A New Multi-dimensional Scaling Methodology for the Analysis of Asymmetric Proximity Data in Marketing Research," *Marketing Science,* Vol. 10 (1991), pp. 1–20.

Wayne S. DeSarbo and Vithala R. Rao, "GENFOLD: A Set of Models and Algorithms for the General Unfolding of Preference/Dominance Data," *Journal of Classification,* Vol. 2 (1984), pp. 147–186.

Donna L. Hoffman and G.R. Franke, "Correspondence Analysis: Graphical Representation of Categorical Data in Marketing Research," Journal of Marketing Research, Vol. 23 (August 1986), pp. 213–227.

Paul E. Green, Frank J. Carmone and Scott M. Smith, *Mulitdimensional Scaling: Concepts and Applications,* (Boston: Allyn and Bacon, 1989).

Paul E. Green and Vithala R. Rao, *Applied Multidimensional Scaling: A Comparison of Approaches and Algorithms* (New York: Holt, Rinehart and Winston, 1972).

Paul E. Green, Donald S. Tull and Gerald Albaum, *Research for Marketing Decisions,* Fifth Edition (Englewood Cliffs, NJ: Prentice-Hall, 1988), Chapters 15 and 17.

Richard M. Johnson, "Market Segmentation: A Strategic Management Tool," *Journal of Marketing Research,* Vol. 8 (February, 1971), pp. 13–18.

Joseph B. Kruskal and Myron Wish, *Multidimensional Scaling,* (Beverly Hills, CA: Sage, 1978).

Allan D. Shocker and V. Srinivasan, "Multiattribute Approaches to Product Concept Evaluation and Generation: A Critical Review," *Journal of Marketing Research,* Vol. 16 (1979), pp. 159–180.

Yoram Wind, "Issues and Advances in Segmentation Research," *Journal of Marketing Research,* Vol. 15 (1978), pp. 317–337.

ADDITIONAL REFERENCES

Carroll, J. Douglas, Paul E. Green, and Catherine M. Schaffer, "Comparing Interpoint Distances in Correspondence Analysis: A Clarification," *Journal of Marketing Research,* Vol. 24 (November 1987), pp. 445–450.

Greenacre, Michael J., *Theory and Application of Correspondence Analyses* (London: Academic Press, 1984).

Lebart, L., A. Morineau, and Kenneth M. Warwick, *Multivariate Descriptive Statistical Analysis: Correspondence Analysis and Related Techniques for Large Matrices.* (New York: John Wiley, 1984).

Nishisato, S. and I. Nishisato, *An Introduction to Dual Scaling.* (Islington, Ontario: MicroStats, 1983).

Punj, G. and D.W. Stewart, "Cluster Analysis in Marketing Research: Review and Suggestions for Applications," *Journal of Marketing Research,* Vol. 20 (May), pp. 134–148.

Srivastava, R.K., R.P. Leone, and A.D. Shocker, "Market Structure Analysis: Hierarchical Clustering of Products Based on Substitution-in-Use," *Journal of Marketing,* Vol. 45 (Summer), pp. 38–48.

William Lazer
Professor Emeritus
Michigan State University
Principal, William Lazer Associates International
East Lansing, Michigan

M. Bixby Cooper
Associate Professor
Marketing and Logistics
Michigan State University
East Lansing, Michigan

CHAPTER 30

DEVELOPING THE ORGANIZATION'S MARKETING MIX

The concept of the marketing mix, which is less than 50 years old, has gained considerable acceptance as a managerial framework for marketing strategies and decisions. The development of the concept is generally credited to two Harvard professors, James W. Culliton and Neil H. Borden. In 1948, Professor Culliton described the business executive as, "A 'decider,' an 'artist,' a 'mixer of ingredients,' who sometimes follows a recipe prepared by others, sometimes prepares his own recipes; he goes along, sometimes adapts a recipe to the ingredients immediately available, and sometimes experiments with or develops ingredients no one else has yet tried."[1]

This characterization of an executive as a mixer appealed to Professor Borden as a way of describing the actions and results of marketing executive decisions. He soon began to use the term "marketing mix" as a way of describing the end results of executive decisions in marketing.[2] The concept filled a void because it not only characterizes critical marketing management activities, but leads to methods of increasing overall marketing efficiency and productivity as well. The marketing mix as a key concept remains firmly embedded in modern marketing management approaches.

Over the years, the marketing mix has been substantially developed and refined. McCarthy offered a simple four-factor classification of marketing mix ingredients or tools that has popularly been described as the *Four P's: product, price, place,* and *promotion.*[3] Sometimes the mix ingredients are listed under different names or are broken down into finer subclassifications. As a general concept, the marketing mix refers to the totality of a company's offering to the marketplace. It is the mix of controllable marketing variables that firms use to pursue the desired level of sales in target markets.

While the concept of the marketing mix is simple to state, the challenge of developing an effective mix is a complex and difficult task. It requires considerable analysis, planning, and creativity. Both those marketing variables controlled by the organization and those influential external forces that are outside of an organization's direct control must be considered.

In this chapter, we will first consider different levels of the marketing mix. Then, attention will be focused on the process of developing the mix. Following this, the challenges offered by today's global competitive environment, marketing mix extension, and nonbusiness marketing mixes are discussed.

LEVELS OF THE MARKETING MIX

Conceptually, the marketing mix exists at several levels of an organization. It varies in connotation depending on whether it is applied to a single business or to a conglomerate, to one product or service, or to several. Basically, the marketing mix may refer to three different organizational levels: the total corporation, the strategic business unit, and the specific product/service level. While the latter often receives primary attention, it must be remembered that for the greatest effectiveness, specific product/service level marketing decisions should only be made within the context of business unit and corporate mix decisions.

Exhibit 1 depicts the character of marketing mix decisions at the three different organization levels: corporate, SBU, and product levels. From the total corporate perspective, the mix may include a host of diverse offerings consisting of a variety of ingredients that make up an extensive array of business, government, and consumer products and services of multi-nation, multi-product conglomerates. Included are strategic decisions concerning fundamental product or service/market opportunities, pricing, promotional, and distribution strategies.

Product strategies—at the corporate level—deal with such matters as the selection and development of product portfolios, research and development, product scope, product design, and quality. Pricing strategies refer to issues such as overall price level choices, price/value decisions, total product-line price relationships, credit, and terms of sale strategies. Promotion focuses on the planning, implementation, and control of persuasive communications with customers, positioning, and image strategies. Included are the total promotional budget as well as guidelines for allocation of the promotional effort among personal selling, advertising, merchandising, sales promotion, and publicity. Distribution strategies at the corporate level are concerned with which distribution functions to perform internally, distribution scope, degree of vertical and horizontal integration, and control over channel activities. The totality of the above—and related decisions—comprise the organization's total marketing mix.

From a strategic business unit, or other divisional or unit perspective, the marketing mix deals with those marketing inputs that collectively comprise the market offerings of that organizational unit. Consider, for example, the small appliance division of a large, diverse manufacturer of electrical appliances. Product decisions must be made that include such factors as policies related to depth and breadth of product line, individual versus family brand policies, market segments and niches, warranty, guarantee, and repair service policies.

Divisional pricing and credit policies must be established to guide more specific decisions for the family of products offered, including new product pricing, price guarantees, skimming and penetration policies, and price flexibility. Promotional policies relate to the extent

EXHIBIT 1. Examples of the Marketing Mix at Different Levels of the Organization

Organizational Level	Product	Price	Promotion	Place
Corporate	• Product portfolio • Research and development • Quality • Scope • Design	• Price strategy • Price/value • Product line Price relationships • Credit and terms strategy	• Total budget • Allocation guidelines • Institutional strategy	• Distribution • Strategy • Scope • Vertical integration
Strategic Business Unit	• Product line depth/breadth • Branding policy • Service policies	• Overall price policy • New product price policy • Price flexibility • Credit and terms policies	• Push versus pull • Promotion themes • Sales organization • Trade promotion policy	• Direct/indirect channels • Locations • Stocking policies
Individual Product	• Specific features Color Size Shape • Brand name • Package design • Warranty • Accessories	• List price • Discounts • Allowances • Terms	• Advertising Media Theme • Trade promotion terms • Personal selling effort	• Specific outlets • Inventory level • Carriers • Locations

of pull versus push promotional themes for the division, and sales and sales management activities. The business unit level must address distribution policies concerning direct versus indirect distribution, strategic alliances with suppliers and customers, and logistics concerns such as full-line versus limited-line distribution centers. Together, such divisional policies are among those guiding the development of the marketing mix for specific products.

The marketing mix is often addressed at the level of specific product offerings. Product decisions consist of such concerns as product features, color, size, brand name, packages, label, warranty and guarantee terms, and servicing of each individual product. The pricing mix pertains to decisions such as list prices, discounts and allowances, trade margins, and terms of credit for each offering. The promotion mix comprises decisions related to advertising media, message content, message timing, personal selling and sales practices, and sales promotion tactics for specific offerings. The distribution mix consists of channel decisions such as which outlets and intermediaries to use as well as such physical distribution concerns as specific transportation modes and carriers, inventory levels, and facility locations. Thus the marketing mix—as applied to the product level—refers to decisions about that unique set of ingredients that comprises a single product or service.

The marketing mix, in a very real sense, is the mechanism by which an organization links itself to its selected target market(s). The alteration of ingredients of the mix is the manner in which the organization adjusts to the marketplace. Developing an effective mix is complex and challenging. It focuses on the most fundamental responsibilities of marketing executives such as the formulation of marketing strategies, the development of marketing plans, and key decision making about marketing activities. The basic challenge is to produce, adjust, adapt, and offer a unique and differentiated product/service that satisfies customer and consumer wants and needs in a superior fashion. The mix links organizations to the market and focuses on adjustments to market change. Dynamic market environments place a premium on marketing management flexibility and its ability to respond by continuously altering the mix in a timely and effective manner.

THE MARKETING MIX AND SYSTEMS THINKING

Fundamental to the development of an effective marketing mix is the application of systems thinking by marketing managers. This mix is not rooted in the consideration of individual marketing ingredients such as the advertising media to employ, prices to establish, or product and packaging features. Rather, it deals with total system performance, with the whole marketing mix, with the effectiveness and profitability of that mix as a totality, rather than with the profitability of individual ingredients or submixes.

As described previously, the marketing mix is often considered in terms of four interrelated subsystems or submixes: the product and service mix; the pricing mix; the promotion mix; and the place or distribution mix. The impacts of each of these submixes must be arranged to be supportive and complementary to each other and the whole system, engendering integration and coordination of the submixes, maximizing the total marketing thrust.

In designing a marketing mix, therefore, two perspectives come into play: each of the individual submixes, and the total overall market mix. Conflicts and tradeoffs are involved at both levels. For example, within the promotional mix, tradeoffs may exist between expenditures for advertising versus personal selling. A higher level of tradeoff may exist between the submixes such as spending more on promotional efforts versus lowering prices. The overriding objective is to design tradeoffs that result in the most effective total mix, often at the expense of a particular component(s). The marketing manager's challenge is the effective application of system thinking to avoid suboptimization—whether at the SBU or specific product level—at the expense of the total system.

In any given industry, competing firms may simultaneously attempt to gain market advantage by adopting quite different marketing mix approaches. However, each must reflect systems thinking to coordinate the mix elements effectively. A typical example is in television sets. General Electric (GE) markets a broad line of relatively low-priced television sets that are distributed nationally through multiple distribution channels, including traditional electronics retailers, mass merchandisers, selected supermarkets, and drugstores. GE compliments this strategy with broad-based mass advertising appeals. Sony, on the other hand, markets a somewhat more limited line of higher-priced television sets with a focus on quality. They are distributed primarily through specialty electronics retailers and upscale department stores. Curtis Mathes emphasizes a very limited line of high-quality products backed by a six-year product guarantee. Curtis Mathes televisions are relatively high priced and are distributed through a limited network of dealers that sell only Curtis Mathes electronics.

This example demonstrates how three successful firms—operating in the same industry—differentiate themselves and link to the marketplace with different combinations of marketing mix elements. They have each employed different strategies successfully, based on different products and services, price, channel, and promotional decisions. Each has achieved significant market share and profitability. Close examination of each firm's strategies reveals the application of systems thinking. Consider, for example, the difficulty Curtis Mathes would encounter with its approach to product and pricing if it chose to distribute through the multiple channels employed by General Electric.

Prior to the explicit recognition and acceptance of systems concepts and systems thinking by marketing managers, marketing decisions were often made on a piecemeal basis. Attention was directed to specific ingredients such as pricing, advertising, merchandising, product development, distribution, or personal selling. Marketing situations were approached as independent entities, as separate pieces, rather than as interrelated components of an integrated whole. Marketing specialists saw their tasks as maximizing the output of particular tasks or functions. The result was less than optimum use of marketing inputs with some being overutilized and others underutilized. Some activities thrived at the expense of overall marketing performance. The marketing mix, by contrast, emphasizes total profitability, investigates returns from alternative commitment of marketing resources, and places the emphasis where it should be—on the performance of the total marketing effort.

THE MARKETING MIX PROCESS

Three components of the marketing mix process are analysis, decision making, and monitoring and adjustment. Analysis begins with the development of an environmental information system that provides critical data relating to the uncontrollable macroenvironment. It extends to competitive analysis, market/customer analysis, and internal analysis. The decision-making process includes decisions related to choices of target market segments and niches, and the formulation of specific mix elements that uniquely appeal to chosen customer needs and wants. Monitoring and adjusting activities—the third component—relate to maintaining the relevance of the mix to its dynamic target markets.

Develop Environmental Information System and Evaluate Macroenvironments

Fundamental to analysis is development of an environmental information system. This system scans the macroenvironmental forces—sociocultural, lifestyle, technological, economic, international, political, legal—that are beyond the control of managers but nevertheless exert a powerful influence on their decisions. They are critical to developing an effective marketing mix because they influence customer needs and wants, competitor's strategies, and the firm itself. The information system extracts key trends and environmental changes that represent new opportunities for marketing success or threats to effective marketing performance.

The sociocultural environment, perhaps more than any other, is directly involved with shaping the nature of consumer needs and preferences. Factors such as changing cultural values and norms, mores, lifestyles, social class structure, and important demographic trends have a major impact on consumer demand for products and services and the way they are promoted, distributed, and priced.

Consider, for example, lifestyle trends that result in greater demand for convenience. These lifestyle changes have manifested themselves in numerous ways across a broad range of industries. In the food industry, an increasing share of the consumer's food dollar has shifted to away-from-home eating establishments, especially fast-food restaurants. Supermarkets have responded by introducing more convenience through frozen prepared meals, in-store salad bars, and deli-prepared food sections. The packaging industry has developed heat and serve packages. The electronic industry created microwave ovens. And there are a host of ready-to-eat single serving items. In other industries, convenience has had similar impacts. Other sociocultural trends such as the aging and greying of the population, single parents, smaller and more mobile families, non-family households, desire for immediate gratification, concerns for health and physical fitness, and changes in family structure all have their implications for marketing mix strategies.

The technological explosion of the post–World War II period is increasing in intensity. The translation of technological developments into new products and services means new means of promotion and distribution. Portable in-home computers, cellular telephones, fax machines, and satellite television once seemed far-fetched—today, they are a reality. Electronic Data Interchange, video shopping, and information technology are changing the basic nature of business relations with customers and consumers.

The economic environment shapes consumers' ability to pay for goods and services. Employment/unemployment, inflation, industry growth/decline, investment, or other economic trends represent major threats/opportunities to industries, products, and services as consumers delay purchases or trade up or down. Economic changes raise opportunities for businesses to adjust their marketing mix elements to respond more effectively to consumer needs.

The political/legal environment impacts the marketing mix decisions from both basic perspectives as regulation and limitation and industry control. Specifically, this may mean packaging and labeling requirements, advertising and pricing regulations, environmental standards, product safety requirements, and the like. Legal parameters vary by industry, product, and market conditions. Marketing managers must remain ever aware of how these parameters affect mix decisions in their specific realm of responsibility.

Identify and Analyze Competition and Competitors

The second major analytic process in developing marketing mix strategies is competitive analysis. No two organizations can compete effectively in the same marketplace for the same consumer dollar utilizing identical strategies. Competitive analysis enables the marketing manager to identify *who* their competitors are and *how* they compete in the marketplace.

Primary competitors are usually easily identified. For example, John Deere Company competes directly in the lawn tractor business with such well known brands as Toro, Lawn Boy, Murrey, Roper, and Cub. However, it is useful to look more closely and broadly at related competitors who fulfill the same generic customer need. John Deere could define its competitors to include all lawn mowers or even lawn maintenance services.

Once the set of competitors is identified, four generic questions must be answered about how each competes in the marketplace:

1. What are their objectives?
2. What are their current strategies?
3. What are their capabilities?
4. What are their likely future strategies?

The challenges of global competition, and an ever-expanding competitive environment, put competitive analysis at the forefront of marketing management concerns in developing a mix that will uniquely satisfy target customer needs and wants.

Internal Analysis

To a very large extent, a company's marketing mix is shaped and influenced by its internal resources: its financial, human, and physical capabilities, both tangible and intangible. The first step is a critical assessment of company capabilities, which can be a demanding and painful process. It forces managers to identify things they have done and can continue to do well and furnishes a realistic assessment of weaknesses and limitations. Without such an assessment, it is not possible to identify objectively an actionable marketing mix strategy. Internal analysis begins with an examination of organizational performance.

The second step is an assessment of strengths and weaknesses in each functional area. For example, the company's reputation and image, market share, financial condition, production capability, and managerial talent must each be assessed in terms of impact on the firm's ability to implement a marketing mix strategy. To be effective, an internal analysis should not ignore any significant aspects of a firm's overall performance.

The internal organization is particularly relevant to the development and implementation of the marketing mix because cross-functional responsibility pervades. Marketing executives are not the only ones whose decisions impact on the mix. This is particularly true of the myriad of decisions regarding product and pricing components.

The product mix is the joint result of decisions made in manufacturing, research and development, engineering, as well as marketing. While marketers may specify product requirements in terms of consumer wants and needs, the design aspect also depends on factors not exclusively in the marketing realm. The technical problems of manufacturing, the ability to service and repair products, the capacity to respond to product changes, and the need to invest in new facilities are not solely within the scope of a marketing manager's authority. They are, however, critical to the development of the marketing mix.

Similarly, price involves executives from fields other than marketing. Even where marketing executives know the "right" price from a marketing standpoint, they consult with other executives whose thinking may be driven by cost or financial considerations.

These above examples serve only to illustrate that marketing mix decisions must be consonant with the framework of overall corporate capabilities. Even in the face of incredible market opportunities, marketing executives must also consider what the firm is able to implement and coordinate realistically with other corporate functions to formulate an effective marketing mix.

Perform Market and Customer Analysis

The fourth—and most critical—analytical process in developing an effective marketing mix is performing effective market and customer analysis—actual and potential. To establish a strategic edge over its competition, management must:

1. identify the broad market it intends to serve;
2. identify segments and niches within that market and understand customer needs, wants, preferences, and behaviors in each segment and niche;
3. assess the macroenvironment, competitive and internal analysis, and their impacts on each segment; and
4. move from analysis to decision making by choosing target segment(s) and formulating specific marketing mix strategy(ies).

Proper market definition is critical to the success of strategies and effective marketing mix specifications. It is a difficult task for markets, and may be defined in many ways. Included are products or product classes such as the "soft drink market" or "the automobile market"; geographic areas such as the West Coast or European market; institutions such as the retail or wholesale market, and so on. The underlying factor in any market definition is customer and consumer needs. Given broad market definitions, the process is to refine and subdivide each market into finer homogeneous segments. Since various buyer segments seek different benefits—in terms of specific product features and in terms of availability, purchasing convenience, service, and price—specific marketing mixes can be developed for them. The mixes must be responsive to the demands of specific customer demand segments.

The wants, needs, and preferences of market segments are the fulcrum on which the development of an appropriate market mix rests.

Understanding customer buying behavior in each market segment is critical because customer behavior is the ultimate driving force behind proper mix decisions. Of particular importance are answers to such questions as: who specifically are the customers in each segment; and how, when, where, and why do they buy. Equally important are answers to questions about the *unmet* needs in each segment. They can be most valuable in the creative design of the marketing mix.

Target Marketing Selection and Formulation of the Mix

Ultimately, the analytical processes described above—the analysis of macroenvironments, competitors, internal resources, and customer analysis—leads to two related decisions: selection of target market(s) and marketing mixes must be formulated. As difficult as it is to gather the data for the aforementioned analysis, the actual decision process may be even more difficult. It is here that managerial creativity, intuition, and insight is brought to bear—the art of designing the marketing mix. Macroenvironmental analysis may reveal trends and opportunities; competitive analysis can furnish information about current and future competitive strategies; internal analysis highlights the firm's capabilities for capitalizing on trends and opportunities and customer analysis reveals needs, wants, behavior, and unmet needs. But matching the output of these analytical processes provides the basis for the creative definition of target markets and leads to the development of a mix to satisfy those markets.

It is in this sense that Professor Culliton referred to the marketing executive as an "artist." While the analytical processes described may result from scientific inquiry and quantification, the decision-making process requires judgment, intuition, and creativity—the touch of an artist.

Over the years, numerous tools have been developed as either guidelines or conceptual frameworks to aid in decision making. Examples include simulations, a variety of multivariate statistical techniques, and sales response functions that attempt to measure how target markets respond to different levels of expenditure for each of the variables. However, such approaches frequently ignore complex interactions among submix variables and fail to recognize that market response varies *between* markets and *within* markets over time.

A number of conceptual marketing frameworks also yield insights. Some examples are product lifecycle models, classification of motives, consumer purchase behavior paradigms, and classification of goods. A danger is that heavy reliance on such broad generalizations may ultimately result in a plethora of non-distinctive, "me too" market offerings that fail to achieve the unique differentiation so fundamental for success.

Consider, for example, the classic case of Hanes and L'eggs hosiery. It is highly unlikely that any existing response function research or frameworks such as the lifecycle concept would have suggested that a one-size-fits-all product, packaged in an egg-shaped container, distributed through (at one time) a totally new distribution channel, and at a price about one-half that of competing products would have any realistic probability of success. Yet, Hanes marketing executives had the creativity and foresight to blend these elements, and consequently reaped the benefits of a remarkably creative new strategy. Similarly, Xerox management put aside the advice of consultants on the limited market for its copiers, and instead created a mix based on the idea that customers would learn to use the service.

Continuous Monitoring and Adjustment

The above examples do not imply that effective marketing mix development is the result of chance or luck. Rather, a premium is placed on proper monitoring and analysis of the externalities and the adjustment of controllable variables to fit the opportunities that exist. It suggests that continuous evaluation of the effectiveness of existing mix components is important. As environments change, competitors enter and exit, customer needs and wants evolve, and organizational capabilities change. They imply that adjustments and reformulations are needed on a continuing basis to be competitive.

We have entered an era in which environmental and marketplace variables are in a state of flux. Market dynamics are forcing marketing managers to remain ever vigilant. Continuously adjusting and improving marketing mix ingredients to meet market changes is a way of business life—a prerequisite of a marketing orientation. Marketing is a change agent for the organization and the marketing mix is the instrument for change. It permits alignment of company offerings with changing customers and consumer needs and wants. And, as companies vie globally for competitive advantage, constant attention to the ever-changing global marketplace and to continuous adaptation of the marketing mix is critical to achieving effective marketing performance.

CURRENT MARKETING MIX CHALLENGES

The current overall business climate is changing in ways that raise special challenges for developing an effective marketing mix. Included are:

1. *Emphasis on value enhancement.* To a major extent, customers now expect to take product quality for granted—it is part of the admission price to the marketplace. The 1980s clearly showed that consumers demand quality, and that quality does not necessarily come at higher costs to sellers or to consumers. The Japanese automobile industry and the phenomenal success of Wal-Mart are but two examples of the value-enhancement approach.

2. *Service quality concerns.* Historically, service was considered to be part of the "augmented" product. Service offered extra benefits to customers but was not perceived as pivotal or central to fulfilling customers' objectives. However, in recent years innovative marketers have realized that providing quality service may be among the most powerful marketing tools available. Companies are realizing that service provides the impetus for generating and maintaining customer loyalty. This is particularly true because physical product quality has improved to meet "the price of admission to the marketplace." Quality service systems then become prime differentiating factors among competitors. Warranties, guarantees, customer assistance in obtaining information, ordering, and resolving problems are all service elements that aid customers in achieving their objectives. When markets are characterized by an overchoice of similar products, quality service systems enhance the firm's competitive edge.
3. *Social and environmental concerns.* While environmental analysis has long been recognized as a critical process in developing the marketing mix, these factors have been more influential in recent years. Such factors as resource and energy conservation and air, water, and noise pollution, for example, present opportunities to rethink existing mix strategies. They focus attention on such elements as packaging, energy consumption, disposability, waste, biodegradability, and the like. Such concerns will continue to have far-reaching effects, ranging from minor modification such as McDonald's reduction in plastic packages to threats to entire product lines such as Procter & Gamble's and Kimberly Clark's disposable diapers.
4. *Impact of an information society.* Pertinent and timely information is available in such quantity and detail as to potentially overwhelm marketing executives. The information age raises numerous marketing mix challenges and opportunities. On one hand, greater understanding of customers' and consumers' needs and wants is more possible today than ever before. Consider the wealth of information concerning consumer preferences and reaction to marketing mix efforts contained in daily retail store scanning data. Detailed, up-to-the minute information makes possible rapid evaluation and continuous adjustment to consumer demand. On the other hand, the information age has been accompanied by shorter product life cycles, more rapid response by competitors to successful strategies, and enhanced customer knowledge of alternative mix choices. The challenge for marketing executives is to find ways to benefit from the information society by being more responsive to customers through more effective mix adjustment. There is also a privacy issue of protecting consumer privacy while using detailed information about consumers for their benefit.

5. *Market fragmentation.* Market segmentation implies that not all consumers want or need the same products, but that customer needs can be aggregated for efficient production and distribution. Currently, some markets are being fragmented into increasingly smaller and smaller segments. While this provides opportunities for niche products and niche competitors, fragmentation also stretches the ability of businesses to meet marketplace demand effectively and efficiently. The challenge is to temper fragmentation with efficient marketing and manufacturing capabilities.

EXTENDING THE MARKET MIX

The marketing mix was described earlier as a linking mechanism, one that links the company to market segment(s). This relationship might be portrayed simply as:

Company → Marketing Mix → Market Segment

Realistically, however, firms do not stand alone in their efforts to link to the consumer marketplace to accomplish the desired linkage. They rely on suppliers, channel members, marketing agency specialists, and others. Thus institutions participating in the linkage must be coordinated somehow, or at least receptive and cooperative to an organization's marketing mix efforts. Two examples illustrate the point:

1. A manufacturer may select a particular chain of retail outlets as an ideal mechanism for reaching target customers. However, the retail chain, as an independent entity, has its own mix strategies to consider. The manufacturer is not assured of obtaining distribution through any given retail store. To gain support, the manufacturer's product must be appealing to both channel members and targeted consumers. Pricing strategies must allow for appropriate retail margins, promotional efforts must be consonant with retail buyer strategies, and retail support must be gained. Target Stores, for example, do not simply accept any product from any manufacturer. Rather, as with most major retail firms, they utilize explicit guidelines for product selection and highly sophisticated processes for designating preferred suppliers.
2. Wholesale and retail intermediaries likewise cannot implement their own mix without explicit recognition of their interface with suppliers' marketing mix strategies. Manufacturers are not required to sell products to any retail firm desiring to distribute them. Manufacturer mix strategies of exclusive or selective distribution may restrict the products available to a given intermediary. Supplier pricing and promotional policies may cause wholesalers and retailers to adjust their programs.

This explicit recognition of the extended linkage among firms has been the driving force in recent years to the development of strategic alliances, partnerships, coalitions, and other networks that multiply the strengths of the participating companies. The basic principle of the extended linkage concept is to coordinate the mix decisions of all parties involved in the value-added process for a given consumer segment—for the benefit of all. The result can be increased consumer satisfaction accompanied by superior financial performance for those involved. The concept of the marketing mix in such situations must then be extended across independent organizations with individual marketing mix decision authority. The resulting marketing mix becomes an overarching concept—one that crosses legal organizational boundaries.

NONBUSINESS MARKETING MIX

The marketing mix as a concept is relevant to nonbusiness applications. It pertains to social causes and ideas, government agencies, symphony orchestras, museums, hospitals, colleges and universities, social welfare institutions, and other nonprofit organizations. Although the organizational objectives of non-profit and profit-motivated entities differ, the principles of developing the marketing mix are similar. Nonbusiness marketers engage in similar analytic and decision-making processes. However, the combination of marketing mix elements differs.

In non-profit settings, the product and service mix relates to the benefits that are delivered to patrons, clients, suppliers, and recipients. The benefits include alleviating hunger, suffering, and pain; generating jobs; uplifting tastes; increasing happiness and well being; advancing educational levels and increasing understanding; absorbing leisure time; and adding to community enjoyment. Nonbusiness marketers may face great difficulty in adjusting their product/service offerings. They often face pressure in pursuing greater segmentation; to do so can mean ignoring some segments. The best product position for the nonbusiness marketer may be unclear since each position may have positive appeals for certain segments but negative appeals for others. Consider, for example, the difficulty faced by the AIDS Foundation in target market selection and product positioning for its campaign promoting "safe sex."

Price in nonbusiness marketing contexts has a variety of meanings. It not only refers to monetary concerns such as donations and contributions, gifts, grants, and other economic values, but also may include psychic, energy, and time costs incurred by patrons, clients, and consumers. The nonbusiness marketer may encounter great difficulty in raising prices. The challenge frequently is to convince target markets that benefits received outweigh added costs.

The nonbusiness promotional mix encompasses a variety of communication tools—both personal and non-personal—to inform, influence, and gain support. Options are usually more limited than those of profit-seeking organizations. Paid advertising may not be feasible due to the high cost of time and space or because social pressures dictate against advertising expenses or particular promotional messages. Some message appeals—such as hard sell—or fear approaches may be prohibited because of the attitudes of target audiences or the nature of the subject itself. (The reaction of some against the Jerry Lewis muscular dystrophy telethons is a case in point.)

Place in the nonbusiness marketing mix refers to the channels used to deliver the benefits to patrons, clients, and customers. Channels are often direct as is the case with museum showings, symphony, opera and ballet performances, hospital services, and charity dispensed by various social welfare agencies. Nonbusiness marketers have difficulty in utilizing and gaining cooperation from intermediaries such as musicians, opera singers, ballet performers, physicians, the media, civic organizations, and other potential facilitators. They normally do not have the funds to build their own distribution channels, are unable to offer the usual monetary incentives, and must rely on appeals to goodwill and social responsibility to gain cooperation. They are at the mercy of the effectiveness of their appeals and the goodwill of channel members to carry out their programs.

Monitoring program effectiveness in a nonbusiness setting can be a trying task. Quantifiable measures such as market share and units sold have limited use in measuring effectiveness of educational, cultural, health, and welfare settings. Frequently, the goals of nonbusiness marketers are long-range and the immediate progress made is imperceptible so that developing measures of ongoing progress is an elusive proposition.

Elements of nonbusiness marketing mix development pose special—but not insurmountable—challenges. They require the same general approach, careful analysis, creativity, and ingenuity necessary in the for-profit sector of the economy. With sound planning and recognition of the challenges, the principles of marketing can be effectively applied in this increasingly important arena.

CONCLUSION

Important marketplace changes are forcing marketing managers to be more attuned than ever to market dynamics. The concept of the marketing mix is an apt framework for reminding executives that ultimately, customers and consumers determine what products and services are to be produced, and how they are to be promoted, distributed, and priced. The marketing mix is a change agent that—properly implemented—establishes and maintains the linkage between an organization and its markets. While the process for developing the marketing mix does not specify the answers to many challenging decisions facing marketing executives, it does, nevertheless, provide a framework for understanding changes in the marketplace and making appropriate adjustments in an organization's offerings.

NOTES

1. James W. Culliton, *The Management of Marketing Costs,* Boston: Division of Research, Graduate School of Business Administration, Harvard University, 1948.

2. Neil H. Borden, "Note on Concept of the Marketing Mix," Boston: Intercollegiate Case Clearing House, Harvard University, 1957.

3. E. Jerome McCarthy, *Basic Marketing,* Homewood, IL: Richard D. Irwin, 1960.

William F. O'Dell
Founder
Market Facts, Inc.
Arlington Heights, Illinois

David K. Hardin
Chairman of the Board
Market Facts, Inc.
Arlington Heights, Illinois

CHAPTER 31

THE MARKETING DECISION

As everyone knows, everyone makes decisions. Some of these decisions are unimportant; others have disastrous consequences when made incorrectly.

So commonplace are decisions that many people make the assumption that the process is largely intuitive in nature, finally resolved by someone pounding a fist on the desk, pronouncing "Go to it!" True, some decisions may be made in this manner, but when the profit or personal consequences are great, the business person must understand the various aspects of the decision-making process.

The development of the right decision criteria may be somewhat more systematic. The company may employ marketing research to uncover data that may prompt new product ideas. Or, the growth of a particular segment of the market revealed by research might lead to the consideration of a reallocation of the total marketing dollar.

The recognition of a significant situation requiring some adjustment is the beginning of the marketing decision. Recognizing significant information may help the marketer recognize a marketing problem.

For example, let us assume that a major breakfast cereal company discovers that its competitor is successfully test marketing an instant breakfast powder. A problem now exists. Should marketing counter with a similar product or, by changing the product concept, seek out a separate market segment? Or, should he or she ignore the product class being created? In any event, a "problem" exists. The question now is: What should be done . . . what adjustment should be made?

MARKETING ALTERNATIVES

It is essential that a complete set of alternative courses of action be developed. The marketing person must first identify the most basic issue. Is the question one of how to allocate the marketing dollar, or how to spend the advertising dollar? The former is more basic. The advertising decision would follow a determination of how large the advertising appropriation is to be.

Often the decision process involves a success in one area and transferring this knowledge to other areas. For example, a successful domestic branch office opening can suggest undertaking overseas expansion. This "discovery" can be termed "environmental."

One marketing environment can result in a multiplicity of separate decision structures—each calling for a different decision. Let's assume that Company A drops the price on a brand in a given product class in which Company B is the leading seller. The apparent tactic of Company A is to garner a greater share of that product class, hoping that Company B's costs will not permit the latter to drop its price for any extended period of time. Here is a *problem* to which Company B must now adjust. The next step is the formation of alternative courses of action. These possibilities are almost without end. Company B could:

1. Maintain its present price level
   Meet the competitive price
2. Add some agreed upon feature to its brand
   Not add the feature to the brand
3. Increase the advertising budget on behalf of this brand
   Not increase the advertising budget
   Decrease the advertising budget in support of this brand
4. Take the brand off the market
   Not take the brand off the market

There are, of course, other possibilities, but the point here is that items one through four represent separate decision structures. Each one has its own set of alternatives. Each one will result in a different decision choice. The profit consequences of each decision structure are quite different; for example, taking the product off the market has greater profit consequences than adding, say, 15 percent to the brand's advertising budget.

Thus, each and every decision structure must have its own set of alternatives, and *one of the stated options must end up as the final decision.* It is vital that the most basic issue be attacked and resolved before attempting to decide on subissues.

CRITERION FOR DECISION

Every business decision is a prediction. If a marketing manager decides to commercialize a new product, he or she is predicting that a sufficient number of units will be sold to produce the required contribution to profit. If the advertising budget is decreased, he or she is predicting that any loss in sales due to fewer advertising dollars will not be as great as the savings resulting from the advertising reduction. If he or she lowers the unit price of one of the products, he or she is predicting that the increase in sales over the long run will more than offset smaller profit per unit.

It is, of course, essential that marketing people know the specifics of their predictions. When a new product is introduced, someone is predicting a given unit sales level or higher. These predictions are in reality criteria for decisions. They are employing what logicians over the years have called syllogisms. Most usable in today's world is the "hypothetical" or "conditional" syllogism, the "if" . . . "then" approach, which is an essential part of the conditional syllogism.

Simply stated, the conditional syllogism states that "*if* 500,000 unit sales a year can be achieved through the commercialization of this new item, then that item will be introduced." The "if" side of the syllogism represents the prediction; the "then" phrase is the course of action under consideration. The "if" side is called the antecedent; the "then" phrase the consequent. The antecedent represents that unknown . . . the uncertainty: "*If* the new product will sell 500,000 units . . . ."

It is not always essential that the criterion be reduced to a syllogistic pattern; however, it is most helpful when it is done. It forces one to think along logical lines. The basis for the decision is set forth *in advance.* The marketing person announces what is expected before the final decision is made.

In today's world, profit, *within the appropriate social context,* is the basic criterion. A new product is introduced, or the advertising effort is altered in some way; those responsible for such actions are really saying that they expect their company's profits to increase as a result of the decisions. If the organization is not-for-profit, of course some other benefit would be substituted.

In making many decisions, one cannot obtain a direct measure of profit. For example, advertising expectations virtually defy measurement of profit. Moreover, in many instances the objective of the marketing effort is not immediate profits. Thus the criterion for the decision would be some other measure.

Monetary Measures

A criterion calling for a monetary measure relates to the outcomes of various alternatives *in terms of dollars.* Let's say that the introduction of a new product is being considered. The alternatives are to introduce the product or not to introduce the product. A sales level that this product is to reach at a given point in time must be stated if the item is to be marketed. If the item will not reach that required level, the product will not be marketed.

A predicted sales figure is used if the organization equates sales with predicted revenue, and ultimately with return on investment. The sales prediction is needed to determine or predict revenue. Product costs are known. The scope of marketing effort has been established. The sales level required if the item is to be profitable is known. So, the criterion is sales. Knowing other costs means that once the uncertain figure (sales to be produced) is agreed on, then it becomes "go or no-go."

Monetary measures are usually required for those decisions having alternative courses of action where the marketing alternatives have diverse costs. Whether to introduce a new product is a diverse cost decision because the cost of entering the item on the market (one alternative) costs more than not marketing the product (the other alternative). Thus, a monetary measure becomes the criterion because a revenue prediction must be made. And a sales prediction is essential because sales are the revenue producer.

Let's assume that increasing the advertising appropriation by 100 percent is under consideration. A total of $1 million is now being spent and the marketing management is suggesting the possibility of doubling that figure for the forthcoming year—at the expense of reducing the sales force in rural areas. In order to make the decision as to which route to follow, a sales-revenue prediction must be made. The criterion, then, is sales (revenue).

Many decisions are more complicated. Perhaps a new product is about to be commercialized, but there is uncertainty as to its price. Assume four alternatives: to market the product at price A, B, or C or not to market the product. Figure 1 illustrates how ten options come into being when three prices and three advertising levels are the alternative courses of action. The criterion would be sales-revenue. It is necessary to predict what the sales would be under each of the ten possible situations posed.

Diverse cost decisions that call for a prediction of sales and revenue are often viewed within some companies as finance decisions. Certainly finance people would participate inasmuch as diverse cost decisions involve alternative uses of funds. For example, in most companies, the alternative of marketing a new product includes discussion by both finance and marketing personnel.

The increasing of an advertising budget is a decision rarely made by the advertising manager alone. He or she may participate in the discussion, but the final decision would be made by those responsible for allocating funds. It is normally desirable to have both the finance and marketing people provide inputs to the decision process, especially in view of the fact that the marketing person will be charged with the task of making the sales and revenue prediction.

FIGURE 1.

Advertising Level	Price		
	A	B	C
X	a	b	c
Y	d	e	f
Z	g	h	i

Nine marketing options (a-i) are presented when this combination of price and advertising level is under consideration. A tenth alternative would be not to market the product.

FIGURE 2.

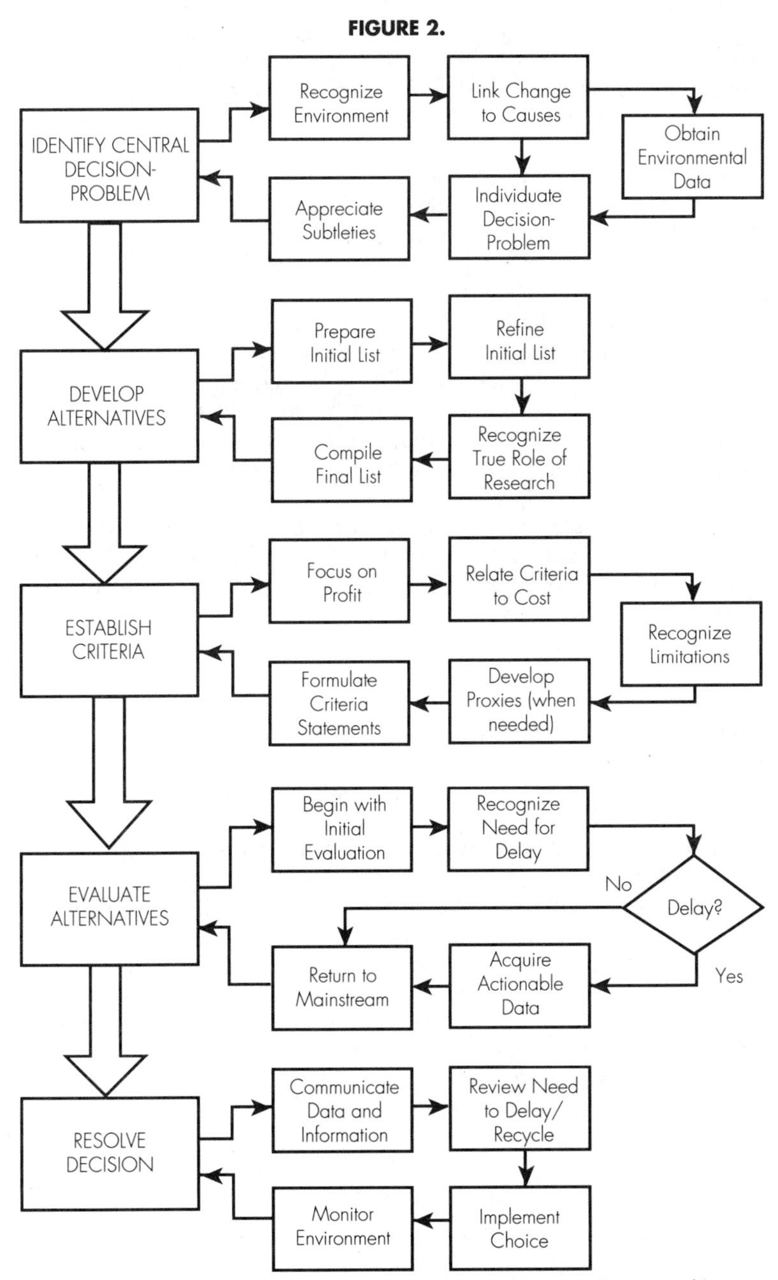

This flowchart of each step in the marketing decision can prove to be invaluable. Reprinted by courtesy of the South-Western Publishing Company from O'Dell, Ruppel, and Trent's *Marketing Decision Making*, 1979.

Nonmonetary Measures

Many contemplated decisions do not seek advance measures of sales and revenue as a basis for determining which alternative will be selected. For example, much advertising is geared to changing the consumers' attitudes toward a given brand, or toward creating greater awareness. To inform the consumer about a given feature or to correct a particular misconception can sometimes be the goal of an advertising campaign.

It is assumed that greater awareness or improved attitudes will ultimately enhance profits. The short-run assignment given to advertising is something short of profits. Much automobile advertising, for example, strives to create a more favorable attitude toward a given make to encourage the prospective buyer to consider that make when in the market for a new car. Automobile advertisers do not urge the consuming public to lunge out of their Sunday night armchairs and rush down to locate a dealer that might be open. On the other hand, a substantial portion of grocery product advertising is aimed at stimulating the shopper to buy a particular brand the next time he or she is in a store.

Therefore, the criterion for identical cost decisions is stated in terms of the objective of the marketing effort: brand awareness, attitude change, awareness of a given feature, etc. Thus, the criterion is stated after the alternatives have been formulated. For many decisions, the nonmonetary criteria are not only acceptable but are preferred over the sales-revenue criteria.

One need only give assurance that one formula will sell better than the other. The criterion can be consumer preference, or stated consumer intention to buy one over the other, or some such nonmonetary measure. It is necessary to know only which of the two is better, not how much better. Assuming that agreement has been reached on two alternatives, it then becomes a matter of determining which of the two is better.

Another example is the decision process when selecting an advertising theme. It costs the same to employ Theme A as Theme B. Thus a nonmonetary measure is desired to determine which of the two themes should be used. The criterion used would depend largely on the objective of the advertising: attitude, awareness, number of people entering a given store, number of people changing their desire to own a given brand, or some other nonmonetary measure. It is not necessary to predict sales for decisions that have identical costs for the various alternatives in question.

DECISION DELAY

Having traveled down the decision path from environment to criteria, it is now appropriate to examine when one should make a decision: without delay or with delay. The extent of the delay before selecting one of the actions being considered is a function of the level of the managerial disagreement and the level of profit consequences of a wrong decision.

If the decision makers quickly decide on which course of action to choose, there is high agreement. When this takes place, the decision makers are saying that they feel there is little question about the criterion being satisfied. Thus there is little disagreement and action is taken; a decision is made easily and quickly.

On other decisions, agreement may not always come readily. The profit consequences of a wrong decision are serious enough that some members of the management group do not agree on whether the criterion figure can be met. Management is saying that it should seek additional information before making the decision. This means a delay until such data can be gathered and analyzed. Such delays are not without cost: opportunity costs as well as costs related to data collection and analysis. In agreeing on a decision delay, management is saying that the decision is too important to make without some reduction in the uncertainty that surrounds the outcome.

In marketing, this information-seeking process is called marketing research. The nature of the research centers around the criterion for the decision. If a diverse cost decision is in the making, the criterion is likely to be sales and revenue. So, the research study would be designed to measure and predict *sales* for the various alternatives in question—in advance of the decision.

How such data would be gathered, what the scope of the research effort should be, and how much time should be allocated to the study would be determined by the marketing researchers and decision makers. This, of course, is the subject of much of this *Marketing Manager's Handbook.* But gathering data through marketing research without first knowing how the information is to be used is not only wasteful but it can be extremely costly when the wrong marketing decision is made. Thus it is good to understand the decision-making process—the specific decision structure—from a recognition of the marketing environment, through the alternative courses of action, the criteria for decision, and a recognition of when marketing research is needed. This will ultimately result in better and more profitable marketing decisions.

IMPLICATIONS

Marketing research information can be maximized considerably when the need for the data is fully understood. Many marketing managers and marketing research people seek data without fully understanding why such data are being sought.

Marketing managers should be prepared to answer the basic question: What would I do with the information if I had it? Until this is answered correctly, there are great chances that inadequate data will be obtained. Or, the data will be overly accurate or not accurate enough.

Often business people will discuss at great lengths the possible courses of action that might be taken, only to realize suddenly that they do not have the power to make the decision; it must be made by someone or some group at a higher level within the company. Or, time is taken to discuss decision possibilities that normally should be handled by a person at a lower level. The marketing vice president, for example, does not participate in the creation of advertising copy. Thus it is a waste of time for the marketing manager to permit a discussion of a review of advertising theme choices. Much time is lost in committee meetings by not recognizing this simple fact.

Real world decisions are often more affected by management personnel changes rather than by logic or systematic analysis. Top management too often blindly focuses on a given decision course that fits its prejudices and does not allow new inputs, new information, or new decisions to alter its decision. For example, some managements in industrial goods are really fearful of committing the front-end money to build a consumer products decision. Consequently, they make decisions based on low front-end investment and patient development—and rationalize out of launching consumer products.

An understanding of the decision structure aids considerably in the resolving of the marketing research issues.

SUGGESTIONS FOR FURTHER READING

Vincent P. Barabba and Gerald Zaltman, *Hearing the Voice of the Market*. Boston: Harvard Business School Press, 1991.

Harvey J. Brightman, *Problem Solving: A Logical and Creative Approach*. Atlanta: Business Publishing Division, Georgia State University, 1980.

George P. Huber, *Managerial Decision Making*. Glenview, Illinois: Scott, Foresman and Company, 1980.

William F. O'Dell, *Effective Business Decision Making and the Educated Guess*. Lincolnwood, Illinois: NTC Business Books, 1991.

William F. O'Dell, et al., *Marketing Decision Making: Analytic Framework and Cases*. Cincinnati: South-Western Publishing Co., 1988.

Alfred R. Oxenfeldt et al., *A Basic Approach to Executive Decision Making*. New York: American Management Association, 1981.

Robert A. Lynn
Former Professor of Marketing
Clark Atlanta University
Atlanta, Georgia

CHAPTER 32

MARKETING STRATEGY

Marketing strategy is the framework on which all marketing actions rest. It guides the whole marketing program.

MAIN CONCEPTS

Marketing strategy is the use of marketing tools to achieve major marketing objectives. Strategy usually considers the long-term situation, although overcoming an immediate crisis can also become a matter of strategic significance.

The Market and the Competition

The two most basic factors for the marketing strategist to consider are the market and the competition. Much of the marketing effort centers on finding and delivering what members of the target market segment want.

If several competitors, however, all have information about buyers' needs and wants and also have adequate resources to meet the needs and wants, coping with competition becomes the major strategic concern.

Marketing strategy in an active competitive environment takes either an offensive or defensive stand. The established market leader usually practices a defensive strategy, while healthy but lower share marketers use offensive strategies.

Marketing and Overall Strategies

Marketing strategy operates under overall corporate strategy, which may include nonmarketing objectives such as maximizing the aggregate long-term value of all the firm's shares or attaining a target rate of return on shareholders' equity. In many cases, marketing strategy goals, are essential means of achieving corporate strategic goals. If marketing strategy does not succeed, corporate strategy may resort to nonmarketing actions, such as plant closings, to preserve financial soundness.

Tactics and Implementation

Tactics are applications of particular marketing techniques to specific marketing projects. The right advertising of a new product properly timed and placed is a tactic. From the viewpoint of a lower-level manager, such tactics are often thought of as their strategies. For example, a marketing strategy might seek a 5 percent sales increase and might raise the sales budget six percent to accomplish this. Or it might consider a "sales strategy" that would achieve the increased goal through bonuses to salespeople.

Implementation is the execution of both strategy and tactics. A strategy based on expanding the sales force rests on the performance ability of the new salespersons to sell as expected; this in turn requires proper selection and training. A potential strategy that cannot be implemented should not be used no matter how attractive it seems.

ORGANIZATION

Marketing strategy is generally conceived by marketing managers with responsibility for attaining marketing goals. In large organizations, marketing vice presidents or senior division executives have obvious strategic responsibility in firms that practice relatively decentralized management. Mid-level personnel may be encouraged to do strategic planning and execution. In other organizations, product managers and store managers may function mainly as skilled implementors of tactics that support overall strategy.

Strategy and Organization Levels

Top management strategy should drive the marketing strategy. In a firm that markets food through supermarkets and operates restaurants, top management may decide to phase out or sell off the restaurants. The marketing strategist for the restaurants would need to know this to avoid the frustration of pursuing a marketing strategy at variance with top management's corporate strategy. In addition, organizational realities affect marketing strategy. The amount of resources available is one of apparent constraint. The level of skill in the production and sales groups will also affect what can be done.

Types of Strategists

Another consideration is various managerial styles or approaches each of which can work especially well under various circumstances. These strategists can be defined as "explorers," "defenders," and "analyzers." Explorers like to try something new. Defenders prefer holding on to the gains made. Analyzers enjoy carefully deliberated moves more than bold intuitive ones.[1]

Good strategy stands on the match between the environmental realities of the marketplace and the organization's capability. Wal-Mart, for example, developed a strategy of exploring smaller markets with weak competitors. Success made growth possible, and growth was made in low-cost locations that would allow low-price strategy to be profitable. The rate of growth was not so fast as to alert longer established retailers to the new competitor's real threat until Wal-Mart had gained a strong market position.

STRATEGIC OBJECTIVES

The terms *objectives* and *goals* are used interchangeably here. The time horizon of objectives can vary. An early leader in a food product may seek a sustained 40 percent market share after 10 years when the product has matured and competitors have found market niches. A motor vehicles marketer who lags behind a competitor with an improved design might consider strategic price cuts or interest subsidies to hold sales losses at a minimum until the marketer's own improved design comes out.

Marketing Goals

Most marketing strategy objectives can and should be expressed in specific quantitative terms. Here are examples:

- Sales: Raise pet food tonnage by 10 percent over last year.
- Share: Raise brand's category market share from 14 to 16 percent.
- Attitude: Make the brand most aspired to by 50 percent of consumers from 30 to 40 years of age in the over $50,000 per year bracket.

These are often the means to attaining corporate objectives. In some cases, profit can be a marketing strategy objective. A new product might be priced for maximum sales volume consistent with profit of $10 million over the first three years of sales.

Setting marketing objectives involves consideration of the marketer's resources, competitor's resources and expected actions, and the environment faced by buyers. If competitors are all financially ailing during an economic upturn, a strong airline might consider a 20 percent passenger-mile increase attainably ambitious. If a flood of well-designed sport utility vehicles hits a recession market, a financially weak firm might base strategy on a goal of holding market share loss to three percentage points. Over a longer time period, this firm might pursue a "niche" strategy of gaining sales and brand loyalty among members of a very narrow market segment, such as buyers from 22 to 29 years of age in the $20,000 to $25,000 income bracket.

Objectives should be attainable and demand the marketing organization's best efforts. Unattainable objectives can demoralize organization members and call forth less than the best use of marketing resources.

Optimal and Incremental Goals

Optimal or maximum levels in goals demand a desired amount of improvement. These are usually applied to profit goals. There is some combination of price and advertising that would yield the most profit.

Most marketing strategists have long-run goals that are attained incrementally. For example, a firm with 10 percent share may seek 15 percent. In each of the next five years, the goal might be to raise share by 1 percent.

STRATEGY CATEGORIES AND APPROACHES

There are various strategy categories that can be used as guidelines.

Marketing Mix Approaches

Some effective strategies are merely based on use of one or more factors in the marketing mix. Successful new products are examples of attaining objective strategies. A powder-plus-skim-milk diet beverage may get a good start in the marketplace. As competitors predictably appear, the innovating strategist can enhance the product by selling precanned liquid, fruit-juice based products, and solid snack foods. This is a product-based strategy. Most marketing strategy is product and brand based. Line extensions (new flavors and forms) and brand leveraging (the use of an established brand name on new products that have a plausible relation to the brand's positioning) are widely effective. "Flanker" brands are brands or models that extend a product to a higher or lower price class or to customers of a younger or older age group. If there is a movement up the price scale, an unprotected upper "flank" is a strategic danger.

Strategists can face a dilemma. Suppose a "high end" flanker would protect against a competitor's future incursion into an upwardly moving market. In the short run, however, the higher end flanker would not be profitable. If such a flanker is a defensive strategy, it could be a wise expenditure.

A margarine may remain the same product but achieve strategic success through advertising of health-related customer benefits. A company can also increase the volume of advertising, which is also a strategic move.

A soft drink may gain sales through intensified efforts to place it in additional fast food outlets. This is a distribution strategy.

It is seldom feasible to pursue all strategic action alternatives. Affordability, skill availability, and estimated comparative effectiveness can guide the strategist's choice. While most marketing mix-based strategies are mainly oriented toward the market, the choice can also be guided by competitive factors.

A good marketing mix member may be one competitors cannot easily match. Competitors without good R&D budgets may not be able to match new line extensions; those with financial problems may not be able to match a price cut.

There is great marketing power in the effective strategic use of marketing mix elements, either used alone or in combination. The following are examples:

- Product (Barbie doll)
- Advertising (Marlboro cigarettes)
- Price and place (Wal-Mart)

A single marketing mix's strength cannot compensate for major perceived weaknesses elsewhere. Yugo entered the United States market in the 1980s with a low price strategy in the tradition of the Model T Ford and the Volkswagen. Weakness in product quality, however, prevented the low price from being an effective tool.

Broad Groups

Among the earliest marketing strategy classification approaches was that of Igor Ansoff in 1957.[2] The variables affected the changes in the product and the market:

- New product, same market: *product* strategy
- New market, same product: *market* strategy
- Same product, same market: *market penetration* strategy
- New product, new market: *diversification* strategy

Another grouping of strategies is build, hold, and pull back. An attractive market environment and weak competitors could encourage a "build" strategy. An already strong position with rising competitors suggests "hold." High uncertainty without much hope to control the situation can make "pull back" advisable.[3] This should usually be accompanied by product innovations or other marketing mix improvements to be effective over the long run.

Competitor-Based Approaches

In the 1980s and 1990s, marketing strategy often centered on actions against competitors which produced "marketing warfare."[4] Such conditions are encouraged when there is slow market growth and when attractive categories are entered by groups of well-financed marketers, often supported by diversified corporations with "cash cow" products.

In a warfare-analogy environment, it is important to know several things:

1. Are you on the defensive posture when an offensive posture is more appropriate? Usually, leaders must defend against attacks while maintaining a willingness to improve their own market offering.
2. How will your strategy affect competitors? If an aggressive strategy sets off a war by a formerly "friendly" or "good" competitor, perhaps it will do more long-run harm than good.
3. What are competitors doing? Careful study of the trade and local press may give clues. The sales force can be used to help monitor and report on competitors' plans (as they may be revealed by customers).

If a competitor is found to be planning a major move, before it actually occurs, the chance for a bold short-run strategy exists. A two-for-the-price-of-one offer may be promoted to help load the trade with inventory and blunt the launch. Trade deals, price cuts, and ad blitzes might also work.

EVALUATION

Since strategy deals with major matters, it must receive careful evaluation. The process is complicated since in a dynamic marketplace things rarely go exactly as planned.

Results

The most obvious way to judge strategy is by the extent to which it achieves its objectives. If you wanted to sell 40,000 of the new car model the first year and you sold 43,000, most marketers would rate the enterprise as a strategic success. If it only sold 10,000, this would indicate something went seriously wrong, even if the market conditions were less than robust.

A long-term measure of strategic success is the extent to which "brand building" occurs. This is the attainment of high share, high brand loyalty, and favorable buyer attitudes. Strong brands can raise the resale value of an entire firm far beyond the value of the equity shown on the balance sheet.

Process

An unpredictable competitive entry or a surprise recession, may affect results and are not necessarily a reflection on strategy. Similarly a competitor's bankruptcy or a shortage of a competitor's product may make a mediocre strategy perform strongly. Strategy can also be judged by its own internal process:

- Did the strategy make a realistic match of the marketer's capability and the whole marketing environment's features?
- Did the marketing organization function effectively to implement the strategy that was planned?
- Did the strategy make use of a systematic monitoring of competitors' actions?
- Did the strategy combine reasonable careful advance planning with changes that "emergent" factors in a dynamic marketplace thrust on managers after the strategic plan was set?[5]

An effective marketing strategy thus should achieve its results, but it also should deserve to achieve them.

REFERENCES

H. Igor Ansoff, "Strategies for Diversification," *Harvard Business Review* (September-October, 1957): 113–124.

Marian C. Burke, "Strategic Choice and Marketing Managers: An Examination of Business Level Marketing Objectives," *Journal of Marketing Research* 21 (November, 1984): 345–359.

Michael D. Hutt, Peter H. Reingen, and John R. Ronchetto, Jr., "Tracing Emergent Processes in Marketing Strategy Formation," *Journal of Marketing* 52 (January, 1988): 4–19.

Stephen W. McDaniel and James W. Kolari, "Marketing Strategy Implications of the Miles and Snow Strategic Typology," *Journal of Marketing* 51 (October, 1987): 19–30.

Al Ries and Jack Trout, *Marketing Warfare* (New York: McGraw-Hill Book Co., 1986).

Gene R. Laczniak
Professor of Business
Marquette University
Milwaukee, Wisconsin

Patrick E. Murphy
Professor of Marketing
College of Business Administration
University of Notre Dame
South Bend, Indiana

Journal of Business Ethics 10: 259–271, 1991.

CHAPTER 33

FOSTERING ETHICAL MARKETING DECISIONS

Most marketing decisions have ethical ramifications whether business executives realize it or not. When the actions taken are "proper," the ethical dimensions go unnoticed and attention centers upon the economic efficiencies and managerial astuteness of the decisions. But such is not always the case. When a marketing decision is ethically troublesome, its highly visible outcomes can be a public embarrassment or sometimes worse. Consider the following examples which are drawn from recent newspaper reports:

1. Between 1982 and 1986, Norelco knowingly sold a water purification system whose filtration mechanisms where contaminated with methylene chloride—a probable carcinogen. Basically, Norelco's so-called *Clean Water Machine* contained a carbonated filtration system which was sealed with a methylene chloride based glue which then seeped into the water. Norelco engineers were quickly aware of the problem but the judgment of the company was that the risk to individual consumers was slight because the leakage was likely minimal. At least, this was Norelco's public posture after questions about the product began to emerge. One wonders whether the company hoped to continue sales while they redesigned the filter, thereby eliminating the negative publicity stemming from the public disclosure of this (ironically) toxic clean water machine.[1]
2. Because of the glut of new products and limited amounts of shelf space, large supermarket chains are demanding upfront payments called "slotting fees" in order to stock new products. Supermarket chains justify this practice primarily because they have very narrow profit margins and because unsuccessful new products are costly to remove from the shelves. Some firms claim that *such practices discriminate* against small manufacturers who are without the ability to pay the large amounts that are demanded. For example, Safeway asked $25,000 from a small Montana specialty foods producer to have its pizzas placed in freezer cases in its California stores. Other manufacturers complain of the practice because many of the slotting fees are privately negotiated and as they are often made in cash, they become especially subject to abuse.[2]
3. Because tobacco manufacturers have been heavily criticized in the U.S. and other developed countries about safety of cigarette smoking, they have looked to the third world as the major source of their growth. Developing countries now consume about one-third of the $200 billion worth of cigarettes sold in the world. Moreover, many

of these developing countries have been targeted as the major sources of tobacco promotion in the immediate future. Often, tobacco companies develop relationships in conjunction with the local government which collects a substantial proportion of the product price in the form of sales taxes. To make matters worse, several tobacco companies admit that many of the brands sold to developing countries contain more tar and nicotine than in cigarette brands sold in developed countries.[3]

4. Manufacturers sometimes "dump" products which are declared unsafe for one reason or another in their initially targeted market and move those products to other areas of the world. In these latter countries regulators have not made the "unsafe" designation or existing regulations haven't caught up to safety standards applicable in the original market. One of the most blatant recent cases of abuse had to do with the output of some Bavarian dairies which had been ordered to destroy their product. The milk was radioactively contaminated by the Cheronobyl nuclear disaster because the German cows had grazed on contaminated grass. In any event, two train loads of milk were intercepted as they were about to be shipped to Egypt.[4]
5. Travel agents have been increasingly accused of not keeping the best interest of their clients in mind. In some cases, they have attempted to capture for their own accounts frequent flyer points which have not been credited to existing customer files. In other cases, the travel agents participated in sweepstakes sponsored by airline or rental car companies. These sweepstakes allow for an improved chance of "winning the game" based on the amount of business directed toward a particular airline or rental car company. The net result is that without the customers knowing it, clients might be steered into higher cost travel options as this is in the best interest of the travel agent.[5]
6. As Americans became increasingly health conscious, advertising stressed the health and nutritionally related benefits of various food products. This has led to numerous cases of misleading or exaggerated claims. For example, ads running in several women's magazines are urging women to drink more milk in order to prevent osteoporosis (the development of brittle bones that can fracture easily). What the ads do *not* say is that many dairy products (e.g., whole milk) are high in fat content and can contribute to high cholesterol levels and as a result, heart disease. Similarly, many cereal manufacturers have now promoted the supposed health benefits of consuming "all bran" cereals. One recent headline for a two page ad about Kellogg's cereals screamed, "Grab a weapon in the war against cancer."[6] This occurred because of the statistical linkage of certain bran and fibrous material consumption to low

rates of intestinal cancer. Yet, what the advertising omits is the fact that there is great debate in the medical community about what the proper level of fiber consumption should be and the fact that an over consumption of fiber—a mistake uninformed consumers might make—can lead to a neglect in the diet of other sources of nutrition valuable for needed vitamins and minerals.[7]

The examples could continue. The items cited above are meant to be illustrative of the point that there are various areas of marketing—including product management, international issues, retailing, advertising, distribution, and pricing—that can raise ethical questions about appropriate marketing practice. The recent spate of business ethics scandals including the Wall Street insider trading scams, the price gouging by numerous defense contractors, and the check overdraft scheme by the former E. F. Hutton brokerage firm has only heightened the skepticism of the American public to business practices.

HOW DOES THE PUBLIC FEEL ABOUT BUSINESS?

Analysts who track the public pulse seem to have established a perception of business and marketing which is less than flattering. Consider the following statistics which seem to show that Americans generally distrust business and business people.[8]

- A *Business Week/Harris* poll indicated that white collar crime is thought to be very common (49%) or somewhat common (41%) and the 46% (most in any category) believe that the ethical standards of business executives are only fair.
- A 1987 *U.S. News and World Report* survey reports that the majority of the American public believes that most business people regularly participate in ethical transgression such as taking home office supplies, padding expense accounts, and using small amounts of organizational funds for personal purposes.
- A 1987 *Time* study suggests that 76% of the American public saw a lack of business ethics in business managers as contributing to the decline of U.S. moral standards.
- A 1988 *Touche Ross* survey of the business community reported that the general feeling (even among business people) is that the problems concerning business ethics which have been portrayed in the media have not been overblown or exaggerated.

From a marketing standpoint, it is even more distressing to realize that among various categories of business professionals those holding marketing positions are viewed to be among the *least* ethical. For example, in a 1983 *Gallup* study judging the ethicalness of various occupations, the categories salespeople and advertising practitioners were ranked at the bottom of the honesty and ethical standards scale.[9] This disturbing public opinion probably developed because of the unethical practices of a minority. Yet, because of data like these all marketers are too often construed as hawkers, pitchmen, con-artists, and cheats. This festers a cancer which gnaws on the integrity of marketing practitioners everywhere.

DOES THE TYPICAL MARKETING MANAGER FACE ETHICAL PROBLEMS?

Over the years, some marketing managers have argued that they are relatively exempt from ethical dilemmas or that such moral pressures do not generally affect them. In reality, most studies confirm that between 65 and 75 percent of all managers do indeed face an ethical dilemma at some point in their career. An ethical dilemma is defined for our purposes as confronting a decision that involves the trade-off between lowering one's personal values in exchange for increased organizational or personal profits. Thus based upon the reports of practicing managers, it appears that most marketing executives are *not* free from dealing with ethical concerns. If anything, the percentages referenced above underestimate the number of marketers who face ethical dilemmas because some may not recognize one when it confronts them. Judging from the questions being raised about the propriety of marketing practices on all its fronts, the proposition that many marketing decisions have significant moral consequences seems a truism.

CAN EMPHASIZING ETHICS MAKE A DIFFERENCE?

The point has sometimes been made that preaching ethics in an organization does not have an effect upon the behavior of managers. This view was captured in the old adage which states "scruples, either you got 'em or you ain't." For years, the Harvard Business School and other colleges of business did not bother to teach business ethics on the supposition that efforts along these lines would most likely prove fruitless. Underlying this approach is a stream of research that indicates moral development occurs at a rather early age and by the time an individual enters a business organization, his/her moral sensibilities are rather established and somewhat immutable.[10] There is evidence that this viewpoint is probably in error as various organizational case studies that have consistently shown the ethical gyroscopes of managers can be spun about by organizational actions and economic pressures.[11]

One way to establish how ethical concern might be of value to an organization is to visualize the archetypal ways in which managers might confront an ethical issue.[12]

First, you have the *crook.* This kind of individual looks at a particular marketing situation, realizes that it has negative ethical consequences, *knows* that taking the action would be morally wrong but consistently goes ahead and takes that action—presumably for personal reward and the (short-term) economic gain of the organization. Such unethical, and often criminal activity, exists in a minority of the population including marketing executives. Most companies will attempt to purge such individuals from the organization when their pattern of action becomes evident. Others, however, may tolerate such behavior if the actions lead to economic rewards for the organization. In any event, concern for ethical issues by the organization will probably not influence the behavior of this type of individual.

A second kind of manager might be called the *good samaritan.* This manager looks at a decision with potential ethical consequences and, based upon some method of moral reasoning and personal principles, generally arrives at what is arguably an ethical and just resolution of the decision. Like the crook, such highly principled good samaritans, who almost always recognize the ethical consequences of their actions and then can reason to appropriate conclusions without respect to the organization, are relatively rare.

The third type of manager might be called the *seeker.* This manager genuinely wants to do the right thing but does not always have the appropriate information or awareness. Seekers may be required to make decisions having ethical consequences but they may not recognize an ethical choice. This type of manager can clearly benefit from ethical education as well as a greater degree of stated ethical concern by the organization. Such managers need to be made aware of the potential ethical consequences of marketing decisions as well as the trade-offs that exist among the alternative actions that are available when making a decision with substantial ethical consequences. We suspect the number of managers falling into the "seeker" category is fairly substantial and especially describes those younger or less experienced marketers.

The fourth type of manager—the *rationalizer*—presents the most difficult situation. The rationalizer recognizes that certain decisions have ethical consequences, but they generally will find a way to justify the most economically expedient solution whether it is ethical or not. That is, they have the ability to recognize that there are moral consequences to particular decisions, but in their mind they can find a reason why in their situation the normal moral cautions do not apply. Obviously, this sort of manager can benefit from heightened ethical concern in the organization. This is particularly true when that concern takes a form which teaches a method of moral reasoning that can be applied to marketing decisions or compels them to act ethically because they fear organizational sanctions.

The upshot of this discussion is that at the extremes, efforts to stimulate ethical concern by organizations will not change managerial behavior. Certain managers (i.e., crooks) will be predisposed to act unethically and others (i.e., good samaritans) will try to do the right thing regardless of the organizational posture. However, in the middle ranges, where one suspects we find most managers, there would appear to be a sufficiently large number either looking for moral guidance (i.e., seekers) or not having the necessary background or fortitude (i.e., the rationalizers) to reason through morally difficult problems. For organizations concerned with improving their ethical climate, the ability to influence seeker and rationalizer type managers becomes a valuable strategic window of opportunity. Those managers who do not regularly recognize the ethical implications of their decision are in need of having their ethical sensitivities raised by ethics education. Those who recognize the situation with moral consequences but cannot properly deal with them are in need of education in the realm of ethical reasoning. It may be that via ethics seminars or even some customized "paper and pencil" tests, organizations can learn what percentage of their managers most likely fall into each category. Then, ethics codes, programs or education can be tailored to fit the ethical needs of the companies' executives.

WHY SHOULD MARKETING ORGANIZATIONS ATTEMPT TO FOSTER ETHICAL BEHAVIOR?

Besides the obvious answer that being ethical is simply the proper thing to do—a point which will be developed later—marketers should be ethical because not to be so will likely generate significant personal, organizational, and societal costs.[13] Consider first the personal costs. If an action is illegal as well as unethical (as many such actions are), the manager who makes the questionable ethical decision can be held personally liable. The case of the Foreign Corrupt Practices Act of 1977 (which applies to U.S. based organizations) that prohibits the bribery of foreign officials to obtain overseas contracts illustrates this point.[14] For each violation—that is, the payment of a bribe—the organization is subject to a $1 million dollar fine. More significant, however, the manager responsible for this payment is subject to a $10,000 fine per violation and a maximum of 5 years in prison. Relatedly, the courts are increasingly disposed to incarcerate executives shown to be responsible for violations of the law which endanger consumers.[15] For instance, a manager who premeditatedly decides to market an unsafe product (the managers responsible for the earlier mentioned Norelco decision come to mind) are subject to criminal and personal liability. Criminal liability, of course, is the harshest of penalties but there are other negative outcomes. Organizations which take their ethical reputation seriously will not hesitate to terminate employees who violate ethical and professional norms. This is an obvious gesture which communicates an organization's seriousness of purpose concerning the maintenance of an ethical culture. Needless to say, such terminations will affect the future career prospects of these individuals, not to mention the personal embarrassment that goes along with being fired.

There are also substantial *organizational costs* resulting from unethical behavior when ethical transgressions by a company become publicized. Typically, these take the form of reduced sales and a loss of goodwill. A classic case is the experience of the Nestlé Company with their marketing of infant formula in Third World countries.[16] In that particular situation, Nestlé attempted to aggressively market infant formula, as a substitute for mothers' breast milk, in less developed countries. Nestlé seemed to pay little attention to the fact that the proper use of infant formula requires sanitary conditions and a fairly high literacy rate on the part of mothers. Because these conditions were not present, infants incurred a substantially higher rate of malnutrition than if they had been fed mothers milk. As these circumstances became known, the result was a public relations nightmare as well as a balance sheet catastrophe for Nestlé. The derogatory publicity along with a substantial loss of sales was due to various boycotts of Nestlé products worldwide.

A similar case involves the Beech Nut Company which continued to sell a cheap, chemical based substitute juice as a real apple juice for babies, primarily to maintain its cash flow.[17] The company denied any wrongdoing even after the evidence had plainly been generated which would find the company guilty of hundreds of counts of premeditated product fraud. In this situation, the reputation of Beech Nut—a company marketing to children and one dependent upon fostering an image of safety and care—has probably become irreconcilably besmirched because of the actions of a few unscrupulous managers.

Finally, there are enormous *societal costs* which are generated by the unethical behavior of organizations. First, a consumer, who is tricked into buying a product that he/she does not need or who ends up paying substantially more for a product or service than is justified, incurs a surplus economic cost as well as some resentment toward the marketing system. Some groups such as the poor, the old, the handicapped, the mentally feeble, children, and recent immigrants are particularly vulnerable to unethical selling practices. Besides the economic or physical pain suffered by victims of unethical marketing practice, there is a general damage to the credibility of the existing economic system which requires a high level of trust to operate smoothly. Whether one believes in a free market economy or a planned economy, most business analysts agree that it is the economically efficient firm with the superior product that should be rewarded, rather than the dishonest firm which gains a preceived advantage via misrepresentation. Yet, when a competitive situation exists wherein an unethical marketing practice generates a short-term benefit for loss efficient firms, the advantages of the supposedly efficient marketplace are shortcircuited and shift toward the unethical firm. If questionable marketing practices continue to a greater extent, further erosion of confidence by the American public occurs.

FRAMEWORKS FOR ETHICAL DECISION MAKING

What standards do marketers use in order to grapple with questions that may have ethical implications? Historically, most marketers and business executives have gravitated toward a utilitarian method of problem solving. Applied to an ethical situation in a marketing context, the reasoning employed by many managers would take the form of a cost/benefit analysis. Businesspeople, because of their training, are naturally prone to talk about concepts such as "maximizing profitability" and "concern for the bottom line." Profitability essentially translates into the excess of revenue over cost. It does not require a great stretch of the marketing manager's imagination to apply a similar sort of thinking to an ethical context. Thus, managers often operate with a rule that essentially says, "make decisions such that the benefits to the firm exceed the costs incurred by the firm to the greatest extent possible." Depending upon how a manager defines "benefits" and "costs" one might arrive at different conclusions. If the emphasis is upon economic criteria (such as short-term profits) it is easy to see how a fair amount of the ethical analysis conducted by business executives gives great weight to economic outcomes which evaluate how various options would benefit stockholders in the near term.

Thus looking at situations from their potential influence upon short run profitability, one can see how an organization rationalizes taking a product (for example, a toy dart gun) which has been declared unsafe in one market and attempts to sell it in another market where the regulation might not apply. The rationale: the organization does not have to write off the inventory—a major cost. The inherent danger of the product might be arguable. Who is to say definitely that a plastic, rubber tipped dart gun is any more or less dangerous than a baseball? The sale of the product is perfectly legal, thereby protecting a revenue stream. In short, economic considerations often prevail over other possible perspectives like whether "toy guns" are a proper plaything or whether a firm should tolerate any product that has a likelihood of severely injuring a child.

This is not to say that there are no other short-hand decision rules besides utilitarian cost/benefit analysis which are used by business people. Other expeditious frameworks for ethical decision making have been articulated as useful. The extent to which these thumbnail frameworks have been utilized by marketers in particular situations has not been systematically studied. Some of the maxims which might aid a marketer facing an ethical dilemma are the following:[18]

The Golden Rule—act in a way that you would expect others to act toward you.

The Professional Ethic—take only actions which would be viewed as proper by an objective panel of your professional colleagues.

Kant's Categorical Imperative—act in a way such that the action taken under the circumstances could be a universal law of behavior for everyone facing those same circumstances.

The TV Test—a manager should always ask, would I feel comfortable explaining this action on TV to the general public?

Some thumbnail rules are difficult to apply in specific situations. At times, the application of one more rule of thumb to the same situation seems to suggest an entirely different solution. For example, if every sales rep pads his/her expense account by 15 percent because customary gratuities (i.e., tips) are not technically reimbursable, the *professional ethic* might dictate the practice is OK despite its variance from the letter of company policy. In contrast, the *categorical imperative* might be interpreted as suggesting that as a "universal rule" padding an expense account is not acceptable.

Still, such maxims can have considerable value. One wonders whether the product manager who permitted the Norelco Clean Air Machine to continue to be sold—knowing that methylene chloride might be leaking into the carbon filtration system—could possibly feel comfortable explaining those actions to the general public on TV. Similarly, the professional ethic can be extremely useful for those sub-specialties in business that have a code of professional conduct which covers certain recurring situations. For example, various groups of professional marketing researchers have developed detailed codes of ethics which cover commonly encountered situations by their peer group. Included, for instance, in many marketing research codes of ethics would be dictums that stipulate that respondent confidentiality should be protected when it is promised, that data which does not confirm the hypothesized findings of the researcher is not suppressed, that the limitations of various statistical methods are identified in the research report, and so forth.

Whatever frameworks are used, the consensus regarding what constitutes proper ethical behavior in a decision making situation tends to diminish as the level of analysis proceeds from the abstract to the specific. Put another way, it is easy to get a group of managers to agree *in general* that a practice is improper; however, casting that practice in a very specific set of circumstances usually reduces consensus. For example, most managers would agree with the proposition that "business has the obligation to provide consumers with facts relevant to the informed purchase of a product or a service." However, let us test this proposition in a specific situation.

Suppose we have a manufacturer of cleaning concentrate whose directions call for mixing one part of the concentrate with four parts of water; suppose further that this cleaning concentrate has been sold in this manner for 25 years. Now, assume that an issue of Consumer Reports *indicates that the product will clean just as effectively if mixed with one part concentrate to eight parts water. Thus, consumers need only use one half as much concentrate. Does the company have an ethical responsibility to inform customers of this fact?*

Again, most managers *agree* that business has the obligation to provide consumers with facts relevant to an informed purchase. But does such an informed purchase include full disclosure of this *new information,* especially if further product testing in different situations would produce different results?

Because of the difficulty of applying such general principles to specific case situations, a number of researchers have begun to investigate what factors account for the particular decisions of managers in an ethical context. In an effort to aid their investigations, some of these researchers have begun to formulate *models* which stipulate the factors which come into play as a marketing manager arrives at an "ethical" decision.

MODELS OF MARKETING ETHICS

The Moral Development Model

This approach draws partly upon the analysis of educational psychologist Lawrence Kohlberg, who studied the moral development of adolescents.[19] Basically, Kohlberg postulated that over time individuals develop moral systems which are increasingly complex although there was no guarantee that any particular individual moves beyond the initial and most fundamental stage of moral development. Essentially, Kohlberg saw three broad levels of cognitive moral development. These were:

- *The preconventional stage* where abiding concern of the individual would be resolving moral situations with the individual's own immediate interests and consequences firmly in mind. An individual at the preconventional level would give strong weight to the external rewards and punishments which would be most likely to affect them. Normally, this stage includes a strong emphasis upon literal obedience to rules and authority.
- *The conventional stage.* Individuals at the conventional stage have progressed to a level where their ethical decision making mode takes into consideration the expectations of some significant referent group and larger society. What constitutes moral propriety has to do with a concern for others, however, still motivated most directly by organizational rules. Such rules are tempered by keeping loyalties and doing one's duty to society.
- *The principled level.*This is the highest stage of moral development. Individuals who reach this level solve their ethical problems in a manner that goes beyond the norms and laws that are overtly applicable to a situation. Proper

conduct certainly includes upholding the basic rights, values, and legal contracts of the society, but beyond that such individuals seem to subscribe to universal ethical principles which they believe that all members of society should follow in similar situations.

What the Moral Development model implies is that the ethical sophistication of managers can increase over time. The major difference among the various stages of moral development according to this approach is that as the manager moves to a higher level of moral development the individual is able to take more factors into consideration, especially factors which go beyond personal self interest. Two major implications of the Moral Development model are that (a) some managers will be less sophisticated than others in terms of the considerations they bring to bear to a decision with potentially moral consequences. At the most basic level, some managers will operate almost totally from the standpoint of egoistic self interest. And (b), perhaps there are interventions that organizations can bring to bear which will compel managers to higher levels of moral development—assuming this is a goal which is seen as in the interest of the organization.

The Contingency Model

Another model has been developed by Ferrell and Gresham.[20] In addition to the usual individual factors that might influence an ethical decision, their approach suggests two major intervening issues that will determine whether a manager acts ethically or not. There are: the *opportunity* to engage in potentially unethical action and the *relative influence* (positive or negative) *of reference groups,* especially peers and top management. With regard to the role of these reference groups, the model stipulates that when contact with peers is great, peers will have a greater degree of influence upon ethical/unethical behavior. Conversely, when the interaction with top management is substantial, the attitudes communicated by top management will have a strong formulative role in shaping the behavior of subordinate managers concerning ethical decisions. For example, sales reps often operate in a fairly autonomous fashion in the field with limited contact with management. In such cases, the attitudes of peers regarding ethical issues would likely be more influential than the opinions of management.

With respect to the *opportunity* to engage in unethical behavior, it is not surprising that the model postulates that the greater the opportunity to engage in such behavior the more likely an individual will do so—all other things equal. The proclivity to favor an unethical option is tempered of course by the rewards and punishments which are operating in a particular manager's environment. That is to say, unethical behavior is discouraged by codes of ethics which prohibit certain activities. Similarly, when punishments are enacted for violation of certain professional conduct, unethical behavior is less likely to occur.

In the absence of such sanctions, the probability of a manager acting unethically increases.

The contribution of the Contingency Model is that it shows individual values are not the sole arbiter of ethical behavior; peer and supervisor influence is also extremely important. With respect to the role of top management, there is an old organizational adage which suggests that the business enterprise is but a lengthened shadow of the person at the top. In all probability, the posture of top management may be the single most important factor determining ethical behavior in an organization.[21] Similarly, the notion of opportunity to act unethically simply underscores the common sense notion that options which are not available will not generally be taken.

The Reasoned Action Model

Other approaches to the study of ethics have taken the "rational man" approach.[22] The basic idea is that a typical individual will approach an ethical problem from a rather calculating perspective. First, the person must perceive that a situation has ethical dimensions. At this point, several evaluations take place. One involves a judgment concerning the inherent rightness or wrongness of the ethical question [at issue]. Either basic or sophisticated principles are used to arrive at this judgment. A second step involves a determination of what the preceived consequences of acting ethically or unethically are. The probability that each of those consequences will occur are then subjectively calculated taking into consideration the importance of each outcome. The ultimate ethical judgment arrived at by the manager is the result of judgment concerning the norms of behavior (i.e., the evaluation regarding the rightness or wrongness of the action) in conjunction with the evaluation of the net gain from each outcome adjusted for the probability of its happening. What all this means is that managers will systematically weigh the possible options and outcomes in light of their individual value system. One of the essential problems of the approach is that it never clearly specifies whether the evaluations are made from the standpoint of the person, the manager as representing the organization or the manager taking into account the various stakeholders (i.e., consumers, employees, etc.) of the firm.

Although this model may seem complicated upon first exposure, it is not terribly complex. Brought down to its essentials, it implies the following:

1. If managers perceive a situation which requires an action which may have ethical consequences they will attempt to elaborate the alternative outcomes of the options available to them.
2. In coming to a decision as to which option to choose, managers will weigh factors including the inherent rightness or wrongness of the

act itself, the probability that acting in a particular way will lead to certain payoffs, and the values of those payoffs.
3. All of this will lead to formation of an ethical judgment which will culminate in the *intention* to take a particular action. Whether the action is actually taken or not can still be mitigated by various situational factors such as the likelihood of getting caught.

Again, the value of models like those described is that they elaborate important issues which bear upon ethical decision making. Whether these factors deal with the moral development of the individual manager, the influence of top management or peer groups, the opportunity to engage in particular actions, or the value of various outcomes to the manager, they are all organizational aspects which can be adjusted to possibly improve the firm's ethical posture. Perhaps the greatest shortcoming of such models is that they are basically descriptive. While they elaborate factors that come into play when managers might take an action with moral consequences, such approaches generally avoid making any moral judgments about the propriety of various actions.

The organization, which is interested in *improving* rather than simply understanding the ethical decisions which take place in marketing, needs (a) an organizational mandated sequence of ethical reasoning that a manager can utilize, and (b) organizational commitment by top management to an ethical culture. Each of these topics are treated briefly below.

A SEQUENCE OF QUESTIONS TO IMPROVE ETHICAL REASONING

One approach to more normatively deal with ethical issues is to require managers to proceed through a sequence of questions which essentially test whether the action that they contemplate is ethical or has possible ethical consequences. A battery of such questions might include the following:[23]

Question 1: Does the contemplated action violate law?

Question 2: Is the contemplated action contrary to widely accepted moral obligations? (Such moral obligations might include *duties of fidelity* such as the responsibility to remain faithful to contracts, to keep promises, and to tell the truth; *duties of gratitude* which basically means that special obligations exist between relatives, friends, partners, cohorts, and employees; *duties of justice* which basically have to do with obligations to distribute rewards based upon merit; *duties of nonmaleficence* which consists of duties not to harm others; *duties of beneficence* which rest upon the notion that actions should be taken which improve the situation of others—if this can be readily accomplished.)[24]

Question 3: Does the proposed action violate any other special obligations which stem from the type of marketing organization at focus? (For example, the special duty of pharmaceutical firms to provide safe products, the special obligation of toy manufacturers to care for the safety of children, the inherent duty of alcohol manufacturers to promote responsible drinking.)

Question 4: Is the *intent* of the contemplated action harmful?

Question 5: Are there any major damages to people or organizations that are likely to result from the contemplated action?

Question 6: Is there a satisfactory alternative action which produces equal or greater benefits to the parties affected than the proposed action?

Question 7: Does the contemplated action infringe upon the inalienable rights of the consumer (such as the right to information, the right to be heard, the right to choice, and the right to redress)?

Question 8: Does the proposed action leave another person or group less well off? Is this person or group already a member of a relatively underprivileged class?

The questions outlined need not be pursued in any lockstep fashion. If none of the questions uncover any potential conflicts, clearly the action being contemplated is quite likely to be ethical. However, if the sequence of queries does produce a possible "conflict," this does not necessarily mean that the action being proposed is unethical *per se*. There may be unusual intervening factors which would still allow the action to ethically go forward. For example, suppose it is determined that the contemplated action is a violation of the law. Perhaps the law is unjust and thus, there could be a moral obligation for an organization to transgress the law. Similarly, suppose there is an alternative action which could be taken which would produce equal or greater good for a larger number of individuals. However, the implementation of this alternative would bankrupt the existing organization. In such a situation, the taking of the alternative action (rather than the contemplated action) is very likely not required.

ORGANIZATIONAL COMMITMENT TO AN ETHICAL CULTURE

The sequence of questions discussed can enhance the moral reasoning ability of managers. However, the organization can take other steps which attempt to shape the *behavior* of managers by virtue of the organizational environment in which they operate. Several possible steps are addressed here. These actions can influence the organizational culture in the long term.[25]

Top Management Leadership

A primary factor in setting a firm's ethical tone is the posture and seriousness of purpose communicated by top managers toward this issue. Most studies of business and marketing ethics make this quite clear.[26] As Deal and Kennedy point out in their book, *Corporate Cultures,* managers give extraordinary attention to those matters stressed in the corporate value system. These values are personified more often than not by the top executive in the organization.[27]

It is commonly accepted that companies are overmanaged and under-led. Leadership is important in all aspects of the firm, but it is critical in the ethics area. Examinations of CEOs' characteristics typically list integrity as an indispensible ingredient. For instance, James Burke, former CEO of Johnson & Johnson, directed managers to evaluate the company's successful corporate credo. These efforts are credited as being responsible for the swift product recall and sensitive reaction to the infamous Tylenol poisonings. Another illustration of leadership and integrity is Lee Iacocca's stance regarding Chrysler's past practice of disconnecting odometers of cars while driven by company executives. Iacocca admitted the firm had made a mistake in judgment and promised that the practice would never happen again.[28]

Codes of Ethics

These statements are ideally the articulation of corporate values in a moral context. One recent report indicated that 75%—80% of all major corporations have established codes of ethics.[29] Such codes can help vitalize the organization, but some are simply "public relations boilerplate" or "motherhood and apple pie" statements. In fact, one study indicated that most existing codes are primarily legalistic in orientation.[30]

Although a few firms, such as the aforementioned example of Johnson & Johnson, have a short and general corporate credo, most companies delineate their ethical stance in a formal and longer code of ethics. These codes commonly address issues like conflict of interest, treatment of competitors, the right to privacy, gift giving and political contributions. Despite their limitations, a recent survey stated that codes are perceived to be *the* most effective way to encourage ethical corporate behavior.[31]

We propose that for codes to have the maximal impact, they should be:

Publicized and Communicated to the Organization. New employees are usually asked to read and sign off on the code during their orientation. However, the code is quickly forgotten if it is never mentioned again. Firms should regularly communicate with marketing personnel about the code and publicize it in departmental memos and meetings. Some firms, including Michigan National Bank, require that employees read and affirm their commitment to the code on an annual basis.

Specific. To avoid vagueness, the code should offer specific guidance to sales and marketing executives. Words that have vague meanings should be avoided. In the gift giving and receiving area, words like nominal, token or modest should not be used. Some firms do follow this type of policy. For example, Waste Management tells employees that gifts should not exceed $100 in aggregate annual value and Donnelly Mirrors' code states "If you can't eat it, drink it or use it up in one day, don't give it or anything else of greater value."

Pertinent. In our examination of codes of ethics, we are continually struck by how similar they are. More thought needs to be given on placing pertinent information in the code. The point is that each organization has certain areas that are particularly likely to encounter ethical abuse, and these concerns are one on which the code should focus. For instance, toy companies must make special provisions for protecting the safety of children. Mail order firms should address the question of their return policy and how they handle merchandise damaged in shipping. Companies that spend millions of dollars on promotion and advertising need to detail their advertising philosophy as well as what program vehicles or media they will or will not use.

Enforced. To gain the respect of managers and their subordinates, the code of marketing conduct must be enforced. Sanctions should be specified and punishments meted out. What the particular sanctions for a given violation would entail depends on the violation. For example, padding an expense account for the first time may result in a salesperson losing his or her commission for a period of time, while a manager who induces employees to use bait-and-switch tactics might be dismissed. Specifically, Baxter's (formerly Baxter-Travenol) code states that violators will be terminated.

Revised. To remain current, codes should be revised periodically. They need to be living documents to reflect changing worldwide conditions, community standards and evolving organizational policies. For example, Caterpillar instituted its code in 1974 and revised it 1977 and 1982. Johnson & Johnson's credo came into being in 1945 and was modified slightly in 1979 as a result of the credo challenge meetings.

Ethics Seminars/Programs

A number of organizations choose to hold periodic seminars for marketing managers that deal with the question of ethics. Each manager might be required to attend one seminar every several years. The purpose of such educational modules is not so much to provide exact answers to particular questions as to sensitize managers to potential ethical problems that fall within the domain of their responsibilities. The programs or seminars may take the form of helping managers develop their capability to morally reason or involve the discussion of hypothetical case situations which treat circumstances that could conceivably arise.

There are several avenues that firms can travel in developing these ethics seminars or programs. One option is a modest effort such as having a speaker or panel at a dealer meeting or corporate conference. For instance, a recent market research conference sponsored by Drakett Company (a Bristol Myers subsidiary) included such an ethics module where several ethically-charged cases were discussed. A second possibility is longer "in-house" conferences or offsite meetings on the subject. Polaroid held a series of ethics conferences several years ago. Probably the most extensive ethics seminar is conducted by Chemical Bank. Their "Decision Making and Corporate Values" program is a two-day, off site, seminar aimed at the VP level. Discussion centers around ethics cases, such as credit approval, branch closings, foreign loans and insider trading—all developed from interviews with Chemical personnel.[32]

A third type of program was undertaken a couple years ago at McDonnell Douglas. The firm distributed three ethics books to all employees of the company. The revised code and other material followed the previously mentioned points for a well-constructed code. The company also instituted a company-wide ethics training program for both white and blue collar employees.[33] Even though McDonnell Douglas undertook this extensive ethics program, some of its marketing executives were implicated in a subsequent defense contractor scandal. Thus, there are no guarantees that ethics programs or seminars will institutionalize ethics within all parts of the firm.

Ethical Audits

Increasingly, firms are finding that unless they monitor their ethical performance, it will be taken for granted. As a result, some companies have developed systematic procedures which allow the organization to determine whether its employees are taking the commitment to ethical and social responsibility seriously. This process can involve the utilization of an outside consultant or perhaps a special ethics committee of the board of directors empowered to periodically evaluate operations against a prescribed set of standards.

Perhaps the company with the longest and most complete ethical audit program is Dow Corning, based in Midland, Michigan. The firm started using face-to-face audits at its plants over a decade ago and holds about twenty of these meetings annually. The number of participants in these four to six hour meetings ranges from five to forty. The auditors meet with the manager-in-charge the evening before so as to ascertain the most pressing issues. Actual questions often come from a relevant section in the corporate code and are adjusted to the audit location. Sample questions are: Do any of our employees have ownership or financial interest in any of our distributorships? Have our sales representatives been able to undertake business conduct discussions with distributors in a way that actually strengthens our ties with them?

A Business Conduct Committee oversees the audits and then prepares a report for the Board. The manager who heads this effort says there are no shortcuts to implementing this program because it requires much time and extensive interaction with the people involved.[34]

CONCLUSION

To return to an earlier point, some managers when given the opportunity to act unethically, especially when that action will lead to *personal gain,* will choose to be unethical. All marketing managers will not behave like saints anymore than one could expect perfect behavior from all doctors, lawyers, or college professors. Nevertheless, for the organization that takes its ethical duties seriously, the provision of mechanisms to help managers better morally reason through ethical problems and the establishment of a corporate culture which will help direct managerial actions toward beneficial ends goes far in the establishment of an ethically enlightened marketing organization.

NOTES

1. 'Norelco Sold Water Purifier That It Knew Could Be Hazardous': 1988, *Milwaukee Journal,* (October 9), p. 13A.
2. Gibson, R.: 1988, 'Space War: Supermarkets Demand Food Firms' Payments Just to Get on the Shelf', *Wall Street Journal* (November 1), Sec. A, p. 1.
3. Mulson, S.: 1985, 'Smoking Section: Cigarette Companies Develop Third World as a Growth Market', *Wall Street Journal* (July 5), p. 1.
4. Tagliabue, J.: 1987, 'Keeping Tainted Foods Off Third World Shelves', *New York Times* (February 2), p. B2.
5. Rose, L.: 1988, 'Travel Agents' Games Raise Ethics Issues', *Wall Street Journal* (November 23), p. B1.
6. 'The Food/Health Supplement',: 1989, *New York Times Magazine* (April 16), Part 2.
7. Morris, B.: 1985, 'Rise In Health Claims in Food Ads Can Help and Mislead Shoppers', *Wall Street Journal* (April 2), p. 33.
8. Reported in Robin, D. P., and R. E. Reidenbach: 1989, *Business Ethics: Where Profits Meet Value Systems* (Prentice-Hall, Englewood Cliffs, N.J.), p. 4.
9. Gallup Poll (1983), 'Honesty and Ethical Standards', Report No. 214 (July).
10. Kohlberg, L.: 1969, 'Stage and Sequence: The Cognitive Developmental Approach to Socialization', in D. A. Gaslin (ed.), *Handbook of Socializations Theory and Research* (hereafter cited as Kohlberg, Stage and Sequence), pp. 347–480 (Rand McNally: Chicago).
11. Brenner, S. and E. Molander: 1977, 'Is The Ethics of Business Changing?', *Harvard Business Review* (January/February), pp. 52–71.
12. Adapted from Martin, T. R.: 1986, 'Ethics in Marketing: Problems and Prospects', *Marketing Ethics: Guidelines for Managers,* Laczniak and E. Murphy (eds.) (D. C. Heath and Company: Lexington, MA). pp. 3–5.

13. Based upon Laczniak, G. R. and P. E. Murphy: 1986, 'Incorporating Marketing Ethics Into The Organization', *Marketing Ethics: Guidelines for Managers* (D.C. Heath and Company, Lexington, MA), pp. 98–100 (hereafter cited as Laczniak and Murphy, *Marketing Ethics*).
14. Kaikati, G. and W. A. Label: 1980, 'Americal Bribery Legislation: An Obstacle to International Marketing', *Journal of Marketing* (Fall), pp. 38–43.
15. Laczniak and Murphy, *Marketing Ethics.*
16. Sethi, S. P. and J. E. Post: 1979, 'The Marketing of Infant Formula in Less Developed Countries', *California Management Review,* Vol. XXI, No. 4, pp. 35–48.
17. Trauk, J.: 1988, 'Into The Mouths of Babes', *New York Times Magazine* (July 24) p. 17.
18. Laczniak, G. R.: 1983, 'Business Ethics: A Manager's Primer', *Business* (January–March), pp. 23–29 (hereafter cited as Laczniak, *Business*).
19. Kohlberg, Stage and Sequence.
20. Ferrell, O. C., and L. Gresham: 1985, 'A Contingency Framework For Understanding Ethical Decision Making in Marketing', *Journal of Marketing* (Summer), pp. 87–96.
21. Baumhart, R. C.: 1961, 'How Ethical Are Businesses?', *Harvard Business Review* (July–August), p. 6.
22. Hunt, S. D., and S. Vitell: 1986, 'A General Theory of Marketing Ethics', *Journal of Macromarketing* (Spring), pp. 5–16.
23. Adapted from Laczniak, G. R.: 1983, 'Frameworks For Analyzing Marketing Ethics', *Journal of Macromarketing* (Spring), pp. 7–18.
24. Ross, W. D.: 1930, *The Right and The Good* (Clarendon Press, Oxford).
25. Partially adapted from: Laczniak and Murphy, *Marketing Ethics,* pp. 100–104.
26. Laczniak, *Business.*
27. Terrence E. Deal and Allen A. Kennedy (1982), *Corporate Culture: The Risks and Rituals of Corporate Life* (Addison-Wesley Publishing Co., Inc., Reading, MA).
28. Patrick E. Murphy, 'Implementing Business Ethics', *Journal of Business Ethics,* December 1988, pp. 907–915.
29. W. Mathews (1987), 'Codes of Ethics: Organizational Behavior and Misbehavior', in Fredrick (ed.) *Research in Corporate Social Performance and Policy* (JAI Press, Inc., Greenwich, CT), pp. 107–130.
30. Donald P. Robin et al., 'A Different Look at Codes of Ethics', *Business Horizons,* January-February 1989, pp. 66–73.
31. Touche Ross, *Ethics in American Business* (Touche Ross & Co., New York) January 1988.
32. Patrick E. Murphy, 'Creating Ethical Corporate Structures', *Sloan Management Review,* Winter 1989, pp. 81–86.
33. Murphy, *Journal of Business Ethics.*
34. Murphy, *Sloan Management Review.*

James M. Hulbert
Professor
Columbia Business School
Columbia University
New York, New York

Bernd Schmitt
Assistant Professor
Columbia Business School
Columbia University
New York, New York

CHAPTER 34

ETHICS IN MARKETING

For marketing managers, ethics in marketing presents some of the most difficult decisions they must make since views on the ethics of marketing practices vary considerably. Senior managers' perspectives often differ from middle managers', while salespeople and public relations personnel hold different views. Likewise, the same individuals may adhere to different ethical criteria when placed in the role of aggrieved consumers than when acting in the capacity of managers for their employers. Perspectives may vary further among such roles as regulator, press reporter, consumer advocate, and "expert" witness, all of whom are typically involved in more widely publicized controversies over marketing ethics. If such variance exists within one country, it is easy to understand how much more complicated the issues become in a world of global competition. Despite disparate legal frameworks, patterns of industrial practice, and cultural difference, managers must wrestle with such issues.

This chapter explores the concept of ethics and the criticisms frequently made of ethics in marketing.

Ethical Decision Making: The Ideal World

Ethics is that branch of philosophy concerned with the rightness or wrongness and goodness or badness of human conduct.[1] Ethics, therefore, provide the basis for deciding whether a particular action is morally good or morally bad. Philosophical approaches to the determination of "good" and "bad" tend to be one or the other of two basic types: the teleological and the deontological.

The teleological perspective judges the moral worth of a behavior by its consequences. It is a pragmatic approach, which is in some ways consistent with the philosophical underpinnings of market-based economies.[2] Even if we agree, however, that ethical marketers should always be concerned with the consequences of their actions, how can all consequences be foreseen? Following the teleological perspective, ethical marketing would seem to require at least a modicum of foresight. One could certainly question the ethics of holding managers accountable because they lack the intelligence—or analytic support—to foresee the consequences of their actions, even though they did what they believed was "right" at the time.

In contrast, deontological reasoning holds that there are universal rules that can and should guide individual behavior. Such reasoning is used to justify many regulatory principles, which establish "rights" and ensure "justice." It is alleged that the world's major religions—Buddhism, Hinduism, Judaism, Islam, and Christianity—all espouse similar values with respect to certain absolute rights of the individual.[3]

Deontological ethics, then, emphasize finding the best set of rules to guide behavior.[4]

The contributions of some moral philosophers, however, are more difficult to characterize, yet are intriguing in their implications.[5] Using a game-of-chance analogy, Rawls, for instance, asks what sorts of rules would rational human beings prefer to establish prior to the game if they were in the position of not knowing whether they would be winners or losers. He argues for the game theoreticians would call the minmax solution—a solution that minimizes the worst possible outcome—since anyone could end up in such a position. From this argument, Rawls derives two basic principles of justice and reaches the egalitarian conclusion that

> *all social primary goods—liberty and opportunity, income and wealth, and the basis of self-respect—are to be distributed equally unless an unequal distribution of any or all of these goods is to the advantage of the least favored. (Rawls, 303)*

While widely respected as a theory of social justice, Rawls's conclusions would raise troubling questions if applied to many "traditional" marketing practices, such as market segmentation, differential pricing, exclusive distribution or even uniform national pricing.

While moral philosophers have generated many interesting ideas on the subject of ethics, their work gives little practical guidance to decision makers. For many marketing decisions, laws represent the only available written standards that might provide guidance. Yet adherence to legal standards alone provides no guarantee of freedom from ethical criticism. Much of the ongoing debate in a democratic society revolves around the adequacies of existing law, and philosophies of minimal conformance are virtually certain to raise ethical concerns. Moreover, the law typically responds slowly to consumers' concerns. Marketers, on the other hand, may well prosper from responding more speedily to such changes.

ETHICAL DECISION MAKING: THE REAL WORLD

Most theorizing on ethics in marketing has been normative, focusing on guidelines or rules that marketers should use to behave in an ethical fashion. But how do marketers recognize ethical dilemmas, how do they make ethical choices, and to what degree do their ethical intentions result in ethical behaviors?

Hunt and Vitell suggest that marketers follow a fairly rational decision-making process.[6] The process starts with the marketer's perception of a situation as one involving ethical issues. The marketer then generates action alternatives and subsequently evaluates the evoked set of alternatives. Both teleological and deontological evaluations occur. As described earlier, teleological evaluations involve perceived consequences for various stakeholder groups, the assessment of the probability and desirability of each consequence, and the importance of each group. Deontological evaluations involve a comparison of each behavioral alternative with a set of deontological norms (e.g., governed by the manager's personal values). For the actual ethical judgment, both teleological and deontological considerations are taken into account. Finally, ethical judgments affect behavior through intentions, and individuals learn by observing the actual consequences of their actions and adding them to their personal experiences.

Hunt and Vitell's model is fairly detailed with respect to manager's thoughts about the ethical decision itself. Yet what situations are perceived as involving ethical issues and under what circumstances do ethical judgments result in ethical behaviors? Their view recognizes that cultural attitudes toward issues such as bribery, honesty, confidentiality, and personnel policies vary significantly; but culture does in fact prescribe situations that individuals will perceive as involving ethical decisions. Moreover, corporate and industry codes fulfill a similar function in defining what does and what does not constitute an ethical issue, and the corporate culture may constrain the range of viable action alternatives.

Despite this, however, situational factors (e.g., incentives and opportunities) may result in actions that are inconsistent with ethical intentions. That is, whether or not a situation is perceived as an ethical problem, what actions are seen as options and what deontological norms and teleological considerations are seen as relevant depends to a large degree not on personal factors but on broader social and situational factors (e.g., culture, industry norms, corporate culture, and peers).

ETHICAL ISSUES AND DILEMMAS

What are the job situations that pose the most difficult ethical or moral problems for marketing managers? According to one survey,[7] the two most often cited ethical issues involved bribery and fairness. Bribery problems included gifts from outside vendors, "money under the table," the payment of questionable commissions, and problems in observing U.S. antibribery legislation when dealing with foreign clients. Issues of fairness included activities such as manipulating others to accomplish tasks, inducing customers to use services they do not need, and leaving customers unclear about the scope of a service.

Although these are the issues marketing managers are most aware of, the fact is that many marketing decisions involve ethical considerations. Is it ethical, a marketing manager may ask, to market a product that is potentially hazardous to people's health to a segment that has a higher-than-average incidence of certain health risks? Are products safe enough, do they perform well enough, are they of the quality claimed? Should we charge a higher price for a comparable product without adding value in service? Is our advertising deceptive? These are issues that marketing managers frequently resolve, with or without conscious consideration of the ethical dimensions of their decisions.

Some of the most serious criticisms of unethical behavior concern product safety and product performance. Auto, toy, and drug manufacturers have been involved in disputes, and the fight over food labels has entered the public debate.

Packaging practices have also incurred critics' distaste. In the past, concern focused on irregularities of package size and shape. More recently, ecological issues have been in the forefront and many companies have adopted "green marketing practices" by using recyclable materials in their package design.

Problems relating to pricing include, for example, differential pricing, charging higher prices for comparable products without adding value in service, and price increases to satisfy corporate goals. The effects of promotional expenditures on price continue to be a focus of criticism.

Advertising has been the target for some of the most vehement criticism. Some advertising has been accused of failing to provide useful information, deceiving the consumer, and unduly influencing particular audiences, such as children and the elderly. Advertising has also been accused of reinforcing nationalist, racist, and sexist values; exhibiting poor taste; and perpetrating the "wrong" values of hedonism and excessive consumption.

REASONS FOR UNETHICAL PRACTICES

Some data suggest that although there seems to be ample opportunity for unethical behavior, few managers admit that they engage in it.[8] The frequency of ethical problems also seems to depend on the size of the firm and the job function. Because unethical behavior is often accompanied by feelings of guilt and stress, it may result in job dissatisfaction and suboptimal performance. The best remedy for these undesirable effects seems clearly to be specific guidelines and open communication within the organization. Moreover, the single best deterrent to unethical behavior is the attitude of top management. When top management takes ethics seriously and discourages unethical behavior, ethical problems decline.

A major reason for practices viewed as unethical by various critics is undoubtedly the pressure of competition. As one marketing executive noted, "If it's profits versus ethics, profits usually come first." In a competitive marketplace, any single firm that refuses to indulge in practices that are profitable but unethical may suffer competitive disadvantage, at least in the short run. Whether or not it turns out to be a competitive advantage in the long run depends on whether the unethical behavior becomes an issue to the public. If a firm believes that it can turn ethical restraint to competitive advantage, it has economic motivation to maintain ethical standards. Moreover, a company may regard differences in ethical values within a society as a segmentation problem or as a means to promote a change process.

Although ethics and profits are not necessarily mutually inconsistent, there is quite often little likelihood of immediate economic benefit to the more ethical competitor. Astute managers, recognizing that there are widespread differences of opinion over what constitutes ethical behavior, may reason that their only safe judgments about their competitors are that they are out to make money and will stay within the law. In short, the nature of competition may produce a system in which reliance is placed predominantly on the law to determine ethical standards.

Another factor bearing on ethical conduct is the prevailing practice in a department, firm, or industry. Indeed, empirical research indicates that while only a minority of marketing managers believe that generally unethical behaviors lead to success in marketing, many believe that successful marketing managers engage in certain specific unethical behaviors.[9]

The time span within which decisions are made may also favor the expedient over the conscientious decision. Even though the marketer may believe that ethical conduct will produce more profit in the long run, emphasis on immediate profits and the short-run focus of managerial objectives and evaluation systems often tend to prohibit a long-run view.

Mitigating against the various pressures toward unethical behavior are opposing forces including, in many cases, the values of managers themselves. Consumer advocates inveigh vigorously against aspects of marketing they believe to be unethical. Religious and consumer groups and the publicity they generate also have an inhibitory effect, as do investigative reports by the media. In addition, government agencies, who are by no means insulated from the pressures of public opinion, are frequently in a position to exert direct influence on marketers to change their behavior. Finally, the attempts by various business leaders, companies, associations, and professional bodies to establish and maintain ethical standards of behavior undoubtedly countervail some of the tendencies toward unethical behavior.

ESTABLISHING ETHICAL STANDARDS

Using the framework developed by Hunt and Vitell[10] enables us to take a broad view of the determination of ethical standards. The broader cultural environment, while it remains beyond the control of an individual firm or marketer, provides important cues. In reviewing the historical literature on ethics in marketing we can observe clear trends. There is, for example, more emphasis on open and clear communication with the customer (although the motivations here are as much commercial as ethical), increased recognition of the firm's obligations in product quality and accompanying issues of safety and health, and a broader awareness generally of issues—like the environmental impact of packaging—that were once regarded as externalities. On the other hand, the morality of advertising to children—once regarded as a serious ethical dilemma—has only recently reemerged as a topic for debate, after years of dormancy.

The cultural milieu might also be reflected in the range of organizations that have attempted to codify standards and, indeed, in the standards themselves. Such codes are usually based on legal standards, Judeo-Christian ethical ideals, and the values professed by developers. Codes of particular relevance to marketers are the Code of Ethics of the American Marketing Association (A.M.A.), the Television Code of the National Association of Broadcasters (N.A.B.), and the code of the National Association of Purchasing Agents (N.A.P.A.).

The A.M.A. code, for example, acknowledges its members' accountability to society as a whole, as well as to the organization for which they work. Further, the members are exhorted to pledge that all presentations of goods, services, and concepts be made honestly and clearly. Unfortunately, definitions of honesty and clarity are not part of the code. As a result, many of the manifest ethical problems mentioned by marketing managers are not specifically addressed in the code.

In some areas, industry, prompted often by fear of increased government regulation, has adopted fairly sophisticated self-regulation. Advertising, for example, typically goes through fairly formal appraisal by agency, client, and media, wherein ethical issues may well arise. Certain industry and trade associations also scrutinize advertising. The best-known body, however, is the *National Advertising Review Council,* formed by four associations,[11] specifically "to sustain high standards of truth, accuracy, morality and social responsibility in national advertising."[12]

The firm itself, of course, is another important source of ethical standards. The same is true of the individual's personal values, which some would hold to be the ultimate arbiter of behavior. It is precisely because of such heterogeneity, we believe, that disputes over morality arise. In such instances, the case for formal (whether self-regulatory or legal) standards, which establish acceptable minima, appear strong.

PRACTICAL CONSIDERATIONS

While it would be impossible to develop a code specifically applicable to every marketing decision problem, the wording of most codes admits wide latitude in interpretation. A first step in developing a system of ethical standards or codes must be to spell out those standards as explicitly and unambiguously as possible. While some discretion will always remain, the provision of examples and operational criteria can do much to reduce the problem of differing interpretations. Members of the organization must also, of course, be familiar with the code's content. Clearly, standards must be communicated before they can be effective.

Many companies have devoted considerable effort to codifying their values—the beliefs that should guide employees' behavior. The domain they cover is frequently broader than ethical standards, but these are often subsumed. During such efforts, some firms have involved a substantial number of people in bottom-up driven exercises, while others have taken a more top-down approach. In most cases, however, the resulting statements of values and beliefs have been quite widely circulated.

Communication, however, is merely a prerequisite for compliance—but not a sufficient condition. Here, two schools of thought might be said to emerge. Traditional management thinking would suggest that to secure adherence to a set of ethical standards, there is no practicable alternative to making those standards part of the performance measurement system. It can be argued that it is precisely because ethical criteria are not used to evaluate performance that many ethical problems arise. If the only standards against which managers are evaluated are short-term profit contribution and market share, there is no incentive to ensure that marketing strategies are ethically acceptable. If management provided a set of specific ethical standards for such areas as packaging, sales promotion, and advertising, for example, and announced that performance would be evaluated against them, there is little doubt that there would be a response.

To provide the organization with "checks and balances" to develop ethical marketing programs, Robin and Reidenbach have argued for the explicit integration of social responsibility and ethics into the strategic marketing planning process.[13] Since the corporate values of profit and efficiency dominate most organizations and members at all levels are rewarded on the basis of achieving profitablility and efficiency, most programs lack ethical elements. To include an ethical perspective, managers must identify not only target markets but also affected publics to examine the anticipated consequences a marketing program may have on these publics. These approaches, while they have merit, fall largely within the domain of traditional management thinking, emphasizing external control measures.

Less traditional approaches to management, however, are focusing on internal or values control, which may be a much more effective approach to resolving ethical issues. Chonko and Hunt affirm that codes of ethics must be integrated into the corporate culture to be effective,[14] while Robin and Reidenbach argue that a major factor in achieving responsible and ethical marketing is management's ability to integrate ethical core values throughout the organization culture.[15] They stress the importance of making these core values actionable, and suggest that they may be formulated in terms of the teleological and deontological maxims discussed earlier (e.g., "Treat customers with respect, concern, and honesty, the way you yourself would want to be treated"). Some large multinationals (especially European) have traditionally favored acculturation as a means of control, while Ouchi has suggested the efficiency and motivational benefit of values control.[16] These approaches are currently being popularized under such mandates as "empowerment" and "trust" and have been promoted particularly vigorously in customer service organizations. The underlying thrust is to delegate authority and permit those in the "frontline" of sales, marketing, and customer service to make decisions. The importance of appropriate values being emphasized in the areas of recruitment, selection, development, appraisal, and reward should be evident. For without effective management of these human resource policies, the potential for unethical—not to say illegal—behavior could rise.

CONCLUSION

Regardless of whether the traditional control model or empowerment and trust is adopted, the firm retains the responsibility for maintaining ethical standards. Further, observing long-term trends in markets, it is becoming increasingly evident that maintaining standards is insufficient. While unethical behaviors do clearly occur, at the same time customers' and society's definitions of desirable ethical standards seem, over time, to be becoming increasingly stringent. This is lending credence to a minority—but increasingly supportable view—that business and morality are not now antithetical. In a stimulating review, Werner argued for self-moralizing corporations, which have "added ethics to their managerial tool boxes as a device to maximize profits over the long-term."[17] This, of course, may be a culturally acceptable way to proselytize a minority view in American society, but interestingly, Werner's conception of the firm places maintenance of moral values as a paramount concern, arguing that values should persist and therefore transcend institutional and structural change.

Society ultimately endows business with a set of ethical expectations. In areas as diverse as environmental protection and conservation, product liability, occupational safety, animal rights, and consumer protection, these expectations are increasing. With such a scenario, we can make a strong case that higher ethical standards in marketing are not just a matter of doing the "right" thing; the likelihood that a firm might obtain competitive advantage from seeking even higher ethical standards is always increasing.

NOTES

1. John Dewey and James H. Tufts, *Ethics* (NY: Henry Holt and Company, 1925), 1.

2. O.C. Ferrell, Larry G. Gresham, and John Fredrich, "A Synthesis of Ethical Decision Models for Marketing," *Journal of Macromarketing*.

3. Shelby D. Hunt and Scott Vitell, "A General Theory of Marketing Ethics," *Journal of Macromarketing* (Spring 1986): 5–16.

4. Donald P. Robin and R. Eric Reidenbach, "Social Responsibility, Ethics, and Marketing Strategy: Closing the Gap Between Concept and Application," *Journal of Marketing* 51 (1987): 44–58.
5. John Rawls, *A Theory of Justice* (Cambridge, MA: Harvard University Press, 1971).
6. Hunt and Vitell, *op. cit.*
7. Lawrence B. Chonko and Shelby D. Hunt, "Ethics and Marketing Management: An Empirical Examination" *Journal of Business Research* 13 (1985): 339–359.
8. Chonko and Hunt, *op. cit.*
9. Chonko and Hunt, *op. cit.*
10. Hunt and Vitell, *op. cit.*
11. The American Advertising Federation (A.A.F.), the American Association of Advertising Agencies (A.A.A.A.), the Association of National Advertisers (A.N.A.), and the Council of Better Business Bureau.
12. George E. Belch and Michael Belch, *Introduction to Advertising and Promotion Management* (Homewood, IL: Irwin, 1990), 706.
13. Robin and Reidenbach, *op. cit.*
14. Chonko and Hunt, *op. cit.*
15. Robin and Reidenbach, *op. cit.*
16. William Ouchi, *Theory Z* (Reading, MA: Addison-Wesley, 1981).
17. Simcha B. Werner, "The Movement for Reforming American Business Ethics: A Twenty-Year Perspective," *Journal of Business Ethics* 11 (1992): 61–70.

H. Keith Hunt
Professor of Business Management
Graduate School of Management
Brigham Young University
Provo, Utah

CHAPTER 35

GOVERNMENT REGULATION AND THE MARKETING MANAGER: DEVELOPING A PERSPECTIVE

Once upon a time, a long time ago, in the narrow strip of land between the edge of the water and the tall dark forest near where the river flowed into the sea, there lived four families, each with several family members and each being located some distance from each of the others. They subsisted on food they grew and on fish and meat they caught. Intermarriage kept the families linked emotionally. All exchange of goods was through a simple barter process. There was no money. No trade credits existed. Occasional violations of what seemed right were handled as family matters, with an occasional battle to assure that each family knew its relative status. Wrongs were quickly taken care of, through some combination of actions ranging from peace gifts to warfare, between parties who knew each other very well. Given the wrong, in most cases the parties knew what was the appropriate combination of actions to restore equilibrium to the simple system. While the system was often brutal, it definitely was simple and effective.

Life has become much more complicated than our "Once upon a time" world. In most cases, we have no idea who makes the products we purchase and consume. We exchange money for products, and we store or borrow money as conditions fluctuate. Many products are so complex that we do not have the capability to evaluate their effectiveness or safety. None of us is an individual life sustainer but rather we are linked for our very survival to most of us doing our own thing well and then exchanging with each other to satisfy needs. Some of our products are so technologically and mechanically complex that it takes whole cities of workers working in concert to efficiently produce the product. This system can be just as brutal as the simple "Once upon a time" system, but instead of simplicity, we have complexity multiplied upon itself. Not only can't individuals directly rectify wrongs, in many cases they are not even aware of the wrong, and in most cases they have no idea how to correct it. The social system is so complex that few people in the society have even a rudimentary understanding of how it operates. Yet all the people, as either consumers or producers or both, try to function within the system to provide an acceptable level of life satisfaction for themselves and their immediate family unit.

As society has become so much more complex, it has gradually invented prescriptions and proscriptions intended to enable the system to work. Which shalt's and shalt not's are in use in a particular society are a reflection of the relative power of the various individuals or associations of individuals existent in the society. Each of the do's and don'ts was specifically introduced into the set of rules to benefit some person or association of persons. Where one person's benefit was another person's detriment, social power and compromise usually determined which rules would hold sway for the current time.

As a marketing manager, you have to operate within this vast, highly-complex set of rules telling you what you must, can, might, cannot, and must not do. If you work a lifetime as a marketing manager in one industry you might not even then understand all the prescriptive and proscriptive regulations that impact on you and on your probability of success. Some things you will do because they seem right to you, never realizing that you are actually required to do them. Other things you will avoid doing because they seem wrong, never realizing there is a rule that you cannot do them.

In still other cases, you will become aware of and come to understand the general and specific rules telling you what you can and cannot do. In each of these cases, whether because you understand the rule or because you are merely doing what seems correct or proper and unbeknownst to you it agrees with the rules, you are behaving in accordance with the standards declared and enforced by society. On the other hand, there will be decisions that to you seem right but that violate some societal rule. If you are aware of the rule and knowingly violate it, you then deliberately risk punishment to gain profit or competitive advantage or whatever your objective might be. Where you are most open to making a serious error is in those decision areas where you are not aware of the societal rules and do not know that you are unaware, not realizing that such a rule might exist.

To the extent that the preceding paragraph is true, as a marketing manager you can get hurt by government rules in only two situations: (1) where you misperceive the risk of violating a rule you are aware of and (2) when you are ignorant of a rule.

The solution to these two situations is the same—it is your responsibility to become fully aware of all the marketing regulations affecting your decision area. You need to know not only the rule, but also the reasoning and history behind the rule so you can correctly judge when and where the rule applies and when and where it does not. You gain this awareness, insight, and understanding through an active, intelligent involvement in professional reading and attending professional meetings. Your competitors, your clients or consumers, and government units will be most willing to point out your mistakes to you.

If you want to avoid those mistakes, or at least know when you are making them and the risk function associated with them, you have to continually add to your knowledge in this area. As you first become aware of a rule or set of rules, you might need some explanation from your legal advisor so you can understand all the ramifications of the rule. Part of becoming knowledgeable about a rule is understanding how the rule came into being and what interest groups wanted it passed. Sometimes the reasons for a rule are obvious. Other times it takes considerable insight and historical understanding to see a rule in its true light. This all becomes critically important if you ever decide that a rule is wrong and you set out to try to get it changed.

Quite simply, then, for trade to freely flow between unacquainted parties and for commerce to operate to the societal good, a wide variety of rules are passed that all parties can rely on in good faith to be the basis for commercial transactions. It is your responsibility as a marketing manager to understand as many of those rules as possible. Spending your time ranting and raving about all the laws working against you that are antibusiness and antifree-enterprise merely marks you as a fool who is unwilling to learn to operate within the set of rules established by society.

Once a marketing manager has internalized the need for understanding the rule system within which he or she operates, two remaining concepts need to be understood: (1) that each rule important to the success of the business needs to be understood from the points of view of all relevant parties, not just from one individual's, and (2) that most of the people involved in the regulation of commerce, except for the marketing managers, have legal backgrounds and espouse the adversary process for resolving conflicts.

It is often the case that a rule, if viewed from only one point of view, is a serious infringement on the free decision making of the one party, maybe even working a serious disadvantage on that party. This is sometimes the case for the marketing manager. A rule requires that you do or do not do something, causing a serious cost or competitive disadvantage to you. Unless you make the extra effort to see that rule from the points of view of the buyer or consumer, of competitors, or of society in general, you will never understand why in the broad sense the rule is good, even though it works a disadvantage on you.

In the previous paragraph, you were urged to understand as many rules as possible. Now, adding to that, it is your responsibility as a marketing manager to not only understand the rule from your point of view, but to recognize the points of view of all other involved parties so you have a full understanding of why all parties feel about the rule as they do. Only then are you in a position to feel you truly understand the rule and to make correct assessments of the risk function associated with violating the rule.

The rules affecting marketing management are developed, formalized, and enforced as part of our system of law. The primary actors, except for the marketing managers, have legal training and are either practicing lawyers or are at least highly familiar with legal proceedings. Scientists use the scientific method in their search. In religion, spiritual feelings and manifestations provide the base for truth. In athletics, winning is truth. In legal matters, truth is arrived at by two or more parties, advocates for each point of view and adversaries in this proceeding, each arranging evidence so as to promote their own point of advocacy and to discredit or destroy their opponent's points of advocacy. A referee or judge hears the arguments and declares which advocate's position is true.

A recognition that most rules affecting marketing managers are developed in an adversary process should alert the marketing manager to at least a couple of things. First, the marketing manager has not been trained to operate effectively in adversary proceedings (indeed, his training and experience are probably highly nonadversarial, whether it is how to operate within the firm's organization or to secure profitable sales from customers), so that marketing manager has about as much chance of being successful in an adversary proceeding as a pro-tour golfer has if one Sunday he or she decides to be a starter for a favorite NFL team. The lack of experience in adversarial proceedings does not mean that the marketing manager should declare a mismatch and give up. Rather, he should seek help from individuals who do have the experience. Also, if he is going to continue to be involved in such matters, he needs to gain his own experience.

The need for help from someone with adversarial experience raises the second alert. Professionals in adversarial domains earn their income from plying their trade in conflict situations. It is to their advantage to generate conflict, to facilitate conflict, to prolong conflict, and to institutionalize conflict. So, while the marketing manager has to use the services of an adversary specialist, he or she needs to continually keep in mind that the specialist is especially attuned to conflict and to operating in the adversary mode, while the marketing manager may be more interested in a conciliatory mode or accommodation mode just to solve the problem so he or she can get on with his or her own specialty of marketing.

The adversary specialist is well grounded in numerous experiences in which the accommodation mode was tried, resulting not only in the accommodation failing but in the adversary base being so compromised that it also failed. Besides, they are comfortable with the adversary process and know how to be successful operating in that mode, and they are substantially less experienced and thus less comfortable operating in any other mode. So, the marketing manager finds himself or herself in the situation where he or she has to have the advice of the regulation expert. At the same time, he or she recognizes that the expert prefers to operate in an adversary mode which tends to formalize the conflict and increase the likelihood of formal legal proceedings. In this damned-if-you-do/damned-if-you-don't situation, the only protection is for the professional marketing manager to develop his or her own knowledge and experience in adversarial processes so he or she can better decide when to fight and when to capitulate, and compare his or her judgment with that of his or her adviser.

Finally, building from the early comments in this chapter, the marketing manager who recognizes that government regulation is necessary for stability in commerce also recognizes that that regulation can be helpful as well as frustrating. Just as regulation forces a marketing manager to incur expenses that benefit the consumer, other regulation protects the marketing manager from the whims of the consumer. Just as regulation protects competitors from an individual or company, so it also protects them from competitors. The marketing manager has the obligation to the firm and society to recognize and use the benefits of regulation for the firm's advantage.

Where new regulation is pending, the uncertainty associated with the new regulation may make the old more desirable, even though the new has much in favor of it. For example, in the late 1970s and the early 1980s, the Federal Trade Commission attempted to make a rule regarding used car sales that would require each used car be inspected by the seller and the condition of specific parts of the car be classified as needing work, being okay, or being uninspected. This information would supposedly help consumers judge which car was most likely to be the best purchase mechanically. However, it would have required used car marketers to develop a formal inspection process, which was a totally new idea. And, there was no evidence that consumers would use the information effectively, if even correctly. So, given the uncertainty, used car marketer associations successfully fought the rule. Most business managers were opposed to the rule because, while the idea was interesting, it was not interesting enough to offset the uncertainty associated with it. This is often the case. Nor can the manager be faulted. The manager knows how to operate successfully under the current rules. Why change? Only when there is considerable consumer outcry against current business practice, such as was novelized by Upton Sinclair in *The Jungle,* does business recognize that the uncertainty of the *status quo* is greater than the uncertainty of the new.

Also, regulation is often used to stifle competition. Rather than changing one's way of doing business, it is sometimes easier to get special interest legislation passed or special regulations passed which protect the endangered business. For example, when chain stores started developing, it was thought easier by many small retailers to urge their states and the federal government to enact special bills discriminating against chains than to revamp their own mode of operation to successfully compete with the chains. In another example, it may make more sense for the small retailer to support the passage and enforcement of a price maintenance program than to attempt to compete head-on on price with chains and large independent stores. In most cases, anticompetition actions will eventually be overturned. But that may take years, even decades, during which the competitive advantage accrues to the special interest group favored by the regulation.

A more frustrating problem is that often the government regulation does not seem to be accomplishing what it was intended to accomplish. Not only is society imposing on the business, but the intended benefit to consumers is not occurring. For example, in the early 1980s, there was substantial talk and action toward requiring various kinds of labels on alcoholic beverages, especially ingredient labels and warning labels regarding fetal alcohol syndrome birth defects. However, preliminary research showed that at-risk people were affected differently by such information—even were differentially perceptive of such information—and that it was highly unlikely that the information program would have any of the planned effects.

On still another front, sometimes consumers do not want to be protected. Pyramid marketing organizations hurt only those who get involved in them, and they want to get involved very badly. Or so the story goes.

Sometimes regulation is needed because consumers cannot be expected to ever know enough to correctly discern whether a product can do what it claims to do. For example, prescription drugs are understood only by thoroughly-trained pharmacists. Even a reasonably-trained medical doctor has only a modest knowledge of pharmacology. Consumers cannot be expected to be able to judge whether a prescription is safe or not. So regulations are imposed to force safety. In providing this safety, individuals wanting unproven drugs and purveyors wanting to sell those people unproven drugs are frustrated.

At a quite different level, a mouthwash product claimed for years that its use reduced the number and the severity of colds and sore throats. Individual consumers had no way to prove or disprove this claim, even with use. Even if one had many bad colds and sore throats, one could only imagine how terribly sick one would have been had one not been a regular user of the mouthwash. If a person had few colds and sore throats, then that was positive evidence that the mouthwash did fulfill its claims, yet most people have few colds and sore throats. When it was found that a large portion of the population believed the product's untrue claims, deceptive advertising law was violated and the advertising was stopped.

And sometimes the regulation exists to protect competitors from each other and from other businesses. Predatory competition is prohibited. Prices must be the same to similar sellers who then resell the goods. Different prices to different wholesalers or retailers must be justified by actual cost differences in servicing the particular accounts. Some anticompetitive actions are punishable by triple damages—that is, the actual damages caused by the illegal action are determined and that amount is tripled, making, in most cases, such actions more expensive than could ever be justified by even the most profitable expected return.

In summary, as life in general, and particularly commerce, has become highly complex, a variety of rules and regulations are needed to keep commerce operating smoothly and fairly. It is the marketing manager's responsibility to be aware of and to understand these rules and regulations, both in facilitating his or her own decisions in a positive sense and in avoiding conflict with the rules and regulations in a negative sense. The rules and regulations can even be used to advantage in some cases. Important rules and regulations need to be understood from the viewpoint of each of the involved parties. Professionals in the world of rules and regulations (often lawyers) are educated and trained in the use of adversary proceedings; most marketing managers are not even aware of how adversary proceedings arrive at truth and thus are unlikely to be able to operate in that mode without the advice of an experienced person. At the same time, such advice is likely to be conservative and may not lead to a quick, simple resolution of a problem. Finally, rules and regulations work for you as well as against you, and the marketing manager needs to recognize how rules and regulations are helpful, learning to use rules and regulations, new or already in place, to better his or her own competitive position.

SUGGESTIONS FOR FURTHER READING

James Bishop, Jr. and Henry W. Hubbard, *Let the Seller Beware* (Washington: The National Press, 1969).

Lewis Anthony Dexter, *How Organizations Are Represented in Washington* (New York: The Bobbs-Merrill Company, 1969).

Earl W. Kintner, *A Primer on the Law of Deceptive Practices* (New York: Macmillan Co., Inc., 1971).

John S. McGee, *In Defense of Industrial Concentration* (New York: Praeger Publishers, 1971).

Louis W. Stern and Thomas L. Eovaldi, *Legal Aspects of Marketing Strategy: Antitrust and Consumer Protection Issues* (Englewood Cliffs, N.J.: Prentice-Hall, Inc., 1984).

U.S. Government Printing Office, *Guide to Record Retention Requirements* (Washington, 1971).

William L. Trombetta, Esquire
Professor of Marketing and Management
Chairman, Department of Management/Marketing
Fairleigh Dickinson University
Madison, New Jersey

CHAPTER 36

SUBSTANTIVE AND PROCEDURAL CHANGES IN ANTITRUST LAW: IMPLICATIONS FOR MARKETING MANAGEMENT

INTRODUCTION

Most marketers are aware that antitrust law has a significant impact on strategic marketing management and decision making. However, they may be unaware that a number of relatively recent United States Supreme Court decisions have created a new legal environment for trade regulation. Specifically, subtle but significant changes have occurred in the evolution of substantive *per se* or horizontal law; a veritable revolution has occurred in procedural law in general as a result of three extraordinary back to back Supreme Court decisions involving the motion for summary judgment. This chapter is designed to provide an overview of these profound changes for the marketing practitioner.

The Antitrust Laws

There are four federal antitrust statutes: the Sherman Act, the Clayton Act, the Robinson-Patman Act, and the Federal Trade Commission Act. In addition, every state, except Pennsylvania, has its own antitrust legislation ("baby antitrust acts") patterned to a great extent on federal antitrust statutes. For the purpose of this chapter, the focus will be on the Sherman Act.

Section 1 of the Sherman Act prohibits contracts, combinations or conspiracies that unreasonably restrain trade. For example, agreements among independent competitors to fix prices or to allocate markets or customers represent classic violations of Section 1. It is very important to note that a Sherman Section 1 violation requires more than one competing entity (the numerosity requirement).

Section 2 of the Sherman Act prohibits any person from monopolizing, attempting to monopolize, or conspiring to monopolize any part of trade. For example, predatory conduct by one competitor to drive another competitor out of business would violate Sherman Section 2. Although Section 2 has a conspiracy provision, it is primarily aimed at predatory or unreasonable *unitary* conduct. In other words, the predatory conduct of a single competitor can run afoul of Section 2 whereas a Section 1 violation requires two or more independent competitors.

Violation of the antitrust laws can be very costly in a number of respects, including criminal as well as civil sanctions, substantial fines, automatic trebling of damages, injunctive relief, and enormous litigation costs in both money and time.

The Basic Antitrust Standards

There are two basic standards of legality in antitrust law: the *per se* rule and the rule of reason. The Supreme Court has held that there are certain types of commercial conduct that are so inimical to competition and so lacking in any redeeming value they are conclusively presumed to be unreasonable and therefore illegal, *per se*. Under this *per se* standard, it is not necessary to inquire as to the harm caused or any market definitions in which the conduct occurred. The courts will not entertain any proposed excuses or justifications for this kind of inherently illegal conduct. Among the practices deemed to be *per se* unlawful are price-fixing and horizontal (within or at the same level of distribution) allocation of customers or markets (*Northern Pacific Railway Co. v. United States,* 1958).

The rule of reason standard is whether a trade restraint is more procompetitive than anticompetitive in the relevant product and geographic markets (*Chicago Board of Trade v. United States,* 1918). Under this standard, reasons and proposed justifications for the challenged conduct will be allowed for consideration. Additional critical issues in a rule of reason analysis will be the existence of a defendant's market power (usually by examining the extent of the relevant product and geographic markets foreclosed) and whether competition was promoted more than it was suppressed.

Recently, a middle ground between the *per se* rule and the rule of reason has arisen, sometimes referred to as the "truncated" approach. Under certain circumstances, courts have refrained from applying the *per se* standard; rather, the challenged conduct has been condemned as unreasonable, but without resorting to a full-blown rule of reason analysis (Proger 1991). This approach encompasses the complementary features of the *per se* and rule of reason approaches. Hence, for our purpose, the focus will be on the two traditional standards: *per se* and rule of reason.

The distinction between the *per se* and rule of reason standards is critical to understanding the change in traditional analysis of the so-called "hard core" *per se* violations, such as price fixing. Depending on the standard being applied, the challenged conduct will receive very different treatment under the law. A plaintiff under the rule of reason will have to prove that the defendant has market power (typically, a surrogate for market power in antitrust cases is high market share) in the relevant product and geographic markets and that the conduct at issue is more anticompetitive than procompetitive. This is very time-consuming and expensive litigation which the plaintiff rarely wins. Hence, it is in the plaintiff's interest to position his case in the *per se* category (Jorde and Lemley 1991). To the extent that the traditional *per se* types of conduct can receive more favorable treatment, from the defendant's perspective, the implications for strategic planning and marketing management are profound. We now turn to the first momentous change in substantive antitrust law.

THE SUBSTANTIVE EROSION IN THE PER SE STANDARD: PRICE-FIXING AND JOINT, COLLABORATIVE BEHAVIOR

The BMI Case

The first Supreme Court decision to retreat from the formal categorization of *per se* conduct is *Broadcast Music, Inc. v. Columbia Broadcasting System* ("BMI") (*Broadcast Music, Inc. v. Broadcasting System* 1979). *BMI* involved a classic *per se* violation; yet, for the first time in nearly ninety years of antitrust law, the Supreme Court accorded *per se* conduct the more lenient (from the defendant's perspective) rule of reason treatment.

BMI involved a challenge to a blanket licensing system by which BMI and American Society of Composers, Authors, and Publishers ("ASCAP") negotiated fees to copyrighted musical compositions on behalf of thousands of authors and composers. Columbia Broadcasting System ("CBS") alleged that this arrangement was illegal price fixing.

Blanket licenses give the licensees the right to perform any and all of the compositions owned by the authors, etc., as often as the licensees desire for a stated period. Fees for blanket licenses are ordinarily a percentage of total revenues or a flat dollar amount, and do not directly depend on the amount or type of music used.

After a trial, the District Court dismissed the complaint holding, among other things, that the blanket license arrangement was not price fixing and, consequently, not a *per se* violation of the Sherman Act. The Court of Appeals reversed holding that the challenged conduct was a form of price fixing illegal *per se*. The Supreme Court held that the issuance of blanket licenses by BMI and ASCAP was not *per se* unlawful price fixing.

SUPREME COURT REASONING

The Court essentially characterized ASCAP and BMI as clearing-houses that made sure if a composition was used, the artist received a royalty. The blanket license system controlled unauthorized use of compositions and negotiated licenses to use the music. Because of the nature of the blanket licensing arrangement, prices for all compositions were necessarily fixed.

The Court rephrased the issue in this case: not, is this price fixing; rather, is the conduct at issue here *per se* price fixing! Prior to *BMI,* any and all agreements on price had no redeeming value and could never be justified (see *United States v. Trenton Potteries Co.* 1927 and *United States v. Socony-Vacuum Oil Co.* 1940).

In *BMI,* the Court made a number of precedent-shattering statements that turned away from formalistic, simplistic labeling of competitive conduct. Now, conduct that does or could affect price will be evaluated according to a new standard: is the conduct such that it "is 'plainly anticompetitive' and very likely without 'redeeming virtue' " (*BMI* 1979). The new threshold inquiry into collaborative behavior, including price fixing (other than overt, naked price fixing where the sole purpose is to eliminate price competition) focuses on "whether the effect and ... purpose of the practice are to threaten the proper operation of our predominantly free market economy; that is, whether the practice facially appears to be one that would always or almost always tend to restrict competition and decrease output" (*BMI* 1979).

The Court used as an example two partners in a firm who agree to set the prices of their goods or services. While this is literally "price fixing," it is not the kind of conduct that is *per se* illegal price fixing (*BMI* 1979).

The Court held that the blanket license was reasonably necessary to make this market work because of the practical difficulties in negotiating with each individual composer. Another critical factor in the *BMI* Court's reasoning was that a "new product" was created here:

> *Here, the whole is truly greater than the sum of its parts; it is, to some extent, a different product. . . . Thus, to the extent the blanket license is a different product, [BMI] is not really a joint sales agency offering the goods of many sellers, but is a separate seller offering its blanket license, of which the individual compositions are raw material. [BMI and ASCAP], in short, made a market in which individual composers are inherently unable to compete fully effectively* (BMI 1979).

The Court also analogized the practice at issue to a joint venture that is typically analyzed under the rule of reason:

> *Not all arrangements among actual or potential competitors that have an impact on price are per se violations . . . or even unreasonable restraints. . . . Joint ventures and other cooperative arrangements are also not usually unlawful, at least not as price fixing schemes, where the agreement on price is necessary to market the product at all* (BMI 1979).

Implications for Marketing Management

BMI puts aside mere labeling and indicates that courts will examine collaborative conduct to determine if procompetitive effects can be demonstrated. The blanket license arrangement resulted in lower costs to licensees of the music by eliminating separate negotiations with thousands of individual composers.

A new product was created through the joint licensing. Finally, the Court analogized the BMI situation to a joint venture: a lawful collaborative undertaking among competitors to achieve a legitimate, superordinate objective beyond the reasonable means of any one joint venturer.

More than ever before, marketing managers will have an opportunity to attempt to justify and demonstrate procompetitive collaborative efforts. Marketing plans will become ever more important as documentary evidence to established legitimate business objectives and the strategies and tactics necessary to achieve them.

For example, the General Motors-Toyota joint venture resulted in a new product that required two competitors to agree on the price of the new car. In health care, networks of competing hospitals and physicians have formed into independent practice associations and preferred provider organizations in response to managed care: systemic alliances among insurers, corporations, and third party payers to manage the delivery of health care by controlling what and when medical services are appropriate and the prices of these services through negotiating price discounts and contracts with health care providers that cap professional fees.

These health care provider formations are fraught with antitrust exposure due to the risk that fee discussions may arise among the competing health care providers. Nonetheless, *BMI* signals, and the antitrust enforcement authorities agree, that the procompetitive benefits associated with competitors coming together to develop a "new product," one that each doctor or hospital acting alone could not offer, a managed care network, outweighs the anticompetitive aspects—independent, competing doctors setting fees among themselves for the convenience of third party payers, insurers and corporations (Trombetta 1987).

In sum, *BMI* suggests that the courts will look to the purpose of the restraint. If the objective is legitimate—lower prices; enhanced quality; improved service; increased consumer satisfaction; or some combination of these procompetitive features—the courts will suffer some ancillary restraints (price fixing or market allowances, e.g.). Hence, the overriding objective and net effect of collaborative efforts among competitors must be procompetitive; any trade restraints must be secondary to the legitimate objective. For the first time in antitrust history, the Supreme Court's message is that it will consider the economic realities of the marketplace in evaluating the legality of heretofore *verboten* practices.

NCAA

National Collegiate Athletic Association v. Board of Regents of the University of Oklahoma ("NCAA") was the second Supreme Court decision that dealt with heretofore strictly forbidden *per se* conduct in a rule of reason fashion (NCAA 1984). *NCAA* involved a complaint by certain colleges over the NCAA's football television regulations. The NCAA contracts specified the total number of games televised in a season, and the maximum number of games that a university could televise.

The NCAA claimed that its controls and contracts were reasonable. They protected gate attendance that might otherwise be adversely affected or destroyed by television. The NCAA claimed that its restraints were not anticompetitive; rather, they enhanced the variety and quality of college football programming.

As in *BMI, NCAA* involved a classic *per se* situation: the restraints raised price and reduced output. Yet, although the Supreme Court found the NCAA program unlawful in the end, that decision resulted after the Court examined the NCAA's preferred procompetitive justifications, typically only allowed in a rule of reason context.

Supreme Court Reasoning. As in BMI, despite the classic *per se* conduct, the Court characterized this industry as one in which horizontal restraints on competition are essential if the product is to be available at all (*NCAA* 1984).

Implications for Marketing Management. Along with *BMI, NCAA* continued the trend away from simplistic pigeon-holing toward more sophisticated analysis of horizontal agreements that may have procompetitive effects.

Indiana Federation of Dentists

Federal Trade Commission v. Indiana Federation of Dentists ("Indiana Federation") involved a group boycott among dentists to refuse to submit x-rays to dental insurers for use in benefits determinations (*Federal Trade Commission v. Indiana Federation of Dentists* 1986). As a result of cost containment pressures in health care, dental health insurers attempted to limit the payment of benefits to the least expensive, yet adequate treatment for patients. Hence, dentists, along with claims forms seeking reimbursement from insurers, were required to submit any dental x-rays in examining patients to assist the reviewers in evaluating questions as to whether a dentist's recommended course of treatment was in fact necessary. The dentists agreed among themselves to withhold the x-rays under the guise that merely sending the x-rays would not provide enough information and could even mislead the reviewers.

Supreme Court Reasoning. Even though the Court characterized the dentists' collective refusal as a group boycott, another classic *per se* violation category, it declined to apply the *per se* rule; "We decline to resolve this case by forcing the Federation's policy into the 'boycott' pigeonhole and invoking the *per se* rule" (*Indiana Federation* 1986).

Even under the more lenient rule of reason, the dentists' collaborative conduct was condemned:

> *Application of the Rule of Reason to these facts is not a matter of any great difficulty. The Federation's policy takes the form of horizontal agreement among the participating dentists to withhold from their*

customers a particular service that they desire—the forwarding of x-rays to insurance companies along with claim forms. . . . Absent some countervailing procompetitive virtue—such as for example, the creation of efficiencies in the operation of a market or the provision of goods and services . . .—such an agreement limiting consumer choice by impeding the 'ordinary give and take of the market place' cannot be sustained under the Rule of Reason (Indiana Federation 1986).

Implications for Marketing Management

The progression from *BMI* through *Indiana Federation* at the Supreme Court level continues at the lower court levels as well as courts factor into their decisions strategic planning, marketing analysis, and economic realities in *per se* contexts. The substantive erosion in the *per se* standard will allow marketers to demonstrate and support legitimate goals in previously foreclosed practices such as agreements on price among competitors in particular.

THE REVOLUTION IN PROCEDURE: THE MOTION FOR SUMMARY JUDGMENT

If the erosion in the *per se* standard was evolutionary, the aggressive use in the procedural motion for summary judgment was revolutionary with perhaps even more profound implications for marketing management.

Definition and Purpose of Summary Judgment

The purpose of the motion for summary judgment is to save courts and litigants from the burden of litigating cases where no genuine dispute exists (Friedenthal 1988). Its purpose is to dispose of useless lawsuits (Levine 1988).

The Old and New Approaches to the Motion

Rule 56 (c) of the Federal Rules of Civil Procedure provides that summary judgment may be granted, prior to trial, through affidavits, depositions, and other materials showing that there is no genuine issue as to any material fact and that the moving party is entitled to relief as a matter of law (Rogers III 1979).

In the "old days," as recently as 1985, the Supreme Court disdained the use of summary judgment in antitrust litigation. Trial judges maintained a rigorous belief of the right of a party to confront and cross-examine witnesses at trial and to have his "day in court."

This thinking is personified in the then landmark *Poller v. CBS* case (*Poller v. CBS* 1962). In this antitrust case, after a certain amount of discovery, the defendant moved for summary judgment. The Supreme Court reversed the trial court's granting of the motion with language that would last for almost twenty-five years: "summary procedures should be used sparingly in complex antitrust litigation" (*Poller v. CBS* 1962). The Court held that:

> *motive and intent play leading roles, the proof is largely in the hands of the alleged conspirators, and hostile witnesses thicken the plot. It is only when the witnesses are present and subject to cross-examination that their credibility and the weight to be given their testimony can be appraised* (Poller v. CBS 1962).

The *Poller* standard is sometimes referred to as "the slightest doubt" standard: when an antitrust claim contains issues of motive or intent, summary judgment is inappropriate whenever the slightest doubt exists whether the motion for summary judgment should be granted (Henninger 1987).

Before we turn to the new era of summary judgment (post-1985), a discussion of one of the most powerful antitrust cases is in order—the *Monsanto* decision.

THE SIGNIFICANCE OF MONSANTO

In 1984, the Supreme Court decided a case with monumental implications for marketing management: *Monsanto v. Spray-Rite* ("*Monsanto*") (*Monsanto Co. v. Spray-Rite Service Corp.* 1984). *Monsanto* was relied on by the Supreme Court in its precedent-shattering 1986 trilogy of decisions revolutionizing the use of summary judgment.

Ironically, *Monsanto* was not a summary judgment case. The case was fully litigated going to trial and decided on its merits. Adding further irony, *Monsanto* was a *vertical* price fixing, dealer termination case, not a horizontal agreement case. Vertical restraints involve agreements between or among different levels of distribution. For example, if a manufacturer terminates a price cutting distributor at the behest of one or more of the discounter's distributor competitors, a vertical price fixing agreement could be alleged. Nonetheless, the language and reasoning in *Monsanto* are critical to the Court's 1986 *Matsushita* decision dealing with summary judgment (*Matsushita Electric Industrial Co. v. Zenith Radio Corp.* 1986) ("*Matsushita*").

Spray-Rite, a Monsanto distributor, began to price discount chemical herbicides. Monsanto terminated Spray-Rite allegedly for failing to comply with a newly instituted distributor policy that required increased push promotions and training salespeople (*Monsanto* 1984). Spray-Rite claimed that it was terminated as a result of complaints about its price discounting from other Monsanto dealers (*Monsanto* 1984).

Vertical price fixing is also a *per se* category of conduct, yet the *Monsanto* Court entertained business reasons for terminating a dealer.

For example, the Court was concerned that a manufacturer could unilaterally and independently terminate a distributor for legitimate business reasons and still be liable for alleged vertical price fixing simply for receiving complaints from its other dealers about a price-cutter.

The Court stressed that a manufacturer has the right to deal or refuse to deal with any distributor on a unilateral and independent basis. The Court reasoned that it was natural for dealers to complain to the manufacturer and for the manufacturer to legitimately entertain those communications. Then the Court expressed a new evidentiary standard for evaluating conspiracy allegations that has become precedent-setting not just for substantive antitrust law but for the procedural motion for summary judgment as well:

> *The correct standard is that there must be evidence that tends to exclude the possibility of independent action by the manufacturers and distributor. That is, there must be direct or circumstantial evidence that reasonably tends to prove that the manufacturer and others had a conscious commitment to a common scheme designed to achieve an unlawful objective* (Monsanto 1984).

Again, even though this language has to do with a fully litigated trial decision on the merits and notwithstanding that *Monsanto* had to do with a vertical price restraint, not horizontal, we will see the power of this language as incorporated into the "new" summary judgment.

THE PROCEDURAL REVOLUTION OF 1986: THE TRILOGY

In 1986, three major, precedent shattering summary judgment cases were decided by the Supreme Court, two of them back to back on the same day! Taken together, these three decisions will have a truly profound impact on marketing strategy, planning, and management.

Celotex

In *Celotex Corp. v. Catrett,* the plaintiff sued on behalf of her deceased husband for wrongful death claiming that he died as a result of exposure to Celotex's *asbestos* products (*Celotex Corp. v. Catrett* 1986) ("*Celotex*"). After a certain amount of discovery had taken place, defendant Celotex moved for summary judgment to dismiss the case on the basis of evidence that the deceased was a heavy smoker. Hence, Celotex argued that it was as probable that the deceased died from smoking as from asbestosis. The Court ruled that the non-moving party (here, the plaintiff), with the burden now shifted to her, had to go beyond her complaint and pleadings with new evidence to show that there was indeed a genuine issue for trial. This the plaintiff failed to do and summary judgment was granted for the defendant, Celotex Corp.

Anderson v. Liberty Lobby

Celotex was a product liability case; *Anderson v. Liberty Lobby* was a libel/defamation case (*Anderson v. Liberty Lobby, Inc.* 1986). Columnist Jack Anderson allegedly published statements about a lobbying organization describing it as racist, anti-Semitic, and neo-Nazi.

In a defamation case involving a public figure such as Liberty Lobby, the plaintiff had to prove with clear and convincing evidence that Anderson and his magazine made the statements with actual malice. After a certain amount of discovery, defendants relied on an affidavit of one of the defendant magazine employees who had written two of the allegedly defamatory articles. The employee testified that he got information about Liberty Lobby from numerous sources believing the information to be accurate.

In ruling in a motion for summary judgment by defendant Anderson, the Court discarded the old summary judgment precedent of "slightest doubt." In deciding what constitutes sufficient evidence to create a genuine issue as to a material fact, the Court held:

> *The question here is whether a jury could reasonably find* either *that the plaintiff proved his case by the quality and quantity of evidence required by the governing law* or *that he did not (*Anderson v. Liberty Lobby *1986).*

Matsushita

The plaintiffs in *Matsushita* were American television manufacturers, including Zenith. The defendants were twenty-one Japanese firms and their American subsidiaries of consumer electronic products. The plaintiffs ("Zenith") claimed that the Japanese firms engaged in a conspiracy to eliminate plaintiffs from the American consumer electronics market by keeping prices artificially high in Japan and artificially low in the United States—in essence, a predatory pricing *conspiracy,* which brought the case within the ambit of Sherman Section 1.

Matsushita was one of the most complex antitrust cases ever, both procedurally and substantively. The case involved massive discovery and time: over one million documents in discovery and ten years in litigation.

The trial court granted the Japanese defendants' motion for summary judgment. The Third Circuit Court of Appeals reversed, holding that it was reasonable that a conspiracy to price predatorily could be found. In a 5-4 decision, the Supreme Court reversed the Court of Appeals.

The Supreme Court reasoned that if there were in fact a conspiracy by the Japanese, it came up woefully short over twenty years. In other words, the Court reasoned that the alleged conspiracy simply made no economic sense and that the evidence was as consistent with independent behavior as with conspiracy.

Relying on *Monsanto,* the *Matsushita* majority held that "antitrust law limits the range of permissible inferences form *ambiguous* evidence in a [Sherman] Section 1 case." (*Matsushita* 1986, emphasis added). Further, "conduct as consistent with permissible competition as with illegal conspiracy does not, standing alone, support an inference of antitrust conspiracy." (*Matsushita* 1986). Again, relying on *Monsanto* for what it takes to survive a motion for summary judgment, the Court held:

> *To survive a motion for summary judgment . . . , a plaintiff . . . must present evidence that tends to exclude the possibility that the alleged conspirators acted independently . . . [Plaintiffs] . . . must show that the inference of conspiracy is reasonable in light of the competing inferences of independent action or collusive action that could not have harmed [plaintiffs].* (Matsushita 1986).

Emphasizing that the alleged conspiracy made no economic sense, the Court went on to hold:

> *The absence of any plausible motive to engage in the conduct charged is highly relevant to whether a 'genuine issue for trial' exists. . . . Lack of motive bears on the range of permissible conclusions that might be drawn from ambiguous evidence: if petitioners [Japanese defendants] had no rational economic motive to conspire, and if their conduct is consistent with other, equally plausible explanations, the conduct does not give rise to an inference of conspiracy* (Matsushita 1986).

The upshot of *Matsushita,* along with *Celotex, Anderson v. Liberty,* and *Mansanto* is that it will be increasingly important for marketers to establish that trade restraints are the result of legitimate business reasons. For marketers, the procedural change in summary judgment means that a marketer will have an opportunity after a certain amount of discovery has transpired to move that a lawsuit is useless or frivolous, that there is no genuine issue to be tried on the merits before the court. The way to do this is to be in a position to offer evidence supporting legitimate business behavior. The other side will then have to come forward with evidence that disproves or excludes the possibility of independent action. If the other side cannot come up with the additional evidence to establish a genuine issue for trial, the suit will be dismissed. We now turn to a more detailed analysis of *Matsushita's* elements.

The "Standing Alone" Element. The decisions just cited, particularly the *Monsanto* and *Matsushita* decisions, make much of the "standing alone" element: i.e., conduct, in and of itself, is not sufficiently conclusive to prove unlawful behavior (Scott 1992). For example, the termination of a dealer along with other dealer complaints about price-cutting, standing alone, does not give rise to an inference of conspiracy. It would be a foolish business that did not consider its distributors' concerns.

On the other hand, if the terminated dealer could show by direct evidence beyond the coincidental timing of complaints by his competitors and his termination (circumstantial evidence) that the manufacturer met with the complaining dealers and assured them that the price-cutter would be persuaded not to discount, the manufacturer's motion for summary judgment should be denied; the additional evidence, the "something more," creates a genuine issue as to whether in fact there was a conspiracy among the manufacturer and the complaining dealers to unlawfully fix prices vertically.

As a practical matter, the defendant, (the manufacturer here) would be wise to be in a position to offer independent business reasons for the termination to demonstrate that the plaintiff's circumstantial evidence (assuming that the terminated dealer could not come up with direct evidence of a vertical price fixing conspiracy) is subject to more than one interpretation, and therefore ambiguous (DeSanti and Kovacic 1990). The manufacturer should be able to *document* that the dealer was not terminated for discounting but for poor service, inferior warranty work, not meeting minimum hours, and any array of typical, legitimate requirements that might be put on a distributor that is related to offering consumers value and satisfaction.

The Economic Plausibility Element. Recall that a key element in *Matsushita* was that the claim had to be economically plausible, i.e., it had to make economic sense. Among other facts, this inference of economic implausibility was supported by the fact that Zenith had not lost any significant market share for over twenty years even though the supposed predatory price conspiracy was in effect since 1953 (*Matsushita* 1986). Hence, it would behoove a defendant in an antitrust action to offer evidence that the conduct complained of makes no economic sense.

This may be easier said than done. In *Matsushita,* the evidence was so extreme in challenging the credulity of the scheme that the economic implausibility aspect was devastating to Zenith. The "standing alone" element is easier to establish through evidence supporting legitimate business objectives and conduct.

Is the "New" Summary Judgment Working?

Any assessment of the "new" summary judgment is to be found at the lower federal court level; and to date, the courts have not been shy about granting the motion, primarily for defendants, particularly in antitrust cases (Note 1989). As of March 1990, a computer search has revealed over 3,000 citations to the Supreme Court's *Celotex* decision in state and federal court opinions (Yamamoto, et al. 1990). One appellate court even stated: "Meet these affidavit facts or judicially die" (*Southern Rambler Sales, Inc. v. American Motors Corp.* 1967).

In *Richards v. Nielsen Freight Lines ("Richards"),* each of the defendant long haul trucking companies were able to establish a legitimate business reason for terminating their interline agreements with the plaintiff trucking company. As in *Monsanto* and *Matsushita,* the *Richards* Court held that each defendant was as likely to have acted independently as pursuant to a boycott conspiracy.

Anderson v. Liberty can be used in an antitrust case to obtain summary judgment where a plaintiff's case is weak. (Soma and McCallin 1991). For example, in *Argus v. Eastman Kodak,* Kodak was granted summary judgment. Using the "implausible claim" language of *Matsushita,* the court also analyzed the sad financial shape Argus was in before Kodak allegedly engaged in predatory pricing conduct to drive Argus out of business. Hence, Argus' poor management could have been equally responsible for its demise as Kodak's "aggressive" pricing. Argus could not offer more evidence and lost on summary judgment as the court relied on *Matsushita* (Soma and McCallin 1991).

In sum, the courts are encouraging the filing of summary judgment motions (Issacharoff and Loewenstein 1990). Even more telling, courts are not reviewing the sufficiency of the defendants' motions. In a sample of 140 contested summary judgment motions in 1988, in the 98 decisions for the defendant, 60 percent of these were entered without any discussion of the sufficiency of the defendant's production in support of the motion; and in twelve of these cases, the courts granted summary judgment for the defendants based solely on the insufficiency of the plaintiffs' efforts early in the cases (Issacharoff and Loewenstein 1990).

CONCLUSION: IMPLICATIONS FOR MARKETING MANAGEMENT

The dramatic changes in substantive antitrust law and procedural law have profound implications for marketing management. For the first time in nearly 100 years of antitrust law, marketers can do things in heretofore strictly prohibited areas such as price fixing and market/customer allocations. Overt, naked attempts not to compete must be avoided, but legitimate, procompetitive undertakings need not necessarily fear simplistic labeling of the conduct. If price fixing and/or market allocations are integral to legitimate efforts to lower prices, improve quality, and increase consumer satisfaction, marketers now have the opportunity to document the procompetitive purposes and effects through strategic planning and marketing research.

The increased availability of summary judgment changes the balance of power between parties in a lawsuit by raising both the cost and risk to the plaintiff and making it easier for a defendant to get out of a sham lawsuit early (Issacharoff and Loewenstein 1990). For the first time, courts can evaluate competing inferences from conduct in the light of legitimate business reasons for the conduct (Henninger 1987).

Matsushita is support to establish through marketing planning and marketing research that claims are economically implausible.

Furthermore, a party can document legitimate objectives and business reasons underlying challenged behavior. The burden is then on the party challenging the conduct to come up with evidence "that tends to exclude the possibility that defendants acted independently" (*Matsushita* 1986). Therefore, marketing planning and marketing research will become increasingly important, in addition to their inherent value as marketing tools, to minimize the risk of becoming mired in time consuming and extremely costly litigation.

REFERENCES

Anderson v. Liberty Lobby, Inc., 477 U.S. 242 (1986).

Argus v. Eastman Kodak, 801 F.2d 38 (2d Cir. 1986), *cert. denied,* 479 U.S. 1088 (1987).

Broadcast Music, Inc. v. Columbia Broadcasting System, 441 U.S. 1 (1979).

Celotex Corp. v. Catrett, 477 U.S. 317 (1986).

Chicago Board of Trade v. United States, 246 U.S. 231 (1918).

De Santi, Susan and Kovacic, William. 1990. *Matsushita:* Its Construction and Application by the Lower Courts. *Antitrust Law Journal* 59 (August): 609–49.

Federal Trade Commission v. Indiana Federation of Dentists, 435 U.S. 684 (1986).

Friedenthal, Scott. 1988. Cases on Summary Judgment: Has There Been a Material Change? *Notre Dame Law Review* 63: 770–804.

Henninger, John. 1987. The Evolving Summary Judgment Standard For Antitrust Conspiracy Cases. *The Journal of Corporation Law* 12 (Spring): 503–34.

Issacharoff, Samuel and Loewenstein, George. 1990. Second Thoughts About Summary Judgment. *Yale Law Journal* 100 (October): 73–114.

Jorde, Thomas M. and Lemley, Mark. 1991. Summary Judgment in Antitrust Cases: Understanding *Monsanto* and *Matsushita. Antitrust Bulletin* 36 (Summer): 271–92.

Levine, Marcy J. 1988. Summary Judgment: The Majority View Undergoes a Complete Reversal in the 1986 Supreme Court. *Emory Law Journal* 37 (Winter): 171–215.

Matsushita Electric Industrial Co. v. Zenith Radio Corp., 475 U.S. 574 (1986).

Monsanto Co. v. Spray-Rite Service Corp., 465 U.S. 752 (1984).

National Collegiate Athletic Association v. Board of Regents of the University of Oklahoma, 468 U.S. 85 (1984).

Northern Pacific Railway Co. v. United States, 356 U.S. 1 (1958).

Note. 1989. Summary Judgment in Federal Court: New Maxims For a Federal Rule. *New York Law School Law Review* 34: 201–24.

Poller v. CBS, 368 U.S. 464 (1962).

Proger, Phillip. 1991. A Primer on Antitrust Law in the Healthcare Field. Paper presented at the Annual Antitrust in the Healthcare Field Conference of the National Health Lawyers Association, Washington, D.C., February 13, 1991.

Richards v. Neilsen Freight Lines, 810 F.2d 898 (9th Cir. 1987).

Rogers III, C. Paul. 1979. Summary Judgment in Antitrust Conspiracy Litigation. *Loyola University Law Journal* 10: 667–712.

Scott, Charity. 1992 Medical Peer Review Litigation and the Healthcare Quality Improvement Act. Paper presented at the Annual Antitrust in the Healthcare Field Conference of the National Health Lawyers Association, Washington, D.C., January 30, 1992.

Soma, John and McCallin, Andrew. 1991. Summary Judgment and Discovery Strategies in Antitrust and RICO Actions After *Matsushita. Antitrust Bulletin* 36 (Summer): 325–39.

Southern Rambler Sales, Inc. v. American Motors Corp., 375 F.2d 932 (5th Cir. 1967), *cert. denied,* 389 U.S. 832 (1967).

Trombetta, William. 1987. Is This The Best Thing Yet in Three-Letter Medicine? *Medical Economics* 64 (August 10): 127–31.

United States v. Socony-Vacuum Oil Co., 310 U.S. 150 (1940).

United States v. Trenton Potteries Co., 273 U.S. 392 (1927).

Yamamoto, Eric; Leonard, Katherine; and Sodersten, Shawna. 1990. Summary Judgment at the Crossroads: Impact of the *Celotex* Trilogy. *University of Hawaii Law Review* 12: 1–45.

Nigel F. Piercy
Professor of Marketing and Strategy
Cardiff Business School
University of Wales
United Kingdom

Visiting Professor
M.J. Neeley School of Business
Texas Christian University
Fort Worth, Texas

William D. Giles
Director
Strategic Management Resource Centre Ltd.
United Kingdom

CHAPTER 37

MANAGING THE MARKET PLANNING PROCESS: THE SEARCH FOR CONTINUOUS COMPETITIVE RENEWAL

INTRODUCTION

The goal of this chapter is to review briefly the conventional model of strategic market planning and to identify some of the shortcomings in providing a basis for managing the planning process. The management agenda identified has as its goal the creation of a culture of continuous competitive renewal, that is the permanent and ongoing search for new advantage and better position in the marketplace.

There are two underlying contentions here. The first of our foundations is that the market planning process is no more than a means to an end—where that end is achieving competitive advantage, not simply producing plans. We start with some cynicism about the value of sophisticated planning, the output of which is disregarded by executives, which changes little of substance in the running of the company or in how it deals with its customers in the marketplace.

The second of our underlying contentions is that while it is only a means to an end, market planning is one of the most powerful means to the end of competitive advantage and the continuous renewal of that advantage, which executives have at their disposal. It is for this reason that what we discuss below is the construction of an agenda for actively and creatively managing the *process* of market planning, rather than the conventional listing and explication of yet more sophisticated analytical techniques.

We will see in this chapter that most authorities and most executive development activity treats the *process* of market planning as an orderly and logical sequence of steps in applying rational-analytical techniques to develop strategies and programs. Their focus is on analysis and modeling sophistication to output carefully constructed strategic and operational plans normally to standardized formats.

Issues like corporate culture, management style, information sharing, organizational structure, influence, participation, and the like, if they are considered at all, are treated as facilitating mechanisms or mere context, to be set aside as trivial compared to the real business of complex analysis and plan writing. This is exactly wrong. These issues are not mere context, they *are* the process.

We will argue that it is success in managing these process issues that determines whether anything useful ever happens as a result of market planning and whether we succeed in tapping the potential for organizational learning and competitive renewal that lies in the planning process.

EXHIBIT 1. The Quality of Output from Market Planning

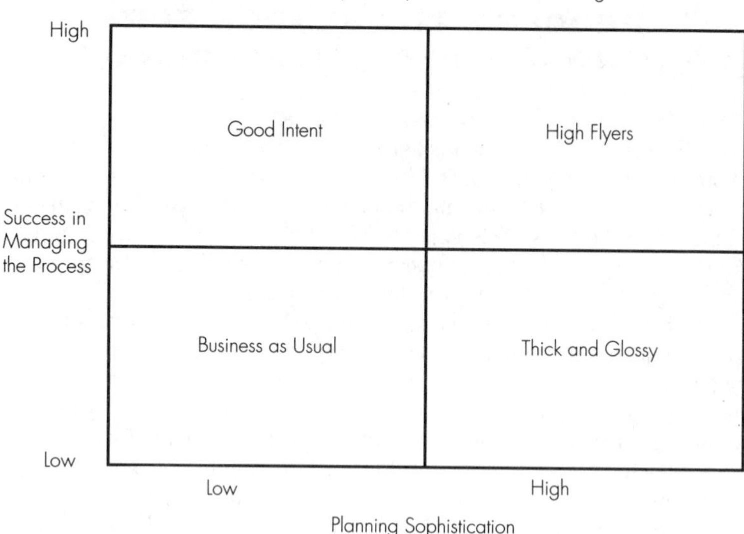

Putting these two contentions together suggests that the real trade-off for management is between planning sophistication and success in managing process issues. This is summarized in Exhibit 1.

The initial question for the managers is whether their market planning avoids the traps of "Business As Usual"—crude plans, but it hardly matters because no one takes much notice of them anyway; "Thick and Glossy"—beautiful plans that everyone ignores; or "Good Intent and Fine Words"—people get excited about planning, but they do not have the tools to put the good intentions into practical effect.

What follows in this chapter focuses on how to manage a way into the "High Flyer" situation, where we achieve both commitment and ownership through the planning process and produce plans that are capable of implementation.

CONVENTIONAL MARKET PLANNING MODELS

It is quite apparent that the marketing literature is replete with widely used prescriptive works that focus on the need for systematic market planning and that describe the procedures, analytical techniques, and format for planning (e.g., Jain 1990; Kerin, et al. 1990). Conventionally these approaches offer flow models of market planning process of the type shown in Exhibit 2. The logic of such models is impeccable.

EXHIBIT 2. A Conventional Model of Market Planning Process

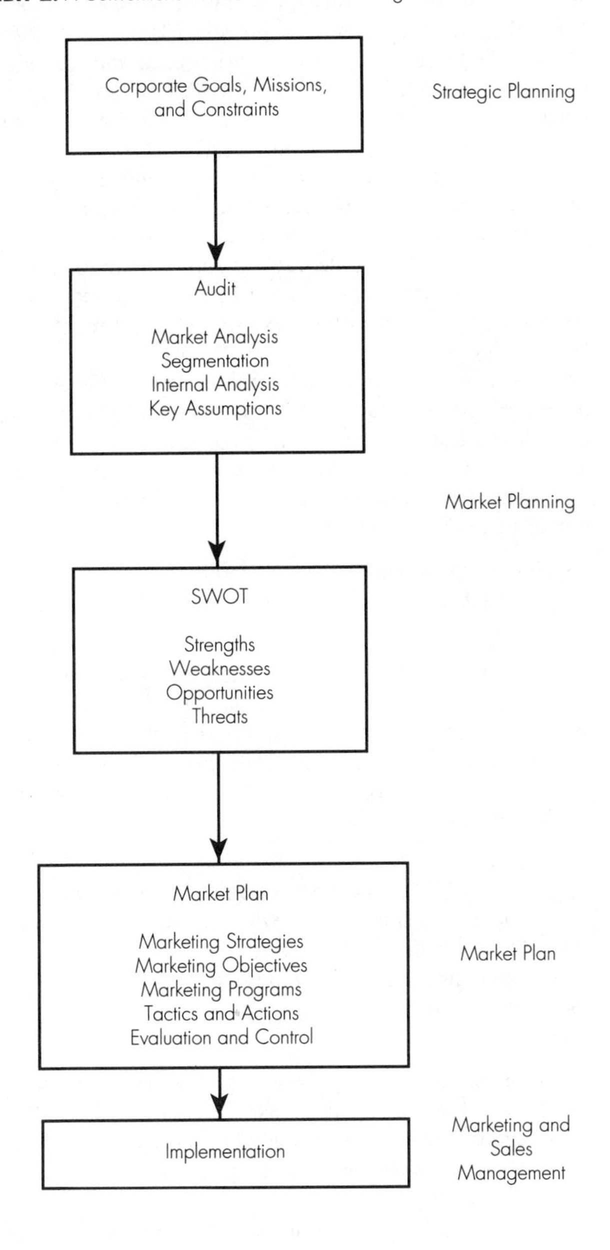

The assumed starting plan for market planning is with a clear statement of corporate mission and goals with any constraints emerging from the strategic planning process. The core activity for market planners is the analysis of the marketplace and the relative competencies and capabilities of the company to arrive at a statement of corporate strengths and weaknesses in the light of opportunities and threats in the marketplace in question. From this a market plan is generated, identifying market strategies and tactics for the market in question over the time period required. Implementation is then a matter for line executives in marketing and sales.

To a reasonable degree of approximation, this type of model describes the conventional view of market planning as it is described in the literature, taught in business schools, and represented in executive training programs.

As a model of building formal systems, for locating market planning in relation to corporate and other functional planning activities, or for providing a framework to identify the points for application of analytical techniques, there is no problem with this type of representation.

There are, however, some minor problems with this conventional model of market planning:

- It almost wholly ignores the real world
- It is inward looking and myopic
- It does not work

A few words of justification for these assertions are probably in order.

Quite simply, the conventional model of a logical, sequential, and analytical planning process ignores two unavoidable characteristics of real planning processes: They are operated by *people,* and they take place in *organizations.* It is worth considering the evidence about how market planning goes wrong.

WHAT GOES WRONG?

Some may think the previous assertions are somewhat exaggerated. The evidence is that there are substantial problems in making market planning effective. A number of studies throughout the world have suggested various conclusions about the practice of market planning:

- Conventional flow models of planning represent a simplistic concept of market strategy and may be positively harmful to performance (Cousins, 1990)
- Conventional models may confuse the issue at stake by presenting legitimate output formats as models of the process required to reach the output (Piercy and Giles 1990)
- The analytical rigor of the planning techniques used may be limited (Wensley 1981, Kiechel 1982)

- Managers report market planning to have failed them and to be inflexible, destructive of initiative, with plans unused in practice, and little more than a meaningless ritual (Greenley 1988, Leppard and McDonald 1987, Verhage and Waartz 1982, Cosse and Swan 1983, Piercy 1992)

These signs that all is not well in market planning as it is practiced are confirmed by some of our own observations and exploratory research.

Much of our current understanding of the real problems of effectively implementing and operating strategic market planning in organizations comes from the responses made by groups of executives in planning workshops and the like to two wholly naive questions that we have asked over a period of several years: "What do you want your market planning process to achieve for your company?" and "What goes wrong with market planning in your company?"

What Do You Want From Market Planning?

Broadly, the answers from managers to this question are as follows.

1. *A Good Market Plan*—a response that generally refers to plans that are achievable, actionable, and capable of being implemented, rather than to technical, analytical sophistication.
2. *Teams and "Ownership" of Output*—a recurring comment that plans that are not "owned" by teams of executives are unlikely to gain implementation, even if they are formally approved and accepted by the company.
3. *A Continuous Process*—while executives typically do not want to spend more time planning, they *do* want planning to operate continuously and not to be a "once-a-year ritual."
4. *A Way to Identify Real Information Needs*—executives answered that planning is a way of isolating and identifying their *real* information needs.
5. *A Way to Understand Strategy and Shake Dogma*—executives said they often do not understand their own companys' strategies and suggested that they had what amounts to culturally based "dogma" rather than genuine strategies for the future—they want to find ways of shaking and testing the beliefs and values of their culture.

On the face of things, anyway, managers seem to want quite surprisingly reasonable things from market planning. This leads directly to our second naive question.

Why Don't You Just Do It?

Perhaps the most outstanding characteristic of the responses to our second question about what goes wrong with market planning in practice was that on no occasion that we have recorded did executives complain of the lack of either formal planning techniques, computerized models, or statistical information systems. The perceived gap is not scientific planning methodology. Rather, the planning pitfalls executives perceive appear to be in the following areas.

1. *Analysis Instead of Planning*—executives have told us frequently that they see planning as bogged down with analytical techniques and models that are far removed from the reality they perceive and that do not lead to actionable plans.
2. *Information Instead of Decision*—in a similar vein, executives have described their planning disintegrating into constant demands for more and better information. Some are cynical enough to suggest that the reason for this is that it is easier than making decisions.
3. *Incrementalism*—at its simplest, executives have described to us many situations where the primary determinant of plan is quite simply the previous plan or at least the previous budget. The planning task then disintegrates into negotiating and arguing about minor departures from the previous year rather than creating new strategies.
4. *Vested Interests Rule*—executives suggest that the powerful people in the company exert undue influence over plans to protect budgets and head counts, to build resource claims, and so on. Many manifestations of this were cited: refusal by key players to participate in planning followed by a rejection of plans by those same players on the grounds of lack of consultation; blockages in the availability of important internal information to planners; side-tracking disputes about jurisdiction and minor company rules and policies; outright, dogged argument against anything that changes the *status quo*; "politicking," bargaining, and "horse trading" outside planning meetings to divert plans from going in unwelcome directions; and so on.
5. *Organizational Mindset*—many executives have suggested that conventional planning processes are by definition inward looking and bounded by "the way we do things here." So, they never produce anything new.
6. *Resistance to Marketing Change*—some executives have suggested that strategic change emanating from the marketing department is seen as threatening—or even unreasonable—and is often successfully resisted by other departments and organizational interest groups.
7. *No Ownership or Commitment*—it seems in many cases that plans are produced (often by staff planners) and accepted, but in the absence of champions determined to make them work, nothing ever happens as a result of the planning effort.

8. *No Resourcing*—executives have pointed out many resource-related pitfalls: the simple refusal by management to provide resources and, perhaps most threatening, approval and acceptance by management of the plan but rejection of the accompanying resource request.
9. *No Implementation*—we have received bitter complaints about situations where planning absorbed resources and management time and even created excitement and support for change but led to nothing more than a report on a shelf, which was never effectively implemented.
10. *Diminishing Effort and Interest*—largely as a result of lack of resourcing and implementation, executives point out that if planning is to be no more than an annual ritual, and managers perceive this, then it is hardly surprising that efforts and interest diminish over time. It becomes a self-fulfilling prophesy that planning is a waste of time.

These pitfalls may not be true of how planning works in *your* organization. The point is that if you look at what managers say they *want* from market planning and the reasons why it goes *wrong,* there is almost no mention of wanting more sophisticated planning techniques and systems.

The trouble with this is that what we really know a lot about is the techniques and the systems. If you look at the conventional market planning textbooks, planning manuals, briefcase planning systems, consultancy advice, management training, and all the rest—they are obsessed with model building, computer systems, and analytical techniques. In contrast to this, what managers seem to be telling us is that we are all missing the point about what really matters in making market planning effective as far as they and their companies are concerned.

We need, then, to rethink how we work on market planning with companies and develop an approach that is about *managing* the market planning *process,* not just the techniques of planning.

DIMENSIONS OF THE MARKET PLANNING PROCESS

The way we present the market planning process to companies now is summarized in Exhibit 3. We suggest that there are at least three dimensions of the market planning process, and if we are in any way serious about *managing* market planning, then we have to address all three of these process dimensions.

Analytical Planning Dimension

There is no doubt that to produce effective market plans we need the tools for the job—the *techniques* to analyze our problems and opportunities and identify the solutions and strategies; the formal

EXHIBIT 3. A Multidimensional Model of Market Planning

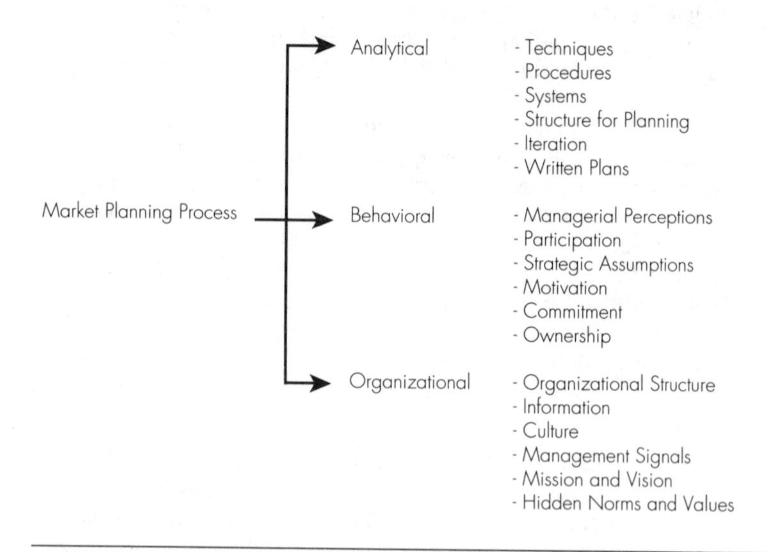

procedures and systems to organize our planning and make it part of running the business; a *structure* for our planning to make it comprehensive and manageable; *iteration* to make our planning dynamic and thorough; and a *written plan* as the output capturing our ideas and strategies as a basis for communicating them.

This is an important element of the planning process, but it has two caveats. First, let us not delude ourselves that this is *all* that planning is about, because then we end up believing that if we can just formalize planning enough and train people in more sophisticated techniques of planning (or perhaps hire professional planners who have this expertise already), then we will improve our performance. There is abundant evidence that it is not so. Second, let us be wary of the trap of creating a planning bureaucracy that actually gets in the way of *doing* things.

Behavioral Planning Dimension

Process means *how* we do things as well as *what* we do. How we do things leads us straight to the problems that our people have in building and using market plans.

The type of issues we have to sort out here have very little to do with formal planning techniques: *managerial perceptions* of planning and the uncertainties they are expected to confront in planning; *participation* levels and types in the planning groups and teams and managers' attitudes towards this; and hidden *strategic assumptions* managers make (and believe) about what the company can and should do and what drives the market; the *motivation* (or otherwise) to make planning effective; the *commitment* to strategic change, or the preference for the status quo; and the *ownership* by individuals of the problem of making things happen, without which it is unlikely that too much will ever happen as a result of market planning.

The sad truth is that we know that these things matter, but many of us ignore them when we try to manage our market planning.

Organizational Planning Dimension

Ultimately, all of this has to be seen in the context of the organization itself: the *organizational structure,* with all this means in terms of formal responsibilities, vested interests, and power to get things done or stop things from happening; the *information issue* and the problems of access and control of information, the inadequacies, and the politics; the *culture* of the organization—"the way we do things here," and all the subcultures in different parts of the organization; the *management signals* that tell us about the real attitudes and beliefs of management rather than the lip service; the existence and direction of *mission and vision* in how the organization is run; and the hidden *norms and values* that really determine what people do in the organization.

We may not know too much about managing people in planning, but we know even less about matching formal planning to organizational attributes of this kind.

The conclusion to which we are drawn is that we know *most* about what matters *least* in planning (the analytical techniques and formal systems), and we know *least* about what matters *most* (the behavioral and organizational dimensions) and that we have not even yet recognized the underlying problem of managing these dimensions of planning to formulate a consistent, managed planning process.

Some Research Evidence

Although it is crude, we have done some exploratory research to substantiate the existence and significance of these hidden dimensions of the planning process. The research was conducted among medium and large UK companies—companies where there is some form of market planning (so you would expect them to be above average in getting the planning act together).

A technical note is available elsewhere (Piercy and Morgan 1990), but the basic question we sought to answer was, "What predicts the credibility and utilization of market plans?" The issue is whether we produce plans that people believe in, and use, to run the business. The predictors of plan credibility and utilization that we found in the study were (1) the formalization of planning and learning of planning techniques; (2) a factor called "planning thoroughness"; (3) the avoidance of behavioral planning problems; and (4) positive signals from the organizational environment.

Formalization and Planning Techniques. The degree to which market planning was formally organized and documented, and the more analytical techniques were brought to bear, the higher the credibility and use was of the plan.

Planning Thoroughness. This factor has to do with three things: the degree to which planning drew on experience and knowledge from all parts of the organization; whether the planning activity was seen to be adequately resourced in time and money; and whether people believed that good planning performance was rewarded in the same way that good operational performance was.

Avoidance of Behavioral Planning Problems. We used a large number of attitude and belief measurements to identify a number of behavioral planning problems at the individual level:

- *Planning recalcitrance*—characterized by people believing that planning was a bore and a ritual and that it was disorganized, with executives mainly picking on the weaknesses in plans and being easily sidetracked into short-term operational issues.
- *Fear of uncertainty in planning*—Executives are seen to resist long-term commitments and to be uncomfortable with long-range forecasting and so emphasize the present, not the future. People resist learning and change and desperately seek a "rational" decision-making technique that will make the decisions for them and take the discomfort away.
- *Political interests*—people see planning as dominated by the vested interests in the company, leading to planning becoming bidding and bargaining for resources, with information sharing precluded and much padding in forecasts and estimates.
- *Planning avoidance*—people are seen to go through the motions in planning and to give compliance, not commitment, so nothing gets challenged because planning is about avoiding responsibility for doing anything.

Organizational Signals. This was a measure of a number of factors to do with the company's attitude toward strategic planning, toward marketing, and the customer philosophy of management (or lack of it), as perceived by the people who do the market planning.

These would seem to be the things that are associated with market plans that are credible and actually used. Where this leads is toward a somewhat different agenda to be addressed in managing market planning—in *all* its dimensions.

MANAGING ALL THE DIMENSIONS OF PLANNING PROCESS

This model of the market planning process with several dimensions provides us with a framework for organizing management efforts to put a handle on market planning.

Managing the Analytical Dimension

This is the most documented element of market planning, and most texts are full of models and sophisticated techniques. However, going back to the basics suggests three areas where we can make a major impact on the real analytical effectiveness of market planning. This may be the starting point in orienting planning to competitive renewal instead of simply producing plans.

Vision. Before we analyze, do we ever communicate and share a clear and existing vision of where we want the business to go? Or do we remain vague and unclear, offering our executives a rehash of last year's goals or impossible wish lists? If our goal is continuous competitive renewal, then sorting out unclear vision is first on the list.

Most senior executives will tell you that they have a mission statement and/or a strategic vision. On the other hand, many middle managers, whose job it is to implement this vision, will tell you that they are working in a vacuum, uncertain about their goals. Oceans of corporate time are spent on word crafting the perfect mission statement to the enormous satisfaction of its authors. The result is a statement that covers every possible eventuality without actually saying anything. Managers scratch their heads and then it is back to business as normal.

It does not have to be like this. Exhibit 4 shows a projection of company performance into the future. The lowest line represents the usual incremental year-on-year approach. The next line represents current expectations based on doing more tomorrow of what we already do today. So within this box lie the expectations of the work force both in terms of how much (performance) and how soon (time). There is nothing very visionary about this, but here is the key.

For a vision to be visionary, it must aim outside both these axes. It should demand both more performance—that gives the organization the stretch it needs—and be further out in time to give people a chance to achieve it. Creating strategy to build this future can now take place in a different environment. The organization sits up here, out in the future, looking back toward the present. The immediate decisions are now very different to the other two conventional approaches.

This is fine in the pictures, but how do we articulate it? The useful vision statement treats hard and soft issues with equal importance. Exhibit 5 shows some sample headings that we can use. Each heading only needs at the most two or three key points to explain it.

The useful vision statement contains some hard goals about markets, customers, products, needs, share, and of course financials. It also contains some soft goals about people, organization, learning, skills, and rewards. And of course, it would not be complete unless we answer the question "By when?"

What is important here is breadth, not depth. These are visionary ideas and goals—not conventional objectives and targets. This is the

EXHIBIT 4. Vision

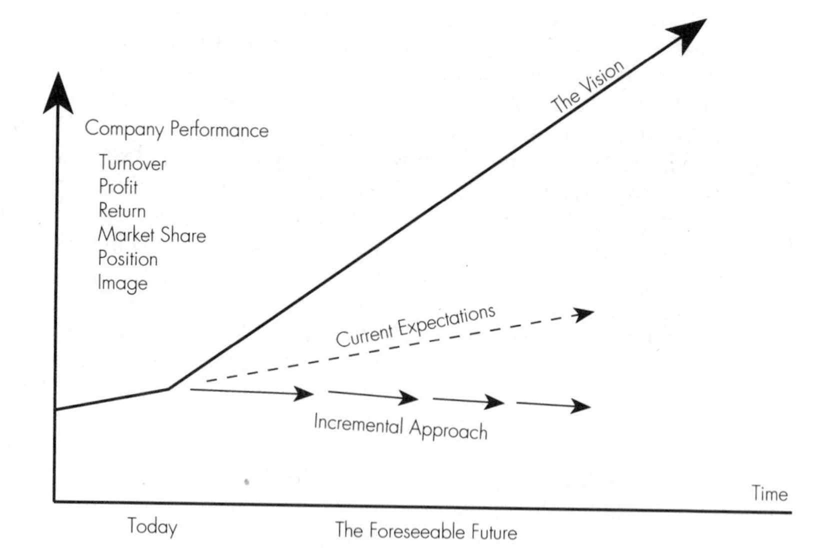

EXHIBIT 5. The "Really Useful Vision" Statement

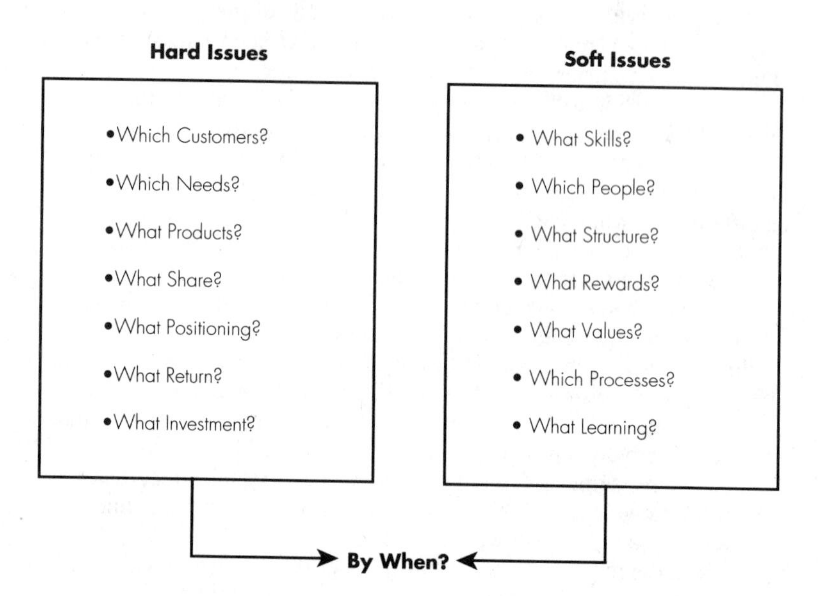

Hard Issues
•Which Customers?
•Which Needs?
•What Products?
•What Share?
•What Positioning?
•What Return?
•What Investment?
Soft Issues
• What Skills?
• Which People?
• What Structure?
• What Rewards?
• What Values?
• Which Processes?
• What Learning?
By When?

EXHIBIT 6. Developing New Ways of Looking at the World

Probability of Events Occurring	Effects of Environmental Changes on the Business: Excellent	Indifferent	Disastrous
High	Utopia		Catastrophe
Medium		Neutral	
Low	Disappointments		To Be Watched

first step in an iterative process for the whole organization. The whole thing fits on two pages. Everyone should know it by heart.

The underlying truth is that clear visions are not about sophisticated analysis or clever presentation. They just have to be simple, memorable, and colloquial.

Developing New Ways of Looking at the World. Corporate culture is not just "the way we do things there." It is also "the way we look at things here." One incredibly simple but very productive analytical technique is to formalize environmental scanning in market planning to produce the type of model shown in Exhibit 6. We can then confront the really big questions.

- Where in our strategies do we explicitly exploit the events that give us "utopia"?
- Where in our planning do we defend against the events in "catastrophe"?
- Do we try to avoid the "disappointments" observing our thinking?
- Does our information system watch the things that matter, or just the things that are easy to watch?

EXHIBIT 7. Make SWOT Analysis Work

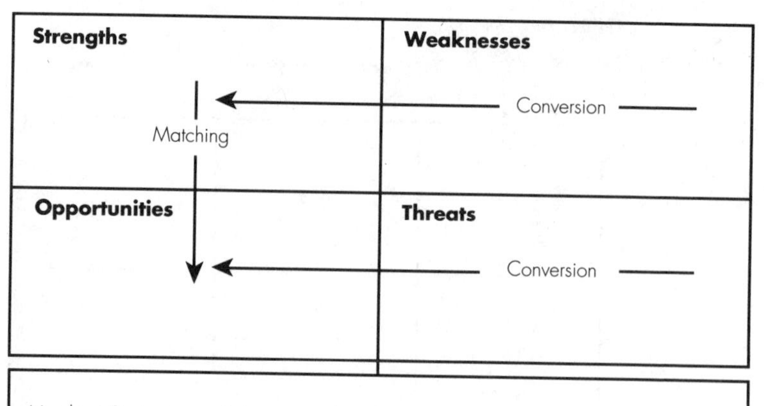
Strengths
Weaknesses
Conversion
Matching
Opportunities
Threats
Conversion
Matching Strategies - Relating our strengths to opportunities in the market
Conversion Strategies - Changing weaknesses and threats into new strengths and opportunities, or at least neutralizing them

Make SWOT Work. To work effectively, SWOT analysis just needs new rules:

- It should focus on specific markets or events
- It should encourage sharing of information and opinions
- It should be customer-oriented—nothing counts as a strength or a weakness unless customers can see it and rate it highly
- It should be environmental—opportunities and threats exist in the market, not in the company

If we follow these rules, then SWOT analysis can be turned back into an effective strategy generator. The goal is to force us to look at ourselves as the customer does and to confront the logic of the match between our capabilities and the marketplace. This is summarized in Exhibit 7.

Managing the Behavioral Dimension

However we deal with the issue of techniques, we cannot avoid the fact that the planning process is about people in terms, for example, of finding the behavioral planning problems discussed above. There is a critical confrontation between analytical technique and formalization

EXHIBIT 8. Commitment versus Complexity

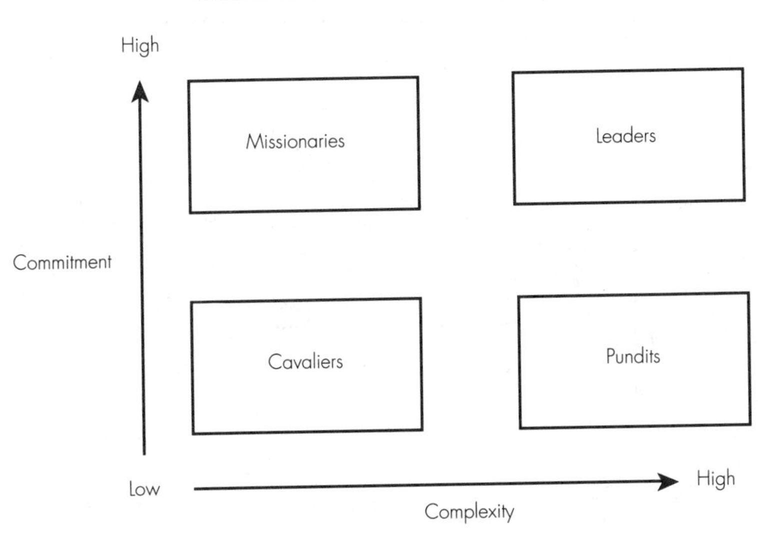

(planning sophistication) and people (in terms of the ownership and commitment to implementation we create or destroy in planning).

We can use the matrix in Exhibit 8 to define the position of companies. It enables us to classify either whole companies or individual business units according to their people's level of commitment and ownership versus the complexity and sophistication of the planning process and strategy generation they use.

Companies, organizations, or business units can be grouped into four categories: Cavaliers, Pundits, Missionaries, and Leaders:

- *Cavaliers* have neither the commitment of their people nor any clear business direction. Their planning systems and processes are superficial. Put another way, no one knows what is going on and nobody cares anyway.
- *Pundits* are typified by large planning departments and ivory tower ideas. Planning is done far away from the operations interface.
- *Missionaries* show great ownership commitment and share values, but as yet their market understanding and business direction have not matured.
- *Leaders,* which is what we would all like to be, have both a high level of commitment and high level of understanding. They exhibit all the hallmarks of sound business direction and effective action.

EXHIBIT 9. Theory versus Practice

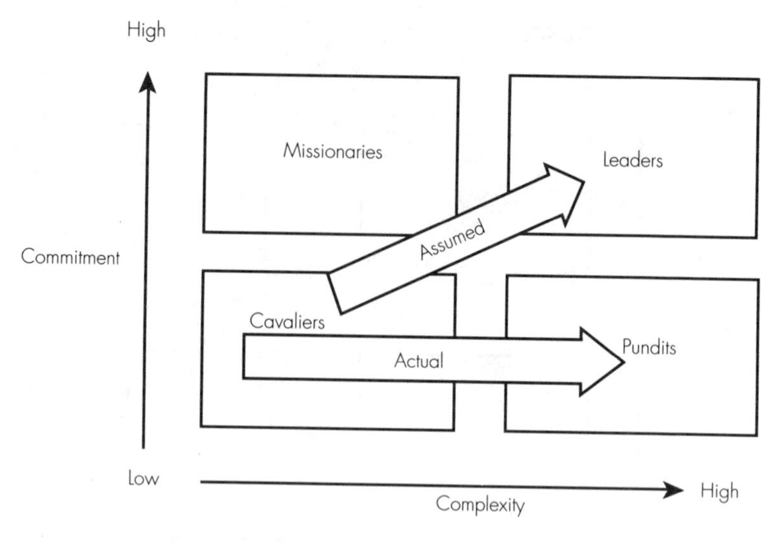

Applying this model to practice has led us to some interesting conclusions.

As suggested in Exhibit 9, the implicit assumption has always been that as organizations get better at producing plans and learn more sophisticated planning techniques, the level of commitment and ownership by the work force would increase correspondingly.

To the contrary, what we have found in practice is that organizations tend to invest in planning specialty as the tangible evidence of their desire to improve. This takes them further and further into the Pundits box. Typically, corresponding investments were not made on the vertical human axis since this was less tangible and harder to measure. This reflects the grand corporate strategy departments that may well have had all the answers but the right people did not understand how to ask the questions.

So just how do we aspire to the Leaders box? Well, there are only a few routes available, as summarized in Exhibit 10.

If we are in the Cavaliers box, we can move into the Missionaries box. But, if we are in the unfortunate position of being in the Pundits box, we may have to backtrack by leaving some of our sophistication behind in order to climb up to the Missionaries box. From the Missionaries box, we can leap into the Leaders box.

What does all this mean? Simply this: In managing the behavioral dimension of market planning, ownership, belief, and commitment all

EXHIBIT 10. Moving to Leadership

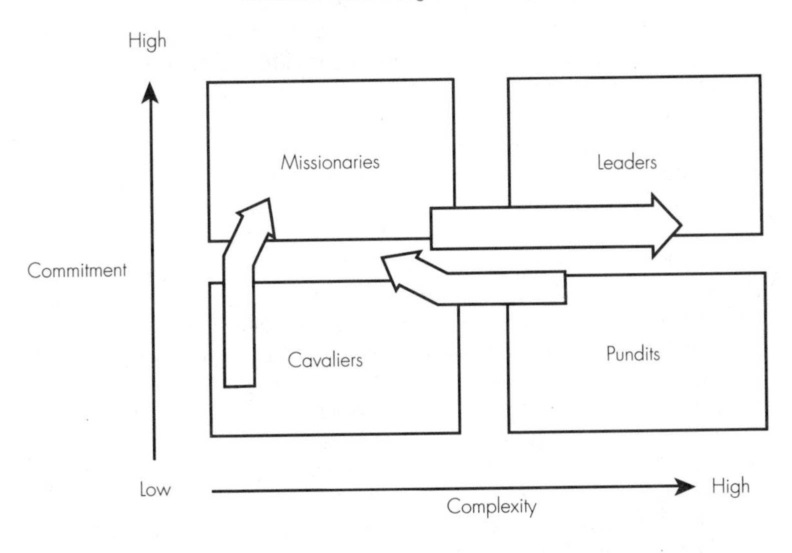

come before sophistication. By investing in this axis first we can get the entire organization pulling in the same direction. Later, we can add the sophistication.

If we go about it the other way, we drift further and further into the ivory tower cul-de-sac. This is all about putting planning back where it belongs: in the hands of the line managers. The role of the manager is changing in the '90s—from doer to facilitator and process designer.

To summarize, if we balance the analytical dimension of planning against the behavioral dimension, we suggest the following:

- *"Better" strategies do not automatically lead to better implementation*—Increasing investment in sophistication without an equal investment in ownership makes planning an ivory-tower activity. The planners become Pundits and implementation fails.
- *Over-sophistication hinders ownership*—Once a Pundit, additional investment in technical expertise is unlikely to turn an organization into a Leader. The behavioral investment that increases ownership is different to the technical expertise that increases sophistication.
- *Ownership can make implementation work regardless of strategy*—An organization can only reach the Missionary stage after a significant human investment in behavior and attitudes of its people. This will be effective if a level of strategy sophistication has not previously been achieved. If it has, it may be necessary to reinvent strategy in order to nurture ownership.

Managing the Organizational Dimension

While it is unavoidable that the planning process is about people, it is also about organization—the real context in which most of us have to operate—with all that this implies about culture, management style, structural inadequacies, information blockages, and so on.

Here the challenge is to evaluate the way the planning activity fits into the organizational context.

The Shape of the Planning Process. One approach to reshaping the planning process to revitalize it amounts to turning it upside down and inside out (Piercy and Giles 1989), as suggested in Exhibit 11. The new model is based on the simple observation that as long as planning is iterative, it matters little where you start in the "logical" sequence. By starting with the marketplace as it is seen and understood by line managers and working backward and forward from this, we may lack sophistication but can gain ownership on the way.

Where Does Planning Fit? Too often we emphasise the ritual of the annual planning pilgrimage. There is too often an assumption that our market planning can be compressed into a month or so each year and the rest of the time is left for us to get on with our "real" jobs.

One of the reasons for this is when we consider who should be doing the planning. Too often planning is given to someone who has neither the authority, responsibility, or experience for the task. Each level of management should be responsible for its own plan and each level, and therefore, requires its own process. Exhibit 12 shows what happens when this goes wrong.

We have here a matrix of management levels on one scale and time scales on the other. This is what happens when senior managers get embroiled in short-term planning when their real responsibility lies in longer-term planning. They lack the detailed knowledge. It is a waste of very expensive time and a poor use of their experience. But most important of all, they rob the implementors of any sense of ownership.

However, the reverse also has its problems when long-term planning is delegated too low down in the organization. The unfortunate incumbents become over-detailed and pedantic. They cannot see the wood for the trees and become hopelessly lost in unwanted detail while missing the big picture elsewhere. Alternatively, they create fantasy plans that cause frustration when they cannot be delivered. Whatever route is taken, unconvincing plans emerge.

This leads us to the conclusion that different levels of management have different planning roles and each requires its own management process. This is the difference between turning planning upside down and inside out as already discussed, or simply attempting to make planning "bottom up."

Exhibit 13 shows how it should work. Senior managers and the trained strategist concern themselves with the longer term—that is, what leadership is all about.

EXHIBIT 11. Turn Planning Process Upside Down and Inside Out

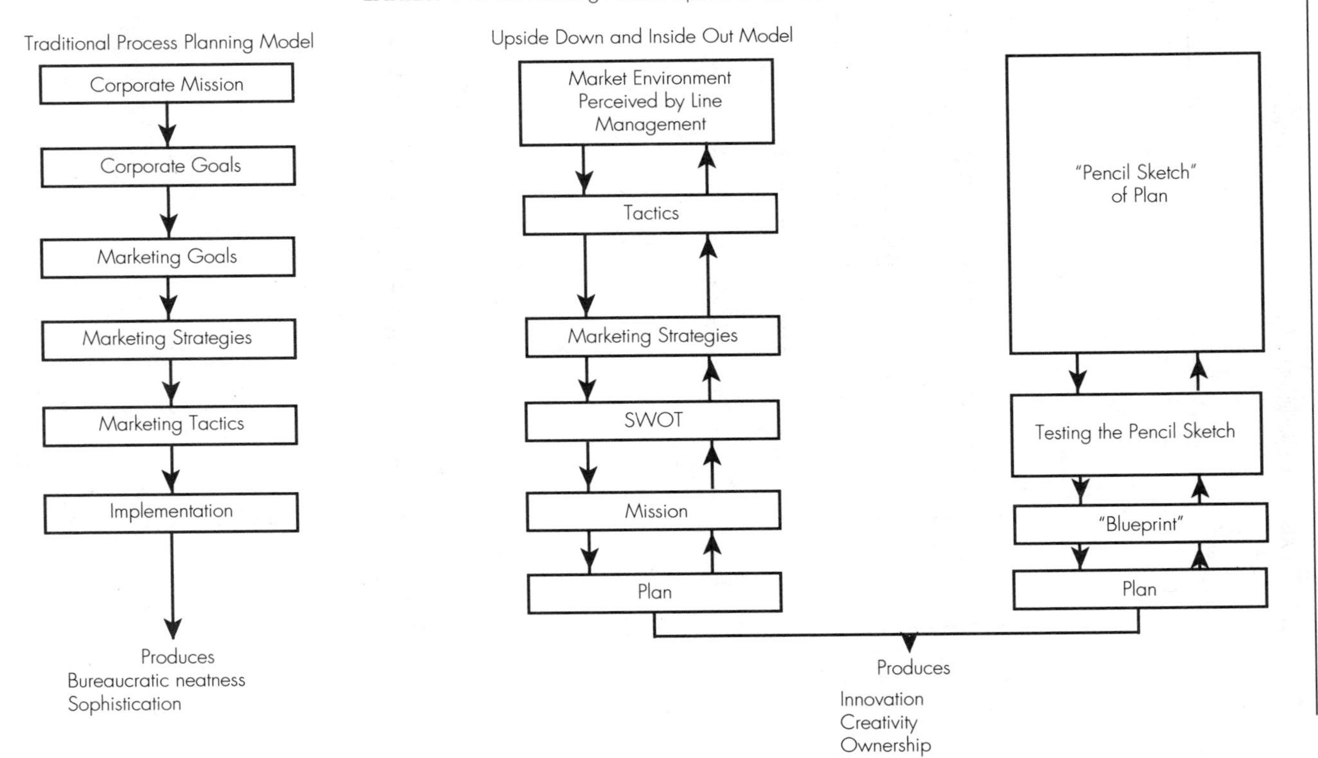

EXHIBIT 12. Confusing Who Does What in Planning

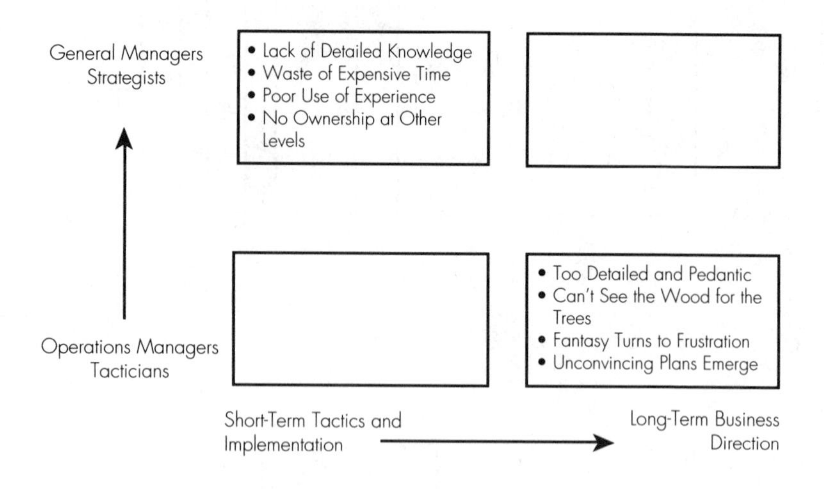

EXHIBIT 13. The Result of Confusing Planning Roles

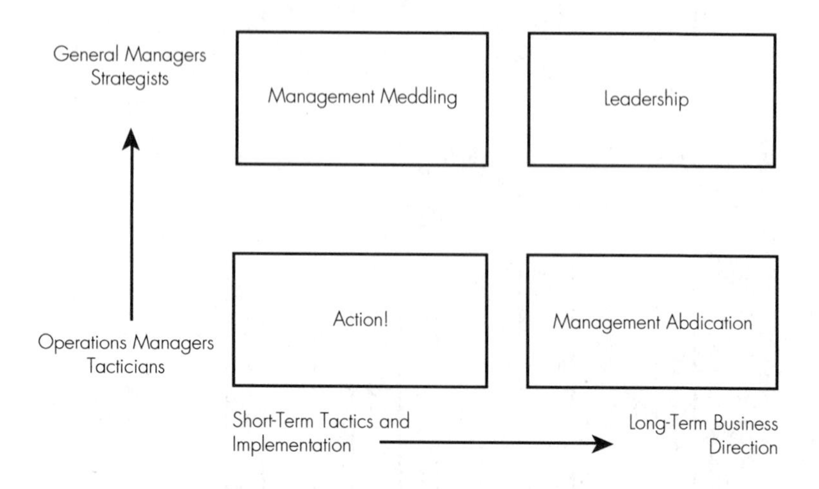

However, many senior managers feel more comfortable in short-term operational planning. After all, as they have risen through the ranks, that is where they have come from. We call this *management meddling.*

Similarly, when the operations people and the tacticians are left to get on with the detailed implementation planning, we achieve some *real* action. Often these same people get forced into long-term planning to fill the vacuum created by lack of leadership. We call this *management abdication,* not delegation as some managers would like to believe.

One further point on this subject is that planning is not a game for individuals, nor is it a spectator sport. Creativity is sparked by the interactions within small work groups or teams tasked to tackle specific issues. Asking individuals to prepare plans for others to tear apart belongs to a punishment culture that helps no one.

How Often Should We Plan? Creativity does not come to order. It leaps up suddenly over long periods of time—hence the idea of continuous competitive renewal. So the short answer to this question is "all the time."

Building the understanding to generate new business direction is a way of life, not a one-time activity. It requires constant iteration.

Exhibit 14 shows an approach that is both top down and bottom up. The only proviso is that the starting point for this process must be

EXHIBIT 14. Top Down-Bottom Up Planning

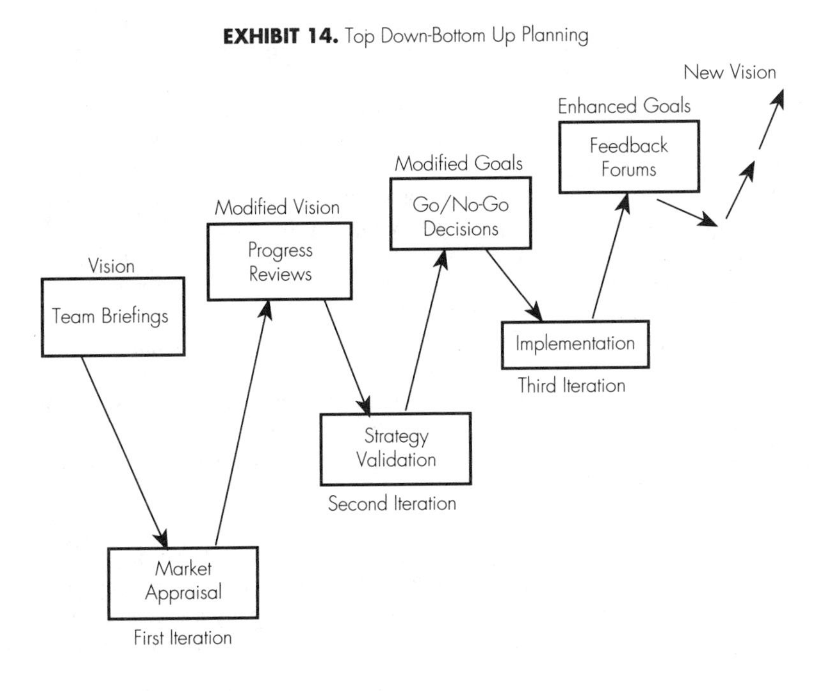

the vision statement discussed earlier. What we see here is a schedule of planned events—team briefings, progress reviews, go and no-go decisions, and feedback forums. Leadership aspirations are traded against the ability and the capacity of the organization to deliver. Through a series of iterations, the two come closer and closer together.

The ultimate aim is to create a new vision standing on the shoulders of the old one. The elapsed time for this process to be worked through may be several years, only to be restarted again at the beginning with a new vision. Several of these processes can overlap each other. This is the essence of continuous competitive renewal; creation and action take place at the same time, each learning from the other. What we are after is that sudden step change in performance. But it does not come to order and it cannot be planned for. Only by a continuous process of improvement can we put ourselves in a position to spot it before our competitors and take advantage of it when it comes.

This brings us back to the annual planning cycle. It is a snapshot in time of the progress we have made so far. It should not be additional work; it should reflect planning that is going on anyway and work that has already been done.

But Does It Match the Organization? The underlying problem we face in confronting the organizational dimension of market planning is designing and managing the process to make planning productive and to get to implementation. This requires that our planning process be comparable with the reality of the corporate culture. In one organization, for example, the debate with executives came down to the issues in Exhibit 15.

Where the corporate culture is supportive of our goals and we manage the dimensions of planning process consistently, we can achieve an effective planning process. Conversely, faced with resistance from the culture and low planning effectiveness, little changes and probably little damage is done. The company in question should have worried more about how to avoid the destructive planning process, where a supportive culture demands results and planning competencies are inadequate, or how to avoid the trap of a conflictual planning process where the planners become committed to implementation and the culture blocks it.

There are no easy answers to these questions, but they have to be confronted in working for consistency between the real corporate environment in which we have to operate and the changes we make to the planning process.

THE REAL MANAGEMENT AGENDA

If we are serious about putting a handle on the market planning process, so we can use it to unleash our company's potential for competitive renewal, then the research evidence and our observations

EXHIBIT 15. Fitting Planning Process to Corporate Culture

Corporate Culture	Technical Planning Effectiveness: High	Technical Planning Effectiveness: Low
Supportive	Effective Planning Process	Destructive Planning Process
Unsupportive	Conflicting Planning Process	Ineffective Planning Process

of practice suggest the real agenda to be addressed has at least four parts: (1) techniques and formalization; (2) behavioral issues in market planning; (3) organizational issues in market planning; and (4) consistency between all these issues.

Techniques and Formalization. It is clear that if we want plans to be credible (the first stage in getting them implemented), then we need to provide a formal system and the appropriate techniques. This seems to be for two reasons: It shows people we are serious about market planning, and it gives executives the tools to do the job. This is necessary but not sufficient, however.

Behavioral Issues. The critical issues here are the *managerial perceptions* of the planning process, with all that this means in terms of their *motivation* to make planning work effectively, and their *commitment* to planning. The variables to be managed here are *training* for the planning job, designing *participation* from a motivational and political viewpoint, and *signals* the organization sends about planning.

Organizational Issues. The critical question is the degree to which the organization is seen to be, and believed to be, *supportive* of the planning effort. Part of the answer is the *example* set by senior management, the resourcing of planning, and the rewards for good performance in planning. Ultimately, these things are important as they have an impact on *planning credibility* in the organization and reflect the surrounding issues of culture, organizational structure, information systems, and so on.

To attack such an agenda, which is an ambitious undertaking after all, we have made the following points:

1. Emphasize *vision* and use it to trigger planning instead of accepting incrementalism and myopia.
2. Use *marketing intelligence* to grow new ways of looking at the world.
3. Use *SWOT analysis* to look at ourselves as the customer does (not how the CEO does) and to face up to the match between our competencies and capabilities and what matters in the market.
4. Actively manage the *people issues* in planning. Choose the trade-off between planning sophistication/complexity and ownership. Work to get to the Leaders box.
5. Adapt for the *culture issue* in the organization. Shape the process to win the hearts and minds of the people who matter, not for bureaucratic neatness and management meddling or abdication. Work for planning as a corporate way of life, not an annual ritual. Match the planning process to the realities of the corporate environment.

To summarize, the *process* of market planning is significant because the way we design and manage the process will have a direct impact on what goes into the market plan, and even more to the point, whether anything useful ever *happens* as the result of planning. Apart from anything else, it is one of the few chances we have to do something constructive to move the company's culture closer to our strategy, rather than *vice versa.* Indeed, it is becoming clear that what a managed planning process offers us is a mechanism to put a handle on organized development because planning process is a form of organizational learning and adaptation. Our goal here is to guide that organizational development and learning toward our market-led goals.

REFERENCES

Cosse, Thomas J. and John E. Swan (1983), "Strategic Marketing Planning by Product Managers—Room for Improvement?" *Journal of Marketing,* 47 (Summer), pp. 92–102.

Cousins, Laura (1990), "The Aims and Process of Marketing Planning," in Proceedings: British Academy of Management, Glasgow.

Greenley, Gordon E. (1988), "Management Perceptions of Marketing Planning," *Journal of Management Studies,* 25 (6), pp. 575–601.

Jain, Subhesh C. (1990), *Marketing Planning and Strategy,* 3rd ed., Cincinatti, Ohio: South-Western.

Kerin, Roger A., Vijay Mahajan and P. Rajan Varadarajan (1990), *Contemporary Perspectives on Strategic Market Planning,* Boston, M.A: Allyn and Bacon.

Kiechel, Walter (1982), "Corporate Strategists," *Fortune,* 27 December.

Leppard, John and Malcolm H.B. McDonald (1987), "A Reappraisal of the Role of Marketing Planning," *Journal of Marketing Management,* 3(2), pp. 159–171.

Piercy, Nigel (1992), *Market-Led Strategic Change,* Oxford: Butterworth Heinemann.

Piercy, Nigel and William Giles (1990), "The Logic of Being Illogical in Strategic Marketing Planning," *Journal of Services Marketing,* 4 (3), pp. 27–37.

Piercy, Nigel and Neil A. Morgan (1990), "Organizational Context and Behavioral Planning Problems As Determinants of the Effectiveness of the Strategic Marketing Planning Process," *Journal of Marketing Management,* 6 (2), pp. 127–144.

Verhage, Branislow and Eric Waartz (1988), "Marketing Planning for Improved Performance: A Comparative Analysis," *International Marketing Review,* 2 (Summer), pp. 20–30.

Wensley, Robin (1981), "Strategic Marketing: Betas, Boxes, or Basics," *Journal of Marketing,* 45 (Summer), pp. 173–182.

John K. Ryans, Jr. William L. Shanklin
Professors of Marketing and International Business
Kent State University
Kent, Ohio

Reprinted by permission of *Harvard Business Review.* "Organizing for High-Tech Marketing," by William L. Shanklin and John K. Ryans, Jr., November-December 1984.

CHAPTER 38

MARKETING TO NONEXISTENT MARKETS

. . . The newer and more innovative a product is the more likely it is that the public might not appreciate it at the beginning. In 1950 our company marketed a tape recorder. Despite the fact that it was a great achievement and a technological innovation for us, at the time it looked like a toy to the general public. Nobody thought about recording speeches or using a tape recorder to learn languages. I believe that in the case of an entirely new product, a market must be created, not surveyed. Another way to say this is that a new product is the creator of a market and a new product cannot survive without the creation of a new market.[1]

—Akio Morita, Chairman and CEO, Sony Corporation

A person perusing most marketing literature, notably academic books on marketing, is told that a company's route to prosperity is the identification and fulfillment of customer needs and desires within the company's strategic competencies or lines of business. In the vast majority of the cases, this is sound advice. A company's commitment to the development and marketing of a product, process or service almost always should be preceded by market demand as identified by marketing research. Yet, there are notable exceptions to this general rule or guideline.

Whenever a product or service is developed in response to perceived market demand, which is normally the case, an appropriate terminology to describe the process is demand-side marketing.[2] In other words, the perceived demand triggers a company's involvement with the product. This sequence is "smart" marketing, because "what profits are there in developing and marketing products for which there is insufficient demand?" Obviously, none.

However, demand-side marketing carried to extreme stifles innovation, entrepreneurship, or intrapreneurship (i.e., entrepreneurship within a going corporation rather than a startup). There are instances when a product, service or process is developed and marketed even though it is highly problematical whether or not market demand is sufficient or can be created. These cases are referred to as supply-side marketing, by which we mean:

> *Supply-side marketing, then, refers to any instance when a product can create a market . . . in other words, a demand . . . for itself in lieu of the conventional other-way-around. Or, put another way, the product is responsible for the demand, rather than the demand being responsible for the product.*[3]

Supply-side marketing is fraught with risk; the two go hand-in-hand. But supply-side marketing—and those entrepreneurs with the tolerance for risk and courage to see their ideas through—is responsible for the technological innovations throughout industrial history. If assorted individuals and companies had waited for customer demand to justify the need for developing and marketing a new product, many technological innovations would have been a longer time coming.

Albeit supply-side marketing is inherently high risk, there are ways to mitigate the risk. Our extensive research among high-technology companies, which resulted in our book *Marketing High Technology,* enables us to make some suggestions along these lines.[4]

FRONTIER MARKETS

One could argue that what appear to be nonexistent markets are really situations of latent demand. However, semantical debates miss this essential point: At the time the revolutionary product or service is being conceptualized and developed, there is no market for it. The existence of a market is contingent upon *both* a demand and a way (an applied technology) to fulfill it.

Obviously, a comprehensive cancer or AIDS cure would have tremendous market demand, but the market for most technological breakthroughs is not so manifest. Consider several supposedly expert opinions regarding the practicality and commercial possibilities of the then-new technologies:

—*"What can be more palpably absurd than the prospect held out of locomotives traveling twice as fast as stagecoaches?"*—The Quarterly Review, *1825.*

—*"I must confess that my imagination, in spite even of spurring, refuses to see any sort of submarine doing anything but suffocating its crew and floundering at sea."—H. G. Wells, 1901.*

—*"The ordinary 'horseless carriage' is at present a luxury for the wealthy; and although its price will probably fall in the future, it will never, of course, come into as common use as the bicycle."*—The Literary Digest, *1889.*

—*"While theoretically and technically television may be feasible, commercially and financially, I consider it an impossibility, a development of which we need waste little time dreaming."—Lee DeForest (American inventor and pioneer in radio and TV), 1926.*

—*"There is not the slightest indication that (nuclear) energy will ever be obtainable. It would mean that the atom would have to be shattered at will."—Albert Einstein, 1932.*

—*"This is the biggest fool thing we have ever done . . . The bomb will never go off, and I speak as an expert in explosives."—Admiral William Leahy, advising President Harry Truman, 1945.*

Imagine a corporate CEO assessing whether or not to proceed with Research and Development (R&D) and commercialization of a new product or process based upon the *negative* recommendation of a Lee DeForest or an Albert Einstein. A CEO might well have said, for instance, "DeForest says the commercial and financial possibilities for this television concept are remote at best. That's good enough for me." Fortunately, for the sake of technological progress and mankind, it was not "good enough" for RCA.

RESEARCHING PIONEER MARKETS

For purposes of market research and planning, we have found it useful, indeed essential, to distinguish between market-driven companies that operate on the demand-side and innovation-driven companies that operate on the supply-side. We have explained the difference between the two as follows:

> *. . . in market-driven high technology, the main directions for R&D are from marketing. R&D's reaction comes in the form of guidance on what is technically feasible and ideas from scientific circles. Formal marketing research, typical to consumer and industrial markets, is helping high-tech managers guide R&D . . . Innovation-driven high technology offers a marked contrast, as R&D provides the stimulus and marketing officials must find applications or simply sell the product. These efforts can help create new markets by applying lab breakthroughs to largely unperceived buyer needs.*[5]

Naturally some companies, especially large ones, simultaneously have R&D projects that are market-driven and others that are innovation-driven.

Market-driven and innovation-driven R&D require different marketing research approaches and techniques. The marketing research techniques most appropriate to commercializing innovation-driven R&D fall mainly in the domain of qualitative rather than quantitative marketing research. Many of the more mathematically-based methods of marketing research used in market-driven ventures (i.e., more mature products and services) require an abundance of data, usually obtained from a random sample of people or firms so that statistical inferences can be made. This requirement is difficult to meet in high-tech industries, for two reasons.

First, whenever markets are being created or obsoleted rapidly by significant product breakthroughs, as they often are in innovation-driven high technology, not much is available in the way of valid historical data. As one executive puts it, "Our company doesn't put much faith in surveys based on what consumers said yesterday."

Second, data obtained from prospective buyers via traditional data collection techniques (telephone interviews, paper-and-pencil mail surveys, and the like) are of dubious value for answering questions about products based on new technologies. Our evidence is overwhelming that in many high-tech markets, consumers are too confused—sometimes even scared or intimidated and not too strong of descriptors—to offer much direction to a company.

The product-education (demonstration) opportunities and indepth probing afforded by qualitative research, such as focus group discussions, temper these kinds of confusion/intimidation problems. Thus, it is not surprising that our research indicates that focus groups and nominal groups, in conjunction with several more sophisticated techniques, are popular means in high-tech companies for generating new product ideas and evaluating potential market demand (see Exhibit 1).

In addition to the marketing research techniques used in innovation-driven ventures, "who to ask" is terribly important in terms of obtaining answers that are truly helpful in making go/no-go decisions and designing "winning" marketing strategies. It is far more desirable to have opinions from 10 buyer-innovator types; opinions, for instance obtained in a two-hour focus group, than to have judgments from a random sample of 1,000 people; most of whom only vaguely can conceive of a new product, its technological benefits and how well it might fit into their work-styles or life-styles.

Another more accurate indicator is the Delphi technique. As used by a jury of six experts, this method is likely to give more correct estimates of how successful dramatically new products may be in the marketplace next year than are the predictions of the most sophisticated econometric model built that must be fed a plethora of historical or cross-sectional data.

We have found that the techniques which use innovative customers, or industrial users in new product research, and methods which use the Delphi method in forecasting are popular among *successful* high-tech companies. For example, in one of our studies, three-fourths of the firms we asked indicated that they have attempted to test new product concepts on innovators; and the vast majority of them reported that

EXHIBIT 1. Assessment of Qualitative Techniques in Generating New Product Ideas

Rank	Usage %		Not Helpful (%)	Helpful/ Extremely (%)
1	78	Brainstorming	13	87
2	58	Focus group	17	83
3	28	Nominal group	14	86
4	46	Attribute listing	26	74
5	42	Forced relationships	38	62
6	20	Morphological analysis	10	90

their "hit rate" on predicting how successful a new product will be in the marketplace was markedly improved.

Another study we conducted, this one specifically in the robotics industry, offered even more corroboration that indepth discussions with current or potential customers is usually the best way for a company to uncover ideas for new products as well as evaluate the feasibility or market potential of technological breakthroughs. We have found that customer-innovators (those who are typically among the first to buy new products) are an especially wealthy source of useful information about new product or application issues.

CUSTOMERS BUY BENEFITS AND VALUE, NOT TECHNOLOGIES

A common error in innovation-driven ventures is that the firm concerns itself with improved technologies rather than improved customer benefits. The reality is, customers buy benefits, not technologies. The relevant question is *not* whether the new technology is superior to the existing technology. Instead, the salient query is whether the new technology provides a bundle of benefits to customers, such that they are eager to abandon the older technology.

Numerous examples can be cited where a new technology did not catch on because customers were comfortable with the existing technology or were not willing to pay an increased price for something technically better. Emerson was wrong; if you build a better mousetrap, people will not necessarily beat a path to your door. Take Emerson's mousetrap adage literally; from a technological standpoint, a better mousetrap can be built than the wire/wood/cheese technology that has been so enduring. Yet, people like the wire and wood trap and are not likely to abandon it for something technologically better, but *more costly.*

So the key to evaluating technological breakthroughs is to ask objectively whether the new technology provides better *benefits* to the customer at a price he or she is willing to pay. Is the new technology more beneficial and a better value than the old technology it will make obsolete or render less useful? For example, most automobile customers could care less whether their cars start with "points" or electronically, just so they start reliably at an affordable price.

Think about the customer benefits of these pairs of products or services: hand-held calculator vs. slide rule; television vs. radio; VCR's vs. purchasing tapes or going to the movies and horseless carriage vs. horse-drawn carriage. In every case, the replacement technology was obviously superior to the older technology. Still, in no instance did a vast market emerge until the *perceived value* was established in enough potential customers. For instance, it took the original Henry Ford to develop the assembly line manufacture of automobiles that broke open the market for cars. Robots will replace human labor only in cases where it can be justified from the standpoint of costs vs. benefits. Because of labor costs, Third World countries may find it difficult to justify robotizing their manufacturing unless this technology can provide inordinate production advantages.

Innovation-driven ventures must meet several tests, then, if they are to hope to obsolete existing products and markets and create new ones: Namely, (1) Is the new technology more beneficial to prospective buyers in terms of improving the quality of their life-styles or work-styles? (2) Will it generally be perceived as such? (3) Will the new technology be seen as a better value (price vs. benefits) than the extant technology? If not, when will it be and what will it take in the way of persuasive marketing to make it so?

Interestingly, at this writing, growth in the in-home personal computer market has slowed considerably. Why? Because the *average* person and household does not see how the benefits of an in-home personal computer are worth the price that must be paid. Obviously, the market will eventually explode, but when? Once the technology yields enough benefits that can be communicated to those in the vast middle-American market so that they are willing to pay the price. And if history repeats itself, the price will be considerably less in inflation-adjusted, real terms than it is today. Color televisions, microwave ovens, autos and other technological innovations followed this pattern.

ESTABLISHING COMMERCIAL PRIORITIES

Opportunity prioritization is—or should be—the high technology company's critical initial step toward commercialization of lab output.[6] By this we mean that, subsequent to indepth marketing research on market potential, the firm must decide which existing or presently non-existent "future" market(s) it is interested in pursuing. When someone says market potential, market demand or market research, it is assumed that a relevant market has been identified and is firmly in mind. For example, the nomenclatures automobile market, or microcomputer market or soap market conjure up clear pictures to most people. But in innovation-driven high technology, this is often not the case.

Take biotechnology. The potential applications of genetic engineering are countless. A biotech company could very well decide *not* to compete in pharmaceutical/medical markets at all, although these are the applications most people think of for biotechnology R&D. A biotech company might, for instance, "create" markets in agribusiness (e.g., disease-free orchids) or environmental pollution cleanup (e.g., oil spills). Similarly, the fields of lasers, robotics and fiber optics have many possible applications (markets) that do not exist today.

Any R&D breakthrough needs to be evaluated within the context of a formal market opportunity identification analysis. In this regard, future opportunities in known and prospective or developing industries are formally assessed. After completing this stage, a company will have identified several possible applications for its new technology, applications that will likely cut across industries. And the firm will have a sense of the future prospects for these industries. At this point, some applications or industries can be eliminated from further consideration, for various reasons.

After a thorough screening, the industries and related applications that remain all will have some potential. Realistically, however, the company will be unable to exploit fully all the potential applications that have been identified, even if all the industries appear to have exceptional prospects. However, before doing the marketing research needed to better target opportunities, it is vital for the company to do some ordering of, or establishing priorities for, the prospective industries. The cost alone of undertaking extensive marketing research necessitates first designating the industry or industries that look to offer the most profitable long-term opportunities.

Once this priority-setting task is achieved, the company can turn its attention to conducting some of the indepth marketing research, particularly qualitative research among potential customers, that we have mentioned. For example, primary (original) research can be carried out to obtain more specific information on possible demand of lasers in the clothing manufacturing business. (Lasers are used to cut patterns.) With the resulting feedback as guidance, more informed choices can be made in the actual ranking and selection of target markets.[7]

Innovation-driven companies must put the "market" in market research. That is, before market research can be undertaken effectively, it must be determined what existing or future market(s) the company has in mind. Under few circumstances should a marketing researcher be turned loose to find an application for an R&D breakthrough without some firm direction as to what market(s) the company has in mind. Otherwise, the researcher is left to flounder about. But is employing good marketing research techniques and establishing commercial priorities sufficient? No, there is an additional ingredient to consider.

ROLE OF ENTREPRENEURSHIP

Indeed, effective marketing to frontier markets requires far more than establishing commercial priorities and corporate reliance on marketing research and market analysis. It also depends on entrepreneurial spirit, the right corporate culture. Marketing research and market analysis can make supply-side marketing more calculated (informed) risk-taking, but there comes a time when management must rely on intuition and fortitude to go ahead with a project. Former ITT CEO, Harold Geneen, makes the point in his book, *Managing,* that almost all large companies which think they are entrepreneurial are, on closer examination, really not. They may fund highly risky projects, but, even if the projects fail entirely, the amount of assets of risk is so small that the net effect on corporate earnings is virtually imperceptible. Because of their fiduciary responsibility to stockholders, most *Fortune* 1000 CEOs must take mainly trustee roles rather than entrepreneurial ones. In Geneen's view, "Betting the Company" is characteristic of startup ventures, but is inappropriate for large going concerns, unless the company is in big trouble. (Which paves the way for a Lee Iacocca, who does bet the company.) And that is precisely why the net job growth in the United States in recent years has come from small business, not from the *Fortune* 500.

Geneen is right; the entrepreneurial spirit embodied in supply-side marketing is rare in large companies. Even so, exceptions exist. There are companies wherein the culture promotes innovation and entrepreneurship. And we know for sure that corporate culture, whether it be a *Fortune* 500 or a startup venture, is crucial if supply-side marketing is to have a fighting chance to succeed.

EIGHT MASTERS LISTED

Fortune magazine, with the help of respected business executives and academics, has identified what are considered to be eight "corporate masters of innovation." Although these companies (American Airlines, Apple Computer, Campbell Soup, General Electric, Intel, Merck, 3M, and Philip Morris) are all large ones, they have managed to retain a culture conducive to innovation and entrepreneurship. We believe that the basic philosophies which pervade these eight companies are essential to effective supply-side marketing, irrespective of company size.

What are some of these philosophies?

- Strong sense of corporate mission.
- Paranoid about change and competitors.
- Devotion to marketing.
- Decentralization (but not anarchy).
- Unpunished subordinates' failures (except for incompetence).
- Mandatory interdisciplinary communications (e.g., between marketing and R&D).[8]

We do not intend to discuss each of these here but do want to elaborate on one characteristic to point out the managerial adroitness it takes to translate an entrepreneurial corporate culture into a functioning system that truly works. A host of recent articles, books and speeches say that a company has to decentralize to encourage and promote innovation and entrepreneurship, which generally is correct. But it is one thing for a CEO to say, "Let's decentralize to promote an entrepreneurial culture," and quite another to implement it.

Take two contrasting examples. IBM has been eminently successful in separating its microcomputer business unit from the remainder of the company, philosophically and physically. In spite of a few setbacks with the PC Jr., the IBM's Boca Raton decentralization was, and is, a great success story. Another computer company, Atari, decentralized with opposite results. When James Morgan became head of Atari, he found tremendous redundancy in R&D that was sapping the ailing company of what strength it had left. When Morgan asked why one engineer lived in Louisville, Kentucky, where Atari had no R&D facilities, he was told the engineer liked living and working there. So, if not properly managed, decentralized can degenerate into near anarchy.

Moreover, decisions about decentralization necessitate considerable thought and study. It might pay to decentralize marketing, but not R&D. For instance, some years ago, Hewlett-Packard mostly centralized its R&D in order to curb R&D redundancy within its divisions and to promote intracorporate R&D sharing.

The point is, there is a great deal of glibness today about how innovativeness and entrepreneurship must start at the top (with the CEO), then pervade the organization, and finally be stimulated through decentralization. We agree with these precepts, but with the caveat that they are hard to implement in practice. Marketing to pioneer markets (i.e., supply-side marketing) requires an entrepreneurial spirit, the right corporate culture, which, in turn, must be achieved through proper incentives to employees, devotion to marketing, carefully orchestrated decentralization and the rest of the aforementioned characteristics of the "masters of innovation." Which is why only a small percentage of all companies are masters of it.

We want to stress that the need for supply-side marketing should not be used by a company as an *excuse* to develop and commercialize a product, service or process. Too frequently, companies devote time, money and effort to products that *realistically* have little or no chance to succeed commercially. Maybe some engineer is enamored with the technology behind the product, or management lets its hope to recoup the company's investment cloud its judgment.

Supply-side marketing is risky, but it is *calculated* risk-taking. Marketing to frontier markets requires strategy and work. It demands a facilitating corporate culture and organization, a focus on potential customers and customer benefits, a healthy dose of (especially qualitative) marketing research guided by lucid market and industry priorities laid down by top management, thorough analysis based on the market research and . . . intuition and fortitude.

Occasionally in this article, we refer to our prior research. During the period 1982-1984, we conducted an extensive formal study among some 125 leading high technology firms. The techniques employed in the various phases of this study included in-person and telephone interviews, questionnaires, and case studies. Augmenting this formal research were our consulting and conference presentation experiences. Since 1984, our formal and informal research activities in high technology marketing, in multiple industries and companies, has continued, thus creating an expanded data base. The data presented in Exhibit 1, for example, were collected in the earlier phases of the ongoing research project.

ENDNOTES

1. Akio Morita, "Creativity in Modern Industry," *Omni,* March 1981, p. 6. Reprinted by permission.
2. William L. Shanklin, "Supply-Side Marketing Can Restore Yankee Ingenuity," *Research Management,* May-June 1983, pp. 20–25.
3. *Ibid,* p. 20.
4. For a more comprehensive discussion, see William L. Shanklin and John K. Ryans, Jr., *Marketing High Technology* (Lexington, Massachusetts: Lexington Books, D.C. Heath and Company, 1984).
5. William L. Shanklin and John K. Ryans, Jr., "Organizing for High-Tech Marketing," *Harvard Business Review,* November-December, 1984, pp. 164–171.
6. See for elaboration, John K. Ryans, Jr. and William L. Shanklin, "High-Tech Megatenets: 10 Principles of High Technology Market Behavior," *Business Marketing,* September 1984, pp. 100–106; and also, John K. Ryans, Jr. and William L. Shanklin, "Positioning and Selecting Target Markets," *Research Management,* September-October, 1984, pp. 28–32.
7. Shanklin and Ryans, *Marketing High Technology,* pp. 64–69.
8. Stratford P. Sherman, "Eight Big Masters of Innovation," *Fortune,* October 15, 1984, pp. 66–84.

REFERENCES

Alavi Maryani, "A Meta Analysis," *MIS Quarterly*, March 1992.

Rajiv K. Sinha, "A Split Hazard Model," *Journal of Marketing Research*, February 1992.

David Mathe, "Influence of Technology and Demand Factors On Firm Size and Industrial Structure," *Research Policy,* February 1992.

Higgins and Shanklin, "Market Acceptance For High-Technology Consumer Products," *Journal of Consumer Marketing,* Winter 1992.

John C. Totten
Vice President Analytical and Technical Products
Nielsen Marketing Research
Northbrook, Illinois

Mike Duffy
Director of Forecasting and Planning
Kraft General Foods, Inc.
Glenview, Illinois

CHAPTER 39

MARKETING TECHNOLOGY AND CONSUMER SCANNING

INTRODUCTION

In this chapter, we will review the uses of data collected from electronic scanning at the point-of-sale (POS). Scanning systems are in place in most major grocery outlets, many drug stores, and major mass merchandisers such as Kmart and Wal-Mart. In addition, a variety of specialty businesses such as video rental outlets use POS systems to capture sales and rental transactions. Our discussion will center on the uses of POS scanning systems by manufacturers and retailers of consumer packaged goods of the type found in grocery or drug stores. However, most of the methods discussed are easily adaptable to any marketing operation able to collect and accumulate transaction data by individual line item in the product line offering.

Information on product sales is collected by manufacturers for a variety of reasons, but there are three major reasons: to assess the level of consumer demand for a product and detect changes in that demand pattern; to assess the strength of competitive products, detect changes in competitive marketing activity, and assess the impact of competitive changes on products of interests; and to provide information that will assist the sales force in obtaining improved treatment of the manufacturers product by the retailer.

The typical distribution system for consumer goods is a complex network of interrelated activities involving manufacturers, distributors, brokers, wholesalers, and retailers. The manufacturer may not have much control over final retail prices because the costs for the intermediate distribution functions must be absorbed into the final retail price. Fluctuations in inventory levels throughout the system generally lead to patterns of manufacturer shipments that when using only manufacturer shipment data may vary significantly from the pattern of consumer demand for the product. The direct link between competitive marketing actions and shipments of a manufacturer's own product is generally so confounded by the number of competitors and the existence of inventory fluctuations throughout the system that little analysis can be done of the link between competitive activity and brand sales.

For manufacturers of consumer packaged goods, the data collection issues were initially addressed in the 1930s with the establishment of audits of retail sales. Art Nielsen established an audit service that used a sample of stores audited approximately every two months and provided estimates of the pricing and sales levels existing for a brand and its competitors. The results of this sample could be "syndicated," or sold to multiple manufacturers in the category at a considerable savings in cost versus the cost an individual manufacturer would incur in collecting similar data. As time passed, a variety of services became available to measure competitive activity, such as newspaper feature advertising, radio and TV advertising, and in-store display activity. Syndicated data from other points in the distribution system, such as warehouse withdrawal data, became available.

In the 1960s, a coding standard for consumer products was established. The Universal Product Code (UPC) system allowed manufacturers to assign a unique code to each of their products that could be read by retail store scanning systems, and used to look up retail prices and to update retail volume movement records. In the late 1970s, grocery stores began to adopt POS electronic scanning systems to read and process the UPC codes. This allowed electronic accumulation of data. In the mid 1980s, several companies announced syndicated data services based on POS scanner data for price and volume information with supplemental audit data on retailer feature ads and in-store display activity. By 1993, Nielsen Market Research and Information Resources, Inc. were the two largest suppliers of such information in the United States, and both were expanding internationally. Major retailers, such as Kmart and Wal-Mart, provide direct sales information to 50 to 70% of their suppliers, but usually do not provide information on competitive sales.

Data on retail store sales performs a useful function, but does not allow examination of the behavior of individual purchasers of a brand or product category. Many important questions exist that require review of individual buyer behavior. For example, in planning an advertising campaign, an important question is often "What fraction of buyers of the product category have purchased my product in the preceding year?" If the answer is a low fraction, then the objective of the advertising campaign might be to persuade non-buyers to try my brand. However, if the answer is a high fraction, then the campaign objective might be to encourage higher rates of repeat buying of the product. Such information might be collected by a survey of consumers, asking a broad cross-section about their recent purchase and usage of products in the category of interest. To examine the behavior of individual consumer purchasing over time, a number of services have been formed to collect and summarize information from consumers via a written purchase diary that is collected and processed on a periodic basis. Such written diaries are most useful when the distribution system is complex and fragmented, or when little POS data capture exists. The workload on the consumer to maintain the diaries restricts data collection to relatively few product categories per panelist.

POS retail scanning systems gave the ability to capture the complete transaction detail of an individual consumer, and the ability to match this information with the list of competitive products stocked in a store and their pricing levels. For marketing activities aimed directly at individual consumers, such as couponing and media advertising, consumer purchase data is combined with information on the activity, such as coupon distribution, coupon redemption, or media exposure in sales estimation models.

In the sections to follow, we shall review some of the common business problems where analyses of scanner data are used, and explore some of the emerging trends that are changing "traditional" analysis methods. The extreme improvements in computing cost/performance in the past decade make possible the processing of large volumes of detail data, and the application of increasingly complex models for data analysis and exception reporting. The discovery of significant differences in consumer response to manufacturer and retailer marketing activity among brands in a category, and across markets for a brand, is now focusing analysis activity on individual retail accounts in a market, and even on individual stores within the account for a truly "micro-marketing" approach.

INFORMATION ON SALES

The Beer Game

MIT's Sloan School of Management has developed a number of management simulation games to illustrate the difficulties management faces in a complex production-distribution environment. In the "Beer Game" reported on by Professor John Sterman, a distribution system consists of retailer, wholesaler, distributor, and factory. Information is limited to analysis of orders and shipments. Consumer demand is not known in advance, and revealed only to retailers on a week-by-week basis as the game proceeds.

Typical experiments start with a steady level of weekly demand and have a simple step function 100% increase in retail demand after about 1/6 of the game weeks have been played. The results reported are that the games almost always exhibit three key patterns: (1) Oscillation—orders and inventories show large amplitude swings on about a 20-week cycle; (2) Amplification—the further removed from retail sales, the greater the swings in orders, with peak orders at factory level usually more than double the peak order rate at retail; and (3) Phase Lag—the order rates peak later and later as you move from retailer to factory. After the game is complete, participants at levels other than the retailer may exhibit complete disbelief when the simple nature of the demand function is revealed. Professor Sterman reports finding similar oscillation, amplification, and phase lag in the U.S. Industrial Production series for materials, intermediate goods, and final products.

Manufacturer Shipments

Most manufacturers maintain detail files on their own shipments. These files usually originated as a by-product of the accounting system, and are used as a basis for production planning, demand forecasting, and inventory management. Shipment data may be difficult to match to consumer demand at levels of detail finer than all-outlet annual sales. There is usually a complete lack of comparable information on competitive brands, so it is difficult to tell from shipment data alone whether increases or decreases in shipments are due to general changes in category sales patterns, or due to a competitive activity change that yields a more or less favorable competitive positioning for your own brand. Retail trade promotion is an important contributor to fluctuations in manufacturer shipments. In recent years, the allocation of funds among trade and consumer activities has been shifting toward a greater and greater proportion of manufacturers' marketing expenditures directed toward retail support activities (see Exhibit 1). Current estimates are that for many manufacturers, over 50% of their total marketing budget is spent on trade promotion activities.

Trade promotion activities generate significant short-term increases of 2 to 20 times normal retail sales on the promoted item. The variability of actual results from the expected average promotional sales is extremely high, causing the retailer to order extra stock for protection against unexpectedly high demand. If there is extra product left after the promotion, the retailer often reprices this product to normal price, and pockets the manufacturers' promotional allowance on this product as additional profit. The manufacturer sees a significant decline in post-promotion orders as this excess inventory is worked off of retail shelves.

A second practice associated with manufacturer trade promotions is "forward-buying." The promotional discounts offered by the manufacturer are usually sufficiently attractive to make it profitable for the retailer to purchase additional inventory beyond that needed for stock-out protection during the promotion. If planned promotional activities are announced in advance, then retailers may delay ordering and deplete normal inventories in order to restock with lower cost promotional product. This behavior leads to a marked decline in manufacturer orders and shipments just prior to the start of the promotion. It is currently accepted that most retailers buy about 90% of frequently promoted consumer package goods on deal, but sell about 60% at the normal price.

A manufacturer in this situation can obtain almost no information from recent shipments about the probable impact of reducing the number of deals at retail. It is also not uncommon to find that the dollar amount of promotional allowances is significantly larger than the manufacturers' pre-tax profit. Conversely, the promotional allowances offered by the manufacturer are currently estimated to amount to between 1/3 and 1/2 of the retailers pre-tax profit. Management of this large dollar transfer between manufacturer and retailer requires detailed information on the impact at retail of the various activities that might be supported by promotional dollars.

EXHIBIT 1. Ad Trade Promotion Expenditure Importance

Share of Expenditures by Type

	1981	1982	1983	1984	1985	1986	1987	1988	1989	1990	1991
Total	$29	$32	$37	$42	$46	$52	$56	$61	$65	$69	$73
Trade Promotion	34%	36%	37%	37%	38%	40%	41%	43%	46%	47%	50%
Consumer Promotion	23%	25%	26%	27%	27%	26%	25%	24%	25%	25%	25%
Advertising Expenditures	43%	39%	37%	36%	35%	34%	34%	33%	30%	28%	25%

Source: Donnelley Marketing
Source: Nielsen Marketing Research Estimates

In summary, manufacturer shipments cover sales from all outlets and account for total movement, but may include promotional volume surges, pre- and post-promotion dips, crowded promotion calendars, and may mask huge inventory stockpiling-depletion swings in the distribution system. Shipment information is difficult to match to consumer demand in geographic subdivisions of total sales area due to diversion, out-of-stocks, and lack of information on competition. Even if these concerns are covered, the oscillation, amplification, and phase-lag relations present in a multilevel distribution system obscures the relation between manufacturer marketing actions and consumer demand.

Retail Sales Data

Retail sales data is close to final demand, but suffers from a number of measurement problems. In the complex distribution system that exists for consumer packaged goods in the United States, products may be sold through many different types of retail outlets including grocery stores, drug stores, convenience stores, and mass-merchandise stores. As population growth has slowed, each outlet type has viewed expansion into products normally handled by other channels as growth opportunities. This channel "blurring" has made it difficult to measure sales across different channels in a consistent and comparable manner.

In order to monitor levels of marketing activities, a number of auxiliary data reporting services are available. These include monitoring of coupon redemption activity, radio, TV, print advertising by the manufacturer, and the feature-ad and in-store display activity by retailers. In most cases, these services provide information on competitive activity in addition to information on the manufacturer's own brand. The increasing popularity of in-store advertising, POS promotional material, and store-specific marketing activity (such as instantly printed coupons or electronic coupons) gives rise to a number of niche opportunities for auditing and syndicating information on new forms of in-store marketing activities.

Syndicated data on store sales available in 1993 combines many of these data collection methods into an extremely comprehensive database. Using POS scanners, data on individual item sales at the store level is captured weekly(or even daily). This data consists of an item code, a count of items moved, and either an item price or total dollar sales amount. To this is added the results of manual audits indicating the presence of retailer ad-features and/or in-store displays. Mathematical models compare current pricing to past pricing to assess whether there is a price reduction from "normal" or "base" price. Other models are employed to estimate the probable level of sales ("baseline" sales) that would have occurred in the absence of any in-store promotion such as price discounts, ads, or displays. Information on the availability of manufacturer supported coupon activity may be supplied from audits of coupon drops, from consumer diary reporting, or increasingly, from POS scanning of the coupons. Media information on TV advertising is measured in gross rating points (GRPs), and may be entered at the product-market-week level from syndicated services that monitor media commercial activity. The product code can be linked to master files containing descriptive information about the product such as brand name, package size, product form, flavor, ingredients, color, and many other attributes. The store identification code can be linked to master files containing descriptive information about the store layout, general pricing policy, and descriptive information about the types of consumers located in the stores trading area (usually based on U.S. census data).

The purchaser of syndicated store data may add additional data, such as shipment and order information for sales to the retailer, the types of promotional incentives and allowances offered to the retailer, and information on marketing activity performed that is not measured by the syndicated data, such as sweepstakes, contests, mail-in offers, product sampling programs, and non-traditional marketing activities, such as in-store television, in-store ads delivered by a variety of different vehicles, production cost or sales margin, and other relevant activity. For the balance of this chapter, we ignore such additions and focus on the data provided in syndicated sales databases, the organizational units of the manufacturer and retailer who might use such data, their issues, and the manner in which the data is reported and analyzed to support decision making on marketing issues.

Consumer Purchase Data

In an electronic consumer panel, data collection on individual purchases is coupled with collection of retail store sales data, with audits of ad features and in-store display data. Usage of coupons is matched with the purchase data. For a subset of households, television viewing is also monitored. The panelist is required to provide demographic information on an annual basis and to show an identification card on each purchase occasion. This low workload leads to lower attrition rates over time among the POS panelists than those experienced in written diary panels.

Databases covering consumer behavior over extended periods of time allow extensive analyses of brand loyalty, and the ability of promotional activity to influence brand switching. Having the store data available allows review of the availability and pricing of brands not chosen when a category purchase was made. The ability of ad-features to shift consumer purchases among competing retailers can be studied. An important study area is the source of increased volume received by a brand when a retail promotion occurred. Analysis of purchase timing allows decomposition of the increased volume sold during promotional periods into that due to stockpiling by loyal brand buyers, that portion due to brand switching, and that portion due to increased category consumption.

Both Nielsen and IRI offer large scale consumer purchase panels with scanner collected data. Panel product purchase data is not normally used for tracking and control purposes, but is used in understanding the impact of various marketing activities, assessing the degree of competitive interaction among brands, and for understanding the nature of seasonal variations in category sales. When there are puzzling results in the retail store sales data, consumer panel data can be an important resource for diagnostic purchases.

DATABASE CONTENTS

Detail Observations

The typical detail observation in a retail store movement database is for a single store, one UPC item for one week. The detail movement data collected directly from scanners for the UPC is:

1. *Unit sales movement*—a count of the number of items sold in the store over the week.
2. *Dollar sales movement*—this may represent actual dollar movement, possibly at several different prices during the week, or may be the most recent price multiplied by unit movement.
3. *Information on usage of retailer coupons may be included*—most probably the number of retailer coupons used on purchases of the UPC item. Average value of retail coupons redeemed may also be included.
4. *To the scanned data, causal detail such as information on the presence and type of retail feature ads and in-store displays may be added from store audits.*

Finally, fields based on proprietary models may be added to the detail data. Both IRI and Nielsen provide:

1. *Base price*—This quantity is the output of models designed to estimate the "normal" or "expected" price for the item in the store week. This field is used together with actual price to generate a model-based classification of some prices as "temporary price reduction" (TPR) pricing, and therefore to classify the week as a "TPR" promotional week.
2. *Base volume*—this quantity is the output of models designed to estimate the "normal" or "expected" unit sales for the item in the absence of retail sales promotional activity (ad-feature, in-store display, or temporary price reduction (TPR). The typical retail grocery store generates about 15,000 to 25,000 observations of detailed movement data a week.

Relational Data

Using relational database methods, a large variety of descriptive information may be merged with the detailed movement data. There are many descriptive elements that can be related to stores. A store is related to its parent organization (chain, independent, etc.), and is related by geography to city, county, market, state, sales regions, and sales divisions. Store format codes may describe the layout of the store, management philosophy (hi-lo versus everyday low price) and stocking policies (full-line stocking versus limited stocking of high-velocity items). Store geodemographics describe the socioeconomic characteristics of consumer households in the store's trading area. Store size is a measure of the relative selling power of a store. Predominant in grocery stores is the all-commodity volume (ACV) measure of store size given by total dollar sales across all items in the store. A related, and easier to generate measure is "scan dollars—the total dollar sales of all items in the store that are UPC coded. While store ACV or scan dollar actually varies on a week to week basis, an annualized number updated on a quarterly or annual basis is often used.

Related to weeks are a number of items such as assignment to months, quarters, and even to year. Weeks may be flagged as "holiday weeks" or "key pay weeks," which allows retrieval, summary, and contrasts of these weeks versus "regular" weeks. Related to the UPC code are many characteristics—manufacturer, brand, size, flavor, special packaging, color, form, ingredient, and assorted nutritional qualifiers (low-fat, low-salt, low cholesterol, etc.). UPCs are usually assigned to competitive product categories, although the exact definition of the UPCs in a category may vary from manufacturer to manufacturer. "Volume equivalency" conversion factors convert a UPC's item movement into a standard category volume measure (quarts, pounds, cups of coffee, etc.). The unit of standard volume may vary from manufacturer to manufacturer within a category, and reflects the individual manufacturers view of the comparability of the individual UPCs.

Selling Conditions

Store-week-UPC detail is often characterized by "selling conditions." These are represented by true/false variables indicating whether the condition is true for the particular store-week-UPC combination. The most common conditions characterize promotional activities that may generate significantly different sales rates. In this class are "any feature," "any display," and "any TPR" (temporary price reduction). These conditions may be further divided; "any feature" may be true if any of the following conditions are true: large (A-size) feature ad, medium (B-size), or small (line ad or C-ad).

Another class of selling conditions is generated by converting continuous variables into ranges. These conditions are usually specific to a product category. Some examples are: unit price at or below $.99, unit price from $1.00 to $1.49; unit price above $1.49; no price discount; price discount below 10%; discount 10 to 24%; or discount above 25%. More complex definitions may involve comparison across several data records. Ranges of price difference versus competition fall into this class. Even with relatively few ranges defined on price discounts or price differences versus competition, the full list of possible conditions may number in the hundreds.

A short list of possible conditions (under 50) will cover most of the mutually exclusive conditions under which sales are made. A popular list of selling conditions is given by pairing a price discount condition list with a list of feature/display conditions. The feature/display list is:

1. "Major Feature" (A or B ad) with no display
2. "All other Features" with no display
3. "Major Display"
4. "Minor Display"
5. "Major Display with Major Feature"
6. "Major Display with A/O Feature"
7. "Minor Display with Major Feature"
8. "Minor Display with A/O Feature"

The price discount list is:

1. Price discount, if any, less than 5%
2. Price discount in the 5 to 15% range
3. Price discount in the 15 to 25% range
4. Price discount in the 25 to 35% range
5. Price discount over 35%

REPORTING SCHEMES

Reporting of the data is organized into a four- or five-dimensional scheme, where an individual number in the report has the following identifiers or indices: geography, product, time, and either fact-condition combined or fact and condition.

A hierarchial summary scheme is often imposed on the data. The lowest level of detail reported is usually not the store-week-UPC information, but some slightly higher level of summarization. The geography dimension is most commonly summarized, with stores combined to give a total for a common store management unit (such as grocery chain) within a market. Low-level reporting then is usually at chain-week-UPC summary of detail, or even summarized to market-week-UPC. The second most common summarization is to combine like UPCs into a brand size summary. Many consumer products have a number of UPC items that are packaged, priced, and promoted similarly, varying only in flavor and color. For business tracking and gross analysis, similar UPCs are summarized into a brand-size-item, the lowest level reported.

Typical summary schemes are:

Geography: Chain → Market → Region → Country
Time: Week → Month → Quarter → Year, or Week → Bimonth → Year
Product: UPC → Size, Form, Flavor → Major Segment → Brand → Manufacturer → Category
As many as 8 to 9 levels commonly exist in the product hierarchy.
Condition: The following minimal set of mutually exclusive conditions are often used, with summarization to "Total all conditions."

No promotion,
TPR with no feature or display,
Any feature without display,
Any display without feature, and
Any feature with display.

FACTS

Auxiliary Facts

To expand the usefulness of the unit and dollar movement data, a number of auxiliary facts may be derived. Some examples are:

1. Discount = base price minus average price
2. % Discount = 100* discount/base price
3. Sales rates = any of the unit or equivalized volume facts may be divided by the outlet coverage fact to give a sales rate fact.
   (eg: Unit sales per million ACV, average sales per store selling)
4. Promotion efficiency index (PEI) = 100 × equivalent volume sales ÷ equivalized base volume sales
5. Incremental volume sales = equivalized volume sales - equivalized base volume sales

The imposition of a hierarchy allows calculation of many new facts that relate an individual cell fact to other facts at the same or higher level in the hierarchy. Examples include:

1. Market share
2. Index versus year ago or versus previous period (for any measure)
3. % change versus year ago or previous period (for any measure)
4. Rank (usually on a product of geography or condition dimension)

Addability of Facts

By adding volume and dollar facts across cells, and then recomputing price facts, many subtotals of facts can be computed from summary databases. For example, a brand's volume is simply the sum of the volumes of the individual brand sizes, even at a market level.

However, there are many facts that require a return to the most basic store-week-UPC level data to create. These are the "non-addable facts," and are associated with classifying "conditions" when multiple product items are combined in a time period, or when multiple time periods are combined. As an example, suppose that Brand A has two sizes—Size 1 and Size 2. In a four-week period in a retail account, Size 1 is featured for two of the four weeks, and Size 2 is featured for two of the four weeks. If they were the same two weeks (both sizes of Brand A featured together), then Brand A was featured in two of the four weeks. But if Size 1 was featured in the first 2 weeks, and Size 2 was featured in the second two weeks, then Brand A was featured in all four weeks. The possibility of overlap means that the feature activity levels for the brand cannot be obtained by adding the activity levels of the individual brands. Similar problems occur in determining the levels of distribution coverage for a brand with multiple sizes, in determining the brand share in stores selling the brand, and in determining the average number of brand sizes carried per store selling.

Market Level Facts

While sales information at retail is collected at the individual store level, and detailed analysis of store conditions versus store sales rates may yield insights, other marketing activities affect consumer groups within a market, and thus all stores in which these groups shop. TV advertising and couponing are such activities.

Typical Syndicated Facts on TV Media and Couponing

TV	Local versus National
	Day part
	Target audience
	Reach
	Frequency
	Share of voice
Coupon	Face value
	Circulation, delivery (FSI, ROP)
	Redemption
	Household inventory of coupons

PROJECTION ISSUES

Retail Sales Sample Data

It is possible to capture data from all stores of a single retailer even if that retailer has hundreds of individual stores. It is seldom possible to capture data for all retail stores in a market, as many smaller outlets are not yet equipped with POS scanners, and even if so equipped, may not be willing to provide detail sales data. Even if complete POS data were available, the costs of processing it and adding manual audits of in-store conditions could raise costs significantly. In 1993, the syndicated services attempted to cover approximately the largest 10% of outlets in a distribution channel (which often account for over 50% of total channel sales), and use statistical sampling methods to project the data to estimates of total sales in the distribution channel. Even if it is easy to capture all of the POS movement data, any additional data to be provided via manual audits may be so expensive to collect that only a sample of the possible universe is used.

When designing an information system based on sample data, experts on statistical sampling theory should be involved. Provision must be made for the closing of outlets in the sample, merging in data from outlets newly added to the sample, and accounting for trends in the total volume of products handled by the distribution system channel being monitored. For example, a recent trend in the United States consumer packaged goods area is for mass merchandisers to add lines of shelf stable items usually found in grocery stores. The projection system must account for growth due to increasing penetration across channel stores and growth due to the increasing use of the mass merchandiser outlets by product purchasers. Simultaneously, sales of such products may be declining in traditional distribution channels.

One of the findings from analysis of detail POS sales data coupled with causal information on detail marketing activities in a retail account or city is that the same marketing inputs may produce significantly different sales results from one geography to the next. In addition, the translation of a manufacturer's marketing activity may vary significantly from geography to geography, so that identical promotional offers to two different retailers may produce completely different pricing and promotional activities being offered to consumers by the two retailers. This supports the current trend by manufacturers toward "micro-marketing," or tailoring marketing actions and programs specific to local regions rather than using a "one size fits all" national program.

Household Purchase Sample Data

Household purchase data by its very nature poses a number of complex problems in projection and interpretation. The data can be kept at finer levels of detail on time of purchase (even down to the hour), but probably represents only a sample of the purchasing by the household. If the data is captured by POS scanners, the data in stores not equipped with POS scanners may be lost. If scanned in the home, then accurate information on the price and in-store promotional conditions may be lost. Accurate recording of usage of coupons on purchases may be a problem in either case. If multiple members of the household participate in purchasing activity, the levels of coverage may be biased (some members may be more faithful in recording purchases than others).

On the other hand, more detailed causal information may be available at the household level. A broad variety of demographic information may be collected, such as the family income; age, education, occupation, and sex of each family member; and information on the type and quality of major possessions such as house and cars. Current research indicates that some 45 to 65 life-stage/life-style groupings aid significantly in projecting household purchasing to store-level purchasing. With such projection, data from the U.S. census at a zip code level can be used to determine the approximate frequency of the groups among an individual store or chain's shoppers. Data on the media portions of a marketing program may be associated with individual households by monitoring TV viewing, receipt of mailed coupons, magazine readership, and use of radios. Additional classifications may be assigned to households based on their purchase histories. Examples are store loyalty, brand loyalty, and "deal" loyalty indices, classification as light, medium, or heavy buyers of various product categories, classification based on type of TV programs used, and propensity to use coupons.

REPORT DESIGN

General Report Design

There are three general management functions that are supported by database reports and analyses. The first of these is the monitoring of current brand performance in the marketplace, and the preliminary selection of sets of performance measures to monitor in more detail. The second is the evaluation of sales performance under various alternative marketing conditions. The third is the projection of analysis results into estimates of sales performance likely to be realized in non-sampled outlets, or estimates of the probable sales performance likely to be realized by a proposed future marketing plan.

An individual report will be prepared for some level of time-product-location, possibly for several levels. A single set of facts will be selected. A report will almost always have one or more measures of sales performance, and one or more causal measures, where the causal measures reflect the marketing actions affecting sales performance. The performance and causal measures may be repeated several times for different conditions.

Sales Performance Measures

The two most common measures of sales performance are volume and share. Volume may be measured in terms of unit sales, dollar sales, or equivalized volume sales. Share is obtained by selecting the volume for an individual product or item, dividing by the total volume for some summary across time, product, or geography, and multiplying by 100. Most often, the summary is across all products in the category to give an items share (market share) of category sales. If the summary is across time, such as a year, the result is the particular periods share of the item's total annual sales. If the summary is across geography, then the result might be the share of U.S sales for the product that is sold in Chicago, or the share of product sales in Chicago that is sold in a particular retailer's chain. Sales performance measures may also be indexed versus previous period, or for the same period a year ago.

Instead of total volume, one might use baseline volume, or incremental volume. This might be converted to share of baseline volume or share of incremental volume. For some applications, an important measure of sales performance is sales rate. This is obtained by dividing volume (unit, dollar, or equivalized) by a measure of the size of the stores in the geography. Common size measures are ACV (millions of dollars of annual sales by stores selling the item), percent of stores in the area selling the product or item, or number of stores in the area selling the product. A recent addition to the list (PEI) is used in evaluating the results of sales generated by retailer promotions compared to the expected value of sales with no retailer promotion.

Causal Measures

The causal measures usually represent the result of sales or marketing activity by manufacturer or retailer. For tracking purposes, only an overall result may be given, but for analysis, the causal measures may be reported by mutually exclusive conditions. When trade promotion activity is the basis for the exclusive conditions, some measures of volume performance are also reported by condition. Where available, data on media and coupon activity may be included to round out the picture of marketing and sales activity. Some of the measures used to track and analyze volume results are:

1. To monitor prices available to consumers, measures include weighted average actual price, weighted average base price, and percent price reduction. Prices may be measured on a unit basis, or on an equivalized volume basis.
2. To monitor the extent of physical distribution of the product, measures include outlet coverage measures such as percent of stores selling, percent of ACV selling, or the total ACV of stores in which the product is sold. If there are multiple items in the product (sizes, flavors, colors, etc), then an important measure might be average number of item carried per store that carries the product.
3. To monitor trade promotion coverage by condition, measures might include outlet coverage measures for the condition (e.g., percent of ACV with an A feature), and time coverage measures (e.g., average weeks of display by stores that had in-store display at least once). These might be combined into a weighted weeks measure that multiplies the outlet coverage and time coverage measures. For example, in a four-week period, one might obtain one weighted week of TPR

performance by any of the following scenarios: 25% of the stores have a TPR for four weeks, all of the stores have one week of TPR (not necessarily in the same week), or in weeks 1 and 2, 50% of the stores have TPR performance, and in weeks 3 and 4, the remaining 50% perform. When trade promotion measures are reported by condition, one or more measures of sales performance are generally also reported by condition, such as volume, share, sales rate, incremental volume or share, incremental volume sales rate, or PEI indices.

4. Media measures possibly reported might include GRPs, reach, frequency, and share of voice. These might be reported in total, or by daypart (specific parts of the programming schedule). For coupons, measures might include circulation, average face value, redemption, share of redemption, or coupon inventory levels (average number of coupons held per household).

In the sections to follow, examples of the use of these measures in constructing reports will be shown. It is important to select measures that are consistent in their definitions. For example, if the sales performance measure chosen is equivalized volume, then market shares should be calculated on equivalized volumes, and prices should be reported in prices per equivalized volume. Sales rates should be calculated by using equivalized volume in the numerator. PEI calculations and sales indices versus a previous period should also be made using equivalized volume.

MARKET POSITION AND DIAGNOSTIC REPORTS

Trend Reports

One of the most basic reports available on most databases is the trend report, which allows a quick comparison of performance over time. The tabular layout often has time periods as columns, although alternative formats exist where time periods are used as rows. In the examples to follow, time periods will be used as columns. Report 1 is a

REPORT 1. Nielsen Scantrack®—Weekly Dollar Share Trend
Category: Bottled Sparkling and Mineral Water
13 Weeks Ending APR2190.1
San Francisco

	Period				
	13 Weeks	**JAN2790.1**	**FEB0390.1**	**FEB1090.1**	**FEB1790.1**
Total Calistoga	23.0	21.3	21.2	22.4	23.4
Total Vittel	0.5	0.6	0.6	0.7	0.6
Total Perrier	0.5	2.5	2.5	1.6	0.1

fact trend report. A single key fact, in this case market share, is displayed across time. In the example shown, the fact is displayed for multiple products in one market so the reader can quickly spot which brands are growing or declining in the market. An alternate format might show all markets for one product in order to highlight areas where the product is growing or declining.

Competitive Monitoring

Report 2, a product profile trend, shows several facts for several brands. This report allows monitoring competitive pricing and promotional activity over time. Such reports can be prepared on an account by

REPORT 2. Nielsen Scantrack®—Product Profile Trend
Category: Bottled Sparkling and Mineral Water
13 Weeks Ending APR2190.1
San Francisco

	Period				
	JAN2790.1	**FEB0390.1**	**FEB1090.1**	**FEB1790.1**	**FEB2490.1**
Total Calistoga					
% Store selling	100	100	100	100	100
% Sales rate	177934	170307	173042	186264	186131
Sales rate	1779.3	1703.1	1730.4	1862.6	186.3
$ Sales w/causal	3408	2465	36916	28424	23766
% Promoted	1.9	1.4	21.3	15.3	12.8
$ Share	21.3	21.2	22.4	23.4	22.7
Display	12	7	22	23	33
Feature ads	0	0	35	33	69
Average price	1.55	1.55	1.41	1.34	1.38
Total Vittel					
% Store selling	70	80	80	76	80
$ Sales rate	5029	4963	5246	4679	4823
Sales rate	71.8	62.0	65.6	61.6	60.3
$ Sales w/causal	0	0	0	0	0
% Promoted	0.0	0.0	0.0	0.0	0.0
$ Share	0.6	0.6	0.7	0.6	0.6
Display	0	0	0	0	0
Feature ads	0	0	0	0	0
Average Price	1.45	1.36	1.41	13.9	1.43
Total Perrier					
% Store selling	93	93	88	12	2
$ Sales	21062	20329	12017	402	150
Sales rate	226.5	218.6	136.6	33.5	75.1
$ Sales w/causal	999	735	365	0	0

account basis as well as at the market level, and allow monitoring of distribution, pricing, and promotional activity. Members of the sales force can use such reports to anticipate competitive threats on an account by account basis.

Report 3 shows an arrangement for many facts for a single brand, trended across time and reported for a single geography. In this last case, all the facts for extremely detailed analysis of sales performance are gathered onto a single page. With the increasing use of spreadsheet programs, hardcopy reports are generated only for simple summary forms like Reports 1 and 2, and detail reporting of facts is handled by loading fact data, as shown in Report 3, directly into the spreadsheet for further analysis.

REPORT 3. Nielsen Scantrack®—Promotion Profile Trend
13 Weeks Ending APR2190.1
Total Calistoga
San Francisco

		Period			
	13 Weeks	**JAN 2790.1**	**FEB 0390.1**	**FEB 1090.1**	**FEB 1790.1**
Share					
Dollar basis	23.0	21.3	21.2	22.4	23.4
Share Volume (Dollars)					
Total	2596269	177934	170307	173042	186264
Total promoted volume	396738	3408	2465	36916	28424
% Promoted	15.3	1.9	1.4	21.3	15.3
W/ad only	144922	0	0	22159	17222
W/display only	164044	3408	2465	1845	11202
W/display and ad	87771	0	0	12912	0
Merchandising Info (% ACV)					
Display		12	7	22	23
Major ads		0	0	35	33
Display and ad		0	0	16	0
Coupon ad		0	0	0	0
Selling Price (per unit)					
Average retail price	1.48	1.55	1.50	1.41	1.34
Feature/display price	1.49	1.93	1.47	0.99	0.95
Non feature/display price	1.48	1.55	1.50	1.60	1.45

Change Reports

Rather than monitor each time period closely, we may wish to review for differences versus year ago. In categories with pronounced seasonal sales patterns, comparison of week to week or month to month is made difficult by the combination of changes due to seasonal effects and changes representing real changes in market position. Report 4 shows a trend change analysis, where market share and volume changes are compared to changes in pricing, distribution, and promotional activity. In this case, the report shows the results for one product, with time period information absorbed into the fact set, and displays the results for multiple markets. An alternative format might show the results for one market, and all major products within the market.

Ranking Reports

If there are more than five to eight rows in the report, it becomes difficult to quickly identify the highs and lows in a column, and to visualize which other facts might follow a related pattern. Any report arranged into a cross-tabular format may have its rows reordered based on the ranking of the contents of any one column. Report 5 shows a change report that has also been ranked. The top and bottom of the report rows are easy to locate immediately, and direct attention to the items with higher than average or lower than average performance on the variable being used for ranking. Instead of all brands in a market, the report might rank all markets for a single brand.

Exception Reporting

For reviewing categories with a large number of items, the ranking report may run to several pages. In an exception report, some cutoff level for inclusion is established, and only those items that meet the cutoff are displayed. Report 6 illustrates such a report. Selection can be based on multiple rankings, such as the top items based on volume increases, the top items based on decreases in base price, and the top items based on percent of volume sold on promotional activity. If longer time periods such as quarters are used, both brands and markets can be combined into a single exception report reporting the largest shifts up and down in market position. Certain exception reports may be produced on a routine basis. Report 7 shows a new product review report that monitors the progress of new items introduced in the market. From reports such as this, management is kept current on the sales progress of new products, and can assess their potential impact in the marketplace.

Workstation Reporting

With the increasing amount of detail available, there is a trend toward minimal use of hard copy reports, and use of workstation software to manipulate the stored data in spreadsheet form for analysis

REPORT 4. Nielsen Scan*Pro® Monitor—Topline Report
Total French Cafe Soluble Coffee
Current Period: 13 Weeks Ending FEB2490.1
Base Period: Year Ago 13 Weeks

Market	Equivalent Share	Change in Share (Point)	Change in Sales (Percent)	Change in Dist. (Point)	Change in % ACV on Deal (Point)	Change in % Volume on Deal (Point)	Change in Regular Price (Percent)	Change in Promoted Price (Percent)	Change in % Price Reduction (Point)
Total United States (over $4 million)	22.5	1.86	1.8	.0	2.9	.4	−3.9	−4.4	.4
Chicago	18.8	2.39	4.5	.4	−8.8	−11.6	−10.7	−14.5	4.0
Denver	9.5	1.64	9.8	−.1	−6.9	−16.2	−5.6	−5.7	.1
Los Angeles	7.1	1.14	5.4	.0	−3.7	−5.7	−6.3	−6.3	.0
New York	25.0	1.15	1.6	.1	−1.9	−2.5	.0	−3.4	2.6

REPORT 5. Nielsen Scantrack®—Brand Ranking Report
Category: Bottled Sparkling and Mineral Water
13 Weeks Ending APR2190.1
San Francisco

Item	$ Rank	Unit Rank	$ Vol	$% Chg vs. Ya	$ Shr	Shr Chg versus Ya	Cum $ Shr	Unit Vol	Unit % Chg versus Ya	Unit Shr	Unit Shr Chg	Cum Unit Shr
Total Calistoga	1	1	2596269	−11.1	23.0	−4.0	23.0	1752790	−11.1	20.6	−3.6	20.6
Total Vittel	2	3	60504	39.1	0.5	0.1	23.6	41067	28.9	0.5	0.1	21.1
Total Perrier	3	2	53959	−79.9	0.5	−2.0	24.1	43089	−82.6	0.5	−2.5	21.6

REPORT 6. *Nielsen Scantrack©—Significant Item Changes*
Category: Oral Antiseptics
Market: Chicago
New Items During the 13 Weeks Ending FEB2391

	Dollar Sales	Actual Change	% Change	Dollar Share	Share Change	% Promo	Pt. Chg.	Last % SS
Top Established Gainers								
Listerine Antsp Yl Oa 48 oz.	100,397	34,941	53.4	4.9	1.7	26.3	26.2	40.0
Listerine Antsp Yl Oa 32 oz.	156,161	32,058	25.8	7.6	1.6	25.3	9.5	67.0
Scope Mw&G Gn Oa 24 oz.	64,472	22,183	52.5	3.1	1.1	13.7	13.7	64.0
Top Established Decliners								
Scope Mw&G Gn Oa 32 oz.	70,338	–22,326	–24.1	3.4	–1.1	26.1	–4.3	49.0
Lmnt Mw&G/F Mt Gn Oa 24 oz.	25,025	–16,186	–39.3	1.2	–0.8	10.6	–7.8	47.0
Act F Trt Lq Cn Rd Or 18 oz.	12,656	–13,743	–52.1	0.6	–0.7	0.0	–5.7	22.0
Top New Items								
Scope Mw&G Gn –.15 Oz 12 oz.	14,483	—	—	0.7	—	22.7	—	17.0
Close-Up Lq Cn Rd Or 6 oz.	3,767	—	—	0.2	—	16.5	—	25.0
Ctl Br Mw Mt Gn 24 oz./8 oz. = 32 oz.	3,473	—	—	0.2	—	66.0	—	2.0

REPORT 7. Nielsen Scantrack©—New Product Highlight
Category: Bottled Sparkling and Mineral Water
Market: Birmingham
New Items During the 13 Weeks Ending JUN1690.1

							Average Weekly			
Item			**# Weeks Selling**	**13 Weeks Unit Sales**	**13 Weeks Sales**	**Max % SS**	**Sales Rate**	**Unit Share**	**Shr in Strs Selling**	**Avg. Price**
Calistoga Spkg Rasp	12	0	6	35	35	2	3.0	0.0	0.4	0.99
Per Pnt Spk	10	0	1	7	15	2	2.7	0.0	0.4	2.08
Per Sk Min Nrb Org	23	0	9	171	118	5	5.7	0.0	0.8	0.69
Calistoga Min Nrb Pch Flv	6.5	0	5	50	34	4	3.8	0.0	0.6	0.69

and exception reporting purposes. Rather than define a specific format for ranking reports and exception reports, any report may be ranked and trimmed to its exceptions. Increasingly sophisticated analysis programs process the movement data against expected values calculated by models using the detail causal facts on marketing activity, and report on those results that are outside the range of values expected, given the marketing changes that have occurred. Some of these models are syndicated by suppliers, and some are built by corporate or retailer analysts based on their particular business knowledge bases, and on the integration of external data such as brand marketing plans, industry trends, and shipments to non-covered channels.

TACTICAL ANALYSIS

Reports 1 thru 7 have illustrated general comparison and evaluation reports that allow management to track the progress of a brand, identify changes in category brand list, and to identify further brand items and/or markets for further analysis. There are three key areas for further analysis: brand distribution, pricing, and promotion (both consumer and trade activity). These areas are monitored by marketing organizations with responsibility for regional or national marketing, and by the sales force with responsibility for executing marketing plans on a tactical basis with local and regional retailers. In the next section, we review some common activities and problems, and the types of reports that might be generated to support these activities.

Sales Force Objectives

A manufacturer's sales force calls on retail accounts and chain buying points to support a number of key activities. The most common and important are: (1) obtaining distribution and shelf space for products not currently carried by the account; (2) obtaining desired shelf price; (3) obtaining appropriate types of retail promotion support; (4) obtaining appropriate frequency of retailer promotion support, and (5) monitoring competitive marketing in the account—distribution, pricing, and promotion. An important consideration for the sales force is that the information they use for presentations is current, for the local market area, and where possible, based almost completely on sales to the account on which they are calling. Many of the reports used by sales are similar to those used by brand management, but have a more local geographical focus.

Obtaining Distribution

Report 8 is typical of the kind of information used to identify those items that are candidates for expanded distribution. The report identifies

REPORT 8. Nielsen Scantrack©—Opportunity Items
Share Basis: Bottled Sparkling and Mineral Water
4 Weeks Ending NOV1288.1
San Francisco

Item	Rate Rank	$ Rank	% SS	4Wk $ Sales	4Wk Op 100%	$ Share	Shr in Stores Selling
Ctl Br Drinking 128 OZ	1	12	31	29697	66100	1.7	5.6
Ctl Br Spring 128 OZ	4	6	54	41061	34978	2.4	4.5
Ctl Br Distilled 128 OZ	6	27	25	17193	51579	1.0	4.0
Ctl Br Drinking 320 OZ	15	26	37	17316	29484	1.0	2.7
K-S R Min W Lmnd Nrb 4P 9.6 OZ	18	32	27	10879	29414	0.6	2.4
K-S R Min W Org/Mng Nrb 25.4 OZ	22	33	27	9654	26102	0.6	2.1
K-S R Min W Org/Psfrt Nrb 25.4 OZ	28	38	24	7405	23449	0.4	1.8
K-S R Min w Lmn/Lm/Org Nrb 25.4 OZ	29	37	25	7461	22383	0.4	1.7
Villar R Min w Lm Nrb 6P 10 OZ	31	35	34	9090	17645	0.4	1.4
Ctl Br Mineral 6P 8 OZ	51	55	21	2864	10774	0.3	1.2
				152620	311908		

those items that do not have 100% distribution, but have high sales rates. The column labeled "4WK OP 100%" is the estimated increase in market dollar sales for the item if it goes from its current distribution level to 100% distribution, and maintains its current sales rate. The column labeled "SHR IN STORES SELLING" is useful in preparing a sales presentation for those retailers not carrying the item. If necessary, the report can be modified slightly to indicate slow moving items whose elimination would result in the least decrease in sales. Often, in order to obtain shelf space for a new item in a category, it is necessary to eliminate an existing item. The slow moving item report will tell a salesperson if any of his items are candidates for delisting, or which items should be delisted in order to make space for the new items desired on the shelf. Retailers use sales rate information to expand or contract distribution of items within a chain, and to make delisting decisions.

Base Pricing

Report 9 is typical of the reports prepared to assist a salesperson in obtaining the desired shelf price for his product. Sales rates might be calculated based on absolute price (as shown), or may be shown as price differences versus a major competitor.

REPORT 9. Sales Rate by Price Point
Product: Calistoga 12 Oz.
Market: New York
Time: 13 Weeks Ending APR2190.1

Price per Unit	Volume	Volume Per MMACV	% Total Volume Sold	Cum % of Total Volume Sold
1.09	5,365	7.76	2.4	2.4
1.14	16,784	7.47	7.6	10.1
1.19	25,476	7.14	11.6	21.7
1.24	41,619	6.61	18.9	40.6
1.27	8,075	6.48	3.7	44.3
1.29	48,231	6.45	22.0	66.3
1.33	4,142	6.11	1.9	68.2
1.34	36,347	6.16	16.5	84.7
1.37	8,653	5.76	3.9	88.6
1.39	24,938	5.80	11.4	100.0

Promotion Frequency

Report 3, the promotion profile trend, would be used by a salesperson to compare an account's performance to a market or region. Comparisons can be made of performance across brands within the retail account, and of performance by a brand in the account versus the region. Often a "fair share" argument can be made for obtaining event frequencies at least as great as those of a major competitor, or for obtaining event frequencies at least as great as those given by major competitors.

Promotion Event Performance

Report 10 summarizes the results of a promotion event. This report could be run for an account, a market, or for a major region. The PEI results can be a very important factor in persuading an account to give desired types of discounting and ad/display support. This particular example shows that combining display with feature ads gave sales rates nearly five times those expected in a week of normal pricing and no support. Such information can be used to significantly improve the chances for obtaining in-store display support from retailers. Collecting such information across many retailers and time periods allows the construction of sales response models that predict the sales increase that might be expected on average for various combinations of price discounts and retailer ad/display support. Exhibit 2 (shown on page 727) shows a typical result of modeling expected PEI performance. The projections from such a model might be used in persuading a retailer to try promotion support combinations that it does not normally use. If cost and margin information is added to such models, projections can be made of the incremental profitability of promotion events to the manufacturer and to the retailer.

Expert Systems

The availability of such information gives a member of the sales force the possibility of anticipating problems with retail accounts, of identifying opportunities for increasing sales, and of preparing focused presentations using a retailer's own sales data and local market data. The drawback is that a full report set on an account's recent activity may run to dozens of pages of detail information. Market research suppliers and individual manufacturers are building expert systems that sift through the data and pinpoint problems and opportunities in exception reporting forms. Other expert systems have scripts for various sales presentations and review the data to select the strongest arguments for obtaining retailer actions and may produce most of the presentation material.

REPORT 10. Scan*Pro®Monitor—Event Analysis
Product: Bradford Caff Sol Coff
Market: Los Angeles
Based on Equivalized Units Sales

Description	Event December 1989	Event February 1990
Summary		
Duration	5	4
Incremental weeks	.6	.1
Total volume	33954	23911
Baseline volume	30502	23064
Incremental volume	3452	847
Efficiency	31.2	18.7
% Volume on Deal		
Any promo	29.6	13.9
TPR only	18.9	13.0
Any feature without display	8.5	.4
Any display without feature	.5	.4
Feature and display	1.7	.0
% ACV on deal (baseline)		
Any promo	22.7	11.7
TPR only	16.0	11.1
Any feature without display	6.0	.4
Any display without feature	.3	.2
Feature and display	.4	.0
PEI		
Any promo	145	123
TPR only	132	122
Any feature without display	157	123
Any display without feature	194	196
Feature and display	493	
% Price Discount		
Any promo	10.8	11.4
TPR only	12.3	11.2
Any feature without display	6.6	31.0
Any display without feature	3.0	1.7
Feature and display	11.2	

EXHIBIT 2. Marketing Response Analysis—Relationship between Marketing Activity and Sales

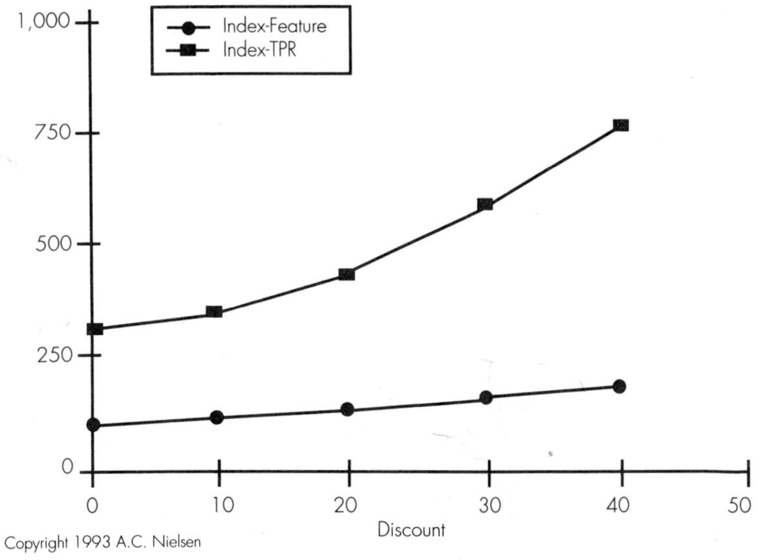

BRAND MANAGEMENT UTILIZATION—STORE DATA

Monitoring Sales and Share

Brand managers will use many of the same reporting tools used by sales managers, but will usually be concerned with higher levels of geography. Trend reports, profiles, and exception reports will be run at the country level. There will be heavy use of reports comparing brand and competitive performance on a market-by-market basis.

Competitive Monitoring

Report 11, a competitive price report, compares a brand's price at regular, and on deal, across many markets. This allows brand management to review their pricing position in both absolute terms and versus key competition on both regular and deal pricing. If extreme deviations are noted, then market level profile and trend reports would be used to identify and characterize the nature of any problems. Trend reports such as Report 1 would be used to monitor brand volume and share in order to track sales progress versus category growth, and versus brand plans. Reports 3 and 8 are used to monitor brand promotion activity and brand distribution.

REPORT 11. Scan*Pro®Monitor—Competitive Pricing Report
Product: Bradford Caff 8 Oz. Sol Coff
Competitor: French Cafe Caff 8 Oz. Sol Coff
For the 13 Weeks Ending FEB2490.1
Merchandising Condition: Any Promo Except Long Sales
Based on Equivalized Unit Prices

Market	Own Reg. Price	Own Deal Price	Own % Price Reduct	Comp Reg. Price	Comp Deal Price	Comp % Price Reduct	Reg. Price Index	Deal Price Index	% Price Reduct Diff
Total U.S. (over $4 million)	33.38	29.76	10.9	22.72	19.08	16.0	147	156	–5.1
Chicago	32.18	25.67	20.2	21.66	19.27	11.0	149	133	9.2
Denver	29.63	25.33	14.5	21.47	18.87	12.1	138	134	2.4
Los Angeles	34.35	28.15	18.1	21.99	19.43	11.6	156	145	6.4
New York	34.08	28.35	16.8	24.23	18.17	25.0	141	156	–8.2

Additional reports might track measures of coupon activity and TV commercial activity to round out the brand managers ability to monitor the brands marketing mix on a market-by-market basis. Suppliers of market research data have recently begun development of software that will integrate both the client's internal data such as shipments and advertising spending and external data such as coupon and media expenditures with the traditional volume and price information provided by syndicated data bases. Report 12, a marketing mix report, illustrates a report layout for reporting marketing mix activities from such data integration.

Strategic Planning

An important use of syndicated data by brand management is in the development of models relating marketing mix decisions and historical sales trends to brand sales levels. Brand managers are responsible for forecasting future brand sales and share levels, particularly when changes in pricing, distribution, or other marketing mix variables are considered. The detail data available in syndicated databases supports many analyses that are of use in the planning/forecasting process. In the simplest forms, trend reports provide a basis for projecting current rates of change in volume or share levels for a brand into a "business as usual" forecast. Sales rate reports such as Report 9 can be used to model the relation between base price and product sales during non-promoted periods. These models can then be used to provide forecasts of the probable impact of future changes in product price. Distribution opportunity reports, such as Report 8, can be used to study the potential for increasing brand distribution, and for modeling the probable impact of gaining increased distribution.

Trend reports may also be used to study the seasonal sales patterns of a brand or category. When examined at a weekly level, we frequently find that the weeks around holidays such as Easter, Thanksgiving, and Christmas exhibit extreme fluctuations in sales levels. Exhibit 3a illustrates the behavior of seasonal indices for a product around Christmas. This product category is not purchased during Christmas/New Year's weeks, although the products continue to be consumed. After the holidays are over, home inventories need to be replenished. Using the average sales indices over a four-week period will almost completely mask the detail sales behavior. For other products, such as diet aids, the holiday dip may occur without a following replenishment spike, as consumption decreases during the holiday periods. Exhibit 3b illustrates such a sales pattern. Identification of such "special" sales weeks can assist the brand manager in targeting television advertising, coupon drops, and promotional activity.

When the brand manager has conducted a major marketing activity such as TV ads, print ads, coupon drops, and/or sweepstakes and contests coordinated with in-store promotional programs, then

REPORT 12. Marketing Mix Performance
Category: Bottled Sparkling and Mineral Water
13 Weeks Ending APR2190.1
Chicago

Product	Total Volume	Volume Share	Avg Base Price/Vol	ACV WT Weeks any Promo	Avg % Dsct on Promo	H.H. Grp	Coupon Circulation	Avb Cpn Face Value
Total Calistoga								
Total Vittel								
Total Perrier								

EXHIBIT 3. Pattern of Weekly Seasonal Sales

(a)

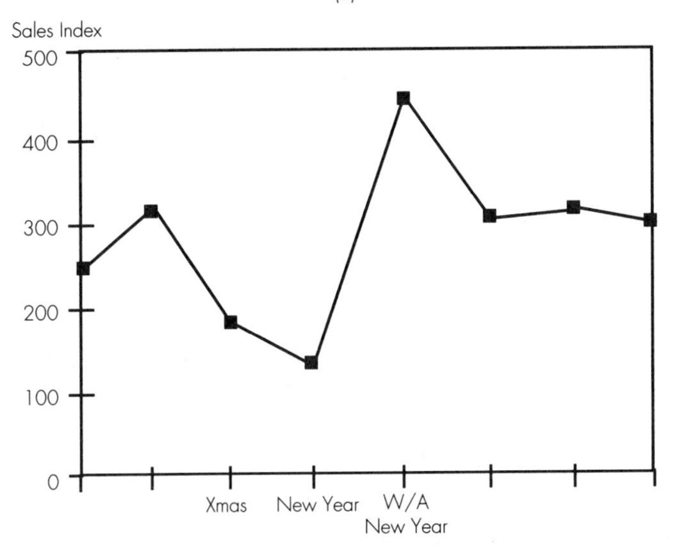

Delay Purchase until After Holiday

(b)

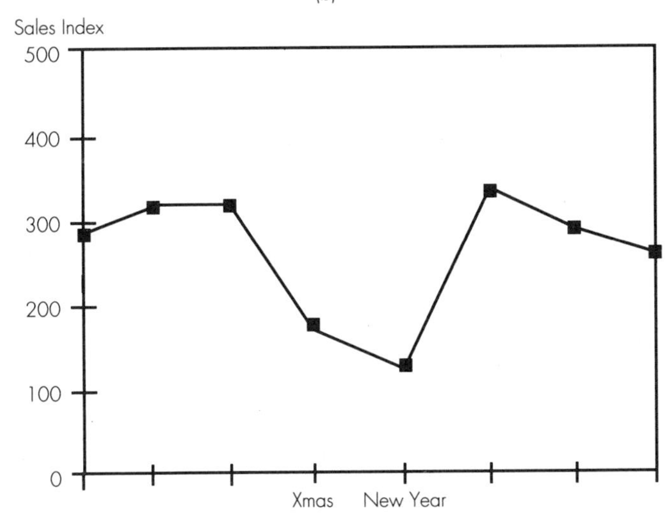

Consumption Decrease during Holiday Period

reports such as Report 10 can be used to evaluate the program's impact on national or regional sales. Detail analysis of the response of individual stores to pricing and promotional conditions will allow preparation of price/promotion response curves such as shown in Exhibit 2. These models allow the brand manager to estimate the probable impact of altering the terms offered with trade promotion allowances to retailers. If feature ads are significantly more effective than temporary price reduction only, then the brand manager might improve sales by obtaining fewer weeks of total promotion, but an increase in feature weeks over current performance. The response models should also aid the manager in determining the value of changing the trade allowances associated with promotional offers. More complex versions of the model allow assessment of the probable impact of changes in competitive pricing and promotion.

Special Studies

Availability of store level detail data permits a large variety of special studies to be conducted. If, for example, the brand manager hypothesises that certain demographic groups are more responsive to promotions on his product than to competitive promotions, then a study can be conducted in which stores are classified by the predominance of the demographic group. The response in "high" rated stores can be compared with the response in "low" rated stores. Many questions of interest to the brand manager can be studied by such store grouping techniques. If the data does not exist in the historical data base, then the brand manager can commission tests, in which elements of the marketing mix are manipulated differently across stores or markets, and the sales results compared both directly and by statistical analysis.

BRAND MANAGEMENT UTILIZATION—PANEL DATA

Panel versus Store Data

Sales data from retail stores shows the brand's relative position in the category and the brand's sales trends, but not the reasons for such trends. In order to evaluate the brand's probable future, one needs to know if changes in sales are due to shifts in the number of brand buyers (household penetration), or in the amount purchased by each buyer (volume per buyer). The fundamental equation in panel analysis is:

$$\text{Brand Volume} = \text{Total Households} \times \text{Household Penetration } (\% \text{ of Total}) \times \text{Volume per Buyer}$$

Marketing mix elements often have the goal of increasing household penetration. Examples are trial-size packages, coupons, and in-store promotional activity. However, such actions may also stimulate sales by increasing the volume per buyer among existing buyers. In order to separate these possibilities, detailed analysis of the purchase behavior of individual consumers is required. When media advertising is targeted to specific groups of consumers, the analysis of panel data can determine if the objectives of the campaign are being met.

New Product Tracking

A critical success factor for new products is their ability to build a successful base of repeat buyers. When the product is initially introduced, its sales are almost totally trial sales to new buyers of the brand. As time passes, some of the initial triers return to make repeat purchases, while the trial sales decay as more and more of the potential buyers have made their trial purchases, leaving a smaller pool of potential triers. There are many examples in marketing history where strong introductory marketing programs gave strong early sales growth composed primarily of trial sales, but where lack of repeat sales among triers led to poor levels of sales after the introductory period. Several services offer tracking and modeling of trial and repeat sales for new or restaged brands.

Panel-Based Analysis Models

Brand management may use detail household purchase information to identify appropriate competitive sets for its products, assess the threat of new products, and to assess the detail impact of various marketing mix activities in consumer behavior. A number of models are available that analyze the sequence of brands purchased by individual consumers over time, and the conditions under which these purchases were made. Typical analyses include:

- *Marketing mix analysis*—Often performed by logit or similar choice modeling techniques, the impact of price, media advertising, coupon, and distribution availability are combined to generate a measure of brand "utility," which is then transformed into a choice probability for individual consumers, and into a simulated market share across consumers.
- *Coupon redemption forecasting*—Following the drop of a coupon, the use of the coupon in brand purchasing is monitored to determine usage by previous brand buyers versus new triers, and to determine at each week of the coupon's life the percentage of total redemptions that will occur in the week.
- *Stockpiling and brand switching associated with trade promotion*—The promotional bump generated in retail stores may come from brand switchers; store switchers who would have bought your brand in other stores; and from stockpiling by a brand's loyal consumers, which reduces future sales. By analyzing detail purchase behavior, the promotional sales may be decomposed to yield net incremental effects.
- *Shopping patterns*—If consumers shop multiple stores, or if they have certain demographics or lifestyles that concentrate heavy buyers in a subset of stores,

then this may imply desired distribution in only high payout stores. Analysis of consumer shopping patterns can assist in determining the appropriate levels of brand distribution.

- *Market structure*—There are models that examine the sequence of brands purchased by individual consumers in order to determine the strength of competition among the various brands and sizes in a category. It is seldom true that all brand sizes in a category compete equally with all other brand sizes in a category. By determining the subset of items most strongly competitive with a brand, the management of that brand will know which brands to monitor most closely in the store data. In addition, knowledge of the items with which their brand does not compete may assist management in developing new products or line extensions that have minimum overlap with their existing products.

Related Data

There are some data sources that bridge the gap between panel and store data. By processing the U.S. Census data (available on a block, census tract, and zipcode basis) into store trading areas, it is possible to assign to each retail outlet the average demographic characteristics of its shopping population. While no substitute for detail individual household level data, such store level consumer data does allow comparison of brand sales and share across stores with significantly different shopping populations. This can be an important consideration for products that appeal to specific demographic groups, such as families with children under age 6, or health aids targeted toward the elderly.

SUMMARY

Since 1988, the availability of detailed weekly data at the level of retail chain and above is leading to significant changes in the way sales and brand management track market performance, identify brand problems and opportunities, and prepare forecasts of future brand performance. The trend toward faster and better price/performance in data collection, storage, and processing devices implies that scanner data will become more broadly available and will be less costly to store and analyze. Some of the trends evident in early 1993 are expanding coverage, as use of POS scanner devices grow from predominately grocery use into broad use in mass-merchandisers, drug, and convenience stores. There is increasing integration of information beyond the machine collected volume and price information, as measures of feature advertising, in-store display, coupon activity, TV, radio, and print advertising, and other marketing mix causal data are merged into the database. Use of panelist identification cards or in-home scanners permits expanded detail on shoppers and their purchasing histories.

For the manufacturer and retailer, there is a greater emphasis on fact-based selling, and creating win-win scenarios between manufacturer and retailer. Timely information on retail sales allows the manufacturer to maintain tighter controls over inventory, and to more accurately schedule manufacturing and shipment activities to minimize stockouts. Research on the impact of marketing activities on sales is establishing a better and closer relationship between the amounts spent on marketing activities and their sales and profitability results. Improved data delivery and information systems will make the data broadly available throughout the sales and brand management functions on a timely basis.

Results of current research on scanner based sales data may be found in *Management Science, Journal of Marketing Research, Journal of Marketing, Journal of Advertising Research, International Journal of Research in Marketing, Marketing Letters, and Journal of Consumer Research.* For general reading on market and sales research, consider the books by Churchill and Farris. John McCann gives a vision of the use of computers in marketing management . For an overview of analysis of store and panel data, the Totten and Block book should be available in late 1993. For detail analysis of store sales data, refer to the books by Blattberg and Neslin and Hassens, Parsons, & Schultz. The works by Assael, Ehrenberg, and Kamakura and Russell provide detail on some types of panel data analysis. Finally, the suppliers of syndicated store and panel sales data, such as Nielsen Marketing Research and Information Resources, Inc. are sources of leading edge analyses and applications software designed for converting the raw data into useful information for marketing decisions.

REFERENCES

Assael, Henry, *Consumer Behavior and Marketing Action*, 3rd ed. Boston: Kent, 1987.

Blattberg, Robert C., and Scott A. Neslin, *Sales Promotion-Concepts, Methods, and Strategies*. Englewood Cliffs, NJ: Prentice Hall 1990.

Churchill, Gilbert A., Jr., *Marketing Research: Methodological Foundations*, 4th ed. Chicago: Dryden, 1987.

Ehrenberg, A.S.C., *Repeat-buying: Facts, Theory, and Applications*. 2nd ed. New York: Oxford Univ Press, 1988.

Farris, Paul W., and John A. Quelch, *Advertising and Promotion Management: A Manager's Guide to Theory and Practice*. Radner, PA: Chilton, 1983.

Hanssens, Dominique M., Leonard J. Parsons, and Randall L. Schultz, *Market Response Models: Econometric and Time Series Analysis*. Boston: Kluwer 1989.

Kamakura, Wagner A., and Gary J. Russell, "Measuring Consumer Perceptions of Brand Quality with Scanner Data: Implications for Brand Equity", Report No. 91–122. Cambridge, MA: Marketing Science Institute, October, 1991.

McCann, John M., *The Marketing Workbench: Using Computers for Better Performance*. Homewood, Il: Dow Jones-Irwin, 1986.

Sterman, John D., "Teaching Takes Off: Flight Simulators for Management Education," *OR/MS Today*, Vol. 19, No. 5 (October 1992) pp. 40–44.

Totten, John C., and Martin P. Block, *Analyzing Sales Promotion*. 2nd ed. Chicago: Dartnell (forthcoming).

Philip Kotler
S.C. Johnson & Son Distinguished Professor
of International Marketing
Northwestern University
Kellogg Graduate School of Management
Evanston, Illinois

Philip Kotler, *Marketing Management: Analysis, Planning, Implementation and Control,* 8e, © 1994, pp. 741–766. Reprinted by permission of Prentice-Hall, Englewood Cliffs, New Jersey.

CHAPTER 40

EVALUATING AND CONTROLLING MARKETING PERFORMANCE

The marketing department's job is to plan and control marketing activity. Because many surprises will occur during the implementation of marketing plans, the marketing department has to continuously monitor and control marketing activities. In spite of this need, many companies have inadequate control procedures. This conclusion was reached in a study of 75 companies of varying sizes in different industries. The main findings were these:

- Small companies have poorer controls than large companies. They do a poorer job of setting clear objectives and establishing systems to measure performance.
- Fewer than half of the companies know the profitability of their individual products. About one third of the companies have no regular review procedures for spotting and deleting weak products.
- Almost half of the companies fail to compare their prices with competition, to analyze their warehousing and distribution costs, to analyze the causes of returned merchandise, to conduct formal evaluations of advertising effectiveness, and to review their salesforce call reports.
- Many companies take four to eight weeks to develop control reports, and they are occasionally inaccurate.

Four types of marketing control can be distinguished (Table 1). We now turn to these four types of marketing control.

ANNUAL-PLAN CONTROL

The purpose of annual-plan control is to ensure that the company achieves the sales, profits, and other goals established in its annual plan. The heart of annual-plan control is *management by objectives.* Four steps are involved (see Figure 1). First, management sets monthly or quarterly goals. Second, management monitors its performance in the marketplace. Third, management determines the causes of serious performance deviations. Fourth, management takes corrective action to close the gaps between its goals and performance. This could require changing the action programs or even changing the goals.

This control model applies to all levels of the organization. Top management sets sales and profit goals for the year. These goals are elaborated into specific goals for each lower level of management. Thus each product manager is committed to attaining specified levels of sales and costs. Each regional and district sales manager and each sales representative is also committed to specific goals. Each period, top management reviews and interprets the results and ascertains whether any corrective action is needed.

TABLE 1. Types of Marketing Control

Type of Control	Prime Responsibility	Purpose of Control	Approaches
I. Annual-plan control	Top management Middle management	To examine whether the planned results are being achieved	Sales analysis Market-share analysis Sales-to-expense ratios Financial analysis Satisfaction tracking
II. Profitability control	Marketing controller	To examine where the company is making and losing money	Profitability by: product territory customer segment trade channel order size
III. Efficiency control	Line and staff management Marketing controller	To evaluate and improve the spending efficiency and impact of marketing expenditures	Efficiency of: salesforce advertising sales promotion distribution
IV. Strategic control	Top management Marketing auditor	To examine whether the company is pursuing its best opportunities with respect to markets, products, and channels	Marketing-effectiveness rating instrument Marketing audit Marketing excellence review Company ethical and social responsibility review

Managers use five tools to check on plan performance: sales analysis, market-share analysis, marketing expense-to-sales analysis, financial analysis, and customer-satisfaction tracking.

Sales Analysis

Sales analysis consists of measuring and evaluating actual sales in relation to sales goals. There are two specific tools in this connection.

FIGURE 1. The Control Process

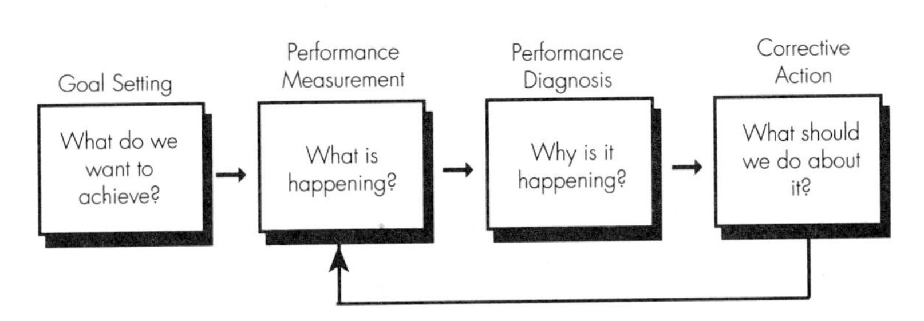

Sales-variance analysis measures the relative contribution of different factors to a gap in sales performance. Suppose the annual plan called for selling 4,000 widgets in the first quarter at $1 per widget, or $4,000. At quarter's end, only 3,000 widgets were sold at $.80 per widget, or $2,400. The sales performance variance is $1,600, or 40% of expected sales. The question arises, How much of this underperformance is due to the price decline and how much to the volume decline? The following calculation answers this question:

Variance due to price decline	= ($1.00 − $.80)(3,000) =	$ 600	37.5%
Variance due to volume decline	= ($1.00)(4,000 − 3,000) =	$1,000	62.5%
		$1,600	100.0%

Almost two thirds of the sales variance is due to a failure to achieve the volume target. The company should look closely at why it failed to achieve its expected sales volume.[1]

Microsales analysis may provide the answer. *Microsales analysis* looks at specific products, territories, and so forth, that failed to produce expected sales. Suppose the company sells in three territories and expected sales were 1,500 units, 500 units, and 2,000 units, respectively, adding up to 4,000 widgets. The actual sales volume was 1,400 units, 525 units, and 1,075 units, respectively. Thus territory 1 showed a 7% shortfall in terms of expected sales; territory 2, a 5% surplus; and territory 3, a 46% shortfall! Territory 3 is causing most of the trouble. The sales vice-president can check into territory 3 to see which hypothesis explains the poor performance: Territory 3's sales representative is loafing or has a personal problem; a major competitor has entered this territory; or GNP is depressed in this territory.

Market-Share Analysis

Company sales do not reveal how well the company is performing relative to competitors. For this purpose, management needs to track its market share. If the company's market share goes up, the company is gaining on competitors; if it goes down, the company is losing relative to competitors.

These conclusions from market-share analysis, however, are subject to certain qualifications:

- *The Assumption That Outside Forces Affect All Companies in the Same Way Is Often Not True:* The U.S. Surgeon General's Report on the harmful consequences of cigarette smoking caused total cigarette sales to falter but not equally for all companies. Companies with better filters were hurt less.
- *The Assumption That a Company's Performance Should Be Judged Against the Average Performance of All Companies Is Not Always Valid:* A company's performance should be judged against the performance of its closest competitors.
- *If a New Firm Enters the Industry, Then Every Existing Firm's Market Share Might Fall:* A decline in a company's market share might not mean that the company is performing any worse than other companies. A company's share loss will depend on the degree to which the new firm hits the company's specific markets.
- *Sometimes a Market-Share Decline Is Deliberately Engineered by a Company to Improve Profits:* For example, management might drop unprofitable customers or products to improve its profits.
- *Market Share Can Fluctuate for Many Minor Reasons:* For example, market share can be affected by whether a large sale occurs on the last day of the month or at the beginning of the next month. Not all shifts in market share have marketing significance.[2]

Managers must carefully interpret market-share movements by product line, customer type, region, and other breakdowns. A useful way to analyze market-share movements is in terms of four components:

$$\text{Overall Market Share} = \frac{\text{Customer}}{\text{penetration}} \times \frac{\text{Customer}}{\text{loyalty}} \times \frac{\text{Customer}}{\text{selectivity}} \times \frac{\text{Price}}{\text{selectivity}} \qquad (40-1)$$

where:

- *Customer penetration* is the percentage of all customers who buy from this company.
- *Customer loyalty* is the purchases from this company by its customers expressed as a percentage of their total purchases from all suppliers of the same products.
- *Customer selectivity* is the size of the average customer purchase from the company expressed as a percentage of the size of the average customer purchase from an average company.
- *Price selectivity* is the average price charged by this company expressed as a percentage of the average price charged by all companies.

Now suppose the company's dollar market share falls during the period. Equation 40–1 provides four possible explanations. The company lost some of its customers (lower customer penetration). Existing customers are buying a smaller share of their total supplies from this company (lower customer loyalty). The company's remaining customers are smaller in size (lower customer selectivity). The company's price has slipped relative to competition (lower price selectivity).

By tracking these factors through time, the company can diagnose the underlying cause of market-share changes. Suppose at the beginning of the period, customer penetration was 60%; customer loyalty, 50%; customer selectivity, 80%; and price selectivity, 125%. According to Equation 40–1, the company's market share was 30%. Suppose that at the end of the period, the company's market share fell to 27%. In checking, the company finds customer penetration at 55%, customer loyalty at 50%, customer selectivity at 75%, and price selectivity at 130%. Clearly, the market-share decline was due mainly to a loss of customers (fall in customer penetration) who normally made larger-than-average purchases (fall in customer selectivity). The manager can now investigate why these customers were lost.

Defining and Measuring Market Share

The first step in using market-share analysis is to define which measure(s) of market share will be used. Four different measures are available.

- *Overall Market Share:* The company's overall market share is its sales expressed as a percentage of total market sales. Two decisions are necessary to use this measure. The first is whether to use unit sales or dollar sales to express market share. The other decision has to do with defining the total market. For example, Harley Davidson's share of the American motorcycle market depends on whether motor scooters and motorized bikes are included. If yes, then Harley Davidson's share will be smaller.
- *Served Market Share:* The company's served market share is its sales expressed as a percentage of the total sales to its served market. Its served

market is all the buyers who would be able and willing to buy its product. If Harley Davidson only produces and sells expensive motorcycles on the East Coast, its served market share would be its sales as a percentage of the total sales of expensive motorcycles sold on the East Coast. A company's served market share is always larger than its overall market share. A company could capture 100% of its served market and yet have a relatively small share of the total market. A company's first task is to win the lion's share of its served market. As it approaches this goal, it should add new product lines and territories to enlarge its served market.

- *Relative Market Share (to Top Three Competitors):* This involves expressing the company's sales as a percentage of the combined sales of the three largest competitors. If the company has 30% of the market, and the next two largest competitors have 20% and 10%, then this company's relative market share is 50% = 30/60. If each of the three companies had $33\frac{1}{3}$% of the market, then any company's relative market share would be $33\frac{1}{3}$%. Relative market shares above 33% are considered to be strong.
- *Relative Market Share (to Leading Competitor):* Some companies track their shares as a percentage of the leading competitor's sales. A relative market share greater than 100% indicates a market leader. A relative market share of exactly 100% means that the firm is tied for the lead. A rise in the company's relative market share means that it is gaining on its leading competitor.

After choosing which market-share measure(s) to use, the company must collect the necessary data. Overall market share is normally the most available measure, since it requires only total industry sales, and these are often available in government or trade association publications. Estimating served market share is harder; it will be affected by changes in the company's product line and geographical market coverage, among other things. Estimating relative market shares is still harder because the company will have to estimate the sales of specific competitors, who guard these figures. The company has to use indirect means, such as learning about competitors' purchase rate of raw materials or the number of shifts they are operating. In the consumer-goods area, individual brand shares are available through syndicated store and consumer panels.

Marketing Expense-to-Sales Analysis

Annual-plan control requires making sure that the company is not overspending to achieve its sales goals. The key ratio to watch is *marketing expense-to-sales.* In one company, this ratio was 30% and consisted of five component expense-to-sales ratios: *salesforce-to-sales* (15%); *advertising-to-sales* (5%); *sales promotion-to-sales* (6%); *marketing research-to-sales* (1%); and *sales administration-to-sales* (3%).

Management needs to monitor these marketing-expense ratios. They will normally exhibit small fluctuations that can be ignored. But fluctuations outside of the normal range are a cause for concern. The period-to-period fluctuations in each ratio can be tracked on a *control*

FIGURE 2. The Control-Chart Model

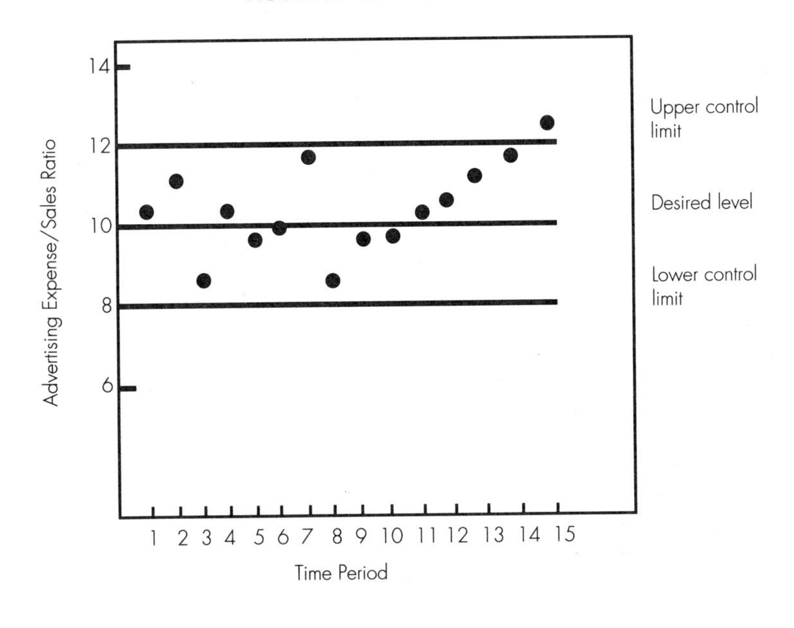

chart (Figure 2). This chart shows that the advertising expense-to-sales ratio normally fluctuates between 8% and 12%, say 99 out of 100 times. In the fifteenth period, however, the ratio exceeded the upper control limit. One of two hypotheses can explain this occurrence:

- *Hypothesis A:* The company still has good expense control, and this situation represents one of those rare chance events.
- *Hypothesis B:* The company has lost control over this expense and should find the cause.

If hypothesis A is accepted, no investigation is made to determine whether the environment has changed. The risk in not investigating is that some real change might have occurred, and the company will fall behind. If hypothesis B is accepted, the environment is investigated at the risk that the investigation will uncover nothing and be a waste of time and effort.

The behavior of successive observations even within the control limits should be watched. Note that the level of the expense-to-sales ratio rose steadily from the ninth period onward. The probability of encountering six successive increases in what should be independent events is only 1 in 64.[3] This unusual pattern should have led to an investigation sometime before the fifteenth observation.

Financial Analysis

The expenses-to-sales ratios should be analyzed in an overall financial framework to determine how and where the company is making its money. Marketers are increasingly using financial analysis to find profitable strategies and not just sales-building strategies.

Financial analysis is used by management to identify the factors that affect the company's *rate of return on net worth.*[4] The main factors are shown in Figure 3, along with illustrative numbers for a large chain-store retailer. The retailer is earning a 12.5% return on net worth. The return on net worth is the product of two ratios, the company's *return on assets* and its *financial leverage.* To improve its return on net worth, the company must either increase the ratio of its net profits to its assets or increase the ratio of its assets to its net worth. The company should analyze the composition of its assets (i.e., cash, accounts receivable, inventory, and plant and equipment) and see if it can improve its asset management.

The return on assets is the product of two ratios, namely, the *profit margin* and the *asset turnover.* The profit margin seems low, while the asset turnover is more normal for retailing. The marketing executive can seek to improve performance in two ways: (1) to increase the profit margin by increasing sales or cutting costs; and (2) to increase the asset

FIGURE 3. Financial Model of Return on Net Worth

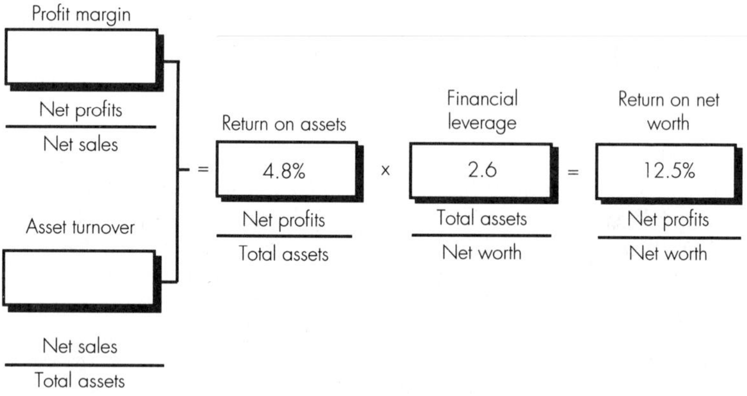

Profit margin
Net profits / Net sales

Asset turnover
Net sales / Total assets

= Return on assets: 4.8% (Net profits / Total assets) × Financial leverage: 2.6 (Total assets / Net worth) = Return on net worth: 12.5% (Net profits / Net worth)

turnover by increasing sales or reducing the assets (e.g., inventory, receivables) that are held against a given level of sales.[5]

Customer-Satisfaction Tracking

The preceding control measures are largely financial and quantitative in character. They are important but not sufficient. Needed are qualitative measures that provide early warnings to management of impending market-share changes. Alert companies set up systems to monitor the attitudes and satisfaction of customers, dealers, and other stakeholders. By monitoring changing levels of customer preference and satisfaction before they affect sales, management can take earlier action.

Corrective Action

When performance deviates too much from the plan's goals, management needs to undertake corrective action. Normally the company undertakes minor corrective actions, and if they fail to work, the company adopts more drastic measures. When a large fertilizer company's sales continued to decline, the company resorted to an increasingly drastic set of remedies. First the company ordered cutbacks in production. Then it cut its prices selectively. Next it put more pressure on its salesforce to meet their quotas. The company then cut the budgets for personnel hiring and training, advertising, public relations, and research and development. Soon it introduced personnel cuts through layoffs and early retirement. Next it cut investment in plant and equipment. The company then sold some of its businesses to other companies. Finally, the company sought a buyer.

PROFITABILITY CONTROL

Here are some disconcerting findings from a bank profitability study:

> *We have found that anywhere from 20 to 40 percent of an individual institution's products are unprofitable, and up to 60 percent of their accounts generate losses.*
>
> *Our research has shown that, in most firms, more than half of all customer relationships are not profitable, and 30 to 40 percent are only marginally so. It is frequently a mere 10 to 15 percent of a firm's relationships that generate the bulk of its profits.*
>
> *Our profitability research into the branch system of a regional bank produced some surprising results . . . 30 percent of the bank's branches were unprofitable.*[6]

Companies clearly need to measure the profitability of their various products, territories, customer groups, trade channels, and order sizes.

This information will help management determine whether any products or marketing activities should be expanded, reduced, or eliminated.

Methodology of Marketing-Profitability Analysis

We will illustrate the steps in marketing-profitability analysis with the following example:

> *The marketing vice-president of a lawnmower company wants to determine the profitability of selling its lawnmower through three types of retail channels: hardware stores, garden supply shops, and department stores. Its profit-and-loss statement is shown in Table 2.*

Step 1: Identifying the Functional Expenses. Assume that the expenses listed in Table 2 are incurred to sell the product, advertise it, pack and deliver it, and bill and collect for it. The first task is to measure how much of each expense was incurred in each activity.

Suppose that most salary expense went to sales representatives and the rest went to an advertising manager, packing and delivery help, and an office accountant. Let the breakdown of the $9,300 be $5,100, $1,200, $1,400, and $1,600, respectively. Table 3 shows the allocation of the salary expense to these four activities.

TABLE 2. A Simplified Profit-and-Loss Statement

Sales		$60,000
Cost of goods sold		39,000
Gross margin		$21,000
Expenses		
Salaries	$9,300	
Rent	3,000	
Supplies	3,500	
		15,800
Net profit		$ 5,200

TABLE 3. Mapping Natural Expenses into Functional Expenses

Natural Accounts	Total	Selling	Advertising	Packing and Delivery	Billing and Collecting
Salaries	$ 9,300	$5,100	$1,200	$1,400	$1,600
Rent	3,000	—	400	2,000	600
Supplies	3,500	400	1,500	1,400	200
	$15,800	$5,500	$3,100	$4,800	$2,400

Table 3 also shows the rent account of $3,000 as allocated to the four activities. Since the sales representatives work away from the office, none of the building's rent expense is assigned to selling. Most of the expenses for floor space and rented equipment are in connection with packing and delivery. A small portion of the floor space is used by the advertising manager and office accountant.

Finally, the supplies account covers promotional materials, packing materials, fuel purchases for delivery, and home-office stationery. The $3,500 in this account is reassigned to the functional uses made of the supplies. Table 3 summarizes how the natural expenses of $15,800 were translated into functional expenses.

Step 2: Assigning the Functional Expenses to the Marketing Entities. The next task is to measure how much functional expense was associated with selling through each type of channel. Consider the selling effort. The selling effort is indicated by the number of sales made in each channel. This number is found in the selling column of Table 4. Altogether, 275 sales calls were made during the period. Since the total selling expense amounted to $5,500 (see Table 4), the selling expense per call averaged $20.

Advertising expense can be allocated according to the number of ads addressed to the different channels. Since there were 100 ads altogether, the average ad cost $31.

The packing and delivery expense is allocated according to the number of orders placed by each type of channel; this same basis was used for allocating billing and collection expense.

Step 3: Preparing a Profit-and-Loss Statement for Each Marketing Entity. A profit-and-loss statement can now be prepared for each type of channel. The results are shown in Table 5. Since hardware stores accounted for one half of total sales ($30,000 out of $60,000), this channel is charged with half the cost of goods sold ($19,500 out of $39,000). This leaves a gross margin from hardware stores of $10,500.

TABLE 4. Bases for Allocating Functional Expenses to Channels

Channel Type	Selling	Advertising	Packing and Delivery	Billing and Collecting
Hardware	200	50	50	50
Garden supply	65	20	21	21
Department stores	10	30	9	9
	275	100	80	80
Functional expense	$5,500	$3,100	$4,800	$2,400
No. of Units	275	100	80	80
Equals	$ 20	$ 31	$ 60	$ 30

TABLE 5. Profit-and-Loss Statements for Channels

	Hardware	Garden Supply	Dept. Stores	Whole Company
Sales	$30,000	$10,000	$20,000	$60,000
Cost of goods sold	19,500	6,500	13,000	39,000
Gross margin	$10,500	$ 3,500	$ 7,000	$21,000
Expenses				
Selling ($20 per call)	$ 4,000	$ 1,300	$ 200	$ 5,500
Advertising ($31 per advertisement)	1,550	620	930	3,100
Packing and delivery ($60 per order)	3,000	1,260	540	4,800
Billing ($30 per order)	1,500	630	270	2,400
Total Expenses	$10,050	$ 3,810	$ 1,940	15,800
Net profit or loss	$ 450	$ (310)	$ 5,060	$ 5,200

From this must be deducted the proportions of the functional expenses that hardware stores consumed. According to Table 4, hardware stores received 200 out of 275 total sales calls. At an imputed value of $20 a call, hardware stores have to be charged with a $4,000 selling expense. Table 4 also shows that hardware stores were the target of 50 ads. At $31 an ad, the hardware stores are charged with $1,550 of advertising. The same reasoning applies in computing the share of the other functional expenses to charge to hardware stores. The result is that hardware stores gave rise to $10,500 of the total expenses. Subtracting this from the gross margin, the profit of selling through hardware stores is only $450.

This analysis is repeated for the other channels. The company is losing money in selling through garden supply shops and makes virtually all of its profits in selling through department stores. Notice that the gross sales through each channel are not a reliable indicator of the net profits being made in each channel.

Determining the Best Corrective Action

It would be naive to conclude that garden supply shops and possibly hardware stores should be dropped in order to concentrate on department stores. The following questions would need to be answered first:

- To what extent do buyers buy on the basis of the type of retail outlet versus the brand? Would they seek out the brand in those channels that were not eliminated?
- What are the trends with respect to the importance of these three channels?
- Have company marketing strategies directed at the three channels been optimal?

On the basis of the answers, marketing management can evaluate a number of alternative actions:

- *Establish a Special Charge for Handling Smaller Orders:* This move assumes that small orders are a cause of the relative unprofitability of dealing with garden supply shops and hardware stores.
- *Give More Promotional Aid to Garden Supply Shops and Hardware Stores:* This assumes that the store managers could increase their sales with more training or promotional materials.
- *Reduce the Number of Sales Calls and the Amount of Advertising Going to Garden Supply Shops and Hardware Stores:* This assumes that some costs can be saved without seriously hurting sales in these channels.
- *Do Nothing:* This assumes that current marketing efforts are optimal and either that marketing trends point to an imminent profit improvement in the weaker channels or that dropping any channel would reduce profits because of repercussions on production costs or on demand.
- *Do Not Abandon Any Channel as a Whole but Only the Weakest Retail Units in Each Channel:* This assumes that a detailed cost study would reveal many profitable garden shops and hardware stores whose profits are concealed by the poor performance of other stores in these categories.

In general, marketing-profitability analysis indicates the relative profitability of different channels, products, territories, or other marketing entities.[7] It does not prove that the best course of action is to drop the unprofitable marketing entities, nor does it capture the likely profit improvement if these marginal marketing entities are dropped.

Direct versus Full Costing

Like all information tools, marketing-profitability analysis can lead or mislead marketing executives, depending upon the degree of their understanding of its methods and limitations. The example showed some arbitrariness in the choice of bases for allocating the functional expenses to the marketing entities being evaluated. Thus the "number of sales calls" was used to allocate selling expenses, when in principle, "number of sales working-hours" is a more accurate indicator of cost. The former base was used because it involves less record keeping and computation. These approximations might not involve too much inaccuracy, but marketing executives should acknowledge this judgmental element in determining marketing costs.[8]

Far more serious is another judgmental element affecting profitability analysis. The issue is whether to allocate *full costs* or only *direct and traceable costs* in evaluating the performance of a marketing entity. The preceding example sidestepped this problem by assuming only simple costs that fit in with marketing activities. But the question cannot be avoided in the actual analysis of profitability. Three types of costs have to be distinguished:

- *Direct Costs:* These are costs that can be assigned directly to the proper marketing entities. For example, sales commissions are a direct cost in a profitability analysis of sales territories, sales representatives, or customers. Advertising expenditures are a direct cost in a profitability analysis of products to the extent that each advertisement promotes only one company product. Other direct costs for specific purposes are salesforce salaries, supplies, and traveling expenses.
- *Traceable Common Costs:* These are costs that can be assigned only indirectly, but on a plausible basis, to the marketing entities. In the example, rent was analyzed in this way. The company's floor space was needed for three different marketing activities, and an estimate was made of how much floor space supported each activity.
- *Nontraceable Common Costs:* These are costs whose allocation to the marketing entities is highly arbitrary. Consider "corporate image" expenditures. To allocate them equally to all products would be arbitrary because all products do not benefit equally from corporate image making. To allocate them proportionately to the sales of the various products would be arbitrary because relative product sales reflect many factors besides corporate image making. Other typical examples of difficult-to-assign common costs are top management salaries, taxes, interest, and other types of overhead.

No one disputes including direct costs in marketing cost analysis. There is a small amount of controversy about including traceable common costs. Traceable common costs lump together costs that would change with the scale of marketing activity and costs that would not change. If the lawnmower company drops garden supply shops, it will probably continue to pay the same rent for contractual reasons. In this event, its profits would not rise immediately by the amount of the present loss in selling to garden supply shops ($310). The profit figures are more meaningful when traceable costs can be eliminated.

The major controversy concerns whether the nontraceable common costs should be allocated to the marketing entities. Such allocation is called the *full-cost approach,* and its advocates argue that all costs must ultimately be imputed in order to determine true profitability. But this argument confuses the use of accounting for financial reporting with its use for managerial decision making. Full costing has three major weaknesses:

- The relative profitability of different marketing entities can shift radically when one arbitrary way to allocate nontraceable common costs is replaced by another. This weakens confidence in the tool.
- The arbitrariness demoralizes managers, who feel that their performance is judged adversely.
- The inclusion of nontraceable common costs could weaken efforts at real cost control. Operating management is most effective in controlling direct costs and traceable common costs. Arbitrary assignments of nontraceable common

costs can lead them to spend their time fighting the arbitrary cost allocations rather than managing their controllable costs well.

Companies are showing a growing interest in using *activity-based cost accounting* (ABC) in interpreting the true profitability of different activities. According to Cooper and Kaplan, this tool "can give managers a clear picture of how products, brands, customers, facilities, regions, or distribution channels both generate revenues and consume resources."[9] To improve profitability, the managers can then examine ways to reduce the resources required to perform various activities, or make the resources more productive or acquire them at a lower cost. Alternatively, management may raise prices on products that consume heavy amounts of support resources. The contribution of ABC is to refocus management's attention away from using only labor or material standard costs to allocate full cost to capturing the actual costs of supporting individual products, customers, and other entities.

EFFICIENCY CONTROL

Suppose a profitability analysis reveals that the company is earning poor profits in connection with certain products, territories, or markets. The question is whether there are more efficient ways to manage the salesforce, advertising, sales promotion, and distribution in connection with these poorer-performing marketing entities.

Some companies have established a *marketing controller* position to assist marketing personnel to improve marketing efficiency. Marketing controllers work out of the controller's office but are specialized in the marketing side of the business. At companies such as General Foods, Du Pont, and Johnson & Johnson, they perform a sophisticated financial analysis of marketing expenditures and results. Specifically, they examine adherence to profit plans, help prepare brand managers' budgets, measure the efficiency of promotions, analyze media production costs, evaluate customer and geographic profitability, and educate marketing personnel on the financial implications of marketing decisions.[10]

Salesforce Efficiency

Sales managers need to monitor the following key indicators of salesforce efficiency in their territory:

- Average number of sales calls per salesperson per day
- Average sales-call time per contact
- Average revenue per sales call
- Average cost per sales call
- Entertainment cost per sales call
- Percentage of orders per 100 sales calls
- Number of new customers per period
- Number of lost customers per period
- Salesforce cost as a percentage of total sales

These indicators raise such useful questions as the following: Are sales representatives making too few calls per day? Are they spending too much time per call? Are they spending too much on entertainment? Are they closing enough orders per hundred calls? Are they producing enough new customers and holding onto the old customers?

When a company starts investigating salesforce efficiency, it can often find areas for improvement. General Electric reduced the size of one of its divisional salesforces after discovering that its salespeople were calling on customers too often. When a large airline found that its salespeople were both selling and servicing, they transferred the servicing function to lower-paid clerks. Another company conducted time-and-duty studies and found ways to reduce the ratio of idle-to-productive time.

Advertising Efficiency

Many managers feel that it is almost impossible to measure what they are getting for their advertising dollars. But they should try to keep track of at least the following statistics:

- Advertising cost per thousand target buyers reached by media vehicle
- Percentage of audience who noted, saw/associated, and read most of each print ad
- Consumer opinions on the ad content and effectiveness
- Before-after measures of attitude toward the product
- Number of inquiries stimulated by the ad
- Cost per inquiry

Management can undertake a number of steps to improve advertising efficiency, including doing a better job of positioning the product, defining advertising objectives, pretesting messages, using the computer to guide the selection of advertising media, looking for better media buys, and doing advertising post-testing.

Sales-Promotion Efficiency

Sales promotion includes dozens of devices for stimulating buyer interest and product trial. To improve sales-promotion efficiency, management should record the costs and sales impact of each sales promotion. Management should watch the following statistics:

- Percentage of sales sold on deal
- Display costs per sales dollar
- Percentage of coupons redeemed
- Number of inquiries resulting from a demonstration

If a sales-promotion manager is appointed, that manager can analyze the results of different sales promotions and advise product managers on the most cost-effective promotions to use.

Distribution Efficiency

Management needs to search for distribution economies. Several tools are available for improving inventory control, warehouse locations, and transportation modes. One problem that frequently arises is that distribution efficiency might decline when the company experiences strong sales increases. Peter Senge describes a situation where a strong sales surge causes the company to fall behind in meeting its promised delivery dates.[11] This leads customers to bad-mouth the company and eventually sales fall. Management responds by increasing salesforce incentives to secure more orders. The salesforce succeeds but once again the company slips in meeting its promised delivery dates. Management needs to perceive the real bottleneck and invest in more production and distribution capacity.

STRATEGIC CONTROL

From time to time, companies need to undertake a critical review of their overall marketing goals and effectiveness. Marketing is an area where rapid obsolescence of objectives, policies, strategies, and programs is a constant possibility. Each company should periodically reassess its strategic approach to the marketplace. Two tools are available, namely, a *marketing-effectiveness rating review* and a *marketing audit.*

Marketing-Effectiveness Rating Review

Here is an actual situation: The president of a major industrial-equipment company reviewed the annual business plans of various divisions and found several division plans lacking in marketing substance. He called in the corporate vice-president of marketing and said:

> *I am not happy with the quality of marketing in our divisions. It is very uneven. I want you to find out which of our divisions are strong, average, and weak in marketing. I want to know if they understand and are practicing customer-oriented marketing. I want a marketing score for each division. For each marketing-deficient division, I want a plan for improving its marketing effectiveness over the next several years. I want evidence next year that each marketing-deficient division is improving its market capabilities.*

The corporate marketing vice-president agreed, recognizing that it was a formidable task. His first inclination was to base the evaluation of marketing effectiveness on each division's performance in sales growth, market share, and profitability. His thinking was that high-performing divisions had good marketing leadership and poor-performing divisions had poor marketing leadership.

Marketing effectiveness is not necessarily revealed by current sales and profit performance. Good results could be due to a division's being in the right place at the right time, rather than having effective marketing management. Improvements in that division's marketing might boost results from good to excellent. Another division might have poor results in spite of excellent marketing planning. Replacing the present marketing managers might only make things worse.

The marketing effectiveness of a company or division is reflected in the degree to which it exhibits five major attributes of a marketing orientation: *customer philosophy, integrated marketing organization, adequate marketing information, strategic orientation,* and *operational efficiency.* Each attribute can be measured. Table 6 presents a *marketing-effectiveness rating instrument* based on these five attributes. This instrument is filled out by marketing and other managers in the division. The scores are then summarized.

The instrument has been tested in a number of companies, and very few achieve scores within the superior range of 26 to 30 points. The few include well-known master marketers such as Procter & Gamble, McDonald's, IBM, and Nike. Most companies and divisions receive scores in the fair-to-good range, indicating that their own managers see room for marketing improvement. Low attribute scores indicate that the attribute needs attention. Divisional management can then establish a plan for correcting its major marketing weaknesses.[12]

The Marketing Audit

Those companies that discover marketing weaknesses through applying the marketing-effectiveness rating review should undertake a more thorough study known as a *marketing audit.*[13] We define *marketing audit* as follows:

- *A* marketing audit *is a comprehensive, systematic, independent, and periodic examination of a company's—or business unit's—marketing environment, objectives, strategies, and activities with a view to determining problem areas and opportunities and recommending a plan of action to improve the company's marketing performance.*

Let us examine the marketing audit's four characteristics:

- *Comprehensive:* The marketing audit covers all the major marketing activities of a business, not just a few trouble spots. It would be called a functional audit if it covered only the salesforce or pricing or some other marketing activity. Although functional audits are useful, they sometimes mislead management as to the real source of its problem. Excessive salesforce turnover, for example, could be a symptom not of poor salesforce training or compensation but of weak company products and promotion. A comprehensive marketing audit usually is more effective in locating the real source of the company's marketing problems.

- *Systematic:* The marketing audit involves an orderly sequence of diagnostic steps covering the organization's macro- and micromarketing environment, marketing objectives and strategies, marketing systems, and specific marketing activities. The diagnosis indicates the most needed improvements. They are incorporated in a corrective-action plan involving both short-run and long-run steps to improve the organization's overall marketing effectiveness.
- *Independent:* A marketing audit can be conducted in six ways: self-audit, audit from across, audit from above, company auditing office, company task-force audit, and outsider audit. Self-audits, where managers use a checklist to rate their own operations, can be useful, but most experts agree that self-audits lack objectivity and independence.[14] The 3M Company has made good use of a corporate auditing office, which provides marketing audit services to divisions on request.[15] Generally speaking, however, the best audits are likely to come from outside consultants who have the necessary objectivity, broad experience in a number of industries, some familiarity with this industry, and the undivided time and attention to give to the audit.
- *Periodic:* Typically, marketing audits are initiated only after sales have turned down, salesforce morale has fallen, and other company problems have occurred. Ironically, companies are thrown into a crisis partly because they failed to review their marketing operations during good times. A periodic marketing audit can benefit companies in good health as well as those in trouble. "No marketing operation is ever so good that it cannot be improved. Even the best can be made better. In fact, even the best *must* be better, for few if any marketing operations can remain successful over the years by maintaining the status quo."[16]

Marketing Audit Procedure. A marketing audit starts with a meeting between the company officer(s) and the marketing auditor(s) to work out an agreement on the objectives, coverage, depth, data sources, report format, and the time period for the audit. A detailed plan as to who is to be interviewed, the questions to be asked, the time and place of contact, and so on, is carefully prepared so that auditing time and cost are kept to a minimum. The cardinal rule in marketing auditing is: Don't rely solely on the company's managers for data and opinion. Customers, dealers, and other outside groups must be interviewed. Many companies do not really know how their customers and dealers see them, nor do they fully understand customer needs and value judgments.

When the data-gathering phase is over, the marketing auditor presents the main findings and recommendations. A valuable aspect of the marketing audit is the process that the managers go through to assimilate, debate, and develop new concepts of needed marketing action.

Components of the Marketing Audit. The marketing audit examines six major components of the company's marketing situation. The major auditing questions are listed in Table 7.

TABLE 6. Marketing-Effectiveness Rating Instrument
(Check One Answer to Each Question)

CUSTOMER PHILOSOPHY

A. Does management recognize the importance of designing the company to serve the needs and wants of chosen markets?

0 ☐ Management primarily thinks in terms of selling current and new products to whomever will buy them.

1 ☐ Management thinks in terms of serving a wide range of markets and needs with equal effectiveness.

2 ☐ Management thinks in terms of serving the needs and wants of well-defined markets and market segments chosen for their long-run growth and profit potential for the company.

B. Does management develop different offerings and marketing plans for different segments of the market?

0 ☐ No.

1 ☐ Somewhat.

2 ☐ To a large extent.

C. Does management take a whole marketing system view (suppliers, channels, competitors, customers, environment) in planning its business?

0 ☐ No. Management concentrates on selling and servicing its immediate customers.

1 ☐ Somewhat. Management takes a long view of its channels although the bulk of its effort goes to selling and servicing the immediate customers.

2 ☐ Yes. Management takes a whole marketing systems view, recognizing the threats and opportunities created for the company by changes in any part of the system.

INTEGRATED MARKETING ORGANIZATION

D. Is there high-level marketing integration and control of the major marketing functions?

0 ☐ No. Sales and other marketing functions are not integrated at the top and there is some unproductive conflict.

1 ☐ Somewhat. There is formal integration and control of the major marketing functions but less than satisfactory coordination and cooperation.

2 ☐ Yes. The major marketing functions are effectively integrated.

E. Does marketing management work well with management in research, manufacturing, purchasing, physical distribution, and finance?

0 ☐ No. There are complaints that marketing is unreasonable in the demands and costs it places on other departments.

1 ☐ Somewhat. The relations are amicable although each department pretty much acts to serve its own interests.

2 ☐ Yes. The departments cooperate effectively and resolve issues in the best interest of the company as a whole.

F. How well organized is the new-product development process?

0 ☐ The system is ill-defined and poorly handled.

1 ☐ The system formally exists but lacks sophistication.

2 ☐ The system is well-structured and operates on teamwork principles.

ADEQUATE MARKETING INFORMATION

G. When were the latest marketing research studies of customers, buying influences, channels, and competitors conducted?

0 ☐ Several years ago.

1 ☐ A few years ago.

2 ☐ Recently.

H. How well does management know the sales potential and profitability of different market segments, customers, territories, products, channels, and order sizes?

0 ☐ Not at all.
1 ☐ Somewhat.
2 ☐ Very well.

I. What effort is expended to measure and improve the cost effectiveness of different marketing expenditures?

0 ☐ Little or no effort.
1 ☐ Some effort.
2 ☐ Substantial effort.

STRATEGIC ORIENTATION

J. What is the extent of formal marketing planning?

0 ☐ Management conducts little or no formal marketing planning.
1 ☐ Management develops an annual marketing plan.
2 ☐ Management develops a detailed annual marketing plan and a strategic long-range plan that is updated annually.

K. How impressive is the current marketing strategy?

0 ☐ The current strategy is not clear.
1 ☐ The current strategy is clear and represents a continuation of traditional strategy.
2 ☐ The current strategy is clear, innovative, data based, and well reasoned.

L. What is the extent of contingency thinking and planning?

0 ☐ Management does little or no contingency thinking.
1 ☐ Management does some contingency thinking although little formal contingency planning.
2 ☐ Management formally identifies the most important contingencies and develops contingency plans.

OPERATIONAL EFFICIENCY

M. How well is the marketing strategy communicated and implemented?

0 ☐ Poorly.
1 ☐ Fairly.
2 ☐ Successfully.

N. Is management doing an effective job with its marketing resources?

0 ☐ No. The marketing resources are inadequate for the job to be done.
1 ☐ Somewhat. The marketing resources are adequate but they are not employed optimally.
2 ☐ Yes. The marketing resources are adequate and are employed efficiently.

O. Does management show a good capacity to react quickly and effectively to on-the-spot developments?

0 ☐ No. Sales and market information is not very current and management reaction time is slow.
1 ☐ Somewhat. Management receives fairly up-to-date sales and market information; management reaction time varies.
2 ☐ Yes. Management has installed systems yielding high current information and fast reaction time.

TOTAL SCORE

The instrument is used in the following way. The appropriate answer is checked for each question. The scores are added—the total will be somewhere between 0 and 30. The following scale shows the level of marketing effectiveness:

0–5 = None	11–15 = Fair	21–25 = Very good
6–10 = Poor	16–20 = Good	26–30 = Superior

Source: Philip Kotler, "From Sales Obsession to Marketing Effectiveness," *Harvard Business Review,* November–December 1977, pp. 67–75.

TABLE 7. Components of a Marketing Audit

PART I. MARKETING-ENVIRONMENT AUDIT	
Macroenvironment	
A. Demographic	What major demographic developments and trends pose opportunities or threats to this company? What actions has the company taken in response to these developments and trends?
B. Economic	What major developments in income, prices, savings, and credit will affect the company? What actions has the company been taking in response to these developments and trends?
C. Ecological	What is the outlook for the cost and availability of natural resources and energy needed by the company? What concerns have been expressed about the company's role in pollution and conservation, and what steps has the company taken?
D. Technological	What major changes are occurring in product and process technology? What is the company's position in these technologies? What major generic substitutes might replace this product?
E. Political	What changes in laws and regulations might affect marketing strategy and tactics? What is happening in the areas of pollution control, equal employment opportunity, product safety, advertising, price control, and so forth, that affects marketing strategy?
F. Cultural	What is the public's attitude toward business and toward the company's products? What changes in customer lifestyles and values might affect the company?
Task Environment	
A. Markets	What is happening to market size, growth, geographical distribution, and profits? What are the major market segments?
B. Customers	What are the customers' needs and buying processes? How do customers and prospects rate the company and its competitors on reputation, product quality, service, salesforce, and price? How do different customer segments make their buying decisions?
C. Competitors	Who are the major competitors? What are their objectives, strategies, strengths, weaknesses, sizes, and market shares? What trends will affect future competition and substitutes for this product?
D. Distribution and Dealers	What are the main trade channels for bringing products to customers? What are the efficiency levels and growth potentials of the different trade channels?
E. Suppliers	What is the outlook for the availability of key resources used in production? What trends are occurring among suppliers?
F. Facilitators and Marketing Firms	What is the cost and availability outlook for transportation services, warehousing facilities, and financial resources? How effective are the company's advertising agencies and marketing research firms?
G. Publics	Which publics represent particular opportunities or problems for the company? What steps has the company taken to deal effectively with each public?

PART II. MARKETING-STRATEGY AUDIT

A. Business Mission	Is the business mission clearly stated in market-oriented terms? Is it feasible?
B. Marketing Objectives and Goals	Are the company and marketing objectives and goals stated clearly enough to guide marketing planning and performance measurement? Are the marketing objectives appropriate, given the company's competitive position, resources, and opportunities?
C. Strategy	Has the management articulated a clear marketing strategy for achieving its marketing objectives? Is the strategy convincing? Is the strategy appropriate to the stage of the product life cycle, competitors' strategies, and the state of the economy? Is the company using the best basis for market segmentation? Does it have clear criteria for rating the segments and choosing the best ones? Has it developed accurate profiles of each target segment? Has the company developed an effective positioning and marketing mix for each target segment? Are marketing resources allocated optimally to the major elements of the marketing mix? Are enough resources or too many resources budgeted to accomplish the marketing objectives?

PART III. MARKETING-ORGANIZATION AUDIT

A. Formal Structure	Does the marketing vice-president have adequate authority and responsibility for company activities that affect customers' satisfaction? Are the marketing activities optimally structured along functional, product, segment, end-user, and geographical lines?
B. Functional Efficiency	Are there good communication and working relations between marketing and sales? Is the product management system working effectively? Are product managers able to plan profits or only sales volume? Are there any groups in marketing that need more training, motivation, supervision, or evaluation?
C. Interface Efficiency	Are there any problems between marketing and manufacturing, R&D, purchasing, finance, accounting, and legal that need attention?

PART IV. MARKETING-SYSTEMS AUDIT

A. Marketing Information System	Is the marketing intelligence system producing accurate, sufficient, and timely information about marketplace developments with respect to customers; prospects, distributors and dealers, competitors, suppliers, and various publics? Are company decision makers asking for enough marketing research, and are they using the results? Is the company employing the best methods for market measurement and sales forecasting?
B. Marketing Planning Systems	Is the marketing planning system well conceived and effectively used? Do marketers have decision support systems available? Does the planning system result in acceptable sales targets and quotas?

C. Marketing Control System	Are the control procedures adequate to ensure that the annual-plan objectives are being achieved? Does management periodically analyze the profitability of products, markets, territories, and channels of distribution? Are marketing costs and productivity periodically examined?
D. New-Product Development System	Is the company well organized to gather, generate, and screen new-product ideas? Does the company do adequate concept research and business analysis before investing in new ideas? Does the company carry out adequate product and market testing before launching new products?

PART V. MARKETING-PRODUCTIVITY AUDIT

A. Profitability Analysis	What is the profitability of the company's different products, markets, territories, and channels of distribution? Should the company enter, expand, contract, or withdraw from any business segments?
B. Cost-Effectiveness Analysis	Do any marketing activities seem to have excessive costs? Can cost-reducing steps be taken?

PART VI. MARKETING-FUNCTION AUDITS

A. Products	What are the product-line objectives? Are they sound? Is the current product line meeting the objectives? Should the product line be stretched or contracted upward, downward, or both ways? Which products should be phased out? Which products should be added? What are the buyers' knowledge and attitudes toward the company's and competitors' product quality, features, styling, brand names, and so on? What areas of product and brand strategy need improvement?
B. Price	What are the pricing objectives, policies, strategies, and procedures? To what extent are prices set on cost, demand, and competitive criteria? Do the customers see the company's prices as being in line with the value of its offer? What does management know about the price elasticity of demand, experience-curve effects, and competitors' prices and pricing policies? To what extent are price policies compatible with the needs of distributors and dealers, suppliers, and government regulation?
C. Distribution	What are the distribution objectives and strategies? Is there adequate market coverage and service? How effective are distributors, dealers, manufacturers' representatives, brokers, agents, and others? Should the company consider changing its distribution channels?
D. Advertising, Sales Promotion, and Publicity	What are the organization's advertising objectives? Are they sound? Is the right amount being spent on advertising? Are the ad themes and copy effective? What do customers and the public think about the advertising? Are the advertising media well chosen? Is the internal advertising staff adequate? Is the sales-promotion budget adequate? Is there effective and sufficient use of sales-promotion tools such as samples, coupons, displays, and sales contests? Is the public-relations staff competent and creative? Is the company making enough use of direct and database marketing?

E. Salesforce	What are the salesforce objectives? Is the salesforce large enough to accomplish the company's objectives? Is the salesforce organized along the proper principles of specialization (territory, market, product)? Are there enough (or too many) sales managers to guide the field sales representatives? Does the sales-compensation level and structure provide adequate incentive and reward? Does the salesforce show high morale, ability, and effort? Are the procedures adequate for setting quotas and evaluating performances? How does the company's salesforce compare to competitors' salesforces?

Example of a Marketing Audit.[17] O'Brien Candy Company is a medium-size candy company located in the Midwest. In the past two years, its sales and profits have barely held their own. Top management feels that the trouble lies with the salesforce; they don't "work hard or smart enough." To correct the problem, management plans to introduce a new incentive-compensation system and hire a salesforce trainer to train the salesforce in modern merchandising and selling techniques. Before doing this, however, they decide to hire a marketing consultant to carry out a marketing audit. The auditor interviews managers, customers, sales representatives, and dealers and examines various data. Here are the auditor's findings:

> *The company's product line consists primarily of 18 products, mostly candy bars. Its two leading brands are mature and account for 76% of total sales. The company has looked at the fast-developing markets of chocolate snacks and candies but has not made any moves yet.*
>
> *The company recently researched its customer profile. Its products appeal especially to lower-income and older people. Respondents who were asked to assess O'Brien's chocolate products in relation to competitors' products described them as "average quality and a bit old-fashioned."*
>
> *O'Brien sells its products to candy jobbers and large supermarkets. Its salesforce calls on many of the small retailers reached by the candy jobbers, to fortify displays and provide ideas; its salesforce also calls on many small retailers not covered by jobbers. O'Brien enjoys good penetration of small retailing, although not in all segments, such as the fast-growing restaurant area. Its major approach to middlemen is a "sell-in" strategy: discounts, exclusive contracts, and stock financing. At the same time O'Brien has not adequately penetrated the mass-merchandise chains. Its competitors rely more heavily on mass-consumer advertising and in-store merchandising and are more successful with the mass merchandisers.*
>
> *O'Brien's marketing budget is set at 15% of its total sales, compared with competitors' budgets of close to 20%. Most of the marketing budget supports the salesforce, and the remainder supports advertising; consumer promotions are very limited. The advertising budget is spent*

primarily in reminder advertising for the company's two leading products. New products are not developed often, and when they are, they are introduced to retailers by using a "push" strategy.

The marketing organization is headed by a sales vice-president. Reporting to the sales vice-president is the sales manager, the marketing research manager, and the advertising manager. Having come up from the ranks, the sales vice-president is partial to salesforce activities and pays less attention to the other marketing functions. The salesforce is assigned to territories headed by area managers.

The marketing auditor concluded that O'Brien's problems would not be solved by actions taken to improve its salesforce. The salesforce problem was symptomatic of a deeper company malaise. The auditor prepared a report to management consisting of the findings and recommendations shown in Table 8.

The Marketing Excellence Review

Companies can use another instrument to rate their performance in relation to the "best practices" of high-performing businesses. The three columns in Table 9 distinguish between poor, good, and excellent business and marketing practice. Management can place a check on each line as to their perception of where the business stands. The resulting profile then exposes the business's weaknesses and strengths. It highlights where the company might move to become a truly outstanding player in the marketplace.

The Company Ethical and Social Responsibility Review

Companies need to use a final instrument to evaluate whether they are truly practicing ethical and socially responsible marketing. We believe that business success and continually satisfying the customer and other stakeholders is intimately tied up with adopting and implementing high standards of business and marketing conduct. The most admired companies in the world abide by a code of serving people's interests, not only their own.

The practices of business are often under attack because business situations routinely pose tough dilemmas as to what is right. One can go back to Howard Bowen's classic questions about the responsibilities of businesspeople:

Should he conduct selling in ways that intrude on the privacy of people, for example, by door-to-door selling . . . ? Should he use methods involving ballyhoo, chances, prizes, hawking, and other tactics which are at least of doubtful good taste? Should he employ "high pressure" tactics in persuading people to buy? Should he try to hasten the obsolescence of goods by bringing out an endless succession of new models and new styles? Should he appeal to and attempt to strengthen the motives of materialism, invidious consumption, and "keeping up with the Joneses."[18]

TABLE 8. Summary of Marketing Auditor's Findings and Recommendations for O'Brien Candy Company

FINDINGS

The company's product lines are dangerously unbalanced. The two leading products accounted for 76% of total sales and have no growth potential. Five of the 18 products are unprofitable and have no growth potential.

The company's marketing objectives are neither clear nor realistic.

The company's strategy is not taking changing distribution patterns into account or catering to rapidly changing markets.

The company is run by a sales organization rather than a marketing organization.

The company's marketing mix is unbalanced, with too much spending on salesforce and not enough on advertising.

The company lacks procedures for successfully developing and launching new products.

The company's selling effort is not geared to profitable accounts.

SHORT-TERM RECOMMENDATIONS

Examine the current product line and weed out marginal performers with limited growth potential.

Shift some marketing expenditures from supporting mature products to supporting more recent ones.

Shift the marketing-mix emphasis from direct selling to national advertising, especially for new products.

Conduct a market-profile study of the fastest growing segments of the candy market and develop a plan to break into these areas.

Instruct the salesforce to drop some of the smaller outlets and not to take orders for under 20 items. Also, cut out the duplication of effort of sales representatives and jobbers calling on the same accounts.

Initiate sales-training programs and an improved compensation plan.

MEDIUM- TO LONG-TERM RECOMMENDATIONS

Hire an experienced marketing vice-president from the outside.

Set formal and operational marketing objectives.

Introduce the product manager concept in the marketing organization.

Initiate effective new-product-development programs.

Develop strong brand names.

Find ways to market its brands to the chain stores more effectively.

Increase the level of marketing expenditures to 20% of sales.

Reorganize the selling function by specializing sales representatives by distribution channels.

Set sales objectives and base sales compensation on gross profit performance.

Source: Adapted with permission from Dr. Ernst A. Tirmann, "Should Your Marketing Be Audited?" *European Business*. Autumn 1971.

TABLE 9. The Marketing Excellence Review: Best Practices

Poor	**Good**	**Excellent**
Product Driven	Market Driven	Market Driving
Mass-Market Oriented	Segment Oriented	Niche Oriented and Customer Oriented
Product Offer	Augmented Product Offer	Customer Solutions Offer
Average Product Quality	Better Than Average	Legendary
Average Service Quality	Better Than Average	Legendary
End-Product Oriented	Core-Product Oriented	Core-Competency Oriented
Function Oriented	Process Oriented	Outcome Oriented
Reacting to Competitors	Benchmarking Competitors	Leapfrogging Competitors
Supplier Exploitation	Supplier Preference	Supplier Partnership
Dealer Exploitation	Dealer Support	Dealer Partnership
Price Driven	Quality Driven	Value Driven
Average Speed	Better Than Average	Legendary
Hierarchy	Network	Teamwork
Vertically Integrated	Flattened Organization	Strategic Alliances
Stockholder Driven	Stakeholder Driven	Societally Driven

Specific issues are further highlighted in Figure 4. Many were reviewed in earlier chapters. Clearly the company's bottom line cannot be the sole measure of corporate performance.

Raising the level of socially responsible marketing calls for a three-pronged attack. First, society must use the law to define, as clearly as possible, those practices which are illegal, antisocial, or anticompetitive. Second, companies must adopt and disseminate a written code of ethics, build a company tradition of ethical behavior, and hold their people fully responsible for observing the ethical and legal guidelines. Third, individual marketers must practice a "social conscience" in their specific dealings with customers and various stakeholders.

The future holds a wealth of opportunities for companies as they move into the twenty-first century. Technological advances in solar energy, home computers, cable television, modern medicine, transportation, recreation, and communication promise to change the world as we know it. At the same time, forces in the socio-economic, cultural, and natural environments will impose new limits on marketing and business practice. Companies that are able to innovate new solutions and values in a socially responsible way are the most likely to succeed.

FIGURE 4. Major Marketing Decision Areas Posing Legal or Ethical Questions

SELLING DECISIONS
Bribing?
Stealing trade secrets?
Disparaging customers?
Misrepresenting?
Disclosure of customer rights?
Unfair discrimination?
ADVERTISING DECISIONS
False advertising?
Deceptive advertising?
Bait-and-switch advertising?
Promotional allowances
and services?
CHANNEL DECISIONS
Exclusive dealing?
Exclusive territorial distributorships?
Tying agreements?
Dealers' rights?
COMPETITIVE RELATIONS
DECISIONS
Anticompetitive acquisition?
Barriers to entry?
Predatory competition?
PRODUCT DECISIONS
Product additions and deletions?
Patent protection?
Product quality and safety?
Product warranty?
Harmful products?
PACKAGING DECISIONS
Fair packaging and labeling?
Excessive cost?
Scarce resource?
Pollution?
PRICE DECISIONS
Price fixing?
Resale price maintenance?
Price discrimination?
Deceptive pricing?

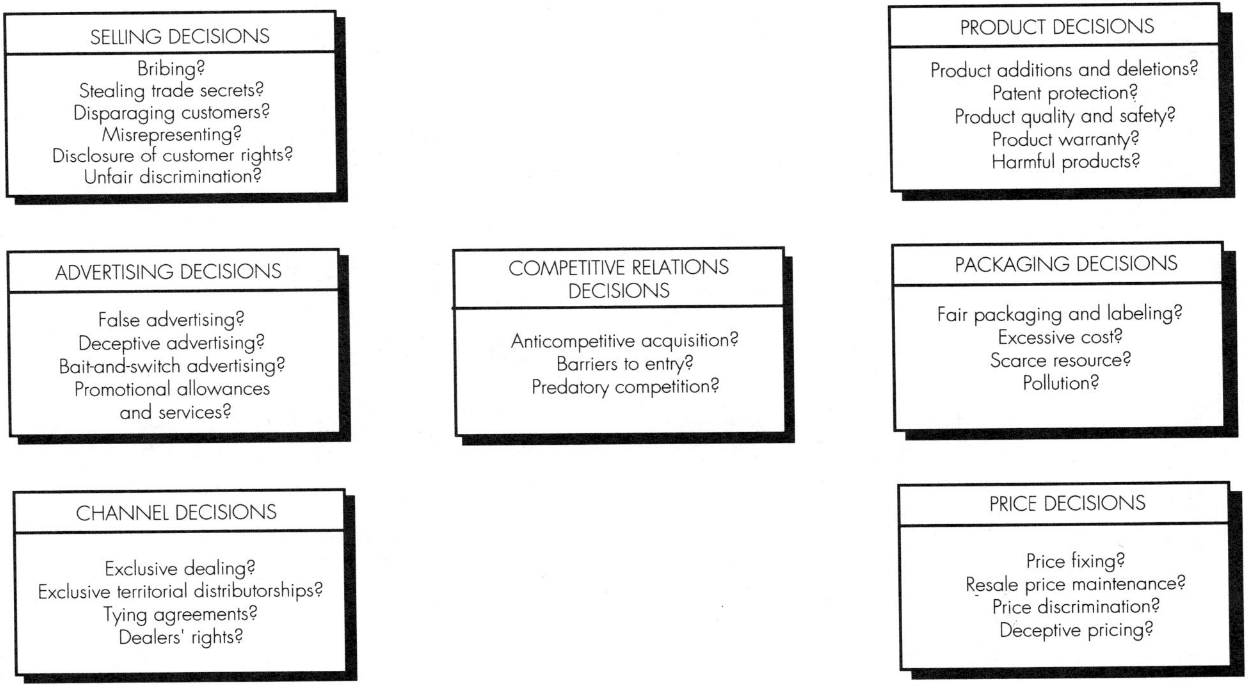

SUMMARY

Marketing control is the natural sequel to marketing planning, organization, and implementation. Companies need to carry out four types of marketing control.

Annual-plan control consists of monitoring the current marketing effort and results to ensure that the annual sales and profit goals will be achieved. The main tools are sales analysis, market-share analysis, marketing expense-to-sales analysis, financial analysis, and customer-satisfaction tracking. If underperformance is detected, the company can implement several corrective measures, including cutting production, changing prices, increasing salesforce pressure, and cutting fringe expenditures.

Profitability control calls for determining the actual profitability of the firm's products, territories, market-segments, and trade channels. Marketing-profitability analysis reveals the weaker marketing entities, although it does not indicate whether the weaker units should be bolstered or phased out.

Efficiency control is the task of increasing the efficiency of such marketing activities as personal selling, advertising, sales promotion, and distribution. Managers must watch certain key ratios that indicate how efficiently these functions are being performed.

Strategic control is the task of ensuring that the company's marketing objectives, strategies, and systems are optimally adapted to the current and forecasted marketing environment. One tool, known as the marketing-effectiveness rating instrument, profiles a company's or a division's overall marketing effectiveness in terms of customer philosophy, marketing organization, marketing information, strategic planning, and operational efficiency. Another tool, the marketing audit, is a comprehensive, systematic, independent, and periodic examination of the organization's marketing environment, objectives, strategies, and activities. The marketing audit seeks to identify marketing problem areas and recommends short-run and long-run actions to improve the organization's overall marketing effectiveness. The marketing excellence review helps a company grade its practices in relation to the "best practices" of high-performing companies. Finally, the company ethical and social responsibility review helps the company assess the quality of its performance along ethical and social responsibility lines.

NOTES

1. For further discussion, see James M. Hulbert and Norman E. Toy, "A Strategic Framework for Marketing Control." *Journal of Marketing,* April 1977, pp. 12–20.

2. See Alfred R. Oxenfeldt, "How to Use Market-Share Measurement," *Harvard Business Review,* January–February 1969, pp. 59–68.

3. There is a one-half chance that a successive observation will be higher or lower. Therefore, the probability of finding six successively higher values is given by $(\frac{1}{2})^6 = \frac{1}{64}$.

4. Alternatively, companies need to focus on the factors affecting *shareholder value.* The goal of marketing planning is to take the steps that will increase shareholder value. Shareholder value is the *present value* of the future income stream created by the company's present actions. *Rate-of-return analysis* usually focuses on only one year's results. See Alfred Rapport, *Creating Shareholder Value* (New York: Free Press, 1986), pp. 125–30.

5. For additional reading on financial analysis, see Peter L. Mullins, *Measuring Customer and Product Line Profitability* (Washington, DC: Distribution Research and Education Foundation, 1984).

6. The MAC Group, *Distribution: A Competitive Weapon* (Cambridge, MA: 1985), p. 20.

7. For another example, see Leland L. Beik and Stephen L. Buzby, "Profitability Analyses by Market Segments," *Journal of Marketing,* June 1973, pp. 48–53.

8. For common bases of allocation, see Charles H. Sevin, *Marketing Productivity Analysis* (New York: McGraw-Hill, 1965).

9. See Robin Cooper and Robert S. Kaplan, "Profit Priorities from Activity-Based Costing," *Harvard Business Review,* May–June 1991, pp. 130–35.

10. Sam R. Goodman, *Increasing Corporate Profitability* (New York: Ronald Press, 1982), Chap. 1.

11. See Peter M. Senge, *The Fifth Discipline: The Art & Practice of the Learning Organization* (New York: Doubleday Currency, 1990), Chapter 7.

12. For further discussion of this instrument, see Philip Kotler, "From Sales Obsession to Marketing Effectiveness," *Harvard Business Review,* November–December 1977, pp. 67–75.

13. See Philip Kotler, William Gregor, and William Rodgers, "The Marketing Audit Comes of Age," *Sloan Management Review,* Winter 1977, pp. 25–43.

14. However, useful checklists for a marketing self-audit can be found in Aubrey Wilson, *Aubrey Wilson's Marketing Audit Checklists* (London: McGraw-Hill, 1982); and Mike Wilson, *The Management of Marketing* (Westmead, England: Gower Publishing, 1980). Also a marketing audit software program is described in Ben M. Enis and Stephen J. Garfein, "The Computer-Driven Marketing Audit," *Journal of Management Inquiry,* December 1992, pp. 306–18.

15. Kotler, Gregor, and Rodgers, "Marketing Audit Comes of Age," p. 31.

16. Abe Schuchman, "The Marketing Audit: Its Nature, Purposes, and Problems," in *Analyzing and Improving Marketing Performance,* eds. Alfred Oxenfeldt and Richard D. Crisp (New York: American Management Association, 1950), report no. 32, pp. 16–17.

17. This case is adapted with permission from the excellent article by Dr. Ernst A. Tirmann, "Should Your Marketing Be Audited?" *European Business,* Autumn 1971, pp. 49–56.

18. Howard R. Bowen, *Social Responsibilities of the Businessman* (New York: Harper & Row, 1953), p. 215.

PART SIX

PUTTING THE MARKETING PLAN INTO ACTION FOR CONSUMER PRODUCTS/SERVICES

PART SIX

INTRODUCTION

Part Six examines a range of issues that become relevant to implementing marketing planning. Here, these issues are taken up in relation to consumers of products and services; the following chapters review the business marketing situation. Focusing on consumers is at the heart of marketing activities, given the importance of end users. Marketing research, as discussed in Part Four, provides insights into opportunities and assists in formulating goals. Implementing these goals requires consideration of how to use the marketing mix of product, place, price, and promotion in interacting with consumers. (Promotion is taken up separately in Part Eight.) Part Six begins with a chapter on the diffusion of innovations, in recognition of the fact that it is the desire to introduce a new product or service that often confronts managers with the need to think about how to address the market.

The next chapters are new contributions to the *Handbook* that reflect the great recent growth of interest in the topic of consumer services. Of course, services always were a significant part of marketing. But the transcendental increase in the part of the economy devoted to services has stimulated much fresh thinking and study of the role of services and how to implement them. At the same time, competitive pressures have led the presenters of traditional products to see the necessity of satisfying consumers by relating to them with greater vigor. The concept of quality—presumably always a desirable aim—was given new vitality by the enhanced conscientiousness that Japan brought to the marketplace. Product quality and service quality have become taken for granted as fostering ever-rising standards for aspiring marketers.

The movement of marketing thinking into areas other than business got under way in the early 1970s. The article, "Broadening the Concept of Marketing," by Philip Kotler and Sidney J. Levy (in the January 1969 issue of the *Journal of Marketing*), awakened an awareness of the need for marketing by all individuals and organizations. The use of marketing by nonprofit organizations and to implement various social goals is now widespread and continues to generate interest. Recognizing that marketing managers are now working in such nonbusiness settings, this development is discussed in the chapter on social marketing.

This edition of the *Handbook* provides an enlarged discussion of the topic of pricing. It is examined as a central marketing strategy, and the chapter on yield management offers intriguing examples of the ingenuity and adeptness with which pricing can be employed. The success of these examples may be debated, given their complexity and the mixed reactions of travelers when faced with the variegated rates of hotels and airlines. However, yield management is just a sophisticated version (made possible by the computer) of the changing prices that go on in bargaining situations, sales, and markdowns, where there is sensitivity and adaptation to the changing worth of products.

The importance of channels of distribution is given attention in this part of the *Handbook* by the chapters on franchising and the role of strategic planning in retailing. Among the many changes in marketing over the past 10 years have been the formidable developments in retailing. These include the proliferation of products and kinds of retail outlets; the growth of shopping strips, centers, and malls; and the intensified power struggle going on among retailers, manufacturers, and distributors.

George R. Frerichs
President
GRFI, Ltd.
Chicago, Illinois

CHAPTER 41

THE DIFFUSION OF INNOVATIONS

It is commonly agreed among product managers and others that eight out of every ten new products or services introduced to the market on a full-scale basis fail in terms of the objectives the product was intended to achieve. With the increasingly important role that new products play in the overall marketing process this high failure rate is very costly. It is vital, then, that marketing practitioners become familiar with past and current research concerning new product and service offerings. This area of research is generally termed the diffusion of innovations area. The exploration of this field is the concern of this chapter. The major phenomena and processes involved in the adoption and diffusion of new ideas, practices, and products are discussed, and the findings of importance to marketing practitioners are presented.

Three basic terms used throughout the discussion need definition. These terms are *innovation, adoption,* and *diffusion.* An innovation is any idea, practice, or product (including services) that is perceived by the consumer as being new. It does not matter how long the product has been in the market, nor does it matter how many other people have adopted it. The important factor is that the consumer sees it as new and consequently is likely to behave toward this product in a manner that differs from the way he behaves toward products that he does not perceive as new. The adoption of innovations refers to the processes whereby an innovation becomes the most acceptable alternative available at that time. Should other things remain constant, and the same need or desire continue or arise again, the same item would be employed once more. The diffusion process is the process whereby an innovation is disseminated and accepted among individuals or other adopter units, such as the family or firm. Innovation decision making is a central phenomenon in the adoption process while dissemination is central to the diffusion process. In the discussion to follow, several key concepts relevant to the adoption and diffusion of innovations in marketing are presented.

THE UNIT OF ADOPTION

Defining the Relevant Units

One of the most critical tasks facing marketers of innovations is to define the potential user of the innovation being placed on the market. In doing this, it is especially important that distinctions be made between four basic roles. First there is the *user* of the innovation who actually practices the innovation or places it into operation and maintains its use. Next there is the *decision maker* who determines whether or not a given innovation is accepted. A third role is that of the *implementer* who carries out the decision and makes the purchase so that the new product is available to users. The fourth role is that of *influencer.* This person may influence the decision-making process, the implementation of the decision, or the way the decision is put into effect and the innovation used. One individual can play all four roles or the four roles may be enacted by different persons. Moreover, there may be more than one person involved in any single role. Several persons may be involved in the decision-making process, for example. This is common in formal organizations. Also, some decisions affecting the family involve the participation of more than one family member. Very often in a specific new product context, people occupying the various roles will be found to have common behavioral factors such as their information seeking and processing. By identifying the relevant roles and determining what behavioral and other characteristics the people involved in those roles share enables the marketer to develop promotional campaigns for each group. This maximizes the likelihood that most people in the various roles will be favorably influenced toward the innovation.

Decision-Making Processes

In addition to segmenting the market for an innovation on the basis of the different functions performed relevant to the ultimate adoption of an innovation by the intended users, it is also important to study the decision-making process individuals engage in when considering an innovation. The discussion to follow takes the perspective of the decision maker who is also the intended user of the innovation. This is one of the most frequently found situations in consumer marketing. The purpose of studying decision-making processes is that the understanding obtained provides a knowledge foundation upon which the marketer can build a more effective promotional campaign. For example, knowing what kinds of information individuals seek at different stages in their thinking enables the marketer to select more knowledgeably the particular information to present to potential consumers and to coordinate this presentation with consumer movement from one stage to another. In this way, the marketer is also able to hasten the overall decision-making process and hence achieve more rapid acceptance of his product.

Many models of consumer innovation adoption decision processes have been presented in the literature.[1] One particular model that integrates the various models into a unified comprehensive scheme is presented here.

Perception. There are two components to perception. First, individuals must perceive or experience a need for the innovation. Secondly, there must be an awareness or perception of an innovation's having the potential capacity to satisfy the felt need. Sometimes the perception of the need comes first and sometimes the perception of the innovation occurs first. There is no rule of thumb to indicate when product perception will precede need perception and vice versa.

Motivation. The perception of a need and an innovation are insufficient to stimulate decision making. The consumer must want to satisfy the need involved. This requires that the strength of the felt need must exceed a certain level of intensity so that the consumer is motivated to satisfy that particular need rather than other competing needs. Also, the consumer must believe that the innovation has a significant probability of satisfying the need so that he or she will be motivated to investigate the innovation. Some researchers add a third condition, namely, that the consumer perceive the innovation as being obtainable within the constraints of available resources.

Attitude. The next stage of the process is attitude. The attitude stage contains three components that have been suggested by numerous sources: cognitive (knowledge), affective (feelings), and behavioral intentions. As the individual moves through the attitude stage, beliefs are developed about the innovation based on information received in interactions with other people, in reading advertisements, in reviewing reports on the product as published in various consumer magazines, etc. Beliefs of this type have been classified as peripheral beliefs. They are based on information supplied by authorities who are viewed by the consumer as being trustworthy.

Legitimation. The legitimation state is when the individual seeks reinforcement for the purchase he or she is contemplating. The appropriateness of the purchase is of prime importance. Appropriateness of the purchase may be determined by observing whether other persons have adopted or are considering adopting the innovations or by seeking affirmation from friends, relatives, or experts. Thus it is important to present new products as being accepted by or acceptable to the relevant people from whom potential adopters seek approval. Interpersonal communication is especially prevalent at this stage and the marketer should seek to influence the important word-of-mouth process.

Trial. The trial stage is when the individual puts the innovations to a personal test. That person may "test" the innovation in three ways. The potential adopter may actually try out the innovation. He may allow others to try the innovation, an act called vicarious trial. Finally, he may only imagine himself using the innovation and attempt to predict the positive and negative consequences. Different types of trial require different marketing approaches. For example, in the first case, it is important to make the innovation readily available for trial, perhaps on a take-home basis, while in the second case it would be desirable in advertising to show others using the product successfully or to gather potential adopters at a place where the innovation is in use. This is sometimes done with major industrial equipment innovations.

Evaluation. Evaluation is a necessary formal step between the trial and adoption or rejection stages. Following trial, the individual will review the pros and cons of continued use. While it is likely that informal or very brief evaluation follows each stage in the adoption process, in order to review the situation to that point, a formal evaluation is probably necessary before a formal commitment is made.

Adoption/Rejection. The stage of adoption represents a level of commitment by the individual involving repeat or continued usage. This is also a stage with knowledge, emotional, and behavioral components. There is, however, a considerable difference between this stage and the attitude stage. Beliefs and feelings in general at this stage are more strongly held than at the attitude stage.

The alternative to adoption, at this point, is rejection. Unsatisfactory outcomes in the process prior to this stage may result in the final beliefs and feelings being negative.

Resolution. The final stage is that of resolution. This concept includes the reduction of postdecision doubt referred to as cognitive dissonance. Dissonance is not the inevitable result of adoption. Some innovations are adopted without regret, even enthusiastically. Dissonance may result when one is forced to choose between two or more attractive alternatives, but some innovations may be far superior to anything previously known, or may be the only known alternative available to solve a problem.

Characteristics of Individuals as Adopting Units

A definition of adopter categories as ideal types includes innovators, early adopters, early majority, late majority, and laggards. The innovators are viewed as venturesome and risk taking, composing about the first 3 percent of those to adopt the innovation. Early adopters are the next 13 percent to adopt. They command respect from their peers and are more integrated into their social system than others, especially more than the innovators who are often at the isolated boundaries of a social system. The early majority are likely to be deliberate and represent 34 percent of the adopting population. Late majority and laggards comprise the remaining 50 percent of the individual adopting units and are either skeptical or traditional about the innovation. They may adopt only after rather strong social pressure or vivid demonstration of the relative advantage of the innovation over other products or services. These classes are definitional rather than fixed through research. They serve to guide the research in determining the characteristics of the adopting unit.

Various market researchers have studied the attitudes of innovators in different contexts as a preliminary step for developing promotional appeals. For example, fashion innovators for women's millinery are more concerned with hair care, are more involved in social visiting, are older, and have more education and higher family income than later adopters. Another researcher studying the characteristics of innovative adopters of touch-tone telephones found innovators to be more venturesome, more socially integrated, more socially mobile, and more financially privileged than noninnovators. Early adopters of color television have been shown to have higher incomes and more group memberships, and are more likely to be involved in professional or managerial occupations. Personality characteristics have an intuitive appeal for describing the different adopter categories. However, marketing researchers have not met with great success. Often only weak relationships have been found.

Once having located and defined innovators, early adopters, and later adopters, it is of interest to determine if the adoption process is different for each group. If it is different, then how can these differences be utilized in formulating more effective marketing strategies? For example, at the later stages of the acceptance process marketers may encourage adoption among nominators by stressing the "social correctness" of the innovation. Testimonial appeals may be effective in gaining legitimation of the innovation by noninnovators.

THE INNOVATION

Given the increasingly important role of innovations in marketing, it is vital for the marketing practitioner to understand the various dimensions of innovations that can be important to potential adopters. Earlier discussion stressed the importance of consumer perception as a factor for determining whether or not an item can be considered an innovation. Product perception factors are also important determinants of acceptance. One market researcher found that product perception factors overall had greater power in predicting innovativeness for the six new products studied than did all several personality variables and such variables as education, age, income, and occupational status.

The important product factors in the study just mentioned were relative advantage, compatibility, perceived risk, divisibility, complexity, and communicability. These product factors or attributes are defined in Exhibit 1, which is a compilation of innovation attributes found to be important in influencing the acceptance of new products. The task for the marketing manager is to determine which attributes are most relevant for a new product and to modify the new product and/or the promotional communications to stress favorable attributes and minimize those that are negative.

The relevance of a particular attribute may depend upon the perspective from which it is viewed. A manufacturer and consumer may define the relevant aspects of an innovation in totally dissimilar ways. The manufacturer may feel the relative advantage of a new product to be labor saving and may develop promotional strategy accordingly. Consumers may not perceive the time saved as significant and thus reject the new product or perhaps adopt it for other reasons, such as the desire for social approval, ease of operation, or low cost.

EXHIBIT 1. Attributes of Innovations

1. *Cost*	The financial and/or social expense incurred in the adoption and continued use of an innovation.
2. *Efficiency*	Time saved and discomfort avoided by the use of an innovation.
3. *Risk*	Uncertainty concerning the functional and dysfunctional consequences of innovation adoption.
4. *Communicability*	The ease and effectiveness with which the idea of the innovation can be disseminated to others.
5. *Clarity of results*	The ease with which the consequences of an innovation can be directly associated with its adoption.
6. *Compatibility*	The similarity of an innovation to an existing product that it may eventually supplement, complement, or replace. Also the ease with which the innovation fits within the general context in which it is used.
7. *Pervasiveness*	The degree to which an innovation requires changes or adjustments by other elements in the social situation.
8. *Complexity*	The ease with which the innovation is understood, implemented, and operated.
9. *Perceived relative advantage*	The function an innovation performs better than any alternative product or service (as viewed by the potential or actual adopter).
10. *Demonstrability*	The facility with which can be shown how the innovation is applied; also the ease with which the benefits of adopting an innovation can be shown.
11. *Structural radicalness*	The degree to which qualities of an innovation bring about alterations in such basic structural elements as communication, authority, and reward systems.
12. *Terminality*	The extent to which there are points in time at which an innovation must be adopted for it to be implemented or to be fully useful.
13. *Reversibility*	The ability and degree to which the status quo ante can be reinstated by ceasing to use the innovation.
14. *Divisibility*	The ability to implement the innovation on a limited basis.
15. *Degree of commitment*	The extent to which attitudinal and/or behavioral acceptance requires full commitment of financial and non-financial resources.
16. *Impact upon interpersonal relationships*	The degree to which social relationships within a social system are affected when an innovation is adopted by it or by some of its members.
17. *Publicness vs. privateness*	The extent to which an innovation, if available to one party in a social system, is more or less automatically and simultaneously available to all members of the social system.

18. *Size of the decision-making body*	The number of individuals involved in making the adoption or rejection decision.
19. *Number of gatekeepers*	The number of channels through which an innovation must travel for the target group to become aware of it.
20. *Susceptibility to successive modifications*	The extent to which an innovation can be refined or modified once in use.
21. *Gateway capacity*	The extent to which the adoption of an innovation opens avenues for the adoption of other innovations.
22. *Ego involvement*	The extent to which a person's beliefs and values are affected by an innovation.

COMMUNICATION AND DIFFUSION

An individual has two main channels of information regarding available innovations, mass media, and interpersonal channels. The mass media of television, radio, magazines, and newspapers provide great quantities of impersonal information sponsored by the marketing organization promoting the innovation and neutral sources such as the news content of the mass media. These impersonal channels are used in conjunction with the personal sources available to the individual. Impersonal and interpersonal channels serve different and often complementary functions during the adoption process. Recently developed communications models have recognized this complementary function.

Distinguishing Characteristics of Mass Media and Interpersonal Channels

There are a number of distinguishing characteristics of mass media and interpersonal channels with regard to message flow. In the communication context interpersonal channels involve face-to-face information flows while the mass media tend to be interposed. High feedback potential characterizes interpersonal communication while it is low for the mass media. The mass media are much speedier in reaching large audiences than are interpersonal channels. In terms of possible effect, interpersonal channels are apt to be more important in attitude formation and change concerning the innovation, whereas the mass media are most important in imparting knowledge about the innovation. The mass media are also relatively more important than face-to-face interaction for early adopters of innovations than for later adopters. The mass media, however, are less able than interpersonal channels to overcome psychological and sociological barriers possessed by the potential adopter.

Interaction of Mass Media and Interpersonal Channels

The mass media and interpersonal channels of communication are believed to enhance each other's impact on the decision to adopt an innovation. In one unpublished study it was found that the possibility of adopting a new product, when the potential adopter was exposed to both mass media and interpersonal channels, was three times greater than when the potential adopter was exposed to only the mass media channels or only interpersonal channels. Interpersonal channels often function to legitimate innovation-related information disseminated through the mass media.

The study of the flow of *influence* (as distinct from information) concerning new products has led diffusion researchers to hypothesize a multistep flow of influence.[2] Recent new product research supports the multistep view. For example, influence may flow through the following steps:

Mass media → innovators → opinion leaders → early majority.

The marketing practitioner needs to identify for a particular product category who the relevant innovators, opinion leaders, etc. are in terms of social psychological characteristics and in terms of communication behavior. This information can be used to develop special appeals for each category to be communicated through channels to which they are most likely to be exposed. The opinion leader concept is particularly appealing for those managing the diffusion of innovations. For example, once new product opinion leaders are located, they represent a point of communication leverage or multiplication in promoting the innovation.[3]

In general, with respect to interpersonal communication, marketers should identify the influential parties involved in diffusion, determine the roles uniquely played by different influential types in the dissemination of information and influence, and profile the influentials as a basis for reaching or approaching them. In doing this, the marketer must be sensitive to the fact that the social psychological characteristics and communication behavior of the influentials may not be the same for all product categories; also that different types of influentials are likely to be differentially effective at different stages of the consumers' innovation decision-making process.

Resistance to Diffusion

The matter of resistance is a major factor to consider in developing diffusion strategies. Resistance forces at least equal the importance of acceptance factors in the innovation decision-making process. The locus of resistance may reside in an individual or in the social system. For the individual resistance is encountered by such factors as habit and dissatisfaction with the present situation, the tendency to expose oneself to information that reinforces presently held attitudes, anxiety about new activities and the unwillingness to take risk. Resistance factors in the social system include general societal norms against change and innovation or norms regarding certain areas as sacred and not to be altered, the rejection of "outsiders," and the incompatibility of the innovation with values and belief systems.

There may also be rejection of innovations because of failures by the marketing organization. Frequent causes of failure related to the marketing organization include the following: failure to comprehend the relevant situation; poorly used or too little communication; lack of guidelines for obtaining and using the innovation; failure to adopt the innovation to unexpected needs or difficulties; improper identification of potential customers' real needs; and not taking into account the potential sources of resistance at the individual and social levels mentioned above.

Implications

A number of marketing implications of studying the adoption and diffusion of innovations have already been cited. Below is a summary of these and some additional considerations:

1. Understanding the dimensions of the consumer's perceptions of newness that are positively related to the adoption behavior in a product category may:
   a. Indicate that market segments vary in their perceptions of an attitude toward product "newness," for example, innovators vs. other consumers, and may require advertising programs directed at key segments over the product life cycle;
   b. Make possible more accurate measurements of the degree of "newness" and the probability of rapid adoption of a particular new product proposal before commercial introduction;
   c. Suggest specific advertising and promotion copy content to maximize positive imagery and minimize negative aspects of a particular product's "newness";
   d. Suggest marked differences in consumer tastes and preferences across adopter groups. The innovator, for example, may report significantly different taste preferences in blind product taste tests than do other consumers.
2. Identifying the innovator and his or her information-seeking and processing behavior, for example, mass media exposure, type of information sought and used, etc. may:
   a. Indicate appropriate combinations of mass media and copy content to accelerate adoption:
   b. Speed total market adoption by increasing the visibility of the product to other consumers, generate product use experience in the market, and provide sales revenues for distribution channels;
   c. Isolate a market segment that should be studied independently as a source of new product ideas and in evaluating new products.
3. Identifying the influential and his/her information-seeking and processing behavior may:
   a. Indicate appropriate combinations of mass media and copy content to accelerate adoption, as in the case of the innovator;

   b. Speed total market adoption by getting the influential's endorsement of the product within a social network, increasing transmission of product trial and other substantive information through the consumer to the social network;
   c. Isolate a market segment that can report those product features that are most likely to be orally transmitted and that should be integrated into mass media copy.
4. Developing research methods for measuring the monitoring of the volume and content of interpersonal communications within the population can:
   a. Indicate perceived product weaknesses or specific information needed by consumers;
   b. Be a partial measurement of the effectiveness of advertising and promotional programs.
5. Regularly monitoring opinions and attitudes of the innovators and influentials through specifically constructed consumer panels may be valuable in:
   a. Monitoring market trends;
   b. Developing and testing new product concepts prior to commercial introductions;
   c. Predicting the probability of new product success early in the product life cycle.

REFERENCES

1. Everett M. Rogers and Floyd Shoemaker, *The Communication of Innovations* (New York: The Free Press, 1971); Thomas Robertson, *Innovative Behavior and Communication* (New York: Holt, Rinehart and Winston, 1971).
2. Everett M. Rogers, *Modernization Among Peasants: The Impact of Communication* (New York: Holt, Rinehart and Winston, 1969).
3. Gerald Zaltman and Ronald Stiff, "Theories of Diffusion," in Scott Ward and Thomas S. Robertson, Editors, *Theoretical Perspectives in Consumer Behavior* (Englewood Cliffs, NJ: Prentice-Hall, Inc., 1973).

SUGGESTIONS FOR FURTHER READING

Lawrence A. Brown, *Innovation Diffusion* (New York: Methuen Inc. 1981).

Gordon R. Foxall, Christopher G. Haskins, "Cognitive Style and Consumer Innovativeness: An Empirical Test of Kirton's Adaption-Innovation Theory in Food Purchasing," *Marketing Intelligence & Planning,* 1986.

Wagner A. Kamakura, Siva K. Balasubramanian, "Forecasting with Innovation Diffusion Models: The Impact of Replacement Purchases," *Journal of Forecasting,* January–March 1987.

G. A. Lancaster, C. T. Taylor, "The Diffusion of Innovations and Their Attributes: A Critical Review," *Quartley Review of Marketing,* Summer 1986.

Vijay Mahajan, Eitan Muller, "Innovation Diffusion and New Product Growth Models in Marketing," *Journal of Marketing,* Fall 1979.

J. J. Masterson, G. Hayward, "Adoption of Innovations: A Concept Attainment View," *Management Decision,* 1979.

Thomas S. Robertson, *Innovative Behavior and Communication* (New York: Holt Rinehart and Winston, 1971).

Everett M. Rogers and Floyd Shoemaker, *The Communication of Innovations* (New York: The Free Press, 1971).

Stanley V. Scott, Salah S. Hassan, "Eclectic Models Best Predict Who Will Buy, and When," *Marketing News,* February 27, 1987.

M. Nawaz Sharif, K. Ramanathan, "Temporal Models of Innovation Diffusion," *IEEE Transactions on Engineering Management,* May 1984.

Christos H. Skiadas, "Two Simple Models for the Early and Middle Stage Prediction of Innovation Diffusion," *IEEE Transactions on Engineering Management,* May 1987.

P. W. Turnball, A. Meenaghan, "Diffusion of Innovation and Opinion Leadership," *European Journal of Marketing,* 1980.

Gerald Zaltman, *Marketing: Contributions from the Behavioral Sciences* (New York: Harcourt Brace Jovanovich, Inc. 1965).

Leonard L. Berry, PhD
Professor of Marketing and
Director of the Center for Retailing Studies
Texas A&M University
College Station, Texas

A. Parasuraman, DBA
Federated Professor of Marketing
Texas A&M University
College Station, Texas

CHAPTER 42

PRESCRIPTION FOR A SERVICE QUALITY REVOLUTION IN AMERICA

The most successful service companies compete with quality service. Through excellent service these companies achieve competitive differentiation, enduring customer relationships, favorable customer word-of-mouth advertising, higher employee morale, and greater productivity.

Conversely, companies with poor service experience marketing difficulty no matter how enticing their advertising or how many calls their salespeople make. All such promotional activity accomplishes is to persuade customer prospects to try a poor service.

The importance of quality service to a company's future is no secret. In a recent American Management Association survey of North American, Western European, and Japanese managers, 78 percent of the sample indicated that improving quality and service to customers is *the* key to competitive success. Unfortunately, concerted efforts to improve service lag behind awareness of its importance. Only 56 percent of the study's respondents state that service quality is a clear and accepted priority throughout their organizations. In only 49 percent of the companies are regular reports on customer satisfaction prepared. And only 38 percent of the respondents indicate that most managers in their firms have attended a learning/training activity on customer service.

In this chapter, we discuss key elements of a service revolution that needs to occur in America and needs to occur now. The luxury of waiting does not exist. From department store retailing to insurance, from the airline industry to the banking industry, the specter of crisis brought by disaffected, value-conscious customers, global, Darwinian competition, and hard economic times demands bold thinking about the meaning of service, and how to deliver it.

The service revolution must occur on two levels. The first level concerns our aspirations for service; the second concerns making service-improvement a habit.

Raising Our Service Aspirations

The process of improving service quality is difficult to begin and difficult to sustain. Firms must undo that which obstructs progress, replace it with culture and tools that foster progress, and drive positive change month after month, year after year. Spending money on service improvement is the easy part; changing the habits, attitudes, skills, knowledge, and systems of human beings in organizations is the hard part.

Although American companies are delivering outstanding service in virtually every industry, and other companies not yet outstanding are making significant progress, these companies are still in the minority. For too many firms quality service is still a soft idea and a low priority.

This is the age of the service economy in America and the rest of the developed world. The stakes for improved service are high. What kind of future can be in store for our service economy if managers tolerate mediocre, uninspired, careless, or incompetent service?

James Cramer of the University of Maryland worked in Japan from 1980 to 1991 before returning to the U.S. In a December 1991 newspaper column he described his impressions of the "new" America he found upon his return:

> *. . . if there is one thing that stands out in sharp contrast to Japan it is the sad state of customer service in America. In attitude toward the customer, America and Japan are separated by more than an ocean. They are divided by a different view of what customers are, and how they should be treated.*

American managers must make some essential attitude shifts to mount the needed service revolution. Each of these attitude shifts involve raising aspirations for service.

From Being Good to Being Excellent

Delivering good service isn't good enough for a firm to reap the full economic benefits of service improvement. Most customers are unlikely to notice or care that one firm is marginally better in service than others. When competing firms are perceived as similar in service quality, then other competitive factors, such as price, usually prevail. These other factors prevail for some customers in any case, but they surely will for most customers if no competitor stands out in service.

Companies develop reputations for outstanding service by consistently meeting customers' service expectations—and, at least some of the time, by exceeding them. Exceeding customers' expectations requires "surprising" customers with uncommon grace, commitment, energy, or competence in delivering the service. It is hard to stand out in service without the element of surprise.

Consider the example of Empire Video, a small chain of video stores in Keene, New Hampshire, that in 1989 was ranked by *Video Store Magazine* as the highest volume-per-store renter in the United States. Empire stores offer a free phone for customers to telephone family or friends to discuss movie choices. Each store features a mini-theater for customers to preview brief movie clips before renting. Movies are displayed in dozens of categories, for example, by actor and country of origin. Computers are available to customers to review movie titles. About 10 percent of the titles at each store are labeled "Our Favorite." These are selected by store employees. If a customer doesn't like one of these videos, the next one is free. Empire has a

"Three Strikes and You're Out" policy. If a customer claims to have returned a movie but the computer disagrees, it is the store's mistake. The same is true the next time. With the third strike, the customer is out.

Empire Video capitalizes on the element of surprise to differentiate itself from competitors. What would Empire Video be, however, if its president, Stuart Skorman, aspired to operate "good" video stores? Would the ambition to be "good" lead to the innovation and strategic investment on behalf of customers that characterizes Empire's strategy? Most likely, the answer is no.

From Quality of Goods to Quality in Everything

Manufacturing companies are also service companies, just less so than the airline, hotel, banking, and other organizations that we are accustomed to thinking of as service companies. Many employees of manufacturing companies are pure service providers, performing accounting, credit analysis, investment, personnel, marketing research, sales, public relations, legal, computer programming, secretarial, and myriad other service functions. They are performers rather than makers. Yet, the quality of their performances influences the value of the "end product." Buyers of computers, automobiles, eyeglasses, prescription drugs, and other goods purchase a total experience, not just a tangible product. Service performers contribute to this total experience.

Progressive manufacturing company executives view the *synergy* of goods and service quality as the true lever of value-adding differentiation. And they view the quality of internal service (service provided to other organizational members) as critical to the quality of goods and services offered to external customers. Quality of goods is too narrow a focus; progressive manufacturing executives seek quality in everything.

The example of Harley-Davidson, the Milwaukee motorcycle manufacturer, is instructive. In 1981, Harley-Davidson was on the brink of extinction. Its market share had fallen from around 70 percent in the mid-1970s to under 25 percent. Yet, by 1990 Harley's market share was back up to 60 percent and the company's biggest problem was that it could not produce enough motorcycles to meet demand.

How did the management team led by Richard Teerlink achieve such an impressive turnaround? The answer is a multifaceted approach to quality. Management made selective technology and product design investments that significantly improved the motorcycles' dependability and styling. They focused on improvements that would count with customers.

Management also focused on promotional quality, using advertising and other promotion to change the image of motorcyclists from tattooed ruffians to individualists seeking a healthy, outdoor life-style. Harley management invested their own time in numerous activities to stay in touch with customers and build a climate of trust. Managers' regular participation in weekend riding rallies is one example. The creation of the Harley Owners Group (H.O.G.) is another. With 140,000 members in 1991, H.O.G. is America's largest affinity group.

Management also invested in distribution quality, forming a dealer advisory council, upgrading dealer training and educational offerings, and implementing a store design program to refurbish and remerchandise the dealerships to reinforce the image strategy. In a 1991 speech, Richard Teerlink commented, "Our goal is to have a mental tattoo." Had Harley-Davidson focused its comeback only on improving the quality of the motorcycles and ignored the service dynamics of the business, the company probably would not have survived. To reiterate, quality of goods is too narrow a focus.

From Management Support to Management Involvement and Leadership

We often hear middle managers complain that senior managers in their companies are not supportive of service improvement. However, this complaint misses the mark. Senior management support is insufficient; senior managers need to be personally involved in service improvement and to lead the charge. Senior managers must sound the trumpet of change; they must be the ultimate teachers, the ultimate role models. They must be knowledgeable, credible, committed quality leaders. Our experience is that without the *involvement* and *leadership* of top management, the service quality bus hardly moves.

Study the most quality-obsessed companies and the personal involvement and leadership of top management surfaces consistently. Indeed it is this personal involvement and leadership role that contributes richly to management's acquisition of essential knowledge, credibility, and commitment.

Chick-fil-A, the successful Atlanta-based fast-food chain noted for its food and service quality, insists that its store operators (who are independent businesspeople) run only one store. No Chick-fil-A store is operated by an absentee owner. To attract first-rate operators who could opt for the competition and the possibility of multiple stores, Chick-fil-A splits store profits with the operators on a 50-50 basis. Chick-fil-A's philosophy is that the owner must be personally involved and lead the charge.

The Stouffer Hotel in Oak Brook, Illinois, assigns each member of senior management a block of rooms to personally inspect from top to bottom every month. These executives are to make sure that everything is in place and working perfectly in their "adopted" rooms.

Virgin Atlantic Airways Chairman Richard Branson regularly travels economy class on his airline to listen to the sounds of his business. For each flight he claims to walk between three and four miles up and down the aisles talking to passengers. A typical flight produced such ideas as special children's meals of peanut butter sandwiches, milk shakes and apples, and more beans in the vegetarian meals.

In these examples, the people in charge of the business are participants in service improvement rather than spectators. They are actively engaged in listening and learning, not just sending out orders from a high perch in a glass house. Managements' personal involvement and leadership give the quality improvement process teeth.

From Errors are Inevitable to Doing It Right the First Time

The core of service quality is reliability. In our studies, customers have consistently indicated service reliability as the most important service dimension. Firms that are unreliable, that routinely break their promises to customers and make frequent mistakes, lose the confidence of customers. And the confidence of customers is a service firm's most precious asset.

Because services are performances rather than objects, they are difficult for customers to evaluate prior to purchase. Customers cannot try on services for fit and feel; there are no tires to kick. Customers buy a service before experiencing it and thus must trust the firm to deliver the promised service.

We have found in our research that friendliness does not compensate for unreliability. Hotel customers expect their guaranteed reservations to be honored; bank customers expect their monthly bank statements to be correct; dry-cleaning customers expect their shirt collars to be folded properly every time. Most customers appreciate a sincere apology when the service breaks down, but the apology does not erase the memory of an unreliable service. If a pattern of failure develops, customers conclude the firm cannot be counted on, friendly or not.

We sometimes hear managers say that it is not practical to try to eliminate mistakes. One problem with this attitude is that it lets managers off the hook, rather than challenging them to boldness and creativity in improving reliability. Customer respondents in our studies rated large, well-known U.S. companies as more deficient on reliability than on any other service dimension. These companies were most deficient on the service dimension most important to their customers.

Another problem with this attitude is that just one mistake can wreak havoc on a company and its customers. In 1991, for example, all 1,400 taxpayers in Norwich, Vermont, were classified by TRW as bad credit risks because a worker mistakenly recorded the names of taxpayers instead of delinquent taxpayers and TRW had no database mechanism to immediately flag such an exceptional occurrence. The negative national publicity resulting from this episode aggravated the image problems of the credit-reporting industry, which is the number one source of consumer complaints in America according to Federal Trade Commission data. More restrictive legislation for the industry seems likely.

A good way to think about a 98 percent reliability rate is as a 2 percent error rate. Better still, managers should calculate the actual number of customers affected by a 2 percent error rate. A company with one million daily transactions undermines the confidence of 20,000 customers each day, for example.

No service attitude in an organization is more important than "doing it right the first time." The true cost of service unreliability includes lost customer confidence, lost customers (and the expense of replacing them with new customers), negative word-of-mouth advertising, possibly negative publicity, and possibly restrictive legislation. In addition are the costs of reperforming the service and placating customers.

Managers should consider every conceivable opportunity to improve service reliability, including teaching the "why" and the "how" of reliability in training sessions, forming reliability teams to search for ways to reduce failures, measuring failure rates, rewarding error-free service, offering service guarantees, and asking employees to sign performance reliability contracts.

Preston Trucking Company, a Maryland-based firm selected in the late 1980s as one of America's ten best companies to work for, has each employee sign a service excellence statement. Posted in each Preston facility, the statement reads in part,

> *Once I make a commitment to a customer or another associate, I promise to fulfill it on time. I will do what I say when I say I will do it . . . . I understand that one claim or one mistake is one error too many. I promise to do my job right the first time and to continually seek improvement.*

De Mar, a Clovis, California plumbing, heating, air-conditioning company went from $210,000 in sales in 1985 to $3.5 million in 1991. How did De Mar do it? One key was guaranteeing a standard of service reliability that customers wanted but could not readily find elsewhere. De Mar decided to guarantee same-day service (addressing customers' number one complaint of plumbers not showing up when they promised). The company also guarantees to the penny its price quote (responding to the second most common customer complaint of surprises in the final bill).

From Recovery as a Problem to Recovery as an Opportunity

Many companies are ill-equipped to recover from service failures. They place weaker people in recovery positions because the role is not viewed as a priority. They tie up employees in rules and procedures, limiting their flexibility in recovery service. They fail to train employees in the art of handling disgruntled customers and nonroutine service situations. They do not invest in the technology and systems needed to facilitate prompt, accurate problem resolution.

Recovery service is often viewed as an expensive nuisance. This is a mistake. Recovery service is critical because preserving customers' confidence in the firm is critical. When a service problem occurs, customers' confidence in a firm may be shaken but probably won't be destroyed except under one of two conditions: The problem reinforces a pattern of failure or the recovery effort fails, compounding rather than correcting the original problem.

Customers usually have higher expectations for recovery service. They have been inconvenienced or worse by an unsatisfactory service and are ready to scrutinize how the firm will handle the situation. In a study of "critical incidents" in which respondents were asked to discuss especially positive and negative service experiences, Bitner and her colleagues found that almost 43 percent of the negative service encounters were poorly handled recovery situations.

Firms that deliver excellent recovery service rebound from service failures much better than firms ineffective in recovery. Our research data show that customers of companies that satisfactorily resolved a recent service problem had higher perceptions of the company's service and were more willing to recommend the company than customers whose service problems were not rectified.

Viewing service recovery as an opportunity means being prepared to respond when problems arise. It also means encouraging customers to complain when they are dissatisfied and regularly monitoring customers' service experiences. The research of the Technical Assistance Research Program (TARP) shows that most dissatisfied customers don't complain because they don't think it will do any good or to avoid a hassle. Instead, unhappy customers may defect to the competition while spreading negative word-of-mouth communications. Thus, it is important to be proactive in identifying unhappy customers. Finally, effective recovery means analyzing where the service system is breaking down and taking corrective measures.

Federal Express, with a three-level recovery system designed to resolve most problems immediately, is one company that views recovery service as an opportunity. The first level of response is customer service representatives who take customer calls in 15 service centers around the country. The representatives receive five weeks of initial training plus monthly training sessions once on the job. They are empowered to spend up to $100 to immediately resolve a customer's problem. Federal Express's telephone system instantly routes calls among the service centers to the next available agent, resulting in less than .005 percent of the calls being abandoned.

If a package is two or more days late, or the customer service representative cannot solve the problem for whatever reason, the problem is referred to trace agents, the second level of recovery. The trace agents' sole responsibility is to locate the missing item and make the necessary amends. The executive services group, the third level of response, is well-versed in the Federal Express system and has the authority to redress any customer problem.

From Service is Shapeless to Service-System Design

Services can be shaped far more than is commonly realized. It is both possible and desirable to design quality into the service system. It is tempting for managers and customers to blame service shortfalls on the people delivering service, but frequently the real culprit is poor service system design.

Consider the following story told by Paul Revere Insurance Company executive Robert Lea and reported in *Productivity Views:*

> *For nearly 30 years, as long as anyone can remember, many group bills the company issued were inaccurate by the time they got to the customer. The customer (a small business) had changed something in their work force: new people came on board, some had left. Due to change, the customer would pay us what they believed they owed us, not what the bill stated. When the customer payment came back, the Premium Collections Department ran it through the computer. Of course, the payment would kick out as an error since the billed amount did not match the paid amount. All errors moved to the Correspondence Section, which researched the problem, wrote to the policyholder, corrected the error, and updated our files. We had built automatic rework into our process.*
>
> *Then the company pulled all customer contact work into a Customer Service unit that did all work for an identifiable set of customers. We put phones on their desks, letting them call customers three days before billing. If the customers had employment changes, say, "X, Y, Z terminated and A, B, C added, and here are their salaries," we could enter them and figure correct premiums. More accurate billing put the Correspondence Section out of business.*
>
> *It was so simple . . . you wonder why we didn't think of it 30 years ago.*

Delivering excellent service requires blending the precision of the engineer, the holistic view of the architect, and the customer-mindedness of the marketer into service system designs. It is important not only to understand the customer, but also the service.

One way to improve service design is "mapping" teams. Mapping teams analyze part or all of an existing service system with the objective of redesigning it to be simpler, more reliable, more efficient, more responsive, or improved in some other way. Their methodology is to draw increasingly detailed pictures of the service process (what happens first, what happens next, and so on) and then ask: "Why do we do it this way?" and "Isn't there a better way?" Mapping teams also can help develop new services by creating pro forma designs.

Customer input is vital in the creation of service maps. The new or improved service has to work for the customer, not simply be more convenient or less expensive for the company. Studying customer complaint and survey data prior to commencing a mapping exercise and obtaining customer reactions to service map drafts are recommended. In some circumstances, it may even be possible to include customers on mapping teams.

Although service mapping adds precision, comprehensiveness, and technical expertise to service system design, the heart and soul of excellent design remains common sense. The Chicago Marriott hotel redesigned its housekeeping service system by placing irons and ironing boards in each guest room, eliminating the source of two-thirds of all guest requests to housekeeping. The hotel dropped from its capital budget color television sets for the bathrooms of VIP guest rooms to fund the acquisition of the irons and ironing boards. No hotel guest had ever requested a color television set for the bathroom.

MAKING SERVICE IMPROVEMENT A HABIT

Raising aspirations for service improvement is insufficient in and of itself; managers must find ways to sustain progress, build on it, and keep the flame lit. The second level of the service revolution concerns making service improvement a habit.

Service excellence comes from integrating the idea of continuous improvement into the fabric of organizational life. Service improvement is not a finite program. A company is never finished with service improvement. Service improvement is hard work and mostly comes in small wins rather than giant breakthroughs. Whereas we need a revolution in mind and spirit, the output of this process will be more evolutionary than revolutionary.

In this section, we discuss five actions companies can take to make service improvement a habit.

Build a Service Quality Information System

Service quality research is most likely to influence decision making when it is performed in multiple ways on an ongoing basis and when research findings are systematically shared with and discussed by managers and by frontline servers. Any given service quality study provides a snapshot of a particular time period. Only when these snapshots are taken regularly—and from different angles—do they tell an insightful story of patterns and trends.

Companies need to install an ongoing service research process that provides relevant comparison data that managers become accustomed to using in decision making. Companies need to build a service quality information system, not just do occasional research studies. Quarterly service quality surveys that include competitors, follow-up calls to samples of customers following service transactions, quarterly "mystery" shopping of service providers, monthly customer focus group interviews, continuous monitoring and analysis of customer complaint and service breakdown data—these are building blocks of a service quality information system.

In addition, a comprehensive service quality information system will include ongoing employee research. Employee research is important for three reasons. First, employees are themselves customers of internal service and thus are the only people who can assess internal service quality. Second, because of employees' intensive exposure to the service system, they can provide insight into conditions that cause service problems. Third, employee research serves as an early-warning system. Employees often see the service system breaking down before customers do. Ask both customers and employees to rate a company's service quality using the same questionnaire and, more often than not, employees will rate the company lower. Why? In part because employees simply know more about a firm's service weaknesses.

Finally, it is also important that managers supplement hard data from the information system with informal feedback and observation. Listening to the voices of customers and employees involves more than reading computer printouts. It also means spending time in the field.

How many airline chief executives walk three to four miles up and down an airplane aisle talking to passengers like Richard Branson does? How many companies have developed an owners' group feedback channel—as Harley-Davidson did with H.O.G.? How many retail chains send their senior managers to visit the stores and shop the competition virtually every week—as Wal-Mart Stores does? Much work lies ahead for many companies in creating the infrastructure of systematic picture-taking, learning how to use it, and supplementing the hard pictures (data) with soft pictures (impressions and feedback from direct contact with customers and employees).

Report Service Quality Performance

Disclosing service quality performance publicly and throughout the organization helps to stimulate and sustain internal interest in quality improvement. Companies measure what is important. When a firm measures a category of performance *and* disseminates results to significant audiences, managers and frontline servers are sure to take note.

Performance reporting practices can reinforce company service priorities, challenge people to greater achievement, celebrate excellence—and embarrass and energize the undercommitted. Accordingly, such practices can be powerful cultural drivers of quality.

Deluxe Corporation (formerly Deluxe Check Printers) discloses in its annual shareholders' report the percentage of orders that it prints without error and ships by its next-day standard. Canadian Airlines International publishes an annual service quality report for each of its divisions—and prints these reports in the same expensive, four-color format as the company's annual corporate report. A Chicago contact lens manufacturer, Wesley-Jessen Corporation, uses service quality bulletin boards to report progress on key service measures to employees. Wesley-Jessen's president sends a monthly letter to all customers informing them of various company efforts to improve service. The letters are also shared with employees. U.S. Healthcare, a Pennsylvania-based health maintenance organization, uses an electronic billboard (called "Vital Signs") in its headquarters to display internal and external service measurements.

Measure the Profit Impact of Poor Quality

One of the best ways to insure a long-term focus on quality in a company is to formally measure the cost of poor quality. These cost data can then be used in analyses of a business unit's profit performance and partial determination of managers' and frontline servers' compensation.

It is not difficult to measure the cost of poor quality. For example, firms can estimate from research the number of customers who defect for service-related reasons, calculate the annual profit contribution of different types of customers, and then calculate lost profit caused by service failures. Reichheld and Sasser conclude from their research that, depending on the industry, companies can increase profits from 25 percent to 85 percent by reducing customer loss by just 5 percent.

Managers who compute the lifetime value of a customer (the total revenue generated by a customer who remains with a company for the equivalent of a lifetime) are unlikely to stray from the commitment of continuous service improvement. Consultant Laura Liswood, who specializes in customer retention strategies, estimates that the lifetime value of a supermarket customer averages $250,000.

Stress Personal Quality

Senior managers should use every opportunity to stress the personal responsibility of each employee for quality improvement. Personal involvement in service improvement fosters insight and commitment. People who are involved experience firsthand how tough it is to change an organization while often becoming more motivated to do just that.

We recommend that all employees (1) be invited to participate on quality-improvement teams on company time; (2) be encouraged to submit quality-improvement suggestions; (3) attend a quality-improvement course within their first few months on the job; (4) devote a predetermined percentage of total work time each year to training and education; and (5) be evaluated on their service quality in performance appraisals.

Good Samaritan Hospital in Cincinnati has all new personnel, regardless of position, attend a service quality training session soon after they start work. De Mar, the California plumbing, heating and air-conditioning company, invests 2 percent of its gross revenues each year in employee training. The company awards a weekly $50 bonus to the employee who suggests the best service-improvement idea. Stew Leonard's, the Connecticut food retailer famed for its service, sponsors a "One Idea Club" in which employees attending seminars and taking field trips must bring back one good idea.

Showcase Service Leadership

In America, the Malcolm Baldrige National Quality Award has provided a strong boost to quality improvement. Participating companies that genuinely seek to improve their quality do improve because the Baldrige process spreads awareness, exposes weaknesses, and energizes the organization. Although only a few companies win the award each year the process of competing is itself beneficial.

All but the smallest of companies could benefit from an in-house quality award. Organizational units could benefit from systematic self-appraisal and the stimulating effects of internal competition in much the same fashion as with the Baldrige Award. Of course, the Baldrige Award offers the potential of external recognition and marketing clout and thus serves a broader set of purposes than an internal award. However, an internal award also has an important bonus to offer: The process usually results in one or more units actually winning an award.

Showering winning units with praise and tribute in the presence of peers showcases service leadership. Winning units set the tone for others in the organization. In telling their story they teach the potential of excellent service and show the way. They become lighthouses for change, helping to sustain the organizational cultural shifts that quality improvement requires.

And in being celebrated within the organization, winners are reminded of the self-satisfaction, energy, and fun that comes with achievement. Peer applause that is genuinely given and richly deserved often transforms itself into the more powerful force of self-applause in which the awardee thinks: "Good for me. Now let's get better." A Mary Kay Cosmetics executive, quoted in *The Service Edge* newsletter, captures with a question the power of peer applause: "If an actor received an Academy Award through the mail, would it have the same impact?"

THE COMPETITIVE ADVANTAGE OF COMMON SENSE AND PASSION

The most successful service companies compete on the basis of great service. There are no exceptions. A service company is defined by its service quality. If the service company's service is mediocre, the company is mediocre.

Excellent service is mostly a function of common sense and passionate leadership. Listening carefully to customers and employees, designing the service system to actually serve, investing in the performers of the service because they in effect are the "product," stressing team play in service delivery, making the service promise inviolate, emphasizing effective recovery service—these are not esoteric ideas. The problem is that common sense is not so common.

Common sense coupled with passionate, hands-on leadership of a service organization is a potent combination. Study closely the leaders and companies mentioned in this article and the common sense/passionate leadership combination is evident.

In the fall of 1990, one of us worked with the senior management of Stew Leonard's in a two-day strategic planning meeting. Of the top 12 executives, 10 are family members and the other 2 are considered "family." To say that Stew Leonard's senior managers are "interested" in excellent service doesn't fit the reality. They are passionate about excellent service—passionate about hiring happy people who will love customers, passionate about creating a "wow" atmosphere in the store, passionate about product freshness, passionate about continuous improvement.

Many stores are operated by dispassionate managers who view their position as "just a job." Stew Leonard's is led by family members who view their work as a "calling." Stew Leonard's taps into the human quest to be part of something special. The company is managed efficiently but its competitive edge lies in passionate leadership.

Excellent service is within grasp in America. Role model companies in every industry are demonstrating that excellent service is more profitable and more fun. But these companies are still too few. In most American firms, service quality is still a soft idea, a vague goal, a peripheral concern. Our collective challenge is to mount a service revolution of higher aspirations and continuous improvement. Large doses of common sense and passionate leadership will help us make the journey.

SELECTED BIBLIOGRAPHY

To learn more about the service quality research findings referred to in this article, see Valarie A. Zeithaml, A. Parasuraman, and Leonard L. Berry, *Delivering Quality Service: Balancing Customer Perceptions and Expectations* (Free Press, 1990) and Leonard L. Berry and

A. Parasuraman, *Marketing Services: Competing Through Quality* (Free Press, 1991).

An excellent article on the importance of service quality to manufacturing companies is James Brian Quinn, Thomas L. Doorley, and Penny C. Paquette, "Beyond Products: Service-Based Strategy," (*Harvard Business Review,* March-April 1990). For a helpful framework to assess a company's level of service quality competitiveness, see Richard B. Chase and Robert H. Hayes, "Beefing Up Operations in Service Firms," (*Sloan Management Review,* Fall 1991).

Recommended articles on the importance of service recovery include Christopher W. L. Hart, James L. Heskett, and W. Earl Sasser, Jr., "The Profitable Art of Service Recovery," (*Harvard Business Review,* July-August 1990) and Mary Jo Bitner, Bernard M. Booms, and Mary Stanfield Tetreault, "The Service Encounter: Diagnosing Favorable and Unfavorable Incidents," (*Journal of Marketing,* January 1990).

An excellent discussion of service quality information systems is Larry Crosby, "Expanding the Role of CSM in Total Quality" (*International Journal of Service Industry Management,* Number 2, 1991). To read more about conducting service quality research, see A. Parasuraman, Leonard L. Berry, and Valarie A. Zeithaml, "Guidelines for Conducting Service Quality Research," (*Marketing Research,* December 1990).

Several of the examples used in this article were adapted from the following newsletters: *The Service Edge* (Lakewood Publications, Minneapolis), Tom Peters' *On Achieving Excellence* (TPG Communications, Palo Alto) and *Martin Stankard's Productivity Views* (Productivity Development Group, Westford, MA). We recommend each of these publications to readers wishing to keep up with the quality movement.

SUGGESTIONS FOR FURTHER READING

Lawrence A. Brown, *Innovation Diffusion* (New York: Methuen Inc. 1981).

Gordon R. Foxall, Christopher G. Haskins, "Cognitive Style and Consumer Innovativeness: An Empirical Test of Kirton's Adaption-Innovation Theory in Food Purchasing," *Marketing Intelligence & Planning*, 1986.

Wagner A. Kamakura, Siva K. Balasubramanian, "Forecasting with Innovation Diffusion Models: The Impact of Replacement Purchases," *Journal of Forecasting*, Jan.–Mar. 1987.

G. A. Lancaster, C. T. Taylor, "The Diffusion of Innovations and Their Attributes: A Critical Review," *Quarterly Review of Marketing*, Summer 1986.

Vijay Mahajan, Eitan Muller, "Innovation Diffusion and New Product Growth Models in Marketing," *Journal of Marketing*, Fall 1979.

J. J. Masterson, G. Hayward, "Adoption of Innovations: A Concept Attainment View," *Management Decision*, 1979.

Thomas S. Robertson, *Innovative Behavior and Communication* (New York: Holt Rinehart and Winston, 1971).

Everett M. Rogers and Floyd Shoemaker, *The Communication of Innovations* (New York: The Free Press, 1971).

Stanley V. Scott, Salah S. Hassan, "Eclectic Models Best Predict Who Will Buy, and When," *Marketing News*, February 27, 1987.

M. Nawaz Sharif, K. Ramanathan, "Temporal Models of Innovation Diffusion," *IEEE Transactions on Engineering Management*, May 1984.

Christos H. Skiadas, "Two Simple Models for the Early and Middle Stage Prediction of Innovation Diffusion," *IEEE Transactions on Engineering Management*, May 1987.

P. W. Turnball, A. Meenaghan, "Diffusion of Innovation and Opinion Leadership," *European Journal of Marketing*, 1980.

Gerald Zaltman, *Marketing: Contributions from the Behavioral Sciences* (New York: Harcourt Brace Jovanovich, Inc. 1965).

Barry Berman
Walter H. "Bud" Miller Distinguished Professor of Business
Hofstra University
Hempstead, New York

CHAPTER 43

DEVELOPING AND IMPLEMENTING AN EFFECTIVE CUSTOMER SERVICE STRATEGY

INTRODUCTION

In this article, we first define customer service through a consumer expectation and experience perspective. We then look at the importance of customer service through examining consumer attitudes and determining the costs associated with poor consumer service. Then, we describe four important models of customer service. Marketers can gain insight into their customer service quality by examining Porter's value chain (an adaptation of Herzberg's theory of job satisfaction model) by using the SERVQUAL measure, and by understanding Jackson's relationship marketing concept. Pitfalls leading to poor customer service are described and common principles of excellent customer service providers are then analyzed. The customer service audit is a valuable tool for evaluating a retailer's customer service strategy. Managers need to be aware of difficulties in developing and implementing a customer service strategy.

Definition of Customer Service

In defining customer service, we need to focus on three dimensions: customers, services, and quality. Customers can be manufacturers, wholesalers, and retailers as well as final consumers. Services can be rendered either before, during, or after the sale. Included within my definition of customer service is personal selling, inventory availability, delivery, instructions, installation, repair, and after-sale follow-up.

Much of the work in customer service involves after-sale effort. Theodore Levitt, professor of marketing at Harvard's Business School and editor of the *Harvard Business Review,* considers the sale the "courtship." How good the marriage is depends on how well the seller manages the relationship. The management of the relationship is customer service; quality can be measured on a number of dimensions. According to research by Professors Zeithaml, Parasuraman, and Berry, the most important "quality" characteristics from the customer's perspective were: tangibles, reliability, responsiveness, assurance, and empathy:[1]

- *Tangibles*—Physical facilities should be attractive and clean; employees should be well-groomed.
- *Reliability*—Customers want companies to perform the desired service dependably, accurately, and consistently. They want companies to keep the promises they make.
- *Responsiveness*—Prompt service is desired.
- *Assurance*—Company employees should be knowledgeable and courteous.
- *Empathy*—Customers want individualized attention, and they want to be heard.

While marketers like to think of services in terms of tangibles such as store hours, credit options, and whether delivery is offered, customers typically measure customer services in terms of expectations and experiences. A consumer-based definition of customer service is based upon the difference between expectations and experiences as judged by consumers; this difference is referred to as a *gap*.

Overall, a consumer's judgment of service quality is based on the size of the gap between his or her expectations and experiences. Exhibit 1 identifies four possible scenarios: two where experiences and expectations coincide, and two where experiences do not match expectations. Where experiences and expectations coincide, consumer expectations are confirmed. In the two where experiences do not match expectations, a consumer encounters either a pleasant surprise (where experiences are significantly above expectations), or an unpleasant surprise (where experiences are significantly below expectations).

Central to a consumer-oriented analysis of customer service is that consumers' judgments of customer service are based upon perceptions. Different consumers may evaluate the same customer service levels quite differently. The same customer may even evaluate a firm's service level quite differently at different times.

EXHIBIT 1. A Customer Service Evaluation Model

	Poor Experience	Excellent Experience
Poor Expectation	No Gap Confirmation of Poor Expectation	Large Gap Pleasant Surprise
Excellent Expectation	Large Gap Unpleasant Surprise	No Gap Confirmation of Excellent Expectation

Consumer perceptions of expectations and experiences apply to both process- and outcome-related activities. Process-related activities accompany a service (such as a store's cleanliness, personnel friendliness, and waiting lines). Outcome-related activities pertain to the reliability of the service (how accurate a repair was made, and whether a repair was done correctly the first time). Both process-related and outcome-related activities are considered by consumers in evaluating their expectations and experiences. For example, while a rental car may be dependable (an outcome measure), poor performance in terms of waiting lines, instructions in use, and a dirty rental facility may result in a less than satisfactory or poor overall customer service judgment. Opinion Research Corp. surveyed 400 executives of the nation's largest companies. The vast majority said that how much an airline cares about its customer (a process measure) is as important to them as prompt baggage delivery and efficient check-in (an outcome measure).[2]

Importance of Customer Service in Marketing Strategy

Research on the importance of customer service quality to firms and on the overall quality of customer service (as judged by consumers) has, for the most part, been conducted by private research organizations, not academics. The number of studies conducted in these areas is not large.

One of the great marketing paradoxes of our time is that many firms have continued to pay little attention to customer service at a time when bankruptcies, too much merchandise similarity among competing marketers, and high price competition characterize many market environments. The lack of interest in customer service among many firms still continues despite the large body of research that cites the direct and indirect costs to marketers that have inferior or "me-too" customer service strategies.

In research conducted for MasterCare auto service centers (a $1-billion-a-year chain owned by Bridgestone/Firestone), the firm found that honest, courteous service was viewed as twice as important to customers as the price of a repair job. According to the firm's senior vice president, "We purported to be the premium provider of auto services in the United States, but we failed. We found we were rude, that mechanics left grease on car seats—all sorts of things."[3]

Studies by the consulting firm of Arthur D. Little suggest that the quality of a company's service can cause it to gain or lose as much as 10 percent of its sales revenues. Service quality also has an effect on buyer loyalty.[4]

The Consumer Service Institute estimates that keeping a customer typically costs only one-fifth as much as acquiring a new one. The same source has found that 7 out of 10 customers who switch from one company to another cite poor service—not price or quality—as the reason. Another research organization, The Technical Assistance Research Programs Institute (TARP), found that 91 percent of unhappy customers will never buy again from the offending company, and will let their dissatisfaction be known to at least nine other people. The multiplier effect can also work the other way when customers enjoy exemplary service. Lastly, increases in consumer service expenditures in such areas as reliability of delivery, or time needed to fill orders, can drastically increase market share and profit margins.

Most of the published studies on the quality of customer service have dealt with store-related experiences by final consumers. There is, unfortunately, little published work relating to industrial products' customer service due to the proprietary nature of the data. Recent surveys confirm that customer perceptions of retailers' customer service is poor. For example, a survey of women shoppers by MAS Marketing, a Chicago-based market research firm, found that 80 percent of its respondents viewed shopping as "annoying but necessary."[5] A *Business Week*/Harris Poll of 1,255 adults found that only 6 percent of respondents stated that they most enjoy shopping as a leisure time activity. Close to half of the respondents agreed with the statement: "Even though from time to time it's a pleasure, mostly it's something I do because I have to."[6]

Robert B. Gill, vice chairman of J.C. Penney, summarizes his opinion of consumers' perceptions of shopping by stating that "shopping used to be an excursion, now it's a job. And not a very pleasant job at that."[7]

The data results can best be summarized by a statement made by a former corporate vice president for marketing at IBM: "It's a shame, but whenever you get good service, it's an exception, and you're excited about it. It ought to be the other way around."

Despite the importance of customer service, only about 10 percent of American service companies have any kind of service quality program, according to a major quality consulting firm.[8]

Marketing managers need to be aware of the significant short- and long-term costs associated with poor customer service. One way to measure the economic impact of poor customer service is to look at the loss in profits due to defecting customers. Mathematically, the loss in income equals the present value of long-term sales potential of a defecting existing customer times the loss in profit margin plus the cost of replacing that customer (in terms of additional advertising, sales promotion, and personal selling expense). Stew Leonard, the founder of the legendary dairy store, stated, "Every time I'm not nice to a customer, $50,000 walks out the door."[9]

Professor Barbara Bund Jackson views each account as an uncertain investment. It is unknown for how long, with what timing, and in what quantity each buyer will purchase. According to this model, the purpose of customer service is to extend the probability of purchase, the length of purchase, and the frequency of purchase to maximize the value of this investment.[10]

Other researchers who have studied the impact of defections on a firm's profits have concluded that "customer defections have a surprising impact on the bottom line." One group of researchers found that reducing the defection rate by just 5 percent generated 85 percent more profits in one bank's branch system, 50 percent more in an insurance brokerage, and 30 percent more in an auto-service chain.[11] Boosting customer retention by 2 percent has the same effect as cutting costs by 10 percent.[12]

Understanding the economics of poor customer service is important to marketers. The economics of poor customer service clearly shows that continuous improvement in service quality is an investment, not a cost, and that a low-cost customer service strategy can easily be overwhelmed by a high customer defection rate.

CUSTOMER SERVICE MODELS

Four important models which depict service quality are Porter's value chain; Herzberg's hygiene factors versus motivators; SERVQUAL, a model of service quality dimensions developed by Professors Zeithaml, Parasuraman, and Berry; and Jackson's relationship marketing concept. According to Michael Porter, buyers seek out suppliers that offer them the greatest added value. An adaptation of Herzberg's theory divides customer satisfaction components into hygiene factors and motivators. SERVQUAL defines service quality on the basis of five dimensions: tangibles, reliability, responsiveness, assurance, and empathy. Relationship marketing evaluates customer service from the perspective of customer switching costs for a firm selling organizational goods.

Porter's Value Chain

Professor Porter developed the value chain as a means of developing and evaluating ways to create added value for buyers. The value chain consists of the collection of activities that are performed to design, produce, market, deliver, and support its products.[13] The chain classifies value activities into primary and support activities. Primary activities include the physical creation of the product, the product's sale, transfer to the buyer, and after-sales assistance. Support activities support the primary activities.

The value chain examines all of the links between a manufacturer and its wholesale customers and retailer and its final consumer buyer in which the channel member can provide a unique competitive advantage. The competitive advantage in terms of wholesale service can be service manuals and procedures, spare parts, technical service, inspection by the vendor, and high quality control. The retail competitive advantage in terms of customer service can be either high reliability, ease of use, product adequacy determination, or ease of repair (see Exhibit 2).

A retailer can increase reliability to a buyer by lowering the risk of product failure. For example, while the furniture industry has a poor record in terms of defects, too few retailers seek to develop a competitive advantage by inspecting furniture before it leaves the retailer's warehouse. Such a strategy would lower the inconvenience of waiting at home for a repair, would increase consumers' quality perceptions of both the product and the service, and would also allow retailers to centrally conduct such repairs (which saves travel time).

Increasing ease of use is a second competitive advantage. Retailers need to recognize that a personal computer is among the most technically complex products that a typical consumer purchases in his or her lifetime. Yet few retailers have developed manuals on computer fundamentals for buyers or offer free half-day workshops for recent buyers. Gateway, a major mail-order computer retailer, for example, increases ease of use by shipping its computers with operating software

EXHIBIT 2. Sources of Customer Service Competitive Advantage Based on Value Chain Analysis

Competitive Advantage Element	Source of Competitive Advantage
High reliability	Increase reliability through selling only products with excellent serviceability and mechanical performance, and products that exceed a marketer's laboratory standards.
	Test all major purchases before they leave the warehouse for shipment to a customer.
Ease of use	Study buyers' level of expertise in use.
	Design effective manuals and instructions for use (beyond instructions provided by manufacturer).
	Offer workshops for recent buyers.
Product adequacy to determination	Produce printed checklists for buyers' use in estimating product needs.
	Train salespeople in identifying consumer needs, in product knowledge, and in matching needs with specific product types.
	Offer on-site product evaluation assistance.
Ease of repair	Sell only those products with excellent manufacturer-supported repair facilities or those where manufacturers offer on-site repair to consumers.
	Own and operate repair facilities.

installed. This enables users to have the computer ready-to-use in as little as two minutes after it is removed from the box. In contrast, competitors' computer systems without the preinstalled software can take as long as 4 to 5 hours to install.[14]

Product adequacy determination is a third source of a competitive advantage. A home improvement center can produce guidelines in estimating air conditioning capacity needs (based on size of area, exposure, degree of insulation, etc.) that are clearly posted in the store. This insures self-service customers that their air conditioner is the most suitable size. These "fact-tags," which can be used in selling other complex items, reduce the level of required sales assistance and can be used to expand the range of goods sold by a self-service retailer.

A fourth source of competitive advantage is ease of repair. A retailer can increase ease of repair by purchasing products only from vendors that offer comprehensive repair services including on-site customer service. Many of these competitive advantages are also applicable to industrial products.

Marketers need to communicate these competitive advantages to increase inquiries, to generate marketer loyalty, and to reduce price competition.

Hygiene Factors versus Motivators: An Adaptation of Herzberg's Job Satisfaction Theory

In his theory of job satisfaction, Frederick Herzberg differentiates between two kinds of satisfiers: hygiene factors and motivators. Hygiene factors are extrinsic to the job (such as pay and supervision); motivators are intrinsic to the job (such as achievement and recognition for performance). Hygiene factors are often labeled as dissatisfiers, meaning that their absence will hinder performance. Motivators are referred to as satisfiers, since motivators increase job performance.[15]

While Herzberg's management theory has been criticized on several counts, it provides a good conceptual framework for our analysis of customer service. Hygiene factors—in terms of customer service—can consist of marketer attributes that are expected by most consumers: on-time delivery, exchange privileges for defective merchandise, credit, hours of operation, and sufficient inventory on-hand. The presence of such variables does not motivate shoppers, nor does it lead to shopper satisfaction. However, the absence of hygiene factors can create ill will. On the other hand, store loyalty and store switching can be generated through such motivators as skilled salespeople, supervised children's playrooms, and responsive service departments (see Exhibit 3).

SERVQUAL Dimensions

An important contribution to the service quality literature was the development of a scale for measuring customers' perceptions of service

EXHIBIT 3. The Role of Hygiene Factors versus Motivators in Customer Service Evaluation

Hygiene Factors: Expectations versus Experiences	Motivators: Expectations versus Experiences
On time delivery	Skilled salespeople
Exchange privileges for defective merchandise	Emergency shipments
	Responsive personnel
Credit	24-hour technical service
Hours of operation	On-site service
Sufficient inventory on hand	Merchandise tested before shipped to consumers

Experiences Don't Meet Consumer Expectations on Hygiene Factors Consumer Dissatisfaction with Customer Service	Experiences Meet Consumer Expectations on Hygiene Factors Absence of Dissatisfaction with Customer Service (Consumer Is Indifferent)	Experiences Meet Consumer Expectations on Motivators Customer Satisfaction with Customer Service

quality. The SERVQUAL customer service measure includes five independent dimensions: tangibles, reliability, responsiveness, assurance, and empathy. Each of these dimensions is defined and illustrated in Exhibit 4.

While Professors Zeithaml, Parasuraman, and Berry found that all of the five dimensions were considered critical by respondents, they

EXHIBIT 4. Service Quality Components of SERVQUAL

Service Element	Definition of Service Element	Examples of Service Element
Tangibles	Appearance of physical facilities, equipment, personnel, and communication materials.	Are the marketer's facilities attractive? Are employees appropriately dressed? Are statements easy to understand?
Reliability	Ability to perform the promised service dependably and accurately.	Will an employee call me back when promised? Are my billing statements correct? Are repairs performed properly the first time?
Responsiveness	Willingness to help customers and provide prompt service.	When there is a problem, will the marketer resolve it quickly? Will the salesperson answer my specific questions? Will I be given a specific time for home delivery?
Assurance	Knowledge and courtesy of employees and their ability to convey trust and confidence.	Are employees able to answer questions? Are employees polite? Does the marketer have a good reputation? Can I be confident that repairs/installations/alterations were properly performed?
Empathy	Caring, individualized attention the firm provides its customers.	How easy is it for me to talk with senior executives when a problem cannot be resolved in the usual manner? Do employees avoid technical language? Am I recognized as a regular customer?

Source: Adapted from Valarie A. Ziethaml, A. Parasuraman, and Leonard L. Berry. *Delivering Quality Service: Balancing Customer Perceptions and Expectations* (New York: The Free Press, 1990), pp. 21–22, 25.

found that the reliability dimension was the most critical in consumers' assessment of service quality. The relative importance of each of the service dimensions in a five-company study (when the total responses are combined) is in order of rank importance: reliability, responsiveness, assurance, empathy, and tangibles.[16] The researchers found that the reliability dimension is primarily a service outcome measure, while tangibles, responsiveness, assurance, and empathy are more concerned with a process outcome measure.

Relationship Marketing

Professor Barbara Bund Jackson popularized a concept called relationship marketing—marketing that is oriented towards developing lasting relationships with accounts.[17] Customer service is a vital part of relationship marketing since high levels of customer service force vendors to have high vendor switching costs. For example, a traditional industrial buyer can easily change vendors on the basis of immediate inducements such as a special price cut. Switching costs are low in this scenario. In contrast, a vendor with a just-in-time inventory system requires a long-term relationship, as well as close coordination with its customers. Customer service increases switching costs for the buyer. It also increases the strength of the customer's commitment to the vendor.[18]

Professor Jackson recognizes that price is generally the shortest-term tool, and that advertising is a short- to medium-term tool. However, general product policy, technological stance, and technical capabilities are especially long-term tools. These are customer service elements.[19]

PITFALLS TO POOR CUSTOMER SERVICE

Customer service has not met with consumer expectations due to poor assumptions by management. These assumptions relate to the operation of the experience curve, the role of technical attributes in customer satisfaction, managers not realizing that there are traps to one-stop shopping, and measurement problems associated with customer service. I call these *customer service traps.*

Trap 1: Managers Assume That the Experience Curve Concept Is All Important

The experience curve is a concept with roots in psychology learning theory and cost accounting. Basically, this concept says that the firm with the highest market share obtains an important cost advantage over its competitors. In a nutshell, it focuses a tremendous amount of attention on being the cost leader, and on having the lowest prices.

The experience curve concept trap clearly creates a climate where the role of cost-cutting and price competition has been overemphasized and customer service is seen as being expendable. An opposing argument is that "customer satisfaction drives market share. The customer is the reason we exist." A Xerox chief executive recently refused to bolster sagging profits by cutting customer service. The feeling was that improved response time on repair calls would help improve long-term market share.

Trap 2: Managers Think That Being Technically Superior Is the Only Thing That Counts

Product reviews, to a large degree, proliferate this trap. A recent computer printer that I purchased was an Editor's Choice from a major magazine. The manufacturer, a major Japanese firm with an international reputation, did not miss a single trick in the design of the printer. The unit can produce six different print fonts, can accept paper three different ways, has three types of printing modes, and handles paper in such a manner as to reduce waste. The manufacturer was so wrapped up in producing a technically-superior product that it assumed that a typical consumer could figure out how to operate all of the features without any difficulty. The manufacturer did not test to see if the directions were understandable by a typical consumer. While the documentation lists a customer service department with a toll-free number, the number is not attended by either an operator or an answering machine. If it were not for the customer service department of a software vendor, I would still be unable to utilize many of the advanced features of the printer.

The review did not mention the difficulty in understanding the directions, and the reviewer did not obviously attempt to contact the firm's customer service department through its toll-free number. To me, the information on the quality of customer service is as least as important as the information on noise level or the number of paper paths.

Technical hubris is not confined to specialized magazines. Major consumer product rating magazines will rate a coffee maker, for example, on a host of technical characteristics yet not include whether the firm has a toll-free telephone number, the hours you can call, whether the firm stocks most of its parts, how long it takes for a part to be shipped, or how reasonable repair costs are after the warranty period.

Trap 3: Retailers Do Not Realize That There Are Pitfalls to One-Stop Shopping Appeals

Retailers commonly engage in what we call scrambled merchandising—the taking on of unrelated lines of merchandise. The strategy is based on one-stop shopping appeals, higher profit margins, greater frequency of customer visits, and self-service merchandising. I was recently startled to see a line of facsimile machines available for sale at my favorite self-service office supply store. Can a sales clerk explain the features of each machine? Or who will be responsible for repairing the machine after the warranty period? Or the kind of telephone line required for the machine to operate properly? Customer service is NOT saying to the customer "Try It, You'll Like It!" or "It's Returnable, Don't Worry!"

Trap 4: Managers Believe That They Can Measure Service Quality by Counting Complaints

This trap can be summarized by the statement: "No one complains, therefore service quality must be high." The truth is that a very limited proportion of dissatisfied customers complain. It is easier to find another supplier. Complaints are like the tip of an iceberg above the water line; there's more of the iceberg below water than what appears above the surface. A good marketer needs to multiply complaints by some factor to measure consumer satisfaction. For example, a study funded by the Office of the Special Advisor to the President for Consumer Affairs found that while 25 percent of all purchases result in some kind of consumer problem experience, approximately 70 percent of those experiencing the problem don't complain. The study indicates that consumers do not complain because (1) they do not believe it is worth the time or effort; (2) they don't know how; and (3) they believe complaining won't do any good. A.C. Nielsen reports that only one unhappy customer out of 50 will complain about purchases valued at $5 or less: "The other 49 just go away mad."

COMMON PRINCIPLES OF EXCELLENT CUSTOMER SERVICE PROVIDERS

In examining the customer service strategies of a large number of firms, I developed a list of eight common principles which the firms with the best customer service records had in common. The best firms have a written customer service policy, regularly monitor customer service levels, define customer service in terms of the customer expectations, make it easy for the customer to complain and for employees to respond to complaints, resolve complaints on the side of the customer, utilize technology in customer service, view customer service personnel as a career path for high caliber personnel, and are concerned about retaining present customers as well as obtaining new business. Let me further explain these principles.

Principle 1: They Have a Written Customer Service Policy Statement

United Services Automobile Association (USAA) is the nation's fifth-largest insurer of privately-owned automobiles and homes. The firm focuses on service quality and its three component parts: customers, workforce, and technology. According to the firm's CEO, Robert F. McDermott, "the mission and corporate culture of this company are, in one word, service. As a company objective, service comes ahead of either profits or growth. . . . But I submit that it's because service comes first at USAA that profits and growth have been so healthy."[20]

Intuit, a microcomputer manufacturer, has this policy: "Intuit stands or falls with what happens in tech support. Do whatever you need to satisfy the customer."[21] The company internalizes importance of customer service by reading customer thank you letters aloud and framing these letters. Customer service statistics for the week are read to employees, even before the firm lists revenue data.

Based on research conducted among a sample of industrial firms in six different industries (silicate, concrete, oil, gases, rubber, and agriculture), firms with a written customer policy were far more likely to use customer service as a competitive weapon than those with no written policy. Only 3 percent of respondents with a written policy did not view customer service as a strategic tool.[22]

Principle 2: They Monitor Customer Service Levels on a Regular Basis

Standardized, ongoing measurement of customer service levels lead to a benchmark against which managers can be evaluated and rewarded. This process also enables a firm to track complaints and to search for a cause. At least one major market research firm has set up a major subsidiary that specializes in customer satisfaction tracking. Another firm visits, on an anonymous basis, its clients' dealers to see if products are properly sold and serviced. Clients range from Sears to the Cadillac division of General Motors.

First National Bank of Chicago studies customer service in terms of 650 service quality measures: 500 that pertain to the bank's commercial customers and 150 that relate to retail services. Measures include how quickly telephones are answered, the number of customers who hang up during a pre-recorded message, the accuracy of check encoding, turnaround time on inquiries, and the speed at which the bank transfers securities.

Federal Express developed a list of service quality indicators; these are weighted to the seriousness they are rated in customer satisfaction surveys. For example, a delivery late by a few hours is weighted as a 1, while a missed pickup or damaged shipment has a weight of 10. These weights give Federal Express personnel something to shoot for, and also explains customer priorities in terms of customer needs and preferences.[23]

Principle 3: They Study Customer Service in Terms of the Customer

Hampton Inns will not charge for a room if it fails to meet the customer's, *not the motel's* standard for cleanliness, comfort, or safety. A survey conducted for the firm estimated that 2 percent of its guests choose to stay at a Hampton Inn on the basis of its "100 percent satisfaction guarantee." The chain has calculated that it has received $8 in revenue for every dollar paid to a dissatisfied guest.[24]

Manpower, a temporary employee agency, does not require that an employer pay for a temporary employee unless the employer is content with his or her services. These firms put their money where their mouth is. They are willing to make adjustments on the basis of customer satisfaction—even if the request may seem subjective and a bit unreasonable.

Principle 4: They Make It Easy for the Customer to Complain and for the Firm to Respond to Complaints

Good customer service departments not only listen, but have discretion to act. Fidelity Bank of Philadelphia recently authorized customer service representatives to resolve problems involving sums up to $1,000 before getting the supervisor's approval. After the change in policy, over 90 percent of customers questioned would recommend the bank to a friend, versus 65 percent before.

A steel manufacturer now has a full-time customer service representative at Honda's Marysville, Ohio plant. Instead of going through multiple channels to resolve a potential complaint, the customer service representative can handle any problem immediately.

According to a TARP (Technical Assistance Research Programs Institute) study, 54 to 70 percent of customers who complain will do business with the target company if the complaint is resolved satisfactorily. When customers felt there was a rapid resolution of the problem, the figure soared to 95 percent.

Principle 5: They Encourage Employees to Resolve Complaints on the Side of the Customer

The owner of a Seattle-based restaurant chain, Satisfaction Guaranteed Eateries, adopted a "replace plus one" philosophy. To compensate for the customer's hassle if an item is late, doesn't taste right, and so on, not only is the item free (with no need for explanation), the patron is also offered a drink or dessert to make him or her satisfied. If consumers wait more than 20 minutes beyond their reservation time, the whole meal might be free. Any employee from the busboy up has the right to placate a dissatisfied guest.[25]

Stew Leonard, the supermarket operator with legendary customer service, has the market's mission statement carved on a big rock in front of his store: "Our policy: Rule 1—The customer is always right. Rule 2—If the customer is ever wrong, reread rule 1."

Principle 6: They Utilize Technology in Improving Customer Services

Federal Express can track a package's location, determine when it was picked up, what plane it is on, what truck will pick it up, and when it will be delivered, based on bar coding of all packages and the use of scanners. This technology gives the firm a major advantage in the fiercely-competitive market for specialized package delivery. Likewise, laptop computers and modems allow a field sales force to quickly log in orders, determine inventory availability, and to generate customized letters to follow-up on recent sales. Four Season's Hotel uses computers to develop and maintain files on guest preferences. It knows when a repeat guest makes a reservation if he or she requires a nonallergic pillow, a low floor, a special newspaper, or has special dietary preferences. Almost 70 percent of guests are repeat visitors.

Principle 7: They Make Customer Service Personnel Part of a Career Path, Not a Dead-End Job

Firms need to position customer service as an important function within the firm, to describe its impact on sales and profits to all employees, and to attract and maintain top caliber people in customer service positions. Customer service cannot flourish in an environment which seeks to minimize costs or where customer service is viewed as an expendable service. For example, Bethlehem Steel sent a positive signal as to the importance of customer service to its employees, customers, and competitors when its chief metallurgist at a major plant was assigned to the customer service department. One of his earliest problems: the alarm on General Time's Big Ben and Little Ben alarm clocks did not match the nice ring of the older models. The solution: increase the hardness of the new steel.

Of 52 large companies surveyed by a New York-based recruiting firm, nearly half have created executive level quality posts since 1988.[26]

Principle 8: They Are Concerned with Customer Retention as Well as Obtaining New Customers

MBNA America, the credit card operation of MNC Financial, holds onto 95 percent of its customers every year, compared with 88 percent for its competitors. A new card member costs $100 to acquire, but a five-year customer brings in an average of $100 in profits annually, and a ten-year customer produces $300. The firm has 68 phone service agents who call every customer who wants to close an account. Agents have broad powers to win customers back, including waiving annual fees. Agents typically rescue one-half of the accounts.[27]

CONDUCTING A CUSTOMER SERVICE AUDIT

This section describes the steps in conducting a customer service audit: who conducts the audit, when and how often it is conducted, the development of audit forms, and recommending changes on the basis of the audit.

Conducting an Audit

A marketer should evaluate its customer service levels through a specialized customer audit on a periodic basis. The audit can be performed by company specialists, department managers, or by outside specialists. While a marketer must decide how often the audit is to be conducted, the topics to be covered, and the time duration of the audit, the most important part of the audit process is the development of the audit form.

Developing Audit Forms

Exhibit 5 applies the material from this article to the development of an audit form for a marketer. Included in the audit are the importance of developing specific standards (for store cleanliness, employee dress, appointment scheduling), communicating standards to employees and customers, the monitoring of performance levels (by questionnaires, waiting line studies, the use of mystery shoppers), and an incentive system for excellence in performance.

A major assumption of this analysis is that product and service standards are interrelated. For example, a good customer service-oriented wholesaler or retailer needs to determine how fast a manufacturer typically repairs a good, whether the manufacturer maintains an 800-customer service number, and how timely repairs are made. Poor manufacturer performance in these areas may transfer over to the retailer's reputation.

EXHIBIT 5. A Sample Customer Service Audit Form

	Strategy and Tactics
	Answer Yes or No to Each Question
Does Your Firm:	
1. Monitor cleanliness of physical facilities on a periodic basis?	________
2. Develop and enforce dress codes for all employees?	________
3. Evaluate retail locations for required maintenance on a periodic basis?	________
4. Sell merchandise that is backed by fair and adequate manufacturer repair service?	________
5. Sell merchandise that your firm is capable of properly evaluating for consumer needs, installing, and trouble-shooting?	________

6. Resist purchasing low-end promotional goods that are shoddy, difficult to repair, and that have high failure rates? __________
7. Key employee compensation to meeting and beating service standard levels? __________
8. Train employees in technical areas relating to selling, installing, and servicing goods? __________
9. Guarantee all services? __________
10. Resolve service problems quickly? If current staff cannot resolve the problem, will the staff contact retailer-based specialists and product manufacturer(s)? __________
11. Make every reasonable effort to maintain scheduled appointments? __________
12. Call customers when service will be late? __________
13. Guarantee all services such as installations and repairs? __________
14. Make guarantees clear and easy to understand? __________
15. Monitor service levels by questionnaires, waiting line studies, use of mystery shoppers, unannounced spot checks by management, and monitoring of complaints? __________
16. Train all technical employees in human relations as well as in technical skills? __________
17. Refuse to sell merchandise that requires special knowledge if salespeople cannot be trained to possess required skills? __________
18. Allow employees to purchase products they sell at cost and/or allow employees to borrow "demo" equipment for home use? __________
19. Encourage employees to be honest in appraisal of service problems? __________
20. Promptly answer all customer service correspondence? __________
21. Train employees to deal with exceptions as well as ordinary service problems? __________
22. Give employees sufficient discretion to "right" service wrongs? __________
23. Encourage employees to seek senior managers for assistance with special problems beyond their discretion? __________
24. Encourage employees to learn names of important customers? __________
25. Train employees in importance of eye contact, the need to express concern, and tone of voice in their relationship with customers? __________
26. Know the cost of losing a steady customer? __________
27. Communicate the costs of losing a steady customer to all employees? __________
28. Provide realistic expectations of customer service in all promotions? __________
29. Conduct periodic customer service audits? __________

Recommending Changes

The customer service audit draws attention to areas requiring additional attention. It is the responsibility of management, not the auditor, to determine these responses. Some appropriate responses may be recommending that the marketer institute a service guarantee program, that the service philosophy be communicated to employees, that the retailer make it easier for customers to complain, and/or that employee compensation be keyed to the levels of customer service and customer retention.

Conclusion

A customer service strategy must be carefully thought out. An effective customer service strategy requires a major support system. Elements of this support system include incentives, measurement of service levels, communication (between management and customers and between management and employees), product testing, and market research on customer satisfaction.

In planning and evaluating a marketer's customer service program, a marketer needs to be careful to avoid general customer service implementation pitfalls. One major pitfall is attempting to get customers to pay extra for services that they expect free-of-charge. A second pitfall is to develop a service mix that includes services that are costly yet not desired by your target market.

These two pitfalls can be avoided by studying the optimal mix of quality and price that exceeds customer expectations and then seeking to deliver it. These pitfalls can also be avoided by segmenting the market by the level of customer service desired and then by establishing separate levels of service and prices that meet those expectations. For example, a furniture retailer can unbundle its pricing strategy for personal computers: basic personal computer ($1,700), installation of software ($100), delivery ($50), and in-office repair ($35). The customer can then pay anywhere between $1,700 and $1,885 for the computer, depending on the cluster of services desired.

A third major pitfall is promoting good service as a differentiating characteristic to consumers before all systems are in place to actually provide such service. In this manner, the marketer is setting an expectation level that it can't deliver on; such unreasonably high expectations might lower consumers' overall customer service quality judgments.

NOTES

1. Valarie A. Zeithaml, A. Parasuraman, and Leonard L. Berry. *Delivering Quality Service: Balancing Customer Perceptions and Expectations* (New York: The Free Press, 1990) 24–28.

2. Patricia Sellers, "What Customers Really Want," *Fortune* (June 4, 1990) 58.
3. *Ibid.,* 62.
4. See Harvey N. Shycon, "Improved Customer Service: Measuring the Payoff," *The Journal of Business Strategy* 13 (January/February 1992) 13.
5. Laura Zinn, Christopher Power, Julia Flynn Siler *et. al.,* "Retailing: Who Will Survive?" *Business Week* (November 26, 1990) 140.
6. *Ibid.,* 144.
7. *Ibid.,* 140.
8. Larry Armstrong and William C. Symonds, "Beyond 'May I Help You?' " *Business Week* (Quality 1991) 100.
9. Barry Farber and Joyce Wycoff, "Customer Service: Evolution and Revolution," *Sales & Marketing Management* (May 1991) 44.
10. Barbara Bund Jackson, *Winning & Keeping Industrial Customers* (New York: Lexington Books, 1985) 5.
11. Frederick F. Reichheld and W. Earl Sasser, "Zero Defections: Quality Come to Services," *Harvard Business Review* 61 (September-October 1990) 107.
12. Armstrong and Symonds, "Beyond 'May I Help You?' " 102.
13. Michael E. Porter, *Competitive Advantage: Creating and Sustaining Superior Performance* (New York: The Free Press, 1985) 36.
14. Gary McWilliams, "Mail-Order Madness," *Business Week* (Quality 1991) 128.
15. Frederick Herzberg, *Work and the Nature of Man* (New York: World, 1971); and Frederick Herzberg "One More Time: How Do You Motivate Employees?" *Harvard Business Review* 39 (January-February 1968) 53–62.
16. Zeithaml, Parasuraman, and L. Berry. *Delivering Quality Service: Balancing Customer Perceptions and Expectations,* 24–28.
17. Jackson, *Winning & Keeping Industrial Customers.*
18. *Ibid.,* 134.
19. *Ibid.,* 168–169.
20. Thomas Teal, "Service Comes First: An Interview with USAA's Robert F. McDermott," *Harvard Business Review* 62 (September-October 1991) 118.
21. John Case, "Customer Service: The Last Word," *Inc.* (April 1991) 92.
22. Myroslaw J. Kyj, "Customer Service as a Competitive Tool," *Industrial Marketing Management* 16 (August 1987) 228.
23. Frank Rose, "Now Quality Means Service Too," *Fortune* (April 22, 1991) 106.
24. Daniel Pearl, "More Firms Pledge Guaranteed Service," *Wall Street Journal* (July 17, 1991) B1.
25. Timothy W. Firnstahl, "My Employees Are My Service Guarantee," *Harvard Business Review* 60 (July-August 1989) 28–30.
26. Gilbert Fuchsberg, "Gurus of Quality are Gaining Clout," *Wall Street Journal* (November 27, 1990) B1.
27. Sellers, "What Customers Really Want," 61.

BIBLIOGRAPHY

Armstrong, Larry and William C. Symonds, "Beyond 'May I Help You?' " *Business Week* (Quality 1991):100–103.

Bund Jackson, Barbara. *Winning & Keeping Industrial Customers* New York: Lexington Books, 1985.

Case, John. "Customer Service: The Last Word." *Inc.* (April 1991):89–93.

Farber, Barry and Joyce Wycoff, "Customer Service: Evolution and Revolution." *Sales & Marketing Management* (May 1991):44–48.

Firnstahl, Timothy W. "My Employees Are My Service Guarantee." *Harvard Business Review* 60 (July-August 1989):28–31.

Fuchsberg, Gilbert. "Gurus of Quality are Gaining Clout." *Wall Street Journal* (November 27, 1990):B1,B7.

Herzberg, Frederick. "One More Time: How Do You Motivate Employees?" *Harvard Business Review* 39 (January-February 1968):53–62.

______. *Work and the Nature of Man*. New York: World, 1971.

Kyj. Myroslaw J. "Customer Service as a Competitive Tool." *Industrial Marketing Management* 16 (August 1987):225–230.

McWilliams, Gary. "Mail-Order Madness." *Business Week* (Quality 1991):128.

Pearl, Daniel. "More Firms Pledge Guaranteed Service," *Wall Street Journal* (July 17, 1991):B1, B4.

Porter, Michael E. *Competitive Advantage: Creating and Sustaining Superior Performance*. New York: The Free Press, 1985.

Reichheld, Frederick F. and W. Earl Sasser. "Zero Defections: Quality Come to Services." *Harvard Business Review* 61 (September-October 1990):105–111.

Rose, Frank. "Now Quality Means Service Too." *Fortune* (April 22, 1991):99–100.

Sellers, Patricia. "What Customers Really Want." *Fortune* (June 4, 1990):58–62.

Shycon, Harvey N. "Improved Customer Service: Measuring the Payoff." *The Journal of Business Strategy* 13 (January/February 1992):13–17.

Teal, Thomas "Service Comes First: An Interview with USAA's Robert F. McDermott." *Harvard Business Review* 62 (September-October 1991):117–127.

Zeithaml, Valarie A., A. Parasuraman, and Leonard L. Berry. *Delivering Quality Service: Balancing Customer Perceptions and Expectations*. New York: The Free Press, 1990.

Zinn, Laura, Christopher Power, and Julia Flynn Siler et. al. "Retailing: Who Will Survive?" *Business Week*, (November 26, 1990):140.

Karen F. A. Fox
Associate Professor of Marketing
Santa Clara University
Santa Clara, California

CHAPTER 44

SOCIAL MARKETING

THE AIMS OF SOCIAL MARKETING

Marketing planning and marketing tools have traditionally been used to encourage consumers to buy goods and services. In the 1970s, the idea emerged that marketing could play a useful role in encouraging people to adopt beneficial practices that would improve their own long-term well being and that of society at large. This new application of marketing has come to be called *social marketing.*

In most cases, social marketing aims to enhance the well being of the adopter while also providing benefits to society. For example, quitting smoking improves the health of former smokers and of their families, and also benefits society by reducing the burden of medical and other costs (covered by insurance or not), including reduced productivity. Where the adopter gains no direct personal benefit (e.g., signing an organ donor card), social marketing focuses on the psychological rewards of altruism.

APPLICATIONS OF SOCIAL MARKETING

A social marketing approach has been used to encourage people to eat less fat; to eat more vegetables, fruits, and whole grains; to quit smoking; to monitor and treat symptoms of high blood pressure; to practice "safe sex" to avoid the spread of AIDS; to sign cards authorizing organ donation; to give blood; and to promote other beneficial practices. Social marketing has also been employed overseas—particularly in developing countries—to encourage adoption of family planning, immunization, breastfeeding, and oral rehydration solution to prevent death from diarrheal dehydration. Social marketing is also relevant outside the area of health and family planning. The principles can be effectively applied to a wide range of issues that require behavior change, for example, energy and water conservation and practices to protect the environment.

SOCIAL MARKETING AND COMMERCIAL MARKETING

A social marketing program is not the same as a public service advertising campaign any more than commercial marketing is the same thing as mass media advertising. While advertising is often a useful, even essential, part of many marketing programs, it is one of several tools that must be integrated and coordinated to produce the desired outcomes. Both social and commercial marketing rely on the "4 P's"—giving attention to product, price, place (distribution), and promotion.

While most social marketing programs are funded by government agencies or not-for-profit organizations, social marketing should also appeal to companies that want to promote causes that benefit the public and that also benefit the company. For example, life insurance companies encourage fire prevention, safety awareness, smoking cessation, and other changes that reduce the incidence of insurance claims. Some beer and spirits companies promote safe driving and the importance of relying on a "designated driver" in order to be responsible corporate citizens and to reduce government and public pressure affecting regulations on selling and serving alcoholic beverages.

Social marketing has partially displaced a number of traditional approaches to encouraging behavior change. In the past, heavy reliance was placed on exhortations by public officials, public and school-based education programs, and public service (donated) advertising. The focus was on telling people the right thing to do, rather than on communicating the value of the change and facilitating its adoption. Social marketing marshals the full range of marketing tools and concepts to enhance the design and implementation of social change programs while continually respecting the right of each individual to decide whether or not to adopt the change.

STEPS IN EFFECTIVE SOCIAL MARKETING

Defining the Problem

Social marketers should first ascertain what the problem is and what it is not, and who is affected and in what ways. The problem statement guides the entire social marketing program, so oversights at this point can derail all subsequent efforts. For example, suppose a group wanting to increase the number of donated hearts for transplantation stated the problem as "we don't have enough donated hearts to meet the demand," when a *behavioral* problem statement might be "neurosurgeons delay or fail to certify brain death, so we are unable to discuss organ donation with family members while tissues are still suitable for transplantation."

Overly facile or incomplete problem statements can lead to simplistic and ineffective programs. For example, a campaign urging the public to "be generous, sign an organ donor card" might not address the actual barriers to increasing numbers of donated organs. Social marketers need to correctly identify and understand the problem, which often calls for extensive interviews with people who can affect or who are affected by the problem, as well as with potential adopters.

Problems need to be understood from the point of view of the person or groups who will be targeted in the social marketing program. For example, campaigns to promote oral rehydration therapy to save the lives of young children with diarrheal dehydration encountered mothers who wanted to "cure" (stop) the diarrhea by withholding food and water, traditional healers who believed in using purgatives, and physicians who prescribed useless antibiotics. The campaign had to teach mothers that dehydration was more dangerous than diarrhea, teach traditional healers how to administer oral rehydration solution instead of harmful purgatives, and teach physicians that oral rehydration therapy was inexpensive and highly effective while antibiotics are expensive and have no effect on diarrheal dehydration.

Selecting the Appropriate Target Audience(s)

The definition of the problem shapes the selection of target audiences. The social marketer segments the potential audience into relatively homogeneous subgroups and then selects one or more segments as a basis for developing the social marketing program. For example, a smoking-cessation program directed at young teenagers might be quite different than one directed at older long-term smokers with health problems. The first program might teach teens to resist peer pressure to smoke, and the second might emphasize behavioral strategies to break a well-entrenched habit and perhaps employ nicotine patches or other pharmacological approaches to reduce the physical effects of withdrawal.

Targeting decisions heavily depend on the social marketers' and/or sponsors' objectives. If the social marketing campaign is funded by the government (as many are), the social marketers may aim to reach the most disadvantaged or affected segments of the population, with the expectation that this will yield the greatest benefit. For example, directing childhood immunization campaigns toward neighborhoods with the lowest immunization rates is good public policy.

But if the program's objective is to immunize the largest number of children in the shortest possible time, other neighborhoods might respond more quickly. In low immunization-rate neighborhoods, there may be greater resistance to government programs, less knowledge about the substantial benefits of immunization, and therefore a greater need to develop contacts in the community and to educate parents about the value of immunization. Only by clearly recognizing the program's goals and objectives can the social marketing program be appropriately targeted.

Conducting Additional Research on the Target Audience

Once selected, the target audience needs to be well understood before developing the marketing plan. At this stage, the social marketers will conduct focus groups, personal interviews, observational studies, or other studies to become fully knowledgeable about this group, its concerns, its attitudes about the proposed behavior change, possible sources of resistance and of attraction to the behavior change, the communication channels they rely on, and other information useful to designing the social marketing program.

Developing a Coordinated, Comprehensive Marketing Plan

An effective social marketing program is laid out with all the care devoted to the best commercial marketing venture. In fact, since social marketing programs often ask people to make difficult changes, such as stopping smoking or changing eating habits, the social marketing plan has to be even more carefully conceived and executed. The social marketing plan details the four components of the marketing mix: the product and/or behavior change to be offered; the "price" involved; where and how the product, information, or other offered resources can be obtained; and the promotional activities to support the marketing plan. (These components are discussed in succeeding sections.) The plan must also specify realistic behavioral outcomes, the time frame, and how the outcomes will be assessed. The overall plan is important because coordinated activities directed at a clearly defined target audience are far more likely to be effective than is a single mass campaign directed at everyone.

Designing the Proposed Behavior Change ("Product")

The social marketers must reflect long and hard on exactly what behavior change should be put forward. For example, a program to create awareness of and attention to early diagnosis of breast cancer could emphasize the need for a periodic mammogram and/or the importance of breast self-examination. Before encouraging mammograms, the social marketers (including medical advisors) must determine who should seek mammograms (all women? all women over 45? those in high-risk groups?) and how often they should have mammograms. Simply saying "get a mammogram" is not a clear proposal for behavior change. If the social marketers decided instead to promote breast self-examination, the program would need to determine the best method of breast self-examination to publicize and how to educate the audience about it, not just urge women to "do breast self-examination."

Extensive research on why people adopt innovations underscores the importance of five factors. New ideas, behaviors, and products are more likely to be accepted when their positive outcomes can be easily understood and observed, and when the new is compatible with adopters' lives and easy to "try out," and offers obvious advantages over the old. Social marketers try to fine-tune the proposed behavior change to simplify, communicate, and facilitate it to increase its likelihood of adoption by the target audience.

Positioning the Desired Behavior Change

Positioning involves influencing how people perceive and think about what is offered. The social marketer aims to encourage behavior change by positioning the behavior change in a positive way. For example, instead of asking people to "consider donating your corneas when you die," signing a donor card might be described as "a small act now that can give others the gift of sight." The latter statement does not mislead the prospective donor in any way, but does place the decision in a more pleasant and altruistic light, focusing on the future benefit to others and the minimal difficulty of the requested action—to sign a donor card.

Developing Tangible Products

While social marketing programs typically aim to influence the acceptability of ideas (such as the value of quitting smoking, donating blood, learning cardiopulmonary resuscitation), they do not rely entirely on promoting intangible ideas that are sometimes difficult to grasp. Instead, whenever possible, social marketers try to come up with some *tangible* product that eases or otherwise encourages the behavior change or heightens its effectiveness.

Selecting, developing, and promoting facilitating products often distinguish social marketing from approaches relying on advertising alone. The Stanford Heart Disease Prevention Program produced and distributed large heart-shaped magnets and a series of small heart-healthy eating posters, and encouraged their target audience to fasten these posters to their home refrigerators as guides and reminders of the importance of heart-healthy eating. Easy-to-understand pictoral record cards encourage illiterate parents to ensure that their children have received all the necessary vaccinations. The availability and high degree of protection provided by latex condoms greatly facilitates the social marketers' already difficult task of promoting "safe sex" to prevent the spread of AIDS. Nicotine patches reduce the physiological craving for tobacco, reinforcing the behavior changes involved in quitting smoking. In each case, the product facilitates the beneficial behavior change.

Controlling the Cost of Adopting the Desired Behavior

In the broadest sense, the price of anything is the cost of obtaining it. The total price includes the time spent shopping; the wear-and-tear on the car; the effort to decide what to buy; and the cost of storing, using, maintaining, and ultimately disposing of the item.

In social marketing, the price is often negligible in monetary terms (e.g., signing a donor card), but the nonmonetary cost in terms of time, effort, or psychological stress may be very high: taking three buses to get one's children to the free immunization clinic, giving up the pleasurable habit of smoking, or facing the reality of one's own mortality are just a few examples.

A marketing approach presumes that people engage in exchange—purchase a product or adopt a new behavior—when they expect to be better off as a result, or at least on a par compared to their previous situation. Social marketers often cannot use price reductions very much because the monetary price of the behavior change is often at or close to zero—for example, taking an aspirin daily to reduce the incidence of stroke. In fact, healthier foods often cost less than unhealthy foods, and quitting smoking saves rather than costs money. The "cost" to the would-be adopter is often in the effort to overcome inertia, to change long-standing habits.

To reduce these costs, social marketers employ two broad approaches. First, social marketers can increase the *perceived value* of what is being offered. Use of modern methods of family planning can help to space the mother's pregnancies, improving her health and that of her children. This is a positive value. Second, social marketers can try to enhance the value of adopting the new behavior by reducing the actual and/or *perceived cost.* Convenient evening and weekend hours, available child care, and a welcoming atmosphere can "reduce the cost" of donating blood, getting immunizations, and obtaining family planning advice.

Pricing can also include setting payment terms that further reduce the (typically modest) financial price. In developing countries, deforestation is caused by population pressure on the land and forests, climatic changes that reduce wood supply, and the reliance on inefficient wood-burning stoves that waste fuel while polluting the air inside the home. Gathering adequate wood also requires searching farther and farther from home and is very time consuming. Social marketers might try to reduce consumption of wood and improve health by promoting the use of more efficient stoves made out of local materials, including clay. If many people cannot afford the price of the new stoves or have little or no cash income, social marketers consider ways would-be purchasers could pay the cost over time or through contributing their work or products toward the cost of the stove. In some areas, villagers are taught how to make their own solar cookers from simple materials, eliminating the need for firewood altogether.

Determining People/Activities That Need to Interact ("Place")

The manufacturer of a product needs to arrange one or more channels of distribution to get the finished product from the place where it is produced to the customer who will buy and use it. Some social marketing programs offer products and rely on channels of physical distribution to get them to customers. For example, overseas social marketing programs to encourage purchase and use of contraceptives strive to make donated products conveniently available to their targeted customer groups by providing distribution through multiple outlets rather than just one, inconvenient type of outlet. Contraceptive products can be made available in public clinics (which often have very limited hours) and private clinics as well as in pharmacies and shops that are open for longer hours each day.

Other social marketing programs involve no physical products but do require the interaction of various groups and agencies to carry out the program. Offering smoking-cessation classes may involve coordination between supporting organizations and may require locating meeting places and handling other logistical matters in addition to promoting the programs to attract participants.

Planning the Communications Program ("Promotion")

The communications or promotional component of a social marketing program can include advertising, public relations, publicity, personal contact, and other promotion activities. Mass-media advertising is often an important vehicle for carrying the social marketing program's message. The appropriate audience must be selected, the appropriate messages must be created, and messages must then be embodied in effective communications that are then presented through appropriate media with adequate reach and frequency to influence the intended audience.

Many effective social marketing programs recognize the value of using multiple types of communications to enhance and emphasize the message. For example, the Egyptian national contraceptive social marketing program includes television, radio, newspaper and billboard ads, bus posters, and informational meetings held in factories and other workplaces. The Stanford Heart Disease Prevention Program used classes, one-on-one counseling, mass-media advertising, booklets, and other promotional tools to reinforce the importance of adopting and maintaining a heart-healthy lifestyle.

Every element of the communications/promotion component needs to be carefully reviewed and pre-tested with a sample from the target audience. If the difficulty is recognized early, an ambiguous message can be modified or replaced. A seemingly obvious message can be misconstrued; for example, when former president Ronald Reagan publicized a little girl's urgent need for a liver, nineteen people telephoned to donate their livers for this child. They were unaware that they would have to be dead to donate their livers; we can assume that these are not the only uninformed people in the United States.

Even when materials are factually correct, they are not useful if the target audience cannot easily understand and apply the message. Although use of pictures can help carry the message, great care is necessary. The Stanford Heart Disease Prevention Program adopted an attractive heart logo without realizing until later that the EKG pattern incorporated into the logo was emblematic of a seriously damaged heart, not a healthy heart. Pictorial flyers demonstrating how to mix oral rehydration solution were distributed throughout the Gambia in Africa before it was discovered that most villagers had never been exposed to pictures and could not interpret the diagrams. Guidelines for pre-testing health and other social marketing messages have been developed and are available from the National Cancer Institute and UNICEF.

Evaluating the Effectiveness of the Social Marketing Program

Social marketing programs require tracking of each component as the program is implemented (formative evaluation) to identify program flaws and unanticipated hurdles, permitting mid-course corrections in the program. For example, when the problem was identified in the Gambia, the flyers were supplemented with radio broadcasts that explained how to interpret the pictures.

The outcomes of the social marketing program should also be carefully tracked to determine the program's accomplishments (summative evaluation). Most social marketing programs are funded by government agencies and by not-for-profit organizations, with limited budgets and many causes to promote. Measuring the costs (including volunteered time and materials) and the outcomes can help guide subsequent social marketing efforts, and help to identify the most promising approaches as well as the ineffective ones.

THE FUTURE OF SOCIAL MARKETING

Social marketing has demonstrated its potential to enhance the effectiveness of social change efforts. As a relatively new approach, few people have been specifically trained to be social marketers. Most people working in this field have backgrounds in public health, education, mass communications, social policy, and—in a few cases—marketing. They have turned to social marketing to provide a more coordinated, targeted, and effective way to help people adopt new practices and behaviors. As the implementation of social marketing programs continues, more professionals will have the background and experience to further extend the application of social marketing.

New discoveries in medicine, diagnostic technology, health promotion, and environmental science will continue to create opportunities to convey valuable new information and practices to selected target audiences and the general public. Organ donation was ineffective before the development of anti-rejection medications; high-resolution mammography permits increasingly early detection; the environmental effects of chlorofluorocarbons (CFCs) as aerosol propellants was only recognized in the 1980s; and the value of aspirin in reducing strokes was only confirmed in the early 1990s. As new developments emerge, social marketing can play a role in informing and motivating people to change their behavior in response.

SUGGESTIONS FOR FURTHER READING

Seymour H. Fine, *Social Marketing: Promoting the Causes of Public and Nonprofit Agencies* (Boston: Allyn and Bacon, 1990).

Karen F. A. Fox, "Social Marketing of Oral Rehydration Therapy and Contraceptives in Egypt," *Studies in Family Planning,* 1988, vol. 19, No. 2, pp. 95–108.

Philip Kotler and Eduardo L. Roberto, *Social Marketing: Strategies for Changing Public Behavior* (New York: The Free Press, 1989).

Richard K. Manoff, *Social Marketing: New Imperative for Public Health* (New York: Praeger, 1985).

Everett G. Rogers, *Diffusion of Innovations,* 3rd. ed. (New York: The Free Press, 1983).

Michael H. Morris, PhD
Associate Professor
Department of Marketing
University of Central Florida
Orlando, Florida

George A. Siragusa
Lubricants Pricing Manager
Mobil Oil Corporation
World Headquarters
Fairfax, Virginia

CHAPTER 45

STRATEGIC PRICING

INTRODUCTION: PRICE AND VALUE

Every product or service sold by a company must be assigned a price. Prices are numerical statements of what a customer must pay for an item; however, the key to effective pricing is to ensure that the price charged reflects the amount of value a customer is receiving. A fundamental principle in pricing is to recognize that *price is a statement of value, not a statement of costs.*

One of the leading causes of new-product failure is a phenomenon marketers refer to as the "price crunch." This happens when a company charges a price that is significantly higher or lower than the amount of value customers associate with a particular purchase. Just as the majority of prospective buyers were not willing to purchase microwave ovens when they cost $600 each, a substantial number of customers might be expected to resist purchasing 100 aspirins for 25 cents. In both cases, the prices may be in line with the seller's costs per unit, but they are out of line with the buyer's value perceptions.

The underlying reason for much of today's ineffective pricing is a preoccupation among those who set prices with the need to cover the costs of running their businesses. Cost coverage—not customer value—is the single most emphasized factor in the pricing policies of most companies. In fact, the most popular method for determining prices is called cost-plus pricing: Cost per unit is determined, usually based on some arbitrary cost allocation scheme, and a profit margin is added. Customer considerations, and especially value to the user, are virtually ignored.

Alternatively, the challenge facing managers who seek to be value-driven is twofold. First, the package of benefits offered for sale must reflect the underlying needs of buyers. Customers vary in how much value they assign to a particular product or service attribute, and are involved in trade-off decisions concerning how much of an attribute is sufficient. For instance, some car buyers place considerable importance on gas mileage, while others are much more concerned with style. In the final analysis, most buyers make some sort of tradeoff between acceptable mileage performance and automobile appearance. This tradeoff defines the value for which they are willing to pay.

The second problem involves assigning a price tag to the attribute package that accurately reflects the value being received by a customer. This problem is complicated because value is perceived in the minds of individual buyers—different customers are unlikely to perceive product value in quite the same way. Further, the subjective nature of value makes it difficult to quantify and measure. And yet the key to enhanced profitability in today's competitive environment lies in dealing with such complications.

The concept of value is always present in the minds of consumers. Such phrases as "value for the money," "best value," and "you get what you pay for," are fairly commonplace. At the most basic level, though, value represents a buyer's overall evaluation of a product or service based on his or her perceptions of the benefits received compared to what must be given up. From this point of view, what must be given up includes not only the monetary price, but also the time and effort that the buyer must invest. Superior value results from either offering customers lower prices for equivalent benefits or providing unique product benefits that more than compensate customers for paying a higher price. Creating and sustaining superior value is crucial for establishing competitive advantage.

PRICE AS A CREATIVE VARIABLE

Implicit in the argument that price must reflect value is the need for flexibility in the methods used to establish prices. While it may seem obvious to some, a fundamental truism in a market-oriented environment is that *price is a variable.* The opposite of a variable is a constant—something that is unchanging. Many managers approach price as a constant. That is, they set prices using a fixed formula, such as determining cost per unit and adding a predetermined margin to arrive at a price. Having applied the formula, they give no further thought to the use of price as a marketing tool. Not only is such an approach naive and overly simplistic, but it causes the manager to lose sight of the real purpose of a price and to miss creative opportunities for realizing profits.

Prices can be varied in many ways. The only requirement is creative thinking on the part of the manager. Examples of ways to vary a price include:

- Keep the same price currently charged but give the customer greater (or lesser) product quality.
- Keep the same price currently charged but give the customer a smaller (or larger) quantity of a particular item.
- Change the time of payment, such as allowing a customer four months to make a payment.
- Offer a rebate or a dollars-off coupon.
- Provide cash, quantity, and/or trade discounts.
- Charge different prices to different types of customers.
- Charge different prices based on the time of day, month, or year.
- Offer to accept a trade-in from the customer.
- Accept partial or full payment in the form of goods and services instead of money.
- Bundle the product or service with other products and services and charge a single price lower than the combined individual prices.

These are but a few of the possibilities. The downside is that price as a variable is a more complicated management task and requires considerably more hard work than does price as a constant or fixed phenomenon. Also, creativity can be dangerous if not properly structured. Pricing decisions should not be made in a piecemeal fashion, but instead should be part of what we will call a "strategic pricing program."

DEVELOPING A STRATEGIC PRICING PROGRAM

Suppose a company faced with stagnating sales growth decides to temporarily reduce the price of its leading product by 5 percent. Such a move might seem commonplace in today's competitive environment, yet pricing decisions such as this are frequently made arbitrarily and prove to be costly mistakes in the marketplace. The company may discover much later that it is giving away margins unnecessarily, alienating middlemen, confusing customers, and inviting aggressive responses from competitors.

Mistakes like this one occur because management has no specific purpose in mind when reducing the price other than increasing sales. To better understand the problem, consider some of the potential underlying reasons for a price cut. A number of possibilities exist, including:

- An attempt to attract new users to the market
- An effort to increase usage rates among existing customers
- A method of taking customers away from competitors
- A means of discouraging current customers from switching to competitors
- An approach for encouraging customers to purchase now instead of later
- A technique for discriminating among different types of buyers
- A means of using the price of one product to help sell other products in the line

Each of these reasons represents an entirely different rationale for the pricing action. That is, the same price cut could be used for a number of distinct purposes.

To be effective, individual pricing moves such as the one just described must be part of a larger program of action. Management must identify a specific purpose for the price change, together with measurable goals for evaluating the effectiveness of the change. Otherwise, the company is, in effect, blindly taking a chance that a particular move is appropriate. This explains why managers are so frequently unsure about whether or not they have made the correct pricing decision.

The program of action that should guide pricing has four key components: objectives, strategy, structure, and levels (tactics). These components can be approached as a logical four-step process.

Step One: The Role of Price Objectives

There is no one best price to charge for a given product. Once the need to set or change a price has been recognized, the manager must determine what he or she is trying to accomplish with this particular price. The answer might seem obvious: to sell more products or services. But this response is too general, and may not even be the case. In fact, companies can have a number of different pricing objectives.

Exhibit 1 provides examples of some of these objectives. The ones cited are not mutually exclusive, and some could be used in combination. For instance, using price to accomplish a particular image, such as that of premier quality provider, may also serve to maximize long-run profitability. On the other hand, some of these objectives conflict with one another. An emphasis on long-term profits may come at the expense of short-term profits, and vice versa. Similarly, charging low prices to discourage market entry may serve to irritate middlemen or detract from the desired image of the firm.

Objectives should be measurable, which generally means they must be quantifiable, otherwise, it becomes difficult to determine how well they are being accomplished and whether or not the pricing program is working. In some cases, quantifying objectives is straightforward, such as with an objective of "increasing market share by two percentage points," or "increasing annual profitability by three percent." Other objectives are more difficult to measure, such as "maintain

EXHIBIT 1. 20 Pricing Objectives

Achieve targeted level of return on investment.
Reach targeted share of the relevant market.
Obtain desired level of long-run profit.
Obtain desired level of short-run profit.
Stabilize the market.
Convey a particular image.
Desensitize customers to price.
Be the price leader.
Discourage entry by new competitors.
Speed exist of marginal firms.
Avoid government investigation and control.
Maintain loyalty and sales support of middlemen.
Avoid excessive demands from suppliers.
Be regarded as fair by customers.
Create interest and excitement for the item.
Use price of one product to sell other products in line.
Discourage others from lowering prices.
Recover investment in product development quickly.
Encourage quick payment of accounts receivable.
Generate volume to drive down costs.

middleman loyalty" or "be regarded as fair." Primary research may be necessary, such as surveys of middlemen or customers before and after the pricing action.

Step Two: Establishing a Strategy

If objectives are the performance levels the manager wishes to achieve, then strategies represent comprehensive statements regarding how price will be used to accomplish the objectives. A pricing strategy provides a theme that guides all of the firm's pricing decisions for a particular product line over a particular time period. Thus it serves to coordinate all of the pricing activities related to the product line. By definition, the strategy adopts a longer-term time horizon, usually from one to three years, and is flexible or adaptable to changing environmental conditions.

To illustrate, Gucci retail shops use a pricing strategy that can be characterized as premium pricing. High prices and margins are charged, with relatively low volume expectations. The central theme is exclusivity. Price is used to reflect the highest quality levels, and the firm is careful not to compromise its image with special deals or discounts.

Pricing strategies generally fall into one of two groups: cost-based and market-based. Cost-based approaches tend to be formula based and focus on variable and fixed costs per unit and some type of standard mark-up. Market-based approaches tend to focus either on the competition, customer demand, or both. Exhibit 2 provides examples of various pricing strategies.

Of these two groups, cost-based approaches are much more prevalent in business. This tendency is one of the great ironies of business and reflects a general level of naivete among managers responsible for pricing decisions. As was emphasized earlier, price is a reflection of value—it is a statement of what the customer is willing to pay. Value and customer willingness to pay are market-based considerations. Costs, alternatively, are frequently unrelated to the amount customers are willing to pay and have more to do with the firm's efficiency and its accounting practices.

The popularity of cost-based strategies reflects the fact that they are easy to implement and manage. In addition, setting a price that covers costs and generates a fixed profit margin makes intuitive sense to the typical manager. Unfortunately, this approach often leads to prices that fail to take advantage of the market opportunities confronting the firm. It ties the hands of the manager and eliminates creativity from pricing management.

Step Three: Developing a Structure

Once a pricing strategy has been selected, the concern becomes implementation. Implementing a strategy requires that the manager develop a pricing structure and then a tactical plan.

EXHIBIT 2. Types of Pricing Strategies

Cost-Based Strategies

Mark-up pricing—variable and fixed costs per unit are estimated and a standard mark-up is added. The mark-up is frequently either a percentage of sales or costs.

Target return pricing—variable and fixed costs per unit are estimated. A rate of return is then taken times the amount of capital invested in the product, and the result is divided by estimated sales. The resulting return per unit is added to unit costs to arrive at a price.

Market-Based Strategies

Floor pricing—charging a price that just covers costs, usually in order to maintain a presence in the market given the competitive environment.

Penetration pricing—charging a price that is low relative to a) the average price of major competitors, and b) what customers are accustomed to paying.

Parity pricing (going rate)—charging a price that is roughly equivalent to the average price charged by the major competition.

Premium pricing (skimming)—the price charged is intended to be high relative to a) the average price of major competitors, and b) what customers are accustomed to paying.

Price leadership pricing—usually involves a leading firm in the industry making fairly conservative price moves that are subsequently followed by other firms in the industry. This limits price wars and leads to fairly stable market shares.

Stay out pricing—the firm prices lower than demand conditions require to discourage market entry by new competitors.

Bundle pricing—a set of products or services are combined and a lower single price is charged for the bundle than would be the case if each item were sold separately.

Value-based pricing (differentials)—different prices are set for different market segments based on the value each segment receives from the product or service.

Cross-benefit pricing—prices are set at or below costs for one product in a product line, but relatively high for another item in the line that serves as a direct complement (e.g., certain brands of cameras and film).

The pricing structure is concerned with: what aspects of each product or service will be priced, how prices will vary for different customers and products/services, and the time and conditions of payment. Many of the managerial questions that should be addressed when establishing the price structure are identified in Exhibit 3. Unfortunately, most of these issues are ignored entirely by those with price responsibility.

The simplest structure involves charging one standard price—with no discounts or variations—for a product or service. Such one-price structures are relatively simple to administer and easily understood by customers and middlemen. This does not suggest all customers or middlemen prefer such a one-price structure; either may feel they deserve price breaks or special concessions for a variety of reasons.

EXHIBIT 3. Key Managerial Questions in Developing a Pricing Structure

1. Should a standard list price be charged for the product or service?
2. Should frequent or large customers be charged the same base price?
3. Can and should separate prices be charged for different aspects of the product or service?
4. How should the time of purchase affect the price charged a customer?
5. To what extent should the price charged be varied to reflect the cost of doing business with a particular customer?
6. Should customers who value the product more be charged a higher price than other customers?
7. What is the nature of any discounts to be offered to the buyer?
8. When and where should title be taken by the buyer?
9. Is it realistic to offer a dual-rate structure, where the same customer has a choice between two pricing options for the same product or service?
10. Should the price structure involve a rental or leasing option?

The biggest problem with such simple structures concerns their lack of flexibility as markets become more competitive and as new profit opportunities arise for the firm. Consider the family restaurant that charges relatively moderate prices on its standard menu items. The restaurant is basically making a tradeoff between the customers who perceive high value from dining at the restaurant and those who perceive lower value. That is, high-valuation customers would likely pay more than the restaurant is asking, while lower-value customers may patronize the restaurant more frequently than if prices were higher. Management may hope, in the process, to maximize revenue.

However, consider how flexibility could be added by altering the price structure. Revenue might be enhanced by giving senior citizens a 10 percent meal discount, especially if they generally fall into the lower perceived value group of customers. Facilities might be more completely utilized by charging less for certain meals during low peak hours, or a premium during high peak hours. Rather than charge a set price for a meal, items might be sold á la carte. Or, alternatively, special "packages" might be put together for a single price, including beverage, appetizer, entrée, and dessert. To facilitate long-term revenue, frequent patrons might be given a discount card or told they can purchase on credit. The structural possibilities are virtually limitless if the manager is creative and knows his or her customers.

A popular means of varying the price structure involves the time and form of payment. Companies (especially industrial firms and firms selling to middlemen) will frequently offer a schedule of cash, quantity, and trade discounts. These discounts result in different prices depending on when customers pay the invoice, the volume that they purchase, and the functions they provide for the manufacturer.

Creative price structures are also critical for companies that sell intangible goods and for companies that sell products that cannot be inventoried indefinitely. This includes most service businesses as well as firms that sell perishable products and products with short life cycles. Airlines, for example, sell asset usage, not the asset itself. They must sell all the seats on a particular flight because those seats cannot be stored and sold at a later time. As a result, an airline may vary price based on the distance to a destination, the popularity of that destination, the time of day, how long a person plans to stay, whether or not the customer is a regular patron (frequent flyer), how far in advance the reservation is made, and whether or not the customer will accept a "no cancellation" penalty. Many of these structural approaches have proven effective in reducing the number of unfilled seats on specific flights. The tradeoffs, however, are the complexity of administering such structures and the potential for confused customers and antagonized middlemen.

Step Four: Determining Price Levels and Related Tactics

Once established, strategies and structures may remain in place for a fairly long period of time. Alternatively, the day-to-day management of prices focuses on setting specific price levels and employing periodic tactical pricing moves.

Price levels refer to the actual price charged for each product or service in the line as well as the specific amount of any types of discounts offered. In determining exact levels, the manager's decisions must not only translate the firm's pricing strategy into specific numbers, but also must reflect a variety of practical considerations. Some of these issues include finding the acceptable range of price levels that convey the desired value perception, determining whether or not to charge odd prices (e.g., $1.95 instead of $2.00), ensuring that price gaps between items within the same line are wide enough to convey meaningful differences in the items, and reflecting tax considerations in setting the final price.

Price levels may require frequent modification in response to changes in production costs, competitor tactics, and evolving market conditions. For instance, costs of a key raw material may increase, a leading competitor may unexpectedly lower prices on a selective basis, supply conditions may change because a competitor has overproduced, or demand sensitivity (elasticity) may change within the current price range.

The ability to manage price levels effectively is heavily dependent on the manager's sense of timing. Price changes must not come across as arbitrary. Customers should sense a degree of consistency and stability in the firm's price levels over time. They must be able to justify paying prices that are higher or lower than before. Otherwise, the company ends up sending conflicting signals regarding the value of its products or services, undermining customer confidence.

Beyond levels themselves, periodic tactical moves can include rebates, two-for-one price deals, cents-off coupons, and any other creative means of temporarily varying price. These tactics are generally promotional in nature, and are usually part of special sales campaigns. They should be used with specific short-term objectives in mind, some of which may be communications-related objectives (e.g., creating product awareness and encouraging product trial). The pricing manager must ensure, however, that such tactics are consistent with the firm's overall pricing program.

PUTTING THE FOUR COMPONENTS TOGETHER

The four components of an effective pricing program (objectives, strategy, structure, and levels) are not independent and should not be approached in an isolated fashion. Rather, they must be closely coordinated, with each element providing direction to the next. Consider two separate examples.

Assume a new car rental agency has entered the market positioning itself as a no-frills, low-cost provider. Price objectives are set with an emphasis on high volume and revenue, low unit profits, and the use of price to convey a bargain image. To implement these objectives, the company selects a penetration strategy, in which price is set low relative to competitor prices and customer expectations. Structure is designed to include a very low price per day and unlimited mileage for each of three classes of cars, with relatively small differences among each car group. An even lower rate is offered to those who rent for five days or more or over a weekend. Levels for the basic car groups are established at $16.95, $19.95, and $25.75, respectively.

This pricing program may serve the car rental agency for a number of years. Pricing objectives and strategy may remain largely unchanged for an indefinite time period. Structure may require periodic modification, such as the addition of a "frequent traveler" program or special price deals for those who fly a particular airline or work for a particular firm. Levels and tactics will require ongoing modification as competitor tactics, production costs, and demand conditions fluctuate.

As a second example, a major manufacturer of quality copiers has found that unit costs have been falling while competition has intensified. At the same time, the product line has proliferated. Product life cycles have been getting shorter—as brief as one year for some models. In response, the firm institutes an entirely new marketing strategy of which price is a central component.

The pricing objective in this case involves maximizing annual profitability across the product and service line. The strategic focus is on selective demand where sales result from replacements and additions sold to the existing customer base and from taking accounts away from competitors. The selected pricing strategy is parity pricing, with the firm attempting to charge base prices at or near the average competitive price. Structure is designed to be flexible, where salespeople are given some leeway in arriving at a final price. This is especially the case with mature products and those with the lowest manufacturing costs. The actual intent is to use the structure to place machines but then to sell customers a service contract for which margins are considerably higher. In addition, significant discounts are provided to customers who purchase multiple machines. Finally, base price levels are established and adjusted monthly to reflect an index of the average prices of the three top-selling machines in each major product category. A discount of 20 percent is provided for each purchase of three or more units.

Again, the four elements of the pricing program are tied intimately to one another. Approached in this manner, price becomes an innovative variable with immense potential for affecting the strategic direction of the firm. Alternatively, if management approaches pricing as an afterthought, concerned only that costs be covered and the firm be reasonably competitive, opportunities are lost and mistakes are much more probable.

THE UNDERLYING DETERMINANTS OF PRICING DECISIONS

When putting together the firm's pricing program and subsequently managing the program over the stages of product or service life, the manager must continually evaluate a number of critical price determinants. These determinants fall into five categories: overall company objectives and strategies, costs, demand, competition, and legal issues. Exhibit 4 provides an illustration of the relationship between the determinants and the strategic pricing program of the firm. Two of these determinants—overall objectives/strategies and costs—can be classified as internal company factors. The remaining three—demand, competition, and legal issues—are external to the company.

Company objectives and strategies constitute a framework within which pricing decisions must be made. They effectively serve to define a role for the price variable. Costs indicate to the manager what the price has to be to break even, or to achieve a given level of profit, and so represent a beginning point in pricing. The concern, though, is only with those costs directly associated with producing, selling, and distributing the product. Demand analysis seeks to determine customer perceptions of value, the relative importance of price when customers make purchase decisions, the size of the market, and the different quantities that are likely to be purchased at different price levels. Competitor assessments focus on evaluating market structure, estimating competitors' cost structures, identifying their current pricing

EXHIBIT 4. Company Pricing Program and Its Determinants

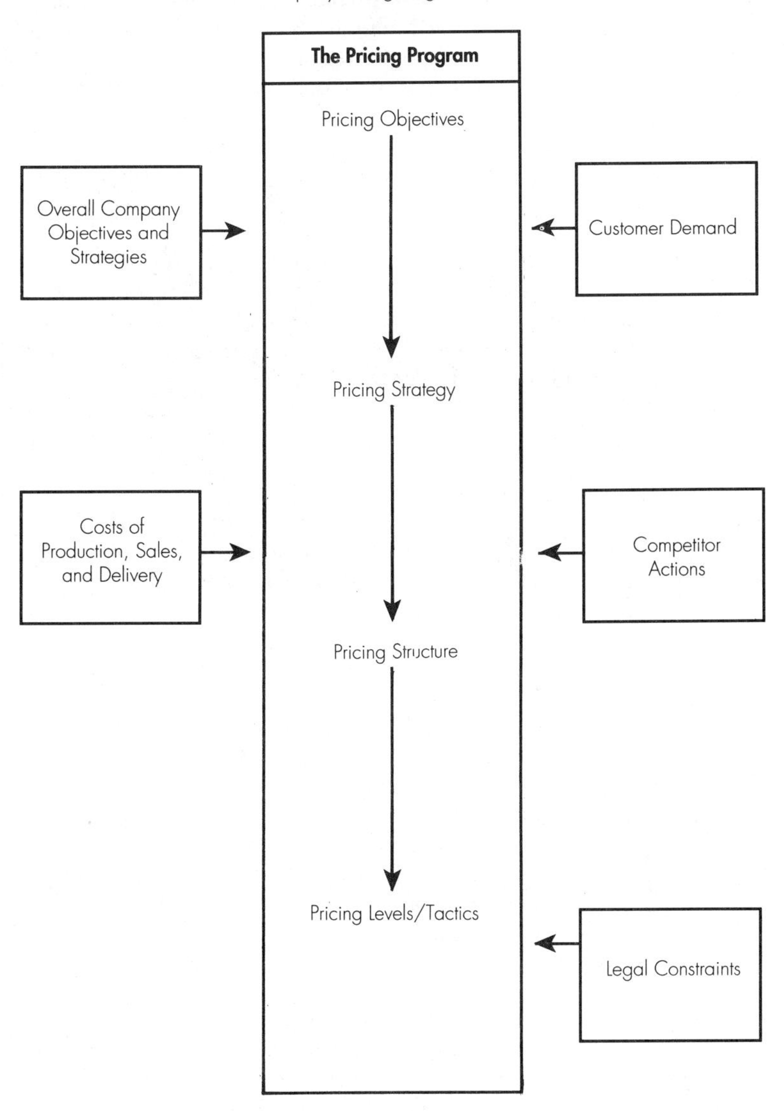

strategy, determining their relative market advantages, and anticipating how they will respond to the various pricing moves of other companies. Lastly, some pricing actions raise serious legal questions and must be evaluated in this context. Unfortunately, jurisprudence is often quite vague in terms of the legality of specific price tactics. However, where pricing actions serve to lessen the amount of competition in the marketplace, are imposed for that purpose, and cannot be justified based on the behavior over time of underlying costs, they are probably illegal.

Importantly, the ability to decipher each of these price determinants involves both art and science. For instance, certain skills are required to properly calculate unit costs or to estimate customer price sensitivity (i.e., elasticity). These analyses can sometimes become quite sophisticated. At the same time, creativity is required in developing realistic estimates of figures for which no data are available, while both insight and experience are invaluable when making hard judgments regarding competitor actions and reactions or assessing customer value perceptions.

The real challenge lies in putting these factors together and drawing implications for price decisions. Consider the case of the Jefferson Chemical Company, a producer of specialty and commodity chemicals for industrial use, including muriatic acid. Based on a decline in profits and market share the past year, the product line manager has proposed that the firm either cut the price of its acid by 10 percent or increase sales and promotional support by $50,000. How would one go about evaluating the price component of this manager's suggestions?

The first step would be to evaluate how the pricing action fits with overall company objectives and strategies. What are the implications of the price reduction for the image of the company? How will the price cut affect the firm's other marketing decision areas, such as its promotional programs or approach to managing channels of distribution? What is the profit goal associated with such a price cut and how does it relate to overall company profit objectives? Much of the remaining analysis follows from objectives in these areas. Assume that the goal is a 5 percent increase in profit and that this increase is the sole objective of concern.

The next step would involve examining costs. A logical approach would be to determine the level of sales necessary to cover the lost unit revenue from the price cut (i.e., to calculate break even on the price cut) plus the sales necessary to increase total profit contribution by a certain percentage, say five percent. This could be accomplished by determining how many dollars the product is currently contributing to overhead and profits after covering its own direct costs (before the price cut) and adding to this a five percent increase in profit contribution. This total figure would then be divided by the new profit margin (price-unit cost) resulting after the price cut. The result would be a required sales figure from which current sales would be subtracted, leaving the required sales increase.

The required increase would next be expressed as a percentage of current sales. Assume it to be 20 percent. This brings us to demand analysis. The company requires a 20 percent increase in sales in response to a 10 percent price reduction, which suggests demand must be fairly elastic, or sensitive. Is this likely to happen? Based on experience and knowledge of the market, management must determine if customers are that price sensitive. Demand tends to be more elastic when a number of acceptable substitutes are available, the purchase is not a necessity, the purchase represents a relatively large percentage of the customer's income or budget, the product is not well-differentiated from those of customers, and the customer must pay for the product immediately. Demand analysis should also raise questions about the importance to customers of price compared to other product attributes, the strength of existing customer loyalties, and the extent to which market potential (both users and usage rates) has already been reached.

Finally, even if the research up to this point indicates the price cut makes sense, management must anticipate competitor reaction. How does the firm's cost structure compare to theirs? How dependent on cash flows from this product are they? How well established are their customer ties in this product area? Do they view this market as growing, mature, or declining? The answers to these questions will provide insight into whether or not competitors will match the price cut.

LINKING PRICING STRATEGY TO MARKETING STRATEGY

Up to this point, the need to systematically approach *pricing* as a strategic variable has been emphasized. However, price is only one of the strategic decision areas facing the manager. As such, it is essential that pricing programs be consistent with the decisions made in these other areas.

Pricing programs should be designed in concert with the other value-related activities of the firm, especially those activities that directly interface with customers. Of primary importance are product programs, sales and promotion programs, and distribution programs. A high price can help convey a quality product image. A special price deal can be an integral part of the firm's promotional program. A trade discount can be an incentive for distributors to provide stronger support in pushing the company's products.

The focal point of all these activities should be the firm's overall *marketing strategy*. Marketing strategies attempt to define where the firm wants to be in the marketplace and how it plans to get there. They provide the larger framework within which pricing and other programs are developed. Accordingly, there should be a clear link between the strategies and the individual programs.

A large number of marketing strategies are available to any company. The appropriate choice requires considerable creativity and keen insight regarding current and future marketplace conditions. One example of a fairly common marketing strategy is called *differentiation.* This is where the company attempts to create unique perceptions in the marketplace of its product offering relative to the offerings of all other competitors in the industry. For instance, IBM differentiates itself on the basis of customer service, while Burger King does so on the basis of its flame-broiled hamburgers, and Caterpillar uses its outstanding dealer network as a source of differentiation.

If a company were to pursue a differentiation strategy, how might the pricing program be designed to reinforce this strategy? As a general rule, successful differentiation allows the manager to charge somewhat higher margins than competitors, reflecting the higher value being delivered to customers. In addition, differentiation encourages brand loyalty, frequently making customers less price sensitive. Customers are likely to perceive fewer acceptable substitutes—the more salient the source of differentiation is to customers, the more brand-loyal they are likely to be.

Another marketing strategy is called *targeting* or *niching*. This involves focusing on a particular market segment, such as a certain type of user, a specific product application, or a single geographic region. Bic ballpoint pens are targeted to the low-end user, while Porter Paints are positioned solely to the professional painter, and the Bryan brand of hot dogs is marketed only in the southern part of the United States. Using the Bic example, price is set well below that of conventional fountain pens to convey the idea that the buyer is getting a reliable but disposable writing utensil. This represents good value for the money to a large segment consisting of students, office workers, and others.

Inconsistencies between overall marketing strategy and product or service pricing strategy frequently produce failure in the marketplace. The company that has positioned itself as a high-end or premium quality provider but then drops prices when confronted with competitive pressures is undermining its own market position, confusing customers, and giving away margins. Similarly, pricing strategies that focus on quickly recouping the initial investment in a product or service often result in prices that are too high given the firm's desired position in customers' minds.

PRICING STRATEGY OVER THE PRODUCT LIFE CYCLE

Perhaps the most widely-known marketing concept is the product life cycle (PLC), which proposes that every product evolves through stages of growth and eventual decline. Put simply, the PLC plots the sales volume and profit curves for an industry (or company brand) over the history of the product. The sales volume curve is generally shown as an S-shaped curve, as found in Exhibit 5.

The PLC is a key tool for market planning and strategy development, including pricing strategy. The basic idea is that strategies should be modified to reflect changing market conditions as a product evolves from its initial introductory stage through growth, competitive turbulence, maturity, and decline.

Consider the range of strategic pricing options presented earlier in this chapter. One of the distinctions drawn in Exhibit 2 was between charging prices significantly lower than competitors (penetration pricing), approximately the same as competitors (parity), or above those of competitors (premium). The questions of which to use—or where on this continuum to operate—must be made at the introductory stage of the PLC. The product is unknown at this time and may require significant customer learning. Price is instrumental in the original positioning of the product. Some of the key considerations in selecting among these alternatives are identified in Exhibit 6.

The initial strategy places constraints on any subsequent pricing decisions. As a case in point, consider the marketer who uses a penetration strategy in anticipation of significant cost savings with large volume production—then does not achieve such economies. Although a price increase may be desirable, the market may strongly resist such a change because it has come to equate a certain amount of value with a given price. It is, in fact, almost always easier to lower price than to raise price.

Also, the manager does not necessarily set a single price for a product in each stage of its life. Different market segments come into play in each stage, perhaps with differing price sensitivities. Charging a high price initially may be related to an initial target segment that views the product as a necessity with few or no substitutes. As other segments enter the market, separate pricing strategies can be tailored to reflect the distinct needs of each.

One danger in introductory stage pricing is attempting to recoup research and development or related start-up expenditures incurred prior to actual product introduction too quickly. These expenditures can be significant and place an undue burden on the new product. Their recovery, together with an acceptable rate of return on the required investment, should be achieved over a product's life cycle.

A product in the growth stage typically is confronting new competitive entries. The benefits of large-scale production economies and the learning curve, if any, are beginning to surface, bringing down costs. A common market price emerges in this stage, with the range of acceptable prices narrowing. The marketer is encountering downward pressure on prices, although this depends on the extent of product differentiation among competitors and the rate at which technological improvements are being made to the product.

EXHIBIT 5. Pricing Over the Product Life Cycle

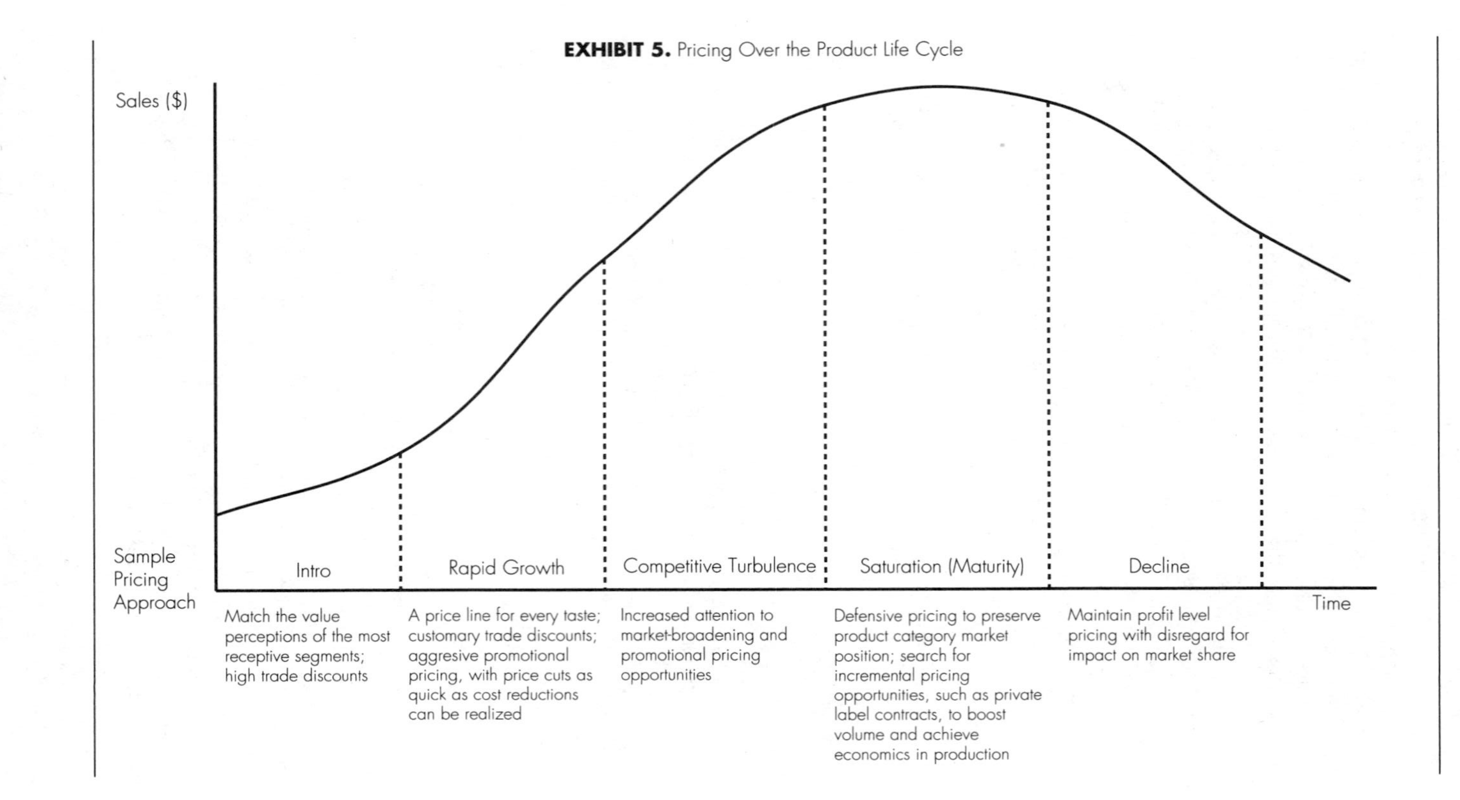

Sales ($)
Sample Pricing Approach
Intro
Rapid Growth
Competitive Turbulence
Saturation (Maturity)
Decline
Time
Match the value perceptions of the most receptive segments; high trade discounts
A price line for every taste; customary trade discounts; aggresive promotional pricing, with price cuts as quick as cost reductions can be realized
Increased attention to market-broadening and promotional pricing opportunities
Defensive pricing to preserve product category market position; search for incremental pricing opportunities, such as private label contracts, to boost volume and achieve economics in production
Maintain profit level pricing with disregard for impact on market share

EXHIBIT 6. Factors in Evaluating Initial Pricing Strategy Options

Factors Favoring Penetration Price	Factors Favoring Parity Price	Factors Favoring Premium Price
Possibility of significant cost reductions with volume production	Well-entrenched competition or presence of a price leader	No cost savings from increased production volume
Sizeable segments with highly elastic demand	Desire to be regarded as "fair" by distributors and customers	Sizeable segments with highly inelastic demand
Low barriers to competitive entry	Moderate barriers to competitive entry	High barriers to competitive entry
Low customer switching costs	Need exists to stabilize the market	High customer switching costs
Ability to use price to convey bargain image	Product or service does not lend itself to non-price differentiation	Ability to use price to convey unique quality benefits or exclusivity
Ability to use low price of one product to sell other products in the line	No differences in cost structures among the various competitors	Clear-cut cost advantage that competitors cannot duplicate

Further, during the growth stage, individual need or benefit segments may surface. A benefit segment is a sizeable group of buyers that places heavy emphasis on a specific product attribute or particular mix of attributes. These segments will often differ in their willingness to pay for specific attributes (e.g., faster delivery, smaller inventories, better service, a special feature), leading the firm to charge different prices to different segments. There may, at this stage, still be a substantial amount of untapped market potential, suggesting the firm need not focus solely on competition-based pricing.

The competitive turbulence stage is the most competitively intense. Aggressive pricing actions result not only because the market leaders are experiencing significant cost reductions, but because new customers are becoming increasingly scarce. Price is pushed further in the direction of costs as firms attempt to run the less efficient producers out of the market. Correspondingly, this period is also referred to as the "shakeout" stage.

With maturity comes an increasingly saturated market and fairly well-entrenched competition. The manager focuses largely on repeat sales to established customers and on ways to achieve internal cost efficiencies. Customers are increasingly apt to see little real difference among competitive offerings. Competition is more heavily price-based, although head-to-head price wars are likely to be dysfunctional.

Frequently, the pricing orientation is to maximize short-term direct product contribution to profit. The manager may use the product as a cash generator, the proceeds of which are used to support newer, growth-stage products.

Market decline presents a number of pricing opportunities. For instance, the firm may raise price to take advantage of any remaining market segments that are very price insensitive. The spare parts business for most products provides a good example of these segments. Alternatively, the strategy might be to cut support expenditures and leave price alone, letting the product die a natural death. Another approach might be to cut the price to the break-even level or lower and use the product as a loss leader to help sell complementary products in the line.

PRICING FOR PRODUCTS VERSUS SERVICES

The design of pricing programs is also likely to be fundamentally different when selling products compared to services. Differences in pricing opportunities exist because of the unique characteristics of services compared to products. Services are intangible and are usually consumed at the time of purchase. Because they cannot be inventoried and sold at a later time, revenue is lost forever if they are not sold during the particular time periods in which they are made available. Since they lack physical qualities, customers may have a tendency to take services for granted, and frequently have a more difficult time assigning values to them. In fact, the customer is often using price as an indicator of service quality.

While some services can be produced efficiently in large volumes, they generally are not as conducive to mass production as are products. In fact, services frequently require a degree of customization when delivered. Further, many services are not transportable, requiring the customer to come to the vendor's place of business.

Managers often encounter difficulties in estimating the actual costs of providing a service to a particular customer. This is due to a number of factors. Two of the principal costs in service delivery are direct labor and depreciation of any machinery or equipment involved. Differing amounts of time and effort may be required to deliver the same service to two different customers. In addition, services are consumed in irregular patterns, often with wide demand fluctuations over time.

Given these characteristics, pricing programs for services permit considerable flexibility and creativity. Pricing for a health spa's services represents a case in point. When purchasing a membership, a customer is paying for an intangible. There are tangible features, primarily the equipment and facilities at the spa, but the customer is paying for use of these assets.

One of the goals of service pricing is to manage demand relative to supply. Assume the health spa charged on a per visit basis. Any time the facilities are open but not being used by customers, revenue is being lost while expense is being incurred. Similarly, any time more customers visit the spa than can be comfortably handled and subsequently leave, revenue is lost.

The need to effectively manage demand has led many spas to charge flat fees for memberships ranging in duration from six months to a number of years. Alternatively, different fee structures can be charged for customers who agree to use the facilities only during limited (low peak) hours. If the health spa has multiple locations, the fee structure can be designed to encourage more traffic at a particular location by a particular patron or group of patrons, or instead to encourage a patron to frequent all locations. In addition, to counter high turnover, renewal rates can differ from initial membership rates.

The services can also be "unbundled," with separate fees charged for individual services. One fee might be charged to use all services, with separate rates for those who want to use only exercise machines or the sauna and pool. Or a flat membership fee might be charged for use of most of the facilities, with a per-use charge for high demand facilities such as racquetball courts.

Service pricing also lends itself to charging price differentials, where two customers pay a different price for the same service. With the health spa, assume a prospective customer visited the club in search of information regarding fees and facilities. The manager can consult with the prospect and glean the nature of his or her needs. Based on responses to questions regarding the prospect's exercise goals, workout habits, weight training experience, type of employment and work schedule, plans to relocate in the foreseeable future, and so forth, the manager can propose a particular "membership plan." The actual fee charged may be somewhat negotiable. The company could have an inventory of 12 to 15 so-called standard plans, with a fee range for each.

Finally, note the difficulty management would have in attempting to determine the cost of delivering the service to a particular client. Customers come in when they want, for as long as they choose. Many engage in different activities on each visit. While costs are important, the prime concern should be determining (a) the break-even level of revenue and (b) the incremental costs incurred if one more customer uses the facility at key time periods. The key point here, however, concerns the need to focus on demand-based pricing, and to capitalize on the innovative opportunities made possible by the unique characteristics of services.

SUMMARY

This chapter examines price as a marketing variable. The central theme is that price is a statement of customer value, not a statement of costs. Value is perceived in the minds of buyers, and value perceptions differ depending on the customer. This suggests pricing must be managed creatively, and should be customized to individual customers or market segments.

Managers are encouraged to move away from purely tactical or reactive approaches and to adopt a strategic perspective on pricing. A strategic pricing program consists of four key components: objectives, strategy, structure, and levels (tactics). Managers must first determine what the price of a particular product or line is meant to accomplish, or price objectives. The strategy is a comprehensive statement regarding how the price will be used to accomplish the objectives. Implementation of the strategy requires managers to develop a pricing structure that details what aspects of each product or service will be priced, how prices will be tailored to different segments, and the time and form of payment. The last component—levels—concerns the daily management of prices and the tactical moves required to achieve the objectives within the strategy and structure. Most important, all four elements must be closely coordinated, with objectives guiding strategy and strategy guiding structure and tactics.

The chapter also discusses the five key considerations that go into formulating a pricing program: overall company objectives and strategies, costs, demand, competition, and legal issues. Company objectives and strategies provide the underlying basis and direction for all pricing decisions. Costs establish a minimum level from which to begin the evaluation of possible price alternatives. Demand analysis attempts to ensure that final price decisions are consistent with customer perceptions of value. Competitive considerations serve to assess the realism of pricing actions given market structures and the resources of firms offering similar or substitute products. Finally, pricing programs must be decided on within the context of current legal and regulatory constraints.

This chapter also discusses the importance of integrating pricing strategy into marketing strategy. The strategic pricing program must be consistent with the direction of the firm's overall marketing strategy. Considerable thought should be given to how the pricing program impacts on and is impacted by the firm's product programs, promotion programs, and distribution programs. Also critical is the need to adapt pricing programs to reflect changes in these other areas over the product life cycle.

REFERENCES

Monroe, K. B., *Pricing: Making Profitable Decisions*, New York: McGraw-Hill, 1992.

Morris, M. H., "Separate Prices as an Industrial Marketing Tool," *Industrial Marketing Management*, 16 (1987): 79–86.

Morris, M. H., and F. E. Morris, *Market-Oriented Pricing: Strategies for Management*, Westport, CT: Quorum, 1990.

Stern, A. A., "The Strategic Value of Price Structure," *The Journal of Business Strategy*, 7 (1986): 22–31.

Donald V. Harper
Professor of Transportation and Logistics
Graduate School of Management
University of Minnesota
Minneapolis, Minnesota

Jack L. Caldwell
Executive Vice-President and General Manager
Glenwood-Inglewood Company
Minneapolis, Minnesota

CHAPTER 46

PRICING

This chapter attempts to provide a very comprehensive treatment of the general subject of pricing from the point of view of the marketing executive. To illustrate various phases of pricing, specific examples are presented from a producer of bottled water marketing in a region consisting of several states. The products of this company include drinking water, distilled water, water coolers, paper cups, and related supplies.

Jules Backman has described three kinds of price making. These are market pricing, administered or business-controlled pricing, and government-controlled pricing.[1]

Market Pricing

Market pricing exists whenever the seller has no control over the price received in the marketplace and price is determined solely by the free play of the forces of supply and demand. The seller either accepts the price determined by this mechanism or refuses to sell. He or she cannot sell at a price higher than that established in the market. Clearly, when market pricing exists, the seller makes no price decisions and needs no price policy.

True market pricing is rare and is found mainly in the organized commodity exchanges, the security exchanges, and in some agricultural markets. Manufacturers and distributors seldom are involved in true market pricing although they sometimes find themselves in situations that approach market pricing. Such situations occur when the product involved is close to being homogeneous, entry into the industry is relatively easy, and there is a fairly large number of sellers.

Administered or Business-Controlled Pricing

Administered, or business-controlled pricing exists when prices are established by business firms at their own discretion. The seller sets the price and the buyers buy or do not buy as they wish. Prices are not fixed automatically by the forces of the marketplace but are, instead, the result of decisions made by sellers. Although the free play of the forces of supply and demand, along with other factors, have an influence on pricing decisions, they do not actually establish the price, as in market pricing.

Most prices in the American economy are administered prices as that term is used here and administered prices are found in all areas of business activity. The amount of control that a seller has over the price of his product or service varies because of variations in the degree of product differentiation, the size of firm, and the number of competitors in the industry. Prices of the bottled water company are administered prices.

Government-Controlled Pricing

Government-controlled pricing exists when the prices of goods and services produced by private business are set by government such as in the transportation and public utilities industries or when wartime or other emergency price controls are instituted. In such cases, public administration of prices replaces or works in conjunction with privately administered prices or market prices.

WHAT IS A PRICE POLICY?

The dominant form of price making in the American economy is administered, or business-controlled pricing, in which the business firm has the right and the responsibility to set prices for its products and services. This means that most business firms need a price policy.

A price policy is an overall guide to action in pricing. It involves general principles or rules that a firm tries to follow in making everyday pricing decisions. There are many examples of price policies that a firm could adopt such as always to "follow the market," that is, to copy competitors' prices; to follow the prices of a particular competitor; to price in order to provide the firm with a given percentage return on investment; never to sell any units of output at prices below fully distributed costs; and to price in such a way as to discourage competitors from entering the market.

The price policies adopted by the bottled water firm include price to maximize volume and share of market; price above variable costs to provide contribution to overhead and profit; price auxiliary products to encourage the consumption of bottled water; establish higher prices where product or service is exclusive, or if competitors are expected to follow price leadership; and allow wholesalers and retailers above normal profit margins to encourage maximum sales volume and geographic distribution.

A firm may need more than one price policy to fit the different kinds of products or services it offers. A firm is particularly likely to have more than one price policy if it is a multi-product or multi- service firm.

Routine daily pricing decisions and procedures should conform to these policies. Thus if a firm has decided as a matter of policy that it will follow the prices of a certain competitor, its routine pricing procedure will simply be to change prices whenever the competitor's prices change. A more complicated routine pricing mechanism is required when a firm's policy is to try to obtain a given percentage rate of return on investment.

No matter what kind of business a firm is engaged in, and regardless of whether the firm's output is a physical product or a service, certain basic factors should be considered in developing a price policy or price policies for the firm. Some of these factors are internal to the firm and some are external to the firm. Internal factors are more easily identified and controlled than are factors that are external to the firm. An understanding of the various internal and external influences on pricing is required before intelligent decisions concerning pricing can be made.

INTERNAL FACTORS

Objectives of Pricing

A sound approach to developing a price policy begins with a clarification of the basic objectives of the firm. The overall objectives of the firm should be synonymous with its pricing objectives. The simplest approach is to assume that the firm's basic objective is to maximize profits. However, various other objectives may exist—at least in the short run—instead of, or in addition to, the objective of maximizing profits. A few examples are (1) the firm may be interested in increasing its market share or its rate of growth, even at the expense of immediate profits; (2) the firm may be interested in some fixed amount of profit as its goal, rather than "maximum" profits; (3) the firm may want to avoid charges of monopolizing an industry and other legal prosecution; (4) and the firm may be interested only in immediate survival.

It would be difficult to find a firm that has only one overall objective. For example, the bottled water company goals are increasing the consumption of bottled water, increasing the firm's share of the market, expanding distribution of the product geographically, and increasing the absolute dollar profit. Usually, a firm has several objectives and in some cases these objectives may conflict with one another. It should also be noted that some firms have never formulated any overall objectives.

Although its importance varies from firm to firm, pricing is one of the tools that a firm has at its disposal in its attempt to reach the stated objective(s). In order to be meaningful and effective, the price policy or policies adopted must be consistent with the overall objective(s) of the firm.

Organization for Pricing

There are two basic kinds of pricing decisions. The first is to decide on the price policy or policies the firm is to follow. The second is to price specific products or services in accordance with the policy or policies. The latter may be referred to as pricing procedure, or mechanics, as distinct from price policy.

In general, since price policy is so closely related to the firm's overall goals, determination of price policy should be the responsibility of those who are in the best position to know and understand those goals and who possess the authority to establish a policy and have it carried out.

On the other hand, the mechanics of pricing, that is, the setting of a specific price, need not be performed at the top of the management ladder. The organizational level at which the mechanics of pricing should be performed depends, to a great extent, on the difficulty in performing the task, and also of the frequency and speed with which pricing decisions must be made. The more the price-setting task is routinized in accordance with fixed formulas or procedures of some kind, the easier it is to delegate price-making authority and the lower on the organizational scale it can go. Also, when a firm must make a large number of pricing decisions quite frequently or must make pricing decisions rapidly, it may be necessary to delegate the pricing function to lower levels in the firm.

The pricing function in the bottled water company is performed by top management because price changes are infrequent and there is a complex and important relationship between pricing and the firm's sales volume, distribution channels, and company goals.

The Role of Price in the Marketing Program

Price is one of the elements in the "marketing mix," which also includes personal selling, advertising, packaging, branding, product development, physical distribution, and the channels of distribution. All the elements in the marketing mix are sales-producing tools available to the firm and they must be combined in the most effective way possible in light of the firm's particular objectives. The marketing manager must determine the specific role of each of the several elements in the mix and must also consider the relationship between the elements. Price can contribute positively to the sales effort only if it coordinates properly with the other elements in the marketing mix. Price decisions cannot be made effectively without due consideration of the role price is to play in the total marketing effort and of the relationship between price and the other elements involved in the marketing program.

Price is considered a dominant factor in the "marketing mix" for bottled water. The characteristics of the product and its uses dictate that the most useful marketing elements are pricing, advertising and packaging. Other examples of industries in which price is a very important marketing factor are the paperback book industry and "discount house" retailing.

Degree of Product Differentiation

One of the most important factors that determines the amount of discretion that a firm has in setting prices is the degree to which its products or services are differentiated from competing products or services in the eyes of buyers. Generally, the more product differentiation a firm enjoys, the more independent it can be in its price-making activities.

Product differentiation may consist of actual physical differences in the offerings of competing sellers, or it may consist of so-called psychological differences based on advertising, brand reputation, colors of packages, and various other intangible emotional factors. In addition, product differentiation often involves delivery terms, credit terms, guarantees, availability of service on a product, and the other elements that comprise the total package being purchased. To the buyer, bottled water products appear to be physically relatively homogeneous. Therefore, differentiation is dependent on intangible emotional factors and convenience of service. The same might be said of product differentiation in the retail gasoline industry. This stands in sharp contrast with the great physical product differentiation that exists in the camera manufacturing industry.

It should be noted that independence in price making based on product differentiation is seldom, if ever, permanent because existing competitors may introduce important changes in their offerings, or new competitors with new products or services to offer may enter the industry.

Costs

Cost is sometimes one of the more important factors considered in pricing. Although costs are usually thought of as a price-determining factor, in practice prices are sometimes a cost-determining factor. This occurs when a firm tries to find out what prices it can reasonably expect to get from its products or services in the marketplace, and then works backward to design or purchase a product or service that is suited to such a price. In this way, price determines the costs of production (or purchasing) and marketing.

Future costs are the most important type of costs in pricing. Past costs have little relevance in a pricing decision unless costs tend to be stable over time. The same is true of current costs. In general, estimated future costs, when reliable, are more useful in pricing decisions than past or current costs.

Many firms make use of full-cost pricing in which the fully-allocated costs, both fixed and variable, associated with the product or service in question, plus a fixed or variable profit margin, are covered by price. Full-cost pricing is a convenient and expeditious method of pricing and can be a proper approach if competitors follow suit. The major limitation of full-cost pricing is that such pricing does not take into account demand considerations, such as buyers' needs and their ability and willingness to pay. It also tends to ignore the activities of competitors in the marketplace. When demand and competitive factors are neglected, only by accident would full-cost pricing produce a price that maximized profit for the firm.

The proper role of costs in a pricing decision is to establish a floor below which a firm will not price its products. The costs that are of crucial importance in a pricing decision are the extra or variable costs associated with producing or distributing additional amounts of a product or service or adding a new product or service. Unless the firm is operating at full capacity, fixed costs can usually be ignored. If the firm has excess capacity and nothing better to do with it, the firm can sell its output profitably at any price that more than covers variable costs. Such prices make at least some contribution to fixed costs and are therefore profitable in the sense that if the product or service had not been sold at the low price, there would have been no contribution to fixed costs at all. However, it must be remembered that, in terms of the firm's overall operations in the long run, all costs must be covered by prices.

Thus in the short run for the firm's overall operations, or in the long run for certain items in the firm's product or service line, prices can be profitable even though they do not cover full costs.

The bottled water company prices all of its products on the basis of their contribution above variable costs. The price for each product must at least cover the direct costs incurred to produce that product and market it through the particular channel of distribution being used. However, the total contribution from all products sold by the firm must cover both variable and fixed costs and produce the desired net profit. The transportation industry prices many of its services below fully-distributed costs under what is called the "value of service" method of pricing. Although this kind of pricing has been used mainly in the freight market, it is also found in the passenger market as is indicated by youth, excursion, military, and other promotional fares offered by airlines.

EXTERNAL FACTORS

Unlike the controllable internal factors discussed above, the external factors that must be considered in developing a price policy are largely out of the control of the business firm. They represent the uncontrollable "environment" within which pricing decisions must be made.

Demand

The nature of the demand for the product or service in question is one of the most important considerations in the pricing decision. This demand is determined by a number of factors, including the price of the offering, the prices and availability of substitutes, the incomes of buyers, the tastes and preferences of buyers, the character of non-price competition (such as advertising), the characteristics of the product or service offered, the number and size of competitors in the industry, and the number and size of buyers. Thus the demand for a product or service is shaped by many factors, all of which are interdependent, and price is only one of these.

It is up to the price maker to determine the precise relationship between changes in price and demand. This can be done only if he or she appreciates the effects of simultaneous changes in other demand influencing factors. To make the best decisions concerning price policy and specific price problems, the price maker should endeavor to learn as much as possible about the character of demand and how demand might be affected by adjustments in price in both the short and the long run.

Market Structure and Nature of Competition

An important external factor is the nature of the market structure in which the firm operates. Each firm must determine what its market structure is like and how it affects price policy determination. The market structure consists of three basic elements. These are the number of competitors, the size of each competitor, and the degree of product differentiation. Other factors that help determine market structure include the ease of entry into the industry by new competitors, their ability to provide effective competition, and the pricing programs they adopt. Together, these elements determine the market structure or, in other words, the nature of competition that a particular firm faces.

In the regional bottled water market example, a dozen smaller competitors of the firms are unable to compete effectively except in terms of price. Entry in this market is not as easy as one might assume because of the technical expertise required and increasing governmental quality control. In contrast with the homogeneity of bottled water and a fairly large number of small firms stands the automobile manufacturing industry with a very small number of large firms and substantial product differentiation.

Suppliers

Although their influence is usually somewhat indirect, suppliers of raw materials, parts, and other industrial goods and labor can have some effect on the pricing decisions of producers. For example, the prices charged for raw materials and parts may have a great influence on the prices established for the goods or services being produced if the raw materials or parts represent a sizable proportion of the total costs of the firm. In fact, it is sometimes necessary for a firm to attempt to negotiate prices with suppliers for the express purpose of keeping the prices of goods and services supplied at a level that will permit the firm to price its offerings at a given price.

The prices of goods supplied play an extremely important role in pricing by wholesalers and retailers. This is because the prices charged by suppliers represent a very large cost element for such distributors and, to a great extent, the prices charged by suppliers are a starting point for pricing over which the distributor has no control. Since distributors sometimes mark up merchandise by well-established, customary percentage amounts, the prices of suppliers can, in such cases, directly determine the prices of distributors.

Buyers

The kind of people and firms that buy a product or service can help shape the price policy of a firm. The number of buyers in the market for a given product or service and their size vary considerably from industry to industry. Even within the same industry, firms may sell their products or services in several different kinds of markets in which the number and size of buyers vary.

As a rule, the more buyers there are in the marketplace, and the smaller each is, the less influence any individual buyer will have on price. Conversely, the fewer the buyers in the marketplace, and the larger they are, the greater the influence the individual buyer has on price. If the buyers are strong enough to produce the item in question themselves, they can wield a great deal of influence on price.

Buyer influence on the price of bottled water ranges from the strong bargaining position of ten large supermarket chains to the relatively weak opposite extreme of thousands of individual business and residential consumers. In the aluminum manufacturing industry, buyer influence on price ranges from that of the small number of large major container manufacturers to that of the many small manufacturers of various hardware items.

Legal Considerations

The legal framework within which pricing decisions are made is an important external factor in pricing. Such legal considerations are apparently becoming more important, and it is crucial that price makers, especially those in large business firms, take account of these factors. At the federal government level, there are several laws with important implications for the price maker. There are the Sherman Antitrust Act of 1890, the Clayton Act of 1914, the Robinson-Patman Amendment to the Clayton Act, enacted in 1936, and the Federal Trade Commission Act of 1914. In addition to the federal laws, the states have enacted a number of similar laws, some of which apply to pricing.

PRICING BY MANUFACTURERS

The above discussion of the internal and external factors to consider in pricing applies equally to all kinds of business firms. The various kinds of pricing problems that confront the firm determine what decisions need to be made concerning price policy and procedure. For manufacturers, certain basic kinds of pricing problems occur concerning which decisions must be made. The manufacturer must decide on the level of prices to charge in terms of pricing "at the market," "below the market," or "above the market." The manufacturer must decide on which segments of the market to appeal to in pricing and how to make price appeals to the several segments. Where a manufacturer has a multi-product line, a decision must be made concerning product-line pricing, i.e., how to price products that are substitutes for one another or are complementary to one another and also how to price replacement parts. Where a manufacturer introduces new products, he or she must deal with the delicate and difficult problem of pricing a new product. In situations where a manufacturer has in the line a product that has reached the state of maturity (an older product), a decision must be made as to what pricing policy to follow. Most manufacturers find that they must rely on distributors of various kinds to perform some of the necessary marketing functions and in making pricing decisions these manufacturers should take into account their relationship with the distributors. Lastly, the manufacturer must usually deal with the problem of accounting for outbound transportation costs in pricing products and, therefore, develop some geographic pricing policy.

PRICING BY RETAILERS

Retail prices are of particular significance because they are the prices that are paid by the ultimate buyers of consumer products. Consequently, the prices attached to products at the retail level are extremely important to the retailer, the wholesaler, and the producer. There are certain kinds of pricing decisions that retailers must make that are similar to those of manufacturers and there are other decisions that are peculiar to retailing. The retailer, like the manufacturer, must decide whether to price "at the market," "below the market," or "above the market." It must be decided whether to practice "price lining"—limiting efforts to products or services that are sold at a limited number of prices rather than attempting to sell products or services at all possible prices. Because retail prices are always subject to change in the form of markdowns, the retailer must be prepared to change prices when necessary and make decisions relative to the timing and size of markdowns. He or she must also decide whether he should use leader pricing—temporarily reducing the price of a product, usually a well-known brand, below its customary level and relying on this "leader" to attract customer traffic into the store with the hope that customers will also purchase other merchandise in his store. The retailer needs to decide to what extent he or she will cooperate with manufacturers in maintaining suggested resale prices. He must also be concerned about state laws called "unfair practices acts" that require that retailers price at no less than a certain minimum level. Lastly, the retailer may be faced with the decision as to whether or not to introduce a private label—a product that bears the trademark, brand, or label of the retailer—and, if so, how to price that private label.

IMPLICATIONS

Since the characteristics and pricing problems of business firms differ considerably, it is not possible to set forth a detailed, universally applicable approach to pricing that any firm can use. However, it is clear that in developing price policies and specific prices a firm should perform the following general tasks.

1. *Define the Objectives of Pricing.* A sound approach to pricing requires that the overall objectives of the firm be articulated as clearly as possible since they are the proper guides to pricing. In order to be meaningful and effective, price policy and procedure must be consistent with the overall objectives of the firm.
2. *Determine the Organization for Pricing.* Responsibility for the establishment of a price policy(ies) and the implementation of such policy(ies) must be clearly assigned.
3. *Determine and Collect the Kind of Information Needed.* The kind of information needed will be determined by the relative importance of the various internal and external factors discussed above. The sources of such information vary widely from firm to firm and include company records, company personnel, outside consultants, research studies done in the field, suppliers, and buyers.
4. *Assign a Role to Price in the Marketing Program.* In developing a price policy, it is necessary to determine what role price is to play in the marketing effort of the firm and how price is to fit in with the other elements in the marketing mix. Price may be a neutral, moderately neutral, moderately active, or an active instrument in the marketing program.

The Role of Judgment in Pricing

Judgment must play a key role in pricing. It is usually impossible to take all of the information that could possibly influence a pricing decision, quantify it, and feed it into a machine or a formula and come up with *the* most desirable price policy or price. Much of this information simply is not of the proper nature to be handled in such a manner. In addition, even if it were, one cannot assume that all of the information desirable for pricing is available or that, when available, it is always accurate.

Like other decision makers in marketing, price makers must operate with imperfect knowledge and under conditions of uncertainty. Although pricing is to some degree an art, not a science, and although judgment is a necessary part of the pricing process, this judgment should be an *informed* judgment, not merely a hunch. The points discussed in this chapter can help the price maker approach the task in an organized and systematic manner with proper consideration given to the objectives of the firm, the organization required for pricing, the kind of information required as a basis for pricing decisions, and the role price is to play in the marketing program.

NOTES

1. Jules Backman, *Price Practices and Price Policies* (New York: Ronald Press, 1953), pp. 3–4.

SUGGESTIONS FOR FURTHER READING

Earl L. Bailey, ed., *Pricing Practices and Strategies* (New York: The Conference Board, 1978).

Donald V. Harper, *Price Policy and Procedure* (New York: Harcourt Brace Jovanovich, Inc., 1966).

Rajshekhar G. Javalgi, "Marketing Financial Services to Affluent Consumers," *Journal of Services Marketing*, September 1992, pp. 33–44.

A. D. H. Kaplan, Joel B. Dirlam, and Robert F. Lanzillotti, *Pricing in Big Business* (Washington, DC: Brookings Institution, 1958).

Robert A. Lynn, *Price Policies and Marketing Management* (Homewood, IL: Richard D. Irwin, Inc., 1967).

Kent Monroe, *Pricing: Making Profitable Decisions* (New York: McGraw-Hill, 1979).

Alfred R. Oxenfeldt, *Pricing for Marketing Executives* (San Francisco: Wadsworth, 1961).

Mel Stein, "The Product Development Shell Game," *Best's Review (Life/Health)*, December 1990, pp. 14–16, 90–92.

Louis W. Stern
John D. Gray Distinguished Professor of Marketing
J. L. Kellogg Graduate School of Management
Northwestern University
Evanston, Illinois

Frederick D. Sturdivant
Senior Vice President
The MAC Group, Inc.
San Francisco, California

CHAPTER 47

GETTING THINGS DONE: CUSTOMER-DRIVEN DISTRIBUTION SYSTEMS

Too often, distribution is the neglected side of marketing. Automobile companies, savvy in many aspects of strategy, have lost huge shares of the parts and service markets to NAPA, Midas, and Goodyear because they resist making changes in their dealer franchise networks. A great many other American companies—Tupperware springs to mind—are reaching their markets in similarly outmoded ways. It is hardly seemly for Tupperware to continue with its "parties" when more than half of American women are working outside their homes.

In contrast, a number of companies have outstripped their competition with imaginative strategies for getting products to their customers—and marketing executives can learn from them. The Federal Express system is so innovative and formidable that it might be considered a model even beyond the small-package delivery industry. American Hospital Supply has gained the edge over its competition by linking up to hospitals and clinics with a sophisticated system of data processing, while Steelcase has set a standard for delivering complex office furniture installations, complete and on time.

Although American companies have been ignoring the ways in which they deliver products and services, their customers are increasingly inclined to demand higher standards of performance. Customers want companies to value their time and trouble.

And so, important opportunities for gaining a competitive advantage through distribution remain, and given the new technology, some companies may, as Federal Express has, achieve a breakthrough. Will the management of American companies (deregulated telecommunications companies included) make use of these opportunities or even recognize them for what they are? Just what process should a company use to select or structure the best possible distribution channels for its products?

We suggest eight steps to design a distribution system that really performs. The word *process* is key here because whatever the result of taking these steps, management will gain by clarifying what its customers want and how to serve them. Managers are always saying that they want their company to be "market driven." In following these steps, they can give substance to what is too often merely corporate rhetoric.

STEP 1: FIND OUT WHAT YOUR CUSTOMERS WANT

Of all marketing decisions, the ones regarding distribution are the most far-reaching. A company can easily change its prices or its advertising. It can hire or fire a market research agency, revamp its sales promotion program, even modify its product line. But once a company sets up its distribution channels, it will generally find changing them to be difficult.

And so, the first step calls for researching what customers want from the buying process and then using their preferences to group customers into market segments. Managers conducting the research concentrate on learning what their ultimate customers—the end users—want in the way of service. It is these people, of course, who actually benefit from the products a company makes.

It is important for the researchers to emphasize that the product's quality is not an issue. Nor should there be any question at this stage of what may or may not be most practical for the company, whether a service company, a manufacturer, or a middleman. Rather, respondents should be encouraged to consider the delivery of the service, the convenience of shopping for the product, and the kind of add-ons that are sold along with either.

There is, of course, no such thing as a truly homogeneous market, in which all customers view the company's offerings in exactly the same way. Yet managers who routinely try to ascertain what market segments are worth preparing for when they design a product rarely try this when they make decisions about how to distribute it. This is a crucial mistake.

The preliminary research is meant to generate an inventory of customers' desires, but it is important to exclude ideas too grand or trivial for consideration. Without restrictions of any kind, who wouldn't ask for the moon? Needless to say, an overarching consideration is price: respondents should be made to realize that for every service (or lack of one) there will be a correspondingly higher or lower price. Equally important, however, respondents must be forced to weigh their preferences not only in relation to price but also in relation to one another.

Consider personal computers. The delivery of service might include such things as a demonstration of the product before sale or the provision of long-term warranties and flexible financing. After the sale, there might be training programs for using the equipment and a program to install and repair it. Customers might appreciate "loaners" while their equipment is being repaired or technical advice over a telephone hot line. They should be prepared to make trade-offs among these inducements.

Services, we've found, usually fall into five categories:

Lot Size. Do customers want to buy in units of one or in multiple units?

Market Decentralization. Do customers value around-the-corner convenience, or are they willing to deal across great distances, say via an 800 number?

Waiting Time. Do customers want immediate delivery, or are they more concerned about the assurance of delivery?

Product Variety. Do customers value having the choice of many related products, or do they prefer the store to specialize?

Service Backup. Do customers want immediate, in-house repair and technical help, or can they wait and choose their own local repair services?

Once customers have traded off, say, demands for convenient location against product variety or variety against expert sales assistance, researchers can group these preferences into market segments and look for links between the segments suggested by the survey and the segments that may be generated by analysis of independent demographic or other marketing data.

We suspect, for example, that a segment of small businesses would be much more concerned about one-stop shopping than large businesses; big companies have purchasing specialists with the time to choose complementary products from different sources and to secure the lowest prices within various quality ranges. If a company sells to people who want one-stop shopping, it might want to know whether this segment coincides with self-employed accountants, for example. This small market segment is likely to be substantial, and it has needs quite different from those of a segment consisting of start-up scientific research companies.

A number of marketing research techniques are available to researchers at this step in the process, among them conjoint analysis, hybrid modeling, and constant-sum scales.[1] Unfortunately, most of these techniques have been developed to elicit choices among the tangible properties of product design: gas mileage versus size of car, size versus model, and so on. The things people want from a distribution system tend to be less tangible and more difficult to visualize and make judgments about (convenience of location versus depth of assortment, for example). Survey instruments ought to be designed with this challenge in mind.

STEP 2: DECIDE ON APPROPRIATE OUTLETS

At this stage researchers focus on the relation between market segments—defined as clusters of demands for service—and the outlets where services are normally delivered. Suppose, for example, that customers for a home computer indicate a desire for "self-service," "a somewhat narrow assortment of merchandise," "limited after-sale service," and "a relatively Spartan atmosphere"—so long as the prices are low. Clearly, this segment consists of people who would put up with a discount store operation—a 47 St. Photo, for instance—and trade off the amenities of upscale service or nearby location.

The fame of a store such as 47 St. Photo can be an asset in the analysis. Using the names of such well-known existing outlets or suggesting a hybrid of two or more kinds of such outlets, researchers can label potential clusters of service attributes. Respondents are asked about the service outlets they visualize, and researchers label the clusters constituting a segment precisely and vividly. On the other hand, labels are merely points of reference. They suggest existing kinds of retail outlets without limiting the possibilities.

For clusters suggesting no existing kinds of outlets, short descriptions of hypothetical outlets may be of help. Researchers may coin new names and, in analyzing the data, position the various segments along a wide continuum. The chemical industry, for example, may have no analog to a discount store or a rack jobber. But if many respondents indicate that they would like to see something along these lines, then the research team might, in the course of the survey, develop an appropriate option, describe it, think of a label for it, and present it to new respondents for consideration.

Venturesome financial institutions such as Merrill Lynch, Bank One, and GE Credit have scored impressive gains with just such distribution ideas. How else did we get to "financial supermarkets" and "discount brokerage"? In contrast, many marketing strategists in the personal computer industry have failed to predict the significance of value-added resellers or retail outlets with multiple but highly focused assortments. Obviously, they did not start by conceiving their distribution channels according to the shopping needs of potential customers.

Do not be hamstrung by industry experience. The more creative researchers are with their labels, the better step 2 will work.

STEP 3: FIND OUT ABOUT THE COSTS

Up to this point, the customer is sovereign: the process aims to determine what customers perceive to be optional shopping conditions among the many pertaining to distribution and related services. In the first part of step 3, however, it is essential to obtain an impartial assessment of whether the things that customers want (more precisely, the "clusters" of things they want) are feasible for the company. This is the first reality check, one that is made before management as a whole gets involved in the process.

It may be made by selected members of the corporation's staff, assuming they are professionals who can be objective about the company's line operations. Otherwise, the company must turn to executives from unaffected wholesaling or retailing enterprises or to academic authorities.

Researchers have already asked customers to trade off their demands for service against price, so that utterly implausible combinations of shopping conditions—outlets combining small-lot purchases and low unit prices, for example—have been eliminated from further consideration. But less obviously implausible combinations may remain. Suppose a group of customers for personal computers claim they are willing to "pay any price" for a hypothetical shopping outlet combining custom tailoring with quick delivery. Are these two shopping conditions ever practical in combination?

The second part of step 3 aims to determine what kind of support will be needed from suppliers or other "up-channel" participants for any hypothetical outlet suggested by the data. Distribution outlets do not operate in isolation; there is always a distribution system backing them up.

For example, if an attribute cluster suggests a "limited line, full function, vertically oriented industrial distributor," the question would be this: What backup system ensures that this kind of distribution will satisfy customers as well as possible? The answers should be concrete: high-technology distribution centers, training programs, catalog expertise. Sometimes existing distribution systems enjoy the necessary support, sometimes not. If not, the division of labor among suppliers will have to be restructured so that what customers desire may be delivered by the most capable up-channel participant.

Step 3 is a good time to get insights from people out in the distributive trades. It is also the time to tap in-house knowledge, the opinions of salespersons and others who stay in contact with customers.

The third and final part of step 3 is to project the cost of support systems feasible for each outlet type, on the assumption that the company may be able to contract with third parties to perform the outlet functions. Researchers cost out the new support systems on an incremental basis, starting with the company's existing distribution system. Costing requires informed guesswork; any change in one element of a distribution system has ramifications for another. But if, for example, the data suggest that customers want rapid delivery, local inventories will have to be maintained. Distribution centers may have to be constructed to support the local inventories. Cost accountants familiar with distribution may provide estimates, although they may have trouble dealing with the more theoretical scenarios. In the end, the question to be answered is this: What increase in market share is required to offset the added costs of the new distribution alternatives?

It is important to collect these cost estimates during step 3 because they are backup material for step 4. The figures may well reveal that certain systems of distribution are prohibitively expensive and should be removed from further consideration. We know one manufacturer of specialty medical supplies and equipment that was losing sales to competitors selling via mail order. But the added cost of establishing a competing catalog system did not make sense, so the company abandoned the option at this stage.

STEP 4: BOUND THE 'IDEAL'

At this point the researchers have come as close as they can to discerning and ideal market-driven system. Top management has been obliged to keep its hands off. Researchers have had a chance to find out, perhaps for the first time, what it really takes to please customers.

Step 4 gives a cross section of the company's executives an opportunity to subject the research findings to their own hard tests. Researchers invite these executives to investigate how any existing or hypothetical channel of distribution would affect company efficiency (costs, revenues, and profits), effectiveness (especially market share), and adaptability (fluidity of capital invested, ability to accept new products or adjust to new technologies). At the same time, executives give their impressions of what distribution is or is not doing. Though this part of the process is meant to generate reliable numbers, discussions with managers should be open-ended. They may even bring up their pet peeves.

Finally, researchers develop a list of company objectives for distribution based on their conversations with top management. They turn this list into a survey instrument and send it to every executive in the company who has a stake in distribution matters. Executives trade off objectives in the same way that customers trade off their requirements for outlet design. The result is a list of weighted objectives that are the constraints bounding the system.

Inevitably, at this stage, some executives want to impose constraints on the distribution design, which they justify not so much by numbers as by industrial tradition. There are rigidities and prejudices in most industries, some of which are reinforced by law, some of which are perceived to have the force of law.

The faltering car dealer system has not been altered for more than 60 years, in part because of peculiarities in the legal structure of auto distribution (franchise laws, dealer-day-in-court laws). But there is also an industry folklore that gets in the way of change, even though auto companies face a shift in power to consolidating dealers. How much longer before the executives of Chrysler, GM, Toyota, and other companies will be forced to compare their old objectives with new options?

The Coca-Cola Company and PepsiCo, in contrast, are consolidating their traditionally independent franchise bottler networks into distribution systems with greater maneuverability. At IBM, distribution by means of a direct sales force had been a sacred principle essentially until the company started making personal computers. It finally began to use third parties but only after great internal strain, after which the personal computer division was accorded the status of an independent business unit.

STEP 5: COMPARE YOUR OPTIONS

With the completion of step 4, company researchers will have a weighted list of management's objectives and constraints on the one hand and on the other a roster of the various ideal, market-driven distribution systems generated earlier in the process. Step 5 requires them to compare these two sets of data with each other and also with the system of distribution already in place. The researchers will, of course, consult with distribution managers about the company's present system: structure, functions performed by various channel participants, costs, discounts, and the like. It may be necessary for researchers to undertake an analysis of volume flows by channels as well as by margins, functions, and value-added at each level. A reasonably detailed map of this type can be very illuminating.

One of three conclusions will emerge from these comparisons. First, the existing system, the management-bounded system, and the ideal system may closely resemble each other. If this is the case, then management knows for sure that the existing system is about as good as it can get. If customer satisfaction is mediocre nevertheless, the message should be clear: the fault lies not in the design of the system but in its implementation.

Second, the existing and management-bounded systems may be similar to each other but substantially different from the ideal. This outcome may mean that the objectives and constraints adopted by management are causing the gap. Such a finding calls for a careful investigation of management's perceptions, the purpose of step 6.

Third and especially sobering, all three systems may be substantially different. Assuming that the management-bounded system is positioned somewhere between the existing and the ideal, it may be possible to improve customer satisfaction without relaxing management's objectives. This is the time to ask if relaxation of certain management constraints might not produce even greater benefits.

By 1980, IBM's direct sales force and sales branches had formed the core of the distribution network for its existing line—mainframe and word processors. These channels could not, however, be cost-effective in delivering personal computers to the small business market—not, in any case, at the standard for customer satisfaction that IBM's executives considered their company's hallmark.

The ideal would have been a network of highly decentralized, service-intensive specialty stores carrying an assortment of personal computer brands and models as well as other types of office equipment. Because some IBM executives were convinced that the company could not maintain control over the quality of service without ownership, the company opened its own retail outlets to sell IBM equipment alone. IBM product centers offered the consumer a variety of equipment, but comparison shopping within them was impossible. In 1986, IBM sold off its product center network to NYNEX. (Interestingly enough, IBM has since come to realize that the small business market is so heterogeneous that it consists of multiple segments.)

And so the ideal system acts as a stake in the ground. If the management-bounded options are not reasonably similar to the ideal, then researchers will ultimately have to confront managers with the fact that the company has been sacrificing customer satisfaction to other objectives.

In the long run, some of these other objectives may be critical and may even supersede the effort to satisfy customers via distribution. When management decides on any new strategy, it will simultaneously establish a hurdle rate—a minimum projected return on investment that justifies going ahead. Managers may, of course, set hurdles incorrectly, not only because they miscalculate costs but because they acquire a prejudice for or against particular channels of distribution. In any case, distribution strategies that do not clear their hurdles should be dropped from consideration in step 5.

STEP 6: REVIEW YOUR PET ASSUMPTIONS

This step is meant to help distinguish a serious constraint from an ordinary prejudice. It entails bringing in outsiders—lawyers, political consultants, distribution experts from other industries—who will call management's assumptions into question. Management often protects the status quo, for example, by claiming that changes might violate the law or encourage shadowy activities. Outsiders can look at the relevant laws and ask if they are what they seem. Can't they be changed? Does holding to one value force the company to sacrifice another?

The automobile industry has clung steadfastly to the dealer franchise system, in part out of fear of legal tangles. Porsche's attempt to implement a more consumer-responsive approach to distribution in the early 1980s turned into a fiasco largely because Porsche's dealers made clear that it would keep the company tied up in the courts for a generation. Alas, Porsche was on the right track.

But the impulse to stand pat does not always stem from anxiety about the law. The use of authorized third-party outlets for personal computers is an example: it often portends gray market activities. Some time ago, top managers at IBM indicated that they had been worried about the price cutting and "footballing" that would result if they authorized third-party outlets—a concern that proved justified. Had they let this serious concern paralyze them, their personal computer division would never have expanded as quickly as it did.

And so during step 6, outside authorities should be called on to check whether legal and other constraints exist and, if they do, whether they can be overcome. Of course reliance on outside experts can be risky. Who is to say top management doesn't know what it is talking about? Who can tell what course a lawsuit will take or what laws Congress and state legislatures will enact?

Business decisions are based on judgments, not certainties. Merrill Lynch would never have launched its highly successful cash management account program if it had not altered its assumptions about how the SEC would enforce federal banking laws. What are other companies missing?

STEP 7: CONFRONT THE GAP

This is the climax of the process. It requires top management to confront the gap between its practices or objectives and the ideal. For the first and only time, managers conducting the research bring together all executives responsible for distribution to determine the shape of a new system. To underline its significance, the company holds the meeting somewhere offsite.

The researchers get things going by presenting the ideal distribution system. Then they share the results of steps 4 and 5. In the course of this discussion, researchers outline for top management the objectives and constraints that were used to bound the ideal and show their effect, if any, in limiting what customers really desire. Next, researchers present the data and expert opinions challenging the validity of management's objectives and constraints—what was gained from step 6.

All this information serves as background for what usually proves to be a provocative discussion. We have found that researchers can prompt openness to it if they use computers to readjust weightings or other data and display the results instantaneously. This session brings top management face-to-face with the folklore restricting its thinking. Executives compare alternatives, weigh opportunity costs in relation to risk and exposure, and consider a host of other quantitative and subjective variables that are all too easily buried under day-to-day affairs. Most important, they make decisions in a new context—one in which an attainable ideal has been delineated, the intervening distance between the ideal and the reality has been measured, and the obstacles to closing the gap have been made explicit.

Such was the case for a personal care products company, whose ideal suggested the elimination of one level in its system—the brokers. It was a big step for managers to contemplate. When the company's brand lacked visibility and strong consumer demand, brokers had played a key role in providing access to the retail trade. Management felt a strong sense of loyalty and indebtedness to them. Over the years the brand had emerged as the best seller in its category; now the brokers contributed little to volume. Indeed, a growing price sensitivity on the part of consumers, coupled with the inefficiency of the broker system, placed the manufacturer in a vulnerable position.

It's not important to know this company's final decision. What is important is how the process teased out the lines of a crucial choice. Apple Computer, for example, would not likely have experimented with mail order channels in its early history had it followed this line of investigation to its conclusion. It would have found that the amount of hand-holding required to make a personal computer plus a software sale is extremely high. Similarly, IBM would not have been so surprised to find that dealers with outbound sales forces have greater staying power than those who simply rely on inbound retail sales. IBM retail showrooms cannot provide the kind of in-depth analysis and training that visits to a customer's premises can.

STEP 8: PREPARE TO IMPLEMENT

The final step in the process modifies the ideal distribution system emerging from step 3 according to the final objectives and constraints established in step 7. What managers are left with is a good system—not ideal, perhaps, but optimal.

This should be the subject of intensive implementation planning. And it is important for senior managers to help implement the system, if for no other reason than to give them a personal stake in the outcome. Besides, having confronted the ideal and having tested it against the other options, management has a full understanding of the trade-offs as well as the obstacles to implementation.

When it comes time to change the existing distribution system or to scrap it entirely, managers should test modifications on a small scale before committing resources to them. The major problem is that word will spread quickly. The gossip network among dealers and distributors is one of the busiest around.

The process we lay out in this article is not a simple one. Managers are required to focus on something as insubstantial as quality, or the ideal system, and then to come up with hard numbers to project a reasonable ratio of return to expense. They must even anticipate how adaptable their ideal might be to changes in the law or the political environment. Clearly, there is as much art here as science.

Still, none of the eight steps we outline should be skipped in the interest of apparent expediency. Managerial sophistication will speed the process along, but sophistication alone will be no substitute for going through it. With all the effort reevaluating the system requires, readers may assume that the process always justifies itself by the constructive changes it brings about. In fact, its real value is in the clarity it brings to a critical aspect of doing business.

Recently a specialty grocery products manufacturer discovered that it was getting its products onto supermarket shelves in ways that on the surface looked Rube Goldbergian. It was using an array of third-party players, including food brokers, grocery wholesalers, and health food distributors, some of whom carried out a remarkable range of functions between the manufacturing and the retail level of the distribution chain. When the company drew a structural diagram, it looked like a bowl of spaghetti. Nevertheless, further analysis revealed that the system met all the criteria of an ideal.

The recommendation? "Don't mess with it! Don't touch a thing!" Sometimes the eight-step process explains precisely why you should do nothing to change the distribution system you already have.

NOTES

1. See Paul E. Green, "Hybrid Models of Conjoint Analysis: An Expository Review," *Journal of Marketing Research,* May 1984, p. 155.

Roger A. Kerin, PhD
Harold C. Simmons Distinguished Professor
of Marketing
Edwin L. Cox School of Business
Southern Methodist University
Dallas, Texas

Dwight R. Riskey, PhD
Vice President, Marketing Research and
New Business
Frito-Lay, Inc.
Plano, Texas

CHAPTER 48

PRODUCT CANNIBALISM

Slowed economic growth, compressed product life cycles, domestic and foreign competition, and consumer desire for variety have placed unprecedented pressures on product management. Properly or improperly, many firms appear to be focusing their efforts on product opportunities that offer minimal market resistance, leverage existing technologies, utilize present manufacturing capability and capacity, and minimize financial investment. These opportunities are often manifested in product line extensions.

It is estimated that 81 percent of new consumer products are extensions of existing products. No product category seems to be immune from the surfeit of product offshoots. In 1990 alone, product line extensions included 64 different sauces, 103 snack chips, 91 cold remedies, and 69 disposable diapers.[1] Line extensions are routinely achieved in a number of ways.[2] Introduction of new sizes (super economy-size toothpaste), forms (deodorant in liquid, powder, spray, and stick forms), compositions (regular Head & Shoulders shampoo and Head & Shoulders shampoo with conditioner), flavors (Jello gelatin, which originally began with six flavors, is now available in more than a dozen), packages (Hi-C fruit flavored drink in glass bottles or paper or metal containers), and varieties (shampoo for dry, normal, and oily hair) are just some of the feasible courses of action.

In general, dominant firms in a product category or industry tend to view product line extension as a relatively low risk means of maintaining or increasing market share, and as an indispensable tool in the fierce struggle for retail shelf space. For example, an Association of National Advertisers study indicated that the majority of line extensions were considered successful. By comparison, only about one-half of new products were deemed successful.[3] On the other hand, low market share firms and potential new entrants tend to view the line extension strategies of dominant firms as a calculated strategy to corner supermarket shelf space, keep out rival brands, and protect their competitive position.

Even though product-line extension strategies pose minimal risk of failure for the product being introduced, potential negative effects on existing products serving existing markets must be considered. These effects can be called *product cannibalism.* While some cannibalism may be planned or expected, considerable amounts of cannibalism may be an unexpected consequence of an improperly managed product development process and line extension program. When Anheuser-Busch launched Michelob Light, it fully expected that 20–25 percent of the new brand would come from its existing base brand because of its low-calorie appeal among current customers.[4] However, despite numerous efforts to differentiate and position Stouffer Food Corporation's Right Course frozen entree, the brand cannibalized the company's popular Lean Cuisine brand. Six months after the introduction of Right Course, it was pulled because, according to a company official, "This brand [Right Course] ended up competing with our Lean Cuisine line."[5]

The purpose of this chapter is to examine several different facets of product cannibalism. We begin by describing the dynamics underlying product cannibalism. Managerial practices and competitive conditions that foster cannibalism are then enumerated. Because cannibalism is sometimes justified on the basis of competitive reality, the strategy of preemptive cannibalism is introduced. The financial consequences of product cannibalism are then illustrated from the perspective of individual products and product line profitability, and approaches for identifying cannibalism potential are briefly described. The chapter concludes with a discussion on the implications of product cannibalism for product line management.

NATURE OF PRODUCT CANNIBALISM

The theoretical roots of product cannibalism can be traced to the theory of cross-elasticity of demand. This theory suggests that the percentage change in the quantity of product A demanded will be influenced by the percentage change in the price of product B. The demand interrelationship between two products may be described as complementary or substitutable. For example, if the price of product B decreases and the quantity demanded of product A increases, the two products are considered to be complements, providing other things remain equal. Common examples illustrating complementary products are razors and razor blades and cameras and photographic accessories. In the case of product substitution, or cannibalism, a lowering of the price on product A will tend to decrease the quantity demanded for product B, providing other things remain equal. Margarine is sometimes viewed as a substitute for butter.

From a marketing standpoint, however, other things rarely remain equal. Accordingly, an expanded interpretation of cross-elasticity of demand is necessary. In addition to price changes, physical and symbolic attributes of products, alternative means of promoting and distributing products, and potential end-use interchangeability between products must be considered. In addition, attention must be given to the potential for variety-seeking by consumers. That is, for some product categories (e.g., snack foods and soft drinks) consumers tend to purchase and consume multiple flavors and sizes.

As shown in Exhibit 1, new entrants and line extensions acquire their sales revenue from three sources: (1) new consumers who were not previously buyers of the product type; (2) consumers of competitive brands within a product category; and (3) consumers of an existing

EXHIBIT 1. Components of New Entrant Sales Revenue

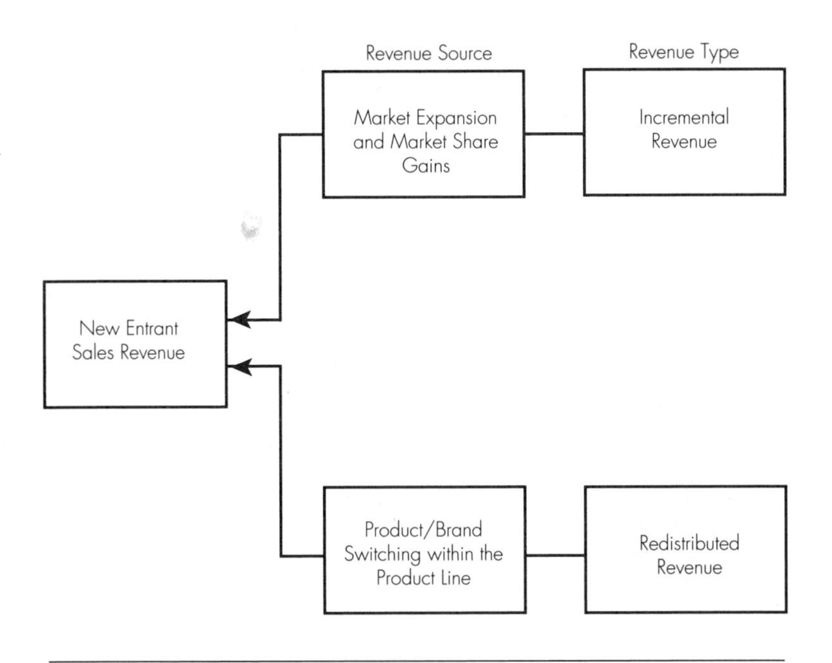

company brand or product who switch to the new entry. The first two sales revenue sources represent, respectively, incremental revenue for the product line because of market expansion and the capturing of competitors' market share or share-building. The remaining sales revenue source represents redistributed revenue, or cannibalization, in that existing buyers are substituting one item for another in the company's product line. Accordingly, product cannibalization can be succinctly defined as the process by which a firm's new entry gains a portion of its sales by diverting them from a firm's existing product(s).

This process of sales diversion or redistribution of revenue has a subtle but managerially important consequence. Assuming that the change in profits earned by the existing product is reduced or negative because of substitution, this amount should be added to the incremental cost curve for the new offering. The implication is clear—sales and profit gains of a new entry at the expense of an existing product do not filter down to the bottom line. Rather, the loss of potential profits from a cannibalized product is real cost that must be absorbed by the new product. The adage "You can't have your cake and eat it, too" applies when cannibalism occurs.

As a generalization, it has been suggested that a product-line extension must gain two market share points for each share point lost by cannibalized products to preserve profit margins. One-half of the gain will come from users of competitors' products and one-half from new users drawn into the category. Therefore, sales revenue for a product-line extension is divided equally among incremental sales volume, cannibalized revenue, and market share gains.[6]

FOSTERING CANNIBALISM

The erosion of an existing product's share of market resulting from cannibalism may stem from management decisions, or it may be a necessary evil, given competitive conditions. Cannibalism becomes a severe problem when it provides no incremental competitive or financial benefit to the firm's product line. Several managerial decisions appear to foster cannibalism of an existing brand's sales volume:

1. management pressure for sales growth from new offerings without full consideration of financial consequences;
2. preoccupation with developing a full line of products in an attempt to achieve increases in overall market share in a product class or category;
3. inadequate positioning of new entries resulting in their seeking the identity of existing products;
4. unrealistic or excessive market segmentation resulting in "two segments" with demands for identical product attributes or end-use needs; and
5. aggressive promotional effort or incentives reflected in sales representatives' overemphasis on new items and neglect of existing products.

Product cannibalism by itself should not be viewed only negatively. Cannibalism sometimes represents an outgrowth of effective and competitive product management. For example, some firms might actively pursue line extensions for the purpose of building a base brand's "brand equity." This rationale has been used by some soft drink producers to justify cannibalism of regular soft drinks by diet and caffeine-free varieties. Even though diet and caffeine-free beverages divert sales from regular drinks, the equity of the base brand name is believed to be enhanced even though cannibalism among line items is present. Additionally, a new item with cannibalism potential may be introduced to eliminate gaps in a product line that might be filled by competing offerings or to neutralize competitive inroads. In other words, it may be wiser to have buyers switching among products and brands within a firm's product line than to have them switching out and purchasing competitive offerings. Viewed in this manner, preemptive cannibalism becomes a viable business strategy.

Preemptive cannibalism is the conscious practice of stealing sales from a company's existing products and brands to keep consumers from switching to competitors' offerings. Two product-line extension strategies are commonly employed in this regard: a flanker brand strategy and a fighting brand strategy.

Flanker Brand Strategy

Bristol-Meyers' introduction of Datril to compete with McNeil Laboratories' Tylenol exemplifies a flanker brand strategy. Bristol-Meyers held a position of strength in the aspirin segment of the analgesic market with its Bufferin and Excedrin brands. However, this segment, while large, had plateaued in the mid-1970s. During the same period, the acetaminophen (noninflammatory compounds) segment of the analgesic market dominated by McNeil Laboratories had grown substantially, with a portion of the growth coming from former and potential aspirin users. Datril's introduction would hopefully attract aspirin switchers (that is, switching away from company brands) and tap existing and potential acetaminophen buyers who would most likely purchase Tylenol. Therefore, even though Datril might cannibalize Excedrin and Bufferin, aspirin switchers would remain in the Bristol-Meyers analgesic product line rather than being attracted to Tylenol.

A similar strategy was recently employed by the Miller Brewing Company with the introduction of Lite Genuine Draft, an extension of Miller's Genuine Draft beer. The company intended to have Lite Genuine Draft compete against Coors Lite and Budweiser Light in the premium segment of the light beer category since Miller Brewing believed Miller Lite users were switching to Coors and Budweiser brands. Even though it was likely that Lite Genuine Draft would steal sales from Miller's Genuine Draft and also Miller Lite, Leonard Goldman, president of Miller Brewing Company said:

> *Miller Lite represents a tremendous presence in the fastest growing segment (light beer), but we are committed to having multiple brands in each segment to give the consumer the broadest array of choices. This is a fancy way of saying that if the consumer is going to defect, we want him to defect to another Miller product."*[7]

Fighting Brand Strategy

A fighting brand is typically introduced when (1) a firm has a high relative share in a product category; (2) its dominant brands are susceptible to having share sliced away by aggressive pricing by smaller competitors; and (3) it wishes to preserve its profit margins on existing brands. The introduction of Santitas® brand Tortilla Chips by Frito-Lay illustrates a fighting brand strategy. As the tortilla chip category leader, managers for Tostitos® brand Tortilla Chips recognized the emergence of restaurant-style tortilla chips (RSTC) as a competitive threat in certain regional markets. Unflavored and typically priced below national and regional tortilla chip brands, RSTC were also lower in quality based on consumer taste tests. Nevertheless, lower pricing coupled with their primary use for dipping with sauces and nacho preparation resulted in RSTC capturing a sizable portion of tortilla chip volume. Frito-Lay introduced Santitas® brand Tortilla Chips at a competitive RSTC price and provided trade promotion to support the brand. This action, while cannibalizing a portion of Tostitos® brand Tortilla Chips, resulted in incremental volume growth and category share-building for Frito-Lay.

ACCOUNTING FOR PRODUCT CANNIBALISM

The previous discussion illustrates the importance of performing a marginal analysis on the new item in the product line within the context of present and forecasted market conditions. Incremental revenue, cost, and investment must be considered.

An analysis of a hypothetical multiproduct firm serves to demonstrate the financial consequences of product cannibalism. This firm has an existing product that was expected to capture 5 percent of a market forecasted at 15 million units, or 750,000 units. At a $2.00 per unit price and a $1.00 per unit gross margin, forecasted sales are $1.5 million with a $750,000 gross margin. Budgeted marketing expenditures plus allocated overhead total $300,000, which will provide a $450,000 profit before taxes and a 10 percent return on investment. An abbreviated pro forma income statement showing these figures is shown in part A of Exhibit 2.

A new offering is introduced that satisfies several, but not all, buyer requirements met by the existing product in addition to providing several other benefits. The new item is value-priced at $1.50 per unit with a $0.75 per unit gross margin. The lower price and modified product benefits are expected to expand the market for this product type by 20 percent to 18 million units. Both products combined are expected to capture 10 percent of the expanded market, or 1.8 million units, which represents a 240 percent increase over forecasted volume for the single existing product. Marketing expenditures plus allocated overhead for the new product are budgeted at $450,000. Incremental investment for the new offering is $1 million. Most of the volume captured by the new product comes from market expansion because of the lower price and differentiated product benefit structure. However, slightly more than 25 percent cannibalism rate occurs from the existing product.

Part B in Exhibit 2 shows the effects of the activities and events described for the existing product and the new item, individually and combined. Also shown is an incremental analysis comparing the existing product alone versus the existing and the new product combined. Given the conditions of the example cited, the apparent new item

EXHIBIT 2. Accounting for Product Cannibalism

	A				B		
	Existing Product Alone	**Existing Product**	**+**	**New Product**	**=**	**Products Combined**	**Incremental Analysis**
Forecast total							
Market units	15,000,000					18,000,000	
Forecast market share	5%					10%	
Forecast unit volume	750,000					1,800,000	
Source of volume:							
New customers	50,000			950,000		950,000	
Competitors' customers	200,000	100,000		100,000		200,000	
Cannibalized customers				200,000		200,000	
Repeat customers	500,000	450,000				450,000	
Total	$750,000	$550,000		$1,250,000		$1,800,000	
Resulting market share		3.1%		6.9%		10%	
Unit price	$2.00	$2.00		$1.75			
Total revenue	$1,500,000	$1,100,000		$2,187,500		$3,287,500	$1,787,500
Gross margin/unit	$1.00	$1.00		$0.75			
Gross margin dollars	$750,000	$550,000		$937,500		$1,487,500	$737,500
Marketing expenditures and allocated overhead	$300,000	$300,000		$450,000		$750,000	$450,000
Profit before tax	$450,000	$250,000		$487,500		$737,500	$287,500
Investment	$4,500,000	$4,500,000		$1,000,000		$5,500,000	$1,000,000
Return on investment	10%	5%		48.7%		13%	28.7%
Less cannibalized volume* (200,000 units × $1.00)				$200,000			
Revised profit before tax		$250,000		$287,500		$537,500	$87,500
Revised ROI				28.7%		9.7%	8.7%

**Note:* Cannibalized volume should approximately be subtracted from gross margin dollars produced by the new product. If this were done, the revised profit and ROI calculations would be inserted into the original profit and ROI computation. The format used here is designed to illustrate critical variances in the analysis.

profit is much less when cannibalized volume is subtracted from the existing product's contribution. The apparent return on investment for the product line with the new offering is inflated; it is actually less than the return on investment for the existing product when cannibalized volume is taken into account. Finally, the incremental analysis reveals that the incremental profit from the new entry is only 30 percent of what it appears to be without consideration of cannibalism's affects.

This example highlights several possible ramifications of product cannibalism:

1. Without accounting for product cannibalism, sales volume and profits for a new item may be more illusionary than real.
2. New-entries examined in an isolated fashion—without also considering cannibalized volume—provides a distorted view of product-line profits and return on investment.
3. Market share growth for a product line resulting from a new entry may represent Pyrrhic victories in terms of product-line profitability and individual item volume.
4. Both the amount and source of potential new item volume must be considered in product-line planning to calculate the impact of cannibalism on product-line profitability.

Effects of Preemptive Cannibalism

This analysis can also be used to illustrate the potential effects of preemptive cannibalism. Suppose in our hypothetical situation that the new item described was used as a retaliatory device (fighting brand) to meet a competitor whose lower-priced product was capturing a portion of the existing product's market share. If one considers the new item's cannibalized volume as potentially lost to the competitor, then these buyers are being kept by the firm, albeit at a lower rate of return. If the new item were not introduced, 200,000 units would be lost, resulting in a five percent return on the existing product's investment. Even with cannibalism considered, the firm's new product will virtually preserve the return on investment percentage, thus showing the benefit of preemptive cannibalism.

Incremental Analysis

It is also possible to calculate the incremental unit volume necessary to overcome the effects of cannibalism. This measure can be used as a benchmark for evaluating market capacity and the quality of introductory marketing programs early in the business analysis stage. The expression is as follows:

$$\begin{array}{c}\text{Incremental volume}\\ \text{to offset}\\ \text{cannibalism effect}\end{array} = \begin{array}{c}\text{Cannibalized}\\ \text{unit volume}\end{array} \times \begin{array}{c}\text{Ratio of the}\\ \text{old and new}\\ \text{product margins}\end{array}$$

Using figures from the hypothetical example, the incremental volume necessary to overcome the effects of cannibalism is approximately 267,000 units: (200,000 units) × ($1.00 margin/$0.75 margin). In other words, at the estimated cannibalism rate, the new item must generate an incremental volume from new and competitors' customers of 267,000 units to offset the loss of margin dollars from the existing product. In effect, for this illustration, a 21 percent increase in incremental volume over forecasted levels would be required. Issues surrounding market capacity and the quality of the market entry program assume a different light in this context.

In some instances, the dollar gross margin of the new item might exceed the dollar gross margin of the existing product that it cannibalizes. In this instance, for each unit of the existing product that is cannibalized, the firm records a higher dollar gross margin. Therefore, the firm would benefit from product cannibalism. It should be emphasized, however, that the incremental costs associated with advertising and promotion or any additions in manufacturing capacity costs must be considered to determine the net effect of cannibalism. If these incremental costs exceed the incremental benefits of higher dollar gross margin, then product-line profitability will suffer.

IDENTIFYING CANNIBALISM POTENTIAL

The importance of identifying cannibalism potential cannot be overemphasized. Cannibalism effects should be considered in light of product-market structure and throughout the product development process, beginning with concept testing and continuing through commercialization.

Analysis of Product-Market Structure

Conventional approaches for defining product-market structure focuses on product segmentation. Exhibit 3 illustrates this approach for chip and vegetable dips sold through supermarkets. As shown, dips divide into two distinct categories. Prepared dips are ready-made and divided into two categories: (1) refrigerated dips such as Marie's and (2) shelf-stable dips such as Frito-Lay's Dips® which are sold in metal cans and require no refrigeration. Dip bases, which require at-home preparation, also divide into two categories: (1) dry soup mixes and (2) dry dip mixes. The implication of this structure is that prepared dips (refrigerated and shelf-stable) compete with each other, but not with dip bases. However, this conclusion might be incorrect when usage situations are considered.

Recent research suggests that attention to usage context offers a broadened perspective on how consumers view products and their substitutability, hence cannibalism potential. The substitution-in-use approach (SIU) simultaneously examines products and their usages to

EXHIBIT 3. Product Segmentation of Vegetable and Chip Dips Sold Through Supermarkets

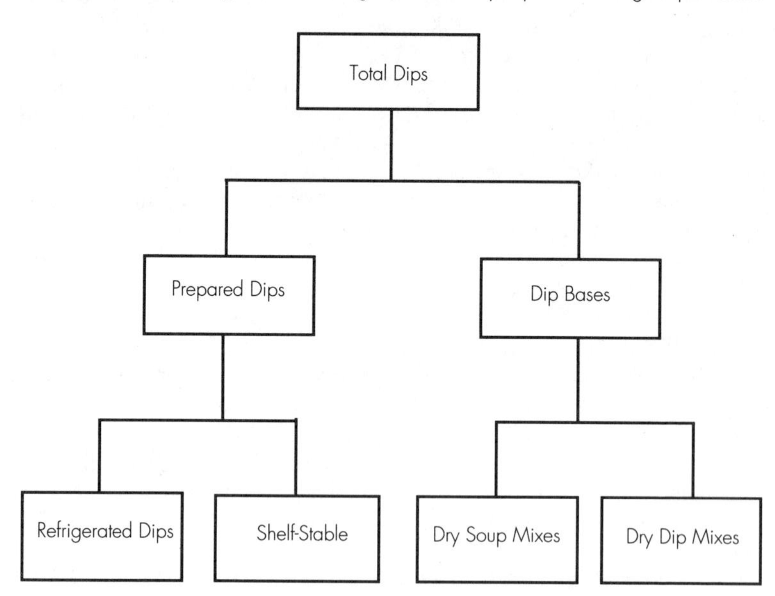

reveal product-market structure. A key assumption underlying this approach is that products represent "benefit bundles" and when grouped on the basis of appropriateness for similar usages are presumed to deliver similar benefit combinations. The SIU approach implies that products perceived to be similar by consumers are considered substitutable as a means for the same ends or usages. Therefore, prepared refrigerated dips could be substitutes for dry dip mixes prepared at home for specific usage situations, e.g., parties. Accordingly, a dry dip mix line extension by a refrigerated dip producer could cannibalize the firm's existing product(s), at least for specific usage contexts.

Applications of the SIU approach result in maps, dendrograms, and other visual depictions that attempt to portray product-market structure in a manner corresponding to consumers' mental representations of a product category (e.g., vegetable and chip dips). The mechanics of this approach are beyond the scope of this discussion.[8] Nevertheless, by directing managerial attention toward consumer perceptions of products as a means to achieving an end inherent in a usage context, the SIU approach provides useful insights into product-market structure, product similarities, and product substitution potential.

Analysis of Product Features, Preferences, and Perceptions

Substitution-in-use analysis offers a useful, although coarse-grain assessment of product comparability in usage contexts. This approach has a "black-box" character in that it does not measure directly the product features sought in a specific usage context nor consumer perceptions of the benefits afforded by individual products. *Conjoint analysis* is typically employed to study the linkage of product features to preferences and the linkage of features to consumer perceptions. This analysis technique is of special value in concept testing where its application is most prevalent.[9]

Conjoint analysis, which actually represents a family of multiattribute choice models, concerns itself with measuring the joint effect of two or more independent variables (e.g., product features) on the ordering of a dependent variable (e.g., preference). Conjoint analysis makes it possible to take a consumer's overall evaluation of a set of concepts and decompose those evaluations into separate scores—utility functions—for the various attributes or features of concepts that led to the consumer evaluating them the way he/she did. Consumer choices based on their individual utility functions can result in estimated share of choices and brand-switching matrices showing the (company or competitive) brands from which any of a number of new concepts (i.e., line extensions) can draw customers. For example, Sunbeam Appliance Corporation routinely uses conjoint analysis to assess new model concepts for its small appliance line both in terms of draw from competitive brands (e.g., Sears, Cuisinart) as well as cannibalization of its own models.[10]

Conjoint analysis also can be used as a tool for product positioning within a product line. For example, applications are possible that can provide insight into the value of a brand name (when brand names are treated as independent variables) as well as the appropriateness of various brands for providing certain types of features and benefits. The latter application treats brands as dependent variables and combinations of product features are sorted according to their similarity to or appropriateness for various brands.

An extended description of the statistical properties and application of conjoint analysis is beyond the scope of this discussion.[11] Nevertheless, it is worth noting that as a concept-testing practice, conjoint analysis does show promise in its ability to predict actual consumer choice and produce valid market share estimates for new concepts.[12] Since actual product sales and market share are often confounded by marketing mix variables such as advertising and distribution and competitive behavior, conjoint analysis as a predictive technique for assessing sources of volume for line extensions—hence, product cannibalism—is not a substitute for pretest market modeling and actual field market tests.

Pretest Market Modeling and Field Test Marketing

Cannibalism potential can be further identified and possibly refined beyond the concept-testing stage. As product ideas evolve from concepts to prototypes, segmentation and positioning strategies become clearer, introductory marketing programs can be drafted, and spending levels can be finalized. At this time, cannibalism potential can be assessed within the context of pretest market models. *Pretest market models* combine executive judgment on marketing strategy, historical data, laboratory data using product preference, and trial and repeat purchase models of buyer behavior to make sales and market share projections for new concepts.[13] Most notably, pretest market models typically incorporate cannibalization estimates that are often based on data gathered from simulated market tests (or laboratory test markets) and preference modeling (e.g., conjoint analysis).

Despite the benefits of pretest market models, they are not without limitations. Their application is limited to studying new brands seeking to enter well-defined product categories. They are not particularly suitable for products with long purchase cycles or products whose benefits are not immediately realized. Consequently, primary use of these models exists in evaluating consumer package goods and food products. Furthermore, these models are limited to the analysis of individual products; they do not provide information on product line dynamics *per se.*

Estimating a new offering's sales volume potential and its tendency to cannibalize existing products can be finally assessed by field test markets. Test markets allow product sales and product item interactions to be observed in an actual—although not always representative—competitive setting. Even in a test market setting, however, assessing cannibalism is not a trivial exercise. Although it is possible to perform product-by-product sales trend analysis to infer levels of cannibalism, trend analysis only uncovers cannibalism effects when they are large. Even then, alternative explanations for an existing product's sales decline can be invoked.

The advent of controlled (scanner) test markets for consumer package goods sold using household panels offers considerable promise in assessing the sources and magnitude of product cannibalism. For example, algorithms for studying household panel data have been developed for analyzing a household's history of purchases before and after the introduction of a new item. These algorithms have proven useful in studying sources of volume for existing products and line extensions. Analysis of household panel data reveals that cannibalism rates ranging from 60 to 70 percent are common for minor line extensions to 10 to 20 percent or less for new offerings with significant, previously unaddressed consumer benefits. A new flavor of potato chip, for instance, typically generates 50 percent incremental volume for its base brand. An altogether new and unique snack chip brand may produce incremental sales volume in the range of 75 to 90 percent.

IMPLICATIONS FOR PRODUCT-LINE MANAGEMENT

The popularity of product-line extensions as a strategy of choice by many firms raises the spectre of product cannibalism. The previous discussion suggests four implications of product cannibalism for product-line management.

First, with companies coming under greater pressure to add new items to their lines, the need to systematically assess the incremental sales and profit contribution of product additions is becoming ever more critical. Specifically, it is important to quantify incremental product-line (versus single-product) profits before deciding whether to add a new item to an existing product line. Such incremental analysis requires an understanding of product cannibalism.

Second, preemptive cannibalism is frequently necessary to confront competitor product development efforts. Nevertheless, product-line filling and stretching efforts to meet competitive inroads need to be assessed by comparing cannibalized sales volume with projected lost volume. If cannibalized volume is substantially larger than projected lost volume, preemptive product cannibalism may not be justified.

Third, understanding demand interdependencies is a necessary first step in assessing cannibalism potential. Traditional notions of cross-elasticity of demand based solely on price are inadequate. Numerous other factors and conditions result in product substitutions. In this regard, effective product-line management must consider a new offering's "substitution-in-use" possibilities and hence its cannibalism potential.

Finally, attention to the sources and magnitude of cannibalism produced by new offerings should be studied throughout the product development process from concept through commercialization. To ignore product cannibalism is to invite unwise product proliferation and its frequent derivative—product cannibalism.

NOTES

1. "New-Product Troubles Have Firms Cutting Back," *Wall Street Journal* (January 13, 1992), p. B1; "Multiple Varieties of Established Brands Muddle Consumers, Make Retailers, Mad," *Wall Street Journal* (January 24, 1992), pp. B1, B5.

2. Roger A. Kerin, Vijay Mahajan, and P. Rajan Varadarajan, *Contemporary Perspectives on Strategic Market Planning* (Boston: Allyn & Bacon, Inc., 1990), pp. 242–243.

3. *Prescription for New Product Success* (New York: Association of National Advertisers, 1984).

4. "Anheuser-Busch, Inc., Has Another Entry in 'Light Beer' Field," *Wall Street Journal* (February 19, 1978), p. 4.

5. Judann Dagnoli, "How Stouffer's Right Course Veered Off Course," *Advertising Age* (May 6, 1991), p. 34.
6. Douglas J. Dalrymple and Leonard J. Parsons, *Marketing Management: Strategy and Cases,* 4th ed. (New York: John Wiley & Sons, Inc., 1986), pp. 381–82.
7. "Miller Brewing to Test-Market New Light Beer," *Wall Street Journal* (April 20, 1988), p. 24.
8. For a recent description of the substitution-in-use approach, see S. Ratneshwar and Allan D. Shocker, "Substitution in Use and the Role of Usage Context in Product Category Structure," *Journal of Marketing Research,* (August 1991), pp. 281–295.
9. Dick Wittink and Philippe Cattin, "Commercial Use of Conjoint Analysis: An Update," *Journal of Marketing* (July 1989), pp. 91–96.
10. Albert L. Page and Harold F. Rosenbaum, "Redesigning Product Lines with Conjoint Analysis: How Sunbeam Does It," *Journal of Product Innovation Management,* 1987, pp. 120–137.
11. For further reading on conjoint analysis and possible applications, see Paul E. Green, Donald S. Tull, and Gerald Albaum, *Research for Marketing Decisions,* 5th ed. (Englewood Cliffs, NJ: Prentice-Hall, 1988).
12. Paul E. Green and V. Srinivasan, "Conjoint Analysis in Marketing Research: New Developments and Directions," *Journal of Marketing* (October 1990), pp. 3–19.
13. For an extended discussion on pretest market models, see Allan D. Shocker and William G. Hall, "Pretest Market Models: A Critical Evaluation," *Journal of Product Innovation Management,* 1986, pp. 86–107.

Joel R. Evans
RMI Distinguished Professor of Business
Hofstra University
Hempstead, New York

CHAPTER 49

STRATEGIC PLANNING IN RETAILING: UNDERSTANDING AND RESPONDING TO A DYNAMIC ENVIRONMENT

INTRODUCTION

Over the last decade, the nature of U.S. retailing has changed dramatically (Zinn 1990). Among the key challenges are these:

- A number of firms have overexpanded, diversified into too many product lines, and/or become saddled with excessive debt—sometimes due to leveraged buyouts. This means that both financial and management resources have been stretched too thin and that company images have been blurred.
- In many areas, retail locations are already saturated and/or extremely expensive—this situation will probably worsen.
- Off-price retailers are growing rapidly and their locations, product lines, and customer service levels are getting closer to those of traditional retailers. At the same time, direct marketing—mostly through mail-order sales—is making significant inroads with customers of traditional retailers.
- The competitive pricing strategies of some of the largest U.S. chains are constraining overall retail profit margins. And consumers today are more price sensitive and more price conscious than ever before. If total U.S. store sales do not rise substantially in the future, the reduced profit margins could have long-run implications for retailers regarding operations, customer service, the use of advertising, etc.
- A phenomenon known as the "free rider" effect is growing, and it has negative implications for full-service retailers. With the free-rider effect, a person first goes to a full-service store to learn about a product, receive advice about the best model to choose, etc., and then visits a discount store, which offers little customer support to keep its costs down and to make a purchase. The discounter gets a free ride at the expense of the full-service firm.
- Marketplace clutter is making it harder for retailers to get their image and advertising messages across to consumers. For example, in overstored areas, many consumers have a tough time differentiating among the available retailers. Thus they may perceive some of the stores that they patronize as interchangeable "me too" outlets; they may be unable to see the subtle differences among stores (or be disinterested in exerting the effort to do so). How well can retailers possibly communicate their images if there so many competing outlets? Also, how can any single firm get customers to pay attention to its ads in such media as the Sunday newspaper? A Sunday paper often contains several inserts, ranging from one page coupon tearsheets to glossy minicatalogs, in addition to regular in-paper ads. Consumers cannot help but be overwhelmed.

- Many consumers have a poor view of retailing and feel that customer service is poor, ads about sales are deceiving, salespeople are too pushy, and retailers are not listening to their needs. Whether these perceptions are right or not, this is what many consumers believe.
- Consumer life-styles are shifting. Over 50 percent of U.S. women with young children are now working, there are more two-income families, the birth rate is low, and there is a fragmented marketplace. One interesting concept is known as a component life-style ("31 Major Trends" 1988): "A consumer may own a BMW but fill it with self-service gasoline. Buy take-out fast food for lunch but good wine for dinner. Own sophisticated photo equipment and low-priced home stereo equipment. Shop for socks at Kmart and suits or dresses at Brooks Brothers." A component life-style can be employed by consumers of any age, income level, or social status.
- Retailers need a large, steady, and eager part- and full-time work force. Yet, many potential employees perceive retailing to be high pressure with long hours and low pay relative to other industries; they do not know or believe that meaningful career ladders exist. Also, a shortage of young workers will persist due to an aging population.
- There is increasing competition from foreign retailers, both through takeovers/mergers with U.S. firms and the entry of foreign firms into the U.S. market, selling everything from furniture to groceries. These firms are often aggressive, innovative, well-financed, and seek to maximize market share.

As the above points indicate, retailing (like all industry, company, and product categories) is evolving. Thus, we should not be distressed if certain types of retailing fall into disfavor and others emerge to replace them. This is natural and to be expected. It is not merely a modern occurrence nor one that should call for undue hand-wringing or overreactions.

We need to understand how and why retailing practices have evolved (and grown or declined) and where they are heading, and adapt strategies accordingly. Any business entity that does not evolve over time will stagnate and become unresponsive to the dynamics of the environment and the marketplace. As the adage goes, "the past is a prologue of the future."

For centuries, each time a major new retail format or practice emerged, the nature of U.S. retailing changed. Better retailers have understood the reasons for the changes and acted accordingly. A look at the present strategy of any successful long-running retailer would show at least several key revisions from its original strategy or in the way in which that strategy is carried out, in response to the dynamics of the environment and the marketplace. Weak or unadapting firms have been, and will continue to be, driven out of the marketplace.

Let us now take an in-depth look at how retailing in the United States has developed and at the current status of retailing in this country.

THE DEVELOPMENT OF RETAILING IN THE UNITED STATES

Since precolonial days, U.S. retailing has made steady progress from trading posts to small general stores to modern formats such as power retailing. The industry, at each stage in its evolution, has become more efficient and effective and better able to serve customers.

In the 1600s, Boston, Newport, Philadelphia, New York, and Charleston emerged as dominant colonial settlements, largely due to their success in becoming market centers:

> *Particular days of the week were set aside as "market days," and semi-annual "fairs" were planned with care. Designated marketplaces were established, with village squares used for this purpose; special buildings were erected for trading activities. The success of these five villages in creating a favorable environment for exchange gave them substantial economic power over surrounding communities, enabled them to regulate wholesale and retail trade, and facilitated their political development (Bridenbaugh 1938).*

During the 1700s and early 1800s, the general store emerged as the leading form of store-based retailing:

> *In the back settlements and western country, rarely was any other kind of store found. While these early stores carried a wide variety of articles, their entire stocks, if the stores of St. Louis were typical, were relatively small. A place occupying a few square feet would contain all of their goods, and, during the period of the first growth of St. Louis, a merchant kept all of his goods in a chest or box, which was opened whenever a purchaser would appear. Sugar, coffee, gunpowder, blankets, paint, spice, salt, knives, hatchets, guns, kitchenwares, hunting shirts, and every variety of coarse dry goods were stored together (Jones 1937).*

Then, in the early to mid-1800s, these events helped to reduce the dominance of the general store:

> *The special knowledge required for drugs was at least a partial explanation for the appearance at this time of the retail drugstore. The retail bookstore had also appeared, but bookstores were probably not so numerous as drugstores. The publisher of the local newspaper often conducted a book and stationery store, but most books were imported and sold by the importer at retail or in odd lots to the general storekeeper. A retail shoe store at the opening of the century was a decided exception, if any were in existence. Shoes were commonly sold at retail by general stores and local shoemakers. This continued to be true until 1860. A jewelry store in the year 1800 was more an artisan's shop than a store. As the industry adopted factory methods, the craftsman manufactured less and repaired more. By 1835, the business of the local jeweler was primarily that of selling at retail and repairing watches (Jones 1937).*

Specialty stores had buying advantages over general stores because owners could purchase in large amounts; by not having as many product lines to manage, these owners could be more adept in finding the best sources of supply. In addition, specialty-store owners had better knowledge of the goods they carried and could sell them more effectively. Since specialty-store proprietors had expertise with regard to the merchandise itself and the sources of supply, risk was reduced. This aided the specialty store in offering lower prices than the general store (Jones 1937). The pioneering U.S. discount stores really emerged in the mid-1800s, not in the 1930s, as often reported.

Then, what appears to have been a general store—evolving into a department store—operated in Springfield, Illinois, in 1851. Instead of heading the different classes of merchandise as dry goods, grocery, hardware, queensware, etc., the different product groups were headed as dry goods department, grocery department, and provision department. Hats, shoes, and furnishings were included in the grocery department. If this store had accounting and controls by departments, it could correctly have been called a department store (Jones 1937).

By the 1860s, Macy's, Wanamaker, Stewarts, and Zion's were operating the first true U.S. department stores. And during the late 1800s, Montgomery Ward and Sears, Roebuck and Co. began their general-merchandise mail-order catalogs.

During the twentieth century, the steady evolution of U.S. retailing has continued. Variety stores began to flourish in the early 1900s, Southland started the first convenience store in 1928, King Kullen opened the first supermarket in 1930, Masters opened the first modern discount store in 1937, and Allied Stores built the first regional shopping center in 1950.

The 1960s saw the birth of Kmart, Wal-Mart, and Target as discounters; the blossoming of fast-food restaurants, led by McDonald's; the growth of franchising; and the introduction of furniture warehouses and catalog showrooms. Since the 1970s, we have seen such retail formats as superstores, "category killer" specialty retailers, membership clubs, factory outlet malls, home shopping networks, and video kiosks.

Just as their predecessors did, present-day retailers are facing challenges, but they have an array of tools with which to deal with them. Insightful, adaptive institutional formats and individual firms should flourish in the period ahead. Nonadaptive institutions and individual firms will have a tough go of it—just as others did 400, 200, and 50 years ago.

THE CURRENT STATUS OF U.S. RETAILING

In the following sections, we will analyze the present state of U.S. retailing by reviewing various fundamental retailing concepts. We will also discuss strategic implications for the future as they relate to each concept.

The Wheel of Retailing

About 35 years ago, McNair and Hollander introduced the wheel of retailing to describe the evolution of institutional formats from discount-oriented innovators to mature medium and upper-end firms. According to the wheel, innovators often begin as low-priced, low-cost, no-frills firms. As they succeed, they add services, upgrade merchandise offerings, and so on to expand their markets and increase profit margins. When they mature and move up the wheel, they leave room for newer low-end innovators to enter (McNair 1958; Hollander 1960; Brown 1990).

The theory relies on four tenets: (1) price-conscious consumers are often willing to forgo services, wide selections, and convenient locations; (2) price-conscious consumers switch stores to secure the best prices; (3) because of operating flexibility and lower fixed costs, many new retail institutions are more efficient than existing firms; and (4) companies want to move up the wheel to broaden their customer base, increase gross profit margins, and enhance store image.

Although critics say that the basic theory is too narrow in focus, that not all retail innovators begin at the low end of the wheel, that some institutional forms have been relatively stable over time (regarding low-end/high-end orientation), and that some retailers (such as Sears) have tried to move back down the wheel, the concept should be understood in the context of the U.S. retailing environment of the 1990s.

As shown in Exhibit 1, there are three fundamental strategic positions along the wheel: low end, medium, and high end. The real value to the concept is not in assessing whether low-end retailers evolve into mature high-end retailers, but in seeing that there are three price/cost/service strategic orientations from which executives may choose.

Each orientation requires that a firm make tradeoffs with regard to customer services, products offered, location, profit margins, and so on. In particular, low-end retailing requires fewer customer services and lower operating costs than high-end retailing. Because different consumer groups desire different retailer orientations, both discount-oriented and upscale firms have opportunities—as long as they are viewed by customers as providing good value or having distinctive offerings. Yet, a growing number of U.S. consumers feel that low-end retailers are better able to address their needs (good quality at "fair" prices) than medium- and high-end retailers.

It is more meaningful for low-end firms to show how they differ from high-end ones—and vice versa—than for them to move along the wheel. In today's price-oriented environment, discounters should be hesitant to move up the wheel.

Retailers with medium strategies are less apt to be seen as distinctive than low- or high-end firms, even if logic might lead us to conclude that most customers would be lured to this strategy. To the

EXHIBIT 1. The Wheel of Retailing

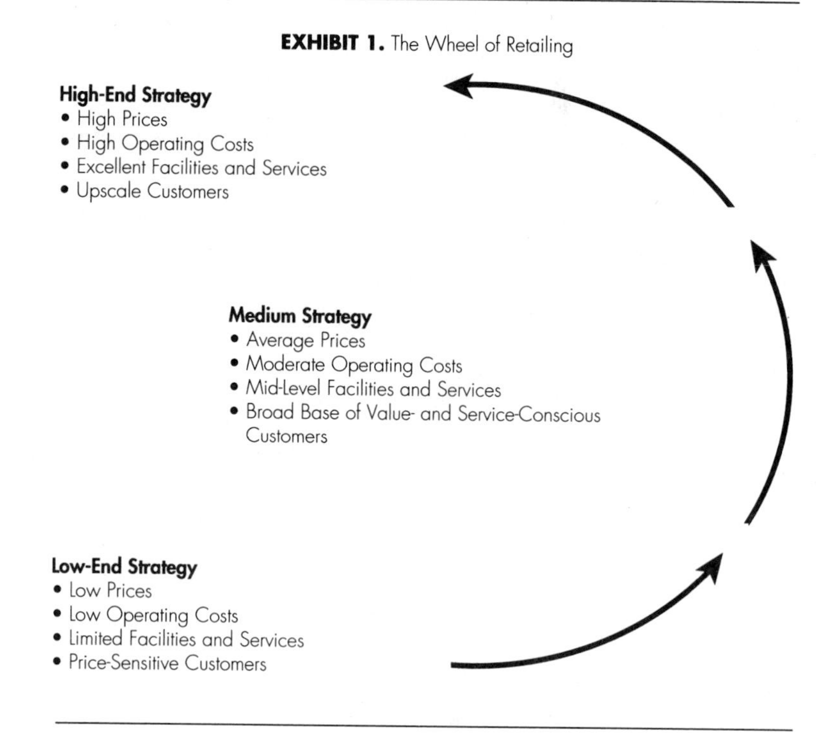

contrary, consumers often think the retailers have a poor value for the dollar and sell "me-too" products.

Multiple store formats can be operated under different names if a single retailer wants to enact both low- and high-end strategies. This is being done by Dayton Hudson, which has traditional department stores as well as the discount-oriented Target and Mervyn's.

A clear and stable position on the wheel will let a firm keep a loyal customer following. Going in either direction along the wheel is more apt to result in confusion and a lack of distinctiveness than a wider customer following. This was illustrated by the demise of W.T. Grant and E.J. Korvette.

Scrambled Merchandising

Firms in the general merchandise category account for about 14 percent of overall U.S. retail sales (excluding groceries). This means that seven-eighths of sales are made by companies classified as specialty retailers. Yet, despite the strength of specialty retailers, a countertrend known as scrambled merchandising has been gaining over the past 20 years. With scrambled merchandising, a firm adds product lines or services not related to one another or the firm's original business.

EXHIBIT 2. The Aggressive Nature of Scrambled Merchandising

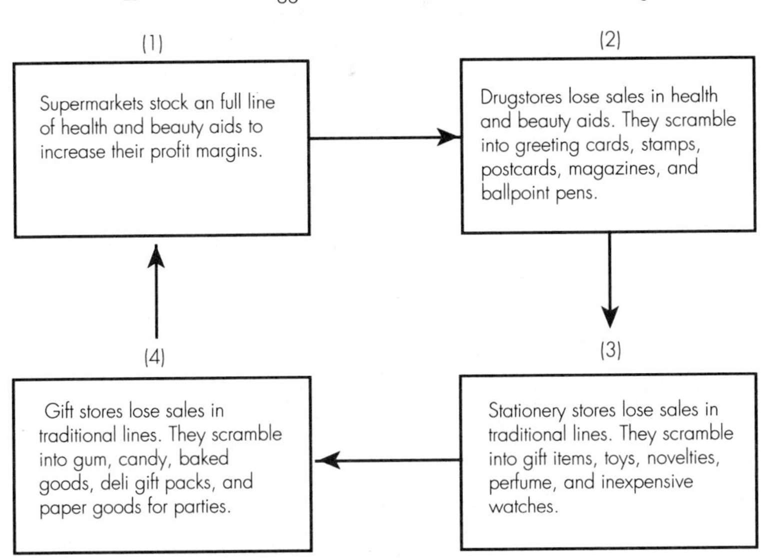

(1)
Supermarkets stock an full line of health and beauty aids to increase their profit margins.
(2)
Drugstores lose sales in health and beauty aids. They scramble into greeting cards, stamps, postcards, magazines, and ballpoint pens.
(3)
Stationery stores lose sales in traditional lines. They scramble into gift items, toys, novelties, perfume, and inexpensive watches.
(4)
Gift stores lose sales in traditional lines. They scramble into gum, candy, baked goods, deli gift packs, and paper goods for parties.

Source: Joel R. Evans and Barry Berman (1992), *Marketing*, 5th ed., New York: Macmillan, p. 413.

All kinds of retailers, such as convenience stores renting videos, have stepped up their use of scrambled merchandising: it raises total store sales; often stimulates impulse purchases; high-markup items are usually added; people spend more per shopping trip; one-stop shopping is facilitated; it is often a defensive tactic brought on by competitors' adding lines; and the effects of seasonality may be lessened.

Shortcomings may be associated with excessive use of this practice. It can be costly because investments rise, and consumers may be turned off and store image blurred if too many unrelated lines are carried. Firms may have a broad assortment without real depth or selection, except in the area of specialization. Firms may add items for which they have no buying or selling expertise. Opportunity costs must be weighed: "If we add item x to the product assortment, we may be unable to afford y." And, scrambled merchandising could be a very aggressive strategy because it may virtually force other firms to scramble in response, with a result similar to a price war (see Exhibit 2).

Power Retailing

In 1987, *Business Week* coined the term power retailing, saying that (Dunkin, Oneal, and Phillips): Power retailers "are fast and focused. Merchandise is well-selected and plentiful. Customers go out of their way to shop at power retailers' stores because they know they'll find what they want with a minimum of hassles. Charles Lazarus of Toys "Я" Us and Leslie H. Wexner of The Limited, Inc., have shown that power retailing can work in specialty formats. Sam M. Walton has applied it to his Wal-Mart discount stores. Now, David C. Farrell of May is showing that power retailing can bring a new nimbleness to the clay-footed giants of retailing—old-line department stores."

Power retailers use a consistent, directed, comprehensive approach. They identify customer needs and pay attention to the marketplace; place orders early and in volume, emphasizing "power assortments" to dominate competitors; and use modern computer and inventory-control systems. Some critics feel the major weakness of power retailing is that management policies are too often standardized and centralized (Dunkin, Oneal, and Phillips 1987): "The key to surviving will be using power systems to usher in new ideas, not to prop up old ones."

Power shopping centers feature a number of power retailers, like Federated Electronics Superstore, Marshall's, Home Depot, Nordstrom Rack, and Wherehouse Entertainment Center. Or, they focus on one product category, such as auto care, with an auto-glass replacement shop, a phone retailer, an oil-change firm, a muffler shop, a foreign car mechanic, an electronics firm, and a radiator installer (Felgner 1988; Razzano 1989).

Every executive should learn this principle from studying the concept of power retailing: to be most effective in the marketplace, a firm needs to be dominant in at least one aspect of its strategy. In the broadest sense, power could result from having the longest store hours, the best delivery policy, and so on. As a result, a small firm could be a power retailer by satisfying an unfulfilled consumer need.

At the same time, a retailer needs to recognize consumers' minimum expectations for each element of its strategy mix. For instance, working women expect stores to have evening hours; this is a minimum requirement. Even if a retailer is dominant in other areas of its strategy mix, it must still satisfy the minimum standards set by consumers.

Here are six ways for a firm to act as a power retailer:

1. be price oriented and cost efficient to appeal to price-sensitive shoppers;
2. be upscale to appeal to full-service, status-conscious consumers;
3. be convenience oriented to appeal to consumers interested in nearby locations, shopping ease, or long store hours;
4. offer a dominant product assortment to appeal to consumers interested in variety and in-store comparisons;
5. be customer service-oriented to appeal to people frustrated by the decline in retail service (as they perceive it); or

6. be innovative or exclusive and provide a unique method of operations (such as video kiosks at airports) or carry products/brands not stocked by other stores to appeal to customers who are innovators, bored, or looking for items not in the "me too" mold.

Two or more of the approaches could be combined to yield even greater power.

Retail firms will probably not succeed in the long run if they are mid-level in all of the six areas just identified; they must do a superior job in at least one. The level of competition will be too intense for them to act otherwise. It should also be noted that a price-oriented strategy may be the easiest for competitors to duplicate, at least in the short run, and that price-sensitive shoppers often have little store loyalty.

The Retail Life Cycle

Davidson, Bates, and Bass introduced the concept of the retail life cycle in 1976. According to this theory, retail institutional types move through identifiable life cycles, comprising four distinct stages:

1. During *innovation,* a new institutional format strongly departs from the strategy mixes of existing formats in at least one key element. The new institution usually has few direct competitors, has an entrepreneurial management style, seeks to generate rapid consumer acceptance, and undergoes a rapid rise in sales—but long-run success is not assured. Video kiosks and hypermarkets are now in the innovation stage in the United States.
2. In *accelerated development,* customer acceptance grows and innovators expand. Direct competitors enter. Sales for the format rise strongly, and investment costs are high. The major goal is to establish preemptive market positions. Large category killer stores and factory outlet malls are in the accelerated development stage in the United States.
3. At *maturity,* there are many direct and indirect competitors for an institutional format. Growth is moderate to slow, and firms face excess capacity, overstoring, and management structures that may be stretched too thin. The key goal is to prolong maturity as long as possible by fine-tuning the basic format in response to new competitors. Traditional department stores and fast-food hamburger outlets are now in the maturity stage in the United States.
4. In *decline,* a format loses popularity. Consumers turn to emerging institutions (indirect competitors). Many firms abandon the old format, thus reducing direct competition. Without major strategy modifications, sales will continue to drop. Variety stores and small conventional supermarkets are now in the decline stage in the United States.

By applying the retail-life cycle concept, the status of a company's institutional format can be assessed and appropriate plans may be developed. If a firm has a format in the introduction or growth phase, it will be able to count on the rising popularity of that format for its own short-term growth, aided by its own strategic efforts. If a firm has a format in the maturity or decline stage, it will need to achieve two goals. First, it must break out of the pack and be viewed as truly distinctive by consumers; the popularity of the format itself will not enable individual retailers to keep growing. Second, strategy revisions must be implemented, combining the best elements of the original format with selected elements from emerging ones.

Executives also can better appreciate the impact of both direct and indirect competitors on their performance and act at the appropriate time if they study the retail life cycle. Direct competitors have the same institutional format. Indirect competitors have different formats but are nonetheless capable of taking sales away from one another. Too often, executives focus on direct competitors and do not recognize the threats posed by new indirect competitors until it is too late. This must change, with the competition being defined more broadly.

Finally, executives need to determine when to turn from stimulating sales growth to managing mature businesses and retaining loyal customers, rather than searching for new ones. Consumers can be bored with mature formats and be motivated to try new ones unless the former become more exciting to them.

Retail Positioning

Retail positioning involves how consumers perceive institutional formats and individual firms and their attributes (Berman and Evans 1992). When an institution or individual firm is new, it must communicate its attributes to consumers: What is its basic strategy mix? What is its marketplace niche? What customers are sought? How is it better than competitors? After a niche is established, a firm must reinforce its image. Once people position a retailer, perceptions may be hard to affect.

A retail strategy should reflect ideal points, competitive positioning, and company positioning. An ideal point embodies the optimal strategy for a given customer group in a given situation. For example, a shopping-oriented clothing customer would stress merchandise selection and salesperson expertise in describing an ideal store. Yet, a shopping-oriented clothing consumer could also be a convenience-oriented dry cleaning consumer. A firm will best succeed if its strategy mix is seen by target consumers as relatively near the consumers' ideal.

Competitive positioning refers to how an institution or individual firm is viewed relative to competitors—the aim is to be more ideal. In the battle between traditional department stores and discount department stores, each is striving for a desirable and unique image in consumers' minds. To be seen as having desirable attributes *or* as being unique would not be sufficient; both factors are necessary for long-run success.

Company positioning refers to how consumers view different strategy mixes within an institutional format (like hamburger versus chicken-based fast-food restaurants) as well as how they perceive different stores operated by the same retailer (like one firm operating both department stores and specialty stores). An institutional format or individual retailer must be aware of how its various entities are perceived and ensure that each offers desirable features, is unique, and does not lead to customer confusion or too much overlap with its other stores. A goal might be to appeal to complementary customer groups and take shoppers from competitors, but not to cannibalize one's own sales. Each store in an institutional format or operated by a single retailer should be positioned near an ideal point and not be clustered too near one another in the consumer's mind.

When undertaking any activities, an executive should ask: Is this action consistent with our image? Are we appealing to customer ideal points? Does the consumer see how we differ from competitors—in a desirable and unique manner? Are our various formats seen as distinct from one another? Exhibit 3 presents an example of retail positioning. In actuality, more than the two factors depicted in this figure go into positioning.

We must remember that *consumer* perceptions of a retailer are critical—not the firm's belief about its position. There are two possible reasons why a consumer may not view a firm in the way intended, and each needs an appropriate action. First, consumers may see a strategy mix as undesirable ("prices are high") or undistinctive ("other stores carry the same items"). The firm must then reposition itself by changing components of its strategy. Second, consumers may misperceive a strategy and thus misposition it. For example, consumers may feel a firm sells conservative clothing when it is really fashion forward. The firm then needs to better communicate with consumers.

These are some ways for retail firms to get positioning messages across in a cluttered marketplace:

- Rely more on mailings and phone calls and less on newspapers.
- Have more special events—not just sales, but theme days, exclusive/special buys, etc. to generate excitement. For example, some shopping centers and individual firms encourage parents and their children to trick-or-treat there during Halloween. This service benefits both retailer and consumer.
- Key some special events to non-holiday and non-prime seasons when competitors may be off-guard.
- Place more emphasis on activities aimed at current customers—private showings of new merchandise, free gifts to acknowledge steady customer patronage, "friendship" phone calls to customers who have purchased a certain amount during a given time period, and "outreach" phone calls to former customers who are no longer shopping there or who are buying infrequently.

Collectively, U.S. retail firms can do much better in communicating with current customers.

EXHIBIT 3. An Example of Retail Positioning

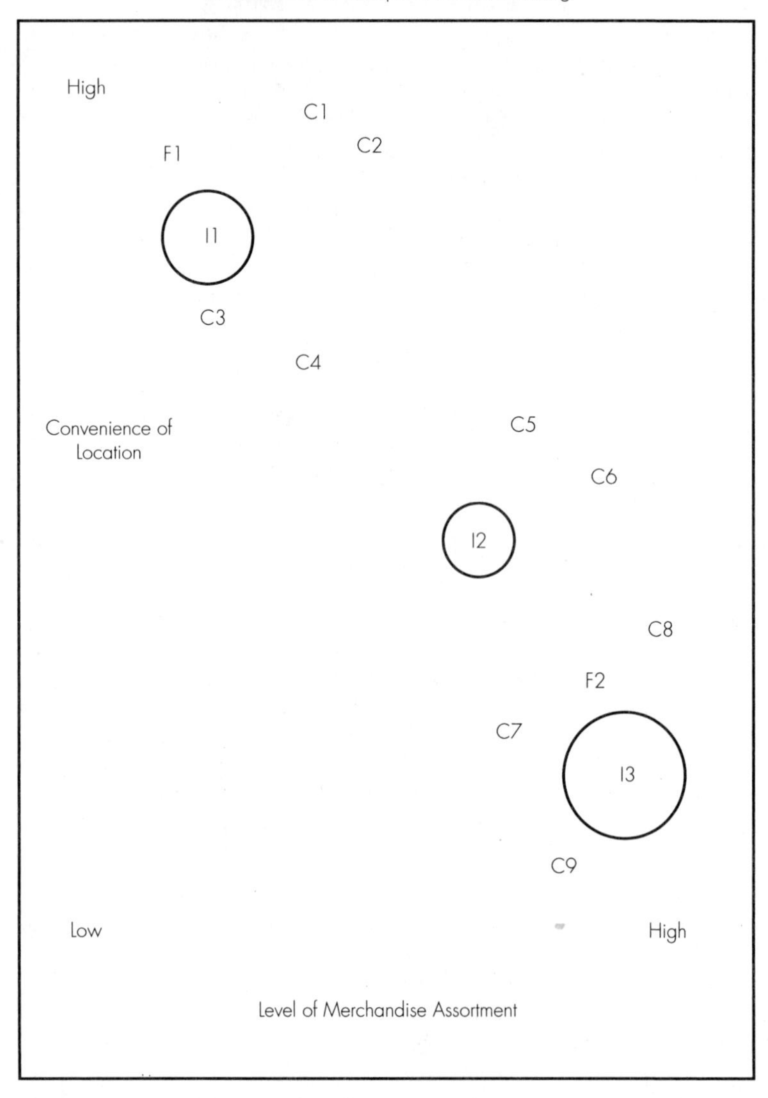

Note: (1) I1 to I3 are consumers' perceived ideal points. The circles' sizes signify the consumers in each segment. (2) C1 to C8 are consumer perceptions of a retailer's competitors. (3) F1 and F2 are the perceptions of the two store formats operated by a single retailer.

In this figure, there are three distinct market segments, with competitors aiming at each. C4 is the poorest positioned of the competitors (being between I1 and I2). The retailer (F1 and F2) has a good approach, aiming at distinct segments with tailored combinations of convenience/assortment.

Expansion/Merger Strategies

The largest U.S. retailers have been steadily increasing their share of total retail sales. In 1960, single-unit firms accounted for two-thirds of the total; they now account for less than half. In 1960, chain retailers operating 100 or more units accounted for about 15 percent of sales. These several hundred retailers now account for 30 percent of the total.

Expansion has taken two forms: internal growth and mergers. With internal growth, companies add stores in new markets, introduce new store formats, become involved in mail-order and telephone sales, construct bigger facilities, and so on. Internal growth has been the more traditional way of expanding. With mergers, expansion is fueled by acquiring other firms. This alternative has grown in popularity in recent years.

Despite the advantages of both types of expansion (in terms of sales growth, retail positioning, economies of scale, and so on), the burgeoning use of expansion strategies among U.S. firms has a number of limitations or potential limitations:

- The emphasis on sales growth has caused some firms to grow too quickly or to place too little weight on other goals.
- Rapid expansion can lead to insufficient availability of senior executives to manage a firm. This is exacerbated with conglomerate expansion, when a firm opens new store formats with which it has little experience or acquires new formats.
- Leveraged buyouts (LBOs) frequently lead to high levels of debt, and resources are used to meet financial obligations rather than invested in the business. LBOs may result in the sale of some superior store divisions to meet short-run debt payments.
- Potential long-run problems with a firm's basic strategy may be overlooked if it is to expansion-oriented. Some retailers pay too much attention to companywide sales growth, obscuring low same-store sales growth, with the companywide increase due to the greater number of stores in a chain.
- Operating flexibility and entrepreneurial drive may fall if a firm expands too much. And previously served small market niches may be ignored if they do not yield enough high sales.
- A firm's positioning may blur if it expands too much, seeks too many market segments, or engages heavily in a middle-of-the-road strategy to stimulate sales volume.
- By opening megastores, larger companies may be giving smaller ones a long-term opening, albeit a narrow one. Many consumers already perceive some chains as impersonal and their stores as too big; these people may be increasingly attracted to the friendly, more intimate ambience of smaller stores.

Executives must carefully weigh how much expansion and how fast. They should consider such issues as their own ability to manage growth, personnel availability, their firms' changing nature as they grow, the firms' ability to handle the debt from expansion, the desirability of internal growth versus mergers, and the focus on sales-driven versus profit-driven goals.

Operational Factors

Today's typical retail firm is far more efficient and its executives and other personnel are far better informed than those of a decade ago—and this will continue in the future.

Strategically, retail companies are now more apt to use a formal budgeting process and plan expenditures by category. For instance, many firms allocate personnel costs so that they have a specified number of employees on the selling floor during different times of the day.

Executives are focusing more on productivity issues than their predecessors did. Their fundamental question is: How can sales and profit goals be reached while controlling costs? Different retail formats have distinct resource requirements regarding store location, fixtures, personnel, and so on; thus, productivity measures must be related to norms for each type of format (like department stores versus discount stores).

With regard to inventory management, many more executives are now quite systematic and thorough in planning and take into account order lead time; stock turnover; demand variability; sales per square foot; and the tradeoffs between a fast-turnover, low-inventory-on-hand approach and a low-turnover, high-inventory-on-hand approach. Lots of firms are applying quick response inventory planning, whereby they have close supplier relations, place frequent small orders, and shift more responsibility for inventory handling to suppliers.

Inventory planning efforts are facilitated by the range of available computer-oriented tools, such as Universal Product Code markings, electronic data interchange, store-based PCs and minicomputers, and low-priced software. Computerization is also enabling firms to be more efficient in virtually all aspects of operations. Chain headquarters readily communicate with branch outlets, data are stored for future use in retail information systems, energy systems are adjusted during the day, employee schedules are coordinated, and payrolls are administered.

In sum, retailers have done an excellent job in improving their operational effectiveness. Yet, many firms could do better in linking their budgets to performance goals and to those tasks required to attain them. Too often, budgets are based on prior year expenditures rather than on performance goals. Firms could also increase their use of the inexpensive and user-friendly computer software that is available. Lastly, firms must be quite careful in one area of operations: self-service. They must weigh the low costs of self-service versus the consumer needs for and expectations of personal attention.

Financial Measures

In analyzing financial performance, U.S. retailers have used a host of measures, ranging from annual sales growth to expense/sales ratios to gross margin return on investment. The industrywide and categorical data provided in various trade publications have eased these analyses. In the context of this chapter, four aspects of financial performance measurement merit discussion.

First, firms should not assess performance by studying just one financial criterion, no matter how important the criterion. To do so could cause executives to overlook opportunities or problem areas. A combination of measures should be used, with each keyed to preset goals or performance standards.

For example, in 1989, *Chain Store Age Executive* and the Management Horizons consulting firm introduced a composite retail performance index (Forseter): "The median performance for all public U.S. companies was assigned an index value. Return on assets, assigned an index value of 100, was weighted at twice the level of sales growth and profit growth, both of which had individual index values of 50. (The overall median performance index for all U.S. retailers was 200.)"

Second, performance needs to be reviewed on a comparative basis, such as year to year, department to department, and firm to industry. Comparing firm performance against industry norms can be particularly valuable.

The *Chain Store Age Executive*/Management Horizons index can further illustrate this point (Forseter 1989): "Each firm's performance can be indexed to the median. For example, if the median return on assets (ROA) for all public retailers was 5.4% and a firm had an average ROA of 11.6%, it would have an ROA index of 215 (11.6/5.4 = 2.15 × 100 = 215). The composite index is the sum of the individual indices." The 1985-1990 medians were compound revenue growth, 11.6%; compound profit growth, 12.4%; and average ROA, 4.2% ("High Performance Retailers Led by Rebounder" 1991). *Chain Store Executive* publishes an annual listing of high performance retailers.

Third, many firms are underusing such emerging measurement tools as direct product profitability (DPP). With DPP, a firm computes the profitability of each merchandise category or unit by determining adjusted per-unit gross margin and assigning direct product costs for warehousing, transportation, handling, selling, etc. Then, the appropriate markup for each category or item is set. Despite DPP's advantages in financial planning, its complexity and the difficulty in allocating costs have deterred executives from using it (Robins 1987; Donegan 1988).

Fourth, the full implications of financial measures must be understood. This may be illustrated by the concept of return on net worth (RNW), which has been misused by some retail firms. RNW consists of three individual measures: asset turnover (net sales/total assets); profit margin (net profit/net sales); and financial leverage (total assets/net worth). RNW equals asset turnover × profit margin × financial leverage.

The error made by some executives is that they do not separate the three components; they just analyze overall RNW. This is a poor approach because a high overall RNW may obscure mediocre performance across all three measures. In the worst case, superior performance in one area may cloud problems in the others. By separately studying asset turnover and profit margin, a firm could also determine whether it is following a relatively consistent strategy (for example, rapid stock turnover with low profit margins). Finally, a high overall RNW may occur simply because a firm is too leveraged. Rather than recognizing that it is debt heavy, a firm might mistakenly feel it is doing well because of its superior RNW.

Labor Force Needs

U.S. retailers employ millions of people; thus, there is an ongoing need to attract new employees as well as to motivate and retain existing ones. Over the last decade, however, the available number of workers aged 16 to 24 has dropped by more than 10 percent. This trend will continue for a while longer.

Retail firms also must deal with a special human resource environment, due to the large number of inexperienced workers and part-time workers, long hours, high employee visibility, and variations in customer demand. These elements can make difficult employee hiring, staffing, and supervision.

To attract and retain good workers, many companies have instituted progressive employment practices. These include paying salaries well above the minimum wage, using financial incentives in compensation (such as commissions rather than salaries alone), providing for transportation to and from the job, setting up child-care arrangements for working parents, seeking out nontraditional workers (such as retirees), and offering bonuses to current employees bringing in new workers.

Although numerous companies have been farsighted in seeking new employees and retaining existing ones, the industry can still do better. Many firms have not been as effective as they should be in luring new college graduates or in developing career tracks that young people will view as long-run "careers" rather than short-run "jobs." Retailers must determine why this is occurring, and they need to interact more with colleges and universities. How many retail companies have surveyed college students to determine their perceptions of retail careers *and* sought to address the issues that such surveys could uncover? When it comes to personnel issues, most retailers are usually internally driven; they do not ask potential members of their labor force what they could do to attract and retain them. Yet many of these same firms conduct regular consumer surveys.

To motivate existing employees, retailers could increase the use of job rotation, where workers are regularly rotated among different positions to reduce boredom. To better deal with the problem of employee scheduling in peak and nonpeak hours, firms could increase the use of cross-training, where employees learn the tasks required to perform two or more jobs and are assigned on an as-needed basis.

Locational Strategies

Let us examine four key aspects of locational strategies in retailing.

First, the concept of retail store saturation has several ramifications besides the negative one arising from excessive competition. Executives must be careful not to reach premature conclusions about particular sites. Although too many overall retail facilities may exist in some locales, the opportunities there may not be poor if (1) individual product categories are underrepresented (such as too many shoe stores but too few restaurants); or (2) certain types of retailers within product categories are underrepresented (such as too many upscale women's shoe stores but too few upscale men's shoe stores).

An understored locale could conceivably yield worse results for a retail firm than an overstored locale because consumer desires for adequate product assortments from which to choose, comparison shopping, one-stop shopping, and other factors may not be satisfied. Accordingly, an understored location may not be appropriate if customer traffic is not drawn to it.

Trading-area overlap, which involves the proximity of two or more shopping areas to one another and the degree to which they interchange customers, has implications when executives study the full range of competition faced by their firms and when they plan sites for new stores. If a single firm locates two or more outlets in close proximity, it may gain efficiency in operations, economies in inventory management, and better use of mass media. However, it could also oversaturate the marketplace and reduce the sales potential for each outlet.

To reduce the effects of market saturation, some retailers are entering understored areas that they avoided in the past, such as rural markets. Others are placing more emphasis on international retailing, unconventional sites (such as outlets on university campuses), and/or opening two or more different stores at one site (a tactic used by various fast-food firms).

Second, in the United States, the planned shopping center has reached the maturity stage of the retail life cycle. For many consumers, shopping centers no longer hold the excitement they once did. In response, more centers are introducing new services and amenities, sponsoring special events, arranging for customer transportation, and so on.

Because a lot of shopping centers have been open for 25 to 30 years or longer, they have recently undergone or will soon be undergoing extensive renovations. Otherwise, newer shopping facilities will take away a lot of their shoppers. Every year, U.S. centers invest heavily to enclose open-air shopping malls, update store premises and pedestrian areas, expand parking, attract "hot" new retailers, and so on. This massive effort is similar to the one undertaken earlier by downtown central business districts (CBDs) and shows how history repeats itself.

Like other formats in maturity, the traditional shopping center has spawned popular derivatives such as off-price centers, power centers, factory-outlet centers, and anchorless centers with no dominant retailer. Each derivative wants to position itself as desirable and distinctive in consumers' minds.

Third, nonstore retailing is more popular among store-based retailers because many firms now look at mail-order and phone sales as essential revenue sources. Nonstore retailing lets the firms easily and inexpensively reach new geographic markets, offers shopping convenience for customers, gains impulse purchases, and improves operating efficiency. Virtually all retailers should look to the potential represented by nonstore sales.

Fourth, there have been exciting advances in the computer-mapping techniques used to portray retail trading areas. For relatively low investments, firms can buy full-color, computer-generated maps depicting population, retailing, and other community traits. The maps provide good data for executive decision making. The Census Bureau's TIGER database of areas' physical characteristics can be quite valuable for retailers.

The Internationalization of Retailing

Two trends involving the internationalization of retailing have received considerable attention: the "invasion" of foreign companies into the United States and the rise of international retailing by U.S.-based firms. Yet, these two trends have been going on for years.

Due to the size and affluence of the United States, foreign firms have been "invading" for decades. For example, Brenninkmeyer of the Netherlands invested in Ohrbach's in 1962. It is the pace of the acquisitions of U.S. retailers by foreign firms that has accelerated recently—this trend will likely continue in the future. Also, such foreign-based firms as Ikea, The Body Shop, and Carrefour will open more of their own U.S. outlets.

Likewise, U.S.-based retailers have had an international presence for years. For instance, in 1972, Southland opened the first convenience store in Japan, and McDonald's has introduced the concept of fast-food into many nations around the world.

U.S.-based retailers now have chances in markets that were previously closed to them. Thus the worldwide opportunities for aggressive U.S.-based firms are enormous. And many are taking advantage of these opportunities by opening outlets in such areas as eastern Europe, the Russian republics, and Latin America. The near future will see explosive retail growth.

Although the influx of foreign firms in the United States is something of a threat to traditional U.S.-based retailers, the latter can learn a lot by studying the practices of such firms as Tengelmann of Germany, Jusco of Japan, and Ikea of Sweden—and then adapt their strategies accordingly.

When operating outside their home markets, retailers must be careful in their approach. Firms should use domestic experts for such key business tasks as selecting store sites, training personnel, and displaying products. Also critical is tracking consumer trends because buying habits vary by nation ("Foreign Retailers Recruit U.S. Talent" 1987; "Foreign Firms Invest in U.S. Retail Chains" 1987): "What similarities, if any, are there between operating a U.S. retailing company and one in a foreign market? How many of the same systems and operating methods can be used by the two different entities?"

GENERAL CONCLUSIONS AND RECOMMENDATIONS

It is imperative that executives understand the dynamics of retailing's environment. Clearly, no one can anticipate all the possible events that may occur or successfully deal with all potential occurrences, such as a competitor starting a price war or a supplier having a strike. Yet, five things can be done to maximize the chances for long-term success in retailing.

Monitor Events

Executives need to systematically monitor any short-run events that could have an impact on immediate performance, such as the consumer price index and the actions of competitors as well as the emerging long-term environmental trends that could have an effect down the road (pending U.S. and state governmental actions, changing consumer demographics and lifestyles, and the influx of new institutional formats).

While doing this, executives should draft contingency plans to deal with best-case, medium-case, and worst-case scenarios. If planning is *evolutionary* (with on-going incremental strategy revisions) and not *stagnant* (with intransigent postures taken) or *revolutionary* (with companies being surprised by changes in the environment and then having to develop procedures to deal with them) in nature, executives will be much better able to respond to customer needs and the outside environment.

Plan Strategically

Retailers need broad strategic plans that regularly address such questions as: What business are we in? Are we satisfying a loyal group of target customers? Where are we positioned now? Where are we heading? What are our *internal* strengths and weaknesses and the *external* opportunities and threats we face?

Executives must be customer oriented; have a coordinated, integrated strategy; and have clear, attainable goals. Since many shoppers feel customer service is the biggest weakness of retailers, perceptions must be improved in this area.

Whether a retail company is upscale or discount oriented, employee courtesy toward shoppers must be the *minimum* customer service offered. Beyond this, a firm must provide the degree of customer service appropriate for its strategy mix.

Be Open-Minded

Executives should be open-minded and not wed to traditional ways of doing business. A poor approach is to say: "We'll never run a sale, never carry private-label merchandise, never accept a bank credit card, never open on Sundays, never use mail-order catalogs, and never add or delete certain product lines." A better approach would be to evaluate each issue separately and reconsider them as environmental factors change.

Project the Proper Position and Image

Each retail company must have a clear, desirable, unique, believable, and relatively stable position and image in the minds of its customers and potential customers.

Develop Customer Databases

More firms should develop customer databases (lists of names and addresses). They can be manually compiled, computerized, or bought from database specialists. Even small firms can set up their own databases.

Databases aid in soliciting possible customers, increasing purchase consumption, improving communications with regular customers, identifying those most apt to buy particular items, and determining how much individual customers spend and the last time that the purchases were made. Mailings can be targeted and even aimed at past customers to win them back.

REFERENCES

Berman, Barry and Joel R. Evans (1992), *Retail Management: A Strategic Approach*, fifth ed. New York: Macmillan.

Bridenbaugh, Carl A. (1938), *Cities in the Wilderness*. New York: Ronald.

Brown, Stephen (1990), "The Wheel of Retailing: Past and Future," *Journal of Retailing*, 66 (Summer), 143–149.

Davidson, William R., Albert D. Bates, and Stephen F. Bass (1976), "The Retail Life Cycle," *Harvard Business Review*, 54 (November-December), 89–96.

Donegan, Priscilla (1988), "DPP: Still Slow Going," *Progressive Grocer* (December), 39–45.

Dunkin, Amy, Michael Oneal, and Stephen Phillips (1987), "Power Retailers," *Business Week* (December), 86–92.

Felgner, Brent H. (1988), "Power Centers Pack Punch in Mature Market," *Marketing News* (December), 1, 10–11.

"Foreign Firms Invest in U.S. Retail Chain" (1987), *Chain Store Age Executive* (September), 58.

"Foreign Retailers Recruit U.S. Talent" (1987), *Marketing News* (March 13), 12.

Forseter, Murray (1989), "High Performance Retailers," *Chain Store Age Executive* (August), 14–17.

"High Performers Led by Rebounder" (1991), *Chain Store Age Executive* (November), 33–36.

Hollander, Stanley C. (1960), "The Wheel of Retailing," *Journal of Marketing*, 25 (July), 37–42.

Jones, Fred M. (1937), *Middlemen in the Domestic Trade of the United States, 1800-1860*. Urbana: University of Illinois.

McNair, Malcolm P. (1958), "Significant Trends and Developments in the Postwar Period," in *Competitive Distribution in a Free High Level Economy and Its Implications for the University*, A. B. Smith, ed. Pittsburgh: University of Pittsburgh Press, 17–18.

Razzano, Rhonda (1989), "Growth of Car-Care Malls Accelerates," *Chain Store Age Executive* (January), 33, 37.

Robins, Gary (1988), "Not Only for Groceries," *Stores* (July), 48–52.

"31 Major Trends Shaping the Future of American Business" (1988), *The Public Pulse*, 2 (1), 1.

Zinn, Laura et al. (1990), "Retailing: Who Will Survive?" *Business Week* (November 26), 134–144.

Norman D. Axelrad
President
The Franchising Board, LTD
Former partner, Axelrad and Edwards
Chairman, Your Own Business, Inc.
Chicago, Illinois

Robert E. Weigand
Professor of Marketing
University of Illinois at Chicago
Chicago, Illinois

CHAPTER 50

FRANCHISING—A MARRIAGE OF SYSTEM MEMBERS

It is nearly impossible to live everyday life in America without dealing with franchises. We eat at Wendy's, sleep in a Marriot hotel, rent cars from Hertz, and primp our hair at Hair Care. We have our lawns manicured by Lawn Doctor, take our work break at Coffee Beanery, meet new friends at Great Expectations, and buy used golf clubs from Play It Again Sports. Franchising—now called an industry—is just about everywhere.[1]

FRANCHISING—VARIOUSLY DEFINED

There are substantial distinctions among types of franchises. First, *product distribution franchise* systems are those where a supplier of goods or services license selected outlets to purchase the supplier's products; the outlets are licensed to use the supplier's trade name and/or trade marks. Franchisors of such systems earn the bulk of their profits by selling goods or services to their outlets. There is no promise of exclusivity on either side; suppliers may sell to several retailers in a particular geographic area while the retailers make no promise they will sell only a single brand.

For example, an electronics store in downtown Cleveland stocks radios, TVs, microwave ovens, and stereos from Sony, Matsushita, Zenith, and General Electric. There are several other retailers within a few hundred yards selling much the same brands. The channel system is rather loose, meaning the outlets are not chosen with great care and the manufacturer provides no powerful incentive for reseller loyalty. Another example is America's automobile manufacturers that sell through retailers who may be licensed outlets for several competing makes. The word "franchising" is used rather loosely, meaning simply that the retailers abide by the sales and service policies established by their suppliers. But they also have divided their loyalties among their various suppliers.

Second, *business format franchises* consist of a tightly knit group of enterprises whose systematic operations are planned, directed, and controlled by the operation's innovator, generally called a "franchisor." The central focus of this chapter is business format franchising.

FORMAT FRANCHISES—THREE TRAITS

Because of early franchising abuses, business format franchises have been subjected to ample government regulations. The result has been a general understanding of the term's meaning. Business format franchises have three widely-accepted criteria, which, if met, will subject the business relationship to federal and state regulations.

Shared Intellectual Property

First, the business format franchisor owns a trade or service mark that it is willing to share with those it has licensed in return for royalty payments. The mark need not be well known when first used, but there is the general expectation that it eventually will gain substantial customer recognition.

Payment for the Right to be a System Member

Second, the franchisee must have paid for the right to be part of the system. Federal law declares that an initial payment of $500 within six months of the agreement satisfies this criterion. However, some state laws are tougher, holding that payment of only $100 brings a business relationship within the "required payment" test of a business format franchise. Indirect payments in the business relationship will also satisfy this test.

Being Part of a Working System

Third, business format franchisors provide their franchise partners with a marketing and operations system for doing business. It is a plan that presumably has been tested and known to work well under the right circumstances. Most franchisors believe that their system works best when all the members follow the system's prescription for success. This includes abiding by the system's policy manuals. It sometimes also presumes an integration of each member's operations into the system. For example, when a particular Holiday Inn is full on a given evening, the front desk immediately is expected to recommend another Holiday Inn a few miles away.

Manufacturers or other sponsors who have devised a distribution system containing all of the above three elements confront the very real likelihood their marketing channel will be defined as a franchise format by both state and federal franchise laws. Consequently, the system is subjected to an unexpected and complex set of marketing regulations.

WHY BUSINESS FORMAT FRANCHISES WORK

There are a number of reasons why format franchises work better than alternative modes of market entry. It is tempting to argue that few manufacturers, wholesalers, inventors, or others who might opt for franchising would want to relinquish to others any part of a juicy product, service, or idea. Vertical integration of the marketing channel—"having it all"—is tempting. Yet there is no powerful evidence that growing downward is necessarily the best use of an entrepreneur's assets. Using other people's money, talent, and energy can be a wise mode of market entry—meaning profitable.

Limited Capital, Limited Human Resources

During the early stages of a company's life cycle, it must usually delegate much of its work to others. It usually does not have either the capital or human resources to make a substantive in-house effort to grow to the next stage. George Stigler once pointed out that functional specialization arises in the marketplace when early entrants learn they cannot do everything at one time.[2] Good managers turn to others because it is expedient and because others do it better or cheaper—those who neglect this lesson often fail. Thus, small franchisors turn to others because they have neither the money nor the people to do everything themselves.

Franchising Is Faster

Franchisors soon learn they can cover a territory in little more time than it takes for each party to sign a contract. Indeed, they may never even need to leave home to gain market presence. While it is not quite so simple, speed of market entry is a major explanation for franchising success.

Even though the franchisor trades off total bottom line profit of a company's operations for a percentage of revenue of its franchisees, the ultimate profit potential of royalties from a network of franchises is much greater. The franchisor can achieve ties with less capital, risk, and human resources than would be needed by the vertically integrated company.

Motivation and Endurance of the Franchisee

The reward system the franchisor offers the franchisee includes the joys—and aggravations—of business ownership. It also includes the financial rewards that often accrue when things go well. No doubt there are naive owners of new franchises who think profits will come easily or that operating a franchise business will avoid hard work and long hours.

Contrast the owner's motives with the employee the franchisor puts into an owned outlet. If our understanding of human behavior is even remotely accurate, the owner shows more entrepreneurial spirit than the "hired hand." The franchisee owner will build a business, and do it better and more profitably than a manager with short-term vision and no long-term responsibility for poor decisions.

The Franchisee—Making Adaptations

America's heterogeneity complicates the marketing process. Its people's needs and tastes clearly differ from region to region, even from one part of a major city to another part a mile away. Most manufacturers, wholesalers, or franchisors who own their own retail outlets can provide ample horror stories about decisions made at headquarters that make no sense locally. Many are astute enough to allow their local managers a degree of decision-making freedom.

Franchise planners sitting at headquarters in Memphis, New York, or Chicago can make similar errors, but the likelihood is less because franchisees generally have more operating freedom than branch managers. A branch manager in Memphis is less likely to have roots in the community, and is less likely to put "Congratulations, Suzie and Don" on the marquee in Minot on Suzie and Don's wedding anniversary. No one in Chicago headquarters would routinely know it is "Avocado Week" in California, nor could a manager in Michigan easily know bar supplies do not sell well in XYZ county in Oklahoma because liquor sales are illegal in that county. This is not to decry the hard-working and intelligent managers at headquarters—they cannot be expected to know the nuances of local life.

This general observation probably is even more true when franchisors move to foreign markets. America's fast-food franchisors present good examples of companies that have been obliged to adapt their menus to local tastes, customs, and demands. Happily, their franchisees are typically nationals of the country and generally have taken on the task.

Many franchisors discourage their franchisees from using their creativity or imagination to alter precise and prescribed business operations. Consistency is paramount. Franchisors commonly provide exhaustive policy manuals that provide the response to virtually every situation a franchisee can expect to confront—deviations are not expected.

Other less structured systems provide a core base of products or services to be offered and encourage franchise initiative and creativity to build sales.

The System's Buying Power Can Be Enormous

Most of us are impressed that McDonald's claims to have sold billions of hamburgers—a fact proclaimed on its exterior signs. It has also sold billions of milk shakes, orders of french fries, and so on. Whether it is McDonald's, Holiday Inn, Hertz, or Meineke, purchase orders for ground beef, bed sheets, automobiles, or mufflers are sure to be enormous. The consequence of aggregated buying power is buying power muscle—the capacity to elicit concessions.

To be sure, retailers need not be part of a franchise system to enjoy the benefits of buying power. Retailer cooperatives consisting of independently-owned and generally small retailers often are little more than buying clubs designed to countervail the power of large manufacturers. One weakness of such groups is that membership is voluntary; there is no assurance that club members will demonstrate the sort of loyalty that elicits manufacturer concessions. However, franchising often has the advantages of powerfully encouraging participation because its members must abide by the strict product specifications prescribed by the franchisor. With this controlled and cohesive buying power, the franchisor and/or franchisee buyer cooperatives can exercise considerable power to neutralize the supplier's strength.

Name Recognition among Mobile Buyers

Americans are mobile—about 17 percent move in a given year. Further, Americans make over a billion business or pleasure trips a year. Anyone who has ever travelled with children knows even the youngest child recognizes good places to eat, places just like back home. Adults are only slightly more sophisticated; we recognize franchised retail outlets in remote places, know we can expect largely the same treatment in Faraway City as in our hometowns. In this respect, franchises are no different in their name recognition than large chains such as Sears or Wal-Mart.

This phenomenon offers a compelling advantage to a would-be franchisee who contemplates the alternative of operating an outlet without benefit of a recognizable franchisor's name. Indeed, some franchisors argue that their franchisees never undergo the agonizing early months of slow sales while the customer either ignores the hoopla associated with the opening or holds back for more information. Established and mature francisors claim that their name recognition often enables their outlets to reach the break even point quickly, in contrast to new, independent start-up businesses.

Foreign Laws—Where Wholly-Owned Outlets Are Not an Option

Few countries welcome foreign capital as openly as the United States. Except for a few industries, European, Canadian, and Japanese and other foreign companies receive national treatment when coming to America; they are accorded non-discriminatory government treatment.

In other countries, more often the less-developed ones, legislation commonly mandates that foreign investors must share their responsibilities with a local partner. In a foreign country where vertical integration—owning and operating retail outlets—is not legally possible, there are two entry options. One choice is a joint venture arrangement that usually requires the sponsor to contribute know-how and some capital in return for part ownership. The other choice is franchising, which sometimes includes the sale of a territory and the right to use marks and know-how, in return for continuing royalties. The sponsor is not expected to contribute capital.

WHY FRANCHISEES JOIN THE SYSTEM

Risk reduction is a central advantage to joining a successful business format system. Four different explanations contribute to reduced risk.

Proved Business

Potential entreprenuers may decide to participate in a franchise system because they are riding a "horse that's already been broke." The difficulties and disasters of the early years have been worked out, and the system is honed to where the worst mistakes have been eliminated. The early entrants, often the franchisor's owned outlets, were the experimenters. The franchisor has paid the tuition for the business experience gained.

Site Location

Large franchisors often operate substantial site selection departments. Such units are expected to know the customer profile of the business, area demographics, and the sales potential of a particular territory. Further, it should know the characteristics, strengths, and weaknesses of nearby rival outlets and real estate costs. While potential franchisees might choose to obtain this information without help, the task would usually be more difficult and costly.

Ongoing Guidance

Franchisees can expect assistance in anticipating problems and solving them. Every large franchisor's regional managers are expected to "mother hen" new franchisees, but they also serve as staff support for mature franchisees.

Easier Financing

Franchisees generally learn it is easier to borrow money when the intent of a loan application is to buy a franchise. Banks and other lending institutions instantly recognize the names of America's larger franchisors, know their history, and discern that most franchisors do not want their franchisees to fail. They understand the big business training and ongoing support that often backs up the small business borrower.

Being One's Own Boss

In addition to risk reduction, there is a lure to "being one's own boss"—not having to obey bosses and bureaucracies. The motive is understandable, but franchising may not always be the proper choice for the individualist or independent person. Business format franchising is generally most successful when its participants slavishly follow the operating manual. Being one's own boss plays out better when such retailers stay free from those highly structured and regimented systems where substantial conformity is expected. Franchising is something of a compromise between succumbing to others and living a free-spirited, entrepreneurial life.

HOW FRANCHISORS MAKE MONEY

There is a variety of ways franchisors may earn their profits—it is a rare franchisor who uses a single avenue.

Sale of Goods and Services

In the earlier years of franchising popularity, the major source of income for many franchisors was selling goods to its franchisees. Franchise contracts commonly carried a clause that required the franchisee to limit its purchases to those products sold by the franchisor.

The "tying contract" issue was tested in America's courts when Elaine and Harvey Siegel argued they could buy supplies for their Chicken Delight outlet at prices well below Chicken Delight's prices.[3] Chicken Delight claimed that a restrictive buying clause was essential to assure product integrity and national sameness, and said dinners should taste just as good in Portland, Oregon, as in Portland, Maine.

The U.S. Supreme Court ruled that Chicken Delight had good reason to maintain product standards, but it also ruled that the Siegels could purchase chicken parts and other supplies from outside suppliers without jeopardizing taste, health, or service. The tying contract was struck down as a restraint of trade.

Other franchisors immediately saw that the Chicken Delight case applied to their own businesses and promptly made changes. The most astute franchisors defined exacting product and service standards for each product its franchises would need—standards that would assure product integrity. They then invited would-be suppliers to demonstrate that their products or services could meet those standards. Finally, they established lists of approved but often unrelated suppliers—vendors who could sell products or services that met exacting quality standards set down by the franchisors.

Franchisors today still earn profits by selling goods and services to their franchisees, but their freedom has been substantially circumscribed by America's antitrust laws. Any franchisor effort to exploit their supplier relationship by reducing their franchisees' buying freedom is sure to attract the trust busters' attention.

The courts have made it clear that franchisors can legally be the sole supplier of products containing bona fide trade secrets. Thus if a secret mixture of ingredients makes fried fish taste better, courts would be sympathetic to the franchisor insisting it should be the sole-designated supplier. Few generalizations can be made here. Whether such products are in fact a secret or simply a scam to generate monopoly profits to the franchisor generally must be tested in the courts.

Selling products to franchisees bears far less legal danger for the more broadly defined franchisor mentioned early in this article. Being a supplier is almost the entire purpose of product distribution franchising.

The electronics retailer in Cleveland would have little chance of successfully pursuing a legal suit against any of its suppliers because such retailers can easily pursue many supplier options.

Initial Franchising Fee

Franchisees must pay a fee to join the system. The amount should roughly correspond to the future value of the business system and its accompanying trade or service marks. This means the initial fee can be low if income expectations are small, however, it can be very high if the expected future benefits are lush. Franchise rights to operate a major hotel in a large city may require a substantial initial fee.

The initial fee and subsequent benefits may not correspond—there is no evidence that franchisors always charge a fee that approximates the value of the benefits sought by the franchisee. Franchisees must be diligent in assessing the value of what they are purchasing.

A major determinant of the initial fee is the territorial exclusiveness the franchisor promises its partner. Each party to an agreement faces a dilemma. On the one hand, both franchisor and franchisee want outlets close enough to each other so the customer is presented with a full system. Customers will not develop expectations about a system if outlets are hundreds of miles apart unless there is good market penetration. The synergism that accrues to franchise systems—synergism that explains most of a franchise's value—is lost. On the other hand, outlets too close to each other engage in unproductive competition. They destroy the benefits of the system. To combat this issue, franchisors may promise in the contract that no other outlet will be franchised within another outlet's market or trading area. This clause can generate problems for a franchisor when an "exclusive" area grows to where it can accommodate several outlets but the franchisee refuses to accept another franchise.

Supplemental Up-Front Fees

The initial fee may only license the franchisee to use the franchisor's intellectual property; it can only do business under its trade name or mark. Supplemental fees may be levied for helping find a suitable site, legal assistance in buying or leasing the location, architectural help in revamping a site so it is suited to its intended use, training employees before opening, and special help with opening day promotions.

Service Fees (Royalties)

A major source of franchisor revenue consists of ongoing fees charged for the continued services it provides its franchisees. Service fees, also called royalties, are rationalized on the presumed value the franchisor adds to the franchisee's business over the years of the agreement. The accumulated service fees over many years of an arrangement may far exceed any other source of income.

Property Leases

Some of America's largest franchisors are both franchisor and landlord. Large franchisors sometimes acquire the prime lease for an acceptable site from a property owner, then sub-lease the location to the franchisee. In addition to a source of revenue, such a practice enhances the franchisor's control over the franchisee. McDonald's goes a step further: it purchases attractive locations, then leases the sites to its franchisees. Thus, it generates a profit on the lease and a percentage of sales rental terms.

Other Sources of Revenue

A few franchisors share computer time with their franchisees, while some provide payroll services for a fee. Problem-solving teams for special difficulties or promotional help for special occasions may generate *per diem* fees.

FRANCHISE EXPANSION TECHNIQUES

There are a number of approaches franchisors may employ in their expansion programs, any one of which may be used in combination with others. There are advantages and limitations to each type of franchise marketing technique.

Unit Franchising

Unit franchising, sometimes called direct franchising, consists of establishing outlets one franchisee at a time. The owner generally is interested in getting deeply involved in operations, being a hands-on owner/operator. For smaller businesses, wife and husband teams are common. There are two major advantages to the franchisor. One is that control over whomever is chosen rests with the franchisor. The second is that no broad territorial rights are conceded to others that may be regretted once the system has become successful.

The major disadvantage to the one-at-a-time approach is that growth is slower than other expansion techniques. Ferreting out, screening, and signing a franchisee for each outlet is costly and time consuming. However, it is the only likely strategy available to the untested and unknown franchisor.

McDonald's Corporation has used this approach—and only this approach—to open new outlets in the United States. Each new restaurant is the result of an individual application and McDonald's careful scrutiny. To be sure, there are multiple unit McDonald's franchisees, but even those McDonald's franchisees who are seeking an additional restaurant must go through an elaborate evaluation procedure.

Conversion Franchising

Conversion franchising, sometimes called affiliation franchising, is a modified single-unit approach. It takes place when an established independent business opts to relinquish its go-it-alone strategy, and become part of the franchise system. The business owner may have conducted business for many years, perhaps quite successfully. However, joining the franchise system is seen as providing even greater benefits. The advantage to the franchisor, of course, is that there are fewer business risks because the applicant has been selected on the basis of a previously successful business—in short, there is a track record.

The major disadvantages to conversion franchising are that formerly independent owners, now franchisees, may resist succumbing to a rigid system, object to paying royalties, and not want to participate in training systems the franchisor demands. In short, teaching an old and experienced dog new tricks may not be easy for the franchisor.

Area Development Franchising

Single-level multiple franchising takes place when the franchisor grants a franchisee the exclusive right to develop outlets in a particular territory for a specified time. Since this can amount to a substantial capital commitment, franchises often consist of investor groups who do not wish to get involved in hands-on management. The developer franchisee agrees to build or convert a specified number of franchise outlets within the defined area and within a certain time—a development fee for the exclusive development rights. Wendy's, Popeye's, and Burger King have used this approach. Area development franchising provides much faster market development than single-unit selection. However, successful and powerful multi-unit franchise operators present a much greater chance of resistance and confrontation to the franchisor than does any single franchisee.

When a franchisor's strategy calls for entry into foreign markets, it may elect a multiple-entry approach even though it opted for single-unit choices in its home market. Sometimes this is because headquarter managers acknowledge they understand very little about the foreign market; they wisely prefer to relinquish broad market development to a local partner who has a better understanding of local culture, law, and politics. In other cases, legislation in the host country encourages strong local partners, making branch offices that would have the task of choosing single outlets difficult to establish. Further, the prohibitive cost of screening and selecting franchises makes unit franchising an unattractive option in many small countries.

Subfranchising

Subfranchising is another type of multiple-unit marketing system, however, it is a two-tiered system. Under this system, the franchisor designates a master franchisee who has the right to appoint single—or even multiple—subfranchises in a particular territory. A contract is signed between the franchisor and the master franchisee, one which establishes this right, defines the territory and performance requirements in developing the territory. The master franchisee then solicits subfranchisee prospects within the area. A second contract is signed between the master franchisee and the subfranchisees.

The master franchisee (now a sub-franchisor) must know the business well, because it is that party to whom subfranchisees—those in the trenches—must look to for support. Since the initial franchisor has no legal or operating relationship with the subfranchisee, the master franchisee must be carefully chosen. To assure a degree of expertise, the master franchisee is often required to own and operate at least one outlet before subfranchising to others. Decorating Den, Molly Maids, and Precision Tune have successfully used the subfranchising approach.

WHAT THE FRANCHISOR MUST TELL

There have been enormous abuses in franchising. Dishonest franchisors have professed to have expertise they did not have or could not convey to others, sold ordinary products at prices vastly higher than their marketplace worth, tied or bundled essential products to less necessary products so the size of the sales package would be higher, and sold too many franchises in territories that could not support those outlets. In some instances, persuasive salespeople claimed to be franchisors with a "can't fail" plan, signed agreements, took the naive party's initial fee, and vanished into the woods.

FTC Disclosure Requirements

Out of this chicanery came a new Federal Trade Commission (FTC) regulation, "Disclosure Requirements and Prohibitions Concerning Franchising and Business Opportunity Ventures." The rule, monitored by the FTC since 1979, requires franchisors to present potential buyers with basic information on 20 subjects. While too voluminous to cover here, the general tenor of what a franchisor must divulge to a prospective franchisee can be summarized:

- A history of the franchisor's business and its predecessors, the business experiences of its directors and officers, including disclosures relating to personal litigation and bankruptcies.
- The fees that must be paid to join the system and whatever continuing royalties or other payments must be made during the course of the franchise business relationship.
- A list of those with whom the system member is required or advised to purchase goods or services and whether the frachisor receives a financial benefit from such a requirement.

- The extent of involvement in the business of any celebrity whose name is associated with it.
- The obligation the investor has in the day-to-day operations of the franchise.
- The circumstances or conditions under which a franchise can be terminated.

Earnings Statements and Claims

Just as important as the above, any promises the franchisor may make about franchisee earnings possibilities must be made with great care. The FTC allows franchisors to say nothing about earnings potential to prospective franchisees. Indeed, most franchisors present no evidence that suggests what franchisees might earn. Unfortunately, this absence of earnings claims disclosures—motivated by a fear of lawsuits—is not helpful in selling franchises. However, if earnings claims are presented, they must be based on evidence that is both current and geographically relevant to the franchise location. If challenged, earning claims must be substantiated.

Franchisors today are legally obliged to provide comprehensive statements about their history, what they do, and what is expected of their franchisees. Such statements may be helpful but do not always reveal the full story. Astute franchisees must conduct a diligent inquiry among existing franchisees to learn whether the promised benefits are true.

State Regulations

Although well beyond the scope of this discussion, about 15 states have legislation pertaining to franchise marketing; other states may only regulate the sales of established business relationships. Much state legislation derives from the slowness of the federal government to take prompt action in curbing alleged franchisor abuses. Each state's laws tends to be a bit different from legislation in nearby states, so franchisors must abide not only by federal disclosure requirements but also by the various state laws. While much progress has been made in attaining disclosure requirement uniformity among states, the process of registering a franchise system in many states and complying with specific laws and regulations is costly and burdensome.

THE CONGLOMERATE DUAL DISTRIBUTOR

Most of the world's largest businesses are multimarketers who pursue a variety of concurrent marketing strategies. This marketing diversity becomes necessary when operating in very complex markets. There are four major bases for their differentiation; these differences are customer types, customers' geographic locations, different purchasing volumes, and product variations—either real or cosmetic. Knowledgeable marketers, particularly in larger firms, know that no single marketing channel is suited to accommodating these differences.

There may be pressures to utilize multi-channel marketing strategies; however, the strategy has the potential for creating conflict between the franchisor's owned outlets and its franchised outlets. A franchisor's strategy to engage in business outside the confines of its franchise operations can intrude on franchisees' rights, at least as seen by the franchisees. Not surprisingly, such issues sometimes wind up in court.

Let us look at some recent examples of how companies adapt to such market diversity and some of the problems such strategies bring:

- McDonald's is accustomed to free-standing restaurants, either the sit-down or walk-in type. In recent years, however, motivated by an America saturated with conventional outlets selling in traditional ways, McDonald's has moved into office buildings, hospitals and universities, airplanes, and most recently into Wal-Mart stores. This move was brought about by either the inability or unwillingness of customers to visit the nearest outlet—McDonald's took its products to its customers.
- Taco Bell bought Hot 'n Now, a hamburger chain, investing a lot of enthusiasm and managerial expertise into making it successful. Many of the Hot 'n Now outlets were asserted to be too near Taco Bell franchisees for comfort. Taco Bell's headquarters claims there is no rivalry because hamburgers and Mexican food are two entirely different products. Taco Bell unit managers claim hamburgers and tacos are competing for the customers' limited dollars, claiming they no longer have an exclusive territory.
- Vie de France managers decided there were too many markets to serve solely via their owned outlets and franchises. This meant multichannel ventures. It sold dough to large retailers and restaurants who had ovens on premises, and it sold baked bread through grocery wholesalers to food stores. Since the products, types of outlets, and volume purchased differed among its customers, so did its marketing channels.
- Ace Hardware is owned by its more than 5,000 retail outlets, making it a retailer cooperative. Its owners are also franchisees, carefully spaced across America so they seldom compete with each other. But when headquarters began selling to One Source Supply, a wholesaler in Hollywood, Florida, a small group of Ace's retailers went to court. The franchisees pointed out that One Source may be a wholesaler, but it also sells to the general public and to nearby apartment complexes and construction companies—markets that traditionally belonged to Ace dealers. Their exclusivity was violated, they said. Ace defended the charges, claiming that One Source is a distributor or wholesaler—not a retailer—as defined by its franchise agreements.
- Pillsbury Company decided franchise shops were the best way to sell its Häagen-Dazs premium ice cream. It also knew that more ice cream was sold in food stores than in walk-in stores. So, when it started a second marketing channel—selling to America's grocery stores—it stepped into legal battles. The franchisees pointed out that on a price-per-scoop basis, they could not compete. Further, it was so much easier for customers to buy a quart at a nearby store than to stop into a Häagen-Dazs outlet.

In sum, much of the conflict derives from the franchisor's inability to keep markets apart, to prevent one market from encroaching into another. McDonald's offered "Happy Meals" for kids on United Airlines flights, comfortable that no franchisee would complain. But, if hungry people see little difference between Hot 'n Now hamburgers and Mexican food, Taco Bell must use enormous imagination to keep them apart. And when ice cream eaters decided they were just as comfortable buying Häagen-Dazs at a nearby supermarket at a lower price and eating it at home, Häagen-Dazs confronted trouble.

A franchisor may keep peace in the family by offering franchisees the right to expand their business with new outlets. For example, franchise contracts sometimes offer franchisees first refusal rights. This means if a new outlet is contemplated—and warranted by ample market studies—nearby franchises are allowed to be first bidders. Since the nearby franchisee already has a performance record, it may also be a preferred bidder.

In one interesting example of keeping peace while expanding into a new market, Domino's Pizza negotiated contracts with about 500 university food services that benefit nearby franchisees. College students like pizza more than dormitory food. But pizza is an out-of-pocket expense to students; dining hall food is generally contracted for the school term. Domino's has arranged so a dorm student can telephone a nearby Domino's, have a pizza delivered, and pay with a coupon that the franchisee can redeem for cash. The student is obliged to eat one less meal in the student dining room.

FUTURE OF FRANCHISING

Franchising is a marriage of entities that need each other. The franchisor brings intellectual property in the form of well-known trade marks and names, a tested format for operations, and human resources to hold it all together. The franchisee brings a capacity for hard work, capital, and the capacity to learn the regime. There are certain truisms that will make some systems prosper while others will wither and die.

Reasons for Staying in the System—Franchisee Inducements

Any franchise's success will heavily depend on its ability to manage what Herbert Simon called the "Inducements–Contribution Balance." Whether individuals participate in an organization is determined by the potential participants' assessment of what they are expected to give—the contribution—weighed against the rewards—the inducements. If inducements exceed contributions, participation occurs. For participation to continue over the years, the rewards of staying in the system must always be greater than the costs of opting out.

Simon's theory particularly applies to franchising because legitimate franchisors hope for lasting franchisee participation. However, the forces making up each side's power shifts during time. Let us look at some dynamics that explain these power shifts.

Franchisee experience often grows substantially after a rather short time. They earn quick acceptance in the market, much of the acceptance attributed to their franchisor's reputation. Yet it is not uncommon that franchisees, having gained market position, discount the future value and benefits that may be delivered by the franchisor. The "break away" scenario is that the franchisor is given notice the franchisee is quitting and the franchisor's marks are eliminated from the business operation. Most important, royalty payments are discontinued.

Franchisors, however, have made unilateral withdrawal from the system difficult. There is the threat of injunctive remedies and damages, and franchise contracts typically specify that franchisees who have withdrawn from the system may not operate competing businesses for a specified time. Well crafted non-compete clauses generally specify reasonable territorial restraints and run about two years, long enough to give the would-be break away franchisee pause. Unilaterally opting out of the system will usually invite litigation.

The short lesson for franchisors is that they must assure their franchisees that the rewards of staying in the system are greater than the advantages of getting out. They must provide continued enhancement of their trade marks and names, volume buying advantages, imaginative promotional campaigns, or such elusive advantages as the personal pleasures and synergy of group membership. Without such inducements, the prospect of avoiding weekly or bi-weeking royalty payments to the franchisor can be very tempting. The franchisor must provide continued reasons for staying in the system. After the first year of operation, franchisees are likely to ask, "What have you done for me lately?" Ancient history does not count.

The Multimarketing Franchisor—Keeping the Games Separate

We have already pointed out that many large firms use a variety of modes for market entry or expansion. Franchisees may unfairly expect their franchisor to keep their techniques well apart. Thus, new franchisees and especially franchisor-owned outlets should not encroach on the trading area of an existing franchisee. Or, multimarketers should not produce and sell similar products through independent distributors that are too similar to the ones sold through their franchised outlets. Perceptions about what is fair will not be the same, and explanations will be difficult or impossible. Successful franchisors are those who do not intrude on what their franchisees—rightly or wrongly—believe is their turf.

Choosing the Franchisee—Getting the Right One

Successful franchisors will be those who carefully select their franchisees and carefully explain the potential rewards of membership. America's recent shift toward fewer middle managers has been good for its businesses, but it has had a gruesome effect on employment. It is tempting to believe that these highly competent people can shift their skills to other endeavors. However, there is little evidence that any particular individual's competence in a large corporate bureaucracy is easily transferred to franchise management. The transition from corporate staff employment to the rigors and "hands on" needs of a small business can be quite difficult for many executives. There are ample accounts of long hours of work and lost lifetime savings incurred by those who could not make the transition. Selecting motivated and informed franchisees who will enjoy and be capable of operating the business is good for both franchisor and franchisee. It is the bedrock of a sound franchise relationship.

NOTES

1. This article is partly based on Norman D. Axelrad and Lewis G. Rudnick, *Franchising: A Planning and Sales Compliance Guide,* (Chicago: Commerce Clearing House).
2. George Stigler, "The Division of Labor Is Limited by the Extent of the Market," *Journal of Political Economy,* (June 1951), pp. 185–193.
3. *Siegel v. Chicken Delight,* 405 U.S. 95 (1972).

SUGGESTIONS FOR FURTHER READING

Axelrad, Norman, *Franchising A Planning and Legal Compliance Guide,* Commerce Clearing House, Inc. 4025 Peterson Ave. Chicago, IL, 60646, 1987.

Brown, Harold, *Franchising—Realities and Realities,* Law Journal Seminar Press 111 Eighth Ave. New York, N.Y. 10011, 1986.

Business Franchise Guide, Commerce Clearing House, Inc.

Franchise Opportunities Handbook, (Washington DC: U.S. Department of Commerce).

Glickman, Gladys, *Franchising,* Matthew Bender & Company, Inc. 1979.

Henward III, DeBanks M. & William Ginalski, *The Franchise Option,* International Franchise Association, 1350 New York Avenue, N.W. Ste. 900, Washington, D.C. 20005.

Kinch, John, *Franchising—The Inside Story,* International Franchise Association, Washington, D.C.

Raab, Steven B., *The Blueprint For Franchising A Business,* John Wiley & Sons, 1987.

Sherman, Andrew J., *Franchising and Licensing-Two Ways To Build Your Business,* American Management Association, 1991.

James C. Makens
Associate Professor
Babcock Graduate School of Management
Wake Forest University
Winston-Salem, North Carolina

CHAPTER 51

YIELD MANAGEMENT: NEW PRICING STRATEGY

No area of marketing offers more potential for immediate and dramatic change to the bottom line than pricing. A new pricing strategy based on microeconomic theory, market segmentation, and knowledge of buyer behavior has proven highly effective within several sectors of the service industry.

Yield management arose out of the airline industry where the strategy was developed and is now employed by virtually all major carriers throughout the world. Other industry users include auto rental firms such as Hertz and Avis; major hotel chains including Sheraton, Hilton, and Westin; cruise lines such as Royal Caribbean Cruise Lines; and railroads including Via Rail Canada and America's Amtrak. The radio broadcasting industry is beginning to embrace yield management in the pricing of advertising time. Experiments have been conducted using yield management in health care by Duke University's Diet and Fitness Center and by EPRI, the research arm of the electric utility industry.

WHAT IS YIELD MANAGEMENT?

Yield management is a managerial pricing tool based on (a) analysis of historical demand trends for a defined product or service; (b) capacity/inventory level management; and (c) booking curve management. Yield management is practiced for the purpose of optimizing revenue.

Demand curve theory from microeconomics serves as the theoretical background for yield management. A demand curve consists of several points at which a number of buyers and sellers agree to close the deal. A low price generates high volume sales while a high price results in decreased sales. Between these two points lie a great number of price/volume points—this is the classical demand curve.

Yield management focuses on a limited number of demand points for the product mix. A hotel with 300 similar rooms could theoretically have 300 product offerings times 365 days. Yield management simplifies the process by selecting a limited number of price offerings for each day's product mix. The price mix available each day depends on forecasted demand for that day as well as other variables such as demand characteristics for days preceding and following that date. The allocation of available rooms per price offering may vary by day and by week.

The data in Exhibit 1 depicts a fictitious hotel with a widely varying price mix and capacity allocation of rooms. A greater percentage of rooms are allocated to high prices on Sunday and Monday when

EXHIBIT 1. Room Allocation by Price by Day—Second Week of March

	Available Rooms						
Price	**Sunday**	**Monday**	**Tuesday**	**Wednesday**	**Thursday**	**Friday**	**Saturday**
$ 60	30	40	50	50	80	150	150
70	40	50	60	60	70	60	60
80	50	60	60	60	60	40	40
90	80	80	80	80	60	30	30
100	100	70	50	50	30	20	20
Total	300	300	300	300	300	300	300

business travelers check in. The mix changes during the week, and by the weekend the majority of rooms are allocated to low prices.

Yield management practitioners are highly conscious of available market segments and the elasticity of price associated with each. Thus, on Sunday a relatively inelastic price segment of business travelers is forecasted while weekends are utilized by price sensitive (elastic) segments such as tourists.

Booking Curve Capacity Management

The goal of yield management is to match available inventory/capacity and demand to enhance revenue. Inventory/capacity allocations are originally set through forecasting techniques, but these often change as the salesforce begins to bring in orders. Booking curve histories are examined to see how sales occurred for this same day in previous years, but last year's booking curve will not be the same as today's.

Therefore, the yield manager or a yield management team will examine sales as they occur. If sales are slower than forecasted, a greater number of rooms will be allocated to the low-priced rooms and vice versa. Sales quotas and incentives can be established to ensure that higher margin times are sold. This is a dramatic change from traditional practices in which sales volume rather than revenue enhancement was the dominant driving force.

Yield management practitioners are quick to warn that product offerings at the high prices must be available because there are always some individuals willing to pay these prices.

Increasing Complexity

Yield management becomes more complex as variables increase in number. An airline may fly five times each day between Chicago and New York. Each flight has different demand characteristics with a different mix of customers who exhibit varying degrees of willingness to pay different prices. Historical demand trends and booking patterns drastically alter as economic or social changes occur. Additionally, competitors continue to have a nasty habit of doing their best to confuse the best laid pricing strategies.

In most industries, marketing or sales managers practice a simplistic version of hand-computed yield management. This becomes impossible in the case of a complex organization such as an airline. Responsibility for making these decisions is generally taken from sales and marketing executives and placed in the hands of a yield management department or multi-department team.

Sophisticated software programs based on algorithms are now commonly used by corporations that employ yield management pricing strategies. These are available from software vendors in the United States and Europe, and range from small entrepreneurial firms to multinational companies such as Andersen Consulting.

MORE THAN A PRICING TOOL

Originally viewed as a method to improve pricing decisions, yield management is increasingly viewed as an effective strategic management tool. Effective yield management requires forecasting, market segment analysis, targeted marketing, inventory/capacity planning, and cross departmental involvement.

British Airways uses the forecasting power of the yield management database as a strategic planning aid for marketing, check-in-desks, cargo loading, catering, and resource management. The management of British Airways strongly believes that there is valuable segmentation and buyer behavior information embedded within pricing information to help determine the service mix the carrier should be offering.[1]

An unexpected but highly welcome outcome of the use of yield management has been an improvement in interdepartment cooperation. Hilton and Hyatt hotels have reported improved interdepartmental relationships after instituting yield management.[2] This appears to be the direct result of visible support from top management. In companies where top management has not given full support, interdepartmental rivalry often exists between yield management and sales, reservations, or financial planning.

A key to success lies in a flexible yield management system that incorporates qualitative and quantitative decision inputs from departments that are immediately affected by pricing decisions. Systems that regard computer-generated pricing decisions as inviolate and not subject to review or modification often result in interdepartmental rivalry and an eventual lack of management support.

INDUSTRY APPLICATION

Yield management may not be applicable in all industries—there are several parameters that define the type of industry best suited to using this pricing tool. According to Dr. Robert L. Philips of Decision

Focus, a yield management consulting firm, six criteria describe industries in which sophisticated yield management is most valuable.[3]

- It is expensive or impossible to store excess production.
- Demand fluctuates substantially over time.
- Commitments need to be made when future demand is uncertain.
- Customers can be discriminated among on the basis of willingness to pay.
- There are many competing products and a complex pricing structure.
- Producers are profit oriented and have broad freedom of action.

Bob Cross, president of Aeronomics Inc., a pioneer in the field, adds two additional parameters.[4]

- The marketplace is diverse.
- The incremental cost of selling and servicing an additional unit is low.

Industries in which yield management is practical tend to have high fixed costs and a customer and practitioner base that has become accustomed to widely varying prices.

The U.S. hospital industry would seem to be a logical candidate for this management tool. Indeed, it is practiced to a limited extent without being defined as such. A major impediment to widespread use within this industry appears to be based primarily in the reluctance of industry administrators to use a system that is clearly "price discriminatory" and may be negatively viewed by the government, physician, and patient.

Initial excitement about yield management led to claims that this was the "pricing breakthrough of the twentieth century." Indeed, for consumer service firms within the travel industry it has proven to be exciting and highly profitable, the revenue potential for these firms can be dramatic. British Airways has determined that a 1% increase in passenger revenue translates into an additional $70 million revenue, much of it profit. For this reason, British Airways invested $26 million in 1991 to upgrade its yield management system.

With costs such as this, yield management has clearly passed from an experimental tool to an essential weapon in the highly competitive travel industry. It remains doubtful if this tool will be adopted by manufacturing. Some observers believe that retailing and banking offer potential, but currently these industries have shown little interest or enthusiasm.

Yield management is an effective pricing tool for select industries. Beyond its role in pricing, all marketing strategies and practices stand to benefit. Sophisticated yield management is built on market segmentation, highly targeted marketing, and marginal revenue-conscious sales strategies. Those using yield management have been forced to sharpen forecasting and consumer behavior tools. All levels of management have found it essential to become market driven and to find new ways to cause departments to work together with improved customer service and well-timed pricing strategies. The end result has been a general strengthening of marketing planning, strategy, and control. That in itself is probably worth the price of admission.

NOTES

1. Bartholomew, Doug, "Yield Management, British Air Stays on Course." *Information Week,* April 27, 1991, p. 40.
2. Orkin, Eric B., "Boosting Your Bottom Line with Yield Management," *The Cornell H.R.A. Quarterly,* May 1989, p. 56.
3. Phillips, Robert L., Ph.D., "What Is Yield Management?" Paper presented in 2nd Multi Industry Yield Management Conference, 1990. Decision Focus Inc., p. 8, 4984 El Camino Real, Los Altos, California 94022.
4. Cross, Robert G., president, Aeronomics Inc., "Yield Management: New Horizons for a Dark Science." Paper presented at 1st Multi Industry Yield Management Conference, 1989, p. 2.

PART SEVEN

PUTTING THE MARKETING PLAN INTO ACTION FOR BUSINESS PRODUCTS/SERVICES

PART SEVEN

INTRODUCTION

There have been some dramatic shifts in the business market over the past 10 or 15 years, and there are certainly more changes to come. The very face of business has changed, with management positions being filled by younger people who bring with them fresh values and attitudes. As the basic personality of American business has evolved, corporate hierarchies have flattened out, with employees on all levels becoming "empowered" with the ability to make decisions once the exclusive responsibility of upper management.

Marketers must now sell to *businesspeople*, not businesses—that is, decision makers who see themselves as individuals rather than cogs in a machine; astute consumers who are themselves wise to the ways of modern-day marketing. More important, organizational buying patterns have changed; many companies now prefer to do business with a smaller, more select group of suppliers. This preference has led to a long-term trend in "partnering," or forming close, collaborative relationships with business customers.

In Part Six, we took an in-depth look at strategies for marketing to consumers. Implementing marketing planning for business customers is an entirely different field. In this section, you'll begin with a broad overview of business marketing, traditionally known as "industrial" marketing, focusing on specific tactical elements that must be considered when planning and executing strategies for business customers. After an exploration of the basic components, further chapters offer a detailed look at several important aspects and subcategories in the field of marketing to business.

A survey of the elements of the industrial marketing mix reveals the essential differences between the worlds of consumer marketing and selling to businesses. In industrial marketing, product selection and development, as well as sales and service support, play larger roles, pricing may be more complex, and advertising is downplayed. Distribution channels are also more complex, and have undergone drastic changes in the past two decades. The recent emergence of information technology has caused a dramatic change in business marketing, enabling marketers to track the profitability of every account, product, and strategy, and to adjust tactics as necessary. Often neglected, marketing implementation or execution—the vital step after planning—is also covered in Chapter 52.

As mentioned above, one of the trends that has emerged in the past decade is that of collaborative relationships between vendors and their business customers. Chapter 53 offers marketing managers a strategic six-step approach to "partnering," as well as guidance on determining which market segments and customers to target as partners. From product development to cooperative pricing to the organization of the seller's sales and marketing efforts, forming partner relationships with customers requires a rethinking of the way an entire company works. The impact, the risks, and the potential involved in making this change are examined in "Partnering as a Focused Market Strategy."

The marketing of raw materials requires special attention, as most marketing techniques are ineffective in this special field in which product development, pricing, and advertising do not apply. Marketing raw materials can be influenced by the following: transportation and storage; industry standards (such as grades of ore); and the inflexibility brought about by factors such as the vertical integration of raw materials, the political and ecological factors involved in global marketing, and the dependency of pricing on the commodities market.

Marketing research in the industrial sector uses a wide variety of investigative approaches and procedures. More and more commonly, studies undertaken by industrial firms are based on the techniques used in behavioral science studies. Due to the facts that industrial customer bases may be quite small and demand is easily influenced, marketing in these fields must give weight to certain factors: customer opinion and judgment, expert opinion, and secondary data. Specific types of studies, steps for conducting a marketing research study, and even ways to organize a company's research teams are explored in Chapter 55.

One of the chief differences between consumer and industrial marketing is the buying process. Organizational buying processes may be composed of several steps and often involve multiple decision makers with various levels of influence. In Chapter 56, author Joseph Bellizzi offers a step-by-step overview of the buying process and makes strong recommendations for the seller staying active at each step. Armed with an understanding of the buying process and the way intrabusiness dynamics may change the outcome of a sale, marketing managers can direct a sales effort aimed at initiating and completing each step of the process. As a potential customer progresses through the steps, the seller can establish a series of contacts and aid in the decision making.

Thomas V. Bonoma
Executive Vice President
Former Associate Professor of Business Administration
Harvard University Graduate School of
Business Administration
Cambridge, Massachusetts

Robert A. Garda
Director
McKinsey & Company, Inc.
Cleveland, Ohio

Sara M. Roche
Director of Client Communications
McKinsey & Company, Inc.
Cleveland, Ohio

CHAPTER 52

MARKETING TO BUSINESS

This chapter is a brief overview of marketing to business and the strategic and tactical considerations that successful marketers take into account in planning and executing strategies for business customers. The traditional descriptive term for the activity of "marketing to business" is "industrial" marketing, and we will use the two interchangeably.

The chapter is divided into eleven sections. The first defines the industrial sector—the regular participants in the business marketing system. The second contrasts marketing to business with marketing to consumers. The next six sections discuss the basic elements of business marketing strategy (sometimes referred to as the marketing mix)—market selection and product policy, pricing, distribution channels, sales force management, advertising and sales promotion, and postsale service. Next is a section on information technology, a marketing tool of rapidly increasing importance. The last two sections turn to a neglected but all-important topic—marketing implementation and performance assessment. Once you have a plan, what are the keys to executing it successfully?

The intent of this chapter is not to give the reader the theoretical underpinnings of marketing to business; they are similar to those in consumer marketing discussed elsewhere in this book. Instead, the intent is to provide practical insights into the business marketing process and to leave the business marketer with some practical hints for carrying out the job successfully.

THE BUSINESS SECTOR DEFINED

Business marketing is concerned with all those marketplace transactions in which the ultimate consumption of what is purchased is not the major goal of the buyer. That is, in business marketing, we are concerned with goods that are acquired for conversion into other forms, or that are themselves used up in this conversion process. This is also sometimes referred to as business-to-business marketing or selling.

Clearly, when the critical criterion for deciding whether we are dealing with business or consumer marketing is the purpose for which a good or service is acquired, one might suspect a bit of fuzziness in the differentiation. That is true. For example, auto batteries, office furnishings, and trucks are purchased by both end-users and by those desiring to employ them in the production of other goods. Advisory services and education are two other examples where the same product can be consumed by both end-users and business users. Where tax help is retained to aid in sheltering investment income by a professional investor, it is hard to know whether we are talking about "consumer" or "industrial" usage. Even though it is hard to tell the two universes apart, we will try to categorize some broad classes of consumption that are usually recognized as marketing to business.

Exhibit A-1 tries to define what we mean by "industrial" using a simple and broad classification scheme.[1] It divides the sources of the GNP into *extractive, manufacturing, support* and *consuming* units. Only consuming units are end-users—the extractive, manufacturing, and some portion of the support industries are industrial sources. Exhibit 1 reflects this fact. Let us look at these categories in more detail.

Extractive industries are those that remove raw materials from the earth to process them. Farming, forestry, and other agricultural pursuits are included here, as are fisheries and mining. These industries all make purchases to carry out their extractive endeavors and to sell their products either to those who will act on them further or to an end-user. A typical bituminous coal-mining operation in Western Pennsylvania, for example, will purchase operating equipment, services, and labor to extract, crush, clean, and transport coal from underground to the market. It will sell this coal either to industrial, commercial, or (rarely) householders for consumption.

Manufacturing industries make up the bulk of the industrial market system. Included here are both durable goods manufacturers (furniture, glass, primary metals, electrical and nonelectrical machinery) and nondurable goods manufacturers (food, tobacco, textiles, apparel, paper, chemicals, and rubber). Fully, 61 percent of manufacturing shipments goes to business buyers. Only 36 percent goes to consumers and the rest goes to various levels of government. Business buyers include food manufacturers, such as Heinz, which buys its glass from three major and several minor suppliers. These in turn buy raw materials from extractive industries. Additionally, both Heinz and its suppliers purchase typewriters, office equipment, trucks and a host of other products from other concerns, both manufacturing and nonmanufacturing companies. On the output side, businesses (such as restaurants), institutions (hospitals), and manufacturing firms (the cafeteria at AT&T) all buy ketchup from Heinz. All of these transactions are correctly placed in the industrial marketing arena.

Regarding *support industries,* these companies sell to both consumer and industrial users of all types. These can be split into three categories: service, construction, and middleman activities. Service companies include financial firms, transportation companies, communications firms, repair shops, and public utilities. All of these businesses may sell directly to "consuming units," or they may have commerce with industrial firms, at home and abroad. The Chase Manhattan Bank, for example, makes auto loans to individuals and to companies, both dealers (floor-plan loans) and those who make the cars (lines of credit

Exhibit A-1

U.S. MARKET FLOW SYSTEM

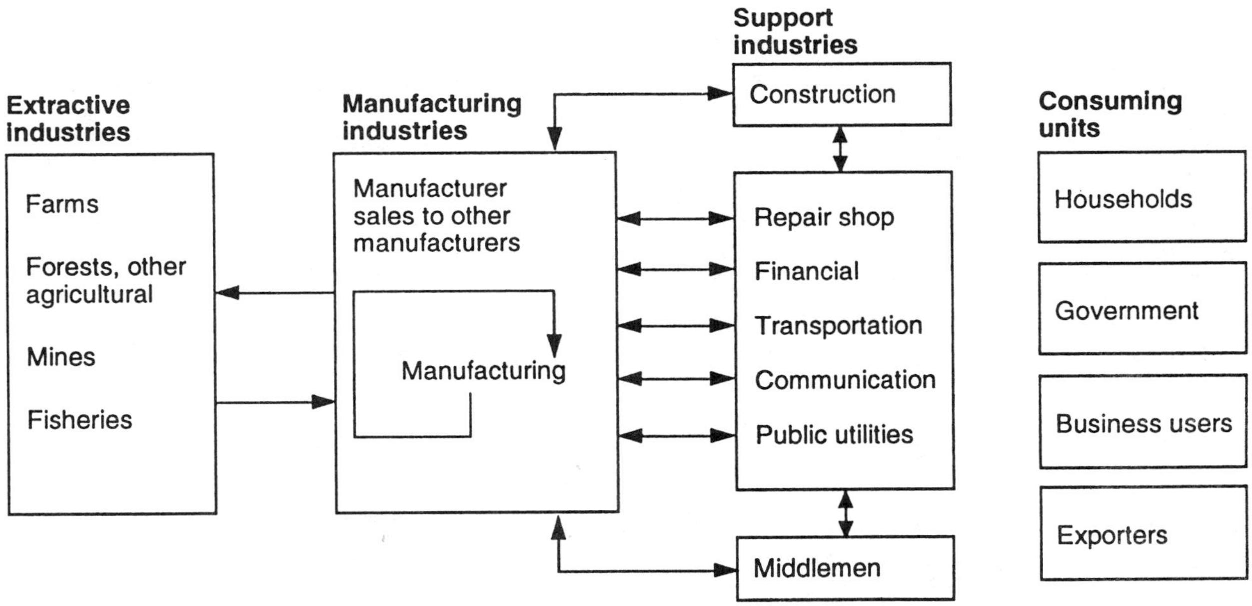

Extractive industries

Farms

Forests, other agricultural

Mines

Fisheries

Manufacturing industries

Manufacturer sales to other manufacturers

Manufacturing

Support industries

Construction

Repair shop

Financial

Transportation

Communication

Public utilities

Middlemen

Consuming units

Households

Government

Business users

Exporters

to component manufacturers). Service businesses buy from and sell to the industrial market, and hence are a critical part of it.

The construction portion of the support sector also serves the consumer, the government, and business, with sales to consumers that are about double those to businesses. The middleman portion of the support sector, which comprises the wholesale trades, turns out to be very important. Of all the manufactured and imported goods sold to business buyers, roughly 60 percent are bought and resold by industrial wholesalers or distributors.

There are three major points to be kept in mind about the business-to-business marketing sector:

1. It consists of extractive, manufacturing, and support (services, construction, and middleman) industries.
2. Profit, not-for-profit, and even religious firms may belong to this sector. The definition rests on the purpose to which acquired goods are put.
3. Even using very conservative assumptions, this sector accounts for about 1.7 times the consumer dollar flow occurring in the end-use sector of the economy.

BUSINESS-TO-BUSINESS VERSUS CONSUMER MARKETING

Why is it so important to have a clear definition of the business-to-business sector as opposed to the consumer goods sector? Because the marketing tasks in the two sectors are different in many respects.

The textbook marketing mix elements—market selection, product, pricing, sales force, channels, after-sales service, advertising, and promotion—are the same in both sectors. And many of the same concepts and principles apply to both. For example, the market should be segmented to create a competitive advantage, and the sales force should cover all key segments of the market with a product/service package designed to fill the customer's needs. Advertising and promotion should stimulate demand, and prices should be set according to the product's value to the customer. Finally, the proper channel should be selected to reach various market segments.

However, business-to-business companies have characteristics that distinguish them from consumer companies; thus they have distinctive marketing requirements. Most of these distinctions are obvious, but the implications are not always so obvious. Recognizing them can make the difference between a successful and an unsuccessful industrial marketer. This section examines the distinctive characteristics of the marketing job.

Nature of Demand

The first important difference is the nature of the demand, which has implications for the marketing mix elements or marketing levers that must be managed. In consumer markets, demand is usually pulled through the channels of distribution by creating brand awareness, building images, and making the product available in many outlets. On the other hand, demand for a typical industrial product is created by developing a product/service package that fills a customer need and by pushing it through the channels of distribution with a strong applications sales effort and/or service network. Together these elements create a company reputation that is equivalent to brand awareness in consumer goods companies. The demand pull in consumer markets is created by advertising, promotion, and packaging. Advertising in industrial markets, in contrast, is usually relegated to a channel support function—helping to push the product/service package through the distributors or the sales force. The key marketing levers in the industrial arena are product selection and development, market/customer selection, pricing, channel selection and management, sales force effectiveness, and service support.

With functions like product development, applications engineering, and after-sales service so fundamental to the demand push, it is clear that successful industrial marketing is a multifunction effort. The impact of nonmarketing functions, such as engineering and manufacturing, is far greater in industrial markets than consumer markets. Most industrial companies have been built around product characteristics or servicing capability (e.g., technical service, applications expertise, delivery, after-sales service, and part availability) rather than marketing skill. In fact, recognition of the importance of marketing is a much more recent phenomenon in industrial companies than in consumer goods companies. Marketing effectiveness evolves in five stages (see Exhibit B-1).[2]

Unfortunately, industrial companies are far behind consumer goods companies, retailing, and electronics companies in marketing effectiveness. Why? Because they are traditionally driven by engineering and manufacturing considerations rather than marketing considerations. The industrial winners of the 1990s will discover the power of industrial marketing and customer satisfaction.

The implication for industrial marketers is that they must learn to collaborate with other functions. Industrial marketers cannot go off in a closet and develop a successful marketing program. They must work with the engineering department on product requirements, with the manufacturing department on cost and delivery, and with the accounting department to assemble cost data. In a sense, successful industrial

Exhibit B-1

EVOLUTION OF MARKETING EFFECTIVENESS

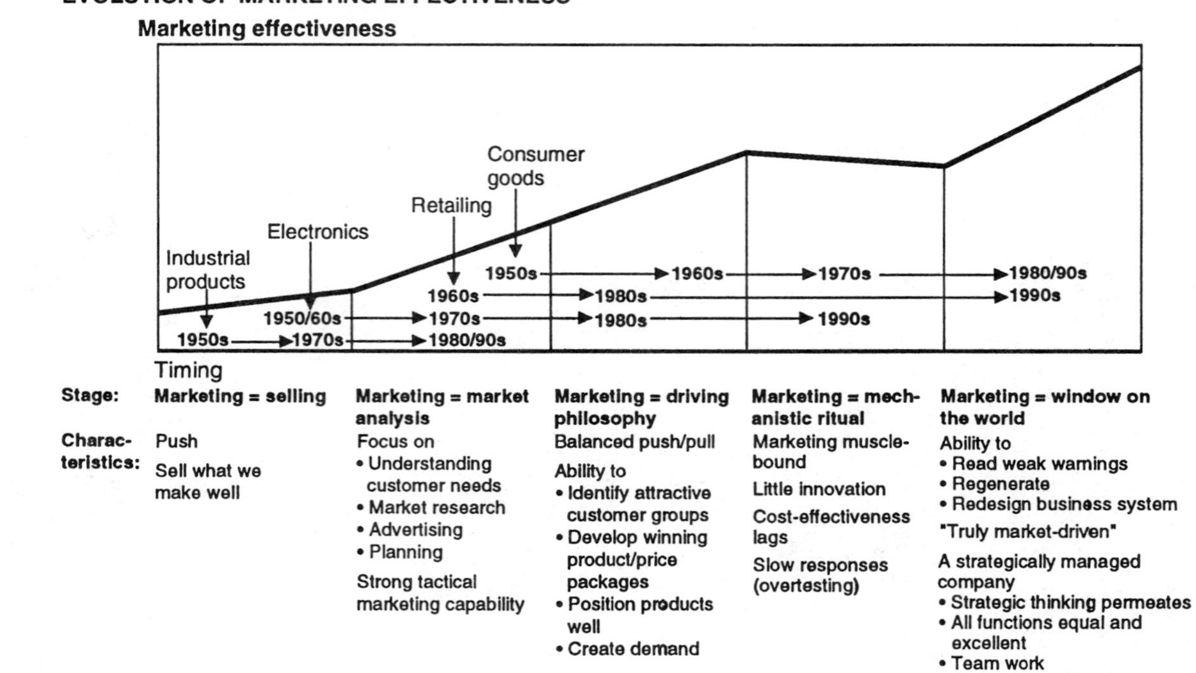

Stage:	**Marketing = selling**	**Marketing = market analysis**	**Marketing = driving philosophy**	**Marketing = mechanistic ritual**	**Marketing = window on the world**
Characteristics:	Push Sell what we make well	Focus on • Understanding customer needs • Market research • Advertising • Planning Strong tactical marketing capability	Balanced push/pull Ability to • Identify attractive customer groups • Develop winning product/price packages • Position products well • Create demand	Marketing muscle-bound Little innovation Cost-effectiveness lags Slow responses (overtesting)	Ability to • Read weak warnings • Regenerate • Redesign business system "Truly market-driven" A strategically managed company • Strategic thinking permeates • All functions equal and excellent • Team work • Cost, service, quality focus • Think entire business system

marketers must be "mini" general managers who rely on all functions to perform their task. Usually top management involvement is necessary to ensure the cross-fertilization of ideas and the cooperation of the other departments.

A multifunction marketing effort is necessary not only for marketing planning but also for selling. The industrial buyer normally employs a more rigorous and sophisticated buying process. Formal evaluations and trials are required before purchase because of the large quantities purchased or the technical specifications that need to be met. As a result, it is not unusual for an industrial products seller to work with several departments in the buying organization—purchasing, engineering, sales, and manufacturing may all be involved.

Market Complexity

The second important difference between industrial and consumer goods companies is the multiplicity and complexity of product, channel, and end-user/influencer combinations. It is not unusual for an industrial company to serve as many as 50 different end-use markets, with multiple products, through several direct and/or distributor channels. Exhibit B-2 shows an example of the typical complexity of an industrial market, in this case metal doors. Consumer marketers would argue that their market is equally complex, with several channels (e.g., drug, food, variety, discount, gas station, specialty, hardware, and department store outlets) and end-user segments, but rarely is a product sold through all channels. In addition, consumer end-user segments are defined according to only a limited number of demographic factors, such as income level, age, fashion preference. Industrial end-user segments, by contrast, can be defined by an unlimited number of buying factors, customer volume usages, geographic regions, user applications, and product characteristics.

The implication of this complexity of products, markets, and channels is that it is rarely possible for an industrial company to be "all things to all customers." Thus, the successful marketer needs to do three things well: identify and segment the market creatively; be selective in the customer groups he or she chooses to attack; and develop multiple marketing strategies, each designed for a specific segment.

Economic Structure

The third major difference between industrial and consumer goods companies is in their economic structures (see Exhibit B-3). Although there are exceptions to any generalization, consumer goods companies have a higher contribution margin (as a percentage of sales) but usually incur higher general, selling, and administrative costs (GSA) because of higher marketing and sales expenses (see Exhibit B-4 on page 956). In

Exhibit B-2

TYPICAL INDUSTRIAL MARKET COMPLEXITY

EXAMPLE

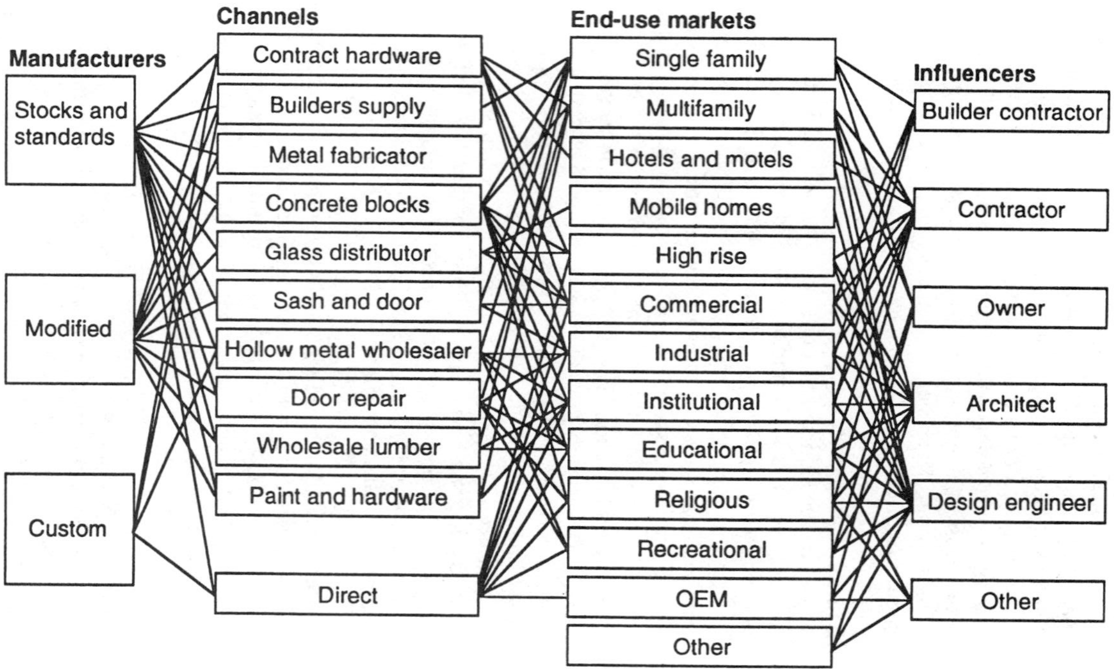

Exhibit B-3

TYPICAL ECONOMIC STRUCTURES

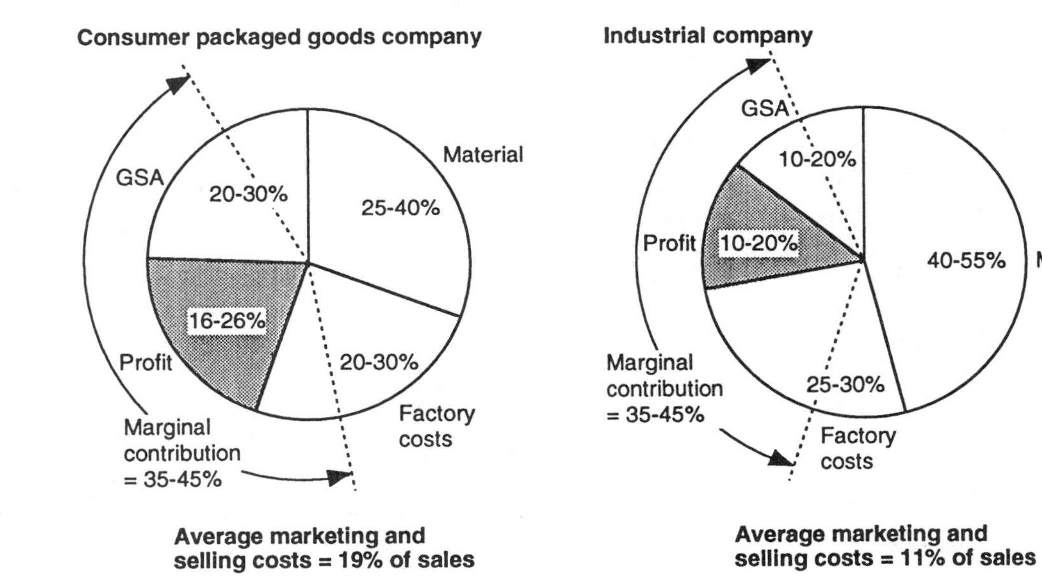

Note: Marginal contribution is defined as sales less all variable costs (including all materials, direct labor, and the variable portion of factory overhead and the variable portion of GSA)

Exhibit B-4

INDUSTRIAL VS. CONSUMER MARKETING AND SELLING COSTS

Average marketing-cost ratios

Marketing costs as a percent of net sales

Marketing-support costs

Selling-related costs

Consumer product classes

Product class	Selling-related costs	Total
Ethical drugs	12.0	32.5%
Prescription drugs	11.2	27.0
Personal care, health & household convenience products	18.0	26.0
All other consumer products	7.6	17.4
Consumer food products	10.6	15.4
Appliances & home electronics	7.3	12.5
Sporting and hobby items	6.5	12.0
Apparel, consumer textile & home furnishings products	3.7	9.4

Average total = 19%

Average marketing = 10%

Selling related = 9%

Nonconsumer product classes

Product class	Selling-related costs	Total
Office equipment	6.7	29.3%
Controls and instruments	5.8	18.0
Metalworking machinery	3.0	16.6
MRO supplies and consumables	3.2	16.3
Communications equipment	3.8	13.2
Farm, construction & mining equip.	3.7	12.1
Fabricated structural metal products	4.1	11.7
AC and heating equipment	3.3	11.6
Abrasives, asbestos & mineral prod.	2.3	11.4
Valves, pumps & compressors	3.3	10.9
Transformers & switchgear	3.1	9.9
Electric lighting & wiring equipment	2.7	9.6
Plastics & rubber products	3.1	9.5
Building materials	2.9	9.5
Industrial chemicals	2.6	8.0
Converted paper products	1.7	6.8
Plastic & synthetic rubber	2.0	6.6
Motor vehicle parts & acces. items	2.2	5.7
Primary metal products	1.2	4.3
Pulp & unconverted paper products	1.0	3.5

Average total = 11%

Selling related = 8%

Average marketing = 3%

Source: Conference Board Study

industrial companies, on the other hand, manufacturing costs are usually higher as a percentage of sales, because of the high raw material content, resulting in lower contribution margins. The net result of the differences in economic structures is that consumer goods companies have the greatest profit sensitivity to volume, price, and GSA; industrial goods companies are sensitive to many more factors, including price, volume, customer mix, product mix, and manufacturing costs (see Exhibit B-5).

The implication for the industrial marketer is that planning has to go beyond merely generating more volume. Each company must build its marketing mix around the economics of its business. And there is room for considerable variety in the industrial sector. Economic structures vary more among industrial competitors than among consumer goods competitors. In almost all industrial markets, there is a wide variation in cost structures owing to differences in production processes, physical distribution setups, levels of integration, channels of distribution, overhead structures, and/or sales efforts. So each marketer must understand her own economics and the economics of the competition.

Illustrations of the importance of this requirement are not hard to find. One small manufacturer of capital equipment who was losing money found that she was unable to compete with high-volume competitors. Top management believed volume was the only answer and urged the marketing department to launch a price campaign to obtain volume. The marketing manager first undertook a competitive cost analysis and learned that the company's contribution margin of 20 percent was well below that of the competition, which ranged between 35 and 45 percent. Furthermore, if the company dropped prices 10 percent to compete, it would require double the present sales volume just to achieve the already poor profit results and would require triple the sales volume to reach management's 20 percent ROI target.

Because the sales task was insurmountable and the competition had more margin with which to retaliate, the marketing manager then decided to study the nature of demand in the market. The field work uncovered a large group of customers who wanted custom, or specialized, machinery and who were willing to pay a premium. These customers were not being served very well by the competitors, all of whom were interested in volume business because of their inflexible, in-line manufacturing processes. Our marketing manager recognized that the company, which had a flexible job shop and skilled engineering applications department, had a special ability to serve the custom segment of the market. Therefore the manager recalculated the economics and determined this specialty niche could provide handsome profits without incurring engineering and sales costs that would offset the margins. The company launched a highly-successful strategy aimed at the specialty niche—so successful, in fact, that competition was forced

Exhibit B-5

DIFFERENCES IN ECONOMIC LEVERS BETWEEN INDUSTRIAL AND CONSUMER COMPANIES

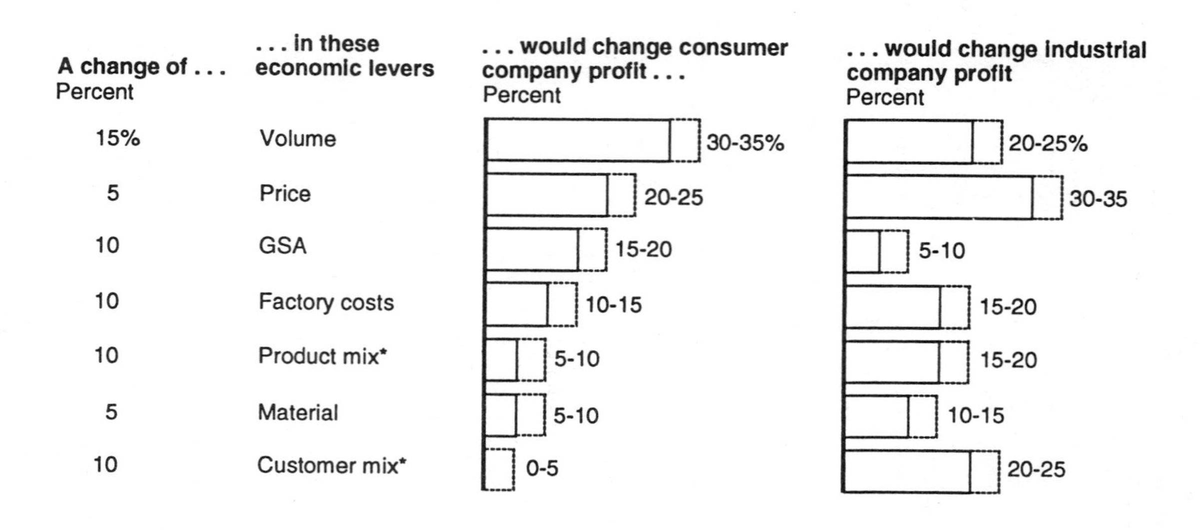

Raising the lowest 10 percent ot the average

to follow five years later as the market migrated toward the specialty product because of its important performance features.

A manufacturer of industrial components also succeeded in using economics to advantage. The dominant manufacturer—with a 65 percent market share—was concerned about selective price cutting from a much smaller competitor. Realizing that the favorable economic structure would be destroyed by meeting the competitor's price, the dominant manufacturer retaliated by beefing up her sales force and physical distribution system to provide more service to her customers. While this strategy added fixed costs, it was far less costly than cutting prices—and it worked.

We have seen that dropping prices to generate volume is sometimes a self-defeating strategy in the industrial sector, and that profits are highly sensitive to price changes. Fortunately, industrial marketers have more latitude with price than their consumer goods counterparts. Pricing constraints under the Robinson-Patman Act are generally less burdensome in the industrial sector because many industrial products are custom made or modified, thus incurring different costs, and/or most industrial buyers do not compete head-on as consumer buyers do. A key element of the Act that is often overlooked is that as long as customers do not compete directly, they can be sold the same product at different prices. Thus pricing is often more flexible in industrial markets. In fact, prices are always negotiated.

Given the importance of negotiated pricing in the industrial environment as well as the varying costs (including sales, application engineering, and distribution) of serving different customers, a successful industrial marketer will give careful consideration to customer profitability in planning the customer mix and pricing strategy. Take the example of the general manager of a motor manufacturer who thought the company was making a reasonable 10 percent profit from sales to its largest customer ($5 million in revenue). The volume from this customer was considered important to the factory. However, when the profitability of this volume was calculated for the first time, it was discovered that the prices to this customer were lower than normal and that costs were significantly higher due to extraordinary applications engineering costs, a distant shipping location, and a large marketing entertainment expense. The net result was a 20 percent net loss on the account and, even more surprising, a negative contribution margin to cover fixed factory overhead.

Justifiably concerned, the marketing manager looked further and learned that the company's brand name was important to the customer's selling effort. Armed with this knowledge, she visited the customer and negotiated a price that was 20 percent higher. So an understanding of economics spurred an industrial marketer to shift from defensive to aggressive pricing to ensure adequate profitability.

Availability of Data

The final important difference between industrial and consumer companies is in the availability of market and cost data, which we have already seen is critical to industrial marketing success. Consumer companies have market and market share data available through the UPC information at checkout counters as well as consumer behavior patterns through well-honed market research. Cost data are usually obtainable in consumer companies because products are fairly standardized and manufacturing operations are not very complex. Profitability by product and channel is also readily available.

In the industrial markets, on the other hand, the key to obtaining economic (profit), market, and competitive data—for selecting market segments to attack, developing profitable growth strategies, managing product and market mix, and determining price levels—is "analytical ingenuity." Market data are often buried or scattered. To get to it, the industrial marketer must segment the market and then develop information on size, growth, customer concentration, and product/service requirements by building up data on individual customers. Market intelligence collected from the sales force and/or in-depth customer interviews are often the only sources of market and competitive data. Forecasting must be derived from end-user market forecasts rather than demographics or gross economic factors.

In most industrial companies, cost data must be reformulated and analyzed before it can be used because corporate financial reporting is aimed at meeting financial requirements or generating product data, not providing decision-making guidelines. Possibly because it is so difficult, few industrial companies add customer-specific engineering, order size, sales/marketing, and physical distribution costs to manufacturing costs. In fact, very few companies generate customer profitability data, an essential ingredient in determining prices and establishing customer priorities. To generate this information, price files must be matched with product costs as well as specific engineering and other costs. The process is easier in consumer companies where products and prices are more homogeneous. Thus the successful industrial marketer must be a skilled, clever market researcher as well as an amateur cost accountant.

Industrial marketers face a more difficult task than the consumer marketer. Their game is more complex, data are less readily available, they must reach a more sophisticated buyer, strategic marketing options are more plentiful, and they are more dependent on the other functions in the organization. Because they generally deal with fewer customers, however, industrial marketers have a better opportunity to understand them, to select the groups to attack, and to talk to customers face-to-face to overcome buying resistance. In contrast to the millions of buyers for a consumer product, most industrial products have fewer than 1,000 buyers—and many have fewer than 300. Equally important, the industrial marketer has more levers to pull in outfoxing the competition and creating customer value.

The essence of a successful industrial marketing strategy was stated best by B. Charles Ames:

> *Marketing in the industrial world is a total business philosophy aimed at improving profit performance by identifying the needs of each key customer group and then designing and producing a product/service package that will enable the company to serve selected groups more effectively than does its competition. This definition is admittedly a mouthful, but it reveals four key dimensions to industrial marketing: (1) aiming for improved profit performance, (2) identifying customer needs, (3) selecting customer groups for whom the company can develop a competitive edge, and (4) designing and producing the right product/ service package or packages.*[3]

MARKET SELECTION AND PRODUCT POLICY

Market selection and product policy cannot be divorced. Over 30 years ago, Wendell R. Smith wrote a classic article showing the connection between these two critical marketing strategy variables.[4] He distinguished between *product differentiation* and *segmentation* as valid marketing strategies. In product differentiation, Smith argued that companies principally attempt to "bend the will of demand to supply" by producing economic quantities of one or a few products. These products are then differentiated from essentially identical competitive offerings by what Smith called a *merchandising strategy*—the appeal through a strong selling effort or other promotional means to the market at large. The aim is to persuade buyers that there is some worthwhile difference between the manufacturer's offering and the competition that would make them decide in its favor. For example, perhaps manufacturer A uses only stainless steel valves in his pumps while competitors B and C use cheaper materials. Manufacturer A also delivers from stock in any of four pump sizes, and is known for its 24-hour service. All of these are differentiating characteristics that manufacturer A could employ through astute selling and promotion to gain market advantage and market share with a fairly limited product line.

Smith asked us to contrast this strategy with one that became possible as production technology allowed smaller production batches to be economically feasible. He defined a *segmentation strategy* as one that isolates subgroups of the whole market that have peculiar or unique needs and then develops products that would be especially satisfying to one or more of these subgroups. Market segmentation, Smith claimed, gives the manufacturer of pumps (who makes a special acid-resistant model) a distinctive and salable advantage with customers who need such a piece of equipment. Smith saw segmentation as "bending supply to the needs of demand."

Although there is nothing inherently better in differentiation or segmentation as product policy strategies, most companies are finding it difficult or impossible to serve the entire market with one or a few offerings. Yet this poses a paradox, for the hallmark of the successful company today is simplicity. The link between reduction of complexity and cost competitiveness is inescapable, and this poses a challenge for the industrial marketer—how to meet the varied needs of multiple customers while controlling product proliferation. The key, as recent research shows, is in the product design strategy. The most successful companies use up to 50 percent fewer parts than their competitors, so their products are faster, simpler, and cheaper to manufacture. They use standard components and gain variety in assembly, thus meeting the internal need for simplicity while also meeting the market need for customization.

Even with a basic differentiation strategy, it may be desirable or necessary to segment customers according to which are easier to serve at a greater profit. Consider the producer of corrugated cartons, a product that cannot be shipped great distances because the freight charges quickly outstrip the product value. Here, the manufacturer would wish to segment the market at the very least into nearer-farther, and it may be wise to consider several other dimensions (e.g., product made by the prospect, company size, etc.).

Segmentation may also enable a company to focus its efforts on those customers where it has a competitive edge. For example, an electrical equipment marketing manager was faced with the complexity of marketing and selling into 35 end-use industries through two traditional sales channels: original equipment manufacturers (who sold the company's electrical equipment on their machines to end-users) and distributors (who sold equipment for maintenance and repair). The marketing manager simplified his task by redefining his markets into three strategic market segments—small maintenance and repair users, large process users, and small new construction users. He arrived at this resegmentation by employing a simple matrix that considered product usage (new construction versus maintenance) and buyer size (large versus small), and by evaluating buying behavior and trends along these dimensions (see Exhibit C-1).

He discovered that the large users, who ran their equipment 24 hours per day, were becoming increasingly concerned with energy consumption and were interested in combining their new construction and maintenance purchases into annual buys to obtain purchasing leverage. This information led him to conclude that he could gain a competitive advantage by developing high-efficiency equipment and launching a direct applications sales effort to serve large users, thus creating a new market segment served by a new channel. In so doing, he could not only provide value for these large users, but equally

Exhibit C-1

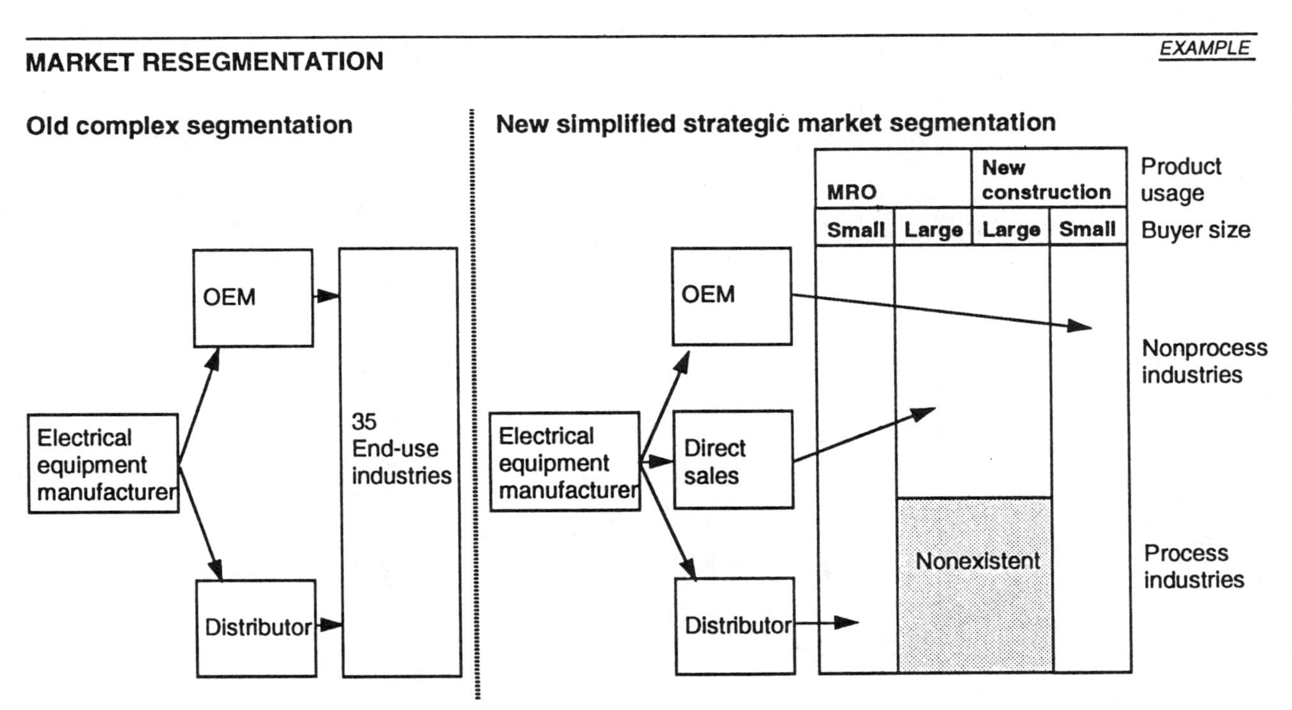
MARKET RESEGMENTATION
EXAMPLE
Old complex segmentation
Electrical equipment manufacturer
OEM
Distributor
35 End-use industries
New simplified strategic market segmentation
Electrical equipment manufacturer
OEM
Direct sales
Distributor
MRO
New construction
Product usage
Small
Large
Large
Small
Buyer size
Nonprocess industries
Nonexistent
Process industries

important, could increase his profit by saving the margins taken by original equipment manufacturers and distributors. He was able to take this volume away from his original equipment manufacturers and distributors without losing their loyalty because the value of the business he generated from the other two groups—the small maintenance and repair user (served by distributors) and the small new construction user (served by original equipment manufacturers)—was substantial.

Segmentation is a necessary part of any industrial marketing strategy because manufacturers usually find that some customers can be served more profitably than others.[5] Segmentation is simply selecting those portions of the market that fall into these categories, and spending scarce marketing resources on them. Thus the two major reasons for segmenting the market are to (1) effectively allocate the firm's scarce marketing resources and (2) provide the basis for niche strategies. Good segmentation occurs when the competitive structure falls out logically and the marketer uncovers a segment where he can gain a competitive advantage. Otherwise, segmentation is only an exercise, rather than a means to a profitable marketing strategy.

There is clear evidence from managers' experiences as well as from the academic literature that industrial market segmentation is practiced more often in breach than in occurrence. Many companies do not segment the market at all, or when they do, they segment it on variables their managers themselves claim are probably not useful. Or the sales force will ignore management's pronouncements about prospecting for one rather than another class of business, and go after "anybody and everybody" in its quest for sales.

The reasons for the lack of market segmentation and clear market selection are simple but seductive. First, many companies have no idea of how much it costs them to serve a given customer. This is one of the most important shortcomings in management practice; firms without a clear idea of their costs by account almost always end up subsidizing unprofitable customers with the profits from more desirable accounts, which would otherwise be available to management for other uses. For example, in the electrical distributing industry, there are essentially two types of customers. The first is the general contractor, who orders in advance in quantity, sticks to a relatively stable line of boxes, cable, and conduit for all homes in a development, and buys primarily on price. The second category of customer is called the "basket contractor," usually a single-home-at-a-time builder who buys over the counter, needs immediate delivery, takes small quantities of many different items, and is not sensitive to price. The mix of business in the typical electrical distributor is at least 80 percent basket business, and often less than 20 percent volume buyers. The profit after taxes in most such enterprises is less than 5 percent. When one distributor computed his contribution margin by account on these basket contractors, he found that over 50 percent of basket orders cost more to pick and fill from inventory than they returned in revenue. He then looked at the same accounts by line item on each order and found that for some frequently purchased items across all basket contractors, he could make money—for several others, he lost money. Thus by segmenting his customers, the distributor was able to adjust prices so that each line item on the basket contractors' orders broke even with the costs of carrying, picking, and selling it. He no longer subsidized the basket accounts with the worthwhile profits of the volume buyers.

Second, there is a great fear in many companies of saying "no" to any business, regardless of its profitability. Companies that are characterized by high fixed-cost structures, such as airlines and primary metals, are the most prone to this disease. Often, the management is afraid to turn down marginally profitable or even unprofitable business because (a) it is afraid that new business may not appear tomorrow and (b) high fixed-cost businesses often benefit from "filling up capacity" and spreading their costs over higher volumes. One manufacturer of prestressed concrete who behaved in this way was trapped by the practice of filling up the order backlog with unprofitable business in poor times. (A minimum of $10 million in unfilled orders was required by the firm in order to have full production runs continually.) In good times, the company found it had little or no production capacity remaining to serve the more profitable accounts that were ready to buy.

Market selection must be done regularly, continually, and unfailingly by every industrial marketer.[6] The principles are simple, but they need to be applied:

1. *Assess the firm's capabilities.* Would a broader line, tailored to more specific market subgroups, allow more profits? Is the line already too broad?
2. *Assess the market.* Start with externally observable and easily available measures, such as company size, location, and industry. Use the SIC data and commercially available data sources (e.g., *Sales and Marketing Management's Survey of Industrial Buying Power*) as a starting point.
3. *Compare sales data from current customers* on such matrices to see if they split the market up into useful groups. Where externally available data does not help, delve deeper into the prospects' or customers' businesses for segmentation "handles." What is their production technology? How is their buying group organized? With key accounts, it may be necessary and worthwhile to prepare individual profiles of each of the buying influences in the prospect firm. Remember, the goal from segmentation is to find market

subgroups that we can serve more profitably than others, and/or that will be more satisfied with what we have to sell than with others.
4. Once a good and small set of segmentation bases have been found, *evaluate the attractiveness of each segment* and set priorities for attracting them. The segment priorities should be determined by such factors as competitive structure, assets required, and the companies' strength in each segment.
5. Once the priorities are established, *develop marketing strategies and programs* for each segment. These strategies should specify customer focus, product offering, pricing, sales force, after-sales service, and distributor management.

Segmentation and market selection cannot be divorced. Most firms do a poor job of selecting those customers who can be most satisfied and yield the greatest profit from service and, hence, subsidize poor business with good business. The job of segmentation is to isolate "good business," either current or potentially available. The use of segmentation may suggest new segments that can be served with current products, or new products that will enable the generation of more profitable business.

In the end, differentiation and segmentation refer to potential *seller* reactions to perceived or real variations in *buyer behavior.* It is not possible in the scope of this chapter to outline the 40 years of work by Tom Bonoma that has been invested in discovering and categorizing buyer behavior, but it is possible to make a brief summary of points he made about the most important discoveries.[7]

1. Buyers in industrial, commercial, and business settings behave very differently from those in consumer or end-user settings. One of the primary reasons for this difference is the fact that the *buying center,* or group of individuals involved in an industrial purchase, is likely to be broader in scope and more varied in purpose than that involved in purchasing something like a breakfast cereal.
2. The *purchasing situation* encountered by the buying center has important ramifications for its deliberations. For instance, buyers facing a routine repurchase of supplies (a "full rebuy," in the literature's parlance) will behave much differently from a buying center attempting to specify and purchase an entirely new production line (a "new purchase").
3. The best way to understand the buying center for purposes of segmentation or differentiation appears to be to probe the individual motivations of the humans coming to form the group and to become familiar with the group dynamics involved in the purchase being attempted. Exhibit C-2 suggests a format for gathering psychological information about the buying center that combines the individual and group approaches. It focuses on buying center composition, the

Exhibit C-2

FORMAT FOR GATHERING PSYCHOLOGICAL INFORMATION

Who's in the buying center and what is the base of their power?	What are their priorities?	What specific benefits does each important buyer want?	How do the important buyers see us?	Selling strategy

power of each of the individuals in the buying center, the perception of those individuals, and the specific benefits sought by each party as a consequence of a purchase.

4. The deliberations of a buying center are not only complex, but change over time and experience with a vendor, implying that buying center analysis and the consequent segmentation/differentiation that occurs as a result is an ongoing need for the selling organization. Shapiro and others, for example, have found that over time buyers "migrate" from high service and willingness to pay high prices for that service in a purchase situation to being more "bargain basement," either doing without technical services or else supplying their own from in-house resources, but expecting thereby to pay much lower prices for their component and other purchases.

PRICING

Many general managers are unhappy with their pricing effort. They feel sure they are leaving money on the table in some cases and missing volume in others. They also have a nagging feeling that there must be some strategic pricing moves they can make to get overall industry prices up and thereby improve their profits. But they are not certain of the legal limits and they are often afraid to raise prices for fear of losing volume.

Pricing is one of the most complex and least understood aspects of industrial marketing. James Nault, in a Conference Board Report, put his finger on the problem when he said:

> *Pricing is a subtle art. Too often it has consisted of black magic—a mixture made up of 1/3 facts, 1/3 myths and elusions, and 1/3 economic theories that are out of phase with reality. If we are smart, we will work to eliminate the black magic and make pricing decisions based on facts.*

In that spirit, we will not dwell on the theoretical aspects of pricing—e.g., price/demand curves, learning curves, penetration versus skim pricing, and marginal pricing that are discussed in any marketing text; we will instead highlight the practical aspects and discuss actual techniques that managers have used to improve their pricing.

The first question often asked is, "How can I determine whether I have a pricing problem and thus take remedial action?" We have found that the use of a simple checklist of ten questions (see Table 1) can assist management in understanding the presence and magnitude of a potential pricing problem. Answering these questions requires detailed understanding of the company's pricing system (i.e., how prices are derived and administered, competitive price level over time, and price/cost relationships by product and customer). If one cannot answer these questions favorably or precisely, chances are there is potential for price improvement.

TABLE 1. Industrial Pricing Strategy Checklist

Ten questions to determine if you have a pricing problem:

1. Are prices falling in real terms, yet share is constant or declining?
2. Do you have the feeling you are leaving money on-the-table, but cannot substantiate it with hard data?
3. Are your salespeople always claiming your prices are 3 to 5 percent high, yet your share is holding steady or rising?
4. Are pricing approval levels acting more as a volume discount mechanism than a control mechanism?
5. Do pricing approval levels reflect real profit levels?
6. Do your prices reflect customer–specific costs (e.g., transportation, off-invoice rebates, all discounts) so that you can obtain true "pocket" prices?
7. Do margins (after customer–specific costs) vary widely by customer?
8. Can you define/describe your competitors' pricing strategies/rules?
9. Can you predict how and when competitors will react to your price moves?
10. Do you have a planned method of communicating price moves to the three key stakeholders—(1) customers, (2) competitors (legally, of course), (3) sales force?

To capitalize on this potential, one must know why there is a problem. Here a distinction must be made between *strategic* pricing and *tactical* pricing. Strategic pricing is principally the pricing image a company establishes for itself—in other words "conventional warfare" pricing. Most industrial managers do a respectable job of strategic pricing, mainly because they are forced to by the marketplace. On the other hand, tactical pricing can be defined as the day-to-day management of the pricing process or "guerrilla warfare" pricing. We have found that the tactical area is often overlooked by management. Yet, because so much industrial pricing is negotiated, guerrilla warfare pricing most often affords management the greatest pricing opportunity.

Strategic Pricing

Strategic pricing consists of three elements: (1) price level vis-a-vis competitive offerings, (2) timing and amount of price changes, and (3) communication of prices to the marketplace.

Determining the price level is well recognized as the most important aspect of strategic pricing. Most companies price their products to meet competition (market-based pricing) and/or to achieve certain profit objectives (full-cost-plus pricing), but few do so with a full understanding or evaluation of the five factors that can make a real difference:

1. real costs/profits;
2. comparative value to the customer;

3. marketing segmentation and demand;
4. likely competitive reactions; and
5. company marketing objectives.

Successful concepts and analyses in each of these will be discussed.

Real Costs/Profits. Most industrial companies use fully absorbed manufacturing costs to determine product line profitability and thus establish the basis for price levels. However, given the high fixed manufacturing costs in most industrial plants and often unreliable allocation methods, many managers have begun to think in terms of contribution margin (i.e., sales less all variable cost) in determining product availability. Contribution margin provides management with a truer profit figure, one that gets around the questionable allocation methods. This view of product profitability enables management to determine which products need price increases (even at the expense of some volume) and which products can afford to have prices shaved to obtain volume. Often referred to as marginal pricing, this method of costing can be dangerous. To ensure that the sales force will not "give away" these seemingly high margins, management often establishes a hurdle rate (which includes fixed manufacturing plus fixed GSA costs) or adds a percentage to cover costs across the board.

The use of contribution margin paid off handsomely for a construction materials company that wanted to expand from one shift to three. Since the plant already had a 40 percent market share in a price competitive market, the marketing manager felt he could not obtain further share in his traditional marketing area without destroying the current price level. Yet the company's accounting system dictated that the product could not be shipped farther than 200 miles and still earn a profit. Faced with this dilemma, the marketing manager first reconstructed the profit economics of the business (see Exhibit D-2) and discovered he could ship 700 miles before incurring an out-of-pocket loss. He then visited customers outside the 200-mile radius and determined that he could "buy" business with a 5 percent price discount. Since the business was on a bid contract basis, he would not upset the price equilibrium in these outlying areas as long as he took only one contract per contractor each year. He then devised a "core-fringe" price strategy in which he changed nothing in the "core" area (200-mile radius) and selectively approached customers in the "fringe" area. Was this a dangerous marginal pricing strategy? Yes. But he did his homework and was very careful not to provoke competitive retaliation. Was it successful? Yes. He filled the plant for three shifts and increased the contribution margin from $4 million to $9 million. As a result, pretax profits went from $2 million to $6.5 million.

Another company in automotive components refined the contribution margin concept and used contribution margin per machine hour as the basis for changing its pricing strategy. The marketing manager

Exhibit D-2

RESTRUCTURED ECONOMICS

EXAMPLE

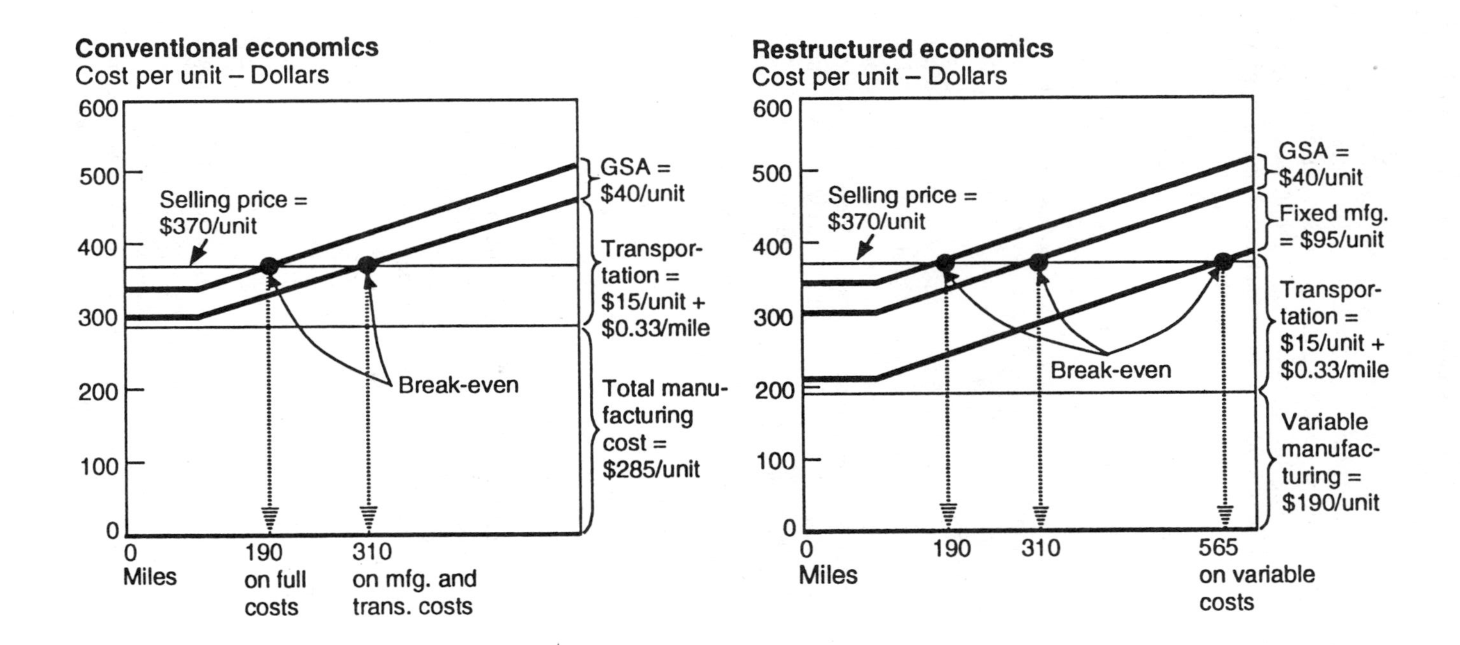

recognized that every product in his plant went through a single machine, which was a bottleneck. He quickly discovered that product profitability viewed in terms of machine time bore no relationship to the traditional, fully-absorbed gross profit indicator (see Exhibit D-3). A recap of individual orders revealed that one seemingly high-profit order was not covering all costs, while a lost order, sacrificed because of its seemingly low profit, would have been a winner even with a 5 percent price discount. Naturally, he changed the quoting system to reflect costs on a machine-hour basis.

The point of these examples is that marketing management must look at real costs in determining prices and profits. In addition to manufacturing and shipping costs, special engineering and marketing costs must be considered. And, as pointed out earlier, a knowledge of customer profitability can assist management in the price negotiation process.

Comparative Value to the Customer. Although most industrial companies give lip service to customer value in pricing, they rarely do a thorough evaluation of their product versus competition, nor do they go beyond the product characteristics or performance to include such things as comparative product lifecycle, operating costs (including maintenance and energy consumption), servicing ability, delivery, prestige, access to product innovation, and personal relationships. One must consider the total product/service package in relation to that of the competitors to maximize price. Two simple competitive analyses can overcome these two shortcomings.

The *price/performance matrix* has been successfully used by a number of companies. The marketing manager for a manufacturer of mobile machinery developed a performance characteristic index on the x-axis, which included a comparative rating of performance features (turning radius, load capacity, and speed between loading and unloading), maintainability (ease of maintenance, average time out of service, and cost of key components), reliability (mean time between failure and average life of key components), and useful life. These data were obtained from used records and company tests. On the y-axis, he plotted prices, his and those of the key competitors (see Exhibit D-4, shown on page 974). He quickly discovered why the major U.S. competitor had a 40 percent market share and the Japanese competitor had 20 percent against his 10 percent share. The U.S. competitor dominated the premium product category and derived a quality image from this product offering. In the standard and low-performance product categories, this competitor had slightly lower prices. In other words, the U.S. competitor was following a "bracket" price strategy that paid off. The Japanese competitor concentrated on the bottom two performance categories and kept prices low, appealing to price-sensitive customers. Given these revealing facts, what did the marketing manager

Exhibit D-3

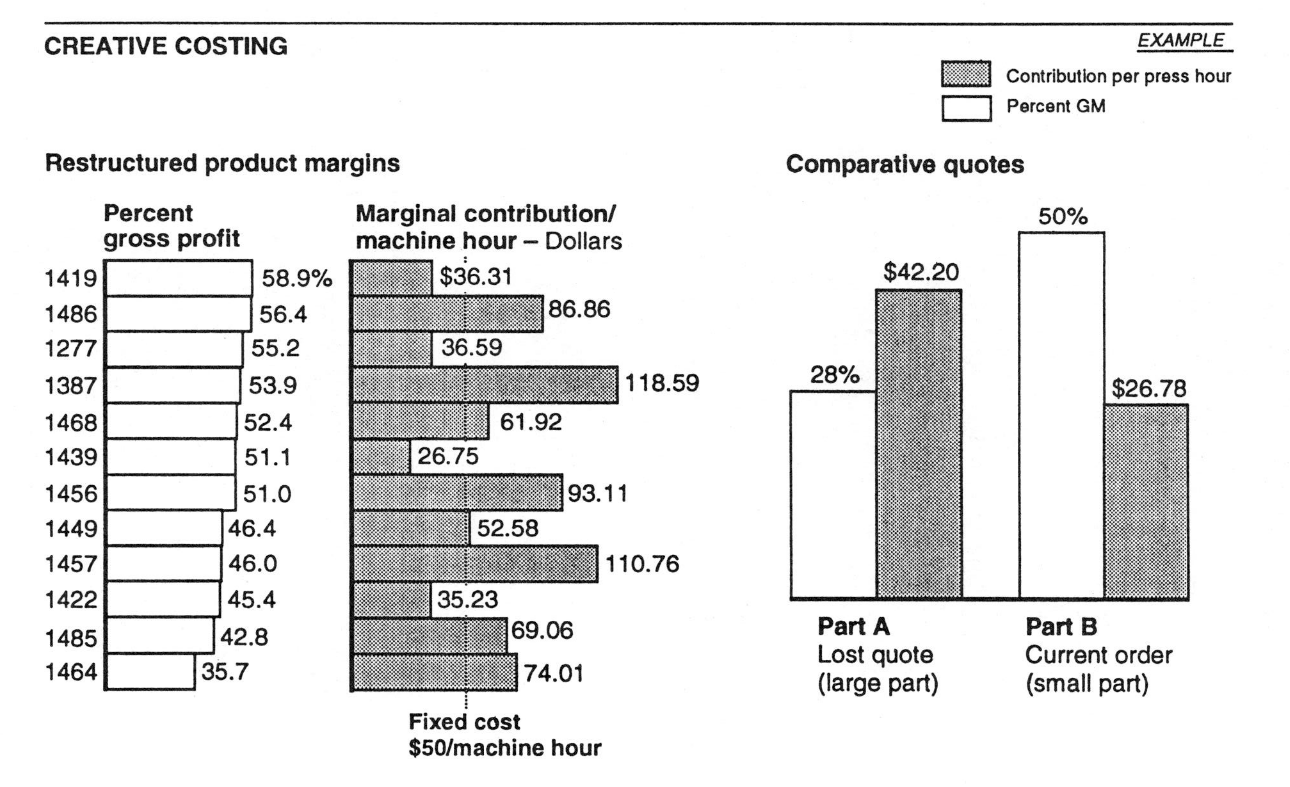
CREATIVE COSTING
EXAMPLE
Contribution per press hour
Percent GM
Restructured product margins
Percent gross profit
Marginal contribution/ machine hour – Dollars
1419
1486
1277
1387
1468
1439
1456
1449
1457
1422
1485
1464
58.9%
56.4
55.2
53.9
52.4
51.1
51.0
46.4
46.0
45.4
42.8
35.7
$36.31
86.86
36.59
118.59
61.92
26.75
93.11
52.58
110.76
35.23
69.06
74.01
Fixed cost
$50/machine hour
Comparative quotes
28%
$42.20
50%
$26.78
Part A
Lost quote
(large part)
Part B
Current order
(small part)

Exhibit D-4

COMPETITIVE PRODUCT POSITIONING

EXAMPLE

Comparative price/benefit grid

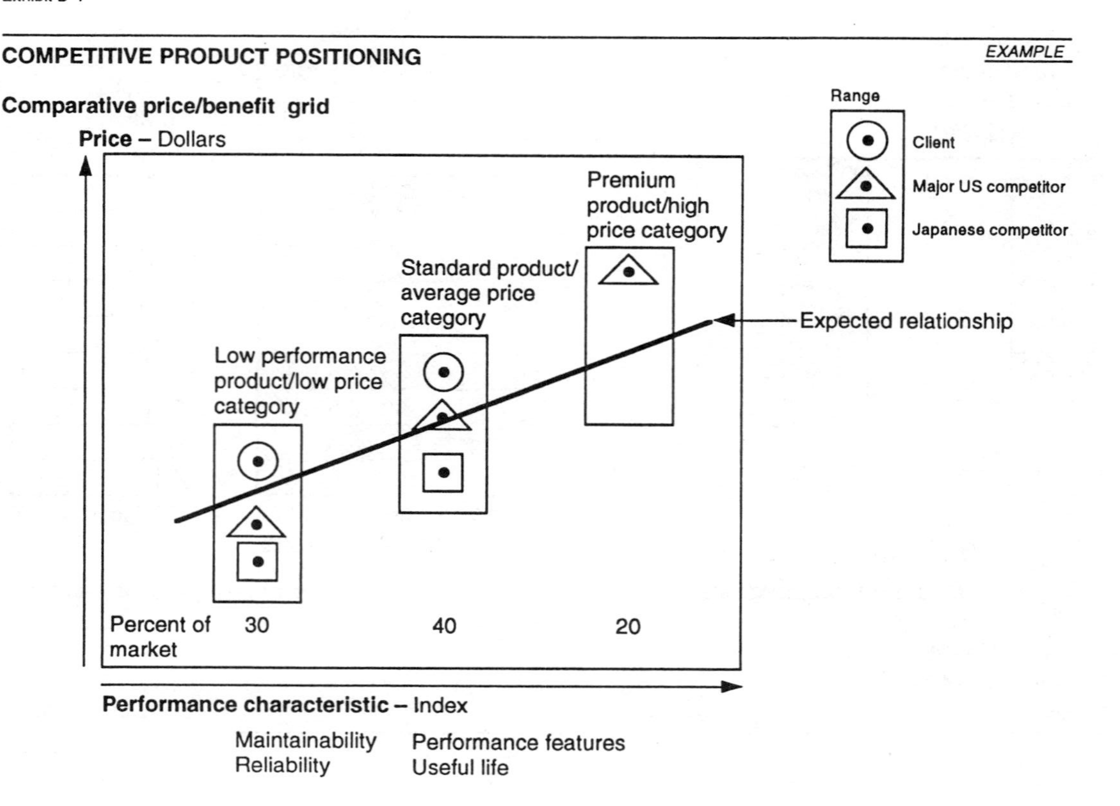

do? He decided to differentiate his product line from the competition by (1) adding important performance characteristics to his existing two products; (2) adding a super-premium product (thus scooping the U.S. competitor's premium image); and (3) adding a stripped-down product priced below both competitors (and thereby appealing to the low-cost segment). It took two years to make these product changes, but in following this strategy, the marketing manager added value (both price and performance) to his product offerings, and achieved a successful competitive advantage. One could argue that this is an example of a successful product strategy. However, as this case points out, product and price are really inseparable.

The second useful comparative analysis is the old standby—*competitive performance* ranked against the key customer buying factors. As shown in Table 2, the marketing manager for a commodity distribution product rated each of the buying factors (based on distributor interviews and surveys), and then ranked the performance of each of the two competitors against his company's. He may have gone a little overboard in quantifying subjective judgments, but he proved that he had a significant performance or value advantage against his competition, mainly in product availability, sales support, and personal relationships (due to his larger sales force); yet his prices were only slightly above his competitors'. To hold his market share, he knew he had to maintain a value advantage (including price), but he judged that it was too high. He determined that he needed only a 5 percent value advantage against his nearest competitor and raised prices to achieve that. As expected, his distributors protested; however, his sales force was able to make the price stick because of other values his company offered.

The point in this section is to price for value to the customer. Too many industrial companies believe they must compete on price alone rather than total value.[8]

Market Segmentation and Demand. Given the negotiated nature of industrial pricing, price differentiation among customer groups is quite common and often the key to profit success. For example, a manufacturer of power transmission devices found it could charge a higher price to an end-user for replacement than to an original equipment manufacturer (OEM) for use on its machines; the value of the device was higher to the end-user (who wants to keep his process running) than to the OEM (who views the motor as a major cost element of his machines).

Although legal price restrictions are less severe in industrial markets, two observations must be made regarding price differentiation schemes. First, there are legal restrictions created not only by the Robinson-Patman Act, but also by the antitrust laws and certain state "loss-leader" laws. Every industrial marketing manager should be aware of pricing practices that might have potential legal pitfalls, e.g.,

TABLE 2. Quantified Comparative Value

Competitive Ranking

Buying Influence	Weight in Buying Decision	Company Rank	Rank x Weight		Competitor A Rank	Competitor A Rank x Weight		Competitor B Rank	Competitor B Rank x Weight	
Price	50	1.00	50.0		1.05	52.5		1.04	52.0	
Availability	20	1.14	22.8		1.00	20.0		1.06	21.2	
Sales effort	10	1.20	12.0		1.00	10.0		1.00	10.0	
Quality	10	1.10	11.0	**62.5**	1.00	10.0	**50.6**	1.10	11.0	**52.2**
Sales support	6	2.00	12.0		1.10	6.6		1.00	6.0	
Breadth of line	3	1.20	3.6		1.00	3.0		1.00	3.0	
Corporate image	1	1.10	1.1		1.00	1.0		1.00	1.0	
Index ranking	100%		112.5			103.1			104.2	
Market share			**50%**			**20%**			**30%**	

	Advantage without Price	Advantage with Price
Company vs. Competitor A	$\frac{62.5}{52.5} = 1.19$	$\frac{112.5}{103.1} = 1.09$
Company vs. Competitor B	$\frac{62.5}{52.0} = 1.20$	$\frac{112.5}{104.2} = 1.06$

resale price maintenance, below-cost reductions, price leadership, price signaling, price discrimination, and new market entry pricing.

Second, within those companies that do have different price levels for different customers or customer groups, there is a strong tendency for the general price level to gravitate to the lowest customer level because of pressures from the sales force. Strong controls must be installed to guard against this.

Notwithstanding the legal and sales force pressures, price differentiation schemes generally result in higher profits because a company can maximize the price/volume trade-offs. As discussed above, however, it is imperative to understand real costs and make effective competitive comparisons.

Likely Competitive Reactions. If all the managers in the cases discussed above had made their pricing decisions in a vacuum without considering potential competitive retaliation, they would have been unsuccessful. For example, the marketing manager who invented "core-fringe" pricing for his construction materials company carefully thought through the competitive ramifications of going after contracts in the fringe area with a 5 percent price reduction. If competitors in the fringe area had retaliated and come after customers in his core area, a devastating price war could have resulted. But he knew the competitors did not want a price war (they had experienced one 10 years previously with a similar product); he knew their economics (each was profitable and near capacity); and he knew the fringe market could absorb another competitor (it was growing and not adequately served). In spite of his confidence, he made his price moves very quietly, carefully, and selectively so as not to arouse the competition.

The marketing manager of the commodity distributor product who raised prices did so only after reviewing how competition had reacted to his past price moves. He discovered that his company (with its 50 percent market share) was the recognized price leader and that in the past the two competitors had raised prices within three months of his company's moves, although not as much. Without these facts (which he had plotted over time), he would not have been as confident of his price increase.

In assessing how competition might react, the industrial marketer must weigh several factors: competitors' cost structures, competitor price changes over time, market demand or lack thereof, the relationship of a competitor's product to other products in his line, and competitor's capacity utilization.

Capacity utilization may be one of the most telling factors. For example, an automotive component supplier with a 70 percent market share was anguishing over a 9 percent price increase. The sales department argued that the major competitor would not raise prices and would thereby take volume from the company; the accounting department claimed they needed a 9 percent price increase to maintain profitability. The marketing manager discovered that the competitor had followed every price increase for the past 5 years; in addition, the competitor only had the capacity for an additional 2 million units. If the marketer lost these 2 million units, he would have to raise prices only 6 percent to offset the profit loss. Thus the 9 percent price rise would net a minimum of 3 percent. Consequently, the price increase was instituted and the competitor followed as predicted. One might say this was a dangerous strategic pricing decision because the competitor might see this as an opportunity to add capacity. However, given the mature nature of this product, that was highly unlikely. The marketer could have rolled prices back very easily if the competitor had not followed.

Company Marketing Objectives. If market demand, real costs, customer value, and competition are accurately assessed, the resulting strategic price levels should maximize profits. However, all of these factors must be weighed against a company's marketing objectives. The impact on the company's other products, the need for short-term profits versus long-term market position, skimming versus penetration objectives for a new product, long-term customer relations, and managing profits over the entire business cycle must be assessed. Pricing should never be done in a vacuum. For example, despite a price-cost squeeze during a recession, a machine tool builder felt it was important to cut prices and match a competitive bid to its major customer to maintain that customer's goodwill. In another example, an electrical equipment manufacturer introduced a new product at a price in line with its other product offerings, even though handsome profits and significant share could have been achieved at a lower price. Management felt the new product introduced at the lower price would have cannibalized its other products. In establishing individual product price levels, the industrial marketer must take into account the marketing objectives for the entire product line.

As to the second element of strategic pricing—the timing and amount of a price change—it is most often better to raise prices once a year rather than several times during a year. Most industrial customers want to lock prices in for their own costing and pricing purposes. Because of the recent persistence of inflation, escalation clauses have become common in some industries; however, if one competitor offers a stable price for a stated period, he is usually assured of being the volume winner.

In all of the above cases, companies tend to be too conservative when it comes to increasing prices. Most companies over-think the competitive reaction. Competitors are usually in the same economic squeeze, and are most often relieved to see the prices rise.

The timing of price changes can be nearly as important as the changes themselves. A simple time lag in following a competitor's price increase can produce the perception of responsiveness to customer cost concerns. The length of the lag is an important consideration because of its effect on profits. One consumer research study showed that a six-week lag in following a competitor's price increase was just as effective as a six-month lag, and choosing the shorter time span resulted in four and a half months of increased profits.

In communicating price changes, the third element in strategic pricing, the industrial marketer must consider three audiences: his sales force, his customers, and his competitors. Salespeople should always be told the rationale for a price change so they can overcome resistance. The same is true of communicating to the customer, whether it be through letters, price lists, etc. However, in many instances it is better *not* to communicate price moves to a customer, especially those who buy the product only occasionally. A purchaser of large machinery is a case in point. Such a purchaser goes out for quotes only when new machinery is needed and does not otherwise keep up with prices; sending him an announcement of price increases would only call attention to the fact and create ill-will.

The most important audience to communicate price increases to is one's competition, so that it will understand your price statesmanship. It is also the trickiest because of legal constraints. Generally speaking, though, it is desirable to publicize price increases, always taking care to inform salespeople and customers in advance—doing so establishes the price leader. Naturally, price moves downward should be as innocuous as possible so as not to encourage retaliation, which could lead to a downward price spiral. It is best to effect price cuts indirectly through changes in terms, service charges, or selective discounts.

In summary, strategic pricing is the cornerstone of an industrial marketer's pricing policy. It consists of price levels, changes, and communications. The key here is to plan the pricing strategy ahead, rather than react to competitive moves.

Tactical Pricing

Strategic pricing is necessary. It is also one way an industrial marketer can gain a competitive advantage if the strategy is carefully thought out. However, we have found that effective tactical, or day-to-day, pricing is where an industrial marketer can really achieve substantial profit improvement. Management's preoccupation with the magic of strategic pricing often causes them to overlook this area of pricing, yet more pricing battles have been won with guerrilla warfare than with conventional warfare.

Astute tactical pricing can yield increases of 5, 10, and even 15 percent in return on sales.[9] A hydraulics manufacturer with annual sales of $210 million increased his return on sales by seven percentage points, yielding increased profits of $15 million. He achieved this in one year by managing daily transaction prices more effectively.

Tactical pricing has four main objectives:

1. Shift the order mix toward more profitable products.
2. Reduce money left on the table in bidding.
3. Gain market share selectively by low-risk price cutting.
4. Apply upward pressure on industry prices.

Consideration of price level, timing, and communication is as important to the achievement of these tactical pricing objectives as it is to strategic pricing.

As discussed above, industrial prices are generally negotiated transaction by transaction. What this means is that the published or list price often is not very useful in determining true profitability. The price that needs to be known is what is actually realized from the transaction—what remains after all the special terms such as volume discounts, delivery, credit arrangements are subtracted.[10] This "pocket" price (so named to denote what the supplier actually puts in his pocket after delivery can vary greatly from transaction to transaction because of differences in the number and size of the special terms that may apply (see Exhibit D-6). Clearly then, it is the pocket price that the marketer should control, since it determines the true profitability of the transaction.

Unlike strategic pricing, tactical price is a day-to-day matter. Two essential elements in a tactical pricing program are appropriate authority levels and pricing decision rules and a complete and up-to-date information base. Because of the multitude of quotes that an industrial company must make, normal day-to-day pricing is handled by a group of product managers who are given guidelines and expected to "get the best price." To go below their approval level to respond to competitive pressures, they must obtain approval from their boss, usually a sales or marketing manager. If the price is below the approval level, they must go to the general manager. This typical system of approval levels leaves the bulk of industrial pricing (usually 80 to 90 percent) in the hands of fairly low-level employees. This system of approval levels is good if adequate systems and safeguards are provided and if authority levels reflect true profit levels. On the other hand, wrong decisions can occur if these safeguards are not provided.

Take the example of a component supplier who had three pricing authority levels. The product manager could authorize up to 35 percent off list price, the marketing manager could go up to 45 percent off, and the general manager could go up to 60 percent off. However, a thorough study of profit levels showed the controller that list prices bore little

Exhibit D-6

POCKET PRICE WATERFALL

Percent

EXAMPLE

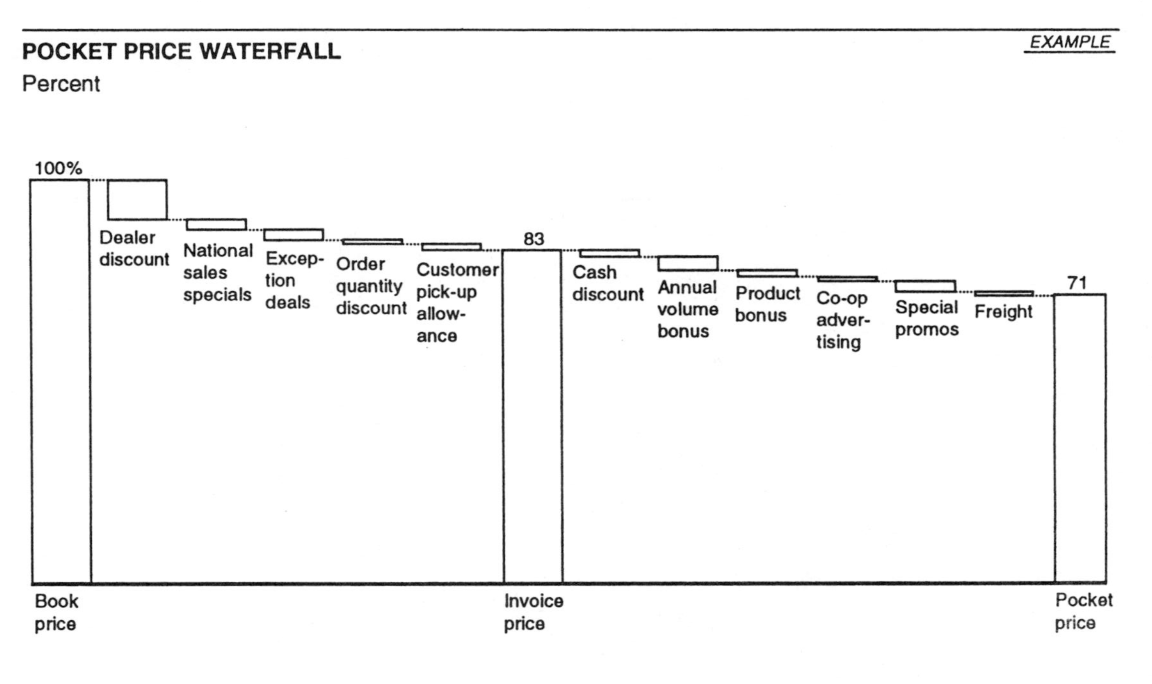

Source: Pricing Administration; interviews

relationship to profits, a common situation in industrial companies. For some products, a 35 percent discount yielded only a 10 percent contribution margin, while in other lines a 60 percent discount yielded a 50 percent contribution margin. In other words, the across-the-board authority levels gave the product manager authority to go well below the company target of 40 percent in some cases, while in other cases the general manager was wasting his time on many relatively unimportant decisions. In no time at all, the authority system was modified to reflect the profitability of each product line. When the authority levels and decision rules have been revised to reflect profit goals, sales incentives must be brought in line to steer salespeople away from bringing in volume at any price.

Regardless of the authority level system in use, the key to success is to provide the lowest authority level with sufficient information to make a sound judgment. Too often, the person making the pricing decision has only two pieces of information to work with: a discount schedule and the salesperson's assessment of the competitive situation with a particular order. The following five pieces of information are essential: (1) costs (including order-specific and customer-specific costs) to provide the basis for determining profitability of the order; (2) price objectives based on profitability targets; (3) latest company "win and lose" quotes to the customer to establish the company's current price position with the customer; (4) most recent prices paid by the customer to establish the account's price threshold; and (5) the current competitive price level (not account specific) to establish the going market price level. Armed with these data, the pricing analyst can then make the proper trade-offs between overall market prices, customer-specific price levels, profitability, and company profit objectives or targets in quoting the best price.

Item number 3 in the above list merits further comment. Knowing how one's price quotes compare to those of competitors—in both lose and win bids—is crucial to effective tactical pricing, yet most companies rarely take the time to learn what the competitive prices were when they win a bid. One company that did found that its winning bids averaged a full 5 percent under those of the nearest competitor. Clearly they were leaving more money on the table than was desirable—or necessary.

These indicators are not easy to come by because often they must be derived from inaccurate cost data as well as sketchy market intelligence. One company tried to put all these data on its center computer but found it unworkable because of the lack of programmers and market intelligence. The marketing manager undertook three programs; she worked with the sales department to obtain competitive price data, bought eleven Apple computers, and taught the pricing clerks how to input the required data and analyze it. Within eight months, they were able to instantly display not only the going market price of a given product, but also the latest quotes by competitors to a

Exhibit D-7

CUSTOMER VISIBILITY/PRICE SENSITIVITY MATRIX

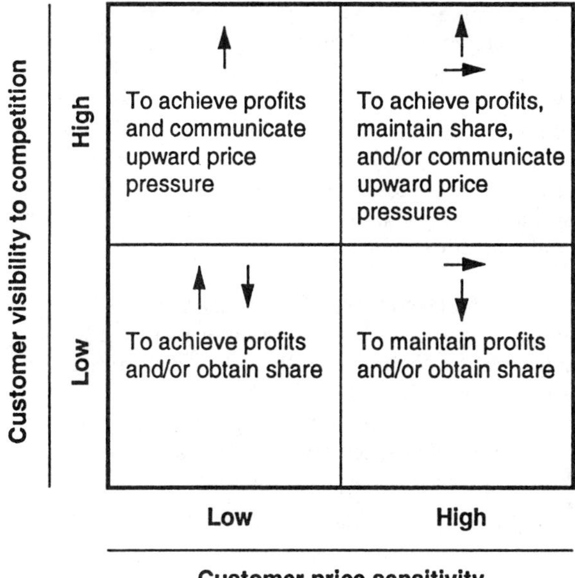

given customer. More important, after a few months, the pricing clerks could forecast what each competitor was likely to bid on a given order for a specific customer. What a powerful tool! Within a year, the marketing manager had raised effective prices 15 percent without even announcing a general price increase. In essence, this process ensured that no money was left on the table. She also increased volume 10 percent by using price to obtain volume in selected customer situations. To aid in customer selection, she also used a matrix that ranked customers by how sensitive they were to prices, how visible they were to competition, and how strong her company was with each customer. By placing each major customer in the appropriate portion of the matrix, she could establish pricing levels vis-a-vis competition that would achieve profit, share, and communication objectives (see Exhibit D-7). This is the epitome of guerrilla warfare pricing, and the competition remained unaware of her tactics.

Customer visibility to competition
High
Low
To achieve profits and communicate upward price pressure
To achieve profits, maintain share, and/or communicate upward price pressures
To achieve profits and/or obtain share
To maintain profits and/or obtain share
Low
High
Customer price sensitivity

In summary, pricing in the industrial environment consists of strategic and tactical pricing. Strategic pricing should be considered a major element in developing a product/market strategy and should be related to the other elements in the mix. The keys to successful development of a profitable pricing strategy are understanding real costs, comparing product/service value to the customer with that of competitive offerings, segmenting the market and assessing demand, predicting likely competitive reactions, and matching pricing strategy with marketing objectives.

Although strategic pricing can often provide an industrial company with a competitive advantage or enhance profits, it is often tactical or guerrilla warfare pricing that can provide the biggest profit boost. Attention to mundane details, such as obtaining competitive quotes for each customer and order-specific costs, plus managing authority levels, can provide a company with a pricing edge.

In short, industrial pricing is a complex subject and fraught with many legal and competitive dangers.

DISTRIBUTION CHANNELS

Over the past 15 to 20 years, market after market has undergone dramatic change in its distribution channels. Exclusive distribution arrangements have fallen, channel options have proliferated, and profits have migrated from the manufacturer to distributors or customers. The distribution complexity that faces many industrial marketers today is the result of two interrelated changes in the market structure:

1. the concentration of market power in the hands of large distributors, customers, or customer groups; and
2. an increasingly diverse set of roles played by the various channel types.

Quantity purchasing is well recognized as a source of advantage by buyers, and the desire for access to this advantage has spurred the trend toward concentration of market power among distributors and end users—i.e., the emergence of distributor chains and buying groups. Beyond this, the emergence of previously unavailable economies of scale is fueling further moves toward channel concentration. Technology can yield substantial economies through more effective inventory management, computer-to-computer ordering, and automated warehousing. But this technology is costly, and only large users can install and sustain these capabilities—a further stimulus for concentration.

Along with this concentration of power has come greater diversity in the roles played by the various channels. A channel can play any mix of many traditional roles: providing geographic sales coverage, maintaining customer contact, defining specific customer needs, negotiating prices and terms, maintaining local inventory, processing goods, delivery, carrying credit, installation, providing postsale service, and gathering market intelligence. Channels vary greatly in their ability to be effective across the range of roles.

For many manufacturers, the restructuring of distribution channels implies a loss of margin to their channels and a loss of control over key elements in their value delivery system—freedom to choose the value they provide and control over the way that value is communicated.

Clearly, today's industrial marketer faces an increasingly complex set of distribution options, with the potential for substantial competitive gains for those who capitalize on channel shifts, and equally substantial losses for those who simply react. It is essential for industrial marketers to address two questions: how to get out in front and capitalize on shifts in the channel structure of the market, and how to respond if someone else moves first.

The objective of distribution strategy is to maximize value to the consumer in terms of product availability and service while maintaining sufficient power over the channels to ensure profitability. Choice of channels is clearly central to the strategy, but beyond this are two other considerations: channel relationship and product allocation.

The way the marketer elects to work with the channel greatly influences the value delivered to the end user. At the most conservative, he might strive for superior execution through training. Alternatively, he might insist on an exclusive relationship in return for such considerations as design service, 10-day restocking, and a limited number of distributors. At the extreme, he might elect some degree of downstream systems integration to ensure the desired sales effort. The more exclusive the relationship (thereby creating a franchise), the greater the control a manufacturer has over its distributors and the less susceptible a manufacturer is to distributor chains.

Another key consideration is the breadth and nature of the product line offered to various channels. Is the entire line to be offered to all channels, a partial line offered to certain channels, or a differentiated product created for each channel? There are no easy answers to these questions. The only way to resolve them is to keep a close watch on the market—regularly test consumer values and assess the fit between emerging price/value profiles and channel structure.

Perhaps the most fundamental statement about the importance of distribution strategy is that the days of stability in channels are over. Globalization, technology, shifting customer values, and a different economic environment are making distribution decisions as critical for most marketers as their choice of the products or basis of competition. Yet sorting through the emerging distribution alternatives provides a major opportunity for the marketer bold enough to get out in front.

SALES FORCE EFFECTIVENESS

Robert Louis Stevenson's comment, "Everyone lives by selling something," is most applicable in the industrial environment. Unlike the consumer market, where advertising and promotion can create

TABLE 3. Sales Force Diagnostic–15 Analyses

Input Measures	Output Measures
• Salesperson turnover versus industry	• Average sales/sales rep versus industry
• Compensation versus industry	• Percent selling costs versus industry
• Age/tenure balance	• Historical sales versus budget
• Supervisory span of control	• Market share trends
• Calls/day versus management expectation	• Key account sales trends
• Evidence of control Call reporting? Account classification? Account records? Call frequency guidelines?	• Customer assessment versus key buying factors
• Territory balance Number of accounts Territory potential	• New account trends
	• Inquiry/tender/bid/order analysis

demand for a product (pull-through), the majority of industrial products must be sold, or pushed, to the buyers. As a result, the industrial salespeople—direct sales rep, manufacturer's agent, or distributor salesperson—are the key link between the manufacturer and the buyer.

The industrial sales job is generally considered to be more demanding and complex than the consumer sales job because it usually entails technical applications selling and requires working with many different functions within a customer's organization. As a result, the average industrial salesperson is more highly educated (50 to 75 percent have college degrees depending on the industry, versus 35 to 50 percent for consumer salespeople) and is paid an average of 10 percent to 15 percent more than a counterpart in the consumer world. Although the industrial salesperson is paid more, the cost as a percent of sales is generally less than that of the consumer salesperson because he or she generally sells a higher dollar volume of goods and services.

Given the more demanding environment, is the industrial sales force doing the job it should? Surprisingly enough, most managers do not know nor do they know how to find out. Not much has been written about the subject.

In diagnosing whether or not management has a sales force problem, 15 quick measures can be used (see Table 3). Half of these measures are output measures (measures of sales results most often sought by management), and the other half are input measures (measures relating to the sales force itself). Although these measures might seem difficult to obtain, they are generally accepted benchmarks in the trade and the raw data can be obtained from readily available sources (industry associations, Dartnell Compensation Surveys, personnel records, and call reports). However, they serve only to raise red flags regarding sales force performance and potential problems. They measure only symptoms and not causes, and thus cannot provide tangible solutions.

Can a company's sales effort in an industrial market become a sustainable competitive advantage? Yes, through either quality or sheer size. While product performance or low manufacturing costs may have provided the original competitive advantage, it is often the sales effort that makes these advantages sustainable, fueling market share growth and providing high profits. Shrewd companies consider their sales forces as strategic weapons of equal weight to the others in their arsenal: product and technology, after-sales services, delivery and cost, pricing, and financial ability.

One capital goods manufacturer transformed itself from an also-ran into a contender for market leadership through selling. After having built product and cost parity, management quietly launched a sales blitz. Within two years, the firm had twice the number of well-trained salespeople as the industry leader; within four years, it challenged the leader for the number one position.

A leading truck component supplier used a sales effort to dominate the fleet segment. Thirty years ago, this manufacturer saw the trend toward fleets by buyers who were beginning to take advantage of the new interstate highway system and recognized an opportunity to create demand around truck manufacturers. Management launched a missionary sales force to inform fleet buyers of the company's product. Within three years, the company had captured 80 percent of the market with this missionary sales force and established the present norm for all successful heavy-duty truck suppliers.

How can an industrial company differentiate its sales effort and achieve the success cited above? By comparing its sales effort with the competition, by understanding the nature of the buying decision and how it might change, and by evaluating its sales effectiveness. In assessing the sales effort, management should ask six questions:

1. Has the role of the sales force been defined appropriately?
2. Is the selling effort structured for effective market coverage?
3. Is the sales force staffed with the right people?
4. Are strong guidance and discipline provided?
5. Is adequate sales support in place?
6. Does the compensation plan provide enough motivation?

As shown in Table 4, there are many areas to probe under each question. We will highlight only a few of these areas in the remainder of this section.

TABLE 4. Six Questions in Assessing Sales Force Effectiveness

What is the role/mission of the sales force?	Is the selling effort structured for effective market coverage?	Is the sales force staffed with the right people?
Products Markets Customers Competition Order characteristics Activities	Organization Size of sales force Territory deployment Market/account coverage	Age/tenure/education profile Interpersonal skills Technical capabilities Selling technique Evaluation system
Is strong guidance/ discipline provided?	**Is adequate sales support in place?**	**Does the sales compensation plan provide the proper motivation?**
Written guidelines Key tasks/mission definition Call frequency Time allocation People to be seen Market/account focus Territory planning and control tools On-the-job coaching	Training Technical backup Inside sales staff Product and applications literature	Total cash Salary/incentive split Incentive design/fit with management objectives Noncash incentives

Role of the Sales Force

The managers of the best sales forces clearly define the role their salespeople play in serving their customers. Should they only sell, or should they sell as well as service the customer (e.g., handle damages or minor repairs)? Should they coordinate sales for a large, multi-location customer or only sell to the headquarters in their territory? This clear definition, in fact, is one of the underlying reasons for consistently higher productivity levels among industry leaders.

The type of sales force you need, of course, depends on the nature of your business. A hand tool manufacturer may simply need efficient order takers, while a controls company will need application engineers to work with the customer on serving his needs. A manufacturer must determine what the sales force needs to do to be successful, e.g., bird-dogging, prospecting, giving presentations, closing, handling complaints, entertaining, networking, customizing product, servicing, chasing delivery, selling, and so on.

Effective Market Coverage

Many industrial companies claim to have national coverage, either through direct salespeople or distributors, because territories are assigned. Yet they discover that they effectively cover only 50 to 70 percent of the market because not all accounts are being called on.

One metals company took a survey of its field sales force to obtain an account-by-account estimate of the potential for one of its product lines. The sales force identified 1,600,000 lbs. of potential and estimated another 200,000 lbs. of unidentified potential. Yet management knew, from industry association shipment data, that 2,300,000 lbs. of that product had been shipped, leaving 500,000 lbs., or 22 percent, unexplained. A thorough re-evaluation of account potential in each territory uncovered that the sales force was too small to cover the potential and that the territories were unbalanced. Ten new salespeople were added and territories realigned to balance the work load. In two years, the company's volume increased 25 percent, while the total market grew only 10 percent.

Why is potential so often underestimated? First, salespeople tend to "skim" in high-potential territories and not do the prospecting necessary to get a handle on true potential. Second, when salespeople are given large geographic territories, they tend to concentrate their efforts on those accounts close to home. Finally, management rarely asks the salespeople to estimate account and territory potential on an annual basis and even more rarely are sales force estimates reconciled with market research estimates. Those who do consistently, and feed the information back to the salespeople, usually receive reasonable estimates.

How can management determine whether enlarging the sales force or redeploying salespeople will pay off? One useful technique is to correlate a salesperson's market share with the potential in the territory. As one sales manager learned, a salesperson's market share tends to be lower in high-potential territories (see Exhibit F-3). He used this simple relationship to determine the payoff (in effect, reducing average territory potential and increasing overall market share). In this case, increasing the number of territories from 25 to 30 reduced the average territory size from $5.1 to $4.2 million and increased the expected market share from 23 to 25 percent. This increase represented $2.5 million in additional company volume, which translated to $1.0 million in additional contribution margin—all this at a total cost of $300,000 for the five salespeople. Actual results outstripped the theory: sales were up $3 million in the first year.

Sometimes coverage can be improved without adding sales representatives but by restructuring the sales force around something other than the traditional geographical territories. Many successful companies have reorganized their sales force around customers, markets, or products to improve sales coverage and customer service (see

Exhibit F-3

CORRELATION OF TERRITORY POTENTIAL WITH TERRITORY MARKET SHARE

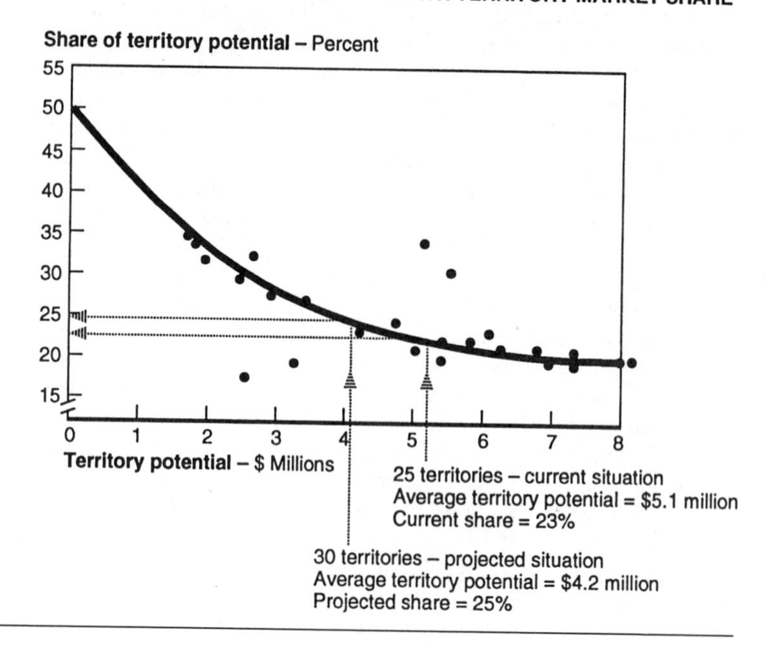

Table 5 for the advantages and disadvantages of various sales force structures).

The Right Salesperson

What management is looking for in its salespeople is *effectiveness*—the ability to relate to the decision makers, solve their problems, and represent the company. What determines the right salesperson obviously depends on the needs of the customer and the competitive situation. Age and education may have a bearing, but they must be accompanied by interpersonal skills, technical expertise, and selling know-how.

One highly successful construction materials manufacturer, who sold largely through distributors, hired MBAs as salespeople to help distributors manage their business better through such methods as computer inventory control, sales management, receivables collection, delivery truck scheduling, and pricing for profit. Using skills acquired in business school, these young MBAs gained a competitive advantage for their company by increasing distributor loyalty and business acumen.

TABLE 5. Advantages and Disadvantages of Various Sales Organizations

	Advantages	Disadvantages
1. Geography	• Clear, simple • Incentive to cultivate local business and personal ties • Travel expenses	• Breadth of customers • Breadth of products
2. Product	• Product knowledge	• Travel expenses • Overlapping territories/customers • Local business and personal ties
3. Customer*	• Market/customer knowledge	• Overlapping territories/products • Local business and personal ties • Travel expenses
4. Common geographic sales force for several SBUs	• Healthy competition • Local business and personal ties • Travel expenses	• Sales management • Breadth of customers • Breadth of products • Different product sales policies
5. Combination	• Maximum flexibility • Travel expenses (?)	• Complexity • Sales management • Product/market/ geography overlap

*By (1) type of industry, (2) size of account, (3) channel of distribution, (4) individual company.

Another company in the specialty chemicals field found that graduate chemical engineers or chemists with 10 to 15 years of experience made the best salespeople for their customers, who required a high level of applications expertise. But highly-educated salespeople are not always the answer. Still another company in the fastener industry found that college graduates were not as effective as less-educated, but experienced, salespeople who had been with the company for years, who could speak the language of purchasing agents, and who could work with inside sales support and manufacturing people to obtain delivery for their customers.

Recruiting standards are obviously an important consideration in ensuring the right kind of sales force, but management has other tools as well. Proper training—both formal and on the job—can do a lot to mold an effective sales force. An equally important and often overlooked tool is a formal evaluation system that not only reinforces quality standards but forces the weeding out of nonperformers. The evaluation form must be tailored specifically to the sales force and should cover such appraisal criteria as familiarity with accounts and prospects, effectiveness of prospecting, accuracy and timeliness of record keeping, quality of quota setting, achievement of target prices, relationships with key accounts, time utilization, and professional and technical skill development. The all-purpose personnel evaluation form used for other employees does not provide effective feedback and motivation, nor does it identify potential for promotion for the sales force.

Strong Guidance/Discipline

Inappropriate sales supervision and control are the biggest deterrents to sales force effectiveness. On the one hand, management must strive for entrepreneurship and independence; on the other hand, it needs to impose discipline and guidance to channel the efforts of the sales force toward achievement of its objectives. The objective here is balance; the key to success is the sales supervisor.

In time studies made of sales force activities, it is clear that the more successful sales forces and the most successful salespeople within a given sales force manage their time more effectively than those who are less successful. For example, in a small aircraft manufacturer, it was not surprising to find that the top six salespeople (13 percent of the sales force) were responsible for 22 percent of all calls made and 28 percent of the total potential seen over a sample survey four-week period. The same survey discovered that these top salespeople spent far more time closing a sale and troubleshooting than the other salespersons, who made a large number of goodwill calls. The successful salespeople simply planned their time better.

In a fabricated metals products company, a three-week time survey revealed that salespeople were spending far too little time in front of the customer (see Exhibit F-5) and that 60 percent of the calls were made on the "comfortable" small accounts that represented only 10 percent of the potential seen. This sales force received little supervision; in fact, supervisors spent only 25 percent of the time with their salespeople.

Admittedly, the first-line sales supervisor has one of the most difficult tasks in the industry, but if he or she executes the role properly, the sales force will be both motivated and disciplined. The sales supervisor must set sales guidelines for call frequency, key tasks, priority accounts and prospects, allocation of time between prospecting and servicing accounts, and people to be seen within an account.

Strong guidance and discipline can also be provided through effective planning and control tools, which permit before-the-fact

Exhibit F-5

TIME UTILIZATION OF SALES REPS
Unit of measure

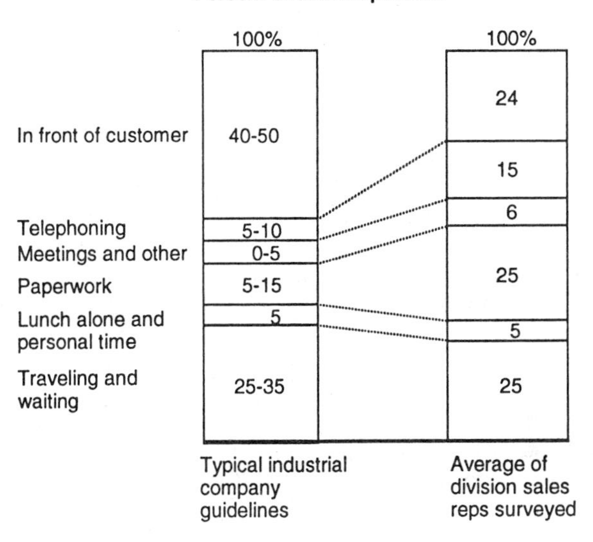

control (usually through a weekly itinerary plan) and a check of call results against plan. These need not be burdensome. Most successful sales forces require only five reports from the field:

1. brief weekly sales plan and call report;
2. account record;
3. annual key account and sales quota plan;
4. expense account record; and
5. lost order report.

The reports themselves should not require a great deal of detail. There is no better way to demotivate a sales force, or lose productive selling time, than to require laborious paperwork. Rarely does anyone need, or even read, the lengthy call report most industrial companies require.

Adequate Sales Support

Adequate sales support is particularly important to the individual salesperson. The typical industrial company fields a sales force of 20 to 60 people to cover the entire United States. The industrial salesperson's time is precious and the demands are great. He or she is, in fact, nine individuals embodied in one: (1) a prospector for new accounts; (2) a qualifier of the accounts for the company's product/service package; (3) a communicator of the company's story; (4) an applications specialist for the product; (5) an order closer; (6) a pricer who tries to obtain the best price, often under bid conditions; (7) an account servicer after the sale to ensure delivery, installation, maintenance, and/or engineering support; (8) a gatherer of market and competitive information for the marketing function; and (9) an allocator of product during times of shortage. With a load like that, any salesperson needs support.

Sales support can take four forms: sales and product training, technical backup to assist with applications and troubleshooting, inside sales staff to provide information and service accounts, and product and applications literature to aid selling efforts. Recent surveys of salespersons revealed that only half feel adequately trained in their company's products, but training goes beyond product and technical training. It includes training in sales techniques, time management, competitive tactics and policies, customer buying characteristics, and the company itself.

Compensation Plan That Motivates

The sales compensation plan can be an effective management tool if its motivational aspects are carefully thought out. Three aspects of the cash compensation package must be considered: the level of total compensation, the proportion of salary to incentive pay (if any), and the design of the incentive portion. Total compensation must be competitive and equitable within the company. As to the makeup of the cash package, the trend is clearly in the direction of salary plus incentive and away from straight commission, but the proportion of companies paying straight salary has remained constant (see Exhibit F-6). Each approach has its advantages and disadvantages and fits certain selling situations (see Table 6). For example, straight salary may be best in situations where selling is low-key and sales reps have many nonselling duties. Straight commission may serve when management wants to apply maximum financial incentives for sales of small-ticket items that require aggressive selling. In the majority of industrial companies, salary plus incentive gains the best of both worlds.

It has been proven time and again that the design of the sales incentive is far more important than the actual dollars paid out. Incentives should be designed to achieve management objectives, whatever they might be. Volume is not the only basis for incentive pay; a balanced product mix, new accounts, and/or long-term relationships can also be rewarded. Although no sales compensation plan can overcome weaknesses in market coverage, sales force or supervisor quality, and sales support, the properly designed sales incentive pro-

Exhibit F-6

TYPES OF SALES COMPENSATION PLAN
Percent

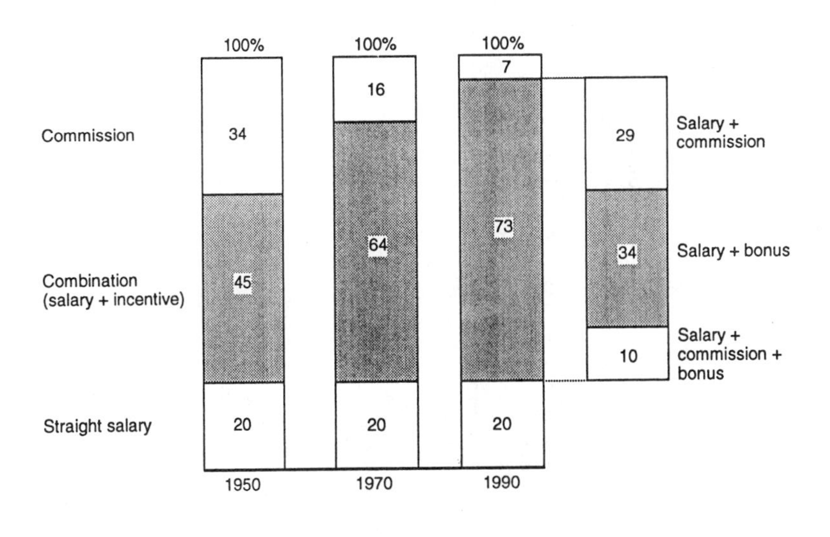

gram can significantly boost the results of a well-managed sales force. It deserves careful study.

In summary, leading companies in the industrial environment recognize the importance of a well-conceived and well-managed sales effort. They strive to structure their sales force to achieve effective market coverage, to select salespeople who meet customer requirements, to provide strong guidance and discipline, to build adequate sales support, and to use incentive pay to achieve management objectives. And in all of these areas, they seek to differentiate themselves from their competition to obtain a competitive advantage.

ADVERTISING AND SALES PROMOTION

In 1990, over $100 billion was spent on advertising in the United States, yet according to American Business Press, less than 10 percent of this amount was spent on business-to-business advertising. Thus it is clear that businesses do not do much advertising to businesses, preferring to allocate most of their communications dollars to other areas of the marketing mix, such as the sales force and product literature.

TABLE 6. Advantages/Disadvantages of Various Incentive Plans

	Advantages	Disadvantages	Representative Industries/Characteristics
Straight salary	• Management direction • Lower sales costs • Stability of income/morale • Low administrative cost • Longer term oriented • Price/volume/mix balance	• No direct incentive to excel • Greater burden on supervision • Inflexible selling expense during downturn • Recruiting of hard chargers	• Capital equipment, chemicals, steel, construction equipment, motors • "Big ticket" items; large buyers; low key selling; many nonselling duties; longer term buys
Straight commissions	• Maximum financial incentive • Constant percent selling expenses • Product/account focus through direct financial incentive • Recruiting of hard chargers • Less burden on supervision • High motivation	• Short-term oriented • Price discounting to obtain volume • Higher administrative cost • Little security/lower morale	• Office equipment, MRO supplies • "Small ticket" items; repeat purchases; aggressive selling; few nonselling duties; on-the-spot buys
Combination salary and incentive	• Best of both can be obtained	• Worst of both can be minimized	• 73 percent of industrial companies

As discussed earlier, however, the industrial buying process is a complex one, involving several individuals depending on the significance of what is bought. For example, Wesley Johnston and Thomas Bonoma found that an average of six to eight individuals were involved even in relatively "mundane" industrial purchases, such as that for a minor piece of capital equipment.[11] Many of the buying influences in the firm cannot be reached very easily through personal selling. The vice-president of information systems, for example, will not be easily accessible to the computer room supplier who wishes to sell work stations. For these two reasons, complexity and accessibility, most managers have found that at least some advertising can be useful. For example, one study of industrial buyers for transportation services found that personal selling reached only one of the 13 individuals regularly involved in transportation buys, but buyers who had been exposed to advertising from the seller, even though they had not been called on, were more likely to recommend the purchase than those that had not.

Advertising can fill a number of functions beyond communication with prospective buyers. It is generally found that industrial firms that advertise have higher awareness and a more positive image among their own employees than those who do not. Similarly, ads can and do convince distribution channels that the selling company management is "backing up" its distributors, and can keep the company image shiny with current customers as well.

A good rule for industrial marketers who need to decide the advertising question is to look for nontraditional selling methods, like advertising, catalogs, direct mail brochures, and pamphlets to "fill in" where the regular marketing program is weak. Therefore, a vendor of $5 million business jets has a very high advertising-to-sales ratio, since the small personal sales force cannot reach the CEOs who buy their planes without at least some initial interest on the potential buyer's part. In contrast, the zinc producer might wish only to engage in a nominal advertising campaign to bolster its galvanizing distributors and to keep its name in front of current and prospective users.

Far greater monies are invested by industrial firms on what is called trade or sales promotion. Trade promotion is generally taken to refer to incentives provided to business partners—like wholesalers or even the sales force—to increase sales. Sales promotion, by contrast, is the broader term, including not only distributor incentives but also any incentives given directly to the customer to induce purchase.

No one knows just how much money is spent annually on sales promotion, but the figure is probably more than double the small advertising expenditures in most industrial firms. As a rough rule of thumb, industrial companies often spend 60 to 80 percent of their marketing dollars on the sales force, 10 to 20 percent on sales promotion, and 9 to 10 percent on advertising. One heavy equipment manufacturer spends almost $600,000 a year on a combination of air trips to prospects who want to see the factory, foreign "business promotion" trips, black golf balls (they're in the coal industry), ties, night lights, digital clocks, and other items designed to build company goodwill and enhance sales. Prospects, customers, and distributors are the recipients of such gratuities.

In addition to gifts and travel, direct price reductions or discounts are often considered part of the sales promotion budget. The W.C. Smith Company, for example, having only one salesperson, essentially placed a $4,196 "cents off" advertisement in candy trade magazines on a new line of cooling tunnels. The promotion was successful in selling 10 additional machines.

Perhaps the most frequently used form of sales promotion is the trade show. Over 10,000 trade shows are held annually in the United States, most of which occur as totally uncontrolled expenditures by the firms attending. Uncontrolled does not mean that money is no object; it means that management has little or no idea how effective the expenditure is as part of the overall marketing program. Additionally, management ordinarily has no sense of whether the monies expended in this way would be better spent elsewhere, for example, hiring several additional salespeople.

As suggested above, advertising and sales promotion need to be carefully planned elements of the firm's communication program. Think of personal selling as the bricks in the industrial firm's wall, and sales promotion and advertising as mortar. The mortar should be mixed in the quantity and consistency to assure that it fills the cracks, but only this. In other words, where the sales force cannot reach foreign prospects, advertise in a publication that does, or attend an international show. If the sales force spends most of its time with current customers, then use trade shows and even response coupons in ads to "beat the bushes" for new customers. The trick with a marketing communications program is to (a) balance the tools available to cover all the marketing communications bases, and (b) to continually assess whether the whole program, and each line item in it, is a worthwhile expenditure in terms of sales generated, prospects reached, or other measures.

POSTSALE SERVICE

It is interesting to note that in many industrial companies, the service function is not considered a formal part of marketing. This is a mistake, not so much because marketing needs more to do, but because it is often after the contract is signed that a customer is born. Management all too often forgets the distinction between a buyer (someone who buys once) and a customer (a repeat and loyal buyer). As customers are always cheaper to serve than buyers (who have attendant segmentation and location costs), it is in management's best interest to pay close attention to service requirements.

One issue of importance to many companies is whether service should be "bundled," or built into the price of the basic goods. In some industries, such as mainframe computers, manufacturers have traditionally bundled the service in with the original sales because of frequent maintenance needs, proprietary technologies, and the amount of expertise needed to fix the equipment. In other businesses, like computer terminals, service is often unbundled from the equipment purchase, and the customer is given extreme latitude in the choice and nature of the service vendor. Although service organization expenses are among the most painful for many industrial concerns, it is important to remember the benefits of continued contact with the buyer for market intelligence purposes and the maintenance of loyal customers.

Another issue of concern is whether service should be proactive or reactive. These terms mean whether service should largely be provided in response to customer complaints of operating problems or whether a fixed and preventative service schedule should be set up regardless of operating problems. Clearly, this choice will depend heavily on what is sold, but there are interesting differences between the two approaches. With the first, the customer essentially only sees the manufacturer's service representative when something has gone wrong. With the second, problems can be avoided altogether if the customer will bear the cost of the schedule.

Perhaps the thorniest issue in postsale service is whether service should be a profit center or just expected to break even. Service operations that lose money or only break even on their operation are less than satisfying to both manufacturers and customers. The manufacturer engages in much effort for no return and the customer invariably experiences the poor service that cost-cutting and understaffing result in. If the manufacturer cannot make a normal "hurdle rate" on the investment in service, the management should reconsider provision of that service, or at least redesign it to be profitable. Much can be done here in terms of providing service, or at least problem diagnosis, long distance over the phone lines.

Another aspect of postsale service is the sale of parts. Most industrial companies make substantial profits on parts. One of the keys here is the sales push provided for parts. All too often, management believes the parts sales will automatically come with the sale of the unit. Taking parts sales for granted can result in the entry of competitors who manufacture and deliver service on a pure price basis (often referred to as "pirates" or "gypsies"). In the continuous miner market, for example, manufacturer refurbishing of a $400,000 mining machine can cost $100,000 and up. Secondary vendors provide a similar service for $50,000, a tempting price to a small "doghole" mine strapped for equipment repairs. Where there are sufficient profit margins, low-end competitors will be drawn into any business. Unfortunately, poor service "fixes" can result in subsequent manufacturer service calls to undo or make right the less-than-complete work that pure price competitors often provide. To overcome this problem, the manufacturer must push parts and service through its sales force.

One equipment manufacturer gained a competitive advantage by training dealer salesmen in parts sales and service. At the end of five years, this manufacturer had 1,300 dealer parts and service salesmen in the field, four times that of the nearest competitor. This strategic move not only kept "parts pirates" away from his customers, but provided additional value to the customers that resulted in increased unit penetration.

The other key to parts sales should go without saying—availability. But availability goes beyond having it in the plant warehouse. Parts must be made available in the field through local warehouses or distributors to meet user emergency demands.

Postsale service should be a major profit contributor to an industrial company, but service needs to be marketed and sold. If parts are not actively pushed, the door can be left open for pirates or gypsies. Thus we have found the most successful service and parts operations are normally under the marketing department and are managed as separate profit centers.

The keys to effective postsales service are contained in two questions:

1. What satisfies the customer?
2. What maximizes profits?

INFORMATION TECHNOLOGY

In some ways, it is inaccurate to write a separate section on information technology (IT) because this topic has become a core thread of modern industrial marketing. Yet, compared to ten years ago, the emergence of IT as a key aspect of marketing strategy has provoked a revolution among the best firms and managers.

Computer technology is not new; but the use of computer technology to inform and change marketing decisions with precision is new among the best-managed marketing companies. One might indeed say that information technology has caused a sea-change in modern industrial marketing in terms of analysis, speed, and strategy.

Take a firm's analytic capabilities: it is now possible for the industrial marketer to know the profitability of each segment, account, invoice, line item on the invoice, and to formulate a customer response strategy accordingly. Indeed, the marketer who does *not* know such information is at a severe disadvantage to his or her competition.

To use the "pocket price waterfall" computations, for instance, the marketer must be able to subtract all transaction-specific decrements to revenues to compute the variable profit from a sales order. Doing so requires computing power for any company other than a very small one, yet the marketer who does not know which orders are priced profitably simply will not exist through the 1990s. The same may be said of all other aspects of the marketing mix, such as what is my share? How much does postsale service cost to large versus small customers?

Another transformation made possible by the computer is that, if used correctly, it offers enough speed to the marketer so that what used to be *post hoc* analysis can become current, allowing marketing decisions to be molded much more closely to the reality that generates them. When account mixes change monthly in a financial printing concern, speed of information makes the difference between guessing about the future from an old past or from a fresh one. While both forecasts will be guesses, the use of *recent* history is worth millions to marketing accuracy.

Even more dramatic, in some companies and industries, the information technology has *become* the marketing strategy. In air freight, for example, the existence of scanned data allowing the shipper to inquire about a package at any step along the way is not only a useful piece of differentiation, but may become a "unique selling proposition" for the marketer, allowing her to dominate a segment or the entire industry. The same may be said of many other industries. In general, the closer an industrial firm is to service provision and the more customers depend on rapid response to make *their* money, the more likely it is that IT will be not an adjunct to, but the core of, marketing strategy.

MARKETING IMPLEMENTATION: GETTING THE MARKETING JOB DONE

The marketing function is long on strategy, but short on good recommendations for how to get the job done once strategic directions have been chosen. This section briefly discusses research findings about effective marketing execution and offers the manager some guidelines for improving the efficiency of that execution in the marketing function.

Skills Needed for Marketing Implementation

Marketing implementation involves four important marketing skills:

1. interacting;
2. monitoring and controlling execution;
3. allocating money and people; and
4. organizing the marketing effort.

Effective marketing action requires good *interaction or people skills,* much as any other management task. The marketing job is one of influencing others, often under conditions where the marketer has no formal power to get his or her own way. For example, how does the product line manager get the sales force to devote more time to the product? How does the marketer get the vice president to kill an ad campaign he or she knows is suboptimal, but the vice president likes? As with all management tasks, the essence of marketing is influence and politics.

Not surprisingly, then, the social intangibles of inside and extra-corporate relationships seem to be the dominant contributory skill to excellence in marketing execution. Marketing, after all, is executed by people with people. But what is surprising is that marketers have generally left the "people" side of the task to other specialists (organizational behavior) and looked for marketing generalizations unaffected by social and political realities. For example, the interaction dynamics between an engineering-oriented chairman and his R&D staff in the mining company cited earlier seemed to have much to do with the company's lateness in getting its new products to market and its less-than-optimal market performance. And the complex interaction patterns in the drainage company, which is a family firm currently containing three generations of fathers, sons, and cousins, has in the past almost totally obscured the firm's marketing mission.

The need for good interaction skills is not limited to influence with company insiders. The marketer needs even sharper interaction skills to deal with the regular parade of "outsiders" used by many firms to help execute the marketing effort: advertising agents, consultants, and a variety of wholesalers, jobbers, and dealers. The task of managing them is often more difficult because their interests may not be completely consistent with those of the firm. Most marketers for example, do not do a good job of managing their distribution network: they fail to take into account the common "love-hate" relationships that arise between distributors and the manufacturer.

Monitoring and controlling skills involve the construction and maintenance of feedback mechanisms that can be used to measure and control the results generated by marketing activities. Here arise a number of questions about execution efficiency to which we now do not have good answers, such as how productivity of the marketing function can be audited. According to one manager, monitoring is best pictured as a control panel with dials and levers on the manager's desk and wires running to the field. The trick, she points out, is to make sure that the gauges and dials give accurate readings and that the wires are "not just dangling off the panel unconnected to anything."

Despite the importance of this skill, marketing groups are generally weak on constructing simple, understandable monitoring mechanisms that do not get corrupted by the politics of the situation or mired in uncomprehensible complexities. Other times, it seems that marketing monitoring mechanisms cannot be divorced from the personnel chosen to fill critical marketing posts. In some marketing jobs that require quick and frequent judgments of business consequence, "monitoring" means trusting the day-to-day calls of the manager put in place to make them. Finally, the companies studied seem best at measuring functions in marketing, but somewhat less capable of evaluating programs and generally uncertain of how to evaluate the marketing function overall, and especially productivity.

Allocating money and people refers to the marketing budgeting process in terms of both financial and human capital. Problems of allocation occur across marketing, from the functional level to that of marketing policy. For example, how much money should be allocated to trade shows? Or from a marketing policy perspective, how can demonstration costs be controlled in selling business jets? The efficient allocation of people to marketing tasks is an even more critical implementation skill—the greatest barriers to effective execution in the companies are these. First, too much money is allocated regularly to mature programs. Second, too little is allocated to risky programs, especially when they are in their infancy and need infusions of staff and cash to succeed. (These two failures together are failures of resolve because they represent a commitment to the easy path of doing things the way they have been done.) And third, people are improperly allocated to the tasks to be done. In many instances, this misallocation was so obvious that the selected candidate or jobholder remarked on it, as did peers and subordinates. Indeed, the misallocation of people across marketing tasks often seemed to be obvious to everyone but the people doing the allocating.

The final marketing skill, *organizing,* is concerned with structure and management of the formal and informal marketing structure in such a way that tasks get done well. Relevant questions regarding organization include what degree of centralization facilities are the firm's marketing objectives, how much the informal organization should be allowed to dominate the formal organization chart, and what the relationship between the two should be. For example, how should a firm in three very different market segments and product lines organize its marketing management, sales force, and research endeavors? How should these program pieces report into top management?

The field observations do not support the great emphasis that has been placed on organization in marketing. Even where marketing structure was inappropriate, the corporations studied seldom found it any impediment to effective execution, choosing instead to accomplish their agendas informally through the stronger but invisible social marketing organization (even when the organization chart did not formally allow this). None of this is to say that marketing organization has no bearing on the effective execution of marketing strategy, only that other marketing skills have a much higher potential of contributing to marketing excellence.

Levels of Execution

Each of these skills can be used to promote effective execution at one of three levels over the total scope of the firm's marketing activities, The first level—*marketing functions*—is concerned with the effective execution of marketing's many subfunctions. An example might be increasing the effective execution of new product development by a mining machine manufacturer, when not enough engineering resources exist to simultaneously rework existing lines, improve its newest machine, and develop a new generation miner.

At the *marketing programs* level, execution efficiency concerns the blending of marketing's functions to market a product or serve a particular segment.

Finally, at the level of executing *marketing policies,* management is concerned with marketing theme, leadership, and commitment. It is more important to have a clear marketing theme that simply and clearly states what the marketing group is about, and a top marketing management that selectively emphasizes policies supporting this theme (and the controls that measure it) than it is to have, for example, effective sales management or new product development activities.

For example, one producer of agricultural drainage tile found that its traditional marketing theme of being the lowest cost, lowest price producer almost cost it the success of a major product innovation that was 180 percent as efficient as the company's current product, but only cost 70 percent as much to make. The firm's marketing theme led it to seriously consider pricing this new pipe on materials costs, a policy that almost certainly would have cannibalized the company's current product sales and brought little new profit.

We have studied companies with much better *functional* execution of new product development and other marketing functions than acknowledged marketing leaders, like IBM or Frito-Lay. Other firms just do not display the focus, determination, and customer/quality orientation so dominant at IBM. Where this focus is absent, market performance seems to be poorer. This is because no matter how well executed each of the marketing subfunctions is, the whole does not "hang together" in a coherent and effective way to serve the market.

If implementing policies dominate implementing functions, then effective execution of marketing's subfunctions appears to dominate the contribution to excellence made by careful program execution. Here, the pattern observed is that the marketing functions (the fundamentals like product management or the selling function) allow programs, like brand or account management ones, to draw on these functional skills for excellent results. Where the reverse is true, however, where there are well-thought-through brand or customer programs but poor functional skills with which to deliver them, excellence does not result. The computer terminals company cited above is one example of a marketing program where poor functional execution dominated programmatic competence.

Thus the potential for improving performance in marketing when levels are considered appears to be counter-intuitive. The policy area is the most critical, involving top management example, a marketing theme, and the clearness of focus that comes from competent leadership. Then, the very bottom of the ladder—marketing's subfunctions—should be brought to technical excellence. With these two contributing the broad and narrow capabilities needed by the firm, the programs seem to take care of themselves.

Diagnosing Implementation Problems

Crossing these four skills with the three marketing levels, we obtain the matrix shown in Exhibit J-1. It appears to categorize the many situations that managers face in getting the marketing job done in a way that allows good specification of many implementation problems. But the questions remain of how to tell when a marketing problem is one of implementation or strategy, and what to do about the implementation problems once they are identified.

Given the close interrelationship between marketing strategy and implementation, diagnostic difficulties are to be expected. When a 50-person computer terminals sales force collectively sells only 39 of the company's new line of "smart" microcomputer terminals during a contest period in which 565 units were expected to be sold without any incentives, is the problem with the compensation plan (execution) or the strategy to move to "smart terminals" in the first place?

Another dimension of importance in diagnosing and remedying marketing problems is determining whether the problem confronting the marketing manager is figuring out what is wrong (problem of diagnosis), or deciding what to do (problem of action) about a known difficulty. Exhibit J-2 maps these two dimensions against each other and serves as a useful diagnostic for either the classroom or the office.

Although it is usually difficult to discriminate implementation problems from problems of strategy in marketing, use of a matrix such as that in Exhibit J-2 allows the problem symptoms to be tentatively allocated to strategy or action categories in the "diagnosis" cells, and then informally tested against the existing facts to make a determination of correct categorization. Of course, no situation is ever *purely* an implementation or strategy problem in marketing.

Guidelines for Implementation Success

On a more practical note, successful implementation of an industrial marketing strategy requires ten interrelated tasks.

1. Ensure middle management participation in the solution of the problem through the use of task forces.

Exhibit J-1

IMPLEMENTATION MATRIX

Marketing implementation can be analyzed at the level of ↓ / Effective implementation is achieved through →	Organizing	Allocating	Monitoring	Interacting
POLICIES	How should the marketing team be reorganized by a company changing its "theme"?	How should resources be allocated to service key accounts by segment and country?	How does a mine machinery company monitor a major trade promotion expenditure?	How should a recall of a defective building component be managed by a major steel producer?
PROGRAMS	How should the sales force be reorganized to emphasize a marketing shift from "dumb" to "smart" terminals?	How should the prospects be selected for demonstration rides in a corporate jet?	How is a successful ad agency team best managed within a brand group for a new product introduction?	How can R&D and marketing effectively collaborate on a new product which will cannibalize almost all existing sales?
FUNCTIONS	How should the new product planning function of a market follower be organized in a high-loyalty business?	How is sales force territory allocation best done by a printing company?	How are salespeople best evaluated and compensated by a bulk chemicals firm?	How are production and R&D colleagues encouraged to devote more time or effort to a single product?

Exhibit J-2

CLASSIFICATION OF MARKETING PROBLEMS

	Strategy	Implementation
Problems of diagnosis		
Problems of action		

2. Hold periodic task force progress reviews with top management to keep the project on track.
3. Allow sufficient time for top management to buy into the recommendations.
4. Identify champions to lead the implementation.
5. Test the key recommendations to ensure buy-in at all levels.
6. Force regular communications/interaction down-the-line to ensure enthusiasm building.
7. Set measurement standards and institute review mechanisms to ensure periodic "wins."
8. Educate those who need to change.
9. Revise compensation incentives to ensure attainment of objectives.
10. Ensure follow-through of the recommendations by evaluating, warning, and separating those who do not comply.

The beginning work completed on execution efficiency in marketing sums up to these recommendations for the manager charged with getting the marketing job done:

1. Work on your organization's marketing theme. Make sure there exists a simple statement of who the company is and what it is about

TABLE 7. Measuring Marketing Muscle

The following checklist provides a quick self-test for a company that wants a rough measure of its marketing capability.

1. Has your company carefully segmented the consumers that it serves?
2. Do you routinely measure the profitability of your key products or services in each of these consumer market segments?
3. Do you use market research to keep abreast of the needs, preferences, and buying habits of consumers in each segment?
4. Have you identified the key buying factors in each segment, and do you know how your company compares with its competitors on these factors?
5. Is the impact of environmental trends (demographic, competitive, lifestyle, governmental) carefully gauged?
6. Does your company prepare and use an annual marketing plan?
7. Is the concept of "marketing investment" understood—and practiced?
8. Is profit responsibility for a product line pushed below the senior management level?
9. Does your organization "talk" marketing?
10. Did one of the top five executives in your company come up through marketing?

If you answered yes to:
9 or 10—you have a strong marketing capability.
6 to 8—you are on the way.
Fewer than 6—you are vulnerable to marketing-minded competitors.

in marketing terms, and that top management knows it, repeats it, and lives it.

2. Work on the fundamentals next. Execute the marketing "blocking and tackling" of functions like sales force management, product development/management, pricing and distribution, and the programs will take care of themselves.
3. Interaction skills are the most important skills necessary to get the marketing job done. The marketers' task is done by people, with people. These "marketing partners," inside and outside the company, need constant management.
4. Finally, the importance of a good set of marketing controls and the ability to allocate money with resolve, and people with artfulness cannot be overemphasized. Controls do not need to be complicated, only consistent and timely. Marketing allocations must reflect the clarity and commitment of the marketing theme.

CONCLUSION

Today, the role of marketing is to be management's window to the world. It is no longer enough to be "marketing oriented." Today, a company must be "market focused." That is, the company's offering must be shaped both to respond to observable needs and opportunities in the marketplace and to energize latent market opportunities. The distinction is not merely semantic: it signifies a shift from sales forecasts to issue-oriented business plans, from a technical marketing approach to a total business approach. Market-focused companies are sensitive to the marketplace and anticipate shifts. They experiment with strategic responses and remain flexible.

The question, "How do you know how well you're doing?" is a tricky one, for research shows its answer has as much to do with expectations as with objective results. However, practice shows that ten factors tend to recur with effective marketing practice. They are listed in Table 7 as measures of "marketing muscle."[12]

Another way to view the motion of marketing effectiveness is given by Bower and Garda, who note the linkage of effective marketing with effective customer and firm strategies. They point out that marketing is effective, in the end, when it contributes toward and even drives the "delivery of value" to the customer. That, after all, is the purpose of business activity.

NOTES

1. Richard M. Hill, Ralph S. Alexander and James S. Cross, *Industrial Marketing* (Homewood, IL: Richard D. Irwin, Inc. 1975 fourth edition).

2. Marvin Bower and Robert A. Garda, "The Role of Marketing in Management," Chapter 1 in Victor P. Buell, *Handbook of Modern Marketing,* McGraw-Hill, NY.

3. B. Charles Ames, "Trappings vs. Substance in Industrial Marketing," *Harvard Business Review,* July-August 1970.

4. Wendell R. Smith, "Product Differentiation and Market Segmentation as Alternative Marketing Strategies," *Journal of Marketing,* July 1956.

5. Robert A. Garda, "Strategic Segmentation: How to Carve Niches for Growth in Industrial Markets," *Management Review,* August 1981.

6. Thomas V. Bonoma and Benson P. Shapiro, *Industrial Market Segmentation* (Cambridge, MA: Marketing Science Institute).

7. Thomas V. Bonoma, "Major Sales: Who Really Does the Buying?" *Harvard Business Review,* May-June 1982.

8. John L. Forbis and Nitin T. Mehta, "Value-based Strategies for Industrial Products," *Business Horizons,* May-June 1981.

9. Robert A. Garda, "Use Tactical Pricing to Uncover Hidden Profits," *Journal of Business Strategy,* September/October 1991.

10. Michael V. Marn and Robert L. Rosiello, "Managing Price, Gaining Profit," *Harvard Business Review,* September-October 1982.

11. Wesley J. Johnston and Thomas V. Bonoma, "Purchase of Capital Equipment and Services," *Industrial Marketing Management.*

12. Edward G. Michaels, "Marketing Muscle," *Business Horizons,* May-June 1982.

James C. Anderson
William L. Ford Distinguished Professor of
Marketing and Wholesale Distribution
Professor of Behavioral Science in Management
J. L. Kellogg Graduate School of Management
Northwestern University
Evanston, Illinois

James A. Narus
Associate Professor of Management
Babcock Graduate School of Management
Wake Forest University
Winston-Salem, North Carolina

CHAPTER 53

PARTNERING AS A FOCUSED MARKET STRATEGY

Partnerships are the way for firms to do business—or so it seems when one reads today's business press. Article after article routinely exhorts both customer and supplier firms to seek close, collaborative relationships with each other. Yet in practice, partnership-building efforts, even when sought by a customer, may not be in the best interests of a supplier firm.[1] Take, for instance, the case of a leading manufacturer of corrugated boxes.

> *Last year, the company's management decided that it was time to jump on the "partnership bandwagon," and it targeted one of the company's largest customers for a collaborative relationship. Believing that the best way to build the partnership was to help the customer enhance its product quality, managers hired a top consulting firm in the area of quality management to put on a two-day seminar at the customer's headquarters. At the end of the seminar, the consultants recommended that the customer establish a "quality circle." Taking the consultants' recommendation to heart, the customer firm established a quality circle and decided to begin by investigating the firm's purchases of corrugated boxes. When they finished deliberations, quality circle members concluded that the firm's annual expenditure for boxes was far too high. Moreover, they recommended that the firm purchase only corrugated box "rejects," which they believed would adequately meet firm requirements. As a result, the corrugated box supplier failed not only in its efforts to build a collaborative relationship, but lost the account as well.*

This anecdote underscores the difficulties that managers can encounter in attempting to cultivate strong working partnerships with their customers. In this article, we present a comprehensive, strategic approach that offers managers guidance on decisions about which market segments and individual customer firms to target for close, collaborative relationships. This approach has six steps:

- Segment the market by product application and customer capabilities.
- Assess the value of the product offering to customers in each segment.
- Target segments, and customer firms within segments, for various kinds of relationships.
- Develop and implement relationship-specific product offerings.

The authors gratefully acknowledge the financial support of the Institute for the Study of Business Markets and Digital Equipment Corporation, and the helpful comments and suggestions of Horst Bender, Richard Clewett, Irwin Gross, Philip Kotler and Frederick Webster, Jr.

- Evaluate relationship outcomes and reassign accounts.
- Periodically update the value of the relationship offering.

We examine the key considerations in accomplishing each of these steps and draw upon examples from firms that have successfully tackled them. As a preface to this approach, a continuum of working relationships that serves as a useful frame of reference for thinking about working relationships is discussed.

THINKING STRATEGICALLY ABOUT WORKING RELATIONSHIPS

All customer and supplier firms that do business together have some sort of working relationship. Jackson has discussed a continuum of working relationships along which industries fall.[2] Purely *transactional relationships,* where the customer and the supplier focus upon the timely exchange of basic products for highly competitive prices, anchor one end. Purely *collaborative relationships,* or partnerships, anchor the other end. This latter kind of relationship comes about through *partnering,* which is a process where a customer firm and supplier firm form strong and extensive social, economic, service, and technical ties over time, with the intent of lowering total costs and/or increasing value, thereby achieving mutual benefit.

The nature of working relationships in business markets suggests that some further elaboration is needed with respect to Jackson's rudimentary premise. Each marketplace, rather than occupying a single point on the continuum, is better characterized as a range of relationships that are more collaborative, or more transactional, in nature relative to that marketplace's norm. We refer to this range as the *industry bandwidth* of working relationships. This bandwidth reflects the explicit or implicit relationship strategies pursued by supplier firms in an industry. Firms either attempt to span the bandwidth with a "portfolio" of relationships, or treat all customer firms more or less alike, thereby having a narrower range of relationships than the industry bandwidth.

Naturally, industry bandwidths for various markets fall along the entire continuum of working relationships. So, even the most transactional relationship in one industry might be more collaborative in nature than the most collaborative relationship in another industry, and vice versa. For example, compare the corrugated box, fiber drum, and programmable controller industries depicted in Figure 1a. Because the underlying technology in the programmable controller industry is the most complicated and is still rapidly developing, collaborative relations in this industry can be all-encompassing, ranging from codesign of manufacturing systems to installation, training, and maintenance. Collaborative relations in the fiber drum industry tend to be more

FIGURE 1. Transactional and Collaborative Relationships

Figure 1a: Industry Relationship Bandwidths

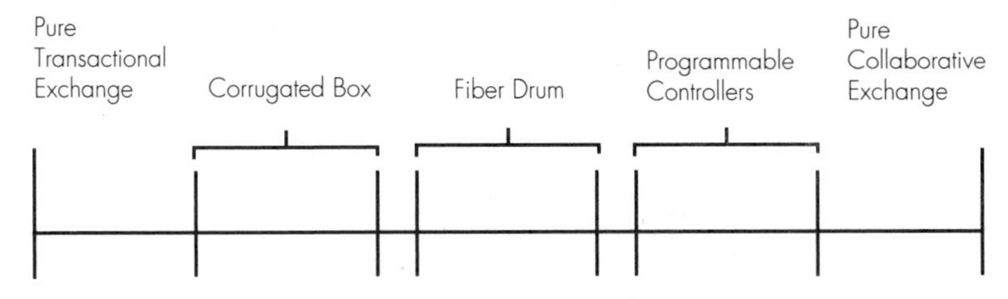

Figure 1b: "Flaring Out" from the Industry Bandwidth

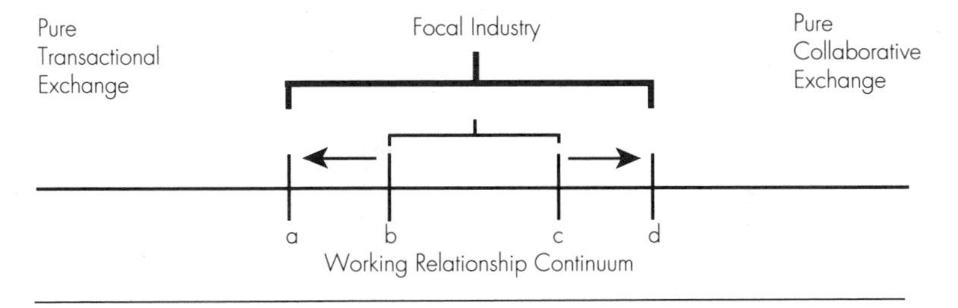

circumscribed and focus on helping customers modify their systems and procedures (e.g., lifting and stacking) to accommodate fiber drums. Finally, because corrugated boxes are considered a commodity by many customers, long-term supply contracts and just-in-time inventory programs generally represent the extent of potential collaboration.

SEGMENT THE MARKET BY PRODUCT APPLICATION AND CUSTOMER CAPABILITIES

The initial task for a supplier firm in formulating a relationship strategy is to partition, or segment, the marketplace into relatively homogenous groups of firms. Business firms segment markets in a number of ways, with demographics such as account size and industry being the most common basis.[3] Although demographics have the advantage of being accessible, they often provide little insight about the way the product is *used* and thus *generates value* for the customer firm. Because value can be regarded as the cornerstone of business marketing strategy, we advocate segmentation of the marketplace based upon the value of the product offering in a given application. This requires that market research be conducted to partition the marketplace into homogeneous application segments; that is, groupings of firms that use the product the same way to add value to the products that they, in turn, produce. The research may also reveal that, within particular applications, subsegments of firms exist that differ significantly in their technical know-how, problem-solving, or other capabilities.

Glen Raven Mills, a manufacturer of acrylic woven fabrics, provides a good example of product application segmentation. Initially, it would appear that Glen Raven Mills has two major segments—the awning market and the marine market. However, careful examination of the marine market demonstrates that there are two distinct applications. Power and sail boat manufacturers can purchase acrylic fabrics for use outside the boat (e.g., for boat covers and canopies) or inside the boat (e.g., seat covers). Moreover, detailed research has shown that acrylic fabrics provide different levels of value inside and outside the boat. As a boat cover, acrylic fiber provides largely functional value; that is, it protects the boat from wind and water damage. Relatively speaking, the total value provided is low because alternate materials ranging from canvas to plastic sheets can do the job. When used internally, acrylic fabric provides greater value because fashion-conscious consumers are willing to pay extra for designs and styles that are feasible only with acrylic fiber. Consumer preferences, in turn, create a greater need for partnerships, as boat manufacturers are anxious to work closely with fabric makers to produce styles that will catch the consumer's eye. Thus, Glen Raven Mills finds that product application is a superior basis for marketing segmentation.

ASSESS THE VALUE OF YOUR PRODUCT TO CUSTOMERS IN EACH SEGMENT

Value refers to the perceived worth in monetary terms of the economic, technical, service, and social benefits received by a customer firm in exchange for the price paid for a product offering. Judgments about value also take into consideration alternative suppliers' offerings and prices. Given the fundamental nature of value in business markets, it is critical for managers to gain estimates of the value of their products in particular applications and learn how it can be enhanced, particularly with relationships. A number of research methods—such as internal engineering assessments, focus groups, or conjoint analysis—can be used to obtain dependable value estimates.[4] In practice, value assessment can be folded in as part of the market research study to identify application segments.

Consider the example of Macfield Texturing Company, a leading producer of texturized, dyed, and spun yarns for the hosiery industry. To gain a more accurate estimate of the value of its products, Macfield has set up production simulation and product testing laboratories at its main plant that have all of the types of textile production equipment used by its customer firms. With this equipment, Macfield personnel can simulate customer production processes and manufacture actual products. In doing so, Macfield can measure precisely the costs a customer incurs by using its products versus those of the competition. Product benefits, in turn, are measured in the product testing lab, where finished goods are examined for wear and tear. Macfield uses its value information to target profitable applications and to create convincing sales presentations.

TARGET SEGMENTS FOR RELATIONSHIP-SPECIFIC EFFORTS

Armed with the information gained in the preceding research, the firm is in a position to make several crucial decisions concerning the targeting of market segments for various kinds of relationship efforts.

Determine the Number of Segments to Be Targeted

The first strategic choice to be made by supplier management is whether to focus on one market segment and develop a narrow range of relationships, or to target a number of market segments and cultivate a "portfolio" of relationships. Many firms either choose or are forced to limit themselves to as few market segments as possible. The C. E. Smith Company, a contract manufacturer of metal parts, provides a prime example. Largely because the company is small, managers of the C. E. Smith Company only pursue high value-added business that requires substantial codesign and custom manufacturing and entails a close, collaborative relationship. As managers point out, the Smith Company could not compete against either the customer's internal manufacturing department or large contract manufacturers for large-volume orders of standardized parts because these operations have economies of scale advantages.

Select Market Segment Candidate(s) for Targeting

Once the number of segments to be addressed has been determined, supplier management should next decide which market segment(s) will be targeted for *collaborative emphasis* versus *transaction emphasis.* We use the term "emphasis" in two key respects. First, "emphasis" is meant to capture our earlier notion that even the most transactional relationship in one industry bandwidth might be more collaborative in nature than the most collaborative relation in another industry bandwidth, and vice versa. Second, we use "emphasis" because some individual accounts within collaborative-emphasis segments should be targeted for transactional relations; similarly, some accounts within transaction-emphasis segments should be targeted for collaborative relations.

Segments where a firm's product offering has superior value relative to the competition are targeted for collaborative emphasis, while segments where its offering does not are targeted for transaction emphasis. Segments where the firm has superior value represent natural places for the firm to allocate resources for relationship-building efforts. Customers in these segments are more likely to be receptive to such initiatives, and in fact, may be proactive themselves in suggesting closer relations. The ways in which the product offering achieves superior value in these segments typically reflect the distinctive competencies of the firm, and close, collaborative relations can spur further development of these as well as facilitate finding ways to buttress elements of the offering where value is presently deficient.

Sonoco Fibre Products Division provides an instructive example of market segment targeting. Its fiber drums can replace stainless steel drums in a multitude of industries ranging from cooking oil manufacturing to gunpowder production. Rather than attempt to serve all of these industries at once, Sonoco has first prioritized and then targeted market segments based on the value of its fiber drums in customer applications. Sonoco knows that its products create the greatest value in situations where highly acidic or alkali products must be stored and transported; the disposal or reconditioning of steel drums presents an environmental hazard; a significant portion of the customer's costs can be attributed to the transportation of heavy steel drums; and customers require "odd-sized" drums. Many of the partnerships in these high-value segments have paid dividends to Sonoco in the form of new product and service ideas. As time has progressed, Sonoco has moved down its priority list to segments with lower value potential, which receive greater transactional emphasis.

Identify Individual Accounts for Collaborative versus Transactional Relations

Having targeted specific segment(s), supplier managers should turn their attention to individual accounts, identifying likely prospects for partnerships versus transactional relations. In doing so, a supplier develops selection criteria based on customer firm and marketplace characteristics. Although these characteristics can be grouped in different ways, one useful way to categorize them is philosophy of doing business, the relative dependence of the supplier firm and the customer firm upon the relationship, and the technological edge contributed by a customer firm.

Philosophy of Doing Business. Sonoco Fibre Drum Division seeks partnerships with customer firms that share a common philosophy of business. The ideal partnership candidate must have a "total cost" orientation. By focusing upon reducing their own total costs, these firms are more likely to seek out and recognize the value provided by Sonoco's fiber drums and accompanying support services. Further, they also are more likely to recognize the benefits of joint programs and activities with Sonoco designed to reduce their total cost of operations. Other accounts that evaluate acquisitions solely on "purchase price" either perceive few benefits from collaboration or are unwilling to pay for the added service. These accounts are better served by steel drum manufacturers.

Relative Dependence on the Working Relationship. Experience suggests that collaborative relations prosper as long as the supplier firm and customer firm each have significant and roughly the same dependence upon the relationship. In this dependence situation, there is mutual interest in cooperating to find ways to add value or reduce cost *and* in equitably sharing these relationship benefits. This cooperative spirit in expanding the "value pie" and sharing equitably predominates over the conflict inherent in a customer-supplier relationship in determining how to split the "pie."[5] Because of this natural tension between cooperation and conflict in the relationship, supplier firms need to be mindful of the relative dependence of each firm upon the relationship.

Switching costs and time horizon are two dependence criteria which have been suggested.[6] Typically, high switching costs serve as barriers-to-exit from a working relationship, and thus motivate a customer firm to actively collaborate with the supplier firm. Value created by continuity or consistency represent two specific sources of switching costs. For instance, customer firms typically make specific investments in "just-in-time" programs. Once in place, these programs and systems are not amenable to using multiple supply sources or to being easily changed. Product offerings from the same supplier can offer greater consistency than products from different vendors. For example, steel coils from the same mill tend to run more uniformly (i.e., less scrap and downtime for minor equipment adjustments) than coils from different mills, even though all coils meet the stated customer specifications. Finally, customer firms whose purchase decisions have long-term consequence (e.g., programmable control equipment for factory automation) are also more likely to collaborate with supplier firms.

The rate of marketplace change is another indicator of dependence. High Point Chemicals sells specialty chemicals to the textile industry. The marketplace for its customers' products is highly volatile because fashion trends dictate product changes at least every two years. As a result, it is in the best interests of both High Point Chemicals and its key customers to have highly collaborative relationships so that they can develop the next generation of dyes and finishing chemicals in advance of changes in fashions.

Technological Edge Contributions. Some firms, even when they are in transaction-emphasis segments, should be targeted for collaborative efforts. Manufacturers of technology-based products should target *lead-user* accounts and *leap-frog* accounts for collaborative efforts as a strategy for improving the value of their product offering in presently designated transaction segments. A lead-user firm is one whose present needs will reflect its segment's needs in future months or years, and one that is therefore positioned to benefit the most from collaborative solutions to those needs.[7] A natural question, though, is "Won't a supplier's competitors that presently have superior value in that segment have already 'locked-up' the lead-user firms in collaborative relationships?" The answer to this is that if the competitors are astute, they will have already engaged the lead-user firms, particularly the large ones, in collaboration.

In this case, a supplier firm's targeting strategy is to focus upon the small, aggressive firms who have the ability to "leap-frog" the present segment leaders with new technology. Such leap-frog firms may be newer entrants that are willing to pursue a riskier development strategy to gain market share. By engaging in collaborative efforts (e.g., codesign), the supplier firm seeks to significantly improve the value of its future offerings in this application.

Needless to say, lead-user and leap-frog firms in designated collaborative segments merit especially close monitoring and involvement by the supplier. To reflect this special status, supplier firms often designate this small subset of collaborative relationships as "strategic alliances." Working closely with these firms enables a supplier to innovate so as to continue to provide superior value over time and remain the offering of choice for that application.

Working with the field sales force, managers of the product-market group within Motorola's Semiconductor Sector continuously seek out lead-users and leap-froggers, using a two-stage identification process. First, they monitor and forecast growth in silicon usage among market segments. Currently, for instance, the automotive market ranks first in silicon technology growth potential while the military, due to projected budget cuts, ranks last. Next, they evaluate companies within each segment based on predicted technological developments within the potential customer firms and then compare this expected progress with Motorola's "Technology Roadmaps." A roadmap is a one-page diagram which charts the anticipated developments in a technology over the next ten years, the steps that Motorola plans to take to secure the technology, and the financial commitments that Motorola has made or needs to make to complete each development step. Companies, large and small, that can aid Motorola in more rapidly and efficiently reaching the goals of a technology roadmap are targeted for partnerships.

With an eye on leap-froggers, Texas Instruments (TI) targets key emerging accounts in each market region and segment. These accounts are smaller clients that are served primarily through electronics distributors, but whose target markets are being principally developed through creatively designed products using TI systems products. TI participates in these firms' product design process as early as possible and, in doing so, suggests improvements that enable these firms to design products that fully capitalize on the strengths and capabilities of TI systems products. Another benefit of this early participation is that TI is able to better anticipate the future needs of its clients and the marketplace, and thus is able to provide better direction to its application development engineers.

DEVELOP AND IMPLEMENT RELATIONSHIP-SPECIFIC PRODUCT OFFERINGS

With segment and individual account targets in mind, supplier managers construct, and then implement, relationship-specific offerings for collaborative and transactional targets. A focal implementation concern is how to handle special cases or problem relationships.

Constructing Relationship-Specific Offerings

As a supplier firm moves from transactional relationships to collaborative relationships, the product offering will change from a "core product," which addresses basic quality, price, and availability requirements of customers, to an "augmented product," which is customized in terms of physical and service attributes to meet more demanding customer needs.[8] As a start in constructing the collaborative and transactional relationship offerings, the supplier firm undertakes market research to determine the extent and intensity of collaborative and transaction efforts currently practiced in the industry. That is, an understanding is gained of the present industry bandwidth.

The supplier firm's strategy is then to extend the present industry bandwidth in both the collaborative as well as the transactional direction. By becoming more collaborative and more transactional, a supplier firm attempts to gain a competitive advantage over other suppliers in both collaborative-emphasis and transaction-emphasis segments. We refer to this strategy as *flaring-out* from the industry bandwidth. By doing this, a supplier firm innovates to provide relationships that more closely meet the disparate requirements of various application segments and customer firms within segments.

As grist for this, a supplier firm can perform "benchmark studies" of other industries in an attempt to learn about collaborative and transactional practices that might be adopted or adapted into their current offerings.[9] Firms also can gain inspiration from a deeper understanding of their customers' needs. Peters and Austin have documented a number of imaginative ways that Milliken Company "gets close to the customer," such as establishing a "customer listening college" that teaches employees how to be more sensitive to customer concerns and problems, and an "internships in manufacturing" program that enlightens sales people on the possibilities and constraints of production.[10] Finally, suppliers can gain insight by drawing on the experiences of their own employees. Milliken gathers and disseminates internal ideas through a program called "Fabulous Bragging Sessions," where every ninety days, work teams are encouraged to give five-minute presentations on how they handle particular problems.[11] This complementary flaring-out is depicted in Figure 1b as offerings *a* and *d*.

Flaring Out by Unbundling. The base transactional offering, *a,* becomes simply the core product itself. The pricing policy for the transactional offering reflects the underlying strategy: *unbundling* of the product offering elements. For each service that is unbundled, the price is lowered, but it is lowered less than the cost of presently performing the service, thereby improving the supplier's profit margin. This requires an accurate understanding of the cost structure of performing each service, something that many firms have neglected.

Augmenting programs and services such as delivery, installation, training, maintenance, and technical assistance are each offered, in menu fashion, on an incremental price basis. A further critical feature of the pricing policy for the transactional offering should be that the sum of the price increments for the entire set of unbundled services should be greater than the price premium granted for the collaborative offering. This should reflect the economies of scope and scale that accrue from being a "full-service" supplier to a customer. Note that this pricing policy is market-oriented in that it allows customer firms to choose the product and relationship offering that *they perceive* provides the greatest value.

Some observations on unbundling the product offering, and competitive response, are needed. Depending upon the industry's bandwidth position on the working relationship continuum, certain augmenting services or programs must be considered as part of the core product. For instance, in the programmable controller industry, initial training on how to use the product is an essential part of doing business with new customers. However, training of alternates or replacements in the customer firms might be a candidate for unbundling. So, for its own industry, a supplier firm first ascertains what the essential core product is, and then successively unbundles the remaining services, programs and systems to arrive at the transactional offering.

Competition or product maturity often forces firms into unbundling. Consider the case of a large chemical company that produces and markets a gasoline additive. Pursuing what they believed was a value-added strategy, over the years, company managers increased the number of services offered with the product until they reached 186. A major consequence of this, though, was to significantly increase the cost of the product. Growing uneasiness led the company to undertake some market research, which revealed that customers typically purchased about a third of their total requirements from the supplier in order to gain access to the services. The remaining two thirds of their requirements for the additive were secured from the other competitors, all of which offered the basic product with minimal services at slightly lower prices. In response, the firm eliminated services that were not being utilized, and unbundled many of the remaining services by charging a surcharge for them, retaining only a minimal set of services as part of the basic offering.

A natural concern that supplier managers have about an unbundling strategy is "How will my competitors respond?" Most often, because they are similarly looking to improve their profitability, the competitors will match the supplier's strategy and unbundle their offerings. In the event that they do not, the supplier is in a position to gain sales at the competitor's expense. In the less likely event that one or more competitors match this lower price, yet continue to offer some services for "free," the supplier must be willing to selectively let some customers "walk." This is particularly difficult for sales-oriented firms to do, where any sale is a good sale no matter what its profitability.[12] Nonetheless, the supplier must remember that: customers in transaction-emphasis segments have been previously designated as ones in which the supplier is not primarily interested; and it is easy to give value away, but it is the role of marketing to receive an equitable return for the value delivered to a customer.

A useful precaution for supplier firms that are anxious about potential negative consequences of unbundling is to "pilot test" this strategy. The firm selects the service that it believes is most amenable to unbundling (e.g., the service judged to be least essential) and then charges a fee for it. By closely monitoring the responses of customers and competitors, and within their own firm, managers can determine the viability of this alternative for the given segment as well as gain some implementation experience.

Supplier firms also need to anticipate some customer, and even sales force, resistance to unbundling. Several years ago, a number of chemical manufacturers unbundled delivery services in response to rapidly escalating transportation costs. The result was a "firestorm" of complaints from distributors and customers alike who thought that delivery was a "free" service. By remaining stalwart, however, these suppliers were able to sustain the policy, although their relations with customers were initially strained. Similarly, some suppliers of programmable controllers have unbundled field technical service by establishing this function as a separate cost/profit center. Charges for field technical service visits are either billed directly to the customer firm in the case of transactional accounts, or to the sales force (or business unit) in the case of collaborative accounts.

Finally, it is worth mentioning that some managers argue that pursuing both unbundling and augmented product strategies at the same time is too difficult and costly. Instead, they recommend that companies market either a core product for the lowest possible price or a fully-augmented product for a premium price. This argument, however, is not supported by recent research which found that for industrial systems (e.g., computer systems), a "mixed bundling" strategy (i.e., offering a core product, an unbundled product, and a fully-augmented product with different price schedules) is, in general, the most profitable.[13]

Flaring Out with Added Augmentation. At the other extreme, the collaborative offering, *d,* becomes the augmented product "wrapped" with whatever collaborative activities, programs, and systems that are valued by the customer firm. Some specific ways in which supplier firms have wrapped their product offerings with collaborative offering elements are summarized in Figure 2. Because collaborative efforts are only undertaken that add value to or reduce the total cost of the exchange between firms, a price premium should be granted in return for the collaborative offering. As an alternative to this, the customer firm may instead offer the supplier a greater share of its business, particularly when the potential cost savings occur in the customer firm's operation. This second alternative is particularly effective when combined with a long-term purchase agreement. Prior to undertaking these efforts, then, frank discussions are needed with a customer firm's management on the potential outcomes of each effort, and consensus should be reached on what would constitute an equitable sharing of achieved outcomes.

As an example of augmentation, look how Leaseway Transportation, a company in the trucking industry, has "flared-out" to create a collaborative offering in a market populated with transactional relationships. As part of its service to General Motors (GM), Leaseway has hired operations researchers to build a model of GM's physical distribution requirements. Based upon this model, Leaseway designed a program to help GM schedule shipping routes, select car models for shipping, and determine the optimal sequence for off-loading cars at GM dealers to minimize potential damage and delivery time. The computer model is highly interfaced with GM's in-house computer systems and can be utilized to troubleshoot emergency problems. Although Leaseway has only a 30-day contract with GM, that contract has been in effect continuously for over 35 years. Leaseway remains a major supplier of trucking services to GM.

A final consideration relating to pricing policy is that long-term collaborative relationships should lead to what can be referred to as "cooperative pricing." Often, design specifications are taken from standard reference sources, which can lead to quoted specs that are unnecessarily stringent for the given application. The trust and cooperation that characterizes long-term collaborative relationships enable a supplier to utilize its expertise and suggest design modifications in return for a lower, delivered price.

FIGURE 2. Ten Ways to Augment the Product Offering for Collaborative Relationships

1. **"Pull" promotional programs** can be directed at the customer firm's customers. This might involve trade journal advertisements touting the value of products made from or with the supplier firm's components.
2. **Warranty, maintenance and repair agreements** can be offered to customer firms to reduce the risk associated with usage of a supplier's products.
3. **Cooperative advertising and promotional allowances** can serve the dual purposes of enabling smaller customer firms to advertise regularly and coordinating customer and supplier market communication efforts.
4. **Joint sales calls** can be utilized to assist customer firms in developing new markets, or to deal with problem accounts.
5. **Coordinated cost-reduction programs** can be implemented to dramatically pare the customer firm's real costs of doing business. Joint material requirements planning (MRP) systems, computer-to-computer order entry systems, just-in-time inventory programs, and statistical process control are some examples.
6. **Technical assistance** can be provided to augment customer firms' technical product and application knowledge. Supplier firm technical and production experts can make suggestions on how the customer firm could gain cost savings through substitute materials and alternative production processes.
7. **Logistics and delivery systems** can be used to create value. For instance, a manufacturer of paint pigments discovered through its customer relationships that offering the pigment in "slurry form" rather than in "dry bag" form created greater value for the customer. This enabled customer firms to reduce costs in the production process because they no longer had to emulsify the pigment before use. As a side benefit, the manufacturer was able to gain logistical cost savings because greater quantities of pigment were ordered at a time and the slurry could be delivered more economically.
8. **Computer networking capabilities** can be used to troubleshoot customer problems from a remote location. For instance, a manufacturer of scientific testing equipment uses its network to solve customer problems more quickly. Data and computer software can be down-loaded from the equipment on-site and transferred to the manufacturer's simulation computers via telephone interlink. The supplier can troubleshoot the software and make corrections in the case of problems. The corrected software can then be sent back to the customer firm via telephone interlink.
9. **Shared expertise programs** in which information is more openly shared between supplier and customer firms is another option. In the marketing area, one manufacturer of chemicals and plastics not only shares information on economic trends with customer firms but also performs market research studies for those customers which lack in-house research expertise. On the technical side, one manufacturing company has a "scientist exchange program" in which its own scientists spend time working in the research and development labs of customer firms.
10. **Value-enhancement and codesign programs** can be put in-place to upgrade the value of present customer firm products as well as to jointly design new products. Considerable value can be added to the product offering at times simply by a reallocation upstream of processing and production functions. For instance, many steel service centers now perform the functions of stamping doors and window panels for the auto makers, resulting in lower overall cost. The assembly of electronic components into modules or boards by electronic component manufacturers is another example of this process.

Implementing Working Relationship Strategy

Creating an Organization that Supports the Relationship Strategy. Companies that pursue a relationship strategy often reorganize their sales and marketing efforts to better serve the different sets of customer requirements. The most common response is to divide the sales force into several units, one each for categories of relationships ranging from transactional to strategic accounts. Each new sales force has different responsibilities and types of participants.

Motorola's Semiconductor Sector provides an excellent example. The division is comprised of three field sales forces: a "Strategic Market or Segment" Sales Force that handles Motorola's partnerships, a "Geographic" Sales Force that has responsibilities for transactional accounts directly served by Motorola, and a "Distributor" Sales Force that deals with distributors of Motorola products. Motorola's Strategic Market Sales Force is composed of "teams" of technical sales engineers, applications engineers, quality engineers, and service personnel, among others, that are assigned to specific partnership accounts. It is the responsibility of these sales teams to deliver the technical and manufacturing know-how needed to make the partnerships successful. Members of the Geographic Sales Force act individually, calling on the thousands of customers that buy Motorola products. They perform traditional selling tasks, such as making periodic customer visits, giving presentations, solving problems, and taking orders. Finally, Motorola's Distributor Sales Force serve as representatives to the trade. Their tasks include encouraging distributors to stock and sell Motorola products, coaching distributor sales personnel on merchandising techniques, and working with distributors to maintain sound, working relationships with the smallest of Motorola customers. As an interesting aside, by carefully matching the skills and personalities of individuals to those needed to flourish in each of the different sales positions, Motorola has managed to avoid the conflict between multiple sales forces that is frequently cited by pundits.

Solving Common Relationship Implementation Problems. In putting the relationship strategy into play, it is inevitable that some special cases or problem working relationships will arise for the supplier firm. The ones of particular concern are customer firms that account for a "significant" proportion of the supplier firm's sales. A supplier's tactics for these large accounts depends upon the targeting for their segment.

Certain large accounts in collaborative-emphasis segments either may not recognize the value of, or are unwilling to pay a premium for, the augmented product offering that they are presently receiving. Marketing communications, supported by value case histories or other results gleaned from the earlier research, should be used by a supplier to persuasively demonstrate the superior value provided. Sonoco Fibre Drum Division has done this with a dramatic set of videos. The videos convincingly show fiber drums outperforming steel drums in a series of Department of Transportation tests.

But some large accounts that tacitly understand this greater value attempt to take advantage of the supplier. Each time some program or system is offered to reduce cost or add value, these accounts opportunistically demand all of the benefits, without granting some price premium in return. An alternate large customer tactic is to "reward" the supplier with a larger share of the customer's business, but then request greater volume discounts. This can be a "hollow bone" if it does not provide enough additional gross profit to cover the costs of the program or system. These opportunistic customers feel that they are "base-loading" the supplier's facility and expect the supplier to make its profits on other, presumably smaller, customers' business.

This is a critical "moment of truth" for the relationship. Suppliers need to respond to such opportunistic accounts by "freezing them" at current levels of service and not offering any new collaborative initiative, such as a codesign program, to them. Should these accounts hear that a new collaborative program has been offered to another customer and question the supplier as to why they have not been offered the program, a supplier needs to firmly respond that they cannot afford to give away the value that such efforts produce, given their incremental cost to the supplier. In response to this inquiry, the supplier should ask: "If we undertook this collaborative effort and it produced the expected outcomes, what would this be worth to your firm?" If the opportunistic customer responds by saying "Nothing!" or some price (or volume) increment less than the cost of the program, the supplier should respond that they cannot undertake the effort at that return. The collaborative product offering for these opportunistic accounts is designated as *c* in Figure 1b.

Turning to transaction-emphasis segments, certain large accounts may want the new, unbundled lower price, but the previous service level. Once again, the supplier faces a moment of truth. If these are truly accounts that the supplier cannot afford to lose, some negotiation is needed. Once compromise is to exchange a basic set of services, such as delivery and technical assistance, for large-volume and longer-term purchase commitments. The transactional product offering for these problematic accounts is designated as *b* in Figure 1b.

EVALUATE RELATIONSHIP OUTCOMES AND REASSIGN ACCOUNTS

Many business marketers, when asked about the success of their relationship-building efforts, respond that they feel the efforts have been successful, but that they have not submitted such efforts to the same scrutiny as they would other marketing programs or systems. This is because often no measurable objectives have been determined, with the results of relationship-building efforts viewed as contributing only to intangible "customer goodwill." However, remembering that the fundamental reason for all relationship-building activities and efforts is to either add value or reduce cost in the exchange relationship, and that there should be an *equitable* sharing of the added value or lowered cost, some formal evaluations of relationship outcomes are needed.

Motorola's Semiconductor Sector provides an instructive example of relationship evaluation procedures. Several years ago, when Motorola began partnering in earnest, senior management devised a one-page "Statement of Partnership Goals" that summarized what Motorola expected to achieve for both itself and key customers from the partnership process. The key objectives spelled out on this statement can be briefly paraphrased as follows:

- *All* partnership programs (e.g., codesign or joint development) will result in profits for both Motorola and its partner firm.
- Motorola's sales to the partner firm will be substantial and/or exhibit significant growth potential.
- Motorola should have a significant, if not exclusive, share of the partner's business.
- The partnership should contribute significantly to achievement of Motorola's "technology roadmap" goals.

Periodically, senior management compares outputs from each of the Semiconductor Sector's approximately 60 partnerships to the goals specified on the partnership statement. Changes in sales and profits as well as the mix of complementary products sold to the partner firms are considered. In order to gauge the benefits of the partnership to the customer firm, managers examine results of Motorola's annual customer satisfaction survey. The survey summarizes Motorola's performance from the perspective of partner firms' managers from such functional areas as manufacturing, engineering, purchasing, and R&D. Following consultation with customer managers, partnerships that do not meet objectives are "downgraded." This is accomplished in two ways. First, responsibility for a downgraded account is transferred from the "Strategic Market or Segment" Sales Force to the "Geographic" Sales Force. Second, Motorola disengages itself from partnership programs (e.g., joint product development). Conversely, promising geographic accounts (i.e., transactional accounts) are upgraded to partnerships.

Another noteworthy example of relationship-outcome measurement is provided by Baxter Healthcare, which uses hospital supply needs per bed as its key relationship measure. Baxter has determined that it could potentially supply $27,000 worth of products and services per bed out of a hospital's total needs each year. Its long-term relationship goal, then, is to supply as much of that $27,000 need as possible. To accomplish this, a target of 15% growth in annual sales volume is established for each customer in Baxter's corporate relationship program, and firms that meet or surpass this target are rewarded with an annual bonus based on their percentage increment in volume. Baxter also works with customers that are having difficulty achieving this growth target to identify mutually beneficial ways for the firms to do additional business together.

A critical question which must be resolved in relationship analysis is "How long should a supplier firm wait to meaningfully evaluate its relationship-building efforts?" Although the answer will vary, it is unlikely that results will begin to appear within the first year, and even two or three years may be needed. Two points can be made with respect to this, though. First, if baseline measures on each account (e.g., sales by product category and profitability) are not available, the supplier firm needs to establish an account information system early on. Second, perceived satisfaction with the supplier firm can serve as a useful intermediate criterion measure. To gain an accurate organizational perspective, and thus avoid being "blindsided," this assessment needs to be taken across several functional areas in the account.

After a suitable period, the supplier firm should make a comparison of results for the collaborative accounts with those for the transactional accounts. Two analyses can be undertaken. First, the averages on the germane relationship measures are compared (e.g., gross margin and number of product modification ideas). If the results do not favor the collaborative accounts, this would suggest that the supplier's augmented product offering is not valued by the targeted accounts, either because of shortcomings in its construction or its implementation. If the results are in the expected direction, the supplier proceeds with an account variance analysis by comparing each account's numbers to the relevant averages. This diagnostic analysis enables a supplier to identify specific accounts that may have been mistargeted due to a misreading of the account characteristics. After further investigation, these accounts might be reassigned for more appropriate relationship efforts.

PERIODICALLY UPDATE THE VALUE PROVIDED IN RELATIONSHIPS

Supplier managers must periodically update the value of their product and relationship offerings in the collaborative-emphasis and transaction-emphasis segments. In this way, they can identify which new services and product modifications can increase customer value as well as which services need to be unbundled or curtailed. Such studies can assess whether developments with lead-user or leap-frog firms should lead the firm to retarget a transaction-emphasis segment as a growth segment for collaborative efforts. At the same time, supplier managers should repeat their benchmark studies to discover new ideas for additional collaborative and transactional practices.

A supplier firm must also anticipate needed reformation of the collaborative relationship offering, based upon customer experience and the product life cycle. Early on, the firm should focus upon adding value through such things as technical and application support. As a product matures or customers gain extensive experience with it, the offering should evolve to emphasize ease of doing business, focusing upon programs and systems for improving the efficiency of exchange. By understanding and anticipating this evolution of the product offering, the firm can proactively reform collaborative programs and systems to remain responsive to customer needs over time.

Most important, firms should strive to avoid complacency, an insidious relationship-killer. They should continuously ask questions in a way that encourages customers to relate problems and shortcomings. The question, "What have we *not* done lately?" should be periodically addressed to each customer.[14] This question's wording is significant in two respects. First, it is phrased in a manner so as to encourage the voicing of problems, rather than simply soliciting a socially desirable response ("Fine"). Second, the inclusion of "lately" recognizes the natural inertia that occurs in relationships and that leads to complacency. Most unhappy customers never complain, and it costs far more to create a customer account than to retain it.[15]

CONCLUSION

Working relationships with customer firms are a significant asset of any supplier's business. Through partnerships, a supplier can leverage its limited resources through joint efforts with customers, gain the benefits of customer ideas and experience, and garner higher profit margins from value-added services. On the other hand, transactional relationships offer the supplier the opportunity to prune elements of the product offering that customers deem superfluous, yielding a more competitively priced offering while at the same time easing pressure on the supplier's profit margin.

To cultivate and sustain these disparate types of working relationships, a coherent strategic approach is needed. The segmentation, targeting, and relationship-building approach that we have advocated has customer value as its cornerstone and adopts the basic premise that not all market segments, or customer firms, want the same working relationship, or value it the same. So, as we have discussed, supplier managers must systematically decide which customer firms are in their firm's best interests to have collaborative relationships with, and then, actively work to keep them "delighted."

NOTES

1. Irwin Gross, "Partnering: Games Businesses Play," *Marketplace: The ISBM Review* (Spring 1989), pp. 1–4.

2. Barbara B. Jackson, *Winning & Keeping Industrial Customers* (Lexington, MA: Lexington Books, 1985), pp. 6–7.
3. Benson P. Shapiro and Thomas V. Bonoma, "How to Segment Industrial Markets," *Harvard Business Review,* 62/3 (May/June 1984): 104–110.
4. James C. Anderson, Dipak C. Jain, and Pradeep K. Chintagunta, "Customer Value Assessment in Business Markets: A State-of-Practice Study," *Journal of Business-to-Business Marketing,* 1/1.
5. Gross, op. cit.
6. Jackson, op. cit.
7. Eric von Hippel, "Lead Users: A Source of Novel Product Concepts," *Management Science,* 32/7 (July 1986): 791–805.
8. Theodore Levitt, "Marketing Success through Differentiation—of Anything," *Harvard Business Review,* 58/1 (January/February 1980): 83–91.
9. Frances Gaither Tucker, Seymour M. Zivan, and Robert C. Camp, "How to Measure Yourself Against the Best," *Harvard Business Review,* 65/1 (January/February 1987): 8–10.
10. Tom Peters and Nancy Austin, *A Passion for Excellence* (New York, NY: Warner Books, 1985), pp. 17–20.
11. Ibid.
12. Philip Kotler, "From Sales Obsession to Marketing Effectiveness," *Harvard Business Review,* 55/6 (November/December 1977): 67–75.
13. Lynn Wilson, Allen Weiss, and George John, "Unbundling of Industrial Systems," *Journal of Marketing Research,* 27/2 (May 1990): 123–138.
14. Theodore Levitt, "After the Sale is Over . . .," *Harvard Business Review,* 61/5 (September/October 1983): 87–93.
15. Frederick F. Reichheld and W. Earl Sasser, Jr., "Zero Defections: Quality Comes to Services," *Harvard Business Review,* 68/5 (September/October 1990): 105–111.

H. Robert Dodge
Professor/Head Marketing Department
Eastern Michigan University
Ypsilanti, Michigan

CHAPTER 54

MARKETING RAW MATERIALS

The focus of this chapter is on the marketing characteristics of raw materials that differentiate this category from the other defined types of industrial goods. This is supplemented by a look at the role of commodity exchanges.

INDUSTRIAL RAW MATERIALS

Raw materials, one of the major categories falling under the broad classification of industrial products, are defined as relatively unprocessed goods emanating from the extraction and agricultural industries. The only processing of raw materials is in response to economies and/or requirements imposed by physical handling. Some examples include ginning and washing to remove waste materials, crushing, as well as drying to remove moisture content.

All raw materials must undergo further processing and so can be viewed as manufacturing or processing inputs into the final physical products. This means that goods classified as raw materials include not only the more obvious ones, such as minerals of either a metallic or nonmetallic nature, crude oil, and forestry products, but over 80 percent of the nation's agricultural output and as much as 70 percent of the fish caught in the world annually. Excluded by definition are the quantities of coal and natural gas that are used as fuel rather than as inputs for the chemical and pharmaceutical industries as well as the fresh fruit and produce that appear in local supermarkets.

Multiple Uses and Allocation Decisions

Crude oil offers a good example of the many uses for a raw material. From a barrel of crude oil, you can obtain gasoline, jet fuel, kerosene, heating oil, ethane, petrochemical feedstocks, naphtha, lubricants, coke, asphalt, and coal oil. While all raw materials do not have this many uses, the fact that they have several uses leads to allocation problems. These allocation problems can be classified as profitability, morality, political, and capacity. In terms of profitability, a log used to produce lumber or plywood will yield a much greater return than if it were used for pulp for newsprint. The most profitable uses of crude oil are gasoline and kerosene, as opposed to fuel oils.

The moral dilemma in allocation of a raw material is illustrated by the question of whether to use corn to make ethanol—an ingredient that will expand our supply of gasoline and make the United States less dependent on foreign sources—or let it remain a foodstuff for starving people around the world. This allocation decision between ethane and foodstuff has political considerations of an international nature. Another example of a political problem is the call by environmentalists to allow the harvesting of Pacific yew trees before other trees on government land. This will allow taxol, a promising cancer drug, to be extracted from the bark of yew trees. The estimates by environmentalists are that at least 50,000 patients could be deprived of the drug because of the loss of bark with uncontrolled cutting of forests.

Conversion capacity—a term used most frequently in the petroleum industry—refers to a refinery's capacity to turn crude oil into the most profitable downstream uses. The obvious problem is that conversion capacity requires large capital outlays that must be matched with future profitable returns.

Marketing Functions

Raw materials are not marketed in the fashion that other industrial products are marketed; with the exception of agricultural raw materials, product development is virtually nonexistent. For example, geneticists throughout the world are finding new ways of improving food products and increasing plant yields through genetic engineering. New foods like tofu, sashimi, and dimsum have been introduced; huge volumes of tomatoes, onions, and lettuce are grown in hydroponic warehouses that permit food production independent of soil and climate; and irradiation is used to reduce harmful bacteria.

To avoid the mushiness of shrimp occasioned by the time span between harvesting and freezing, shrimp are fattened to market size in shrimp feedlots where they swim into a flash freezer. High fructose corn syrup is another example of product development. As a substitute for sugar, it has the sweetness of sugar, is easily handled in bulk systems, and offers increased economy plus simplified storage.

Pricing is largely outside the control of marketers of raw materials. On the supply side, attempts such as OPEC have not met with a great deal of success. What gains there have been are largely short term in nature. The initial increase in the price of crude oil was buffered by increased exploration and development of oil reserves in other parts of the world, lessening use of crude oil, and the shift to alternate products. Thus the pricing of raw materials tends to approximate perfect competition. The prices of iron ore and bauxite fall because mini-mills use scrap metal rather than iron ore and the global slowdown in aluminum consumption has depressed demand for bauxite. On the other side, the price of nickel could rise over 20 percent by the end of 1992 due to its use in the making of stainless steel that in turn becomes part of pollution-control equipment.

Seldom—if ever—are advertising and personal selling employed to stimulate demand. Competition is priced-based in relation to specified quality levels. There have been scattered cooperative promotional efforts directed at the final consumer. Advertising has been placed to impress on final consumers the desirability of seeking out and purchasing consumer products made from raw materials such as leather hides, cotton, wool, and steel.

Transportation and storage are the two most important marketing functions. Of somewhat lesser importance is the function of standardization that plays an essential role in the buying and selling of raw materials by description.

The importance of low cost transportation such as water stems from the fact that raw materials frequently move great distances to the point of consumption. This is true of domestic shipments as well as international movements. As an example of the former, more than 90 percent of the nation's potash is mined in a small area near Carlsbad, New Mexico, a location somewhat isolated from most of the makers of commercial fertilizer who consume almost all of this raw material. To make a ton of steel in Cleveland will take ore from Minnesota or Nova Scotia, limestone from Ohio, coal from West Virginia, manganese from Brazil, scrap from anywhere, and ferroalloys from across the world.

The bulkiness of raw materials and generally a low value per cubic foot makes low-cost transportation all the more important. The requirement for an economical means of handling bulk over long hauls indicates water carriers, pipelines, and railroads as principal modes of transportation. For example, pipelines carry 75 percent of all the crude oil transported in the United States. Using 1,000 foot ore carriers, each one equivalent to about 920 railroad cars, Japanese steelmakers are able to ship iron ore from Brazil for about the same price per ton as iron ore imported into the United States from Venezuela. This is startling in that the distance from Brazil to Japan is some 11,500 miles, or roughly three and one-half times the 3,200 miles separating the United States and Venezuela.

This same bulkiness plus production and transportation characteristics necessitate extensive and low-cost storage facilities for raw materials. Seasonal production such as experienced with agricultural raw materials and continuous consumption by processors will occasion the need for storage to bring about an adjustment of supply to demand. Storage is also required for production surpluses such as are experienced with agricultural raw materials. In fact, to get a price-support loan from the government, grain must be placed in storage.

Stockpiling of raw materials may be indicated to accumulate economical shipping quantities or to adapt productive capacity to interruptions in shipping schedules resulting from weather conditions. The winter stoppages of iron ore freighters on the Great Lakes is an example of the latter.

Standards are basic to the marketing of raw materials. For practically all raw materials there are one or several standard deliverable grades. In trade parlance, the term "specification" may be substituted for standard. Various ores, crude oils, etc., are sold on the basis of specification (examples: low sulfur crudes versus high sulfur crudes, and higher concentrate phosphate ores versus lower concentrate phosphate ores). The principal advantage in utilizing standards is buying and selling by description. This method of exchange is faster, less risky, and more economical than either inspection or sampling. Additionally, standard grades of raw materials permit futures trading, which in turn helps to reduce market risk and enhance the value of market information. The governmental agencies interested in the development and control of standards are the U.S. Department of Agriculture for agricultural goods and the Commodity Standards Division of the U.S. Department of Commerce for nonagricultural goods.

Cost considerations in moving raw materials have also seen processing plants move closer to the source of raw materials. Iowa Beef Packers and Monfort have livestock slaughtering operations located adjacent to feedlots. Frozen food packages have moved closer to areas where crops are grown, and paper mills are situated near logging operations. For example, P&G's Flint River plant processes 5,000 tons of wood a day in making disposable diapers.

RAW MATERIAL MARKETS ARE GLOBAL MARKETS

The markets for raw materials are international in scope, rather than national. As an example, the price of copper on the world market has been affected by the significant reduction in mining in Zaire resulting from political, economic, and geological problems in this central African country. For the United States, the exportation of agricultural raw materials in food-loan programs has a significant impact on the prices of such materials as corn, wheat, and soybeans. Typically, the United States imports minerals and exports agricultural raw materials.

The United States as well as other industrially-advanced countries depend on less-developed countries for the bulk of the world's supply of raw materials, particularly those of a mineral nature. Industry in the United States, for example, depends on imports for 23 of the 36 minerals classed as essential. The political repercussions of the inability of the less-developed countries to effectively utilize their natural wealth has led to ever-increasing economic and political retaliations. The most obvious has been OPEC. Established in 1960, OPEC is dedicated to reducing the power of the Western World by strategic use of the members' oil reserves. World prices of raw materials have also been affected by the economic-political seesaws prevalent in the Middle East, other parts of Asia, and Africa.

The breakup of the USSR into republics signals opportunities for Western nations. The various republics need enormous amounts of investment and are willing to make deals such as generous terms for

EXHIBIT 1. Resources in Soviet Political Entities

Republic	Resources
Russia	iron, coal, oil, gold, platinum, copper, zinc, rare metals
Ukraine	iron, coal, chemicals, rich farmland
Uzbekistan	coal, oil, gas, copper
Kazakhstan	coal, oil, tungsten, manganese, copper, lead, zinc
Byelorussia	peat, timber
Azerbaijan	iron, oil, gas, bauxite, copper, zinc, gold, silver
Georgia	coal, oil, manganese, timber
Tadzhikistan	coal, oil, lead, zinc, rare elements
Moldavia	lignite, gypsum
Kirghizia	oil, timber
Lithuania	timber, peat, amber
Turkmenia	oil, coal, sulfur, magnesium
Armenia	copper, zinc, bauxite
Latvia	peat, amber
Estonia	oil, shale, timber

Paul Hofheinz, "Let's Do Business," *Fortune*, September 23, 1991, pp. 62–66.

mineral rights to obtain funding. Georgia has invited foreign companies to bid for mineral water concessions. Kazakhstan and Azerbaijan are negotiating with foreign firms for oil exploration rights (see Exhibit 1).

Vertical Integration

The flow of raw materials from their source through production and distribution levels can best be described as a vertical chain. Vertical integration is the absorption of one or more levels by another level. Integrating backward to the raw material source by the manufacturer or processor is advantageous for several reasons. One reason is desired quality; another is assured supply or self-sufficiency, while still another is lower costs. Banquet is a major poultry producer because its branded frozen-foods business is heavily dependent on frozen chicken.

The impact of vertical integration on the cost structure of a firm can be highly significant. The timber costs for a forest-products firm that draws on its own resources are only a small fraction of those incurred by a competitor that is buying timber from the government.

A major disadvantage of vertical integration is a lack of flexibility. Integrated firms experience difficulty in adjusting to fluctuations and perceived opportunities in the markets for their finished products. Another major disadvantage is an obsession with the exploration for and the processing of raw materials. This in turn distracts from the other vital concerns of the firm, most notably the marketing of finished products. Chemical companies that have integrated backward to oil and phosphate reserves have learned that this can be a dilution of their efforts without a meaningful return on their capital investment.

Common examples of backward vertical integration are the mining properties owned and operated by steel, aluminum, and copper producers, and the oil wells belonging to petroleum companies. Acquisition of timberlands is viewed as vital to growth in the forest-products industry. In fact, newsprint is largely made from trees grown as a crop.

Vertical integration involving the raw material source is also found in agriculture. A partial answer to how extensive is the estimate that all broilers and nearly 90 percent of the vegetables destined for processing are products of integrated firms. Perdue Farms, Inc.—the fourth largest chicken processor in the nation—delivers seven million chickens a week from eight locations in Maryland, Delaware, Virginia, and North Carolina.

A decided interest in the vertical integration of the raw-material source can also be found in agriculture. A partial answer to how extensive is the estimate that all broilers and nearly 90 percent of the vegetables destined for processing are grown by integrated firms.

Minute Maid owns a significant number of citrus groves in Florida, and J. M. Smucker makes extensive use of contract growers. An objective of Tenneco's agricultural operations is integration from "seedling to supermarket." This integrated system includes the jet-freight movement of tree-ripened and vine-ripened fruits and vegetables to the nation's markets.

In the agricultural industry, various forms of strategic partnering are emerging. One form might be a joint venture involving a food producer and biotech company. Another form is the combination research/marketing partnerships where a biotech research company joins with a food producer to market a genetically engineered product. An example is the agreement between Bio Technica International Inc., of Cambridge, Massachusetts and the Seagrams Company Ltd. of Canada.

Firms involved with raw materials may also be involved in the transportation of the commodity. Two mining companies, Hanna Mining and Cleveland-Cliffs Iron Company, are ranked second and fifth respectively in the worldwide shipment of iron ore. One steel firm operates its own railroad line to ship iron ore from a lake port to its inland mills.

Middlemen

Functional middlemen are involved in the marketing of raw materials that flow through nonintegrated channels. For agricultural and nonagricultural commodities, the most important middleman is the broker. Tending to represent the seller rather than the buyer on a transaction-by-transaction basis, brokers offer their principals several advantages. The main advantage is extensive market knowledge that is utilized in the negotiation of prices for highly standardized products such as raw materials that are bought and sold largely by description. Another factor favoring the broker is that the seller or buyer of raw materials may not need continuous market representation. Finally, the anonymous nature of representation by a broker permits "testing out" the market for price without risk of commitment.

Among the other types of functional middlemen are selling agents, who are found in the marketing of nonagricultural raw materials, and commission merchants, who handle sales of grain and livestock at terminal markets. Brokers and a number of export agents will be found in the international markets for raw materials.

Merchant middlemen are of little economic significance in the marketing of raw materials. Assemblers have a decidedly limited role in the distribution of agricultural goods. Drop shippers handling raw materials can be found in both the domestic and export markets. Another merchant middleman in the export market is the raw materials merchant.

ENVIRONMENTAL CONSIDERATIONS

Ecology has added still another dimension to the marketing of raw materials. The shipment of oil by tanker and pipeline, domestic mining operations, and the use of public lands are but a few of the examples of the conflict between environmental values and the economics and/or availability of raw material production. Without doubt, the environmental dimension has cast a pall over the costs and risks associated with raw-material production. Safer and more costly ways of handling raw materials will have to be developed and implemented. Source locations will be shifted from troublesome areas to environmentally safer areas, and accessibility and exploration costs will rise disproportionately as will the involved risks. Perhaps the most worrisome risk for U.S. industry is that of decreasing self-sufficiency in raw materials and increasing reliance on the resources of other nations. The likely results are higher prices and/or shrinking profit margins coupled with a lessening of control over the flow of raw materials.

The ecological equation is much more complicated than the simple tradeoff of a cleaner environment for increased material costs. For instance, stiff pollution controls have led to cuts in output and even the closing down of marginal operations. As a direct result, unemployment in the small adjacent communities has soared many times to disastrous proportions. Thus, the ecological values of a clean environment must also be weighted against the social costs accruing from a potential loss of worker livelihood.

Comparable usage of an area such as a coastal zone for oil wells and recreation might best be solved by setting up standards for environmental protection. If the project met the standards, then it would be approved. If it did not, then it would not be approved.

COMMODITY EXCHANGES

In the domestic and world markets for both agricultural and extractive raw materials, an immense volume flows through organized commodity exchanges. One of the most important is the Chicago Board of Trade (CBT), which executes contracts in agricultural commodities, notably wheat, livestock, and soybeans. In all, there are 10 exchanges in the United States and Canada. Some exchanges are located near the major production centers such as Minneapolis and Kansas City for wheat, while others may be located in major trade centers. An example of the latter is the New York exchange where trading involves cocoa, coffee, sugar, potatoes, and orange juice. Aluminum, tin, copper, lead, nickel, and zinc are traded on the London Metal Exchange.

The CBT was formed in 1848 to alleviate the market stress of violent price fluctuations and the cyclical nature of grain surpluses and shortages. During the early years of its existence, merchants used forward contracts or cash commitments to buy and sell grain for delivery at some date in the future. The major disadvantage of the forward contract was the lack of standardization in regards to quantity and delivery. This was corrected in 1865 when the CBT formalized grain trading by developing standardized agreements called futures contracts and initiating a margining system to eliminate the problem of buyers and sellers not fulfilling their contracts.

Today, future contracts are actively traded on government-debt instruments, stock indexes, energy, precious metals, and foreign currencies, as well as the more traditional commodities such as wheat. The CBT has responded to the emergence of worldwide financial markets by developing relevant contacts linked to international business activities, expanding trading hours to accommodate overseas business hours, opening branch offices to facilitate its marketing and educational efforts, and increasing communication with foreign-based exchanges. The business mission of the CBT is to provide business with a forum and the tools with which to manage the price risk inherent in cash market transactions.

More specifically, the economic functions of the CBT are to:

1. *Provide price discovery.* As trades between buyers and sellers are executed, the fair market value (price) of a given commodity is discovered and the information disseminated throughout the world.
2. *Provide price-risk management.* The most common method is hedging. Hedging is the practice of offsetting the inherent price risk in any cash market position by taking an equal but opposite position in the futures market. Its purpose is to protect against adverse price changes.

IMPLICATIONS

The political and environmental dimensions of the global markets for raw materials complicate and heighten the inherent risks in already

EXHIBIT 2. Fiber Consumption by U.S. Textile Mills

	Total Mill Consumption (Million Pounds)	Percent of Total Mill Consumption		
		Cotton	Wool	Man-made Fibers
1977	11,515.2	27.5	1.0	71.5
1978	11,650.8	26.1	1.0	72.9
1979	11,891.1	25.9	1.0	73.1
1980	11,223.3	27.1	1.1	71.8
1981	10,715.8	25.3	1.3	73.4
1982	9,378.8	26.5	1.3	72.2
1983	11,122.4	25.2	1.3	73.5
1984	10,822.7	25.1	1.3	73.6
1985	11,152.6	25.2	1.0	73.8
1986	12,317.4	26.4	1.2	72.4
1987	12,961.7	29.0	1.1	69.9
1988	12,848.6	27.3	1.0	71.7
1989	13,398.4	30.2	1.0	68.8
1990	13,283.2	30.9	1.0	68.1

U.S. Department of Agriculture, Economic Research Service.

intensely competitive buying and selling situations. The simple economics of supply and demand more often than not are overwhelmed by political and environmental considerations. The interplay of diplomatic relations such as the granting of favored-nation status and nationalization aspirations are two political considerations. Ecological considerations center on safety in the production and distribution of raw materials as well as the diversion of land for other purposes and the protection of various species of animals or birds.

The dynamics of the markets for raw materials stem not only from supply and demand figures, currency exchange rates, inflation rates, and weather forecasts, but also from the political and environmental dimensions plus the impact of science and technology. The latter has already become a major consideration with agricultural raw materials. Vertical integration—already a dominant market factor—will likely take on even greater significance in the future and affect basic structural changes in tomorrow's markets. This can be seen happening with agribusiness and the management of timberlands. The future will also see increasing pressures to lower transaction costs, integrate raw materials into marketing systems, and use scientific research to make changes in raw materials that improve their usage or widen their usage. For example, man-made fibers are a major constituent of textile production in the United States (see Exhibit 2). Of further interest is the increase in relative importance for cotton at the expense of man-made fibers.

SUGGESTIONS FOR FURTHER READING

"The American Revolution in Food," *World* (Fall 1987), pp. 21–29.

Paul Hofheinz, "Let's Do Business," *Fortune* (September 23, 1991), pp. 62–66.

Peter Huber, "Man Versus Nature," *Forbes* (December 13, 1991), p. 160.

"The Not So Peaceful Word of Greenpeace," *Forbes* (November 11, 1991) p. 174.

Gary McWilliams, "Plastics as High as an Elephant's Eye?" *Business Week* (August 19, 1991) pp. 110–111.

Richard M. Hill
CSIDA Professor
Department of Business Administration
University of Illinois at Urbana-Champaign

CHAPTER 55

RESEARCH ON INDUSTRIAL PRODUCTS AND SERVICES

Research that is focused on industrial products and services encompasses a considerable array of investigative techniques and methodology. These are briefly identified to acquaint the reader with their nature and scope. The major share of attention is given to the application of research to decisions regarding the products and services to be offered by industrial firms. This approach is developed in three phases: the organization of market research in industrial firms, commonly used methods of investigation and analysis, and some examples of research studies.

Types of Studies

The most common types of research conducted by industrial firms regarding products and services include (1) market share analysis; (2) brand preference studies; (3) competitive pricing; (4) measurement of market and sales potential; and (5) sales forecasts. Other significant, but less common, categories of product and service research pursued by industrial firms are product satisfaction measurements, cost/profit analysis, and concept development and testing.

A list of the various kinds of research projects pertaining to products and services undertaken by a sample of industrial firms belonging to the American Marketing Association is shown in Exhibit 1.

Performing studies of this scope and variety has required industrial researchers to make increasing use of techniques drawn from the behavioral and physical sciences. The choice of methods is strongly influenced by the characteristics of industrial markets. Many of these markets are relatively small. Buying firms number only the hundreds, and a few large firms account for a large share of total purchases.

Industrial marketers also face a demand that is derived from the demand for products and services. This characteristic, combined with the organizational context of accountability in which customers' buying decisions are reached, often render opinion and judgment as important as data. The relatively small number of buying firms and a tendency of a few large ones to dominate their markets means that a substantial amount of knowledge needed by industrial marketers is in the hands of a relatively few managers in customer firms.

As a result of these market characteristics, industrial market researchers tend to place considerable reliance on secondary data and expert opinion. Efforts to apply rigorous procedures to secondary data have brought such techniques as multiple regression analysis, multiple discriminate analysis, factor analysis, cluster analysis, non-metric

EXHIBIT 1. Representative Types of Industrial Product and Survey Research

Business/corporate level

Industry/market characteristics and trends
Acquisition and diversification
Market share

Pricing

Cost analysis
Profit analysis
Price elasticity
Demand
Comparative pricing

Product

Concept development and testing
Brand name generation and testing
Test market
Packaging design
Competitive product

Distribution

Warehouse location
Channel performance
Channel coverage
Export and international

Promotion

Motivation
Media
Copy
Advertising
Competitive advertising
Public image
Sales force compensation
Sales force quotas
Sales territory structure
Premiums, coupons, deals

Buyer behavior

Brand preference
Brand attitudes
Product satisfaction
Purchase behavior
Purchase intentions
Brand awareness
Segmentation

Source: 1988 Survey of Marketing Research, Chicago: American Marketing Association 45.

multidimensional scaling, and conjoint analysis into wide usage. Efforts to improve the identification of knowledgeable experts have given increased emphasis to such techniques as sociogram analysis and key informant techniques. Cross-impact analysis also appears to be a technique that is being increasingly adopted by industrial market researchers to estimate the impact of environmental developments that knowledgeable experts expect and on which they agree.

ORGANIZATION AND OPERATION OF RESEARCH DEPARTMENTS

Industry practice appears to support the view that marketing research is a staff function of the director, who should report to a top marketing executive. Within the staff concept, there are at least three ways to organize market research in multidivision companies:

1. A single, corporate-level department. Depending on the size and diversity of the company, the activities of centralized research departments may be structured in one of two patterns: (a) research teams, which specialize in the problems of one of the company's operating divisions, or (b) branch departments located in each of the divisions but reporting to the central department.
2. Semi-autonomous research departments in each division. Under this arrangement, department directors report to their respective division managers, but are subject to general guidelines and technical directives established by the corporate level marketing research staff.
3. Completely autonomous divisional marketing research departments responsible only to division headquarters.

The arguments advanced in favor of centralized departments include the opportunity for greater specialization of research personnel and the refinement of research techniques that usually accompanies specialization. Other advantages that may accrue to centralized research departments are greater stature for marketing research within the company, and consequently, a stronger voice in the formulation of corporate strategy and policy.

However, a centralized arrangement itself does not assure that research personnel will be used efficiently. If marketing problems vary significantly among different divisions, or if division managers hesitate to refer problems to the corporate marketing research staff, specialized research personnel are likely to be underutilized. Hesitancy to seek assistance from a corporate level department may result if division managers have been unable to get the help they needed when they needed it in the past, if they resent the necessity of competing with other divisions for research service, or if they prefer not to have corporate members "snooping around" their divisions.

Completely autonomous divisional research departments offer the advantage of close contact with the division's operations and specialized attention to its problems. However, it may be difficult to fully utilize personnel in such departments unless the problems calling for research studies are unique to that division and the workload is not subject to wide fluctuations.

Divisional departments reporting to divisional management but operating within the guidelines and under the technical direction of the corporate marketing research staff frequently offer an advantageous middle ground. The corporate staff can assist in unusually difficult assignments, aid in recruiting and screening personnel, and exercise a degree of persuasive quality control over the work performed by divisional departments. This type of assistance is unavailable to the autonomous decentralized research operations or to research departments often found in small and medium-sized companies. When such departments are assigned studies—the time frames or technical demands of which exceed the capabilities of their staffs—there is often no alternative to the use of consultants. While this is often a more practical alternative than expanding the research staff for peak loads, the frequent use of consultants is not without its risks and pitfalls.

Specialized marketing research firms have enjoyed substantial growth since the early 1950s and many companies make extensive use of their services. The experience of these firms with many types of client problems gives them a breadth of knowledge that is an important ingredient in the services they render. The number of free-lance consultants also has grown substantially in the last few decades as the complexity of data collection and interpretation has demanded novel approaches and more rigorous procedures. It is unfortunate that the proportion of consulting firms and consultants with extensive experience in industrial marketing is still relatively small. Consequently, more than usual care needs to be exercised in selecting a firm to undertake an industrial market research study.

METHODS OF INVESTIGATION AND ANALYSIS

There are several steps that should be taken to ensure the success of a marketing research study. They may be identified as problem definition and statement of objectives; planning the investigation; data collection; data analysis; presentation of results; and careful follow-up.

Problem Definition and Statement of Objectives

It is often claimed that a problem accurately defined is half-solved. While this may be an exaggeration, a statement of ends to be achieved that clearly separates the unknowns from the knowns and relates them to the general purpose of the study can head off much muddled thinking and wasted effort. Although problems frequently arise without warning, and available information is often obscure (sometimes conflicting) as well as difficult to appraise, research effort should begin with the formulation of as simple and concise a statement as possible of what is to be accomplished. It is almost always necessary to conduct an exploratory investigation before such a statement can be formulated.

An exploratory investigation normally begins with a search of the company files or pertinent past studies or reports. Sales records can be a particularly revealing source of information and should often be supplemented with interviews of company executives, division sales managers, salespersons, and trusted customers. When appropriate, interviews should be extended to trade paper editors, well-informed distributors, and market research personnel in related but non-competitive businesses as well as to government officials. While such interviews should possess some structure, the questions should be open-ended so as not to preclude discussion of any aspect of the problem. Moreover, there are few areas of marketing investigation that have not been the subject of published articles in the trade or academic press. A search of this literature is an integral part of exploratory studies.

The results of such initial probing may substantially confirm one's original hypotheses and assumptions as well as permit a much more precise definition of them. Conversely, results may require a complete revision of one's original conception of the problem because it is more complex than it initially appeared to be. It also is recommended that the researcher learn who is asking for the study, who must approve it, who will ultimately use its results, how the results will be employed, what kinds of decisions may be based on the results, when the results may be completed, and what level of resources (funds and staff personnel) can be justified in pursuing the project.

Planning the Investigation

The exploratory phase of study should produce a final statement of objectives and reveal the best way of attacking the problem. With a precise statement of objectives, it is possible to plan in detail the types of information needed, the sources from which it should be collected, how the information is to be collected, a timetable to be followed, and an estimate of costs likely to be incurred.

Type of Information Needed. Secondary data are generally preferred by researchers for reasons of cost and availability. However, the limitations inherent in their use often make primary data the preferred choice.

Using Secondary Data. Secondary data are often the major sources of information for both the exploratory and the principal investigations. In addition to a firm's internal records, the published reports of government agencies, trade associations, commercial directories, and commercial research services represent the chief secondary sources. Much of the data available from secondary sources are organized on the basis of the Standard Industrial Classification (SIC) system.

Despite the reliance that is customarily placed on secondary data, they suffer a number of limitations:

1. *Age of the data.* Due to the time consumed in the collection, assembly, and verification process, secondary data often are several years old when published.
2. *Questionable accuracy.* When first published, much secondary data are identified as "preliminary," which means that they are subject to subsequent revision. Unfortunately, the user of the data has no way of knowing whether the revisions will be upward or downward and by how much. Even the revised data may be biased as the result of different accounting methods and the presence of captive plants. Reporting data on an establishment basis introduces inaccuracies into measures of territorial demand, particularly for production materials. This results from the inclusion of corporate headquarters in territories as establishments as well as manufacturing plants.
3. *Lack of detail.* The smallest geographical subdivision for which data are generally available is the county. Yet, a number of counties are quite large and include a variety of industrial outputs that are simply lumped together. The smallest output classification is the establishment, and establishments are assigned to industries on the basis of their primary product or service. Information regarding the output of secondary products and services by multiproduct firms, of which there are a substantial number, is unavailable.

Depending on the nature of the problem, objectives of the study, the degree of accuracy required, and the opportunity for compensating adjustments, the limitations inherent in the use of secondary data may not seriously compromise the validity of results. If this is not the case, then secondary data must be replaced by or supplemented with primary data.

Using Primary Data. Primary data can be developed from three different sources: field surveys, observation, and experiments. Due to the widespread use of field surveys, their importance as sources of primary data, and limitations of space, the application of observations and experiments will not be considered here.

When information has to be collected from the field, as opposed to published sources or internal company records, it is usually necessary to design a sample. Samples are necessary when time and expense do not permit a complete census of the group being studied. In order to interpret the results of a sample with any degree of reliability, it must be so designed that each unit in the market being studied has an equal chance of being included in the sample, or at least a known probability of being included. Before designing the sample, however, one must define the market and product boundaries. As a general rule, this definition should be based on the principles of product substitutability. A sampling frame, i.e., a list of sampling units, usually can be developed from industrial or commercial directories, many of which are published by state departments of commerce. The concentration of demand typical of industrial markets and the concentration of information among a relatively few individuals that accompanies it argue strongly for nonprobability sampling in general and judgment sampling in particular.

At least four factors have a bearing on sample design for industrial markets:

1. *Variation in the number of buyers.* Some industrial products, such as nuclear turbine-generators and jet aircraft engines, are purchased by relatively few buyers. Others, such as abrasives and electric majors, are purchased by thousands of different firms.
2. *Wide variation in product use.* Substantial differences may exist among manufacturing establishments in the extent and nature of their use of identical products. This is the result of differences in technical experience and manufacturing methods that exist even among firms in the same industry.
3. *Distribution of purchases.* It is very common for a few companies to account for the major share of purchases of a commodity A half-dozen firms may buy as much as 70 to 90% of all the materials and specialized equipment used in an industry.
4. *Use of multiple sources for the same product.* Despite the growing practice of sole sourcing, and the prevalence of supplier-buyer partnerships that encourage it, splitting orders among several different suppliers is widespread among industrial companies. Unless this practice is recognized in the interviewing procedure, sampling is apt to produce biased results.

In view of these characteristics, it is customary to stratify an industrial sample according to size of firms and to include all of the largest firms in the upper stratum. A probability sample should be drawn from the strata containing firms of small and medium size. A complete census of the large companies is essential because of the proportion of total industry purchases they usually account for and the variability in purchasing practices likely to exist among them.

Due to the difficulty of predicting variations in purchasing practices and attitudes, even after the exploratory phase of a study, it is advisable to examine carefully the initial results of an industrial market survey for any indications of faulty sample design. For example, it may be discovered that certain industries thought to have genuine need for a new product have little, if any, interest in it. These can be eliminated from the study. It also may be discovered that other industries whose constituent firms were thought to be homogeneous are, in fact, very diverse in manufacturing techniques and hence product usage. In the latter instance, it would be advisable to increase the number of interviews in such industries to be sure the results are representative. On the other hand, if initial interviewing indicates an unexpected degree of uniformity in a given industry, it might be feasible to reduce the number of interviews planned.

Data Collection

Four methods may be used in collecting data from samples: personal interviews, telephone interviews, mail questionnaires, and focus groups.

Personal Interviews. Since the selection of respondents within each firm chosen for a sample depends on the organizational structure of the firm, personal interviews play a key role in industrial surveys. They are used whenever time and budget permit thorough coverage of a subject. They permit maximum interaction, exploration, and probing, not only for data but for opinions, conjectures, and projections.

The interviewer often has the prerogative of selecting the appropriate respondent(s) within each firm. There are usually some genuine experts who know specifically what characteristics a product must possess to succeed in the marketplace. It is reasonable to assume that many of these experts are willing to contribute to a research effort because results may be beneficial to them personally or to their company. Identifying these experts among company personnel can be difficult. In some instances, the difficulty is finding an expert who is authorized to speak for his or her company. If this is the situation, it may be necessary to contact a company officer, division manager, or staff director who can give a knowledgeable person permission to respond to questions.

Interviewing industrial respondents requires a relatively high level of knowledge, intelligence, and conversational skill on the part of the interviewer. This is due in part to the experience and practical know-how of buyers, engineers, plant managers, or other persons who are likely to be interviewed. It also is due to the difficulty of developing a questionnaire form that can be used uniformly throughout a survey. Variations in production methods and purchasing procedures make it virtually impossible to formulate a standardized set of questions of the type used in consumer surveys. An interview guide that outlines the topics to be discussed is much more common. Its use requires more initiative, skill, and understanding on the part of the interviewer than simply repeating a series of questions in the prescribed order.

Depending on the number of interviews involved, time limitations, and other constraints, interviewing may be done by members of the marketing research department, part-time interviewers hired and supervised by department personnel, research firms that specialize in marketing surveys, and, in some cases, by salespeople or other company employees. Personnel of the marketing research department or of a marketing research organization should be sufficiently well acquainted with the needs and problems of industrial respondents to conduct effective interviews.

The use of sales personnel as interviewers is generally regarded as a poor use of their time and abilities. Salespersons are extroverts by nature. There is a considerable amount of evidence that such personality types are not inclined to analyze situations objectively or in detail, generally dislike paperwork, and usually resist additional demands for it. Moreover, good salespersons are costly, both in terms of salaries and expenses, and should be used to increase company sales and build customer goodwill. Diversion of their time to market survey work can be justified from a cost standpoint only when they have idle time. When demand for a product line is seasonal, there may be an opportunity to use salespeople for interviewing without compromising their primary responsibilities.

Firms that have successfully used salespeople for field interviews customarily limit the information requested to what the salesperson views as important and what can be secured readily in the course of his or her regular calls. Even in these instances, however, it is necessary to be sure the salesperson understands the objectives of the study, how the desired information should be obtained, and how it should be recorded. This is no small task and has been known to challenge the abilities of the best communicators.

Telephone Interviewing. Along with personal interviewing, telephone interviewing has the merit of making possible controlled contact with the sample selected. It is useful when the number of respondents is too great to justify travel and/or the questions are relatively few and understandable with little or no explanation. Moreover, there seems to be little significant resistance on the part of business to telephone interviewing. The telephone is so much a way of life to many executives that this approach seems normal to them. Moreover, it often requires less of the respondent's time than would a personal call.

Unlike personal interviews, telephone interviewing suffers from at least three significant disadvantages.

1. It becomes awkward when the information needed requires interviews with several persons jointly so as to record their reaction to each other's views.
2. It is an impractical medium when the interview involves a long or detailed discussion. An interview involving discussion of product techniques or technical problems, for example, can extend over a considerable period of time.

3. It is inappropriate when the respondent must consult company records to provide the information requested. Even in personal interviews, this may require a great deal of skill on the part of the interviewer, and persuasion is much more difficult in a telephone conversation. However, some researchers have experienced good results by writing to respondents in advance of the telephone interview, asking for their cooperation in assembling the needed information.

Mail Questionnaires. Virtually all mail surveys are plagued with the problem of nonrespondents. Even mail surveys, which yield returns as high as 50 to 75%, cannot be accepted without further evaluation. The nonrespondents may consist almost entirely of companies with little or no interest in the subject under study.

Methods for estimating the characteristics of nonrespondents also rely on sampling. In designing the sample of nonrespondents, a suitable range in size and business characteristics should be included. A good practice is to design two identical samples and separately analyze the results from each. If the variability between the results of the two samples is low, additional sampling would not be needed. If variability is high, additional sampling would be needed to get a reliable indication of the characteristics of nonrespondent companies.

In sampling the nonrespondent group, personal interviews and telephone interviews probably would yield more reliable results than would mail questionnaires because returns from additional mailings would be subject to the same bias as were the original returns. If the survey concerns the conditions under which a product is used or the amount of it that is used, the proportion of users to nonusers among the nonrespondent group is an important piece of information.

Since mail surveys are far less costly than either personal or telephone interviewing, results must be weighed against the cost of obtaining them. A mail questionnaire also has specialized uses in studies designed to determine market opportunity for a commodity or line of products. For example, when the Dewey and Almy Chemical Company expanded the production capacity of its plants for making synthetic rubber sealing compounds, additional markets were needed to use the excess capacity. To identify these markets, a preliminary exploratory questionnaire was prepared. This was sent to 1,500 companies with 100 or more employees, selected from the *New England Directory of Manufacturers.* It was believed that the New England area included a sufficiently broad range of industry that this exploratory questionnaire would reveal most, if not all establishments, that used adhesives in significant volume. It included the following questions: (1) Do you use adhesives? (2) What types? (3) What average monthly consumption? (4) For what end use? (5) What are your major sources of supply?

Questionnaires were returned by 43% of the manufacturers, of whom nearly three-quarters used some type of adhesive. About one-quarter of the companies that used adhesives had need for the types manufactured by the Dewey and Almy Chemical Company. The marketing research director selected 14 industries that appeared to be important enough to warrant more detailed study. These were then analyzed carefully by personal interviews and further mail questionnaires.

Another example of the exploratory use of mail questionnaires was a double postcard sent to several thousand companies throughout the United States, asking whether they used rope and, if so, in what quantities and for what purposes. Data supplied by the returns were used to develop detailed plans for a study of the uses of rope.

Focus Groups. Focus groups rely on group interaction to produce information and insights that would be difficult to obtain without the interaction unique to a group environment. They are useful either as a self-contained means of collecting data or as a supplement to other methods. Since group interviews can provide the trained observer with clues to underlying but fundamentally unobservable motivations, they are particularly helpful in preliminary or exploratory investigations.

At present, the two principle means of collecting qualitative data are one-on-one personal interviews and participant observation in groups. Focus groups not only combine elements of both methods but possess an identity of their own. While they cannot really be substituted for data collection formats well suited to personal interviews or participant observation, they can provide access to types of data not easily obtained through either of these methods.

The chief advantage focus groups offer is the opportunity to observe extensive participant interaction on a topic in a limited period of time. Group interactions are well suited to analysis of attitudes as well as motivations and in this respect are preferable to personal interviews. When properly conducted, they can produce revealing and spontaneous responses from participants.[1] Hearing how participants respond to each other provides insight not only into their familiarity with a topic but also what leads them to raise and respond to challenges. A key prerequisite, however, is one's control over the selection of group participants and the conduct of their sessions.

Focus groups also offer some economies of time compared to personal interviews. Not only can the same number of participants be interviewed in less time in a group format, but the time required for analysis is less because there are fewer transcripts. The other side of this coin, however, is that typically less data is collected than with the same number of personal interviews.

The practical strength of focus groups lies in the comparative ease with which they can be conducted. In many instances, data collection can be done quickly and economically. This is not to say that all focus group research is a bargain—some projects can involve considerable complexity. However, when time and/or money are important considerations, it is often possible to design investigations using focus groups that would be prohibitively expensive using other methods.

In many situations, focus groups are an unsurpassed means of exploring topics and generating hypotheses. They offer a real advantage to one who is relatively new to a topic under investigation, or does not wish to rely on conventional assumptions. Compared with other interviewing techniques, focus groups can produce useful data with little direct input. When all goes well, focusing group discussion on a single topic often brings forth information that is not likely to result from either participants' own casual conversations or an interviewer's preconceived questions.

The downside is that in comparison to individual interviews, one's degree of control over a group discussion is less. If there is a clear set of predefined issues, or a strong need to maintain strict confidentiality across separate interviews, focus groups would not be the preferred technique. This is particularly true if it is more important to discover individual reactions than group reactions because individual reactions are often subject to group influence.

Those who advocate focus groups as a technique emphasize that their essence is lively conversation about a topic among peers or associates and that conversations need to be continued until points of agreement and disagreement emerge. Participants not actively involved in the discussion must be questioned by the moderator sufficiently to draw out their reactions. However, if the reason for a person's reticence is that he or she does not know enough about a topic to discuss it, what responses do come forth are apt to be of dubious value. This of course could be the result of inadequate procedures for participant selection. It could also be an indication that personal interviews would be more effective.

The simplest test of whether focus groups would be appropriate is to ascertain how actively and easily participants representing the target group would discuss the topic under consideration. Whether participants meet this criterion depends on their experience and perspective. Relevant experience is clearly preferable to opinions that have an unknown basis. Evidence suggests that people generally are much more willing to exchange experiences than to challenge or comment on someone else's opinion.

Compared with mail questionnaires, which present difficulties when issues are posed about which respondents have no well-formed opinions, focus groups are a good way to observe the process of opinion formation. Moreover, they can be effectively used with personal interviews and mail questionnaires. A small number of focus groups can be conducted prior to a survey to generate ideas for questions. Several authors have suggested such a procedure to facilitate questionnaire item and scale construction.[2]

Group discussion should provide ample evidence regarding how respondents typically talk about a topic to be investigated and reveal the terminology customarily used in discussing it. This is most helpful, of course, when it is important to ensure that a topic is being investigated from the participants' points of view, or if an outside consultant is being used who is suspected of having ignored some key issues. An equally important contribution of preliminary focus groups to survey research is the assurance that one has as complete an understanding of participants' thinking as reasonably possible.

Focus groups also may be useful beyond the preliminary phase of an investigation. They are an easy way to discover whether participants are likely to interpret questions as they were intended. Pretesting with focus groups not only enables one to unearth potential problems of interpretation, but provides an avenue for exploring how to correct them. Presenting a final pretest version of a questionnaire to a focus group also can be enlightening because live respondents may react quite differently to proposed questions than those who formulated them assumed. Even the IRS now pretests its forms using focus groups.[3]

Focus groups can be useful in selecting persons for personal interviews, particularly if one's objective is to compare different segments of the same population. Additionally, they may be useful after survey data have been assembled and analyzed if results are puzzling. Group interviews are often helpful following personal interviews when it is important to explore and/or clarify issues that surface only during interviews. Moreover, asking participants to explain the reasons for some of their answers and whether they considered factors about which they were not asked may render analysis more revealing.

This review of ways focus groups can be linked to other methods should not detract from their potential as a primary method of data collection. What is being suggested is that it may be useful to conduct focus groups before and after surveys or even alternate back and forth between the two methods. The end result should be higher quality information.

When pursued as a primary research technique, focus groups demand the same attention to detail as any other means of data collection.

Number of Groups. Logically, the first planning issue that needs to be confronted is the desired number of focus groups to be conducted. Since the practical duration of a focus group is usually fixed at one or two hours and only a relatively narrow range of group size is practical, the number of groups that would be appropriate is a basic consideration. Although several factors have a bearing on the appropriate number of groups, the chief one is the research objective. Research that is exploratory in nature or simply intended to reveal some population's perspective, would probably require only a few groups with a relatively high degree of moderator-imposed structure. However, if the research goal is detailed content analysis, with a modest degree of moderator-imposed structure, six to eight (or more) groups might be necessary.

A second factor influencing the appropriate number of groups is the number of different population subgroups required by the research objective. The more homogeneous the population in background, experience, and perspective, the fewer groups one should need. Since focus groups offer few economies of scale, a good rule of thumb is to organize only as many groups as the information needed requires. However, one group is seldom enough. Even though the dynamics of only a single set of participants is being observed, one is on much safer ground conducting two focus groups rather than one. One group may fail to produce useful results.

Number of Participants. Available evidence suggests that the smallest practical size for a focus group is four and the upper limit is about 12. Smaller groups, of course, demand a greater contribution from each participant. This circumstance often produces a high level of involvement in group discussion. If the investigation calls for a clear sense of each participant's reaction to a topic, small groups are apt to be more productive than large ones.

Unfortunately, small focus groups have a high level of sensitivity to the dynamics of individual participants. The functioning of a group can easily be disrupted by friendship pairs, those who regard themselves as experts, and the uncooperative. The logical antidote for this weakness is to conduct a number of small groups to obtain a larger number of participants. This adds to costs, however, particularly in the additional time required for travel as well as for the coding and analysis of additional transcripts.

On the other hand, large groups do not always promise efficiency. A high level of moderator involvement may be required to manage discussions and prevent them from breaking up into small conversations among neighbors around the table. The latter may result in significant loss of data as such conversations are very difficult to tape. Also, it requires an experienced moderator to control a group of 12 or more participants.

Source of Participants. Since researching industrial products and services would very likely not involve a broad population, sample bias in selecting participants should not be a problem. It is evident that what one hears from 40 or so participants cannot be interpreted as representing a full spectrum of experience and opinions. However, in many industrial situations, specific categories of participants are needed and locating them can involve a substantial amount of effort.

When recruiting participants from narrowly-defined groups, recruitment procedures should be specific. Even if only one focus group member fails to share some crucial characteristic, keeping the discussion on track can be very difficult. Telephone interviewing a random sample of persons drawn from the target group, or using a short questionnaire can be useful in identifying those who both fit the category and are interested in participating.

In some instances, it may be necessary to offer substantial cash incentives if the target population is composed of top level executives or others with unusual expertise. Payments of $50 to $100 per person per session are not unusual. If the investigation has an external sponsor that is genuinely respected by the participants, they might be willing to serve in the focus group without a specific incentive.

An accepted fee for focus group participation has been established by precedent in some industries. Since sales of prescription drugs depend so much on the recommendation of physicians, they are frequently targeted for focus groups by pharmaceutical companies and expect to be paid handsomely for their participation.

A perennial question in recruiting participants for focus groups is whether strangers should be preferred over friends. As a general rule, it is better to work with strangers, unless friendship is an important element of the research topic, or the topic is something that would normally be discussed only among friends, such as the quality of executive talent or placing the blame for product failure. Using friends may also present practical problems since it may be difficult to recruit friends who form a single group. Mixing friendship groups can produce complicated group dynamics that can defeat even the skilled moderator.

Moderator Involvement. The level of moderator involvement can be thought of as a continuum. At one end of the spectrum, moderators exert only a minor influence on the content of group discussion. Their comments are purposefully nondirective. At the other extreme, the moderator controls both the topics discussed and the dynamics of the discussion. The latter situation is reinforced by the emphasis on videotaped presentation of results to clients as well as the common practice of having the client observe group discussion from behind a one-way mirror.

As a general rule, low levels of moderator involvement will be preferred for issues of an exploratory nature. If the intent is to learn something new from participants, it is probably best to let them speak for themselves. High levels of moderator involvement are recommended when one has a specific agenda for discussion, such as comparing the responses of a new set of participants with the responses obtained from a previous set of participants, or obtaining answers to a specific set of questions. The highly involved moderator is also advantageous if there is a need to restart a discussion that is lagging, or if "groupthink" threatens to stifle opinions that differ from the majority.

Analysis of Data

Since the number of interviews in a typical industrial marketing study is far less than that in the usual consumer survey, it is essential that the information secured in each interview be completely utilized. A small number of large companies typically represent large shares of the industry market, and their influence must be carefully evaluated in analyzing and interpreting the data. Particular attention should be given to the variability of practices between companies and markets. An industrial market that initially appears to be relatively homogeneous may in fact consist of several segments, each of different importance and with somewhat different requirements.

Presentation of Results

Since market research is undertaken to help solve management problems, the researcher owes management a complete statement of the information that has been discovered and his or her analysis of it. The report may also contain the researcher's opinion as to what the data mean in terms of action and the reason for that opinion. This is not to imply that a marketing research report should be like a lawyer's brief, emphasizing the facts and analysis that support the conclusion the researcher has reached and ignoring or deprecating any finding that does not. Instead, the report should present impartially all the information the study has disclosed, indicating the significance of data that do not support the conclusions as well as those that do.

Computers have made possible the use of a number of statistical techniques in the analysis of survey data. Those that appear to have won the widest acceptance and provide particular insights are multiple regression analysis, discriminate analysis, and factor analysis.

Multiple regression is probably the most commonly used of these techniques. It can be employed to develop sales forecasts and measures of market potential as well as prepare estimates of customer preference and loyalty. Discriminate analysis is particularly useful in identifying customer characteristics that differentiate market segments. It can also be used as a predictive technique for identifying profitable account and successful products.[4] Factor analysis has been useful in determining the reasons underlying buyer attitudes as well as finding bases or classes for grouping industry, market, or company characteristics.[5]

Follow-Up

A systematic follow-up procedure is needed to ascertain how a recommendation is working out in practice and to test the validity of the original analysis. At least three important reasons can be cited in support of a systematic follow-up procedure:

1. to bring to light any significant factors that were either not recognized or not given adequate attention in the original study;

2. to identify any significant changes in the industry or industries under study that may have taken place after the collection of data was begun, and consequently not reflected in the data; and
3. to identify any deficiencies in planning or implementing the study that should be corrected in future studies.

BASIC TYPES OF MARKETING RESEARCH STUDIES

Although industrial marketing research departments may be called on to conduct many types of studies, most probably belong to one of five types: (1) market size measurements, (2) sales analysis, (3) sales forecasts, (4) customer analysis, and (5) analysis of competition.

Market Size Measurements

Measuring the size of domestic industrial markets involves at least three phases: the national market, territorial sub-divisions, and the special case of new products.

The National Market. In the simplest case, market size refers to total sales by all sellers of a particular type of product to industrial users throughout the United States. Imports should be included in these figures, and exports, of course, excluded. Provided the time lag between the occurrence of sales and distribution of data concerning them is not excessive, monthly data are preferred. They are the most helpful in following industry movements, especially during shifts from a sellers' to a buyers' market, or vice versa.

Territorial Subdivisions. There are several ways of developing territorial measurements.

1. Develop some index or series of indexes by which the total market can be broken down into geographical units small enough to use in laying out sales territories.
2. Break down the total market into different industry markets by using the Standard Industrial Classification system. It should then be possible to determine the number and size of companies within each industry class, and hence, each geographical unit from governmental and trade association sources. Many state industrial directories, for example, list manufacturers by SIC classification as well as by city and county. Most directories also indicate the sales size and number of employees for each listed company.[6]
3. Search company records for the names and locations of firms in the using industry or industries. If company records contain this information, they probably also contain enough clues about each customer to enable experienced sales executives to make a reasonable estimate of the needs of each. These estimates can then be summed by counties, standard metropolitan areas, or states to get territorial-size estimates.

A major manufacturer of metal-forming equipment uses capital expenditures as a basis for estimating territorial potentials. Total capital investment by all establishments in the metal fabricating industry is multiplied by the proportion of total U.S. employment in this industry that is accounted for by metal fabricating establishments in the Chicago area. The resulting figure represents total dollar expenditures for plant and equipment by metal fabricating firms in this area.

If total U.S. employment in the metal-fabricating industry were 1,000,000, and employment in this industry in the vicinity of Chicago were 90,000 (9% of the national industry total), a capital investment of $1.5 billion by all metal-fabricating establishments in the United States would indicate an expenditure of almost $135 million by metal-fabricating establishments in the Chicago area. A survey of building permits issued by municipalities in this part of the state indicates which part of the local expenditure represents outlays for new construction. The remainder represents spending for new equipment.

Information on employment and capital investment is taken from the *Annual Survey of Manufacturers* and *County Business Patterns.* Although data in these publications are usually two to three years old, the company's commercial research department extrapolates the data on capital investment and employment, using information contained in sales call reports together with data in the "U.S. Industrial Outlook" and current releases of the Bureau of Economic Analysis.

The underlying assumption, of course, is that the expenditure-per-employee ratio in a territory is the same as the national average for the metal-fabricating industry. An analysis of historical data has enabled the firm's research staff to derive an adjustment factor that takes into account the deviation of expenditure-employee ratios in the territories from the national average. This factor is then applied to the expenditure value determined for each territory in arriving at the territorial market potential.

Market Measurements for New Products. Total sales alone of a new product do not accurately reflect market opportunities for it because of the time that usually must elapse before the new product is accepted and assimilated into the production process. In this situation, the concept of market potential is useful. It represents the total possible purchases of a product—within a given time period—of all industrial buyers who might have use for it and purchase it if effectively brought to their attention.

Several approaches may be used to arrive at an estimate of the potential volume of new product sales. One is to identify the possible end uses of the product or service and the principal market segments in which these uses are likely to be found. If the level of business activity in each segment can be determined, such as end-product output, a usage rate for the new product or service can be calculated for each market segment based on the expected use for the product per unit of activity. The market potential for each segment can then be estimated by multiplying the usage ratio by the level of business activity of the segment and summing these values for each segment.[7]

An alternative method is to identify the type of establishment that should have a bona fide use for the new product and the establishments that conform to this type. The latter can be surveyed to ascertain the extent to which the product would be used. The volume of possible usage for each establishment over the selected time period—e.g., a year—would then be summed.

A third method is based on the assumption that new products and services are substitutes for existing products and services. Determining their market potential, therefore, is a matter of estimating the rate at which they will be substituted for the old by applying the concept of the product life cycle. While this method has been employed with apparent success by some researchers, it is criticized as being of little value by others.[8]

The need for estimating market potential is greatest during the early stages of a product's life cycle when decisions have to be made concerning new plant and equipment or additions to the sales force. Once a product is well into its growth phase, actual sales of it by all sellers would approximate its market potential. Even for well-established products, though, estimates of market potential are helpful in alerting management to the possibility of untapped opportunities resulting from technological developments and environmental changes.

Sales Analysis

One of the most important factors affecting company profits is sales volume. The profit figure can be made more meaningful by classifying sales so that the most profitable products, the most profitable customers, the most profitable territories, and the most productive salespersons can be identified.

The basic unit of information is the sale of a specific product to a specific customer. While the number of physical units sold is the measure least subject to distortion, value of shipments in either current or constant dollars is frequently employed. A typical invoice may contain several lines, each giving the number of units sold, a description of the item sold, the price per unit, and the total value of sales—unit price × quantity. These data, with other items of information on the invoice, may be classified and cross-referenced to give almost any breakdown of sales results desired.

The comparison of sales performance with cost experience reveals whether or not the desired level of profit has been realized for each marketing activity or market segment. Measuring sales performance against costs requires decisions on how costs will be assigned.

While some authorities have a strong preference for direct costing and limit the allocation of indirect costs to long-term considerations, others argue for full costing.[9]

A key issue in profitability measurement is how to determine the return on investment in a market segment. Two studies provide insights and useful approaches to this question. The first is a report on cost and profitability analysis for marketing published by the American Accounting Association. It discusses various approaches to the measurement of return on investment in marketing activity. The other is the analysis of marketing cost ratios pioneered by The Conference Board. It identifies and discusses 12 significant determinants of the ratio of marketing costs to sales. Although both contributions to the literature were published over a decade ago, each can still be helpful in gauging the profit impact of marketing activity.

Sales Forecasting

The difficulty and uncertainty that accompanies attempts to forecast sales in no sense lessens the significance of this task. In fact, concern for accuracy often elevates it to the highest management levels to assure a proper balance of quantitative and qualitative inputs. Even though a high order of accuracy is often well beyond one's grasp, making decisions about the level of tomorrow's business can be done with greater confidence if an orderly and systematic approach is followed.

A widely-accepted procedure among industrial enterprises consists of two major steps or phases: (1) an estimate of what sales are expected to be under the assumption of an unchanged pattern of company activities, and (2) an adjustment of this estimate in light of changes management plans to introduce in its products or marketing effort during the period to which the forecast applies. There are two general approaches to this effort. The first is to estimate the general level of business activity expected during the period to which the forecast pertains in each of the markets the enterprise serves. One can derive from this figure the sales volume expected by using some index or benchmark such as anticipated market share. This value can then be adjusted for known factors likely to affect future sales among different customer groups as well as in different geographical areas.

The second approach is to build up a forecast by estimating sales of each product in each market in which the company is active. It may even be desirable to estimate sales for each account served by the company. The sum of these individual estimates equals the company sales forecast.

The complexity of the various social and economic forces that affect the level of sales have been responsible for increased interest in the use of econometric models and the forecasting services that specialize in their application (e.g., Chase Econometrics, Inc.). An equal amount of interest appears to be in developing statistical modeling of the adaptive process as it applies to the substitution of new products as well as new technology.[10] Increased interest is also apparent in subjective methodology such as the Delphi method and cross-impact techniques.[11]

Due to both the economic and technological instability characteristic of many industrial markets, it is generally advisable to employ two forecasting methods, each of which utilizes a different database. If a variety of inputs is desirable, reconciliation of these forecasts probably should be done within a group or committee of executives to gain the benefit of their insight and business acumen.

Customer Analysis

The practices and attitudes of industrial buyers are another important category of intelligence for the marketing executive. Buying practices and policies may vary not only among different industries, but among different companies within the same industry as well. Buyer attitudes and preferences regarding desirable vendor attributes and responses can vary within the same company. Among the more important questions regarding the buying decision process and the influences that shape it are:

1. Who participates in the purchasing decision?
2. What part in the purchasing procedure does each play?
3. What is the nature of their primary responsibility?
4. What appeals are most likely to influence them?
5. What is the most effective and efficient way to communicate with these persons, to get messages to them as well as information from them?
6. What specifically is needed—JIT delivery, technical assistance, market information?
7. What are the customary discount structures and credit terms?
8. How important are reciprocity and barter?
9. How do participants in the buying process react to abrupt, discontinued, and accelerated change?

Such information must usually be developed through field investigation. Calls on a sample of companies in each industry—with special attention to those buying in large quantities—may be sufficient. If a small fraction of the firms in an industry account for a large portion of total purchases of a given product or material, say 80 to 90%, it may be advisable to include all of them in the sample because their buying practices may differ considerably. Sellers of noncompetitive products purchased by the same industry also are important sources of information.

An interest in modeling buying decisions has resulted in the application to industrial situations of nonmetric multidimensional scaling and its extension, conjoint analysis. Unfortunately, discussion of the validity and usefulness of this technique to organizational purchasing decisions is beyond the scope of this chapter.

Analysis of Competitors

The most basic category of information about competitors is what share of a given market they command. This statistic can often be determined in the process of measuring the size of a market. Of particular importance, however, is how this share has been achieved—whether through unusually well-designed product lines, good distribution service, effective advertising, aggressive selling, excellent technical service, or some other means. Information concerning the goals and objectives of competing companies, their pattern of organization, pricing policies, acquisition and diversification plans, financial structure, and expenditures on R&D all help round out the picture of competitors' strengths and weaknesses.

Unfortunately, assembling reliable information on competitors requires a great deal of ingenuity and patience. Not all companies are willing to supply detailed information to reporting organizations like Moody's or Dun & Bradstreet. This is particularly true of firms in which ownership is closely held. Reports of congressional hearings, testimony before regulatory agencies, and court cases may supply revealing information. Reports filed by company salespeople often contain detailed accounts of competitors' activities and useful insights into their strengths and weaknesses. Trade journals are another common source of information about competitors, as are customers, prospective customers, and distributors.

IMPLICATIONS

The role of marketing research as the intelligence arm of an operating organization gives it a unique responsibility for the analysis of competitors. The researcher needs more than technical competence to conduct this analysis in a way that provides management with the information and insight sound decisions require. Research personnel need a good understanding of what effective marketing involves. The researcher who comprehends the context of a marketing problem will be better able to design an investigation that "fits" its dimensions than one who does not. The investigator who understands marketing will be able to wring from his or her data a meaningful evaluation and make an important contribution to the search for product and marketing innovation on which so much of a firm's competitive vitality depends.

NOTES

1. Fern, E. F. 1982. The use of focus groups for idea generation: The effects of group size, acquaintanceship, and moderator on response quantity and quality. *Journal of Marketing Research.* 19: 1–13.
2. Rossi, P. H., Wright, J. D. and Anderson, A. B. 1983. Eds. *Handbook of Survey Research.* New York: Academic Press; Converse, J. M. and Presser, S. 1986. Survey questions: Handcrafting the standardized questionnaire. *Sage University Paper, Quantitative Research Methods Series.* 63. Beverly Hills, CA: Sage Publications Inc.
3. Morgan, D. L. 1988. *Focus Groups As Qualitative Research.* Newbury Park, CA: Sage Publications Inc. 35.
4. An interesting example of discriminate analysis can be found in Spekman, R. E. 1988. Perceptions of strategic vulnerability among industrial buyers and its effect on information search and supplier evaluation. *Journal of Business Research.* 17: 313–26.
5. An interesting example of factor analysis can be found in Miller, E. M. 1990. The effect of factor price changes on factor intensities: The case of the marginal machine. *American Economist.* 34: 75–8.
6. Further discussion of this issue may be found in Blankenship, A.B. and Breen, G. E. 1992. *State of the Art Marketing Research.* Chicago: American Marketing Association. 37-42; Proctor, R.A. 1991. Marketing information systems, *Management Decision.* 29: 55–60.
7. For example see Lancioni, R. A. and Coyle, M. P. 1992. A comparison of two methods for measuring motor carrier market potential. *Transportation Journal.* 22: 63–74.
8. Short, T. K. 1985. Industrial product life cycle analysis. *Planning Review.* 13: 18–23.
9. Ajinkya, B., Antiase, R. and Bamber, L. S. 1986. Absorption versus direct costing: Income reconciliation and cost-volume-profit analysis. *Issues in Accounting Education.* 86: 268–81; Chen, J. T. 1986. Full and direct costing in profit variance analysis. *Issues in Accounting Education.* 86: 282–92.
10. Urban, G. L. and Katz, G. M. 1983. Pre-test-market models: Validation and managerial implications. *Journal of Marketing Research.* 20: 221–34.
11. Woudenberg, F. 1981. An evaluation of Delphi. *Technological Forecasting and Social Change.* 40: 131–50.

Joseph A. Bellizzi
Professor and Marketing Program Coordinator
Arizona State University
Phoenix, Arizona

CHAPTER 56

BUSINESS-TO-BUSINESS SELLING AND THE ORGANIZATIONAL BUYING PROCESS

Like all selling tasks, business-to-business selling requires a solid understanding of product knowledge, communication skill, persuasiveness, and knowledge of customer needs. However, the most successful salespeople are those who understand the organizational buying process and the way organizational dynamics can affect purchase outcomes. This chapter examines the organizational buying process and describes how sales effort needs to be directed as potential customers progress through the buying process. This approach to selling views the selling process as a *series* of sales calls and communication links between buyers and potential sellers that take place over an extended period (over the course of the entire buying process). Furthermore, it recognizes the organizational needs of buyers and the organizational realities that are associated with group decision making. Understanding this process allows sellers to plan individual sales calls and better predict buyer needs and actions as the process moves from start to finish.

THE BUYING PROCESS

The buying process is described in many business-to-business marketing texts as consisting of several steps or stages.[1] The identification of these stages is the pioneering work of Patrick Robinson, Charles Faris, and Yoram Wind.[2] These stages (modified) are listed in Exhibit 1. As the buying process moves from the first stage to the last stage, selling activities need to be matched accordingly. When sellers understand the process, they are able to make necessary adjustments. Furthermore, understanding how organizations function and the way in which individual and group decisions are made within organizations will help sellers match their efforts with the buying process.

Organizations are often interpersonally complex. Therefore, organizational buying can also be described as interpersonally complex. It is well recognized that organizational buying involves joint or group decision making. The group process further complicates the buying task, hence the selling task too. The remainder of this chapter describes the stages in the buying process and selling suggestions appropriate for the various stages. The suggestions take into account not only the specific task being performed at each stage but also the organizational dynamics—interaction of people and departments, individual motivations and behaviors, organizational policies and practices, etc.—likely to affect purchase at each stage.

EXHIBIT 1. Stages in the Buying Process

1. Recognition of a need
2. Determining the charateristics of needed item
3. Search for/qualification of potential supply sources
4. Acquisition of vendor information/proposals
5. Analysis and evaluation of vendor information
6. Carrying out the order routine
7. Performance evaluation

Stage One: Recognition of a Need

Buying begins when customers recognize that a need exists. As with all the stages, the process can end at any time. It does not always continue on to the next stage. In order for the buying process to continue on to the next stage, buyers must believe that the need they perceive can be at least partially satisfied through purchasing. Since many organizations are partially self sufficient, a decision to make rather than to buy is a plausible course of action. Selling at this stage, therefore, may have to address the pros and cons of a make versus a buy decision. While a make decision provides sellers with control and confidentiality, it is also associated with greater investment, loss of operating flexibility, and the forfeiture of sellers' combined expertise. To sell effectively at this stage, sellers need to be prepared to discuss the pros and cons credibly and objectively with prospective buyers. Unprepared sellers who rely exclusively on discussing specific brand attributes vis a vis competing brands may be providing buyers with inappropriate information—information that may be more wisely inserted later in the process.

In this stage, sellers also need to be active in the recognition of the need itself. That is, sellers should not be content to wait for notification from buyers that a need has been recognized. In many instances, buyers may not be aware of problems that can be solved with a purchase. They may not recognize waste or operating inefficiency or opportunities that may be available through purchase. Sellers should play active roles here for this reason but there may be another good reason for becoming an active seller at this stage. For sellers who wait for buyer notification of needs, such notification is usually communicated to sellers with a considerable time lag between need recognition (stage one) and notification (stage four). The time lag often eliminates sellers from the next two stages and could reduce the chances of obtaining the order for several sellers to zero as a result. Discussion of the next stage explains the seriousness of not being involved from the beginning.

Stage Two: Determining the Characteristics of Needed Item

At this stage, buyers decide what specific item is needed to satisfy their need. They go beyond a basic generic product statement to a more complete description of characteristics the needed item must possess. In doing this, buyers may state product and/or service *performance* standards (i.e., pull-out strength for a construction fastener or *design* requirements. Alternately, to speed up a purchase or to make a purchase easier for some individuals, buyers may specify a needed item by *brand name* or come up with a *sample* of what is needed. This is an important stage for would-be sellers. The product specification will eliminate some sellers while including others. What is important for sellers is to avoid *unnecessary* elimination resulting from specification setting.

Clearly buyers have the responsibility to set specifications in any way they deem appropriate. However, buyers may not be in the best position to make optimum specification statements. Buyer familiarity with a needed item may be limited. Sellers, on the other hand, are usually experts in their product category. It is not uncommon for buyers to either overspecify (specify a product that surpasses need) or under specify (specify a product that falls short of need). Both under- and overspecifying are not in buyers' best interests, yet due to limited knowledge of and experience with the needed item, under and over-specifying frequently occur.

Sellers can provide needed assistance to buyers by helping buyers set appropriate specifications consistent with buyers' needs. The sellers' knowledge and insight may be particularly valuable. The special knowledge and insight of sellers can serve as consultative advice when provided objectively and professionally. Sellers should attempt to influence spec setting with the buyers' interests in mind much like a doctor recommends medical treatment based on what the patient needs, not what the doctor needs. This assistance will help ensure that sellers are not eliminated unnecessarily by setting specifications that rule out a seller's product but are also set inappropriately inconsistent with real buyer need because of buyers' inability to set specs properly on their own.

The key here is to help buyers *and* be objective. Provide information and insight regarding product application, alternate applications, and alternate solutions to buyers' problems. Help buyers reconcile differences among their personnel and their departments. Become a problem solver for the buyers while making sure you are not eliminated as a potential vendor when your product can actually benefit buyers.

Being active on the first two stages requires regular contact with potential customers. The beginning of the buying process needs to be monitored or even stimulated by providing timely information to buyers that causes them to question their current practice (and associated purchases). This requires regular contact with user departments in buying firms rather than purchasing departments. Purchasing departments often become part of the process after need recognition and in some cases after the specifications have been set. Monitoring user departments is critical. For inventoried items purchased regularly, the buyer departments that monitor inventory levels may be the first to spot an upcoming need. Regular contact with inventory monitoring personnel is required here, but user contact is also critical since users play a key role in judgments concerning loyalty (placing repeat orders for items previously purchased) or vendor switching precipitated by user recognition that a better solution exists. Seller contact with user departments can trigger this recognition.

Unfortunately for sellers, users are not the only critical group to monitor. Users tend to be narrow in their viewpoint concerning products and/or services purchased and are most concerned with how products and services perform, how they are used, and how they affect their specific range of activity. Users are not particularly concerned with prices paid for items or related costs of ownership unless these charges are applied to user department budgets or users are directly affected by these costs. Departments responsible for budget administration also need to be monitored through regular seller contact. In addition, other departments may also be affected by a particular purchased item. If the product to be purchased becomes part of the buyer's finished product, the buyer's marketing department may be involved since marketing has the task of selling the finished product and the task of merging market needs with product strategy. In such cases, these other departments are likely to play a role in both need recognition and specification setting. Seller contact here is important also.

As need recognition moves into specification setting, satisfaction with previous purchases from among affected departments could result in stating the specification in terms of a brand name. Such a spec rules in one seller and rules out all others. Obviously, this is attractive to only one seller, the in-supplier. The others—the out-suppliers—will work to replace the brand name spec with a design spec or performance spec that would not automatically rule them out. Both in-suppliers and out-suppliers can influence the specification setting by being in contact with users and other affected departments during the first two stages. In addition, should the user department need technical assistance in writing a specification in technical performance and/or design terms, engineering departments will also be involved. Sellers will need to maintain contact at this level also. The critical message is that selling must begin early in the buying process and seller-buyer contact must go beyond distant contact with only one buyer department or individual.

Stage Three: Search for/Qualification of Potential Supply Sources

When specifications are set, buyers begin a search for potential sources of supply. Purchasing departments usually conduct this search, although other affected departments as discussed above will also get involved. Potential vendors are qualified on the basis of their ability to provide products and/or services that fit the specifications that have been previously set. Potential vendors are selected based on prior information buyers have accumulated about sellers including product literature, catalogs, prior purchase experiences, and sales calls. Trade press information and publications like *Thomas's Register,* a business-to-business "Yellow Pages," are also useful sources of vendor information. Only sellers deemed able or likely to fulfill buyer needs as stated in the specifications are designated as qualified.

At this stage, sellers need to make sure buyers have sufficient information to make appropriate vendor qualification decisions. Contact with user departments and purchasing departments will aid sellers in their attempt to be designated as qualified. Without proper contact, buyers will make decisions on whatever information is available or readily attainable. Unfortunately for sellers, this information may not be sufficient, accurate, or up-to-date. Successful sellers are not willing to leave the qualification decision to chance based on limited information concerning their ability to match buyer specs; they aggressively supply such information.

Stage Four: Acquisition of Vendor Information/Proposals

Sellers who have been designated as probably or most likely qualified to fulfill buyer requirements are now asked to provide evidence to demonstrate such ability. Sellers will be asked to be specific regarding how they would meet buyer needs with regard to all purchase conditions and specifications that may include not only aspects of product/service design or performance, but also delivery dates, quantities, price, credit terms, and other transaction-related matters. The entire package of transaction-related matters could be quite extensive. Buyer interest in these matters is spread throughout a buyer's organization, therefore, sellers need multiple contact points with buyers. Users, marketing, engineering, and purchasing may be interested in performance and design matters. Accounting/finance/control and purchasing may be concerned with price and credit terms; users, purchasing, and manufacturing may be most preoccupied with delivery dates. Sellers should communicate appropriate information to appropriate departments and personnel.

Stage Five: Analysis and Evaluation of Vendor Information

At this stage of the process, buyers review acquired information related to all aspects of vendor performance. The information is analyzed, studied, and judged. Since the information covers many aspects of the transaction from product performance data to financial considerations, the task is often very difficult. Since many different departments and individuals are often involved, the task becomes more difficult as different opinions and judgments need to be addressed and reconciled.

At this stage, selling should stress a product's attributes with regard to customers' stated specifications. Demonstrations, performance test data, spec sheets, product samples, and other data need to be presented to clearly show a product's conformance with customer specifications.

It should be noted that the buying process can move backward from any particular stage to any other stage. For example, stage three—vendor qualification—could result in a movement back to step two—specification setting—rather than a movement forward to step four. This step backward may be the result of a failure to qualify any vendor because product or service specs may have been stated beyond the capabilities of *all* sellers, or because buyers realize that the specifications set earlier were not appropriate. A return to specification setting can revise the specs so that they are more realistic with product/service availability or buyers' real needs. However, while backward moves can occur throughout the process, they appear more frequently in stage five. It is very common for buyers to temporarily move away from analysis and evaluation of information and go back to acquisition of information, stage four. In addition, buyers may also conclude from analysis and evaluation that they need to revisit the vendor qualification stage (stage three), or the specification stage (stage two), or even the need recognition stage (stage one) if they wish to reassess the make/buy decision.

Going back is not always easy and is not done without expense on the part of buyers. It delays purchase, takes up more executive time, and delays a number of chain-related activities in the buyer's organization that could range from manufacturing and distribution schedules to marketing and personnel decisions, depending on the item being purchased. Going back may not be in the best interest of all sellers. If it strengthens a particular seller's position, it is welcomed; if it weakens a seller's position, it is resisted. For example, a seller whose product fits specs very well will encourage buyers to make a decision and move forward by selecting a supplier. However, sellers whose products do not conform completely with buyer specs may advocate a return to spec setting, hoping for a spec rewrite. Given the cost of moving backward, sellers may be at a disadvantage to advocate a move backward in the process. Therefore, playing an active role during spec setting will benefit sellers as the process continues.

Sellers need to monitor this stage to make sure that sliding back to any previous stage does not undermine their position. They are in a better position to do this if they can anticipate buyers' needs to revisit prior decision stages and be ready to place additional (position strengthening) information in the hands of buyer personnel in a timely fashion. As stated above, the key is to monitor the entire process carefully and become an active participant with buyer personnel in whatever departments they are found. Do not assume that buyers will naturally gravitate in your direction. By monitoring their buying steps, sellers can initiate informative, consultative, and timely information exchanges that help ease buyers in your direction. While this stage may move backward to other stages, it can only move forward if a decision is made to award a contract or place an order with at least one of the potential suppliers. For many purchases, this outcome requires a *group* decision.

Organizational Dynamics Affecting Stage Five. Decision making in organizations can be quite difficult and complex. In moving a decision to any particular conclusion, buying participants are attempting to satisfy a variety of organizational, professional, and at times, purely personal objectives. Agreeing on a strategy to achieve organizational objectives may become particularly difficult since individuals consider objectives from a variety of organizational positions that may not always be consistent. Often there will be disagreement within organizations regarding the likelihood of meeting objectives through any particular action (i.e., a purchase). In addition, individuals may be more concerned with achieving their own departmental objectives despite the fact that they may not be totally consistent with the objectives of other departments because they may view their departmental objectives as more important to the organization than the objectives of other departments. This usually results in differences among buying personnel regarding the importance of various product or service features and the way in which alternate suppliers are evaluated.

While organizational objectives—albeit confusing and potentially inharmonious—should predominate decision making, other factors also play a role in the final decision. Individuals who influence buying decisions may be motivated by a desire to gain *professional* stature or competence. A particular purchase decision can either enhance or diminish professional objectives. Purely *personal* matters play a role also as individuals may support or oppose a potential vendor on the basis of a purchase's impact on them personally. For example, an executive nearing retirement may resist the purchase of new computers hoping to delay purchase until retirement to avoid an uncomfortable last year with the company learning new computer routines. And while organizational objectives should, they do not always predominate, however, the *appearance* that they do will be prevalent. Individual buyers will send mixed signals, they will say one thing and do another, they may provide limited information to sellers, and could rely on political activity to induce a preferred outcome. It is within this setting that sellers must navigate as they interact with buyers and present their selling messages.

Since individuals will at least appear to give priority to organizational goals, especially their own departmental objectives, sellers must constantly sell to these goals. However, sellers should be prepared to address other professional or personal objectives of individual buyers. More importantly, if buyers are motivated by professional and personal objectives but prefer to give the appearance of achieving higher organizational goals, sellers may need to address professional and personal objectives obliquely. Not only will sellers have to support the merits of their products as a means of achieving a number of organizational objectives, they may also have to avoid having other organizational, professional, or purely personal objectives sway an order to a competitor.

As employees and other representatives of the buying firm work to complete this stage of the process and make a supplier selection decision, sellers should be aware of the manner in which buyers will proceed and the forces within an organization that can affect the outcome. This includes knowledge of the formal *and* the informal processes that are likely to emerge as an organization tries to make one decision from many voices.

Formal Process. The formal process likely to be utilized is not exceedingly difficult to predict—formal levels in an organization are usually well-documented and recognized. Sellers with any experience with a buyer should be able to identify the formal leaders. Power to shape an outcome, like a purchase decision, is related to formal organizational level; the higher the level, the greater the formal power. However, it does not mean that this power will always be used—formal leaders may delegate or otherwise rely on the wisdom of lower-level individuals. Should consensus be difficult to achieve or strong differences of opinion exist among those involved in making a supplier selection decision, those with formal authority could become pivotal. While sellers need to communicate with many individuals and departments during the buying process, those in higher level positions who perhaps play key roles along the way should be critical targets for selling messages.

Informal Process. Decision making in organizations does not always follow formal authority processes. In many cases, group decision makers may be positioned on the same organizational level. As a result, informal devices will play an important role. Despite an equality of formal power, real power to affect a decision outcome will usually vary in an organization. Individuals and departments (business functions) that are highly valued within an organization will often possess more control in decision making. Furthermore, individuals and departments that are most affected by a decision outcome may attempt to influence outcomes regardless of the amount of power they possess and in many cases can be expected to aggressively pursue particular decision outcomes. In many cases, others will often defer judgment to those who are affected most—users.[3] Sellers are advised to study the informal power structure that exists within buying organizations and to adjust their sales tactics to fit the structure.

As sellers make sales presentations to various individuals, they should recognize which individuals feel positive about their sales proposal. These positively-inclined individuals should be considered *inside crusaders* who can help bring selling messages to others in the organization. Relationships with those who are leaning positively should be nurtured carefully. Sellers may not have a full range of motion within selling organizations and the presence of inside crusaders can gain access to others and provide valuable information to sellers regarding the progress of the buying process. Inside crusaders become especially valued if they possess high levels of formal and informal power to affect buying decision outcomes.

Formal levels of power are easy to spot, but informal levels are more difficult to observe, however, a few clues exist. As mentioned above, group decision makers (organizational buyers) are often positioned on the same organizational level. However, some departments may be more closely linked to organizational success. Usually these departments and their key personnel are afforded a greater deal of organizational power and influence in decision making. Sellers should look carefully for individuals who seem to be listened to at meetings despite speaking infrequently, or seem to have a good understanding of how their organization operates. These are usually signs of organizational influence and power. In some instances, those with above-average levels of decision-making influence are those in an organization who are permitted to exercise exceptions to company policy. With experience, sellers will be able to identify those in the buying organization who are likely to dominate decision making. Selling messages should be expressly directed toward these individuals.

Decision Process. As the various buying participants interact in an attempt to reach a decision, sellers need to be prepared to provide more information—if needed by buyers—and to maintain communication links with key contact personnel, i.e., inside crusaders, to monitor buying progress. The members of the purchase decision group who have the most to gain or lose from a purchase can be expected to act more aggressively to influence the outcome. For any given seller, an ideal situation would include developing organizationally powerful inside crusaders who have a lot to gain through purchase of the seller's product. Selling effort should strive to create such situations since the probability of obtaining the order is high under these circumstances. On the other hand, sellers may fail to develop any inside crusaders (or only a few), or they may develop inside crusaders who possess only modest levels of organizational influence. In the event that no further insider crusader development is possible, sellers will have to rely on tactics that are designed to strengthen the modest levels of influence possessed by their inside crusaders. These tactics are discussed below and can also be used to further strengthen the influence of any inside crusader.

Information in organizations is powerful.[4] It is essential that inside crusaders possess sufficient information to present purchase-related facts clearly and convincingly. Ideally, sellers would like to present this information personally throughout the buying organization; however, they may not always be permitted to do so. Therefore, they must arm their inside crusaders sufficiently for this task. They should also provide inside crusaders with information necessary to refute competitive claims they receive from competitors' inside crusaders. This point may be particularly important since competitive claims received in this way may be potentially distorted, or at least filtered. This information can strengthen an inside crusader's position relative to other purchase decision makers.

As the purchase decision process continues, sellers should monitor the decision-making protocol that could undermine their inside crusader, especially a less powerful one. Given equal levels of formal power, which is common in this type of decision making, informal struggles may arise. If additional information fails to break a deadlock among the purchase decision makers, organizational politics could be introduced into the process. Active sellers who monitor the purchasing process can help inside crusaders gain power and avoid loss of power as a result of political activity within buying organizations in a number of appropriate and ethical means. First, sellers can help inside crusaders *build coalitions,* which are usually more powerful than individuals. Since active sellers will present their selling messages throughout the buying organization, they may be in a good position to help inside crusaders identify each other and to recognize their common preference for a purchase decision.

Second, sellers need to work around those in buying organizations who attempt to *control the flow of information.* As stated above, information is powerful; in an attempt to limit power, information may be withheld. The organizational literature usually refers to those who control the flow of information as gatekeepers. Sellers should work within existing organizational protocol—appointment making, appointment keeping, security sign-in, etc.—but they need to verify the receipt of information they expect to travel from gatekeepers to other members of the purchase group. It is usually best to present information to all relevant individuals personally, but when not able or permitted to do so, sellers will have to rely on purchaser's personnel to deliver information. Delivery is not automatic—it could be accidentally delayed or derailed as well as purposefully lost, held up, or modified. Seller verification of the quantity and quality of information delivery through gatekeepers should be carried out.

Third, astute sellers also help inside crusaders detect political *gamesmanship* and diminish possible adverse effects. In group decision making, individuals may attempt to influence a decision by use of game playing—staying within organizational rules but using them to attain a desired outcome. There are a number of game tactics that can be used to reduce the influence of a seller's inside crusader, and sellers can help reduce their impact. In many cases, sellers may see a tactic being used before it is identified by their inside crusader. Conscientious sellers do not assume their inside crusader can spot these games, although pointing them out must be done carefully and professionally to avoid embarrassment and humiliation for themselves as well as their inside crusader. For example, an important meeting could be arranged by the purchase influence team during a period when your inside crusader is scheduled to be out of town. Notification of the meeting to your inside crusader may be delayed intentionally, thereby reducing the probability that changes in his or her travel plans can be made or that a qualified replacement can be sent to this important meeting. In a political game designed to reduce the decision-making power of your inside crusader, a seller may learn of the scheduled meeting before the inside crusader. A quick phone call to an inside crusader offering to provide additional information prior to the important meeting could make a big difference.

Selling in stage five requires monitoring the vendor evaluation process; making sales presentations at various levels and to various departments; and demands that sellers recognize the differences among buying participants and how their specific and diverse views of the organization and their personal objectives affect their evaluations of potential suppliers. It also requires insights regarding group decision making and the formal and informal mechanisms that are used to produce a supplier decision from many, often disparate, voices.

Stage Six: Carrying Out the Order Routine

When a decision has been made to award a contract or place an order with a particular supplier, a variety of administrative procedures need to be accomplished. The successful seller should help customers carry out these tasks smoothly. These procedures include such matters as preparing the order paperwork, monitoring shipment, order verification, order receipt, order inspection, order adjustment, and customer payment. Customers will evaluate vendor performance on these matters. Therefore, it is in the seller's best interest to provide appropriate levels of assistance to permit these tasks to be carried out satisfactorily from the customer's point of view.

Although a number of vendor personnel will be involved with these tasks, the salesperson continues to be the contact person with the customer. Salespeople should remain in the information loop so that customers can be informed in an accurate and timely fashion regarding their status inquiries. Computerized sales forces will enhance sellers' ability. Salespeople and customers will appreciate order routine support.

Sellers should attend to these order routine tasks and provide adequate training, incentive, and motivation to employees who carry out this process. Furthermore, outside contractors that assist sellers with these tasks (i.e. common carriers) should be selected and monitored accordingly—customer satisfaction and future business will depend on the way these functions are performed. Outside contractors should be considered extensions of a seller's business for which the seller *is* responsible.

Stage Seven: Performance Evaluation

During the final stage of the buying process, customers evaluate the performance of their suppliers. On the surface, this may seem like a task that is performed exclusively by the customer; however, sellers can play an important role in assisting customers. This assistance can result in a greater chance of receiving a positive supplier evaluation and continuing business. Sellers should recognize that customers may not be familiar with product usage, operation, and maintenance during the early period of ownership. As a result, early experience with the product is often associated with utilization delays, underutilization (infrequency of use *and* use below performance peak), and misuse.

Care and attention to customer training can prevent unnecessary negative evaluations. Installation, set up, and user training are also important as are maintenance contracts and user-friendly service and operating manuals. Suppliers need to anticipate customer problems and expect customers to encounter some operating difficulties during the early ownership period. Seller assistance on this stage must be timely. Adequate resources—personnel—need to be made available during this time and sellers can benefit by developing capabilities for prompt response to customer problems. An 800 customer phone line staffed with technical and/or application knowledgeable personnel makes sense. Many problems may be solved over the phone, however, field assistance may be necessary for some difficulties. The goal should be to ensure customer satisfaction by playing an active role during the customer's early use experience with the product.

CONCLUSION

The selling process recommended in this chapter is a continuous selling process that encourages sellers to be active in each buying stage. Such a selling process requires ongoing and regular contact with potential customers so that appropriate selling messages can be directed to appropriate individuals at the right time. The process also requires selling effort beyond the sale to improve the likelihood of customer satisfaction—and future business. Sellers can help themselves by being active throughout the buying process, but customers also benefit. In fact, sellers should not view this recommended aggressiveness as purely self-serving. To maximize customer benefit, sellers need to be driven by customer interest. If they do, customers will welcome their efforts throughout the buying process and better long-run relationships between buyers and sellers will emerge.

NOTES

1. Hutt, Michael D. and Speh, Thomas W. *Business Marketing Management.* Fort Worth: The Dryden Press, 1992.

2. Robinson, Patrick J.; Faris, Charles W.; and Wind, Yoram. *Industrial Buying and Creative Marketing.* Boston: Allyn & Bacon, 1967.

3. Patchen, Martin. "The Locus and Basis of Influence on Organizational Decisions." *Organizational Behavior and Human Performance* 11 (1974): 195–221.

4. Griffin, Ricky W. and Moorhead, Gregory. *Organizational Behavior.* Boston: Houghton Mifflin, 1986.

PART EIGHT

PROMOTING PRODUCTS AND SERVICES

PART EIGHT

INTRODUCTION

The main challenges in promotion can be boiled down to these three points: what to say, how to say it, and where to say it. Many of today's successful advertising messages—"what to say"—are those that tell the target audience what it wants to hear. Once the marketer can determine what motivates individuals in a given market, the next step is easy: Give the people what they want. The trend today is to "sell" the customer, rather than the product, by getting more of the customer profile into the marketing message. Sell a line of convertibles to freedom-loving young affluents with commercials that let them feel the wind in their hair. Convince the new generation of businesspeople that they need a particular computer system because they are creative, freewheeling thinkers. Today, more than ever before, consumers are conscious of their feelings—the emotional pull of advertising. If they are predisposed to buy a certain product or service, the promotion strategy that pushes the right emotional buttons is likely to get the sale.

Moving on to the subject of "how to say it," we must take into account two factors that have greatly influenced the consumer of the 1990s: time and trust. It is true for both individual and business consumers that their time or, more accurately, their lack of time, will dictate how they buy. Shoppers in dual-income families, single parents, overloaded managers in "downsized" companies, and just about everyone else in today's society doesn't have "enough" time. This means less time for comparison shopping, meeting with sales representatives, or researching big-ticket items. Instead of these steps in the old buying process, customers are relying more and more on promotion, such as television and radio advertising, print ads, direct mail—and, in the case of busy businesses, sales brochures, mailings, and other business communications—to stay informed.

There are ways to position a company, a product, or a service in this fast-track, snap-decision market, and one of these ways is trust. If one can successfully convey a company's or brand's *trustworthiness*, consumers are more likely to choose that product over the competition's. Whether that trust is built by using a celebrity spokesperson, a well-known company name or brand name, or an image that exudes reliability and solidity, trust can make all the difference.

Where to say it? A good marketing promotion will take into account both time and trust. By integrating the available marketing tools in such a way that the strengths of each element are exploited, a marketer can reach different marketing niches, hitting each with the appropriate message. Public relations can play a big part; this powerful marketing element can stretch dollars farther than advertising and, if used effectively, get equally impressive results.

Chapter 57 demonstrates how today's marketer will blend all types of marketing communication vehicles to touch a target audience. There are more and more "revolutionary" media today, and all can be very effective for marketing—for example, various channels of direct marketing, including home shopping via television, the growth of cable television, and telemarketing.

In Part Eight, too, the major aspects of marketing promotion are examined. There have been major shifts in the components and the approaches of promotions in recent years, and this part of the *Handbook* reflects that change with seven entirely new contributions. We begin by tracing changes in advertising communications—and consumers—from the simpler times of the 1950s and 1960s until today. The splintering of markets, the separate booms in direct marketing and event marketing, and the explosion in the number of television channels—all of these changed the "big picture" of marketing drastically over the past 30 years. They, in fact, shape how we do business today.

The marketing of a business has also changed; successful business communications now call for an "attack on many fronts" in order to reach the many people who influence buying decisions—from industry movers and shakers to employees to the community in which the business resides.

Part Eight also covers a variety of other topics on promotion, including creating, building, and maintaining an image for a company or a brand; what solid sales promotion objectives can and cannot do; and how to plan public relations activities.

Ronald B. Kaatz
Associate Professor of Integrated
Marketing Communications
Medill School of Journalism
Northwestern University
Evanston, Illinois

CHAPTER 57

CUSTOMER CONTACTS IN AN INTEGRATED MARKETING COMMUNICATIONS ENVIRONMENT

We lived in a much simpler communications environment in 1960 when Ted Turner was only 22 and Chris Whittle hadn't yet reached his teens. Long before CNN, home video, place-based media, interactivity, and micromarketing, Gunsmoke was the nation's number one TV show—seen in 40 percent of our homes each week. Media planning was easy and an advertiser only had to buy six issues of *Life, Look,* and the *Saturday Evening Post* to reach 77 million people.

In a 1961 study of the issues involved in evaluating media effectiveness, the Advertising Research Foundation recognized just five basic media types—newspapers, magazines, radio, television, and outdoor (ARF Audience Concepts Committee, "Toward Better Media Comparisons").

The task of the marketer was far simpler in 1961 than it is now. You wrote an ad and you bought time and space in which to communicate your message.

Mass Media Domination

During the 1960s, mass media marketing flourished in the United States—bigger was always better. The most popular magazines emphasized broad circulation and general editorial content that appealed equally to men and women across the country. Their battles for readers and circulation were so intense that subscriptions sold for as low as 8 cents a copy—magazines would lose money on circulation that they hoped to make up in advertising revenue.

The emphasis on reaching a homogeneous mass audience was even evident in magazines aimed at women. *Good Housekeeping, McCalls,* and *Ladies' Home Journal* were still focusing on the nonworking wife and mother with helpful information on cooking, home decorating, child care, entertaining, gardening, and home management. Little thought was given to single or working women.

Throughout history, the dominance of one medium always gave way to the arrival of another. At each stage, the focus was on reaching larger and larger audiences with more and more information about more and more different products, services, and ideas. So it was with the arrival of newspapers, followed by the growth of magazines in the late 1800s, radio in the 1920s, and the most mass of mass media—television—in the post-World War II era.

In the 1960s, magazines and television fought fiercely for advertising dollars. The larger the audience, the more that could be charged for time and space. Bigger was *always* better!

The emphasis on mass media was evident in the early 1960s, when the average American home received less than six television stations and most viewing was confined to ABC, CBS, and NBC. In fact, during the evening hours, families spent 95% of their viewing time with the (generally) all family, all white, all middle class network schedules.

CHANGES IN THE MARKETPLACE

As we moved beyond the 1960s, changes were taking place with the consumer, within the marketplace, and in the media environment. These changes created vast problems and opportunities for every company that was concerned with how best to reach its customers in an increasingly complex and cluttered communications environment. Consumers were no longer part of the typical American "nuclear" family where father went to work, mother kept house, and there were 2.2 children. Society saw the development of a host of new living structures involving all combinations of singles, marrieds, formerly marrieds, about-to-be marrieds, about-not-to-be marrieds, etc. Women went to work in record numbers either because they had to financially, because they wanted to, or because they worried what their friends might think of them if they simply stayed home and kept house. Between 1959 and 1991, the percentage of women with jobs grew from 37 to 57%. The once sacred evening meal where the entire family gathered together to discuss the day's events gave way to "grazing." Like a cow in a pasture, you ate a little bit here and a little bit there.

While marketers for years had been fixated on youth, they suddenly began to notice that the population was aging. The once singularly popular 18 to 49-year-old market now gave way to a new 25 to 54-year-old market. And looking beyond the 1980s, many predicted the key demographic group for the 1990s would be the 35 to 60-year-olds. Special interest groups proliferated, and fitness and well being came into vogue.

As the consumer changed, advertisers actively sought more selective niches where they could profitably target their sales efforts. These niches represented segmentation not only by demographics, but by psychographics, lifestyle, and media behavior patterns.

1. We had teenagers who were influenced by the motion pictures of Hollywood and the music of MTV.
2. There was the growing Hispanic market with wide differences between the Puerto Rican, Cuban, South and Central-American, and Mexican-American segments.

3. The impact of the African-American consumer was found at the cash register, the ballot box, and in movies.
4. And to the young urban professionals, success was measured in terms of their jobs, money, cars, condos, vacations, and the labels in their clothes. Although yuppies were less than 7% of the population, their share of media coverage was far greater!

As consumers changed, so did the marketplace in which they would be met and (hopefully) sold a product, a service, or an idea.

In the United States, there was a proliferation of new products. *New Product News* reported that prior to 1980, 75 new brands or categories of products were introduced each month. After 1980, the number had jumped to 170. If you considered all sizes, shapes, colors, flavors, etc., nearly 500 new products were introduced each month in 1992. Unfortunately, 83% of the new products brought to market would fail to reach their business objectives (1992 Group EFO Limited Innovation Survey).

To compete for a share of the consumer's pocketbook, companies in the late 1970s began to spend an increasingly large portion of their marketing budgets on consumer and trade sales promotions. Coupons, contests, premiums, rebates, sampling, trade deals, and slotting allowances were but a few of the techniques that gained favor as more and more dollars shifted from image and brand-building advertising to action-oriented, short-term, promotional efforts.

In 1992 alone, more than 300 billion coupons were distributed throughout the United States. This represented an average of 3,200 coupons per household—or more than 60 every week of the year! Mergers and takeovers encouraged this promotional focus as companies sought to maximize their short-term sales and profits, hoping that long-term growth would take care of itself. And, through in-store scanners, stores received far faster and more accurate reports on their customers' shopping behavior.

The fastest growing avenue of marketing communications has been direct marketing. Specialized catalogs, shopping at home, interactive television, telemarketing, and databases focused on the best prospects for every conceivable product and service. Each medium benefited in one way or another from direct marketing as companies sought new venues in which to target their prime customers, communicate with them more effectively, and build with them a long-term relationship.

This desire to create an even tighter bond between a company and its customers also created a boom in event marketing. In 1992, more than 4,000 firms spent over $3 billion to sponsor everything from the Boston Marathon to the Decatur, Illinois' Terminex Great American Cockroach and Rat Race.

EXPANDING MEDIA OPTIONS AS MEDIA HISTORY IS REVERSED

These changes with the consumer and within the marketing climate all took place in an environment of expanding media options that would shape communications of the 1980s and 1990s as well as the ways in which media would be looked at and evaluated.

A host of new and different media all were pulling on the consumer and advertiser from many different directions. For the first time, the entire direction of media history seemed to be reversed. Instead of large audiences replaced by larger ones, they were being replaced by smaller ones, more and more sharply defined by each individual's interests and attitudes. For radio, this began in the 1950s when television replaced it as the medium of choice for family home entertainment. As radio audiences declined, stations focused on reaching highly-targeted listening segments with very selective programming formats. Thus, in Chicago, more than 50 different stations now appeal to every musical, sports, ethnic, and information taste. In 1965, FM radio was in only 25% of all U.S. homes. Today, nearly everyone can listen to FM on one of more than five sets in their homes and cars.

Since the mid-1960s, the number of major consumer magazines jumped from 500 to more than 1,800. There is not a magazine today that does not cover either in whole or in part a subject that someone wants to read about. For example, *Standard Rate and Data* lists 46 magazines dealing with boating and yachting, 49 computer magazines, 34 health magazines, and 142 sports magazines.

While newspaper readership—especially among young people—declined over this period, their size and weight increased enormously. As Andy Rooney said on *60 Minutes,* "If they have to deliver the Sunday *New York Times* to my home in two parts over two days, how can they expect me to read it all in one day!" Perhaps, however, this is the wrong way to look at the newspaper of the 1990s. Readers may no longer be interested in all of the newspaper. Rather than viewing it as a single, compact "department store," they may see it as an attractive "shopping mall" of many different boutiques. They can spend as much time as they want with some shops (sections) and totally skip those in which they have no interest. Instead of regarding the newspaper as a single source vehicle, readers and advertisers would view each individual section—sports, business, arts and entertainment, women, automotive, home and garden, and general news—as a separate information source tailored to their individual wants and needs.

An example of what might be a new role of newspapers was seen in a California study of young adults in their twenties. While they said that newspapers were "dull and boring" and that they would not pay 25 cents for them, they would pay 25 cents just for the weekend entertainment guide—if it were sold separately.

As great as were the changes taking place with radio, magazines, and newspapers, what was taking place with television was even more enormous. The American love affair with the television set was well documented in a late 1980s survey of 1,550 adult men and women conducted by D'Arcy, Masius, Benton and Bowles advertising agency. When asked "What gives you a great deal of pleasure and satisfaction?" the winner was watching television—checked by 68% of the respondents. It beat out being with friends, helping others, vacations, hobbies, reading, marriage, sex, food, money, sports, and religion. *TV Guide* took this a step further in a 1992 nationwide survey of 1,007 adults. One in four would refuse to "give up watching absolutely all types of television" for the rest of their lives—even for $1 million! This impact of television on the nation has been a cause of concern for many.

According to a 13-year study of viewers conducted by two University of Chicago professors and released in 1990, Americans will spend an average of two hours per day—the equivalent of seven years over a lifetime—in front of the TV set. While many viewers turned to the tube to feel better, the study said that they usually wound up feeling worse after watching. Viewers reported becoming drowsy, bored, sad, lonely, and hostile. At the same time this study was released, the American Academy of Pediatrics said that too much television contributed to childhood obesity and could cause violent or aggressive behavior.

To a certain extent, television has always been a medium that people have loved, hated, or loved to hate.

Television in the 1980s and 1990s was not the same as television in earlier decades. Certainly, the sets themselves had changed. They became both cheaper (as low as $50 for a ten inch black and white set) and more expensive ($10,000 for a ten-foot custom designed wall unit.) They became small enough to carry around and even gave you a picture within a picture so you could watch two or more shows at once. The changes that most impacted on the consumer and advertiser, however, resulted more from what came out of the television set than from the set itself.

In the mid-1960s, only 17% of all Americans owned more than one television set; 4% could receive more than ten stations; 2% subscribed to cable; and only television engineers knew what a VCR was. By 1994, 65% of the population had two or more television sets; 61% could receive 30 or more channels; cable was in two out of three homes; and more than 80% viewed what they wanted with home video.

Television of the 1980s had become channels of choice. New video options gave the consumer both a greater variety of what to watch and more freedom as to when to watch. And with cable, advertisers discovered new and highly-targeted channels on which to reach their customers.

With such a vast array of video options, and with the new Fox network and strong syndicated programming, the three major television networks saw their shares of the viewing pie grow smaller and smaller. During the 1992–93 television season, the A.C. Nielsen Company reported that ABC, CBS, and NBC attracted less than 60% of the available primetime audience. This had declined from 90% in 1979–80. Because of the increase in viewing options, the consumer also began to watch television in new ways. Instead of sitting contently throughout a single show, they began to "graze the dial" and flip from one program to another. Cable allowed viewers to tune into a few minutes of music, news, sports, and weather—52 or more different options in many cases—during a commercial break in their favorite show. They might tape a program and play it back at a later, more convenient time, perhaps even skipping through the commercials. Watching television also came to include viewing rental movies, playing games, and shopping from home. And the phenomena of "zipping and zapping" added further to the worries advertisers already had about audience declines.

Still another concern was brought about by commercial overload. In the 1950s and early 1960s, most television commercials were 60 seconds long. To fight rising costs, advertisers in the mid-1960s turned to 30-second messages and by the mid-1970s, 95% of all network commercials were 30s. Although advertisers grew increasingly concerned about commercial clutter, this didn't stop the trend to still shorter messages. As costs continued to soar, advertisers in the latter half of the 1980s turned to 15-second commercials. Today, this popular "mini-message" represents one-third of all network spots.

Journeying through the last decade of the 20th century, still further developments in the video environment are taking shape and will change the television medium from what it once was. Direct broadcast satellites will make direct transmission to an inexpensive home satellite dish easy and convenient, and high-definition television will deliver a stunning, movie-quality picture. Pay-per-view is making more programs available on a watch-when-you-want, pay-as-you-watch basis. And with video on demand, the television set will act as a video jukebox. Through computer storage, you will be able to retrieve and view almost every program ever made.

The important point to remember is that all the latest technology (hardware) is of absolutely no value without the programming (software) that will create consumer demand and sustain consumer interest. If it does this, the traditional television medium will become even further fractionalized, but with more and more options for the advertiser.

IN SEARCH OF CUSTOMER CONTACTS

The fight for consumers' attention has not been confined to the traditional media. Hardly a day goes by that there is not some report on a new means of communicating with consumers. Marketers are searching for and discovering a whole host of new ways to reach their customers, at all times and in all locations. New, alternative media hit consumers at airports, in doctor's offices, in the classroom, on ski slopes, on their computer screens, and at ball parks. There are moving billboards on 18-wheel trucks, commercials on videos, and computer diskettes that let you play games while learning all about an automobile manufacturer's cars. Campbell Soup Company even put fish recipes calling for the company's soups on the back of Roman Catholic church bulletins during Lent.

In this new marketing communications environment of the 1990s, the task of the marketer is far more complex than it once was. Business as usual means *no* business to companies who must deal with a changing consumer who is

1. expressing doubts and fears about the future;
2. becoming a tougher customer;
3. being more and more price-driven;
4. looking for lasting relationships, someone they can trust;
5. barraged by claims and counterclaims; and
6. living in an environment of increasing media fragmentation.

Companies want something that *works!* It is not simply advertising. It is not merely a media message. It is not just another sales promotion. Neither is it a communications effort measured in terms of the number of "warm bodies" they reach. For example, Nike may know exactly how many young men see its commercial in the Super Bowl or read about its new running shoe in *Sports Illustrated.* These numbers say precisely nothing, however, about what this really accomplishes for Nike. What Nike and all other marketers are searching for are customer contacts that will move consumers to action and grow their business.

The concept of customer contacts goes back to the early days of the peddler and the country store, when the only two media were personal contact and word-of-mouth. Customers learned about a product from the person who made it, sold it, or had tried it. But the selling world grew larger and more complex. More stores competed to sell more products to more people scattered across more areas—this encouraged the growth of mass media.

Sophisticated techniques, developed by large advertising agencies, were used to analyze these media opportunities. A new language known as "MediaSpeak" referred to such things as

- reaching 80% of all men, an average of five times each; and
- delivering 400 GRPs at a cost of $20 per 1,000.

Media flow charts were neatly laid out and attached to page after page of statistical analyses. Unfortunately, no mass medium ever matched the effectiveness of personal contact and word-of-mouth. Neither did the "mass" distribution of advertising ever make a sale.

Effective marketing communications has nothing whatsoever to do with GRPs, CPMs, reach, or frequency. MediaSpeak is a placebo for sales—the only thing a business cares about. And with rising marketing costs, increasingly fragmented media audiences, and a consumer who controls more than ever before what he or she reads, hears and watches, business as usual means no business at the cash register.

Effective marketing communications means getting right down under the skin of the consumer to find out what makes them tick. Consumers do not receive advertising in the same nice, neat way it is laid out in a media schedule. They receive it on their own schedules, in the context of a multitude of activities, and among hundreds of ads from other marketers all fighting for a share of their spending. For example, a television schedule may reach 80% of your prospects an average of five times each. But these same prospects also have 500 other TV messages aimed at them each week. What media people refer to as "impressions" never impress the consumer and a company can only put real money (not a $20 cost per 1,000) in the bank.

SEVEN FACTS OF LIFE

In the real world of consumers, the focus must first be on discovering real insights into what makes them tick. Then, the marketer must deliver contacts that touch and communicate with these *consumers* and turns them into *customers*. Rather than focusing on how many million impressions he delivers, the smart marketer wants to know how *effectively* he is communicating

- One message to—
- One prime prospect at—
- One point in time.

For the 1990s and beyond, "Seven Marketing Communications Facts of Life" will help us to accomplish this.

Fact of Life Number 1

Every consumer has his very own communications clock. It covers 365 days of the year and extends from when he gets up in the morning until he goes to sleep at night. The effectiveness of a company's attempt to sell him depends on the consumer's needs and desires at the time of exposure. It is highest when what a company is selling is at the top of the consumer's mind and when distractions are at a minimum.

The ideal "sales call" occurs when people are using your product, thinking about it, or able to buy it right now. Thus, the simple little sign you spot in a restaurant window can do more to sell you breakfast than their expensive, 30-second commercial you see on TV that night.

To maximize communications' impact, today's challenge is to reach prospects at both the most productive time and in the most productive place (see Exhibit 1). For example, what is the consumer most receptive to

- at 7:30 am?
- in his car that is stuck in traffic?
- when the temperature is below freezing?
- when she is on a long airplane flight?

Fact of Life Number 2

Rarely does a business view its advertising within the same media environment as does its customers. A marketing director may decide whether or not to go with a campaign after carefully scrutinizing a newspaper or magazine layout on the wall of a comfortable conference room. He will screen a television commercial all by itself on a $2,000 professional monitor. In contrast, his customers will hopefully see the newspaper ad in the middle of page 16, 26, or 36. They may or may not see the magazine ad as they flip through a 140-page publication with 70 other pages of advertising. And they may catch that TV spot on a modestly priced set, perhaps not well tuned, with their children fighting

EXHIBIT 1. The Right Time and the Right Place

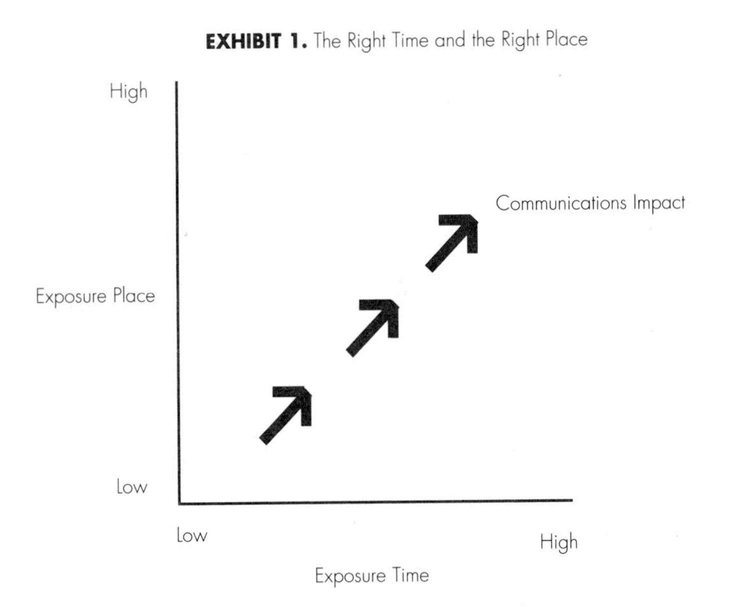

in the background. This commercial will also appear in a pod with five or six other commercials.

It is not enough just to plan your marketing communications strategy from the consumer's point of view. You must actually view your advertising just as your consumers will see it.

Fact of Life Number 3

Marketing communications decisions must reflect a selection from among all possible options on the media menu. Unfortunately, most companies make their choices from among only the "major" traditional print and broadcast options. But what about nontraditional media in today's nontraditional communications environment?

If a business wanted to reach young people with music, they might immediately think of MTV and radio. But what about sound trucks on college campuses, cinema advertising, summer music festivals, and shopping mall music videos?

A business with a large amount of information to convey might automatically opt for newspapers and reject a television commercial as being too short and too expensive. The sales manager of a Cadillac dealership wasn't worried about this, however, when he bought an hour of time, brought five cars into the TV studio, spent eight minutes pitching each car, offered great prices, received 200 calls, and sold $200,000 worth of autos. That was selling cars in a nontraditional, but highly cost-effective manner.

Fact of Life Number 4

When a company wants to uncover real consumer insights, it must talk to consumers. A business cannot learn what will impact on its customers simply by studying research reports. To gain true consumer insights, this author designed and conducted over 25 original studies of media consumption and behavior. For example,

- A television station ran four six-minute commercial breaks in a movie instead of ten shorter breaks. Because viewers liked this, the movie ratings went up and the station began charging more for its spots. However, when I asked viewers why they liked having fewer breaks, they said it gave them more time to leave the room at commercial time.
- The president of a large corporation said that top executives never read magazines—he believed that their secretaries simply clipped articles for them. Personal conversations that my associates and I had with 30 top executives documented that this was not true and that the executives all read magazines.
- A soft drink company's marketing director questioned the value of radio for the brand. By observing their teenage customers on a beach listening to radio, however, I could demonstrate the value of the medium in a way the marketing director believed.

Simple research such as this in which marketers talk to their customers about their media exposure can effectively show what motivates them and in what ways.

For example, the manager of a computer store regularly asked its customers where they saw the store's advertising. One week, a number of customers responded "on TV" although the store ran only radio commercials and newspaper ads. The customers had put together the radio sound and the newspaper sight, and imagined that they had seen a television commercial. The store learned something new about a radio/newspaper combination that had never previously occurred to them.

Fact of Life Number 5

A marketing communications plan may look just fine on a flow chart, even though it ignores a perfect opportunity to reach customers. Year after year, a leading food company saved money by eliminating advertising for its pancake and waffle mixes between Christmas and New Years. They argued that brand sales were low then. Unfortunately, the company forgot about all the people who took a week off at year end and would enjoy very leisurely breakfasts. While they wouldn't run out to the store to stock up on pancake and waffle mixes, they did move it from their kitchen cabinets into their stomachs. Once the company recognized what was happening, they developed a year-end promotion that continues to this day.

Fact of Life Number 6

Marketers constantly judge the quality of a media vehicle's environment and how this will impact on the response to their advertising. The problem is that such judgments are usually based on their own subjective definitions of quality. But what *is* quality? A company's customers do not feel that their favorite magazines, newspapers, or television shows are of a lesser quality than those media vehicles that are the favorites of others. The reader of one paper doesn't feel it is "trash" while the reader of another paper feels his is "class."

The consumer is the judge of the quality of a media vehicle to which he is exposed, and the only way to learn how he feels is by talking to him. The marketer cannot and should not judge media quality solely on the basis of their own tastes.

Fact of Life Number 7

For years, astute marketers have tried to determine how best to reach their customers for the least amount of money and with the least amount of waste. Some companies wisely developed ways of using their product's own package. They could promote themselves on the coffee container or cereal box that sits on the kitchen counter every morning. They could even do something as simple as having a message near the end of a roll of tape saying, "You're almost out!"

Such communication opportunities

- reach a guaranteed customer with no waste;
- reach the customer at the key time of product use or interest; and are almost 100% *free.*

INTEGRATED MARKETING COMMUNICATIONS AND THE CONSUMER

These "Seven Marketing Communications Facts of Life for the 1990s" are not just about advertising as we traditionally think of it. They are about advertising, sales promotion, public relations, events, displays, direct marketing, packaging, and everything else that creates a bond between a company and its customers.

This involves an integrated approach in which the traditional and the nontraditional, the familiar and the unfamiliar, the well known and the lesser known marketing communications vehicles all work together to engage the consumer in a genuinely meaningful sales conversation. The pieces of the program all are based on a single consumer-focused strategy to achieve maximum productivity for a product or service.

The American Association of Advertising Agencies has defined integrated marketing communications as

> *A concept of marketing communications planning that recognizes the added value of a comprehensive plan that evaluates the strategic role of a variety of communications disciplines, e.g. general advertising, direct response, sales promotion, and public relations, and combines these disciplines to provide clarity, consistency, and maximum communications impact.*

In their 1992 book, *Integrated Marketing Communications,* Don Schultz, Stan Tannenbaum, and Bob Lauterborn refer to integrated communications as

> *The process of managing all sources of information about a product or service to which a customer is exposed, which behaviorally moves the customer towards a sale and maintain customer loyalty.*

Integrated marketing communications is reflected at three key levels of the planning process (see Exhibit 2). At that stage when objectives are set, it requires that there be an achievable, measurable customer response. When setting strategy, it requires the establishment of a singularly focused communication/action goal that encompasses all elements of the program. At the tactical level, it insists on zero-based vehicle selection with the ability of each marketing communications vehicle to effectively touch the customer.

EXHIBIT 2. Three Levels of Integration

Objectives

an achievable, measurable response

Strategy

a singularly focused communication/action goal

Tactics

zero-based vehicle selection
+
the ability to effectively touch the customer

THE CUSTOMER CONTACT CONNECTION

An effective integrated marketing communications program aims beyond a one-time sale. It seeks to build lasting relationships with its customers that extend over the years. It accomplishes this through the "customer contact connection" (see Exhibit 3).

This begins with a solid understanding of consumers—insights into what makes them tick, what turns them on, what turns them off, and what are the most productive ways in which to touch them. From these insights, the marketer reaches out to deliver his offer or proposition. If successful, what the marketer offers will make it through the communication barriers of indifference, preoccupation, competitive noise, and commercial clutter to make contact with the consumer.

But this is only the beginning. To turn a consumer contact into a successful customer contact demands a measurable response for the marketer—the consumer must take the bait to become a customer. This might be in the form of making a purchase, responding to an offer, attending an event, or taking some other action. And just as there are communication barriers to making contact with the consumer, there are activation barriers to securing a customer response. The consumer

EXHIBIT 3. Building Relationships via the Customer Contact Connection

Consumer Insights

Delivery

Communication Barriers

Consumer Contact

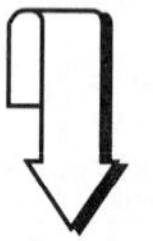

Activation Barriers

Customer Response

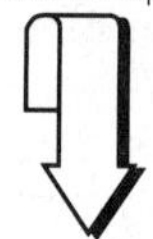

Customer Relationship

New Consumer Insights

may simply lack interest in what the marketer says or offers, be satisfied with his or her existing product or service (or even political candidate), or be unconvinced of the value of what the marketer has to say.

If the consumer does respond, and becomes a customer, the marketer still has one task remaining. He must hold onto the customer and retain his loyalty month after month and year after year. It is far more costly to be constantly in search of new customers than it is to focus on satisfying existing ones. Thus, the marketer must build a long-term customer relationship by delivering on what has been promised. Through the establishment of such a lasting customer relationship, the marketer is then in a position to gather more knowledge as to what makes his customers tick. He then builds this into a database that provides new consumer insights and the process goes on. In this way, the marketer learns from experience and profits from what he learns at each step in the process.

In focusing on the customer contact connection, a marketer must be prepared to accept an unfortunate fact of marketing life. The vast majority of people theoretically reached by the marketing communications program will be neither touched, moved, nor influenced by it. Consider the experience of one major high-tech equipment manufacturer. Out of every 100 target prospects, 90 were reached (in the media sense of having an opportunity for exposure) by its marketing communications program. Of these, 68 prospects became at least marginally aware of the company's message. Unfortunately,

- only nine prospects really learned what the company was proposing;
- only seven liked the proposition;
- only five showed a preference for it over other options;
- only three felt a strong conviction that they would take action; and
- only two actually made a purchase.

There should actually be nothing surprising in this example. For most products or services, it is doubtful that any more than 2% of those regarded as target prospects will become purchasing customers. Most target "prospects," especially those identified in advertising media plans, are actually only "suspects."

In Exhibit 4, the large square represents all women aged 18–49 who are a TV plan's target "suspects" for a new product. Unfortunately, once the marketer makes it through the communication and activation barriers of indifference, preoccupation, competitive noise, commercial clutter, low interest, product satisfaction, and lack of conviction, he will be left with the smaller square of true customers on whom the success of his brand depends. The cost per 1000 of reaching all 18 to 49-year-old suspects may have been only $10. However, the cost of making the true customer contacts would have been closer to $500 per 1000, or 50 cents each.

EXHIBIT 4. Customers versus Suspects

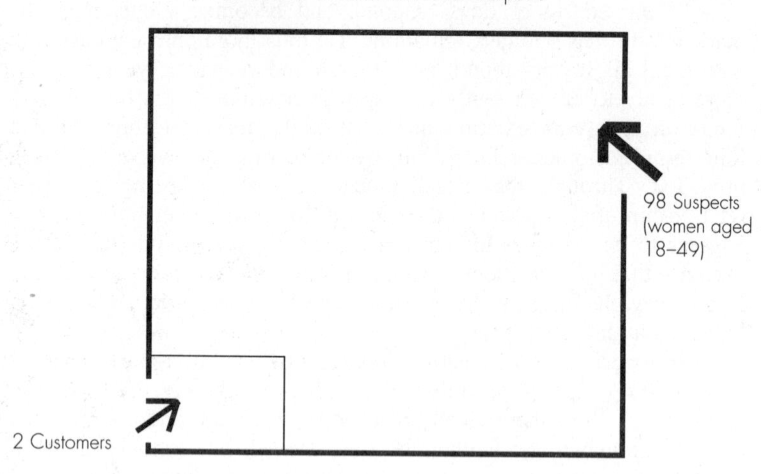

The astute marketer who seeks to maximize the effectiveness of a marketing communications program does not accomplish this by focusing on how to reach more suspects. He or she must maximize the effective delivery of true customer contacts. In accomplishing this, he or she asks

1. what response do I want a single customer contact to produce?
2. what is the best way to deliver this single customer contact?
3. what is the most effective blend of advertising, sales promotion, direct marketing, events, packaging, displays, and public relations to turn this one customer contact into a significant mass?

INTEGRATED CUSTOMER CONTACTS

The delivery of integrated customer contacts via a blend of marketing communications systems can be looked at in several ways. In Exhibit 5, we begin with our consumer insights. They provide us with the knowledge to develop a consumer marketing communications strategy that can be executed in a well-integrated manner using one or more of all possible marketing communications venues.

EXHIBIT 5. Integrated Customer Contacts — Part I

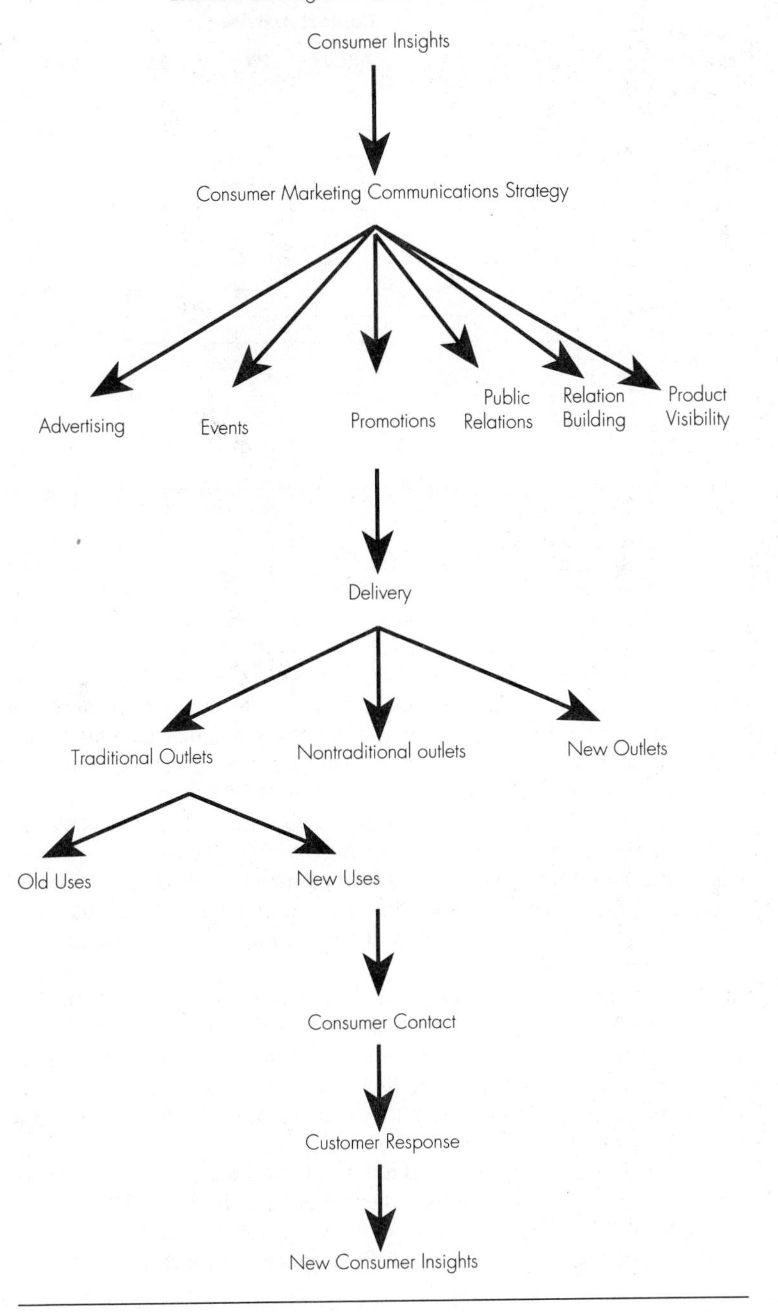

EXHIBIT 6. Integrated Customer Contacts—Part II

Contact Vehicles	Contact Activities					
	ADV	EV	PROM	PR	RB	PV
Broadcast TV	____	____	____	____	____	____
Cable TV	____	____	____	____	____	____
Radio	____	____	____	____	____	____
Magazines	____	____	____	____	____	____
Newspapers	____	____	____	____	____	____
Out-of-home	____	____	____	____	____	____
Direct mail	____	____	____	____	____	____
Telemarketing	____	____	____	____	____	____
Yellow Pages	____	____	____	____	____	____
Home video	____	____	____	____	____	____
Computers	____	____	____	____	____	____
On-site	____	____	____	____	____	____
The package	____	____	____	____	____	____
What else?	____	____	____	____	____	____

It may be delivered via traditional outlets (newspapers), nontraditional outlets (home video), and new media outlets (an interactive vehicle). Even with traditional outlets, consideration is given to new uses (product sampling in a magazine) as well as old uses (a full-page magazine ad). This delivery then results in the consumer contacts from which will come the customer response and the new consumer insights to use in future planning. The process then grows and evolves over time.

In Exhibit 6, the delivery of integrated customer contacts is looked at in still another way. Along the top are six contact activities that a marketer can utilize—advertising (ADV), events (EV), promotions (PROM), public relations (PR), relationship building (RB), and product visibility (PV). Down the left are contact vehicles that can deliver these actions. Integrated marketing communications requires the consideration of all options in the initial stage of planning. Thus if a marketer is considering relationship building via direct marketing, he must consider all consumer contact vehicles that can possibly deliver this relationship-building program. Or, if cable TV represents a desirable consumer contact vehicle, the marketer should consider how a variety of consumer contact activities can use cable TV to maximize the delivery of these contacts.

Finally, an integrated marketing communications system can be looked at as a chain of events, where there can be no weak link. For example, Exhibit 7 shows how multiple consumer contacts might be delivered smoothly and seamlessly across seven venues from network

EXHIBIT 7. Integrated Customer Contacts—Part III

Network TV	Delivers strong brand identity
Direct response TV	Offers more information
Brochure	Provides the information
Radio	Reminds consumers to act
The store display	Triggers action at the point-of-sale
The package	Keeps the brand "top-of-mind"
Toll-free number	Gathers customer feedback

television to a product's package and a toll-free number to gather customer feedback.

This system permits the logical introduction and flow of messages on the computer via Prodigy, in the doctor's office, at the airport, in the classroom on Channel One, and at every decision-making point. It is based on the ability of one communications force to enhance and reinforce another.

WHAT DOES THIS ALL MEAN?

In planning and executing marketing communications programs, there is never a 100% money-back guarantee of success. However, one thing is certain. The company that fails to seek new approaches, that fails to innovate, and that fails to recognize the constant change that is taking place in the consumer marketplace will fail.

A business must investigate every possible avenue to assure that its propositions find their way into the minds of their intended consumers, turning them into long-term customers. A key element of the process is recognition that these propositions must be delivered via whatever vehicles and in whatever venues will most effectively motivate the consumer. At the same time, all elements of the program must be well integrated through a consistent, singularly focused strategy. A successful marketer must not confuse the consumer by sending out conflicting messages. Consider the company whose television commercials focus on the top quality of one of its brands. It then runs a price promotion that says "$1 off." The consumer may say to himself, "If this product is as great as they say, why do they have to knock a buck off the price to get me to buy it?"

In today's changing marketing communications environment, marketers can successfully develop new consumer insights and turn these into the delivery of profitable customer contacts if they break down existing barriers. Rather than operating as islands unto themselves, advertising people, direct marketers, public relation experts, sales promotion specialists, event marketers, and package designers must join together to seek those integrated marketing communications programs that will move us productively and profitably into the next century.

SUGGESTIONS FOR FURTHER READING

Lisa Fortini-Campbell, *"Hitting the Sweet Spot,"* (Chicago; The Copy Workshop, 1991).

Ronald B. Kaatz, *"Advertising & Marketing Checklists,"* (Lincolnwood, IL; NTC Publishing Group, 1989).

August B. Priemer, *"Effective Media Planning,"* (Lexington, MA; Lexington Books, 1989).

Stan Rapp & Thomas L. Collins, *"MaxiMarketing,"* (New York; McGraw-Hill, 1987).

Al Ries & Jack Trout, *"Bottom-Up Marketing,"* (New York; McGraw-Hill, 1989).

Don Schultz, Stan Tannenbaum & Robert Lauterborn, *"Integrated Marketing Communications,"* (Lincolnwood, IL. NTC Publishing Group, 1992).

Jeff Slutsky, *"Street Smart Marketing,"* (New York; John Wiley & Sons, 1989).

Frances B. Emerson
Director of Communications
Honeywell Inc.
Minneapolis, Minnesota

CHAPTER 58

ATTACK ON MANY FRONTS: BUSINESS COMMUNICATIONS

These days, having a "better mousetrap" simply is not enough to bring you marketing success. No one "beats a path to your door" anymore.

Like it or not: It is not necessarily those with the best ideas who succeed; rather, it is those who best communicate their ideas.

So, how do you "best communicate" in a highly competitive, global marketplace? How do you effectively reach multiple influencers and decision makers in a complex, business marketing environment? How do you capture positive attention, differentiate your ideas, and sustain interest in your products and services over a selling cycle that could take months—even years? How do you make people want to buy things on behalf of their company—expensive things that might affect their own career?

THE MANY FRONTS

To be effective, business communications requires an attack on many fronts. That is, you must reach and persuade a variety of key publics:

1. key influencers;
2. buyers;
3. sales and distribution channels;
4. technology partners/alliances;
5. employees; and
6. the community.

Communications with these audiences occur in three segments over the lifecycle of your product: pre-launch, the launch itself, and an extended period of sustaining interest. The communications media available to meet these needs also vary considerably. This chapter will provide an overview of ways to attack on many fronts, familiarize you with the arsenal of media available to you, and help you determine if you are "winning the battle."

Key Influencers

Key influencers in a business marketing environment include industry analysts and consultants; editors of business and trade journals; and securities analysts. These individuals *do not* buy your products; rather, they *evaluate* your products and your company to advise those people who do buy your products—these are the people who can make you or break you. To extend the battle analogy further, influencers are troops who can fight for you *or* against you. You want them in your camp, helping you stave off the competition. How do you do that?

Industry Analysts and Consultants. First, let us consider the industry analyst or consultant. This person usually represents a firm that has a regular set of reports or a newsletter for clients who pay dearly for the service. They also perform customized research. These are the individuals to whom trade and business editors turn for expert opinions after reading your press releases. These are the individuals who want to interview your most senior management, get direct access to your product developers, try product demonstrations, and even do comparative testing.

An effective strategy to deal with these influential sources is to keep them in the loop all the time. After they sign non-disclosure agreements, let them know about any new directions you are taking, important decisions being made, and the impact you believe new developments will have on the industry you serve. These people hate surprises. Their value to their clients is their purview of the industry. Invite these people to your company at least once a year. Meet with them at trade shows, conferences, and exhibits. Ensure they have access to your management when an interview is important. Put analysts in touch with satisfied customers who can corroborate your story. Certainly, do not pander to these people. However, they should feel comfortable that you are an honest and open source of information for them. Best yet, because these people are likely to ask very tough questions before your products come to market, you may be in a position to make adjustments before any damage could be done.

Industry analysts will reward you with coverage in key reports related to your product areas, and they will ask you for background information when doing research reports. You will become a valuable source to them and they will not want to alienate you with poor or inaccurate coverage. You will know if you are winning the battle if you are regularly featured in their reports, receive positive coverage, and find your own sales force using these reports with customers and prospects.

Editors. A second, very important influence within the business marketing environment are the editors of business or trade journals. While these individuals will vary dramatically in their degree of expertise, readers of their media will take their opinions quite seriously. It is up to the marketing manager to make certain that an editor understands your product, its newsworthiness, and the value it has to the readers of the journal. To ensure that you establish a positive relationship with all major trade and business publications, it is important to do the following:

- Have a professional public relations specialist on staff who acts as the primary point of contact.
- Identify the most important media in your industry and the most important editors on their staffs.

- Match the editorial requirements of these publications with your marketing objectives.
- Provide newsworthy materials and valuable articles to these publications.
- Track exposure of your company and your products in these media.

The first point needs no elaboration. However, once you have identified the most important media in your industry, it is critical to evaluate them as objectively as possible in light of the following criteria:

- timeliness of articles;
- level of detail and length of articles;
- tone of articles (scholarly, technical);
- objectivity;
- mix of topics;
- graphics and types of examples;
- mix of advertising to editorial;
- mix of staff-written versus contributed articles;
- quality of production;
- circulation figures;
- years in business; and
- number of experts on staff.

You will be interested in working with publications with long-lived reputations for fair journalistic practices, topical and incisive editorial content, and technical accuracy. Undoubtedly, your resources will be limited, therefore, select only the best publications for your concentrated efforts. As you establish a stronghold in these publications, lesser media will begin to contact you.

In the pre-launch phase of your product cycle, you want to create editorial opportunities. Work with one of the top magazines in your industry and offer them an exclusive cover story that can break simultaneously with the actual launch. They will want a scoop, and you will want that prized cover position.

For major product announcements, you may wish to conduct a media tour one month prior to the launch. Your public relations manager should do all the advance work as well as participate in the tour. This individual will ensure that questions remain on track during your meetings, that all follow-up information is sent out in a timely manner, and that all editorial opportunities are pursued. On the tour, a marketing manager and a product development expert should make formal presentations and perform product demonstrations. Let the editors know when they can expect the announcement materials to arrive so that they can plan their publications.

During the launch phase of your product, several important media are available:

- press conference;
- press kit;

- press release; and
- interviews.

A press conference should last no more than an hour if there is no breakfast or luncheon included. Press people do not want to have their time wasted. Therefore, be certain you have identified all the newsworthy elements of your story: What is new? How does it differ from what is already available from you or your competition? Who has already used it and what do they say about it? How much does it cost? Does it use breakthrough technologies? Does it have a unique application?

If possible, schedule a brief but high-impact demonstration. Senior marketing management and product developers should be on hand to answer questions at the end of the announcement. Prepare a set of likely questions and appropriate answers before the conference so that all of your company's participants are fully briefed and comfortable with the "party line." The hand-out material at the conference should be the press kit. The press kit should be sent via overnight mail to any major publications that were unable to attend.

The press kit should contain the press release announcing the product, photographs of the product (suitable for reproduction), an application or testimonial article if possible, and a background article on your company. It should also include brief biographies of any of the speakers at the conference. If appropriate, copies of speeches or presentations also can be included.

The announcement press release is a simple document whose purpose is to disseminate information in ready-to-publish form. It should enable editors to relay new content easily. Main facts should be stated succinctly in the opening paragraph of a release for quick recognition. A press release faces fierce competition when it arrives on an editor's desk. Here are some tips for getting your releases "picked up":

1. *Don't bury the lead.* The first sentence should state the most important point of the story.
2. *Be concise.* Edit the copy to remove all extraneous words. Keep the release to one or two pages.
3. *Be accurate.* Make certain that every fact, figure, name, and title is correct and verifiable.
4. *Provide substance.* Do not waste editors' time with stories that lack news—no one is interested in promotional angles.
5. *Issue releases in a timely manner.* No editor is interested in old news.
6. *Tailor information to the needs of your specific contacts.* When the corporation sends out a story, customize it to ensure that the importance to your part of the business or the impact on your industry is clear.

If you have handled the conference, kit, and/or press release well, you will undoubtedly get requests for interviews from editors. If the decision to grant an interview has been made and you are the spokesperson, make sure you and the editor have a clear understanding of the topic, the deadline, the thrust of the story being covered, and anyone else who may have been or will be interviewed.

Preparation is the key to the successful interview. It is important to anticipate as many of the questions that might be posed as possible. In addition to the important documents related to the story being covered, review corporate documents such as the annual and quarterly reports, recent major organization announcements, and key position papers recently published.

During the interview, follow these tips for effective answers:

1. Keep your marketing objective in mind at all times.
2. Stress the benefit to the readers of the journal.
3. Eliminate all jargon; rely on simple language.
4. Use positive language.
5. Use concrete, accurate examples to illustrate your points.
6. Practice the tough questions so that these answers are as smooth as your answers to the easy questions.
7. Make certain your answers do not raise additional questions.
8. Pause before you answer to make certain you have heard the question accurately. If you have doubts, ask the editor to repeat it.
9. Short answers are better than long ones.
10. If an editor asks for information you cannot release, do not be evasive. State simply that you cannot release it and explain why.
11. If you do not know the answer to a question, say so, but offer to find out.
12. *Never* lie to an editor.

During the third phase in your product life cycle—sustaining interest—your ability to understand the journals in your field is critical. Here you will need to examine editorial calendars to determine opportunities for feature stories, testimonials, case histories, and unique applications. You will have to contact the editors and reporters often because they will not know that you have these stories.

A good feature story is one that matches the editorial focus of the journal for that issue. It will provide concrete examples of the theme being explored. For example, a magazine featuring the effects of new legislation on industry would jump at a story where a new product or service helps companies comply with the regulation. Generally, the journal will write the feature, but you will provide the contacts and source material. Usually, a journal will send an advance copy of a feature for your comments and approval.

Testimonial articles are hard to come by. Customers, even if completely satisfied with your products, will be reluctant to put in the time and energy required to write an article. As important, your customers are not always sure that an article will be approved by their management. Hence the simplest way to get these type of articles published is for your own company staff to develop them, work with the customer to secure approval, and then submit it to the journal.

Case histories generally are developed by a third party who is conducting research. They will do the work and contact you and your customer for background information, comments, and approvals. Very often such stories are contracted for by the magazine with the industry analysts and consultants mentioned above.

Application stories need not be about a particular customer's use of the product; rather, they can be about breakthrough ways to use the product or service. These stories are usually developed within your company and later placed with the magazine. If you can get the journal to develop the story for you, it will carry greater credibility than if the story is contributed by the vendor.

The way to know if you are winning the battle with the press is to follow the coverage you receive. Is it ample? Accurate? Favorable? Well-positioned in the journal? Do articles generate qualified inquiries? Hire a "clipping service" to save yourself the drudgery of accumulating this data.

Securities Analysts. An audience often overlooked by marketing professionals is that of securities analysts. These individuals can affect your corporation based on their understanding of or appreciation for a major product announcement. Most investment firms have specialists assigned to specific industries and each is quite expert in the areas served. These people always want to know things that you may feel squeamish about telling them because they will hold you to the promises you make and they demand proof of the claims you make.

This group is likely the toughest you will face. It is advisable to work with your corporate investor relations specialist, who knows each firm well, is likely to anticipate their questions, and can fend off probes that have broader ramifications than an evaluation of your new product. Securities analysts will want to know available market size, your anticipated share, the ramp-up curve for profits, your profit margins—all things you have likely covered in your business plans, but are not quite willing to share. Decisions to divulge such matters should be made by the investor relations specialist rather than the marketing manager.

You will know if the "street" is pleased with your announcement if your stock stays steady or goes up, if the stock becomes a "buy" recommendation, if credit ratings are re-evaluated, or if articles appear in *The Wall Street Journal, Barrons, Fortune* or *Forbes.*

Buyers

Three types of buyers exist in a business marketing environment. *User buyers* actually use the product, such as a computer, stationery, circuit board etching equipment, etc. These kinds of buyers will care about ease-of-use, design, or durability. *Technical buyers,* oftentimes engineers or scientists, may also be users, but these individuals are relied on by their companies to determine the technical efficacy of major purchases. The *economic buyer,* often a manager or financial officer, evaluates the return on investment in terms of increased productivity, profitability, flexibility, or in terms of improved time to market, quality, safety, etc.

In the sale of "big ticket" items like corporate jets, process control computers, or manufacturing lines, buyers often form committees who must be approached both individually and *en masse*. The sales cycle is long—often months or years. In all cases, these individuals will rely on the opinions of the analysts and editors mentioned above. They will also require a variety of promotional media.

During a pre-launch phase of your product lifecycle, a selected group of buyers may be communicated with to test your product. Research may take the form of focused group discussions, product sampling, and alpha and beta testing. You may prepare presentations, draft promotional documents and specification sheets, as well as instruction manuals, training materials, and demonstration packages.

The launch phase of a product is perhaps the most exciting for the marketing manager. Here you have at your disposal such promotional "weapons" as

- advertising;
- brochures and flyers;
- catalogs;
- data sheets;
- direct mail;
- multimedia presentations;
- overhead presentations/slides; and
- trade show exhibits.

Within the confines of a single chapter on business communications, it is quite difficult to do any of these media justice. The best we can hope for in this overview is a taste of what works and what does not for some of the most important ones. The set of references at the end of the chapter will help you learn more about each medium.

Advertising. Advertising can be the most expensive medium to produce and distribute; however, it can reach the broadest audience and create the greatest impact. In the business environment, usually only print advertising is used. According to the ABP/ARF 1991 report, this type of advertising can

1. make contact;
2. generate leads;

3. build awareness;
4. build preference;
5. increase sales;
6. lower costs;
7. increase share; and
8. increase profits.

Advertising is best used for familiarizing your key contacts with your products or services, helping your sales channels get sales opportunities (people are more likely to entertain a visit from a familiar company), and keeping the customer sold. It helps create enthusiasm for the salesperson's visit and reduces the risk of rejection. When a company does not advertise in an important trade or business journal (while its competitors do), the company can be conspicuous by its absence. Its long-term goal is usually to affect buying behavior and preference. Short-term goals must be explicit and involve a singular action, such as "generate 1,500 sales inquiries each time the ad runs for the first six months." Note that in the case of expensive and/or complex products, advertising is rarely used solely for generating sales leads. However, for inexpensive or simple products, it can actually be used as the direct distribution channel by means of coupons, toll-free numbers, or order forms.

Advertising works best when it speaks to a specific audience and addresses their greatest need(s). It should differentiate the product and company from the competition, and should be as clear, direct, and simple as possible. Although there is not a foolproof formula for developing memorable and effective advertising, the key elements to consider are:

- headlines;
- graphics;
- body copy; and
- layout.

Headlines are the most important element of any print advertisement. If you do not catch your reader's attention with the headline, you might not have a second chance. Therefore, your "take-away" message (what you want readers to remember) must be apparent in the headlines. Here are some tips for writing effective headlines:

1. Promise a benefit to readers. Tell them what to expect from your product:

   Protect application investments with OpenUSE

2. Reveal exciting news to readers. Use key words—announcing, introducing, new, revolutionary, or innovative—that identify the newsworthiness of your announcement:

Introducing SmartJet—the plane that lands itself

3. Tell readers something of interest to them or how something has been done. This headline establishes a tutorial tone:

How to decrease energy consumption

4. Offer advice to your readers. Most readers are always looking for helpful tips. Be certain you provide valuable help so readers feel rewarded for the time they spend with the ad:

Guidelines for simple system configuration

5. Use an imperative verb to motivate readers to action. Although this kind of ad connotes confidence, it is a stance that can frighten some readers away:

Compare our capabilities to your current system

6. Feature a special offer, event, or price. The offer must not be misleading, although important details and qualifications can be reserved for the body copy:

Buy now. Train Free.

The *graphics* of an advertisement—line art, photographs, or drawings—must work in harmony with the copy, headline, and layout of the ad. The illustration often occupies more space than any other element in the ad; it should work just as hard to sell the product or tell your story as the text. It should telegraph the same promise as the headline. To create effective graphics:

1. Illustrate in color whenever possible.
2. Keep illustrations simple, uncluttered.
3. Use captions underneath or at the side if possible (this tactic gets reader's attention).
4. Represent the product accurately.
5. Let the photography or art tell a story.

The *body copy* of an ad is read by only about five percent of the total number of readers of a trade or business journal. This might sound like an insignificant number, but when you consider the readership of *Control Engineering* magazine (97,000), that percentage equals more than 4,800 people. Those who do take the time to read body copy are far more likely to be real prospects than those who do not. Therefore these readers should be rewarded for their interest with informative, stimulating material. Here are some tips to help you develop interesting body copy:

1. Tell readers what the product will do for them.
2. Tell a story.

3. Present a testimonial.
4. Answer a question posed by the headline.
5. Discuss a special offer.

The *layout* of the ad (i.e., the way in which headline, graphics, and body copy are arranged) can enhance an ad's readability and effectiveness. Poor layout, in contrast, can make an ad fail. Usually, the layout is the domain of an art director, but you should know the basic principles of layout so that you can evaluate the ads presented to you for your review.

The amount of space an ad will occupy is an important consideration. An ad that looks good in a two-page spread will not necessarily work in a quarter-page corner. It is also important to consider the context in which the ad will appear. Will it be opposite the editorial content of the journal? If so, white space will be very important to provide readers with visual relief from the text-heavy environment.

The placement of headlines, copy blocks, graphics, subheads, photo captions, and logos must be balanced and distributed in an eye-pleasing, inviting way. Keep in mind the concepts of unity and proportion: Unity is the degree to which the entire ad holds together as a single, integral piece. In general, the simpler the layout, the more unified the look of the ad. Proportion is the relationship of elements to each other. In an ad containing a headline, a photo, and copy blocks, one or more of these elements will be dominant.

Once an ad is created, it must be placed in the most appropriate publications for the marketing and sales objectives to be satisfied. The ad should appear between four and seven times *in the same publication* to be noticed and remembered. Do not disperse your advertising—select the most important publication and ensure that it receives sufficient exposure. Do not expand your advertising into additional publications until you can satisfy this initial requirement.

Base your decision on the importance of the publication on its audited circulation statement, making certain the people you want to reach are covered. Test your own customers with a readership survey that will indicate to you the publications they read most often and respect the most.

Brochures and Flyers. The marketing manager plays a significant role in the development of brochures and flyers. You will want to make sure your product has the brochure it deserves. These glossy, attractive pieces will be the flagship for the product. They will be used in sales calls, sent as fulfillment to inquiries, and displayed at trade shows. Brochures say as much about the company as they do about the product. A brochure that is done sloppily will imply that the product itself is shoddy.

Brochures are designed to motivate customers and prospects to make a purchase. This objective is accomplished through their content, language and format.

Because readers usually approach a brochure wishing to learn more about a product or service, it is essential that the document provide a clear, concise, accurate description of that subject. Using the needs of the audience as a guideline, organize the description to emphasize the most important features, functions, and benefits of the product. These six steps will help you develop successful brochures:

1. Address the audience's needs, interests, and goals explicitly. For instance, a brochure might begin with a scenario of a problem facing the reader.
2. Describe the product or service so that its ability to serve a need or solve a problem is emphasized.
3. Clearly identify the key benefits or solutions provided by this product or service.
4. Link each benefit or result with a specific product feature or function.
5. Stipulate limitations that apply to the product or its use. These might include availability, warranty duration, exception conditions, or prerequisites.
6. Close the brochure with a call for action. Suggest, for instance, that the reader call a sales representative to find out more about the product. List local sales offices to make this action easy.

Ideally, the language of a brochure should involve readers. Emphasize direct address and avoid passive constructions. Make your language rhythmic by alternating long and short sentences. Sentences should be concise, with important ideas placed in the independent clauses. Rely on jargon only when all of your readers will be certain to understand it. Finally, avoid unpleasantries: "Never pitch from the negative" is a basic tenet of sales promotion. Choose positive, believable words and phrases. The tone should be casual yet respectful, as if you are speaking comfortably to the reader. The personal voice should be used to demonstrate that the reader is important to your company.

The way in which a brochure will be used will affect its design. For instance, if it is to be part of a direct mail campaign, it may need to be small enough to fit into a standard business envelope. If it is to be distributed personally during sales calls or at trade shows, it can have the dimensions of a typical magazine (not necessarily thickness).

Graphic aids are a must in all brochures because they help engage the interest of the reader. Work closely with the art director to establish a careful balance between visuals and the text. Graphic aids should corroborate information presented in the text. "Art for art's sake" does not go over very well with the serious business reader.

Wherever appropriate, captions should be used for photographs and drawings to explain what is being depicted. Researchers have determined that 90% of a brochure's readers will read the captions, but only 30% will read the entire document. Therefore, be certain that captions are informative and that by reading *only* the captions, readers will still have a good idea of the product. Use the captions as well as the graphic aids to reinforce key points being made in the text.

Headlines, main headings, and subheadings are also important design elements. They move readers along in a logical sequence as key points are made. Many readers look only at the headings of a document, reading sections of interest but not others. Therefore, headings should not only be eye-catching, they also should impart valuable information. To maintain the direct address of the document, headings should emphasize benefits to the reader.

Direct Mail. Direct mail is actually a form of advertising sent directly through the mail to targeted individuals. It is designed to motivate recipients to respond in a specific way (e.g., request additional information, try a demonstration, have a sales representative call, or make a purchase). Its effectiveness depends on its use in appropriate situations and on its ability to complement other media in a marketing campaign.

Direct mail has several different uses. It can help convey product information to prospects before a salesperson visits. In the case of an established customer, sales work may be reduced or eliminated through direct purchasing by mail. As a follow-up to a sale, direct mail can help maintain customer satisfaction and continue to keep your company's name in the recipient's mind. Key advantages include:

1. *Elimination of wasted appeals.* Direct mail communicates with only those people most interested in a product; an accurate mailing list is essential. The cost of communicating with prospects via direct mail usually is lower than through print advertising.
2. *Establishment of a personal tone.* Effective direct mail personalizes each letter or package with the properly spelled name and title of the recipient. Frequently, the sales representative's signature appears at the bottom of the letter, and a business card is enclosed. Recipients feel they are getting special attention and are thereby more inclined to make purchases from your company.
3. *Elimination of competitive distractions.* When it is read, direct mail is not in competition with the advertising or editorial content found in other print media, such as journals.
4. *A means of communicating regularly with your target audience.* A periodic newsletter, magazine, letter, or promotional package keeps your company's name in front of the customer.

The most noteworthy *disadvantage* of direct mail is that it arrives unrequested; thus the recipient may have no interest in the message. Chances of ignoring average kinds of direct mail packages are high. Catchy techniques and careful identification of prospects are required. Getting past the executive assistant's mail-screening procedures to the desk of the actual target reader requires crafty, creative packaging.

Recently, a private jet manufacturer launched a direct mail campaign for its private executive jet line by sending very large posters in mailing tubes to the chief executive officers of major companies (the sort of people likely to be interested in such a product). The posters were life-size reproductions of the cockpits of the planes as seen from the pilot's position, including a breathtaking view of a landing field lit up at night. Because the poster was so spectacular, the mailer was taken into the executives' offices. The executives, in turn, so enjoyed the poster that they took the time to read the accompanying letter. Executives soon called the sales representatives to request additional copies of the posters for friends and family members. The sales representatives used the occasion of personally delivering additional posters to discuss the product with the executives. The representatives initiated the calls, of course, if they did not hear from the executives. Sales figures soared as a result of this effective direct mail campaign.

How can you, as a marketing manager, help create an equally effective direct mail campaign? Let us look at the components of a solid direct mail package and its contents.

The *sales letter* is used as a lead-in to the other materials included in the direct mail envelope or package. These letters can be used to

- make direct sales;
- announce products and special offers;
- generate good will;
- describe changes in the marketplace or organization; and
- solicit information.

To satisfy the purpose of the mailing, the sales letter must attract and keep the reader's attention. Thus sales letters are usually held to a single page. Because you are writing to people who have not asked you to do so, you cannot take up too much of their time while making your points.

Start the letter with a statement that really grabs the reader. Although not set apart from the letter the way a headline might be in an advertisement, your first sentence should play the same role as a headline. You can use some eye-catching techniques such as underlining, italics, a different color ink, capital letters, etc. In addition to the same techniques mentioned regarding headline approaches, other tips apply to starting a sales letter.

1. Make the reader feel unique, significant:

   As a member of the XXX, your opinion is especially important.

2. Present a startling fact:

   Seventy-five percent of all children who have died in car accidents were not wearing seat belts.

3. Negate a commonly held belief:

   Dieting is not the best way to lose weight.

4. Refer to an upcoming or recently held event:

   September 8th marked the 35th anniversary of the invention of the integrated circuit—a day that changed the world.

The first paragraph of the sales letter should tie the "punchy" lead-in to the rest of the letter. It should be no more than two or three sentences.

The rest of the letter gets down to business and stays there. For instance, the second paragraph should create a desire for the product in accordance with customer needs (e.g., adventure, comfort, return on investment, quality). Above all, when you are advertising products to business audiences, the appeal should be as informative and factual as possible.

The final paragraph of the letter should motivate readers to complete a specific action. These might include

- calling a toll-free telephone number;
- clipping a coupon;
- answering a questionnaire;
- filling in an order blank;
- returning a postpaid card;
- taking a trial offer; and
- logging on to an electronic service.

The letter should also point to the other enclosures in the package (e.g., brochure, flyer, demonstration diskette, videotape). Letters are far more effective when the action is spelled out. Do not leave it to the reader's imagination or initiative to follow the course you desire.

Close the letter with a signature, and the typed name and title of an individual. Use a postscript to reinforce a particular message, if possible, because the eye is drawn to such a final note.

Enclosures within the direct mail package are unlimited in their variety. Entire companies offer complete lines of specialty promotions that can be included in a direct mail campaign. For example, Honeywell Inc. recently conducted a campaign for an advanced control software package for oil movement and storage at large refineries. The package itself looked like a storage tank. Within the mailer was a letter, a small rear-view mirror that could be mounted on the side of a personal computer, and a brochure that talked about the "danger of running a refinery through the rear-view mirror." Real-time information is critical—only this software can provide it.

In any direct mail campaign, the enclosures, though unlimited in their variety, should tie together in theme and closely support the marketing story. The more likely the item will remain at work with the recipient, the more likely your campaign will be successful.

In addition to specialty items, direct mail packages often include "old standbys" like catalogs, demonstration diskettes, product samples, an audio or videotape, a brochure, a working model, or a gift. Stand-alone mailings such as newsletters and magazines must have a professional, serious tone. The more they resemble paid-subscription media, the more likely they will be read.

Catalogs have an irresistible quality. Rarely is one tossed out without the recipient at least peering inside. No other medium provides you such an opportunity to portray depth and breadth of your product line. Some catalogs enjoy a long "shelf life;" people keep them around until they are ready to make a purchase.

Demonstration diskettes, samples, videotapes, and working models let the recipient experience the product. There is no more convincing argument than the recipient's own judgment of the product's performance or ability to meet specific needs.

Free gifts are also powerful attention getters. Sending a personalized pen and pencil set, a coffee mug, key chain, book, or paperweight usually ensures that a good portion of your message will be read. Naturally, you must stay within the legal limits of the Internal Revenue Service for gifts (or recipients will have to declare their value at tax time).

Most direct mail should include a response device (e.g., an order form, a postpaid card, a list of sales offices and phone numbers, or a toll-free number). Even better, carefully planned follow-up should always accompany direct mail campaigns. Sales personnel should know who will be receiving mail and when, the nature of the mail, and the specific advised follow-up behavior. Tracking results will also depend on good field work.

The *package* itself can make or break a campaign. If curiosity is not created or if a benefit is not promised, it is quite possible all of the wonderful contents will remain inside a sealed package. Three-dimensional packages work best in making it past the screening process. Overnight delivery or express mail almost guarantees the package will make it to the executive's desk because the assistant will assume it was requested. An eye-catching graphic or headline on the package itself will further inspire the recipient to open the package. Ensure that the statement or graphic is consistent with the contents and the marketing objective and that it does not over promise.

Multi-media Technologies. Business communications are beginning to take advantage of the latest technologies to tell the story and attract attention. Multi-media technologies incorporate video, music, narration, animation, hierarchical arrangement of information, interactive scenarios, photographs, computer simulations, and more on computer diskettes and CD ROM. These technologies can be used in a number of exciting ways. Honeywell, for instance, uses multi-media kiosks at its major trade shows so visitors can conduct a self-paced tour of the booth, ask questions, and request literature. The same technology is used at the front of the trade show booth for interactive presentations of the products or services being demonstrated at the show. The company also uses these diskettes in direct mail campaigns and has been able to dramatically increase sales opportunities. Technical training courses are also using the technologies to make materials more interesting and to accommodate self-pacing and self-testing mechanisms into the curricula. System simulations also have been developed to limit the amount of expensive hardware and software required to present demonstrations.

These media are so exciting, especially because they are easy to deliver: via a laptop computer, on a standard screen via an overhead projector (with a special read-out pad from the computer), at a desktop computer, or via video conference. Using technology to sell technology quickens the sale and establishes an image of innovativeness.

The true value of multi-media technology in meeting a company's presentation requirements is only just being recognized by leading edge companies. Within a few years, it is predicted computer-driven technologies will completely replace standard overhead and slide presentation media.

Trade Shows and Exhibits. Trade shows and exhibits are a must for the business marketing manager. They provide a superb forum for making major announcements and for reinforcing existing product lines. Nowhere else can your customers and prospects "kick the tires," familiarize themselves with your offerings, and compare them to the competition. *Booth structure* should be open, simple, and inviting. To be effective, the booth must be distinctive—it need not necessarily be big. Plot traffic flow through the booth to ensure that access to your most important products is intuitively obvious.

A word of caution: Do not bring very much *literature* to the trade show. Research shows that more than 80% of the literature handed out at trade shows winds up in the trash bin. Instead, establish a means of securing qualified leads from booth visitors. If the trade show does not provide computerized badges that gather this information for you via card-reader in your booth (a service many shows do provide), then create a three-part form that can be run through an imprinter or filled in manually. List a range of topics for which visitors can receive additional information. Leave space to provide comments. These inquiries should be routed to the appropriate salesperson, the inquiry handling service, or your in-house facility, and a copy should be retained by marketing to track the show's effectiveness.

Signs in the booth should tout benefits to the passerby. Just by looking at the signs, visitors should get a good sense of what is being displayed and why it is unique, beneficial, new, etc.

Booth personnel should be trained on ways to stand, meet, and greet visitors; provide succinct demonstrations; route them to other parts of the booth; secure their name and contact information for follow-up; and answer as many questions as possible. Booth personnel should be gracious, patient, and calm. Whenever possible, staff the booth with knowledgeable employees rather than external agency personnel.

Demonstrations in the booth should be brief and provide a clear picture of the product's benefits, its differentiators, and its ease of use. The purpose of the trade show is to titillate, to create interest in learning more. Do not conduct full-blown product demonstrations at the booth; this preempts your sales force. Rather, work toward securing permission to have a salesperson call on the visitor to show him or her more.

In the final phase of a product's life cycle, it is critical to maintain your customers' and prospects' interest in your company and your product(s). All of the above media can be used in this "sustaining" cycle; however, several other exciting media can be added to the list:

- application notes and white papers;
- conferences/events;
- electronic bulletin boards;
- presentations, papers, and speeches; and
- videotape.

These media lend themselves well to the reinforcement of your product's virtues because each can provide detailed proof of use. Let us touch briefly on each.

Application Notes/White Papers. Much like the application story, a note or white paper can explore the specific application of your product in considerable technical detail. Providing corroborative evidence of the benefits your more promotional documents claim, this serious-toned document can be used effectively with the technical buyer. This individual wants to understand the product thoroughly before recommending it to his or her company. The application note or white paper serves this purpose.

Conferences and Events. Conferences and special events help maintain contact with customers and prospects and reinforce your company's image. A users group forum, for instance, enables users of your products to share ideas, learn from one another, and provide much-needed feedback to the marketing manager on product requirements. In these sessions, users present papers, provide demonstrations, or conduct discussions.

An executive conference sponsored by your company regarding a topic important to economic buyers (e.g., global competitiveness, the impact of environmental regulations on the process industries), enables you to maintain good will and foster a leadership image. These types of conferences usually provide a slate of professional speakers, and are conducted in a resort atmosphere, wherein the selling is very soft and low key. Attracting the top management of your customer base to such conferences helps build long-term relationships and sponsorship.

Electronic Bulletin Boards. Many companies are out-marketing their competition by providing a free electronic bulletin board service that helps customers stay current with product offerings. Such a service also puts customers directly in touch with product developers for quick answers to technical questions. Questions of interest to many users can be "posted" for all users.

In addition to company-sponsored bulletin boards, many software news services are available from a host of sources. Some are pure news services; however, they allow sponsors to advertise on opening screen displays. Other services provide up-to-the-minute product release information by industry. Still others enable users to scan catalogs and order directly from the manufacturer. As these electronic media become more widely used, it will behoove the savvy marketing manager to stay abreast of them.

Presentations, Papers, and Speeches. One of the most unnerving experiences anyone can have is making a presentation, giving a speech, or presenting a paper in front of a group. Nonetheless, the business environment demands that serious "contenders" actively participate in this environment through meetings, conferences, and seminars. Those who are not making presentations can be conspicuous by their absence. Nothing helps sustain a leadership image more than making a presentation, delivering erudite papers, or having your company's management present keynote speeches at major events.

A presentation, paper, or speech is given to inform, instruct, solve a problem, motivate, and persuade. In the case of formal oral presentations, such as customer meetings, conferences, symposia, keynote speeches and lectures, it is usually a good idea to prepare a complete written copy of your talk. A written speech differs from other forms of writing:

1. It reflects the cadence and word choice of spoken language. Avoid multi-syllable words, highly complex sentences, and tongue-twisting phrases.
2. Its structure is more repetitive. Your audience is listening rather than reading; hence, they cannot go back to earlier points in the text. For points to be remembered, they must be presented emphatically and reiterated.

3. It is less technically detailed. The speech format does not allow your audience to retain complicated facts, figures, or concepts as well as a white paper.
4. It allows for audience input. Depending on the forum, you can entertain questions during or after your talk. Naturally, a written document is static.

Often the organization sponsoring the conference or lecture prints a set of proceedings that includes the text of presentations. Even if your speech will not be published, a complete written statement allows you to develop a clear, focused presentation. Edit and revise your speech until you are confident it is the most effective it can be. However, the written speech should not be memorized, nor should it be read verbatim. Once the speech has been mastered, rely only on note cards.

Keep the speech simple in both the order of information and sentence structure. Provide a clear introduction in which you tell the audience the subject of the speech and the key points you will be making. Provide a clear discussion section in which you develop the points you need to make and provide a clear conclusion in which the key points are reinforced.

Even the most exciting speaker must work hard to maintain the audience's interest (which drops off sharply after three to five minutes). To keep momentum going:

1. Use vivid examples.
2. Cite personal experience.
3. Use graphic aids (simple, uncluttered overheads, slides, or multimedia screens).
4. Ask rhetorical questions (use this tactic sparingly).
5. Demonstrate the point being made (with the product).
6. Use colorful language (i.e., metaphors, similes, analogies, not "off-color").
7. Use active, logical transitions.
8. Modulate your voice to emphasize key points.
9. Use your hands to gesture appropriately.
10. If possible, move about freely—even walk into the audience to engage them.

Videotapes. Videotape is an exciting medium that allows the marketing manager to actually show customers how a product is used. Videotape can be expensive, but its paybacks are significant. No other medium, short of a live demonstration, enables customers to learn so much about your product so quickly. Tape can be used to train users, to provide an overview of the product, or to visit with an existing user who vouches for the product.

Plan your videotape well. The more time spent in preparation, the less expensive and the higher quality the final tape will be. Work with a professional videographer who will use good camera and audio equipment, lighting, makeup, and tape. Perform a walk-through of the site or demonstration before any taping takes place. Work from a storyboard of events. Script the tape whenever possible and use a teleprompter for people who are not used to having "lines" to recite. The final product should mix in music, professional narration, and special effects to cut in and out of different scenes. Customers have been spoiled by television and movies. Their expectations of corporate videos are very high—do not disappoint them.

While videotapes can be extremely effective, getting people to watch them is tricky because equipment must be available. You may want to send the tape in a special mailer to customers along with other literature. The package is sure to be opened and many individuals will take the tape home to view. When used for training purposes, the tape will probably be viewed on video monitors provided by the customer or manufacturer to the person being trained. Finally, sales personnel can set up meetings and bring video equipment with them or secure it for the meeting.

Packaging for the tape should complement the subject matter enclosed. Labels should be clear. Because a viewer may receive the tape without benefit of a sales call, insert a letter or small flyer explaining the nature of the tape and the reasons the person will benefit from watching it. Provide a postpaid card whenever possible so you can receive feedback on the tape from viewers.

Tracking Mechanisms. You will know if you are winning the battle with customers and prospects if your sales increase—it is that simple. However, tying communications efforts directly to sales is not at all simple in the business environment. Very few media generate direct sales (e.g., coupons, catalog order forms); rather, most are part of an overall marketing mix. We must satisfy ourselves with tracking inquiries—in terms of number generated, followed up on by sales force, and converted to sales; number of visitors to a trade show; number of attendees at conferences; number of direct mail orders; awareness benchmarks; and timing of sales activity (e.g., sudden increases after an advertising blitz).

Despite this seemingly inexact science, all those involved in marketing and communications will testify that advertising and sales promotion materials and events are essential parts of the selling effort.

Sales and Distribution Channels

Within the business marketing environment, channels to the ultimate customer can be varied. Your company may have a cadre of sales personnel who call directly on the customer. It may have a group of manufacturers' representatives, value-added resellers, original equipment manufacturers, dealers, or distributors. It may have any combination of these elements, or all of them.

You, as the marketing manager, must look on these resources as your "battalions." These are forces that will deliver the messages you create, impress the customer, and keep the customer happy. These people will fight your battles—it is your job to make sure they are adequately prepared and armed to win.

No matter how effective your advertising and promotional materials may be, if your selling channels cannot follow up on them effectively or reinforce these media, your efforts will be undermined. Conversely, a solid selling organization—one that is well-trained, professional, and service-conscious—can win battles even when communications programs fall short of the mark. The ideal situation is one in which both the media and the human resources complement one another.

Too often in the business marketing environment, emphasis is placed on the external launch of a product, and little attention is paid to ensuring that sales channels stand at the ready. To avoid this potentially costly mistake,

1. prepare a thorough sales release guide;
2. conduct training with key sales resources;
3. provide appropriate sales tools; and
4. create appropriate incentives.

Sales Release Guide. Whether in electronic or paper format, a good sales release guide is available in sufficient advance of the external launch for sales channels to become acquainted with it. Contents should answer the following questions.

1. What is being launched?
2. Who are the customers and why would they need it?
3. How is it differentiated from the competition?
4. How does it work?
5. When will it be available?
6. How is it ordered?
7. What is its cost? Discount rate?
8. What support is available for it?
9. What is the commission structure?
10. Who are the key contacts (internal and reference sites) for further information?

The better the organization of the sales release guide, the easier it will be for your channels to access the information they need. Do not get bogged down in technical details. Keep the information succinct and readable. Once you establish a particular format for a sales release guide, stick to it. People get used to receiving information in particular ways and find uniformity very efficient.

Sales Training. Not every product launch will require training, but whenever a major new type of product or service is introduced, training makes a great deal of sense. Your sales channels must come to understand "fit," that is, the positioning of the new offering within the context of other products and services. They must learn the types of questions customers are likely to ask. In the case of a product that creates a technological discontinuity (e.g., personal computers, jet engines, compact disc players, video cassette recorders, microwave ovens), it is essential they understand technical differences between these products and less advanced ones.

Training may be regularly scheduled events, such as annual kick-off meetings, or periodic occurrences on an as-needed basis. However, because time away from the selling process is expensive, training media are becoming far more varied than traditional classroom settings where salespeople had to congregate for an education. A sample of media available includes

1. *"Train the trainer" courses.* Here, top-notch salespeople are brought in for a concentrated course. They are then sent out to the other sales channels to "proselytize."
2. *Multi-media self-paced instruction.* These media include branched instruction and testing that enable individuals to study on their own time, at their own pace. "Students" can review material as often as necessary or skip ahead whenever they have qualified in a specific area.
3. *Videotape.* Either in groups or individually, sales personnel can learn directly from the engineers or marketing manager in a convenient way. Time and travel costs are significantly reduced. Videotapes should be packaged with printed highlights to reinforce the messages.
4. *Audiotape.* Especially in cases where representatives spend time traveling to reach the customer, audiotapes can be very effective. Again, package tapes with printed highlights.
5. *Demonstrations.* Either in electronic media (e.g., diskette, CD ROM), videotape, or live media, a demonstration serves the same purpose for your sales channels as it does for customers. It enables them to become familiar with the product and it builds their confidence. The demonstration, if properly constructed, can also serve as a sales tool.
6. *Modular printed instruction.* Tutorial materials, refresher courses, and basic skills can be taught or reinforced through a classic textbook approach. Keep material up-to-date and develop a solid index.

Sales Tools. The media appropriate for buyers are the sales tools your direct sales channels will use. The sales organization must know what is available and how it should be used in the sales cycle. Several media are especially helpful to indirect selling channels such as manufacturers' representatives, distributors, dealers, and value-added resellers:

- direct mail;
- cooperative advertising programs;
- point-of-purchase displays; and
- telemarketing services.

In the case of direct mail, each of these sales channels will want to be able to customize standard materials your company has prepared so that their customers can respond directly to them for follow-up. This may require your company to supply art films, do the address customization for them, or affix special stickers or labels.

In the case of advertising, many dealers, representatives, and distributors do their own in regional journals and newsletters. Most companies supply their indirect channels with camera-ready artwork for use in these channel-specific ads. Additionally, cost-sharing programs ensure that your products are regularly featured by these resources. Programs vary from 25 to 75% of the advertising costs being borne by the marketing budget of the manufacturer.

Original equipment manufacturers (OEMs) and value-added resellers (VARs) require a different approach than these other indirect selling channels because they manipulate or alter your product in some way. For instance, an oven manufacturer may embed temperature control products within its ovens. These controllers may make the product more reliable, cost-effective, etc. The VAR, on the other hand has coupled or "bundled" your product with others and with some services to provide a specific solution or a broader scope offering. Your challenge is to provide OEMs and VARs with materials that can be modified to appear in their own promotional media. These might include spec and tech sheets, photographs, or line art.

Incentives. Most companies have clear, standard compensation and incentive programs that are negotiated with their sales channels on at least an annual basis. They know what percentage their commission will be based on what revenue, order level, and margin. However, in the case of a specific product launch, the marketing manager is wise to consider ways to provide additional incentive for that item. These motivational tactics can include

1. *Sales contests.* Rules must be clear and fair. Be certain you have legal approval, especially in the case of interstate commerce. Usually a single large prize is awarded (e.g., a car, a dream vacation.)

2. *Promotional catalogs* (wherein points or credits are earned toward rewards). These work best when sent to the homes of the sales personnel. Family members add peer pressure that works to your company's advantage.
3. *Recognition programs.* These establish special titles and cliques that distinguish successful individuals.
4. *Bonus compensation.* In addition to the established incentive programs, extra compensation may be awarded (usually for a limited time) for this product.
5. *Special discount rates.* For indirect selling channels who purchase products from your company and then sell, these programs allow a special discount for these products (again, for a limited time and usually associated with a high volume order).

For any of these motivational tactics to work well, they must be communicated effectively. Use merchandising tactics such as flyers, posters, and direct mail to capture the attention and imagination of your sales channels.

Technology Partners and Alliances

With the rapid increase in global competition, the acceleration of time-to-market for new products, and the rise in customer expectations, many companies are willingly (or unwillingly) forging development and marketing alliances to achieve growth and stability. Very often these relationships are formed with competitors. The latest marketing literature likes to call this concept the "virtual corporation;" i.e., one that comes together for a focused business purpose and may later disband, each party free to pursue other relationships.

Communicating with these partners is a new kind of challenge for the marketing manager. Communication takes place in the same three phases: pre-launch, launch, and sustaining.

In the pre-launch or "sounding" phase, it usually is the marketing manager who defines the need to create such a bond. This person identifies likely prospects, puts out feelers, reports back to management, and then may pursue likely candidates on behalf of the company. At the sounding stage, you will need to supply this potential partner with background material about your company. Presentations, the annual report, and product catalogs will feature big in this phase. Similarly, your potential partners will need to provide this kind of information about their companies. Confidentiality is critical at this stage. Documents should be clearly marked as proprietary, the list of people with whom communications are conducted should be limited and known by both parties. Non-disclosure agreements should be reached very early in the process.

If a partnership or alliance is formed, it should be launched publicly in a jointly developed press release or a joint press conference (see above for details on these media). Promotional materials may be developed jointly as well for follow up after the announcement. The review process is complicated insofar as two companies are creating and approving the documents. However, if marketing and communications staffs from both companies plan together from the outset, things should go smoothly.

The sustaining phase is especially important regarding partnerships. It takes time for the marketplace to associate the change with the parties involved, to feel confident about the relationship, and to accept it. To the degree possible, plan joint articles, presentations, trade shows, etc.—media that prove your "togetherness." Knowing if you are winning the battle with technology partners and alliances is critical to knowing whether you should be continuing the relationship. In addition to tracking sales and share of mind, keep track of the "comfort level." Do personnel who have been working jointly on teams still feel separate or have they bonded? Do people use the future tense when they are working together, or do they reflect a much more limited time frame? Do individuals initiate discussions of additional ways to cooperate?

Employees

Until now, we have been discussing forms of communication targeted toward external audiences; however, it is essential that a company's employees be able to embody a company's image in their own attitudes and behaviors. Often, a company will forget to keep its employees posted. The net effect is a disenfranchised organization, one that cannot meet its objectives as easily as an informed body, and worst case, one that may undermine the credibility of messages being sent out into the marketplace.

Employees should know how their company is perceived in the marketplace, how products are positioned, what the competition does or says, who the customers are, and what their needs might be. Vehicles for providing this level of information include news services, meetings, sales promotion materials, and demonstrations/events.

It is also important for employees to have feedback mechanisms such as suggestion boxes, surveys, or telephone hotlines. Questions or comments of interest to many employees can be distributed via the media listed above. The media discussed in this section can and should be used in the pre-launch, launch, and sustaining phases of a product's life cycle.

News Services. Internal news media are varied, ranging from traditional newsletters to electronic mail systems, voice mail, video programs, and bulletin boards. In all cases, the content should be timely, written objectively, and should be as open and detailed as possible. Do not *market* to your employees. Employees must be able to trust the information they receive from their management if you want to consistently keep them in your camp. In times of trouble, the worst thing you can do is go silent with employees; rather, keep the information flowing. This stream helps buoy up morale, quells rumors, and prepares individuals for changes that might affect them (e.g., the need for layoffs in light of competitive pressures).

Meetings. A variety of meetings can keep employees informed. Certainly, senior management should mix with "the people" on a regular basis to share the mission and objectives of the business—the more people are included, the more they can contribute. Coffee talks and brown bag lunches with other levels of management are also an excellent means of reinforcing key strategies with employees. Celebrations of work done well is another key means of demonstrating elements of success. People need to know what the preferred behaviors and accomplishments are to pursue them effectively.

Sales Promotion Materials. While it is not necessary to share all sales promotion materials with employees (that would be prohibitively expensive in large companies), it is a good idea to position display cases of materials in prominent places throughout your building. Employees take pride in seeing their company advertised and promoted. With major announcements, share materials with managers, who in turn, can share them with individuals in their departments. Post advertising schedules, major marketing initiatives, and key customer visits so that employees have a sense of the vibrancy of your marketing efforts.

Demonstrations/Events. Many people who work for industrial companies do not know much about the products and services they provide to the marketplace. Marketing managers are often blind to this fact because they are so immersed in this side of the business. Demonstrations, exhibits, and open houses help fill this gap. After a major trade show, consider bringing the event "home" to employees so they can share in the excitement. Participate in "Engineers Week," hold customer fairs, and invite employees to visit guest service centers—all of these provide employees with a chance to learn and take ownership for the products they help create.

The Community

The marketing manager has one last front to think about before he or she can feel confident of success: the community. Each company is a corporate "citizen." With today's emphasis on "good neighbors," no company can afford to have its community uninformed about what it does, how it does it, or why its presence is beneficial. On the other hand, it is as important for you to work with community leaders, legislators, and local business press to affect regulations (e.g., taxes, zoning restrictions).

Regular meetings with the community in the form of open houses work well. Factory tours and speeches, demonstrations, or presentations by product developers will go a long way toward making neighbors feel comfortable with the responsible company next door. Coverage in local newspapers regarding major orders, new product announcements, promotions of individuals, and major contributions to the community is also important.

Volunteerism is a key way that your company becomes involved in its community. Each employee acts as an ambassador for your marketing messages and corporate image. (Hence, another reason good internal communications programs are valuable.) Monetary contributions, while important, should be focused on a few key charities where your dollars can make a noticeable difference. Your company should stand for something specific: the arts, special olympics, education, or health reform.

Crisis Communications Plan. Every company and every physical site within that company should have a crisis communications plan developed in the rare event that anything should go wrong that affects the community. Examples include fire, murder, industrial accidents, contamination, hostages, and product liability.

While no plan can cover every contingency, prepare yourselves in advance by identifying spokespersons, off-campus meeting sites (in case site is dangerous), key experts, and major corporate policies. This plan will most likely be developed by your communications director. However, because the way crises are handled will be judged by your community, your employees, and your customers, the marketing manager should be part of the review cycle and should be one of the people contacted in case of an emergency.

The best advice to offer about community relations is that the more positive things you can do on a regular basis, the more accepted your company will be. If and when a crisis should occur and if it is handled well, the community will be forgiving. However, if a community does not hear from your company except in crisis, you can expect a poor reception to your messages and the strong possibility of litigation. Good community relations make for good business.

MANY FRONTS MEAN MANY OPPORTUNITIES

Before reading this chapter, you may have been a typical marketing manager, believing you only had customers and prospects to reach with your marketing messages. By now, you realize there are several fronts on which you must launch a coordinated attack to be successful.

The more carefully planned your communications efforts are, the more likely they will support your marketing objectives. Work closely with the communications experts in your company to ensure your investments of time, money, and energy are well spent. Understand the timing, human resources required, and potential roadblocks in the process of getting your story to market. Be realistic about budgets—if you are not making sufficient investment on the marketing side of a product, it would not matter how many dollars you spend on the development side of your product. After all, it is not necessarily those with the best ideas who succeed—it is those who best communicate their ideas.

SUGGESTIONS FOR FURTHER READING

American Business Press, *It Pays to Advertise.* Report of ABP/ARF, Chicago: 1991.

Arnold M. Barban, et al. *Essentials of Media Planning.* Chicago: Crain Books, 1976.

Alec Benn. *The 17 Most Common Mistakes in Advertising.* New York: American Management Association, 1978.

Jim Bessen. "Riding the Marketing Information Wave." *Harvard Business Review.* September–October 1993, pp. 150–160.

Thomas Bivins and William E. Ryan. *How to Produce Creative Publications.* Chicago: NTC Business Books, 1991.

Burson-Marsteller. "Communications Challenges of the '90s." A Survey of Corporate Communications Officers, 1993.

William H. Davidow. *Marketing High Technology: An Insider's View.* New York: Free Press, 1986.

Frances B. Emerson. *Technical Writing.* Boston: Houghton Mifflin, 1987.

Penton Publishing, Cleveland, "Know the Buyer Better." A Motivational Research Study Conducted for Penton Publishing. George R. Frerichs, Inc. 1991.

Ann Keding and Thomas Bivins. *How to Produce Creative Advertising.* Chicago: NTC Business Books, 1991.

Jim Kobs. *Profitable Direct Marketing.* Chicago: Crain Books, 1979.

Theodore Levitt. *The Marketing Imagination.* New York: Free Press, 1983.

Charles Patti, et al. *Business to Business Advertising.* Chicago: NTC Business Books, 1991.

Don E. Schultz, et al. *Strategic Advertising Campaigns.* Chicago: Crain Books, 1984.

Sidney J. Levy
Professer Emeritus of Behavioral Science in Management
J. L. Kellogg School of Management
Northwestern University
Evanston, Illinois

Ira O. Glick
President
Ira O. Glick & Associates, Inc.
Evanston, Illinois

CHAPTER 59

IMAGERY AND SYMBOLISM

The concept of *imagery* is an important one in marketing. The term is widely used, both casually and technically, and often in misleading ways. The purpose of this chapter is to explain what imagery is, and how it is conveyed and received. After indicating its meaning, the discussion will take up the role of this concept in marketing planning and communications. How symbolism functions in relation to imagery is then explored, followed by analysis of imagery and symbolism from the viewpoints of participants in the marketing system.

THE MEANING OF IMAGERY

The concept of brand image was introduced in 1955[1] and was widely seized upon[2] because it aptly summed up the idea that consumers buy brands not only for their physical attributes and functions, but also because of the meanings connected with the brands.

The notion of imagery reminds us that action in the marketplace is based on impressions and interpretations that people derive from their experience of a broader sort than that which narrowly relates to the objects they buy or sell. They cannot learn all the facts available, and they cannot keep in mind all those they do learn. In addition, there are various influences pressing them to have one opinion or another about the product, service, and company at issue.

The Content of Images

The image is a result of all these facts and influences, reduced to manageable proportions. Drawn from many sources, the image includes such ideas as these.

1. *Knowledge about technical matters* helps people define a brand. For example, the image of a Hewlett-Packard computer might include the fact that it uses the DOS program; or the image of Jell-O might say it is high in protein.
2. *Awareness of other characteristics* that are somewhat more subjective, that seem like facts, but may or may not be supported by experience, is part of imagery. Here might be included the idea that a certain fabric will launder well, or that a certain movie is funny.
3. *Beliefs about the value of the object* come to be part of its image. For example, the conviction that a Rolls-Royce is worth the cost, that Budweiser is indeed a premium beer, that Pepsi-Cola has a lot to give—such ideas become bound up in the image of those brands.
4. *Judgments about the suitability of the brand* are influences added to the image. Brands acquire a greater sense of appropriateness for

some kinds of people than for others. It is part of the image, then, that one brand is thought to be a cigarette mainly smoked by men, a beverage preferred by teenagers, or a food that is too spicy for American tastes.

As these points suggest, imagery is a mixture of notions and deductions, based on many things. It is fundamentally subjective, a fact that troubles those who believe marketing decisions should be made only on hard facts and in accordance with their ideas about what is rational or economically sound. The harder fact is, however, that people live by their images—images that are governed by their individual experiences and values and how they interpret what comes across to them.

Illusions and Facts

At times, imagery is indeed largely an illusion—the belief that some product is highly nutritious when it is not, that eating a carrot will contribute significantly to improved vision, that a particular automobile make is near-perfect in quality, or that another offers the degree of "functional" transportation believed to be the case. Other images are debatable: will a sports car enhance one's sexuality and youthfulness? Will flying on a particular airline imply a higher status level or a more attractive lifestyle? No, say some, a deodorant or toothpaste will not make one more alluring to the opposite sex; on the other hand, say others, bad breath and dingy teeth *are* offensive and of no help in social relations, as the advertisements claim.

The idea of imagery is not restricted to mean only those aspects of products or communications that are misleading or that try to make things seem more attractive or valuable than they really are. It also refers to any inferences drawn about qualities that seem well-grounded—the image of diamonds as hard and durable, of prices as rising, of refrigerators as noisy, of candy as sweet, of tires as safer than they used to be, and of Mercedes-Benz cars as socially impressive.

Long-Range and Short-Range Imagery Goals

There is much discussion among marketers about setting objectives, and planning has first to consider where the enterprise wishes to go. Commonly, however, objectives are thought of in concrete terms relating to sales volume, profit level, or getting customers to be aware of some facts about the product. More recently, marketing managers have been giving attention to what kinds of imagery goals they should have and how to achieve them.

There are many problems involved. Often, managers do not realize how a given action will affect the imagery about their brand or their company, as when an emphasis on stylishness or an upgrading of quality unexpectedly modifies customers' views of a product's value or desirability, or their feelings about a company's suitability to their own habits, tastes, and identities. Managers may not know how to bring about the imagery they want to present—what precise ideas to present, the context in which these are appropriately dealt with, and the channels of communication where this might be best accomplished. Their imagery goals may have elements that are in conflict. An example of how inadvertent imagery might come about is the frequent running of sales, whereby the manager is surprised to discover that the product is coming to be regarded as inferior in quality. When a brand creates imagery that boasts of the brand's popularity, there may be difficulty in trying also to suggest it is an intimate brand. Brands that seem large tend thereby to seem impersonal.

Thus it is that a marketing action—running a sale, designing a package, selecting an advertising theme—is both a short-run effort and an investment in the brand's long-run reputation. If short-run decisions are made without reference to long-run implications—as is commonly the case under competitive pressures and the varied demands of dealers, advertising agencies, and package designers—the results may be haphazard and confused so that over time, the brand image is not well oriented to its market segments, or it turns out to be an image that is different from what the seller would like.

Recently, the growth of sales promotional activities and the power of some retailers has pressed manufacturers in the direction of offering products that seem more like commodities in the lowered level of brand loyalty shown by customers. Anxiety about this shift has increased the awareness of the importance of brand imagery. Procter and Gamble demonstrates this apprehension in its recent decision to back away from sales promotion in order to re-emphasize the stature of its brands. This re-emphasis on brand imagery is shown in the volume on brand equity by David Aaker,[3] and in the surge of interest in integrated or "total marketing" approaches to creating imagery.

Corporate Imagery

An important instance of imagery is that which affects the company as a whole. The corporate image refers to the kinds of ideas and impressions people have of the organization in general. Reputation of its specific products and brands will play a role, but other factors are also relevant. Such knowledge, awareness, beliefs, and judgments—including the size of the company, its personnel, incidents in its history, its value as a stock, and its contribution to the life of the community or the country—are used in reacting to the company.

The corporate image may be of significance to consumers of the specific products by reassuring them of the responsibility and quality of the manufacturer. It affects the buyers of company shares and influences the government in its relations with the enterprise; suppliers to the company will be guided by their image of it.

Appreciation of the power of corporate imagery has led many companies to give special thought to communicating with their various publics. Public relations, institutional advertising, community-oriented programs, training programs, corporate literature, the name of the company and its logogram, and marketing activity within the trade are increasingly evaluated for their effects on the corporate image as well as their immediate practical functions.

Imagery and Symbolic Communication

An image is an interpretation—a set of inferences and reactions. It is a symbol because it is not the object itself, but refers to it and stands for it. In addition to the physical realities of the product, brand, or corporation, the image includes their meanings, that is, the beliefs, attitudes, and feelings that have come to be attached to them.

These meanings are learned or stimulated by the component experiences people have with the product, and these components are particular symbols whose significance is grasped. For example, part of the "real" experience of riding in a convertible is the wind blowing in one's hair. This experience becomes symbolic of the convertible, a component with such meanings as freedom, youthfulness, and irresponsibility. As a rider, one feels a release from conventional restraints, and watchers see the riders visibly showing (probably flaunting) their disorderly hair. As a result, Ernest Dichter interpreted that a convertible symbolized a mistress.

Similarly, all other component symbols communicate aspects of the image, acting as messages to the observer. A new package design might be made to serve as a more efficient container than the old one. Symbolically, the new package could also imply a more modern product inside, a company concern with beauty, or an enhanced femininity, depending on the shape, colors, graphics, and illustrations.

Symbols in Advertising and Promotion

The symbolic actions in marketing are pervasive and inescapable. They are most noticeable and are given most specific attention in advertising and promotion. The structure of a company's office lobby plays a symbolic marketing role, but architects are often either unaware of or indifferent to that fact. However, people in promotional work are apt to be sensitive to the more intangible aspects of their efforts, the possible effects on imagery.

Advertising as an activity is itself symbolic. To advertise is usually understood as a way of being proud and boastful, as something one may do hard or softly. Advertising contrasts with personal selling by usually being some kind of public announcement—a fact that suggests an openness, a prevalence, a quality of being larger than life. It seems democratic—potentially for everyone—and often enjoyable because it is bold, colorful, fantasy-arousing, and exaggerated. On the same grounds, it is adversely criticized because it may symbolize deception or distraction from the true facts, and may seem demanding and intrusive or insufficiently informative.

Whether appreciated or demeaned, advertising is powerful in presenting symbols that help to form people's images. It does this even when the symbolism is resisted. Commercials used to show white doves and white tornadoes in the kitchen, giants' fists in washing machines, and white knights transforming laundry, which were frequently criticized as meaningless and insulting to intelligence. At the same time, the symbolic vigor of these messages was pronounced, absorbed attention, aroused astonishment and amusement as well as irritation, and created imagery concerning brand effectiveness. Figures such as Mr. Clean and the women representing Land-O-Lakes or SunMaid products personalize and reassure their offerings.

Symbolic Form and Movement

Such results come about because people are not literal-minded nor do they respond only to the most obvious, explicit statements in advertising. This is evident if one examines the various kinds of advertising symbolism and how they gain their effects.

Viewers of television commercials may come to learn the messages well because they usually have several opportunities. In doing so, they are often especially influenced by such elements of form as animation, music, special word choices, particular forms and shapes, the sequence of events, their pace, and so on. Some of this influence is difficult to describe and to specify, attesting to the subtle symbolic factors at work. Examples might be the emotional situation aroused when mothers and daughters discuss using sanitary products, and the irritation some people feel at the smug tone of the announcer extolling the virtues of Volvo's cars or the nudity shown in Calvin Klein's ads.

The less deliberate or self-conscious reactions to symbolism are also demonstrated by the effects of movement. The kinds of movement used in television commercials are themselves a vocabulary, contributing to imagery in an intricate fashion. Some examples are

1. Rotation—a movement that suggests the three-dimensional form of the television tube and a showing off of all sides.
2. Approach and retreat—a movement indicating arriving and departing, bringing something to the viewer, or the yearning feeling elicited by a fading away.
3. Unifying movement—occurs when parts are shown that come together to form a whole. The movement is dynamic, leading the audience to want to see the resolution.
4. Staccato movement—such as achieved by stop-motion photography. The effect is one of stylization, a quirkiness, a watch-and-wait idea that is sometimes annoying because viewers vary in their rates of ability to integrate such visual material.

The Manager's Point of View

The position of the marketing manager trying to promote his brand is not an easy one because the creation of a desired brand image is a complex activity. It draws on all the symbolic elements discussed briefly above, in a situation that is in constant flux. There is no simple recipe for the symbolic mix that will produce a specific brand image. The problems vary. Perhaps the brand is on the rise and needs to be kept aloft, conveying a sense of confidence, of having a sturdy place in the contemporary market, and a suitability for everyday lifestyles. Perhaps the brand is declining—this is an agonizing situation for marketers, since what is wrong is often not apparent, leading to some flailing around and blaming in all directions.

Introducing a new brand is an exciting challenge and opportunity. Customarily, the focus on the product is so great that the manager may neglect the fact that he is engaged in creating a brand image almost from scratch because he may be constrained by existing imagery about the company and by other products in the line. If he forgets to realize that pricing policy, channels of distribution, media employed, timing, and all the myriad marketing decisions will each be saying something about the brand, defining it and symbolizing it, as well as offering it in practical ways, he may miss the audience.

The Buyer's Point of View

The world of marketing symbolism and imagery is composed of individual events—products, prices, coupons, advertisements, salespeople, media—and each is handled in some particular way when encountered. Together, these individual events come to form a substantial part of the daily environment. As people move through the day, the multitude of objects and messages that remind them about consuming and buying is almost inescapable and relentless. The manager's problem is to make himself or herself seen, heard, and noticed among all the communications; the people being marketed to have the problem of sorting out their experience, learning from it, and finding in it the things and the meanings that will satisfy them. They constantly process the symbols they are exposed to, deciding how much attention to give to them, making inferences about the product and the form in which it is presented, and about how well it fits into their goals.

An example of how this goes on in a particular area of marketing is found in consumer incentives. Managers may not realize the extent to which housewives reason and draw imagery from different promotional approaches. When such devices as coupons, contests, premiums, and miscellaneous deals are used, these can be interpreted positively or negatively, not only as means of gaining advantage but for suggesting something about the company or brand. On the positive side, incentives have such meanings as the following.

- a large, well-established company;
- an aggressive marketer; and
- a generous, friendly company.

On the other hand, negative inferences may be drawn.

- The company is in trouble.
- The product is poor or overstocked.
- It is normally overpriced.

Additionally, each type of incentive has its own symbolic character and appeal. Samples are almost always welcome, seeming truly free and fair. Sweepstakes are fun and get large numbers of entries, but they seem frothy and are usually forgotten quickly and do little to enhance the reputation of the brand. Then again, there are always exceptions when an activity is done well or the source seems especially reliable—for example, *Reader's Digest.*

Symbolism in Industrial Advertising

Imagery is often thought to be less important in industrial marketing than in consumer marketing. This is a misunderstanding that comes about when the image is taken to refer only to the "nonrational" mood aspects of communications, which seem more prevalent in consumer marketing. This view overlooks the fact that industrial organizations and their brands also have images, even if the content of those images has to do with reliability, service, delivery dates, and competitive pricing. Imagery is not merely frivolity, as a company can have a stodgy image as well as a stylish or even phony one.

Part of the imagery of industrial communication is a sense of dull technical emphasis, of old-line companies relying on their salespeople, being heavy and serious to the point of depression. Where advertising is used, it tends to be traditional, conventional messages with relatively straightforward reassurances that the company and product can provide the performance the user needs. The product is illustrated, or one of its applications is shown, and a request for inquiries winds it up. The people shown, if any, are often earnest, stiff representatives of the seller or users, or both, in "show and tell" situations.

Changing Imagery

Some organizations are unhappy with this, feeling the result is an imagery that is static, old-fashioned, and false to the energetic character of the company. As newer symbols are used to modify the industrial and commercial scene, the advertising becomes more emotional and colorful, and the imagery changes toward greater subtlety. Humor has come to the fore, taking many forms. Verbal and visual puns are common. A bank in New York says to its commercial customers, "The American capitalist. When his needs are financial, his reactions are chemical." An ad for Canteen Corporation showed a drinking straw, with the headline, "Are you keeping this management pipeline open?" The sense of humor starting to pervade industrial advertising may show R&D workers exaggeratedly achieving their marvels. It finds expression in cartoons, whimsy, and many kinds of fantasy. The purpose is to show that the company is not conventional and routine. The use of humor symbolizes that the company has some modern self-awareness, that it is "with it," and that it is not just plodding along doing the same dull, unamusing things. An engineer shows his appreciation of more vital industrial advertising:

> *The photograph is modern, the catch phrase is up-to-date, suggests a modern, today, ad approach. This all comes over to the company . . . I'd expect to see cylinders and fittings—I've seen one that showed all the fittings that were available. I appreciate this. This is an eye-catcher. I like the unusualness of the ad. It's far from the workaday world ads.*

Implications

From the point of view developed in this chapter, the main overall task of the marketing manager is to relate all the symbols possible to the general thrust of the company or the product responsibility. He or she can do this by asking and exploring the following questions.

1. What does he have to sell? The manager should *understand* what is sold in a fundamental way. That is, he or she should learn about the symbolic significance of what is being offered in the marketplace. The meaning of the offering is the central message sent out.
2. What is the symbolic suitability to the audience? In studying markets, the manager needs to understand more than the conventional descriptions of market segments. Part of modern study is to learn about the lifestyle of the customers because the imagery of the brand will be seen through the eyes of people living in diverse ways.
3. What can the manager say? All that the manager has to present to current and potential customers constitutes a repertoire of symbols from which he or she can draw to put together the image he would like to have. He has to work complexly with what the ideal imagery goals might be; what would be believable given the product, his history, and what the contemporary period allows; and what he or she can control in the face of competition.
4. How do subsymbols relate to the goal? If the image the company offers of itself and its brands is a large symbol, the specific actions taken in the marketplace are subsymbols that comprise the total. The accumulation of symbolic meanings produces more intense imagery. Each action should be analyzed not only for its immediate value (e.g., reducing inventory, making more people aware of the name), but for what it contributes to the accumulating imagery.

NOTES

1. Burleigh B. Gardner & Sidney J. Levy, "The Product and the Brand," *Harvard Business Review,* (March-April, 1955), pp. 33–39.
2. David Ogilvy, "The Image and the Brand," *Advertising Age,* (Oct. 17, 1955), p. 1.
3. Aaker, David, *Managing Brand Equity,* Free Press, 1990.

SUGGESTIONS FOR FURTHER READING

David Aaker, *Managing Brand Equity*, (New York: The Free Press, 1990).

Kenneth Boulding, *The Image* (Ann Arbor: University of Michigan Press, 1968).

I. J. Dolich, "Congruence Relationships Between Self Images and Product Brands," *Journal of Marketing Research*, (February, 1969), pp. 80–85.

Henry Dreyfuss, *Symbol Sourcebook* (New York: McGraw-Hill Book Company, 1972).

Erving Goffman, *The Presentation of Self in Everyday Life*. (New York: Doubleday Anchor, 1959).

Sidney J. Levy, *Promotional Behavior* (Glenview, IL: Scott, Foresman, & Co. 1971).

Sidney J. Levy, *Marketplace Behavior—Its Meaning For Management* (New York: AMACOM, 1978).

Joseph P. Flanagan
President and CEO
IMPACT
Chicago, Illinois

CHAPTER 60

SETTING PROMOTIONAL MARKETING OBJECTIVES

Advertising builds value. Promotion builds volume. And the linchpin of all promotional marketing efforts is the promotion objective. This chapter will examine its place in the marketing plan, what a sales promotion objective really is, what it can and cannot help to accomplish, *how to prepare for developing it,* and finally how to craft meaningful objectives.

Sales promotion objectives are rooted in the marketing plan. The development of sales promotion objectives and strategies is an important ingredient in a strategic marketing plan. A marketing plan is essentially a road map, guiding the way to properly achieve the volume, share, and profit goals for the product. Any marketing plan worth its salt will include the means for understanding the brand's overall marketing goals with respect to brand spending, advertising, pricing, and promotion.

Another way of looking at it is marketing plans establish a "who, what, where, when, and how" for the brand. Who you are (and whom you serve), what you offer them, where you are today (and where you want to be tomorrow), and when and how you get from here to there. It is in the realm of the "when and how" that sales promotion plays such an important role.

After the overall goals of the marketing plan are set, both short and long term, it is time to pay attention to the specific sales promotion objectives. It is in the basic nature of marketing plans to start big and become more focused as the plans go from the general to the specific. In this sense, sales promotion objectives are the most acute of all the marketing plan elements.

Sales promotion objectives are pointed, measurable statements that guide and support specific sales velocity and frequency goals for the brand. Simply put, sales promotion objectives are the desired achievements for buying action. But before we look at how sales promotion objectives are assigned or what they say, it is important to examine what sales promotion can and cannot achieve in the first place.

WHAT CAN BE EXPECTED FROM SALES PROMOTION?

We certainly know that sales promotion has no place in Newtonian physics. For while every action has an equal and opposite reaction in the real world, the world of sales promotion is far less pat. There are just so many things promotion can do. What promotion does, it does well—but its role is very specific. Sales promotion can accomplish the following:

1. It can cause a consumer who is unfamiliar with a product to try it. This applies whether the product is new or the consumer is new to the product.
2. It can keep current users loyal to the product and convince them to use even more of it. Loyalty is simply any brand's biggest reward, and promotion can and does intensify it.
3. It can encourage consumers to buy more of the product. This, of course, is significant as both an offensive and defensive marketing tool.
4. It can add value to the product as well as strengthen or reinforce the advertising message. This may involve offering a quality premium to enhance the brand rather than a price-off coupon. For example, a running shoe marketer might include a sweatshirt with a purchase. This would be a classic use of promotion, and today savvy promotion people are learning to get even more mileage out of merchandising the brand image. It recognizes that brand equity is the factor that often allows sales promotion to work effectively.
5. It can generate trade support. Promotional activity is proof positive to the trade that a brand is going somewhere.
6. It can supercharge a sales force. There is no better way to freshen a salesperson's perspective than to give him or her a promotion to work with.

Sales promotion cannot accomplish the following:

1. It cannot overturn a negative perception of a product. It's just like the saying for advertising: a consumer will try something once, but if the product doesn't live up to its promise, it's all over.
2. It cannot turn around a product in decline. Similarly, sales promotion just can't revive a brand that's no longer viable or has lost consumer acceptance.
3. It cannot create a brand image. By its very nature, sales promotion is a short-term, in-out plan of action. Image building requires a long-term plan. And that's that.
4. A single promotion cannot motivate a consumer to purchase a product over an extended period of time. It's the rare product that can thrive long term on a single burst of sales support. Go ahead. Try to think of one that has.

PREPARING THE SALES PROMOTION PLAN

The most comprehensive way in which a marketing professional might look at setting sales promotion objectives, and then strategies, is to skillfully analyze all the aspects that will affect the product's success. This may seem somewhat broad in its definition. But in today's world, sales promotion is becoming so widely used that even something as remote as the quality of the raw material used to make the product's package may control the success or failure of a sales promotion program. This is an extreme example, but it makes the point. Consider for instance, time-dated products. If better packaging materials are purchased, they may facilitate lengthening the product's end purchase date and thereby accommodate a promotion tactic that otherwise couldn't be used, such as pantry loading.

BE AWARE OF PROMOTIONAL POWER

The late 1980s and early 1990s have been times in which the world has experienced a global recession. Not all businesses have been negatively affected, but they certainly have been affected enough to result in the short-term mentality of getting sales as quickly as possible as the *modus operandi*. From top management to middle management, meeting sales objectives is of utmost importance. CEOs need marketing tools that generate sales fast to create jobs and sometimes to save their own.

At the next level, the CEO had better not make a mistake in estimating quarterly earnings per share, or the financial community will punish the stock. The marketing director needs sales today in order to keep the distribution system healthy and the brand manager views the fast return that sales promotion can deliver as a viable springboard for career advancement.

The quick-result nature of sales promotion feeds the corporate fire. On the flip side, the mindset of today's consumers is "instant gratification isn't fast enough." Sales promotion fuels this appetite, too.

The point to be made is that even as the economy turns around, corporations and consumers have been so acclimatized to the benefits of sales promotion that it will never again revert to its position as a secondary marketing tool. Unless, of course, it is used that way. But the alert marketing professional will recognize the power of a promotional plan versus a single-burst promotion. In any event, sales promotion has had an addictive effect on the manufacturer as well as on the consumer.

CONSIDER THE "BIG THREE" TARGETS

Here is another dimension to consider. Sales promotion affects not only the consumer but also the trade distribution and sales force. Generally speaking, brand-image advertising affects only the consumer, which in today's marketing world is like trying to win a triathalon with one arm tied behind your back. Attention must be paid to the trade and the sales force as well.

Each of the three big targets can also have somewhat different objectives. Traditional consumer objectives, for example, might be to (1) reach new customers, (2) hold current customers, (3) load the pantry or build consumer inventories, (4) increase product usage, (5) trade consumers up to larger sizes or more expensive lines, (6) introduce a new product, or (7) reinforce other franchise-building activity such as advertising. Traditional trade objectives might be to gain distribution or shelf space, build retail or store inventories, secure trade support for merchandising activity such as displays and feature advertising, and launch a new product. Sales force objectives might include boosting morale and productivity and prioritizing the sales effort.

The proper use of sales promotion to produce the desired action by the consumer, trade, and sales force is a powerful marketing tool. If focused objectives and strategies are established up-front to get these three audiences moving in the right direction, the program will be a winner. That's the good news. The bad news is that the next program will have to do better next quarter or next year. Success begets success.

FOCUS ON THE BIG PICTURE

Up to this point, we have addressed the emerging importance of sales promotion as a key marketing tool and how a variety of business conditions will have an effect on its success. It is because of these issues that the proper planning of a sales promotion campaign is rooted in clearly stated and well-documented objectives and strategies.

The planning process to properly set sales promotion objectives and strategies is a line management activity centered on getting the right people, resources, and information together in order to make decisions.

Before the sales promotion planning process even begins, marketers should challenge themselves to raise their sights, to look beyond the obvious. Here are several tips for thinking about the "Big Picture":

- Question the value and need to have sales promotion as part of the marketing program. Is that where the brand is going? Is it in keeping with current momentum? Is the brand in big demand?
- Look for the largest context and audience for sales promotion. As things stand now, whom is the brand reaching successfully? Who has been left out? How badly does the company want to "convert" them? How easy can it be?
- Seek contributions from other specialists who may bring new thinking to the process. What does the advertising director say that the advertising strategy doesn't? What vision does the production person have? Take the research director to lunch.
- Commit yourself to an action orientation. Be mindful that advertising—along with other vehicles for delivering marketing messages—provides people with a *reason* to do business with that brand or company. It stimulates consumer desire. In contrast, promotion gives people an *incentive* to buy, generally in the short term.
- Center the success of a sales promotion program around end uses—the consumers, the trade, and the sales force. Consider them to be like a three-legged stool. Each is pivotal to the success of the whole.

- Accept that accountability and end results will be the final judgment. Numbers don't lie, but they do educate. Whether or not a promotion is a success on paper, it will be easy to know where to go from here. And soon.

If this type of "objectivity" can be addressed up-front, the planning process to reach the most rewarding company sales promotion objectives and strategies will not be filled with management bias.

GET THE KEY FACTS TOGETHER

Even though there are a number of steps in the sales promotion objectives and strategic planning process, the lines between each step are blurred. When one step is complete, the next one doesn't automatically start up. In fact, if the successive tasks were charted, they would appear to be a matrix of overlapping lines.

For this reason, the sales promotion planning process should be viewed as an ongoing one, with decision points that are deadline driven.

Here are the steps that will help get the key facts together and keep one's sights focused:

Analyze the Customer

- This activity should include identifying the customer (consumer, trade, sales force) and how this customer audience is prioritized based on the current situation.
- This is also the point to determine how the buying decisions are made and what the customer needs are, and in what order.

Analyze the Market

- Determine the market potential for the brand (short, mid- and long-term for a sense of direction) and gain an understanding of what is achievable now and later. Being realistic is important.
- Examine the structure of the market and determine what regional differences may exist. Are they exploitable? Should the focus be regional rather than national?
- Explore the breadth and scope of the market in terms of its segmentation and what differences may influence sales promotion objectives and strategies. Are buying patterns universal? Are there any demographic shifts or considerations?

Analyze the Competition

- Identify the key competitors and understand what and why they are doing what they are doing. Look at types of promotion, time frames, and other elements. Now's the time to get the sales force to play supersleuth.
- Assess the strengths and weaknesses of the competition. How does the company's brand measure up to the competition? Be realistic. Better still, be critical.

- From this understanding, planners will then be able to set objectives and strategies that attack the competition as well as understand their cost structure.

Analyze Past Sales Promotion Programs

- Determine the program's strengths and weaknesses. Don't forget, no promotion, no matter how flawless in design, ever meets every single expectation. If a program was 60% successful, it may still be viable.
- Assess the results and determine if the expectations were realistically set in the first place. Here again, give the brand the benefit of the doubt. Even if a promotion was a dismal failure, never say never again.

Examine the Distribution System

- Identify the priorities at the three key levels of consumer, trade, and sales force. Then try hard to meet them.

Determine if Testing Is Necessary

- Talk to the research people. Look at test market viability for now and later. Maybe what is needed is a promotion plan that "holds its own" while the company regroups and tests bigger issues. For example, it may be necessary to support the retail distribution or other trade channels in the interim.

Determine Budget Levels to Achieve Desired Results

- Establish realistic expectations for all three levels. Don't underestimate production and media needs. If these budgets will be small, take another look at the marketing plan.

Determine the Fit with the Overall Marketing Plan

- Above all else, make doubly certain the plan is in sync with the overall direction of the brand. It is a lot easier to harm the brand than help it.

After this information has been prepared, organized, and understood, the sales promotion objectives can then be prepared. The sales promotion objectives also need to be considered in the context of other elements of the marketing communication mix.

SALES PROMOTION AND MARKETING COMMUNICATION

There is a variety of factors which influence the amount of relative spending on consumer promotion. It is important to note that these factors represent a traditional view that sees consumer promotion as an activity that does not build the brand or the consumer franchise. This is simply not true. Much sales consumer promotion activity builds the brand and the consumer franchise. Consumer sales promotion does much more than merely stimulate short-term sales.

It is worthwhile to examine the traditional view briefly. Exhibit 1 shows three categories of factors: consumer factors, brand factors, and category factors. Instances in which consumer promotion spending has been traditionally higher usually have resulted from high price sensitivity or elasticity and low brand loyalty. Promotion spending tends to be lower when there is less price sensitivity and stronger brand loyalty. Consumer promotion is also associated with products that require little information and have low perceived risk. It is interesting to note that this may be the opposite for trade promotion. Products with high risk and information needs generally require considerable trade support.

Brand factors associated with consumer promotion spending include the later stages in the product lifecycle, particularly maturity and decline. Products in the growth stage are less associated with promotion spending. New products, however, require considerable promotion support to get them established. Also, consumer promotion spending is associated with more competitive or lower share brands. Nevertheless, promotion spending is often a good way for a dominant or a high share brand to fend off competitive challenges from smaller brands.

Category factors play a role as well. Seasonal products need to use promotion to regain their position on the store shelf and in the consumer's mind when their selling season returns. Also, a category with high share private label or generic brands may require additional promotion support to maintain its position.

EXHIBIT 1. Traditional Factors Guiding Promotion Spending for a Brand

	Low Promotion	**High Promotion**
Consumer Factors		
Price sensitivity	Low	High
Brand loyalty	High	Low
Purchase planning	High	Low
Information needs	High	Low
Perceived risk	High	low
Brand Factors		
Lifecycle stage	Growth	Maturity
Market position	Dominant	Competitive
Seasonal pattern	Uniform	Seasonal
Category Factors		
Product differentiation	Strong brands	Commodity
Private brands	Limited	Extensive

GETTING STARTED

Now that the planners are armed with the marketing facts, a sense of direction, and a laundry list of everyone's biases, the real fun begins—writing the promotion objectives.

Actually, writing objectives is a discipline that gets easier with practice. And like the proverbial skill of riding a bicycle, there are sure to be a few skinned knees along the way. But once a marketer learns to master the logic of it, it will only enhance the brand's performance, if not the marketer's career.

What Promotion Objectives Are

As we saw earlier, sales promotion objectives are the desired achievements for sales action. For all the drama and mystery of what they mean, they are quite simple. In fact, there are very few things the writer actually needs to remember about them.

Sales promotion objectives are simple, concise, and crystal clear. They are not a mission statement; they do not have subsets, subtexts, or sidebars. They are a bare bones statement of what must be done.

Sales promotion objectives are action oriented. Sales promotional needs demand action. So the objective should be written that way. It should always, *always* lead to results.

Sales promotion objectives operate in a defined time frame, a very short one. Think in terms of weeks, not months. As a quick rule of thumb, a typical promotion takes from two to eight weeks from start-up to wind-down. The timetable behind the objectives should reflect this.

Here are some examples of sales promotion objectives that work:

- Generate a 5% increase in sales during the Jan. 1–Feb. 15 launch.
- Create awareness and trial of the new product.
- Encourage multiple purchases prior to competitive relaunch.
- Increase display and ad features by 10% for July 4 sales blitz.
- Motivate the sales force to attain a 24% sell-in.

Notice that each of these examples is short and precise; they all demand action and include a keen sense of timing and urgency. Plus there is one other unifying element. Every sales promotion objective should ultimately be measurable. If the writers start out focused on accountability, chances are they will end up with a promotion that is accountable for itself.

Tips for Writing Objective Objectives

Finally, here are some well-founded pointers for writing sales promotion objectives that are realistic yet aggressive, accountable yet flexible.

1. **Use 10 words or less.** This exercise will help the writer stay as focused as the objective should be. Plus, the fewer words used, the less chance there will be for miscommunication, misdirection, or loopholes.
2. **To get action, use action verbs.** This may be a good time to dig out that 8th grade grammar book. Words such as *create, attain, increase, motivate,* and *generate* have a sense of direction to them. There is no mistaking their meaning.
3. **Establish a time frame.** Don't let the promotion be accountable for anything that happens before or after it is supposed to take place. And be realistic about how long it can really keep its energy and momentum.
4. **Assign one objective per target segment.** Don't get carried away. A single consumer promotion cannot possibly create awareness, generate trial, increase multiple purchase occasions, and encourage repeat purchase. The more you ask for, the less you'll get. If one main objective is written for the consumer, one for the trade, and one for the sales force, that in itself is a tall order.
5. **Write objectives with specific results in mind.** Each objective should always answer the question: "What should be accomplished as an end result of this promotion?" That is what a promotion objective is all about. It is then up to the promotion strategy to determine how to get it accomplished.

SUGGESTIONS FOR FURTHER READING

Aaker, David A., *Managing Brand Equity,* New York: The Free Press, Macmillan, 1991.

Abraham, Magid M. and Leonard M. Lodish, "Getting The Most Out of Advertising and Promotion," Harvard Business Review, May-June 1990.

Blattberg, Robert C. and Scott A. Neslin, *Sale Promotion: Concepts, Methods, and Strategies,* Englewood Cliffs, NJ: Prentice-Hall, 1990.

Strang, Roger A., "Sales Promotion—Fast Growth, Faulty Management," *Harvard Business Review,* July-August 1976.

Schultz, Don E. and William A. Robinson, *Sales Promotion Essentials,* Lincolnwood, IL; NTC Business Books, 1987.

Tuck, R.T.J. and W.G.B. Harvey, "Do Promotions Undermine the Brand?" ADMAP, January 1972, pp. 29-33.

Quelch, John A., *Sales Promotion Management,* Englewood Cliffs, NJ: Prentice-Hall, 1989.

S. Watson Dunn
Professor Emeritus
University of Missouri-Columbia
Columbia, Missouri

Arnold M. Barban
Chairman and Professor of Advertising
University of Alabama
Tuscaloosa, Alabama

Dean M. Krugman
Professor
University of Georgia
Athens, Georgia

Leonard N. Reid
Department Chair of Advertising and Public Relations
University of Georgia
Athens, Georgia

CHAPTER 61

DEVELOPING ADVERTISING MESSAGE STRATEGY

Advertising creativity, the force that drives message strategy development and execution, is the one aspect of advertising that has defied mathematical treatment. Gordon E. White, a former creative director, calls creativity the *X* factor in the advertising planning equation because, unlike media planning and budgeting decisions, the potential efficacy of various creative approaches cannot be plugged in as the "message" variable of some advertising formula.[1] As experience has taught advertising practitioners, different creative approaches will produce different results even when backed by the same number of advertising dollars in the same media. Yet, though message strategy is indisputably the least scientific aspect of advertising, it is the most important. As so poetically described by creative genius Leo Burnett in his famous speech, "Finally Somebody Has to Get Out an Ad," the life, core, and heart of the advertising business is making ads.[2]

This chapter will provide guidance for working out the message strategy for an advertising campaign. It will show how message strategy is built and the role that such important inputs as creativity, marketing decisions, and message characteristics play in working out that strategy. Message strategy is an extension of the marketing plan and must be coordinated with media and budgeting strategies to provide a blueprint for executing the specifics of an advertising campaign.

WHAT IS MESSAGE STRATEGY?

In theory, creating effective advertising would seem a simple business—getting the right message to the right audience at the right time. In practice, however, the business of advertising is not so simple; other advertisers are trying to reach the same audience.[3] To overcome competing voices as well as the audience's general defensive tendencies, the key to effective advertising—getting people's attention and then motivating them to process the sales message—is the development and execution of the right message strategy. According to John O'Toole, former chairman of one of the world's largest agencies, an advertising campaign cannot succeed with the wrong message strategy.[4]

Message Strategy as Differentiated from Tactics

Message planning involves two interrelated decisions: the determination of message strategy and of message tactics. Message planning has been defined in a variety of ways by advertisers. Some call it copy strategy; others call it creative strategy. However, regardless of what it is called, all agree that message strategy involves the determination of "what the advertising is to say" and that message tactics involve the matter of "how the strategy is executed." As a basic component of campaign planning, message strategy provides a logical progression from marketing to communication objectives to message content to tactics for conveying the advertising message in the form of finished advertisements.

The "what to say" decision involves the formulation of a main message idea that will communicate the benefit or problem-solving capabilities of the advertising object—the product, service, or idea—to the identified target audience. It spells out what advertising is expected to communicate, but it does not specify how the message will be delivered. To one agency creative head it is "a kind of route map laying down how we will get from Point A to Point B—Point A being what our prospects think today, Point B being what we want them to think one, two, three years from now."[5] Put another way, it is the "Big Idea," described in the accompanying Ad Insights, that captures the want-satisfying qualities or benefits of an advertised object, which is translated into attention-getting and memorable ads.

Consider, for example, the message strategy of the recruiting campaign of the U.S. Army.[6] First introduced in 1981, "Be All You Can Be" was chosen as the main theme to communicate the benefits of personal growth and development that could be derived through Army enlistment. Since then only minor changes in some lyrics and subthemes have been necessary, mainly to reflect subtle changes in message targeting. For the first two years of the campaign, the subtheme "Because We Need You in the Army" was paired with the main theme to reflect a "your country needs you" attitude. Two years later, the subtheme was changed to "You Can Do It in the Army," a claim more in line with the "individual development" emphasis of the campaign's main strategy. In 1985, "Find Your Future in the Army" became the subtheme, a theme that reflected individual challenge and career training.

Today, the Army's campaign strategy is still alive and well, using the subtheme "Get an Edge on Life" as an extension of the "Find Your Future" idea. The campaign is testimony to the fact that, once the right message idea is determined, it can be retained and built on for years.

Determining the Message Idea

The most effective message idea is the product of an accumulation of facts—about products, markets, consumers, and competitors. The common denominator of all advertising creative efforts is background information.[7] Writers, artists, and others involved in the creation of advertising need to understand such things as how the consumer sees the product in relation to competitive offerings; what specific attributes, usage situations, or user characteristics are important to the consumer when considering purchase; what competitors are saying about their products in their advertising campaigns; and whether particular product attributes or usage situations have been overlooked by competitive advertising messages.

The necessary information comes from two sources: (1) intuition and acquaintance with the product or service and (2) scientifically collected research data, which is often detailed in the situation analysis and strategies of the marketing plan. Intuition and acquaintance are the accumulation of facts through firsthand experiences with the product and its users or reliance on professional judgment and familiarity. Research data is the accumulation of facts through secondary analyses of published data or through commissioned consumer surveys, in-depth interviews, observations, or *focus groups.* Neither information source can determine the best answer to the message idea question; however, both can provide valuable insight that may lead to the "Big Idea"—that one idea, like "Be All You Can Be," that will guide a campaign for years.

What the advertising planner is searching for is what Kenneth Longman calls the differential-copy advantage—the characteristic or set of characteristics, either real or perceived, that will allow advertising to differentiate the product or service from the competition.[8] A real advantage exists when something is actually different about the product or service, such as superior performance, a special ingredient, or a cost-saving feature. A perceived advantage, on the other hand, exists when the consumer sees a difference, although in actuality the difference is slight or even nonexistent. Both types of advantages are natural outgrowths of the fact that all products and services consist of objective and subjective features. For example, when women buy perfume, they do not buy just a fragrance; they buy psychological and interpersonal benefits. Beer drinkers do not buy simply liquid refreshment; they buy a reward for a hard day's work; they buy a lifestyle. Once found, that differentiation will become the basis for the campaign's message idea.

A differential-copy advantage is based on three differences that exist in all products and services:

1. *Physical differences:* the actual composition of the product or service, such as ingredients, styles, or features.
2. *Functional differences:* the operational consequences of product/service consumption, such as ease of operation or performance.
3. *Characterizational differences:* the psychological consequences of product/service consumption, such as how it makes consumers feel or see themselves in relation to the product/service or in relation to others.

FIGURE 1. Determining a Differential-Copy Advantage: An Analysis of Colombian-Grown Coffee Beans

Product: Colombian-grown coffee beans

Physical Features:

100% Colombian coffee
Full-bodied flavor
Rich aroma

Functional Features:

Fewer poor pots of coffee
Please spouse or guests
Please self
Relaxing and soothing

Characterizational Features:

Coffee-growing tradition
From mountains of Colombia
Early morning enrichment

Source: Kenneth A. Longman, *Advertising* (Orlando, Fla: Harcourt Brace Jovanovich, 1971), 172.

How a differential-copy advantage is determined is shown in Figure 1. Three things that should be noted about this example are true of all approaches to message idea development:

1. All products and services have many physical, functional, and characterizational differences that can be generated; however, not all are unique or relevant to the target audience. For example, although Colombian coffee is rich in aroma, the attribute may not be very important to the coffee buyer. Or another major brand of coffee may have based its advertising campaign on rich aroma for years. As a result, no opportunity exists for message differentiation, unless a "me-too" message strategy is desired.
2. Physical, functional, and characterizational differences are interrelated; the decision to focus on one or any combination must be determined by relevancy and opportunity. For example, drinking pleasure is derived from the knowledge that Colombian coffee, with its full-bodied flavor, is grown and harvested under special and unique mountain conditions.
3. The targeted consumer is the final judge of which physical, functional, or characterizational differences are important; therefore, any differential-copy advantage must be selected based on how the consumer sees the product, not how advertising professionals or clients see the product.

The Copy Platform: The Creative Blueprint

In practice, the differential-copy advantage that is selected is expressed as part of a copy platform. Although creative managers do not necessarily agree on the form of the copy platform, most would agree on at least the following:

1. The copy platform should be consistent with the marketing plan's strategies and objectives.
2. The copy platform should state clearly and specifically the message or creative objectives (advertising communication objectives).
3. The creative objectives should include a statement of which market segments are to be targeted and which product/service/idea attributes are to be communicated.
4. The copy platform should be coordinated with media and budgeting strategies.
5. The copy platform should provide guidelines for creating the ad executions.

An example of one agency's creative work plan is shown in Figure 2. McCann-Erickson, another major advertising agency, refers to its plan format as a creative contract. Regardless of what it is called, a good copy platform should address five specific points, each of which must be consistent with the previously formulated marketing plan:[9]

1. *Creative objectives:* what the message strategy should accomplish. How does the advertiser want targeted consumers to think, feel, or act as the result of exposure to the message?
2. *Target audience:* the individual that the advertising should directly address. Based on market statistics, who is the typical targeted consumer?
3. *Key benefit:* why the consumer should buy or lease the product/service or adopt the advocated idea; that is, the selected differential-copy advantage. What want-satisfying feature differentiates the product from the competition?
4. *Tone:* the manner or direction the message idea should convey. Should the message be strong and forceful or understated and implicit? Should it be humorous or serious?
5. *Message idea statement:* a terse and precise statement of what the advertising should say and how it should be said. In essence, the message idea statement brings together the other four points of the platform.

The objectives specify exactly how the key benefit—the selected differential-copy advantage—is related to the desired responses from the target audience. The tone gives direction to the differential-copy advantage, and the message idea statement provides a summary position.

FIGURE 2. Example of a Creative Work Plan

CLIENT: STAR APPLIANCE COMPANY

PRODUCT/SERVICE: Star Line of Cordless, Rechargeable Aplicances

PLANNING PERIOD: Fall 1989 DATE: April 18, 1989

I. KEY FACT *(The one most important fact upon which the creative strategy will be based.)*
Research indicates a strong consumer interest in cordless, rechargeable appliances; Star line will include: handmixer, knife, and can opener.

II. CONSUMER PROBLEM THE PRODUCT SOLVES *(Problem consumer is having in buying or using the product or service. It's a problem the client's product solves and advertising can address.)*
Consumers believe that cordless products do not provide the power that is required to complete their intended tasks.

III. COMMUNICATION OBJECTIVE *(What the advertising needs to do to solve the consumer problem and the response desired from the consumer.)*
—Introduce Star's New Freedom line of cordless appliances
—Convince consumers that Star's products offer superior benefits

IV. CREATIVE STRATEGY DEVELOPMENT

A. Target Group Definition *(The characterization of the target consumer.)*

1. Demographics: —women ages 25–54
—college educated
—HH income $20M+

2. Psychographics: —convenience oriented
—organized
—likely to try new products

B. Principal Competition *(The market segment which the product will be positioned against.)*
—Black & Decker (knife and mixer)
—Norelco (can opener)
—Hamilton Beach (knife)

C. Consumer Benefit *(What the product promises to do for the consumer that* ***solves*** *the consumer's problem.)*
An entire line of new cordless appliances that always provides the power you need and the freedom you want

D. Reason Why *(The key ideal(s) or fact(s) that justify the consumer benefit allowing the advertising to make the product's claim.)*
—Products are powerful
—Exclusive interconnect system
—Products are stored in recharging stands
—Freedom from cord restriction

E. Tone of Advertising *(The feeling the advertising should convey.)*
Introductory–implied superiority

V. Requirements *(All elements that are required to appear in the advertising.)*
—Strong Star brand indentification
—Legal requirements: A. ® Star TM Interconnect System disclaimer
B. ©1985 Star Appliance Company
C. Star Logo

As noted by Michael Ray, a tone statement should deal with three broad questions:[10] (1) whether and to what extent advertising should be emotional as opposed to rational; (2) whether and how competition should be considered in advertising; and (3) how strong the advertising message should be. The question of emotional tone involves deciding where to situate the advertising on the factual–feeling continuum. In today's terminology, the continuum is anchored by two forms of advertising:[11]

- *Informational advertising,* which provides consumers with factual, relevant information in a clear and logical manner so that they have greater confidence in their ability to make reasoned purchase decisions.
- *Transformational advertising,* which associates the experience of consuming the product or service with psychological characteristics so that emotions and feelings are experienced.

Whether factual- or feeling-based, tone can be positively or negatively directed. One of the most recognized forms of feeling-based tone is the use of fear appeals in advertising.

Competitive tone deals with the decision of how to treat the competitive environment encountered by the advertising campaign. One option, of course, is to employ a positive, noncompetitive tone in advertising. The use of this option ignores the potential countervailing effects of competitive claims. If the decision is made to address the competitive environment, the advertising strategist has two viable options:[12]

1. Position the product or service in relation to competitive offerings by implicitly or explicitly mentioning competitors.
2. Use a refutational approach to attack consumer-held beliefs that are counter to the established message strategy or competitive counter-claims.

The question of message strength involves deciding how strongly the message should be communicated. Advertisements can be designed with great intensity, moderate intensity, or little intensity. In advertising terms, they can be hard sell, soft sell, or somewhere in between the two extremes. The optimal degree of message strength stimulates interest, but not incredulity.[13]

The message idea, often expressed as a theme, serves as a written guide for the creation of ads and as a gauge for measuring whether the creative output of the campaign is on strategy. As a rule, numerous theme alternatives should be generated and tested among representatives of the target audience in focus group sessions or in-depth interviews to determine the best campaign theme.[14] As with the search for the differential-copy advantage, the generation and selection of a theme must be based on the consumers' perspective—what the theme communicates to them. Later in the chapter we will return to the role of message strategy in evaluating effective advertising.

Message Tactics: Elements of Ad Execution

Once the message idea has been selected, tactical decisions must be made about the verbal and visual character of ad executions. An advertisement is composed of verbal and visual signs—words, pictures, and sounds—that are arranged by copywriters, composers, directors, and artists. As shown in Figure 3, tactics form the creative mix, which flows from the campaign's objectives.

Which is more important—message strategy or tactics? Some experts have argued that strategy is more important on the grounds that strategy directs executions. In John O'Toole's view, it is possible to get by with mediocre executions if the strategy is on target, but not possible to get by with brilliant executions if the strategy is wrong.[15] On the other hand, brilliant executions could turn a mediocre strategy into a winner; or a brilliant strategy could be diminished by weak executions. All things considered, the answer to the question is simple: they both are important. Like all aspects of advertising planning, both strategy and tactics must work together. They must build on the marketing and advertising strategies and complement each other.

TYPES OF MESSAGE STRATEGIES

A number of classification schemes have been developed as a means of identifying various types of message strategies. One of the most useful, developed by Charles Frazer, is shown in Figure 4. As in other classification schemes, Frazer's seven alternatives are neither exhaustive nor mutually exclusive. However, the scheme does provide a useful way of looking at and evaluating the general nature and character of message approaches.

CLASSIC CREATIVE APPROACHES

Over the past half century, advertising has been influenced by six distinct and enduring approaches to message strategy: Leo Burnett's inherent drama, Rosser Reeves's unique selling proposition, David Ogilvy's brand image, William Bernbach's execution emphasis, Jack Trout and Al Reis's positioning, and Richard Vaughn's message matrix.[16] Five of the six approaches are dealt with in Frazer's classification scheme. The exception is Bernbach's execution emphasis. All of the others focus on the "what is said" component of message strategy.

Burnett's Inherent Drama

Leo Burnett, founder of the Leo Burnett agency and father of the Chicago School of Advertising, believed that the secret to effective advertising was finding the inherent drama in a product. To him, this

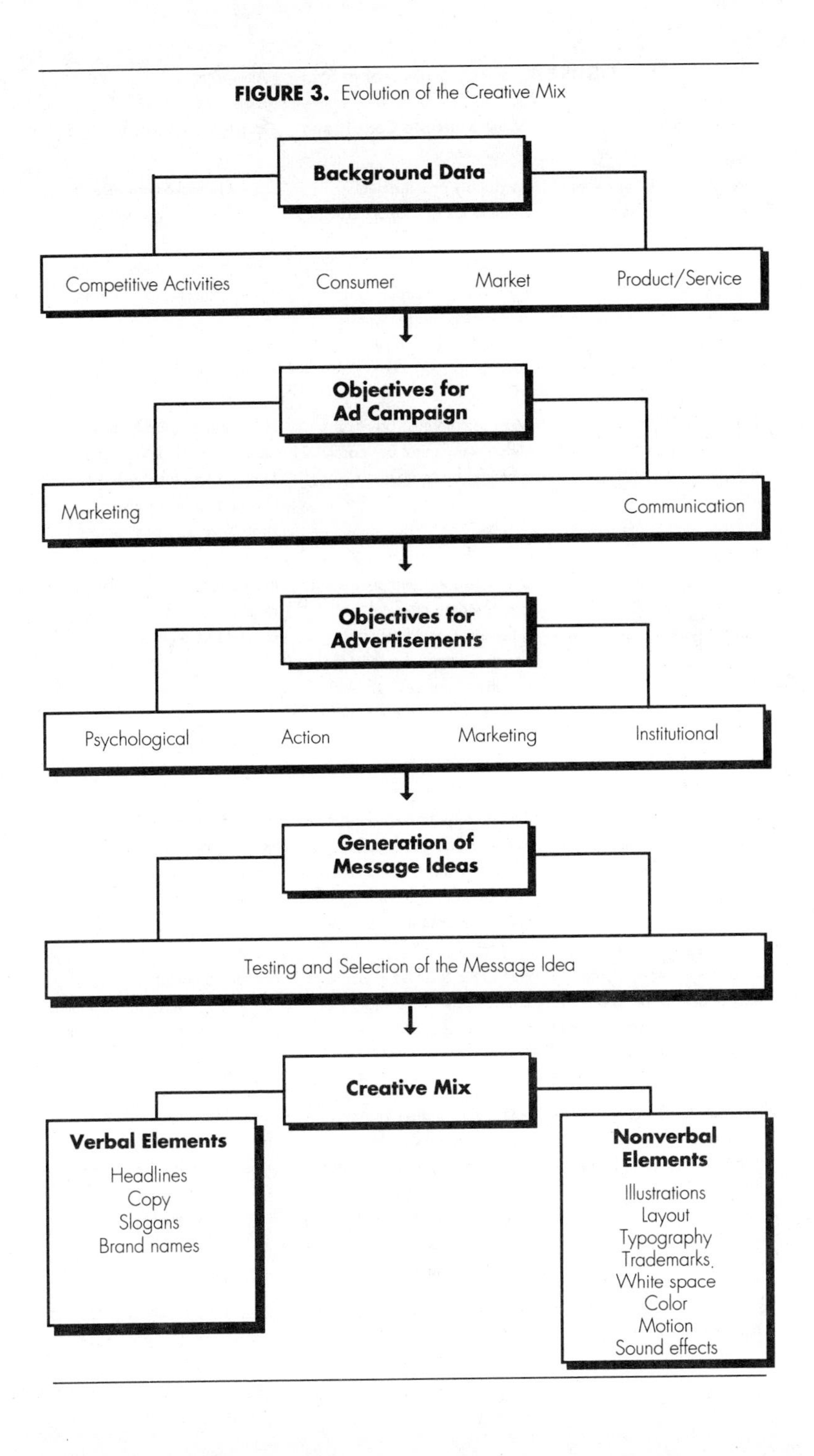
Background Data
Competitive Activities
Consumer
Market
Product/Service
Objectives for Ad Campaign
Marketing
Communication
Objectives for Advertisements
Psychological
Action
Marketing
Institutional
Generation of Message Ideas
Testing and Selection of the Message Idea
Creative Mix
Verbal Elements
Headlines
Copy
Slogans
Brand names
Nonverbal Elements
Illustrations
Layout
Typography
Trademarks
White space
Color
Motion
Sound effects

FIGURE 3. Evolution of the Creative Mix

FIGURE 4. Summary of Creative Strategy Alternatives

Alternative	Most Suitable Conditions	Competitive Implications
Generic Straight product or benefit claim with no assertion of superiority	Monopoly or extreme dominance of product category	Serves to make advertiser's brand synonymous with product category; may be combated through higher order strategies
Preemptive Generic claim with assertion of superiority	Most useful in growing or awakening market where competitive advertising is generic or nonexistent	May be successful in convincing consumer of superiority of advertiser's product; limits response options for competitors
Unique Selling Proposition Superiority claims based on unique physical feature or benefit	Most useful when point of difference cannot be readily matched by competitors	Advertiser obtains strong persuasive advantage; may force competitors to imitate or choose more aggressive strategy (e.g., "positioning")
Brand Image Claims based on psychological differentiation, usually symbolic association	Best suited to homogeneous goods where physical differences are difficult to develop or may be quickly matched; requires sufficient understanding of consumers to develop meaningful symbols/associations	Most often involves prestige claims, which rarely challenge competitors directly
Positioning Attempts to build or occupy mental niche in relation to identified competitor	Best strategy for attacking a market leader; requires relatively long-term commitment to aggressive advertising efforts and understanding consumers	Direct comparison severely limits options for named competitor; counterattacks seem to offer little chance of success
Resonance Attempts to evoke stored experiences of prospects to endow product with relevant meaning or significance	Best suited to socially visible goods; requires considerable consumer understanding to design message patterns	Few direct limitations on competitor's options; most likely competitive response is imitation
Affective Attempts to provoke involvement or emotion through ambiguity, humor or the like, without strong selling emphasis	Best suited to discretionary items; effective use depends upon conventional approach by competitors to maximize difference; greatest commitment is to aesthetics or intuition rather than research	Competitors may imitate to undermine strategy of difference or pursue other alternatives

Source: Charles F. Frazer, "Creative Strategy: A Management Perspective," *Journal of Advertising* 12 (1983): 40. Reprinted with permission of CtC Press, 1994.

meant the identification of the "reason" why a manufacturer made a product and why the consumer purchased it. Once it was found, the job of advertising was to take the Inherent Drama—the product–consumer interaction—and produce arresting, warm, and believable ads without relying on gimmicks, tricks, or borrowed interest.[17]

One of the best examples of the inherent-drama approach is Burnett's work for Green Giant peas. To communicate the special care taken in the company's harvesting and packaging process and the consumer's desire for freshness, Green Giant peas were advertised as "harvested in the moonlight." A more contemporary example is Starkist's "Charlie, the tuna," who is not good enough for Starkist, but who nevertheless keeps trying to get caught. Charlie knows, as the advertising campaign has driven home for decades, that Starkist uses only the "best" tuna in its product.

Reeves's Unique Selling Proposition

Neil Borden emphasized the importance of looking for the differentiating qualities of product to determine how advertiseable it is. The more product differentiation possible, the more advertiseable the product will be. Rosser Reeves, then of the Ted Bates agency, put Borden's notion in action as the "unique selling proposition." To his way of thinking, a successful advertising campaign had to be built on the product's USP, which he described as having three parts:

1. Each advertisement must make a proposition to the consumer. Not just words, not just product puffery, not just show-window advertising. Each advertisement must say to each reader, "Buy this product and you will get this benefit."
2. The proposition must be one that the competition either cannot, or does not, offer. It must be unique either in the brand or the claim.
3. The proposition must be strong enough to move the mass millions, i.e., pull new customers to your product.[18]

Once it was identified, Rosser believed that the USP should be hammered away at repeatedly in advertisements and retained indefinitely in a campaign. One of Reeves' most famous USP's was M&M candies' claim, "melts in your mouth, not in your hands."

Ogilvy's Brand Image

Product personality is the total impression people have of a product, and it is commonly called an image. It is what comes to mind upon hearing the names IBM, Sears, Delta Airlines, Transamerica Corporation, or UPS. David Ogilvy, one of the most respected creative people in the history of advertising and cofounder of the agency Ogilvy & Mather, believed that a brand image could be developed or cultivated through advertising for every product. He based his approach on the belief that images are not inherent in products, but are instead qualities that the consumer associates with them. To Ogilvy, people buy physical and psychological benefits, not products, and advertising should therefore be built on the long-term investment in the development and retention of a brand image, even if the approach meant short-run sacrifices.

> *Every advertisement should be thought of as a contribution to the complex symbol which is brand image. The manufacturer who dedicates his advertising to building the most sharply defined personality for his brand will get the largest share of the market at the highest profit. By the same token, the manufacturers who will find themselves up the creek are those shortsighted opportunists who siphon off their advertising funds for promotions.*[19]

Over the years, brands such as Betty Crocker foods, Marlboro cigarettes, and Budweiser beer have conjured up strong images in the public mind as their advertising has built on unique and well-defined brand images. Marlboro was, at one time, a filter-tipped cigarette with definite feminine appeal. Then a new campaign set out to build an image of Marlboro as the cigarette for outdoor men "who came up the hard way." Illustrations and other visuals showed only rugged-looking men, cowboys, tattooed laborers, and in print or on television each told something of his outdoors life and explained why he chose Marlboro. Although the Marlboro man appears only in print in America today, he continues to ride the range in some foreign countries where television commercials for cigarettes are not banned.

Bernbach's Execution Emphasis

In the early 1950s, William Bernbach began creating advertising based on an approach quite different from the approaches of Burnett, Reeves, and Ogilvy. Bernbach, one of the founders of the then Doyle Dane Bernbach agency, believed that execution—the "how you say it" component of message strategy—could become content in and of itself. To him, execution style was the dominant feature of advertising, and he believed that the secret to effective advertising was taking a problem and turning it into an advantage with dramatic visuals and honesty. Sound execution had to be based on four points:

1. The audience must be respected; ads should not talk down to the people they are trying to reach.
2. The approach must be clean and direct.
3. Advertisements must stand out from others; they must have their own character and style.
4. Humor should not be ignored; it can be effective in gaining attention and providing a listening, viewing, or reading award.[20]

One of the best-known examples of Bernbach's Execution approach is his early work for Volkswagen. When first introduced in the United States, the VW had four negative features: it was small, ugly, rear-engine powered, and foreign produced. Bernbach took these negatives and created humorous and distinctive advertisements that are regarded as some of advertising's all-time best creative output.

Trout and Reis's Positioning

In 1972, Jack Trout and Al Reis, founders of the Trout & Reis agency, introduced the Positioning approach to message strategy. They believed that advertising should be created to gain a perceptual foothold in the consumer's mind by establishing something memorable and distinctive about the product relative to competition. To support their approach, they offered Crest's ADA Seal of Approval, Avis' "We're No. 2, but Trying Harder" theme, and Michelob's "first American-made premium beer" claim as evidence of effective perceptual positioning through advertising. Like the approaches of Burnett, Reeves, and Ogilvy, the positioning approach is based on "what should be said," and once identified and communicated should be recalled every time the consumer needs the kind of benefit or problem solution the product offers.

The problem is to decide which positioning strategy is most likely to be successful. David Aaker and John Myers suggest the following as possible approaches to the positioning strategy:

1. Product characteristics or customer benefits (Miller beer's cold-filtering process)
2. Price–quality relationship (Sears as a family-oriented, middle-class store offering top value)
3. Use or application (IBM PCs for desk-top publishing and graphics)
4. Product user (positioning Busch as the heavy-drinking, working man's beer)
5. Product category (positioning domestic wines as an alternative to foreign wines)
6. Cultural symbols (American cowboy as the symbol of Marlboro cigarettes)
7. Competitor (Avis positioning itself as the number-two rental car company)[21]

The positioning approach is sometimes confused with the brand-image approach but is actually a broader concept. Positioning involves "identifying competition, relevant attributes, competitor position, and market segments."[22] In effect, it is the logical outgrowth of image analysis in that it involves applying what is known about the brand's image, the competition, the audience the advertiser is to reach, and how members of the audience are motivated to respond. As a consequence, it is helpful to analyze brand image before it is converted to a

FIGURE 5. Vaughn's Message Matrix: A Modern Creative Approach

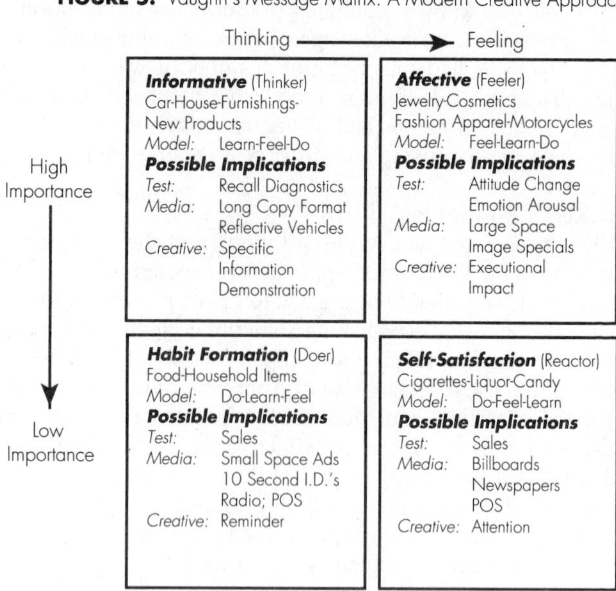

Thinking
Feeling
High Importance
Low Importance
Informative (Thinker)
Car-House-Furnishings-New Products
Model: Learn-Feel-Do
Possible Implications
Test: Recall Diagnostics
Media: Long Copy Format
Reflective Vehicles
Creative: Specific Information
Demonstration
Affective (Feeler)
Jewelry-Cosmetics
Fashion Apparel-Motorcycles
Model: Feel-Learn-Do
Possible Implications
Test: Attitude Change
Emotion Arousal
Media: Large Space
Image Specials
Creative: Executional Impact
Habit Formation (Doer)
Food-Household Items
Model: Do-Learn-Feel
Possible Implications
Test: Sales
Media: Small Space Ads
10 Second I.D.'s
Radio; POS
Creative: Reminder
Self-Satisfaction (Reactor)
Cigarettes-Liquor-Candy
Model: Do-Feel-Learn
Possible Implications
Test: Sales
Media: Billboards
Newspapers
POS
Creative: Attention

Source: How Advertising Works: An FCB Strategy Planning Model, Foote, Cone & Belding Communications, Inc., 1979.

positioning strategy, which states how the product position is to be communicated.

Vaughn's Message Matrix

In 1979, Richard Vaughn outlined Foote, Cone & Belding's approach to the planning, creation, and execution of advertisements.[23] The approach, called the FCB Strategy Planning Model, has been refined over the years and is now utilized by many agencies and advertisers, although it is often called something else. The model consists of a "message matrix" anchored on two continuums: thinking/feeling and high/low importance (involvement). We refer to the model as the message-matrix approach because it forces the planner to match product characteristics with consumer styles when searching for the "Big Idea"—the differential-copy advantage.

The matrix, with its four planning quadrants, is depicted in Figure 5. Each quadrant relates the type of product to consumer involvement; suggests how advertising should be processed; and offers creative, media, and testing implications. According to Vaughn, the purpose of the approach is to identify the information, emotion, or action leverage for a particular product; build the appropriate model for the advertising situation; and then execute it.[24]

CREATIVE OBJECTIVES

Without knowing the objectives of an advertisement, it is impossible for copywriters and artists to produce a successful advertisement or to judge how good it is on the criterion of communication effectiveness. Creative expert David Deutsch notes that the most valuable contribution one can make to enhance creativity is to succinctly define what the ad is supposed to communicate to the target audience.[25] (Kenneth Roman, whose somewhat different approach to creativity is presented in the Ad Insights, believes that outstanding advertising is the product of the right to be wrong.)

Objectives provide planning guidance and a means of evaluation. When restated in the copy platform, advertising objectives serve a guidance purpose: They allow creative people to see the response an advertisement is supposed to evoke and to design content and format to best bring about the desired response.

In this section, we will visit advertising objectives once again to show how communication response is related to message strategy. Creative objectives are discussed on three dimensions: long-range versus short-range, hierarchical character, and general versus specific communication response.

Long-Range versus Short-Range Objectives

When planners emphasize communication, their focus is primarily on short-range objectives. But when sales are emphasized, planners are adopting a long-term outlook, because they realize that it takes time for advertising to affect sales even though it can produce communication effects in the short term.

Agency executive William Wells urges advertising practitioners to be more sensitive to the differences between communication and marketing objectives.[26] He believes overemphasis on marketing objectives causes creative people to sacrifice "creative sensitivity" in their haste to cram as many claims as possible into an advertisement, without proper regard for the ad's communicative role in the larger marketing plan. To Wells, the trick is to decide in the short term how advertising can contribute to long-term marketing success.

Hierarchy of Creative Objectives

Michael Ray maintains that advertising creatives use a hierarchy of objectives, however inadvertent that use may be.[27] He analyzed the philosophies and style of Rosser Reeves, Leo Burnett, David Ogilvy, and William Bernbach. Ray discovered that Reeves worked predominantly in the low-involvement hierarchy of objectives with products in the mature stage of the life cycle. Ogilvy dealt more with the learning hierarchy in his early work with products such as Rolls-Royce and Hathaway shirts, but later in the low-involvement hierarchy as he moved more to mass-consumption products. Like Ogilvy, Burnett favored the learning hierarchy, trying to get across the naturally involving nature of products, which he called inherent drama. Bernbach, in contrast to the others, had no implicit allegiance to any hierarchy; instead, he relied on tactics and executional devices such as humor and format to communicate the virtues of products. The hierarchical nature of objectives are built into Vaughn's message-matrix approach and guide all creative thinking at Foote, Cone & Belding. Based on his analysis, Ray notes that objectives must be response-oriented and that message content and tactics must be adapted to each advertising situation using research findings as a guide.

General versus Specific Objectives

To say that we want to create awareness, increase comprehension, build conviction, or move people to action is not enough. Sound advertising objectives must specify the exact nature of the desired responses and in a manner that they can be measured. They must also, as we have previously discussed, be ordered on the basis of how we think advertising-presented information will be processed: from comprehension to action to conviction as suggested by the "learn-do-feel" model or from comprehension to conviction to action as suggested by the "learn-feel-do" model.

Awareness. A fundamental objective of most advertisements is to create immediate awareness of a theme or a brand name. But planners must decide on the awareness they hope to achieve and with what target audience. They must specify what they want the audience to be aware of, and to what extent they will appeal to the audience's predisposition to attend encountered advertising.

Often consumers select stimuli in one quick glance or after hearing a few syllables. In that instant, an advertisement either creates awareness or loses the prospect. In less time than it takes to turn a page or flip a dial, an advertisement must engage the prospect's interest. The power to create awareness is the power to distract, and then arrest, an audience.

How, then, can we determine whether an advertisement will create awareness or be ignored? We know from communication research that people are stopped by a message either because they see in it some promise or reward or because it is easier to notice than to ignore (the principle of least effort). Awareness created by advertising comes from a sound message idea dramatically presented and from the right media environment.

We know that awareness is a relative quality. Most advertisements achieve some level of awareness with some people. Others attract mass attention. The question is not, Will this advertisement create awareness? It is, Will the advertisement create all the awareness about the theme, brand name, or product feature that it should? The question is not presence, but power; not general awareness, but specific awareness.

Awareness is also influenced by the inherent interest of products. Some products are simply more interesting than others. For example, a BMW is more appealing to most people than a Pontiac LeMans; and if both are advertised in the same publication, chances are that the BMW ad will attract more attention than the LeMans ad, all things being equal. A major function of message strategy is to make sure that the other things are *not* equal. It is the job of strategists, copywriters, and artists to create attention-grabbing advertising that makes a product more interesting.

Comprehension. The process of learning from an ad is complex. What elements must the creative person include to make comprehension easy and thorough? To a considerable extent, the key is knowing how much information the audience has and is likely to seek. Research has shown that people look for market information, but that they do not usually work too hard to find it. The decision facing creatives is to identify what the advertiser specifically wants the audience to comprehend and then to decide how to best present the information—in a highly structured executional format or in a loosely structured format.

A highly structured format takes the audience by the hand and leads them through the ad in an effort to reduce subjective interpretation and miscomprehension. A loosely structured format allows for some desired level of audience interpretation, so that the audience projects their experiences and knowledge when processing the ad. Miscomprehension is a real problem for advertisers, and ads must be created and designed to enhance comprehension in the direction and manner stated in the advertising plan.

Conviction. Most creative people would like to create in an audience a favorable disposition (emotional or rational) toward the purchase of the advertised product or brand. However, there is no unanimity on how to achieve it, other than to say that it is difficult to do through advertising alone. Advertising can create awareness and convey information; but conviction is generally built from experience, not advertising. What advertising usually does is reinforce conviction, which is acquired more readily through experience or from information obtained from more objective and personal information sources. As a consequence, the question facing advertising creatives is, Will the specific content and format elements contribute to creation or maintenance of conviction?

Action. In judging an advertisement for impulsion to act, the key question is, Will this advertisement move people we are trying to reach to behave in the desired manner? Advertising is only one of the host of marketing and nonmarketing factors that influence sales, and it is much more important in some marketing mixes than in others. Its impelling action must therefore be coordinated with other marketing and communication elements. There must be some reason to believe that advertising will contribute, either directly or indirectly, to consumer action; otherwise, the money spent for advertising should be allocated to another element of the promotion mix.

Consumer motivation is a complex and sometimes perverse process. Consumers sometimes behave on impulse; at other times, they behave on reason. Sometimes they know why they behaved in a certain way; at other times, they cannot articulate a reason. However, in most situations, the impulsion to act comes from one basic force: a conviction that an advertised product or brand will satisfy one or more of their basic needs or wants.

In product trial situations, content and format must be designed to get people to take some initial action; for example, to get them to pick up a brand of beer because it has that "original draft taste." In commitment situations, on the other hand, message strategy and tactics must work to reinforce or legitimize how consumers already see products and themselves.

JUDGING MESSAGE IDEAS AND EXECUTIONS

Not all individuals are blessed with the ability to look at message ideas and executions and know that they are winners. Some have the ability by instinct. Others have to develop it. Fortunately, for those without instinctive ability, rules can be applied in judging advertising creativity. Message ideas can be judged on seven criteria:

1. *Strategy fit.* Is the idea consistent with the already established marketing and advertising strategies? Can the idea be established with the allocated number of media dollars? Will it cause consumers to act in the desired manner? Does it fit the company's image?
2. *Target segment fit.* Is the idea aimed at the appropriate segment? Is it consistent with the problems and language of the target audience? Does it speak to the buyer that the advertiser wants to reach?
3. *Total promotion mix fit.* Is the idea coordinated with the message of other promotion elements? Is the idea conveying "exclusivity" while sales promotion is communicating "cheap"?
4. *Leverage.* Will the idea stand out under competitive media conditions? Does it have the power to grab the attention of the target segment?
5. *Specificity.* Is the idea to the point? Or is it too generic?
6. *Resistance to counterattack.* Is the idea vulnerable to competitive claims?
7. *Durability.* Does the idea have legs? How long will it last before it wears out?[28]

Ad executions can be evaluated on four dimensions:

1. *Strategy adherence.* Make sure the ads adhere to the stated message idea.
2. *Single-mindedness.* Make sure the ads convey the main benefit, attribute, function, or character of the product in a succinct and simplistic manner.
3. *Message dominance.* Make sure the ad tactics do not overpower the product message.
4. *Image consistency.* Make sure the ads do not change the product's image, unless image change is the strategic objective.[29]

Strict adherence to these rules is not a guarantee of creative success. The perfect message idea or the unique ad execution comes with ability and experience. A checklist for identifying the creative thinker is provided in the Ad Insights.

CREATIVITY AND MESSAGE STRATEGY

No other aspect of advertising is quite so surrounded by myths as the subject of creativity. Some contend that highly creative advertisements result from pure inspiration. Others contend that creativity requires a certain standardized way of thinking. And still others contend that the secret ingredient is hard work, an open mind, and ungovernable curiosity.[30]

All of these views, as well as others, certainly contain some truth. But what does the research tell us? Five basic propositions can be gleaned from the research on creativity.

An organized approach helps but does not ensure creative success. For example, many have praised the idea-generating approach of James Webb Young, a pioneer in creative thinking. Leo Burnett thought it the finest spur to creativity, and David Ogilvy identified Young as one of the five giants in the history of advertising copywriting. The organized approach is still regularly used and has influenced thousands of working ad people.[31]

The Young model has five distinct states:

- *Immersion:* the collection and analysis of information pertinent to the communication problem
- *Digestion:* the "turning over in the mind" of bits of information
- *Incubation:* the placing of the problem on "conscious hold" to let the subconscious work
- *Illumination:* the point when the light goes on, with creative ideas surfacing as the result of the first three stages
- *Verification:* "the cold grey dawn of the morning after," when doubt creeps in

As shown in Figure 6, Young's approach is an integral part of the way creativity is conceptualized by advertising scholars and is grounded in the notion that research is an important antecedent to creativity.

FIGURE 6. Young's Technique for Producing Ideas

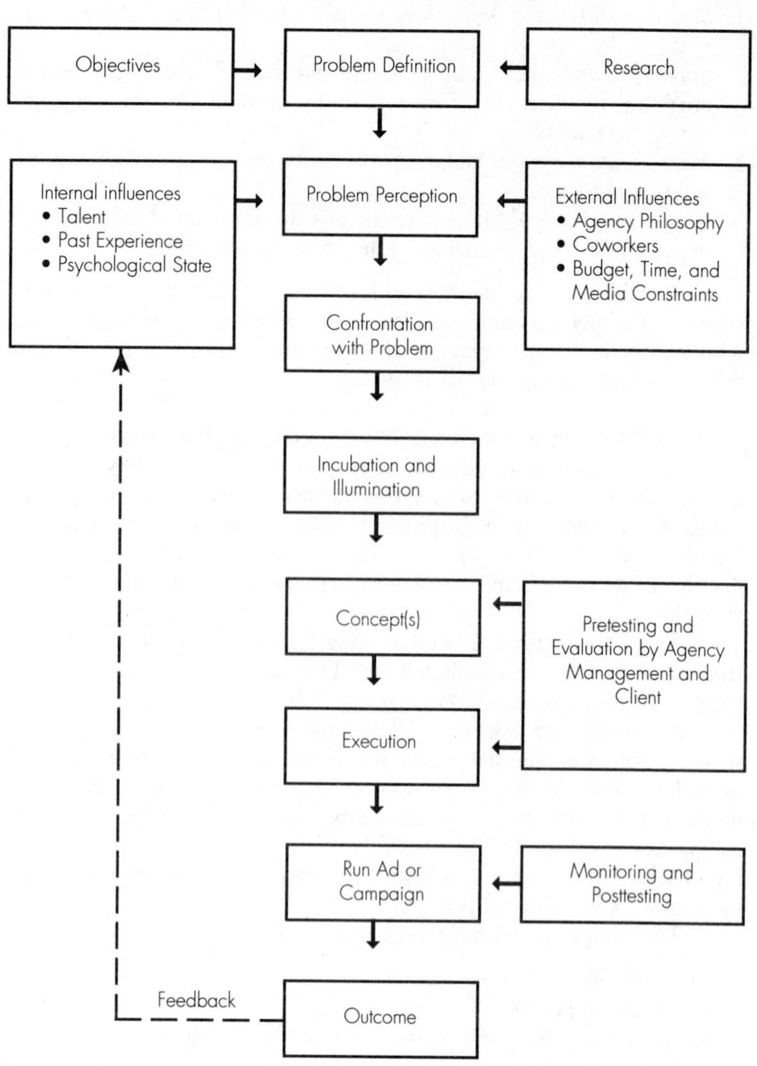

The brainstorming technique was developed by another famous advertising agency executive, Alex Osborn. The key to his approach is the generation of ideas by a group and deferred judgment of the generated ideas—the separation of idea generation and idea evaluation. Some studies have validated the brainstorming approach; others have raised doubts.

Some types of individuals are more likely to be creative than others. Successful creative types are significantly more open to experience, more flexible, more unconventional, more playful, more aggressive, more independent, more inner-directed, and rank higher on self-image, sense of humor, risk taking, and curiosity than less creative individuals. No direct relationship, however, has been found between intelligence and ideation, or creativity.

Creative people produce better ideas when they are in a structured group than when they participate voluntarily in unstructured groups. Groups of up to 12 members help to stimulate creativity. Individuals in group situations seem to be more fluent, more flexible, and more original than when they are in individual situations. To a certain extent, this explains why most large agencies use creative planning or creative review boards to judge both components of message strategy: "what is said" and "how it is said."

Training tends to increase the production and quality of ideas. In spite of the widely held belief that creativity cannot be taught, some evidence suggests that training definitely helps. Studies indicate that people in training programs significantly differ from comparable individuals in their ability to produce and evaluate ideas.

The desire to create is more important than the environment. Some work best under pressure; some create their own pressure. But all good creative people have an inner compulsion to create. As William Marsteller put it in his observations about the great creative people in advertising:

> *They did not need a certain kind of office, certain time of day, phase of moon, soft music, sharp pencils, three martinis or light covering of dandruff in order to be inventive. Their fame is rooted in their ability to be fresh and interesting and relevant and original over a long period of time for a wide variety of purposes.*[32]

IDENTIFYING SYMBOLS

Trademarks, brand names, trade names, and slogans are symbols that, over time, come to stand for a product, organization, or concept. Once created and accepted, they often become the one consistent and unifying feature of all forms of marketing communication, including advertising. Because of their enduring nature, here we will examine the communicative functions of the four identifying symbols and the principles involved in integrating them in message strategy.

Trademarks, Brand Names, and Trade Names

As defined by the Lanham Trade-Mark Act (1946), which regulates registration of identifying marks, a trademark is "any word, name, symbol, device or combination thereof adopted and used by a manufacturer or merchant to identify the origin of a product and distinguish it from products manufactured or sold by others." The mark need not be physically affixed to the product. The Lanham act also covers service marks (used to distinguish services rather than products), certification marks (used by persons other than the owner to certify geographical origin, grade, or quality), and collective marks (used to indicate membership in some organization) as well as product marks.

A trademark is a broader term than brand name, store name, or trade name because it is protected by law and subsumes these other related terms under its legal umbrella. Its basic intent is to protect owners from the unlawful use of their property by others and to protect the public from being deceived.

A registered trademark is the name by which the manufacturer has branded a product to distinguish it from competitors' products. In marketing terms, it is called a brand name. The brand name is often paired with a graphic or pictorial design, which is called a *logotype,* or logo.

The term *trademark* should not be confused with the term *trade name.* A trade name is the name under which a company does business. For example, Nestlé is the trade name of an international company that markets tea under the brand name of "Nestea." Winn-Dixie is the trade name (store name) of a retailer that markets food products under its store brand, Thrifty Maid.

Trademarks, brand names, and trade names may come from many sources. Generally speaking, they are likely to come from one or some combination of the following, although, as will be pointed out later, some of the sources should be avoided.

Source	Examples
Dictionary Word	United Airlines, Dial soap, Crest toothpaste, Sure anti-perspirant.
Coined Word	Exxon gasoline, Amtrak rail service, Gleem toothpaste, Ultima II cosmetics, Xerox information services.
Personal Name	Ford automobiles, Calvin Klein clothing, Campbell's soup, Heinz foods.
Geographical Name	USAir, Pittsburgh paint, Altanta diaries, California Cooler.
Foreign Word	Ciara perfume, Monte Carlo automobile, Popov vodka.
Initial and Numbers	IBM computers, 3M tape, MGA electronics, A-1 steak sauce.

Identifying symbols perform four important communication functions:

1. Buyers of most mass-produced merchandise have little or no direct contact with manufacturers or sellers of products and look for some sign indicating reliability and quality. Trademarks, brand names, and trade names signify these two features.
2. Many products have qualities that are hidden by packaging or are too complex to judge by appearance. Trademarks, brand names, and trade names identify products that may be trusted.
3. Many products are sold by self-service retailers. Trademarks, brand names, and trade names often presell products before purchasers go into the store.
4. Mass communication makes it possible for manufacturers and sellers to capitalize on identifying marks. Trademarks, brand names, and trade names are used inexpensively in advertising and other forms of promotion to build and maintain name recognition and to unify marketing communication messages.

Licensed Names

A special kind of identifying symbol is the licensed name. In recent years, there has been an increase in the use of "rented" names in advertising and other forms of promotion—NFL football teams, Disney characters, and movie characters (E.T., Roger Rabbit), to name a few. Advertisers who use licensed names capitalize, of course, on the wide acceptance and popularity of that name, but they must pay a fee for using the name and must conform to certain licensing standards.

Trade Characters

Another visual identifying symbol often associated with advertising is the trade character. The trade character can be registered as a trademark and is often an animal, cartoon character, distinctive personality, or inanimate object. Once adopted, a trade character can build product, company, or brand recognition, sometimes even after the particular trade character has been abandoned. (Remember the Campbell's twins or Speedy Alka-Seltzer?) Examples of popular and enduring trade characters are the Prudential Rock, Exxon's Tiger, McDonald's Ronald McDonald, Budweiser's Clydesdales, and Juan Valdez.

Slogans

Slogans are repeated creations of advertising people that are utilized to establish or perpetuate some basic idea or theme over a long period of time. Like trademarks, they serve to identify advertisements with products, manufacturers, or sellers. To be effective, slogans must be consistent with the purpose of campaigns and must be changed or

FIGURE 7. Some Widely Used Slogans

Suggestion: Cover the right-hand column and see how many slogans you can name without peeking.

Brand or Company	Slogan
Hallmark	When you care enough to send the very best.
Delta Air Lines	We love to fly and it shows.
Maxwell House Coffee	Good to the last drop.
American Express card	Don't leave home without it.
Hyundai	Cars that make sense.
Advil	Advanced medicine for pain.
American Airlines	Something special in the air.
Volvo	A car you can believe in.
DuPont	Better things for better living.
McDonald's	Good time. Great taste.
BMW	The ultimate driving machine.
Allstate Insurance	You're in good hands.
Bud Light	Everything else is just a light.
Northwestern Mutual	The quiet company.
Sure deodorant	Anything less would be uncivilized.
ESPN	The total sports network.
Toyota	Who could ask for anything more.
JCPenney	You are looking smarter than ever.
Lee jeans	The brand that fits.
Texaco gasoline	Star of the American road.

modified when campaigns drastically change their message strategies. Some widely used slogans are listed in Figure 7.

In structure, slogans are similar to headlines. Many slogans, in fact, evolve from headlines that prove successful; but the slogan's purposes are generally different from those of the headline. The two most common purposes of slogans are: (1) to provide continuity for a campaign, perhaps for a year, perhaps for many years, and (2) to crystallize in a few memorable words the message idea [theme] that the advertiser wants to associate with the product.

The two main types of slogans are those that emphasize a product (institutional) reward and those that emphasize action to be taken.

Reward Emphasis
"You're in goods hands" (Allstate)
"K mart . . . the savings place" (S.S. Kresge)
Action Emphasis
"Don't leave home without it" (American Express card)
"The right choice" (AT&T)

Advertising research indicates that slogans are more effective when aimed at product users and adolescents and work best with products of the impulse type—like beer, soap, and potato chips—that are low in price and are purchased without much thoughtful deliberation.

From the various studies of slogans, certain general rules for slogan writing seem to emerge:

1. Make the slogan easy to remember and unlikely to confuse.
2. Make it help differentiate the product from the competition.
3. Make it provoke curiosity, if possible.
4. Make it emphasize a reward or an action.
5. Use rhyme, rhythm, or alliteration.

OBTAINING AND RETAINING PROTECTION FOR IDENTIFYING SYMBOLS

The big problem with using any identifying mark is how to avoid conflict with earlier users. No complete directory exists of brand names, slogans, trademarks, and other identifying symbols, but trademark lawyers have access to a number of sources of information, including Patent Office records and trade directory listings. Reports and opinions can be obtained indicating whether a proposed trademark will be considered confusingly similar to one already in use.

Any identification symbol should be registered. If the mark meets the legal requirements for registration, it will probably also "stand up" in court if necessary. If a trademark is registered, it is considered that everyone has access to information regarding the trademark, whether or not the records are actually checked.

An ever-present danger is that a brand name may become so successful that it comes to represent a whole class of products and appears in the dictionary as a generic name. Aspirin, zipper, linoleum, and escalator are examples of brand names that became generic. The American Thermos Company said in its catalog in 1910 that "thermos is a household word." More than 50 years later, the company found that it had indeed made the brand a household name, when the courts offered no protection from competitors. By contrast, General Motors has successfully defended its right to exclusive use of "Frigidaire" and Minnesota Mining and Manufacturing (3M) its rights to "Scotch Tape."

To avoid the loss of trademarks and related identifying symbols, trademark expert Sidney Diamond advises that a trademark always must be identified on packaging, in advertising, and wherever else it may appear and that infringers be sued. He writes that a trademark can be protected in five ways:

1. Use the generic name of a product in association with the trademark (for example, Q-tips cotton swabs).

2. Provide notice that the brand name, character, or slogan is a trademark by using an ® symbol or a line specifying ownership.
3. Use a special typographical design—a particular typeface, italics, or color combination.
4. Present the trademark in the correct grammatical form; a trademark should not be used as a noun, in the plural, as a verb, or in the possessive.
5. Monitor competitive marketing activities for possible infringements.[33]

GUIDELINES FOR USING IDENTIFYING SYMBOLS

Although trademarks, brand names, trade names, slogans, and other identifying symbols differ in format, certain principles apply in the creation and utilization of all of them. Some of these stem from legal requirements and some from the principles of effective communication.

1. Avoid using confusing visual and verbal elements.
2. Avoid names that describe the product.
3. Avoid family names.
4. Avoid geographical names.
5. Make symbols easy to identify.
6. Avoid unpleasant connotations.
7. Make symbols applicable to all media.
8. Make symbols international.

SUMMARY

Advertising message planning consists of two related decisions: "what to say" in advertising and "how to say it." The first decision is called message strategy and involves the formulation of a main message idea that will communicate the benefits or the problem-solving capabilities of a product or service. The second decision is called message tactics and involves how the visual and verbal elements, the tactical tools of advertising, are utilized to most effectively communicate the message idea.

A number of schemes exist for classifying message strategy. The six best-known strategic approaches are Burnett's inherent drama, Reeves's unique selling proposition, Ogilvy's brand image, Bernbach's executional emphasis, Trout and Reis's positioning, and Vaughn's message matrix.

The message idea is the product of the accumulation and analysis of facts—about products, markets, consumers, and competitors. In these facts, the advertising planner hopes to find the "Big Idea," or differential-copy advantage, that will become the basis for the campaign's copy platform. The copy platform is a managerial device that serves to guide and evaluate creative efforts. It consists of five basic components: (1) statement of creative objectives, (2) definition of target audience, (3) key benefit to be communicated, (4) tone of message delivery, and (5) statement of the main message idea.

Message strategy is determined to a great extent by the already formulated marketing and advertising strategies, especially by established communication objectives. Every ad is supposed to influence how the consumer behaves, and it is expected to accomplish certain steps outlined in a specific and hierarchical fashion—awareness, comprehension, conviction, and action. Creative objectives, because they are communication objectives, tend to be short-range in nature.

The force that drives message strategy is creativity. Increased research on creativity in recent years has provided more understanding about how creativity works and how it may be encouraged. However, creativity still remains the most unscientific aspect of advertising, even though its creations are the most important products of advertising people.

Trademarks, brand names, trade names, slogans, and trade characters are identification symbols that advertisers incorporate in their advertisements and other forms of promotion. These identifying symbols are important communication assets that can be legally protected as specified by the Lanham Act of 1946 and various state trademark laws.

NOTES

1. Gordon E. White, "Creativity: The *X* Factor in Advertising Theory," *Journal of Advertising* 1 (1972): 28–32.
2. Leo Burnett, "Finally Someone Has to Get Out an Ad," in *The Role of Advertising,* eds. Charles H. Sandage and Vernon Fryburger (Homewood, Ill.: Irwin, 1960), 352.
3. Don Schultz, *Essentials of Advertising Strategy* (Chicago: Crain Books, 1981), 8.
4. John O'Toole, *The Trouble with Advertising* (New York: Chelsea House, 1981), 121.
5. Norman Berry, in Annual Report, Ogilvy & Mather, 1983.
6. William H. Harkey, Leonard N. Reid, and Karen Whitehill King, "Army Advertising's Perceived Influence," *Journalism Quarterly* 65 (Fall 1988): 719–725, 732.
7. Sandra E. Moriarty, *Creative Advertising: Theory and Practice* (Englewood Cliffs, N.J.: Prentice-Hall, 1986), 13.
8. Kenneth Longman, *Advertising* (New York: Harcourt Brace Jovanovich, 1971), 167–177.
9. W. Keith Hafer and Gordon E. White, *Advertising Writing: Putting Creative Strategy to Work,* 2d ed. (St. Paul, Minn.: West, 1977), 3–4; Kenneth Roman and Jane Mass, *How to Advertise* (New York: St. Martin's Press, 1976), 3.

10. Michael Ray, *Advertising and Communication Management* (Englewood Cliffs, N.J.: Prentice-Hall, 1982), 250–272.
11. John R. Rossiter and Larry Percy, *Advertising and Promotion Management* (New York: McGraw-Hill, 1987), 165–191.
12. Ray, *Advertising and Communication Management,* 256–265.
13. Ibid., 270.
14. Bruce G. Vanden Bergh, Leonard N. Reid, and Gerald A. Schorin, "How Many Creative Alternatives to Generate," *Journal of Advertising* 12 (1983): 46–49.
15. O'Toole, *The Trouble with Advertising,* 121.
16. Ray, *Advertising and Communication Management,* 284–290; Al Reis and Jack Trout, *Positioning: The Battle for Your Mind* (New York: McGraw-Hill, 1981); and Richard Vaughn, "How Advertising Works: A Planning Model," *Journal of Advertising Research* 20 (October 1980): 27–33.
17. Denis Higgens, *The Art of Writing Advertising* (Chicago: Crain Books, 1965), 44.
18. Rosser Reeves, *Reality in Advertising* (New York: Alfred A. Knopf, 1961), 47–48.
19. David Ogilvy, *Confessions of an Advertising Man* (New York: Atheneum, 1964), 100–102.
20. See Ray, *Advertising and Communication Management,* 288–289.
21. David A. Aaker and John G. Myers, *Advertising Management,* 2d ed. (Englewood Cliffs, N.J.: Prentice-Hall, 1982), 134–141.
22. David L. Kurtz and Louis E. Boone, *Marketing,* 3d ed. (Hinsdale, Ill.: Dryden, 1987), 645.
23. Vaughn, "How Advertising Works: A Planning Model," 27–33.
24. Ibid.
25. "The Sources of Invention: Top Creatives Talk about Ideas—How They Become Ads That Are Remembered," *Advertising Age,* December 29, 1980, S-2.
26. William Wells, "Creative Sensitivity Called Missing in Ad Education," *Advertising Age,* November 13, 1980, 164.
27. Ray, *Advertising and Communication Management,* 284–290.
28. Ibid., 212–215.
29. John Kiel, "Can You Become a Creative Judge?" *Journal of Advertising,* 4 (1975): 29–31.
30. Ogilvy, *Confessions of an Advertising Man,* 28.
31. Timothy A. Bengston, "Creativity's Paradoxical Character: A Postscript to James Webb Young's Technique for Producing Ideas," *Journal of Advertising,* 11 (1982): 3.
32. William A. Marsteller, *Creative Management* (Chicago: Crain Books, 1981), 37.
33. Sidney A. Diamond, "Protect Your Trademark by Proper Usage," *Journal of Marketing* 26 (July 1963): 17–22.

SUGGESTED READINGS

Hafer, W. Keith, and Gordon E. White. *Advertising Writing: Putting Creative Strategy to Work.* 2d ed. St. Paul, Minn.: West, 1977. Chapter 1.

Moriarty, Sandra E. *Creative Advertising: Theory and Practice.* Englewood Cliffs, N.J.: Prentice-Hall, 1986.

Ray, Michael. *Advertising and Communication Management.* Englewood Cliffs, N.J.: Prentice-Hall, 1982. Chapters 7–9.

Roman, Kenneth, and Jane Maas. *How to Advertise.* New York: St. Martin's Press, 1976.

Schultz, Don E., and Stanley I. Tannenbaum. *Essentials of Advertising Strategy.* 2d ed. Chicago: NTC Business Books, 1988.

Zeigler, Sherilyn K., and J. Douglas Johnson. *Creative Strategy and Tactics in Advertising: A Managerial Approach to Copywriting and Production.* Columbus, Ohio: Grid, 1981. Chapter 5.

Jack Z. Sissors
Professor Emeritus
Medill School of Journalism
Northwestern University
Evanston, Illinois

James Surmanek
Executive Vice President and Media Director
McCann Erickson
Los Angeles, California

CHAPTER 62

CONTEMPORARY ADVERTISING MEDIA PLANNING

The main purpose of media planning is to devise a course of action that will deliver advertising messages to selected "targets." These targets can be consumers who individually buy a product or service, or businesses that purchase, or influence the purchase of products or services. The former target requires the use of consumer media—the kind of media you use primarily in your personal life, such as entertainment television, magazines, etc. The latter, which is referred to as a business-to-business plan, may require the use of the same media *form,* but different vehicles within that form. For example, a consumer media plan may include the use of *Conde-Nast Traveler,* while a business-to-business plan would incorporate *Travel Agent* magazine.

Just as the advertising message, which is usually referred to as the "creative," must communicate to targets what advertisers want to say about their products, so must the media plan recognize these same targets and determine which media forms are best suited to deliver the creative. Both the creative and media plan reflect what the client has set forth as the advertising challenge. This challenge usually takes the form of a marketing plan in which the marketing problem—or marketing opportunity—is completely spelled out.

As important as media planning might be in the marketing process, it is not the only element. Manufacturing, packaging, pricing, and distribution, also play a critical role in the success of a product. A media plan alone, no matter how effective or brilliant it might be, cannot solve marketing problems nor take advantage of marketing opportunities.

Nevertheless, the starting place for media planning is in an advertiser's marketing plan. Thoroughly written marketing plans will contain much of the background material and basic direction that media planners need to take about constructing a media plan. The starting place for creative development also is in the marketing plan. Media and creative therefore, are the two faces of the same coin, working together to fulfill marketing goals.

The Starting Place for Media Planning

The following material highlights the activities involved in media planning.

Marketing Problems

The starting place for media planning is an in-depth study of the client's marketing problems. Often, solutions are more easily found if the problems are spelled out in detail. Media personnel usually have a thorough background in marketing principles that helps them understand those problems. When advertising is recommended in a marketing plan, it is the planner's responsibility to find the best ways to get these messages to target audiences and at reasonable costs. The targets that planners should seek are individuals who are the best prospects for purchasing the brand.

Marketing Goals and Strategies

A study of marketing goals and strategies is a logical next step. After the problem is studied, the most significant parts of that plan for media planners are *marketing goals and strategies.* The client, in conjunction with the advertising agency's account representatives, usually recommends which marketing actions need to be taken to solve the problem, and these more or less guide all media decisions. Once a planner knows what direction media will probably take, it is also possible to make rough estimates of media costs. While media planners may have a role in making marketing recommendations, it is usually the client's responsibility. Therefore, planners must follow recommendations of the marketing plan rather closely.

Studying Competitors' Strategies

Determining how important certain competitors are and planning to meet their advertising and marketing efforts is the next step. Planners who disregard competitors' marketing and advertising efforts assume they are unimportant. But competitors have marketing power of various sorts that a media planner must be able to nullify. Strategies can be devised for combatting competitors' advertising by placing a brand's messages in the same geographic markets, in larger quantities, with more repetition, and perhaps with more impact than competitors.

Determining How Much to Spend

The cost of achieving marketing goals at this step in the planning can be more accurately estimated and become part of the total cost picture, subject to the client's acceptance. There are many methods of determining how much to spend for advertising. Here are some:

1. *Advertising/sales ratios.* The advertiser might conclude that five percent of sales can be spent to advertise the product. If sales are predicted to be $20 million, the advertising budget is therefore $1 million.
2. *Historical experience.* Many advertisers budget the same amount of money they spent in the past, adjusted possibly for cost inflation, changing marketing dynamics, etc.
3. *Task orientation.* This method sets out the communication objectives, such as how many people should be exposed to advertising, and then "costs-out" a media plan that achieves those objectives.

4. *Affordability.* This is also called the "what's left" method. This budgeting device merely allocates to advertising the amount of money left over after all other costs and a profit margin are calculated.

Choosing Target Markets

Choosing a target market involves determining whom to advertise to in terms of demographic and psychographic statistical data. These are the targets for the copywriter and art director who will create the advertising message, as well as the targets for the media planner. The planner must know to whom the advertising will be directed in order to choose the best media vehicles. A raft of statistical data is usually available—either from the advertiser's own knowledge or market research, or from proprietary research commissioned by advertisers, advertising agencies, or media suppliers, or from syndicated marketing/media research companies.

Two popularly used syndicated studies are *Simmons* (Market Research Bureau) and *MRI,* (Mediamark Research Incorporated). Each conducts national surveys among thousands of consumers to report their media consumption habits (e.g., how many people read a particular magazine), and product/service consumption patterns (e.g., how many people eat a particular candy bar). All of the data is available across multiple demographic cells, such as by age, household income, and family size. Furthermore, all of the data can be cross-tabulated whereby the media planner can assess the media and/or product consumption patterns of a demographic segment.

Psychographic data (also called "lifestyle" data) is becoming increasingly popular and increasingly available from syndicated researchers. Psychographic information allows media planners to analyze people in terms other than basic demographics, and provides a richer, more enhanced description of the target audience. For example, one might select a demographic target of people aged 18–34 to whom to advertise an upcoming movie, and a psychographic target of people aged 18–34 who are successful, sophisticated, active, take-charge people with high self-esteem. This psychographic description is of "actualizers—one of the eight segments reported by *VALS 2*, a syndicated research study that defines fundamental contrasts in consumer attitudes and behavior.

Beyond demographic and psychographic information is a growing resource of geo-demographic segmentation data that combines the information previously described with actual population accounts based on U.S. Census, and which places people within one or another cluster. Four systems currently used by many advertisers are *ACORN, Cluster-Plus, Micro-Vision* and *PRIZM.* Each of these systems is capable of slicing the U.S. population into approximately 50 distinct demographic/

lifestyle segments and providing product/service and media consumption patterns for each of these segments—either on a national basis, or in specific geographic places.

Determining Where to Advertise

Every product or service has geographic pockets of sales strength or weakness. Toothpaste A might sell well in markets 1, 3, and 5 while toothpaste B garners proportionately more sales in markets 2 and 4. The challenge facing a media planner is how much advertising should be directed in each of these five markets? Providing the same level of advertising to all markets might not allow for enough message weight in high development areas (e.g., markets 1, 3, 5) or might provide proportionately too much weight in weaker markets (2, 4). One assumption could be to add more media delivery in weaker markets to improve, i.e., take market share away from the competitor. Funding these weaker markets takes available advertising dollars away from stronger markets, which might weaken a brand's position in the stronger markets. Conversely, the possible gains in the weaker markets could offset any possible loss in the stronger markets. The idea, nevertheless, is that the planner must be armed with sufficient marketing information from the marketing plan to properly analyze the alternatives and make astute decisions on how to allocate advertising dollars and media audience delivery across geographic markets.

Evaluating the Creative Message

Evaluating the creative message vis-à-vis its effectiveness in various media forms is a step that often occurs before some of the others mentioned above, but certainly is critical during the media selection process. Some media, by their very nature, offer attributes that may enhance the effectiveness of the creative message. For example, if sight, sound, and motion are considered important elements of what needs to be communicated to consumers, then television is best. If color fidelity is more important, then magazines are automatically considered. Likewise, creative executions that require lengthy explanation are better served by placement in newspapers than on outdoor poster panels.

Setting Reach and Frequency Levels

Reach is a term that means the total number of targets exposed to the chosen vehicles at least once, and *frequency* means the average number of repetitions to the vehicles. Both are parts of media strategy. Levels of each are determined on how well these meet the media objectives and strategies to be written. Each of the two also have different cost effects on the entire plan. Reach and frequency levels can be related to various kinds of marketing strategies. New product introductions most often require high reach, and products sold in highly competitive markets usually require high frequency. Added to this idea is the concept of *effective frequency,* which suggests that different levels of frequency are more or less effective for different product categories. However, the research on this subject leaves a lot to be desired, and effective frequency levels turn out to be decided on a highly subjective basis.

Writing Media Objectives and Strategies

At this point, a planner should be prepared to write media objectives and specific strategies so that everyone—the client, the advertiser, the agency creative teams—is in sync with what must be accomplished through the use of media. Objectives and strategies are marching orders for the direction the media plan will take and the goals that need to be achieved. Just as the marketing plan is an organized tool for providing all the needed information about a product/service, and setting the overall goals for the brand, the media objectives and strategies reflect the marketing strategy but flesh-out the specifics that relate to media selection.

Evaluating All the Media Choices

At this point, an evaluation of all media choices are made relative to the objectives of the media plan. There is a plethora of media to choose from: magazines, newspapers, out-of-home, radio, television, etc., and within each of these forms are thousands of choices: nearly 12,000 magazines; 1,600 daily metropolitan newspapers; 9,000 commercial radio stations; and over 1,000 television stations. Furthermore, within each of these offerings are subsegments of media choices, such as regional or demographic editions of magazines, different sections of newspapers, and hundreds of radio and television programs. The planner must set forth the ingredients to be used to evaluate all of these choices and state the priority order of these ingredients. For example, one evaluation device is assessing the cost versus delivery relationship of each vehicle. This is a calculation known as "cost-per-thousand" (CPM) analysis, and shows the *relative* cost of one vehicle versus another, with the lowest CPM representing the most cost-efficient choice. CPMs alone, however, do not include consideration for *how many* people will be exposed to the vehicles (i.e., "reach"), only how much it will cost per thousand people delivered. While both reach and CPM should realistically be evaluation ingredients, each needs to be given an order of priority so the planner can decide whether to choose a more efficient vehicle before one delivers the audience, or vice versa.

Putting It Together into a Media Plan

All of the decisions are now organized and assembled into one document. This is the media plan, which contains all of the pertinent information needed by the advertiser to decide if this plan will achieve the marketing and media goals. At a minimum, it should contain statements of media objectives and strategies and the rationales for these statements, a schedule of the recommended media (also called a flow chart), a rationale and/or statistical analysis for these media choices, required timing for actually buying media, the cost of the media, and the total media budget.

Executing the Media Plan

The next natural step is buying media. Often advertising agencies have specialists who deal with one particular media form for selecting media vehicles. For example, one person might be an expert in network television while another is an expert in cable network TV. One might be a specialist for local TV while another for local radio. These specialists are commonly called *buyers.* They are media experts who work hand-in-glove with media planners to ensure that the details of the plan are accomplished.

Post-Analysis Is the Final Step

In the media planning/buying process, a final analysis is made after the advertising has run to make sure that what was planned was actually delivered. The dynamics of the media marketplace often cause changes between the purchased media schedule and the media activity that actually ran. For example, a buyer might have purchased a commercial in Program A and later find that the commercial inadvertently was aired on Program B. A post-analysis of the final aired schedule—as provided by the TV network or TV station—would reveal this discrepancy. Likewise, an advertisement in a newspaper or magazine might have been misplaced or improperly reproduced. Only through a careful post-analysis can the planner know how much and what type of media delivery was provided, and at what final cost.

SOME MAJOR PROBLEMS IN MEDIA PLANNING

Segmented Media Replacing Mass Media

Mass media is giving way to segmented media. In bygone years, it was customary for national advertisers to utilize several national media forms and direct their advertising messages to the masses, seldom distinguishing between geographic markets or demographic segments. It was quite usual, for example, for an advertiser to focus media delivery to "adults" or "housewives" or "households." The basic strategy was to expose the advertising message to as many people as possible throughout the United States. This strategy was driven by the complexion of the consumer marketplace, the lack of definitive marketing information, and the stability and consistency of available media vehicles at that time. All of this has changed—the consumer marketplace is more complex and more segmented. Marketing information is much more available because more research information is generated and computers store and analyze the information. Media choices have proliferated and have fragmented consumer audiences.

For example, in the situation of selling high-fidelity radio equipment, there may be one segment that perceives the brand on the basis of a piece of fine furniture. Another segment may want high-fidelity sound. Another segment may want one piece of multi-media equipment that includes radio, television, videotape equipment, and perhaps, digital sound. Presumably, these segments arose as the culture became more affluent and consumers could afford to choose products that more distinctly represented their personal needs. The use of mass media to reach all of these groups may simply not be an optimum strategy that it once was.

The Problem and the Opportunity

The problem and the opportunity is how to precisely describe the best consumer targets geographically, demographically, and psychographically. Although there is more market research than ever before, there is never enough statistically-reliable information on which every advertiser could comfortably hang his hat on and be totally confident that the targets selected were the best targets.

Media Proliferation

Media proliferation has fragmented audiences, making it harder than ever to reach all important consumer target groups. When there were three TV networks and few other entertainment alternatives, advertisers were able to air a commercial in primetime and reach 30 percent or more of consumers. Now, with an increased number of TV program choices, especially in homes that have cable TV, the average TV program primetime is viewed by only 10 percent of the people. Similar phenomena has occurred in magazines, radio, out-of-home, and various other media. Additionally, new media forms have emerged that attempt to reach consumers in unique ways (e.g, advertising on computer screens via *Prodigy* or TV advertising in health clubs) that further fragment audiences. The overall fragmentation problem is exacerbated by the lack of definitive audience information—either for small demographic segments of traditional media, or in total for the new emerging (nontraditional) media forms.

An article in *Advertising Age* tells the problem in its title: "Execs Resort to Gut Feelings Despite Hunger for Data; Ad Recommendations Often Guesswork.[1] Media planners who want to use nontraditional media have some difficulty when working with some of these newer media. They have been given almost anything the publisher can find that may substitute for measured data such as "cash register receipts, ski lift tickets, rider counts—to prove audience exposure."

A second problem related to media proliferation is whether the smaller sizes of market segments delivered by these media are large enough to accomplish marketing and media objectives. When high reach was required for many media plans, the size of media delivery was felt to be worth the dollars spent as cost-per-thousand comparisons could show. But now, the newer media often have high cost-per-thousands that is sometimes being sold as being worth the price because the segments will be more valuable in selling the product than in the large and relatively undifferentiated audiences of the past.

Integrated Marketing Communications

Integrated marketing communications may result in new ways of planning media. There are many people, including some of the leading names in advertising such as John O'Toole, president of the American Association of Advertising Agencies, and Keith Reinhard, president of DDB Needham advertising agency, who strongly recommend that advertising agencies think in terms beyond advertising alone and include public relations, sales promotion, direct marketing plus advertising to solve marketing problems. But because media has proliferated so much, the old way of planning for it just will not do. Now a new media concept may have to come before the creative has been done to plan for "seamless communication." The term "seamless" suggests that even though four different communication techniques are used in one campaign, they will have to be presented so consumers will see this as a single message, not four different messages. And the media cannot be traditional because there are better ways of avoiding the clutter brought about by proliferation. Media planning therefore may start even before creative and will set the tone for all the synthesized marketing communication that will follow.

Media Creativity

Media creativity is also a challenge facing media planners. Creativity can be viewed in several ways, such as finding more cost-efficient alternatives than were used in the past, or finding ways to "break through" the clutter of advertising to which consumers are exposed. The problem with media creativity is one of risk. Using previously used media strategies and tactics to deliver media audiences offers a comfort level that these strategies *will probably work.* Using untried strategies might offer breakthrough communication devices, but their effectiveness will not be known until after the plan is implemented and paid for.

SUMMARY

Media planning is an increasingly important part of the overall marketing plan. There is more research data available than ever before to help the planner make astute decisions, but that is coupled by a dynamically changing media arena—proliferation of media outlets, audience fragmentation, new media, etc. Having an *attack plan* that spells out media objectives and strategies, the recommended schedule of the media used, etc. is of paramount importance.

Although there continues to be problems facing media planners in terms of available data, if overcome, all the solutions to these problems become significant opportunities for advertisers.

NOTES

1. *Advertising Age,* August 27, 1990, p. S–4.

Harold A. Bergen
Executive Vice President
Ruder-Finn Inc.
New York, New York

CHAPTER 63
PUBLIC RELATIONS

While public relations has almost as many definitions as definers, the general consensus is that it is a form of communication to mass and special audiences in which payment is not required for appearance. The concept includes communication about things and events that already exist or that are created for the purpose of generating messages.

Public relations is an essential element (and, sometimes, the only affordable option) of marketing programs on behalf of products, services, and concepts—if only because much of the competition probably is using it already. Recognizing that publicity is almost always the chief end-product of public relations programming in support of marketing, a marketing program devoid of publicity forfeits opportunities for placing marketing messages in the editorial space and broadcast programming that the competition is getting. So the absence of public relations means the absence of a strategic component of any marketing plan that the competition may well be using.

PUBLICITY

While many like to think that public relations is more than publicity, the fact is that publicity is most of public relations. For marketers, the reputation of their organizations accompany their products, services, and/or concepts to the marketplace whether this is acknowledged or not. Examples abound where product sales are encumbered by negative publicity arising out of product recalls, environmental disasters, charges of false claims, boycotts, and the like. So marketers not only have a direct stake in the public perceptions of what they are trying to market, but also in the effects of all publicity about their organizations. The ideal, of course, is to minimize the negative and maximize the positive through a proactive public relations effort.

Targeting Is Crucial

For marketers, publicity should be much more than reaction to events that they cannot control directly. Generating publicity, within the total context of public relations, should be an aggressive, proactive, planned program to gain exposure for the positive attributes of products, services, and concepts in the minds of those who can make a difference in the marketplace. And they are more than just the ultimate users; they include sales, distributors, and dealers as well as those who influence the buying decisions of end-users—doctors, nurses, consultants, bartenders, beauticians, pharmacists, purchasing professionals, teachers, and so on. For example, an importer of a branded frozen meat product determined that food brokers and butchers were simply essential for product introduction and ongoing position protection in the freezer case as well as for delivering preparation tips and recipes to consumers. These links in the distribution chain were publicity targets—and as important as supermarket shoppers.

As with paid media advertising and/or direct mail, effective and cost-efficient public relations programs must play to the psychographic and demographic parameters of the intended marketplace. Selling electric motors in the original equipment market calls for a much different media mix than does selling suntan lotion to teenagers.

Another factor to recognize is that publicity for branded products is much harder to generate than for unbranded ones. Therefore, manufacturers should lean harder on non-publicity public relations techniques than on associations who represent suppliers on the generic level. Also, associations and professional societies are looked on by media as news sources that are less commercial and more objective than those who are representing branded interests.

Research

To be cost-effective, the first task is to research the marketplace. Who affects, influences, and/or recommends purchase decisions to the ultimate buyers? What kinds of people are in the distribution chain between producers and buyers, and how important are these intermediaries in providing access to what is being marketed? How do we reach everyone from producers to buyers in this chain—through print media, broadcast media, trade shows, professional meetings, direct mail? How should public relations interface with other, chiefly paid, communications components of the marketing program?

Then, what are the messages to be communicated? How do we position the products, services, and concepts against the competition, against our own shoulder lines, against the popular causes of the day that might be relevant—environmentalism, product safety, sexual mores, labeling, animal rights, discrimination issues, fiscal responsibility, and so on?

Often, much of the research required will already be at hand as the result of marketing research and consumer testing already done for other aspects of the marketing program. In addition, much information is readily available from industry associations, government, and media.

But add to all of this some direct contact with editors and broadcasters who reach the target audiences for their perceptions as well; a 30% return is not at all unusual for a well-constructed, two-page questionnaire that not only addresses the media's perceptions but also asks for preferences in subject matter and format for public relations materials.

Another application of research is to provide newsworthy information about human behavior specifically for its publicity value.

Professionally sound research about consumer attitudes, business peoples' perceptions, or any other group's feelings or acknowledged action all can be converted into publicity—perhaps to be released at a press conference if sufficient media interest can be expected.

Creating Publicity

Publicity in support of marketing programs can be created in several forms, all of which generate media coverage that builds awareness of the products, services, or concepts to be sold. Even mere mention of the people and producers in the marketing chain reminds prospective buyers about what's being marketed and reassures actual buyers that they made wise purchase decisions.

What creates publicity? Consider:

- *News releases.* These are mailed widely to all media reaching target audiences about such subjects as new products, new literature, significant sales or installations, open houses, anniversaries, executive appointments, significant orders, milestone events, new facilities or production capabilities, charitable contributions, mergers, divestments, research results, and significant policy changes. Whether marketing to business or consumer buyers, news releases also can cover "how-to-select," "how-to-use," or "how-to-maintain" aspects of products and services. Distribution can be by mail over lists maintained in-house, through mailing houses that specialize in publicity mailing (and maintain their lists on a daily basis), and/or fax networks. Broadcast media can be reached similarly through in-house lists or through firms that specialize in creating and distributing radio and video news releases. In all cases, but especially with consumer media, be very sparing in brand name mentions so that the material does not become too commercial for editorial use. And, if at all possible, send along high-quality, relevant illustrations to the media; do not stint on quality because anything less than truly professional visuals is a total waste.
- *Captioned photographs.* Print media in particular are always looking for attractive, attention-getting photographs. Even newspaper business page editors make room for high-contrast photographs with a whimsical approach that are based on strong geometric patterns, closeups, or some other visually magnetic element. All that is needed are good photographs with informative or intriguing captions, without a logo or label showing blatantly. Distribution generally is widespread as with news releases.
- *How-to features.* Perhaps the most welcomed publicity material is how-to features. These can range from how to cook something (recipes) to how to dress, how to travel, how to select the best fasteners, how to maintain machinery, and how to handle money. The list is endless. As with all features, these should not be broadcast as widely as news releases. They are better distributed as an "exclusive-in-your-field" to non-competing publications. Again, professional visuals will make features more desirable and, of course, generate more space or time.

- *Success stories.* While bad news seems to be the staple of the editorial world, room still is available for success stories about people and things. Particularly with business publications, success stories are welcomed that document how something reduces costs or saves time. Personal achievements, especially on behalf of causes, can generate coverage. Success stories can be handled as widely distributed news releases or selectively targeted features, depending on the appeal and the nature of the media selected for approach.
- *Cause marketing.* Perhaps the most rapidly growing mechanism for creating publicity is cause marketing. While the concept of tie-ins with other entities has been around for a long time, the notion really took hold in the 1960s when tobacco advertising was banned from broadcast and advertisers aggressively sought other venues for their advertising dollars. Public relations practitioners spent great efforts to identify outlets for sponsorships of worthy causes as well as sports and the arts as vehicles for generating publicity. The practice quickly spread to health and environmental related causes. Relevance to the cause and/or the target audience is essential.
- *Teaching materials.* Educators at almost all levels welcome materials for classroom that promote awareness of products, services, and concepts if the materials are educationally sound and not at all commercial. This means that generic references are much more acceptable than brand-name identification. This means that material coming from associations generally will be more welcome. Associations, in particular, are using educational materials to help students and their school counselors become more aware of career opportunities in the fields they represent.
- *Created events.* While many events are created for such audiences as shareholders or employees, they all have a marketing component in the pubilicity they can generate. These can range from annual shareholder meetings to anniversaries, community open houses, new facilities dedications, awards presentations, ground breakings, topping out ceremonies, convention opening ceremonies, and mayoral or gubernatorial proclamation photo opportunities. Proclamations generally tie into special days, weeks, or months declared usually by associations or other nonprofit groups. (See *Chase's Annual Events Directory.*)
- *Spokesperson tours.* Although mail and and commercial publicity distribution services are the most frequently used means for distributing publicity, the most effective is the spokesperson tour. Whether it be publicists alone or publicists accompanied by organizational spokespersons, calling on the media for face-to-face presentations of editorial resources is by far the most effective placement technique. Spokespersons can be corporate or elected leaders or authority figures in the fields, and editorial calls by spokespersons can be tied into their appearances at local or national meetings.

In all cases, calling on key editors, writers, and broadcast producers once or twice a year establishes personal relationships that last all year. Make appointments in advance, of course, initially with a letter outlining what the spokesperson can talk about and follow up by telephone. Not only can your resources be discussed in an hour or so, but the valuable opportunity arises to ask media people about what they are working on, what they would like to get, and what the marketers can come up with that the media would like to have.

DIRECT MAIL

Direct mail can greatly leverage the value of time and money invested in publicity by reinforcing it through reprise in a controlled format. Most often taking the form of newsletters and sometimes magazines, all of the publicity material generated for marketing programs can be converted into a newsy format for mailing to known prospective and current buyers as well as the media. Of course, lists can be bought to extend the reach of the mailings, and the lists should include field sales forces, distributors, legislators, dealers, directors, contributors, campaigners, and leaders of local units. Once into production, the unit cost is low for reaching all these target audiences with appropriate direct mail. Just be sure that newsletters specifically created for sales organizations do not go outside the organizational family.

In addition to newsletters, individual articles can be reprinted and mailed. A series of related articles can be compiled into freestanding booklets for mailing, too. In some instances, the major value of articles is in reprints; for example, a story about the unique design of a professional power tool can be placed in a design magazine reaching product designers (who would never use the tool) and then reprinted (with permission) for distribution to building contractors (who could use the tool).

All direct mail materials can also be distributed by the field sales force on sales calls or at meetings and conventions. In addition, some organizations even include their annual reports in response to requests for bids or in funds solicitation programs.

CRISIS COMMUNICATIONS

The corporate reputation of all organizations is vital to its success in marketing their products, services, and concepts, so the effects of crises are a valid concern of marketing professionals. Crises can come in many forms: product failure or tampering, allegations of fiscal mismanagement, protests by activists or constituents, accidents, storm damage, allegations of personal rights violations, and government pronouncements. Such crisis situations typically are complicated by inaccurate reporting early on and by organizations' lawyers insisting that nothing be said for fear of jeopardizing their legal standing with respect to claims and litigation that may follow. Denials and/or withholding information may be viewed as a coverup by the outside world—an almost automatically assumed admission of some responsibility or guilt. Therefore, legal and marketing interests must be balanced.

The first rule of responsible communication is to confirm facts as quickly as possible from the highest possible level in the organization, preferably with the chief executive going to the site to meet the media to give the facts, not necessarily the explanations. The marketplace will look more kindly on organizations whose leaders demonstrate instant concern and prompt revelation of the actual facts, followed up with a commitment to set things right as soon as possible. Instances abound where the marketplace turns on organizations whose leadership seemed uncaring. Rare are the cases in which organizations are upfront from the very beginning—but they win in the marketplace when all is said and done.

Marketers must advocate that their organizations anticipate all manners of crises that could come and be prepared with a crisis communications program. This program should identify all possible crises, designate who should call whom to report internally that something has gone awry, who is the designated coordinator of communications so that the truthful story is told, and who should be the organizational spokesperson (so that the story is told with consistency).

PUBLIC RELATIONS TRIGGERS

A wide variety of situations can trigger public relations support of the marketing effort (see Exhibit 1). Be alert to the kinds of opportunities to publicize and promote products, services, and/or concepts.

EXHIBIT 1. Public Relations Triggers

- New product, service, concept
- New marketing/promotional channels, plans
- Special themes (geographic, seasonal)
- New, unusual, prestigious applications
- New packaging, colors, features, sizes
- New literature, booklets
- Milestones (millionth unit)
- Significant orders (large, international)
- Anniversaries
- Changes in industry rankings, recognition
- Special events (construction; dedication of new facilities; seminars; learned papers; VIP visitors; trade shows, public exhibits; sampling; testing)
- Unique shipment, packaging, delivery
- How-to features (how to select, specify, design, troubleshoot, maintain)
- User/consumer research (into attitudes, applications, perceived values)
- Photographs (interesting applications, production processes, testing, training, delivery)
- Corporate support (trade programs, dealer incentives, promotional specials, advertising, quality control, financing, training)
- People news (appointments, honors, public appearances)
- Direct mail (newsletters, reprints, annual reports)
- Sponsorships (arts, sports, education, community service)

CONCLUSION

Public relations, whether ignored or cultivated, is a part of all marketing programs. If ignored, opportunities to increase awareness are lost while competitors fill the void. If cultivated, the marketing program is enhanced and the organization is more successful. It behooves marketers to identify all the public relations potential that already exists in their organizations as well as to create new possibilities.

SUGGESTIONS FOR FURTHER READING

Cutlip, Scott M., Allen H. Center, and Glen M. Broom, *Effective Public Relations,* 6th ed., Englewood Cliffs, NJ: Prentice-Hall, 1985.

Dilenschneider, Robert L. and Dan J. Forrestal, *Public Relations Handbook,* Chicago: The Dartnell Corporation, 1987.

Harris, Thomas L., *The Marketer's Guide to Public Relations,* New York: Lexington Books, 1993.

Lewton, Kathleen L., *Public Relations in Health Care: A Guide for Professionals,* American Hospital Association Services, 1991.

Barkgelt, James D., *The Complete Book of Product Publicity,* AMACOM, 1987.

Goldman, Jordan. *Public Relations in the Marketing Mix,* Lincolnwood, IL, NTC Business Books, 1992.

Arch G. Woodside
Tulane University
New Orleans, Louisiana

CHAPTER 64

DIRECT MARKETING: MODELLING CUSTOMER-MARKETER RELATIONSHIPS IN INTEGRATIVE MARKETING COMMUNICATIONS

According to the Direct Marketing Association (*Direct Marketing* 1993), direct marketing is "an integrative system of marketing that uses one or more advertising media to effect a measurable response and/or transaction at any location, with this activity stored on database." About two-thirds of all advertising in the United States, Canada, the United Kingdom, and other developed nations include one or more ways for viewers, listeners, or readers to respond directly to receive additional information or to buy the product/service being promoted. In the United States, this two-thirds amounts to $142 billion in 1991 (*Direct Marketing* 1993). Direct response mechanisms include telephone numbers, coupons, reader service (bingo) cards, free-standing-insert coupons, and telefax numbers.

Most direct marketing strategies include combinations of three or more advertising vehicles to achieve a measurable response from prospects. For example, a television commercial might include the offer of a free brochure if the viewer will telephone the toll-free number on the screen, or complete and mail a postcard. Thus, an effective communication process usually involving more than three media needs to be designed to complete the planned exchange: *television* to make the offer; the *telephone* and *postcard-mailing* response media; the *brochure;* the *computer* to create/store/retrieve the customer-product-firm database; the *marketer reply medium* to send the brochure (often via mail) to the customer; *people* to process responses, stuff envelopes, and/or talk on the telephone; and the *products/services* in the brochure (a product is always a communication medium as well as combination of attributes that provides benefits).

Given the impact of combining—that is, integrating multiple media—to make direct marketing strategies effective, it should not be surprising that direct mail expenditures represent less than 20 percent of the total direct marketing expenditures. However, to say that direct marketing is much more than direct mail misses the really important point: the use of multiple media needs to be integrated well to make direct marketing work.

Integrated marketing communication (IMC) programs include designing and implementing a dynamic, interactive, marketer-customer system that incorporates multiple media, measured customer responses, and immediate access and use of customer databases. Many details of why IMC programs are needed and how to design them are described by Roman's (1988) *Integrated Direct Marketing;* Rapp and Collins' (1987) *Maxi-Marketing;* Schultz, Tannenbaum, and Lauterborn's (1993) *Integrated Marketing Communications;* and Shepard's (1990) *The New Direct Marketing.* Thus, several advocates have made compelling cases for IMC programs.

In this chapter, the major opportunities and problems with direct marketing and IMC programs are reviewed briefly. Next, a model of the early stages in customer-marketer information search and responses in integrative marketing communications is described; some research findings related to the model are reviewed. Finally, based on the discussion of the model, direct marketing implications for designing and implementing effective IMC programs are offered. The aim here is to start to detail all the important behavioral steps that need to be integrated and assessed in interactive systems known as direct marketing.

MAJOR OPPORTUNITIES/BENEFITS AND PROBLEMS WITH DIRECT MARKETING STRATEGIES AND IMC PROGRAMS

Both opportunities/benefits and problems are associated with designing and implementing effective direct marketing strategies and IMC programs. Substantial increases in marketing effectiveness and efficiency have been documented in case studies of IMC programs (see monthly issues of *Direct Marketing Magazine,* the industry trade publication in the United States). Unfortunately, the problems that always occur with starting and running IMC programs receive little attention in the literature. Three major opportunities and benefits gained from an effective IMC program are described; two major problems that almost always occur with designing/implementing IMC programs are then discussed.

Opportunities/Benefits

Building Close, Long-Term Relationships with Customers. Effective direct marketing and IMC programs permit the building of long-term, close relationships linking the marketer and customer; this feature of direct marketing is the most important benefit of effective IMC programs. The marketer is able to respond to customers individually through the marketer's IMC program; thus, the first of Tom Peter and Nancy Austin's (1985) two sustainable strategic advantages can be achieved via effective IMC programs: creating and maintaining an obsession with customers (the second is to constantly innovate). Individual service designed to meet the personal needs of a customer who the marketer communicates with by name, is a useful description of relationship marketing. Relationship marketing is achieved by effective direct marketing and IMC programs.

A well-designed and implemented IMC program prevents relationships from going stale. Levitt (1983) points out that relationships tend to grow stale without continual attention:

> *The sale merely consummates the courtship, then the marriage begins. How good the marriage is depends on how well the relationship is managed by the seller. . . . The natural tendency of relationships, whether in marriage or in business, is entropy—the erosion or deterioration of sensitivity and attentiveness. . . . A healthy relationship requires a conscious and constant fight against the forces of entropy. (Peters and Austin 1985).*

The argument might be offered here that dramatic increases in marketing costs will occur from designing and implementing an IMC program. Contrary to this conventional wisdom, decreases in total marketing expenditures often occur from effective IMC program for two reasons. First, because of technological advances in using computers and databases, data handling and customer contact costs continue to fall. Second, with an effective IMC program, marketers start spending substantially less money on trying to reach prospects who will never buy or who become unprofitable customers. Also, such improved allocations of marketing funds result in higher net returns per dollar spent because specific marketing actions can be targeted to reach customers most likely to buy. Thomas Roger, a U.S. producer of software for direct marketing, offers the following example, "We tell people, 'you can mail 1,000 letters, or you can use one of these [IMC database] systems and mail 100 letters and get the same results' " (quoted from Bulkeley 1993). Thus, contrary to conventional wisdom, embracing direct marketing and an IMC system need not—should not—increase marketing costs substantially.

Using "Frequency-Marketing" to Increase Sales to Best Customers. We know that all customers are not alike: for both consumer and industrial firms, 5 percent of a firm's customers often provide more than 20 percent of total sales and more than 30 percent of net profits (see Dubinsky and Ingram 1984; Dwyer 1989). This knowledge is leading more firms to create and maintain frequency marketing (FM) programs.

Frequency marketing is "to identify, maintain, and increase the yield from best customers, through long-term, interactive, value-added relationships" (Colloquy 1991).[1] A firm's best customers (e.g., the customers above the 90 percentile in total purchases among all customers in a firm's customer base) usually are the most sensitive to the firm's new product offerings, special promotional offerings of the firm, and tend to buy products from the firm that provide the highest contribution to overhead and profits (for a detailed example see Woodside and Soni 1991). Even though very few customers are loyal 100 percent of the time, an enterprise can often capture a larger share of the available business among its best customers by creating frequency marketing programs. Frequent traveler membership programs among airlines are early examples of such FM programs.

Often, it is much cheaper and more profitable to persuade established customers (especially best customers) to respond to a specific marketing action than it is to bring in new customers. James Pisz, the national direct response manager for Toyota Motor Corporation in the United States, estimates that it is "three-to-five times more expensive to attract a new customer than a repeat customer" (in Bulkeley 1993). Pisz uses a computer workstation to locate best customers among a seven million U.S. customer database. When Toyota dealers plan "tent sales," Pisz provides mailings to local residents who have bought new Toyotas three years before.

Certainly an enterprise needs to design/implement marketing strategies to attract new customers. Most firms do not have explicit strategies directed toward their best customers; FM programs are made possible by well-developed direct marketing and IMC programs.

A Mighty Dog Example. A pre-emptive competitive strategy by Mighty Dog provides a packaged-product example of initial steps toward an FM strategy (from "Trend Setters" 1992). In 1992 Mighty Dog wanted to defend its brand and market share against a larger competitor about to launch a national campaign for a new dogfood entry (Heinz's Reward). The problem was that Reward's spending levels could not be matched. The strategy was to use a targeted mailing to pull known Mighty Dog households out of the market prior to Reward's roll-out. Mighty Dog wanted dog owners to stock up on their product before Reward's campaign hit.

Mighty Dog sent a direct mail piece to 526,291 households, the majority of which came from Mighty Dog's own database of names generated from previous promotions. Tactics included timing the mailing to be in consumer's homes two weeks prior to the Reward launch and deliver ten time-sensitive, personalized, sequentially dated coupons to the user households. The direct mail package included $5 worth of Mighty Dog coupons and the chance for consumers to purchase a dog's personalized bowl and blanket once they sent in the appropriate number of UPC symbols from Mighty Dog Products.

A total of 6.7 percent of the coupons distributed were redeemed. Premium redemption was 13 percent: 71,000 households redeemed the UPS symbols for either the bowl or blanket. The Mighty Dog used coupon values forcing high-purchase commitment (saving $1 on 10 cans) and attracted known customers to complete a program of having enough UPC symbols to redeem for a personalized bowl or blanket. Mighty Dog's market share increased .5 percent during the first two weeks of the promotion. The promotion minimized Mighty Dog's market share loss—only .2 percent—to Reward in the first eight weeks.

EXHIBIT 1. Tennessee Squire Letter

December 19, 1991

Dr. and Dr. Jerome D. Wilson
North Hills Court
Rural Route 2, Box 467-C
Hodges, South Carolina 29653

Dear Dr. and Dr. Wilson,

Well it's a shame you couldn't make it down for the coonhunt this year, because we sure had a good time. And like I said in my note to you, we didn't hurt your property much at all since the dogs went off in the other direction and never did circle back to your place. When they finally did tree a coon, it was the only one we saw the whole hunt. There was quite a discussion as to who's dog actually did the treeing, since the commotion was so loud and two or three of the dogs sound just about alike.

Well I finally settled the question by declaring everybody's dog a winner, which seemed to satisfy everybody except Roger, but he calmed down after a spell. And after a little Black Label.

It was a clear night, but a bit chilly and we were glad we had our long handles on. There were a few out-of-towner Tennessee Squires along this year, and I tried to take a picture of the whole group. Unfortunately I had some camera trouble. By the time I got it working most everybody had gotten tired and left, including the dogs, and the few that were still hanging around weren't very cooperative as you can see.

What with these hunts getting bigger every year, Dr. and Dr. Wilson, I sure hope you can figure a way to join us one of these times. Just drop me a line if your plans look hopeful, and I'll be glad to add your name to the list.

Cordially yours,

Bill Weaver

Bill Weaver

The Jack Daniel's Tennessee Squires Example. The "Tennessee Squires" is an FM customer association—club—founded by Jack Daniel's to create brand loyalty among the firm's best customers. Each member of the club receives a deed to a small plot of land owned by the distiller, invitations to local raccoon hunts, updates on "municipal" business, a Squire card, and a certificate of membership.

The letter shown as Exhibit 1 helps create and maintain a strong sense of being a Tennessee Squire, "belonging" to the club, and likely helps maintain top-of-mind-awareness and preference for Jack Daniel's whiskey among club members.

Note the informal, enjoyable tone of the letter, for example, "we didn't hurt your property much at all since the dogs went off in the other direction and never did circle back to your place." Accompanying the letter was an out-of-focus, color photograph showing 24 club members, one child, and four coon-hunting dogs. The photo explains the sentence in Exhibit 1, "Unfortunately I had some camera trouble." (The club members are posed with no rifles in the photograph, a thoughtful tactic given the negative connotations that might come to mind with drinking alcohol and guns.) Note that the letter ends with a personal reference to the Wilsons in the last paragraph. This illustrates the personalizing feature of effective FM programs and direct marketing.

Assessing Performance and Building Forecasting Models. Advertising budgets and other marketing expenditures are much easier to justify to senior management when sales can be linked directly—and accurately—to money spent. Thus the beauty of direct marketing: a performance tracking system can be created to continually monitor relationships with customers, including how customers respond to specific advertising executions. Thus *measurable response,* in the DMA definition of direct marketing, is particularly noteworthy.

A particularly strong case for designing-in a measurable response in almost all advertising executions, including image ads, appears in *Maxi-Marketing:*

> *Most advertisers of products, services, and establishments who devote their advertising to building their favorable awareness can, at the very least, incorporate a direct-response element as an index of performance. Inviting a direct response of some sort can measure comparative creative impact, comparative positioning effectiveness, and comparative media performance. (Rapp and Collins 1987)*

Performance tracking systems can be developed at different levels of sophistication, for example, from low (say, Stage 1) to high (Stage 5):

Stage 1: one-time, conversion studies
Stage 2: one-time, true experiments
Stage 3: continual monitoring and relationship building
Stage 4: continual monitoring/relationship building with true experiments
Stage 5: continual monitoring/relationship building, true experiments, with forecasting models of consumer response functions

Stage 1: One-Time, Conversion Studies. In Stage 1, the performance of ads and ad placements in competing media vehicles in delivering inquirers (prospects) is measured for an ad campaign. The conversion power of ad and ad placements is measured; conversion is the proportion of inquirers who convert into buyers. Also, revenues and the net profits associated with each ad and ad placement can be monitored. Conversion rates can be tracked by surveying inquirers to learn if they purchased the brand or service for which they requested information.

CPI, RPI, and ROI are index values of performance used often to compare impact in direct marketing campaigns. CPI is cost per inquiry, calculated by dividing all costs assignable to a particular ad placed in a given media vehicle (e.g., ad space cost and expenses in fulfilling the prospect's inquiry, including fulfillment literature expenses) by the total number of inquiries generated by this ad placement. RPI is the revenue per inquiry, calculated by dividing the revenues to the advertiser from the ad placement by the total number of inquiries generated by this ad placement. ROI is return on investment, calculated by dividing revenue net of assignable costs by assignable costs.

A tracking system developed by the state of Louisiana for assessing advertising performance for attracting tourist visitors provides details of such a Stage 1 tracking system (Woodside and Soni (1990). In the Woodside and Soni report, the conversion proportion of visitors-divided-by-inquirers for ads placed in 1987 ads in *Southern Living* magazine was very high (.46) compared to the conversion proportion from ads in *Bon Appetit* (.11).

However, conversion rates are only one measure of performance. Similar to a medical doctor examining a patient, multiple-method measurements should be included to assess well-being, that is, ad performance. Exhibits 2 and 3 are examples of RPI, CPI, and profit measures of performance for the 1987 Louisiana ad campaign (Tables 7 and 8 in

EXHIBIT 2. Revenue and Cost Analysis of Advertising in Competing Magazine Vehicles

Category	Magazine	Revenue per Inquiry (RPI)	Cost per Inquiry (CPI)	CPI as a Percent of RPI
Life cycle	*Magazine X*	$240	$49.51	20.6
	Magazine Y	35	15.16	43.3
Food	*Gourmet*	256	14.28	5.6
	Bon Appetit	89	6.60	7.4
Women's service	*Family Circle*	159	7.60	4.8
	Ladies Home Journal	105	4.18	4.0
Regional focus	*Southern Living*	237	5.99	2.5
	Texas Monthly	227	18.15	8.0
Travel related	*Travel & Leisure*	446	12.27	2.8
	N. G. Traveler	180	7.59	4.2

Source: Woodside and Soni (1990, p. 63).

EXHIBIT 3. Profitability Analysis of Advertising by Magazine Vehicles

Category	Magazine	Advertising Total Cost	Total Tax Revenue*	Net Profit to State and Local Governments
Life cycle	*Magazine X*	$ 24,856	$ 10,843	–$ 14,013
	Magazine Y	12,524	2,602	–9,922
Food	*Gourmet*	26,616	42,947	16,331
	Bon Appetit	29,934	36,293	6,359
Women's service	*Family Circle*	91,480	172,292	80,812
	Ladies Home Journal	30,108	68,059	37,951
Regional focus	*Southern Living*	46,968	166,564	119,596
	Texas Monthly	21,581	24,184	2,603
Travel related	*Travel & Leisure*	38,516	125,994	87,483
	N. G. Traveler	32,396	69,158	36,762
Total		$354,979	$718,936	$363,957

*Estimated using 9 percent of total revenue.
Source: Woodside and Soni (1990, p. 63).

Woodside and Soni 1990). Note in Exhibit 3 that profits associated with the *Bon Appetit* ads are positive; thus, the Louisiana ad performance associated with *Bon Appetit* might be judged to be pretty good, even with the low conversion rate. (Magazines X and Y are not named in Exhibits 2 and 3 because of their poor profit performance for the advertiser.)

Data evaluation is a critical issue in Stage 1 and other stages in performance monitoring. Managers looking at the study and evaluating the evaluation should ask how the data variables are defined in the study. What are the details of the procedures with which the data were collected? What factors were controlled and not controlled in obtaining the data? What are the statistical properties of the data? In what direction will data problems bias the results? (Clarke 1993).

In several respects, data evaluation of the 1987 Louisiana study lead to the conclusion that the data looked pretty good. The study was designed to achieve a high response rate (52 percent) for the questionnaire sent to inquirers; the data included questions on buying competing brands (i.e., visiting other states); and the questionnaire and cover letter did not reveal the sponsor of the study (to reduce sponsor-identity-biases in responding to the questions). Most tourism conversionresearch studies report high conversion rates, overall for example, above 45 percent. Such reports make the advertising expenditures look good, even if the estimates are unrealistic (i.e., invalid estimates of reality). One reason such high conversion rates are estimated often is that multiple attempts are not made to reach non-respondents in sampled households. Non-respondents are usually different from respondents in surveys—not in their demographic profiles but in their product use profiles (see Woodside and Ronkainen 1994).

Stage 1 performance evaluations have two major shortcomings: (1) relationship marketing is not done and (2) the basic question of advertising effectiveness (does advertising cause sales) is not answered adequately. A major shortcoming with Stage 1 performance tracking is that no long-term relationships are developed with inquirers. After the inquiry is fulfilled by sending some literature—possibly a brochure or an information kit that might include a video or offers for additional information—that is the end to the relationship. No additional contacts with the customer by the marketer are attempted; the marketer discards the names, addresses, and other information provided by the inquirers. Hard to believe, isn't it? Yet, many marketers using direct marketing do only Stage 1 performance evaluation; they do not attempt additional sales calls by telephone, personal visits, or through the mail. Almost all state travel offices in the United States and Canadian Provincial tourism agencies do Stage 1 type performance evaluations of their advertising programs, even though they are marketing a high-ticket service (*average* expenditures in a state by overnight, visiting travel parties are typically above $1,000).

Stage 1 tracking does not answer this basic question: how many sales (how much revenue was gained) because of the advertising? As a research tool, Stage 1 research is unscientific in learning valid answers to cause-and-effect relationships, even if customers respond favorably when asked if the advertising and literature they requested influence them to buy. Scientific research to learn cause-and-effect influence requires a *direct comparison of results between two equal groups, one exposed to a treatment (say, advertising) and one not exposed.* Such comparisons are known as "true experiments" (see Banks 1965).

Stage 2: True Experiments. Doing true experiments to estimate cause-and-effect relationships between advertising and sales are more sophisticated than conversion research studies. While Stage 1 may provide useful information of the relative performance of alternative ad executions and media vehicles, they cannot answer the more basic questions: Did the advertising cause sales beyond what would have occurred without the advertising? Did the sales performance of the new ad beat the sales performance of the old ad?

Stage 2 provides useful answers to the question of whether or not advertising causes sales. *True experiments* are creating two, three, or more equal groups of subjects (e.g., prospects) and exposing one group to treatment A and a second group to treatment B, and other groups to other treatments. Treatment A might be a new ad and treatment B might be the standard ad being used often by a firm; the executives in the firm want to know if the new ad performs better than the standard ad in generating inquiries, new customers, sales, and profits. Equal groups are created by randomly assigning a sample of subjects (say, 20,000) from a representative population to each group (10,000 to group A and 10,000 to group B) in the study; demographic and buying behavior characteristics of the groups can be checked to insure that the random assignment worked to create two or more groups that do not differ (Banks 1965).

Treatment A might be tested against treatment B, where treatment B is no advertising; one group of subjects is assigned randomly to be exposed to ad A and the second group is exposed to no advertising. This test is designed to examine how much impact is caused by advertising exposure versus no exposure: thus, how much, if any, does advertising cause sales?

True experiments are used in medical research to test the effectiveness of new drugs versus a placebo in double-blind designs; the administrators of the drug and the patients receiving either treatment A versus treatment B do not know which of the treatments are being administered. Thus care is taken to avoid false reports of impact often made because subjects know they are being tested.

True experiments are known as *split-run tests* in advertising and direct marketing. A split-run is an old newspaper term referring to splitting a publication run by removing an ad, or newspaper section, and adding a second ad or newspaper section. Split-run testing and other forms of true experiments can be used in testing the cause-and-effect influence of advertising versus no advertising, newspapers versus television, station A versus station B, magazine X versus Y, appeal M versus R, and headline T versus U. Here is one example (Caples 1974) of split-run testing two headlines, the copy and illustrations were identical in both ads except for a change in headline wording:

Headline of Ad A: Save one gallon of gas in every ten
Headline of Ad B: Car Owners! Save one gallon of gas in every ten

Ad B pulled 20 percent more inquirers; although the sales results were not in this test, most likely ad B pulled more total sales orders than ad A.

John Caples' (1974) book continues to be the best source to read to learn about true experiments—and wisdom—in advertising. A famous quote appears in his book:

> *I have seen one mail order advertisement actually sell, not twice as much, not three times as much, but 19 1/2 times as much goods as another. Both advertisements occupied the same space. Both were run in the same publication. Both had [the same] photographic illustrations. Both had carefully written copy. The difference was that one used the right appeal and the other used the wrong appeal.*

David Ogilvy makes a telling observation about direct marketing in the Foreword to Caples' (1974) book, "Experience has convinced me that the factors that work in mail order advertising work equally well in *all* advertising. But the vast majority of people who work in [advertising] agencies, and almost all their clients, have never heard of these factors. That is why they skid helplessly about on the greasy surface of irrelevant brilliance. They waste millions on bad advertising, when good advertising could be selling 19 1/2 times as much." In 1993, Don Schultz's report stated that most advertising agencies still are unable to embrace direct marketing and IMC programs; unfortunately Oglivy's observations about advertising agencies still holds true as we enter the mid 1990s (Schultz 1993). Schultz (1993) reports two problems many ad agencies perceive about direct marketing: it's a bit tacky and less profitable for the ad agency compared to placing image advertising on television.

Workable solutions to transforming advertising from image communicating to integrated marketing communications have to be started in client firms—not with their advertising agencies. Advertising and marketing managers need to insist on creating relationship marketing strategies with customers (i.e., IMC programs) because (1) IMC programs are more effective than image advertising; (2) IMC programs provide the hard evidence demanded by senior management on *how much* advertising and marketing cause sales; and (3) most advertising agencies will not do it unless they are forced to do it. The real problem is that many advertising and marketing managers lack the knowledge/ability and conviction needed to create IMC programs; we return to this issue in the next section.

The best technical reading on true experiments in marketing continues to be Banks' 1965 book. Banks offers detailed numerical examples of simple true experiments as well as sophisticated research designs to test cause-and-effect relationships. The book is out-of-print but well worth finding because it is readable and provides the technical training needed by advertising and marketing managers.

Stage 3: Continual Monitoring and Relationship Building. Two important features of relationship marketing are (1) creating unique products/services for distinct groups of customers in a firm's customer database and (2) communicating the offer only to these distinct groups. For example, Cindy Lay used her personal computer to find 1,400 Southern women who buy Anne Klein dresses only on sale. Evaluating their past purchases, she discovered that when they waited until the second markdown, they "cost me an additional $75 per person." So before the first markdown period ended, she spent $850 to notify these customers of a "special sale" on the clothes they wanted. The two-day event increased volume on the dresses by 97 percent in a normally slow period (Bulkeley 1993). Ms. Lay is the director of market research for

Proffitt's Inc., an Alcoa, Tennessee, department store chain that has recently created an IMC program.

All firms in some industries have transformed themselves into relationship marketers by creating IMC programs: direct marketing, financial investment firms, for example, Fidelity Investments; credit card companies, for example American Express; airlines for customers in their frequent flyer programs, for example Delta Airlines; direct marketing, clothing companies, for example, L. L. Bean; and mail order seed companies, for example, Burpee. Some firms and whole industries have yet to start IMC programs, for example, marketing departments in state and Canadian provincial governments, most banks, and many department stores.

With an IMC program, most marketers are able to keep and use a customer database of the complete buying history of each customer. Customer demographic and lifestyle information often can be included in such databases. Individual customer account databases often begin by including the following information: how many years the customer has been buying from the company; what was purchased each year; how the customer responded to each marketing communication to reach this customer; customer complaints and how the firm responded; the total dollar amount purchased by the customer per year; and how frequently the customer buys each year.

The "SALES" model developed by Pareto, a Cincinnati-based database marketing company, is an example of a database system that provides department store marketers with the capability to target customers with unique buying histories to receive marketing communications especially designed for them. The SALES model is based on five key indicators of customer activity and value. Sales data are processed through the SALES model and customer/department summary entries are created. For each unique relationship between a customer and a department in the store, a numeric indicator value is computed ("A Database . . ." 1991). The indicators are:

S Sales history—sales volume for this customer, in this particular department
A Across department—cross buying in other departments
L Last purchase—last purchase in days in this department
E Extent of the relationship—how long a customer
S Shopping frequency—frequency of buying in this department

Here is an example of the SALES model: If a retailer decides to invite 1,000 of its best customers to a special preview of the men's fall suit selections, customers can be selected by criteria based on the entries in the SALES model for the menswear department. A typical

EXHIBIT 4. Sales System Women's Wear

Name	Account Number	S	A	L	E	S
Joe Smith	1434528	8	2	7	3	7
Melanie Jones	1417076	4	1	4	9	3
Carrie Loftus	1381154	6	4	8	6	6

Note: The example above illustrates three partial database entries from the SALES system for a particular department. Melanie Jones has a 4 under the first S (Sales History), which indicates that she falls somewhere between the 40th and 49th percentile in "sales history" (year to date spending in this department). The 1 under A indicates that she falls into the lowest of four equal sized groups in terms of "tendency to buy across departments." The 4 under L indicates that she falls somewhere between the 40th and 49th percentile in terms of "days since the last purchase in this department." The 9 under E indicates that Melanie is one of the customers with the longest "history of purchase activity in this department." She falls at or above the 90th percentile in terms of "extent of relationship" with the women's wear department. And finally, the 3 under the second S indicates that she falls somewhere between the 30th and 39th percentile in terms of "frequency of purchase" in this department.

selection criteria might be to select all customers in the top 20 percent for sales history in menswear (S); in the top quartile for buying across departments (A); in the top 20 percent for last menswear purchase in days (L); in the top 30 percent for extent of relationship (E); and in the top 40 percent for menswear shopping frequency (S). The first criterion (the first S requirement) selects the biggest spenders in the department for the year.

If the count turns up less than 1,000 customers, the criteria for an indicator may be revised, and the selection computer run made a second time. Exhibit 4 is a summary of entries in the customer database in the SALES model.

The biggest problem in creating the customer database needed for relationship marketing is that firm's management information systems (MIS) are programmed only to meet the needs of the finance and accounting departments. For example, banks generally have customer account databases for each product—mortgages, car loans, savings and credit cards, and savings accounts. The databases may even identify the same customer differently—without a middle initial, for example, or last name first. Marketers want one customer database that includes all details of the firm's relationship with each customer.

The most workable solution to this problem is *not* in trying to transform a firm's existing MIS to a complete customer database; given the substantial decreases in costs of customer database software programs and computer workstations, the faster and most workable solution is to create a customer database from scratch. This is done by selecting from several high-quality, spreadsheet software programs and using a workstation or personal computer with the necessary hard drive memory. A critical point related to this approach: The time is now for the marketer to develop finger-tip computer capability to mine her own customer database on her personal computer.

> *For years, marketing gurus have been preaching the merits of "mining" corporate databases. But the databases used for billings, deposit records, and installment plan payments usually have been inaccessible except to the programmers who maintain them. Marketers designing direct-mail campaigns have had to stand in line to ask programmers to search for particular types of customers. Now the marketing experts themselves [programmers not needed] can get at the data. High-end PCs with two-gigabit hard drives—20 times larger than the 100 megabyte drives most home users buy now—can hold several million customer names on hardware that costs about $10,000 now. The software to manage such data starts as low as $15,000 (Bulkeley 1993).*

Given that the marketer is willing to invest some time, he or she is now able to have the technical capability and wisdom to create and handle a customer database to fulfill the two major benefits of direct marketing: (1) relationship marketing, including forecasting net profit contributions of marketing tactics using customer response functions and financial data; and (2) hard evidence measuring of how much advertising and marketing influences sales.

Before the 1990s, low cost approaches for high-quality relationship marketing (IMC) programs were not widely available. The situation has finally changed. The best technical introduction to customer database management and relationship marketing is likely to be Clarke's (1993) second edition of *Marketing Analysis and Decision Making.* Reading Clarke (1993) provides the marketer with basic training and wisdom of handling databases to make better marketing decisions.

Stage 4: Continual Monitoring/Relationship Building with True Experiments. Stage 4 is including true experiments (Stage 2) in relationship marketing programs (Stage 3). Thus, Park Seed, a mail-order seed company, might test a special high-price bulb offer designed to be purchased by the firm's best customers (identified using a SALES-type software program) by assigning a randomly selected sample of best customers to two groups: one group receiving the special offer (treatment A), and the second group *not* receiving the special offer (treatment B). Note the two types of randomization are used: (1) random selection to achieve representativeness of the sample to the population of best customers, and (2) random assignment to achieve equality between the two groups on all variables so that only the marketing offer (treatment A versus B) is available to explain any difference in sales response.

Quasi-experiments can also be performed in Stage 4 IMC programs. Quasi-experiments are looking at changes in customer responses to the presence and absence of marketing offers through time, without equivalent test and control treatment groups. Quasi-experiments do not meet the two requirements of true experiments for testing cause-and-effect relationships, but examining database relationships between marketing actions and customer responses through time provides useful information, even when true experiments are not planned. Customer response models can be considered and tested to learn which models, if any, are useful for explaining customer responses among some groups of customers to particular marketing actions. The best reading on quasi-experimentation is the book by Cook and Campbell (1979); reading Banks (1965) is helpful preparation for reading Cook and Campbell (1979).

Stage 5: Continual Monitoring/Relationship Building, True Experiments with Forecasting Models of Customer Response Functions. Stage 5 relationship marketing is what David Shepard (1990) means by the phrase, "The New Direct Marketing." In Stage 5, the marketer uses the customer database, develops and tests customer response functions, and does financial payback ("what if") sensitivity analysis of different marketing strategies and tactics. For example, with useful customer response models developed from insight and tested using the database, a catalog company might examine if its business was built on the assumption of three catalog mailings to customers per year instead of two. Instead of using a third catalog mailing, what would be the net contribution to profit if the firm spent the available marketing funds on attracting new customers? A lifetime value analysis of new customer marketing can forecast useful answers to this question, based on the valid customer response functions. Shepard (1990) is a very useful introduction to Stage 5 relationship marketing.

Equation 1 is an illustration of a customer response model. In this model, unit sales for product X are influenced by four variables: price of the product, advertising, customer annual household income, and age of household head. The two marketing variables are advertising and price. The model was developed and tested against other possible models from data in the firm's customer database.

Equation 1

$$\text{unit sales} = 320\,[1 + ((1/250{,}000)\,(\text{advertising})^{1.5})\,((1/12)\,(\text{price})^{-0.9})] + (.065)(\text{income}) + (.86)(\text{age}).$$

This hypothetical model indicates that increasing advertising has a positive influence on unit sales; increasing price has a negative influence; increases in income has a positive effect; and increases in age have a positive effect. Unit sales forecasted from Equation 1 can be used with revenue and cost of goods sold equations to forecast net contribution for different prices and advertising combinations.

If the firm wants to consider the impact on net contribution of four prices at each of three levels of advertising, then twelve (4 prices by 3 advertising) combinations of specific prices and advertising expenditures can be included in Equation 1 in a computer spreadsheet program to forecast sales for each combination. Equations 2 and 3 can then be used to estimate the net contribution for each pricing-advertising mix.

Equation 2

revenue = (unit sales) (price).

Equation 3

COGS = ($8.00) (unit sales).

Airlines, mail-order seed companies, credit card companies, and many firms in several industries are now using such customer response functions to provide specific forecasts of results of specific marketing actions.

Problems with Direct Marketing Strategies and IMC Programs

Two major problems almost always occur in designing and implementing IMC programs: (1) not planning and coordinating deeply enough to accomplish Stage 1 direct marketing; and (2) the advertiser's and marketer's lack of knowledge and technical ability in modelling customer/marketer information search and relationships in IMC programs. Problems include (a) marketing team members refusing to contact new customers (i.e., not responding to inquiring prospects who reply to an advertising offer); and (b) no follow-up to learn if prospects have received the information they requested and to prompt purchase.

Not Planning and Coordinating Deeply Enough. Two independent studies confirm that about 20 to 40 percent of customer requests for product/service information offers in direct response advertising go unanswered. The conclusion would be reasonable that some marketers refuse to fulfill customer requests for the information offered in the marketer's own advertising.

In a five-year study, Performark researchers—pretending to be potential customers—mailed in thousands of reader-response cards, the kind found in business and trade publications with offers of more information on goods and services. They responded to solicitations from hundreds of companies selling industrial products costing at least $5,000.

> *What happened? It took an average of 58 days for the requested pamphlets or brochures to arrive. Nearly one out of four inquiries went unanswered. Only one in eight generated a follow-up call by a sales representative, and those contacts came an average of 89 days after Performark's initial indication of interest. ("Poor Handling . . ." 1993).*

The president of Performark, Joseph Lethert, reports, "The problem is sales and marketing aren't working together. No one has responsibility for making sure prospects are converted to customers."

Too often marketing people blame the sales force for not pursuing leads, while salespeople are loath to share information about their customers ("Poor Handling . . ." 1993).

Similar findings are reported in a second study of business-to-business and consumer marketers responses to inquiries (Woodside, Brose, and Trappey 1991). Acting as customers, inquiries were sent to 90 direct marketers (47 businesses and 43 consumer firms). After eight weeks, 25 percent of the business marketers and 28 percent of the consumer marketers had yet to respond in any manner. However, the proportion of responses did vary according to media used to make the inquiry. Overall, 80 percent of the marketers responded to telephone inquiries; 80 percent to direct mail inquiries; and only 60 percent responded to reader-response inquiries. Follow-up calls after responding to the inquiries were made by only 34 percent of the business marketers and 25 percent of the consumer marketers.

Besides many advertising agencies not supporting direct marketing and IMC programs (Schultz 1993), many advertising and marketing team members within firms with active IMC programs fail to implement the program and/or fail to design in IMC steps for effective relationship marketing. One specific example serves to illustrate the problem: In 1984, the sales manager of an office furniture distributor in Greenville, South Carolina, did *not* want area customers interviewed for the company's customer newsletter because photographs of the customer executives using the product were always run with the news stories, and the newsletter is direct response advertising for the company. The sales manager's reasoning was that too many people in companies who would not be buying might call him and tie him up on the phone; this problem was not occurring in the other four company sales territories participating in the program. The Greenville sales manager also reported, "I know all customers in the Greenville-Spartanburg area and they know me; there's no reason for sending them a newsletter or advertising to them."

Part of this first problem is not creating a database to store each marketing contact-attempt and customer response within each customer's file record. Unfortunately, most companies in Stage 1 direct marketing are probably not operating an on-line, customer database that includes marketing contacts and customer responses.

Part of the solution to this serious problem is creating and continuing to use an on-line, customer/marketer computer database to help create and maintain relationships with new and established customers. Given the continuing lowering of software and data handling and storage costs, this solution is feasible in the 1990s. Since relationship marketing includes knowing the customer by name and the nature/quality of your current contacts and responses with this customer, storing such information in the heads of a few persons and on paper is inadequate for designing active marketing strategies and building valid marketing response models. Monitoring the execution of planned marketing contacts with customers (including follow-up calls) and customer responses can occur systematically with an on-line customer/marketer database.

To make on-line entries and analysis of such databases and to achieve widespread acceptance and enthusiasm for IMC programs, senior executives need to be technically competent in handling the database and to understand customer response functions and "what if" sensitivity analyses of marketing moves. The time has come to put away the old solution to the problems on failing to deliver the literature offered and not following up on inquiries by educating sales people on the importance of direct marketing. The new solution is in leading by behavioral example by the CEO and other executives in contacting customers and hands-on ability in handling a customer/marketer database.

Lack of Knowledge and Skills for Modelling Customer/Marketer IMC Relationships. Up until the mid-1980s, creating and running an effective and efficient IMC program (and achieving Stage 5) was very difficult to accomplish for three reasons. First, low-cost help was unavailable for managers to develop and test explicit and useful market response models for estimating how much marketing actions affect customer responses—low priced computer software programs and inexpensive personal computers. As discussed, this problem now has been eliminated.

Second, skill-building books and manuals have not been widely available for combining useful marketing response models and financial spreadsheet analysis into decision models for forecasting net contribution impacts of alternative marketing actions. With the availability of skill-training books such as Clarke (1993) and Shepard (1990), this problem now has been eliminated. The unique moment of the mid-1990s is captured well by Clarke:

> *Developments in the fields of statistics, mathematical marketing models, and marketing research have advanced by slow increments over the years to provide finally a meaningful, critical mass of useful knowledge. Parallel developments in computer technology, computer software, and commercially available software, which have advanced at a fantastically rapid rate, have converged to provide an analytical capability for marketing managers that could only have been dreamed of ten years ago. In terms of both power and accessibility, these developments have the potential to greatly expand the manager's knowledge of how the marketplace works, as well as to explode old myths and increase the manager's ability to exploit his or her knowledge.*

This second problem includes not fully describing, understanding, and modelling the search and choice processes involved in customer/marketer IMC programs. For example, the substantial possibilities are usually not included in such models that customer requests for information offered in ads may *not* be fulfilled and customers may *not* receive or notice they have received the information requested and sent to them. This issue is discussed more fully in the next section.

Third, illusion of knowledge may be the last major obstacle for advertisers and marketing managers to overcome. All successful marketing managers have an intuitively insightful model of customer responses for making decisions and implementing actions. "The result is that most marketing managers base their decisions on conceptual models of the marketplace that are part fact and part imagination. Like Christopher Columbus, who died believing that the island of Cuba was the east coast of Asia, the misconceptions of marketing managers will never be corrected by monitoring the same data in the same way as they have in the past." (Clarke 1993). The goal is not to replace marketing imagination with database decision models but to combine them to achieve better decisions.

MODELLING CUSTOMER/MARKETER INFORMATION SEARCH AND RELATIONSHIPS IN INTEGRATIVE MARKETING COMMUNICATIONS

Effective IMC programs require deep understanding and database entries of the multiple give-and-take responses between the customer and marketer. Exhibit 5 is an overview of two-way responses that may occur in using direct marketing for starting an IMC program with customers. Exhibit 5 is intended to be a model of the sequence of steps that occur often in direct marketing and to emphasize the many possibilities for recurring communication breakdowns/failures. The model is intended to be relevant for both business and consumer marketing. The steps in the model and some research findings related to these steps are summarized in this section.

In Exhibit 5, this direct marketing model begins with asking whether or not the customer is exposed to an advertisement that includes a direct response offer. Prior media steps, such as vehicle distribution and customer exposure to the vehicle, are described in the Advertising Research Foundation's model for evaluating media (ARF 1961; Phelps 1993).

Mere Exposure Effects of Advertising

Given that customer exposure to an advertisement containing a direct response occurs (box 1), the advertisement may have an influence even if the customer does not notice the ad (boxes 2 to 3). Thus including box 3 in the model is to include the hypothesis supported by empirical evidence that mere exposure can influence attitude and purchase choices (Krugman 1965; Zajonc 1968; Fazio, Powell, & Williams 1989; Petty, Unnava, & Strathman 1991). Thus the sequence

EXHIBIT 5. Model of Customer/Marketing Information Search and Use of Direct Response Advertising

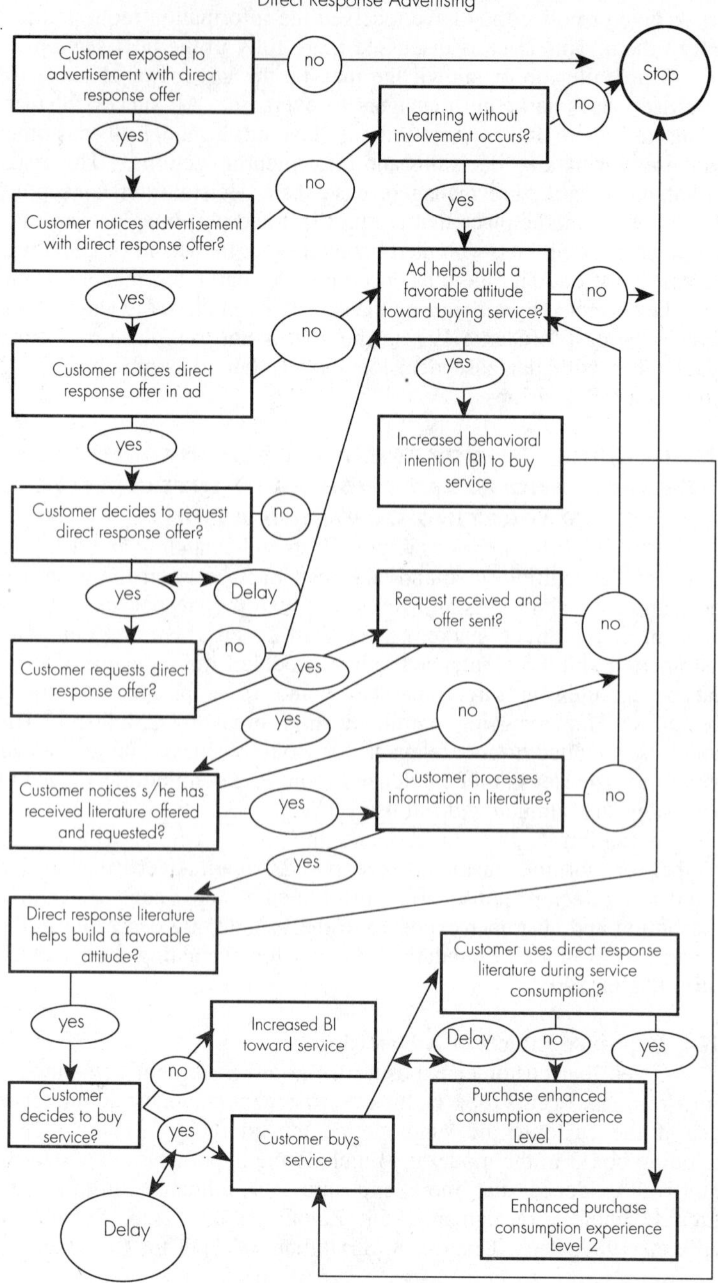

of moving through boxes 1-2-3-5-7-15 is to indicate the peripheral route to persuasion described by Petty and Cacioppo (1986), and the possible impact of perception without awareness (Bornstein and Pittman 1992).

The Central Route to Persuasion

The central route to persuasion described (Petty and Cacioppo 1986; Petty, et al. 1991) applied to direct marketing is reflected in the customer noticing and being motivated to request the direct response offer (linking of boxes 4 and 6), or increases customer awareness of the advertising, affecting favorable attitude toward the brand (linking of boxes 4 and 5).

$TOMA_a$ and $TOMA_b$ Linkage: To Box 5 and Beyond. Image advertising effects are accounted for in the model by linkage between boxes 4 and 5 as well the mere exposure effect. $TOMA_a$ is the customer's top-of-mind-awareness for an ad in a product category. Shares of $TOMA_a$ for different brands in different product categories are reported in *Advertising Age* from monthly U.S. household surveys sponsored by Gallup and *Advertising Age.* Unaided $TOMA_a$ by brand is measured by asking sample members to name the advertising that first comes to mind from all they have seen, heard, or read in the previous 30 days. The hypotheses are supported empirically that increasing $TOMA_a$ is associated with increasing $TOMA_b$, top-of-mind-awareness toward the brand; $TOMA_b$ is associated positively to building preference (box 5), intentions (box 7), and sales (box 15) (Woodside and Wilson, 1985).

The Customer Direct-Response-Route to Persuasion. Rapp and Collins (1987) emphasize that advertisements can and should "do double-duty by inviting a [direct] response from your best prospects while increasing general awareness of your product or service." Rapp and Collins (1987) then advocate that "advertising a high-price, high-involvement product should focus first on getting a response from prime prospects rather than on creating an image. Then, convert that response to a sale by providing powerful linkage (the fulfillment literature)."

The active noticing a direct response offer is a central route to persuasion that may lead to deciding to request the offer in the ad, for example, request a free catalog or brochure offered in a television commercial, magazine, or newspaper ad (linking boxes 4 and 6). Note in Exhibit 5 that a delay is indicated between boxes 6 and 8; customers may decide to request the direct response offer but never get around to doing so. Advertisers sometimes attempt to reduce the delay by reducing the effort and time necessary for the customer to respond; such attempts include placing a telephone number in the ad (sometimes toll-free), using free-standing-inserts (FSIs), and suggesting that a number be circled on the reader-service card. There are systematic differences in buying behavior, according to the mode customers use to request information (Manville 1987; Woodside and Soni 1988). For example, when advertising a high-involving service—vacation destination travel—the proportions buying the service varied from a low of .26 for reader-service card inquirers to .36 for direct-response coupon inquirers to .43 for toll-free telephone inquirers.

Marketers' Responses to Customer Inquiries. According to the DMA, direct marketing is "an interactive system." Thus, two-way customer/marketer communications are planned for implementation. However, as described earlier, substantial numbers of marketers do not fulfill requests made by customers to offers included in the marketers' ads. Thus the marketing activity of getting back to the customer (boxes 8 to 9 to 10) is not a given; it has to be built-in and monitored actively in the IMC program. This first fulfillment step is often subcontracted out by the advertiser or the advertising agency to a fulfillment house. Such a marketing strategy has the advantage of bringing in the expertise of fulfillment experts, but also increases the need for careful coordination and attention to customer requests.

Unfortunately, in most directing programs, little attempt to gain information and to build a relationship are designed into the initial linkage of customer-response and marketer-fulfillment. As a test of this proposition, make ten telephone calls in response to television commercials and magazine ads and record the number of questions asked by the person fulfilling your request beyond asking for your address. Also, record persuasive attempts to encourage readership included in the fulfillment package, and record whether or not the advertiser calls you back to learn if you received the fulfillment linkage and to ask for your order. The proposition is that most marketers are missing the opportunity to build relationships with new customers at the first moment-of-truth, even for high-priced products and services.

Customer Use of Fulfillment Materials. What happens after customers receive the fulfillment literature they request? Customers vary considerably in how they process fulfillment literature; some are not aware of receiving it; some do not report ever asking for it when later asked; and some do use the materials extensively for making buying decisions.

In a study, 45 percent of inquirers who were sent the literature they requested did not report either asking for nor receiving the literature (Woodside and Soni 1991). Thus customers may not process information they request and receive. Reaching box 11 in Exhibit 5 is not a certainty; monitoring this step in the direct marketing process is necessary to ensure customer usage of fulfillment literature. "Great advertising creative work that results in high inquiry rates is not good enough; the direct-response offer may have to be even better to get through the second level of clutter—all the competing advertising brochures and catalogs being received by the inquirer" (Woodside and Soni 1991).

Customer information processing of the fulfillment materials often may be helpful in convincing the customer to buy (box 13), and her/his purchase choices (box 15). Note that a delay is shown in Exhibit 5 between boxes 13 and 15; this indicates that the effects of direct-marketing fulfillment on buying behavior may be long term and not immediately visible in one advertising campaign. Monitoring the impact on direct marketing on sales should include assessing the effects over several time periods beyond the immediate advertising-and-buying time frame. The term "enhanced purchase consumption experience" is used in box 17 to express the proposition that the customers' experiences in using the product or service is affected by processing the fulfillment literature before purchase—versus not requesting, receiving, or processing such literature.

In some industries, customers may refer to the fulfillment materials while using the product or service (box 18). For example, consumers buying seeds and plants through mail-order may refer to their catalogs for planting information and recipes for preparing vegetables grown; vacation travelers may refer to destination visitor guides to learn about places to visit, things to do, and products to buy during their visit. In one tourism advertising study of visitors to Prince Edward Island in Canada (Woodside, MacDonald, & Trappey 1993), total dollar purchases more than doubled among customers using fulfillment literature compared to expenditures using the literature only before visiting PEI (comparing sales results between box 17 and 18).

Limitations. For many customer-marketing interactions, the model summarized in Exhibit 5 is a simplification of the first stages in an IMC program. Multiple two-way contacts may occur between the customer and marketer before the first purchase-sale. In the U.S. office furniture industry for example, customer response to a direct mail or newspaper ad is often followed by several telephone conversations, sales calls, and customer visits to the marketer's showrooms—all before the first purchase! The recent and long-term history of interactions with many established customers may exist only in the long-term memories of one or two persons in the marketing firm—no computer database may yet be developed for such relationships in many firms.

However, some firms and entire industries have accomplished IMC programs with long-term customers that meet the DMA definition of direct marketing. Handling a database built on such long-term interactive systems, and estimating customer response functions to marketing actions in such systems, are more than a possibility. Such interactive systems and the use of decision models for sensitivity analysis is now more than the future promise of direct marketing. However, building and using computer databases for forecasting net contribution effects of marketing decisions is still time-consuming, expensive, and requires management science expertise. The good news is that computer software, hardware tools, and modelling skill-training have become available in the 1990s.

DIRECT MARKETING IMPLICATIONS FOR DESIGNING AND IMPLEMENTING EFFECTIVE IMC PROGRAMS

In 1986, Stan Rapp predicted, "When the light of a new day dawns on January 1, 1990, I believe that all service companies and many product manufacturers will be spending as much time and money maximizing their relationships with known customers as they now do on their brand-image advertising to the world at large" (Rapp and Collins 1990). The review here of some of the empirical studies in direct marketing indicates that this prediction has not come to pass. However, substantial strides have been made in achieving the opportunities and benefits of direct marketing by some marketers.

The transformation from the illusion of knowledge into marketing wisdom is now occurring in many IMC programs because of (1) advances in computer software/hardware tools in creating and handling databases and (2) marketers' use of customer response functions in decision models for "what if" analyses. The model and empirical findings described here of the initial stages in customer-marketer, direct-marketing interactions indicate that monitoring of each of the multiple points-of-contact needs to occur for an IMC program to be useful.

Transforming marketing away from image-advertising towards relationship marketing—that is, an effective, working IMC program—requires technical computer software and skill-training by marketers. The tools and skill-learning materials are now available. Creating and using decision models from such IMC programs will enable marketers to justify their marketing strategies and tactics with hard evidence; senior management continues to demand nothing less. Recommendation: Let each of us make the transformation before the year 2000.

NOTES

1. *Colloquy* is a free quarterly newsletter published by Frequency Marketing Inc., P.O. Box 3920, Milford, Ohio 45150.

REFERENCES

"A Database Designed Especially for Department Stores (1991)," *Colloquy,* October, 12–13.

ARF (1961), *Toward Better Media Comparisons,* New York: Advertising Research Foundation.

Banks, Seymour (1965), *Experimentation in Marketing,* New York: McGraw-Hill.

Bornstein, Robert F., and Thane S. Pittman (1992), Eds., *Perception Without Awareness,* New York: Guilford Press.

Bulkeley, William M. (1993), "Marketers Mine Their Corporate Databases," *The Wall Street Journal,* June 14, B6.

Caples, John (1974), *Tested Advertising Methods,* Englewood Cliffs, NJ: Prentice-Hall.

Clarke, Darral G. (1993), *Marketing Analysis and Decision Making,* South San Francisco, CA: The Scientific Press.

Colloquy (1991), "Calling All Tennessee Squires," *Colloquy,* Milford, OH: Frequency Marketing, Inc., October, 3.

Cook, Thomas D., and Donald T. Campbell (1979), *Quasi-Experimentation,* Chicago: Rand McNally.

Direct Marketing (1993), "Direct Marketing . . . An Aspect of Total Marketing," *Direct Marketing Magazine,* April, p. 2.

Dubinsky, Alan J., and Thomas N. Ingram (1984), "A Portfolio Approach to Account Profitability," *Industrial Marketing Management,* 13 (February), 57–62.

Dwyer, Robert F. (1980), "Customer Lifetime Valuations to Support Marketing Decision Making," *Journal of Direct Marketing,* 3 (Autumn), 8–15.

Fazio, R. H., M. C. Powell, and C. J. Williams (1989), "The Role of Attitude Accessibility in the Attitude-to-Behavior Process," *Journal of Consumer Research,* 16, 280–288.

Gibson, Richard (1993), "Poor Handling Turns Leads into No-Sales," *The Wall Street Journal,* March 31, B1.

Krugman, Herbert (1965), "The Impact of Television Advertising: Learning without Involvement," *Public Opinion Quarterly,* 29, 349–356.

Levitt, Theodore (1983), *The Marketing Imagination,* New York: Free Press.

Manville, Richard (1987), "Does Advertising—or Product 'Publicity'—Pull More Inquiries? Which Ones Are More Valuable?" *BPAA Communicator,* New York: Business and Professional Advertising Association.

Peters, Tom, and Nancy Austin (1985), *A Passion for Excellence,* New York: Warner Books.

Petty, Richard E., and J. T. Cacioppo (1986), *Communication and Persuasion: Central and Peripheral Routes to Attitude Change,* New York: Springer/Verlag.

Petty, Richard E., Rao Unnava, and Alan J. Strathman (1991), "Theories of Attitude Change," in *Handbook of Consumer Behavior,* ed. by Thomas S. Robertson and Harold H. Kassarjian, Englewood Cliffs, NJ: Prentice-Hall, 241–280.

Phelps, Stephen P. (1993), "A Media Evaluation Model for the 21st Century," *Proceedings of the 1993 Conference of the American Academy of Advertising,* ed. by Esther Thorson, Columbia, MO: School of Journalism, University of Missouri-Columbia, 60–72.

Rapp, Stan, and Tom Collins (1988), *Maxi-marketing,* New York: McGraw-Hill.

Rapp, Stan, and Tom Collins (1990), "Special Report: The Great Marketing Turnaround," *Direct Marketing Magazine,* October, 57–60.

Roman, Ernan (1988), *Integrated Direct Marketing,* New York: McGraw-Hill.

Schultz, Don E., Stanley I. Tannenbaum, and Robert E. Lauterborn (1993), *Integrated Marketing Communications,* Chicago: NTC Business Books.

Schultz, Don E. (1993), "Why Ad Agencies Are Having So Much Trouble with IMC," *Marketing News,* April 26, 12.

Shepard, David (1990), *The New Direct Marketing,* Homewood, IL: Business One Irwin.

"Trend Setters," (1992), *Direct Marketing Magazine,* November, 41.

Woodside, Arch G., Frederick C. Brose, and Randolph J. Trappey III (1991), "Assessing Performance of Business-to-Business and Consumer Direct Marketing Fulfillment Strategies," working paper, New Orleans: Freeman School of Business, Tulane University.

Woodside, Arch G., Roberta MacDonald, and Randolph J. Trappey III (1993), "Effects of Knowledge and Experience on Purchasing Behavior and Consumption Experiences, Working Paper, New Orleans: Freeman School of Business, Tulane University.

Woodside, Arch G., and Ilkka A. Ronkainen (1994), "Improving Conversion Research Studies," in *Travel, Tourism, and Hospitality Research,* 2nd Edition, ed. by J. R. Brent Ritchie and Charles R. Goeldner, New York: Wiley, forthcoming.

Woodside, Arch G., and Praveen K. Soni (1988), "Assessing the Quality of Advertising Inquiries by Mode of Response," *Journal of Advertising Research,* 28 (August/September), 31–37.

Woodside, Arch G., and Praveen K. Soni (1990), "Performance Analysis of Advertising in Competing Media Vehicles," *Journal of Advertising Research,* 30 (February/March), 53–66.

Woodside, Arch G., and Praveen K. Soni (1991), "Direct-Response Advertising Information: Profiling Heavy, Light, and Nonusers," *Journal of Advertising Research,* 31 (December), 26–36.

Woodside, Arch G., and Elizabeth J. Wilson (1985), "Effects of Consumer Awareness of Brand Advertising on Preference," *Journal of Advertising Research,* 25 (August/September), 41–48.

Barbara B. Stern
Associate Professor of Marketing
Rutgers, The State University of New Jersey
Newark, New Jersey

CHAPTER 65

ADVERTISING TO THE "OTHER" CULTURE: WOMEN'S USE OF LANGUAGE AND LANGUAGE'S USE OF WOMEN

Culture is male. . . . What it does mean (among other things) is that the society we live in, like all other historical societies, is a patriarchy. And patriarchies imagine or picture themselves from the male point of view. There is a female culture, but it is an underground, unofficial, minor culture, occupying a small corner of what we think of officially as possible human experience. Both men and women in our culture conceive the culture from a single point of view—the male (Russ 1972).

Men and women occupy separate cultural spheres as well as separate biological ones. Cultural differences between the sexes occur in all known societies (Gilly 1988) and are made manifest in language, the shaper of human reality. Shulamith Firestone, in *The Dialectic of Sex,* argues that "the sex role system divides human experience; men and women live in these different halves of reality; and culture reflects this" (1971). Marketing and advertising researchers have studied several cultural domains in reference to women: stereotypes of women in advertising (Courtney and Whipple 1983; Gilly 1988), feminine themes and values (McLuhan 1951; Marchand 1985), and pictorial depictions of gender roles (Goffman 1979). The focus is ordinarily on *visual* images and depictions of typical characters, settings, and occupational roles. Most advertising studies rely on content analysis and count denotative elements in the visual imagery to assess depictions of women (Ferguson, Kreshel, and Tinkhan 1990). While some research efforts have incorporated more connotative message elements, these are characteristically conducted outside the advertising discipline (Williamson 1978).

Even advertising studies of "latent" content, requiring not simply observation of what is "manifest" in the visuals but also interpretation of what the images mean, do not ordinarily focus on language (Ferguson, Kreshel, and Tinkhan 1990). Although feminist critics since Robin Lakoff (1975) have identified a dichotomy between male and female language, the impact of genderization on the language used in advertising messages has not yet been widely studied. However, research on advertising verbals is necessary because language is the vehicle through which culture is transmitted. This chapter thus adopts the perspective of feminist language-based criticism—the discipline that focuses on women's experience as a proper subject for study in its own right (Register 1975). It draws specifically from feminist literary criticism to examine advertising's *words* to clarify how women use language and how language uses women (Lakoff 1975). The purpose is to adapt another methodology from a different discipline to enrich our understanding of the nature of role portrayals. Literary criticism can contribute to advertising research by rendering women's language visible. In so doing, it may assist advertisers to design persuasive appeals with greater verisimilitude to position or reposition products more effectively to men's and women's markets.

The chapter begins by discussing some cultural differences between men and women that give rise to three qualities characteristic of women's language: propriety, hesitancy, and verbal excess. It next describes the influence of sex-specific language on advertising dialogue and male/female role portrayals. Last, it discusses two contributions that awareness of women's language can make to better advertising. First is the creation of realistic scenarios for dramatic advertisements, those in which characters speak (Wells 1989). Second is the development of copy language for product positioning where male and female characters speak and/or are spoken about. The chapter views advertising as one kind of creative text (Stern 1989), and relies primarily on feminist literary criticism as the interpretive filter. It is limited to the verbal parts of advertising, and thus excludes elements such as pictures, scenery, or music. Additionally, it does not deal with other cultural factors such as age, race, or social class likely to interact with sex and treated fully by other researchers.

LANGUAGE AND WOMEN'S CULTURE

Examination of women's language as a special and separate entity begins with an overview of the pervasiveness of male norms in a patriarchal society (de Beauvoir 1953). The gender asymmetry that characterizes male-dominant society (Ortner 1974; Staton 1987) went unquestioned for a millenia. It was not until the 1960s that feminist critics brought to light the hidden assumptions of male-centered culture in which "female" is defined by negative reference to "male" as the human norm (Abrams 1988). For most of human history—read by feminists as "his story"—women internalized civilization's reigning patriarchal biases and accepted the cultural constructs defining masculinity and femininity (Abrams 1988). Although debate continues as to whether men and women are different—and if so, why—(Deaux and Major 1987), consensual beliefs about the stereotypical personality traits that characterize and differentiate the average man and woman have remained consistent for nearly two decades (Broverman, et al. 1972; Deaux and Major 1987).

Stereotypical maleness and femaleness are built into the patriarchal culture and expressed in the language of both art and life. Language is now widely viewed as basic to the constitution of social life—a dynamic social phenomenon—(Maynard 1986) rather than a stable neutral medium of communication. Feminist theorists pointed out that language categorizes and structures one's concept of oneself, others, and society, and amassed evidence indicating the male bias encoded in our linguistic conventions (Berman 1988). For example, the nouns "man" or "mankind" are used to define all human beings, and the pronouns "he" and "his" often refer to ostensibly gender-neutral nouns such as God, inventor, author, poet—and the advertiser as well (McConnell-Ginet, Borker, and Furman 1980). Lacan states that women's relationship to language must be seen in terms of the traditional cultural construction of language "around the male term [the "phallic" term] . . . or the privileging of that term" (Mitchell and Rose 1982). The gender identification created and maintained in language was based on the male as a normative model of the self, and the female as a deviant "other," first identified in Simone de Beauvoir's landmark book, *The Second Sex* (1953). Since that time, feminist critics have brought to light the almost unthinkable acceptance of male norms and female opposites hidden beneath the surface.

By the 1960s, feminist researchers had begun to uncover the extent to which male dominance is so rooted in our terminology that it is accepted as "normal" language (Abrams 1988). Feminism—also called "women's studies"—has taken as its domain the study of women's "place" in many disciplines (Ellmann 1968; Millett 1969; Showalter 1985). Its foundation is acceptance of women's role as cultural "other" (de Beauvoir 1953): the largely invisible subculture unexamined for centuries. Feminist scholars were the first organized school of criticism to recognize the presence of women (albeit their official invisibility), the kinship among them, and the differences between this *sub rosa* group and that of the male mainstream (Register 1975). Feminist criticism always examines cultural factors because to understand a woman's point of view (as a character in a novel or in an advertisement), a critic must take into account the social, legal, and economic status of women in society.

To do justice to the female point of view, feminist criticism in America began by investigating the concept of an appropriate cultural "place" for each sex (Welter 1966). Linguists and literary critics set out to expose the hitherto unquestioned assumptions embedded in language as a result of place (Lakoff 1975). American society, like most others, has traditionally assigned a different "place"—an appropriate sphere of activity—to men and women. Women historically assumed the role of homemaker, and men that of provider (Bullough 1974). In at least one consumer behavior text, sex-linked traits are treated as subcultural differences (Schiffman and Kanuk 1991), and the argument is made that since sex roles are culturally determined, gender as a subcultural category is appropriate. Interestingly, this consumer-oriented definition of subculture as a "distinct cultural group which exists as an identifiable segment within a larger, more complex society" (Schiffman and Kanuk 1991) parallels the feminist view of women's culture. In this view, women exist as an identifiable segment within the larger, more complex male society that dominates American life.

In post-Industrial Revolution America, the distinction in place became more rigid. By the mid-nineteenth century, the new manufacturing economy and its attendant prosperity led to a more sharply schismatic differentiation between male and female roles than had existed in the past. When men and women both worked at home—a common pattern in society based on an agrarian economy (Beard 1946)—their experiences were centered in the same sphere, although role differences existed. Once men left the home, however, and went into the workplace, their paths diverged. Man's place became the factory, later generalized into the "work place," and woman's place became the home. Victorian society solidified the separation, and idealized the woman enshrined within her home as a "lady"—pure, dedicated to her husband and children, and untouched by the rough and tumble of the external world. This pedestalization was commonplace in American thought in the nineteenth century, evident in literature and language as well as social life. The nature of women's language was, for the most part, circumscribed by the limitations associated with her place in society.

THREE CHARACTERISTICS OF WOMEN'S LANGUAGE

Beginning with Lakoff (1975), feminist critics have set out to specify the impact of place on "woman's language," that distinctively feminine *style* of speaking and writing. They have focused on sentence structure, diction (word choice), organizational flow, and characteristic images (Showalter 1977) to ascertain how women select and combine words in everyday life. This usage is related to the covert messages that culture sends about women's place. Women's speech reflects cultural imperatives calling for niceness, politeness, ladylike expression, and concern for the feelings of others. Women's style is described by Firestone as "personal, subjective, emotional, descriptive" in contrast to men's "vigorous, spare, hard-hitting, objective" expression (1971). Women externalize society's message to be "nice" in their speech, just as men externalize society's permission to be "rough": male talk can be powerful, hard, intellectual as a result of man's place from childhood on—the ballfield, the army, the factory. But women are expected to speak more softly. Three characteristics that mark women's language as special are its propriety, hesitancy, and verbal excess (Lakoff 1975).

Propriety

Propriety in word choice (diction) and grammar reinforces the dual sexual standard. First and foremost, women are expected to talk "like ladies." This entails avoiding obscene words, curses, and angry expletives. Sexual or scatological terms are taboo for women (Johnson and Fine 1985), while men who curse are considered "one of the guys."

One reason why obscenity is off-limits for women is that some "four-letter" words are expressions of anger historically associated with male hostility. When a woman uses certain expletives, she expresses a degree of rage that threatens the social order, for women are expected to soothe angry words, not hurl them. Powerful Anglo-Saxon curse words are deemed unladylike, and when women do use curses in literature, they are labeled as either rebels (intellectual bluestockings; defiant temptresses) or outcasts (whores, addicts, illiterates).

In addition to sanitized diction, women are also expected to use hyper-correct grammar and any polite forms of address the language possesses. The expectation of perfect correctness harks back to women's role as the keeper of the cultural flame: while men went off to work and war to protect society, women stayed home to preserve its cherished values for transmission to future generations. Women have traditionally been regarded as guardians of the language, primarily as mothers teaching their children informally, but also in more formal occupational roles as elementary school teachers and librarians. Women were thus conventionally cast as conservators of language deemed proper in reference to dictional choice and grammatical structure.

Hesitancy

Women's language also avoids the taint of impropriety by displaying hesitancy or tentativeness (Lakoff 1975). This hesitancy is expressed in two ways: a tendency to make assertions using tag-question form, and a reliance on "hedge" or filler words. Women are likely to state things tentatively either by appending a question to a declarative sentence or by turning a statement into a question. For example, a simple declarative sentence reads: "It's a nice day." This is made tentative by a tacked-on question: "It's a nice day, isn't it?" or by the interrogative, "Isn't it a nice day?" Women are thought to avoid commitment to a point of view that declarative statements imply in order to avoid potential conflict with those who might disagree. Conflict, like anger, is unladylike, and women who declare themselves in no uncertain terms are considered at best unfeminine, at worst aggressive and pushy.

A second way to express uncertainty is to circumlocute, and women tend to use "filler" and "hedge" words that undercut ideas so that they may be stated, but not strong enough to provoke disagreement. Empty adjectives, long stripped of substantive meaning, such as "divine, charming, cute" (Lakoff 1975) are all-purpose descriptors attached to nearly any noun. Additionally, meaningless filler expressions such as "well," "you know," "sort of," or "like" punctuate sentences. The avoidance of assertive language is entertainingly demonstrated in a short parody by Veronica Geng (1979), repeating a conversation overheard in a restaurant:

> *Valerie: "Their sole amandine sounds* nice."

Man: "I would quarrel with that, Valerie, I'm afraid. Though you are free to disagree. I'd like nothing more than to hear you disagree. Show some spine, Valerie, for a change."

Valerie: "Well, to be honest—maybe *I'm* way out of line *on this one, but I'm* pretty *positive that I* probably *don't want the sole, I* almost *think."*

Man: "Among aware, intelligent people there will always be some difference of opinion. You should have the sole Valerie, even if it is the wrong choice. Nobody's keeping score."

Valerie: "Well, *your willingness to discuss this has* meant a lot. *I* really *appreciate it. I* guess *I'll* just *have the gravy." [emphasis added]*

Verbal Excess

Related to women's use of tentative expressions and filler words is the last characteristic: a tendency to verbal excess. One kind of excess is sheer verbosity—constructions that use more words than necessary to express a thought. This, of course, inevitably accompanies reliance on filler phrases, and is a means of softening direct assertions by circumlocution, or beating around the bush. Another kind of excess is hyperbole or overstatement. Language is hyperbolic when frequent underlining or italicizing of words and expressions occurs, when unremarkable comments end with exclamation points, and when emphatic words are sprinkled throughout. While advertising in general is often condemned for puffery, it is important to note that some forms of overstatement are more characteristic of women's usage patterns than of men's. For example, women's language often attaches words describing excessive emotions to mundane things. McLuhan was one of the first to point out that technology provided the "ever intenser thrills" (1951) that characterized advertising depictions of the "mechanical bride's" sexuality. This particular kind of excess is still with us, for a 1989 advertisement for Alberto Culver's Bold Hold hair spray says: "Go ahead . . . give your hair a *thrill!*" Here, a hype-word, an underlining, and an exclamation point are used all at once. Despite the changes that have occurred in the last generation, women's language is still deeply etched with cultural patterns that lend legitimacy to hesitancy and hyperbole.

ADVERTISING AND WOMEN'S LANGUAGE

How Women Use Language in Dramatic Scenarios

An understanding of women's language is necessary for the creation of realistic scenarios in dramatic advertisements—those in which the characters speak to an audience or to each other (Wells 1989). These mini-dramas often use everyday speech, and verisimilitude is enhanced when the characters sound "right." One example of a slice-of-life print drama using realistic dialogue is Talbot's announcement of the 1989 opening of its main New York store (see Exhibit 1).

EXHIBIT 1. Talbot's Advertisement

[WOM 1]	"Look at that brick building . . . I've never noticed it before. What do you think it's going to be?"
[WOM 2]	"I think . . ."
[WOM 1]	"It's so classic . . . like this blazer of mine. I've had it for so long. It's starting to wear out. Where do you think I can find a new one?"

Tag-line: A new tradition in classic women's clothing is coming soon to 525 Madison Avenue.

The ad reveals several characteristics of women's language in spoken dialogue. WOM 1 asks naive and self-doubting questions (what is that building? where can I get a new blazer?) and twice repeats the intensive "so," another typical hedge word (Lakoff 1975). Neither WOM 1 nor WOM 2 completes a thought, for the elliptical periods (". . .") indicate a trailing off of ideas expressed by a long pause. WOM 1 is garrulous—she allows WOM only two words before resuming speech—and her train of thought appears disconnected. She moves from contemplation of a new building to a metaphorical comparison of the building to her blazer, based on the common dimension of "classic." The characters' questions and incomplete thoughts demonstrate the mildly tentative and inoffensive women's language that lend verisimilitude to advertising as well as to literary dialogue. This newspaper ad relies on words alone to delineate the characters by letting them speak in a language recognizable by other women, the sex-linked target market for a new women's clothing store.

It is essential for advertisers who seek to create convincing dramatic scenarios to put suitable language into a character's mouth. Verisimilitude requires sensitivity to differences between appropriate language for men and women. An example of typically male language is found in a Perry Ellis ad for men's cologne, the first instance of a speaker using the "F" word in a nationwide print ad (although the word was not spelled out in full) (Stern, Gould, and Barak 1987). When women do use obscenity, their curses are milder and less sexually explicit. For example, a Paco Rabanne men's cologne ad features an unseen woman talking on the telephone to a scantily dressed man. She describes her fantasy of him "wearing that Paco Rabanne cologne—and damned little else." "Damned" is not a very strong expletive, and is categorized as a profanity rather than a reference to scatological or sexual activity (Johnson and Fine 1985). The word suggests that the woman is a sexually frank, "liberated" partner—something stronger might imply that she is a whore. Advertisers who are sensitive to women's language can strike a note of authenticity in dramas, even those where visual images are not present.

How Women Are "Read": Language and Cultural Roles

Women both use and are used by language, for cultural roles, values, and constraints can be read in language that describes and defines women whether or not they speak directly (Lakoff 1975). Feminist critics point out differences between the way male and female characters are read, for most readers—men and women—interpret the male experience as dominant and the female experience as peripheral or subordinate (Schumacher 1975). It is important to understand that these norms are almost automatically called into play when people come into contact with male and female characters in a text. Literature—like advertising—is a textual mirror that reveals the realities of the men's and women's lives (Bishop 1979; Donovan 1975). Some advertising critics feel that it is a "distorted" mirror (Pollay 1986), and feminist theoreticians often adopt a prescriptive agenda for ameliorating what they judge to be predominantly negative stereotypes of women (Register 1975).

A contribution of feminist literary criticism to decoding how language uses women has been the revelation of the existence of sex-linked readings by pointing out the underlying "masculinist" assumptions. The methodological process at the heart of feminist theory is the simple act of reversing the sex roles of characters to highlight underlying norms (Schumacher 1975). Feminists suggest that one way to test the assumptions that we take to be the "natural" order of things is to imaginatively reverse the positions of commonly paired binary opposites such as man and woman (Fetterley 1977). This enables us to see that what we take for natural is socially conditioned. These societal norms are invoked when people "read" about male and female characters. Goffman sums up the method as follows: "By imagining the sexes switched and imagining the appearance of what results, one can jar oneself into awareness of stereotypes" (1979).

Stereotyping pervades literary images of women. Women characters are described in positive terms when they behave appropriately *as women*—when they embody socially-approved feminine traits such as kindness, tactfulness, patience, and selflessness (Richmond-Abbott 1979). If women embody masculine traits such as aggressiveness, independence, or leadership, they may be judged negatively and stereotyped as "bitch," "ball-buster," and so forth. Feminist critics point out that masculine traits are ordinarily culturally rewarded to a greater extent than feminine traits, but only when men display them (Fox and Hesse-Biber 1984). Cultural changes in sex roles in the past 20 years have been associated with the change in woman's place from home to work site. Nevertheless, despite the 1970s call for androgyny (Heilbrun 1973) and re-readings of cultural texts based on a man's or a woman's conformance to generally-valued human traits (autonomy, unselfishness, humaneness), a traditional trait-dichotomy still differentiates the sexes (Gilly

1988). Even *Ms.* magazine, despite an explicit commitment to nonstereotypic portrayals of women, presents substantial levels of "sexism" in the course of its 18-year history (Ferguson, Kreshel, and Tinkhan 1990). With few exceptions, the androgynous or non-sexist ideal did not become popular reality, and men and women characters are still likely to be read differently.

Reading Women in Advertising

Culturally held beliefs about the sexes can also be read in ads, for as McLuhan pointed out, "ad agencies express for the collective society that which dreams and uncensored behavior do in individuals. They give spatial form to hidden impulses, and when analyzed, make possible bringing into reasonable order a great deal that could not otherwise be observed or discussed" (1951). Since advertisements present advertisers' views of how men and women can be profitably pictured (Goffman 1979), they are likely to show the culturally approved version of maleness/femaleness.

Advertisers often devise male/female characters as spokespersons when it is necessary to position or reposition a product on the basis of sex. Marketers now feel that a wide range of products can be targeted to both sexes. Although the Advertising to Women ad agency, for example, positioned itself in the 1970s as an agency for "women's products," its philosophy shifted in the 1980s: "We feel that you can take almost every product that's traditionally marketed to men and now market it to women" (Kent and Fitch 1985). Products that were formerly marketed to men (Jockey and Calvin Klein underwear, for example) have been repositioned for women, just as products once marketed to women only (Clinique skin treatments, Sebastian hair gel and mousse) have been repositioned for men. The question that arises is, should there be one ad with one spokesperson to appeal to both sexes, or separate ads, one with a male spokesperson and one with a female spokesperson? Strategic decisions as to the superiority of single versus dual approaches can be made more knowledgeably if more can be learned about how audiences read the men and women who speak for products and services.

The feminist method of reading by role reversal is well-suited to an advertising example of perfectly matched Merrill Lynch (ML) print ads from the same issue of the same periodical (*The New Yorker,* September 15, 1986). The ads take up the same amount of space (one page), feature the same product/service, and use the same title ("Financial Consultant") for the spokesperson. The only difference is that one has a male spokesperson, and the other a female. The ad thus permits an unusually clear reading of masculinity and femininity, since the reversal has in effect been performed by the advertiser (see Exhibit 2).

Each ad presents a spokesperson, using the individual's own words (in quotation marks), followed by a narrator's comment (last two

EXHIBIT 2. Merrill Lynch Advertisements

Male Spokesperson	**Female Spokesperson**
Picture of Jere Goldsmith (man)	Picture of Saly Glassman (woman)
"I have to earn my reputation every day."	"My clients work hard for their money. So I work hard to invest it right."
"I'm not one to rest on my laurels. My goal is to give you better service than you could get from anyone else."	"I feel my clients deserve nothing less from me than total commitment."
"I start by looking at your long-range goals and how much risk makes you comfortable. Together we'll find the best way to meet your basic financial needs, like asset management, credit management, insurance, and tax minimization."	"That's why we sit down together first and talk about your long-range goals and what level of risk is right for you. Then we'll see how best to handle your basic financial needs, including asset management, credit management, insurance, and tax minimization."
Jere has the resources to put his own reputation, plus that of Merrill Lynch, behind every recommendation he makes.	With all of Merrill Lynch behind her, Saly has the resources to help you make the right investment decisions.
Want a professional financial consultant like Jere Goldsmith, and the strength of Merrill Lynch on your side?	Put a professional financial consultant like Saly Glassman—plus the strength of Merrill Lynch—to work for you.

paragraphs). The ads reveal several underlying assumptions about culturally conditioned male and female norms that result in different readings of Saly versus Jere. To begin, Saly's headline is nearly twice as long as Jere's. She is more talkative, and focuses on her clients; he is more laconic, and talks about himself. In the headline, Saly emphasizes hard work for her clients, while Jere stresses his reputation among peers. Saly's first copy sentence reiterates her nurturance (she uses the words "feel" and "commitment"), while Jere's echoes his competitiveness (he will not "rest on his laurels," a reference to the winners of Olympic games, and his "goal" is "better service"). Next, Saly says that "we" will sit down and talk, while Jere says that "I" will start by looking at your goals, and then "we'll" find the best way to manage your finances. The narrator says that Saly needs "all of Merrill Lynch behind her," but Jere "has the resources to put his own reputation" ("plus that of ML" as an afterthought) behind his recommendations. The narrator then commands the reader to "put" Saly "to work for you," but asks the reader to put Jere "on your side."

The ads can be read as illustrations of prevailing mid-1980s norms for masculinity and femininity. Traits related to instrumentality, dominance, and assertiveness are believed to be more characteristic of men, and those related to expressiveness, warmth, and concern for other people are believed to be more characteristic of women (Deaux and Major 1987). Jere's language reveals aggressiveness, competitiveness, and self-confidence; Saly's reveals nurturance, cooperativeness, and reliance on the strength of Merrill Lynch.

Masculine rivalry has long been identified as a popular advertising theme (McLuhan 1951), and competition for financial success was especially prevalent in the money-oriented 1980s. However, women's progress in the male workplace caused profound changes in the financial services market. Once women embarked on lifelong careers and gained sufficient education to compete for lucrative positions, they began earning salaries that made them a tempting target for financial vendors (Bartos 1989). Merrill Lynch's marketing strategy, which formerly targeted financial planning to men, now repositioned the services bundle to attract women.

The Saly ads appear to be designed to appeal to women by depicting a female financial consultant who displays traditionally feminine traits such as caring, commitment, and patience. Men and women are thought to differ in their interpretation of the desirability of particular behaviors: women judge communality more desirable than do men, while men judge self-assertive acts more socially desirable (Buss 1981). Jere and Saly appear to conform to the stereotypical cultural norms that expect women to be modest and self-effacing, and men to be heroic and non-conformist (Deaux and Major 1987). While women as financial advisers may now be a commonplace modern role, the language they use relies on traditional concepts of how women are expected to sound.

This may relate to financial industry wisdom, suggesting that women are not as confident in financial management as men, and rely more on their advisers. Proprietary research found that women were more likely to respond unfavorably to "hard sell" than to offers of advice and assistance, for they want someone with whom they can "talk about financial services" (Conklin 1986). Saly personifies the "personal, subjective, emotional, descriptive" style that women are said to prefer (Firestone 1971). Thus, the reading of Saly as feminine and Jere as masculine appears to be part of Merrill Lynch's positioning strategy in using a female spokesperson for the new women's market and retaining a male spokesperson for the men's segment.

However, even though male and female consumers read text through the filter of sex-specific concerns, much additional research on stereotyping is necessary. Several questions arise in reference to the creation of effective product appeals in an age of evolving target markets and to the role of advertising as an agent for social change. The question of advertising effectiveness requires more informed understanding of whether women ought to be set apart as a distinct market segment in situations where this does not seem warranted by specific relationships between gender and product (Astroff 1991). This requires further examination, for at present it is unclear whether women do indeed respond more *favorably* to a woman financial adviser than to a man (Milner 1991). It is at least arguable that women may read authoritativeness in a male character as preferable because women may not yet be conditioned to accept their own self-sufficiency (Donovan 1975). Recent research in social psychology using reader response theory suggests that when readers are faced with a narrator, they have been culturally conditioned to expect the narrator to be male. This is based on previous reading experience (more stories are told by men than women) and on general cultural beliefs (Howard and Allen 1989).

The issue of cultural conditioning leads to the need for more careful examination of whether (or how) advertising perpetuates/changes sex-role stereotypes. Despite objectively similar roles that can be taken by men or women nowadays, stereotypes about sex-linked appropriate behaviors—including language—persevere and are embodied in advertisements (Deaux and Major 1987). Even though women have entered the work force and educational institutions in record numbers in the past decades, old habits built into the traditional cultural heritage die hard. The construct of appropriate role behaviors (Ferguson, Kreshel, and Tinkhan 1990) may be changing more slowly than the actual sociocultural changes in role performance. Habitual usage of language—the vehicle for transmitting the beliefs and values that make up a culture—is one of the most significant definers of sexual identity. Advertisers can benefit from greater sensitivity to the way women use language and are used by it to create messages that talk to the contemporary consumer in a language she understands. However, since advertising seems less an agent for social change than a reflection of the cultural context, its language concretizes societal norms. Nevertheless, both norms and language change over the course of time, and advertisers keep pace with the ongoing cultural flow to create effective appeals. As Goffman says, (1979)

> *By and large, advertisers do not create the ritualized expressions they employ; they seem to draw upon the same corpus of displays, the same ritual idiom, that is the resource of all of us who participate in social situations, and to the same end: the rendering of glimpsed action readable. If anything, advertisers conventionalize our conventions, stylize what is already a stylization.*

REFERENCES

Abrams, Meyer H. (1988), *A Glossary of Literary Terms,* Fifth Edition. New York: Holt, Rinehart and Winston, Inc.

Astroff, Roberta (1991), "Advertising, Anthropology, and Cultural Brokers: The Commodification of Latino Culture," in *Global and Multinational Advertising,* eds. Basil G. Englis and D. Frederick Baker, Hillsdale, NJ: Lawrence Erlbaum Associates, Inc.

Beard, Mary R. (1946), *Women as Force in History: A Study in Traditions and Realities.* New York: Collier Books.

Berman, Art (1988), *From the New Criticism to Deconstruction: The Reception of Structuralism and Post-Structuralism.* Chicago: University of Illinois Press.

Bishop, Nadean (1979), "Women in Literature," in *The American Woman: Her Past, Her Present, Her Future,* ed. Marie Richmond-Abbott. New York: Holt, Rinehart and Winston, 48–70.

Bullough, Vern L. (1974), *The Subordinate Sex: A History of Attitudes Toward Women.* Baltimore: Penguin Books, Inc.

Buss, D. M. (1981), "Sex Differences in the Evaluation and Performance of Dominant Acts," *Journal of Personality and Social Psychology,* 40, 147–154.

Broverman, I. K., Vogel, S. R., Broverman, D. M., Clarkson, F. E., and Rosenkrantz, P. S. (1972), "Sex-role Stereotypes: A Current Appraisal," *Journal of Social Issues,* 28 (No. 2), 59–78.

Conklin, Michele (1986), "Purses and Portfolios," *Madison Avenue,* 28 (October), 25–26.

Courtney, Alice E. and Thomas W. Whipple (1983), *Sex Stereotyping in Advertising.* Lexington, MA: D. C. Heath and Company.

de Beauvoir, Simone (1953), *The Second Sex,* trans. H. M. Parshley. New York: Alfred A. Knopf, Inc.

Deaux, Kay and Brenda Major (1987), "Putting Gender into Context: An Interactive Model of Gender-Related Behavior," *Psychological Review,* 94 (No. 3), 369–389.

Donovan, Josephine (1975), *Feminist Literary Criticism: Explorations in Theory.* Lexington, KY: University Press of Kentucky.

Ellmann, Mary (1968), *Thinking About Women.* New York: Harcourt, Brace, Jovanovich.

Ferguson, Jill Hicks, Peggy J. Kreshel, and Spencer E. Tinkham (1990), "In the Pages of *Ms.:* Sex Role Portrayals of Women in Advertising," *Journal of Advertising,* 19 (Number 1), 40–51.

Fetterley, Judith (1977), *The Resisting Reader: A Feminist Approach to American Fiction.* Bloomington: University of Indiana Press.

Firestone, Shulamith (1971), *The Dialectic of Sex: The Case for Feminist Revolution.* New York: Bantam Books.

Fox, Mary Frank and Sharlene Hesse-Biber (1984), *Women at Work.* Boston: Mayfield Publishing Company.

Geng, Veronica (1979), "Lobster Night," *The New Yorker,* (February 26), 30–33.

Gilly, Mary C. (1988), "Sex Roles in Advertising: A Comparison of Television Advertisements in Australia, Mexico, and the United States," *Journal of Marketing,* 52 (April), 75–85.

Goffman, Erving (1979), *Gender Advertising.* New York: Harper & Row.

Heilbrun, Carolyn (1973), *Toward a Recognition of Androgyny.* New York: Alfred A. Knopf.

Howard, Judith A. and Carolyn Allen (1989), "Making Meaning: Revealing Attributions Through Analyses of Readers' Responses," *Social Psychology Quarterly,* 52 (No. 4), 280–298.

Johnson, Fern L. and Marlene G. Fine (1985), "Sex Differences in Uses and Perceptions of Obscenity," *Women's Studies in Communication,* 8 (Spring), 11–24.

Kent, Debra and Ed Fitch (1985), "Honey, is this your aftershave or mine?" *Advertising Age,* (September 12), 17.

Lakoff, Robin (1975), *Language and Woman's Place.* New York: Harper & Row.

Marchand, Roland (1985), *Advertising the American Dream: Making Way for Modernity, 1920–1940.* Berkeley: University of California Press.

Maynard, Douglas W. (1986), "A Review of John Heritage, *Garfinkel and Ethnomethodology,* 1984," *Contemporary Sociology,* 15, 346–349.

McConnell-Ginet, Sally, Ruth Borker, and Nelly Furman (1980), *Woman and Language in Literature and Society.*

McLuhan, Marshall (1951), *The Mechanical Bride.* Boston: Beacon Press.

Millett, Kate (1970), *Sexual Politics.* Garden City: Doubleday.

Milner, Laura M. (1991), "Multinational Gender Positioning: A Call for Research," in *Global and Multinational Advertising,* eds. Basil G. Englis and D. Frederick Baker, Hillsdale, NJ: Lawrence Erlbaum Associates, Inc.

Mitchell, Juliet and Jacqueline Rose (1982), *Feminine Sexuality: Jacques Lacan and the Ecole Freudienne,* trans. J. Rose. New York: Norton.

Ortner, Sherry B. (1974), "Is Female to Male as Nature is to Culture?" in *Women, Culture, and Society,* eds. M. Z. Rosaldo and L. Lamphere. Stanford: Stanford University Press, 67–87.

Pollay, Richard W. (1986), "The Distorted Mirror: Reflections on the Unintended Consequences of Advertising," *Journal of Marketing,* 50 (April), 18–36.

Register, Cheri (1975), "American Feminist Literary Criticism: A Bibliographical Introduction," in *Feminist Literary Criticism: Explorations in Theory,* ed. Josephine Donovan, Lexington, KY: University Press of Kentucky, 1–28.

Richmond-Abbott Marie (1979), "Stereotypes of Men and Women in the American Culture," in *The American Woman: Her Past, Her Present, Her Future,* ed. Marie Richmond-Abbott. New York: Holt, Rinehart and Winston, 71–95.

Russ, Joanna (1972), "What Can a Heroine Do? or Why Women Can't Write," in *Images of Women in Fiction: Feminist Perspectives,* ed. Susan Koppelman Cornillon, Bowling Green, OH: Bowling Green University Popular Press.

Schiffman, Leon G. and Leslie Lazar Kanuk (1991), *Consumer Behavior,* Fourth Edition. Englewood Cliffs: Prentice-Hall, Inc.

Schumacher, Dorin (1975), "Subjectivities: A Theory of the Critical Process," in *Feminist Literary Criticism: Explorations in Theory,* ed. Josephine Donovan, Lexington, KY: University Press of Kentucky, 29–37.

Showalter, Elaine (1985), *The New Feminist Criticism: Essays on Women, Literature, and Theory.* New York: Pantheon.

—— (1977), *A Literature of Their Own: British Women Novelists From Bronte to Lessing.* Princeton: Princeton University Press.

Staton, Shirley (1987), *Literary Theories in Praxis.* Philadelphia: The University of Pennsylvania Press.

Stern, Barbara B. (1989), "Literary Criticism and Consumer Research: Overview and Illustrative Analysis," *Journal of Consumer Research,* 16 (December), 322–334.

——, Stephen J. Gould, and Benny Barak (1987), "Baby Boom Singles: The Social Seekers," *The Journal of Consumer Marketing,* 4 (Fall), 5–22.

Wells, William D. (1989), "Lectures and Dramas," in *Cognitive and Affective Responses to Advertising,* eds. Patricia Cafferata and Alice M. Tybout, Lexington, MA: D. C. Heath and Company, 13–20.

Welter, Barbara (1966), "The Cult of True Womanhood: 1920–1960," *American Quarterly,* 18 (Summer), 151–174.

Williamson, Judith (1978), *Decoding Advertisements,* London: Marion Boyars.

PART NINE

GLOBAL MARKETING

PART NINE

INTRODUCTION

The dramatic changes and trends that can characterize the types of marketing we have examined in the first eight parts are magnified in the field of global marketing. Corporations planning to enter the global arena may find themselves in a seemingly unpredictable new world, where marketing data is not always available or reliable, and their existing marketing mix goes right out the window.

As Illka Ronkainen points out in Chapter 66, market conditions in the United States over the past decade have encouraged corporate international expansion. Factors such as the trade deficit, an increase in U.S. investment by foreign companies, and the state of the U.S. economy have led more and more companies to look to other nations—particularly European countries and the Far East—for bigger and better markets.

This growth in global trade has come at a time favorable to international business. Recently, the potential for overseas profits has been greatly increased by the opening up of the former Soviet Union and, to a lesser extent, the North American Free Trade Agreement and the Single European Act (the goal is *to create* a single economy in Europe).

Part Nine begins with an overview of global marketing, providing insights on why a company may consider international expansion; the role that governments play; and some of the major challenges in dealing with differing economic, cultural, and political systems. Based on its particular goals, forecasts, and needs, a corporation may choose several ways to initiate global activities, ranging from manufacturing goods domestically and exporting them, to owning and operating production facilities on foreign soil.

Throughout Part Nine, the importance of carefully planning an entry into the global market is stressed. Chapter 67 offers an in-depth look into the class of information needed before entering any foreign market. The time investment and dollar costs of collecting market data can be high, and the resulting information may not be compatible with that of other nations. But spending time and money to painstakingly research unknown foreign markets can save a company untold hours and dollars in later recouping losses from incomplete planning. Once a firm is established as a global entity, the need for information does not stop. In addition to using the information already collected, it is necessary to monitor any changes in the marketing environment for areas of expansion and improvement.

Chapter 68 examines the rules and regulations that govern exports from the U.S., covering controls such as the Export License Application and Information Network (ELAIN) and various export documents. The authors go on to address various import restrictions and regulations, common methods of payment, and other mechanics of marketing abroad. Chapter 71 unveils the machinations of setting prices in a global environment. Factors range from corporate goals and competitive pressures to exchange rates and government regulations. There are basically three pricing strategies an export company may follow. These strategies are based on how much emphasis a corporation puts on its overall costs.

When marketing goods or services in several national markets, it may be necessary to adapt the product, as well as the marketing strategy, to individual markets to ensure success. On the other hand, an increasing number of companies hold that the world's cultures are becoming more homogeneous, and that what interests consumers in one country will interest buyers across the world—particularly in the triad of Europe, North America, and Japan. These "global corporations" treat their various national markets as a single market. Chapter 69 explores variations on this global view, looking at everything from organizational structure to product planning to pricing.

The barter system is still alive and well in major markets. Chapter 70 reveals how international marketers are more likely to trade goods and services than their domestic counterparts are. The terminology of bartering, how arrangements and compensation are made, and how to avoid getting stuck with unsellable goods are all covered.

Expanding into international arenas is both enticing and frightening; the opportunities are excellent, but the hurdles may seem daunting. Whether your company is considering initial entry into the global market, or you're already established as an international entity, the plethora of information in Part Nine should prove useful in sizing up the hurdles and learning how to leap them—or get around them.

Illka A. Ronkainen
Faculty of Marketing and International Business
Georgetown University
Washington, D.C.

Docent of International Marketing
Helsinki School of Economics
Helsinki, Finland

CHAPTER 66

INTERNATIONAL MARKETING CONCEPTS

Between 1970 and 1991, world exports increased sharply from $315 billion to $3,486 billion, or 1,006%. During the same period, however, U.S. exports increased only by 879% from $43 billion to $421 billion. As a consequence, the U.S. share of world exports declined from 15.3 to 12.3% of the total, a reduction of 20%. In spite of the decline in world market share, U.S. exports as a share of GNP have grown substantially in the recent years and was 7.4% in 1991. However, this increase pales in comparison to the trade performance of other nations; for example, Germany has consistently maintained an export share well over 20% of GNP. In interpreting these figures, the large size of the U.S. internal market has to be kept in mind. When exports are scrutinized on a per-capita basis, the United States places last among industrialized nations ($1,565 in 1991), amounting to less than one-fourth of Germany's figure and one-third of the per-person exports of Canada. Even though imports per capita are also relatively low ($2,056), the figure still points out to imports exceeding exports with a trade deficit as a result. The United States has sustained trade deficits during the last decade; the highest deficit was in 1987 at $171 billion. Even though the 1991 figure is lower ($66 billion), these deficits are not sustainable in the long run.

In the same time frame, U.S. foreign direct investment has increased from $75.5 billion to $421 billion, while foreign direct investment in the United States has increased from $13 billion to $404 billion with the major trading partners of the United States leading the way. The share of U.S. investments as a percentage of U.S. and foreign investments has dropped from 85 to 51. For decades the United States was the leading foreign direct investor in the world. In the last ten years, acquisitions in the United States by foreign entities (especially from Europe and Japan) have accelerated due to a low value of the dollar, the attraction of the large internal market of the United States, as well as fears of being excluded from trade by governmental action.

THE INTERNATIONAL MARKETING IMPERATIVE

Both the trade and the investment figures point out to the critical importance of international competitiveness for U.S. firms. On the one hand, they have to be able to sell more abroad; on the other hand, they have to remain competitive in their own domestic market against foreign competitors. Never before has the need to sell to the world been as important: exports have been one of the few bright spots in the overall economic situation of the United States, accounting for 2.2%

growth in an economy that would have otherwise declined 0.4%. To some extent, foreign direct investments substitute for trade activities. Firms operating only in the domestic market may be surprised by the onslaught of foreign competition, and, if unprepared to respond quickly, may lose market share. However, the substitution for trade is far from complete. In many instances, foreign affiliates themselves are major participants in trade. They may import raw materials or components and export some of their output. For example, U.S. affiliates of foreign corporations accounted for over 34% of U.S. merchandise imports and more than 23% of U.S. merchandise exports.

The international marketing operations of a firm evolve over time to take advantage of both the internal resources (such as accumulated experience) and external opportunities (such as the opening of new markets). The explosive changes of the past five years have made international markets more accessible and the advances in technology are shaving the once formidable costs of doing business abroad. The process of a company changing from a domestic-only marketer to one involved with globally-coordinated products and programs is presented in Exhibit 1.

INTERNATIONALIZATION[1]

While over 100,000 U.S. firms are at the minimum infrequent exporters, over 80% of U.S. exports are still accounted for by the 250 largest export firms. The share of U.S. firms engaged internationally is substantially smaller in comparison to countries elsewhere. The reluctance of U.S. business people to seek overseas business opportunities has been attributed to a number of factors such as the relatively large size and self-contained nature of the domestic market and a prevailing attitude that exports are a marginal business. Those who have not pursued business opportunities abroad perceive international marketing as dissimilar from domestic marketing and therefore difficult to cope with, much too risky, and too unprofitable. They also tend to be unfamiliar with foreign market data resources, and the international marketing services, public and private, that are available.

Internationalization Drivers

The internationalization of a firm may be driven by home country factors, target market factors, or firm-specific factors. For many firms around the world, their own markets are far too small to guarantee sustained growth opportunities. As more and more markets are becoming open, foreign competition may make internationalization a necessity as well. In some industry segments in the United States, small and medium-sized firms have opted for growth abroad rather than attempt to increase market share at home. For Boeing, the largest U.S. exporter, overseas sales have helped it avert disaster: In 1991, when U.S. airline

EXHIBIT 1. Adjustment of Marketing to Internationalization

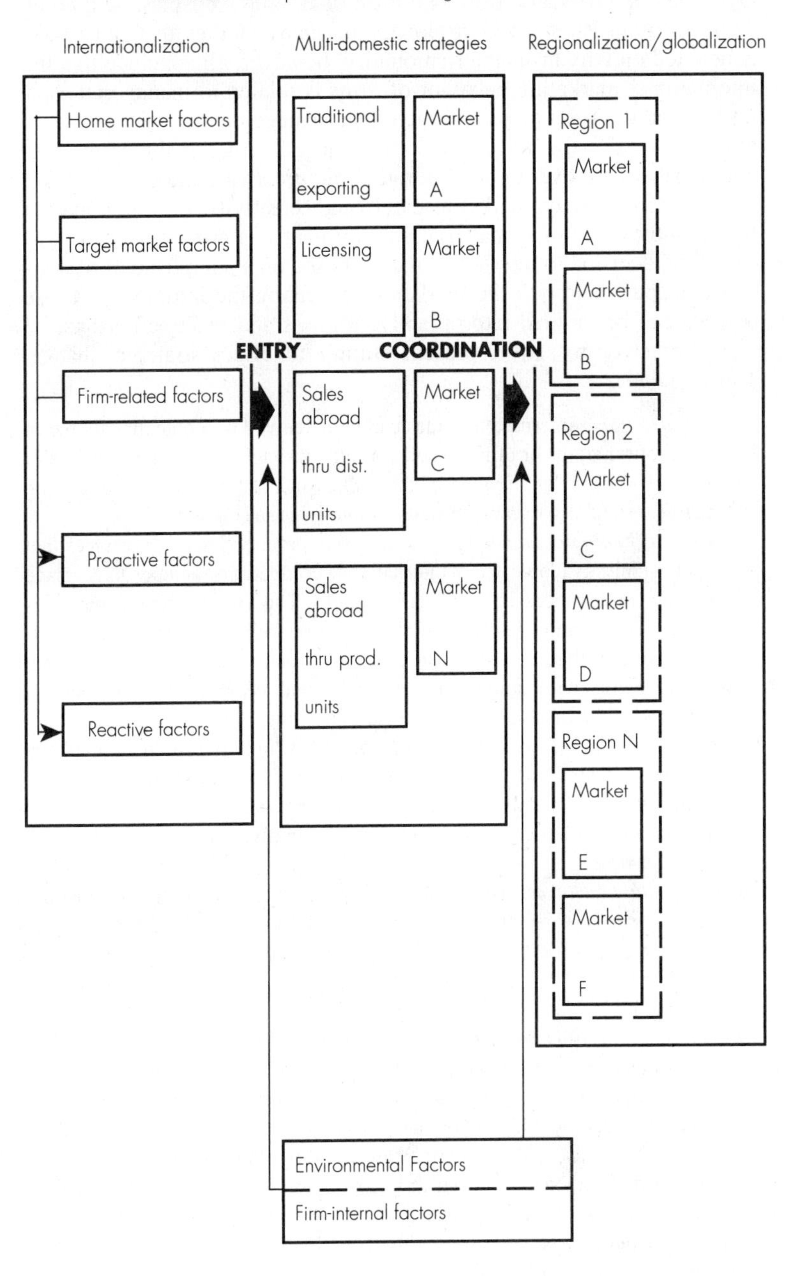

sales dried up, a full 80% of Boeing's orders came from foreign airlines. Over the next 20 years, fully one-third of Boeing's business will come from the Asia-Pacific region alone. The many studies that have been conducted on why firms internationalize, however, all conclude that the international marketing behavior of firms is related to managerial aspirations and the level of commitment that management is willing to give to the international marketing effort. Because international markets cannot be penetrated overnight—but rather require a vast amount of market development activity, market research, and sensitivity to foreign market factors—the issue of managerial commitment is a crucial one. In most cases, the decision to internationalize is based on a composite of reasons that both push and pull the marketer into taking the initial step. These reasons can be divided into proactive reasons and reactive reasons.

Proactive reasons represent stimuli to effect strategic change. These include:

- *Profit advantage.* International sales can be perceived as a potential source of higher profit margins or of more added profits through achieved economies of scale. The lower relative value of the dollar since 1985 has made exporting attractive, especially to new entrants to international markets.
- *Product/technological advantage.* A firm may produce goods or services that are not widely available from international competitors or may have made technological advances in a specialized field. The environmental market is providing U.S. companies with tremendous opportunity especially in developing countries that, in their rush to create wealth, ignored the ecological concerns. Firms with unique products may find geographic diversification more attractive than diversifying their product line.
- *Exclusive market information.* Knowledge about foreign customers, markets, or market situations that is not widely shared by other firms may provide the marketer with a competitive advantage. Such special insights may be based on international research, special contacts, or simply being in the right place at the right time.
- *Government incentives.* The public sector's role in providing information, financing, and tax benefits may provide the boost to export efforts. In countries such as Germany and Japan, public support is provided by the national and regional governments, often in cooperation with universities and private banks.
- *Potential/opportunity.* Perhaps the most obvious driver to internationalize is in the tremendous opportunity in foreign markets. While the traditional trading partners of the United States are buying more (for example, exports to Canada increased by 49% to Germany between 1988 and 1991), old markets are reopening (e.g., Latin America) and new markets (such as the newly-emerging democracies of Central Europe) are opening up. The General Agreement on Tariffs and Trade estimates that a successful completion of the Uruguay Round would boost world trade flows by $200 billion, creating further opportunity to international marketers.

Reactive reasons motivate firms that are responsive to environmental changes and adjust to them by changing their activities over time.

- *Competition.* A firm may be losing market share to competing firms that benefit from their international operations through economies of scale or experience. Some may perceive competition to be less severe abroad than it is in the domestic marketplace and, if not properly prepared, may find quite the opposite to be true.
- *Following customers/competitors.* Many firms become international because they have to. Suppliers may want to follow their customers abroad to secure their domestic accounts in the long term. Further, some may fear losing foreign markets permanently to rivals who have a more international outlook.
- *Overproduction/excess capacity.* International marketing activity motivated by getting rid of overproduction or utilizing excess capacity for foreign markets does not represent full commitment by management, but rather safety-valve activity. If customers or intermediaries perceive a lack of commitment to international markets, they may not commit themselves either, making foreign-market entry difficult.
- *Domestic market conditions.* If the domestic market is saturated or if domestic sales are declining due to the product approaching the end of its life cycle, international markets may become attractive to the firm. Success, however, will be predicated on the degree of preparation and appropriate adjustment of the marketing mix to the new market conditions.
- *Geographic proximity.* Physical and psychological closeness to an international market can often play a role in the export activities of the firm. While most European firms automatically become international marketers because their neighbors are so close, U.S. firms do not have the same circumstances. Firms often seek markets that they perceive to be closest on the psychological scale for initial market entry.

In order for the change to take place for a firm to transform from a domestic to a internationally-oriented firm, someone or something within or impacting on the firm must initiate it and see it through implementation. This change agent can be internal to the firm such as new management, or it can be external such as other firms, intermediaries, banks, or governmental agencies. The desire to increase participation in international trade and investment and to improve competitive positions has led nations to engage in major promotional efforts for and on behalf of firms.

The Governmental Role

Governments participate in international trade and investment decision making through policies of promotion and restriction. To take advantage of the new world order, many believe that the U.S. government should make trade a national priority in the 1990s. This would mean developing a coherent strategy involving information, financing, and environmental facilitation. The U.S. Department of Commerce, for example, has added new information services that provide U.S. companies with data on foreign trade and marketing developments. Also, the U.S. & Foreign Commercial Service provides an inward and outward link for U.S. businesses in terms of information and market assistance. In export financing, the Export-Import Bank of the United States has been charged with a new mission of aggressively meeting foreign-financing conditions. Proposals have been made to have state governments offer loan guarantees to regional banks that would take the lead in trade financing. This in turn would foster the relations between banks and small local businesses. Tax benefits through tax deferrals are provided to exporters through a mechanism called the Foreign Sales Corporation. A specific export promotion effort was the passage of the Export Trading Company Act of 1982. This legislation encourages and permits firms to work together to form export consortia. The basic idea was to provide the foreign buyer with an opportunity for one-stop shopping with a group of U.S. firms offering a wide variety of complementary and competitive products. In terms of comparative efforts, however, U.S. export promotion activities still lag far behind the support provided by most industrialized nations. Export promotion spending in the United States was $294 million in 1988, while the figure for France was $340 million and $547 for Canada in the same year. Furthermore, the Export-Import Bank covers less than 2% of export-finance transactions versus an average of 15% in the developed world.

An important task for the government is to make sure it facilitates the entry and operations of its firms in foreign markets. This environmental facilitation is performed through multilateral and bilateral negotiations to ensure that free trade is also fair trade. For example, the service sector now accounts for 53% of the U.S. economy but only 29% of exports. While deregulation is taking place around the world, U.S. industries with significant export potential such as insurance, banking, airlines, and engineering are still facing protectionist barriers abroad. Free trade arrangements around the world are increasing and U.S. firms are already taking advantage of the free trade agreement with Canada as well as the future joining of Mexico into the deal to form the North American Free Trade Agreement (NAFTA). Discussions are already on the way for a hemispheric free trade area from Point Barrow to Tierra del Fuego. Although firms themselves can develop networks of cooperation across borders, political decision making is still needed to guarantee the viability of such alliances.

INTERNATIONAL MARKET ENTRY[2]

International marketing is concerned with planning and conducting transactions across national borders to satisfy the objectives of individuals and organizations. In its many forms, it ranges from export-import trade to licensing, turnkey operations, and strategic alliances to wholly-owned subsidiaries. International marketing very much retains the basic marketing tenet of satisfaction. The fact that a transaction takes place across national borders highlights the difference between domestic and international marketing. The international marketer is subject to a new set of macroenvironmental factors, to different constraints, and quite different conflicts resulting from different laws, cultures, and societies. The basic principles of marketing apply but their application in the attempt to achieve a long-term sustainable competitive advantage will vary. This is reflected in the entry mode chosen for a particular market and in the adjustments to the marketing program for the new target market.

Environmental Challenges

While firms marketing internationally may benefit from experience and scale economies resulting from operations in multiple markets, they are also faced with many challenges not experienced by domestic firms. These challenges are the consequence of marketing in different countries with different environments ranging from different economic systems to different cultural beliefs.

Sovereign Entities. Marketing internationally means marketing either between nations or within foreign nations. To do this, marketers must comply with a wide variety of national economic and political policies. These range from the imposition of restrictions in the form of tariffs, quotas, and exchange controls on inputs brought across the national boundary to domestic restrictions on advertising appeals, marketing organizations, and the products themselves—all designed to achieve some desired domestic policy. Countries, furthermore, have different legal systems, of which the most important are the Common Law of the English-speaking countries, Code Law of the European Continent and countries that have been influenced by it, and the Islamic Law of the Muslim counties. Important for decision making are variations in taxation and other elements of regulation; for example, the Value Added Tax system in Europe or the nonavailability of certain mass media for advertising purposes in some countries.

Monetary Systems. Each nation has its own monetary system with its own currency value relative to other currencies. The exporter will not only have to worry about getting paid for exports but also about the amount of money actually received for the foreign transaction especially in periods of major exchange-rate fluctuation. This will lead to utilization of methods of payment seldom used domestically. Most important are the use of letters of credit and documentary draft financing. Should payment be stipulated in a foreign currency, the exporter needs to acquire protection against foreign-exchange risk by hedging. In cases when the international marketer has to deal with cashless buyers or buyers who are faced by exchange controls, countertrade transaction have to be prepared for.

Physical Environment. Climate and geography will usually have an effect on the total product offering as well as the logistics aspects of distribution. The geographic distance between production site and target market will necessitate careful packaging for both the longer transit time and for protection of the product during its physical movement. Seasonal differences between markets (for example between the Northern and Southern hemispheres) will allow marketers of certain products such as farm or sports equipment to balance their marketing efforts during the off-season for one of the markets.

Political Environment. Marketers typically want to conduct their business in a country with a stable and friendly government, but political risk does not only mean dramatic adverse moves against business operations. As a matter of fact, most of political risk today is a result of policy changes that have a negative impact on the firm's bottom line. For example, the imposition of price controls (i.e., maximum prices for products) to combat rampant inflation may force a firm to close down its operations in a market especially if its inputs are not under such price controls. While many of the policy changes affect all companies equally with no intention to discriminate against foreign companies, some policy changes may target a particular foreign company and result in what is known today as "creeping expropriation."

Cultural Environment. Culture reflects the social, political, and religious heritage of the country, often presenting the international marketer the hardest variable to change and adjust to. The elements of culture that have to be adjusted to are language, both in verbal and nonverbal form, religion, values and attitudes, manners and customs, aesthetics, educational level, and social institutions. The international marketer will have to be aware of the availability and adequacy of the basic economic, social, financial, and marketing infrastructures. The example of Western footwear highlights a situation in which a competitive advantage (i.e., made in the U.S.A.) may be squandered if appropriate cultural sensitivity is not observed. The sales of Western footwear have been boosted dramatically in Europe by a fashion theme emphasizing the West and the outdoors. Germans, for example, buy 500,000 pairs annually but hardly a pair made by a U.S. manufacturer. The main reason cited is that the toes of the U.S. boots are not pointed enough. U.S. boots are practical but not interesting in a market where the boots are a fashion statement.

Macroeconomic Environment. The assessment of the foreign market environment often starts with the evaluation of economic variables relating to the size and nature of the market to establish an estimate of market potential. The main dimensions of a market can be captured by considering variables such as those relating to the population and its various characteristics. Low levels of macroeconomic development—the less-developed areas of the world—preclude the sale of products developed for the industrialized markets except for certain narrow segments who may portray very developed-market features due to high income levels, for example. Some of the data indicate potential for the international marketer. A large number of telephones, and their even distribution among the population or a target group, may make market research via telephone interviewing a possibility barring any cultural barriers to it. While data abound on this dimension of the environment, the international marketer needs to be careful in making assessments of potential for a product; for example, refrigerators in European households are far smaller than their U.S. counterparts.

Microeconomic Environment. This environment refers to the ways of doing business in a market; i.e., its business culture. Typically, the differences in conducting business transactions may present subtle but yet very powerful challenges to the international marketer. A 1990 report by the U.S. government's International Trade Commission concluded that "the end result of the close, sometimes overlapping relations and practices in Japan's distribution chains is that it may be unusually difficult and expensive for foreigners to break into the system." Similarly, U.S. marketers who, in entering new markets in Europe, have continued their marketing practices unchanged have encountered government restrictions after local competitors have complained about excessive marketing expenditure by the U.S. firms.

In dealing with environments, the international marketer may look for government assistance in creating conditions abroad more palatable to its needs. Governmental action, especially trade negotiations, can work in areas that the target market's government can control; e.g., protecting intellectual property. However, in most cases, international competitiveness can be assured by improved business procedures: thorough market research before entry, responding to research findings by adaptation of products and procedures, emphasizing a service-orientation, entering strategic alliances when necessary, and nurturing a long-term orientation within the firm. Those companies that have been acknowledged as excellent exporters (e.g., by winning export awards) have shown long-term commitment to export-market development, adopted integrated strategies of carefully defined target markets and adapted marketing mixes, as well as had dynamic partners, such as freight forwarders or advertising agencies, in the effort.

International Marketing Planning

The need for sound planning is the same regardless whether the firm is a domestically-oriented firm with infrequent exports or a multinational corporation looking at expanding its operations. However, the initial phase requires great care because a failure in market entry may cause long-term problems in reputation or cause the firm to cease its internationalization drive altogether. The objective in the planning effort is to identify the most attractive opportunities to leverage the firm's competitive advantage whether it is in product or process technologies, marketing skills, or economies of scale.

Central to the planning effort and the control effort to evaluate the effectiveness of implementation is the development of an international information system. Information about the differences in environmental, market, and competitive conditions is needed to make the initial choice of market(s) as well as future modification or expansion efforts. The firm has to also decide on the appropriate organizational structure for international efforts to ensure the firm is optimally positioned in the short term and ready for future. Investment in the preliminaries (market research and personnel) will indicate the commitment the firm is willing to put forth.

The key decisions involved in the planning process include the markets to be entered, the timing and sequence of entry, as well as the entry mode to be used for each product and market. The choice of market(s) will be a function of the firm's perceptions of opportunity and risk. Opportunities relate to the market and sales potential that research has indicated in a market as well as the degree of comfort management feels in possibly doing business there. The degree of comfort usually correlates heavily with the distance from the market, whether geographic, psychological, or economic. Risk, on the other hand, is a function of the commercial, financial, and political dimensions of the market. Higher risk may be tolerated should the expectations of returns be high as well. A central issue for exporters is the timing and sequencing of market entry. Conventional wisdom would have a firm enter one closed market initially and only after success there and accumulated internal experience would new markets be entered. However, diversification may be needed if a strategic window is open for a limited time. For example, if a firm with unique technology has only a short lead on its competition, it may choose to enter as many markets as possible to preempt competition. In these cases, the importance of planning is emphasized.

Entry Modes

The planning period for the entry mode should be long enough to compel managers to raise and answer fundamental questions about the future direction and the scope of the firm's operations domestically and internationally. Without such elaboration, a firm may withdraw from a market at the first sign of adversity; for example, as a result of the dollar appreciating against the local currency, thus making competition tougher.

There are several alternative methods for foreign market entry. The method selected is dependent on the management's views as to the

EXHIBIT 2. Market-Entry Modes

Production in home market		Production in foreign market	
Indirect exports	**Direct exports**	**100% ownership**	**Alliances**
• Domestic purchase by foreign customer • EMCs • Trading companies • Cooperative exports • Complementary marketing	• Foreign interm. -Agent -Distributor • Sales subsidiary	• Manufacture • Assembly	• Mfg/Mgmt contract • Licensing • Equity joint venture

firm's future activities internationally, its current resources and experiences, and the selected market's characteristics. The basic modes are presented in Exhibit 2. International companies usually evolve through a sequence of entry strategies with the present strategy (e.g., indirect exports), preparing the firm for different entry strategies (e.g., production abroad) later. Some companies, however, may remain in one entry mode but intensify their efforts by increasing the share of exports as a percentage of total sales. The sequence can be reversed when a firm decides to disinvest in a particular market (e.g., South Africa in the 1980s) because of political and/or economic reasons.

Production in Home Market. Many export efforts start with an unsolicited inquiry about a company's product from a domestic export intermediary or directly from a prospective foreign buyer. There may be very little special international activity carried on within the firm with those activities performed by export management companies in exchange for a commission. The firm using this service gets the performance of an export department without the cost and time delays incurred in establishing one within the firm. The more than 1,000 export management companies in the United States provide an attractive alternative for many smaller firms considering international market entry. While most EMCs act as agents, some act as distributors. The domestic firm selling to the EMC is now in the comfortable position of having sold its merchandise and received its money without having to deal with the complexities of the international market. However, it is unlikely to gain international marketing experience and may thus relegate itself to remaining a purely domestic firm. In some important markets (e.g., Japan, South Korea, and Brazil), indigenous trading companies perform the majority of export-import functions. The non-trading company giants of Japan in 1991 acted as intermediaries for about half of the country's exports and two-thirds of its imports.

Cooperative exports are another way to enter foreign markets without the full commitment of having an export department. Legislation enacted in 1918 led to Webb-Pomerene Associations, which permit firms to cooperate in terms of sales allocation, financing, and pricing information regarding their international sales. By 1991, only 22 associations were active and accounted for less than 2% of U.S. exports, mainly in agricultural and commodity areas. The passage of the Export Trading Company Act of 1982 was designed to improve the export performance of small and medium-sized firms. To improve export performance (and to emulate the success in Germany), bank participation in trading companies was permitted and antitrust threat to joint efforts was reduced. The cost of developing international markets would be shared and bank participation would allow for better access to capital. The success of U.S. export trading companies is still uncertain. By 1992, only 130 individual ETCs had been certified by the U.S. Department of Commerce. Yet these certificates covered more than 4,800 firms, mainly because of trade association sponsorship. While some believe that businesses and banks simply are not interested in joining forces to penetrate international markets, the concepts of synergism and cooperation make sense in terms of enhancing the international competitiveness of U.S. firms.

Complementary marketing ("piggybacking") refers to an arrangement whereby one manufacturer obtains distribution of its products through another manufacturer's overseas marketing facilities. For the rider, the arrangement provides entry to a foreign market through established facilities without exorbitant expenses. The carrier gains better utilization of its system and, provided that carried products are chosen carefully, synergistic benefits.

At some point, it may become evident that the firm's export business has become a significant part of its overall activities, and closer supervision of foreign market activities is required. Direct export means that the firm itself performs the export task rather than delegating it to some outside entity. Usually, an export manager is assigned with a small staff. With further growth, a full-service export department is established to operate at the same level as the domestic sales department. Further growth will justify the establishment of foreign sales subsidiaries to replace or more closely control foreign agents and distributors.

Foreign Production. Many exporters prefer to stay out of foreign production because of perceived risks and the increased investments required. At some stage, however, exporting may become insufficient to achieve the firm's objectives in foreign markets (or at home as well). A manufacturer can decide to enter foreign markets by means of foreign production under one or more arrangements with a foreign partner or through a wholly-owned assembly or manufacturing unit.

Any interfirm cooperation that goes beyond exporting and importing can be defined as a strategic alliance in that the relationship is long term and based on more broad-based cooperation. Alliances that are not equity-based include contractual agreements on manufacturing or management. Joint efforts might include licensing, cross-licensing, or cross-marketing activities. Under a contract manufacturing arrangement, the firm's product is produced in a foreign market by another producer under contract with the firm. This arrangement is attractive if the firm's competitive advantages are in areas other than production, such as marketing. This alternative is feasible only when appropriate foreign manufacturers are available. In some cases, companies may enter management contract agreements, in which companies sell their business expertise and know-how. For high-technology firms especially, licensing provides foreign market entry. Although licensing, or the transfer of intellectual property (patents, trademarks, or copyrights) may also be considered exporting activity, licensing deals that involve serious internationalization (rather than merely revenue-generating activity) are long-term cooperative arrangements. A more involved version is cross-licensing where the two parties to the deal exchange intellectual property. Cross-marketing is a two-way form of complementary marketing in that each partner provides the other access to its markets for a product. Increasingly, firms worldwide are also participating in joint research and development activities to avoid the high cost of developing next-generation solutions; for example, a new drug may cost $200 million or a new telecommunications switch $1 billion to develop and bring to market. With government support, a number of R&D consortia—joint efforts involving more than two partners—have been established around the world. In the United States, these include MCC and Sematech, and in Europe ESPRIT and RACE.

An equity joint venture can be defined as the participation of two or more companies in an enterprise in which each party contributes assets, owns the new entity to some degree, and shares risk. Joint ventures may be the only way in which a firm can profitably participate in a particular market; for example, although India restricts equity participation in local operations to 40%, other operations may be even more restricted by barriers such as high tariffs or restrictions on royalty payments. The advantages of joint venture strategy are the sharing of risk and the ability to combine strengths such as better technology and market experience. The main disadvantages are loss of absolute control and problems with coordination. An example of this arrangement is New United Motor Manufacturing (NUMMI), the joint venture between General Motors and Toyota. Toyota needed more direct access to the U.S. market, while GM benefited from the technology and management approaches provided by the Japanese partner.

The most extensive form of foreign market entry is through wholly-owned production facilities. Usually companies achieve this status either through direct expansion or acquisition. Acquisition is employed when quick entry is required (for example, to enter European markets before 1992), labor is scarce, or existing competition preempts the establishment of a new business. In some cases, the firm may produce domestically all or most of the components/ingredients and ship them to foreign locations to be assembled as a finished product. Assembly operations are justified when transportation costs of a finished product are high or when tariffs on assembled products are higher than for the unassembled parts as a whole. It should be noted, however, that products assembled in a region may not satisfy country-of-origin requirements; for example, the French have been opposed to accepting products assembled in Europe (in so-called "screw-driver" factories) as products with EC-origin.

As foreign-market involvement increases through learning and entry to more diverse markets, the firm faces a need to become more involved in all of its individual markets. This means more attention to product and process adaptation for both external, market-related reasons and internal, firm-specific reasons. Individual local market conditions warrant the development of a multi-domestic strategy within the firm; i.e., planning will be done predominantly on a market-by-market basis.

Standardization versus Adaptation

As the firm moves from exporting to more involved entry modes and as the objective becomes to penetrate existing markets further, the focus and often the locus of decision making shifts to the individual markets. This results in adaptation of products and processes for optimal market-specific results. In many cases, new products and brands are acquired or developed within individual markets based on unique potential. Even in exports, studies have found that only one out of ten products is transferred abroad without modification. In the multidomestic stage of the firm's internationalization development, localization pressures become even more significant.

Factors that affect adaptation can be divided into three general categories: (1) market, (2) product/program, and (3) firm/system characteristics. These include factors that make adaptation either mandatory or discretionary. Typically, the market environment mandates the majority of product modifications or product forms. The most stringent requirements result from government regulations, be they to protect the consumer or to protect the local producers. Product decisions made by marketers of consumer products are especially affected by local behavior, tastes, attitudes, and traditions—all reflecting the marketer's need to gain the customers' approval. In terms of the product and the marketing program, care has to be taken that no legal requirements or customs are violated. For example, U.S.-style consumer promotions have been considered by Japanese consumers as wasteful, expensive, and not very appealing. New product variants may be developed to better cater to local market preferences, such as smaller size of homes, or by industry that the firm caters to in a particular market. The firm's position in a given market will determine the degree of adaptation needed. In many European markets, for example, distribution power rests with the trade (in England with retail multiples, in Finland with wholesale cooperatives) compared with the United States where the manufacturer may still be calling the plays. Even if a firm aims for consistency in its marketing efforts, it may be difficult to attain in some areas such as warranties. Warranties can be uniform only if use conditions do not vary drastically and if the firm is able to deliver on its promise anywhere it has a presence.

However, as the last example indicates, the international marketer may want to start coordinating activities across national borders, especially if cross-border similarities are minor or if the nation-by-nation programs cause inefficiencies in the overall marketing system. The marketer's choice is to pursue globalization as a strategy.

GLOBALIZATION[3]

Globalization is a business initiative based on the belief that the world is becoming more homogeneous; furthermore, distinctions between national markets are not only fading but, for some products, will eventually disappear. As a result, companies need to globalize their international strategy by formulating it across markets either on a regional or completely global basis.

Globalization Drivers

Both external and internal factors will create the favorable conditions for development of strategy and resource allocation on a global basis. These factors can be divided into market, cost, environmental, and competitive factors.

Market Factors. A new group of consumers has been identified that is emerging in the triad of North America, Europe, and the Far East whom marketers can treat as a single market with the same spending habits. Approximately 600 million in number, these consumers have similar educational backgrounds, income levels, lifestyles, use of leisure time, and aspirations. One reason given for the similarities in their demand is a level of purchasing power (ten times greater than that of LDCs or NICs) that translates into higher diffusion rates for certain products. Another reason is that developed infrastructures—ownership of telephones and an abundance of paved roads—lead to attractive markets for other products. Products can be designed to meet similar demand conditions throughout the triad. These similarities also enhance the transferability of other marketing elements.

At the same time, channels of distribution are becoming more global; i.e., a growing number of retailers are now showing great flexibility in their strategies for entering new geographic markets. Some are already world powers (e.g., Benetton and McDonald's), while others are pursuing aggressive growth (e.g., Toys "Я" Us and IKEA). Also noteworthy are cross-border retail alliances that expand the presence of retailers to new markets quite rapidly. The presence of global and regional channels makes it more necessary for the marketer to rationalize marketing efforts.

Cost Factors. Avoiding cost inefficiencies and duplication of effort are two of the most powerful globalization drivers. A single-country approach may not be large enough for the local business to achieve all possible economies of scale and scope as well as synergies, especially given the dramatic changes in the marketplace. Take, for example, pharmaceuticals. In the 1970s, developing a new drug cost about $16 million and took four years to develop. The drug could be produced in Britain or the United States and eventually exported. Now developing a drug costs about $250 million and takes as long as 12 years with competitive efforts close behind. Only a global product for a global market can support that much risk. Size has become a major asset, which partly explains the many mergers and acquisitions of the past few years in the business. In the heavily-contested consumer goods sectors, launching a new brand may cost as much as $100 million, meaning that companies are not going to necessarily spend precious resources on one-country projects.

Environmental Factors. Governmental barriers have fallen dramatically in recent years to further facilitate the globalization of markets and the activities of marketers within them. For example, the forces pushing towards a pan-European market are very powerful: the increasing wealth and mobility of European consumers (favored by the relaxed immigration controls), the accelerating flow of information across borders, the introduction of new products where local preferences are not well established, and the publicity surrounding the 1992 process itself all promote globalization. Also, the removal of physical, fiscal, and technical barriers as a result of 1992 are indicative of the changes that are taking place around the world on a greater scale.

At the same time, rapid technological evolution is contributing to the process. For example, Ford Motor Company is able to accomplish its globalization efforts by using new communications methods, such as teleconferencing and CAD/CAM links, as well as travel, to manage the complex task of meshing car companies on different continents.

Competitive Factors. Many industries are already dominated by global competitors who are trying to take advantage of the three sets of factors mentioned earlier. To remain competitive, the marketer may have to be the first to do something or to match or preempt competitors' moves. Products are now introduced, upgraded, and distributed at rates unimaginable a decade ago. Without a global network, a marketer may run the risk of seeing carefully researched ideas picked off by other global players. This is what Procter & Gamble and Unilever did to Kao's Attack concentrated detergent, which they mimicked and introduced into the United States and Europe before Kao could react.

Market presence may be necessary to execute global strategies and to prevent others from having undue advantage in unchallenged markets. Caterpillar faced mounting global competition from Komatsu but found out that strengthening its products and operations were not enough to meet the challenge. Although Japan was a small part of the world market, as a secure home base (no serious competitors) it generated 80% of Komatsu's cash flow. To put a check on its major global competitor's market share and cash flow, Caterpillar formed a heavy equipment joint venture with Matsushita to serve the Japanese market.

Globalization Dimensions

Decisions need to be made how to best utilize the conditions set by the four dimensions driving globalization. Decisions will have to be made in terms of five areas: market participation, the product offering, marketing approach, location of value-added activities, and competitive moves.

Market Participation. The conventional wisdom of globalization requires a presence in all of the major triad markets of the world. In some cases, markets may not be attractive in their own right but have some other significance, such as being the home market of the most demanding customers (thereby aiding in product development) or being the home market of a significant competitor (a preemptive rationale). In its challenge of IBM, Fujitsu has acquired a substantial presence both in North America (through Amdahl Corp., the $2.2 billion-a-year Silicon

Valley maker of IBM-compatible mainframes) and in Europe (through International Computers Ltd., Britain's largest computer manufacturer at $2.7 billion in annual sales).

Product Offering. Globalization is not equal to standardization except in the case of the core product or the technology used to produce the product. The components used in a personal computer may to a large extent be standard with the localization needed only in terms of the peripherals; e.g., IBM produces 20 different keyboards for Europe alone. Product standardization may result in significant cost savings upstream. For example, Stanley Works' compromise between French preferences for handsaws with plastic handles and "soft" teeth with British preferences for wooden handles and "hard teeth" to produce a plastic-handled saw with "hard teeth" allowed consolidation of production and resulted in substantial economies of scale. Local preferences may change the product somewhat; e.g., CPC International Inc. sells 15 versions of minestrone soup in Europe.

Marketing Approach. Nowhere is the need for the local touch as critical as in the execution of the marketing program. Uniformity is sought for especially in elements that are strategic (e.g., positioning) in nature, while care is taken to localize necessary tactical elements (e.g., distribution). This approach has been called globalization. For example, Unilever achieved great success with a fabric softener that used a common positioning, advertising theme, and symbol (a teddy bear), but differing brand names (e.g., Snuggle, Cajoline, Kuschelweich, Mimosin, and Yumos) and bottle sizes.

Location of Value-Added Activities. Globalization strives at cost reductions by pooling production or other activities or exploiting factor costs or capabilities within its system. Rather than duplicating activities in multiple, or even all country organizations, activities are concentrated. For example, Texas Instruments has designated a single design center and manufacturing organization for each type of memory chip. To reduce high costs and to be close to markets, two of its four new $250 million memory chip plants are in Taiwan and Japan. To reduce high R&D costs, it has entered into a strategic alliance with Hitachi.

Competitive Moves. Companies with regional or global presence will not have to respond to competitive moves only in the market where it is being attacked. A competitor may be attacked in its profit sanctuary to drain its resources, or its position in its home market may be challenged. When Fuji began cutting into Kodak's market share in the United States in the mid-1980s, Kodak responded by drastically increasing its advertising in Japan and created a new subsidiary to deal strictly with that market. Cross-subsidization, or the use of resources accumulated in one part of the world to fight a competitive battle in another, may be the competitive advantage needed for the long term. One major market loss may mean losses in others resulting in a domino effect. Jockeying for overall global leadership may result in competitive action in any part of the world. An example of Nokia Mobile Phones, one of the leading manufacturers of cellular telephones in the world (1990 market share 10%, second only to Motorola's 22%), highlights globalization as a strategy. The company's focus is on cellular mobile telephones (manufactured in Finland, Germany, and South Korea). The objective is to be a volume manufacturer; i.e. provide products for all major systems through a presence in all major markets. A global product range with customized variation for different distribution channels assures local acceptance.

Challenges of Globalization

Marketers who have tried the global concept have often run into problems with local differences. Especially in the 1980s, global marketing was seen as seen as a standardized marketing effort dictated to the country organizations by headquarters. Procter & Gamble (P&G) stumbled badly in the 1980s in Japan when customers there spurned its Pampers in favor of rival brands. P&G's diapers were made and sold according to a formula imposed by Cincinnati headquarters. Japanese consumers found the company's hard-sell techniques alienating. Pitfalls that handicap global marketing programs and contribute to their suboptimal performance include market-related reasons, such as insufficient research and tendency to overstandardize as well as internal reasons, such as inflexibility in planning and implementation.

Market Factors. Should a product be launched on a broader scale without formal research as to regional or local differences believing in transferability as such, the result may be failure. AT&T has had its problems abroad because its models are largely reworked U.S. models. Even after spending $100 million adapting its most powerful switch for European markets, its success was limited because phone companies there prefer smaller switches. Often the necessary research is only conducted after a product or program has failed.

Internal Factors. Globalization by design requires a balance between sensitivity to local needs at the same time they deploy technologies and concepts globally. This means that neither headquarters nor independent country managers can call the shots alone. If country organizations are not part of the planning process or if adoption is forced on them by headquarters, local resistance in the form of the *not-invented-here* (NIH) syndrome may lead to the demise of the global program, or worse, to an overall decline in morale. Subsidiary resistance may stem from resistance to any idea originating from the outside or may be based on valid concerns about the applicability of a concept to that particular market. Without local commitment, no global program will survive.

Localizing Global Marketing

The successful global marketers of the 1990s will be those who can achieve a balance between country managers and global product managers at headquarters. This balance may be achieved by a series of actions to improve a company's ability to develop and implement global strategy. These relate to management processes, organization structures, and the overall corporate culture, all of which should ensure cross-fertilization within the firm. In the multidomestic approach, country organizations had very little need to exchange ideas. The best approach against the emergence of the NIH-syndrome is utilizing various motivational policies such as (1) ensuring that local managers participate in the development of marketing strategies and programs for global brands; (2) encouraging local managers to generate ideas for possible regional or global use; (3) maintaining a product portfolio that includes local as well as regional and global brands; and (4) allowing local managers control over their marketing budgets so that they can respond to local customer needs and counter global competition (rather than depleting budgets by forcing them to participate only in uniform campaigns).

SUMMARY

Although international marketing makes use of the same marketing tools, techniques, concepts, and principles as does domestic marketing, it deserves special attention for several vital reasons. First, overseas markets are growing in importance as opportunity areas. The continued growth in worldwide trade—now exceeding $4 trillion—economic interdependence, and the emergence of large multinational firms of diverse origins provide pull to overseas markets and competitive challenge at home. Second, the risks and uncertainties in marketing overseas are initially more pronounced than in marketing domestically because of the lack of experience of most marketers with the international environment as well as the environments of other national markets. Third, the economic, cultural, social, political, and legal dimensions of overseas markets all work together to necessitate varying degrees of modification to the domestic marketing mix, the policies and procedures adopted for the marketing function, and even the management style used. Finally, even though environmental differences call for market-specific adaptations, convergence of differences along market and governmental dimensions as well as cost and competitive forces are calling for increased coordination of strategies across national borders.

When the decision has been made to enter an attractive overseas market, it is then necessary to select the appropriate mode of entry.

To maintain optimal strategy over time, managers need to continually monitor and evaluate changes in the target market(s). While the marketing mix in the initial internationalization stage follows that of the domestic market closely, local-market adaptation becomes the guiding principle as marketing efforts expand in the markets chosen. As the inefficiencies of operating different marketing mixes in each market escalate, the need for increased coordination finally results in the firm's adaptation of the globalization strategy.

NOTES

1. For a more detailed discussion, see Michael R. Czinkota, Pietra Rivoli and Ilkka A. Ronkainen, *International Business* (Hinsdale, IL: The Dryden Press, 1992), Chapters 11–12.
2. For a more detailed discussion, see Hans B. Thorelli and S. Tamer Cavusgil, *International Marketing Strategy,* (Oxford, England: Pergamon Press, 1990).
3. For a more detailed discussion, see George S. Yip, "Global Strategy . . . In a World of Nations," *Sloan Management Review* 31(Fall 1989): 29–41; Susan P. Douglas and C. Samuel Craig, "Evolution of Global Marketing Strategy: Scale, Scope, and Synergy," *Columbia Journal of World Business* 24(Fall 1989): 47–58; George S. Yip, Pierre M. Loewe, and Michael Y. Yoshino, "How to Take Your Company to the Global Market," *Columbia Journal of World Business* 23(Winter 1988): 28–40; and John A. Quelch and Edward J. Hoff, "Customizing Global Marketing," *Harvard Business Review* 64(May–June 1986): 59–68.

SUGGESTIONS FOR FURTHER READING

Czinkota, Michael R. and Ilkka A. Ronkainen. *International Marketing* (Fort Worth, TX: Dryden/HBJ, 1993).

Lewis, Jordan D. *Partnerships for Profit: Structuring and Managing Strategic Alliances* (New York: NY: The Free Press, 1990).

Ohmae, Kenishi. *Triad Power: The Coming Shape of Global Competition* (New York, NY: The Free Press, 1985).

Porter, Michael E. *The Competitive Advantage of Nations* (New York, NY: The Free Press, 1990).

Quelch, John A., Robert D. Buzzell, and Eric R. Salama. *The Marketing Challenge of 1992* (Reading, MA: Addison-Wesley, 1990).

Rodkin, Henry. *The Ultimate Overseas Business Guide for Growing Companies* (Homewood, IL: Dow Jones-Irwin, 1990).

Susan P. Douglas
Professor of Marketing and Business
Stern School of Business
New York University
New York, New York

C. Samuel Craig
Professor of Marketing and Business
Stern School of Business
New York University
New York, New York

CHAPTER 67

RESEARCHING GLOBAL MARKETS

INTRODUCTION

Just like domestic marketing decisions, international marketing decisions must be based on a thorough understanding of the context in which they will be implemented and played out. Without adequate information regarding the market environment, its infrastructure, potential consumers, and competitors, the firm cannot hope to formulate an appropriate strategy. Once implemented, information is needed to monitor a strategy carefully to ensure it remains effective.

In international markets, systematic collection of information is especially critical due to frequent lack of familiarity with overseas markets. While management often has experience and an intuitive understanding of domestic market conditions, the sheer geographic distances and cultural dissimilarities characterizing many overseas markets pose substantial barriers to management comprehension of a foreign market environment. Thus when a firm begins overseas expansion, information collection is crucial to avoid mistakes typically generated by an ethnocentric or domestic market orientation.

As the firm expands its operations in international markets, these geographic and cultural distances coupled with rapid rates of change in many overseas markets make continued attention to information collection imperative to keep abreast of the latest environmental and market developments. In particular, monitoring the competitive situation and the firm's own performance is crucial to continued success.

This chapter is designed to guide the information requirements and data collection efforts of firms contemplating entry into, as well as those actively participating in international markets. It begins by identifying general information requirements for international marketing decisions. Next, the generic problems associated with data collection in the international environment are considered. The majority of the chapter is organized around two main sections. The first deals with information required for initial entry into international markets. The second looks at information requirements from the perspective of the firm already in international markets seeking to expand its activities. The chapter ends with a brief discussion about the ongoing need for information to coordinate and control global operations.

INFORMATION REQUIREMENTS

Information requirements for international strategy development vary depending on the extent of involvement in international markets. To make decisions regarding initial entry into international markets, information is required to assess marketing opportunities worldwide to determine which product markets appear to offer the most attractive opportunities and what mode of operation and competitive strategy to adopt in these markets. Secondary data sources are important resources and allow extrapolation of information relating to one market or environment to predict potential and likely success in another.

As the firm expands and develops local markets, emphasis shifts and greater reliance is placed on primary data collection to probe ideas for new products, to examine the feasibility of transferring products and marketing ideas from other countries, and to test how far products, advertising copy, or pricing need to be adapted (Douglas and Craig 1989). Here, a central issue, especially in conducting multi-country research to coordinate strategy across countries is the comparability of data and research results from one country to another.

As the firm gains extensive experience in international markets, attention shifts to global rationalization and integration of strategy. This requires collection and coordination of internal company data to assess and compare operations across countries as well as continued use of secondary and primary data. Development of a global information system to assess performance of business units, functions, and products etc in different areas of the world is important. This provides a key input into decisions relating to improved integration and coordination of strategy across countries, regions, and business units to ensure optimal allocation of resources worldwide.

Thus the information requirements for strategy formulation differ depending on the degree of experience and involvement in international markets. Yet, regardless of the type of information required, a common problem is its accuracy and interpretation. Lack of comparability of data in different countries may cause market opportunities to be overestimated or underestimated. Approaches to collection of primary data may have to be different in each country to produce comparable results. Even internal company data are not immune to problems of comparability. Accounting standards differ from country to country, requiring adjustments to be made to ensure comparability.

These generic problems associated with data collection in the international environment are next examined in more detail.

DATA COLLECTION PROBLEMS

In international markets, the abundance and diversity of information available as well as its variability pose a number of specific conceptual and organizational issues. Costs of data collection are often high in international markets relative to market size, and hence the economics of information decisions differ substantially from domestic markets. Collection of information in multiple and highly diverse contexts and relative to different types of operations gives rise to problems of data comparability and equivalence across markets. Such problems are further compounded by differences in the accuracy and reliability of data from one country and from one source to another. Organization, integration, and interpretation of information for global strategic decisions is thus extremely complex.

Cost of Data Collection

Data availability and information costs differ from country to country. In industrialized countries, information is readily available, ranging from data on population demographics and income, industrial production and growth, to company reports, consumer lifestyle studies, and store audit data. In developing countries, however, difficulties may be encountered in obtaining basic population or income data or even production statistics. In such countries, there is often no well developed infrastructure for collection of economic or market-related information, and little experience in conducting market research. Consequently, substantial costs are incurred to obtain basic information in order to, for example, develop sampling frames to conduct a survey, or alternatively, to train qualified interviewers and researchers to collect and analyze data. Further, potential market size may be considerably smaller than in the industrialized nations.

Even among industrialized countries, research costs may vary substantially. In some countries, costs of conducting in-depth interviews tend to be high, as psychologists trained in in-depth motivational analysis are used, rather than focus group moderators.

As a result, the economics of international market information decisions differ substantially from comparable domestic market decisions. In the first place, the lack of familiarity with foreign environments and of operations within these environments implies that information collection expenditures and research, especially in the initial entry stages, should be viewed as an investment, rather than as a current expense. This aids in avoiding costly entry mistakes and enables the development of more effective long-run international market expansion strategies.

Second, the appropriate time horizon for evaluating these expenditures should be considerably longer. Often, initial market size or potential may seem small or even non-existent. However, long-run potential may be much greater. This is in part due to rapid rates of growth and change in many international markets (for example, the Far East or Eastern Europe). Furthermore, it is often important to consider entry at an early stage of market development to avoid allowing the market to be captured by competitors.

Thus the payoff period for evaluating the costs associated with collecting international market information is considerably longer than for comparable domestic projects. While in the domestic market, a payoff period of one year might be appropriate for research conducted to aid in developing the marketing plan, in international markets, a period of five years might be more appropriate.

Data Comparability and Equivalence Across Markets

Collection of information relating to multiple country markets poses a number of issues with regard to the comparability and equivalence of the information collected in different countries. Comparable information may not be available in all countries. For example, studies or reports relating to a given product such as those conducted by the U.S. Department of Commerce or the Economist Intelligence Unit may not be available for all countries. Similarly, in many countries, companies are not required to publish annual reports.

The relevant base unit may not be defined in the same way or be equivalent in all countries. For example, in the case of motor vehicle registration, in some countries a company car may be provided to management and sales representatives as a fringe benefit, and hence is counted as a commercial vehicle. It may, however, also be used for personal transportation. Similarly, the counterpart of SIC code data may not be defined in the same way. A television set, for example, may be included as a recreational and entertainment item rather than as furniture and household equipment.

Data collection procedures may also affect the reliability and comparability of data. For example, production statistics may be based on company tax records. Companies or local operating units may, however, underestimate production levels in order to minimize tax liabilities. Manipulation of transfer pricing, i.e., prices charged to subsidiaries for different components, may also affect productivity or profitability figures.

Also, in primary data collection, many of the concepts, measurement instruments, and procedures to administer these have been developed and tested in the United States. Their relevance and applicability in other countries is, however, far from clear. Explicit administrative and analytic procedures for modifying and testing the relevance of concepts and measures developed in one country to another should thus be incorporated into the research design. In addition, such procedures should enable the identification of concepts and measures unique to a specific country or culture (Douglas, Broadman, and Craig 1992).

Establishing the comparability of data administration procedures poses further difficulties. In one country, a certain method of data collection, for example, mail questionnaires, may be known to have a given level of reliability. In another country, personal interviews rather than mail questionnaires may have an equivalent level of reliability. Levels of reliability associated with comparable research techniques thus differ and suggest the desirability of using techniques with equivalent levels of reliability rather than techniques that are strictly comparable.

Organizational Issues in Information Collection

An important consideration in collecting data for global marketing strategy is to determine by whom and where information should be collected, i.e., internally or externally, at corporate headquarters, or by local country management; and how information is integrated into decision making, i.e., through the establishment of a global information bank, internal reports, etc. While these are also considerations in collecting information for domestic markets, they assume greater significance in international markets due to the hierarchical nature of decision making, the interdependence of operations in multiple markets, and hence, the desirability of coordinating information from different countries.

Whether information is collected in-house or purchased from an external organization is likely to depend on the type of information required as well as the size of the organization and its research staff and the comprehensiveness of its information system. Relatively few companies are likely to maintain their own field staff, and hence, primary data are likely to be purchased from an outside supplier. If the company has an extensive information system and qualified research staff, secondary data may be collected and analyzed internally, for example, company or market data and reports.

The way in which information collection and analysis is organized, and more particularly, by whom, is often closely related to the organizational structure of the company. If international marketing operations are under the control of an International Division or product division staff at corporate headquarters, information collection may be directed from this location. Within-company coordination problems are likely to be minimized, except that in the case of the product division structure, there may be some danger of lack of coordination between divisions and duplication of country environment information by different product divisions within a country. If, on the other hand, the company has a geographical organizational structure, then information collection is likely to be decentralized and conducted by local operating units. In this case, the main problem is likely to be attention to the collection of comparable information in different countries and product markets to make appropriate decisions with regard to strategy development and resource allocation across countries and product markets.

INFORMATION FOR INITIAL MARKET ENTRY

Information to assess opportunities and risks in different markets worldwide is required in order to select which markets to enter, the mode of operation, and what competitive strategy to adopt in these markets. It is particularly important to collect information *prior* to international market entry to avoid costly mistakes that may occur due to lack of familiarity with local market conditions and structure or customer interests and desires. A Taiwanese manufacturer of jeans, for example, in entering the U.S. market, remembered to lengthen the jeans in order to fit the taller U.S. figure, but forgot that with longer legs go bigger feet, and consequently made the ankle width too small for the American foot.

In collecting information for initial entry decisions, data need to be collected relating to 1) the national investment climate and environment, assessing, for example, prospects for economic growth, financial and political stability, the nature of the market infrastructure, etc.; and 2) the specific product market(s) in which the company is involved, including, for example, market sales and rate of growth, substitute and competing products, and the strength of competition.

The high costs of primary data collection relative to potential market size in many international markets imply that substantial reliance may be placed on the use of secondary data. Secondary data are relatively inexpensive to collect and, particularly in the case of government sources, typically widely available. Often the key problem here is the plethora of data available and the need for selectivity in identifying appropriate and reliable sources.

The Business Environment

At the level of the business environment, two major dimensions need to be examined, namely, potential opportunities and threats, or risks associated with entering a given country. Here, information is required relating to the macroenvironment, for example, *political* factors such as possible expropriation or political unrest; the *economic* and *financial* climate, such as the likelihood of economic growth or depression; and *legal* and *regulatory* factors, such as restrictions on foreign ownership or import-export restrictions. In addition, business and market growth potential can be assessed from information on factors such as population and income growth and sociocultural and lifestyle trends. Each of these types of information is next discussed in more detail.

In assessing opportunities and threats associated with operating in a specific national or country environment, management requires information relating to the political, financial, economic and legal environments. While such factors are commonly viewed as constituting different types of risks, they may also provide opportunities or incentives to market entry (for example, tax advantages or favorable product regulation). The types of information likely to be required in relation to each of these aspects are next examined. It is, however, important to note that management needs to determine the specific information to be collected based on management objectives, the nature of the product, and the type of company.

Political Environment. Collection of information relating to the political climate such as the number of expropriations, attitudes toward foreign investment, internal political stability, and external political relations helps in assessing the likelihood of confiscation of assets or the imposition of restrictions on foreign corporations by host governments, insurrection, or the outbreak of war. The importance of assessing risk does, however, vary with the company and industry as well as the mode of entry envisaged.

Financial and Foreign Exchange Data. Examination of financial and foreign exchange risk factors, such as the rate of inflation, currency depreciation, restrictions on capital flows, and repatriation of earnings, is important insofar as these have a critical impact on overall levels of profitability and expected ROI. Such factors are thus a major consideration in making international investment and resource allocation decisions.

Assessment of foreign exchange risk is particularly critical where foreign-based production is concerned and goods or services will move across national boundaries. A manufacturer of color TV sets, planning to establish a plant in the United Kingdom to supply European markets, will need to make a careful evaluation of the anticipated movement of the pound relative to other European currencies. Similarly, the movement of inflation and interest rates may be an important factor for companies with high credit exposure (for example, consumer credit card companies or retailers).

If a company wishes to make its own evaluation of financial risk, data on many of the relevant variables can be found in International Financial Statistics. With the advent of floating exchange rates this has become increasingly complex. Consequently, a number of commercial services for predicting different types of financial risks have been established. These include service for predicting foreign exchange rates in the long run, such as those provided by the major international banks, or specialized econometric forecasters as well as a number of smaller organizations.

Legal and Regulatory Data. Information on legal and regulatory factors, such as import-export restrictions on various forms of ownership, modes of operation, tariff barriers, taxation, and product regulation and legislation, must also be collected. These are often a major impediment to market entry and limit the modes of operation that can be used. They also affect the extent to which modification in products or in marketing strategies will be required.

Information on product standards and regulations also has to be obtained. These often vary from one country to another, and are especially critical for industries such as pharmaceutical, food, and agricultural products. Recently, environmental standards have become more stringent in many industrialized nations.

Information about such factors must generally be analyzed on a country-by-country basis for a specific product category and can be found in sources such as the *Price Waterhouse Information Guides,*

Dun and Bradstreet's *Exporter's Encyclopedia,* or Business International's *Investment Licensing and Trading Conditions Abroad* series.

Indicators of Market Potential

The second aspect that needs to be considered at a macro-level is the favorability of the business climate and prospects for growth. This is a critical factor in country entry decisions insofar as market size and growth are key factors influencing rates of return. This may be assessed based on a variety of characteristics such as demographic trends, population size, population growth, degree of urbanization, or economic factors such as GNP per capita, growth of GNP, steel and energy consumption, income distribution/concentration, or sociocultural factors.

In some instances, management prefers to develop its own assessment of market potential in a country, based on characteristics tailored to specific corporate objectives and product businesses. Exhibit 1 presents a listing of the types of variables that might be used to evaluate market potential. These are intended chiefly as guidelines to the selection of appropriate measures. The relevance and operational definition of each indicator will vary with the product category. In each case or problem context, the specific variables used and their appropriate measurement will need to be determined.

Demographic Characteristics. Demographic characteristics are often an important indicator of market size since they provide an upper bound of market potential for products oriented to the mass population and also for certain industrial goods. Specific demographic characteristics, such as the composition of the population, may also be critical for products that are directed toward particular segments of the population. Information may therefore be required relating to factors such as population size, the rate of population growth, the age structure and composition of the population, as well as the degree of urbanization and population density.

Geographic Factors. The physical and topographical features of a country comprise a further set of characteristics that affect demand for specific product categories. The physical size of a country, measured in terms of square miles or kilometers of terrain, determines in large measure the scope of opportunities open to the firm. While topographical characteristics are particularly critical for products associated with transportation and communication, climatic conditions also affect consumption patterns and production technology as well as demand for certain types of industrial and consumer products.

Economic Factors. Economic factors are also crucial in evaluating demand for both consumer and industrial goods and are the most commonly used predictors of market potential. Interest in products and

EXHIBIT 1. Sample Indicators of Market Potential

Demographic Characteristics

- Size of population
- Rate of population growth
- Degree of urbanization
- Population density
- Age structure and composition of the population

Geographic Factors

- Physical size of a country
- Topographical characteristics
- Climate conditions

Economic Factors

- GNP per capita
- Income distribution
- Rate of growth of GNP

Technological and Educational Factors

- Level of technological skill
- Existing production technology
- Existing consumption technology
- Education levels

Sociocultural Factors

- Dominant values
- Lifestyle patterns
- Ethnic groups
- Linguistic fragmentation

willingness to buy must be backed by ability to pay. Aggregate statistics on indicators such as GNP, growth of GNP consumer expenditures, and buying power and capital investment are readily available.

Technological and Educational Factors. The importance of technological factors in evaluating demand varies according to the specific product category and particularly its technical complexity. Such factors are often especially critical in evaluating potential for industrial goods. Various aspects of a country's technology may be considered including the level of technological skills, production technology, consumption technology, and education.

Sociocultural Factors. Dominant social and cultural patterns in a country constitute further criteria for evaluating target countries and are particularly relevant for consumer goods, such as clothing, leisure items, and household furnishings that may be used to express a

EXHIBIT 2. BI Market Indexes: Size Growth, and Intensity of 21 Largest Markets

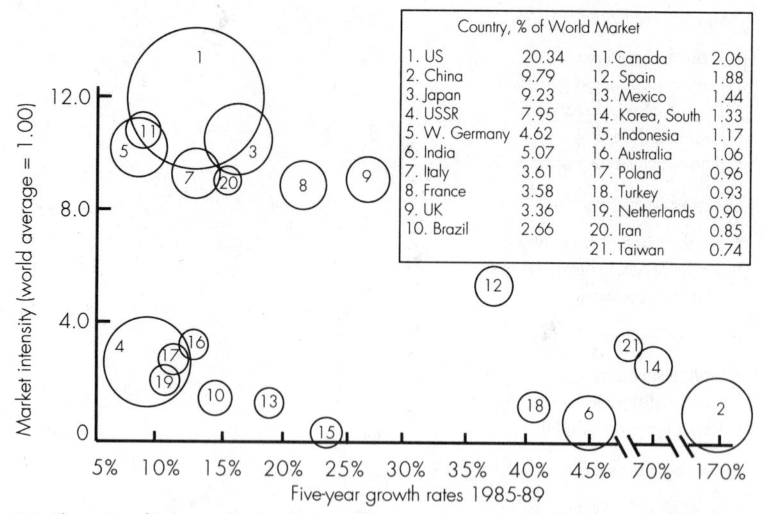

Note: The position of the center of each circle shows the intensity of the market (when measured against the vertical axis) and its cululative growth over the 1985-89 period (when measured against the horizontal axis). The size of the circles indicates the relative size of the markets as a percentage of the total workd market. See text for definitions and methodology.
Source: Business International Corp.

lifestyle or personality. Various aspects of sociocultural patterns may be examined depending on the specific product, including dominant sociocultural values, lifestyle patterns, religious and ethical beliefs, ethnic groups, etc.

As in the case of the macroeconomic assessment, ratings or composite indices evaluating business potential in a country are published by various organizations. Business International, for example, publishes three indexes each year: 1) market growth, 2) market intensity, and 3) market size for countries in Western and Eastern Europe, the Middle East, Latin America, Asia, Africa, and Australia. A summary of these regional analyses for the 21 largest markets in the world is shown in Exhibit 2. The specific variables included in each of these indexes vary somewhat from region to region, reflecting different market characteristics.

The principal limitation of these indexes is that they focus on macro-country indicators. They provide surrogate indicators or proxy variables for evaluating the general business climate. As such, they are useful as a first step in identifying countries that are likely to be attractive candidates for initial entry or expansion of international operations. Individual companies will, however, need more detailed analyses, tailored to corporate objectives and the specific product markets in which they are involved. Consequently, their use is somewhat limited, particularly for companies that wish to make a serious commitment to international operations.

Costs of Market Operation

The third set of variables includes factors relating to the infrastructure that affect the costs of operating in a specific country environment: (1) *integrative networks,* which affect the feasibility or desirability of utilizing specific types of marketing programs and strategies and (2) *basic resource requirements,* which affect the feasibility or costs associated with different modes of operation within a given national market.

Integrative Networks. A variety of factors are important here, for example, the availability of television advertising, commercial radio networks, and supermarkets or other self-service outlets; the development of the transportation network and the communication system; and the existence of banking, financial, and credit services, advertising agencies, or market research organizations. Information on these factors can be obtained from a variety of sources, including standard international information sources as well as international or national trade associations (for example, the International Advertising Association (IAA), or national chambers of commerce).

Basic Resource Requirements. The requisite infrastructure and basic resources are essential for success. These fall into three basic categories:

1. *physical resources,* such as electricity, energy, or water;
2. *human resources,* such as the availability of labor, work skills, management training, and attitudes; and
3. *capital resources,* such as financial and capital resources and technology availability and sophistication.

Information on these factors can be obtained from international data sources such as UN Statistical Yearbooks and International Financial Statistics, but availability for specific regions or industries will require more explicit investigation.

Product Market and Company Performance

Wherever feasible, data relating to the specific product market should be collected. These should include information with regard to product usage, usage of complementary and substitute products, and competitive market structure. The relevant types of variables are essentially the same as those that would be used to assess potential market size and structure in relation to the domestic market.

Product-Usage Data. Here, information relating to levels of product ownership for durable products or sales-purchase and repeat-purchase rates for non-durables is desirable. Availability of such data is likely to depend on the development of the product market and the specific country. Nielsen data can, for example, be obtained for most major industrialized countries. The Economist Intelligence Unit also publishes studies relating to different products such as shoes, confectionery, and radios in various European countries. In developing countries such as the African countries or the Asian markets, greater difficulty is likely to be encountered in obtaining such data.

Usage of Complementary or Substitute Products. Data relating to usage of complementary products such as automobiles for tires and cameras for film, or substitute products such as margarine for butter may be useful. For example, data on bourbon consumption might be collected by companies marketing Scotch whiskey. Similar difficulties are likely to be encountered in collecting such data as in relation to product usage. Data for some industries are readily available. In relation to consumer goods such as soft drinks or electronic toys, much may depend on the degree of market development.

Competitive Market Structure. Data relating to the competitive market structure should also be collected. This might include the number and size of competitors in the marketplace, their sales volume and rates of growth, relative market share, and so forth. Again, the feasibility of obtaining such data is likely to vary significantly with the specific product. In industrial markets, some data may be obtained from company reports or trade sources. In developing countries, these may be scanty. In consumer-goods industries in general, greater difficulty is likely to be encountered because firms often have diverse product lines and do not break down aggregate figures on this basis.

Using Information to Make Market Entry Decisions

Once the information required to make market entry decisions has been determined, the next step is to establish procedures to analyze the information and select the most attractive markets for the firm. Here, a wide variety of procedures can be adopted, depending on the volume of data, the level of precision, and analytical sophistication required (Papadopoulos and Denis 1988). The degree of management input and its integration into the evaluation procedure is also an important consideration. Approaches ranging from qualitative evaluation and/or ranking of data to the development of elaborate simulation models can be adopted. The appropriate procedure depends to a large extent on the budget and time available for collecting and evaluating information and on the role that the evaluation plays in the management decision-making process.

Regardless of the specific procedure adopted, a *systematic* evaluation of potential opportunities on a worldwide basis is important in order to avoid haphazard market entry decisions based on familiarity with a particular country or market, a chance encounter, or solicitation of interest. A systematic evaluation of all countries and markets worldwide often helps to reveal new or unexpected opportunities and provides a key input in long-range planning for international market involvement and in determining priorities for international market entry.

INFORMATION FOR LOCAL MARKET EXPANSION

In selecting international markets to enter, heavy reliance is typically placed on secondary data. Once certain markets have been selected, based on secondary data, the firm may engage in the collection of primary data to develop marketing strategies appropriate to the specific country. The initial issue is how far strategy has to be adapted to the local market. In many instances, such as export and licensing, the firm assumes a rather passive role, simply providing someone else with the opportunity to sell the product in a different country. However, where the firm is actively involved in a particular country, it will need to collect primary data. In addition to issues related to adaptation of strategy to local market conditions, primary research may be used to identify opportunities for new products and to assess the extent to which similar opportunities and segments exist across countries and can be targeted using the same products, brand names, product positioning, advertising themes, or copy.

While in principle, similar types of information and similar research techniques apply as in domestic market research, in practice, a number of issues arise specific to international markets. In the first place, lack of familiarity with overseas markets may necessitate collection of preliminary information to aid in research design and determine appropriate research questions and methods. Second, differences in the research infrastructure affects organization of research and cost-effectiveness of alternative research methods. Issues of data comparability and equivalence across countries and markets should also be considered in research design, especially where multi-country studies are conducted or when results are to be compared across countries. Each of these issues are next examined in more detail.

Preliminary Data Collection

Often limited management knowledge and research experience in an overseas market coupled with a paucity of secondary data sources or prior research relating to a market mandates a preliminary phase of information collection. This is intended to aid in formulating research specifications and also in research design.

This preliminary phase may include collection of background information, relating, for example, to the product market, complimentary or substitute products, existing attitudinal and behavior studies, competitive analyses, etc. Information on the research infrastructure may also be collected, for example, availability of trained interviewees, reliability of mail services, levels of telephone or fax ownership, etc.

Qualitative research may also be helpful in providing input for the design of a market survey. Such research may enable identification of constructs, product class definitions, or relevant attitudes and behavior to be examined in subsequent phases of research. Qualitative data collection techniques are appropriate in these instances as they are unstructured in character. Rather than imposing a specific response format on the respondent, as in a questionnaire, they focus on probing how people think, feel, and react in response to specific situations or stimuli. They thus avoid the imposition of a cultural bias, since no conceptual model is prespecified by the researcher. The researcher thus gains insights into the problems to be studied and into differences as compared with the domestic market. Often this helps in revealing the impact of sociocultural factors on behavior and response patterns in the marketplace. They can therefore be used to pinpoint relevant aspects to be further examined and to identify appropriate concepts and constructs.

Lack of Market Research Infrastructure

In some countries, the research infrastructure may not be as well developed as in the domestic market. It is likely to be particularly problematic outside the Industrial Triad. Following trade patterns, most marketing research is conducted within the Industrial Triad countries and investigation of markets outside these countries is relatively recent. Consequently, research organizations qualified to conduct field research are often scarce. In some instances, international research companies have established their own field operations and hence may provide coverage.

If qualified research organizations are not available, management may prefer to organize research in-house and develop their own research capabilities. These may include development of in-house databases, hiring of research personnel, and establishment of facilities to conduct concept or new product testing. Greater reliance may also be placed on collection of information from sales personnel or distributors. Establishment of in-house research capabilities is however, likely to entail significant costs, and hence may only be feasible for a firm with substantial operations in a country. Consequently, in some countries management may have to make decisions based on relatively sketchy and less reliable information than is typically available in the domestic market.

Limited availability of secondary data and of government and trade sources of information may also imply that difficulties may be encountered in developing a sampling frame. In the case of consumer research (telephone books and electoral or municipal lists) that is frequently used to develop sampling frames in industrialized countries may not be available or not provide adequate coverage. Similarly, in industrial markets, directories, lists of companies, or organizations may not be available. Consequently, sampling frames may need to be developed from scratch. In some cities, street maps may not be available, or a certain part of the population may live on boats, thus further complicating the research task.

The communications infrastructure may also not be well developed, or may be inefficient. This can significantly hamper information collection and survey administration. For example, the quality of the mail service may be poor, resulting in lengthy delays, or, in some cases, non-delivery of a significant proportion of mail. Similarly, telephone communications may be difficult, and telephone networks may not be well developed. While the spread of modern telecommunications has considerably expanded the scope and quality of communication in many parts of the world, others still remain poorly served, thus hampering collection and transmission of market-related information.

Data Equivalence and Comparability

A final issue concerns the equivalence and comparability of the data collected. As far as possible, the data should have the same meaning or interpretation and the same level of accuracy, precision of measurement, or reliability in all countries and cultures. This is important insofar as international marketing decisions are concerned with the development of strategic and tactical decisions relative to several countries, as opposed to a single national market. Comparability in research design and data is crucial where research is conducted, to determine how far to integrate strategies across different countries and product markets, for example, whether to adopt a standardized advertising strategy. Yet even where research is only conducted in a single country, it is important to bear in mind that research relating to a similar product or service may subsequently be conducted in another country. Consequently, it is important that research designs are developed in such a way that findings from different markets can be compared.

The need for comparability gives rise to a number of issues in the design of primary data collection. These stem in large measure from the conduct of research in different and highly diverse sociocultural environments. In particular, their diversity in language and in levels of literacy can give rise to difficulties of communication between researcher and respondent.

This diversity implies that different behavioral and attitudinal phenomena may occur or be relevant to a specific problem. Consequently, the issue of whether similar research designs can be used or are relevant in different environments arises. In this regard, a number of different types of equivalence or comparability have to be considered. These include the functional, conceptual, and category equivalence of constructs; the linguistic and metric equivalence of the measurement instruments; and the equivalence and comparability of samples. Finally, the establishment of control procedures to reduce cultural bias in data interpretation is needed to limit nonequivalence arising in the administration and interpretation of the research instrument. Each of these issues is next discussed in more detail.

Construct Equivalence. In determining what information to collect, it is important to determine whether a given concept or behavior serves the same function from country to country (that is, its *functional* equivalence), whether the same concepts or behavior occur in different countries, and whether the way in which they are expressed is similar (that is, their *conceptual* equivalence).

In the first place, concepts, objects, or behaviors studied may not necessarily be *functionally* equivalent, that is, have the same role or function in all countries studied (Berry 1969). For example, while in the United States, bicycles are predominantly used for recreation, in the Netherlands and in various developing countries, they provide a basic mode of transportation. This implies that the relevant competing product set must be defined differently. In the United States, it will include other recreational products, while in the Netherlands it will include alternative modes of transportation.

Yet, even where the same concept or construct is identified, it may be expressed by different types of behavior in different cultural settings. Innovativeness, for example, may be a relevant concept in both the United States and France. In the United States, this is reflected not only in the purchase and trial of new products, but also in conversations and in providing information to friends and neighbors about new products and brands. In France, however, to be innovative is not socially valued, and consequently, those who purchase new products will rarely discuss these products with others (Green and Langeard 1975).

Similarly, in many Western societies, social interaction and sociability is frequently reflected in having dinner with friends, going to parties, bars, and so on. In other cultural contexts, such as developing countries, dining with friends may not be a common practice, as meals are taken almost exclusively with family; similarly, parties may not be given. Social interaction may take other forms such as participation in communal dancing or other festivities.

Category Equivalence. The category in which objects or other stimuli are placed may also vary from country to country. Relevant product class definitions may, for example, differ from one country to another. In the soft drink and alcoholic beverage market, forms of soft drinks such as carbonated sodas, fruit juices, and powdered and liquid concentrates differ significantly from one culture to another, and hence, how these are defined and delineated differs. In Mediterranean cultures, beer is considered to be a soft drink (Berent 1975). Similarly, in the dessert market, items that are included will vary substantially, ranging from apple pie, jellies, and ice cream, to baklava, rice pudding, and zabaglione. In some societies, cakes or cookies are included as desserts, while in China, sweet items do not form part of the meal. This implies that what is included in the relevant competing product set will vary. Careful attention to such factors is thus an important consideration when developing product-related measures. In addition, the characteristics or attributes perceived by consumers as relevant in evaluating a product class may differ from one country to another. In France, the hot-cold continuum is a key attribute in characterizing consumers' perceptions of fragrance. In the United States and the United Kingdom, however, this is not an attribute that is perceived as relevant by consumers.

Calibration Equivalence. In developing a research instrument, equivalence has to be established with regard to the calibration system used in measurement. This includes not only equivalence with regard to monetary units and measures of weight, distance, and volume, but also other perceptual cues, such as color, shape, or form, which are used to interpret visual stimuli.

While the need to establish equivalence with regard to monetary and physical measurement units is clearly apparent, more subtle differences in instrument calibration, which are particularly relevant in the case of nonverbal instruments, relate to perceptual cues such as color, form, or shape. Interpretation of the meaning attached to various colors varies from one culture or cultural context to another. White, for example, is a color of mourning in Japan, while in Chinese culture, red is a symbol of happiness and plays a focal role in weddings—from invitations being printed in red and monetary gifts given in red envelopes to the red dress worn by the bride. Awareness of such nuances is thus an important consideration in instrument design and development, especially in relation to visual stimuli.

Translation Equivalence. Questionnaires or other stimuli have to be translated so that they are understood by respondents in different countries and have equivalent meaning in each research context. The need for translation of questionnaires and other verbal stimuli into different languages is readily apparent. The need to translate nonverbal stimuli to ensure that they evoke the desired image and to avoid problems of miscommunication is less widely recognized.

Translation of verbal stimuli frequently helps to pinpoint problems with regard to whether a concept can be measured by using the same or similar questions in each cultural context and whether a question has the same meaning in different research contexts. If different questions are used, then issues arise with regard to whether these can be considered the same and how equivalence can be established.

Translation of nonverbal stimuli requires attention to how perceptual cues are interpreted in each research context. Misunderstanding may arise because the respondent is not familiar with a product or other stimulus or with the way in which it is depicted. Alternatively, respondents may misinterpret stimuli because the associations evoked by the stimuli differ from one country or culture to another.

Sampling Equivalence. The comparability of samples from one country to another should also be considered both in terms of relevant respondents and representation of the population of interest. First, the question arises as to whether or not the respondents should be the same in all countries. In the United States, it is not uncommon for children to exercise substantial influence in the purchases of cereal, toys, desserts, and other items. In other countries, where families are less child oriented, children have much less influence. Similarly, with the increasing proportion of working women in many Western nations, men participate to an increased extent in grocery shopping activities, while in other countries, a single person (the housewife or maid) may be primarily responsible.

In organizational purchasing decisions, in addition to buyers, several other managers may play a key role in purchase decisions, especially where there is a buying committee. Differences in relevant participants in the buying process from one country to another will need to be determined and may vary depending on propensity to delegate or centralize decision making.

A second issue to be considered in sampling is the extent to which samples are comparable and representative of the population of interest from one country to another. Here, a basic dilemma arises. Probability samples of the population of a country, although representative, are unlikely to be comparable with regard to their composition on characteristics such as income, education, or other sociocultural factors that may influence customer response. If, on the other hand, samples are matched so as to ensure comparability on relevant characteristics, other confounding effects may be introduced, and representativeness is lost. For example, if, in studying interest in a new product in different countries, probability samples are drawn, mistaken inferences relative to the difficulties of standardization may be made due to differences in sample composition.

Data Collection Equivalence. Telephone, mail, or personal interviews differ from country to country in terms of their potential biases and reliability due to factors such as the communications infrastructure, the degree of literacy, and the limited availability and adequacy of sampling frames. Consequently, it is not clear that use of the same procedure is necessarily appropriate.

In the United States, telephone surveys enable coverage of a broadly distributed sample as well as facilitating control over interviewers. Telephone ownership is widespread, and hence telephone directories or listings provide reasonably accurate sampling frames. In other countries, however, low levels of telephone ownership and poor communications limit the coverage provided by telephone surveys. In addition, telephone costs are often high and volume rates may not be available. Consequently, telephone surveys are most likely to be appropriate where relatively upscale or affluent socioeconomic segments are to be sampled.

Similarly, while in the United States mail surveys provide a low-cost means of reaching a broad sample without necessitating a field staff, in other countries they may not be as effective. Particularly in developing countries, use of mail surveys may give rise to some problems. Mailing lists comparable to those in the domestic market may not be available, or not sold, and sources such as telephone directories may not provide adequate coverage. In addition, in some countries, the effectiveness of mail surveys is limited not only by low levels of literacy, but also by the reluctance of respondents to respond to mail surveys. Consequently, as in the case of telephone surveys, mail surveys may only be appropriate in industrialized countries in which levels of literacy are high and mailing lists available.

The problems encountered with the use of both telephone and mail surveys in developing countries implies that, in this context, data are best collected through personal interviews. This does, however, require the availability of trained interviewers who are fluent in the relevant language. Furthermore, factors affecting the interviewer/interviewee interaction need to be considered.

Although American consumers are accustomed to the notion of being interviewed, in other countries suspicion about the interviewer's motivations—and feelings that interviewing constitutes an invasion of privacy as well as negative attitudes toward questioning by strangers—often exist. This affects the willingness of respondents to participate or cooperate in both industrial and consumer surveys and also the extent to which respondents will deliberately conceal information or give false answers.

Similarly, respondents in various countries differ in the extent to which they may desire to be socially acquiescent to provide the socially acceptable response in responding to specific items in the questionnaire. Social acquiescence is particularly marked, for example, in Asia. Dominant cultural traits may also affect the nature of the response. The Japanese are more humble, which leads them to undervalue assets or property while the Middle Eastern consumers tend to vaunt their possessions.

Willingness to respond to different types of questions, such as questions relating to income or age, also varies from country to country. Such factors suggest that use of similar procedures in different countries will not always generate comparable results, and hence be appropriate. Accumulated experience from previous research is thus in many cases helpful in providing indications of different sources of bias.

In particular, knowledge of the research infrastructure, i.e., the level of telephone ownership, the reliability of the mail service, the level of literacy, and the willingness and ability of respondents to respond to different questions, as well as the availability of trained interviewers in a given country or culture, may suggest which procedures are likely to be most effective and generate equivalent results in different countries and sociocultural contexts.

Data Interpretation and Cultural Bias

In international marketing research, problems of misinterpretation can arise due to differences in the cultural background of the researcher and the phenomena studied. In particular, there is a danger of cultural self-referent bias (Lee 1966). In other words, there is always a tendency for a researcher to perceive or interpret phenomena or behavior observed in other countries and cultures in terms of his or her own cultural self-referent.

Cross-cultural bias can affect various stages of the research process. It can arise in research design, in communication between researcher and respondent, and in interpretation of the data. Such bias is likely to be particularly acute where a researcher is investigating an unfamiliar sociocultural environment or where he or she lacks experience with sociocultural patterns. As the researcher builds up experience and familiarity with different markets, however, he or she is likely to develop increased sensitivity to sociocultural specificities. This experience may carry over to other similar markets. Study of the United Kingdom market may, for example, aid in understanding reactions in the Netherlands. Similarly, experience in the French market may prove valuable in investigating the Italian or Spanish markets.

CONTINUING NEED FOR INFORMATION

Once the firm is established in international markets, it begins to look for ways to effectively coordinate and control global operations. As the firm grapples with issues related to global rationalization, it faces new information requirements as well as the need to make more effective use of data already collected. Secondary data that helped guide country entry decisions are now also used to monitor changes in the firm's operating environment. Countries that were politically stable or welcomed foreign investment at one time can become unstable and hostile to foreign investment. Economic growth can slow down or accelerate. Inflationary pressures may rise and foreign exchange rates fluctuate. Similarly, information about consumer tastes and preferences gathered on a country by country basis needs to be consolidated to identify commonalities across countries as well as emerging trends.

While emphasis on local market expansion generated a need for primary data to examine local market characteristics and to assess response to products and marketing stimuli, concern with improved coordination and integration of strategy and management systems across countries requires consolidation of data collected on a country by country basis. Information relating to each product business and marketing function needs to be collected and coordinated across countries. Integration of data from various international sources with external sources suggests the desirability of designing an international information system to monitor performance and to determine how best to allocate resources on a global basis.

Central to the integration and coordination of operations on a transnational basis is the identification of opportunities for the harmonization of products and product lines across countries. This requires information relating to external market characteristics as well as performance of different products, product lines, their production, distribution and marketing costs, and performance of various marketing functions in each market or country in which the firm operates. In addition to financial measures of performance such as profits, costs, etc., other types of measures, relating to market share, growth, brand image, customer satisfaction, shared marketing activities, and product line synergies need to be collected. The sheer volume of data required and the organizational complexity of assessing and comparing performance across multiple country and operating units suggests the desirability of building an interactive computerized information system. Data can thus be fed into the system by local operating units by sales representatives, delivery or warehouse personnel, and retail outlets providing up-to-date information on performance for local national, regional, or corporate headquarters. This can provide invaluable input to production, distribution scheduling, and pricing and promotional decisions, enabling rapid adjustment to changes in market demand as well as strategy decisions relating to product lines, product elimination, logistics, etc.

CONCLUSION

Information is a critical ingredient in the formulation of international marketing strategy. Firms contemplating expansion into overseas markets need information regarding market potential and operating climate. Once established in international markets, the firm needs information to fine tune the marketing mix and seek new marketing opportunities. Firms with extensive operations in international markets need information to help coordinate and control far flung activities. This chapter examines the information requirements of firms at various levels of international market development. While the types of information required at each stage of involvement vary, the fundamental problems of comparability and equivalence remain. This represents a formidable challenge for the manager seeking to develop global marketing strategy.

REFERENCES

Berent, Paul-Howard, "International Research is Different," in Edward M. Mazze, ed., *Marketing in Turbulent Times and Marketing: The Challenges and the Opportunities—Combined Proceedings,* pp. 293–97, Chicago: American Marketing Association, 1975.

Berry, J. W. "On Cross-Cultural Comparability," *International Journal of Psychology,* Vol. IV (1969), pp. 119–128.

Douglas, Susan P., Maureen Broadman, and C. Samuel Craig, "Cross-National Consumer Research Traditions," paper prepared for Conference on Research Traditions in Marketing, Brussels. January 8–10, 1992.

Douglas, Susan P. and C. Samuel Craig, *International Marketing Research,* Englewood Cliffs, N.J.: Prentice-Hall, 1983.

Douglas, Susan P. and C. Samuel Craig, "Evolution of Global Marketing Strategy: Scale, Scope and Synergy," *Columbia Journal of World Business* (Fall 1989).

Green; Robert and Eric Langeard, "A Cross-National Comparison of Consumer Habits and Innovator Characteristics," *Journal of Marketing,* 49 (July 1975), pp. 34–41.

Lee, J. A. "Cultural Analysis in Overseas Operations," *Harvard Business Review,* Vol. XLIV (1966), pp. 106–114.

Papadopoulos, N. and J. Davis, "Inventory, Taxonomy and Assessment of Methods for International Market Selection," *International Marketing Review,* Vol. 5, No. 3 (1988), pp. 38–51.

Philip R. Cateora
Professor of Marketing
University of Colorado
Boulder, Colorado

Linda J. Shea
Associate Professor of Marketing
University of Massachusetts
Amherst, Massachusetts

CHAPTER 68

EXPORT MARKETING

A large majority of American companies actively engaged in foreign marketing manufacture products in the United States and export them to foreign customers. Some of these companies maintain elaborate marketing departments abroad that are responsible for the sale of products; others maintain no foreign sales staff but rely exclusively on export middlemen to market the products in the foreign country. These middlemen are, in essence, their customers. Increasingly common are companies engaged in manufacturing activities in several countries, a situation that involves them in worldwide exporting.

Whether a foreign marketer maintains marketing control over the product until it reaches the intended customer or sells to an intermediary early in the distribution chain, the marketing program is basically the same. A target market must be studied, a product designed, a price established, a promotional program planned, and a distribution channel developed that reflects country market requirements and uncontrollable environmental elements. Essential requirements unique to export marketing that must be considered relate to required documents, conditions of tariff systems, means of payment, and other impediments to the free flow of goods between independent sovereigns. The mechanics of export marketing are the special concern of this chapter. While the mechanics should not be viewed as comprising the major task of foreign marketing, a clear understanding of them is essential in successfully completing foreign marketing transactions.

REGULATIONS AND RESTRICTIONS OF EXPORTING

All countries impose some form of regulation and restriction on the exporting and importing of goods; such restrictions are placed on the movement of goods in foreign markets for many reasons. Export regulations may be designed to conserve scarce goods for home consumption or to control the flow of strategic goods to actual or potential enemies. Import regulations may be imposed to protect health, conserve foreign exchange, serve as economic reprisals, protect home industries, or provide revenue in the form of tariffs. To comply with the various regulations, the exporter may have to acquire licenses or permits from the home country and be certain that the potential customer has the necessary permits for importing goods.

U.S. Export Restrictions

Although no formal or special license to engage in an export business is required, permission or a license to export most goods from the United States is required. Most items that require special permission or license for exportation are under the control of the Department of Commerce. Other departmental responsibilities for product categories include (1) arms and implements of war, Department of State; (2) atomic and fissionable energy material, Atomic Energy Commission; (3) gold and U.S. silver coins, U.S. Department of Treasury; (4) narcotic drugs, Department of Justice; (5) natural gas and electric energy, U.S. Federal Power Commission; and, (6) endangered wildlife, Interior Department.

The exporter must consult the Department of Commerce to determine whether a specific license to export a product is required. The export licensing controls administered by the Department of Commerce apply to (1) exports of commodities and technical data from the United States; (2) re-exports of U.S.-origin commodities and technical data from a foreign destination to another foreign destination; (3) U.S.-origin parts and components used in foreign countries to manufacture foreign products for export; and, (4) in some instances, the foreign-produced direct product of U.S.-origin technical data.

All regulations imposed by the Department of Commerce are published in the Export Administration Regulations which is periodically revised and supplemented by the Current Export Bulletin. The respective departments of bureau should be contacted for the current control regulations.

Types of Licenses. Licenses are required for movement of goods outside the United States except for U.S. territories and Canada. There are two types of licenses for exporting to foreign destinations; a general license and a validated license.

A *general license* is a privilege permitting exportation within limits without requiring that an application be filed or that a license document be issued. The exporter merely records the correct general license symbols on the export declaration form. A *validated license* is a document authorizing exportation within the specific limitations it sets forth; it is issued only upon formal application.[1] Application must be made in accordance with procedures set forth in Export Administration Regulations. Most commodities can be exported from the United States to free-world countries under a general license, but a validated license is required when exporting strategic goods and when exporting to unfriendly countries. The type of export license required by the Department of Commerce is determined by the type of product being exported, country of destination, the end use, and the final user.

Country Classification. All countries except Canada are classified into seven groups designated by the symbols Q, S, T, V, W, Y, and Z. The most stringent license requirements are set for Group Z (North Korea, Vietnam, Cuba, and Cambodia), with validated licenses required on almost all commodities going to those countries.

Commodity Control List. In the United States, commodities are classified according to their availability for export. Exporting scarce or strategic goods to foreign countries is either prohibited altogether or restricted as to quantity. All commodities under the export control of the Department of Commerce and all country classifications are found in the Commodity Control List and Country Groups Supplement of the Export Administration Regulations. By consulting these lists, an exporter can determine whether a validated or general license is required for shipment of a particular commodity to a specific country. If a validated license is required to export a commodity to a particular country, the exporter must acquire the appropriate license before export shipment will be allowed. For shipments not requiring a validated license, the exporter must supply a specific notation in the "Shipper's Export Declaration" as to what kind of general license is applicable.[2]

Export controls are considered one of the reasons why many U.S. companies hesitate to export. The system of controls often results in lost sales due to delayed shipments and increased costs. In an effort to increase exports, the Department of Commerce has instituted several changes to expedite completion of export licenses.

Elain and Stela

Two innovations designed to reduce paperwork and time necessary to acquire export licenses are the Export License Application and Information Network (ELAIN) and the System for Tracking Export License Applications (STELA). ELAIN is an electronic network enabling authorized exporters to submit export applications for most commodities for all free-world destinations. The licensing decisions are electronically conveyed back to exporters via the same network. STELA is a computerized voice answering service that provides exporters with information on the status of their applications as well as the authority to ship goods for those applications approved without conditions.

These and other changes have enabled the Department of Commerce to reduce in-house processing time for free-world destinations from an average of 46 days to 14 or fewer. With the worldwide move away from socialist-based to market-driven economies and the recent organization of the Commonwealth of Independent States (CIS), export controls for a significant number of goods traded with Western countries have been eliminated.[3]

Export Documents

Various documents are necessary for every export shipment to satisfy government regulations controlling exportation and to meet the requirements for international commercial payment transactions. The most frequently required documents are the export declaration, the consular invoice or certificate of origin, the bill of lading, the commercial invoice, and the insurance certificate. In addition, such documents as import licenses, export licenses, packing lists, and inspection certificates for agricultural products are often necessary.

The paperwork involved in successfully completing a transaction is considered by many to be the greatest of all non-tariff trade barriers. There are 125 different types of documents in regular or special use in more than 1,000 different forms. A single shipment may require as few as five or more than 50 documents and involve as many as 28 different parties and government agencies. Preparation of documents can be handled routinely but their importance should not be minimized. Incomplete or improperly prepared documents may lead to delays in shipment. In some countries, penalties, fines, or even confiscation of goods can result from errors in some of these documents. Export documents result from requirements imposed by either the government from where the product is exported or by the government where the product is imported by commercial procedures. Following is a description of the principal export documents.

Export Declaration. To maintain a statistical measure of the quantity of goods shipped abroad and to provide a means to determine whether regulations are being met, most countries, including the United States, require shipments abroad to be accompanied by an export declaration. Usually, such a declaration, presented at the port of exit, includes the names and addresses of the principals involved, the final destination of the goods, a full description of the goods, and their declared value. If a validated license is required to ship a particular commodity from the United States, the export license must be presented with the declaration for proper certification thus serving as the principal means of control for regulations by agencies of the U.S. government.

Consular Invoice or Certificate of Origin. Some countries require consular invoices and are typically very exacting about the manner in which the invoices are prepared. Proper forms must be obtained from the country's consulate and returned with two to eight copies in the language of the country. Copies of other required documents, such as an import license, commercial invoice, and bill of lading must also be sent before certification is granted. Of these documents, the consular invoice probably involves the most red tape. Preparation of the document should be handled with extreme care because fines are levied for any errors uncovered. In most countries, the fine is shared with whomever detects it, so few errors go undetected.

Bill of Lading. The most important document required to establish legal ownership and facilitate financial transactions is the bill of lading. It serves the following purposes: (1) as a receipt from the carrier for shipment, (2) as a contract for shipment between the carrier and shipper, and (3) as a certificate of ownership, or title to the goods. Bills of lading are issued in the form of straight bills, which are nonnegotiable and are delivered directly to a co-signer, or order bills, which are negotiable instruments. Bills of lading are frequently referred to as being either clean or foul. A clean bill of lading means that the items presented to the carrier for shipment were properly packaged and clear of apparent damage when received; a foul bill of lading means that the shipment was received in damaged condition, and this fact is noted on the bill of lading.

Commercial Invoice. Every international transaction requires a commercial invoice, that is, a bill or statement for the goods sold. This document often serves several purposes in that some countries require a copy for customs clearance, and it is also one of the financial documents required in international commercial payments.

Insurance Policy or Certificate. The risks of shipment due to political or economic unrest in some countries and the possibility of damage from the sea and weather make it absolutely necessary to have adequate insurance covering loss resulting from damage, war, or riots. Typically, the method of payment or terms of sale require insurance on the goods, so few export shipments are uninsured. The insurance policy or certificate of insurance is considered a key document in export trade.

Licenses. Export or import licenses are additional documents frequently required in export trade. In those cases where import licenses are required by the country of entry, a copy of the license or license number is usually required to obtain a consular invoice. Whenever a commodity requires an export license, it must be obtained before an export declaration will be properly certified. Sanitary and health inspection certificates attesting to the absence of disease and pests may be required for certain agricultural products before a country will allow the goods to cross its border. Packing lists with correct weights are also required in some cases.

IMPORT RESTRICTIONS

In any analysis of the feasibility of exporting to a foreign country, it is necessary to examine not only the export restrictions of the home country but also the import restrictions and regulations of the foreign country. Although the responsibility of import restrictions generally rest with the importer, they are an important consideration to the exporter in terms of the feasibility of conducting business with a particular foreign customer.

The import tariff imposed by the foreign country is a major impediment to trade although there are many other types of trade restrictions. Examples of some of the barriers to exporting include (1) import licenses, quotas and other quantitative restrictions; (2) currency restrictions and allocation of exchange at unfavorable rates on payments for imports; (3) devaluation; (4) prohibitive prior imports deposits and prohibition of collection-basis sales and insistence on cash letters of credit; (5) arbitrarily short periods in which to apply for import license; and (6) delays resulting from pressure on overworked officials or from competitors' influence on susceptible officials.

Of all trade restrictions, the most frequently encountered are tariffs and such non-tariff barriers as exchange permits, quotas, and import licenses.

Tariffs. Tariffs are the taxes or customs duties levied against goods imported from another country. Almost all countries have tariffs for the purpose of raising revenue or protecting home industries from foreign competition. Tariff rates are based on value or quantity or a combination of both. In the United States, for example, the types of custom duties used are classified as (1) ad valorem duties, based on a percentage of the determined value of the imported goods; (2) specific duties, a stipulated amount per unit weight or some other measure of quantity; and (3) a compound duty that combines both specific and *ad valorem* taxes on a particular item, that is, a tax per pound plus a percentage of value. Tariffs are subject to change and an exporter should have the most recent information available from each country.

Exchange Permits. Especially important to the exporter are the exchange restrictions placed on the flow of currency by some foreign countries. In order to conserve scarce foreign exchange and alleviate balance of payment difficulties, many countries impose restrictions on the amount of their currency they will exchange for the currency of another country. In effect, they ration the amount of currency available to pay for imports. Exchange controls may be applied in general to all commodities or, as is frequently the case, a country may employ a system of multiple exchange rates based on the type of import. Essential products might have a very favorable exchange rate, whereas nonessentials or luxuries would have a less favorable rate of exchange. In some cases, no exchange permits are issued for certain classes of commodities.

In countries that utilize exchange controls, the typical procedure is for the importer to apply to the control agency of the importing country for an import permit; if the control agency approves the request, an import license is issued. Then, through the proper government agency, the import license can be used to have the local currency exchanged for the currency of the seller.

When local currency is in short supply (as frequently happens in some countries), other means of acquiring home-country currency are necessary. For example, in a transaction between the government of Colombia and a U.S. truck manufacturer, there was a scarcity of U.S. currency to exchange for the 1,000 vehicles Colombia wanted to purchase. The problem was solved through a series of exchanges. Colombia had a surplus of coffee which the truck manufacturer accepted and traded in Europe for sugar, the sugar for pig iron, and finally the pig iron for U.S. dollars.

This rather complicated but effective transaction is increasingly being used. In fact, an international marketing middleman, sometimes called an intermerchant, has evolved as a result of these switch or triangular trades in which several principals from different countries are involved. In some countries where no exchange permits are issued, an increasing amount of trade is conducted on a barter basis. This is especially true in trade with Eastern European countries, China, and republics of the former U.S.S.R. where nearly 40 percent of trade is conducted with some form of countertrade. The dissolution of the U.S.S.R. and the subsequent establishment of the CIS will most likely result in increased countertrade arrangements. Since exchange procedures are sometimes complicated, the exporter should seek the advice of a banker or some other informed source when questions of foreign exchange arise.

Quotas. Countries may also impose limitations on the quantity of certain goods imported during a specific period. These quotas may be applied to imports from specific countries or from all foreign sources in general. The United States, for example, has specific quotas for importing some products, such as sugar, wheat, cotton, tobacco, textiles, and peanuts. In the case of some of these items, there are also limitations on the amount imported from specific countries.

Quotas are set for a variety of reasons, the most important being to protect domestic industry and to conserve foreign exchange. Some importing countries also set quotas to insure an equitable distribution of purchases among friendly countries.[4]

Import Licenses. As a means of regulating the flow of exchange and the quantity of particular commodities imported, countries often require import licenses. The fundamental difference between quotas and import licenses when used to control the quantity of a commodity brought into a country is the greater flexibility of the import license. Quotas are generally set for a specific amount over a specific period of time, but licensing can limit quantities to be imported on a case-by-case basis.

Other Restrictions. Many other kinds of restrictions may also be imposed on imports, such as regulations affecting the importation of harmful products, drugs and medicine, and amoral products and literature. Products must also comply with all government standards set for health, sanitation, packaging, and labeling. For example, in the Netherlands, all imported hens' and ducks' eggs must be marked in indelible ink with the country of origin; in Spain, imported condensed milk must be labeled to show its fat content when less than 8 percent fat is involved; and in Mexico, all animals imported from the United States must be accompanied by a sanitary certificate issued by an approved veterinary inspector and a visa secured from a Mexican consulate. Exhibit 1 is a comprehensive list of non-tariff barriers an exporter may encounter. Non-tariff barriers can result in delays, severe fines, and penalties. Since requirements vary from country to country, regulations

EXHIBIT 1. Common Non-Tariff Barriers

Import quotas
Minimum import pricing
Port-of-entry taxes or levies
Import licensing requirements
Complex customs procedures
Technical standards
Arbitrary product classification
Safety and health requirements
Packaging and labeling requirements
Local content requirements
Discriminatory government procurement requirements
Voluntary export restraints
Channel restrictions

for each country must be consulted.[5] Overseas Business Reports, issued periodically by the Department of Commerce, provides the foreign marketer with the most recent foreign trade regulations of each country as well as the U.S. regulations regarding each country.

The various market barriers that exist among members of the European community create a major impediment to trade. One study of 20,000 EC firms indicated that the most troublesome barriers were administrative roadblocks, frontier delays, and capital controls. As the Single European Act became a reality after 1992, the elimination of many existing barriers among member countries occurred.[6] The Single Market will no doubt make trade easier among its member countries, but there is a rising concern that a fully integrated EC will become a market with even stronger protectionist barriers toward nonmember countries.[7]

FOREIGN COMMERCIAL PAYMENTS

The sale of goods in other countries is further complicated by additional risks encountered when dealing with foreign customers. Risks result from inadequate credit reports on customers, problems of currency exchange controls, distance, different legal systems, and the cost and difficulty of collecting delinquent accounts all of which require different emphasis on payment systems utilized. In U.S. domestic trade, the typical payment procedure for established customers is an open account—the goods are delivered and the customer is billed on an end-of-the-month basis. The most frequently used term of payment in foreign commercial transactions for both export and import sales is by letter of credit, followed closely in importance by commercial dollar drafts or bills of exchange drawn by the seller on the buyer. Open accounts are reserved for well-established customers, and cash in advance is required only for new customers whose credit worthiness has not been established, the poorest poorest credit risks, or when the character of the merchandise is such that failure to pay may result in heavy loss. Because of the time typically required for shipment of goods from one country to another, advance cash payment is an unusually costly burden for a potential customer and places a seller at a definite competitive disadvantage.

Terms of sale are typically arranged between the buyer and seller at the time of the sale. The type of merchandise, the amount of money involved, business custom, the credit rating of the buyer, the country of the buyer, and whether the buyer is a new or old customer are all items to be considered in establishing the terms of sale. The two most commonly used payment arrangements—letters of credit and bills of exchange—are discussed next.

Letters of Credit

Most American exports are handled on the basis of export letters of credit opened in favor of the seller by the buyer. Letters of credit shift the credit risk of the buyer to the bank issuing the letter of credit. When a letter of credit is employed, the seller can ordinarily draw a draft against the bank issuing the credit and receive dollars with the presentation of the proper shipping documents. Except for cash in advance, letters of credit afford the greatest degree of protection for the seller.

The procedure when using a letter of credit generally begins at the completion of the contract when the buyer goes to the local bank and arranges for the issuance of a letter of credit; the buyer's bank then notifies its correspondent bank of the seller's country that the letter has been issued. After meeting the requirements of the letter of credit, the seller can draw a draft against the credit (in effect, the bank issuing the letter) for payment of the goods. The precise conditions of the letter of credit are detailed in it and generally require the presentation of certain documents with the draft before the correspondent bank will honor the draft. The usual documents required are (1) the commercial invoice, (2) the consular invoice (when requested), (3) a clean bill of lading, and (4) an insurance policy or certificate. Upon presentation of the proper documents and a draft, the correspondent bank will then honor the draft under the terms of the letter of credit.

Since all letters of credit must be very exact in terms and considerations, it is important for the exporter to check its terms carefully to be certain that all the necessary documents have been acquired and properly completed. There are numerous omissions, oversights, and other defects that result in delays when drafts or letters of credit are presented for collection. Some of the more common are:

- *Insurance.* Defects in insurance include inadequate coverage, no endorsement or counter-signature, and dating later than the bill of lading.

- *Bill of lading.* Defects in the bill of lading include no "on board" endorsement, no signature of carrier, a missing endorsement, or failure to specify prepaid freight.
- *Letter of credit.* Defects in letters of credit include missed expiration dates, the credit amount exceeds the invoice amount, or unauthorized or disproportionate charges.
- *Invoice.* Defects in the invoice include missing signatures or failure to designate terms of shipment (C&F, CIF, FAS, etc.) as stipulated in letter of credit.
- *Other.* Other defects occur when documents are missing, stale, dated, or incorrect.

Bills of Exchange

Another important form of international commercial payment is handled through the use of sight or time drafts drawn by sellers on foreign buyers. In letters of credit, the credit of one or more banks is involved; in the use of bills of exchange (or dollar drafts), the seller assumes all risks until the actual dollars are received. The typical procedure followed is for the seller to draw a draft on the buyer and present it with the necessary documents to the seller's bank for collection. The documents required are principally the same as those required for letters of credit. Upon receipt of the draft, the U.S. bank forwards the draft with the necessary documents to a correspondent bank in the buyer's country; the buyer is then presented with the draft for acceptance and immediate or later payment. With the acceptance of the draft, the buyer receives the properly endorsed bill of lading, which is used to acquire the goods from the carrier.

Bills of exchange or dollar drafts generally have one of three time periods—at sight, arrival, or time. A sight draft requires that acceptance and payment be made upon presentation of the draft and often before arrival of the goods. An arrival draft requires that payment be made upon arrival of the goods. Unlike the other two kinds, a date draft has an exact date for payment and in no way is affected by the movement of the goods. There may be time designations placed on the sight and arrival drafts which stipulate a fixed number of days after acceptance when the obligation must be paid. Usually this period is from 30 to 120 days, thus providing one means of extending credit to the foreign buyer.

Dollar drafts have advantages for the seller because an accepted draft frequently can be discounted at the bank for immediate payment. Banks, however, usually discount drafts only with recourse, that is, if the draft is not honored by the buyer, the bank returns it to the seller for payment. An accepted draft is also much sounder evidence in case of default and necessary litigation than an open account would be.

INTERNATIONAL TRADE TERMS

International trade terms often sound similar to those used in domestic business but generally have different meanings. To avoid one source of misunderstanding in documentation, the exporter should become familiar with the common export trade terms detailed in Exhibit 2.

A complete list of terms and their definitions can be found in Incoterms, a booklet published by the International Chamber of Commerce, 801 Second Avenue, Suite 1204, New York, NY 10017. It is important for the exporter to understand exactly the meanings of terms used in quotations. A simple misunderstanding regarding delivery terms may prevent the exporter from meeting contractual obligations or make that person responsible for shipping costs he or she did not intend to incur. Exhibit 3 indicates who is responsible for a variety of costs under various terms.

PACKING AND MARKING

Special packing and marking requirements must be considered for shipments destined to be transported over water, subject to excessive handling, or destined for parts of the world with extreme climates. Packing that is adequate for domestic shipments often falls short for goods subject to the conditions mentioned above. Protection against rough handling, moisture, temperature extremes, and pilferage may require heavy crating which increases total costs for packing as well as freight rates because of increased weight and size. Since some countries determine import duties on gross weight, packing can add a significant amount to import fees. To avoid the extremes of too much or too little packing, the marketer should consult export brokers, export freight forwarders, or other specialists.

All countries impose import regulations for marking goods and containers and severe penalties can result from noncompliance. The exporter must be careful that all marking on the container conforms exactly to the data on the export documents because discrepancies are often interpreted by custom officials as an attempt to defraud. A basic source of information for American exporters is the Department of Commerce series of pamphlets entitled, Preparing Shipment to (Country), which details the necessary export documents and outlines pertinent U.S. and foreign government regulations regarding such matters as labeling, marking, packing, and customs procedures.[8]

FREE-TRADE ZONES

To facilitate international trade and lessen the difficulties caused by various import restrictions, some countries have established free-trade zones (FTZs) or ports. There are more than 200 of these facilities

EXHIBIT 2. Common Export Trade Terms and What They Include

Quotation	Cost of Goods at Factory	Transportation to Dock	Loading onto Vessel	Ocean or Air Freight Charges	Shipping Insurance	Unloading at Foreign Port
Ex factory	X					
Free alongside (f.a.s.)	X	X				
Free on Board: Name of home port (f.o.b.)	X	X	X			
Cost and freight: Name of foreign port (c & f)	X	X	X	X		
Cost, insurance, freight, name of overseas port (c.i.f.)	X	X	X	X	X	
Ex dock	X	X	X	X	X	X

EXHIBIT 3. Who's Responsible for Costs under Various Terms?

Cost Items/Terms	FOB (Free on Board) Inland Carrier at Factory	FOB (Free on Board) Inland Carrier at Point of Shipment	FAS (Free Along Side) Vessel or Plane at Port of Shipment	CIF (Cost, Insurance, Freight) at Port of Destination
Export packing*	Buyer	Seller	Seller	Seller
Inland freight	Buyer	Seller	Seller	Seller
Port charges	Buyer	Buyer	Seller	Seller
Forwarder's fee	Buyer	Buyer	Buyer	Seller
Consular fee	Buyer	Buyer	Buyer	Buyer[†]
Loading on vessel or plane	Buyer	Buyer	Buyer	Seller
Ocean freight	Buyer	Buyer	Buyer	Seller
Cargo insurance	Buyer	Buyer	Buyer	Seller
Customs duties	Buyer	Buyer	Buyer	Buyer
Ownership of goods passes	When goods onboard an inland carrier (truck, rail, etc.) or in hands of inland carrier	When goods unloaded by inland carrier	When goods alongside carrier, in hands of air or ocean carrier	When goods on board air ocean carrier *at port of shipment*

*Who absorbs export packing? This charge should be clearly agreed on. Charges are sometimes controversial.

[†]The seller has responsibility to arrange for consular invoices (and other documents requested by buyer's government). According to official definition, buyer pays fees, but sometimes as a matter of practice, seller includes in quotations.

in operation in the United States alone. A free port or trade zone can receive shipments of goods for importation to be stored or processed in some manner without paying the required import duties until they enter the country from the free-trade zone area. Thus exporters can ship in large quantities to such free ports as Shannon Airport, Ireland, or Barcelona, Spain for storage and processing and then supply other areas with smaller quantities as demand arises.[9] A free-trade zone is in essence an enclave and not considered a part of the country to which it is contiguous as far as import regulations are concerned. If an item leaves a free-trade zone area for distribution and is imported into the country where the free-trade zone is located, all duties and regulations are imposed.

In recent years, U.S. free-trade zones have extended their services to over 1,000 firms engaged in a spectrum of international trade related activities ranging from distribution to assembly and manufacturing. More than 50 free-trade zones are located in a large number of areas throughout the United States, including New York, New Orleans, San Francisco, Seattle, Toledo, Honolulu, Mayaquea (Puerto Rico), Kansas City, Little Rock, and Denver. Goods subject to U.S. custom duties can be landed in these areas for storage or such processing in repackaging, cleaning, and grading before being brought into the United States or re-exported to some other country. In those cases where goods are imported into the United States to be combined with American-made goods and re-exported to another country, the importer or exporter can avoid payment of U.S. import duties on the foreign portion and eliminate the complications of applying for a "drawback"—a request for a refund from the government of 99 percent of the duties paid on imports that are later re-exported. Other benefits for companies utilizing free-trade zones include (1) lower insurance costs due to greater security required in an FTZ; (2) more working capital since duties are deferred until goods leave the zone; (3) the opportunity to stockpile products when quotas are filled or while waiting for ideal market conditions; (4) significant savings on goods or materials rejected, damaged, or scrapped for which no duties are assessed; and (5) an exemption from paying duties on labor and overhead costs incurred in a zone which are excluded in determining the value of the goods.

Maquiladoras

Maquiladoras, a more elaborate variation of a free-trade zone exists on the Mexican–U.S. border. In 1971, the Mexican and U.S. governments established an "In-Bond" program[10] which created a favorable opportunity for U.S. companies to use abundant, low-cost Mexican labor.

The Mexican government allows U.S. processing, packaging, assembling, and/or repair plants located in the "In-Bond" area to import parts and processed materials without import taxes provided the finished products are re-exported to the United States or to another foreign country. In turn, the U.S. government permits the re-importing of the packaged, processed, assembled, or repaired good into the United States with a reasonably low import tariff applied only to the value added while in Mexico. More than 1,700 U.S. companies in electronics, health care, automotive, furniture, clothing, and toy manufacturing participate in the "In-Bond" program.[11]

Special Economic Zone

China's variation of the maquiladora is the *special economic zone* (SEZ). Average manufacturing labor costs in China run between $60 and $95 per month, including benefits. Higher labor costs in the United States and other developed countries have led multinational corporations to search worldwide for low-cost labor.

Information about free-trade zones, free ports, and similar customs-privileged facilities abroad may be abstained from the Foreign Trade Zones Board, U.S. Department of Commerce.

THE FOREIGN FREIGHT FORWARDER

A foreign freight forwarder is an indispensable agent for an exporting firm that cannot afford a specialist to handle paperwork and other export trade mechanics. Even in large companies with active export departments capable of handling documentation, a forwarder is useful as a shipment coordinator at the port or at the destination. Besides arranging for complete shipping documentation, the full-service foreign freight forwarder provides information and advice on routing and scheduling, rates and related charges, consular and licensing requirements, labeling requirements, and export restrictions. Further, the agent offers shipping insurance, warehouse storage, packing and containerization, and arranges for ocean cargo or air freight space. Both large and small shippers find freight forwarders wide range of services useful and well worth the fees normally charged.

NATIONAL TRADE DATA BANK

The single best source of information for the exporter is the International Trade Administration (ITA)/US&FCS District Offices. Found in all 50 states and Puerto Rico, the ITA office can provide technical help for the new exporter and is an important source of export information. Additionally, information on the National Trade Data Bank (NTDB) is provided by ITA district offices.

The Omnibus Trade and Competitiveness Act of 1988 mandated the Commerce Department to collect in one place the U.S. government's extensive offerings of information on international trade and export. Thirteen other federal agencies that collect trade information were directed to cooperate with the Commerce Department to provide all federal trade information available in electronic form.

The NTDB which resulted from the mandate is designed to bring over 100,000 different documents—the equivalent to three complete sets of the Encyclopedia Britannica—to the user. Updated monthly, the NTDB compact disc-read only memory (CD-ROM) contains information from 15 U.S. government agencies. The CD-ROM works with common microcomputers and contains the complete data bank and two user-friendly software packages, BROWSE and ROMWARE, which allow a user to access the data in a variety of ways.[12] New information is constantly being added. Projected to be included in the future are the Department of Commerce's Background Notes, information on Eastern European countries, and possibly United Nations' trade information and data from the International Monetary Fund.[13] The NTDB is available in Commerce Department district offices, at all 700 Federal Depository Libraries, and is for sale to the public.[14]

SUMMARY

An awareness of the mechanics of export trade is indispensable to the foreign marketer who engages in exporting goods from one country to another; these mechanics, however, should not be considered the essence of foreign marketing since they are only one aspect that must be incorporated in a total marketing plan. Although most marketing techniques are open to interpretation and creative application, the mechanics of exporting are very exact; there is very little room for interpretation or improvisation with the requirements of export licenses, quotas, tariffs, export documents, packing, marking, and the various types and uses of commercial payments.

The very nature of the regulations and restrictions surrounding importing and exporting can lead to frequent and rapid change. In handling the mechanics of export trade successfully, the manufacturer must keep abreast of all foreign and domestic changes in requirements and regulations pertaining to the product involved.

NOTES

1. A summary of the U.S. Export Control Regulations (Washington, D.C.: U.S. Department of Commerce, 1990).
2. For a complete discussion of export controls and the most recent changes in country classifications and licensing requirements, consult the current issue of the Export Administration Regulations, International Trade Administration, Office of Export Administration, U.S. Department of Commerce, Washington, DC.
3. "Fewer Licenses Required for Exports to the West," *Business America,* July 2, 1990, pp. 20–21.

4. "What Free Trade Will Mean to Different Industries," *Fortune,* August 26, 1991, p. 91.
5. For a comprehensive review of non-tariff barriers, see Earl Naumann and Douglas J. Lincoln, "Non-Tariff Barriers and Entry Strategy Alternatives: Strategic Marketing Implications," *Journal of Small Business Management,* April 1991, pp. 60–69.
6. "Preparing for the Europe of Tomorrow," *Business America,* February 24, 1992, p. 2.
7. "Protectionism Is King of the Road," *Business Week,* May 13, 1991, pp. 57–58.
8. "Five Steps To Export Success," *Business America,* May 4, 1992, p. 2.
9. "Free Trade Zones in Europe: A Boom in the East, A Burden in the West," *EuroSphere,* KPMG Peat Marwick, August/September 1991, pp. 2–3.
10. For a profile of a maquiladora see: "Twin Plant Briefs," *World Trade,* March 1991, p. 98.
11. "Mexico Strength of In-Bond Industry," *Institutional Investor,* June 1990, pp. 24–26.
12. An explanation of what NTDB CD-ROM is, how to use it to explore and access the information stored in the NTBD can be found in "ABCs of Exporting" a special issue of *Business America,* January 28, 1991.
13. Mark W. Plant, "The National Trade Data Bank: A One-Year Perspective," *Business America,* September 23, 1991, pp. 2–5.
14. Annual subscription is $360 for 12 CD-ROMS, or single-month for $35.

SUGGESTIONS FOR FURTHER READING

U.S. Dept. of Commerce, *A Basic Guide to Exporting,* International Trade Administration, Washington, D.C.

Philip R. Cateora, *International Marketing,* (Homewood, IL, Richard D. Irwin, Inc, 1993).

Gerald S. Albaum
Professor of Marketing
University of Oregon
Eugene, Oregon

Gordon E. Miracle
Professor of Advertising
Michigan State University
East Lansing, Michigan

CHAPTER 69

INTERNATIONAL DISTRIBUTION AND SELLING

"The world is my market. As an international marketing person, I make no distinction between home and overseas markets." This point of view is being voiced by an increasing number of business executives, and is a major theme underlying the *internationalization* activities that were popular in business firms in the 1980s and still are going strong in the 1990s. Statements like this indicate that increasing numbers of companies throughout the world are emerging (or trying to emerge) as global marketers serving global markets.

The extreme case of a global marketer has been called the global *corporation,* defined as a company operating with such consistency—at low relative cost—it would appear the world, or major regions of the world, were a single entity.[1] Such a company would be selling the same product(s) the same way everywhere. In contrast, the "old-style" multinational corporation (MNC) operates in a number of countries and adjusts its products and practices in each—at high relative costs. These two extremes represent standardization and adaptation/individualization. A major premise of the global corporation is that as the world evolves, nations, people, and markets become increasingly homogeneous and people are willing to sacrifice preferences in product features, etc. for good quality at lower prices. Indeed, it is argued that the global corporation seeks to hasten what already occurs, to force standardized products and practices throughout the world because that is what the world will accept, particularly when aggressive low pricing is linked to quality and reliability. Opponents argue that there is no evidence the world is becoming homogeneous such that market response functions across countries are uniformly similar or that consumers are becoming more price sensitive at the expense of product features and functions.

To an extent, the issue is one of semantics. Companies who are internationalized have been called international, transnational, world, multinational, and global companies. Often, the distinctions made between these are not very many, nor large. Moreover, not everyone defines each the same way. The "truth," if there is one, probably lies between the extremes. Regardless of what it is called, the key for many companies is taking a global view with respect to

1. the assessment of the relative promise of market opportunities;
2. the assessment of investment opportunities and the allocation of investment funds;
3. the purchasing of raw materials, components, equipment, and supplies;

4. the recruitment of personnel; and
5. the procurement of capital.

In short, a company with a global view operates without regard for national boundaries except as they affect the relative desirability of one course of action over another.

In some instances, standardization may be appropriate when there is a global market segment. Benetton, for example, seems to operate this way. Under other conditions, adaptation needs to occur. To successfully market an automobile in Japan, for example, the product needs to be right-hand drive, an adaptation that United States manufacturers choose not to make.

INTERNATIONAL MARKETING MANAGEMENT

International marketing management includes management of marketing activities for products that cross national boundaries. It also includes marketing activities of companies that manufacture, assemble, and/or sell within a given foreign nation *if* certain conditions are met: (1) the firm is a part of an organization or enterprise that operates in other countries or (2) there is some degree of influence, guidance, direction, or control of such marketing activities from outside the country in which the firm operates. The major dimensions of international marketing are *exporting* and *managing marketing operations* in foreign countries. International marketing involves marketing to and in foreign countries.

In Chapter 66, "International Marketing Concepts," the basic similarities and differences between domestic and international marketing were discussed. Regarding differences, three basic dimensions emerge: (1) the environment, (2) the crossing of national borders, and (3) the marketing in two or more countries at the same time. Therefore, a company often must tailor marketing decisions to different environments, or transfer effective marketing policies and procedures across national borders when appropriate. In addition, when a company markets its products simultaneously in more than one national environment, it should relate its activities in multiple nations to each other such that the effectiveness of the individual nation marketing programs is enhanced as well as the effectiveness of the total world marketing effort.

Interest in international marketing activities can be attributed in large part to different and shifting demand and supply characteristics in markets throughout the world as well as to the ever-changing competitive environment. Companies that have been serving domestic markets often find that they are reaching the point where supply, in terms of productive capacity, is exceeding demand. This is due to the slowing down, or perhaps, the leveling off, of growth in national markets and to increased competition from other domestic firms and from foreign firms. Or it may be that the home market is small *per se*. Another reason may be that a company views expansion to foreign markets as a way to diversify or spread out risk. Behavior for these "reasons" represents *reactive* behavior in that a firm is responding to internal or external pressures (i.e., push factors), and is acting more or less passively. In contrast, underlying motivations may lead to more *proactive* and/or aggressive behavior based on a company's desire to exploit unique competencies or market opportunities (i.e., pull factors).

INTERNATIONALIZATION

As suggested earlier, internationalization or a call for it, is becoming increasingly common within the business community. But, is internationalizing a process, an end-result, a way of thinking, or a philosophy of doing business? The answer is that it is all of these.[2] From the viewpoint of the individual firm, the internationalization process can be defined as *the successive development in a firm's international involvement in terms of the geographical spreading in markets, products and operation forms, and the changes in international management philosophies and organizational behavior from the beginning of the process to the actual situation.*

Thus the evolutionary process must then be seen as a time-phased function of the foreign experience gathered so that the international marketing firm successively accumulates organizational learning over time. The learning cycles include processes by which the firm adjusts itself defensively to foreign markets as well as processes by which knowledge and experience are used offensively to improve the fit between the firm and its foreign market environment. International marketing development can be described as a stimulus-response process in which experimental learning has been considered as an important determinant. Information activities, willingness to commit resources and the expectations of the favorability of international marketing activity, and managerial risk-taking behavior are all essential in describing the process.

How should one measure the individual firm's degree of internationalization? Several measurements have been proposed. In general, the degree of internationalization has been measured by quantitative indicators, such as the number of countries in which a firm is doing business; characteristics like foreign earnings, sales, or assets; the number of employees engaged in foreign activities; and so on. The quantitative characteristics may be measured either absolutely or relatively. The absolute component gives an indication of the amount of resources a firm commits to foreign operations. The relative measure shows that a firm is strongly dependent on its foreign activities if it has committed a significant portion of its financial, technological, and human resources to foreign market operations.

The firm's degree of internationalization can also be described by qualitative indicators. Behavioral characteristics like top management's "international orientation," the degree of foreign experience, and so on are very appealing, but the use of such characteristics involves many measurement problems and they are difficult to operationalize. It is almost impossible to ascertain exactly what is meant by top management "thinking international" or "looking at the world as our marketplace." Whether a company weighs alternative marketing possibilities on a worldwide basis or does not discard a marketing opportunity abroad simply because it is not in the country where it has its production is of importance in understanding a company's international behavior; such distinctions, however, are very difficult to make in practice.

It is important to consider what type of operations the company is engaged in. In some cases, the activities of a firm may be international by definition—for instance, the operations of major airline companies like SAS, KLM, and QANTAS. There are also distinct differences between an automobile company with manufacturing subsidiaries in dozens of countries; a mining company with operations in several countries all supporting the company's manufacturing activities in, for instance, Germany; an oil company that owns and operates oil fields in several countries and transports and markets oil; a machinery company with manufacturing operations in one country and an export network and sales and service outlets all over the world; and a textile company that only sells its products overseas through indirect exports. The problems faced by these companies and their solutions differ, which means that it is difficult to define their degree of internationalization.

Change processes are the starting point for any investigation of company internationalization: How can the international marketing process be characterized concerning changes in strategies, functions, and structures? Which factors determine this process? What are the managerial and organizational consequences of the adoption process? The international marketing development process can be viewed as a product of environmental forces or as a product of managerial behavior on the part of those within the firm who decide on strategies. There is no consensus emerging from the research on this issue to support one view only.

STRUCTURE OF INTERNATIONAL OPERATIONS

Examples of companies in which a significant share of earnings comes from international operations are not difficult to find: Coca-Cola, IBM, International Harvester, Procter & Gamble, CPC, N.V. Philips Gloelampenfabrieken, Sony, Nestlé, C. Itoh, Daimler-Benz, and Toyota, to name a few. For many companies, the bulk of foreign earnings comes from foreign-based operations rather than export sales.

Entry strategy for international markets involves a comprehensive plan including the objectives/goals, resources, and policies that will guide a company's international marketing operations over a future time period that is of sufficient length that the company can achieve sustainable growth in foreign markets.[3] There is no set time period for all companies, but 3–5 years seems to be adequate for most companies. Rather than view entry strategy as a simple plan, in practice it is actually a summation of individual product/market plans. International marketing managers need to develop an entry strategy for each product in each foreign market. While the end result of this process may exhibit similarities, one cannot assume that market response to a particular entry strategy will be the same for different product and country markets.

An entry strategy consists of an entry mode and a marketing plan. The mode of entry is what is used to penetrate a target country while the foreign marketing plan is used to penetrate a target market. The entry mode is important as it determines the degree of a company's control over the marketing mix (program) in the target market. Without an entry strategy for a given product/market, a company will follow only a "sales" approach to foreign markets. Differences between the "sales" and "entry-strategy" approaches are shown in Exhibit 1. While a sales approach may seem proper for a newcomer to international marketing, it hardly fits a company that wants to internationalize.

An international market entry mode is an institutional arrangement necessary for the entry of a company's products, technology, and human and financial capital into a foreign country/market. There are seven major alternative strategies for entering a foreign market.

Exporting

Perhaps the simplest and easiest way to meet the needs of foreign markets is by exporting. This approach generally has minimal effect on the ordinary operations of the firm, and the risks involved are less than other alternatives. At the same time, many companies long involved in foreign markets still export on a regular and permanent basis. Exporting may be conducted through export middlemen, foreign import middlemen, or by a company's own overseas sales branches, subsidiaries, or salespeople.

Licensing

One of the first means a manufacturer can take in expanding international operations beyond exporting is licensing agreements. Licensing includes arrangements for the foreign licensee to pay for the use of manufacturing, processing, trademark or name, patents, technical assistance, marketing knowledge, trade secrets or some other skill provided by the licensor.

EXHIBIT 1. Entry Strategy Approach versus "Sales" Approach to International Markets

	"Sales" Approach	**Entry Strategy Approach**
Time horizons	Short run	Long run (say, 3 to 5 years)
Target markets	No systematic selection	Selection based on analysis of market/sales potential
Dominant objective	Immediate sales	Build permanent market position
Resource commitment	Only enough to get immediate sales	What is necessary to gain permanent market position
Entry mode	No systematic choice	Systematic choice of most appropriate mode
New-product development	Exclusively for home market	For both home and foreign markets
Product adaptation	Only mandatory adaptations (to meet legal/technical requirements) of domestic products	Adaptation of domestic products to foreign buyers' preferences, incomes, and use conditions
Channels	No effort to control	Effort to control in support of market objectives/goals
Price	Determined by domestic full cost with some *ad hoc* adjustments to specific sales situations	Determined by demand, competition, objectives, and other marketing policies, as well as cost
Promotions	Mainly confined to personal selling or left to middleman	Advertising, sales promotion, and personal selling mix to achieve market objectives/goals

Source: Franklin R. Root, *Entry Strategies for International Markets* (Lexington, MA: D. C. Heath and Company, 1987, p. 5).

Licensing is a viable means of developing investment footholds in overseas markets and a complement to exporting and direct investment in manufacturing facilities. It often constitutes a prelude to a more permanent equity investment. Probably the main appeal of this strategy to the potential licensor is the ease and low cost of entering an overseas market. For example, one of the reasons Gerber Products Company, a manufacturer of baby food, entered the Japanese market through licensing was that it did not have enough bilingual people to operate a foreign subsidiary.

Sometimes licensing is the only potentially profitable avenue open in a desirable overseas market area, if imports and direct investments are severely restricted or prohibited. The major drawbacks to the licensor are (1) a potential competitor is established, (2) there is a lack of control over production, and (3) there is a loss of flexibility. It is often difficult to coordinate a licensee into a worldwide marketing plan.

Contract Manufacturing

This strategy involves contracting for the manufacture or assembly of products by manufacturers established in overseas markets while still retaining the responsibility for marketing. Under certain circumstances, e.g., in the book publishing field, the contractor firm may distribute the products through its own outlets. This method allows a company to break into international marketing without making the final commitment of setting up complete manufacturing and selling operations; yet, the way is kept open for implementing a long-term development policy at the appropriate time.

Management Contracting

In management contracting, a local investor in a foreign market provides the capital for an enterprise while a company from "outside" provides the necessary know-how to manage the company. Such an approach to entering international markets is low risk if used with some type of purchase option. It allows a company to manage another company without equity control or legal responsibility. There is a "guaranteed" minimum income, and unlike other types of joint overseas operations, the return is quick. Also, exchange or other types of remittance controls often are avoided. One significant drawback to this strategy is that future management and investment decisions may be limited, depending on the terms of the contract and the possibility of a conflict of interest arising.

Manufacturing

The decision to manufacture abroad may be forced on a company because of competitive pressure, market demands, government restrictions on imports, or government actions that would result in imports being at a disadvantage. For example, the completion of the European Community's internal market on January 1, 1993 (resulting from the Single European Act of 1987) will put companies outside the EC at a greater disadvantage than now exists. Or the decision may be part of a company's long-run plan to strengthen its international operations. Rarely should a company establish manufacturing facilities as its first international business operation. Exceptions exist, however, if the policies and regulations of the foreign government are such that the best way to enter the market is through direct investment in a manufacturing facility.

In this case, it is desirable that the particular market offer great sales potential or that it be situated so that it serves as a good base from which surrounding market areas can be served. Direct investment in manufacturing requires significant capital. Yet, if properly managed, investment in manufacturing can be the most profitable means of entering and thus serving a foreign market.

Once the decision to manufacture abroad has been made, a company has three basic questions to answer: (1) where the manufacturing facility is to be located, (2) what percentage of ownership should be held—wholly owned or only partially owned, and (3) what is the best way to implement its decision—start from scratch or acquire an existing firm in the selected market. These three questions are interrelated, since the answer to one will affect the answers to the others.

Assembly Operations

The establishment of assembly facilities represents a cross between exporting and overseas manufacturing. When following this strategy, a manufacturer exports components or parts. At the overseas assembly site, these parts are then put together to form the complete product. When a product is exported in this manner, savings may be realized in freight charges, various foreign government fees and in some countries (for certain products) custom duties.

By assembling products overseas, a manufacturer is in a position to buy some components from local, low-cost sources of supply. It is desirable to use local sources if the nature of the overseas market requires product modification in such a way that key component parts with the necessary operating characteristics are not normally available in the home country. To illustrate, most U.S. manufacturers of farm machinery, such as plows and tillage implements, must alter designs to suit farming practices in Europe that are different from those in the United States. Although there are substantial costs of operating an assembly facility, capital investment is usually less than that needed to establish and operate a manufacturing facility.

Joint Venture

This strategy is followed in an overseas market when a foreign company joins with local interests. A joint venture may be started by forming a new company, by investing in an existing local company, or by a local company acquiring an interest in an existing operation of the foreign company. The central feature of a joint venture is that ownership and control are shared. A company may be forced into a joint venture in a specific overseas market because of local government policies, nationalistic feelings, or intense competitive pressures. Yet, some companies select this approach voluntarily because it is more profitable in the long run than other approaches.

Joint ventures sometimes are the best way to get started in an overseas market because they allow a company with limited capital and manpower resources to enter more overseas markets than would be possible if the company established wholly-owned subsidiaries. Because of the resource savings and the potential ability to enter more markets, business risks can be minimized. Risk is also minimized because management skills and experience from a local partner allow easier adaptation to the particular dangers of an unfamiliar business environment. Moreover, risks are reduced because the project is generally less subject to the danger of adverse action by that government. Sales and profits of the joint venture may be greater than those of a wholly-owned subsidiary because the operation is looked upon with more favor by nationalist-oriented consumers than would be the case if it were considered a foreign operation.

Although there are significant potential advantages associated with using joint ventures, certain limitations may also appear. The profit potential may be less because all profits must be shared. Also, there are many things that can lead to disagreements between the partners, such as a dispute over dividend policies or differences in management philosophies, as in several Japanese-U.S. joint ventures.

STRATEGIC ALLIANCES

Licensing, contracting, and joint ventures are three types of activity between companies from two or more countries that have come to be known as *strategic alliances.* Other types include R & D consortia and partnerships, cross-marketing agreements, cross-manufacturing agreements, and cross-distribution agreements. All of these can be considered strategic marketing alliances as they enhance marketplace leverage. Such alliances are increasing in incidence and will be prominent through the 1990s as a way to operate in global markets. Examples include Boeing joining with the Japanese companies Mitsubishi, Fuji, and Kawasaki Heavy Industries to develop, manufacture, and market a small jet aircraft. Similarly, during the 1980s, Texas Instruments reported agreements with many companies including Fujitsu, Philips/Signetics, Hyundai, and Ericsson. A final example comes from the international airline industry where USAir and Air France have a marketing program to coordinate schedules, marketing, and joint facilities.

A strategic alliance is defined formally as a mode of interorganizational relations in which the partners make substantial investments (of human, financial, and/or technological capital) in developing a long-term collaborative effort and common orientation toward common and individual goals.[4] A fundamental purpose of such an alliance is to enhance the long-run competitiveness of the strategic partners. A global strategic alliance is founded on a belief that each party has something unique to contribute—e.g., technology, managerial know-how, market access, etc. This requires that power and control be shared in the interest of mutual benefit.

Any strategic alliance has certain core dimensions. If any of these are lacking, problems can arise and there can be conflict between individual company goals and alliance goals. These core dimensions are:[5]

1. *Goal compatibility*: each party's goals must be compatible to the extent that both alliance and individual party goals can be achieved.
2. *Strategic advantage*: there must be a perceived benefit.
3. *Interdependence*: each partner will be dependent on the other and the relationship must be managed such that conflict is held to a minimum while cooperation emerges victorious.
4. *Commitment*: trust is crucial to the long-run viability of an alliance and is vital to the pledge of relational continuity between partners that underlies commitment.
5. *Communication and conflict resolution*: partners need to communicate with each other and there is a need to have a mechanism, other than legal, to resolve conflicts that inevitably will arise.
6. *Coordination of work*: it is clear that work among the partners be coordinated without a bureaucracy and costs of ownership.
7. *Planning*: the first things to plan are the structure and processes of exchange; then, the substance of exchange can be tackled.

Although these critical elements for the successful operation of a strategic alliance have been described individually, they are, in fact, interrelated with each other.

EUROPE AND THE EUROPEAN COMMUNITY

Two major events have led to a major restructuring for Europe. First, in the late 1980s, the 12 nations of the European Community (EC) approved the Single European Act. This Act formed the basis of a program known as Europe 1992 which called for the implementing of 285 accords by January 1, 1993. The end result was to be the creation of the *internal market.* Although there already is free movement of products and resources within the community, Europe 1992 is designed to close all gaps. Moreover, all border controls and technical borders to trade are to be removed, government purchasing is to be opened to non-nationals, and financial services are to be opened up competitively. On the horizon is the creation of a common currency (ECU) for the community.

The long-run goal of EC leadership is to expand membership to other countries. The countries of the European Free Trade Association (EFTA) are those most likely to be admitted first. Austria has made formal application and Sweden and Finland will do so soon. The others in EFTA will follow, such that the future for EFTA as an entity is dim. In the interim the EC and EFTA will agree on an alliance—European Economic Association (EEA).

The second major event was the breakup of the communism-based countries in Eastern Europe. Established governments were replaced by new governments embracing capitalism. The EC has looked eastward and the most likely candidates for admission, hopefully by the year 2000, are Hungary, Poland, and Czechoslovakia.

The dissolution of the Soviet empire also seems likely to have a major impact on future trade in Europe, Russia, Belorus, Estonia, Latvia, Lithuania, and Ukraine. There is a distinct possibility that they will also seek admission to the EC eventually.

The emergence of the internal market and the expansion of the EC have a definite impact on international marketing activities of a company. Outsiders will find themselves to be at a greater disadvantage due to the increased competition from, and preference for, inside companies. Thus outsiders will be forced to explore investment and strategic alliances as entry modes. Insiders themselves will find the competitive situation changed as there could be fewer, but stronger companies as a result of Pan-European mergers.

All in all, there are exciting times ahead for Europe and for all companies wanting to do business there.

PRODUCT PLANNING AND PRODUCT POLICIES

In international marketing, there are four major forms of product development:

1. new product development or addition;
2. changes in existing products;
3. finding new uses for existing products; and
4. product elimination.

All of these decision areas are important to the success of managing the international product mix, although primary attention is frequently given to the problem of developing, adding, and modifying new products. Since any product may be at different stages in its lifecycle in different national markets, concern for potential new uses and product elimination is as necessary as concern for the other facets of product development if a company is to operate effectively in foreign markets.

Decisions must be made on products offered for sale in multiple national markets regarding (1) characteristics of the products offered, (2) breadth of product lines, (3) characteristics of packages, and (4) multiple versus family branding. In each of these policy areas, the questions may be reduced to standardization versus individualization. Should a company sell the same product, product line, brand, and package in all markets? Or, should the product, product line, brand, and package be adapted to the needs of each market? Product adaptations range from simple changes to conform to specific foreign conditions to basic modifications of the character of the product.

The "total product" includes the entire "bundle of utilities" which the buyer receives—not only quality, design and other physical characteristics, but also such utilitarian aspects of the "total product" as the package, the warranty, a service policy, credit, a pleasant store in which to purchase, the service of clerks—even information about the product, or how to use it, so the consumer can receive maximum benefit.

If a seller is to provide satisfaction desired by customers, the seller needs to know a great deal about those customers. Since analysis of customers in diverse foreign markets is complex and will differ from one product to another, there can be no comprehensive list of factors that will be appropriate for all sellers.

Often it is possible to standardize products offered in multiple foreign markets if (1) the products are used essentially in the same way in each market, e.g., razor blades, automobile tires, ball-point pens, electric irons (except for easily-made modifications to adapt for different voltage), and (2) the markets are similar with respect to such factors as customer income, education, occupations, attitudes and customs, e.g., as in certain strata of societies in the United States, Australia, Canada, Japan, or the developed countries of Western Europe.

For many products, the world should be divided into segments that transcend political or geographical boundaries. For example, the musical tastes of teenagers in Tokyo are more nearly like the tastes of teenagers in London or Rome than they are like the tastes of their parents. The tire buyer in Michigan is more like the tire buyer in Finland than the one in Florida. A particular model of automobile may satisfy a market segment in many countries, although the share of market of that segment may differ substantially in each country.

Products requiring artwork or creative designs often are universal within certain market segments in numerous countries, for example, Rosenthal-Porzellan china. The company employs artists and designers from a number of countries to turn out products that meet both a high international level of taste and all of the variations of taste within that level.

One of the most difficult products to standardize is food, since preferences vary widely and are deeply ingrained. For example, U.S.-style cake mixes were introduced unsuccessfully in England. Campbell Soup reportedly lost $10,000,000 in West Germany trying to change wet soup habits. Dehydrated Knorr Soups did not sell as well as anticipated in the United States. Government regulations, taxes, and political conditions can also be a factor. When Orange Fanta was introduced around the world, it was discovered that there were many different legal requirements on the percentage of real orange juice that food products must contain if the word "orange" is used. The differing regulations by the respective ministries of health required that Orange Fanta must vary either the product formula, the name of the product, or the advertising messages. Pharmaceutical companies frequently encounter varying legal requirements of purity or tests of efficiency before a product can be introduced to a market.

The issue usually does not involve one extreme or the other. Standardization is common for certain agricultural products, raw materials, and processed commodities sold to industry. Likewise, individualization of products or services is common for certain kinds of buildings, plants, and equipment, as well as for certain services. But, although a policy may be primarily one of standardization or individualization, international product decisions usually have to be a compromise between these extremes. Adaptation can be mandatory or voluntary. Mandatory adaptation may be required because of such things as language differences, differing electrical systems, differing measurement systems and product specifications, and government regulations. Voluntary adaptation occurs when the international marketer decides solely to modify one or more products. Even supposedly global (i.e., standardized) products need some adaptation.

Product	Adaptation
Sony TV	Voltage, broadcast standard
McDonald's	Menu, decor of restaurant
Levi jeans	Size mix, fabric, cut
Coca-Cola	Brand name (China), package

There seem to be numerous conditions under which a policy of either standardization or individualization is desirable. And, there seems to be no way to generalize on this matter, except that the desirability of the policy depends on analysis of the market, buyer behavior, competition, government or legal regulations, and other factors in the relevant economic, social, and political environment. One approach is illustrated in Exhibit 2.

The internal market of the European Community, while not constituting a single market, still has major implications for standardization or adaptation of products, packages, and brands. An increasing number of companies are examining the use of a standardized approach resulting in a Euro-brand, Euro-package, and/or Euro-product strategy. Procter & Gamble has attempted to use Vizir detergent as a Euro-brand. Similarly, Oxford Biscuits A/S of Denmark uses a Euro-package for its cream crackers—the ingredients are printed in 10 languages on a single package.

EXHIBIT 2. Factors to Consider for Standardized Product Strategy

	Standardize When:	Adapt When:
Competitive factors		
Strength of competition	Weak	Strong
Market position	Dominant	Non-dominant
Market factors		
Homogeneity of consumer preferences	Homogeneous	Heterogeneous
Potential for growth of currently small segments	Low	High
Consumer purchasing power	Uniform	Varied
Willingness of consumers to pay for differentiated products	Low	High
Need satisfied by product in markets served	Shared	Individual
Conditions of use	Uniform	Varied
Product factors		
Importance of scale economies in manufacturing	High	Low
Opportunities to learn from small-scale production of innovative products	Low	High
Type of product	Industrial	Consumer
Codes and restrictions	Uniform	Varied
Company factors		
Scope of international involvement	Many or large markets	Few or small markets
Company resources (financial, personnel, production)	Limited	Abundant

Source: Adapted from B. N. Rosen, "Global Products: When Do They Make Sense?" *Advances in International Marketing* (S.T. Cavusgil, ed.) Greenwich, CT: Jai Press, 1989.

PRICING POLICIES

International pricing policies must be established for (1) exported products and (2) products produced or marketed locally but with some centralized guidance, direction, or control from outside the country. Such decisions include setting initial prices, changing the price of established products from time to time, and coordinating pricing policies with foreign channels of distribution, licenses, and one's own subsidiaries, joint ventures, or strategic alliance partners. This discussion will assume general familiarity with the extensive literature on pricing and therefore will be devoted only to those aspects of pricing that are relevant to international pricing.

Price decisions must be made for different classes of purchases, that is, prices must be set for sales that are made to

1. consumers or industrial users;
2. wholesalers, distributors, or importing agencies of all types;
3. licensees (when parts or components are exported); and
4. one's own subsidiaries or joint ventures, whether minority or majority interest or wholly-owned subsidiaries; that is, *transfer prices.*

Other pricing decisions include

1. determining the relationships between prices of individual products in the product line;
2. deciding, in larger companies, on the type and amount of central control to be exercised to ensure that the price to ultimate consumers and users is maintained at a certain level; and
3. establishing a geographic pricing policy, for example, whether or not to quote uniform delivered prices, or FOB factory prices.

Due to widely varying market and competitive conditions, pricing decisions are complex. For example, markets segmented effectively by barriers to the movement of products from one market to another may permit a low price policy in some countries and a skimming policy in others. There are also reasons for coordinating international pricing policies into a carefully considered global pattern and strategy. For example, when dealing with customers who travel frequently or by other means have an intimate knowledge of prices in world markets, there must be a reasonable relationship between prices from one country to another. A key determinant, of course, is what management wants to achieve by using price as a marketing tool. There are many possible objectives in pricing, including

- satisfactory return on investment;
- maintaining market share;
- meeting a specified profit goal;
- largest possible market share;
- meeting a specific sales goal;
- highest return on investment;
- meeting competition; and
- profit maximization.

There are also many possible strategies in pricing, including pricing at the high end of the price range, and prices that are set at a high level and then lowered after a certain period has elapsed.

FACTORS THAT INFLUENCE THE ESTABLISHMENT OF INTERNATIONAL PRICES

The factors to take into consideration when solving international pricing problems can be classified into five groups.

Costs

Costs are useful in setting a price floor. In the short run, when a company has excess capacity, the price floor may be out-of-pocket costs, that is, such direct costs as labor, raw materials, and shipping. However, in the long run, full costs for all products must be recovered, although not necessarily full costs for each individual product. The actual cost floor, therefore, may often be somewhere between direct cost and full cost. For example, a large chemical company sometimes sells products abroad on an incremental cost basis whenever excess domestic capacity exists. The company's price floor is direct cost, since every unit sold at a price in excess of direct cost will contribute to net profit.

Market Conditions

The utility or value placed on the product by purchasers sets the price ceiling. The factors that are helpful in assessing how the market will evaluate a product include demographic factors, customs and traditions, and economic considerations, all of which may be related to customer acceptance and use of a product. Diverse religions, differences in the cost of borrowing, varying attitudes on family formation and living habits, to mention a few factors, create wide differences in the willingness and ability of customers to pay a given price.

Competitive Conditions

While costs and demand conditions circumscribe the price floor and ceiling, competitive conditions help to determine where within the two extremes the actual price should be set. For example, a large U.S. manufacturer of explosives, recognizing that explosives cannot be sold abroad at domestic prices, meets foreign competitors' low prices. The company covers its variable costs and receives some contribution to overhead, but not as much as contributed by domestic products.

Generally, consumer branded products (e.g., automobiles, household detergents, cigarettes, shoes, packaged foods) must be priced competitively, that is, quite close to competing substitutes. In the automobile industry, for example, consumers in most countries try to weigh each product against competing models, and it is important that prices be comparable to those of competing models offering similar economy, luxury, comfort, durability, quality, performance, and styling.

In contrast, one manufacturer of capital equipment for mining and earth-moving operations sells primarily on a cost plus "fair profit" basis. The company sells abroad at domestic factory list prices plus costs of exporting. It pays little attention to the "utility" of the equipment and to competitors' prices, mainly because foreign products are not good substitutes and the product is in a commanding position in the marketplace.

Legal and Political Conditions

Executives with international pricing responsibility usually must accept the legal and political situation as it exists, taking account of antidumping legislation, tariffs, and important restrictions covering earnings and profit remittances.

Most industrialized countries have antidumping legislation that prohibits the practice of selling in foreign markets at prices below those of the domestic market. Thus, antidumping legislation sets a price floor.

Officials of some countries will not issue import licenses if they feel that the price is too high or low. One company in Brazil needed a product that Brazilian manufacturers were unable to supply due to lack of capacity. Brazilian authorities, presumably to foster local production, would not permit importation of the product from Japan or the United States because it was available at a *lower* price than ordinarily charged by Brazilian manufacturers.

Tariff levels vary from country to country. Thus in countries with high custom duties, when price for the product is elastic, the base price may have to be lower than in other countries if the product is to achieve satisfactory volume. Under these conditions, the profitability of the product may be reduced. On the other hand, if demand is inelastic, the price may be set at a high level with little loss of volume, unless competitors are selling at lower prices.

Corporate Policies

If a company utilizes the international division structure with relatively autonomous subsidiaries, primary foreign pricing authority may be delegated either to the international division or to subsidiary management. Under these conditions, especially if delegated to subsidiary management, it is likely that the prices of similar products will vary from country to country to a greater extent than if prices were set centrally.

Under the geographic or product line organization structure, when such divisions have worldwide responsibility and authority, both divisional and top management may be involved in the formulation of prices. Top management might set basic policy and divisional management might determine the actual price schedules. Thus a coordinated and unified price policy and structure for regions or for the entire world may be established with sufficient flexibility to permit adaptations for local requirements.

The channel of distribution also affects price. Certain channels such as export merchants may require a higher operating margin than a manufacturer's export agent. Thus if dual channels are used and if the price to middlemen is uniform, the price to ultimate users probably will vary.

Utility of a product depends not only on its physical characteristics but also on how it is sold and serviced. For example, in the past, a manufacturer of a diversified line of electrical control products and other electrical equipment has found that in most, if not all, instances they would have to sell at or below their factory cost in order to be competitive. Nevertheless, the company has found the price disadvantage often can be overcome by (1) careful selection and training of technical representatives; (2) continued analysis and comparison of product features with competitors' products and exploitation of design advantages by demonstrating superior performance characteristics, ease and low-cost of maintenance, long life, and ease of installation; and (3) prompt delivery, which is in some cases facilitated by maintaining inventories abroad. Plus, such factors as type of channels selected, the relations with foreign representatives, dealers, or partners, the distinctiveness of the product, and the services provided determine the price customers are willing to pay.

SALES AND DISTRIBUTION POLICIES

International channels of distribution are the modes by which foreign markets are entered, and include

1. the methods used or channels through which the products are sent to overseas markets—i.e., *channels between nations.*
2. the means by which these products reach the target, final user or consumer in the overseas markets, assuming the importers are not the final users or consumers—i.e., *channels within nations.*

Typically, a company will develop a foreign market entry strategy.

Regarding channels between nations, there are many different alternatives, as shown in Exhibit 3. The first decision that must be made concerns where the production base should be located—in the home country or overseas. There are many different ways a manufacturer can reach the consumers or users of a product after it arrives in an overseas market area—through distributors, agents, wholesalers, and retailers.

A large manufacturer of farm equipment has a wholly-owned subsidiary as its exporting entity. The subsidiary has about 60 sales and service representatives located throughout the world who sell through about 200 distributor outlets in more than 140 countries. Each of the 60 representatives is authorized to sell the products of any of the company's manufacturing subsidiaries or divisions anywhere in the world except in the United States or other countries where manufacturing or

EXHIBIT 3. Outline of Alternative Basic International Marketing Channels

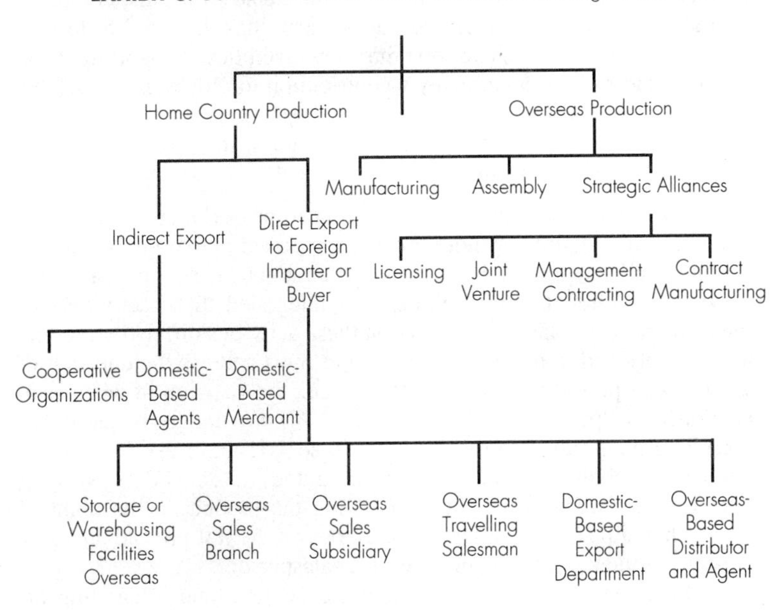

sales operations exist. Manufacturing or sales subsidiaries have responsibility for handling sales of their own products as well as exports to their own market areas.

Each of the 60 sales and service representatives has a catalogue that lists the products of all divisions and subsidiaries. All manufacturing operations are obligated to provide the export subsidiaries and its 60 representatives with all necessary sales and service information, including operations manuals.

Sales policies vary widely and are interrelated with overall marketing communication and promotion activities and policies. In a broad sense, there are five major forms of international marketing promotion.

1. *Personal selling:* Salespeople are used to communicate primarily face-to-face with prospective customers.
2. *Advertising:* A non-personal presentation of sales messages through various 'mass' media, paid for by the advertiser.
3. *Sales promotion:* All sales activities that supplement and strengthen personal selling and advertising. Activities usually are non-recurrent and have a relatively short-run "life."

4. *Public relations:* Any kind of news about a company or its products that is reported by some media and is not paid for by the company. Public relations also includes various activities designed to lead to media coverage such as opening new facilities, supporting local civic causes, and a company's contribution to employment and the local economy.
5. *Direct marketing:* Through mail, catalogues, in-home shopping in television, and so forth.

The above activities, when coordinated properly, are often called integrated advertising, or more broadly integrated marketing communication. Such integration is much more common in recent years then previously, although some sellers have integrated these activities for many years. The relative emphasis on these activities differs by product and market conditions. Initially, the seller must address the question of what mix of promotion activities to use, i.e., the question of whether to emphasize a "push" or a "pull" strategy. A *pull* strategy is defined as preselling the product so that buyers will seek it out or ask for it at the point of purchase. In contrast, a *push* strategy is defined as working with resellers or assisting them in selling the product at the point of sale. When a push strategy is required, buyers are not presold and they depend on the advice or guidance of a salesperson.

Planning, directing, coordinating, executing, and integrating effective advertising, sales promotion, public relations, and direct marketing are complex functions. They require the use of specialized creative people, media planners, and others found in advertising agencies and other service organizations. Since these subjects are covered elsewhere in this book, they will not be discussed further here.

The objective of any international marketing operation in the final analysis is only achieved through people. It is the personal aspect of marketing that can least readily be duplicated by competition. A company must rely on survival and progress on the personal qualifications of those who make up its personnel and direct its destinies. These include managers of advertising, sales promotion, public relations, and direct marketing (when relevant) as well as managers of the sales force.

A well-selected, well-trained, and well-compensated salesperson can, and in most instances will, make the difference between successful and unsuccessful foreign sales volume. Sales promotion, public relations, and advertising can arouse interest in the company or the product. But the final sales will not be closed until the actual purchasing decision is made, and personal contact is often essential for this.

There are three basic functions that all salespeople operating in foreign markets must perform.

1. The actual selling activity to be performed: that is, the communication of product information to customers, and obtaining orders.

2. A salesperson is always deeply involved in customer relations. He or she must at all times be concerned with maintaining and improving the company's position with customers and the general public.
3. A salesperson is an information gatherer and communicator. The salesperson is often able to provide information that might be useful in planning advertising and trade promotion programs.

COMMUNICATION POLICIES

Effective communication between domestic and foreign operations, or between a manufacturer and foreign distributors or retailers in multiple countries is difficult because of the many obstacles posed by cultural differences. Although one can recognize such differences, their full meaning may not be obvious to the inexperienced.[6]

Language differences are one of the most readily apparent problems. Although many foreign businessmen have some knowledge of several languages, their capacity to understand them may be considerably lower than appears on the surface. They may understand only a part of what they read or hear and sometimes they will say they understand when they do not.

The question of how effective communication takes place has occupied the attention of social psychologists and communication scientists for many years. One explanation that is widely accepted involves the process of empathy. If Ms. A wishes to communicate effectively with Mr. B, Ms. A and Mr. B must somehow put themselves in each other's shoes. Effective communication requires that they have a common set of meanings and definitions. Such a common set of meanings derives not only from the language, but refers more broadly to the pattern of beliefs, codes, and feelings on the basis of which persons learn to live with their environment.[7]

In some countries, the lone-wolf secretiveness of the merchant-trader is essential to the capacity to outbargain and outmaneuver other businesspeople (typical in certain Middle Eastern or Latin American countries). But, in the large U.S., Japanese, or European corporation, it is important for executives (as a group) to produce results. Thus such executives must have the attitudes of the group-oriented personality.

Difficulties in communication styles come from differences in religious, educational, and family backgrounds, especially values based on differing moral codes. There may be beliefs in one country particularly relevant to communication that may be disturbing to a businessperson from another country: There is the tendency in many cultures for subordinates and others to give weight to politeness, form, and agreeableness at the expense of accuracy and directness, which may be emphasized in other cultures.

Another barrier to communication is social or class structure. In societies where social status attitudes are quite rigid, a salesperson from the middle class is usually not effective if the job requires selling to upper-class factory owners, since he or she will not know how to behave in the new social environment.

Communication is important with respect to controlling, directing, or guiding the selling activities of foreign operations or channels of distribution. With rapid air transportation, it is often feasible for home office executives to make regular visits abroad to communicate top management views, knowledge, or skills. A regular flow of information to foreign units on selling methods, advertising techniques, product changes, and new developments in other foreign units is often important. Likewise, headquarters must keep informed about foreign operations to make plans, advise foreign units properly, and keep foreign managements from deviating from company policies. Written and telephone communication may suffice for routine matters, but regular personal visits often are necessary to overcome the substantial barriers to communication. Personal computers and FAX technology are changing how companies communicate to others.

MANAGEMENT OF INTERNATIONAL MARKETING OPERATIONS

The task of international marketing management is to formulate and implement a marketing mix that will enable a company to adapt to the international environment in such a way that its goals are achieved. Measurement of results against goals is the essence of control and controlling international marketing activities requires information via constant communication.

The approach to the solution of international marketing problems requires, first, a global outlook—viewing the world or relevant parts of it as a single market consisting of a number of segments, defined in a manner appropriate to the product and not necessarily along national boundaries. Second, market targets must be realistically assessed, and the segments of the "world market" to be exploited should be selected. Third, the relevant environmental factors in the market segments must be assessed. Fourth, a marketing program must be formulated. In going through this process, the size and extent of foreign markets must be evaluated, domestic and foreign competition must be assessed, legal and political factors must be reviewed, and costs must be calculated. Success will go to those who systematically plan and organize their efforts to

1. identify and produce products needed to satisfy customers, relating production to market requirements, and using marketing research information to guide production decisions; and
2. select an appropriate international marketing program, which involves careful planning, organization, and coordination.

Planning, organization, and coordination problems—and their solutions—do not recognize national boundaries. Thus such potential problem areas as vertical and horizontal communication, line-staff relationships, span of control, and delegation of authority and responsibility are found in any type of business firm, regardless of the nature of its operation or location.

Some companies integrate their foreign operations into their existing organization structure, but many do not. One important consideration that helps explain the reason for differences in organization patterns adopted by different companies is the extent, type, and duration of experience with overseas operations. Three basic organization structures have evolved:

1. Variants of the traditional *international division structure,* all displaying a shift of responsibility for policy and worldwide strategic planning to the corporate level.
2. The *geographic structure,* replacing the international division with line managers at the top-management level, who bear full operating responsibility for subsidiaries in assigned geographic areas.
3. The *product structure,* replacing the international division with executives at the top-management level who bear worldwide responsibility for development of individual product groups.

In practice, such forms are rarely found; rather, a combination is more common. Since companies differ with respect to product lines, management orientation, company history, and other internal factors, it is not to be expected that any two companies will or should be identical. There is variation in the manner in which functions are performed and in the assignment of functions to personnel.

One of the more common types of "combination" organization structures is the *matrix* organization. Often geographic and product structures are superimposed on each other to form the matrix. Many globally-oriented companies have structured themselves in this way. The success of an international matrix organization depends on how the interacting forces between strategic and regional managements are coordinated and balanced. Asea Brown Boveri Ltd., the world's largest electro-technical corporation, is a federation of national companies organized in a group matrix structure. Worldwide business activities are grouped into eight business segments that oversee fifty business areas. The company is also organized into geographical markets. Managers in each country and region conduct operations in line with the global strategies of business segments.

IMPLICATIONS

A few hundred companies, largely based in the triad area of Europe, Japan, and the United States, are taking a global outlook such that basic decisions concerning their operations are made in terms of opportunities available throughout the world. Many companies look to overseas markets as a means of achieving growth and stability.

NOTES

1. See T. Levitt, *The Marketing Imagination* (New York: Free Press, 1986), Chapter 2.
2. See J. Strandskov, "Toward A New Approach of Studying the Internationalization Process of Firms." Working Paper 4/1986, Institute of International Economics and Management, Copenhagen Business School, 1986; J. Johanson and J. E. Vahlne, "The Internationalization Process of the Firm—A Model of Knowledge Development and Increasing Foreign Commitments," *Journal of International Business Studies,* 8 (Spring/Summer 1977), pp. 23–32.
3. See Franklin R. Root, *Entry Strategies for International Markets* (Lexington, MA: D. C. Heath and Co., 1987, Chapter 1).
4. R. E. Spekman and K. Sawhney, "Toward A Conceptual Understanding of the Antecedents of Strategic Alliances," Marketing Science Institute Working Paper 90–114, August 1990. Also see R. S. Achol, L. K. Scheer, and L. W. Stern, "Designing Successful Transorganizational Marketing Alliances," Marketing Science Institute Working Paper 90–118, September 1990.
5. Spekman and Sawhney, pp. 6–9.
6. One source of information on difficulties of communication is the work of cultural anthropologists. See Edward T. Hall: (1) "The Silent Language in Overseas Business," *Harvard Business Review,* 38 (May–June 1960), pp. 87–96, (2) *The Hidden Dimension,* New York: Doubleday, 1966, (3) *Beyond Culture,* Garden City: New York, Anchor Press/Doubleday, 1976, (4) *The Dance of Life: The Other Dimension of Time,* Garden City: Anchor Press/Doubleday, 1983.
7. For a more complete discussion of this topic, see Vern Terpstra and Kenneth David, *The Cultural Environment of International Business* (Cincinnati: Southwestern Publishing Co., Second Edition, 1985).

SUGGESTIONS FOR FURTHER READING

Gerald Albaum, Jesper Strandskov, Edwin Duerr and Laurence Dowd, *International Marketing and Export Management* (Wokingham, England: Addison-Wesley Publishing Company, 1989).

Warren J. Keegan, *Multinational Marketing Management* (Englewood Cliffs, NJ: Prentice-Hall, Inc., Fourth edition, 1989).

Stefan H. Robock, Kenneth Simmonds and Jack Zwick, *International Business and Multinational Enterprises* (Homewood, IL: Richard D. Irwin, Inc., Fourth Edition, 1989).

Robert E. Weigand
Professor of Marketing
University of Illinois at Chicago
Chicago, Illinois

CHAPTER 70

BARTER AND BUYBACKS—DOING BUSINESS THE OLD-FASHIONED WAY

Vignettes describing the way international managers do business in various parts of the world can be fascinating. For example,

> *When NEC, the huge Japanese electronics company, tried to sell television sets to Egypt, it agreed to take part of its pay in airline tickets. About 5,000 NEC employees were scheduled to buy package tours to Egypt on special Egyptair flights. NEC would get its money for the TV sets when its employees, mostly young and single, paid about the yen equivalent of $1,400 for the eight-day trip. The deal suggests everyone would be happy. Egypt got its TV sets and full airplanes, NEC made a sale that probably would not otherwise have happened, and NEC workers saw the pyramids.*

> *Westinghouse sold an air defense system to Jordan. But Jordan did not have $100 million to pay cash. So Westinghouse agreed to take phosphate for its pay. Not knowing what to do with so much phosphate, it turned to Mitsubishi for help. The large Japanese trading company sold the phosphate to customers all over the world.*

> *North Korea and South Korea fought each other forty years ago; neither side much trusts the other. Yet the antagonism may give way to the reality that they are neighbors and must more or less get along. The first hint came when South Korea bartered 5,000 tons of its rice for 40,000 tons of North Korea's coal.*

> *The Russians know about Pepsi Cola, and many of American's vodka lovers drink Stolichnaya vodka. The carefully orchestrated barter arrangement called for the amount of eastbound Pepsi syrup and bottling know-how to pretty much match the amount of westbound Stolichnaya. But to increase the trade, Pepsi Wines and Spirits now imports and promotes Priviet brand vodka. The lower-priced brand should increase vodka imports from Russia, and allow more Pepsi syrup into Russia.*

Back of these stories lie weeks or months of tedious negotiations, careful monitoring to assure compliance with the agreements, and occasional disappointments. Yet the size of such transactions sometimes is stunning, amounts that cannot be ignored by today's global companies. Doing business where each side takes back goods or services rather than hard currency is hardly new. It is an old-fashioned practice, preceding recorded history. Yet it appears to be an increasingly important tool for modern world trade.

This chapter focuses on how such trade arrangements occur, trade terminology, why such agreements are so popular even to the point of being necessary, how barter and buybacks are priced, the content of contracts between the parties, and the marketing channels through which unwanted goods taken back in trade may be sold.

TERMINOLOGY AND DEFINITIONS

Every profession has its own lexicon. Those who engage in trade without money—which, by the way, is not quite correct—are no exception. Exact definitions sometimes differ among practitioners, but the following terms and strategies are used in this article.

Barter Arrangements

Barter consists of two sales and purchase transactions that occur simultaneously, the values of each transaction usually being the same. Each side contractually agrees to sell specific merchandise (or services) to its customer. But it also agrees to purchase merchandise (or services) from its customer, meaning that its customer becomes its supplier.

In some instances, the sales contract may be straightforward and may not contain a full explanation that the sale presumes reciprocity. It looks like any standard sales contract, one that will be transacted in a hard currency such as dollars, yen, or marks. However, reference is made in the contract to an accompanying protocol. The protocol spells out each side's responsibilities.

The purpose of the reference is to alert outsiders that the sale is not a standard contract but is subject to reciprocal duties the seller must perform, meaning the seller must purchase goods or services from the customer. Banks or factors, for example, may be more skeptical of a barter-like transaction than a straight sale for hard currency. They often want to know—something of a warning—that the transaction is not a straight sale and purchase transaction. The protocol provides that information.

A protocol is unnecessary when one of the partner's buy-back effort is voluntary. Perhaps surprisingly, Western partners sometimes try to take back a portion of their pay in goods rather than hard currency, more to show good will than because of any legal obligation.

Barter arrangements are particularly useful when the parties do not trust each other or when neither party seeks a long-term commercial relationship.

Counter-Purchase Agreements

Counter-purchase agreements are similar to barter deals, but they take place over a longer time and are less specific about what goods will be traded. One side may have agreed to a specific export transaction, meaning the type of goods and value are explicit. But it may also have agreed to be paid in an assortment of goods not specified in the initial contract but whose import value will match its exports.

For example, when Philip Morris and RJR Nabisco, in separate transactions, agreed to sell more than 37 billion cigarettes to the (then) Soviet Union, neither company was sure what it would take back. But both companies assured the public that they knew what sort of goods were eligible for the reciprocal arrangement and the goods taken back could handily be sold in the West or diverted to other markets.

Counter-purchase arrangements have the advantage of flexibility, meaning the partner need not accept a specific product at a particular time. Rather, at the time the transaction is signed, the partner receives what amounts to a shopping list from which selections can be made when the time is opportune. The shopping may be delayed for months or may be taken in a series of purchases so the marketing channel will not be disrupted with a sudden spurt of purchases. But because of the time value of money, purchases are more likely to start early.

Astute negotiators know they should learn early in the discussions that reciprocal purchases are an obligatory part of the transaction. The simplest way is for the free market partner to ask openly if the transaction is to be for cash or part of a sales and purchase agreement. The seller will be provided with a list of products or services they will be allowed to take back in trade. Thus wrist watches or musical instruments may be eligible for purchase but not petroleum or timber. Further, the list should include a hard currency price list, explaining unit value of the wrist watches or musical instruments.

When selling into some cash-short countries, astute Western traders may simply assume that a reciprocal purchase will be obligatory. Reciprocal obligations have become so common that the Western partner may submit what amounts to an anticipatory purchasing plan, suggesting to its customer what it would be willing to take for its pay.

For example, aircraft manufacturers generally know well in advance of negotiations that they will not be paid in hard currency for the full value of any airplanes they sell in some countries. They will be paid partly in cash, the balance in goods or services. Thus they routinely keep, and regularly update, what amounts to "fact books" containing a list of products their customer countries might supply for part payment. Indeed, aircraft manufacturers are so astute at such marketing strategies they are said to know more than their customers what goods or services their customers can submit as payment and the value of those take-back products.

There are ample stories of shopping lists chock full of goods that are unmerchantable in sophisticated markets. The stories come from companies that did not do their homework.

Compensation Agreements

Compensation agreements are contracts in which one party agrees to take its pay in the proceeds of a project it has helped start. One expression tells the story: "I will teach you to fish. Later I will collect my teaching fee in fish you have caught." For example, General Motors gained access to the Hungarian market—and perhaps other eastern European states as well—when it entered a joint venture with that country's truck and engine manufacturer. General Motors will own two-thirds of the plant. RABA, the state-owned Hungarian Railway Carriage and Machine Factory, will hold the other one-third. The American company will take its pay in engines. In particular, within a few years, about 100,000 engines will be exported to go into Opels and Vauxhalls. The rest will go into Kadett automobiles assembled by RABA; they will stay in Eastern Europe.

The Swing

The values of the goods or services traded by the two sides need not match. The swing describes the difference between the amount taken back by one of the parties and its market value; the difference is paid in hard currency. In some instances, the side holding the strongest bargaining position may insist that part of its trading partner's pay be in hard currency. The stronger partner may take back, say, 80 percent of its pay in goods but the remaining 20 percent must be paid in dollars, francs, marks, yen, or some other hard currency. The hard currency difference is the Swing.

The percent of each party's contributions in both goods and hard currency should be defined early in the negotiations and carefully written into the contracts or protocol between the two parties.

Why Old-Fashioned Ways Are the Best Ways

Bartering probably precedes recorded history. Long before disparate groups found ways to communicate with each other and before money became a common denominator, tribes engaged in trade. Often called "the silent trade," such commercial ventures consisted of one group leaving an assortment of merchandise in a forest clearing for others to assess and leave what they were willing to trade away. The first group would return and decide if the offer was good enough. If so, they took the offering; if not, they returned with their own goods.

In some respects, the reasons for today's barter and compensation agreements are similar. Indeed, such old-fashioned arrangements are not just the best way to do business in some parts of the world; they are the only way. There are several reasons why non-hard currency reciprocal arrangements take place.

Shortage of Hard Currency. First, and most obvious, many countries lack hard currency. Thus they cannot use their limited foreign exchange to purchase imports with dollars, francs, marks, Yen, and so on. Further, the creditworthiness of such countries commonly is scant.

Thus their imports must be paid for by nearly simultaneous exports, virtually forced on reluctant foreign suppliers.

Tough-to-Market Products. Second, many of the products eligible for export on a barter or buyback basis are too poor to be sold in free markets. The only reliable way they can make their way into foreign markets is through reciprocal trading deals. Absent such arrangements, the goods would go largely unsold. There are, of course, many high quality products—petroleum, firs, caviar, for example—coming from such countries. However, superior products that can be easily sold for hard currency seldom are eligible for reciprocal contracts; only the tough-to-sell products make the list.

Undeveloped International Channels. Third, some of the countries using barter and buyback arrangements have not yet developed the sort of sophisticated marketing network necessary for selling a vast assortment of goods into other countries. Thus they must rely on the international marketing channels of their trade partners. They are channel hitchhikers. (Many years ago I visited with the manager of a Soviet buying office in New York City who explained he had never heard of RCA, General Electric, or several other American companies I mentioned).

PRICING THE DEAL—BARTER ARRANGEMENTS

Barter arrangements—a simple swapping of goods or services of equal value—are easiest to price. This is true for two reasons. First, since the transactions are simultaneous, it is unnecessary to forecast the traded goods' values. Second, each side enters the negotiations knowing the open market value of the goods it will trade away and the value of the goods it will take back. This is because the goods often are commodities whose prices are widely known and commonly published in daily newspapers or industry price sheets.

In barter arrangements, market price becomes the shadow price for the traded goods. Thus, when South Korea traded away its rice for North Korea's coal, the value of the trade was heavily influenced by the world market price for the two commodities at the time the agreement was completed. Further, both rice and coal are widely enough traded so there is less dispute about price than there would be for a one-of-a-kind manufactured good. The generally accepted ratio—one ton of rice is worth about eight tons of coal—becomes the starting point for the haggling.

When differentiated goods are taken back for pay—toys, cosmetics, television sets, women's blouses—pricing is more difficult. However, industry experts generally can submit advice about the value of such products. In this respect, the problem is no different from a standard purchase of such products in a non-reciprocal transaction.

PRICING THE DEAL—COMPENSATION ARRANGEMENTS

In more sophisticated arrangements, price negotiation, the time value of money, estimating the market value of the goods or services taken back, forecasting the direction of currency changes, price fudging, discounting revenue to its present value, and amortization become vital tools for completing the deal.

Let us suppose a Japanese trading company has agreed to invest 160 million yen to build a copper smelter in the Peoples' Republic of China. The Chinese negotiators insist that a lack of foreign exchange precludes payment in yen or any other hard currency. It is willing to pay the Japanese in copper, once the mill comes on stream. The Japanese agree to negotiate on this basis.

Agreeing on the Currency

Perhaps the first step is for the two parties to agree on the currency—yen, marks, francs, dollars—to be used for the life of the contract. The 160 million yen to be invested by the Japanese comes to about 1,224,000 American dollars at the time the contract is signed, or 2,027,000 German marks, or 6,934,000 French francs. This is important because each side knows that the contract will last several years. The Chinese—theoretically, at least—would like to denominate the contract in a currency that will decline in value and cost them less in foreign exchange when the Japanese later ask to be paid. The Japanese—again theoretically—would like to pick a currency that will gain value during the life of the contract. But in reality, perhaps neither side opts for speculation and hopes to choose a currency that will remain stable.

To complicate our example, suppose the Chinese insist on the Swiss franc as the contractual currency which means the Japanese are making an upfront investment of 1,780,000 Swiss francs, a translation of 160 million yen into Swiss francs at signing time. Believing in the stability of the franc, the Japanese agree. Each is using the franc—a third country currency—as a surrogate for its own national currency.

Minimum Return on Investment, Maximum Payment

The second step is for the Japanese party to determine the minimum return on investment it will accept. Further, the Chinese must decide the maximum they will pay. And the two sides must agree on the duration of the payback period. There is nothing to distinguish these discussions from any other bargaining table. Each side can point to its options, threaten to pull out, make counter-proposals, submit what is purported to be "our last offer," and so on. All are standard bargaining tactics, postures taken to weaken the other side's resolve.

Suppose each side agrees the smelter will take two years to build, the Japanese are entitled to a 15 percent ROI, and the agreement will run for twelve years. No payments will be made during the first two years because the plant has not yet come on stream. Even so, the Japanese company is entitled to a return on its investment during the time the plant is being constructed. Thus the Peoples' Republic of China will owe the Japanese company 2,354,000 francs at the end of the two years when the plant begins to produce. An amortization table tells us that the Chinese would pay the equivalent of 37,977 Swiss francs each month for the rest of the contract, beginning with the third year.

Fixed Volume, Fixed Price

The third step in the negotiations consists of the two parties deciding whether a fixed amount of copper will be delivered each month or if the amount delivered will be a function of the product's world price. If the first option is chosen during the negotiations and if the price of copper was $1.10 per pound at the time the contract was signed, the Chinese will deliver 1,112,727 pounds of copper every month for ten years.

If the second option is chosen, the amount the Peoples' Republic delivers each month will depend on the world price of copper. The Chinese must deliver more copper if the price declines, less if it rises. When negotiating this step, each side is no doubt forecasting what will happen to copper prices in the years ahead.

Fudging the Price

Finally, it may be necessary for the seller to fudge its own invoice price upward. This is an important strategy when (a) the goods taken back cannot be sold at the price the supplier insists is the proper price and (b) when the company taking back the goods wants to earn a full margin on its goods. Unhappily, there commonly is a difference between claimed value and market value. Suppose a chemical company has agreed to sell specialty chemicals to a controlled currency country and has agreed to take back bicycles for its pay. If the trading partner insists the bicycles are worth, say, $60 each, but even the most casual observation makes it clear their market price is only $45, the chemical company has two strategic choices. It can either fudge its sales price upward to adjust for the discrepancy—without admitting to doing so—or quietly resolve that it is making a heavily discounted sale.

Merchantable Products. As in all commercial transactions, the goods taken back may not match the promises made or some other provision of the agreement may go wrong. Contracts generally contain provisos that warrant the goods taken back will conform to samples provided during the negotiations and are merchantable in the markets for which they are intended.

Dispute Resolution. Contracts often provide that disputes will be resolved by the American Arbitration Association, International Chamber of Commerce, or some other dispute resolution body. More specifically, such contracts may mention the name of the arbitration association that will be used, the number of arbitrators and how they will be chosen, and the site for such decisions. For example, in a recent counter-trade arrangement, Merchant Ivory (U.S.A.), an American movie maker company, agreed to provide Paritet (a Russian venture) with three movies to be shown in and around Moscow. Paritet could not pay in hard currency; none was available. However, it agreed to pay rubles to a production company in Moscow that would provide Merchant Ivory with facilities to produce movies that would be exported to Western markets. Things went wrong. One of the movies arrived too late for the important winter season when Russians like to go to movies. Further, one of the copies was damaged, perhaps in transit. Finally, Merchant Ivory's movies were sent with an optical soundtrack rather than a magnetic soundtrack, making language dubbing more difficult. The American Arbitration Association resolved the matter, largely favoring the Russian side.

Product quality and on-time delivery are probably the two most contentious issues in cross-national disagreements, but there is almost no end to the number of matters that can be disputed. In this respect, reciprocal contracts differ very little from standard sales arrangements made for hard currency.

MARKETING CHANNELS FOR TAKE-BACK GOODS

In both barter and compensation arrangements, it is essential to find a use for the goods taken back. In a sense, this is the first step because astute traders know they should not enter a transaction without seeing how it will end. There are ample horror stories about companies that take back goods merchantable only at such low prices that the transaction loses money. Several outlets are available.

In-House Use

First, the products taken back can sometimes be used in-house, meaning they become part of the manufacturer's own product. For example, a major American automobile manufacturer sold new automobiles to a South American country, taking its pay in tanned leather. The leather made its way into leather seats in some of the manufacturer's luxury cars. This approach is easiest when the goods taken back are commodities whose quality can be easily discerned. The contract may call for "acceptable international market standards" or some other such terminology. Evaluations can be made by independent test laboratories or professionals to discern quality levels.

Taking back fabricated parts and equipment is more difficult, particularly if the exporting country's products do not meet free market standards. However, many companies work carefully with their potential suppliers to assure the supplied products meet acceptable standards, roughly similar to what is produced in-house. Since compensation agreements sometimes last for many years, each partner generally is willing to commit the time and money necessary to assure each other's satisfaction. The problem is not insurmountable.

On-site inspection of fabricated parts and equipment—seldom welcomed by the supplier—is nonetheless appropriate because it may substantially reduce a variety of costs. In particular, transport and tariff costs have not yet been incurred if the goods have not left the maker's factory. If the unsatisfactory products have already been delivered (and have already incurred transport and tariff charges) and must be returned to the producer, return transport costs must be negotiated and paid.

Fabricated parts and equipment that are used in-house generate two problems if they are below the receiving company's acceptable standards. Much like a chain is no stronger than its weakest link, an assembled product is no stronger than its weakest component. The potential for consumer dissatisfaction is obvious. The long-term implications in terms of sales and market share need not be spelled out. Further, where imported components are used, the company opens itself to product liability suits if health or safety are jeopardized.

Adding to the Line

A second alternative is simply to add the new imports to the company's product line, marketing them alongside the firm's other products. This is particularly attractive if the imports supplement rather than compete with the company's own products. American liquor importers routinely sell foreign wines through their well established distribution channels. The wines often have come to them as part of a barter or compensation arrangement.

Exclusive Dealer Proviso. The partner taking back goods may ask to be the exclusive dealer in a particular territory. Thus if an American company takes back, say, Polish language phonograph records, it can insist that it have no rival sellers in the United States. This forecloses the Polish seller from entering into a second arrangement with a different American company either on a reciprocal or cash basis.

American Antitrust Laws. This particular proviso should be used with care. Under American antitrust law, it is susceptible to challenge if it restricts commerce and tends to create a monopoly. And, of course, this is exactly the intent of the exclusive territory provision.

Fobbing Off to New Customers

Take-back products can be sold to users or buyers who are not normally part of the receiving company's customer base. For example, a pharmaceutical company, anxious to make a sale into a Middle Eastern controlled currency country, agreed to take back leather clothing—dresses, jackets, belts, and coats. The company initially sold some of the goods to their employees at steep discounts; their own employees were not part of their regular customer base. Ultimately, the manufacturer turned to a broker who found a large discounting department store that bought what was left. This particular story had an unhappy ending because the revenue earned did not come close to what had been expected. The company knew very little about how to value leather goods, substantially overestimating their resale worth. Rather than turn to experts, they relied on their own judgment, which turned out to be quite poor. However, there are ample stories where cautious traders know how they will exit a transaction before they get into it. These are the profitable ones.

Enter the Specialist Middleman. Specialized institutions have arisen to help companies market products they cannot use in-house or market through their own distribution channels. In particular, trading firms, barter houses, and Japanese *sogo shosha* routinely match sellers and buyers in geographically disparate parts of the world. Such companies—sometimes acting as agents, sometimes as merchants—know where virtually anything can be sold, but only if the price is right.

Diversion Rights. During the contractual negotiations, the two parties must decide whether the party taking back goods is obliged to limit its marketing efforts to its home market or is commercially and legally free to divert the goods to other markets. Thus an American company may determine that the cosmetics it takes in trade cannot be sold in its own fiercely competitive market but can be sold in a less developed country at a substantially discounted price.

Diversionary rights or limits are commonly written into the contract, particularly if the two parties hope that other agreements will be signed in the years ahead. The foreign partner might resist such a clause, hoping to sign similar agreements with other parties in other areas. Third country parties would be much less attracted to such an agreement if the American company had already diverted some of the merchandise into its own potential territories.

Most Favored Customer Rights. Finally, the Western party will want assurance it is receiving terms at least as good as others—if there are others—who may be in a similar situation. The contract will contain what amounts to a "most favored customer" provision, meaning it will pay prices at least as low as other parties. Terms of trade will be subjected to similar contractual arrangements. Such provisos are unnecessary, of course, if the Western partner has negotiated an exclusive dealer arrangement.

END NOTE

Americans who do not know about barter have forgotten their history. In mid-1775, the country's first Congress issued two million

Continental dollars to finance the revolution. The step was so easy to take. Indeed, the temptation to turn on the printing presses was too great. In a series of bills during the next five years, Congress turned on the printing presses—it authorized the distribution of almost a half billion dollars. The consequence was inevitable. The dollar's value deteriorated so badly that by 1781 it had no value. It was no longer accepted as medium of exchange. A time came when it cost more to print a single dollar than the dollar was worth. Thus we have the expression, "Not worth a Continental." In those early years, Americans turned to barter.

Today, much of the world trusts goods more than it does many currencies. Goods and services have more value. The world's largest enterprises now routinely swap goods and services in enormous quantities. Some things never change.

SUGGESTIONS FOR FURTHER READING

International Counterpurchase Contracts, (Geneva: Economic Commission for Europe, 1989).

Robert D. Kase, "Petroleum Perestroika," *Columbia Journal of World Business,* (Winter 1992), p. 17.

Marcie Marino, "Bartering with the Bolsheviks," *Dickinson Journal of International Law,* (Winter 1990), pp. 269–289.

Arnold Reisman, Duu-Cheng Fuh, and Gang Li, "Achieving and Advantage With Countertrade," *Industrial Marketing Management,* 17 (1988), p. 55.

"Short-Term Compensation Transactions in East-West Trade. . ." (United Nations Economic and Social Council, (October 1985).

Joseph J. van Dort and Eilard Friese, "The Counterpurchase Contract and Their Contractual Issues," *Dickinson Journal of International Law,* (Fall 1987), pp. 45–59.

Robert E. Weigand, "International Trade Without Money," *Harvard Business Review,* (November–December 1977), p. 28.

Robert E. Weigand, "Reciprocal Trading: Putting Numbers to Prices," *Columbia Journal of World Business,* (Fall 1993), pp. 62–74.

S. Tamer Cavusgil
Executive Director
International Business Center
Professor of Marketing and International Business
The Eli Broad Graduate School of Management
Michigan State University
East Lansing, Michigan

CHAPTER 71

UNRAVELING THE MYSTIQUE OF EXPORT PRICING

In recent years, hundreds of U.S. companies have become involved in international business. The initial foreign activity is typically exporting. Perhaps the most puzzling part of international business for these firms is making pricing decisions.

What role should pricing play in the exporting company's marketing efforts? Can pricing be used as an effective marketing tool? Or would that practice expose the firm to unnecessary risks? What considerations affect the choice between incremental and full-cost pricing strategies? What approach should management take when setting export prices? How can the firm cope with escalations in international prices? What strategies are appropriate when a strong currency impairs overseas competitiveness? These are only a few of the many questions international marketing managers must answer.

Export pricing is a complex issue, and simple decision rules are often inadequate. The complexity lies in the large number of variables that affect international pricing decisions and the uncertainty surrounding them. These variables can be classified as either internal or external to the organization. The internal group includes corporate goals, desire for control over prices, approach to costing, and degree of company internationalization. The external group includes competitive pressures, demand levels, legal and government regulations, general economic conditions, and exchange rates.

Despite export pricing's importance and complexity, very little empirical research has been conducted that might give managers norms to follow.[1] This article attempts to illuminate this important area of international marketing management. The overall purpose is to provide a better understanding of export pricing issues and to identify propositions that can be tested by more definitive, large-scale surveys, as well as to generate findings and implications useful to export managers.

Personal interviews, two to three hours in length, were conducted with one or more executives at each of 24 firms. Most of the firms studied were exporters of industrial or specialized products. The typical firm employed about 500 persons. Background information about each firm was collected with the use of a structured questionnaire either prior to or during the interview. All firms were located in the Midwestern United States.

PRICING LITERATURE

Price is the only marketing variable that generates revenue. Top marketing executives call pricing the most critical pressure point of the 1980s.[2] Recently, with accelerating technological advances, shorter product life cycles, and increasing input costs, price changes have become more common. Despite these developments, academic research on pricing has been modest at best.[3]

The neglect of international pricing is even more serious.[4] Intracorporate (transfer) pricing issues received attention during the 1970s, when study of multinational corporations (MNCs) was intense, but other pricing topics remain relatively unexplored.[5]

Other studies have focused on pricing practices under floating exchange rates,[6] location of pricing authority within MNCs,[7] price leadership of MNCs,[8] multinational pricing in developing countries,[9] and uniform pricing.[10] Several studies have had a regional/industry focus. One found a relatively high degree of export price discrimination among industrial firms in Northern England.[11] Another compared the pricing practices of chemical and construction industries in South Africa.[12] A third, on the other hand, studied price-setting processes among industrial firms in the French market.[13]

This last study is particularly important, because it represents an effort to systematically describe and compare the processes used by firms to set prices. Through in-depth analyses of price decisions made by companies, the authors were able to develop flowcharts as well as indices of similarity, participation, and activity. They contend that decision-process methodology can help people gain insights into the dynamic activities of firms. The decision-making model for export pricing discussed in this article employs a similar approach.

The discussion here focuses on three major issues. First, those factors which have a bearing on export pricing are examined, and each factor's relevance is illustrated with company examples. The next section reveals that companies appear to follow one of three export pricing strategies. Finally, a decision framework for export pricing is offered.

FACTORS IN EXPORT PRICING

Export pricing is not a topic that lends itself easily to generalization. As with domestic pricing, any consideration of policies for setting export prices must first address the unique nature of the individual firm. Company philosophy, corporate culture, product offerings, and operating environment all have a significant impact on the creation of pricing policy. In addition, export marketers face unique constraints in each market destination.

The interaction of the internal and external environments gives rise to distinct—yet predictable—pricing constraints in different markets. These to a large extent determine export price strategy. For example, negotiation is normally required in the Middle East, so Regal Ware, a producer of kitchen appliances and cookware, uses a higher list price in such markets to leave a margin for discretion. But D. W. Witter, a manufacturer of grain storage and handling equipment, doesn't make price concessions in the Middle East. Witter is convinced that once a price becomes negotiable, the Middle Eastern buyer will expect and demand future concessions, making future negotiations interminable.

In Algeria, the interest rate is limited by the government. To counter this one company, a manufacturer of mining and construction equipment, builds the additional cost of capital into the price.

Six variables have important influences on export pricing. They are:

1. nature of the product/industry;
2. location of the production facility;
3. chosen system of distribution;
4. location and environment of the foreign market;
5. U.S. government regulations; and
6. attitude of the firm's management.

A brief discussion of each factor is presented below.

Nature of the Product/Industry

A specialized product, or one with a technological edge, gives the firm flexibility. There are few competitors in such cases. In many markets there is no local production of the product, government-imposed import barriers are minimal, and importing firms all face similar price-escalation factors. Under such circumstances, firms are able to remain competitive with little adjustment in price strategy. Firms with a technological edge, such as the Burdick Corporation (hospital equipment) and Nicolet Instruments (scientific instruments), enjoy similar advantages, but both experience greater service requirements and longer production and sales lead times.

A relatively low level of price competition usually leads to administered prices and a static role for pricing in the export marketing mix. Over the years, however, as price competition evolves and technological advantages shrink, specialized and highly technical firms must make more market-based exceptions to their uniform export pricing strategies.

Many firms' export pricing strategies are also influenced by industry-specific factors, such as drastic fluctuations in the price of raw materials and predatory pricing practices by foreign competitors (most notably the Japanese). The presence of such factors demands greater flexibility in export pricing at some companies: Ray-O-Vac adjusts export prices frequently according to current silver prices. Other companies negotiate fixed-price agreements with suppliers prior to making a contract bid.

Location of Production Facility

Many U.S. companies produce exported products only in the United States. These U.S. exporters are unable to shift manufacturing to locations that make economic sense. Purely domestic companies are tied to conditions prevailing in the home market, in this case the United States.

Those companies with production or assembly facilities abroad, often closer to foreign customers, have additional flexibility in overseas markets. These companies find it easier to respond to fluctuations in foreign exchange. Cummins Engine, for example, supplies Latin American customers with U.S. production when the U.S. dollar is weak. When the dollar is relatively strong, U.K. plants assume greater importance.

A number of factors may have impeded the global competitiveness of U.S. manufacturers in recent years. These include lagging productivity in many sectors of the economy and, until recently, reluctance to seek global sources of supply for materials, parts, and components. Also, strong unions and a high standard of living in the United States have contributed to higher labor costs. Naturally, these comparative disadvantages are reflected in the quotations submitted to overseas buyers.

Chosen System of Distribution

The channels of export distribution a company uses dictate much in export pricing. For example, subsidiary relationships offer greater control over final prices, first-hand knowledge of market conditions, and the ability to adjust prices rapidly. With independent distributors, control usually extends only to the landed price received by the exporter. As one might expect, many of the executives interviewed spoke of the difficulty of maintaining price levels. These firms report that distributors may mark up prices substantially—up to 200 percent in some cases.

When a firm initiates exporting through independent distributors, many new pricing considerations arise. Significant administrative costs stem from the selection of foreign distributors and the maintenance of harmonious relationships. Discount policies for intermediaries must be established. Also, the costs of exporting (promotion, freight service, and so forth) must be assigned to either the intermediaries or the manufacturer. To minimize the administrative, research, and travel expenses involved in switching to direct exporting, most firms use a relatively uniform export pricing strategy across different markets. Gross margins are then increased to account for additional levels of distribution. In other cases, companies establish prices on a case-by-case basis.

The use of manufacturers' representatives offers greater price control to the exporter, but this method is used less frequently. Finally, sales to end users may involve negotiation or, in the case of selling to governmental agencies, protracted purchasing decisions. List prices are not used in these circumstances.

Firms often attempt to establish more direct channels of distribution to reach their customers in overseas markets. By reducing the number of intermediaries between the manufacturer and the customer,

FIGURE 1. Strategic Options to Deal With Price Escalation

- Shortening channels of distribution by reducing number of intermediaries or engaging in company-sponsored distribution. Fewer intermediaries would also have the effect of minimizing value added taxes.
- Reducing cost to overseas customers by eliminating costly features from the product, lowering overall product quality, or offering a stripped-down model.
- Shipping and assembling components in foreign markets. Popularity of the free-trade zones in Hong Kong, Panama or the Caribbean Basin is due to companies' desire to minimize price escalation.
- Modifying the product to bring it into a different, lower-tariff classification. The Microbattery division of Ray-O-Vac Corporation, for example, ships bulk to foreign marketing companies who then repackage. Another company, through consultations with local distributors, places products in "proper" import classifications. Proper wording is used for initial import registration to qualify for lower duties.
- Lowering the new price (landed price) to reduce tariffs and other charges by the importing country. This can be accomplished through the application of marginal cost pricing or by allowing discounts to distributors. Nicolet Instruments, a producer of scientific instruments, for example, compensates its distributors for the cost of installation and service. Western Publishing Company compensates its distributors for the differences in import duties between book and nonbook exports.
- Going into overseas production and sourcing in order to remain competitive in the foreign markets. Dairy Equipment Company located in Wisconsin, for example, supplies the European market with bulk coolers made at its Danish plant as a way of reducing freight costs.

they offset the adverse affects of *international price escalation.* Excessive escalation of prices is a problem encountered by most exporters. Aside from shorter distribution channels, the firms studied had developed other strategies to cope with price escalation. These alternatives are listed in Figure 1.

Location and Environment of the Foreign Market

The climatic conditions of a market may necessitate product modification. For example, a producer of soft-drink equipment must treat its products against rust corrosion in tropical markets. Another company, an agribusiness concern, must take into account climate, soil conditions, and the country's infrastructure before making any bid. Economic factors, such as inflation, exchange-rate fluctuations, and price controls, may hinder market entry and effectiveness.[14] These factors, especially the value of U.S. currency in foreign markets, are a major concern to most of the firms interviewed. Consequently, several companies have introduced temporary compensating adjustments as part of their pricing strategies. The unusually strong value of the U.S. dollar during the first half of the 1980s was a significant factor in pricing strategy.

Since currency fluctuations are cyclical, exporters who find themselves blessed with a price advantage when their currency is undervalued must carry an extra burden when their currency is overvalued. Committed exporters must be creative, pursuing different strategies during different periods. Appropriate strategies practiced by the firms studied are outlined in Figure 2.

It must be noted that, while exporters can implement some of these strategies quickly, others require a long-term response. For example, the decision to manufacture overseas is often a part of a deliberate and long-term plan for most companies. And while some strategies can be used by any exporter, others, such as countertrade and speculative currency trading, are limited to use by the larger, more experienced exporters. In fact, most managers interviewed said that high-risk propositions such as countertrade deals should be used only by multinational companies.

FIGURE 2. Exporter Strategies under Varying Currency Conditions

When domestic currency is WEAK. . . .	**When domestic currency is STRONG. . . .**
• Stress price benefits	• Engage in nonprice competition by improving quality, delivery and aftersale service
• Expand product line and add more costly features	• Improve productivity and engage in vigorous cost reduction
• Shift sourcing and manufacturing to domestic market	• Shift sourcing and manufacturing overseas
• Exploit export opportunities in all markets	• Give priority to exports to relatively strong-currency countries
• Conduct conventional cash-for-goods trade	• Deal in countertrade with weak-currency countries
• Use full-costing approach, but use marginal-cost pricing to penetrate new/competitive markets	• Trim profit margins and use marginal-cost pricing
• Speed repatriation of foreign-earned income and collections	• Keep the foreign-earned income in host country, slow collections
• Minimize expenditures in local, host country currency	• Maximize expenditures in local, host country currency
• Buy needed services (advertising, insurance, transportation, etc.) in domestic market	• Buy needed services abroad and pay for them in local currencies
• Minimize local borrowing	• Borrow money needed for expansion in local market
• Bill foreign customers in domestic currency	• Bill foreign customers in their own currency

The cultural environment and business practices of the foreign market also play a large role in export pricing. Some countries abhor negotiation, others expect it. As previously noted, D. W. Witter has successfully overcome the expectation of price negotiation in the Middle East market. In some markets, a subtle barrier to foreign imports is erected in the form of procurement practices which favor domestic companies.

U.S. Government Regulations

Government policy also affects export pricing strategy. While the majority of the firms interviewed are not directly affected by U.S. pricing regulations, they feel that U.S. regulations such as the Foreign Corrupt Practices Act put them at a significant competitive disadvantage. One company often receives "requests" by overseas customers to add over $100,000 to the contract price and make appropriate arrangements to transfer the money to private accounts abroad. Interestingly, such requests are sometimes openly made. Submission to demands for "grease payments" appears to be the only option if businesses want to compete in certain countries.

Attitude of the Firm's Management

Many U.S. firms still view exporting as an extension of the domestic sales effort, and export pricing policy is established accordingly. Smaller companies whose top management concerns itself mostly with domestic matters have major problems setting export prices. Price determination of export sales is often based on a full-costing approach. The preference for cost-based pricing over market-oriented pricing reflects the relative importance given to profits and market share. This is particularly notable with firms that are unconcerned with market share and require that every quote meet their profit expectations. Other companies are more concerned with selling one product line at any price, even below cost, and reap longer-term benefits from the sale of follow-up consumables and spare parts. Producers of expensive industrial equipment, scientific instruments, and medical equipment fall into this category.

ALTERNATIVE APPROACHES TO PRICING

Firms typically choose one of three approaches to pricing. These can be called the rigid cost-plus, flexible cost-plus, and dynamic incremental pricing strategies.

Rigid Cost-Plus Strategy

The complexity of export pricing has caused many managers to cling to a rigid cost-plus pricing strategy in an effort to secure profitability. This strategy establishes the foreign list price by adding international customer costs and a gross margin to domestic manufacturing costs. The final cost to the customer includes administrative and R&D overhead costs, transportation, insurance, packaging, marketing, documentation, and customs charges, as well as the profit margins for both the distributor and the manufacturer. Although this type of pricing ensures margins, the final price may be so high that it keeps the firm from being competitive in major foreign markets.

Nevertheless, cost-plus pricing appears to be the most dominant strategy among American firms. Approximately 70 percent of the sampled firms used this strategy. Over half of the firms using a cost-plus strategy adhered to it rigidly, with no exceptions. This approach may be typical of other exporting firms in the United States. The following company examples illustrate the popularity of the rigid cost-plus pricing approach.

Autotrol is a Wisconsin manufacturer of water treatment and control equipment. The firm employs about 80 people, and exports account for about 60 percent of its estimated $14 million annual sales. Principal markets include Western Europe, Japan, Australia, New Zealand, and Venezuela. Autotrol sets export prices 3 percent to 4 percent higher than domestic prices to cover the additional costs. Such costs include foreign advertising, foreign travel, and all costs incurred when shipping the product from the factory to the foreign distributor. The firm has successfully exported for the past 15 years by using a rigid cost-plus strategy.

Chillicothe Metal Co. is a solely owned manufacturer of generator sets, pump packages, engine enclosures, controls, and spare parts. The firm has recently lost a significant portion of its foreign business. Sales dropped from $5 million in 1982 to $3 million in 1984, and the current employment of 40 is down from its 1982 high of 100. The company had successfully exported for more than 15 years, but current exports are down 40 percent from the 1982 level. Principal foreign markets are the Middle East, North Africa, and the Far East. The company adheres to a rigid cost-plus pricing strategy that includes a built-in margin ranging from 5 percent to 15 percent. However, the president has recently taken efforts to control costs, extend credit, and reduce margins for cash-in-advance customers in an attempt to counter the effects of the slow business cycle.

Dairy Equipment Co. produces milk machines, bulk coolers, and other high-quality equipment for the dairy industry. The company's annual sales are about $40 million, with current employment at 400. Although the company has exported continuously over the past decade, export earnings have become negligible. This has been caused by a significant drop in sales in the company's primary foreign market—West Germany. Gross profit has remained the company's primary export goal, but the rigid cost-plus pricing strategy has not yet proved to be effective. The company has always sought equal profitability from foreign sales, although fierce competition in some markets has forced it to consider lower profit margins. The company's export pricing policy remains a static element of the marketing mix.

These examples demonstrate that a rigid cost-plus pricing strategy may or may not be effective. They also imply that just because a strategy has been successful in the past, there is no guarantee that it will be successful in the future. Competitive pressures often force firms to reevaluate their pricing decisions and consider new alternatives.

Flexible Cost-Plus Strategy

One such alternative is a flexible cost-plus strategy. This is also the most logical strategy for companies that are in the process of moving away from their traditionally rigid pricing policies.

Flexible cost-plus price strategy is identical to the rigid strategy in establishing list prices. Flexible strategy, however, allows for price variations in special circumstances. For example, discounts may be granted, depending on the customer, the size of the order, or the intensity of competition. Although discounts occasionally are granted on a case-by-case basis, the primary objective of flexible cost-plus pricing is profit. Thus, pricing is still a static element of the marketing mix. The following cases are good examples of companies that use a flexible cost-plus pricing strategy.

Baughman, a division of Fuqua Industries, manufactures steel grain-storage silos and related equipment. The company currently employs about 125 people, and annual sales are around $6 million. The company has traditionally exported about 30 percent of its sales over the past ten years, but recently exports have grown to over 50 percent of annual sales. Baughman's products are of high quality, and pricing has not often been an active element in the marketing mix. The firm's export sales terms consist of an irrevocable confirmed letter of credit in U.S. currency with no provisions for fluctuating exchange rates. Export and domestic prices are identical before exporting costs are added. However, Baughman will make concessions to this policy to secure strategically important sales.

Nicolet Instrument Corporation designs, manufactures, and markets electronic instruments that are used in science, medicine, industry, and engineering. The firm employs more than 500 people and has annual sales of over $85 million. Exports account for about 42 percent of total sales, and the firm has been exporting for the past ten years. Major foreign markets include Japan, Germany, France, Canada, England, Mexico, Sweden, and the Netherlands. Foreign and domestic prices are calculated according to full cost. Since Nicolet has held a technological edge, it has not been affected by competition in foreign markets. However, the competitive gap has been slowly closing, and the company now varies from administered prices more frequently.

Badger Meter manufactures and sells industrial liquid meters. The company employs 700 people, and its annual sales are estimated at $60 million. The company has sold internationally for more than 50 years, but export sales only account for 9 percent of total sales. Major markets include Europe, Canada, Taiwan, and the Philippines. The company owns a production facility in Mexico and has licensees in Ecuador and Peru. Cost-based list prices are used for both domestic and foreign markets. Although prices usually remain fixed, the company has, at times, offered special discounts to regain market share or to offset unfavorable exchange rates.

Flexible pricing strategies are useful to counter competitive pressures or exchange-rate fluctuations. They help firms stay competitive in certain markets without disrupting the entire pricing strategy. However, if competitive pressures persist and technology gaps continue to close, the company could face losing its export market. This is when a company may consider the third alternative.

Dynamic Incremental Strategy

The dynamic incremental pricing strategy was used by approximately 30 percent of the firms studied. Most firms using this strategy had sales well over $50 million with exports ranging from 20 to 65 percent of total sales. In the dynamic incremental strategy, prices are set by subtracting fixed costs for plants, R&D, and domestic overhead from cost-plus figures. In addition, domestic marketing and promotion costs are also disregarded.

This strategy is based on the assumption that fixed and variable domestic costs are incurred regardless of export sales. Therefore, only variable and international customer costs need to be recovered on exported products. This makes it possible for a company to maintain profit margins while selling its exported products at prices below U.S. list. It is also assumed that unused production capacity exists and that the exported products could not be otherwise sold at full cost. Companies can thus lower their prices and be competitive in markets that may otherwise be prohibitive to enter or penetrate. The following examples illustrate this strategy.

Flo-Con Systems, a subsidiary of Masco Inc., manufactures high-quality and sophisticated flow-control valves for molten-steel-pouring applications. The company employs 500 people and has sales between $50 and $60 million, of which 25 percent result from exports. A plant located in Canada produces final products, and an additional plant in Mexico is being considered. Flo-Con finds the nature of its markets very competitive. The firm's export prices are based on competitive prices in the local market. Management is often forced to temporarily overlook costs and margins to remain competitive and secure orders.

Ray-O-Vac, a producer of batteries and other consumer goods, has been exporting successfully for over 30 years. Its Micro Power Division employs 250 and has estimated annual sales of $100 million. The major products in this division include batteries for hearing aids and watches. Exports account for 20 percent of total business, and major markets include Europe, Far East, and Japan. These markets are entered through wholly-owned subsidiaries strategically located around the world. Each subsidiary may be treated as a cost or profit center depending upon the market circumstances. Competitive pressures demand flexible pricing, and discounts are often granted to gain market share or secure OEM business. Branch managers may adjust prices on a day-to-day basis to counter exchange-rate fluctuations. Export pricing is a very active ingredient in the firm's marketing mix.

Econ-O-Cloth is an independent manufacturer of optical polishing cloths and a wholesaler of related goods. Although the company has traditionally exported around 25 percent of its sales volume, this figure has slipped to around 5 percent over the past five years. Major markets include Canada, Mexico, and Western Europe. Econ-O-Cloth reduced export margins to compensate for the strong dollar in the early 1980s, and it considers pricing an active instrument for achieving marketing objectives. The firm continually monitors the foreign environment and at times modifies its prices and products to blend with foreign consumer demands. Econ-O-Cloth has been squeezed hard by competition, and it is still waiting for its dynamic pricing strategy to pay off.

The above examples demonstrate that pricing strategies are complex and that no single strategy suits a firm at all times. There is no guarantee that pricing strategies that work successfully today will continue to do so in the future. Many traditionally successful exporters have recently experienced sales downturns in their foreign markets. One can only speculate on whether a change of pricing strategies could have prevented these downturns. Also, it is not known to what extent other factors (poor market intelligence, weak distribution networks, no product modifications when they were needed, slow delivery, or poor image) were responsible.

The uncertainties of international business make it difficult for executives to select the pricing strategy that is best for their firm. As a result, most firms use the rigid cost-plus strategy until external pressures force them to reconsider. This strategy makes managers feel secure, and it is frequently used when a firm enters the export market. As competition and other external variables grow more intense, however, the firm typically makes exceptions to its pricing policy, moving from rigid to flexible cost-plus pricing. Few firms have attempted to price their export products according to the dynamic conditions of the marketplace. For these firms, the dynamic incremental strategy is usually required, and prices may change frequently in response to competition, the prevailing exchange rate, and other variables.

Most exporting firms appear to establish their pricing policies reactively, changing only when external pressures force the issue. In working this way, however, these firms lose valuable sales and market share during the transition period. Although this strategy may be defensible, three types of lags may result in irreversible damage. The recognition lag is the amount of time between an actual change in the environment and a company's recognition of that change. Reaction lag is the amount of time between the company's recognition of the problem and its decision to react to it. Finally, effectiveness lag is the amount of time needed to implement the decision.

One might conclude that if executives were proactive in their pricing strategy, they might avoid many of the headaches associated with exporting. But how can executives be sure which pricing policy is best for their firms? Considering all the variables that affect price, it is reasonable to assume that different pricing policies should exist for different markets. Furthermore, considering the volatility of foreign markets, one would suspect that these policies should be continuously reviewed and updated. It is not surprising, then, that most executives resort to setting their pricing policies reactively.

A DECISION FRAMEWORK FOR EXPORT PRICING

Most companies lack a systematic procedure for setting and revising export prices. The absence of a formal decision-making procedure that incorporates and weighs relevant variables has led to the development of the framework described here. It is not intended to replace management judgment, since the business executive is usually in the best position to assess the suitability of various strategies and policies, but simply to provide a systematic framework for arriving at export pricing decisions.

Figure 3 illustrates the steps involved in a formal export price determination process. A brief description of each step is presented below.

Verification of Market Potential

The first step in the analysis gives firm information on the market potential in specific countries. The company can identify market potential for its products by using both formal and informal sources. Formal sources include market-research firms, the U.S. Department of Commerce, banks, and other agencies that provide information on foreign countries. Informal sources include trade shows, local distributors, international trade journals, and business contacts.[15] During this process, those countries that do not demonstrate adequate market potential are dropped from the list of possible markets.

FIGURE 3. Decision Process for Export Price Determination

Verify export market potential
↓
Estimate target price range: floor, ceiling, and expected prices
↓
Determine company sales potential at given prices
↓
Analyze import, distribution and transaction barriers
↓
Examine corporate goals and preference for pricing strategy
↓
Select suitable pricing strategy:
1. Rigid cost-plus
2. Flexible cost-plus
3. Dynamic incremental

↓
Check consistency with current price setting
↓
Implementation: Select tactics, distributor prices, and end user prices
↓
Monitor export market performance and make adjustments as necessary

Estimating Target Price Range

Once it is determined that a market has sufficient potential, the firm observes the price ranges of substitute or competitive products in the local market to find its target price range. This consists of three prices:

- The floor price, that price at which the firm breaks even;
- The ceiling price, the highest price the market is likely to bear for the product; and
- The expected price, the price at which the firm would most likely be competitive.

Estimating Sales Potential

Assuming that a high enough level of sales potential exists to warrant market entry, management then identifies the size and concentration of customer segments, projected consumption patterns, competitive pressures, and the expectations of local distributors and agents. The landed cost and the cost of local distribution are estimated. The potential sales volume is assessed for each of the three price levels, taking into account the price elasticity of demand.

Analyze Special Import, Distribution, or Transaction Barriers

If adequate sales potential exists, management then assesses any special import barriers not accounted for in its earlier efforts. These barriers include quotas, tariffs and other taxes, anti-dumping, price-maintenance, currency-exchange, and other governmental regulations that affect the cost of doing business in that country. In addition, internal distribution barriers must also be assessed. Lengthy distribution channels, high margins, and inadequate dealer commitment may present difficulties for the exporter. Finally, currency supply, payment terms, and financing availability should be reviewed. Is it customary for prices to be negotiable? Do customers expect certain credit or payment terms? Once again, sales potential, market share, and profitability should be analyzed in light of the above information in order to confirm the desirability of market entry.

Corporate Goals and Preference for Pricing

After deciding on a target market, some companies may not wish to consider anything but full-cost pricing (either rigid or flexible cost-plus). If desired margins can be achieved, this pricing policy can be implemented. If, however, the desired margins cannot be achieved, the firm can either abort market entry or resort to some form of marginal costing approach. If the firm's management is willing to consider pricing strategies that focus on market rather than profit objectives, it may continue the analysis with a systematic identification of the optimal pricing strategy.

Systematic Selection of Appropriate Pricing Strategy

The company needs to arrive at a strategy choice by systematically considering all relevant variables. Management faces a basic choice between a dynamic incremental pricing strategy and a cost-plus pricing strategy (either rigid or flexible). Dynamic incremental pricing implies a marginal costing approach, while cost-plus pricing implies full costing.

Figure 4 identifies 15 criteria that help management make choices between the two pricing strategies. Some criteria are derived from the general environment of the firm, while others are unique to the specific export opportunity being considered. Management may choose to weigh each group, as well as individual criteria, in arriving at a choice. Figure 4 spells out the conditions that call for incremental pricing.

Checking Consistency with Current Pricing

If a firm is already in the targeted market, the recommended pricing strategy should be compared to the strategy currently in place. If deviations exist, they should be explained and justified. If they cannot be justified, the firm should seriously consider adopting the recommended pricing strategy in order to achieve marketing goals more

FIGURE 4. Criteria Relevant to the Choice between Full and Marginal Costing

Conditions favoring . . . Marginal Costing/ Aggressive Pricing	Criteria	Conditions favoring . . . Full Costing/ Passive Pricing
	(a) Firm-Specific Criteria	
Low	Extent of product differentiation	High
Committed	Corporate stance toward exporting	Half-hearted
Long term	Management desire for recovering export overhead	Short term
Sufficient	Company financial resources to sustain initial losses	Insufficient
Wide	Domestic gross margins	Narrow
High	Need for long-term capacity utilization	Low
High	Opportunity to benefit from economies of scale	Low
	(b) Situation-Specific Criteria	
Substantial	Growth potential of export market	Negligible
High	Potential for follow-up sales	Low
Continuous	Nature of export opportunity	One-time
High	End-user price sensitivity	Low
High	Competitive intensity	Low
Likely	Opportunity to drive out competition	Unlikely
Favorable	Terms of sale and financing	Unfavorable
Low	Exchange rate risk	High
Low	Cost of internal distribution, service and promotion	High

effectively. It is also important to check for consistency of export pricing policies across export markets to minimize any conflicts (such as inter-market shipping by competing middlemen).

Implementation

The exporter will determine specific prices for distributors and end users, in accordance with the recommended pricing strategy, and decide on specific pricing tactics. A strategy may fail in a specific market if execution is not effective or if reaction to change is slow. For example, distributors may vary their margins as a response to price changes. Similarly, distributors may hold a large inventory of products at the old price, creating a lag before the new pricing policy actually becomes effective.

Monitoring

Exchange rates can be one of the more volatile variables in international business, especially in developing countries. These rates should be monitored continuously, and the effect of their changes on pricing policy should be evaluated. Variables such as competition, regulations, and price sensitivity can be monitored periodically. As these variables change, the firm can adjust its pricing strategy appropriately. The proposed decision process, therefore, provides a proactive means of establishing pricing policies.

A major implication of this analysis is that no export pricing strategy will fit all of a company's products and markets. International pricing issues are extremely complex, and pricing decisions are fueled by many variables. It is important that the company establish a systematic and periodic approach in selecting a pricing policy. The approach should account for both internal and external variables affecting the firm's export efforts. This framework for export pricing is one such approach. Executives may wish to modify the model in order to better blend it with their firms' perspectives.

A second implication is that many U.S. firms may be overlooking lucrative foreign markets because of their strict adherence to the full-cost pricing approach. Furthermore, this rigid practice may hinder effective market penetration in existing foreign markets. A complete reassessment of the firm's market-share objectives may be needed. Committed exporters will allocate the resources needed to accomplish this task if it becomes necessary.

Finally, there is no guarantee that those pricing policies that are suitable today will work in the future. Changing business trends, exchange rates, consumer preferences, and competition are only a few of the variables that have caught successful exporters off guard. Therefore, a method for monitoring changes in the pricing policy variables should be established. The most volatile variables, such as exchange rates and competitive transaction prices, should be monitored more frequently. Once again, committed exporters will recognize the need for this and allocate the appropriate resources to establish an adequate monitoring system.

Although no best pricing strategy exists, most American firms have adhered to a full-cost approach, often disregarding conditions that are particular to their targeted foreign market. Many companies have abandoned lucrative foreign markets because of seemingly unattractive potentials. Other firms have relinquished sales and market share to local or more aggressive foreign competitors. The full-cost approach is a major deterrent to improving the exports of American businesses.

The establishment of international pricing policies is a dynamic process. Success with one strategy does not guarantee that the same strategy will continue to work. Many companies react passively when global changes make their traditional pricing policies obsolete. Such companies are usually forced to either abandon the market or adapt their pricing strategy to the new conditions. The lag times associated with recognition, reaction, and effectiveness can cause an irreversible deterioration in a company's sales, profits, and market share in the foreign country.

A proactive stance on establishing pricing strategy can often reduce or eliminate these lags, enhancing the firm's flexibility and responsiveness to changing business conditions. To develop a proactive stance, businesses need to establish systematic methods to monitor and evaluate the variables associated with an international pricing policy. Firms that are committed to international business will quickly recognize this and allocate resources accordingly.

The guidelines and decision process discussed in this article have been derived from the experience of exporting firms. Such an empirically-based approach to developing managerial guidelines is appropriate, given the current dearth of export pricing literature. Insights obtained from the field can rip away the shroud of mystery that surrounds export pricing decisions. At the same time, it should be noted that the managerial guidelines offered here are appropriate for a given set of conditions. The seasoned executive will realize that these recommendations are not substitutes for good business judgment. The proposed strategies may need minor modifications to better reflect a company's perspectives and constraints on international pricing.

NOTES

1. Vern Terpstra, "Suggestions for Research Themes and Publications," *Journal of International Business Studies,* Spring/Summer 1983, pp. 9–10.

2. "Pricing Competition is Shaping Up as 84's Top Marketing Pressure Point," *Marketing News,* November 11, 1983, p. 1.

3. Vithala R. Rao, "Pricing Research in Marketing: The State of the Art," *Journal of Business,* January 1984, pp. 539–559.

4. See: James C. Baker and John K. Ryans, Jr., "Some Aspects of International Pricing: A Neglected Area of Management Policy," *Management Decision,* Summer 1973, pp. 177–182; S. Tamer Cavusgil and John R. Nevin, "State-of-the-Art in International Marketing: An Assessment," in B. M. Enis and K. J. Roering, eds., *Review of Marketing 1981* (Chicago: American Marketing Association), pp. 195–216; and Terpstra (see note 1).

5. See: Jeffrey S. Arpan, "Multinational Firm Pricing in International Markets," *Sloan Management Review,* Winter 1973, pp. 1–9; M. Edgar Barrett, "Case of the Tangled Transfer Price," *Harvard Business Review,* May-June 1977, p. 21; Seung H. Kim and Stephen W. Miller, "constituents of the International Transfer Pricing Decision," *Columbia Journal of World Business,* Spring 1979, pp. 69–77.

6. Llewellyn Clague and Rena Grossfield, "Exporting Pricing in a Floating Rate World," *Columbia Journal of World Business,* Winter 1974, pp. 17–22.
7. Baker and Ryans (see note 4).
8. Donald J. Lecraw, "Pricing Strategies of Transnational Corporations," *Asia Pacific Journal of Management,* January 1984, pp. 112–119.
9. Nathaniel H. Left, "Multinational Corporate Pricing Strategy in Developing Countries," *Journal of International Business Studies,* Fall 1975, pp. 55–64.
10. Peter R. Kressler, "Is Uniform Pricing Desirable in Multinational Markets?" *Akron Business and Economic Review,* Winter 1971.
11. Nigel Piercy, "British Export Market Selection and Pricing," *Industrial Marketing Management,* October 1981, pp. 287–297.
12. Russell Abratt and Leyland F. Pitt, "Pricing Practices in Two Industries," *Industrial Marketing Management,* 14: 301–306.
13. John U. Farley, James M. Hulbert and David Weistein, "Price Setting and Volume Planning by Two European Industrial Companies: A Study and Comparison of Decision Processes," *Journal of Marketing,* Winter 1980, pp. 46–54.
14. Victor H. Frank, Jr., "Living with Price Controls Abroad," *Harvard Business Review,* March-April 1984, pp. 137–142.
15. S. Tamer Cavusgil, "Guidelines for Export Market Research," *Business Horizons,* November-December 1985, pp. 27–33.

INDEX

A

Aaker, David, 1169

Accessibility and market segmentation, 176

Accounting for product cannibalism, 886-89

Ace Hardware and franchising, 931

ACORN, 1189

Acquisitions, role of marketing research in, 242-43

Action audits, 353

Activity-based cost (ABC) accounting, 753

Adaptability test, 98

Adaptation
- and global marketing, 1266-67
- mandatory, 1330
- voluntary, 1330

Administered pricing, 857

Adopting units, characteristics of individuals as, 778-79

Adoption
- definition of, 775
- unit of, 775-79

Adversary specialist, and government regulations, 640-41

Advertising, 538, *See also* Media planning
- body copy of, 1115-16
- direct mail, 1118-21
- efficiency of, 754
- exposure effects of, 1223, 1225
- graphics in, 1115
- headlines in, 1114-15
- image in, 1225
- in industrial markets, 951
- informational, 1163
- in international marketing promotion, 1337
- latent content in, 1233-34
- in layering strategy, 69-70
- layout of, 1116
- in marketing industrial raw materials, 1032-33
- in marketing to business, 995-98
- placement of, 1116
- purpose of, 1113-14
- symbols in, 1140-41, 1143
- theoretical stages in, 403-4
- transformational, 1163
- and women's language, 1238-45
  - in dramatic sceneries, 1238-40
  - reading women in, 1241-44

Advertising message strategy, 1157-58
- classic creative approaches, 1164
  - Bernbach's execution emphasis, 1168-69
  - Burnett's inherent drama, 1164, 1167
  - Ogilvy's brand image, 1167-68
  - Reeves's unique selling proposition, 1167
  - Trout and Reis's positioning, 1169-70
  - Vaughn's message matrix, 1170-71
- copy platform in, 1161-64
- creative objectives, 1171
  - general versus specific, 1172-74
  - hierarchy of creative, 171-72
  - long-range versus short-range, 1171
- creativity in, 1157, 1175-77
- definition of, 1157
- determining message idea, 1158-60
- differential copy advantage in, 1159-60
- differentiation from tactics, 1157-58
- elements of ad execution, 1164
- guidelines for using identifying symbols, 1182
- identifying symbols, 1177-81

brand names, 1178
licensed names, 1179
slogans, 1179-80
trade characters, 1179
trademarks, 1178
trade names, 1178
judging message ideas and executions, 1174-75
durability, 1174
image consistency, 1175
leverage, 1174
message dominance, 1175
resistance to counterattack, 1174
single-mindedness, 1175
specificity, 1174
strategy adherence, 1175
strategy fit, 1174
target segment fit, 1174
total promotion mix fit, 1174
obtaining and retaining protection for identifying symbols, 1181-82
types of, 1164

Advertising research and measurement, 399-416
attention, communication, and comprehension, 406-8
background considerations regarding copy and commercial testing, 403
basic aims of, 400, 402
basic considerations, 399
choosing method of testing and evaluating, 409-10
consumer preferences and attitudes, 408-9
copy testing in, 399, 403, 404, 410
definitions and planning, 399-400
direct and indirect sales measures in, 404-6
focus of, 399
implications of, 415-16
laboratory testing of, 409
measuring media profitability, 414-15
media measurement in, 410-11
place for scientific sampling, 402
qualitative evaluation of media in, 414
quantitative evaluation of media in, 411-14
scientific method in, 400, 402
theoretical stages in, 403-4

Advertising-to-sales ratio, 744

Aeronomics, Inc., 940

Affiliation franchising, 928

Affirmative action, 97, 98

After-sales customer satisfaction activities, 387-88

Agriculture, U.S. Department of, and marketing of raw materials, 1034

Airline industry. *See also specific airlines*
asset usage in, 842
yield management in, 937

Albaum, Gerald S., 1318

Alka Seltzer, trade character use by, 1179

All-commodity volume (ACV) measure of store size, 707

Alliances, 1265

Allocation criteria, profitability measures as, 138-39

Allocation models, 363

Allport, Gordon W., 278

Alphanumeric keypad, 256

Ambiguity, eliminating, 74-75

Amdahl Corp, 1269-70

American Airlines
advertising tactics of, 6
marketing tactics at, 19
as master of innovation, 694-96
and product positioning, 16
use of information technology by, 490-91, 499-500

American Association of Advertising Agencies, 1194

American Electric Power (AEP)
and green marketing, 231
proactive strategy of, 225-26

American Express, use of direct marketing by, 1216

American Hospital Supply and distribution, 869

American Marketing Association, ethics codes of, 190, 632

American Thermos Company, 1181

Amirani, Shahrzad, 552

Amtrak, and yield management, 937

Analytical planning dimension, 667-68
managing, 671-74

Analytic approach to qualitative research, 273

Anchorless centers, 914

Andersen Consulting, 939

Anderson, James C., 1010

Anderson v. *Liberty Lobby,* 654, 657

Anheuser-Busch, and product cannibalism, 881

Announcement press release, 1110-11

Annual-plan control, 739-40

Annual Survey of Manufacturers, 1060

Anonymity, perceived, in survey research, 313

Ansoff, Igor, 603

Antitrust law, 645-58
basic standards, 646-47
per se rule, 646
rule of reason, 646
truncated approach, 646
implications for marketing management, 657-58
motion for summary judgment, 651
definition and purpose, 651
old and new approaches, 651-52
procedural revolution of 1986, 653
Anderson v. *Liberty Lobby,* 654
Celotex Corp. v. *Catrett,* 653
Matsushita Electric Industrial Co. v. *Zenith Radio Corp.,* 652, 654-56
significance of *Monsanto* v. *Spray-Rite Service Corp.,* 652-53
substantive erosion in the *per se* standard, 647
summary judgment, 656-57
and take-back goods, 1353

Apple Computer
and distribution, 877
as master of innovation, 694-96

Application notes, 1123

Application stories, 1112

Approach and retreat, 1141

Aptitude in sales performance, 108

Area development franchising, 928

Argus v. *Eastman Kodak,* 657

Asea Brown Boveri Ltd., 1341

ASI Market Research, 266

Assembly operations, 1326

Asset turnover, 746

Asset usage in airline industry, 842

Atomic Energy Commission, and U.S. export regulations, 1302

AT&T, and globalization, 1272

Attitude research, 399, 408-9

Audience
qualitative research on, 278
target
conducting research on, 827
selecting appropriate, 827

Audimeter, 412

Audiotapes in sales training, 1128

Audit
action, 353

customer service, 817-20
marketing-environment, 760
marketing-function, 762-63
marketing-organization, 761
marketing-productivity, 762
marketing-strategy, 761
marketing-systems, 761-62
store, 405

Audubon House, and recycling, 228

Austin, Nancy, 1206

Authority seekers, 179

Autotrol, export pricing by, 1364

Avis
positioning by, 1169
and yield management, 937

Axelrad, Norman D., 918

B

Backward vertical integration, 1035-36

Badger Meter, and export pricing, 1366

Baldrige, Malcolm, National Quality Award, 798

Bank One, and distribution, 872

Barabba, Vincent P., 328

Barban, Arnold M., 1156

Barometric measurements, 240

Bartels, Robert, 536

Barter and buybacks, 1345-55
barter arrangements, 1346
compensation agreements, 1347-48
counter-purchase agreements, 1346-47
marketing channels for take-back goods, 1352
adding to the line, 1353
fobbing off to new customers, 1353-54
in-house use, 1352-53
old-fashioned ways in, 1348-49
pricing the deal, 1349-52
swing, 1348

Baseline sales, 704

Base price, 706, 724

Base volume, 706

Bash, Dan, 283

Basket contractor, 964

Baughman, and export pricing, 1365

Baxter Healthcare
ethics code of, 622
and relationship-outcome measurement, 1026-1027

Bayesian analysis, 295
classical assumptions, 295-97
and direct marketing, 1216

Bean, L. L., 442

Beardon, William O., 370

Beech Nut Company, and ethical behavior, 613

Beer game, 701

Behavior
adopting desired, 829-30
controlling cost of, 829
purchase, 13-15

Behavioral issues, 683

Behavioral planning dimension, 668-69
managing, 674-77

Behavior change
designing proposed, 828
positioning desired, 828-29

Bellizzi, Joseph A., 1066

Benefit segmentation, 510
in analyzing sensory data, 531
phases of, 524

Benetton, and globalization, 1268

Berelson, Bernard, 278

Bergen, Harold A., 1196

Berman, Barry, 802

Bernbach, William, 1168, 1171, 1182

Berry, Leonard L., 786

BHS, 498

Bias
  data interpretation and cultural, 1296
  nonresponse, in survey research, 312
  potential for interviewer, in survey research, 313-14
  sample, 290

Bic ballpoint pens, 848

Bill of lading, 1304-5

Bills of exchange, 1310

Bio Technical International Inc., 1036

Blattberg, Robert C., 418

BMW, and value marketing, 47

Body Shop, 914

Boeing
  and global sales, 1254, 1256
  and strategic alliances, 1327

Bonoma, Thomas V., 946

Bonus compensations, 1130

Booth, Charles, 278

Borden, Neil, 571, 1167

Boston Consulting Group, 140-41

Bowen, Jack, 283

Boxes, 55

BRAD (British Rate and Data), 487

Brainstorming technique, 1177

Brand dominance, 163-72
  competitive advantage, 169
    competitive implications, 169-70
    perceptual distinctiveness, 169
    persistence, 170
  consumer preference formation
    consumer learning, 164-65
    consumer learning and preference, 165-66
    preference structure, 166-68
  strategic implications, 170-71

Brand factors in sales promotion, 1153

Brand identity profile, 21-22

Brand image, 21-22, 1169

Brand loyalty, 182

Brand management utilization
  panel data
    new product tracking, 733
    panel-based analysis method, 733-34
    panel versus store data, 732-33
    related data, 734
  store data
    competitive monitoring, 727-29, 730
    monitoring sales and share, 727
    special studies, 732
    strategic planning, 729, 731-32

Brand managers in monitoring sales and share, 727

Brand names, 1177

Brand preference studies, 1043

Brand size summary, 708

Brand-switching models, 364

Break-even models, 362

Bristol-Meyers, and flanker brand strategy, 885

British Airways, and yield management, 939-40

Britt, Steuart Henderson, 283

Broadcast for database marketing, 430-31

Broadcast Music, Inc. v. *Columbia Broadcasting System,* 647-49

Brochures, 1116-18

Brooks, John, 333

BROWSE, 1316

Bryan brand of hot dogs, 848

Bryson, John, 226

Bubbles, 55

Budget for media planning, 1188-89

Budweiser

and competitive advantage, 171
trade character use by, 1179

Bundle pricing, 840

Bundling of services, 999

Burdick Corporation, and export pricing, 1359

Burger King
and area development franchising, 928
marketing strategy of, 848

Burnett, Leo, 283, 1157, 1164, 1167, 1171, 1172, 1175, 1182

Burpee, and direct marketing, 1216

Burton group, 498

Busch, positioning by, 1169

Business, public perceptions of, 609-10

Business communications, 1107-34
buyers in, 1112-26
community in, 1132-33
employees in, 1131-32
key influencers in, 1107-12
opportunities in, 1133-34
sales and distribution channels in, 1126-30
technology partners and alliances in, 1130-31

Business-controlled pricing, 857

Business definition, 142
dimensions of, 142-44
scope of, 145-47

Business environment in global markets, 1282-84

Business environmental scanning, 53

Business format franchises, 919

Business International's *Investment Licensing and Trading Conditions Abroad,* 1284

Business sector, definition of, 947-50

Business-to-business plan, 1187

Business-to-business selling, 1067-79
buying process, 1067
acquisition of vendor information/proposals, 1071
analysis and evaluation of vendor information, 1071-77
carrying out the order routine, 1077-78
determining the characteristics of needed item, 1068-70
performance evaluation, 1078
recognition of need, 1068
versus consumer marketing, 950

Buybacks. *See* Barter and buybacks

Buyers
in business communications, 1112-26
and pricing, 864

Buying decisions, and sizing markets, 479-80

C

Cabalistic symbolism, 231

Cable television for database marketing, 431

Caldwell, Jack L., 856

Calibration equivalence, and local market expansion, 1293

California Psychological Inventory, 98

Campbell Soup Company
as master of innovation, 694-96
and reaching consumers, 1091
and trade characters, 1179

Canteen Corporation, advertising by, 1144

Cantril, Hadley, 278

Capacity utilization, and pricing, 977-78

CAPI. *See* Computer-assisted personal interviewing (CAPI)

Caples, John, 1214

Captioned photographs, 1199

Carlson, Chester, 335

Carrefour, 914

Case histories, 1112

Catalogs. *See also* Direct mail; Direct marketing
- in business communications, 1121
- in database marketing, 433
- promotional, 1130

Category dominance, 169

Category equivalence, and local market expansion, 1292-93

Category factors in sales promotion, 1153

Cateora, Philip R., 1300

Caterpillar, 1269
- ethics code of, 622
- and global marketing
- marketing strategy of, 848

CATI. *See* Computer-assisted telephone interviewing (CATI)

Catlin, John, 283

Causal measures, 713-14

Cause marketing, 120

Cavaliers, 675

Cavusgil, S. Tamer, 1356

Celotex Corp. v. *Catrett,* 653, 656

Census data in sizing markets, 454

Central control unit (CCU), 155

Certificate of origin, 1304

Chain retailer, marketing system using, 33-34

Chain Store Age Executive/ Management Horizons index, 911

Change
- acceptance of, 60
- and internationalization, 1322
- management of, in marketing concept cycle, 51-52

Change reports, 717, 718

Channel of distribution. *See* Distribution system

Chase Manhattan Bank, 948, 950

Chemical Bank, ethics programs at, 623

Cheskin, Louis, 283

Chicago Board of Trade (CBT), 1038

Chicago Board of Trade v. *United States,* 646

Chicago Marriott Hotel, 795

Chicken Delight as franchise, 925

Chick-fil-A, 790

Chillicothe Metal Co., export pricing by, 1364

Chrysler
- and distribution, 874
- and recycling, 228

Ciba-Geigy Pharmaceuticals, use of information technology by, 481

Clayton Act (1914), 645, 864

Clean Air Act, 225

Cleveland-Cliffs Iron Company, 1036

Cluster analysis of joint-space coordinates, 565-67

Clustering, 291

Cluster-Plus, 1189

Coca-Cola
- and cola wars with Pepsi, 163
- and distribution, 874
- and global marketing, 1322

Collaborative emphasis, 1015

Collaborative relationships, 1012

Commerce, U.S. Department of
- and data collection, 1280
- and information services, 1258
- and marketing of raw materials, 1034
- and U.S. export regulations, 1302, 1303

Commercial invoice, 1305

Commercial testing, background considerations regarding, 403

Commodity Control List and Country Groups Supplement of the Export Administration Regulations, 1303

Commodity exchanges in marketing raw materials, 1038

Communication. *See also* Business communications
- continuous measurement instruments in research, 255-66
- crisis, 1133, 1201-2
- integrated marketing, 1194
  - and the consumer, 1096
- policies, in international distribution and selling, 1339-40
- in staffing the marketing function, 103-5

Community in business communications, 1132-33

Company ethical and social responsibility review, 764, 766

Company marketing objectives, and pricing, 978-79

Comparative value to the customer in pricing, 972

Compensation agreements, 1347-48

Compensation plan for sales force in marketing to business, 994-95

Competition
- analysis of, in marketing mix, 577-78
- and establishment of international prices, 1334-35
- as factor in globalization, 1269
- government regulation of, 641-42
- in information technology, 497-98
- marketing strategy, 603-4

Competitive advantage
- of common sense and passion, 799
- competitive implications, 169-70
- ease of repair in, 809
- gaining, 500
- in marketing, 6-7
- perceptual distinctiveness, 169
- persistence in, 170

Competitive monitoring, 715-16
- and brand management utilization, 727-29

Competitive positioning, 906

Competitive pricing, 975, 1043
- strategies for, 897

Complaints
- counting, 814
- encouraging employees to resolve, 818
- and measuring service quality, 814
- responding to, 816

Complementary marketing, 1264
- in global marketing, 1288

Component life-style, 898

Composite retail performance index (Forseter), 911

Comprehensive Environmental Response, Compensation, and Liability Act, 223

Comp-U-Card, 498

Computer-assisted personal interviewing (CAPI), 304
- bias in, 313
- control of field force in, 311
- cost of, 314
- data collection environment in, 310
- diversity of questions in, 308
- flexibility of data collection in, 306
- perceived anonymity in, 313
- physical stimuli in, 308
- potential for interviewer bias in, 313
- quantity of data in, 312
- sample control in, 308
- social desirability/sensitive information in, 313
- speed of, 314

Computer-assisted telephone interviewing (CATI), 302-3
  control of field force in, 311
  cost of, 314
  data collection environment in, 310
  diversity of questions in, 308
  flexibility of data collection in, 306
  in international marketing research, 315-16, 321
  perceived anonymity in, 313
  physical stimuli in, 308
  potential for interviewer bias, 314
  quantity of data in, 312
  response rate in, 313
  sample control in, 308
  social desirability/sensitive information in, 313
  speed of, 314

Computerized sales force in business-to-business selling, 1077-78

Computer literacy in the marketing organization, 440-41

Computers
  and database marketing, 420-21
  and growth of statistical sophistication, 421
  in information technology, 480-82
  in management science, 359

Concept testing, 240

Conferences, 1123-24

Conglomerate dual distributor, 930-32

Conjoint analysis, 991

Conner Peripheral, 1270

Conservation, and green marketing, 227

Construct equivalence and local market expansion, 1292

Consular invoice, 1304

Consulting Psychologists Press
  California Psychological Inventory, 98
  Holland Vocational Preference Inventory, 98

Consumer
  determining wants and needs, 151-59
  input/output of, 36-37
  and integrated marketing communications, 1096
  preference formation
    consumer learning, 164-65
    consumer learning and preference, 165-66
    preference structure, 166-68
  role of, 151
    in improving marketing management, 152-53
    industrial producer in, 153-54
    in understanding society needs, 151-52

Consumer affairs office in handling consumer complaints, 383

Consumer behavior, theory of, 543

Consumer factors, 1153

Consumer goods, vertically integrated, 32-33

Consumer marketing
  advertising and sales promotion, 995
  versus business-to-business, 950
    availability of data, 960-61
    economic structure, 953-59
    market complexity, 953
    market selection and product policy, 961
    nature of demand, 951-53
    pricing, 968-69
  distribution channels, 984-85
  information technology, 1000
  marketing implementation, 1001
  sales force effectiveness, 985
  segmenting, 180

Consumer media plan, 1187

Consumer-oriented analysis of customer service, 804

Consumer preferences and attitudes in advertising research, 408-9

Consumer purchase data, 705-6

Consumer satisfaction
organizing for, 382-83
in perspective, 371-72
consumerist goals, 372
extent of consumer satisfaction/dissatisfaction, 373-80
forces behind consumer dissatisfaction, 373
summary model of, 380-82
monitoring consumer satisfaction, 384-85
operational response mechanisms, 383-84

Consumer scanning, 699-735
brand management utilization—panel data, 732
new product tracking, 732, 733
panel-based analysis models, 733-34
panel versus store data, 732-33
related data, 734
brand management utilization—store data, 727
competitive monitoring, 727-29, 730
monitoring sales and share, 727
special studies, 732
strategic planning, 729, 731-32
database contents, 706
detail observations, 706
relational data, 707
selling conditions, 707-8
facts, 709
addability of, 709-10
auxiliary, 709
market level facts, 710
information on sales, 701
beer game, 701
consumer purchase data, 705-6
manufacturer shipments, 701-4
retail sales data, 704-5
market position and diagnostic reports, 714
change reports, 717, 718
competitive monitoring, 715-16
exception reporting, 717, 720, 721
ranking reports, 717, 719
trend reports, 714-15
workstation reporting, 717, 722
performance, 725, 726, 727
projection issues, 710
household purchase sample data, 711-12
retail sales sample data, 710-11
report design, 712
causal measures, 713-14
general, 712
sales performance measures, 712-13
reporting schemes, 708-9
tactical analysis, 722
base pricing, 724
expert systems, 725
obtaining distribution, 722-24
promotion event performance, 725, 726, 727
promotion frequency, 825
sales force objectives, 722

Consumer Service Institute, 805-6

Consumer survey research, 531

Content theories of motivation, 117

Contingency model of marketing ethics, 617-18

Continual monitoring and relationship building, 1215-18
with true experiments, 1218-19

Continuity, 433

Continuous competitive renewal, 661-84

Continuous measurement instruments, 255-66
deciding what to test, 263-64
history of, 255-57

instrument reliability and
construct validity, 257
construct validity, 257
reliability, 257
management applications, 258
diagnostics, 258-63
validating with links to other
response variables, 264-66

Continuous monitoring and adjustment and marketing mix, 581

Contract manufacturing, 1325

Contribution margin, 970

Control chart, 744-45

Controlled growth rate (CGR), 54-55

Conventional flow models of planning, 664

Conversion capacity, 1032

Conversion franchising, 928

Co-op marketing, 432

Cooper, M. Bixby, 570

Cooperative exports, 1264

Cooperative pricing, 1022

Copy testing in advertising research, 399, 403, 404, 410

Corbin, Arnold, 238

Corning, Inc., and value marketing, 47

Corporate imagery, 1139-40

Corporate policies, 1335-36

Corrective action, 747
determining best, 750-51

Correlation analysis, 295

Correspondence analysis, 554, 563, 567

Cost-based approaches to pricing, 839, 840

Cost coverage in pricing policies, 835

Cost/effectiveness, improving, in green marketing, 230-31

Cost-plus pricing, 835
exports, 1365-66
flexible, 1365-66
rigid, 1363-65

Costs
consideration of, in pricing, 861-62
and customer-driven distribution systems, 872-73
direct, 752
and establishment of international prices, 1334
as factor in globalization, 1268
nontraceable common, 752
and sizing markets, 448-49
traceable common, 752

Counter-purchase agreements, 1346-47

Country classification in export regulations, 1302

County Business Patterns, 454, 455, 1060

Coupons, growth of use, 1087

CPC International Inc., 1270, 1322

CPI, 1211

Craig, C. Samuel, 1276

Crawley, Alan, 478

Created events, 1200

Creative message, evaluating, 1190

Credit, 538

Crest, positioning by, 1169

Crisis communications, 1201-2
plan for, 1133

Critical incident method, 102

Critical Path Method (CPM), 363, 364

Crocker, Betty, 71

Cross-benefit pricing, 840

Cross-classification analysis, 294

Cross-cultural bias, 1296

Cross-distribution agreements, 1327

Cross-impact analysis, 1045

Cross-licensing, 1265

Cross-manufacturing agreements, 1327

Cross-marketing, 1265
  agreements, 1327

Cross-subsidization, 1270-72

CRT interviews in international market research, 318-19, 321

Culliton, James W., 571

Cultural conditioning, 1244

Cultural differences between the sexes, 1233-34

Cultural environment and global marketing, 1260

Cummins Engine, and global marketing, 1360

Currency
  agreeing on, in compensation arrangements, 1349
  shortage of hard, and bartering, 1348-49

Curtis Publishing Company, marketing research at, 277

Customer
  analysis of in research on industrial products and services, 1063-64
  assessing value of product to, 1014-15
  database marketing, in acquisition and retention of, 441-42
  in determining marketing concept, 60
  lifetime value of, 424-25
  market segmentation by capabilities, 1013-14
  measurement and management of affinity, 442
  model for determining wants and needs, 154
    alternative evaluation, 158
    choice processes and outcomes, 159
    decision process approach, 154-55
    implications, 158-59
    individual's psychological make-up, 155
    perceptual process, 152-61
    post purchase and further behavior, 158
    problem recognition, 157-58
    search processes: information processing, 158

Customer contacts, 1090-92
  in integrated marketing communications environment, 1085-1103
    changes in the marketplace, 1086-87
    customer contact connection, 1097-1100
    expanding media options as media history is reversed, 1088-90
    facts of life in, 1092-96
    integrated customer contacts, 1100-1103
    integrated marketing communications and the consumer, 1096
    mass media domination, 1085-86
    meaning of, 1103
    searching for customer contacts, 1090-92

Customer-driven distribution systems, 869-79
  bounding ideal, 873-74
  comparing options, 874-76
  confronting gap, 877-78
  costs in, 872-73
  deciding on appropriate outlets, 871-72
  finding out what customers want, 869-71
  preparing to implement, 878-79
  reviewing pet assumptions, 876-77

Customer groups, definition of, 491-92

Customer information, acquisition of, in database marketing, 439-40

Customer loyalty, 743

Customer orientation, and marketing concept, 43

Customer penetration, 743

Customer retention, 817

Customer satisfaction
- closing expectations/performance gap, 392-93
- diagnosing shortfalls, 388-91
- and marketing, 26-28
- strategic dimensions of, 385
  - after sales, 387-88
  - culture, 388
  - product, 385-87
  - sales activity, 387
- tracking, 747

Customer selectivity, 743

Customer service, 803-20
- consumer-oriented analysis of, 804
- definition of, 803-5
- monitoring on regular basis, 815
- traps in, 812-14
- written policy statement in, 814-15

Customer service audit, 817-20
- career path for personnel, 817
- competitive advantage based on value chain analysis, 808
- models of, 807
  - audit, 818-19
  - conducting, 818
  - hygiene factors versus motivator, 809
  - pitfalls to poor, 812
  - Porter's value chain, 807-9
  - principles of excellent providers, 814-17
  - recommending changes, 820
  - relationship marketing, 812
  - SERVQUAL dimensions, 809, 811-12
  - studying in terms of customer, 815-16

Customer set, identification of, 55-56

D

Daimler-Benz, international operations of, 1322

Dairy Equipment Co.
- and change management, 52
- export pricing by, 1364-65

Data. *See also* Information
- analysis of, 294-95
- availability of, in business-to-business versus consumer marketing, 960-61
- comparability and equivalence across markets for global markets, 1280
- equivalence and comparability and local market expansion, 1291-96
- evaluation in performance monitoring, 1212-13
- interpretation and cultural bias, 1296
- limitations due to quantity and quality of in database marketing, 440
- quantity of in survey research, 311-12

Database marketing, 419-45
- antecedents of, 419-20
- case studies in, 435-39
- versus conventional marketing, 424-28
- dawn of new era, 421-22
- definition of, 422-24
- economics of, 433-35
- efficiency and effectiveness of marketing expenditures, 427-28
- elements of programs, 428
  - media of, 428-32
  - offer in, 432
  - package in, 432-33
- emergence of computer technology, 420-21
- growth of statistical sophistication, 421
- inhibitors to success, 439
  - acquiring customer information, 439-40

computer literacy in the marketing organization, 440-41
limitations due to the quantity and quality of data, 440
slowness to change, 441
organizational impact of, 441-45
agency retention and acquisition, 443-44
customer retention and customer acquisition specialists, 441-42
installed-base marketing, 444-45
knowledge-based systems experts, 442-43
lifetime value of customer, 444
measurement and management of customer affinity, 442
relationship marketing, 421

Data collection
control of environment in survey research, 310-11
cost of, 1279
flexibility of, and survey research, 306
in global markets, 1279-80
and local market expansion, 1294-96
preliminary, in local market expansion, 1289-90
problems of, in global markets, 1278-81
in researching industrial products and services, 1050-57

Datastart, 486

Datastream, 486

Dayton Hudson, 902

DDB Needham advertising agency, 1194

Decision framework for export pricing, 1368-73

Decision Labs, Ltd., 256

Decision process approach in determining customer wants and needs, 154-55

Decision support systems and information provision, 485

Decision-theory models, 361-62

Decorating Den, 929

Delphi technique, 690

Delta Airlines, 1216

Deluxe Corporation, 797

Demand
in business-to-business versus consumer marketing, 951-53
and pricing, 844, 862-63

Demand curve theory
booking curve capacity management, 938
and yield management, 937

Demand-side management program, 226

Demand-side marketing, 687

De Mar, 792, 798

Demographics in global marketing, 1284
in sizing markets, 456
in segmentation, 177-78

Demonstration diskettes, 1121

Demonstrations in sales training, 1128, 1132

Deontological reasoning, 627-28

Depth interviews, 281, 402

Descriptive mathematical model, 361

Deterministic mathematical model, 361

Deutsch, David, 1171

Developing countries
mall interviews in, 319
personal survey research in, 317-18
telephone interviewing in, 316

Development committee and organizing for marketing, 194

Dialogue, women's language in spoken, 1239

Dichter, Ernest, 279, 280, 282, 283

Differential advantage, theory of, 542

Differential-copy advantage, 1159-60

Differentiation, 145
as marketing strategy, 6-7, 848

Diffusion of innovations, 775
communication and diffusion, 781
distinguishing characteristics of mass media and interpersonal channels, 781
implications, 783-84
interaction of mass media and interpersonal channels, 781-82
resistance to diffusion, 782-83
unit of adoption, 775
characteristics of individuals as adopting units, 778-79
decision-making processes, 776-78
defining the relevant units, 775-76

Digestion, 1175

Direct costs, 752

Direct mail, 1118-21. *See also* Direct marketing
advantages of, 1118
catalogs in, 1121
for database marketing, 430
demonstration diskettes in, 1121
enclosures in, 1120-21
gifts in, 1121
package in, 1121
and public relations, 1201
response device in, 1121
sales letter in, 1119-20

Direct marketing, 1205, 1206. *See also* Direct mail
definition of, 1205
growth of, 1087
implications for designing and implementing effective integrated marketing communications programs, 1228
in international marketing promotion, 1338
opportunities/benefits in, 1206-20
performance tracking systems for, 1210
problems with, 1220
strategies in, 1205

Direct product profitability (DPP), 911

Direct response mechanisms, 1205

Discount Shopping Service, 498

Discover credit and value marketing, 47

Discriminate analysis in analysis research of industrial products and services, 1058

Disneyland, 9

Disney World, 9

Dispute resolution, 1351-52

Distribution efficiency, 755

Distribution strategies, 572

Distribution system, 1360-61
customer-driven, 869-79
bounding ideal, 873-74
comparing options, 874-76
confronting gap, 877-78
costs in, 872-73
deciding on appropriate outlets, 871-72
finding out what customers want, 869-71
preparing to implement, 878-79
reviewing pet assumptions, 876-77
as factor in export pricing, 1360-61
in marketing to business, 984-85
and sizing markets, 450
for take-back goods, 1352-54

Diversification, and change management, 52

Dodge, H. Robert, 1030

Dollar drafts, 1310

Dollar sales movement, 706

Dominant brands, 169
Domino's Pizza, 932
Donnelley, Reuben H., 420
Donnelly, James H., Jr., 356
Douglas, Susan P., 1276
Dow Corning, ethical audit at, 623-24
Doyle Dane Bernbach agency, 1168
Drakett Company, ethics programs at, 623
Dramatic scenarios, women's use of language in, 1238-40
Duffy, Mike, 698
Dumping, 608
Dun and Bradstreet, 1064
  Exporter's Encyclopedia, 1284
Dunn, S. Watson, 1156
Du Pont, 753
Dutka, Sol, 238

E

Econ-O-Cloth, and export pricing, 1367
Economic activity in sizing markets, 456-58
Economic buyer, 1113
Economic factors of global markets, 1284-87
Economic objectives, 137
Economic order quantity (EOQ), 363
Economic Statistics, 455
Economic structure in business-to-business versus consumer marketing, 953-59
Economist intelligence unit and data collection, 1280
EDIFACT (electronic data interchange for administration, commerce and transport), 497
Editors, 1108-12
Edsel, failure of, 333, 334
Edwards Personality Inventory, 282
Edwards Personal Preference Schedule, 98
Efficiency, 274
Efficiency control, 740, 753
Efforts to improve, 797
EFTPOS, 498
Ehrman, Chaim M., 446
Electronic bulletin boards, 1124
Electronic data interchange, 577
Electronic data process (EDP) systems and information provision, 485
Electronic markets in information technology, 492-93
Electronic media for database marketing, 432
Emerson, Frances B., 1106
Empire Video, 788-89
Employees
  in business communications, 1131-32
  commitment of, and consumer complaints, 384
  comparisons of, 100
  encouraging, in resolving complaints, 818
  motivation of, 58
Enclosures in direct mail packages, 1120-21
Entrepreneurship, 693-94
Entry strategy for international markets, 1323
Environmental changes, marketing research in, 242
Environmental considerations in marketing of raw materials, 1037
Environmental factors in globalization, 1268-69

Environmental information system in marketing mix, 576-77

Environmentalism and adaptivity, theory of, 541-42

Equal Employment Opportunity Commission (EEOC), 96-97

Equity joint venture, 1265-66

Ericsson, 1327

Error, random, 290

ESPRIT, 1265

Estimation problems, 289

Ethical audits, 623-24

Ethical behaviors, reasons for fostering, 612-13

Ethical culture, organizational commitment to, 620-24

Ethical decision making, 607-24
- contingency model in, 617
- emphasizing ethics in, 610-12
- establishing standards in, 631-32
- ethical issues and dilemmas in, 629-30
- frameworks for, 614-16
- ideal world in, 627-28
- issues and dilemmas in, 629-30
- marketing ethics in, 616
- methods of fostering ethical behavior in, 612-13
- moral development model in, 616
- practical considerations in, 632-34
- and public perception of business, 609-10
- real world in, 628-29
- reasoned action model in, 618
- reasons for unethical practices, 630-31
- role of marketing manager in, 610
- sequence of questions to improve reasoning in, 619-20

Ethics
- codes of, 190, 621-22, 632
- effect of, on managerial behavior, 610-12
- establishing standards in, 631-32
- in professional marketing, 188-89
- seminars/programs, 622-23

Ethnographic approaches, 284

European Community, 1331

European Economic Association (EEA), 1329

European Free Trade Association (EFTA), 1328-29

Evaluative criteria, and consumer wants and needs, 155

Evans, Franklin, 282

Evans, Joel R., 896

Event marketing, growth of, 1087

Exception reporting, 717, 720, 721

Exchange permits, 1306-7

Exclusive dealer proviso, 1353

Expansion in retailing, 909-10

Expectations/performance gap, closing, 392-93

Expenses-to-sales ratios, 746-47

Experimental design, 292-93

Experiment units, 292

Expert panel method of preevaluating style merchandise, 520, 523

Expert systems, 725

Exponential smoothing in sizing market, 459

Export declaration, 1304

Export-Import Bank, 1258

Exporting, 1323

Export License Application and Information Network (ELAIN), 1303

Export management companies, 1263-65

Export marketing, 1301
- foreign commercial payments, 1308-9
  - bills of exchange, 1310
  - letters of credit, 1309-10

foreign freight forwarder, 1315
free-trade zones, 1311, 1314
maquiladoras, 1314-15
special economic zone, 1315
import restrictions, 1305-8
international trade terms, 1311, 1312-13
national trade data bank, 1315-16
packing and marking, 1311
regulations and restrictions of exporting, 1301
export documents, 1303-5
Export License Application and Information Network (ELAIN), 1303
System for Tracking Export License Applications (STELA), 1303
U.S. export restrictions, 1301-3

Export pricing, 1357-73
alternative approaches to, 1363
dynamic incremental strategy, 1366-68
flexible cost-plus strategy, 1365-66
rigid cost-plus strategy, 1363-65
decision framework for, 1368
analyze special import, distribution, or transaction barriers, 1370
checking consistency with current pricing, 1370-71
corporate goals and preference for pricing, 1370
estimating sales potential, 1369
estimating target price range, 1369
implementation, 1371
monitoring, 1372-73
systematic selection of appropriate pricing strategy, 1370
verification of market potential, 1368
factors in, 1358-59
attitude of the firm's management, 1363
distribution system of, 1360-61
location and environment of the foreign market, 1361-63
location of production facility, 1359-60
nature of the product/industry, 1359
U.S. Government regulations, 1363
literature, 1357-58

Export promotion spending, 1258

Exports
cooperative, 1264
growth in world, 1253
U.S., 1254

Export trading companies, 1264

Export Trading Company Act (1982), 1258, 1264

Extractive industries, 948

Exxon, and trade characters, 1179

F

Factor analysis
in analysis research of industrial products and services, 1058
and consumer satisfaction, 28

Factory-outlet centers, 914

Fanta, 1330-31

Faris, Charles, 1067

FCB Strategy Planning Model, 1170

Feature story, 1111

Federal Express
and customer service, 815
and distribution, 869
and information technology, 488
recovery service of, 793

Federal Trade Commission
disclosure requirements for franchising, 929-30
and used car sales, 641

Federal Trade Commission Act (1914), 645, 864

Federal Trade Commission v. *Indiana Federation of Dentists,* 650-51

Federated Electronics Superstore, 904

Feedback in marketing concept, 59

Feminism, 1235-36. *See also* Women's language
- and reading by role reversal, 1241
- and women's language, 1240

Fidelity Investments, 1216

Field force, control of, in survey research, 311

Field-test marketing, 892-93

Fighting brand strategy, 885-86

Financial analysis, 746-47

Financial and foreign exchange data in global markets, 1283

Firm, objectives of, in setting prices, 859

First mover advantage, 458

First National Bank of Chicago
- in conducting personal interviews, 304
- and customer service, 815

Fisk, George, 220

Flanagan, Joseph P., 1146

Flanker brand strategy, 885

Flaring out, 1019
- with added augmentation, 1022-23
- by unbundling, 1020-22

Fletcher, Keith, 478

Flo-Con Systems, and export pricing, 1366

Floor pricing, 840

Flyers, 1116-18

Focus group
- in advertising message strategy, 1159
- in motivation research, 283-84
- in quantitative research, 271
- in researching industrial products and services, 1053-57
- in researching pioneer markets, 690
- and scientific sampling, 402

Forced-choice checklist, 100, 102

Ford Motor Company
- advertising slogans of, 66
- and global marketing, 1269
- use of market information at, 333-34

Forecasting
- Delphi technique in, 690
- in sizing markets, 456-60

Foreign commercial payments, 1308-9

Foreign corporations, as U.S. affiliates, 1254

Foreign Corrupt Practices Act (1977), 612

Foreign direct investment, growth in U.S., 1253

Foreign exchange risk, assessment of, 1283

Foreign freight forwarder, 1315

Foreign investments, and sizing markets, 448

Foreign market, location and environment of, as factor in export pricing, 1361-63

Foreign production, 1265-66

Foreign Sales Corporation, 1258

Format franchises, 919
- reasons for success of, 920-23
- trails of, 919-20

47 St. Photo, 871

Forward-buying, 702

Fox, Karen F. A., 824

Franchising, 919-34
- conglomerate dual distributor, 930-32
- definition of, 919
- earnings statements and claims, 930
- expansion techniques, 927
  - area development franchising, 928
  - conversion franchising, 928

subfranchising, 926-27
unit franchising, 927
format, 919
reasons for success of, 920-23
traits of, 919-20
FTC disclosure requirements, 929-30
future of, 932
choosing the franchisee, 934
inducements, 932-33
multimarketing franchisor, 933
product distribution in, 919
profits in, 925
initial franchising fee, 926
per diem fees, 927
property leases, 927
sale of goods and services, 925-26
service fees (royalties), 926-27
supplemental up-front fees, 926
reasons for joining systems, 923-24
state regulations, 930

Frazer, Charles, 1164

Free-form essay method, 102

Free-rider effect, 897

Free-trade zones, 1311, 1314

Frequency, 431, 1190

Frequency marketing, 1207-8

Frerichs, George R., 774

Frontier markets, 688-89

Fuji
and globalization, 1270
and strategic alliances, 1327

Fujitsu
direct foreign sales force of, 56-57
and globalization, 1269
and strategic alliances, 1327

Full-cost pricing, 752-53, 861

Future contracts, 1038

Future costs, and pricing, 861

G

Gallup, George, 255

Gamesmanship, 1076-77

Garda, Robert A., 946

Gardner, Burleigh B., 280, 283

GE Credit, and distribution, 872

General Agreement on Tariffs and Trade (GATT), 1256

General contractor, 964

General Electric Company (GE)
and identification of marketing concept, 7-8
marketing mix for, 575-76
as master of innovation, 694-96
and sales force size, 754

General Foods Corporation
and change management, 52
and efficiency control, 753
qualitative research at, 278
use of mall-intercept interviews by, 312
use of sensory panels by, 514

General marketing, 538

General Motors
and distribution, 874
and globalization, 1348
implementing inquiry center at, 347
reactions to environmentalists' concerns, 224

Generic names, 1181

Geographic mobility, 152

Geographic factors of global markets, 1284

Geographic segmentation, 177-78

Geographic structure, 1341

Gerber Products Company in Japanese market, 1324

Gifts, free, 1121

Giles, William D., 660

Gill, Robert B., 806

Glick, Ira O., 1136

Global corporation, 1319

Globalization, 1267-73. *See also* Global marketing; International distribution and selling; Internationalization
- challenges of, 1272
  - internal factors, 1272-73
  - market factors, 1272
- competitive moves, 1270, 1272
- location of value-added activities, 1270
- marketing approach, 1270
- market participation in, 1269-70
- product offering, 1270

Global marketing, 1249. *See also* Globalization; International distribution and selling; Internationalization
- barter and buybacks in, 1345-55
- export marketing, 1301-16
- export pricing, 1357-73
- international distribution and selling, 1319-42
- international marketing concepts in, 1253-74
- localizing, 1273
- raw materials in, 1034-35
- researching markets in, 1277-98
  - continuing need for information, 1296-97
  - data collection problems, 1278-81
  - information for initial market entry, 1281-89
  - information for local market expansion, 1289-96
  - information requirements, 1277-78

Glue, 75-76

Goal dimensions, and sales performance, 117-18

Goals, versus marketing objectives, 136-37

Goldman, A. E., 284

Goods, marketing characteristics of, 181-82

Good Samaritan Hospital, 798

Goodyear, and distribution, 869

Government, role of, in internationalization, 1257-58

Government-controlled pricing, 858

Government regulation, and marketing manager, 637-43

Grant, W. T., failure of, 902

Graphic aids in brochures, 1117-18

Green, Paul E., 552

Greenlining, 223

Green marketing, 221-33
- advantages of, 222
- blending elements of, 226-30
- conservation in, 227
- definition of, 221-24
- designing and launching strategy, 224-26
- evaluation of efforts in, 232-33
- impact audit of, 222-24
- improving cost-effectiveness in, 230-31
- pollution control in, 229
- principles in distinguishing from non-green marketing, 222
- proactive strategy in, 225-26
- recycling in, 227-29
- steps in developing program in, 222-24

Green movement, 372

Gross rating points (GRPs), 705

Group appraisal method, 102

Growth maximization, 82

Guerrilla warfare pricing, 969

Gunn, Sandy, 283

Gwynn, Robert, 283

H

Häagen-Dazs, and franchising, 931, 932

Habitat, 498

Haeckel, Steve, 340, 344

Haley, Russell I., 508

Hanna Mining, 1036
Hardin, David K., 588
Harley-Davidson
  and feedback, 796
  and measuring market share, 743-44
  service quality of, 789-90
Harper, Donald V., 856
Hathaway, 1172
Head & Shoulders, and product cannibalism, 881
Health care industry, yield management in, 937
HealthLine Products Incorporated, 23-25
  and niching, 26
  and product concept, 22-23
Henry, Harry, 281
Henry, William E., 280
Heritage positioning strategy, 71
Hertz, and yield management, 937
Herzberg, Frederick, job satisfaction theory of, 803, 809
Herzog, Herta, 283
Hesitancy in women's language, 1237-38
Heterogeneous market, 447
Hewlett-Packard Co., marketing research of, 329
Hierarchical summary scheme, 708
High Point Chemicals, 1017
Hill, Richard M., 1042
Hilton Hotels, and yield management, 937, 939-40
Holistic approach to qualitative research, 273
Holland Vocational Preference Inventory, 98
Home Depot, 904
Home market, production in, 1263-65
Homogeneous market segments, 447
Honda, and value marketing, 47
Honderich, Beland, 283
Honeywell Inc., 1120, 1122
Horizontal communications, and consumer satisfaction, 391
Hospital industry, use of yield management by, 940
Hot 'n Now, and franchising, 931
Household purchase sample data, 711-12
How-to features, 1199
Hughes, G. David, 254
Hulbert, James M., 626
Hunt, H. Keith, 636
Hyatt Hotels, and yield management, 939-40
Hygiene factors versus motivator, 809
Hypochondriacs, 179
Hypothesis testing, 289
  problems in, 289
Hyundai and strategic alliances, 1327
  international operations of, 1322
  marketing strategy of, 695
  and market participation, 1269, 1270
  sales force of, 58

I

IBM
  and distribution, 875, 876
  marketing strategy of, 848
  positioning by, 1169
IKEA, and globalization, 914, 1268
Illumination, 1175
Image advertising, 1225
Imagery, 1137
  changing, 1143-44
  content of, 1137-38
  corporate, 1139-40

illusions and facts, 1138
implications of, 1144
long- and short-range goals in, 1138-39

IMC programs. *See* Integrated marketing communications

Immersion, 1175

Impact audit in green marketing, 222-24

Imports. *See also* Export marketing
licenses for, 1307
restrictions on, 1305-8

In-bond program, 1314-15

Incentives, 1129-30

Incremental analysis, and product cannibalism, 888-89

Incrementalism, 666

Incremental pricing strategy in export pricing, 1366-68

Incremental volume sales, 709

Incubation, 1175

Individual differences, and job satisfaction, 127

Inducements for franchisee, 932-33

Industrial advertising, symbolism in, 1143

Industrial marketing. *See also* Marketing to business
segmenting in, 180-81

Industrial producer, role of, 153-54

Industrial products, marketing systems for, 31-32

Industrial raw materials, 1031
marketing functions, 1032-34
multiple uses and allocation decisions, 1031-32

Industry as factor in export pricing, 1359

Industry analysis and consultants, 1108

Industry bandwidth of working relationships, 1012

Information. *See also* Data; Data collection
adequacy of, 274
and consumer complaints as feedback in, 384
continuing need for, 1296-97
determining and collecting in pricing, 866
for initial market entry, 1281-89
in making market-entry decisions, 1288-89
organizational issues in collection of, 1281
requirements of in global markets, 1277-78

Informational advertising, 1163

Information technology, 479-505, 577
buyer/supplier power during exchange, 494-97
competition in, 497-98
computers in, 480-82
creation of new businesses within old, 498-500
definition of, 479
electronic markets in, 492-93
elements in, 479
firm-level impact of, 493-94
industry-level impact of, 489-90
information provision, 485-88
issues and problems in information use, 482-85
and just-in-time delivery, 495-97
and marketing, 479-80, 488-89
in marketing to business, 1000-1001
role of business in, 490-92
strategy-level impact of, 500-503

In-home interviews in international market research, 317-18

In-house use, 1352-53

Initial franchising fee, 926

Inner Response, Inc., 256

Innovation
attributes of, 780-81
definition of, 775
diffusion of, 775-84

Innovation decision making, 775
Innovation-driven companies, and market research, 693
Innovation-driven ventures, tests of, 692
Input/output of marketing system
consumer, 36-37
and control, 38-39
and marketing planning, 40-41
participants, 36
retailer, 37-38
Inquiry center, 338
fundamental value of, 345-49
Inside crusaders, 1075-77
Installed-base marketing, 425-26, 444-45
Institute for Personality and Ability Testing's Sixteen Personality Factors Questionnaire, 98
In-store consumer consultants, and consumer complaints, 384
Insurance policy or certificate as export documentation, 1305
Integrated customer contacts, 1100-1103
Integrated marketing communication (IMC), 1194, 1205-6, 1223-27
customer contacts in, 1085-1103
direct marketing implications for designing and implementing effective, 1228
opportunities/benefits, 1206-20
problems with, 1220
Integrative networks, 1287
Intel as master of innovation, 694-96
Internal analysis in marketing mix, 578-79
Internal barriers to practice marketing, 211-14
Internal market, 1328
International Advertising Association (IAA), 1287
International Computers Ltd., 1270
International distribution and selling, 1319-42
communication policies, 1339-40
Europe and the European community, 1328-29
factors that influence the establishment of international prices, 1334
competitive conditions, 1334-35
corporate policies, 1335-36
costs, 1334
legal and political conditions, 1335
market conditions, 1334
implications, 1341-42
internationalization, 1321-22
international marketing management, 1320-21
management, 1340-41
pricing policies, 1332-33
product planning and product policies, 1329-32
sales and distribution policies, 1336-39
strategic alliances, 1327-28
structure of international operations, 1322-23
assembly operations, 1326
contract manufacturing, 1325
exporting, 1323
joint venture, 1326-27
licensing, 1323-25
management contracting, 1325
manufacturing, 1325-26
International division structure, 1341
International Harvester, international operations of, 1322
Internationalization, 1254-56, 1321-22. *See also* Globalization; Global marketing
activities in, 1319
competition in, 1257
domestic market conditions in, 1257
exclusive market information in, 1256
following customer/competitors in, 1257

geographic proximity in, 1257-58
government incentives in, 1256
governmental role in, 1257-58
international market entry, 1258-59
entry modes, 1262-66
environmental challenges, 1259-61
international marketing planning, 1261-62
marketing management, 1320-21
overproduction/excess capacity in, 1257
potential/opportunity in, 1256
product/technological advantage in, 1256
profit advantage, 1256
retailing in, 914-15
standardization versus adaptation in, 1266-67
survey methods in, 315-20
evaluation of methods in, 320-23
survey methods in, 315

International Trade Administration (ITA), 1315

International trade terms, 1311, 1312-13

Interviewer bias, potential for, in survey research, 313-14

Interviews
depth, 281, 402
mail, 305
cost of, 314
data collection environment in, 311
diversity of questions in, 308
flexibility of data collection in, 306
in international marketing research, 319-20, 321, 322
perceived anonymity in, 313
physical stimuli in, 308
quantity of data in, 312
questionnaires, in researching industrial products and services, 1052-53
response rate in, 312-13
sample control in, 309-10
speed in, 314
non-directive, 281
personal
computer-assisted, 304
bias in, 313
control of field force in, 311
cost of, 314
data collection environment in, 310
diversity of questions in, 308
flexibility of data collection in, 306
perceived anonymity in, 313
physical stimuli in, 308
potential for interviewer bias in, 313
quantity of data in, 312
sample control in, 308
social desirability/sensitive information in, 313
speed of, 314
in-home, 304
control of field force in, 311
cost of, 314
data collection environment in, 310-11
diversity of questions in, 306, 308
flexibility of data collection in, 306
perceived anonymity in, 313
physical stimuli in, 308
potential for interviewer bias, 313-14
quantity of data in, 311-12
response role in, 312
sample control in, 308
social desirability/sensitive information in, 313
speed of, 314
mall-intercept, 304
control in, 308
control of field force in, 311
cost of, 314
data collection environment in, 310
diversity of questions in, 306, 308
flexibility of data collection in, 306

perceived anonymity in, 313
physical stimuli in, 308
potential for interviewer bias in, 313-14
quantity of data in, 312
response role in, 312
sample control in, 308
social desirability/sensitive information in, 313
speed of, 314
and recruitment, 122
telephone methods of
computer-assisted, 302-3
control of field force in, 311
cost of, 314
data collection environment in, 310
diversity of questions in, 308
flexibility of data collection in, 306
in international marketing research, 315-16, 321
perceived anonymity in, 313
physical stimuli in, 308
potential for interviewer bias, 314
quantity of data in, 312
response rate in, 313
sample control in, 308
social desirability/sensitive information in, 313
speed of, 314
traditional, 302
control of data collection environment, 311
control of field force in, 311
flexibility in data collection, 306
quantity of data in, 311, 312
response rate in, 312
sample control in, 308-9

Inventory models, 362-63

IRS-Dialtech, 486

Itoh, C., international operations of, 1322

Ivancevich, John M., 356

Ivory Soap, and green marketing, 231

J

Jackson, Barbara Bund, 806-7

Jacobs Succhard A.G., and change management, 52

Jack Daniels, and brand loyalty, 1209-10

Japanese companies, advertising strategy of, 57

Jim Beam Brands, and change management, 52

Job analysis, and effective recruitment, 119-20

Job satisfaction, 121-25, 122
antecedents of, 125-27
organizational commitment, 124
and sales performance, 122-23
theory of, 809
turnover, 124-25

Job-task variables, and job satisfaction, 126-27

John Deere Company, and competitive analysis, 578

Johnson & Johnson
and efficiency controls, 753
ethics code of, 621, 622

Joint venture, 1326-27
equity, 1265-66

Judgment, role of, in pricing, 866

Junior professional, and organizing for marketing, 194

Jury of execute opinion in sizing market, 458

Just-in-time (JIT) delivery, and information technology, 495-97

K

Kaatz, Ronald B., 1084

Kassarjian, Hal, 283

Katona, George, 280

Kawasaki Heavy Industries, and strategic alliances, 1327

Kelly Tires, 71

Kerin, Roger A., 880

Keynote speeches, 1124-25

Key performance indicators (KPIs), 91

Kidvantage, and value marketing, 47

King Kullen, 900

Kleid Company, 420

Kleining, Gerhardt, 283

KLM, international operations of, 1322

Kmart, 900
  point-of-sale scanning at, 699

Knorr Soups, 1330

Kodak
  and competition, 1270
  and use of marketing research, 245
  recycling program at, 228-29

Kohlberg, Lawrence, 616

Komatsu, and globalization, 1269

Korvette, E. J., failure of, 902

Kotler, Philip, 738

Kraft
  and change management, 52
  marketing strategy of, 71

Krugman, Dean M., 1156

Kuder Preference Record Vocational Form CP, 98

L

Labor force needs in retailing, 912-13

Laczniak, Gene R., 606

Land-O-Lakes, 1141

Language
  hesitancy in, 1237-38
  verbal excess, 1238
  women's, 1234-36
    and advertising, 1238-45

Lanham Trade-Mark Act, 1178

Latent content, advertising studies of, 1233-34

Launch decision, and sizing markets, 448

Lay, Cindy, 1215-16

Layering, as marketing strategy, 68-71

Lazer, William, 570

Lazersfeld, Paul F., 255-57, 278, 279

Lazersfeld-Stanton system, reliability of, 255

Leaders, 675

Lead-user accounts, 1017-18

Leap-frog accounts, 1017-18

Learning
  consumer and brand preference, 164-65
  role of, in purchase behavior, 15

Leaseway Transportation, 1022

Legal and regulatory data in global markets, 1283-84

Legal considerations in pricing, 864, 1335

Leonard, Stew, 798, 799

Leonhard, Dietrich, 283

Lethert, Joseph, 220

Letters of credit, 1309-10

Leveraged buyouts (LBOs), 909

Levy, Sidney J., 270, 1136

Licensing, 1265, 1323-25
  as export documentation, 1302, 1305
  of names, 1179

lifestyle data, 1189

Limited, Inc., 904

Linear programming model, 363

Literacy
  and international marketing research, 322
  and use of mail interviews, 319, 320

Locational strategies in retailing, 913-14

Lockheed Dialog, 486

London Metal Exchange, 1038

Longman, Kenneth, 1159

Long-range monitoring, 240

Lot size, 870

Lucas, Darrell B., 398

Lynn, Robert A., 598

M

Macfield Texturing Company, 1014-15

MacNab, Bruce E., 536

Macroeconomic environment and global marketing, 1260-61

Macroenvironmental analysis, 580

Macy's, 900

Magazine, for database marketing, 430

MAGIC (Marketing and Advertising General Information Centre), 487

MAID (Media Analysis and Information Database), 487

Mail order copy, testing of, 404

Mail panels, 305
- cost of, 314
- data collection environment in, 311
- diversity of questions in, 308
- flexibility of data collection in, 306
- in international marketing research, 320, 321
- physical stimuli in, 308
- quantity of data in, 312
- response rate in, 313
- sample control in, 310
- speed in, 314

Mail surveys, 302, 305
- cost of, 314
- data collection environment in, 311
- diversity of questions in, 308
- flexibility of data collection in, 306
- in international marketing research, 319-20, 321, 322
- perceived anonymity in, 313
- physical stimuli in, 308
- quantity of data in, 312
- questionnaires, in researching industrial products and services, 1052-53
- response rate in, 312-13
- sample control in, 309-10
- speed in, 314

Makens, James C., 936

Makers Mark Distillery, 52

Malhotra, Naresh K., 300

Mall intercept, 304
- control in, 308
- control of field force in, 311
- cost of, 314
- data collection environment in, 310
- diversity of questions in, 306, 308
- flexibility of data collection in, 306
- perceived anonymity in, 313
- physical stimuli in, 308
- potential for interviewer bias in, 313-14
- quantity of data in, 312
- response role in, 312
- sample control in, 308
- social desirability/sensitive information in, 313
- speed of, 314

Management
- attitude of, as factor in export pricing, 1363
- commitment to ethics, 621
- marketing, 43-46, 50-51, 152-53
- role of, in marketing campaign, 468-69

Management by objectives, 102, 739

Management contracting, 1325

Management information systems (MIS), 1217-18

Management program, demand side, 226

Management science, 357-69
boundaries of, 358-59
constructing models, 365-68
growth of, 358
popular models in, 361
allocation, 363
brand-switching, 364
break-even, 362
decision-theory, 361-62
inventory, 362-63
network, 363-64
simulation, 364
waiting-line, 364
practical value of mathematical models for marketers, 359-60
role of the computer in, 359
traditional bases for marketing decisions in, 357-58
types of mathematical models, 360-61

Managerial behavior, effect of ethics on, 610-12

Mandatory adaptation, 1331

Manufacturers, pricing by, 864-65

Manufacturer shipment, sales information from, 701-4

Manufacturers' representatives, and export pricing, 1360

Manufacturing, 948, 1325-26

Mapping teams in improving service design, 794-95

Maquiladoras, 1314-15

Market
complexity of, in business-to-business versus consumer marketing, 953
conditions of, in establishing international prices, 1334
definition of, 175, 447

Market and customer analysis, in marketing mix, 579-80

Market-based decisions, 329-54
inquiry center, 338
connections in, 345
creating new solutions in, 345
fundamental value in, 345-49
law of the lens, 339-94
logical analysis, 344-45
voice of the market, 338
management dilemma in, 331
factors discouraging better information use, 331-32
need for better information use, 331
myths of information use, 332-37
perspectives of information acquisition and use, 337-38
in pricing, 839
steps to ensure value need of, 350
anticipating unwelcome results, 353-54
asking managers to predict important data outcomes, 350
determining comfort zones of managers, 350-51
developing simulated data, 352
identifying likely areas of uncertainty, 351-52
performing action audits, 353

Market-based strategies, 840

Market Compilation and Research Bureau, 420

Market coverage, role of sales force in, 989-90

Market decentralization, 870

Market-driven behavior, encouraging, 394

Market-driven quality (MDQ), 47

Market entry, information for initial into global market, 1281-89

Market expansion, information for local, 1289-96

Market factors in globalization, 1268

Market gaps, theory of, 539-40

Marketing
cause, 120
commercial, 825-26
customer satisfaction and, 26-28
definition of, 8, 463
demand-side, 687

differentiation and competitive advantage in, 6-7
ethics in. *See* Ethical decision making
evolution of modern, 7-8
export, 1301-16
frequency, 1207-8
green, 221-33
of industrial raw materials, 1032-34
information technology in, 479-80
installed base, 425-26
linking quality to, 45-47, 60
Maslow's hierarchy of needs in, 11-12
myths about, 6-7
needs and wants in, 12-13
one-on-one, 426-27
purchase motivation in, 9-11
questions about, 5-6
relationship, 812, 1206, 1219, 1228
social, 825-32
supply-side, 687-88, 694-95
tactical, 19-21
value, 46-47
to women, 44, 45

Marketing and sales productivity systems (MSP), and information technology, 500

Marketing audit, 197-98, 756-64
characteristics of, 756-57
components of, 757, 760-63
definition of, 756
example of, 763-64
procedures in, 757

Marketing campaign, 463-76
attitude, 474-75
background or historical data, 472
definition of, 463-66
elements of the campaign strategy, 468
external situation in, 466
feedback and adjustment, 468
flip-chart presentation, 475-76
internal situation in, 466
new market facts, 472
objectives of, 464-65, 472-73
preparation of plan in, 466-76
preparatory data, 471-72
reader benefit, opportunity, and reward, 470-71
role of management in, 468-69
role of retailer in, 469
selling the plan, 468
sequence of events, 473-74
thoroughness, 473
writing style, 475

Marketing change, developing coordinated comprehensive, 828

Marketing channels for take-back goods, 1352
adding to the line, 1353
fobbing off to new customers, 1353-54
in-house use, 1352-53

Marketing communication, and sales promotion, 1152-53

Marketing concept, 43-61
acceptance of change and environmental orientation, 60
customer determination, 60
definition of, 43
determining nature of company's business, 54-55
feedback in, 59
foundation, 43
linking quality and marketing, 46-47
marketing management in, 43-46
social responsibility in marketing management, 50-51
strategic alliances, 47, 50
identification of customer set, 55-56
importance of disciplined planning, 61
linking quality and marketing, 60
management of change in, 51-52
market intelligence system, 61
marketplace environment, 52-54
monitoring and measuring the results, 58-59, 61
organizing the effort and applying resources, 57-58
product, sales, and distribution strategy, 56-57

product planning and development, 61
social responsibility, 61
strategic alliances, 61
theory of, 542-43

Marketing control, types of, 740

Marketing decision, 589-96
criterion for decision, 590-91
monetary measures, 591-93
nonmonetary measures, 594
decision delay, 594-95
ethical. *See* Ethical decision making
implications, 595-96
marketing alternatives in, 589-90

Marketing-effectiveness rating instrument, 758-59

Marketing-effectiveness rating review, 755-56

Marketing entities, assigning functional expenses to the, 749

Marketing-environment audit, 760

Marketing excellence review, 764

Marketing executives, and marketing planning, 40-41

Marketing expense-to-sales analysis, 744-45

Marketing expense-to-sales ratio, 744

Marketing failure, cost of, 463

Marketing-function audits, 762-63

Marketing-function staffing. *See* Staffing the marketing function

Marketing information system (MIS), and information provision, 485

Marketing intelligence system, 61

Marketing management
improving, 152-53
in marketing concept, 43-46
social responsibility in, 50-51

Marketing manager, emphasis on ethics for, 610-12

Marketing mix, 15-16, 571-86
competition analysis in, 577-78
continuous monitoring and adjustment in, 581
at corporate level, 572
current challenges in, 581-83
definition of, 571
environmental information system in, 576-77
extending, 583-84
internal analysis in, 578-79
levels of, 572-74
market and customer analysis in, 579-80
and marketing strategy, 602-3
new, 28
nonbusiness, 584-85
at product level, 574
at strategic business unit perspective, 572
and systems thinking, 574-76
target marketing selection in, 580-81

Marketing objectives, 135-48

Marketing organization
commitment to ethical culture, 620-24
reasons for fostering ethical behavior, 612-13

Marketing-organization audit, 761

Marketing performance, 739-68
advertising efficiency
annual-plan control, 739-40
corrective action, 747
customer-satisfaction tracking, 747
defining and measuring market share, 743
financial analysis, 746-47
marketing expense-to-sales analysis, 744-45
market-share analysis, 742-43
sales analysis, 740-42
company ethical and social responsibility review, 764, 766
corrective action, 747
customer-satisfaction tracking, 747
defining and measuring market share, 743

determining best corrective action, 750-51
direct versus full costing, 751-53
distribution efficiency, 755
efficiency control, 753
advertising efficiency, 754
company ethical and social responsibility review, 764, 766
distribution efficiency, 755
marketing audit, 756-64
marketing-effectiveness rating review, 755-56
marketing excellence review, 764
salesforce efficiency, 753-54
sales-promotion efficiency, 854
financial analysis, 746-47
marketing audit, 756-64, 757
marketing-effectiveness rating review, 755-56
marketing excellence review, 764
marketing expense-to-sales analysis, 744-45
market-share analysis, 742-43
methodology of marketing-profitability analysis, 748-50
profitability control, 747-48
determining best corrective action, 750-51
direct versus full costing, 751-53
methodology of marketing-profitability analysis, 748-50
sales analysis, 740-42
salesforce efficiency, 753
sales-promotion efficiency, 754
strategic control, 755

Marketing plan, 549
business-to-business selling, 1067-79
developing, 206-10
coordinated, 828
implications of marketing systems for, 40-41
international, 1261-62
marketing decision in, 589-96
marketing mix in, 571-86
in marketing raw materials, 1031-39
marketing strategy in, 599-604
in marketing to business, 947-1009
market position analysis in, 549-67
partnering in, 1011-28
research on industrial products and services, 1043-1064

Marketing planners in planning marketing campaigns, 466

Marketing position analysis, 553-67
cluster analysis of joint-space coordinates, 565-67
computer firm images in, 554-55
correspondence analysis, 554, 563, 567
drug products in, 555
high-nutrition cereals in, 555
illustration of, 556
analyzing the data, 558
clustering results, 562
method in, 556-57
scaling results, 558-62
implications of, 562
multidimensional scaling, 553-54
recent developments, 563-67
soft drink slogans in, 554

Marketing-productivity audit, 762

Marketing-profitability analysis, methodology of, 748-50

Marketing program, assigning role to price in, 866

Marketing programming, improving, 153

Marketing research, 239-50, 301
See also International marketing research
continuous measurement instruments in, 255-66
differences between market research and, 245-46
manager-researcher relationship in, 246-50
market-based decisions in, 329-54

nature and scope of, 243-46
primary orientation, 239
qualitative research in, 271-84
role of, 239
acquisitions, 242-43
control function, 240, 242
developmental function, 240
monitoring environmental changes, 242
relationship of goals and objectives to research strategy and functions, 239-40
survey methods of data collection, 301-2
classified by mode of administration, 302
comparative evaluation of survey methods, 305-14
control of field force in, 311
control of the data collection environment, 310-11
cost, 314
diversity of questions in, 306, 308
flexibility of data collection in, 306
mail interviews, 319-20
mail methods, 305
mail panels, 320
mall intercept and CRT interviews, 318-19
perceived anonymity in, 313
personal interviews, 317-18
personal methods, 304
potential for interviewer bias in, 313-14
quantity of data in, 311-12
response rate in, 312-13
sample control in, 308-10
selection of survey method, 314
social desirability/sensitive information, 313
speed, 314
telephone interviewing and CATI, 315-16
telephone methods, 302-3
use of physical stimuli in, 308

Marketing research-to-sales ratio, 744

Marketing role behavior, theory of, 543-44

Marketing segmentation, developing, 153

Marketing strategies, 15, 65-76, 599-604
competitor-based approaches, 603-4
customer service in, 805-7
evaluation, 604
generic strategy articulation, 71-72
in-depth analysis, 72
implementation as communication, 65-75
importance of, 805-7
and information technology, 488-89
internal strategic focus, 66-68
maps, 66-67
site visits, 67-68
managerial communication as strategic glue, 75-76
market and the competition, 599
marketing goals in, 601
marketing mix in, 15-16, 602-3
marketing tactics, 19-21
optimal and incremental goals, 601
and organization levels, 600
and overall strategies, 599
positioning in, 17-18
primacy of implementation, 68-71
strategic objectives in, 600-3
success in, 16-17
tactics and implementation, 599-600
types of strategists, 600
unfocused and ambiguous strategy language, 72-75

Marketing-strategy audit, 761

Marketing systems, 31-41
analysis, 39-40
chain retailer in, 33-34
implications for marketing planning, 40-41
industrial products in, 31-32

input/output and system control, 38-39
input/output participants, 36
consumer, 36-37
retailer, 37-38
with one independent middleman, 33
structure interrelationships, 35-36
with two independent middlemen, 34
vertically integrated consumer goods in, 32-33

Marketing-systems audit, 761-62

Marketing tactics, 19-21

Marketing theory, 537-39
of consumer behavior, 543
differential advantage, 542
environmentalism and adaptivity, 541-42
implications of, 545-46
market gaps, 539-40
of marketing role behavior, 543-44
nature and origin of, 537-39
of social responsibility, 544-45
of specialization and integration, 540-41
of marketing concept, 542-43
of value, 540

Marketing to business, 947-1009
advertising and sales promotion, 995
availability of data, 960-61
business-to-business versus consumer marketing, 950
availability of data, 960-61
economic structure, 953-59
market complexity, 953
nature of demand, 951-53
definition of business sector, 947-50
distribution channels, 984-85
economic structure, 953-59
information technology, 1000
market complexity, 953
marketing implementation, 1001
diagnosing implementation problems, 1005
guidelines for implementation success, 1005, 1007-9
levels of execution, 1004-5
skills needed for marketing implementation, 1001-3
market selection and product policy, 961-68
nature of demand, 951-53
postsale service, 998
pricing, 968-69
strategic, 969-79
tactical, 979-84
sales force effectiveness, 985

Marketing to nonexistent markets, 687-96
American Airlines in, 694-96
Apple Computer in, 694-96
Campbell Soup in, 694-96
customer benefits and value in, 691-92
establishing commercial priorities in, 692-93
frontier markets in, 688-89
General Electric in, 694-96
Intel in, 694-96
3M in, 694-96
masters of innovation in, 694-96
Merck in, 694-96
Philip Morris in, 694-96
researching pioneer markets in, 689-91
role of entrepreneurship in, 693-94

Market intelligence system, 55-56

Market level facts, 710

Market operation, costs of, in global markets, 1287

Marketplace
changes in, 1086-87
clutter in, 897
environment in, 52-54

Market planning process, 661-84
agenda in, 682-84
continuous competitive renewal, 661-84
conventional market planning models, 662, 664

dimensions of, 667
analytical, 667-68
behavioral, 668-69
organizational, 669
research evidence, 669-70
managing dimensions of, 670
analytical, 671-74
behavioral, 674-77
organizational, 678-82
problems in, 664-67

Market position and diagnostic reports, 714
change reports, 717, 718
competitive monitoring, 715-16
exception reporting, 717, 720, 721
ranking reports, 717, 719
trend reports, 714-15
workstation reporting, 717, 722

Market potential
indicators of, in global markets, 1284-87
verification of, and export pricing, 1368

Market pricing, 857

Market program, role of price in the, 860

Market research
differences between marketing research and, 245-46
implications, 1064
on industrial products and services, 1043-64
basic types of studies, 1059
customer analysis, 1063-64
market size measurements, 1059-61
sales analysis, 1061-62
sales forecasting, 1062-63
lack of infrastructure in, 1290-91
measurement in, 245
organization and operation of, 1045-46
analysis of data, 1058
data collection, 1050-57
follow-up, 1058-59
planning the investigation, 1047-50
presentation of results, 1058
problem definition and statement of objectives, 1046-47
pioneer markets in, 689-91
types of studies, 1043-64

Market restructuring, 53

Market saturation, and retailing, 913

Market segmentation, 175-83. *See also* Segmentation
of consumer markets, 180
definition of, 175-76, 447
demographic, 177-78
framework for, 25-26
geographic, 177-78
of industrial markets, 180-81
marketing characteristics of goods and services, 181-82
and marketing mix, 579-80
in pricing, 975, 977
principle of, 176
by product application and customer capabilities, 1013-14
psychographic, 178-79
by rate of product usage, 178
requirements for meaningful, 176-77
ultimate consumers and industrial users, 179-81

Market selection and product policy, in marketing to business, 961-68

Market share
defining and measuring, 743-44
determination of, 139-40
overall, 743
served, 743-44
use of, as objectives, 141

Market-share analysis, 742-43, 1043

Market-share measures, 147-48

Market size measurements in researching industrial products and services, 1059-61

Market strategy, linking pricing strategy to, 847-48

Market structure and nature of competition, 863

Marks and Spencers, 498-99

Markup pricing, 840

Marlboro, positioning by, 1169

Marshall's, 904

Martineau, Pierre, 281, 283

Mary Kay Cosmetics, 798

Maslow's hierarchy of needs, 11-12

MAS Marketing, 806

Mason, J. Barry, 370

Mass media. *See* Media

Mass media marketing, 1085-86

MasterCare auto service centers, 805

Masters, 900

Master strategy, 81-83

Mathematical models
- practical value of, for marketers, 359-60
- types of, 360-61

Matrix organization, 1341

Matsushita Electric Industrial Co. v. *Zenith Radio Corp.*, 652, 654-56, 657-58

May, 904

MBNA America, and customer retention, 817

MCC, 1265

McCann-Erickson, 1161

McCollum/Spielman Research, 256

McDonald's Corporation, 900
- and franchising, 931, 932
- and globalization, 915, 1268
- and green marketing, 223-24
- and trade characters, 1179
- and unit franchising, 927

McDonnell Douglas, ethics programs at, 623

McIntyre, O. E., 420

McKay, Edward S. (Ted), 8

McMennamin, John L., 552

McMillan, Hugh, 283

MEAL (Media Expenditure and Analysis Ltd.), 487

Measurability, and market segmentation, 176

Measurement of market and sales potential, 1043

Measuring media profitability, 414-15

Media
- creativity in, 1194
- in database marketing, 428-32
- evaluating choices in, 1192
- expanding options in, 1088-90
- measurement of, 410-11
- measuring profitability of, 414-15
- proliferation of, 1193-94
- qualitative evaluation of, 414
- quantitative evaluation of, 411-14
- replacement with segmented media, 1192-93
- writing objectives and strategies, 1191

Media creativity, 1194

Media flow charts, 1091

Media planning. *See also* Advertising
- budget for, 1188-89
- choosing target markets, 1189-90
- determining where to advertise, 1190
- evaluating media choices, 1191
- evaluating creative message, 1190
- executing, 1192
- marketing goals and strategies, 1188
- marketing problems in, 1187-88
- post-analysis in, 1192
- problems in, 1192
  - integrated marketing communications, 1194
  - media creativity, 1194
  - media proliferation, 1193-94
  - problem and the opportunity, 1193
  - segmented media replacing mass media, 1192-93
- purpose of, 1187

putting it together into media plan, 1191-92
setting reach and frequency levels, 1190-91
studying competitors' strategies, 1188
writing media objectives and strategies, 1191

Media research, focus of, 399

Meetings, 1132

Mellon Bank, 498

Mercedes Benz, and value marketing, 47

Merchandising, scrambled, 813-14

Merchandising strategy, 961

Merchantable products in compensation arrangements, 1351

Merchant middlemen in marketing of raw materials, 1037

Merck, as master of innovation, 694-96

Merge/purge programs, 420-21

Mergers in retailing, 909-10

Merrill Lynch
and distribution, 872, 876-77
positioning strategy of, 1243

Merton, Robert K., 278

Mervyn's, 902

Message planning, 1157-58

Michelob Beer
positioning by, 1169
promotional campaign of, 69, 71

Michigan National Bank, ethics codes of, 621

Microeconomic environment and global marketing, 1261

Microsales analysis, 741-42

Micro-Vision, 1189

Midas, and distribution, 869

Middleman
in marketing of raw materials, 1036-37
marketing system with one independent, 33
marketing system with two independent, 34
specialist, 1353

Mighty Dog, 1208

Miles, Virginia, 283

Miller Brewing Company
and competitive advantage, 171
and flanker brand strategy, 885
and product positioning, 1169

Milliken Company, 1019

Mills, Glen Raven, 1014

Minnesota Multiphasic Personality Inventory, 98

Mintel, 487

Minute Maid, 1036

Miracle, Gordon E., 1318

Missionaries, 675

Mitsubishi, 1327

Mobility
geographical, 152
psychic, 152-53
social, 152

Modular printed instruction in sales training, 1128

Molly Maids, 929

Monetary measures for marketing decision, 591-93

Monetary systems and global marketing, 1259-60

Monsanto Co. v. *Spray-Rite Service Corp.*, 652-53

Montgomery Ward, 419, 900

Moody's, 1064

Moore, Harriett Bruce, 283

Moral development model of marketing ethics, 616-17

Moral dilemma in allocation of raw material, 1031-32

Morita, Akio, 335

Morris, Michael H., 834

Most favored customer rights, 1354

Mothercare, 498

Motivation in sales performance, 109, 116-17

Motivation research, 281-84

Motorola, 1018
 Semiconductor Sector of, 1024, 1026

Moving averages in sizing market, 458-59

Mr. Clean, 1141

MRI (Mediamark Research Incorporated), 1189

Multidimensional scaling, 553-54

Multimarketing franchisor, 933

Multi-media self-paced instruction in sales training, 1128

Multi-media technologies, 1121-22

Multinational corporation (MNC), 1319. *See also* Globalization; Global Marketing; International distribution and selling; Internationalization
 pricing by, 1358

Multiple goal achievement, testing of, 84

Multiple regression in analysis research of industrial products and services, 1058

Multistep promotion, 433

Murphy, Patrick E., 606

Myers, John, 1169

N

Names, licensed, 1179

Narus, James A., 1010

Narver, John C., 329

National Advertising Review Council, 632

National Association of Purchasing Agents
 and distribution, 869
 ethics codes of, 632

National Collegiate Athletic Association v. *Board of Regents of the University of Oklahoma,* 649-50

National trade data bank, 1315-16

Nault, James, 968

NEC, 1345
 direct foreign sales force of, 56, 57

Needed items, determining characteristics of, in business-to-business selling, 1068-70

Needs
 identifying, in marketing, 12-13
 Maslow's hierarchy of, 11-12
 recognition of, in business-to-business selling, 1068

Nestlé Company
 and ethical behavior, 613
 international operations of, 1322

Network models, 363-64

Newman, Joseph W., 281

New products
 market measurements for, 1060-61
 price crunch as cause of failure, 835
 proliferation of, 1087
 tracking of, 733

Newsletters and public relations, 1201

Newspapers for database marketing, 431

News releases, 1199

News services, 1131-32

New United Motor Manufacturing (NUMMI), 1266

Niche marketing, 5, 26
 and marketing concept, 44
 as marketing strategy, 848

Nicolet Instrument Corporation, and export pricing, 1365

NICs (newly industrialized countries), telephone survey research in, 315-16

Nielsen, Art, 699

Nielsen Market Research and Information Resources, 700

NIH-syndrome, 1273

Nike, and customer contacts, 1091

Nokia Mobile Phones, and globalization, 1272

Nonbusiness marketing, place in the, 585

Nonbusiness setting, monitoring program effectiveness, 585

Non-directive interview, 281

Nonmonetary measures in marketing decisions, 594

Non-profit setting, product and service mix in, 584

Nonresponse bias in survey research, 312

Nonstore retailing, 914

Non-tariff barriers, 1307-8

Nontraceable common costs, 752

Nordstrom Rack, 904

Norelco, and ethical decision making, 607

Normative mathematical model, 361

North American Free Trade Agreement (NAFTA), 1258

Northern Pacific Railway Co. v. *United States,* 646

Not-invented-here (NIH) syndrome, 1272

N.V. Philips Gloelampenfabrieken, 1322

NYNEX, and distribution, 875

O

Objectives
- corporate, 135
- economic, 137
- marketing, 135-48

O'Brien Candy Company, 763

O'Dell, William F., 588

Offer in database marketing, 432

Off-price centers, 914

Off-price retailers, 897-916

Ogilvy, David, 1167-68, 1171, 1172, 1175, 1182, 1215

Ogilvy & Mather, 1167-68

Ohrbach, 914

Old American Insurance, 420

Omnibus Trade and Competitiveness Act (1988), 1315

One-on-one marketing, 426-27

One Source Supply, and franchising, 931

On-time conversation studies, 1210-13

OPEC, 1034

Optimum reorder point, 363

Order routine, carrying out, in business-to-business selling, 1077-78

Organizational commitment, and job satisfaction, 124

Organizational dimension, managing, 678-82

Organizational mindset, 666

Organizational planning dimension, 669

Organization restructuring, 53

Organoleptic testing, 515

Original equipment manufacturers (OEMs), 1129

ORTEK Labs, 256

Osborn, Alex, 1177
O'Toole, John, 1157, 1164, 1194
Outcome-related activities, 805
Overall market share, 743

P

Package in database marketing, 432-33
Packard, David, 329
Packard, Vance, 281
Packing for foreign shipment, 1311
Panel-based analysis models, 733-34
Panel data, brand management utilization of, 732-34
Parasuraman, A., 786
Parity pricing, 840
Partnering, 1011-28
  assessing value of product, 1014-15
  developing and implementing relationship-specific product offerings, 1019-25
  evaluating relationship outcomes and reassigning accounts, 1025-27
  market segmentation and assessing value of product to customer, 1014-15
  periodically updating value provided in relationships, 1027-28
  segmentation in, 1013-14
  strategical thinking in, 1012-13
  targeting segments for relationship-specific efforts, 1015-19
Partnerships, 1327
Parts, sale of, 999-1000
Paul Revere Insurance Company, 794
PEAC/Viewfacts system, 256, 258
  reliability of, 257
Penetration pricing, 840
Penney, J. C., 806
Pepsi Cola
  cola wars with Coca-Cola, 163
  and distribution, 874
  and globalization, 1345
Perceived cost, 830
Perceived value, 830
Perception, components to, 776-78
Perception Analyzer, 256
Perceptual process, consumer wants and needs, 155-61
Perdue Farms, 1036
Performance evaluation in business-to-business selling, 1078
Performance monitoring, data evaluation in, 1212-13
Performance potential, reaching, 88-89
Performance tracking systems for direct marketing, 1210
Pergamon-Infoline, 486
Per se rule, 646
Per se standard, substantive erosion in, 647
Personal attributes in sales performance, 108
Personal interviews, 302
  computer-assisted, 304
    bias in, 313
    control of field force in, 311
    cost of, 314
    data collection environment in, 310
    diversity of questions in, 308
    flexibility of data collection in, 306
    perceived anonymity in, 313
    physical stimuli in, 308
    potential for interviewer bias in, 313
    quantity of data in, 312

sample control in, 308
social desirability/sensitive information in, 313
speed of, 314
in-home, 304, 314
control of field force in, 311
cost of, 314
data collection environment in, 310-11
diversity of questions in, 306, 308
flexibility of data collection, 306
perceived anonymity in, 313
physical stimuli in, 308
potential for interviewer bias, 313-14
quantity of data in, 311-12
response role in, 312
sample control in, 308
social desirability/sensitive information in, 313
speed of, 314
mall-intercept, 304
control in, 308
control of field force in, 311
cost of, 314
data collection environment in, 310
diversity of questions in, 306, 308
flexibility of data collection, 306
perceived anonymity in, 313
physical stimuli in, 308
potential for interviewer bias in, 313-14
quantity of data in, 312
response role in, 312
sample control in, 308
social desirability/sensitive information in, 313
speed of, 314
in international marketing research, 317-18, 321-22
in researching industrial products and services, 1050-51
Personal selling in international marketing promotion, 1337
PERT (Program Evaluation and Review Technique), 363-64
Peter, Tom, 1206
Phenomenological perspective in qualitative research, 275-77
Philip Morris Inc., 1347
and change management, 52
as master of innovation, 694-96
Philips Lighting and British Gas, and use of information technology, 481-82
Philips Petroleum, 498
Philips/Signetics, 1327
Photographs, captioned, 1199
Physical environment, and global marketing, 1260
Physical stimuli in survey research, 308
Piercy, Nigel F., 660
Piggybacking, 1264-65
Pillsbury Company
and franchising, 931
and motivation research, 282
PIMS (Profit Impact of Marketing Strategies), 140
PIMS report, 147
Pioneer markets, researching, 689-91
Pisz, James, 1208
Place
determining for social marketing, 830-31
as motivation for sizing markets, 450
Planned shopping center, and retailing, 913-14
Planning. *See also* Marketing plan; Media planning; Strategic planning
in staffing, 95-96
Planning credibility, 683

Planning thoroughness, 669

Polaroid, ethics programs at, 623

Political environment
  in global markets, 1260, 1282-83
  impact on marketing mix, 577

Polk, R. L., 420

Poller v. *CBS,* 651-52

Pollution control, and green marketing, 229-30

Pontiac, advertising campaign of, 72

Popeye's, and area development franchising, 928

Population mean, 296

Porter Paints, 848

Porter's value chain, 803, 807-9

Positioning approach, 1169

POS retail scanning systems, 699-701

Power centers, 914

Power retailing, 903-5

Practice administrator, and organizing for marketing, 194

Practice positioning statement, developing, 207

Precision Tune, 929

Predatory competition, prohibition of, 642-43

Preemptive cannibalism, 893

Preference Analyzer II system, 256

Preference asymmetry, 171

Preference formation, 163

Premium pricing, 840

Presentations, 1124-25

Press conference, 1110-11

Press releases, announcement as, 1110-11

Preston Trucking Company, 792

Pretest market modeling, 892-93

Price. *See* Pricing

Price crunch, 835

Price elasticity, total revenue test in measuring, 449-50

Price fixing, vertical, 652-53

Price leadership pricing, 840

Price levels, developing, 842-43

Price/performance matrix in pricing, 972, 975

Price policy, 858-59

Price selectivity, 743

Price/value decisions, 572

Price Waterhouse Information Guides, 1283

Pricing, 857-66. *See also* Strategic pricing
  administered or business-controlled pricing, 857
  in barter arrangements, 1349
  bundle, 840
  and buyers, 864
  in compensation arrangements, 1349-52
  cooperative, 1022
  costs in, 861-62
  as creative variable, 836-37
  cross-benefit, 840
  defining objectives of, 866
  determining organization for, 866
  export, 1357-73
  external factors in, 862-64
  factors influencing establishment international, 1334-36
  floor, 840
  fudging, 1351
  full-cost, 861
  government-controlled, 858
  influence of suppliers on, 863
  internal factors in, 859-62
  international policies, 1332-33
  judgment in, 866
  legal considerations in, 864
  by manufacturers, 864-65
  market, 857

in marketing to business, 968-69
in marketing program, 860
and market structure, 863
mark-up, 840
in nonbusiness marketing, 584
objectives of, 859
organization for, 859-60
parity, 840
penetration, 840
premium, 840
price leadership, 840
and product differentiation, 860-61
by retailers, 865
and sizing markets, 449-50
stay out, 840
strategic, 835-54, 969-79
strategies in, 572
structures in, 839-42
tactical, 979-84
target return, 840
value-based, 840

Primary data
in researching global markets, 1278
in researching industrial products and services, 1048-50

PRIZM, 1189

Probabilistic mathematical model, 361

Probability sampling, 402

Problem psychology, and professional service environment, 191-92

Problem recognition, and consumer wants and needs, 157-58

Process-related activities, 805

Procter & Gamble
and database marketing, 426
and globalization, 1269, 1272, 1322, 1334
green marketing strategy of, 225

Producer/service unity, 192-93

Product
distribution strategy for, 56-57
as factor in export pricing, 1359
market segmentation by application, 1013-14
motivation for sizing markets, 448-49
pricing of, 852-53
testing, 240

Product adequacy determination, 809

Product and selling expertise, and sales performance, 117-18

Product cannibalism, 881-93
accounting for, 886-89
effects of preemptive, 868
fostering, 884-86
identifying potential, 889-93
implications for product-line management, 893
incremental analysis, 888-89
nature of, 882-84

Product concept, 21-23

Product development, and installed-base marketing, 444-45

Product differentiation, 9
degree of, 860-61
distinguishing between segmentation and, 961

Product distribution franchise system, 919

Production facility, location of, as factor in export pricing, 1359-60

Production in home market, 1263-65

Product lifecycle
final phase of, 1123
launch phase, 1109-11, 1113
pre-launch or phase, 1109, 1113, 1130-31
pricing strategy over, 848-52
sustaining phase of, 1111-12, 1131

Product-line management, implications of product cannibalism for, 893

Product market and company performance in global markets, 1287-88

Product market structure, analysis of, 889-90
Product market system, 23-25
Product mix, 578-79
Product planning, 61
  and product policies, 1329-32
Product review, and customer service, 813
Product strategies, 572
Product structure, 1341
Product-testing, 240
Product-usage data in global marketing, 1288
Product variety, 871
Professional marketing, 187-216
  client analysis and opportunities, 200-201
  control and evaluation, 206
  developing marketing plan, 206-10
  ethical and practical considerations, 188-89
    client analysis and opportunities, 200-201
    control and evaluation, 206
    personal communication, 203-4
    philosophy, positioning, and targeting, 201
    practice environment, 198-200
    professional fees, 202-3
    service mix, 201-2
    written communication, 204-6
  internal barriers to practice marketing, 211-14
  marketing audit, 197-98
  organizing for marketing, 193-97
  personal communication, 203-4
  philosophy, positioning, and targeting, 201
  practice environment, 198-200
  professional fees, 202-3
  professional service environment critical service characteristics, 189-93
  rainmakers in, 214-16
  service mix, 201-2
  written communication, 204-6
Professionals, identifying, 188
Professional service environment, critical service characteristics of, 189-93
Profitability
  as allocation criteria, 138-39
  measuring future, 139-41
Profitability control, 740, 747-48
Profit-and-loss statement, preparing, for marketing entity, 749-50
Profit impact, measuring for poor quality, 797
Profit margin, 746
Profit maximization, 81-82, 137
Profits, and sizing markets, 448-49
Program Analyzer, 255
Projective techniques in qualitative research, 280
Promotion, 572. *See also* Sales promotion
  business communications, 1107-34
  contemporary advertising media planning, 1187-95
  customer contacts in integrated marketing communications environment, 1085-1103
  developing advertising message strategy, 1157-83
  direct marketing, 1205-28
  imagery and symbolism, 1137-44
  as motivation for sizing markets, 450-51
  planning, in social marketing, 831-32
  public relations, 1197-1203
  setting marketing objectives for, 1147-55
  symbols in, 1140-41
  women and language, 1233-44
Promotional catalogs, 1130
Promotional marketing, 1147
  analyzing customer in, 1151

analyzing past programs in, 1152
analyzing competition in, 1151-52
analyzing market in, 1151
determining budget in, 1152
determining need for testing in, 1152
determining fit in, 1152
examining distribution system in, 1152
expectations of, 1147-48
tips for writing objectives in, 1154-55

Promotional mix, nonbusiness, 584-85

Promotion efficiency index (PEI), 709

Promotion event performance, 725, 726, 727

Promotion frequency, 725

Promotion-from-within policy, 97

Property leases, and franchising, 927

Propriety in women's language, 1236-37

Protocol in barter arrangements, 1346

Prudential Rock, 1179

Pseudo-clairvoyance, 350

Psychic mobility, 152-53

Psychographic data, 1189

Psychographic segmentation, 178-79

Psychological Corporations'
Edwards Personal Preference Schedule, 98

Wechsler Adult Intelligence Scale and Wesman Personnel Classification Test, 98

Publicity, 1197

Public relations, 1197-1203
crisis communications, 1201-2
direct mail, 1201
in international marketing promotion, 1338
publicity, 1197
targeting as crucial in, 1197-98
creating publicity, 1199-1201
research in, 1198-99
triggers in, 1202

Pull strategy, 1338

Pundits, 675

Purchase behavior, 13-15
role of learning in, 15
understanding, 13-15

Purchase motivation in marketing, 9-11

Push strategy, 1338

Pyramid marketing organizations, 642

Q

QANTAS, 1322

Quaker Oats Company, and market segmentation, 178

Qualitative evaluation of media, 414

Qualitative research, 271-84
analytic approach in, 273
comparing approaches in, 271-75
in designing market surveys, 1290
history of, 277
growth of surveying, 278
indirectness and depth, 280-81
motivation research, 281-84
rise of qualitative analysis, 279-80
holistic approach to, 273
phenomenological perspective in, 275-77

Quality
linking to marketing, 46-47, 60
measuring, 803
profit impact of poor, 797
stressing personal, 797-98

Quantitative data in sizing market, 458

Quantitative evaluation of media, 411-14

Quantity purchasing, 984

Quartile analysis, 96

Quasi-experiments, 1218-19
  designs of, 293-94

Questions, diversity of, in survey research, 306, 308

QuickTally, 256

Quilford-Zimmerman Temperament Survey, 98

Quotas, 1307

R

RABA, 1348

RACE, 1265

Rainmakers, 214-16

Random digit dialing (RDD) technique, 309

Random error, 290

Random sample, 290-91

Ranking reports, 717, 719

Rapp, Stan, 1228

Rating scale, 100, 518-19

Raw materials, 1031-39
  commodity exchanges, 1038
  environmental considerations, 1037
  global market for, 1034-35
  implications, 1038-39
  industrial, 1031
    middlemen, 1036-37
    vertical integration, 1035-36
  marketing functions, 1032-34
  multiple uses and allocation decisions, 1031-32

Ray, Michael, 1163, 1171-72

Ray-O-Vac, and export pricing, 1359-60, 1367

R & D consortia, and strategic alliances, 1327

Reach, 431, 1190

Realists, 179

Reasoned action model of marketing ethics, 618-19

Recall, measurement of, 407-8

Recognition programs, 1130

Reconciliation, 86-88

Recovery service, 793

Recruiting, 96-97

Recruitment, guidelines for effective, 119-21

Recycling, and green marketing, 227

Reeves, George, 283

Reeves, Rosser, 1167, 1171

Regression analysis, 295

Reid, Leonard N., 1156

Reinhard, Keith, 1194

Reis, Al, 1169, 1182

Relational data, 707

Relationship marketing, 812
  definition of, 812
  in direct marketing, 1206, 1219
  in IMC program, 1206, 1228
  shift of database marketing to, 421-22

Repair, ease of, in computer, 809

Reporting schemes, 708-9

Representative sampling, 406

Research, 538. *See also* Advertising research and measurement; Marketing research; Market research
  in public relations, 1198-99

Resistance to marketing change, 666

Response device in direct mail, 1121

Response homogeneity, 176

Response rate in survey research, 312-13

Responsibility for staffing, 95

Retailer
  input/output of, 37-38
  in marketing campaign, 469
  pricing by, 865

Retailing, 538
current status of U.S., 900
expansion/merger strategies, 909-10
financial measures, 911-12
labor force needs, 912-13
locational strategies, 913-14
operational factors, 910
power retailing, 903-5
retail life cycle, 905-6
retail positioning, 906-8
scrambled merchandising, 902-3
wheel of retailing, 901-2
developing customer databases, 916
development of, in the United States, 899-900
internationalization of retailing, 914-15
monitoring events in, 915-16
open-mindedness in, 916
planning strategically, 916
projecting the proper position and image, 916
strategic planning in, 897-916

Retail life cycle, 905-6

Retail positioning, 906-8

Retail sales data, 704-5, 710-11

Return on assets, 746

Return on net worth (RNW), 911-12

Reward compensation, 81-92
consequences, 91
dichotomy between short and long view, 83
master strategy, 81-83
participation, 84, 86
pitfalls, 89-90
program design, 90-91
reaching performance potential, 88-89
reconciliation, 86-88
transition to multiple goals, 83-84

Reynolds, William, 333

Rice, Craig S., 462

Richards v. *Nielsen Freight Lines*, 656-57

Riskey, Dwight R., 880

RJR Nabisco, 1347

Robinson, Patrick, 1067

Robinson-Patman Act, 645, 975
pricing constraints under, 864, 959

Roche, Sara M., 946

Rodkin, Henry H., 288

Roger, Thomas, 1207

Role ambiguity, and consumer satisfaction, 391

Role perceptions
and job satisfaction, 125
and salesperson performance, 109

Role reversal, feminist method of reading by, 1241

Rolls-Royce, 1172

Roman, Kenneth, 1171

ROMWARE, 1316

Ronkainen, Ilka A., 1252

ROP (run on paper), 431

Rotation, 1141

Royal Bank of Scotland, 503

Royal Caribbean Cruise Lines, and yield management, 937

Royalties, in franchising, 926-27

RPI, 1211

Ruch, Dudley, 283

Rule of reason, 646

Ryans, John K., Jr., 686

S

Safeway, and ethical decision making, 607

Sales administration-to-sales ratio, 744

Sales analysis, 740-42
in research on industrial products and services, 1061-62

Sales and distribution channels, 1126-30

Sales contests, 1129

Sales force
- effectiveness of, in marketing to business, 985-95
- efficiency of, 753-54
- objectives of tactical analysis, 722

Sales force-to-sales ratio, 744

Sales forecasting in research on industrial products and services, 1062-63

Sales forecasts, 1043

Sales letter, 1119-20

Sales management, 538

Salesmanship, 538

SALES model, 1216-17

Sales performance
- determinants of, 107-8
- measures of, 712-13

Salesperson performance, 107
- behavioral variables, 118-19
  - direction, 118
  - effort, 118
  - interpersonal role implementation, 118-19
- business definition, 142
  - dimensions, 142-44
  - scope of, 145-47
- cognitive and psychological-state variables, 116-18
  - content theories of motivation, 117
  - goal dimensions, 117
  - motivation, 116-17
  - product and selling expertise, 117
  - self-efficacy beliefs, 118
- developing better understanding of, 111-14
- economic objectives, 137
- goals versus, 136-37
- guidelines for effective recruiting, 119-21
- job satisfaction, 121-25
  - antecedents of, 125-27
  - organizational commitment, 124
  - and sales performance, 122-23
  - turnover, 124-25
- measuring future profitability, 139-41
- personal characteristics and personality traits, 116
- profitability measures as allocation criteria, 138-39
- sales performance, 107-8
  - aptitude, 108
  - conclusions on performance determinants, 109-11
  - motivation, 109
  - organizational and environmental variables, 109
  - personal attributes, 108
  - role perceptions, 109
  - selling skills, 108-9
- sales work outcomes, 121

Sales potential, estimating, in export pricing, 1369

Sales promotion. *See also* Promotion
- brand factors in, 1153
- category factors in, 1153
- consumer factors in, 1153
- efficiency in, 754
- focus on the big picture, 1150-51
- in international marketing promotion, 1337
- in marketing to business, 995-98
- and marketing communication, 1152-53
- materials in, 1132
- objectives in, 1154
- power of, 1149
- preparing plan, 1148-49
- setting objectives in, 1147
- targets of, 1149-50

Sales promotion-to-sales ratio, 744

Sales rate reports, in strategic planning, 729

Sales rates, 709
Sales-related activities, and consumer satisfaction, 387
Sales release guide, 1127-28
Sales support in marketing to business, 993-94
Sales testing, 405-6
Sales tools, 1129
Sales training, 1128
Sales-variance analysis, 741
Sample bias, 290
Sample control, in survey research, 308-10
Sample design, 290-92
Sample frame, 290
Sample mean, 295-96
Sampling
- probability, 402
- representative, 406
- scientific, 402

Sampling equivalence, and local market expansion, 1294
Santitas Tortilla Chips, 885-86
SAS, international operations of, 1322
Savacentre, 498
Schlitz Beer, and competitive advantage, 171
Schmitt, Bernd, 626
Schoner, Bertram, 288
Schultz, Don, 1215
Schwerin, Horace, 255
Schwerin test, reliability of, 257
Science Research Associates
- Adaptability Test, 98
- Kuder Preference Record Vocational Form CP, 98

Scientific method, 400, 402
Scientific sampling, 402
Scott Paper Company, 5-6
- and positioning of product, 17-18

Scrambled merchandising, 813-14, 901-3
Screw-driver factories, 1266
SDC-Orbit, 486
Sears, 498, 900
- positioning by, 1169
- and value marketing, 47

Sears, Richard Warren, 419
Secondary data
- in researching global markets, 1278
- in researching industrial products and services, 1047-48

Securities analysis, 1112
Segmentation. *See also* Market segmentation
- benefit, 510, 524, 531
- distinguishing between product differentiation and, 961
- strategy of sensory, 510, 524-31

Selection ratio, 121
Self-efficacy beliefs, and sales performance, 118
Selling agents in marketing of raw materials, 1037
Selling conditions, 707-8
Selling skills in sales performance, 108-9
Sematech, 1265
Senior partner, and organizing for marketing, 194
Sensory merchandise
- definition of, 509
- predicting preferences, 509-10

Sensory panel, 510, 513-15
- nature of voting, 518-19
- operating, 517-18
- selecting common touch members, 515-17
- track record of, 520-24

validating performance of members, 520

Sensory segmentation, 510, 524-31

Sequential brand entry, 165

Sequential consumer entry, 165

Served market share, 743-44

Service aspirations, raising, 787-95

Service backup, 871

Service fees in franchising, 926-27

Service leadership, showcasing, 798

Service quality information system, building, 795-96

Service quality performance, reporting, 796-97

Service quality revolution, 787-800
competitive advantage of common sense and passion, 799
making service improvement a habit, 795-98
raising our service aspirations, 787-95

Services
marketing characteristics of, 181-82
pricing for, 852-53
unbundling of, 853

SERVQUAL dimensions, 803, 809, 811-12

Shanklin, William L., 686

Shea, Linda J., 1300

Sheraton Hotels, and yield management, 937

Sheridan Psychological Services' Quilford-Zimmerman Temperament Survey, 98

Sherman Antitrust Act (1890), 645, 864

Shipper's Export Declaration, 1303

Shops, Richard, 498

Shotgun approach to targeting, 73

SIC system in sizing markets, 455

Silent trade, 1348

Simmons (Market Research Bureau), 1189

Simulation models, 364

Single European Act (1987), 1308, 1325, 1328

Siragusa, George A., 834

Sissors, Jack Z., 1186

Size, definition of, 447

Sizing markets, 447
appropriate unit for, 479
identifying the key input, 452-53
inputs affecting buying decisions, 479-80
prerequisites for, 453-54
definition of, 447
methods for, 447-48
motivation for, 448
place, 450
price, 449-50
product, 448-49
promotion, 450-51
using census data in, 454
SIC system, 455
sizing future markets, 455-60

Skeptics, 179

Slater, Stanley F., 329

Slogans, 1177, 1179-80

Slotting fees, 607

Smith, C. E., Company, 1015

Smith, C. Theodore, 246

Smith, George Horsley, 281

Smith, W. C., Company, 998

Smith, Wendell R., 961

Smucker, J. M., 1036

Social desirability, 313

Social intelligence, 116

Social marketing, 825-32
aims of, 825-32

applications of, 825-32
commercial marketing, 825-26
future of, 832
steps in effective, 826-27
conducting additional research on target audience, 827
cost of adopting desired behavior, 829-30
defining problem, 826-27
designing proposed behavior change, 828
determining people/activities that need to interact, 830-31
developing coordinated, comprehensive marketing plan, 828
developing tangible products, 829
evaluating effectiveness, 832
planning communications program, 831-32
positioning desired behavior change, 828-29
selecting appropriate target audience, 827

Social mobility, 152

Social Research, Inc., 280

Social responsibility
in marketing concept, 61
in marketing management, 50-51
theory of, 544-45

Sociocultural factors of global markets, 1285-86

Sonoco Fibre
Drum Division, 1016, 1024-25
Products Division, 1015

Sony, 1322

Southern California Edison, and green marketing, 226

Southern Rambler Sales, Inc. v. *American Motors Corp.,* 656

Southland, and globalization, 915

Sovereign entities, and global marketing, 1259

Special discount rates, 1130

Special economic zone, 1315

Specialist middleman, 1354

Specialization and integration, theory of, 540-41

SpeedBack® system, 256, 258-62, 264
construct validity of, 257
reliability of, 257

Spiegel, 426
database marketing by, 438-39

Split-run tests, 1214

Spokesperson tours, 1200

Staccato movement, 1141

Staffing the marketing function, 95-105
appraising and rewarding performance, 100-3
communication in, 103-5
determining what kinds of personnel are needed, 96
induction and assimilation, 99
planning for personnel needs, 95-96
recruiting, 96-97
responsibility for staffing, 95
screening, selecting, and testing, 97-99
training and development, 99-100

Standardization
and global marketing, 1266-67
of product, 1330-31

Stanford Heart Disease Prevention Program, 829, 831-32

Stanford University Press's Strong-Campbell Interest Inventory, 98

Stanley Works, 1270

Stanton, Frank, 255-57

State, U.S. Department of, and U.S. export regulations, 1302

Statistical Abstracts, 455

Statistical and experimental designs, 289-98
analysis of data, 294-95
Bayesian analysis, 295
Bayesian versus classical assumptions, 295-97
experimental design, 292-93
quasi-experimental design, 293-94
sample bias, 290
sample design, 290-92

Stay out pricing, 840

Steelcase, and distribution, 869

Stereotyping
literary images of women in, 1240-41
maleness and femaleness in, 1234-35

Sterman, John, 701

Stern, Barbara B., 1232

Stern, Louis W., 868

Stewart, George, 283

Stewarts, 900

Stockpiling of raw materials, 1033

Store audits, 405

Storecard, 498

Store data, brand management utilization of, 727-32

Stouffer, Samuel A., 278

Stouffer Food Corporation's Right Course, and product cannibalism, 882

Stouffer Hotel, 790

Strategic alliances, 1327-28
in marketing concept, 47, 50, 61

Strategical thinking in partnering, 1012-13

Strategic business units (SBUs), 87

Strategic control, 740, 755

Strategic information systems (SIS), and information provision, 485

Strategic planning
and brand management utilization, 729, 731-32
and information provisions, 485-86
in retailing, 897-916

Strategic pricing, 835-54. *See also* Pricing
developing program for, 837
determining price levels and related tactics, 842-43
developing structure for, 839-42
establishing strategy for, 839
role of price objectives, 838-39
linking pricing strategy to marketing strategy, 847-48
in marketing to business, 969-79
over product life cycle, 848-52
price as creative variable in, 836-37
for products versus services, 852-53
putting components together, 843-44
underlying determinants of pricing decisions, 844-47

Stratification, 291

Stratified sampling, 291

Strong-Campbell Interest Inventory, 98

Structured-direct survey, 301-2

Sturdivant, Frederick D., 868

Style merchandise
predicting market responses to, 509
background, 509-10
nature of the voting, 518-19
operating the panel, 517-18
selecting common touch panel members, 515-17
sensory panel, 513-15
sensory segmentation, 524-31
track record, 520-21
validating the performance of panel members, 520
problems of marketing, 511-13

Subfranchising, 926-27

Subjective data in sizing market, 458

Substantiality, and market segmentation, 176

Substitute products, in global marketing, 1288

Substitution-in-use approach (SIU), 889-90, 891

Success, measuring marketing, 16-17

Success stories, 1200

Summary judgment, 656-57, 657

Sunbeam Appliance Corporation, use of conjoint analysis by, 991

SunMaid, 1141

Supervisory behaviors, and job satisfaction, 125-26

Supplemental up-front fees, 926

Suppliers, influence of, on pricing, 863

Supply-side marketing, 687-88, 694-95

Supply sources, qualification of potential, in business-to-business selling, 1070-71

Support industries, 948, 950

Surmanek, James, 1186

Surveying, growth of, in qualitative research, 278

Survey methods, 301-2. *See also specific method*
- comparative evaluation of, 305-14
  - control of field force in, 311
  - control of data collection environment in, 310-11
  - cost, 314
  - diversity of questions in, 306, 308
  - flexibility of data collection in, 306
  - perceived anonymity in, 313
  - potential for interviewer bias in, 313-14
  - quantity of data in, 311-12
  - response rate in, 312-13
  - sample control in, 308-10
  - selection of survey method, 314
  - social desirability/sensitive information in, 313
  - speed, 314
  - use of physical stimuli in, 308
- computer-assisted, 304
- in-home, 304
  - control of field force in, 311
  - cost of, 314
  - data collection environment in, 310-11
  - diversity of questions in, 306, 308
  - flexibility of data collection, 306
  - perceived anonymity in, 313
  - physical stimuli in, 308
  - potential for interviewer bias, 313-14
  - quantity of data in, 311-12
  - response role in, 312
  - sample control in, 308
  - social desirability/sensitive information in, 313
  - speed of, 314
- in international marketing research, 315-16
  - mail interviews, 319-20
  - mail panels, 320
  - mall intercept and CRT interviews, 318-19
  - personal interviews, 317-18
  - telephone interviewing and CATI, 315-16
- mail
  - interviews, 305
  - panels, 305
- mall-intercept, 304
  - control in, 308
  - control of field force in, 311
  - cost of, 314
  - data collection environment in, 310
  - diversity of questions in, 306, 308

flexibility of data collection in, 306
perceived anonymity in, 313
physical stimuli in, 308
potential for interviewer bias in, 313-14
quantity of data in, 312
response role in, 312
sample control in, 308
social desirability/sensitive information in, 313
speed of, 314
personal, 304
selection of, 314
telephone, 302-3

Survey Research Center, 280

Swing, 1348

SWOT analysis, 674, 684

Symbolism
in advertising message, 1171-81
buyer's point of view, 1142-43
implications of, 1144
in industrial advertising, 1143
manager's point of view, 1142
obtaining and retaining protection for identifying, 1181-82

Symbols
in advertising and promotion, 1140-41
guidelines for using, 1182
identifying, 1182

Syndicated data on store sales, 704-5

Systematic error, 290

System for Tracking Export License Applications (STELA), 1303

Systems thinking, and the marketing mix, 574-76

T

Taco Bell, and franchising, 931

Tactical analysis, 722
base pricing, 724
expert systems, 725
obtaining distribution, 722-24
promotion event performance, 725, 726, 727
promotion frequency, 825
sales force objectives, 722

Tactical marketing, 19-21

Tactical pricing, in marketing to business, 979-84

Take-back goods, marketing channels for, 1352-54

Tangibility, and professional service environment, 189-91

Tangible products, developing, 829

Target, 900, 902

Target audience
conducting research on, 827
selecting appropriate, 827

Targeting, 5, 26
marketing mix in, 580-81
as marketing strategy, 848
of segments for relationship, specific efforts, 1015-19

Target market
definition of, 447
in marketing mix, 580-81

Target population, 289-90

Target price range, estimating, in export pricing, 1369

Target return pricing, 840

Tariffs, 1306

TARP (Technical Assistance Research Programs Institute) study, 816

Task force, and organizing for marketing, 194-95

Taste test, 308

Teaching materials, 1200

Technical Assistance Research Program (TARP), 793, 806

Technical buyers, 1113

Technical hubris, and customer service, 813

Technological and educational factors, 1285

Technological Edge Contributions, 1017-18

Technologically driven substitution, 227

Technology, utilizing, in improving customer services, 816-17

Technology partners and alliances, 1130-31

Technology Roadmaps, 1018

Telemarketing for database marketing, 428-29

Teleological perspective of ethical decision making, 627

Telephone interview
- computer-assisted, 302-3
  - control of field force in, 311
  - cost of, 314
  - data collection environment in, 310
  - diversity of questions in, 308
  - flexibility of data collection in, 306
  - in international marketing research, 315-16, 321
  - perceived anonymity in, 313
  - physical stimuli in, 308
  - potential for interviewer bias, 314
  - quantity of data in, 312
  - response rate in, 313
  - sample control in, 308
  - social desirability/sensitive information in, 313
  - speed of, 314
- in international marketing research, 315-16
- perceived anonymity in, 313
  - cost in, 314
  - potential for interviewer bias, 314
  - social desirability/sensitive information in, 313
  - speed in, 314
- in researching industrial products and services, 1051-52
- traditional, 302
  - control of data collection environment, 311
  - control of field force in, 311
  - flexibility of data collection in, 306
  - quantity of data in, 311, 312
  - response rate in, 312
  - sample control in, 308-9

Television Code of the National Association of Broadcasters, ethics codes of, 632

Temporary price reduction (TPR) pricing, 706, 707

Territorial subdivisions in market size measurements, 1059-60

Testimonial articles, 1111-12

Testing, and recruitment, 120-21

Test marketing, 240
- field, 892-93

Texas Instruments (TI)
- and partnering, 1018-19
- and strategic alliances, 1327
- and value-added activities, 1270

Theater systems in communication research, 256

Thematic apperception technique, 280

Thomas's Register, 1071

Thompson, J. Walter, 283

3M
- auditing services at, 757
- as master of innovation, 694-96
- and use of marketing research, 245

Time-Life, 427-28

Time series data in sizing market, 458-59

Tobacco companies in developing countries, 607-8

Top box method of scoring rating scales, 518

Total Revenue (TR) test, in measuring price elasticity, 449-50

Totten, John C., 698

Tough-to-market products, 1349

Toyota
and direct marketing, 1208
and distribution, 874
international operations of, 1322
and value marketing, 47

Toyota Motor Corporation, 1208

Toys "R" Us, 904, 1268

Traceable common costs, 752

Tracking mechanisms, 1126

TRADACOM (Trading Data Communications), 497

Trade characters, 1179

Trademarks, 1177

Trade names, 1177

Trade show
in business communications, 1122-23
in marketing to business, 998-1000

Trading-area overlap, and retailing, 913

Training and development, 99-100

Train-the-trainer courses in sales training, 1128

Transactional relationships, 1012

Transaction emphasis, 1015

Transformational advertising, 1163

Translation equivalence, and local market expansion, 1293-94

Treasury, U.S. Department of, and U.S. export regulations, 1302

Trend reports, 714-15, 727

Triangle test, 514, 532n

Trombetta, William L., 644

Trout, Jack, 1169, 1182

True experiments
continual monitoring/relationship building with, 1218-19
in performance monitoring, 1213-15

Truncated approach, 646

Tupperware, and distribution, 869

Turnover
and job performance, 123
and job satisfaction, 124-25
reasons for, 95

Twelve-month prune rule, 419

Tying contract, 925

U

Unconscious devices in communication research, 256-57

Undeveloped international channels, 1349

Unethical practices, reasons for, 630-31

Unfair practices acts, 865

Unglaub, Lynn C., 418

Unifying movement, 1141

Unilever, 1269, 1270

United sales movement, 706

United Services Automobile Association in database marketing, 435-37

United States v. *Socony-Vacuum Oil Co.,* 647

United States v. *Trenton Potteries Co.,* 647

Unit franchising, 927

Universal Product Code, 700
and inventory planning, 910

U.S. Census of Manufacturing, 455

U.S. & Foreign Commercial Service, 1258
Federal Power Commission, and U.S. export regulations, 1302
government regulations, as factor in export pricing, 1363

U.S. Time Company, use of marketing research by, 245

User buyers, 1112-13

USSR
breakup of, 1034
and market for raw materials, 1034-35
Utility, definition of, 540

V

Valdez, Juan, 1179
Validated license, 1302
VALS 2, 1189
Value
assessing, for product to customer, 1014-15
concept of, 46-47
in pricing, 835-36
marketing, 46-47
theory of, 540
Value added by marketing, 540-41
Value-added data services (VADS), and information technology, 486, 487
Value-added resellers (VARs), 1129
Value-based pricing, 840
Value chain, 807-9
Value concept in marketing, 540
Value creation, 540
Vaseline, and competitive advantage, 170
Vaughn, Richard, 1170, 1172, 1182
Vendor information/proposals
acquisition of, in business-to-business selling, 1071
analysis and evaluation of, in business-to-business selling, 1071-77
Veraldi, Lewis, 334
Verbal excess in women's language, 1238
Verification, 1175
Verisimilitude, 1239
Vertical integration in marketing of raw materials, 1035-36
Vertically integrated consumer goods, 32-33
Vertical price fixing, 652-53
Vertical restraints, 652
Vested interests rule, 666
Via Rail Canada, and yield management, 937
Vicary, James, 282
Video shopping, 577
Videotape, 1125-26
in sales training, 1128
Vie de France, and franchising, 931
Virgin Atlantic Airways, 790-91
Volkswagen, positioning by, 1169
Volume equivalency conversion factors, 707
Voluntary adaptation, 1331
Volunteerism, 1133

W

Waiting-line models, 364
Waiting time, 870
Walk around management, 65
Waller, Robert, 345-46
Wal-Mart discount stores, 900, 904
and competitive analysis, 796
point-of-sale scanning at, 699
and value marketing, 47
Wanamaker, 900
Wants, identifying, in marketing, 12-13
Warner, W. Lloyd, 280
Wave theory of advertising scheduling, 465
Wear out phenomenon, 520
Webb-Pomerene Associations, 1264
Wechsler Adult Intelligence Scale, 98

Weigand, Robert E., 918, 1344

Weighted checklist, 100

Wells, William D., 283, 1171

Wendy's, and area development franchising, 928

Wesley-Jessen Corporation, 797

Wesman Personnel Classification Test, 98

Westin, and yield management, 937

Wherehouse Entertainment Center, 904

White, Gordon E., 1157

White Papers, 1123

Whiteside, Henry O., 283

Wholesaling, 538

Wholly-owned production facilities, 1266

Wilson, Joseph, 335

Wind, Yoram, 1067

Witter, D. W., 1358-59

Women, marketing to, 44, 45

Women's language, 1234-36
- and advertising, 1238-45
  - in dramatic sceneries, 1238-40
- characteristics of, 1236
  - hesitancy, 1237-38
  - language and cultural roles, 1240-41
  - propriety, 1236-37
  - reading women in advertising, 1241-44
  - verbal excess, 1238

Women's studies, 1235

Wonderlic Personnel Test, 98

Woodside, Arch G., 1204

Work orientation, 117

Workstation reporting, 717, 722

X

Xerox, use of marketing research by, 245, 335

Y

Yield management, 937-41
- booking curve capacity management, 938
- definition of, 937-38
- goal of, 938
- increase complexity of, 938-39
- industry application of, 939-41
- as more than pricing tool, 939
- origin of, 937

Young, James Webb, 1175

Yugo, 603

Z

Zion's, 900